International Business Dictionary

国際ビジネス

英和

活用辞典

菊地義明 編

国際取引 | Global Transactions
貿　易　Trade
為　替　Currency
証　券　Securities

日外アソシエーツ

International Business Dictionary
Global Transactions,
Trade, Currency & Securities

Compiled by

©Yoshiaki KIKUCHI

Nichigai Associates, Inc.

Printed in Japan, 2015

●編集担当● 簡 志帆
装丁：赤田 麻衣子

はじめに

　本書は、国際取引文書や国際ビジネス関連記事等を読み解くうえで必要とされる基本的な用語と重要語句を、幅広く収録したものです。

　収録分野は、主に貿易（輸出入取引）、為替、保険、契約書、ビジネス・レター（商業文）のほか、商品・金融・証券等の各種取引、知的財産権［所有権］、国際取引関連法やカレント・トピックスなど多岐にわたっています。

　また本書は、基本的に見出し語、見出し語の多様な語義のほか、見出し語の関連語句と文例（英文とその日本語訳）とで構成されています。

　豊富な文例には文例の文脈に応じた的確な訳例が示してあるため、ビジネス実用用語辞典、翻訳事典として利用することができるのも、本書の特長です。

　国際間の商取引は、企業や政府、個人が主体となって国境を越えて行われるモノ（goods）、金（money）、サービス（services）と情報（information）の取引と言えるでしょう。これらの国際ビジネスを展開する上でまず考慮しなければならないのは、契約書です。契約用語は極めて専門性が高いため、慣れないと訳出するのが困難です。そこで本書には、契約関連用語も重点的に収められています。

　これらの文例を、とくに翻訳の実務面で活かしていただくのが、本書のねらいです。

　国際取引・ビジネスの対象分野は幅広く、まだまだ収録し切れない部分が多いのが実情で、これらは今後の課題として努力を重ねるつもりです。

2015 年 4 月

菊地 義明

本書を利用するにあたって

1．本書の内容

　　本書は、国際取引で多用される用語の多様な語義と関連語句、文例を網羅した実用ビジネス英和辞典です。

2．本書の基本構成

　　以下に示すように、基本的に見出し語、見出し語の語義のほか、多用される見出し語の重要語句と文例（英文とその日本語訳）で構成されています。

　　また、必要に応じて適宜、語義の後のカッコ内に見出し語の説明も添えてあります。

　　例）

　　recourse（名）遡求（そきゅう），償還請求，償還請求権（手形などの振出人または裏書人に支払いを請求する権利），第二次的請求，依頼，頼みの綱，手段

　　　endorsement without recourse　遡求に応じない裏書き

　　　without recourse　償還請求に応ぜず（振出人、裏書人が手形に書く文句），遡求に応じない

　　　without recourse credit　償還請求権なき信用状

　　　without recourse to　〜に頼らずに，〜に訴えることなく

　　　◆ ABC shall have no recourse against XYZ for any obligations under the original agreement assigned pursuant to this assignment agreement.

　　　ABC は、この譲渡契約に従って譲渡された原契約上の債務については、XYZ に履行の請求を一切求めないものとする。

3．収録基準

　　国際取引文書や国際ビジネス関連記事を読み解くうえで欠かせない国際

(4)

取引の基本的用語、重要語句と最新用語を幅広く収録。

4．語彙の収録分野

収録分野は、主に貿易（輸出入取引）、為替、保険、契約書、ビジネス・レター（商業文）のほか、商品・金融・証券等の各種取引、知的財産権［所有権］、国際取引関連法やカレント・トピックスで、国際事業としての合弁事業や業務・資本提携、M＆A（合併・買収）、国際投資なども含まれています。

5．収録語数

収録語数は、見出し語約 4,200 語、関連語句約 12,900 項目で、文例は約 4,700 件に達しています。

6．構成要素

1）見出し語と副見出し語

見出し語は、基本的にアルファベット順に配列してあります。ただし、とくに単数形と複数形で意味が異なる名詞や同音異義語については、それぞれ別個に見出しを立ててあります。

また、見出し語を含む関連語句は、副見出し語としてアルファベット順に配列してあります。

2）品　詞

品詞の略記は、以下のとおりです。

（動）動詞	（副）副詞	（接）接続詞
（名）名詞	（自動）自動詞	（関代）関係代名詞
（前）前置詞	（代）代名詞	
（形）形容詞	（助動）助動詞	

3）語　義

見出し語の後に表示してある語義は、基本的に国際取引・ビジネス分野の多様な語義で、文脈に応じて適切な語義を選択できるようできるだけ広範に網羅されています。

4）参照事項

見出し語の語義の後に表示してあるカッコ内の語句は、基本的に見出し語の簡単な説明と参照事項です。ただし、漢字の読みを示す振り仮名の場合もあります。

カッコ内のイコール記号（＝）で示される語句は、見出し語の同義・同意表現です。また、矢印（⇒）の後の語句を参照すると、見出し語を含む文例や関連語句が掲げてあります。

例）

advanced technology　最新技術，先進技術，先端技術，
高度技術（＝ high technology, sophisticated technology,
state-of-the-art technology；⇒ intellectual property）

5）文例と訳例

見出し語には、その語義と用法の理解に役立てるため、できるかぎり文例とその訳例が添えてあります。訳例中のカッコ（　）内は基本的に説明語で、カギカッコ［　］内は同意語または同意表現として示してあります。

6）解　説

重要な見出し語に関しては、解説を見出し語の末尾に付してあります。

A

AB〔ABS〕 米国船級協会（American Bureau of Shippingの略）

ab initio 初めから，当初から，遡及的に，遡（さかのぼ）って（=from the beginning）

abandon （動）廃止する，中断する，中止する，断念する，（権利や財産を）放棄する，廃棄する，遺棄する，除却する，（船舶や積み荷を）委付する，訴訟を取り下げる

abandon efforts to rehabilitate itself　自力再建策を断念する

abandon low-price competition　安値競争と決別する

abandon one's duties　職務を放棄する

abandon one's plan to merge　合併計画を断念する

we abandon to you our interest in the undermentioned by the said vessel　同船所載の下記積み荷に対する当社の権利を御社に委付する

◆Shinsei and Aozora banks have abandoned their plan to merge. 新生銀行とあおぞら銀行が，両行の合併計画を断念した. ◆The firm has been struggling after it abandoned low-price competition at mass retailers to pursue greater profits. 同社が苦戦しているのは，量販店の安値競争と決別して，収益重視路線に舵を切った結果だ.

abandonment （名）放棄，委付

abandonment clause　（保険証券の）委付条項

abandonment method　除却法

abandonment of a cargo　積み荷の委付

abandonment of equipment　設備の廃却

abandonment of voyage　航海放棄

notice of abandonment　委付の通知，委付通知，委付申込み書

property abandonment　財産放棄

abandonment and consolidation 統廃合
◆The business tie-up does not include the firms' sales divisions or the abandonment and consolidation of refineries. 今回の業務提携に，両社の製油所の統廃合や販売部門は含まれていない.

abate （動）緩和する，軽減する，無効にする，弱まる，和らぐ，衰える，減少する，低下する

abated currency inflows　資金流入の減少

abated inflationary pressures　インフレ圧力の低下

continue on an abated decline　引き続き減少傾向にある

◆There have been no signs of a rebound in the amount of outstanding loans, which continue on an abated decline. このところ引き続き減少傾向にある銀行の貸出残高に，反転の兆しは見えない.

abatement （名）緩和，軽減，低下，減少，減価，減額，値引（き）

abatement claim　減額請求

show some abatement　低下の兆しを見せる

Abenomics （名）安倍政権の経済政策，アベノミクス
◆Benefiting from the yen's depreciation which resulted from Abenomics, the Abe administration's economic policies, the earnings environment for export-oriented companies has greatly improved. 安倍政権の経済政策「アベノミクス」による円安効果で，輸出企業の収益環境が大幅に改善した. ◆Thanks to the yen's depreciation and other tailwinds brought about by Abenomics, the latest interim financial results of many listed companies have improved. アベノミクスによる円安などの追い風で，多くの上場企業の最新中間決算は改善している.

abide by 〜に従う，〜を遵守（じゅんしゅ）する，〜を守る
◆The parties hereto agree to abide by and perform in accordance with any award rendered by the arbitrator in such arbitration proceedings. 本契約当事者は，上記の仲裁手続きで仲裁人が下した判断を遵守し，その判断に従って履行することに同意する.

abolish （動）廃止する，撤廃する（scrap），放棄する，廃絶する，解散する

abolish minimum commissions　最低手数料を廃止する

abolish the holding companies　持ち株会社を解散する

abolish tariffs 関税を撤廃する
◆Prime Minister Abe said that at a summit meeting with U.S. President Barack Obama, the two leaders confirmed abolishing tariffs on all items was not a prerequisite for joining the TPP negotiations. 安倍首相は，「オバマ米大統領との首脳会談で，両首脳は全品目に対する関税の撤廃がTPP（環太平洋経済連携協定）交渉参加の前提条件ではないことを確認した」と語った.

abolition （名）廃止，撤廃，廃絶

abolition of trade barriers　貿易障壁の撤廃

gradual abolition of tariffs　関税の段階的撤廃

◆As a member country of the WTO, Moscow should first improve Russia's investment climate, including the abolition of trade barriers. 世界貿易機関（WTO）加盟国として，ロシアはまず貿易障壁の撤廃など投資環境を改善する必要がある. ◆Washington and Brussels will conditionally accept an abolition of subsidies to farmers in the United States and the EU who grow agricultural products for export. 米国や欧州連合（EU）は，それぞれ国内の輸出用農産物栽培農家に対する補助金の撤廃を条件付きで受け入れる方針だ.

above （前）〜を上回る，〜より上の，〜以上の，アバブ（形）上記の，上述の（=stated above）

above and below the exchange rate　為替相場

の上下の

above date　上記日付

above-mentioned　上記の, 前記の, 前述した, 以上の

above par（value）　額面超過, 額面以上で, 打ち歩（ぶ）で（at a premium）, 額面以上の状態, 割増し, 水準以上, オーバー・パーの

◆The express warranty stated above is in lieu of all liabilities or obligations of ABC for damages arising from or in connection with the delivery, use or performance of the licensed program. 上記の明示保証は, 許諾プログラムの引渡し, 使用または履行から生じる損害, またはこれに関連して発生する損害に対するABCの債務または責任に代わるものである。

above notification　上記通知

◆Full written notice of the purchaser's claim accompanied by a licensed surveyor's report when the quality or quantity of the products is in dispute shall be sent by registered airmail by the purchaser to the seller within 20 days after the above notification. 本製品の品質または数量について争いがある場合, 買い主は, 上記通知後20日以内に, 買い主のクレームを詳細に記載した通知書に公定鑑定人の報告書を添付して, 書留航空郵便で売り主に送付するものとする。

above right　上記権利

◆In case any dispute arises in connection with the above right, the seller reserves the right to terminate unconditionally this agreement or any further performance of this agreement at the seller's discretion. 上記権利に関して紛争が生じた場合, 売り主はその裁量で, 本契約または本契約のその後の履行を無条件で終了させる権利を留保する。

above-written　（形）上記の, 前記の, 以上の

◆We confirm our agreement to the contents of the above-written letter. 上記レターの内容に対する当方の同意を確認します。

abroad　（副）海外に, 外国に, 流布（るふ）して, 広がっている（around）, 知れ渡っている

◆As the domestic market is tapering off, the company will aggressively expand its business abroad. 国内市場が先細り状態なので, 同社は今後, 事業の海外展開を積極化する。◆Japanese companies can hedge exchange risks and improve their business image abroad through external bond financing. 日本企業は, 外債発行による資金調達で, 為替リスクを回避するとともに海外での企業イメージアップを図ることができる。◆Japan's foreign assets include investment in companies, securities, loans and savings Japanese made abroad as well as the nation's foreign reserves. 日本の対外資産には, 日本人（日本の政府・企業・個人）が海外で行った企業や有価証券に対する投資, 融資や貯蓄のほか, 日本の外貨準備高などが含まれる。◆The Chinese economy will become anemic and the world economy could suffer immense damage if China is faced with an unabated flight of capital due to speculative investments that its economic bubble has lured from abroad. 中国で, 中国のバブル景気で海外から流入した投機マネーが大量に流出したら, 中国経済は活気を失い, 世界経済は甚大なダメージを受けることになろう。

absence　（名）欠席, 不在, 欠勤, 留守, 欠如（けつじょ）, 欠乏, ないこと

absence of certain changes　変更の不存在

absence of new products　新製品の欠如

absence of registration　未登録

in the absence of　〜がないので, 〜がないときは, 〜がない場合

◆Date of marine bill of lading shall be proof of the date of shipment in the absence of the evidence to the contrary. 海上船荷証券の日付は, 反対の証拠がない場合, 船積み日の証拠となる。◆Japanese people are becoming difficult to find jobs and maintain their quality of life in the absence of competitive manufacturers at home. 競争力の高い製造業者が国内から消えたため, 日本人は雇用を求め, 生活の質を維持するのが困難になっている。

absence fee　不在補償費, 日当, アブセンス・フィー（=daily allowance）

◆ABC agrees to pay XYZ a daily absence fee in the amount of 300 United States dollars per person, or such other amount as may be mutually agreed upon between the parties. ABCは, XYZに対して1人当たり1日300米ドル, または両当事者間で別途合意する金額のアブセンス・フィーを支払うことに同意する。

absolute　（形）絶対の, 安全な, 純粋な, 無条件の, 絶対的な, 全面的な

absolute acceptance　売り申込みの無条件での承諾, 手形の単純引受け（clean acceptance）（=clear acceptance）

absolute contract　無条件契約

absolute cost advantage　費用の絶対的優位性

absolute endorsement　単純裏書き

absolute liability　絶対責任, 厳格責任, 無過失責任, 確定債務

absolute majority　絶対多数, 過半数

absolute monopoly　完全独占, 絶対独占

absolute order to pay　単純支払い指図

absolute title　絶対的権原, 無疵（むきず）の権利

absolute total loss　絶対全損, 絶対海損（=actual total loss）

in absolute terms　金額ベースで, 絶対ベースで, 絶対値で

absolute assignment［**conveyment**］　無条件譲渡

◆In life insurance, absolute assignment refers to the type of legal transfer of ownership rights that transfers complete ownership of a policy permanently. 生命保険での無条件譲渡とは、法的所有権移転の一種で、契約の全所有権を恒久的に移転することを指す。

absque （前）〜なしで（ラテン語で英語のwithoutに相当）

absque hoc これなしでは

absque injuria 法的権利の侵害なしで

A/C No. 口座番号（A/C=account）

accelerate （動）加速する, 加速させる, 促進する, 推進する, 拍車をかける
◆Hostile mergers and acquisitions have been increasing rapidly as the dissolution of cross-shareholding ties among companies accelerates. 企業間の株式持ち合い関係の解消が加速するにつれ, 敵対的M&A（企業の合併・買収）の件数は急増している。◆The decline in China's exports accelerated in February as a slump in global demand worsened. 世界的な需要冷え込みの悪化で, 中国の2月の輸出減少は加速した。◆The government's policy of ending reliance on nuclear power generation will accelerate the hollowing-out of industry and hamper nuclear power plant exports. 政府の原発ゼロ方針［原発への依存度をゼロにする政府方針］は, 産業空洞化を加速し, 原発輸出を妨げることになる。

acceleration （名）加速, 回復, 期限の利益喪失

acceleration clause［provision］ 加速条項, 期限の利益喪失条項

acceleration demand 期限前返済要求

acceleration of payment 期限の利益喪失

subjective acceleration clause 一方的に支払い条件の繰上げを認める条項

accept （動）承諾する, 受諾する, 同意する, （手形や注文などを）引き受ける, （貨物を）引き取る

accept a bill 手形を引き受ける, 手形の支払いを引き受ける

accept a bill of exchange 為替手形を引き受ける

accept a cargo 船荷を引き受ける

accept a risk 危険を引き受ける

accept an offer オファーを引き受ける［受ける, 受諾する］, 申込みを受諾する

accept such assignment and delegation 当該譲渡と委託を引き受ける

accept the goods very soon 貨物を至急受け取る
◆ABC accepts such appointment and undertakes to use its best efforts, at its own expenses, to promote the sales of the products throughout the territory at all times during the term of this agreement. ABCは当該指定を受諾し, 本契約期間中つねに, その自己負担で, 契約地域全域で本製品の販売を促進するため最善の努力をすることを約束する。◆The Exporter grants the Distributor and the Distributor accepts to be the exclusive distributor for the sale and distribution of the products of the Exporter in the defined sales territory. 輸出者は, 販売店が指定販売地域内で輸出者の製品販売の総代理店となることを認め, 販売店はこれに同意する。

accept your buying offer 貴社の買いオファーを引き受ける, 貴社の買いオファーを受諾する
◆We are glad to accept your buying offer of March 15. To confirm this business, we are sending our Sales Note No. 120. 貴社の3月15日付け買いオファーを受諾します。この成約を確認するため, 当社の売約書第120号をお送りします。

accept your offer 貴社のオファーを引き受ける, 貴社のオファーを受ける, 貴社の申込みを受諾する
◆We accept your offer subject to immediate confirmation by letter. 書簡での至急確認を条件として, 貴社のオファーを引き受けます。◆We will accept your offer if you assure us of an order for at least 1,000 pieces per quarter for one year. 1年間, 四半期ごとに最低1,000個のご確約いただければ, 貴社のオファーをお受けします。

accept your order 貴社の注文を受ける［受諾する］, 貴注文を受ける
◆We are pleased to accept your order unconditionally and are sending you our sales note. 貴社の注文を無条件で快諾し, 当社の売約書をお送りします。◆We fear that we may not accept your order as the production of these products has been suspended for some time. この製品の生産がしばらく中止となっておりますので, 貴社の注文はお受け致しかねます。

acceptable （形）承諾できる, 受諾できる, 容認できる, 引き受けられる, 受領できる, 許容範囲にある, 一般に認められている

acceptable environmental limit 環境容量

acceptable level 容認できる水準

acceptable price 受入れ可能価格, 支払い可能価格

acceptable quality 合格品質

apply an acceptable actuarial（cost）method 一般に認められている保険数理法［保険数理上の原価計算法］を適用する

be acceptable subject to May shipment 5月積みの条件なら引受け可能である
◆If you find the terms of payment acceptable, please confirm the order subject to the modifications above. この支払い条件がのめるなら, 上記の変更を条件として本注文の確認をお願いします。◆The quality and quantity of the products shall be determined by a mutually acceptable surveyor at the expense of the seller prior to loading. 本製品の品質と数量は, 売り主の費用で, 相互に受諾できる検査人が積込み前に決定するものとする。

acceptable to 〜が承諾できる, 〜が許容できる, 〜が引き受けられる, 〜が受領できる（⇒in favor［favour］of）

ACCE 4

◆The Buyer shall establish in favor of the Seller an irrevocable letter of credit issued by a first-class international bank acceptable to the Seller. 買い主は, 売り主のために, 売り主が承諾できる [同意できる] 第一級の国際銀行が発行する取消不能の信用状を開設するものとする。

acceptance （名）申込み [オファー] に対する承諾, 承認, 商品の受領, 手形の引受け, 検収

absolute acceptance 売り申込みの無条件での承諾, 手形の単純引受け (clean acceptance)

acceptance advice 引受通知, 手形引受通知書, 引受通知書

acceptance bank （手形）引受銀行

acceptance bill 引受手形

acceptance business 手形引受業務

acceptance by intervention （第三者による）手形の参加引受け (=acceptance for honor)

acceptance commission 引受手数料

acceptance credit 引受信用状

acceptance house 手形引受業者 (=merchant banker)

acceptance inspection 受入れ検査

acceptance line 手形引受限度

acceptance of an order 注文の引受け, 受注

acceptance of an order at below-cost 出血受注 (=accepting orders at a sacrifice)

acceptance of bill (of exchange) 手形引受け

acceptance of offer オファー [申込み] の受諾, 申込みの承諾

acceptance on security 担保付き手形引受け

acceptance payable 支払い手形

acceptance quality level 合格品質水準

acceptance rate 手形決済相場, 輸入決済相場 (一覧払い輸入手形の決済に適用)

acceptance receivable 受取手形

acceptance sampling 受入れ抜取り検査, 合格判定サンプリング

acceptance supra protest 引受拒絶証書作成後の参加引受け

acceptance without security 無担保手形引受け

conditional acceptance 条件付き承諾

customer's acceptance 得意先引受手形

dollar acceptance ドル貸引受け, ドル払い引受け

facultative acceptance 任意再受

letter of acceptance 承諾書, 注文請書

qualified acceptance 制限付き引受け

◆Any amounts exceeding the limits of automatic cover shall be offered to the Reinsurer for facultative acceptance. 自動再保険の適用限度を超え

る額は, 任意受再のために再保険会社に申し出るものとする。 ◆The seller shall be liable for latent defects of the products at any time after delivery to the purchaser of the products or any subsequent purchaser, notwithstanding the inspection and acceptance of the products by the purchaser or any subsequent purchaser. 売り主は, 本製品の隠れた瑕疵（かし）については, 買い主またはその後の購入者による本製品の検収にかかわらず, 本製品の買い主またはその後の購入者への引渡し後, いつでも責任を負うものとする。

acceptance testing procedures 検収試験手続き, 受入れ検査手続き, 合格判定試験手続き

◆Payment is not conditioned upon Products meeting any acceptance testing procedures Distributor may have. 支払いは, 販売店が行う受入れ検査手続きに本製品が適合することを条件とするものではない。

accepting bank 引受銀行 (=acceptance bank)

accepting house 手形引受業者 (=acceptance house, merchant banker)

access （動）接続する, 利用する, データを検索する, 閲覧する, 入手する, 参加する, 参入する, 加入する, 立ち入る, 接近する, アクセスする

access cash 資金を調達する

access external sources of cash 外部から資金調達する (=access external sources of funding, access external funding sources)

access foreign technology 海外技術を導入する

access information on ～の情報を入手する

access the capital markets 資本市場で資金を調達する, 資本市場で調達する

access the market 起債する, 市場で資金を調達する

access （名）接近, 立入り, 出入り, 通行, 通行権, 加入, 参加, 参入, 参入機会, 利用, 取得, 閲覧, アクセス

access code 暗礁番号

access to capital 資金調達, 資金調達力

access to information 情報の入手, 情報の閲覧

access to records and books of account 会計記録と会計帳簿の閲覧

access to the market 市場への参入, 市場への参入機会, 市場進出, 市場アクセス, 市場へのアクセス (=market access)

foreign access zone 輸入促進地域, FAZ

market access barriers 市場参入障壁

unauthorized access 不正アクセス

◆The United States will continue to actively address anticompetitive activity, market access barriers, and or market-distorting trade practices. ア

メリカは、非競争的行為や市場参入障壁、市場を歪める商慣行に引き続き取り組んで行く方針だ。

access for foreign rice 外国産米の輸入枠
◆In the agricultural negotiations at the World Trade Organization, Japan has been under strong pressure from rice exporters to lower import tariffs on rice and to expand access for foreign rice. 世界貿易機関（WTO）の農業交渉で日本は、コメ輸出国から、コメの輸入関税率引下げや外国産米の輸入枠拡大への強い圧力を受けている。

access to capital 資金調達, 資金調達力
◆Our plans, which require significant investments, are at risk because of limited access to capital. 大幅投資が必要な当社の計画は現在、資金調達力にも限界があるため、危機にさらされています。

access to genetic resources 生物遺伝資源の利用
◆Access to genetic resources requires prior informed consent of the country of origin. 生物遺伝資源を利用する場合は、資源原産国の文書による事前の同意・承認を得なければならない。

accident （名）事故, 偶発事故, 災難, 思いがけない出来事, 偶然, アクシデント
a serious accident 重大事故
accident beyond control 不可抗力事故
accident incidental to voyage 航海に関する事故
accident insurance 障害保険, 災害保険
accident of navigation 航海の事故
accident scene［site］ 事故現場
by accident 偶然に, 思いがけなく
nuclear accident 原子力事故, 原発事故
personal accident insurance 傷害保険
traffic personal accident insurance 交通事故傷害保険
◆The Landlord shall effect insurance by itself or have other tenants effect insurance against such accidents as aforementioned and indemnify the Tenant within the extent covered by the insurance. 「貸主」は、前記の事故などに対して自ら保険を付けるか他のテナントに保険を付けさせ、その保険でカバーされる範囲内で「借主」に損害の補償をするものとする。◆Under the Civil Aeronautics Law, the airlines of joint services must share responsibilities in terms of ensuring safety and compensation in the event of an accident. 航空法によると、共同運航の航空会社は、安全管理と事故時の補償について責任を分担しなければならない。

accommodate （動）収容する, 適合させる, 合わせる, 準備する,（金を）融通する, 用立てる,（紛争などを）調停する
accommodate a ship for transporting bulk cargo 散荷（ばらに）輸送のための船を準備する
accommodate our production schedule to yours 当社の生産計画を貴社に合わせる

accommodated party 被融通者
accommodating monetary policy 景気刺激型の金融政策
accommodating stance 緩めのスタンス

accommodation （名）融通, 融通手形, 弁護供与, 貸金, 和解, 調停, 施設, 宿泊, 宿泊施設, 適応
accommodation acceptance 融通手形引受け
accommodation acceptor 融通手形引受人
accommodation address 郵送物受領用の宛先
accommodation bill［note］ 融通手形
accommodation birth 停泊埠頭
accommodation drawer 融通手形引受人
accommodation endorsement 融通裏書
accommodation line 営業政策的引受け, 小口火災保険
accommodation maker 融通手形振出人
accommodation paper 融通手形, 融通証券
accommodation party 融通当事者, 融通署名者
financial accommodations 資金融通
official credit accommodation 公的輸出信用供与
travel and accommodation 出張費

accompanied by ～を添えて, ～を添付して（⇒authorized surveyor）
◆Full written notice of the purchaser's claim accompanied by a licensed surveyor's report when the quality or quantity of the products is in dispute shall be sent by registered airmail by the purchaser to the seller within 20 days after the above notification. 本製品の品質または数量について争いがある場合、買い主は、上記通知後20日以内に、買い主のクレームを詳細に記載した通知書に公定鑑定人の報告書を添付して、書留航空郵便で売り主に送付するものとする。

accompany （動）～に同行する, ～に同伴する, ～に重なる, ～に付随して起こる, ～と同時に起こる, ～に添える［加える］, ～に付属する
◆An increase in transactions that brokerages handle has accompanied the brisk stock market business. 証券会社が扱う取引の増加は、そのまま株式相場の盛況と重なる。

accompanying by the satisfactory proof 満足できる証拠を添えて
◆Provided that the purchaser notifies the seller of such defect, within 14 days from the date the purchaser finds such defects, in writing, accompanying by the satisfactory proof. ただし、買い主が当該瑕疵（かし）に気づいた日から14日以内に、買い主は満足できる証拠を添えて売り主に当該瑕疵の通知をするものとする。

accord （動）与える, 捧げる, ～を許す, 許容する, 容認する, 調和させる, 一致させる,（敬意などを）示す［表する］ （自動）～と一致す

る［調和する］, 〜と合う, 合意する, 同意する

accord a person respect　人に敬意を表する

accord due praise　しかるべき賞賛を与える

accord with　〜と一致する, 〜と合う, 〜と和解する

accord with reason　道理に合う

◆We have valued upon you today for the amount specified above, at sight, and ask you to accord our draft your due protection. 当社は本日, 貴社宛てに上記金額に対する一覧払い手形を振り出しましたので, この手形のお引受けをお願い致します。

accord　（名）合意, 同意, 合意書, 合意文書, 協定, 条約（treaty）, 意見の一致, 和解, 代物弁済

a basic accord　基本合意

Basel Accord　バーゼル合意, BIS規準

be in full accord with　〜と完全に一致している

conclude an investment accord　投資協定を締結する

of one's own accord　自分の判断で, 自発的に, 自ら進んで, ひとりでに

Plaza Accord　プラザ合意

production accord　生産協定

put an accord into action　合意を実行する

reach an accord　合意に達する

sign a historic accord　歴史的協定に調印する

with one accord　いっせいに, 気持ちを一つにして

◆Citigroup will buy back the auction-rate securities from investors under separate accords with the Securities and Exchange Commission and state regulators. 米シティグループは, 米証券取引委員会（SEC）や州規制当局との個々の合意に基づいて投資家から金利入札証券（ARS）を買い戻す。

account　（名）勘定, 勘定書, 計算, 計算書, 決算, 決算書, 預金, 口座, 取引関係, 取引先説明, 報告, 理由, 考慮, 重要性　（⇒at one's account, bank account）

Account to be credited with　受取人取引銀行名

accounts receivable and inventory　売掛金と在庫品

at one's account　〜の勘定で

for account of　〜の勘定で, 〜の負担で　（=for one's account）

personal account　個人用口座, パーソナル・アカウント

profit and loss accounts　損益計算書

special accounts　特別取引先

Web account　ウェブ口座

◆All payments to XYZ shall be made to the account of XYZ at a bank in the city of San Francisco designated by XYZ and shall be made in U.S. dollars. XYZに対する支払いは, すべてXYZが指定するサンフランシスコ市内のXYZの銀行口座宛てに, 米ドルで行うものとする。◆Mitsubishi UFJ Financial Group Inc. agreed to pay \$8.6 million to the Treasury Department's Office of Foreign Assets Control to settle alleged U.S. sanction violations related to the transfer of funds to client accounts in Myanmar, Iran and Cuba. 三菱UFJフィナンシャル・グループは, ミャンマーやイラン, キューバなどの顧客口座に行った送金に関して, 米国の経済制裁規制に違反した疑いで, 米財務省外国資産管理局に860万ドルの和解金を支払うことで合意した。◆With a personal account, ordering will be faster and easier. パーソナル・アカウントがありますと, 注文も速くて簡単にできます。

account for　〜を占める, 〜に達する, 説明する, 計上する, 処理する, 会計処理する

◆Because of soaring labor costs, the Japanese maker of small and midsize televisions lowered its production ratio in China that previously accounted for 90 percent of its total output. 人件費が高騰しているため, 中小型テレビを生産しているこの日本企業は, これまで総生産の9割を占めていた中国生産比率を引き下げた。◆By starting talks on a comprehensive partnership agreement, the EU and the United States will take the first step toward creating a giant free trade zone that would account for about 50 percent of the world's gross domestic product. 包括的連携協定の交渉を開始することで, 欧州連合（EU）と米国は, 世界のGDP（国内総生産）の5割近くを占める巨大な自由貿易圏の創設に一歩踏み出すことになる。◆Interbank trading between the U.S. dollar and the Chinese currency yuan accounts for 99.3 percent of the Shanghai foreign exchange market. 米ドルと中国の通貨・人民元の銀行間取引［銀行間為替取引］が, 上海外国為替市場の99.3%を占めている。

accounts　（名）財務書類, 財務諸表, 計算書類　（=financial statements）

accounts settlement ending in March　3月期決算

annual accounts　年次財務諸表

closing of accounts　決算　（=closing of books）

consolidated accounts　連結財務書類, 連結財務諸表（group accounts）, 連結決算

external accounts　対外収支

final accounts　決算報告書, 決算, 年次財務書類, 年次財務諸表

group accounts　グループ財務諸表, グループ財務書類, 連結財務諸表［財務書類］（=consolidated accounts）

income and expenditure accounts　収支計算書

interim accounts　中間財務諸表, 中間財務書類, 半期財務書類　（=interim financial statements, interim statements）

midyear accounts　中間決算

profit and loss accounts　損益計算書

statement of accounts　決算, 決算報告, 決算報告書
the half-year closing of fiscal 2015 accounts　2015年度中間決算
◆The revision of the firm's assumed exchange rate will translate into an additional ¥150 billion loss in its consolidated accounts for the six-month period through March 2015. 同社の想定為替レートの修正に伴って、同社の2014年度下半期(2014年10月～2015年3月)の連結決算では、追加で1,500億円の為替差損が生じることになる。

accredited representative　信認する代理人
accreditee　(名)信用受領者(信用状の受益者で、一般に輸出者が信用状の受益者となる)
accrue　(動)生じる, 発生する, 付加する, 付与する, 増加する, 計上する, 見越し計上する
accrued income taxes　未払い法人税等
accrued liabilities　未払い負債, 未払い債務, 未払い費用, 見越し負債
◆Interest shall accrue on any delinquent amounts owed by Distributor for Products at the lesser of 18% per annum, or the maximum rate permitted by applicable usury law. 利息は、販売店が負っている本製品の延滞金について発生し、年18%の利率と適用される利息制限法で認められる最高利率のうちいずれか低いほうの利率によるものとする。

accrued interest　発生済み利息, 発生利息, 未払い利息, 未収利息, 経過利息　(⇒grace period)
accrued interest receivable　未収利息
accrued interest thereon　その発生利息, その経過利息
◆If ABC defaults in the performance of any term, condition or agreement contained in this loan agreement, the Lender may by notice to ABC, declare the Loan together with all accrued interest to be forthwith due and payable. ABCが本融資契約に定めるいずれかの条項、条件または合意事項の履行を怠った場合、貸主は、ABCに通知して、本融資金[貸付け金]とそのすべての発生利息について即時支払い[返済]義務を宣言することができる。

acknowledge　(動)認める, 確認する, 同意する, 承諾する
acknowledge and agree that　～を確認しこれに同意する、～を認めこれに同意する
acknowledge and agree to　～を確認し同意する、～することを認めこれに同意する
Acknowledged and agreed to:　上記を確認し、これに同意する。
◆No orders shall be binding unless acknowledged by the seller. どんな注文も、売り主が承諾しなければ拘束力がないものとする。

acquire　(動)取得する, 購入する(buy, purchase), 導入する, 引き受ける, 買収する, 身に付ける, 培う(つちか)う
(⇒cash tender offer, obligation of secrecy)
acquire a stake in　～の株式を取得する、～に出資する
acquire and learn skills and knowledge　技術と専門知識を取得・修得する
acquire capital in　～に資本参加する
acquire full ownership　完全子会社にする
◆Chinese companies are looking to enhance the value of their products in the market by acquiring Japan's state-of-the-art technology and brand names. 中国企業は、日本の先端技術やブランド力を得て、市場での自社製品の価値を高めようとしている。◆Ripplewood Holdings will use the fund to acquire Japan Telecom's shares from Japan Telecom Holdings Co., Japan Telecom's holding company. リップルウッド・ホールディングスは、その資金を使って、日本テレコムの持ち株会社「日本テレコム・ホールディングス」から日本テレコムの株式を取得する。◆Sanyo Electric Co.'s unprofitable businesses including production of solar power generation panels and lithium-ion batteries were acquired for about ¥670 billion by Panasonic Corp. 三洋電機の太陽電池パネルやリチウムイオン電池の生産などの不採算事業を、パナソニックが約6,700億円で買収した。◆The company acquired six firms via a share swap in 2008. 同社は、2008年に株式交換で六つの会社を買収した。◆Toshiba will be given priority in negotiations for the right to acquire Westinghouse, British Nuclear Fuels PLC's U.S. nuclear power plant arm. 東芝に、ウェスチングハウス(英核燃料会社の米原発子会社)買収権獲得のための優先交渉権が与えられることになった。

acquired　(形)既得の, 獲得した, 入手した, 取得した, 買収した, 取得された, 買収された, 後天的な
acquired business　買収した事業
acquired firm[company]　被取得企業, 被買収会社
acquired right　既得権
acquired surplus　獲得剰余金

acquirer　(名)買収会社, 買収企業, 取得者, 購入者, 買取り手
corporate acquirer　企業買収者, 買収企業
friendly acquirer　友好的買収者
hostile acquirer　敵対的買収者
potential acquirer　買収者候補
would-be acquirer　買収希望者, 買収側
◆A "white knight" is a friendly acquirer sought by the target of an unfriendly takeover. 「ホワイト・ナイト」とは、非友好的買収の標的企業が探し求める友好的買収者をいう。◆Many of listed companies are set to adopt measures to counter corporate acquirers, such as increasing their authorized capital or reducing the quorum of directors. 授権資本(株式発行可能枠)の拡大や取締

役の定数削減など、買取防衛策を導入する上場企業も多い。◆The three steelmakers are considering preventing acquirers from using the acquired company's non-shared patents without the other two firms' permission. 鉄鋼3社は、他の2社の許可がなければ、相互利用の対象となっていない買収された会社の特許を買収者が使えないようにすることも検討している。

acquisition (名) 取得, 獲得, 習得, 購入, 買取り, 買付け, 買収 (takeover), 企業取得, 企業買収, 事業買収, 購入所蔵品, 新収集品

acquisition cost　買収コスト, 取得原価

acquisition date　取得日　(=date of acquisition)

acquisition group　買収グループ

acquisition of business　企業買収 (=business acquisition)

acquisition of competitors　競争相手の買収

acquisition of foreign assets　海外資産の買収

acquisition offer　買収の申込み, 買収提案

acquisition plan [planning]　買収計画

acquisition price　取得価格, 買付け価格, 取得原価, 買収価格

acquisition strategy　買収戦略

acquisition talks　買収交渉

acquisition value　取得価格, 取得価額

add-on acquisition　既存事業拡大のための企業買収, アドオン型企業買収

climate for acquisition　買収の条件

debt-financed acquisition　外部負債による買収

diversification via acquisition　買収による多角化

finance an acquisition　企業買収の資金を調達する　(=fund an acquisition)

friendly acquisition　友好的買収

high-leverage acquisition　多額の借入れを伴う買収, 多額の借入れによる買収

high-yield funded acquisition　高利回り債による買収

hostile acquisition　敵対的買収

international acquisition　海外企業買収

launch a frenetic acquisition binge　買収路線をひた走る

major acquisition　大型買収 (=significant acquisition)

make an acquisition　買収を行う, 買収する

merger and acquisition　企業買収, M&A

neutral acquisition　中立的買収

pursue disastrous acquisitions　危険な買収に突っ走る

significant acquisition　大型買収

stock acquisition　株式取得 (=share acquisition)

strategic acquisition　戦略的企業買収

undertake a large acquisition　大型買収に乗り出す

◆Nonmonetary balance sheet items and corresponding income statement items are translated at rates in effect at the time of acquisition. 貸借対照表の非貨幣性項目とこれに対応する損益計算書項目は、取得日の為替レートで換算されています。◆Suntory Holdings Ltd. is expected to use about ¥500 billion in estimated proceeds from the listing of its beverage and food unit to finance mergers and acquisitions abroad. サントリーホールディングスは、清涼飲料・食品子会社の上場により推定で5,000億円程度の資金を調達して、海外企業の買収に充てる見込みだ。◆We make an acquisition when that seems to be the most effective way to take advantage of a particular market opportunity to further our growth goals. 当社が企業を買収するのは、特定の市場機会を利用して当社の成長目標を推進するうえで、それがいちばん効果的な方法であると思われるときです。

act (動) 行動する, 行動を起こす, 動く, 活動する, 取り組む, 決定する, 決議する, 役割を果たす, 作用する, 効果を発揮する, 出演する, 舞台に立つ, 演技する, 演じる

◆An improving trade deficit can act to boost the economy. 貿易赤字の改善は、景気浮揚の一因になる可能性がある。◆If Japan is acting weak in currency intervention, speculators will try to capitalize on that. 日本が為替介入に弱腰なら、投機筋に付け込まれることになる。◆The board of directors may act at a meeting at which a quorum is present by the affirmative vote of a majority of those present at such meeting. 取締役会は、定足数の取締役が出席した会議で、出席取締役の過半数の賛成投票により決議することができる。

act (名) 作為, 行為, 行動, 法律, 条令, 制定法　(⇒trade act)

Act Against Unfair Competition　不正競争防止法

act and omission　作為・不作為

act of bankruptcy　破産行為

act of fraud or dishonesty　詐欺行為または不正行為, 詐欺または不正行為

act of indemnity　免責法

act of insolvency　（銀行の）支払い不能状態を示す行為（手形の支払い拒絶や預金の払戻し拒否など）

act of law　法の作用, 裁判所の行為

act of providence　神の行為, 不可抗力, 自然現象　(=act of God)

act of public enemies　内乱

act of sale　（公式の）売買記録

acts of destruction　破壊行為

acts or omission of any government 政府の作為もしくは不作為

Community Reinvestment Act 地域社会再投資法

Consumer Credit Protection Act 消費者信用保護法

Export Administration Act 米国の輸出管理法

illegal act 不法行為

Restrictive Trade Practices Act 制限的取引慣行法

Section 301 of the Trade Act of 1974 （1974年）米通商法301条，スーパー301条

Uniform Sales Act 統一売買法

◆ABC's obligation under this Article shall not apply to any information relating to the licensed products that is or becomes available without restriction to the general public by acts not attributable to ABC or its employees. 本条に基づくABCの義務は、ABCまたはその従業員が引き起こしたと考えることができない行為によって一般公衆に制限なく知られている、または知られるようになった許諾製品に関する情報には適用されないものとする。 ◆Some Japanese-affiliated companies and Japanese restaurants have been forced to suspend their factory operations or close their outlets due to the acts of destruction by Chinese demonstrators. 一部の日系企業や日本料理店は、中国のデモ隊による破壊行為で、工場の操業停止や店舗の休業に追い込まれている。

act as ～を務める[勤める]，～として働く，～として行為する （⇒agent）

◆Distributor desires to act as an independent distributor of Products under the terms and conditions set forth herein. 販売店は、本契約書に記載する条件に従って本製品［契約品］の独立した販売店になることを希望している。 ◆The third arbitrator shall act as the chairman of the arbitration panel. 第三仲裁人が、仲裁機関の議長を務めるものとする。

act [Act] of God 天災，不可抗力，天変地異 （⇒force majeure clause）

◆If performance of this agreement is interfered with, for any length of time, by an Act of God, war, civil commotion, epidemics, or other similar occurrences which are beyond the control of either party, neither party shall be held responsible for non-performance of this agreement for such length of time. 本契約の履行が天災、戦争、動乱（内乱）、流行病や各当事者が支配できないその他の同種の事態で一定期間妨げられた場合、当該期間の本契約の不履行に関しては、いずれの当事者も責任を負わないものとする。

act or failure to act 作為または不作為

◆The confidential information shall not include information which is or becomes generally known or available through no act or failure to act by ABC. この秘密情報は、公知であるか一般に入手することができる情報、またはABCの作為

または不作為によらずに公知となるか一般に入手することができる情報を含まないものとする。

act or omission 作為または不作為 （⇒representation）

◆ABC shall not be liable for any representation, act or omission of XYZ. ABCは、XYZの表明、作為または不作為については責任を負わないものとする。

action （名）訴訟（suit），訴え，行政上の処分，決議，決定，裁判の判決，行為，行動，活動，措置，対抗措置 （⇒appropriate action, belong to）

action number 訴訟番号

action or inaction of governmental, civil or military authorities 政府・文民・軍当局の作為または不作為

all rights of action すべての提訴権

◆ABC releases XYZ, subsidiaries and affiliates of XYZ, and all purchasers, licensees and users of the Software, from all claims, demands, and rights of action which ABC may have on account of any infringement or alleged infringement of the copyrights by manufacture, use, sale or other disposition of the Software. 本ソフトウエアの製造、使用、販売または他の取扱による著作権の侵害または侵害の申立てによってABCが持ち得るすべての請求権、要求および提訴権から、ABCは、XYZとその子会社および関連会社と、本ソフトウエアのすべての購入者、ライセンシーとユーザーを開放する。 ◆ABC shall have the sole right to conduct or defend any action relating to the Trademarks set forth above. ABCは、上記商標に関する訴訟を起こすまたは防御する単独の権利を持つものとする。 ◆The following actions require the unanimous written approval of all the shareholders of the new company. 次の決議は、新会社の全株主の書面による全員一致の承認を必要とする。 ◆The guarantor hereby waives, and agrees not to assert by way of motion as a defence or otherwise, in a suit, action or proceeding pursuant to this guarantee, any claim that this guarantee or the subject matter hereof may not be enforced in or by such courts. 保証人は、本保証書に従う訴訟、裁判または手続き［訴訟または訴訟手続き］で、抗弁として申し立てることによりまたは他の方法により、本保証書またはその主題を上記裁判所でまたはその裁判所が強制することはできないとの主張をここに放棄し、これを主張しないことに同意する。 ◆The licensor will, to the extent it considers necessary, take at its expense all appropriate actions. ライセンサーは、ライセンサーが必要と判断する範囲で、すべての適切な対抗措置をライセンサーの費用で取るものとする。 ◆We may not have to add that we do not hold ourselves responsible for the corresponding delay in shipment if your actions should not be taken in time. 言うまでもなく［申すまでもなく］、貴社の打つ手が遅れたら、それに伴って生じる船積みの遅延に対して、当社は責任を負いません。

ACTI　　　　　　　　10

action or proceedings　訴訟または法的手続き
◆The parties, and each party of them, hereby consent to and confer nonexclusive jurisdiction upon any court in the State of New York over any action or proceedings arising out of or relating to this agreement. 全当事者および各当事者は、本契約からまたは本契約に関して発生する訴訟または法的手続きについては、すべて本契約によりニューヨーク州内裁判所の非専属管轄権に服するものとする。

action, suit or proceeding　訴訟または法的手続き（actionもsuitも「訴訟」という意味）
◆There is no action, suit or proceeding to which the Company is a party（either as a plaintiff or defendant）pending before any court or government agency. 対象会社が当事者（原告か被告かは問わない）となって裁判所または行政庁で継続している訴訟や法的手続きは、存在しない。

activity　（名）活動, 動き, 働き, 活動範囲, 活動度, 操業, 事業, 業務, 業務活動, 取引, 活気, 活況, 景気, 好景気
acquisition activities　企業買収活動
business activities　事業活動
commercial activities　商業活動, 営業活動
core activities　中核事業, 主力事業
　（=main activities）
economic activity　経済活動, 景気, 経済動向
financing activities　財務活動, 資金調達活動, 金融活動, 資金調達と返済に関する活動
hedging activities　ヘッジ取引
investing activities　投資活動
marketing activities　マーケティング活動
operating activities　営業活動
pick-up in activity　景気回復
production activity　生産活動
sales activities　販売活動
statement of activity　営業報告書, 活動報告書
trading activities　業務展開
◆Falling activity in the biggest economies of the eurozone could lead to a technical recession. ユーロ圏最大の経済国（ドイツやフランス、イギリス）の景気低迷［景気減速］は、定義上の景気後退［2四半期連続のマイナス成長］につながる可能性がある。

actual damages　実損額, 現実的損害賠償, 現実的損害賠償金
◆In the event of the breach of this agreement by the seller, the limit of the seller's liability shall be for the actual damages directly sustained by the purchaser from such breach. 売り主が本契約に違反した場合、売り主の責任限度は、買い主が当該違反から直接被った実損額とする。

actual demand　実需
◆Service charges or tax on crude oil futures trading should be raised to curb the inflow of specu-

lative money not related to actual demand. 実需に関係ない投機マネーの流入を抑えるため、原油先物取引の手数料の引上げや課税強化をすべきだ。

actual number of days elapsed　実際に経過した日数
◆The borrower shall pay to the lender an interest on the loan for each interest payment period applicable to the loan at the floating rate of the LIBOR（British Bankers Association Interest Settlement Rate in U.S. Dollars）plus 1.625 percent per annum, calculated on the basis of actual number of days elapsed and a year of 360 days. 借主は、1年を360日として実際に経過した日数に基づいて計算した、ロンドン銀行間取引金利（米ドルでの英国銀行協会金利決済レート）に年1.625%を加算した変動金利で、この借入れに適用される各利払い期間の借入金の利息を貸主に対して支払うものとする。

actual payment date　実際の払込み日, 実際の支払い日
◆If the buyer fails to pay any amount under this agreement when due, the buyer shall be liable to pay to the seller overdue interest on such unpaid amount from the due date until the actual payment date at the rate of 15% per annum. 買い主が支払い期日に本契約に基づく代金の支払いを怠った場合、買い主は、支払い期日から実際の払込み日までの当該未払い金額に対する年率15%の遅延金利を、売り主に支払わなければならない。

add　（動）加える, 追加する, 加算する, 合計する, 付加する, 付け加える, 増す, 強化する, 高める, 押し上げる
◆The price of regular gas has gone up for six weeks because oil wholesalers have added their import costs, which have been going up due to the weak yen since the end of last year, to the retail price. レギュラー・ガソリンの価格は、昨年末からの円安で上昇している輸入費用の増加分を元売り各社が小売価格に転嫁しているため、6週間連続で上昇した。

added value　付加価値
◆To increase exports, Japanese manufacturers must develop attractive products of high added value and find ways to capitalize on growing markets in the emerging economies of Asia and other regions. 輸出を拡大するには、日本の製造業各社が、付加価値の高い魅力的な商品を開発して、アジアなどの地域の新興国の成長市場を積極的に取り込む方法を見つける必要がある。

addendum　（名）追加契約, 追加条項, 契約書の別紙, 付属書類, 添付書類, 補遺, 付録, 増補（複数形＝addenda）
◆The Company agrees to cede to the Reinsurer such shares of all insurances covered by this Agreement as are set forth in the annexes（Schedule and any Addenda）to this Agreement. 元受会社は、本協定対象の全保険のうち、本協定の補遺（特別条項や追加条項）に明記した部分を再保険会社に出再することに合意する。

ADOP

additional royalty 追加ロイヤルティ, 追加のロイヤルティ
◆Licensee shall have a right to use such development or improvement of the proprietary information made and disclosed by Licensor without payment of any additional royalty. ライセンシーは、ライセンサーが開発して開示した専有情報の開発または改良版を、追加ロイヤルティを支払わないで使用する権利を持つものとする。

adherence (名)遵守[順守], 固守
◆The failure of either party to insist upon strict adherence to any terms or conditions of this agreement on any occasion shall not be considered a waiver of any right thereafter to insist upon strict adherence to that term or condition or any other term or condition of this agreement. いずれかの機会に当事者の一方が本契約の条件または条項の厳格な順守を要求しなくても、これは本契約の当該条件・条項または他の条件・条項の厳格な順守を要求するその後の権利を放棄したとは見なされないものとする。

adjudicate (動)宣告する, 判決を下す
be adjudicated bankrupt 破産宣告を受ける
(=be adjudicated a bankrupt)

adjudication (名)破産宣告

adjustment (名)調整, 修正, 整理, 処理, 清算, 査定, 損害査定, 共同海損清算, 調停, 決算整理, 期末整理
bunker adjustment factor バンカー課徴金, BAF (=bunker surcharge: 燃料費割増料)
currency adjustment factor 通貨変動課徴金, CAF (海上運賃に加算して徴収される割増料)
◆Such adjustment shall be made prior to the payment by ABC of such tax. この調整は、ABCが当該税金を納付する前に行うものとする。◆The prices stated in this agreement shall not be subject to any adjustment on account of increase or decrease in costs of materials or labor by reason of severe shortage or oversupply thereof or substantial change in exchange rate or market. 本契約書に記載する価格は、原材料または労働力の深刻な過不足による当該コストの増減または為替レートもしくは市場の大幅な変動を理由にした調整は行わないものとする。

administration (名)経営, 経営管理, 経営陣, 理事会, 執行部, 管理, 運営, 運用, 統括, 監督, 事務, 事務管理, 業務, 執行, 執務, 実行, 実施, 政権, 政府, 行政, 政府部局, 行政当局, 政権運営, 政権担当期間, 任期, 投薬, 投与, 治療
import administration 輸入管理
the Bureau of Export Administration (米商務省の)輸出管理局
the Farmers Home Administration 農業住宅局
the Federal Housing Administration 米連邦住宅局

the Food and Drug Administration 米国食品医薬局
the General Services Administration 調達庁
the International Trade Administration (米商務省の)国際貿易局
◆Before the G-20 meeting, representatives from emerging economies expressed concern that the Abe administration's economic policy dubbed as Abenomics, which involves bold monetary easing and an active fiscal stimulus package, is aimed at the depreciation of the yen. G20(主要20か国・地域)会議前に、新興国の代表らは、「大胆な金融緩和や積極的な財政出動を含む安倍政権の経済政策「アベノミクス」は、円安誘導ではないか」との懸念を表明していた。◆Egypt's Morsi administration has concluded a basic agreement with the IMF on loans totaling $4.8 billion, with strings attached, in an effort to avert a default on debts. エジプトのモルシ政権は、債務不履行を回避するため、付帯条件付きで、国際通貨基金(IMF)との間で総額48億ドルの融資を受けることで基本合意した。

administrative complaint FTCの審判開始決定書

administrator (名)遺産管理人, 管理者, 保全管理人, 管財人

admission of infringement of the copyrights 著作権侵害を認めること
◆The execution of this agreement shall in no way constitute an admission of infringement by ABC of the Copyrights or its liability. 本契約の締結は、どんな意味でも、ABCによる本著作権の侵害またはその責任を認めることにはならないものとする。

admission of liability 責任を認めること

admit (動)認める, 承認する, 資格を付与する, 許可する, 許容する, 自白する

adopt (動)採用する, 採択する, 決定する, 決める, 導入する, 選出する, 指名する
◆Under the revised Commercial Code, only large companies with capital of more than ¥500 million would be qualified to adopt the U.S.-style board structure. 今回の商法改正では、資本金5億円以上の大企業だけが米国型の取締役会制度を導入することができる。

adopt a road map toward ～の工程表を採択する
◆Leaders of the Asia-Pacific Economic Cooperation forum adopted a road map toward an envisioned regional free trade area which would cover about 60 percent of the world economy. アジア太平洋経済協力会議(APEC)の各国首脳は、世界経済の6割をカバーする地域自由貿易圏構想の工程表を採択した。

adopt global safety criteria for ～の国際安全基準を採用する
◆The ISO, a private organization that sets international standards for industrial products, will adopt Japan-led global safety criteria for

nursing-care robots. 工業製品の国際規格を定める民間組織の「国際標準化機構 (ISO)」は、日本政府が主導する介護ロボットの国際安全基準を採用する方針だ。

adopt measures　対策を講じる
◆Since the poisoned gyoza case came to light in 2008, some Japanese companies in China have adopted measures to prevent toxic substances from contaminating their products by setting up security cameras at their factories and requiring workers to wear pocketless working uniforms. ギョウザ中毒事件が2008年に発覚して以来、中国に進出している日系企業の一部は、工場に防犯カメラを設置したり社員にポケットのない作業服の着用を義務付けたりして、製品への有害物質の混入を防ぐ対策を講じている。

ADR　代替的紛争解決手段
（⇒alternative dispute resolution）

advance　(動) 前払いする, 前貸しする, 立て替える, 貸し付ける, 融資する, 資金を提供する
◆The loan shall be advanced by the lender to the borrower wholly or partially in an amount of ten million Japanese Yen（￥10,000,000）or its integral multiple upon request by the borrower. 貸付け金は、貸主の要請に基づき、貸主が借主に対してその全額または一部を1千万円またはその倍数の金額で提供する。

advance　(名) 貸付け, 貸付け金, 借入れ, 借入金, 前払い, 前払い金, 前渡し, 前渡し金, 前貸し金, 前受け金, 仮払い金, 進歩, 前進

advance pricing agreement　事前確認制度, APA（企業内取引の形で海外子会社に輸出される製品の価格について、事前に企業と税務当局が話し合っておく方法）

make a written notice in advance　予め書面で通知する

the request for advance　借入れの要請
◆Comparative advantage in this new global market depends not only on superior R&D, but also on speed in making management decisions, finding unique applications for research advances and delivering them to customers ahead of competitors. この新しいグローバル市場で比較優位性を確立できるかどうかは、高度な研究開発だけでなく、経営の意思決定を迅速に行えるかどうかと、研究を進めるうえで独創的な適用範囲［用途］を素早く確認して、それを競合他社に先駆けて製品化できるかどうかにかかっている。◆Such request shall be made by the borrower to the lender within 10 years from the date first above written by giving to the lender the request for advance in the form attached to this agreement as Exhibit B, five business days prior to the respective advance date. この要請は、本契約締結日から10年以内に、付属書類Bとして本契約書に添付する書式で借入れの要請を各借入日の5営業日前に貸主に通知して、借主が貸主に対して行うものとする。◆

The interest rate to be paid by the borrower to the lender on the loan hereunder shall be five percent（5％）per annum on the balance of the loan from time to time outstanding calculated from each respective advance date to and including the date of maturity of the loan on the basis of a 365-day year, for the actual days elapsed. 本契約に基づいて借主が貸主に対して支払う借入金の金利は、1年を365日として各借入日から借入金の返済期日まで実際に経過した日数についてそのつど計算した未決済の借入金残高について、年5％とする。

advance date　貸付け日, 融資実行日, 借入日
◆The borrower shall repay the loan in an amount of each of the individual sums to the Lender on the third anniversary date of the respective advance date. 借主は、個別の各借入金について、その各融資実行日から3年経過した日に貸主に対して返済するものとする。

advance notice　事前通告, 予告
◆The licensee shall make its records and accounts available for inspection by the licensor or its duly authorized representatives upon reasonable advance notice. ライセンシーは、(ライセンサーから) 合理的な事前の通知を受けたときは、ライセンサーまたはその正当な権限を持つ代理人の検査のためにライセンシーの記録と帳簿を提供するものとする。

advanced　(形) 進んだ, 進歩・発展した, 先端の, 最新の, 最新鋭の, 高度な, 高等の, 上級レベルの, 前渡しの, 期限前の, 繰上げの

advanced composite material　先端複合材料, 先進複合材料, ACM

Advanced Energy Projects　米政府の先端エネルギー・プロジェクト, AEP

advanced GDP figures　GDP速報値

advanced industrial economy［nation］　先進工業国（=advanced industrialized nation）

advanced information society　高度情報化社会, 高度情報社会

advanced liquid processing system　多核種除去設備, ALPS

advanced materials　新素材

Advanced Planning & Scheduling　先端的プランニング・スケジューリング・システム, APS

advanced processing　二次加工, 川下部門

advanced redemption　繰上げ償還（=early redemption）

advanced telecommunications features　先端通信機能

advanced television　高品位テレビ

advanced thermal reactor　新型転換炉, ATR
◆The most advanced market economies of Japan and the Unites States, if bound together, would put a powerful brake on protectionism. もっとも高度に進化した市場経済の日本と米国が手を結べ

ば、保護貿易主義化に強力な歯止めをかけること
になろう。

advanced country 先進国
(=advanced economy, advanced nation)
◆In light of complaints from emerging
economies that a glut of speculative funds due
to monetary easing measures taken by advanced
countries have caused the appreciation of their
currencies and asset inflation, the G-20 participants agreed that they will monitor and minimize
the negative ripple effects of their respective financial policies. 先進国の金融緩和策でだぶつい
た投機マネーが新興国の通貨高や資産インフレを
招いているという新興国の不満に配慮して、G20
参加国は、それぞれ金融政策の負の波及効果を監
視し、最小化することで合意した。

advanced technology 最新技術, 先進技術,
先端技術, 高度技術 (=high technology,
sophisticated technology, state-of-the-art
technology; ⇒intellectual property)
◆Information about advanced technologies is
sold to overseas rivals in industrial espionage,
which has become a common threat for Japanese
manufacturers. 産業スパイでは先端技術情報が海
外のライバル企業に売り渡されるので、日本のメー
カーにとって産業スパイは、共通の脅威となって
いる。

advantage (名)有利, 利点, 長所, 強み, メ
リット, 利益, 優勢, 優位, 優位性, 競争力, 優遇
措置, 好都合, アドバンテージ
comparative advantage 比較優位, 比較優位
性 (=relative advantage)
comparative location advantages 比較立地
優位
competitive advantage 競争上の優位, 比較優
位, 競争力の高まり
cost advantage コスト面での競争力
economic advantages 経済的優位
relative advantage 比較優位
take advantage of insolvency laws 支払い不能
に関する法律の恩典を受ける
trading advantage 取引上の優位性
◆Due to the IT revolution and trade liberalization, product specialization now is determined
by comparative advantages not in finished products but in work unique to each country or region in the context of global value chains. 情
報通信技術 (IT) 革命と貿易自由化で、製品の特
化は、「最終財」の比較優位ではなく、国際的価
値連鎖との関連で国・地域にそれぞれ特有の「仕
事」の比較優位で決まるようになった。◆European
automakers have launched low-interest loan and
cost-free repair campaigns by taking advantage
of the yen's strength against the euro. 欧州の自動
車メーカーは、円高ユーロ安を背景に、低金利ロー
ンや修理費無料のキャンペーンを展開している。
◆The development of cross-border infrastruc-

ture in the Greater Mekong Subregion (GMS)
has prompted a number of multinational corporations to transfer some of their manufacturing
processes to Laos, Cambodia and Myanmar to
take advantage of cheaper labor costs. 大メコン
圏での国境を越えたインフラ整備に伴い、多くの
多国籍企業が、安い人件費[低賃金]の利点を生か
して生産工程の一部をラオスやカンボジア、ミャ
ンマーに移転している。

adverse (形)逆の, 反対の, 逆向きの, 不都合
な, 不利な, 不利益な, 意に添わない, 不運な,
不幸な, 批判的な, 有害な
adverse balance 国際収支の赤字
(=adverse balance of payments)
adverse balance of trade 輸入超過, 貿易の入
超 (=adverse trade balance)
adverse budget 赤字予算
adverse economic conditions 経済情勢の悪化
adverse effect 逆効果, 不利な影響, 悪影響,
マイナス影響, 弊害, 悪材料, 逆境
(=adverse impact, negative effect)
adverse environment 厳しい環境
adverse exchange 逆為替, 下げ相場
adverse factor 悪材料
adverse selection 逆選択 (=anti-selection,
selection against insurer: 保険事故発生の可
能性が高い保険に保険契約者が進んで入り
たがる傾向や、保険会社に不利な保険の申
込みのことをいう)
adverse situation 困難な状況
be bond-adverse 債券相場に打撃を与える
be under adverse circumstances 逆境にある
adverse change 不利益を与える変更
◆Since March 31, 2010 there has not been any
material adverse change in the results of operations, financial conditions, assets, or liabilities of
the Company. 2010年3月31日以降、契約対象会社
の経営成績、財務状態、資産や負債に重大な不利
益を与える変更は生じていない。
adverse claim 反対主張, 異議申立て, 不利益
を及ぼすクレーム
adverse claims or rights 不利益を及ぼす
クレームや権利
◆Seller has good and marketable title to the
Shares, free and clear of any and all covenants,
conditions, restrictions, voting trust arrangements, liens, options and adverse claims or
rights. 売り主は、一切の約束、条件、制約、議
決権信託契約、担保権、選択権、不利益を及ぼす
クレームや権利をまったく負担しない本株式を売
買できる正当な権原を持っている。
adversely impact 悪影響を及ぼす, 悪影響
[マイナス]を与える (=adversely affect)
◆Adverse impacts on Japanese companies' business are spreading due to anti-Japan demonstrations and a campaign to boycott Japanese prod-

ucts. 反日デモや日本製品の不買運動などで、日本企業のビジネスに悪影響が広がっている。◆Currency wars will cause turmoil in global markets and adversely impact the world economy if the wars become common practice. 通貨安戦争［通貨安競争］が広がれば、世界の市場の混乱を招き、世界経済に悪影響を及ぼすことになる。

adversity （名）逆境, 困難, 災難
◆Japanese electronics makers are needed to shrug off the adversity of economic slowdowns overseas, a strongly appreciating yen, and ever-intensifying competition with foreign rivals by wielding their latent power. 日本の電機製造業各社は、底力を発揮して、海外経済の減速、超円高、海外勢との競争激化などの逆境を跳ね返す必要がある。

advertise （動）宣伝する, 広告する, 売り込む, 告知する, 公示する, 公にする, 強調する, 誇示（こじ）する, ～を際立たせる
advertise a house for sale　売家の広告をする
advertise one's wares in a newspaper　新聞で商品を宣伝する
promote and advertise　宣伝広告活動をする
the advertised sale price　広告の特価
◆ABC shall bear and pay for expenditures necessary to promote and advertise the products in accordance with the marketing and advertisement plan of ABC approved by XYZ. ABCは、XYZが承認したABCのマーケティング・宣伝計画に従って本商品の宣伝・広告を行うのに必要な費用を負担し、支払うものとする。◆Abe advertised Japan at the New York Stock Exchange by explaining that introduction of a high-speed railway system using Japan's superconducting magnetic levitation technology could connect New York and Washington in less than an hour. 安倍首相は、ニューヨーク証券取引所で、「日本の超電導リニア技術を用いた高速鉄道を導入すれば、ニューヨークとワシントンは1時間足らずで結ばれる」と説明して、日本を売り込んだ。

advertisement （名）宣伝, 広告, 宣伝広告 (=advertising)
◆All the expenses for advertisements, incidental to selling Products in Territory, shall be paid by Licensee. 契約地域内での契約品の販売に伴う宣伝広告費は、すべてライセンシーが支払う。

advertising （名）広告, 宣伝, 広告宣伝
◆Upon expiration or termination of this agreement, Distributor will immediately cease all display, advertising and use of all of Supplier's names, trademarks and logos. 本契約が満了または終了したときは、販売店は、直ちに供給者の一切の名称、商標とロゴの陳列、宣伝と使用をすべて止める。

advertising campaigns　広告キャンペーン, 広告宣伝活動
◆Samples of all promotional materials or plans of advertisements referring to the Trademarks

for intended use by the licensee shall be submitted by the licensee to the licensor for its prior approval before the commencement of the licensee's advertising campaigns to the public. ライセンシーが使用する予定の本商標にかかわるすべての販促資料の見本または広告宣伝計画書は、ライセンシーが一般公衆に対する広告宣伝活動を開始する前にライセンサーに提出して、その事前承認を受けなければならない。

advice （名）助言, 勧告, 忠告, 通知, 通知書, 案内, 案内書, 報告, 情報
acceptance advice　引受通知, 手形引受通知書, 引受通知書
acting under [on] your advice　お指図に従って
advice and pay　通知払い
advice note　通知書, 案内状, 発送通知書, 発送案内
advice of arrival　着荷通知
advice of bill [draft]　手形振出案内
advice of credit　信用状開設通知, 信用状の通知, 入金通知書
advice of delivery　引渡し案内
advice of payment　支払い通知
advice of receipt　受取通知
advice of shipment　発送通知, 船積み通知, 出荷案内 (=shipping advice)
advice sheet [slip]　手形振出案内票
credit advice　信用状の通知(書), 入金通知書
letter of advice　通知状, 荷送り通知書, 手形振出し通知書, 積み荷通知書
payment advice　支払い通知, 払い込み通知書, 保険金支払い通知書
remittance advice　送金通知書, 送金案内書
◆The credit advice reached us on June 8. 信用状の通知は、6月8日に届きました。

advisable （形）適切な, 賢明な, 得策な

advise （動）助言を与える, 忠告する, 通知する, 通告する, 知らせる, 勧告する (⇒obliged to)
be advised of　～を知らされる, ～を知る
be fully advised and informed of　～を十分知らされる, ～を十分知る
so advise　その旨通知する, その旨連絡する
◆In no event shall XYZ be liable for incidental, consequential or tort damages of any kind, including damages resulting from any loss of profits, loss of use or loss of data, even if XYZ is advised of the possibility of such damages. 逸失利益、使用の喪失またはデータの喪失により生じる損害を含めて、あらゆる種類の付随的、派生的または不法行為による損害については、たとえXYZがその損害の可能性を知らされていても、XYZは一切責任を負わないものとする。◆We are very sorry indeed to have to advise you of a delay in the ex-

ecution of your order. 貴社注文の履行が遅れたことを、お知らせしなければなりません。◆We fear we have to advise you that we may not be able to dispatch in full your order due to the shortage of shipping space. 不本意ながら、船腹不足のため、貴社の注文が一部積み残しになる可能性があることをお伝えしなければなりません。

advisory agreement アドバイザー契約

aerospace exhibition 航空宇宙展
◆A real-size cabin mock-up of the Mitsubishi Regional Jet（MRJ）was put on display at Japan International Aerospace Exhibition 2012. MRJ（三菱リージョナルジェット機）の実物大の客室模型が、2012年国際航空宇宙展で展示された。

affiliate （名）関係会社, 関連会社, 子会社, 支社, 支部, 加入者, 提携者, 参加者, アフィリエイト
　affiliate agreement アフィリエイト契約, アフィリエイト契約書
　affiliate license agreement アフィリエイト・ライセンス契約, アフィリエイト・ライセンス［契約書］
◆ABC releases XYZ, subsidiaries and affiliates of XYZ, and all purchasers, licensees and users of the Software, from all claims, demands, and rights of action which ABC may have on account of any infringement or alleged infringement of the copyrights by manufacture, use, sale or other disposition of the Software. 本ソフトウエアの製造、使用、販売または他の取扱いによる著作権の侵害または侵害の申立によってABCが持ち得るすべての請求権、要求および提訴権から、ABCは、XYZとその子会社および関連会社と、本ソフトウエアのすべての購入者、ライセンシーとユーザーを解放する。◆Affiliates can earn a 10% commission on every item sold through their websites. アフィリエイトのウェブサイトを通じて販売した商品については、アフィリエイトはすべて10%のコミッションを受け取ることができます。

affiliated company 関係会社, 関連会社, 系列会社
◆Japanese-affiliated companies operating in China will have to be aware of "China risks" such as rising production costs as well as the stronger Chinese yuan and anti-Japan riots. 中国に進出している日系企業は今後、生産コストの上昇のほか、人民元高や反日暴動などのような「中国リスク」を意識せざるを得ない。◆Some Japanese-affiliated companies and Japanese restaurants have been forced to suspend their factory operations or close their outlets due to the acts of destruction by Chinese demonstrators. 一部の日系企業や日本料理店は、中国のデモ隊による破壊行為で、工場の操業停止や店舗の休業に追い込まれている。

affiliated with 〜と提携している, 〜と資本関係がある

affirmative vote 賛成投票

◆All resolutions of the board shall be adopted by the affirmative vote of four directors. 取締役会の決議は、すべて取締役4名の賛成投票により採択するものとする。◆The board of directors may act at a meeting at which a quorum is present by the affirmative vote of a majority of those present at such meeting. 取締役会は、定足数の取締役が出席した会議で、出席取締役の過半数の賛成投票により決議することができる。

affix one's duly authenticated seal 正当に認証された社印を捺印する
◆This agreement shall become effective on the date when both parties hereto affix their duly authenticated seals. 本契約は、本契約の両当事者が正当に認証された社印を捺印した日に発効する。

affordable （形）（値段が）手頃な, 手頃な価格の, 安価な, 低コストの, 入手可能な, 買うことができる, 都合がつけられる, 負担可能な
　affordable housing 安価な住宅
　affordable quality 値段が手頃で［安価で］質が高いこと
　at affordable prices 手ごろな値段で
◆A prerequisite for the continued existence of industry in Japan is an affordable and stable supply of high-quality electricity. 日本の産業が生き残るための必要条件として、良質な電力の安価で安定した供給が挙げられる。

aforementioned （形）前述の, 前記の, 上述した, 上記の
◆The Landlord shall effect insurance by itself or have other tenants effect insurance against such accidents as aforementioned and indemnify the Tenant within the extent covered by the insurance. 「貸主」は、前記の事故などに対して自ら保険を付けるか他のテナントに保険を付けさせ、その保険でカバーされる範囲内で「借主」に損害の補償をするものとする。

after execution of this agreement 本契約締結後, 本契約の締結以降
◆As promptly as practicable after execution of this agreement, Supplier shall provide Distributor with information, materials, manuals and other technical documents necessary to enable Distributor to perform its obligations under this agreement. 本契約締結後できるだけ速やかに、供給者は、販売店が本契約に基づく販売店の義務を履行するのに必要な情報、資料、マニュアル、その他の技術文書を、販売店に提供しなければならない。

after receipt of 〜の受領後
　after receipt of a written notice specifying the default （債務・契約の）当該不履行を明記した書面による通知を受領した後, （債務・契約の）不履行を明記した通知書の受領後
　after the execution of this agreement 本契約締結後
◆If within 30 days after receipt of said notice the defaulting or breaching party cures the said de-

fault or breach, then said notice shall not be effective. 不履行当事者または違反当事者が上記通知の受領後30日以内に当該不履行または違反を改めた場合、当該通知は効力を生じないものとする。

against （前）対 (=versus)，〜に対して，〜と交換に，〜と引換えに，〜に不利な，〜に比べて （⇒endorsement）

against all risks　全危険担保 （=AAR, all risks）

against your paying our draft　貴社による当社手形の支払いと引き換えに

cash against documents　書類引換渡し，船積み書類引換現金渡し，CAD

delivery against B/L　船荷証券引換渡し

documents against acceptance　手形引受渡し，手形引受書類渡し，引受渡し，引受渡し条件，D/A

documents against payment　代金引替え書類渡し，手形支払い（書類）渡し，支払い渡し，支払い渡し条件，D/P

negotiable against a draft at sight signed by　〜が振り出した一覧払い手形と引換えに買い取られる

supply against remittance upon arrival of goods with 1% discount　着払い送金ベース1％引きで供給する

◆During the period when Products are in the custody of ABC, ABC shall keep Products insured at ABC's account for the benefit of XYZ against loss or damage by fire, theft or otherwise with extended coverage. 本製品［契約品］をABCが保管している期間中、火災、盗難、その他による滅失や損害を拡張担保するため、ABCはその勘定で、XYZを保険金受取人として本製品に付保するものとする。◆Since electronic money requires safeguards against unauthorized use and counterfeiting, encryption technology, on the software side, and IC cards, on the hardware side, represent essential technologies. 電子マネーには不正使用や変造を防ぐ技術が必要で、ソフト面では暗号化技術、ハード面ではICカードが、その代表的な技術とされている。◆The letter of credit set forth above shall be negotiable against a draft at sight signed by the seller upon the presentation of the following documents: 上記の信用状は、次の船積み書類の提示がある場合には、売り主が振り出した一覧払い手形と引換えに買い取られるものとする。◆To ensure fair international commercial trade, the law against unfair competition stipulates that both individuals involved in bribery and the corporations they belong to should be punished. 公正な国際商取引を確保するため、不正競争防止法には、贈賄（外国公務員への贈賄）に関与した個人と法人を罰する規定（両罰規定）がある。

agency （名）代理，代理権，代理行為，代理業，代理店，代理関係，行政機関，行動，行為，作用，働き，仲介，世話

advertising agency　広告代理店，広告代理業

affiliated advertising agency　専属広告代理店

affiliated agency　提携代理店

agency commission　代理店手数料

agency contract　代理店契約

agency relationships　代理店契約

exclusive selling agency　一手販売代理店

general agency　総代理店

granting agency　認可機関

hold agency for　〜の代理をする，〜の代理店をする

human agency　人間の行為

maker's export agency　輸出代理店

paying and conversion agency agreement　支払い・転換代理契約

principal paying agency agreement　主支払い代理人契約

secure agency　代理権を獲得する

sole selling agency　一手販売代理店

special advertising agency　特殊広告代理店

undertake exclusive agency for　〜の代理業を一手に引き受ける

◆Distributor is an independent contractor and is not the legal representative or agent of Supplier for any purpose. 販売店は独立した契約当事者であり、どんな目的であれ供給者の法律上の代表者または代理人ではない。◆Distributor shall not be given any agency, express or implied, by Company for any purpose whatsoever. 代理店に対して、会社は明示・黙示を問わずどんな目的であれいかなる代理権も付与しないものとする。

agency relationship　代理関係

◆This agreement shall not create a partnership or agency relationship among the parties hereto. 本契約は、本契約当事者間にパートナーシップまたは代理関係を創設するものではない。

agent （名）代理店，代理人，代行業者，仲介業者，斡旋業者，担当者，保険外交員，セールスマン，捜査官，工作員，手先，スパイ，諜報機関員，情報機関員，主因，動因，要因，因子，作用因子，作用物質，作用薬，試薬，薬剤，〜剤，エージェント

a buying［purchasing］agent　買付け代理人，買付け代理店

a commission agent　委託販売人，問屋

a forwarding agent　運送店，運送業者，海運業者

a general agent　総代理人，総代理店

a house agent　不動産業者

a land agent　土地周旋業者

a landing agent　陸揚げ代理人，陸揚げ代行業者

a listing agent　上場代理人

a literary agent　著作者代理人

a mercantile agent　商事代理人
a nonexclusive agent　非独占的代理店
a personal agent　購買代理店企業
a process agent　送達受取人
a purchase agent　買入れ代理人
a real estate agent　不動産業者
　(=an estate agent)
a remarketing agent　再販売代理人
a revenue agent　税務当局
a sales agent　販売代理人
a security agent　受託行, 担保管理人
a selling agent　売込み代理店, 販売代理店
a shipping agent　回漕業者, 海運業者, 船積み代行業者
a sole agent　総代理店
a transfer agent　名義書換え代理人
a travel agent　旅行代理店, 旅行案内業者, 旅行業者
a universal agent　総代理店
an ad [advertising, publicity] agent　広告代理店
an agent bank　幹事銀行, エージェント行
　(=lead bank, lead manager)
an exclusive agent　一手販売代理店, 専属特約店, 独占的代理店, 専売代理店
an exclusive exporter's selling [buying] agent　輸入総代理店
an exclusive selling agent　一手販売代理店
an FBI agent　FBI (米連邦捜査局) 捜査官
an insurance agent　保険外交員
an intelligent agent　情報の代理人
principal obligations of the agent　代理店の基本的義務
　◆The company is not entitled to act as XYZ's agent except as provided in this agreement.　同社は, 本契約で規定する場合を除いて, XYZの代理人として行為する権利を持たない。　◆The firm acted as an agent between U.S. pork exporters and Japanese importers.　同社は, 米国の豚肉輸出業者と日本の輸入業者の仲介をしていた。

aggregate amount　総額, 合計額
　◆In case the aggregate amount of the net wholesale price during any contract year exceeds ＿＿＿＿ United States dollars, Licensee shall pay to Licensor an additional running royalty of 4 percent of the aggregate amount of the net wholesale price of the licensed products as set forth below;　契約年度中の純卸売り販売額の合計額が＿＿＿米ドルを超えた場合, ライセンシーは, 追加のランニング・ロイヤルティとして許諾製品の純卸売り販売額の合計額の4%を下記のとおりライセンサーに支払うものとする。

agree　(動) 同意する, 合意する, 合意に達する, 承認する, 承諾する, 賛成する
as agreed　合意に従って
effectively agree to conclude an accord　協定の締結で実質合意する
It is hereby agreed that　ここに〜することに合意する
　◆Commodity loans are used to import commodities such as industrial machinery, industrial raw materials, fertilizer, agricultural chemicals and machinery, and other various kinds of machinery, which are agreed upon beforehand between the Japanese and recipient governments.　商品借款は, 日本政府と借入国政府が前もって合意した商品 (工業資本財 [工業用機械], 工業用原材料, 肥料・農薬, 農機具, 各種機械など) の輸入のために使用される。　◆Six executives of Kobe Steel Ltd. agreed in an out-of-court settlement to pay back ￥310 million to the company.　神戸製鋼の幹部6人が, 示談による和解で3億1,000万円を会社に返済することで合意した。　◆The parties hereby agree that any disputes arising out of this agreement shall be brought to before the Tokyo District Court of Japan for the first instance.　本契約により両当事者は, 本契約から生じる紛争はすべて日本の東京地方裁判所を第一審の管轄とすることに合意する。

agree in writing　書面で同意する
　◆A party hereto may sell all or any portion of the shares of the new company then owned by it to a third party only on condition that such purchaser agrees in writing, concurrently with such sale, to be fully bound by the terms and conditions of this agreement.　本契約当事者は, 当該当事者がその時点で保有する新会社の株式の全部または一部を第三者に売却することができる。ただし, これは, 当該購入者が売買時に本契約の条件に全面的に拘束されることに書面で同意した場合にかぎる。

agree to　〜することに合意する, 〜することに同意する
　◆Takeda Chemical Industries Ltd. and Kirin Brewery Co. have agreed to join in developing next-generation medicines, including anticancer drugs.　武田薬品工業とキリンビールが, 制がん剤など次世代新薬の開発で提携することで合意した。

agreed　(形) 同意した, 合意した, (合意して) 決めた, 協定した, 所定の, 納得して, 意見が一致した
agreed between the parties hereto　本契約当事者が合意する
agreed between the parties in writing　契約当事者が書面で合意する, 当事者が書面で合意する
agreed charges　約定料金, 協定料金
agreed insured value　協定保険価額, 保険評価額
agreed price range　協定価格帯
agreed upon between the parties in writing　契約当事者が書面で合意する, 当事者が書面

で合意する

agreed-upon limits　約定基準

agreed-upon rate　約定金利

agreed value　協定価格, 約定［協定］保険価額, 保険評価額

agreed value insurance　協定価格保険

an agreed amount　協定金額

an agreed bid［takeover］　合意による株式公開買付け

an agreed range　所定の変動幅

be agreed on　～で意見がまとまっている［一致している］, ～で同意見である

international agreed specialization　合意的国際分業

the agreed date　決めた日にち, 解禁日

the agreed rate　協定率

the agreed time　決めた時間

◆An employment agreement in the past became toothless due to the practice of "aotagai" (green harvest) which refers to starting recruiting activities earlier than the agreed date. かつての就職協定は, 就職活動の解禁日より早く就活を開始する「青田買い」の慣行で, 骨抜きになった。

agreement　(名)契約, 契約書, 同意, 同意書, 合意, 合意事項, 合意内容, 合意書, 協定, 協約, 規約, 取決め（契約書は, 英語でagreementまたはcontractという。その違いは, 基本的にはagreementが単なる「合意・合意書」であるのに対して, contractは約因(consideration: 契約を成立させるための理由・主要要因)を備えた合意文書を指す。英米法(英文契約書のもとになる法律)では, この約因があってはじめて法律上, 義務の履行を強制できる契約書となる, と考えられている。）

affiliate agreement　アフィリエイト契約

agency agreement　代理店契約

agreement among managers　幹事団契約

agreement for resources development　資源開発契約

agreement jurisdiction court　合意管轄裁判所

agreement of articles　基本定款

agreement of bank transactions　銀行取引約定書

agreement of general terms and conditions　一般取引条件協定書

agreement of IMF　IMF協定

agreement on commerce　通商協定

agreement on trade terms　貿易条件協定書

agreement or instrument　契約書または証書, 契約書

bank credit agreement　銀行融資枠

breach of the agreement　本契約違反

broad agreement　大筋合意, 大筋での合意

buy-sell agreement　売買契約

come to an agreement　合意に達する, 合意する

commercial agreement　商業契約書

consent agreement　同意書

consulting agreement　コンサルティング契約

contractual agreement　契約上の取決め, 契約上の規定, 契約上の責務

credit agreement　融資契約［契約書], 与信契約(書)

cross licensing agreement　クロス・ライセンス契約

currency swap agreement　通貨スワップ協定, 通貨交換協定, 通貨スワップ契約

customer agreement　顧客合意書

dealer agreement　販売店契約

debt agreement　借入契約

depositary agreement　事務委託契約

distributor agreement　販売総代理店契約(書), 販売店契約, 販売店［輸入代理店］契約

double taxation agreement　二重課税防止条約

draft agreement　契約案文

draw up an agreement　契約書を作成する

employment agreement　雇用契約

enter into an agreement　契約を結ぶ, 契約を締結する

exchange a written agreement　合意文書を取り交わす

exchange clearing agreement　為替清算協定

financing agreement　借入契約

General Agreement on Tariffs and Trade　関税と貿易に関する一般協定, ガット, GATT

international agreement　国際協定, 国際合意

international commodity agreement　国際商品協定

International Foreign Exchange Master agreement　国際外国為替標準契約

joint venture agreement　合弁事業契約

license agreement　使用許諾契約, 実施権許諾契約, 特許権実施契約, 実施権契約, 技術援助契約, ライセンス契約

licensing agreement　ライセンス契約, ライセンス供与契約, 使用許諾契約, 実施権契約

loan agreement　貸付け契約, 融資契約, 借入契約

maintenance agreement　保守契約, メンテナンス契約

manufacturing consignment agreement　製造委託契約, 製造物委託契約

margin agreement　証拠金契約

master agreement　標準契約, 基本協約, 基準協定, マスター契約

master sales agreement　基本売買契約

memorandum of general agreement　一般取引条件協約書

multilateral trade agreement　多角的貿易協定

option agreement　オプション契約

Orderly Marketing Agreement　市場秩序維持協定

original agreement　原契約

original equipment manufacturing agreement　相手先商標製品製造契約, OEM契約

participation agreement　参加契約

partnership agreement　連携協定, 組合規約, 組合契約, 組合約款・定款 (articles of partnership), パートナーシップ契約

plant export agreement　プラント輸出契約

price agreement　価格協定

purchase agreement　購入契約

reach a broad agreement　大筋で合意に達する, 大筋で合意する

reach an agreement　合意に達する, 合意する

redemption agreement　償還契約

reimbursement agreement　保証契約

renew the agreement　本契約を更新する

repurchase agreement　現先取引, 現先, 売戻し条件付き買いオペ, レポ

resale agreement　売戻し契約, レポ取引

reverse repurchase agreement　逆現先, リバース・レポ取引, リバース・レポ

revolving credit agreement　回転信用契約

revolving loan agreement　回転融資契約

sale and purchase agreement　売買契約

settlement agreement　和解契約

sign an agreement　契約書に署名する, 合意書に署名する, 基本合意する

software license agreement　ソフトウエア使用許諾契約, 使用許諾契約, ソフトウエア・ライセンス契約 (書)

support agreement　支援契約

tacit agreement between A and B　AとBの暗黙の了解

tax agreement　租税条約

technical assistance agreement　技術援助契約, 技術援助契約書, 技術指導契約

terminate an agreement　契約を解除する

terms of service agreement　利用規約

trade agreement　通商協定, 貿易協定

trade by agreement　協定貿易

tri-party agreement　三者契約

user agreement　利用規約, 利用契約

◆A subcommittee on fundamental issues at the Tax Commission reached an agreement on the streamlining and consolidation of various types of tax deductions from income. 税制調査会の基礎問題小委員会は、各種の所得控除 (所得税額控除) を整理・統合することで合意に達した。◆Japan and the United States will sign the open skies agreement, and carriers in both countries will be able to apply for U.S. antitrust immunity. 日米両政府がオープンスカイ協定を締結することによって、両国の航空会社は米国独占禁止法の適用除外申請が可能になる。◆Nippon Steel Corp. and Shanghai Baoshan Iron & Steel Co., China's largest steelmaker, signed an agreement to set up a joint venture to manufacture sheet steel for automobiles. 新日本製鉄と中国最大手の鉄鋼メーカー、上海宝山鋼鉄が、自動車用の鋼板を生産する合弁会社を設立する合意書に署名した。◆The broad agreement to establish the stock-purchasing organization was reached among the financial institutions through coordination efforts by the bank. 同行の調整努力により、各金融機関は株式取得機構を設立する大筋の合意に達した。◆The cross licensing agreement will allow the two firms to save time and costs for developing digital consumer electronics. クロス・ライセンス契約で、両社はデジタル家電製品の開発期間とコストを削減することができる。◆The leasing contract was signed because the agreement with U.S. forces was still valid. 米軍との合意事項がまだ失効していないため、この賃貸借契約が締結された。◆THIS AGREEMENT is made on the first day of March, 2003. 本契約は、2003年3月1日に締結した。

agricultural　(形) 農業の, 農産物の, 農政の

agricultural chemicals　農薬 (⇒quality control)

agricultural commodity　農業製品, 農産物

agricultural demand　農産物需要

agricultural disarmament　保護主義的農業政策の撤廃

agricultural import　農産物輸入, 農産品輸入

◆Commodity loans are used to import commodities such as industrial machinery, industrial raw materials, fertilizer, agricultural chemicals and machinery, and other various kinds of machinery, which are agreed upon beforehand between the Japanese and recipient governments. 商品借款は、日本政府と借入国政府が前もって合意した商品 (工業資本財 [工業用機械]、工業用原材料、肥料・農薬、農機具、各種機械など) の輸入のために使用される。

agricultural exports　農産物輸出, 農産品輸出, 輸出農産品

◆The LDP aims at doubling agricultural income and the value of agricultural exports, but its road map to achieve this target is unclear. 自民党は農

業所得や農産品輸出額の倍増を目指しているが、この目標実現への道筋は曖昧だ。

agricultural imports　農産物輸入, 農産品輸入, 輸入農産品
◆If agricultural imports become cheaper due to the lowered tariffs, consumers will greatly benefit. 関税の引下げで輸入農産品が安くなれば、消費者の利点も大きい。

agricultural negotiation　農業交渉
◆In the agricultural negotiations at the World Trade Organization, Japan has been under strong pressure from rice exporters to lower import tariffs on rice and to expand access for foreign rice. 世界貿易機関 (WTO) の農業交渉で日本は、コメ輸出国から、コメの輸入関税率引下げや外国産米の輸入枠拡大への強い圧力を受けている。

agricultural product　農産物, 農産品
◆Japanese agricultural and marine products have been seriously damaged by harmful rumors. 日本の農産物や海産物［日本の農水産物］は、風評被害で大きな打撃を受けている。

agricultural products for export　輸出用農産物
◆Washington and Brussels will conditionally accept an abolition of subsidies to farmers in the United States and the EU who grow agricultural products for export. 米国や欧州連合 (EU) は、それぞれ国内の輸出用農産物栽培農家に対する補助金の撤廃を条件付きで受け入れる方針だ。

air parcel post　航空便小包み

air waybill　航空運送状, AWB

airmail with brief preliminary cable advice　開設された信用状の概要を開設銀行 (発行銀行) が通知銀行に電信で先ず知らせ、その後信用状の原本を航空郵便で通知銀行に郵送する方法。

all elements rules　オール・エレメンツ・ルール（特許クレーム記載の構成要件をすべて実施した場合に、権利侵害が認定されるとするルール）

all of which together　全部合わせて
◆This agreement may be executed in any number of counterparts, each of them shall be deemed an original, but all of which together shall constitute single instrument. 本契約書はいかなる部数の副本も作成することができ［本契約はいかなる部数の副本でも締結することができ］、その副本はそれぞれ正本と見なされるが、全部合わせて唯一の証書を構成するものとする。

all or any part [portion] of　〜の全部または一部　(⇒obliged to)
◆In case there is delay in delivery of all or any part of the Goods on the time as stipulated in this agreement, the buyer is entitled to claim liquidated damages at the rate of one-half of one percent (0.5%) of the amount of the delayed Goods for each complete week of delay. 本契約で定める期限に本商品の全部または一部に引渡

し遅延が生じた場合、買い主は、遅延対象の各1週間につき引渡し遅延商品の代金の0.5%を損害賠償予定額として請求することができるものとする。

all risks　すべての危険, 全危険担保, オールリスク担保, 全危険担保条件, オールリスク（⇒CIF value）
◆In case of individual contracts on a CIF basis, marine insurance covering All Risks shall be effected by the seller on behalf of and in the name of the purchaser, in respect of the products purchased by it under an individual contract unless the parties agree in writing to the contrary. CIF条件での個別契約の場合、両当事者が書面で別途合意しないかぎり、買い主が個別契約で購入した製品については、売り主が買い主に代わって買い主の名前で全危険担保条件による海上保険をかけるものとする。◆Marine insurance policy shall cover all risks and be endorsed in blank. 海上保険証券は、全危険担保条件を付保し、無記名裏書き［白地裏書き］するものとする。◆The purchaser shall assume all risks and liability for the damages or loss of third parties, lives or properties resulting from the use of the products which are delivered under this agreement. 買い主は、本契約に基づいて引き渡された製品の使用により生じる第三者、生命または財産に対する損害または損失にかかわるすべての危険と責任を引き受けるものとする。◆User shall, at its expense, keep the Equipment insured against all risks until returned to Lender. ユーザーは、「機器」を貸主に返還するまで、ユーザーの費用負担で「機器」にオールリスク保険をかけなければならない。

all risks of loss or damages　損失または損害の全危険
◆Pursuant to concerned provisions of Contract, all risks of loss or damage to Machines shall be directly transferred from Supplier to Customer. 本契約の関連規定に従って、本機械に関する損失または損害の全危険は、サプライヤーから顧客へ直接移転するものとする。

allegation of breach　違反の申立て, 違反の主張
◆In the event of any allegation of breach or question of interpretation relating to this agreement, the parties shall meet and negotiate in good faith to settle the matter amicably. 本契約に関して違反の申立てが行われた場合または解釈の問題が生じた場合、当事者は誠実に交渉して、友好的に問題を解決するものとする。

alleged infringement　申し立てられた侵害, 侵害の申立て
◆Supplier shall be responsible for any claim of infringement or alleged infringement of patents, designs, trademarks, copyrights or other rights brought by a third party in relation to Products. 本製品に関して第三者が提起する特許、意匠、商標、著作権またはその他の権利の侵害または申し立てられた侵害の請求については、供給者がすべて責任を負う。

alleging that 〜と主張する、〜と申し立てる、〜として　(=asserting that)

alliance （名）提携、提携関係、連携、連合、統合、同盟、同盟関係、同盟国　(=tie-up)

alliance strategy　提携戦略

comprehensive alliance　包括的提携、包括提携　(=broad alliance)

dissolve one's alliance with　〜との提携関係を解消する

equity alliance　資本提携関係

form a capital and business alliance　資本・業務提携を結ぶ

form a search engine alliance　検索で提携する

four-way alliance　4社提携

maintain one's capital alliance with　〜との資本提携を維持する

producer-retailer alliance　製販同盟

strategic alliance　戦略提携、戦略的提携

◆Following the tie-up of Volkswagen AG and Suzuki Motor Corp., the alliance of Nissan and Renault SA of France announced a strategic partnership with Daimler AG. フォルクスワーゲンとスズキの提携に次いで[続いて]、日産・仏ルノー連合が、独ダイムラーとの戦略的提携を発表した。

allocate （動）割り当てる、配分する、配賦（ふ）する、割り振る　(=allot)

◆Hokuetsu Paper Mills Ltd. decided to allocate 50 million new shares to trading house Mitsubishi for ￥607 per share and form a business tie-up with the trading house. 北越製紙は、三菱商事に1株607円で新株5,000株を割り当て、三菱商事と業務提携することを決めた。

allocation （名）割当て、配分、配賦（ふ）、割振り、配当　(=allotment)

allocation to a third party　第三者割当て、第三者割当て増資　(=third-party allotment)

◆U.S. equity fund KKR is likely to procure shares to be issued by Renesas as an allocation to a third party to become the biggest shareholder, with an equity holding of more than 50 percent. 米投資ファンドのコールバーグ・クラビス・ロバーツ（KKR）は、半導体大手ルネサスが第三者割当て増資で発行する株式を引き受け、ルネサス株の50%超を得て、筆頭株主になる[経営権を握る]見通しだ。

allow （動）許す、認める、許容する、容認する

◆In the joint venture with an Indian investment bank, Tokyo Marine Holdings Inc. put up about 26%, the maximum a foreign investor is allowed in an Indian company, of the new firm's capital. インドの投資銀行との合弁事業で、東京海上ホールディングスは、新会社の資本金の約26%（外資の持ち分比率の上限）を出資した。◆Our quotations do not allow us any concession. 当社の建て値には、値引きの余地がまったくありません。◆Please inform us what discount you will allow us for quantities. 大口取引に対してどれだけの値引きを

認められるか、お知らせください。

allowance （名）値引（き）、控除、割引、手当て、報酬、給付、割当量、割当額、増減許容数量、許容誤差、公差

make a special allowance of 5%　5%の特別割引をする

pay the allowance claimed very soon　請求された値引きを早急に支払う

◆We are prepared to make the special allowance of 6%. 当社は、とくに6%の値引きをする用意があります。◆We ask you to kindly favor us with a large allowance. 大幅[多額の]値引きを、お願いします。

alternative dispute resolution　代替的紛争手段、代替的紛争処理、裁判によらない紛争解決方法、裁判外紛争処理（制度）、ADR

◆Alternative dispute resolution（ADR）for the revitalization of a business is a procedure that uses an intermediary from the private sector. 事業再生ADR（裁判外紛争解決手続き）は、民間の仲介機関[第三者機関]を活用する再建手続きだ。

alternative electricity source　代替電源

◆As long as Japan depends on thermal power generation as an alternative electricity source, LNG imports will continue to increase and the nation's wealth will flow to countries rich in natural resources. 日本が代替電源として火力発電に依存するかぎり、天然液化ガス（LNG）の輸入額は増え続け、国富は天然資源の豊富な国に流出する。

amalgamation, reorganization, or merger or consolidation　合併、会社更生、または吸収合併もしくは新設合併

◆For the purpose of this agreement, any change of corporate identity of one of the parties, such as by amalgamation, reorganization, or merger or consolidation, has not been agreed to by the other party. 本契約の目的上、合併、会社更生または吸収合併や新設合併といった当事者の一方の法人格の変更については、相手方当事者が同意していない。

amend, modify, alter or change　訂正・修正・改変または変更する、訂正・修正・変更する

◆This agreement may be amended, modified, altered or changed only by a written instrument duly executed by the authorized representatives of both parties. 本契約は、両当事者の権限のある代表者が正当に作成した証書によってのみ、訂正、修正、改変または変更することができる。

amendment agreement　修正契約

◆The seller shall, for its own account, effect marine insurance only free from particular average（FPA Institute Cargo Clause）for the amount of CIF value of the products plus 10 percent. 売り主は、売り主の自己負担で、本商品のCIF価格プラス10%の保険金額により単独海損[分損]不担保条件（FPA協会貨物保険約款）の海上保険を付けるものとする。

amount （名）金額, 総額, 合計, 総計, 総数, 総量, 額, 量, 高

additional amount　加算金, 追加金額

aggregate amount　総額, 合計額

amount covered　保険金額, 付保金額

amount equal to　〜に相当する金額

amount in arrear　未払い金額

amount insured　保険金額, 付保金額

amount owed by　〜の未払い金額, 〜が支払う義務のある金額

amount withheld　源泉徴収された金額

amounts brought to account　計上される金額

full amount　満額, 全額

in a total amount of　総額〜, 合計額〜

insurance amount　保険金額

net amount　正味金額

overdue amount　延滞金, 期限経過の金額

the amount of the licensed products manufactured, sold and used　許諾製品の製造・販売・使用数量

the outstanding amount of the loan　融資残高, 借入金の残高

total amount　総額

unpaid amount　未払い金額, 未払い額

◆ABC agrees to pay XYZ a daily absence fee in the amount of 300 United States dollars per person, or such other amount as may be mutually agreed upon between the parties. ABCは、XYZに対して1人当たり1日300米ドル、または両当事者間で別途合意する金額のアブセンス・フィーを支払うことに同意する。◆Any amounts exceeding the limits of automatic cover shall be offered to the Reinsurer for facultative acceptance. 自動再保険の適用限度を超える額は、任意受再のために再保険会社に申し出るものとする。◆If the buyer fails to pay any amount under this agreement when due, the buyer shall be liable to pay to the seller overdue interest on such unpaid amount from the due date until the actual payment date at the rate of 15% per annum. 買い主が支払い期日に本契約に基づく代金の支払いを怠った場合、買い主は、支払い期日から実際の払込み日までの当該未払い金額に対する年率15％の遅延金利を、売り主に支払わなければならない。◆In case there is delay in delivery of all or any part of the Goods on the time as stipulated in this agreement, the buyer is entitled to claim liquidated damages at the rate of one-half of one percent（0.5%）of the amount of the delayed Goods for each complete week of delay. 本契約で定める期限に本商品の全部または一部に引渡し遅延が生じた場合、買い主は、遅延対象の各1週間につき引渡し遅延商品の代金の0.5%を損害賠償予定額として請求することができるものとする。◆Subdistributor discount means the amount below the prices set forth in the price list, at which the subdistributor may purchase the products from

Distributor.「二次代理店割引」とは、価格表に記載する価格より低い金額のことで、二次代理店はこの金額で代理店から本製品を購入することができる。

amount due　満期支払い高, 満期決済額, 期限到来債務, 支払い金, 支払わなければならない金額, 未払い金　（⇒amount of such claim, on demand）

amount due under this agreement　本契約に基づく満期支払い高, 本契約に基づく満期決済額, 本契約に基づく支払い金

◆The license granted hereunder may be canceled by Licensor if Licensee is in default in payment of any amount due under this agreement for a period of 30 days. 本契約に基づいて付与されたライセンスは、ライセンシーが本契約に基づく満期支払い高の支払いを30日間履行しない場合、ライセンサーが解除できるものとする。

amount of payment　支払い額

◆Licensee shall calculate the amount of payment based on the preceding Article four times a year. ライセンシーは、前条に基づいて年4回、支払い額を計算しなければならない。

amount of such claim　当該請求額

◆In the event of any claim being made by ABC against XYZ, ABC shall not be entitled to withhold any amount due under this agreement or any individual contract or to set off the amount of such claim against any amount due under this agreement or any individual contract. ABCがXYZに対して請求を申し立てる場合、ABCには、本契約または個別契約に基づいて支払わなければならない金額の支払いを保留する権利がなく、また本契約または個別契約に基づいて支払わなければならない金額と当該請求額を相殺する権利もないものとする。

amount of taxes　税額

◆ABC shall furnish XYZ within sixty days of the end of each term of license of this agreement with all documentation as shall be necessary to establish the amount of taxes actually paid. ABCは、本契約の各ライセンス期間終了後60日以内に、実際に納付した税額を立証するのに必要な書類をすべてXYZに提供するものとする。

amount owing to　〜に対して支払う義務のある金額, 〜に支払われる金額

◆Except as otherwise expressly provided for in this agreement, ABC shall not be entitled to set off or withhold any amount owing to ABC under this agreement, against any payment to XYZ for the performance by XYZ of this agreement. 本契約に別に明文の規定がないかぎり、ABCには、本契約に基づきABCに支払われる金額を、XYZによる本契約の履行に対するXYZへの支払い金と相殺する権利も、またその支払いを保留する権利もないものとする。

amount specified above　上記金額

◆We have valued upon you today for the amount specified above, at sight, and ask you to accord our draft your due protection. 当社は本日、貴社宛てに上記金額に対する一覧払い手形を振り出しましたので、この手形のお引受けをお願い致します。

amounts payable 支払い期限が到来した金額
◆Forthwith upon termination of this agreement for any reason, ABC shall immediately pay all amounts payable under this agreement. 理由のいかんを問わず本契約の終了後直ちに、ABCは、本契約に基づいて期限が到来したすべての金額を直ちに支払うものとする。

annex （名）付属書類、添付書類、別紙、補遺、付加物
◆The Company agrees to cede to the Reinsurer such shares of all insurances covered by this Agreement as are set forth in the annexes (Schedule and any Addenda) to this Agreement. 元受会社は、本協定対象の全保険のうち、本協定の補遺（特別条項や追加条項）に明記した部分を再保険会社に出再することに合意する。

anniversary date 応答日、ある時点から一定期間が経過した日
◆The borrower shall repay the loan in an amount of each of the individual sums to the Lender on the third anniversary date of the respective advance date. 借主は、個別の各借入金について、その各融資実行日から3年経過した日に貸主に対して返済するものとする。

annual anniversary of this agreement 本契約1年後の応答日
◆The price of the products for any subsequent year commencing on the annual anniversary of this agreement shall be such as may be negotiated and agreed upon between the parties not later than 30 days prior to the commencement of such year. 本契約から1年後の応答日に始まる次年度の本商品価格は、当該年度が始まる30日前までに当事者間で交渉して合意する価格とする。

annual financial statements 年次財務書類, 年次財務諸表
◆The annual financial statements for the financial year ending on December 31, 2015 present a true and fair view of the financial position as of the date thereof. 2015年12月31日に終了する事業年度[会計年度]の年次財務書類は、同日現在の財政状態について真実かつ公正な見方を提示している。◆The auditor of the Chinese company, listed on the TSE's Mothers market for start-up firms, refused to certify its annual financial statements. 東証の新興企業向け市場「マザーズ」に上場している中国企業の監査法人は、同社の年次財務諸表の正確さに対する保証を拒否した。

annual report 年次報告書, 年次決算報告書, 年次営業報告書, 有価証券報告書, 年報, アニュアル・レポート（[年次報告書]は、英国ではannual report and accountsともいわれるが、アメリカの場合はSEC（米証券取引委員会）向け年次報告書と株主向け年次報告書がある。SEC向け年次報告書は、SECに登録している企業が株式、社債などの証券を発行した後、決算期ごとに毎年提出する報告書で、その様式は米国企業がForm 10-K（様式10-K）、外国企業がForm 20-F（様式20-F）となっている）

annual report and accounts 年次報告書

annual report on Form 10-K 様式10-Kに基づく年次報告書

Annual Report on the Japanese Economy and Public Finance 経済財政白書

annual report to stockholders [shareholders] 株主向け年次報告書, 年次報告書
◆The Annual Report on Form 10-K is available from the date of its filing with the Securities and Exchange Commission in the United States. 様式10-Kに基づく当社の年次報告書は、米国の証券取引委員会（SEC）への提出日以降に入手できます。

annul （動）法令や契約などを無効とする, 取り消す
◆The revised Investment Deposit and Interest Rate Law annuls contracts for loans whose interest rates exceed 109.5 percent per annum—the maximum interest rate permitted on loans extended and received by individuals. 今回改正された出資法では、金利が個人間の貸し借りの上限である年利109.5%を超える融資契約を無効としている。

Answerback: アンサーバック・コード:

anticipated final shipping date 最終出荷予定日
◆This letter of credit shall be opened not less than 30 calendar days before the first scheduled shipping date for each order and shall be 90 days beyond the anticipated final shipping date. この信用状は、各注文の最初の出荷予定日から30暦日以上前に開設するものとし、最終出荷予定日から90日を超えて有効でなければならない。

anticompetitive activity 非競争的行為
◆The United States will continue to actively address anticompetitive activity, market access barriers, and or market-distorting trade practices. アメリカは、非競争的行為や市場参入障壁、市場を歪める商慣行に引き続き取り組んで行く方針だ。

antidumping （名）反ダンピング（不当廉売）, ダンピング防止, 不当廉売防止, アンチダンピング

antidumping actions 反ダンピング措置

antidumping investigation 反ダンピング調査

antidumping law 反ダンピング法, ダンピング防止法, 不当廉売防止法, アンチダンピング法

antidumping measure 反ダンピング措置

antidumping order 反ダンピング命令

antidumping procedures 反ダンピング手続き

antidumping rule 反ダンピング・ルール

antidumping tariff 反ダンピング関税, ダンピ

ング防止関税 （=antidumping duties）

apply an antidumping law　反ダンピング法を適用する

implement antidumping measures　反ダンピング措置を発動する

the 1916 U.S. Antidumping Act　米国の1916年反ダンピング法［ダンピング防止法］

antidumping duties　反ダンピング関税, ダンピング防止関税, 不当廉売防止関税（⇒Byrd Amendment）
◆If antidumping duties are imposed on cold-rolled steel, this will amount to a virtual ban on imports of the products. 冷延鋼板に反ダンピング関税が課税されると、同製品の輸入は事実上、禁止されることになる。

antidumping probe　反ダンピング調査
◆In the United States, a provisional ruling on dumping is usually issued about six months after launching antidumping probes. 米国では、ダンピング（不当廉売）の仮決定をするのは通例、反ダンピング調査の開始から半年程度である。

anti-Japan demonstration　反日デモ
◆Adverse impacts on Japanese companies' business are spreading due to anti-Japan demonstrations and a campaign to boycott Japanese products. 反日デモや日本製品の不買運動などで、日本企業のビジネスに悪影響が広がっている。◆The Chinese government allowed people to stage a campaign to boycott Japanese products following anti-Japan demonstrations. 中国政府は、反日デモに続いて、中国人の日本製品の不買運動をも容認した。

anti-Japan demonstrators　反日デモ隊
◆The attack on a Panasonic Corp. factory which has played a pioneering role in expanding its operations in China by a violent mob of anti-Japan demonstrators symbolizes the current bleak state of Japan-China relations. 中国進出で先駆的役割を果たしてきたパナソニックの工場が、反日デモ隊の暴徒に襲われた事件は、日中関係の寒々しい現状を象徴している。◆To prepare for unpredictable events by anti-Japan demonstrators, the Japanese government will strongly press the Chinese government to ensure the safety of Japanese people and Japanese-affiliated companies in China. 反日デモ隊による不測の事態に備えて、日本政府は、在留邦人や日系企業の安全確保を中国政府に強く求める方針だ。

anti-Japan riot　反日暴動
◆Japanese-affiliated companies operating in China will have to be aware of "China risks" such as rising production costs as well as the stronger Chinese yuan and anti-Japan riots. 中国に進出している日系企業は今後、生産コストの上昇のほか、人民元高や反日暴動などのような「中国リスク」を意識せざるを得ない。

Antimonopoly Law　独占禁止法
◆The Antimonopoly Law stipulates that documents submitted to FTC hearings may be disclosed to certain concerned parties upon their request. 独占禁止法は、「公正取引委員会の審判に提出された書類［記録］は特定の利害関係人の請求に基づいて利害関係人に開示することができる」と定めている。◆The bank was found to have forced corporate borrowers to buy financial products in violation of the Antimonopoly Law. 同行は、独占禁止法に違反して融資先企業に金融商品を無理に購入させていたことが判明した。

antitrust immunity　独占禁止法の適用除外, ATI
◆Japan and the United States will sign the open skies agreement, and carriers in both countries will be able to apply for U.S. antitrust immunity. 日米両政府がオープンスカイ協定を締結することによって、両国の航空会社は米国独占禁止法の適用除外申請が可能になる。

antitrust law　独占禁止法, 反トラスト法（米国の場合、独占禁止法の基本法であるシャーマン法（Sherman Act）、クレイトン法（Clayton Act）連邦取引委員会法（Federal Trade Commission Act of 1914）とそれを補完・修正する法律からなる）
◆The contractual clause is a violation of the Antimonopoly Law. この契約条項は、独占禁止法違反である。◆The U.S. Federal Trade Commission（FTC）concluded there was not enough evidence that a Sony-BMG merger would violate U.S. antitrust laws. 米連邦取引委員会（FTC）は、ソニーとBMG（独複合メディア大手ベルテルスマンの音楽事業部門）の統合が米国の独占禁止法に違反することを示す十分な証拠はない、との結論を下した。

antitrust regulators　反トラスト規制当局
◆U.S. federal antitrust regulators have cleared the way for the proposed merger between Sony Music Entertainment and BMG, the music unit of the German media conglomerate Bertelsmann AG. 米連邦反トラスト規制当局（米連邦取引委員会）は、ソニーと独複合メディア大手ベルテルスマンの音楽部門のBMGとの事業統合案を承認した。

antitrust violation　反トラスト法（米独占禁止法）違反
◆Auto parts supplier Yazaki Corp. agreed to pay a $470 million fine, the second-largest criminal fine obtained for an antitrust violation. 自動車部品メーカーの矢崎総業は、罰金4億7,500万ドル（反トラスト法違反では過去2番目に大きい罰金）を支払うことで合意した。

any　（形）いくつかの, いずれかの, どんな〜でも　（代）どれか, いずれか, 各〜

any of the parties hereto　いずれかの本契約当事者, いずれかの当事者, 本契約の各当事者, 本契約のいずれの当事者も

any or all agreements contained herein　本契約に定めるいずれかの合意事項またはすべての合意事項

any part, provision or covenant of this

agreement 本契約のいずれかの部分、条項または約束

any partner いずれのパートナーも
◆Any claim by the purchaser, except for latent defects, shall be made in writing as soon as reasonably practicable after the arrival, unpacking and inspection of the products, whether by the purchaser or any subsequent purchaser of the products. 買い主によるクレームは、隠れた瑕疵（かし）を除いて、買い主によるか本製品のその後の購入者によるかを問わず本製品の到着、開梱および検査後、合理的に実行可能なかぎり速やかに書面で行うものとする。◆Any failure, whether willful, through neglect or otherwise, of either party to perform or fulfill any of its duties, obligations or covenants in this agreement shall constitute a breach of this agreement. 故意であれ、怠慢またはその他によるものであれ、本契約における各当事者の責務、義務または約束ごとを各当事者が履行または達成できない場合、これは本契約の違反を構成するものとする。◆In case any dispute arises in connection with the above right, the seller reserves the right to terminate unconditionally this agreement or any further performance of this agreement at the seller's discretion. 上記権利に関して紛争が生じた場合、売り主はその裁量で、本契約または本契約のその後の履行を無条件で終了させる権利を留保する。◆The guarantor hereby waives any right it may have as surety which may be at any time inconsistent with any of the provisions of this guarantee. 保証人は、本保証書［保証状］の条項にどんな時でも矛盾する可能性のある、保証人が保証人として持つことができる一切の権利をここに放棄する。

any and all あらゆる、すべての、一切の
◆The parties hereto shall keep in strict confidence from any third party any and all important matters concerning the business affairs and transactions covered by this agreement. 本契約当事者は、本契約の対象である営業上の問題や取引に関するすべての重要事項については、どんな第三者に対しても一切極秘にする。

APEC アジア太平洋経済協力会議、エイペック（⇒adopt a road map toward, Asia-Pacific Economic Cooperation (forum)）
◆APEC groups 21 economies, including Japan, the United States, China, South Korea, Russia, Southeast Asian countries, Canada and some Latin American nations. APECには、日本、米国、中国、韓国、ロシア、東南アジア諸国、カナダ、中南米諸国など21の国・地域が参加している。◆The APEC's special statement came out in favor of the promotion of free trade. アジア太平洋経済協力会議（APEC）の特別声明は、自由貿易推進を打ち出した。◆The APEC's special statement sounded the alarm about the rising protectionist sentiment. アジア太平洋経済協力会議（APEC）の特別声明は、保護主義の台頭に警鐘を鳴らした。

APEC Summit アジア太平洋経済協力会議（APEC）の首脳会談
◆In a joint statement released after the two-day APEC Summit in Beijing, the leaders of the 21 APEC member economies said that they would aim to realize a Free Trade Area of the Asia-Pacific (FTAAP) at the earliest possible time. 北京で行われた2日間のアジア太平洋経済協力会議（APEC）の首脳会談後に発表された共同声明で、加盟21か国・地域の首脳は、できるだけ早期に「アジア太平洋自由貿易圏（FTAAP）」構想の実現を目指すと述べた。

APEC's Early Voluntary Sectoral Liberalization program 早期自主的分野別自由化

apparent （形）明らかな、明白な、はっきりした、明瞭な、目に見える、上辺の、外見上の、見せかけの、表面上の、見たところ、他人に奪われることのない相続権を持った

an apparent fact 明白な事実

an heir apparent 法定推定相続人

in apparent good order and condition 外見上［外観上］良好な状態で

appeal （名）懇願、懇請、要請、要求、訴え、抗議、異議申立て、不服の申立て、高等裁判所への控訴・抗告、最高裁判所への上告・上訴、魅力、人気、アピール
◆China lost an appeal at the WTO in a case about its export restrictions on raw materials including bauxite, magnesium and zinc. 中国によるボーキサイトやマグネシウム、亜鉛などの鉱物資源［原材料］輸出規制に関する問題で、中国は世界貿易機関（WTO）で敗訴した。

appellate （形）上訴の、上訴事件を扱う、控訴［上告］事件を審理する権限のある、上級の

appellate body 上級委員会

appellate court 上訴裁判所

applicable （形）適用される、適用できる、応用できる、配賦可能な、妥当な、適当な、適切な、適格な、対応する

applicable fees 適用料金

applicable grace period 適用猶予期間（⇒grace period）

applicable income taxes 適用所得税, 当該所得税

applicable interest rate for the loan 融資に適用される金利, ローン適用金利

applicable tax rate 適用税率
◆The borrower shall pay to the lender an interest on the loan for each interest payment period applicable to the loan at the floating rate of the LIBOR (British Bankers Association Interest Settlement Rate in U.S. Dollars) plus 1,625 percent per annum, calculated on the basis of actual number of days elapsed and a year of 360 days. 借主は、1年を360日として実際に経過した日数に基づいて計算した、ロンドン銀行間取引金利（米ドル

APPL 26

での英国銀行協会金利決済レート）に年1.625%を加算した変動金利で、この借入れに適用される各利払い期間の借入金の利息を貸主に対して支払うものとする。

applicable interest rate 適用される金利
◆The applicable interest rate for the loan will be 5.375 percent p.a.［per annum］. このローンに適用される金利は、年率で5.375%です。

applicable law 適用法, 準拠法, 適用される法律 （=governing law; ⇒manage）
in accordance with applicable law 適用法に従って
◆Any tax arising out of the separate business activities conducted by XYZ and ABC pursuant to this agreement shall be born and paid by the party upon whom such tax is imposed by applicable law. 本契約に従ってXYZとABCが行う営業活動から発生する税金は、適用法によりその税金が課される当事者が負担して支払うものとする。◆Dividends are declared at a general meeting within the scope of such sum as is permitted under applicable law. 配当は、適用法により許される金額の範囲内で、株主総会で宣言される。

applicable laws and regulations 適用法令
◆The new company shall be managed under the provisions of this agreement, the articles of incorporation and the applicable laws and regulations of Japan. 新会社は、本契約の規定、定款と日本の適用法令に従って運営する。

applicable requirements 適用要件
◆All goods were produced in compliance with the applicable requirements of the Fair Labor Standards Act. 商品は、すべて米国の公正労働基準法の適用要件に従って生産された。

applicable tax law 適用される税法
◆Licensor shall bear any tax to be levied under applicable tax laws on the income of Licensor arising under this agreement. ライセンサーは、適用される税法に基づき、本契約に基づいて生じるライセンサーの所得に課される税金を負担する。

applicable usury law 適用される利息制限法
◆Interest shall accrue on any delinquent amounts owed by Distributor for Products at the lesser of 18% per annum, or the maximum rate permitted by applicable usury law. 利息は、販売店が負っている本製品の延滞金について発生し、年18%の利率と適用される利息制限法で認められる最高利率のうちいずれか低いほうの利率によるものとする。

applicant （名）申請人, 申請者, 申立て人, 仮処分申請の債権者

application （名）適用, 応用, 利用, 実用, 充当, 使途, 運用, 申込み, 申請, 出願, 申込み書, 申請書, 願書，（⇒R & D）
application for amendment L/C 信用状変更依頼書
application for extension of time-limit 時効延長願い

application for extra-work 時間外貨物取扱い申込み

application for forward exchange contract 先物為替の予約申込み書

application for insurance 保険申込み書

application for irrevocable documentary credit 取消不能の荷為替信用状の開設依頼書, 信用状開設依頼書

application for marine insurance 貨物海上保険申込み書

application for new warrant （税関に対する）倉荷証券再下付願い

application for opening bonded warehouse 臨時保税倉庫願い

application for remittance and notice 外国送金依頼書兼告知書

application for remittance with declaration 外国送金依頼書兼告知書

application for shipment 船積み申込み書

application for ship's space 船腹予約申込み書

application form 申込み書, 申込み用紙, 申請書, 願書

application money 申込み金,（株の）申込み証拠金

application number 登録申請番号

application of payment 支払いの充当

application slip 申込み票, 保険申込み書

application therefor その出願

application to open a current a/c 当座取引申込み書

application to unload 荷卸し申請書

drawback application 戻し税申請

electronic application 電子出願

electronic patent application 電子特許出願, 電子出願

extraterritorial application 域外適用

file an application for ～を申請する

foreign exchange application 外国為替申込み, 外国為替申告

letter of application 申込み書

license application 免許申請

listing application 上場申請 （=application for quotation）

loan application 融資申込み

patent application 特許出願

pay-on application 請求払い, P/A

shipping application 船積み申込み, 船積み申込み書

source and application of funds 資金の源泉と使途

◆Soshisha Publishing Co. filed an application with the Tokyo District Court for protection from creditors under the Civil Rehabilitation Law. 草思社は、民事再生法に基づく資産保全［民事再生法の適用］を東京地裁に申請した。◆The licensor warrants that it will submit an application for trademark registration of the Trademarks covering the products in the territory immediately after the execution of this agreement. ライセンサーは、本契約締結後直ちに許諾地域で製品に使用する本商標の登録出願をすることを保証する。◆The parties agree to exclude the application of the United Nations Convention on Contracts for the International Sales of Goods（1980）. 両当事者は、国連物品売買統一法条約（1980年）の適用を排除することに合意する。

application or the improvement the licensed products 許諾製品の利用と改良
◆ABC hereby grants to XYZ during the term of this agreement, an exclusive and nontransferable right and license, with the right to grant a sublicense, to use the information and the proprietary rights, for the purpose of manufacturing, having manufactured, using and developing and the application or the improvement of the licensed products at one or more plants located in the territory. 本契約期間中ABCは、契約地域に所在する一つまたは複数の工場で許諾製品を製造するおよび製造させる目的と使用、開発および利用・改良する目的のために、本情報と財産権を使用する独占的で譲渡不可能な権利とライセンスを、サブライセンスを付与する権利とともに、本契約によりXYZに付与する。

apply （動）適用する, 応用する, 利用する, 運用する, あてはめる, 配賦する （自動）申し込む, 志願する, 依頼する, 問い合わせる
◆A counselor to the Japan Research Institute warned that under the current trade structure, the yen's depreciation might apply downward pressure on the Japanese economy. 現状の貿易構造では、円安で日本の景気が押し下げられる懸念がある、と日本総研の理事が警告した。◆For reimbursement, we have applied to our bankers for an L/C to be opened. （本注文に対する）代金支払いのため、当社は銀行に信用状の発行を申請しました。◆The consumption tax rate for goods is currently uniform at 8 percent, whether applied to food or nonessentials such as jewelry. 商品の消費税率は、食品でも宝石などすぐには必要でないものでも、今は8パーセントで同じだ。

apply for or register 出願または登録する
◆Distributor shall not apply for or register any industrial property right in connection with Products except the prior written consent of Company. 代理店は、会社の書面による事前の同意がないかぎり、本製品（契約品）に関する工業所有権の出願または登録は一切しないものとする。

apply for product approval 製品の承認を申請する
◆Because of the domestic lengthy process of approving production and sales of medical devices, some domestic medical device makers have been applying for product approval in Europe and the United States first. 国内での医療機器の製造販売承認手続きの遅れから、国内医療機器メーカーの一部は、製品の承認申請を欧米で先に行っている。

apply for registration of ～の登録出願をする
◆Licensee shall not apply for registration of Trademarks in whole or in part or other trademark similar thereto with respect to Products or any other products in Territory or otherwise. ライセンシーは、契約地域またはその他で、本製品または他の製品に関して本商標の全体または一部、あるいは本商標に類似するその他の商標の登録出願をしてはならない。

apply for U.S. antitrust immunity 米国独占禁止法の適用除外を申請する
◆Japan and the United States will sign the open skies agreement, and carriers in both countries will be able to apply for U.S. antitrust immunity. 日米両政府がオープンスカイ協定を締結することによって、両国の航空会社は米国独占禁止法の適用除外申請が可能になる。◆The licensee's obligation under this Article with respect to confidential information shall not apply to information which may be acquired hereafter by the licensee from any third party without any obligation of secrecy. 本条に基づく秘密情報に関するライセンシーの義務は、秘密保持義務なしに第三者からライセンシーが今後取得する情報には適用されないものとする。

apply to ～に適用される, ～に当てはまる, ～に照会する
◆The licensee's obligation under this Article with respect to the confidential information shall not apply to information which is already in the possession of the licensee prior to the disclosure by the licensor and was not acquired by the licensee directly or indirectly from the licensor. 本条に基づく秘密情報に関するライセンシーの義務は、ライセンサーが開示する前にライセンシーがすでに保有していて、ライセンシーがライセンサーから直接または間接的に取得しなかった情報には適用されないものとする。◆The licensee's obligation under this Article with respect to the confidential information shall not apply to information which is part of the public domain at the time of disclosure by the licensor, or thereafter becomes part of the public domain without fault on the part of the licensee. 本条に基づく秘密情報に関するライセンシーの義務は、ライセンサーによる開示の時点で公知であるか、その後ライセンシー側の過失なしに公知となる情報には適用されないものとする。

appoint （動）指名する, 指定する, 任命する, 選任する
◆Subject to the terms and conditions herein provided, Company hereby appoints Distributor as its exclusive distributor. 本契約に定める条件に

従って、会社は、本契約により代理店を会社の一手販売店 (総代理店) に指名する。◆Supplier hereby appoints Distributor as its sole and exclusive distributor to sell Products in Territory subject to the terms and conditions set forth herein. 本契約により供給者は、販売店を、本契約に定める条件に従って契約地域内で本製品を販売する独占的な販売店に指名する。

appointment （名）指名, 任命, 選任, 官職, 任務, 地位, 取決め, 約束, 法令, 条例

appointment of an exclusive distributor 一手販売店の指定

set up an appointment with ～と面会の約束を取り付ける

◆ABC accepts such appointment and undertakes to use its best efforts, at its own expenses, to promote the sales of the products throughout the territory at all times during the term of this agreement. ABCは当該指定を受諾し, 本契約期間中つねに, その自己負担で, 契約地域全域で本製品の販売を促進するため最善の努力をすることを約束する。◆Distributor's appointment does not transfer any right to title to or interest in Products to Distributor. 販売店の指名は, 本製品の所有権の権利または利権を販売店に移転するものではない。

apportionment （名）損害填補額の分担

appraisal （名）評価査定

appreciate （動）上昇する, 騰貴する, 相場が上がる, 高く評価する, 好感する, 正しく認識 [理解] する, 鑑賞する, 感謝する

appreciate across the board 全面高となる

appreciate against [relative to] the US$ 対米ドルで上昇する, 米ドルに対して [米ドルと比べて, 米ドルに照らして] 上昇する

highly appreciate one's best cooperation ～のご協力に感謝します

◆It would be appreciated if you could make the partial shipment. 分割船積ができれば, 嬉しい。◆The dollar appreciated relative to the euro and the yen. ドルが, ユーロや円より上昇した。◆We appreciate your inquiry. お問い合わせ, ありがとうございます。◆We would appreciate your immediate reply as time is running short. 時間がないので至急, ご返事をいただきたい。◆Your prompt reply would be highly appreciated. 早急にご返事いただきたい, 有り難い。

appreciating yen 円高

◆Japanese electronics makers are needed to shrug off the adversity of economic slowdowns overseas, a strongly appreciating yen, and ever-intensifying competition with foreign rivals by wielding their latent power. 日本の電機製造業各社は, 底力を発揮して, 海外経済の減速, 超円高, 海外勢との競争激化などの逆境を跳ね返す必要がある。

appreciation （名）価格・相場の上昇, 騰貴, 急騰, 増価, 平価切上げ, 正当な評価, 理解, 認識, 鑑賞, 感謝

a letter of appreciation 感謝状

appreciation of currencies 通貨高

appreciation of the yen 円高

appreciation of the yen against the dollar 円高・ドル安

appreciation pressure on the yen 円高圧力

benefits of the yen's appreciation 円高差益

capital appreciation キャピタル・ゲイン

equity appreciation 株価上昇

in appreciation of ～に感謝して, ～を認めて

sharp yen appreciation 急激な円高

the yen's appreciation against the dollar 円高・ドル安, ドルに対する円相場の上昇

the yen's excessive appreciation 行き過ぎた円高

the yen's sharp appreciation 急激な円高

the yen's sharp appreciation against the U.S. dollar 急激な円高・ドル安

◆Eurozone countries whose economies are suffering from the euro's appreciation likely will criticize Japan if the yen falls further at a faster pace again. 今後も速いスピードで円安が進めば, ユーロ圏の経済はユーロ高に苦しんでいるため, ユーロ圏は再び日本を批判する可能性がある。◆In appreciation of your past custom, we made this proposal for you. 御社の従来のご愛顧に感謝して, 当社は御社にこの提案をしました。◆Losses from fluctuations of the currency market due to the yen's steep appreciation have added to Toyota's plight. 急激な円高による為替差損で, トヨタの経営状況が深刻化した。◆Sony has suffered from declining export profits due to the yen's sharp appreciation. ソニーは, 急激な円高で, 輸出の採算悪化に見舞われている。◆Speculative money has poured into emerging economies, causing an appreciation of their currencies and asset inflation because of drastic monetary easing by Japan, the United States and Europe. 日米欧の大胆な [大規模な] 金融緩和で, 投機マネーが新興国に流れ込み, 新興国の通貨高や資産インフレを招いている。◆The recent yen's appreciation is not so painful as to deal a heavy blow to export-oriented industries. 最近の円高は, 輸出企業に大きな打撃を与えるほどの痛手 [大きな打撃を与える水準] ではない。

appreciation of currencies 通貨高

◆By being vigilant against excessive volatility in exchange rates, the G-20 will reduce the risk of speculative money causing appreciation of currencies and inflation in emerging countries. 為替相場の過度な変動を監視して, 世界 [主要] 20か国・地域 (G20) は, 投機マネーが新興国の通貨高やインフレを招くリスクを軽減する方針だ。◆In light of complaints from emerging economies that a glut of speculative funds due to monetary easing measures taken by advanced countries have caused the appreciation of their currencies and asset inflation, the G-20 participants agreed that they will monitor and minimize the negative ripple effects of their respective financial policies. 先進国の金融緩和策でだぶついた投機マネーが新興国の通貨高や資産インフレを招いているという新興国の不満に配慮して、G20参加国は、それぞれ金融政策の負の波及効果を監視し、最小化することで合意した。

appreciation of the yen 円高, 円の騰貴, 円為替相場の上昇 (=the yen's appreciation)
◆Business sentiment and the willingness of household to spend may cool and stall the economy unless the sharp appreciation of the yen is checked. 円の急騰を止めないと、企業の心理や家計の消費意欲が冷え込み、景気が腰折れしかねない。◆The hyper-appreciation of yen that had afflicted the Japanese economy was corrected after the launch of the Abe Cabinet. 日本経済を苦しめてきた超円高は、安倍内閣の発足後、是正された。

appropriate (形)適切な, 妥当な, ふさわしい, きちんと合った, 特有な, 固有の
an appropriate example 適切な実例
appropriate tax authorities 所轄の税務当局
appropriate to the occasion 時宜(じぎ)を得た, その場にふさわしい
deem necessary and appropriate 必要で適切と考える
take appropriate measures 適切な措置を取る
◆Commencing on the date of this agreement until the Closing, Buyer shall be permitted to perform such due diligence investigation related to the transactions contemplated by this agreement as Buyer deems necessary and appropriate in its discretion. 本契約締結日からクロージングまで、買い主は、本契約で意図した取引に関して買い主が買い主の判断で必要かつ適切と考えるデュー・ディリジェンス調査を行うことができるものとする。

appropriate action 適切な措置
◆In the event that any third party infringes any of the proprietary rights or the trademark of the licensor in the territory, then the parties hereto shall cooperate to take appropriate action against such third party. 第三者が契約地域でライセンサーの財産権または商標を侵害した場合、本契約当事者は協力して当該第三者に対して適切な措置を取るものとする。

approval (名)認可, 承認, 承諾, 確認, 許可
obtain shareholder approval 株主の承認を得る
without prior written approval of ～の書面による事前承認を得ないで
◆Because of the domestic lengthy process of approving production and sales of medical devices, some domestic medical device makers have been applying for product approval in Europe and the United States first. 国内での医療機器の製造販売承認手続きの遅れから、国内医療機器メーカーの一部は、製品の承認申請を欧米で先に行っている。
◆Citibank Japan Ltd. is arranging to sell its retail banking business by the end of March 2015 if it can obtain approval from the Financial Services Agency, while it will maintain its corporate banking business. 米金融大手シティグループの日本法人「シティバンク銀行」は、金融庁の承認が得られれば、2015年3月末までに個人向けの小口取引銀行業務の売却を打診しているが、企業との取引を行うコーポレート銀行業務は続ける方針だ。◆Companies should obtain shareholder approval when introducing methods to counter hostile takeover attempts. 敵対的買収への対抗策を導入する場合、企業は株主の承認を得なければならない。◆Nissan Motor Co.'s board of directors gave its approval for exploratory talks on a proposal for struggling U.S. auto giant General Motors Corp. 日産自動車の取締役会は、経営再建中の米自動車大手ゼネラル・モーターズ(GM)に対する提携提案の事前協議を承認した。

arbitral award 仲裁判断, 仲裁裁定
◆The arbitral award may grant any relief deemed by the arbitrators to be just and equitable, including, without limitation, specific performance. 仲裁判断は、特定履行などを含めて、仲裁人が正義かつ衡平と見なす救済を認めることができる。◆The arbitral award shall be rendered in writing, and shall state the reasons for the award. 仲裁判断は、書面で行い、その判断理由を明示するものとする。◆The arbitral award shall state the reasons for the award and relief granted. 仲裁判断は、その判断の理由と認められた救済理由を明らかにするものとする。

arbitral proceedings 仲裁手続き

arbitral tribunal 仲裁裁判所, 仲裁機関
◆Each party shall bear its own expenses but the two parties shall share equally the expenses of the arbitral tribunal. 各自の費用は各当事者が負担するが、仲裁機関の費用は両当事者が均等に負担する。

arbitration (名)仲裁, 裁定, 仲裁機関, 国際裁判
American Arbitration Association 米国仲裁協会, AAA
arbitration agreement 仲裁契約, 仲裁裁定, 仲裁合意, 仲裁合意書
arbitration before a single arbitrator 単独仲裁人による仲裁
arbitration board 仲裁人団, 仲裁人の合議体 (=arbitration panel)
China International Economic and Trade Arbitration Commission 中国国際経済貿易仲裁委員会, CIETAC
commercial arbitration 商事仲裁
Court of Arbitration, International Chamber of Commerce 国際商業会議所仲裁裁判所

demand for arbitration 仲裁の請求, 仲裁申立て書

final and binding arbitration 最終的で拘束力のある仲裁

if arbitration is brought by ～によって仲裁が申し立てられたときは

Japan Commercial Arbitration Association 日本商事仲裁協会, JCAA（旧称：国際商事仲裁協会。2003年1月1日から名称変更）

London Court of International Arbitration ロンドン国際仲裁裁判所

submit ～ to arbitration ～を仲裁に付す, ～を仲裁に付託する

the parties to the arbitration 仲裁当事者

◆Any and all disputes arising from or in connection with this Agreement or a transaction conducted under this Agreement shall be settled by arbitration in Tokyo in accordance with the Commercial Arbitration Rules of the Japan Commercial Arbitration Association. The award of the arbitration shall be final and binding upon the parties. 本契約もしくは本契約に基づいて行われる取引から生じる, またはこれに関連して生じる紛争は, すべて日本商事仲裁協会の商事仲裁規則にしたがって東京での仲裁により解決する。仲裁の判断は, 最終的なもので当事者を拘束［法的に拘束］するものとする。◆Exhibit D sets forth a complete and accurate list of all claims, suits, actions, arbitrations, legal or other proceedings or governmental investigations to which the Company is a party or which is, to the knowledge of ABC, threatened against the Company. 付属書類Dには, 本会社が当事者である, またはABCが知るかぎり本会社が当事者になる恐れのある［本会社に対して提起される恐れがある］すべての請求, 訴訟, 仲裁, 法的手続きもしくはその他の手続き, または政府調査の完全かつ正確なリストが記載されている。◆The party initiating arbitration shall appoint its arbitrator in its demand for arbitration. 仲裁を申し立てた当事者が, 仲裁申立て書でその仲裁人を指名するものとする。

arbitration costs 仲裁費用
◆Each party shall bear its own arbitration costs; provided that the arbitration panel, at its discretion, may grant the prevailing party its attorney's fees and expenses. 各当事者が, 各自の仲裁費用を負担するものとする。ただし, 仲裁の合議体は, その裁量に従って, 勝った当事者にその弁護士費用［代理人費用］の賠償を受けさせることができる。

arbitration panel 仲裁人の合議体, 仲裁人団, 仲裁機関 (=arbitration board)
◆The arbitration panel shall consist of three arbitrators. 仲裁機関は, 仲裁人3名で構成するものとする。◆The third arbitrator shall act as the chairman of the arbitration panel. 第三仲裁人が, 仲裁機関の議長を務めるものとする。

arbitration proceedings 仲裁手続き
◆All direct costs of the arbitration proceedings

under this Article, including fees and expenses of the arbitration, shall be borne equally by the parties. 本条に基づく仲裁の手続きの直接費用は, すべて仲裁の手数料と仲裁費用を含めて両当事者が均等に負担する。◆The parties hereto agree to abide by and perform in accordance with any award rendered by the arbitrator in such arbitration proceedings. 本契約当事者は, 上記の仲裁手続きで仲裁人が下した判断を遵守し, その判断に従って履行することに同意する。

arbitrator （名）仲裁人
（⇒abide by, production of documents）
a panel of three arbitrators 3名の仲裁人団
sole arbitrator 単独仲裁人
third arbitrator 第三仲裁人
（⇒arbitration panel）
◆If the Respondent fails to appoint an arbitrator within such 60 day period, the arbitrator named in the Demand shall decide the controversy or claim as a sole arbitrator. 被申立て人が上記60日の期間内に仲裁人を指名しない場合には, 申立て書［仲裁申立て書］で指名された仲裁人が, 単独仲裁人として紛争または請求を判断する。◆The arbitrators failed to clarify the matter. 仲裁人は, 本件を解明できなかった。

area （名）地域, 地方, 地帯, 地区, 区域, 分野, 領域, 範囲, 面積, 部分, 部位, エリア （⇒free trade area）
ASEAN Free Trade Area アセアン自由貿易地域, AFTA
assisted area 開発助成地域
bonded area 保税地域, BA
commodity areas of the industry 汎用品分野
development area 開発地域
dollar area ドル地域
free trade area 自由貿易地域, 自由貿易圏
integrated hozei area 総合保税地域
key areas 中核業務, 主要セクター
leading-edge area 先端分野
market area 営業地域, 商圏
trade area 商業区域, 商圏, 貿易圏
◆Apple and other foreign electronics companies are able to obtain high-tech parts at low prices as they hold large market shares in the area of smartphones. アップルなどの海外家電メーカーは, スマートフォンの分野で高いマーケット・シェア（市場占有率）を占めているので, 高性能部品を安く仕入れることができる。

arise （動）生じる, 発生する, 立ち上がる, 蜂起する, 迫る, 大きく見えてくる
◆In case any dispute arises in connection with the above right, the seller reserves the right to terminate unconditionally this agreement or any further performance of this agreement at the seller's discretion. 上記権利に関して紛争が生じた場合, 売り主はその裁量で, 本契約または本契

約のその後の履行を無条件で終了させる権利を留保する。

arise from ～から生じる, ～に起因して生じる, ～を原因とする
◆The express warranty stated above is in lieu of all liabilities or obligations of ABC for damages arising from or in connection with the delivery, use or performance of the licensed program. 上記の明示保証は, 許諾プログラムの引渡し, 使用または履行から生じる損害, またはこれに関連して発生する損害に対するABCの債務または責任に代わるものである。

arise out of ～から生じる, ～に起因して生じる, ～を原因とする
◆Any dispute arising out of this agreement or any individual contract hereunder shall be subject to the exclusive jurisdiction of the Tokyo District Court. 本契約または本契約に基づく個別契約から生じる紛争は, すべて東京地方裁判所の専属管轄権に服するものとする。

arm （名）子会社, 部門, 部局, 支店, 行政部, 管理部, 武器, 兵器, アーム （⇒unit）
brokerage arm　証券子会社, 証券会社, 証券部門
consulting arm　コンサルティング部門, コンサルティング会社
financial arm　金融子会社, 金融部門
（＝finance arm, financing arm）
long-arm jurisdiction　域外適用管轄権
research arm　研究所, 研究部門
treasury arm　財務部門
◆General Motors Corp. has reached an agreement to sell a 51 percent stake in its finance arm. ゼネラル・モーターズ（GM）は, 金融子会社（GMAC）の株式の51％を売却することで合意した。
◆Toshiba will be given priority in negotiations for the right to acquire Westinghouse, British Nuclear Fuels PLC's U.S. nuclear power plant arm. 東芝に, ウェスチングハウス（英核燃料会社の米原発子会社）買収権獲得のための優先交渉権が与えられることになった。

arms export restrictions　武器輸出規制
◆Japan once provided patrol vessels to Indonesia as an exception to Japan's three principles on arms export restrictions. かつて日本は, 日本の武器輸出規制［武器輸出］3原則の例外として, インドネシアに巡視船を供与したことがある。

arm'slength [arm's-length]　（形）公正な, 独立した, 独立当事者間の, 独立企業間の, 独立第三者間の, 第三者間取引にかかわる, 商業ベースの
arm's length basis　純然たる商業ベース, 商業ベース
arm's length price　第三者間との取引価格, 独立企業間価格, 独立当事者間の価格
arm's length sale　独立企業間の売買, 対等の立場での販売

arm's length transaction［bargaining］　第三者間の公正な取引, 独立当事者間の取引, 対等取引
◆Transfers between geographic areas are based on "arm's length" prices. 地域間の1商品の売買は, 第三者間との取引価格に基づいて行われている。

around-the-clock [around the clock]
（形）24時間ぶっ通しの, 丸1日ぶっ通しの, 24時間休みなしの, 24時間営業の　（副）24時間営業で, 24時間休みなしで
around-the-clock operation　24時間営業, 24時間操業, 24時間運用
around-the-clock watch　24時間警戒態勢
◆In FX margin trading, investors can trade around the clock via the Internet. 外国為替証拠金取引の場合, 投資家はインターネットで24時間取引できる。

arrange （動）手配する, 準備する, 打診する, 打ち合わせる, 取り決める, 取りまとめる, 手はずを整える, 解決する, 同意する, 調停する, アレンジする
arrange a dispute　紛争［争い］の調停をする, 争いの仲裁をする
arrange a term loan facility　ターム・ローン（有期貸付け）案件をアレンジする
arrange all transportation of Products　本製品の運送の手配をする
arrange an initial public offering　株式公募を取りまとめる
arrange swap between two end-users　二当事者間のスワップ取引をアレンジする
arrange with a person about　人と～について打ち合わせる
arrange with a person to do　人と～するよう打ち合わせる
arranged total loss　妥協全損
as arranged　取決めどおり［取決めのとおり］, 打ち合わせどおり
be sold at arranged price　取り決めた価格で売却される, 同意した価格で売却される
◆Citibank Japan Ltd. is arranging to sell its retail banking business by the end of March 2015 if it can obtain approval from the Financial Services Agency, while it will maintain its corporate banking business. 米金融大手シティグループの日本法人「シティバンク銀行」は, 金融庁の承認が得られれば, 2015年3月末までに個人向けの小口取引銀行業務の売却を打診しているが, 企業との取引を行うコーポレート銀行業務は続ける方針だ。◆Distributor shall be responsible for arranging all transportation of Products. 販売店は, 本製品の運送の手配に関してすべて責任を負うものとする。◆Please arrange to send your samples to us as soon as possible. できるだけ早く貴社の見本を送るよう, 準備していただきたい。◆The firm appointed Deutsche Bank AG and Daiwa Securities SMBC

to arrange an initial public offering to raise about ¥100 billion. 同社は、約1,000億円を調達するため、ドイツ銀行と大和証券SMBCを株式公募の取りまとめ役に指名した。◆We have already arranged with our bankers for an L/C to be established by the end of this month. 今月末までに信用状を開設する件については、当社が当社の取引銀行にすでに手配してあります。

arrange for 〜の手配をする、〜するよう手配する、〜を準備する、〜を取り決める
  arrange for A in writing　Aを文書で取り決める
  arrange for ocean freight of the products　本商品の海上輸送を手配する
  arrange for shipment　積み出しの手配をする
  arrange for the goods shipped immediately　商品の即時積み出しを手配する
  ◆In case of a CIF contract, the seller shall, at its own expenses, arrange for ocean freight of the products from the port of shipment stated in this agreement to the port of destination of the products. CIF契約の場合、売り主は、本契約に定める船積み港から本商品の仕向け港までの本商品の海上輸送の手配を、自己負担でするものとする。◆In case of a FOB contract, the purchaser will, at its own expenses, arrange for ocean freight of the products from the port of shipment stated in this agreement to the port of destination of the products. FOB契約の場合、買い主は、本契約に定める船積み港から仕向け港までの本商品の海上輸送の手配を、自己の費用で手配するものとする。

arrangement （名）手配、手はず、準備、打合せ、措置、取決め、申し合わせ、協定、合意、契約、取りまとめ、調整、解決
  according to arrangement　打ち合わせどおり
  arrangement committee　準備委員会
  arrangement plan　設備配置計画
  arrangements for export　輸出手配
  arrive at［come to］an arrangement　話し合いがつく、示談になる、協定に達する、協定が成立する
  barter arrangement　バーター取引
  borrowing arrangement　借入協定
  business arrangement　業務協定、業務契約、業務提携
  by arrangement　申し合わせて、協定して
  conditional arrangements　条件付き協定
  formal arrangement　正式取決め
  in arrangement　整然と
  internal arrangement　内部での取決め
  make arrangements for　〜の手はずを整える、〜の手配をする、〜の準備をする
  monetary arrangement　通貨協定
  our arrangements with you on　〜に関する貴

社［御社］との協定
  reciprocal trade arrangement　互恵通商協定
  revolving credit arrangement　回転信用契約
  store arrangement　店舗配列
  swap arrangement　スワップ協定
  ◆The government has upgraded currency swap arrangements with India and South Korea. 政府は、インドや韓国と（それぞれ互いの通貨をやり取りする）通貨スワップ（交換）協定を強化した。◆The retail stores which form chain-store contracts with a large manufacturing firm deal with all the products of the manufacturer and receive various services such as design of stores, store arrangement and free supply of samples. ある大手メーカーとチェーン店契約を結ぶ小売店は、そのメーカーの全製品を取扱い、そのメーカーやり店舗のデザインや店舗配列、サンプルの無料供給などの各種サービスを受ける。◆The two airlines have agreed to enter into a code-sharing arrangement on international routes. 両航空会社は、国際線の共同運航協定を結ぶことで合意した。◆The two firms have built a relationship during a three-year business arrangement. 両社は、3年前からの業務提携で信頼関係を築いた。◆We hope these arrangements would in no respect bind our company. この取決めは、決して当社を拘束するものではないと思います。

array （名）整理、整頓、整列、陳列、展覧、配置、配列、列、陳列品、展示品、配列盤、勢ぞろい、軍勢、軍隊、（陪審員の）召集、陪審員総員　（動）整列させる、配備する、並べる、盛装させる、美しく着飾らせる、（陪審員を）列席させる、召集する
  a considerable array of protectionist methods　数々の保護主義的措置
  a wide［huge, vast］array of imported foods　多種多様な輸入食品
  an array of　〜の勢ぞろい、ずらりと並んだ〜、並べ立てた〜、一連の〜、大量［多数、多量］の〜
  ◆In Japan, ensuring a stable supply of the fuel for thermal power generation and importing the gas from a wide array of countries have become important issues since the accident at the Fukushima No. 1 nuclear power plant. 日本では、福島第一原発事故以来、火力発電用燃料の安定供給確保［安定調達］とガス輸入先の多様化が重要な課題となっている。

arrears （名）延滞、遅滞、遅れ、後日、滞り、延滞金、滞納金、未納金、未払い金
  account in arrear　残金勘定
  arrear coupon　繰延べ利札
  arrears sanctions　延滞した場合の制裁措置
  be in arrears with one's interest payments　利息の支払いが遅れている
  call in arrears　払込み請求残高
  fall into arrears　滞納状態［履行遅滞］に陥る

ARTI

in arrears　遅れて, 延滞して, 遅滞して, 後払いで
interest for arrears　遅延利息, 延滞利子
people in arrears　未納者
settle arrears　未払い金の決済をする, 未払い金を払う, 未払いを解消する
shall be payable in arrears　後払いとする
arrival　(名)到着, 到達, 到来, 訪れ, 登場, 出現, 出生, 誕生, 赤ん坊, 新生児, 新着品, 新着書, 到着した人, 到着便, 就任, 赴任
after arrival of cargo　積み荷到着後, 船積み荷物到着後
an arrival list　到着船客名簿
arrival bill　着荷払い手形
arrival contract　先物契約
arrival draft　到着後一覧払い手形, 着荷後一覧払い手形
arrival in port　入港
arrival list　入港船表
arrival notice　(輸入書類や輸出信用状の)到着案内, 船積み書類到着案内, 着船案内, 着船通知(書), 着荷通知, 貨物の到着通知, 貨物到着案内
arrival notice of import bill　輸入為替到着案内
arrival sale　先物売買, 到着渡し売買
arrival terms　到着条件
belated arrival　延着
cash on arrival　着荷払い
estimated time of arrival　到着予定日, ETA
ex-quay port of arrival　着地払い運賃
for arrival　到着渡し
new arrival　新着品, 新着荷
on［upon］(one's) arrival　着き次第, 着くとすぐ, 到着時に, 到着した時点で, 搬送された時点で
order arrival　引合い
pay on arrival　到着払い, 着荷払い
payment on arrival　着払い, 着荷払い
port of arrival　到着港
safe arrival　安着
supply against remittance upon arrival of goods with 1% discount　着払い送金ベース1%引きで供給する
the date of arrival　到着日
arrive　(動)到着する, 到達する, 届く, 配達される, 運ばれる, (行事が)行われる, 開催される, ～に至る, やって来る
arrived ship　着船
arriving and sailing schedule　配船表
goods［merchandise］to arrive　未着品
to-arrive［to arrive］contract　未着品契約, 未着品取引
◆We shall not hold ourselves responsible for the corresponding delay in shipment if the credit should fail to arrive in time.　万一信用状が間に合わない場合、その結果として起こる［それに伴って生じる］船積みの遅延に対して、当社は責任を負わないものとする。
article　(名)(契約などの)条項, 条文, 箇条, ～条, 項目, 定款, 規約, 記事, 論説, 論文, 物件, 物品, 品物, 物, 商品, 品目, (海事関係の)雇用契約, (事務弁護士や会計士の)実務研修
a choice article　精選品
a hand-made article　手作り品
article titles　条項の表題, 条項の見出し
Article 1 of the Sherman Act　シャーマン法第1条
articles consigned　委託積送品
articles durable　耐久品　(=durable articles)
articles free　無税品
articles in custody　保管品
articles not for sale　非売品
articles of agreement　契約書, 契約覚書, (社団の)規約, 協定規約, 基本定款
articles of amendment　修正条項
articles of company　(英国の)通常定款
articles of consolidation　合併届出書
articles of consumption　消耗品
articles of export　輸出品
articles of furniture　家具
articles of luxury　贅沢(ぜいたく)品
articles of trade　商品
articles on order　注文品
articles subject to taxation　課税品
branded article　有標品
contraband articles　禁制品, 密輸品
domestic articles　家庭用品
free articles　無税品
gift articles　贈答品
home-made articles　国産品, 国内製品
Japanese Article Number　日本商品コード, JANコード
manufactured articles　加工品, 製品, 工業品
memorandum and articles　定款
proprietary articles　専売品, 特許薬品
ship's articles　船員雇用契約書, 船員名簿
similar articles　類似商品, 同類商品
staple articles　主要品目
stock articles　在庫品, 手持ち品
tax-exempt［tax-free］articles　免税品
the Article 301 of the Trade Act　米通商法第301条
the genuine article　本物, 真正品
the headings of Articles used in this agreement　本契約書で使用する条項の見出し

the interpretation of the respective Articles of this agreement　本契約の各条項の解釈

the numbered Articles hereof　番号を付した本契約条項

toilet articles　化粧品

trade-in articles　下取り品

uncustomed articles　未通関品目

◆Diplomats are prohibited from engaging in commercial activities for the purpose of their personal profits under the Vienna Convention's Article 42. ウイーン条約42条で、外交官は個人の利得を目的とした商業活動を禁止されている。◆Generally speaking, every imported article must be marked in a conspicuous place as legibly, indelibly and permanently as the nature of the article will permit so as to indicate to an ultimate purchaser in the United States the English name of the country of origin of such article. 一般に、輸入品にはすべて輸入品の性質に応じてできるだけ永続的に消えない形で、また識別できる形で目立つ箇所にマークをつけて、当該輸入品の原産地の英語名を米国の最終購入者に示さなければならない。◆Licensee shall, concurrently with the royalty payment under subparagraph d) of Article 5, furnish Licensor quarterly with an auditor's statement of the royalty due hereunder for the preceding calendar quarter. ライセンシーは、第5条d) 項に基づくロイヤルティの支払いと同時に、直前の暦四半期 (四半期) に関して本契約に基づき支払い義務のあるロイヤルティについての監査人の報告書を、四半期ごとにライセンサーに提供する。◆The headings of Articles used in this agreement are inserted for convenience of reference only. 本契約書で使用している条項の見出しは、参照の便宜のためにのみ挿入してある。◆The licensee's obligation under this Article with respect to the confidential information shall not apply to information which is part of the public domain at the time of disclosure by the licensor, or thereafter becomes part of the public domain without fault on the part of the licensee. 本条に基づく秘密情報に関するライセンシーの義務は、ライセンサーによる開示の時点で公知であるか、その後ライセンシー側の過失なしに公知となる情報には適用されないものとする。◆The payment to Company under Paragraph 1 of this Article shall be made in Japanese Yen and remitted to such a bank account as Company shall have specified by written notice. 本条1項に基づく会社への支払いは、日本円で行い、会社が書面による通知で特定した銀行口座に送金するものとする。◆This in no way changes the validity of this Article. これは、決して本条の効力を変更するものではない。◆We fear we may not supply exactly the same articles you want as they are not in our lines. 貴社お望みの商品は扱っていませんので、当社としてはお望みの品とまったく同じものを提供することはできないと思います。◆We would assure you of our best cooperation in realizing business if you can secure these articles. これら

の商品をすべて確保できれば、当社は成約に最大限の協力を致します。

articles of association　米国の会社の基本定款 (articles of incorporation), 英国の会社の通常定款 (英国の会社の基本定款 ＝memorandum of association), 団体規約
◆Pursuant to the terms of the articles of association of the Joint Venture Company, ABC will have an initial ownership interest of forty percent of the voting shares of the Joint Venture Company. 合弁会社の定款の規定に従って、ABCの当初の出資比率は、合弁会社の議決権付き株式の40％とする。

articles of incorporation　基本定款, 設立定款, 定款　(＝articles of association: 会社の方針を定めたもの。日本は単一定款制度をとっているのに対して、欧米では基本定款 (articles of association, articles of incorporation) と付属定款 (bylaws) の二つの定款制度をとっている。)

revised articles of incorporation　変更定款
◆At TEPCO's shareholders meeting, the Tokyo metropolitan government as a major shareholder in the utility, proposed to include in the articles of incorporation a provision stipulating that putting customer service first is the company's mission. 東電の株主総会で、同社の大株主として の東京都が、「顧客サービス第一を会社の使命とする」との規定を定款に盛り込むよう提案した。◆The new company shall be incorporated pursuant to the Articles of Incorporation in the form attached hereto as Exhibit D. 新会社は、付属書類Dとして本契約書に添付する書式の定款に従って設立するものとする。

as　(接) 〜するとき、〜するにつれ、〜するような、〜なので　(関代) 〜するような、〜する　(前) 〜として、〜と、〜のときに、〜のような　(副) 同じくらい、同様に、〜のように

as against　〜に対して、〜に比べて、〜に関して、〜との関係では　(＝as between)

as agreed　合意に従って

as between　〜との関係では、〜に比べて、〜に関して　(＝as against)

as hereinafter defined　本契約の以下に定める、以下に定義する

as referred to in the preceding section　前項に定めるとおり、前項に定めたように

as stated in the preceding Article　前条に定めるとおり、前条の規定どおり

as the case may be　場合に応じて、場合次第で、随時、事情により

as a matter of right　権利として
◆The confidential information shall not include information which is hereafter furnished to ABC by a third party, as a matter of right and without restriction on disclosure. この秘密情報は、本契約締結後、第三者が権利として、また開示制限な

しにABCに提供した情報を含まないものとする。

as a requirement for　〜の条件として、〜の抱き合わせに
◆Distributor shall not, without Supplier's written permission, require its customers to purchase other goods or services as a requirement for the purchase of Products. 販売店は、供給者の書面による許可なしに、本製品の購入の抱き合わせに［購入の条件として］他の商品またはサービスの購入を顧客に要求してはならない。

as amended　修正された、改正された、改訂された、修正［改正］済みの
◆The trade term CIF shall be interpreted in accordance with INCOTERMS 2010 as amended. 貿易用語のCIFは、2010年版インコタームズ（改訂版）［インコタームズ2010（改訂版）］に従って解釈する。

as among A and B　AとBとの間で
◆The parties hereto believe it to be their best interests and the best interests of the New Company as defined in Article 1, that they provide for certain rights, duties, and restrictions as among themselves and others who may become shareholders of the New Company, all as provided in this agreement. 本契約当事者は、すべて本契約に規定するとおり、両当事者と第1条に規定する新会社の株主になる他の者との間で一定の権利、義務と制約について定めることが、両当事者にとって最上の利益となり、新会社にとっても最上の利益となる、と考えている。

as amount equal to　〜に相当する金額
◆At least the licensee shall in each year spend on advertising and promoting the licensed products as amount equal to ＿＿% of the total net sales amount of the licensed productsinvoiced in the previous year or ＿＿U.S. dollars, whichever is greater, in accordance with the advertisement plan to be approved by the licensor. 少なくともライセンシーは毎年、前年度に仕切った許諾製品の純売上総額の＿＿%に相当する金額と＿＿米ドルのうちいずれか多いほうの金額を、ライセンサーが承認する宣伝計画に従って宣伝と販売促進に使うものとする。

as and for one's own obligation　自己の義務として
◆Guarantors hereby guarantee jointly and severally as and for its own obligation, until full payment and performance are effected by ABC in accordance with the terms and conditions of the agreement, the due and punctual performance by or on behalf of ABC, of all obligations under the agreement. 保証人は、契約の条件に従ってABCが当該支払いと履行を完全に行うまで、ABCによるまたはABCに代わる契約上のすべての債務の適正かつ期限どおりの履行を、自己の義務（債務）としてここに各自連帯して保証する。

as defined below　以下に定義する、以下に定める、以下に定義するとおり
◆Licensee is engaged in the business of manu-

facturing, distributing, and selling software devices as defined below. ライセンシーは、以下に定義するソフトウエアの記憶媒体の製造・流通および販売業務に従事している。

as defined in　〜に定義する、〜に定義するとおり
◆Company has a right to grant Distributor a distributorship for the said products in the territory as defined in Article 1 hereof. 「会社」は、代理店に対して本契約第一条に定義する地域での上記（当該）製品の販売権を付与する権利を持っている。

as designated by　〜が指定する
◆The royalty shall be paid to Licensor by Licensee in Japanese currency by wire transfer remittance to Licensor's account at a bank in Japan as designated by Licensor. ロイヤルティは、ライセンサーが指定する日本国内銀行のライセンサーの口座に日本国通貨で電信送金して、ライセンシーがライセンサーに支払う。

as follows　次のとおり、以下のとおり、下記のとおり
◆In reply to your inquiry of March 5, we are pleased to quote you our prices as follows: 貴社の3月5日付け引合いに対して、下記のとおり当社の価格見積りについてご回答申し上げます。

as herein used　本契約で使用する
◆"Trademarks" as herein used shall mean the trademarks described in the following schedule. 本契約で使用する「商標」とは、以下の付属書類に表示する商標を意味する。

as is　現状有り姿の、現状有り姿で、現状有り姿のままで、現状のままで、そのままで、無条件で、無保証で　（=as seen, without any changes）
◆All information is provided as is. 情報は、すべて現状のままで提供されています。

as is, where is　現状のまま、現状有り姿で、無条件で、無保証で
◆The product is being sold and delivered to the purchaser under this agreement "AS IS, WHERE IS". 本製品は、現状のまま、本契約に基づいて買い主に販売され引き渡される。

as long as　〜するかぎり、〜であれば
◆Copyrighted materials can be used freely under the U.S. law as long as it is considered "fair use." 著作権のある著作物は、「公正な利用」であれば、米国の法律では自由に利用することができる。
◆This agreement shall remain in force as long as the joint venture company continues to exist, unless earlier terminated as provided for in this agreement. 本契約は、本契約に定めるとおり中途終了する場合を除いて、合弁会社が存続するかぎり有効とする。

as of　〜現在で、〜の時点で、〜現在の、〜の日付で、〜の日付に、〜から、〜以降

as of the date first above written　冒頭に記載した日付で［日付に］、冒頭記載の日付で

as of the date hereof　本契約日現在、本契約の

AS

日現在, 本契約の締結日現在

as of the date of signature of this agreement　本契約の署名日現在

◆As Abenomics, the economic policy by the Abe administration, has drawn global attention to the Japanese economy, the ratio of foreign holders of Japanese equities reached a record high of about 30 percent as of the end of March 2013. 安倍政権の経済政策「アベノミクス」で日本経済が世界に注目されたため、外国人株主の日本株保有比率が、2013年3月末の時点で過去最高の約3割に達した。

as of the date of this agreement　本契約締結日の時点で, 本契約締結日に

◆Any orders or debts which exist as of the date of this agreement shall be enforceable in accordance with the terms thereof. 本契約の締結日時点で存在する注文や債務は、その条件に従って強制執行できるものとする。

as of the date thereof　同日現在の, 同日時点の

◆The annual financial statements for the financial year ending on December 31, 2015 present a true and fair view of the financial position as of the date thereof. 2015年12月31日に終了する事業年度［会計年度］の年次財務書類は、同日現在の財政状態について真実かつ公正な見方を提示している。

as per　～に従って, ～によって, ～のように, ～のとおり

a model as per the enclosed specifications　同封仕様書どおりの機種

as per attached copy　添付の写しのように

as per one's instructions　～の指示に従って, ～の指示どおり

as per the enclosed copies of the shipping documents　同封の船積み書類のとおり

as promptly as practicable　できるだけ速やかに, 可能なかぎり速やかに, 可及的速やかに

◆As promptly as practicable after execution of this agreement, Supplier shall provide Distributor with information, materials, manuals and other technical documents necessary to enable Distributor to perform its obligations under this agreement. 本契約締結後できるだけ速やかに、供給者は、販売店が本契約に基づく販売店の義務を履行するのに必要な情報、資料、マニュアル、その他の技術文書を、販売店に提供しなければならない。

as provided　定めるとおり, 規定するとおり, 明記するとおり

as provided above　上記の

as provided for in this Section　本項に定めるとおり, 本項で定めるとおり, 本項に規定するとおり

as provided elsewhere in this agreement　本契約の他に規定するとおり, 本契約の他の条項に定めるとおり

◆This agreement shall continue to be effective for 5 years thereafter unless earlier terminated as provided elsewhere in this agreement. 本契約は、本契約の他に規定するとおり早期終了しないかぎり、その後も引き続き5年間有効とする。

as provided herein　本契約に定めるとおり, 本契約の規定どおり

◆The term of this lease shall continue for a period of sixty（60）months unless sooner terminated as provided herein. 本リースの期間は、本契約に定めるとおり早期終了しないかぎり60日間存続するものとする。

as provided in this Article　本条で定めるとおり, 本条で規定するとおり

◆Unless notice is given as provided in this Article, Distributor shall be deemed to have accepted such Products and to have waived all claims for shortages, defects, or damage. 本条で定めるとおり通知が行われなかった場合、販売店は、当該製品を受け入れ、不足、瑕疵（かし）または損傷に関する一切のクレームを放棄したものと見なされる。

as set forth above　上記の, 前述の, 前述した, 前項に定める, 上記のとおり

as set forth below　下記の, 以下に定める, 以下に明記する, 後述する, 次のとおり

◆In consideration for the license of the trademark and the technical information granted under this agreement, Licensee shall pay to Licensor the minimum royalty for each contract year as set forth below. 本契約で付与する商標と技術情報の使用許諾の対価として、ライセンシーは、下記の各契約年度のミニマム・ロイヤリティをライセンサーに支払うものとする。

as set forth in　～に定める［規定する］とおり, ～に明記するとおり

◆ABC warrants that the licensed program, when properly used, will operate substantially as set forth in the documentation subject to the conditions stated in this agreement. 許諾プログラムは、正しく使用した場合は、本契約で規定する条件に従って文書に明記するとおり実質的に稼動することを、ABCは保証する。

as set forth in a formal agreement　正式契約書に定めるとおり, 正式契約書に規定するとおり

◆The parties' legal obligations will be as set forth in a formal agreement, if and when such formal agreement is signed by the parties hereto. 両当事者の法的義務は、（本覚書の）両当事者が正式な契約書に署名した場合には、その正式契約書に定めるとおりとする。

as soon as reasonably practicable　合理的に実行可能なかぎり速やかに, 合理的にできるだけ速やかに, できるだけ速やかに

◆Any claim by the purchaser, except for latent defects, shall be made in writing as soon as reasonably practicable after the arrival, unpacking and inspection of the products, whether by the purchaser or any subsequent purchaser of the products. 買い主によるクレームは、隠れた瑕疵（かし）を除いて、買い主によるか本製品のその後の購入者によるかを問わず本製品の到着、開梱および検査後、合理的に実行可能なかぎり速やかに書面で行うものとする。

as stipulated in this agreement 本契約の規定どおり
◆If Distributor should have failed to cause to be established a letter of credit as stipulated in this agreement, Company is entitled to immediately cancel this agreement and such sales contract. 代理店が本契約の規定どおりに信用状を開設させることができなかった場合、会社は直ちに本契約と当該売買契約を解除する権利を持つものとする。

as such そのようなものとして（suchは反復の代名詞で、次の文例ではTerritoryを指す）
◆The Territory means Japan, Singapore, South Korea and other Asian countries upon which the parties herein agree as such from time to time. 「契約地域」は、日本、シンガポール、韓国と、両当事者が（契約地域として）随時合意する他のアジア諸国を意味する。

as used in this agreement 本契約で使用される場合
◆As used in this agreement, Licensed Products means the software products listed on Schedule B attached hereto together with all enhancements and modifications thereto as may from time to time be made by the licensor. 「使用許諾製品」とは、本契約で使用する場合には、本契約書に添付する付属書類Bに記載したソフトウエア製品と、ライセンサーが随時行うその改訂および変更をすべて意味する。

ASEAN アセアン, 東南アジア諸国連合（Association of South-East［Southeast］Asian Nationsの略）
ASEAN Free Trade Area アセアン自由貿易地域, AFTA
ASEAN summit ASEAN首脳会談, アセアン首脳会談
Japan-ASEAN ties 日本とアセアンとの関係
◆Japan-ASEAN ties are meaningful in ensuring regional security, particularly freedom of navigation at sea. 日本とアセアン（東南アジア諸国連合）との関係は、地域の安全保障、とりわけ航海の自由を確保するうえで重要である。◆Japan's imports from and exports to ASEAN members have doubled over the past decade. 日本のアセアン加盟各国との輸出入額は、ここ10年間で倍増している。

ASEM アジア欧州会議, アジア欧州首脳会議（Asia-Europe（summit）meetingの略。1996年3月、アジアと欧州の関係強化を目的としてバンコクで第一回首脳会議を開いて発足。日本、中国、韓国、東南アジア7か国と欧州連合（EU）、欧州委員会が参加）
Asia-Europe（summit）meeting アジア

欧州会議, アジア欧州首脳会議 ASEM（⇒ASEM）

Asia-Pacific Economic Cooperation（forum） アジア太平洋経済協力会議, エイペック, APEC （⇒APEC）
the Asia-Pacific Economic Cooperation forum アジア太平洋経済協力会議（APEC）
the Asia-Pacific Economic Cooperation forum summit meeting アジア太平洋経済協力会議（APEC）首脳会議
◆Leaders of the Asia-Pacific Economic Cooperation forum adopted a road map toward an envisioned regional free trade area which would cover about 60 percent of the world economy. アジア太平洋経済協力会議（APEC）の各国首脳は、世界経済の6割をカバーする地域自由貿易圏構想の工程表を採択した。

Asian countries［nations］ アジア諸国, アジア
◆As many domestic manufacturers have moved their production sites from Japan to Asian nations and elsewhere, the Japanese economy benefits less and less from the weak yen which lowers export costs. 国内製造業の多くが生産拠点を日本からアジアなどに移しているため、日本経済は、輸出コストが下がる円安メリットを享受しにくくなっている。

Asian-Pacific region アジア太平洋地域
◆An important role of the NIEs is to act as a nucleus or center in the promotion of export-oriented industrialization in the Asian-Pacific region. 新興工業経済地域（NIEs）のひとつの重要な役割は、アジア太平洋地域における輸出志向型工業化の中核あるいはセンターとして機能することにある。

assailing thieves 強迫行為

assemble （動）組み立てる, 生産する, 集める,（集めて）整理する （自動）集まる, 集合する, 終結する, 機械語に変換する
◆Japan and China have established a system of international division of labor in which China imports industrial parts from Japan to assemble into finished products in China and these are marketed domestically or exported to the U.S., Europe and elsewhere. 日本と中国は、中国が日本から工業部品を輸入して中国で最終製品に組み立て、中国国内で販売したり欧米などに輸出したりする国際分業体制を築いてきた。◆MMC's Outlander sport-utility vehicles produced in the Netherlands are currently assembled at its Dutch plant with parts imported from Japan. オランダで生産されている三菱自動車の多目的スポーツ車「アウトランダー」は現在、部品を日本から輸入してオランダの自社工場で組み立てている。

assembling drawings 組立図面

assembly （名）組立て, 組立部品
assembly service 集荷サービス
assembly shop 組立工場

ASSE 38

assembly work 組立作業

assembly plant 組立工場 (=assembling plant)
◆Nissan Motor Co. is considering building an assembly plant in Russia. 日産自動車は、ロシアに車両組立工場を建設する計画を検討している。

assert (動)主張する、断言する
◆Seller shall waive any claim against Buyer under the Uniform Commercial Code or otherwise, with respect to a claim asserted against Seller or Buyer for patent, trademark or copyright infringement or the like. 売り主は、特許・商標・著作権の侵害等について売り主または買い主に対してなされる請求に関しては、買い主に対する米国統一商事法典その他に基づく請求権をすべて放棄する。
◆The guarantor hereby waives, and agrees not to assert by way of motion as a defence or otherwise, in a suit, action or proceeding pursuant to this guarantee, any claim that this guarantee or the subject matter hereof may not be enforced in or by such courts. 保証人は、本保証書に従う訴訟、裁判または手続き［訴訟または訴訟手続き］で、抗弁として申し立てることによりまたは他の方法により、本保証書またはその主題を上記裁判所でまたはその裁判所が強制することはできないとの主張をここに放棄し、これを主張しないことに同意する。

assess (動)査定する、算定する、資産などを評価する、税金・罰金などを課す
◆ABC shall pay all import duties or sales, use, value added or property taxes or any other taxes of any nature, assessed upon any Product or Service purchased by ABC from XYZ. ABCは、ABCがXYZから購入した本製品またはサービスに課されたすべての輸入関税、売上税、使用税、付加価値税、資産税または他のあらゆる種類の税金を支払うものとする。

assessment (名)査定、評価、査定額、評価額、株金払込み請求、保険などの賦課金、追徴金損失賠償額の決定、損失補償額の決定

assessment contract 賦課式契約

asset value assessment 資産評価

credit assessment 信用評価

economic assessment 景気判断

rating assessment 格付け評価

risk assessment リスク評価、リスク査定
◆All transportation costs after shipment, insurance and import duties, fees, taxes and similar assessments or charges shall be for the account of Distributor. 船積み後の輸送費、保険料と輸入関税、料金、税金および類似の賦課金、または諸経費は、すべて代理店の勘定とする。◆As a basis for its economic assessment, the report referred to increases in exports, progress in inventory adjustment and the bottoming out of industrial production. 景気判断の根拠として、同報告書は輸出が増加し、在庫調整が進展して、鉱工業生産も底を打ったことを挙げている。◆The EU's stress test

criteria for assessing the banks' assets were not sufficiently rigorous. 銀行資産を査定するためのEU（欧州連合）のストレス・テスト（特別検査）の基準は、甘かったと言える。

asset (名)資産、財産、アセット

asset assessment 資産査定、資産評価 (=asset appraisal, asset evaluation)

asset-backed securities 資産担保証券、商業用不動産証券、アセットバック証券、ABS（銀行の貸出債権や企業の売掛債権などを担保に発行される証券）

asset base 資産基盤、資産構成

asset erosion 資産の目減り、資産価額の低下

asset sales 資産売却

asset value 資産価値、資産価格、純資産

assets purchase agreement 資産購入契約、資産譲渡契約、営業譲渡契約、資産買収契約

capital assets 資本的資産、固定資産

current assets 流動資産 (=liquid assets)

excess of liabilities over assets 債務超過

external assets 対外資産、対外資産残高（日本の政府や企業、個人が海外に持っている資産）

fixed assets 固定資産

foreign assets 対外資産、海外資産

freezing terrorist-related assets テロ関連資産の凍結

hidden assets 含み資産

intangible assets 無形資産、無形固定資産

out-of-book assets 簿外資産

quick assets 当座資産

real assets 不動産

securitized assets 証券化資産、証券化した資産

tangible assets 有形資産、有形固定資産

total assets 総資産
◆Great rotation refers to the shift of investment money from low-risk assets such as U.S. Treasuries and the yen into riskier assets such as stocks. 「グレート・ローテーション（大転換）」とは、投資資金を米国債や円などの低リスク資産［安全資産］から株式などリスクの高い資産に移すことを言う。◆Gross foreign assets held by Japanese in the form of direct investment, securities investment, financial derivatives, loans and export credits, deposits, other investments and official foreign reserves came to ¥379.78 trillion. 直接投資、証券投資、金融派生商品、貸付け金や輸出信用、預金その他の投資と政府の外貨準備高の形で日本の政府や企業、個人が保有する海外資産の総額（対外資産残高）は、379兆7,800億円に達した。◆In a global carry trade, hedge funds borrow low-interest yen funds to invest in dollar-denominated assets. グローバル・キャリー・トレード［グローバル・キャリー取引］では、ヘッジ・ファンドなどが、低利の

円資金を借りてドル建て資産に投資している。

asset inflation 資産インフレ
◆Speculative money has poured into emerging economies, causing an appreciation of their currencies and asset inflation because of drastic monetary easing by Japan, the United States and Europe. 日米欧の大胆な［大規模な］金融緩和で、投機マネーが新興国に流れ込み、新興国の通貨高や資産インフレを招いている。

assign （動）割り当てる，配分する，課する，任命する，指定する，選定する，定める，決める，与える，譲渡する，委託する
  accounts receivable assigned　売掛金の割当て
  amount assigned　担保提供額
  assign a deadline for　〜に締切りを定める
  assign a person for　人を〜に選任する
  assign a prospective AAA rating to　〜にAAA（トリプルA）の予備格付けを付与する［与える］
  assign a rating of AA　AAの格付けを付与する
  assign a trademark　商標を譲渡する
  assign limits to　〜に制限を課す，〜に制限を設ける
  assign swaps　スワップを譲渡する
  assign the contrary to a third party　本契約を第三者に譲渡する
  assign the property to　財産を〜に譲渡する［譲る］，財産を〜に委託する
  assign the work to　この仕事を〜に割り当てる
  the rating assigned to the issuer　発行体に与えられた格付け
◆ABC shall have no recourse against XYZ for any obligations under the original agreement assigned pursuant to this assignment agreement. ABCは、この譲渡契約に従って譲渡された原契約上の債務については、XYZに履行の請求を一切求めないものとする。◆Except as otherwise expressly provided herein, neither party hereto shall assign, transfer, sell or otherwise pledge all or any portion of its shares in the New Corporation to any third party. 本契約に別に明文の規定がないかぎり、いずれの当事者も、新会社の株式の全部または一部をいかなる第三者にも譲渡・移転、売却または入質してはならない。◆Standard & Poor's assigned a negative outlook to the rating on Spain's debt, but it could be further downgraded if Spain's economic conditions erode further. スタンダード・アンド・プアーズ(S&P)は、スペインの国債格付け見通しを「ネガティブ(弱含み)」としたが、スペインの経済状態がさらに悪化すれば、さらに引き下げられる可能性もある。

assignable （形）譲渡可能な，明記できる，列挙できる，特定できる，はっきりした
  assignable cause　はっきりした原因，除去可

能な原因
  assignable credit　譲渡可能信用状
  assignable debt　譲渡可能債権
  assignable subscription warrant　譲渡可能新株引受権証書

assigned （形）割り当てられた，指定された，譲渡された，〜の割当て，〜の譲渡
  assigned account　（融資を受ける場合に担保に差し入れられる）売掛金勘定，担保勘定
  assigned accounts receivable　割当債権
  assigned counsel　国選弁護人，州選弁護人
  assigned debt　譲渡された債権，債権の譲渡
  assigned in blank　株券などの白地式譲渡
  assigned risk　危険の割当分担，割当危険負担，割当危険，割当物件
  assigned risk plan　危険割当方式，不良物件割当制度

assignee （名）譲受人，被譲渡人，受託者，代表，代理人
  an assignee of Licensor　ライセンサーの譲受（ゆずりうけ）人
  assignee in bankruptcy ［insolvency］　破産管財人　(=trustee in bankruptcy)
◆A party hereto proposing to effect a sale of any shares of the new company (the Offerer) shall give a written notice to the other parties hereto, or their assignee, who are then shareholders of the new company (the Offerees), of the Offerer's intention, the identity of the prospective third party purchaser, and the terms and conditions of the proposed sale. 新会社の株式の売却を申し出る本契約当事者（「申込人」）は、他の当事者またはその時点で新会社の株主である譲受人（「被申込人者」）に対して、申込人者の売却意思、予定される第三者購入者の住所・氏名と申し出をした売却の条件を、書面で通知するものとする。

assignment （名）譲渡，譲渡条項，譲渡証書，選任，任命，派遣，管財人，割当て，assignment and delegation，譲渡と委託，譲渡と委任
  assignment and pledging of policy　保険金請求権の譲渡
  assignment of accounts receivable　債権譲渡契約
  assignment of agreement　契約の譲渡，契約譲渡
  assignment of rights and obligations　権利と義務の譲渡
◆Any such assignment shall not release the assigning party from its duties, liabilities or obligations hereunder. このような譲渡は、本契約上の義務、責任と債務から譲渡当事者を解放しないものとする。◆No assignment of this agreement or any right hereunder shall be made, in whole or in part, by either party, without the prior written consent of the other. 本契約と本契約に基づいて

発生した権利は、その全部か一部かを問わず、相手方の書面による事前の同意を得ないでいずれの当事者も譲渡してはならない。

assignment agreement 譲渡契約, 契約譲渡契約

copyright assignment agreement 著作権譲渡契約

patent assignment agreement 特許権譲渡契約

trademark assignment agreement 商標権譲渡契約

◆The assignment under this assignment agreement shall not relieve ABC of any of its obligations under the original agreement. この譲渡契約に基づく契約の譲渡によって、ABCはその原契約上の債務履行の責任を免除されないものとする。

assignment and delegation 譲渡と委託, 譲渡と委任

◆ABC hereby accepts such assignment and delegation and agrees to assume and perform all of the obligations of XYZ under the original agreement. ABCは、ここに、当該譲渡と委託を引き受け、原契約に基づくXYZのすべての義務を引き受けて履行することに同意する。

assignment, conveyance and transfer 譲渡

◆After the closing, Seller, upon request of Purchaser, shall take such action and execute and deliver such further instruments of assignment, conveyance and transfer as may be necessary to assure, complete and evidence the full and effective assignment, conveyance and transfer to Purchaser of the Shares. クロージング後、買い主は、買い主の要求に基づいて売り主は、本株式の買い主に対する完全かつ効力のある譲渡を保証、実行し、証明するのに必要な行動を取り、追加の譲渡証書を作成して交付するものとする。

assignment for the benefit of creditors 債権者のための財産譲渡, 債権者の利益のための譲渡, 債権者のための財産の信託譲渡(倒産手続きの一種。債権者がある人に全財産または財産のほとんど全部を信託し、信託された人がその財産を処分して債権者に配当を行うこと)

◆This agreement terminates automatically, with no further act or action of either party, if a receiver is appointed for Distributor or its property, Distributor makes an assignment for the benefit of its creditors. 本契約は、販売店またはその財産に管財人が選任され、販売店が債権者のために財産の信託譲渡を行った場合には、各当事者の別段の行為を要しないで自動的に終了する。

assignor (名)譲渡人, 委託者

◆The assignor shall remain in all respects responsible to the nonassigning party for the performance of the assignor's obligations set forth in this agreement. 譲渡人は、本契約に定める譲渡人の義務の履行について、引き続きすべての点で非譲渡当事者に対して責任を負うものとする。

assistance (名)援助, 支援, 協力, 助力, 斡旋(あっせん), 指導

◆The particulars of the services and assistance are set forth in Exhibit A hereto. サービスと指導の詳細は、本契約書の付属書類Aに定める。

associated (形)～と関連した, ～と関係した, ～と結びついた, ～がらみの, ～に伴う, ～に伴って［～に関連して］発生する, ～系の, 連合の, 協賛の, 共有株の

associated gas 随伴ガス

associated peripheral devices 関連周辺機器

associated trademark 連合商標

be associated in ～に関係している

◆Two investment funds associated with Lenovo will join the second round of bidding to choose a company to support the corporate rehabilitation of chipmaker Elpida Memory. レノボ系の投資ファンド2社が、半導体メーカー大手エルピーダメモリの企業再建支援企業を選定する二次入札に応札する［参加する］予定だ。

associated with ～にかかわる, ～に関連する, ～に付随する

be closely associated with ～と密接に関わっている［係わっている］, ～と密接に関連している

costs associated with originating loans 貸付け［貸出］の実行に関連して発生した費用, 貸付け実行関連費用

credit risks associated with privatization 民営化に伴って発生する信用リスク

◆ABC represents and warrants that it owns and possesses all rights, title, interest, in all of the Software Products, and any trademarks, logos, trade secrets and proprietary rights associated with the Software Products. ABCは本ソフトウエア製品の全部に対するすべての権利, 権原, 権益と、本ソフトウエア製品に関連する一切の商標、ロゴ、トレード・シークレットおよび財産権を所有していることを、ABCは表明しこれを保証する。

◆Licensor is the owner of the well-known trademark and of the substantial goodwill and reputation associated with it. ライセンサーは、有名な商標の所有者であり、それに付随する多大な信用と営業上の名声の所有者でもある。

assume (動)任務や義務・債務を引き受ける, 負担する, 責任を負う, 引き継ぐ, 占有する

assume and agree 同意する, 合意する

assume the obligation of ～の義務を負う

◆Distributor agrees and assumes such appointment. 代理店は、当該指名に同意し、これを引き受ける。◆The purchaser shall assume all risks and liability for the damages or loss of third parties, lives or properties resulting from the use of the products which are delivered under this agreement. 買い主は、本契約に基づいて引き渡された製品の使用により生じる第三者、生命または財産に対する損害または損失にかかわるすべての危険

と責任を引き受けるものとする。

assume and perform　引き受けて履行する
◆ABC hereby accepts such assignment and delegation and agrees to assume and perform all of the obligations of XYZ under the original agreement. ABCは、ここに、当該譲渡と委託を引き受け、原契約に基づくXYZのすべての義務を引き受けて履行することに同意する。

assume or create any obligation or responsibility　債務、責任を負担するまたは負担させる
◆Distributor will not have, and will not represent that it has, any power, right or authority to bind Supplier, or to assume or create any obligation or responsibility, express or implied, on behalf of Supplier or in Supplier's name, except as herein expressly provided. 本契約に明文の規定がある場合を除いて、販売店は供給者を拘束する権能、権利または権限も、また明示・黙示を問わず供給者のためにまたは供給者の名義で債務・責任を負担するまたは負担させる権能、権利または権限も有しておらず、これらを有する旨表明することもしない。

assume the defence thereof　その防御を引き受ける
◆If any claim shall be asseted or brought against the licensee, in respect of which indemnity may be sought under Section 1 of this Article from the licensor or its successor thereto, the licensee shall give a prompt written notice of such claim to the licensor which may assume the defence thereof. ライセンシーに対して請求がなされるか起こされ、それについて本条第1項によりライセンサーまたはその承継人に補償を求めることができる場合、ライセンシーはライセンサーに対して当該請求の書面による通知を迅速に行い、ライセンサーはその防御を引き受けることができるものとする。

assumed exchange rate　想定為替レート
（企業が決算見通しを策定するにあたって、事前に予想するドルなどの外国通貨に対する円の為替レートのこと。輸出企業の場合、想定より円高になれば為替差損が生じ、想定より円安になれば為替差益が出る）
◆An exporter company will incur losses if the yen rises above the assumed exchange rate, but benefit if the yen declines. 輸出企業では、その想定為替レートより円高になれば為替差損が生じ、（想定為替レートより）円安になれば為替差益が出る。
◆The revision of the firm's assumed exchange rate will translate into an additional ¥150 billion loss in its consolidated accounts for the six-month period through March 2015. 同社の想定為替レートの修正に伴って、同社の2014年度下半期（2014年10月〜2015年3月）の連結決算では、追加で1,500億円の為替差損が生じることになる。

assumption of risk　危険の引受け

assurance　（名）保証、確約、確信、確実性、自信、言質（げんち）、保険（insurance）

assurance company　保険会社
assurance of bill　手形保証
assurance policy　保険証券
firm assurance　確信
quality assurance　品質保証

assure　（動）安心させる、保証する、請けあう、確実にする、確信させる、納得させる、〜に確信をもって言う、保険をかける（insure）、保険を付ける
assure A of　Aに〜を保証する、Aに〜を請けあう、Aに〜を確信をもって言う
assure oneself against　〜に保険をかける、〜に保険を付ける
be already assured of　すでに〜を確信している
have one's life assured　生命保険をかける
◆We will accept your offer if you assure us of an order for at least 1,000 pieces per quarter for one year. 1年間、四半期ごとに最低1,000個の注文をご確約いただければ、貴社のオファーをお受けします。◆We would assure you of our best cooperation in realizing business if you can secure these articles. これらの商品をすべて確保できれば、当社は成約に最大限の協力を致します。

assured　（形）保証された、確実な、保険をかけた［付けた］　（名）被保険者
assured amount　保険金額、保険金
　（=amount insured, amount of insurance, insured amount）
assured person　被保険者、保険金受取人
the assured　被保険者

assurer [assuror]　（名）保険者（insurer, underwriter）、保険業者、保証者

at　（前）〜に、〜で、〜の、〜するときに、〜の状態で
at all reasonable hours　合理的な時間に
at all times during the term of this agreement　本契約期間中つねに
at any point in time　いつでも
at any reasonable time　合理的な時間にいつでも、合理的な時間内にいつでも
at any time during the term of this agreement　本契約の有効期間中いつでも
at any time or place　いかなる時であれいずれの場所であれ
at any time thereafter　その後いつでも
at less frequent intervals　それより頻繁でない間隔で
at no charge　無料で
at one's burden of cost　〜の費用負担で
　（=at the cost of, at the expense of, for account of）
◆ABC shall, at all times during the term of this agreement, maintain an adequate stock of the products so as to enable it to meet the require-

ment and supply promptly all orders reasonably anticipated in the territory. ABCは、本契約の期間中つねに、合理的に予想される契約地域内の必要量をみたすことができるようにするため、またすべての注文品を迅速に供給できるようにするため、本製品の十分な在庫を維持するものとする。

at one's account 　〜の勘定で
◆During the period when Products are in the custody of ABC, ABC shall keep Products insured at ABC's account for the benefit of XYZ against loss or damage by fire, theft or otherwise with extended coverage. 本製品［契約品］をABCが保管している期間中、火災、盗難、その他による滅失や損害を拡張担保するため、ABCはその勘定で、XYZを保険受取人として本製品に付保するものとする。

at one's discretion 　〜の裁量で，〜の自由裁量で，〜の（独自の）判断で
at one's sole discretion 　〜の単独の裁量で，〜の独自の判断で，〜のみの判断で
◆In case any dispute arises in connection with the above right, the seller reserves the right to terminate unconditionally this agreement or any further performance of this agreement at the seller's discretion. 上記権利に関して紛争が生じた場合、売り主はその裁量で、本契約または本契約のその後の履行を無条件で終了させる権利を留保するものとする。

at one's option 　〜の選択で，〜の裁量で，随意に，自由に，任意に
◆Quantity is subject to a variation of 5% more or less than the contracted quantity at Seller's option unless otherwise specified. 数量は、他にとくに明記しないかぎり、売り主の裁量で契約数量より5％増減の変動が生じることがある。

at one's own expense 　〜の費用で，〜の自己費用で，〜の自己負担で
◆For the purpose of display, demonstration and distribution, Distributor shall maintain at its own expense a stock of the Products. 展示、宣伝と販売のため、販売店は、本製品の在庫を自己費用で［自己負担で］維持するものとする。◆The purchaser shall effect, at its own expense, marine insurance on each cargo of the products from the point where such cargo passes the rail of the vessel of the port of the shipment. 買い主は、買い主の自己費用で、本製品の各貨物が船積み港の本船の舷側欄干を越える時点から、当該貨物に海上保険を付けるものとする。

at one's sole option 　〜の単独の選択で，〜の単独の裁量で
◆In the event of any such violation of this Article, the party whose conduct does not violate this Article may, at its sole option, terminate this agreement. このような本条違反の場合、本条に違反していない行為の当事者（本契約に違反する行為をしていない当事者）は、その単独の裁量で本契約を解除することができる。

at or prior to 　〜以前に

◆The obligations of Purchaser to effect the transactions contemplated hereby shall be, at the option of Purchaser, subject to the fulfillment, at or prior to the closing date, of the following additional conditions: 本契約で企図されている取引を実行する買い主の義務は、買い主の裁量で、クロージング日以前に以下の追加条件を達成することを条件とする。

at par 　額面で，パーで
be paid off at par 　パーで償還される
be priced at par 　パーで値決めされる
conversion at par 　額面転換
debenture convertible at par 　額面転換社債
issue at par 　パー発行
stock at par 　額面株
◆The parties hereto shall subscribe for, at par, shares of the common stock of the New Company to be issued at the time of its incorporation as follows: 本契約当事者は、新会社の設立時に発行される新会社の普通株式を、額面で次のとおり引き受けるものとする。

at sight 　一覧払いの，一覧次第，A/S
a draft at sight 　一覧払い手形
a draft at sight signed by 　〜が振り出す一覧払い手形，〜が振り出した一覧払い手形
draw a draft at 30 day's sight on you 　貴社宛てに一覧後30日払い手形を振り出す
◆Such letter of credit shall be transferable and having the clause of definite undertaking by the issuing bank for unconditional payment against a draft at sight. この信用状は、譲渡可能で、一覧払い手形に対する無条件支払いに関して発行銀行が明確に約束した文言が入っているものとする。◆The letter of credit set forth above shall be negotiable against a draft at sight signed by the seller upon the presentation of the following documents: 上記の信用状は、次の船積み書類の提示がある場合には、売り主が振り出した一覧払い手形と引換えに買い取られるものとする。◆To cover this shipment, we have drawn upon you at sight for the invoice amount under the L/C opened by ABC Bank. この船積みに対して、当社はABC銀行発行の信用状に基づいて、一覧払い送り状額面金額の手形を貴社宛てに振り出しました。◆We have drawn a draft at 30 day's sight on you through ABC Bank for $1,000. ABC銀行経由で1,000ドルの一覧後30日払い手形を、貴社宛に振り出しました。◆We have valued upon you today for the amount specified above, at sight, and ask you to accord our draft your due protection. 当社は本日、貴社宛てに上記金額に対する一覧払い手形を振り出しましたので、この手形のお引受けをお願い致します。

at such time as may be agreed upon by 　〜が合意する時期に
◆Provided, however, that the purchaser shall have the right to inspect the products by an independent inspection company designated by the

purchaser at the premises of the manufacturer of the products at such time as may be agreed upon by the seller and the purchaser prior to loading. ただし、買い主は、積込み前に売り主と買い主が合意する時期に、本製品製造者の構内で、買い主指定の独立した検査会社により本製品を検査する権利を持つものとする。

at the latest　遅くとも
◆We need to have the goods by the end of October at the latest, so punctual shipment is essential. 同品は遅くとも10月末には入手しなければならないので、積み期に遅れないことが肝要です。

at the option of　～の選択で、～の裁量で
◆In the event any such assignment or transfer is attempted without the prior written consent of the other party, this agreement and all the rights conferred hereunder shall, at the option of the other party, immediately terminate. 当該譲渡または移転が相手方の書面による事前の承諾を得ないで企てられた場合、本契約と本契約に基づいて付与された権利はすべて、相手方の選択で直ちに終了するものとする。◆The obligations of Purchaser to effect the transactions contemplated hereby shall be, at the option of Purchaser, subject to the fulfillment, at or prior to the closing date, of the following additional conditions: 本契約で企図されている取引を実行する買い主の義務は、買い主の裁量で、クロージング日以前に以下の追加条件を達成することを条件とする。

at the premises of　～の構内で
（⇒at such time as may be agreed upon by）

at the rate of　～の料率で、～の割合で
◆If the buyer fails to pay any amount under this agreement when due, the buyer shall be liable to pay to the seller overdue interest on such unpaid amount from the due date until the actual payment date at the rate of 15% per annum. 買い主が支払い期日に本契約に基づく代金の支払いを怠った場合、買い主は、支払い期日から実際の払込み日までの当該未払い金額に対する年率15%の遅延金利を、売り主に支払わなければならない。

at the time subsequent thereto　その後に
◆During the life of this agreement and thereafter Distributor shall not divulge any confidential information which it may acquire in connection with Products, this agreement or performance thereunder, except insofar as such information is or becomes generally known or publicly available at the time of disclosure under this agreement or subsequent thereto. 本契約期間中とその後も、代理店は、本契約に基づく開示時点とその後に公知または公用となる場合を除いて、本製品（契約品）、本契約または本契約に基づく履行に関連して取得することができる一切の秘密情報を漏洩しないものとする。

at will　自由に
◆Distributor or Supplier may terminate this agreement at will, at any time during the term of this agreement, with or without cause, by writ-ten notice given to the other party not less than 30 days prior to the effective date of such termination. 販売店または供給者は、この契約終了の効力発生日の30日以上前に相手方に書面で通知して、本契約中いつでも理由の有無を問わず自由に本契約を解除することができる。

ATA　米国航空運送協会（Air Transport Associationの略）

ATA Carnet　通関手帳、ATAカルネ（ATA ＝仏語のadmission temporaireと英語のtemporary admissionの合成語）

ATI　米独占禁止法の適用除外（antitrust immunityの略。⇒antitrust immunity）

attached　(形)添付の、添付した、付属の
attached copy　添付の写し
attached documents　添付書類
attached hereto as　～として本契約書に添付する、～として本契約書に添付した
in the form attached to this agreement　本契約書に添付する［添付した］書式で
with strings attached　付帯条件付きで
◆As used in this agreement, Licensed Products means the software products listed on Schedule B attached hereto together with all enhancements and modifications thereto as may from time to time be made by the licensor. 「使用許諾製品」とは、本契約で使用する場合には、本契約書に添付する付属書類Bに記載したソフトウエア製品と、ライセンサーが随時行う不の改訂および変更をすべて意味する。◆Egypt's Morsi administration has concluded a basic agreement with the IMF on loans totaling $4.8 billion, with strings attached, in an effort to avert a default on debts. エジプトのモルシ政権は、債務不履行を回避するため、付帯条件付きで、国際通貨基金（IMF）との間で総額48億ドルの融資を受けることで基本合意した。

attachment　(名)差し押さえ、逮捕、付属書類、別紙、付属品、付属装置　（⇒sovereign immunity）

attempt　(名)企(くわだ)て、企画、計画、策、措置、試み、努力、行為、挑戦、攻撃、襲撃、攻勢、未遂
a coup attempt　クーデター未遂事件
（＝attempted coup）
a hostile takeover attempt　敵対的な買収攻勢
a takeover attempt　買収劇、買収攻勢
an attempt to prop up a company　企業支援策
fail in an attempt　計画が挫折する
in an attempt to　～しようとして、～するため
◆In an attempt to recapitalize itself, the bank raised ¥15 billion through a third-party share allotment. 資本再編のため、同行は第三者株式割当てで150億円を調達した。◆The parties hereto will enter into bona fide discussions in an attempt to

solve any issues or dispute which may arise from the interpretation or performance of this agreement. 本契約当事者は, 本契約の解釈または履行から生じる一切の問題または紛争を解決するための試みとして, 善意の話し合いを行うものとする。

attention （名）注意, 注目, 興味, 関心, 焦点, 集中力, 好意, 配慮, 気配り, 世話, 治療, 修理, 修復, 手入れ, ～宛, 気付, 担当者, 担当部課

add special attention to　～に特に注意する

arrest attention　注意を引く

attention deficit　注意欠陥

attract considerable [great] attention　多大の注目を集める, 大いに注目を集める

be the center [focus] of attention　関心の的となる

by careful attention to　～に細心の注意を払って

consumer attention　消費者の注目

draw one's attention　～の目を引く, ～の注意を引く

gain attention　注目される

get the attention of　～の関心を引く

give full attention to　～に細心の注意を払う, ～に全神経を集中する

investment attention　投資先, 投資の関心

pay as much attention as possible　細心の注意を払う

pay close attention to　～に細心の注意を払う, ～に（とくに）注目する, ～にとくに留意する, -に十分注意する, -をよく注視する, ～を警戒する

pay courteous attention to　～を丁重に取り扱う

receive a lot of attention from　～から大いに注目される

to the attention of the person who executed this agreement on behalf of such party　当該当事者を代表して本契約に署名した人を気付として

with best attention　最善の注意を払って

◆The firm received a lot of attention from investors as an emerging company. 同社は, 新興のベンチャー企業として投資家から大いに注目された。◆The weaker yen helps exporters, but close attention must be paid to the fact that the excessive depreciation of the yen will further increase the prices of imports of LNG and other foreign products. 円安は輸出企業にはプラスだが, 円安が行き過ぎると, 天然液化ガス（LNG）など海外製品の輸入額が一段と増えることにも, 警戒が必要である。◆We will execute the order with best attention upon receipt of your L/C. 貴社の信用状を受け取り次第, 当社は最善の注意を払って注文を履行します。

attorney （名）弁護士, 代理人, 検事

a district attorney　地区（首席）検事

a letter [warrant] of attorney　委任状

an attorney-at-law　弁護士

an attorney in fact　代理人

Attorney General　米国の司法長官, 英国の法務長官, 検事総長

by attorney　（代理人による）委任状でもって

consult an attorney　弁護士に相談する

power of attorney　委任権, 代理権, 委任状

retain an attorney　弁護士に依頼する

U.S. Attorney　米連邦検事

◆California's Attorney General Bill Lockyer has sued the six largest U.S. and Japanese automakers for damages related to greenhouse gas emissions. 米カリフォルニア州のビル・ロッキャー司法長官は, 自動車が排出する温室効果ガスについて日米の大手自動車メーカー6社に損害賠償を求める訴訟を起こした。◆To seek information on cyber attacks, U.S. Attorney Preet Bharara has sent subpoenas to bitcoin exchanges including Mt.Gox and businesses that deal in bitcoin. サイバー攻撃に関する情報を得るため, プリート・バララ米連邦検事は, マウントゴックス社などビットコイン（仮想通貨）の取引所やビットコインの取扱い業者に対して, 召喚状を送った。

attorney [attorney's] fee　弁護士費用, 弁護士報酬, 弁護士料, （仲裁などの）代理人費用

◆Each party shall bear its own arbitration costs; provided that the arbitration panel, at its discretion, may grant the prevailing party its attorney's fees and expenses. 各当事者が, 各自の仲裁費用を負担するものとする。ただし, 仲裁の合議体は, その裁量に従って, 勝った当事者にその弁護士費用［代理人費用］の賠償を受けさせることができる。

attorney's fees and expenses　弁護士費用, 代理人費用

◆Each party shall bear its own arbitration costs; provided that the arbitration panel, at its discretion, may grant the prevailing party its attorney's fees and expenses. 各当事者が, 各自の仲裁費用を負担するものとする。ただし, 仲裁の合議体は, その裁量に従って, 勝った当事者にその弁護士費用［代理人費用］の賠償を受けさせることができる。

attractive product　魅力的な商品

◆To increase exports, Japanese manufacturers must develop attractive products of high added value and find ways to capitalize on growing markets in the emerging economies of Asia and other regions. 輸出を拡大するには, 日本の製造業各社が, 付加価値の高い魅力的な商品を開発して, アジアなどの地域の新興国の成長市場を積極的に取り込む方法を見つける必要がある。

attributable to　～に起因する, ～に帰属する, ～による　（=be attributed to, be caused by, be due to, be traceable to, result from）

AB is primarily attributable to CD　ABは主にCDに起因する, ABの主な要因［主因］はCDである, ABは主にCDによる

AUDI

income attributable to ordinary activity　経常損益（正常な営業活動から生じる損益）
losses attributable to credit defaults　信用デフォルトに起因する損失
losses attributable to dilution　減額による損失, 減額に起因する損失, 受取債権の減額による損失
◆ABC's obligation under this Article shall not apply to any information relating to the licensed products that is or becomes available without restriction to the general public by acts not attributable to ABC or its employees. 本条に基づくABCの義務は, ABCまたはその従業員が引き起こしたと考えることができない行為によって一般公衆に制限なく知られている, または知られるようになった許諾製品に関する情報には適用されないものとする。

auction　（名）競売, 競り売り, 公売, 入札, 公募入札, オークション　（動）競りで売る
auction business　オークション事業, オークション・ビジネス
auction date　入札日
auction dealer　競売取引員
auction event　オークションの入札
auction house　競売場, 競売専門会社, 競売企画専門会社
auction market　競り売り市場
auction notice　競売通知　（=auction sale notice）
auction off　競りで売る
auction participant　オークション参加者
auction period　入札期間
auction price　入札価格
auction procedure　競売手続き
auction rules　オークション規定
auction sale　競売
auction sale catalogue　競売カタログ
auction system　競売制度
be up for [to] auction　競売に出ている, 競り [競売] に出される　（=come up for auction）
buy a thing at [by] auction　物を競売で買う
competitive auction　競争入札
compulsory sales by auction　強制競売
double auction　二重競売
Dutch auction　逆競り, ダッチ・オークション　（=Chinese auction: 売り主が売り値を付け, 買い主が買ってくれるまで値下げして行く競り売りの方法）
e-auction　eオークション
government bond auction　国債入札
monthly auction　月次入札
Net auction　ネット・オークション　（=Internet auction）
online auction　オンライン・オークション, ネット・オークション
open auction　公開競売
public auction　公共の競り, 公開入札
put a thing up for auction　物を競売に出す, 物を競りに出す
quarterly auction　四半期入札, 四半期ごとの入札
reverse [reversal] auction　逆オークション, リバース・オークション
sell a thing at [by] auction　物を競売で売る, 物を競りにかける
sell by auction　競売で売却する
Treasury note auction　Tノート入札

auction-rate security　金利入札証券, ARS　（=auction-rate debt: 米国の地方自治体や美術館などの文化施設が資金調達のために発行する満期20年以上の長期債で, 定期的に行われる入札で金利が変わるのが特徴）
◆Federal and state regulators have been investigating marketing of the auction rate securities by a number of big banks. 米連邦と州の規制当局は, 一部の大手金融機関による金利入札証券（ARS）の販売方法について調査している。

auction site　オークション・サイト, 競売サイト（売り手が出品した品物を, 買い手が落札するホームページのこと）
◆The firm's auction site auctioned off $15 billion worth of merchandise last year. 同社オークション・サイトのオークションでの商品販売額は, 昨年は115億ドルに達した。

auctioneer　（名）オークション業者, 競売人
◆This online auctioneer has been asking sellers for pertinent information, including credit card numbers to reduce fraudulent transactions. 不正取引を防ぐため, このオンライン・オークション業者は, クレジット・カード番号などの関連情報を売り手に求めている。

audit　（動）監査する, 会計検査する, 審査する, 検査する, 目を通す, 聴講する　（名）監査, 会計検査, 審査, 検査, 聴講
an internal audit　内部監査
audit expenses　監査費用
audited balance sheets　監査済み貸借対照表
conduct an audit of　～の検査をする
safety audit　安全検査
◆Companies with more than ¥500 million in capital are required to be audited by an auditing firm or a certified public accountant in addition to internal auditors. 資本金5億円以上の会社は, 内部監査役（監査役）のほか, 監査法人か公認会計士の監査も受けなければならない。

auditing firm　監査法人　（=audit corporation, audit firm, auditing house, auditor: 「監査法人」は, 5人以上の公認会計士が共同で設立する法人。会計基準などに照らして企

業決算が適正かどうかを第三者の立場で審査して、監査証明書（監査報告書）を出す。4大監査法人（みすず（旧中央青山）、あずさ、トーマツ、新日本）が、上場企業の8割を監査している）

auditor （名）監査人, 監査法人, 監査役, 会計検査官

external auditor　外部監査人

independent auditor　独立監査人

internal auditor　内部監査人

outside auditor　社外監査人

statutory auditor　法定監査人, 常勤監査役, 監査役

◆The auditor of the Chinese company, listed on the TSE's Mothers market for start-up firms, refused to certify its annual financial statements. 東証の新興企業向け市場「マザーズ」に上場している中国企業の監査法人は, 同社の年次財務諸表の正確さに対する保証を拒否した。

auditor's statement　監査人の報告書

◆Licensee shall, concurrently with the royalty payment under subparagraph d）of Article 5, furnish Licensor quarterly with an auditor's statement of the royalty due hereunder for the preceding calendar quarter. ライセンシーは, 第5条d）項に基づくロイヤルティの支払いと同時に, 直前の暦四半期（四半期）に関して本契約に基づき支払い義務のあるロイヤルティについての監査人の報告書を, 四半期ごとにライセンサーに提供する。

authority （名）権限, 権力, 権能, 代理権, 職権, 権威, 威厳, 迫力, 公共機関, 公的機関, 関係組織, 当局, 権威者, 専門家, 許可, 先例

◆Finance ministers from the European Union's 27 countries agreed to give the European Central Bank the authority to supervise eurozone banks from March 2014. 欧州連合（EU）27か国の財務相は, 2014年3月から, 欧州中央銀行（ECB）にユーロ圏の銀行を監督する権限を与えることで合意した。

◆The arbitrators shall have the authority to order such discovery and production of documents, including the depositions of party witnesses, and to make such orders for interim relief, including injunctive relief, as they may deem just and equitable. 仲裁人は, 当事者の証人の宣誓証言［証言録取書］を含めて文書の開示と提出を命じる権限と, 差止救済を含めて仲裁人が正義かつ衡平と見なす暫定的救済を命じる権限を持つものとする。

authorization [authorisation] （名）承認, 承諾, 認可, 許可, 公認, 権限, 権限付与授権, 検定, 委任, 委任状

authorization code　承認番号

authorization of agent　委任状

credit authorization network　信用照会ネットワーク

credit authorization terminal　信用照会端末装置, 加盟店端末機, クレジット専用端末, CAT

credit card authorization　クレジット・カードの認証

governmental authorization　政府の承認, 政府の認可, 政府公認

interim authorization　仮認可

legal authorization　法的裏付け

letter of authorization　授権書

prior authorization　事前の許可

signed authorization form　署名入り委任状

written authorization　書面による権限付与, 授権書

◆Deliberations on the bill to revise the Pharmaceutical Affairs Law to simplify screening procedures for regenerative medicine products to speed up government authorization have been carried forward to the next sitting of the legislature. 再生医療製品の審査手続きを簡素化して政府承認の早期承認を目指す薬事法の改正法案は, 継続審議となった。

authorized （形）権限を与えられた, 権威のある, 認可された, 許可された, 認定された, 公認の, 検定済みの, 正当な, 正当な権限のある

an authorized aged　指定代理人

an authorized agency　公認格付け機関

an authorized dealer　認可業者, 指定販売店, 正規販売店

authorized but unissued common stock　未発行の授権普通株式

authorized capital provided for in the articles of incorporation　会社定款に定められている授権資本

authorized common stock　授権普通株式数

authorized depository　公認保管業者

authorized distributor　正規販売店

authorized foreign exchange bank　外国為替公認銀行, 外為公認銀行

authorized, issued or paid-up capital　授権資本, 発行済み資本または払込済み資本

authorized shares　授権株式 （=authorized issue, authorized stock: 会社がその基本定款に基づき発行できる株式の総数）

authorized signatory　正当な署名人

authorized signature　権限のある者の署名

authorized capital　授権資本

◆Many of listed companies are set to adopt measures to counter corporate acquirers, such as increasing their authorized capital or reducing the quorum of directors. 授権資本（株式発行可能枠）の拡大や取締役の定数削減など, 買収防衛策を導入する上場企業も多い。

authorized capitalization　授権株式総数

◆The authorized capitalization of the Company consists solely of 50,000 authorized shares of Common Stock, 30,000 shares of which are issued to Seller and outstanding on the date hereof.

契約対象会社の授権株式総数は、普通株式50,000株の授権株式だけであり、このうち30,000株は本契約日現在、売り主に対して発行済みとなっている。

authorized representative 授権された代表者, 権限のある代表者, 正当な代表者
◆The terms of this agreement may be modified only in writing signed by authorized representatives of both parties. 本契約の条項は、両当事者の正当な代表者が署名した書面によってだけ修正することができる。

authorized surveyor 公認鑑定人
◆The purchaser shall forward full particulars of such claim, accompanied by an authorized surveyor's certificate of inspection of quality and quantity of the products delivered in dispute, to the seller by registered airmail within 30 days after such notification. 買い主は、当該通知後30日以内に、引き渡された問題の製品の品質と数量に関する公認鑑定人の検査証明書を添付して、当該クレームの詳細を記載した書面を書留航空便で売り主に送付するものとする。

automated transaction 自動取引
◆Two factors responsible for the recent market plunge are speculative moves intended to drive down stock prices and high-speed, automated transactions. 最近の株安を招いた二つの要因は、売り崩し（大量の売りを出して相場を崩すこと）を狙う投機筋の動きと、（瞬時に売買が成立する）コンピュータでの高速の自動取引である。

automatic cover 自動再保険
◆Any amounts exceeding the limits of automatic cover shall be offered to the Reinsurer for facultative acceptance. 自動再保険の適用限度を超える額は、任意受再のために再保険会社に申し出るものとする。

automatic damages 自動的損害賠償請求権

automatically （副）自動的に, 無意識に, 器械的に, 何気なく
automatically terminate 自動的に終了する, 自動終了する, 自動的に解除し終了する
◆The new small car "up！" released by Volkswagen has a standard collision-avoidance feature that automatically stops when a collision is imminent. 独フォルクスワーゲンが発売した新小型車「up！（アップ）」には、（前方の車と）衝突しそうになると自動的にブレーキがかかる衝突防止装置が標準装備されている。

automatically extend 自動延長する, 自動更新する
be automatically extended for additional consecutive periods of two（2）years each さらに2年ずつ自動的に延長（更新）される
◆The said term of this agreement shall be automatically extended for additional consecutive periods of three years each, unless terminated by either party hereto by giving the other party a written notice to that effect at least three months prior to the end of original term of this agree-

ment or any extended term thereof. 本契約の上記期間は、少なくとも本契約の当初期間またはその延長期間が満了する3カ月前までに、本契約の当事者の一方が相手方に対して本契約を終了させる旨の書面による通知をして本契約を終了させないかぎり、さらに引き続き3年間ずつ自動的に延長するものとする。

automatically renew 自動更新する
◆This agreement shall be automatically renewed from year to year for one year term hence expiration of the initial term of this agreement. 本契約は、本契約の最初の期間満了後は、1年単位で年毎に自動更新されるものとする。

availability （名）有効性, 有効期間, 効力, 利用可能度, 可用性, 可用度, 使用可能度, 提供可能性, 提供, 確保

available （形）有効な, 利用可能な, 利用できる, 使用可能な, 入手可能な, 手に入る, 提供できる, 確保できる, 手配できる, 閲覧可能な, 求めることができる, 請求できる, 適用される
（⇒act or failure to act, comparable）
all other remedies available at law or in equity コモン・ロー上またはエクイティ上有効な他のすべての救済, 法律上有効な他のすべての権利

available funds 手元の資金

available properties 不動産の物件

be available till 〜まで有効

in immediately available funds 直ちに引き出せる資金で

money available for investment［to invest］ 投資に運用可能な金

products available for export 輸出可能製品

publicly available 公然と入手できる

ship the goods by the earliest available vessel 手配できる第1便で船積みする

the approximate quantity available 手配可能な概略数量
◆ABC's obligation under this Article shall not apply to any information relating to the licensed products that is or becomes available without restriction to the general public by acts not attributable to ABC or its employees. 本条に基づくABCの義務は、ABCまたはその従業員が引き起こしたと考えることができない行為によって一般公衆に制限なく知られている、または知られるようになった許諾製品に関する情報には適用されないものとする。◆In the event the seller should have quantities of the products available for sale, the seller shall notify the purchaser of such quantities. 売り主が販売に提供できる本製品の余裕数量を持ち合わせている場合、売り主は買い主に当該数量を通知するものとする。◆Larger discounts are available due to the additional expense of handling trade-ins. 下取り品を扱うのに追加費用がかかるため、大幅な割引率が適用される。◆The L/C shall be available for at least fifteen days after the

latest date for shipment stipulated in the contract. 信用状は、本契約指定の積み期の後、少なくとも15日間は有効である。◆The licensee shall make its records and accounts available for inspection by the licensor or its duly authorized representatives upon reasonable advance notice. ライセンシーは、(ライセンサーから)合理的な事前の通知を受けたときは、ライセンサーまたはその正当な権限を持つ代理人の検査のためにライセンシーの記録と帳簿を提供するものとする。◆The licensor and the licensee agree that damages, costs, and attorney fees arising from breach are available in an action for material breach by either party. 契約違反から生じる損害賠償、費用と弁護士料は、一方の当事者による重大な違反に対する訴訟で請求できることに、ライセンサーとライセンシーは合意する。◆There is a discount available for a large order. 大量注文には、割引の恩典があります[値引も適用されます]。◆This article is available for immediate shipment. 本品は、直積み可能です。

average （名）平均, 海損　（形）平均の, 海損の

average adjuster［stater, taker］　海損清算人

average adjustment　海損清算

average bond　共同海損盟約書

average claim　海損賠償要求

average clause　海損分担条項

average common shares outstanding　発行済み普通株式の平均数, 発行済み普通株式の平均株式数

average general claim　共同海損賠償要求

average loss settlement　分損計算法

average rate of profit　平均利益率

average rate of return　平均資本利益率

average return on investment　平均投資収益率, 平均投資収益

average shares outstanding　期中平均発行済み株式総数

average tare　平均風袋

compound yield based on weighted average　加重平均利回り

general average　共同海損, G.A.

general average clause　共同海損約款

general average deposit　共同海損供託金

overall average　総平均

particular average　単独海損

petty average　小海損

stock price average　平均株価

weighted average price　加重平均株価

with（Particular）Average　単独海損担保, W. A.

◆Concerns over the safety of Chinese food products are rising in Japan, but the percentage of safety violations involving food imports from China fell below the overall average for all imported foods in fiscal 2012. 日本では中国産食品の安全性への懸念が強まっているが、中国からの輸入食品のうち安全面での違反件数の割合は、2012年度は輸入食品全体の総平均を下回った。

avoid （動）取り消す, 撤回する, 無効にする, 回避する

◆ABCD's obligations under Article 5 shall terminate when the party seeking to avoid its obligations under such Articles can document or otherwise prove that: 第5条に基づくABCDの義務は、当該条項に基づくその義務の回避を求める当事者が以下を文書その他で証明できる場合には、終了するものとする。◆To avoid the high costs of operating domestically, Japanese companies are moving their production overseas. And this leads to the rapid hollowing-out of the domestic manufacturing industry. 国内操業のコスト高を回避するため、日本企業が生産拠点を海外に移転しており、これが国内製造業の急速な空洞化を招いている。

avoidance （名）回避, 忌避（きひ）, 無効, 取消し

legal tax avoidance　合法的な課税逃れ

tax avoidance　節税, 租税回避, 税金逃れ, 課税逃れ

◆In a report released by the U.S. Senate Permanent Subcommittee on Investigations, Apple was held up as an example of legal tax avoidance. 米上院行政監察小委員会が公表した報告書で、米アップル社は、合法的課税逃れの典型例と指摘された。

award （名）賞品, 賞金, 賞, (裁判官などの)判断, 裁定, 仲裁判断, 仲裁裁定額, 裁定金, 審査, 審判, 判定, 奨学金, 賞与, 昇給

a damage award　損害賠償裁定金

accept the arbitration award　仲裁裁定を受け入れる

award rendered by arbitration　仲裁による判断, 仲裁による裁定, 仲裁判断

judgment upon the award　仲裁判断に基づく判決

◆Judgment upon the award rendered by the arbitrator（s）may be entered in any court having jurisdiction thereof. 仲裁人が行った仲裁判断に基づく判決は、その管轄権のある裁判所の記録に正式に登録することができる[仲裁人による仲裁裁定の執行判決は、その管轄権のあるいずれの裁判所でも受けることができる]。

award rendered by arbitrator（s）　仲裁人による判断, 仲裁人による仲裁判断, 仲裁人が下す判断, 仲裁人が行う仲裁判断　（⇒abide by）

◆The award rendered by arbitrator（s）shall be final and binding upon both parties. 仲裁人が行った仲裁判断は、最終的なもので、両当事者を拘束するものとする。

B

BAF バンカー課徴金（bunker adjustment factorの略。bunker surchargeともいう），燃料費割増料

bag for fresh-water transport 淡水輸送用大容量バッグ

balance （名）収支, 貿易収支（trade balance）, 差額, 残高, 勘定残高, 残金, 残り, 貸借勘定, 帳尻, 不足額, 繰越金残存価額, 均衡, 釣合い, バランス

 balance due 差引不足額, 支払うべき差引残高, 支払い金の差額, 請求額

 balance of accounts 勘定残高

 balance of capital account 資本収支, 資本勘定収支, 資本勘定残高

 balance of current account 経常収支

 balance of invisible trade 貿易外収支（保険、船舶・航空運賃、対外投資の利子・配当など、サービス取引の収支尻）

 balance of payment constraint 国際収支の天井

 balance of payment figures 国際収支統計

 balance of payment risk 国際収支リスク

 balance of transfer account 移転収支（政府の対外無償援助や個人の海外送金など、対価を伴わない外国との一方的取引の収支尻のこと）

 balance renewal バランス更新, 書換え, 再融資

 bank balance 預金残高

 bring bilateral trade into balance 2国間の貿易を均衡の取れたものにする

 external balance 対外収支

 external balance of payments 対外収支

 fiscal balance 財政収支

 invisible trade balance 貿易外収支

 overall balance of payments 総合収支（=overall balance）

 service balance 貿易外収支

 strike a balance はかりにかける, 清算する

 total balance 総合収支

 trade balance 貿易収支

◆Due to the turmoil that followed the regime change, Egypt's external balance of payments deteriorated and foreign reserves dropped sharply. 政変による混乱で、エジプトの対外収支が悪化し、外貨準備は激減した。◆Japan's 2012 trading balance, or exports minus imports, ran up a record deficit of ¥6.9 trillion, 2.7 times more than the 2011 figure, the first trade deficit in 31 years due to the negative effects of the Great East Japan Earthquake. 輸出額から輸入額を差し引いた日本の2012年の貿易収支は、過去最大の6.9兆円

の赤字で、東日本大震災の悪影響で31年ぶりに貿易赤字に転落した2011年と比べて2.7倍に増えた。◆The interest rate to be paid by the borrower to the lender on the loan hereunder shall be five percent （5%）per annum on the balance of the loan from time to time outstanding calculated from each respective advance date to and including the date of maturity of the loan on the basis of a 365-day year, for the actual days elapsed. 本契約に基づいて借主が貸主に対して支払う借入金の金利は、1年を365日として各借入日から借入金の返済期日まで実際に経過した日数についてそのつど計算した未決済の借入金残高について、年5%とする。

balance of capital account 資本収支

 balance of long-term capital account 長期資本収支

 balance of short-term capital account 短期資本収支

balance of current account 経常収支

 balance of invisible trade 貿易外収支（保険、船舶・航空運賃、対外投資の利子・配当など、サービス取引の収支尻）

 balance of trade 貿易収支

 balance of transfer account 移転収支（政府の対外無償援助や個人の海外送金など、対価を伴わない外国との一方的取引の収支尻のこと）

balance of exports and imports 輸出入のバランス, 輸出と輸入のバランス

◆If we consider a good balance of exports and imports, a desirable exchange rate between the yen and the U.S. dollar would be ¥95-¥105 to the dollar. 輸出と輸入の妥当なバランスを考えるなら、円とドルの望ましい為替相場は、1ドル=95～105円程度だろう。

balance of international payments 国際収支

◆Changes in exchange rates are a result of multiple factors, including the balance of international payments and market supply and demand. 為替相場の変動は、国際収支や市場の需給など複数要因によるものだ。

balance of payments 国際収支, 支払い差額, 支払い残高, BOP （=balance of international payments, international balance of payments; ⇒international balance of payments）

 adjustment process of balance of payments 国際収支調整過程

 balance of payments constraint 外貨不足

 balance of payments deficit 国際収支の赤字

 balance of payments equilibrium 国際収支均衡

 balance of payments, foreign trade and foreign exchange 国際収支

 balance of payments statement 国際収支表

balance of payments statistics　国際収支統計

balance of payments surplus　国際収支の黒字

解説 国際収支とは：国際収支は経常収支（balance of current account）と資本収支（balance of capital account）で構成され、この二つを合わせたものを総合収支（overall balance of payments）という。また、経常収支は貿易収支（balance of trade）と貿易外収支（balance of invisible trade）、移転収支（balance of transfer account）から成り、資本収支は長期資本収支（balance of long-term capital account）と短期資本収支（balance of short-term capital account）から成る。なお、総合収支から短期資本収支を除いたものを基礎収支（basic balance of payments）という。

balance of power　勢力均衡

◆The U.S.-led TPP framework, which excludes China, has a strategic meaning to create a multilateral balance of power system. 中国を除外した米国主導の環太平洋経済連携協定（TPP）の枠組みには、多角的な勢力均衡体系を作るという戦略的な意味合いがある。

balance of trade　貿易収支, 貿易尻, 貿易差額　（=trade balance: 製品類の輸出入取引の収支尻）

adverse balance of trade　輸入超過, 貿易の入超

balance of invisible trade　貿易外収支（保険, 船舶・航空運賃, 対外投資の利子・配当など, サービス取引の収支尻）

balance of trade without L/C［letter of credit］信用状なしの貿易収支

balance of visible trade　貿易収支

favorable balance of trade　貿易収支の黒字, 輸出超過

unfavorable balance of trade　貿易収支の赤字

◆The international competitiveness of companies and a country's balance of trade with the rest of the world are affected not by nominal exchange rates but by real exchange rates, so we need to follow real exchange rates. 企業の国際競争力や国の他国との貿易収支などの動きは、名目為替レートではなく、実質為替レートの影響を受けるので、われわれは実質為替レートの動きを見る必要がある。

balance of trade in goods and services　モノとサービスの貿易収支

◆The balance of trade in goods and services logged a surplus of ¥3.43 trillion in the April-September period. 4〜9月期のモノとサービスの貿易収支は、3兆4,300億円の黒字を記録した。

balance on services　サービス収支

◆The balance on services saw a ¥255.8 billion deficit as the appreciation of the yen deterred tourism to Japan. サービス収支は、円高で日本への観光客が減ったため、2,558億円の赤字となった。

balance sheet　貸借対照表, バランス・シート　（=position statement: 財務諸表の一つ）

balance sheet growth　資産の増加

balance sheet management　財務管理

closing balance sheet　クロージング貸借対照表, クロージング時現在の貸借対照表

nonmonetary balance sheet items　貸借対照表の非貨幣性項目

off-balance-sheet asset　簿外資産

post-balance sheet date　決算日後

post-balance sheet event　後発事象

projected balance sheet　見通し貸借対照表

◆Nonmonetary balance sheet items and corresponding income statement items are translated at rates in effect at the time of acquisition. 貸借対照表の非貨幣性項目とこれに対応する損益計算書項目は、取得日の為替レートで換算されています。◆The balance sheet, operation statement and profit and loss statement and the statement of changes in the fiscal position of the Company as at December 31, 2014 prepared by the Company, heretofore delivered to the Buyer, are in accordance with the books, records and accounts of the Company. 本会社が作成してこれまで買い主に引き渡した2014年12月31日現在の本会社の貸借対照表、営業報告書と損益計算書および財務状態変動表は、本会社の会計帳簿、記録と勘定に従って作成されている。

ban　（動）禁止する, 停止する　（⇒grain export）

ban A from doing　Aが〜するのを禁止する

ban imports　輸入を禁止する

ban job discrimination against women　女性に対する仕事上の差別を禁止する

be banned from doing　〜するのを禁止される, 〜するのを一生禁止される

Egypt's banned Muslim Brotherhood　エジプトの非合法組織「ムスリム同胞団」

◆Bitcoin, an online currency, is illegal in Thailand and financial services involving bitcoin are banned in China, but the virtual currency has been spreading around the world online. ネット通貨のビットコインはタイでは違法で、ビットコイン関連の金融サービス［ビットコインを使った金融サービス］は中国では禁止されているが、この仮想通貨はネット上で世界に拡散している。◆Mister Donuts outlets sold imported nikuman (Chinese steamed meat buns) that contained an antioxidant banned under the Food Sanitation Law. ミスタードーナッツのチェーン店が、食品衛生法で禁止されている酸化防止剤を使った輸入肉まんを販売していた。

ban　（名）禁止, 停止, 廃絶, 禁止令　（⇒blanket ban on）

ban on arms exports　武器輸出禁止

blanket ban　全面禁止

BANK

import ban 輸入禁止, 輸入停止
(=ban on imports)

lift the ban on ～を解禁する, ～の禁止を解除する

put a ban on ～を禁止する
(=impose a ban on, place a ban on)
◆Japanese deluxe wagyu beef has started to hit the market in Europe due to the lifting of a ban on beef exports from Japan to the European Union. 日本からEU（欧州連合）への牛肉輸出の解禁で、日本の高級和牛が欧州の市場に出回り始めた。◆The safety of U.S. beef must be confirmed before lifting the import ban. 輸入禁止を解く前に、米国産牛肉の安全性を確認する必要がある。◆The three principles on arms exports add up to a de facto arms export ban. 武器輸出3原則とは、要するに事実上の武器輸出禁止を意味する。◆With the import ban, there is a danger of triggering a shortage of beef, along with price increases. 輸入停止で、牛肉の品不足や価格上昇を招く恐れがある。

ban crude oil imports 原油輸入を禁止する
◆Washington will not ask Japan to ban crude oil imports from Iran. 米政府は、イランからの原油輸入禁止を求めない方針だ。

ban imports 輸入を禁止する
◆The Customs Tariff Law bans imports that infringe on patent, design and commercial brand rights. 関税定率法で、特許、意匠権、商標権などの侵害品の輸入は禁止されている。

ban on imports of ～の輸入禁止［停止］
◆The company considered switching purchases of chicken from Thailand to China following the ban on imports of Thai chicken. 同社は、タイ産鶏肉の輸入停止で、鶏肉の調達先をタイから中国に切り替えることを検討した。

bank （名）銀行, バンク （⇒negotiate）
advising bank 信用状の通知銀行
(=notifying bank, transmitting bank)
bank commission 銀行手数料
bank guarantee 銀行保証, 銀行支払い保証
（銀行が輸出業者に対して輸入業者の支払いを保証すること）
bank hours 銀行営業時間
bank letter of credit 銀行信用状
(=banker's credit)
bank reference 銀行照会, 銀行信用照会先
bank remittance 銀行送金為替, 送金為替
clearing bank 決済銀行
commercial bank 商業銀行, 普通銀行, 市中銀行, 都市銀行
confirming bank 信用状の確認銀行
e-bank e銀行, eバンク
establishing bank 信用状の発行銀行, 開設銀行 (=issuing bank, opening bank)

Internet bank インターネット銀行
issuing bank 信用状の発行銀行, 信用状開設銀行 (=opening bank)
L/C issuing bank L/C発行銀行
national bank 国法銀行, 全国銀行
negotiating bank 信用状の買取り銀行, 手形買取り銀行, 買取り銀行（外貨建ての荷為替手形を買い取る銀行）
notifying bank 信用状の通知銀行
opening bank 信用状開設銀行, 発行銀行
(=establishing bank, issuing bank)
paying bank 支払い銀行
presenting bank 手形の提示銀行
prime bank 優良銀行, 主力銀行, 一流銀行
principal bank 主要取引銀行
remitting bank 仕向け銀行
state bank 州法銀行
virtual bank 仮想銀行, バーチャル銀行
wholesale bank 法人向け銀行
◆Business Day is a day on which commercial banks are open for international business in Tokyo and San Francisco. 「営業日」とは、商業銀行が国際業務のために東京とサンフランシスコで営業している日のことをいう。◆For the purpose of this agreement, the prime rate shall mean that rate announced by the principal bank of the seller as its prime commercial lending rate from time to time. 本契約の目的上、プライム・レートとは、売り主の主要取引銀行が最優遇商業貸出金利として随時発表する利率を意味する。

bank account 銀行口座, 銀行勘定, 銀行当座勘定
◆A major Internet shopping mall program which began in March 2000 allows payments to be made immediately through the bank accounts of users. 2000年3月にスタートした大規模なインターネット上の仮想商店街プログラムは、利用者の銀行口座から即時決済できる。◆All payments shall be made in Japanese Yen and to the bank account in Japan designated by Licensor. 支払いは、すべてライセンサーが指定する日本の銀行口座に対して日本円で行わなければならない。◆Money laundering is the practice of legitimizing money gained through illegal drug and gun sales or other crimes by putting it through bank accounts. マネー・ロンダリングは、麻薬や銃器の不正販売やその他の犯罪で得た資金を銀行口座を経由させて合法的に見せる行為だ。◆Payment for each delivery of the Products shall be by the purchaser in United States Dollars by means of telegraphic transfer remittance to such bank account in the City of San Francisco, as the seller may designate from time to time, no later than 30 days after the date of the bill of lading for each such delivery. 本製品の引渡しに対する支払いは、当該引渡しにかかわる船荷証券の日付から30日以

内に、売り主が随時指定するサンフランシスコ市内の銀行口座に買い主が米ドルで電信為替で送金して行うものとする。

bank charge 銀行手数料, 銀行費用
◆All bank charges, commissions and other costs associated with a bank wire transfer or establishing and maintaining a letter of credit associated with payments under this agreement shall be for the account of ABC. 本契約に基づく支払いにかかわる銀行の電信送金または信用状の開設・維持にかかわる銀行費用、手数料、その他の費用は、すべてABCの負担とする。

banker （名）銀行家, 銀行経営者, 銀行員, 銀行マン, 銀行, バンカー

banker's acceptance 銀行引受手形, BA手形 （=bank acceptance, banker's acceptance bill）

banker's bank 銀行の銀行, 中央銀行 （=central bank）

banker's bill 銀行手形

banker's check 銀行小切手 （=bank check, cashier's check）

banker's clearing house ロンドン手形交換所

banker's commercial credit 銀行信用状

banker's deposits 銀行預金

banker's discount 銀行割引

banker's draft 銀行手形, 銀行為替手形 （=bank draft）

banker's guarantee 銀行保証状

banker's (letter of) credit 銀行信用状

banker's opinion （銀行照会に対する）銀行の意見

banker's order 定額自動送金, 自動振替依頼, 自動引落しの依頼

banker's reference 銀行信用照会先 （=bank reference）

be paid by banker's order 自動引落しで支払われる

central bankers and supervisors from major nations [countries] 主要各国[主要国]の金融監督当局

eligible banker's bill 適格銀行手形

investment banker 投資銀行 （=investment bank）

merchant banker 引受銀行, マーチャント・バンク （=merchant bank: 証券発行業務などを手がける）

◆For reimbursement, we have applied to our bankers for an L/C to be opened. （本注文に対する）代金支払のため、当社は銀行に信用状の発行を申請しました。◆We have already arranged with our bankers for an L/C to be established by the end of this month. 今月末までに信用状を開設する件については、当社が当社の取引銀行にすでに手配してあります。

Banking Law 銀行法
（⇒business improvement order）
◆The FSA has ordered Mizuho Bank to rectify its business practices on the Banking Law as the bank had extended a total of ￥200 million in loans to members of crime syndicates. 金融庁は、みずほ銀行が暴力団員らに計2億円を融資していたため、みずほ銀行に対して銀行法に基づく業務改善命令を出した。

bankrupt creditor 破産債権者

bankruptcy, insolvency or debtor's relief law 破産、支払い不能または債務者救済法
◆This agreement terminates automatically if any proceedings are commenced by, for or against Distributor under any bankruptcy, insolvency or debtor's relief law. 販売店のためにまたは販売店に対して破産、支払い不能または債務者救済法の手続きが開始された場合、本契約は自動的に終了する。

bankruptcy, insolvency or voluntary dissolution 破産、支払い不能または任意解散, 破産、支払い不能または自発的解散
◆In the event of the bankruptcy, insolvency or voluntary dissolution of either party, the nondefaulting party may terminate this agreement immediately upon written notice to the defaulting party. 当事者の一方に破産、支払い不能または任意解散の事態が発生した場合、不履行に陥っていない当事者は、不履行当事者に書面による通知を行って本契約を直ちに解除できる。

banned chemicals 無認可の化学薬品
◆Supermarkets, convenience stores and other retailers throughout the country were busy removing from their shelves food products containing the banned chemicals. 全国のスーパーやコンビニなどの小売店は、無認可の化学薬品を使用した食品の棚からの撤去作業に追われた。

bargain （名）取引, 交渉, 協議, 取引契約, 売買契約, 相互の契約, 契約, 協定, 取決め, 特価品, 格安品, 掘り出し物, バーゲン （動）契約する, 契約で取り決める, 取引する, 交渉する

at a good bargain 格安の値段で

bargain basement [counter] 値引き商品特設売場, 特売場, 特価品売場

bargain buying 押し目買い

bargain hunter 割安株ねらいの投資家, 特売品を買いあさる人

bargain-hunting 安値拾い

bargain sale 特売, バーゲン・セール

drive a hard bargain 有利に交渉を進める, 有利な取引契約を結ぶ

forward bargain 先物取引, 先渡し取引

strike a bargain with ～と契約[協定]を結ぶ （=make a bargain with）

◆We have no intention to sitting down and bargaining again. われわれは、再び席に着いて交渉するつもりはない。

bargaining （名）交渉, 取引, 労使の契約, 団体交渉

bargaining cost　契約費用

bargaining leverage　交渉力

bargaining partner　交渉相手

bargaining representative　交渉代表
　　(=bargaining agent)

bargaining table　交渉のテーブル

collective bargaining　団体交渉

diplomatic bargaining　外交的な駆け引き

have a bargaining session with　〜と交渉する

◆A business combination is a significant economic event that results from bargaining between independent parties. 企業結合は、独立した当事者間の取引から生じるひとつの重要な経済事象である。

bargaining power　交渉力, 購買取引力, 買付け交渉力

reinforce [enhance] bargaining power　交渉力を強める[強化する]

strengthen bargaining power　交渉力を強化する

◆Itochu Corp. formed a tie-up with Chinese food firm to strengthen bargaining power in the global food market. 伊藤忠商事は、世界の食料市場での交渉力[買付け交渉力]を強化するため、中国の食料企業と提携した。

barrel （名）バレル（石油の単位：米国では42ガロンで159リットル、英国では42ガロンで191リットル）, 円筒形のもの, 政治資金, 運動資金, 多量

barrel per day　日量〜バレル, 日産〜バレル, 1日当たり〜バレル, bpd

make barrels of money　しこたま儲（もう）ける

on the barrel　即金で

per-barrel price　1バレル当たりの原油価格

◆Crude futures soared to $135 per barrel on the New York market. ニューヨーク市場の原油先物価格が、1バレル＝135ドルに急騰した[1バレル＝135ドルの高値を付けた]。◆In the crude oil contract market of the New York Mercantile Exchange（NYMEX）, the price of January WTI, the benchmark U.S. crude oil, fell below $60 a barrel for the first time since June 2009 on December 11, 2014 due to the forecast of rising global oil production. 2014年12月11日のニューヨーク商業取引所の原油先物市場では、指標となる米国産原油WTI（テキサス産軽質油）の1月渡し価格が、世界的な石油増産見通しから、2009年7月以来5年5か月ぶりに1バレル＝60ドルを割り込んだ。◆The U.S. light crude front month contract rose a further 36 cents a barrel in after-hours electronic trading to top $50. 米国の軽質原油の翌月渡し価格は、時間外の電子取引で1バレル当たり36セント上伸して、1バレル＝50ドルを突

破した。

barrier （名）障壁, 障害, さえぎるもの, 壁, 障害物, 関門, 関所, 妨げ, 境界

barriers to entry　参入障壁

barriers to exit　流出障壁

barriers to free trade　自由貿易への障壁[障害]

customs barrier　関税障壁

entry barriers　参入障壁　(=barriers to entry)

erect import barriers　輸入障壁を設ける[築く]

heavy import barriers　高い輸入障壁

indirect barriers　間接的障壁

inflation barrier　インフレ障壁

intangible barriers　無形障壁

liberalize investment barriers　投資障壁を撤廃する

market barriers　市場障壁

nontariff barrier　非関税障壁
　　(=nontraded barrier)

overcome trade barriers　貿易障壁を乗り越える, 貿易障壁に対応する

production differentiation barriers　生産物差別化障壁

psychological barrier　心理の壁

regulatory barriers　規制上の障害

tangible barriers　有形障壁

tariff barrier　関税障壁

tax barrier　関税障壁

the abolition of trade barriers　貿易障壁の撤廃

trade barriers　貿易障壁　(=barriers to trade)

◆As a member country of the WTO, Moscow should first improve Russia's investment climate, including the abolition of trade barriers. 世界貿易機関（WTO）加盟国として、ロシアはまず貿易障壁の撤廃など投資環境を改善する必要がある。◆The domestic market has been shrinking due to an aging population and declining birthrate, so Japan must expand its economic cooperation agreements with other countries to have overseas markets act as quasi-domestic markets where there are no barriers to entry for Japanese companies. 少子高齢化で国内市場が縮小しているので、日本は他国との経済連携協定を拡大して、海外市場を日本企業が垣根なしで参入できる準国内市場にする必要がある。◆The United States will continue to actively address anticompetitive activity, market access barriers, and or market-distorting trade practices. アメリカは、非競争的行為や市場参入障壁、市場を歪める商慣行に引き続き取り組んで行く方針だ。

base rate　基準金利, 基準貸出金利

◆Late payment shall incur an interest charge of 2 percent over the base rate current in XYZ Bank at the time the charge is levied from the due date

BASE 54

to the date of payment in full. 支払いが遅延した場合、支払い期日から全額支払い日まで、支払い利息（遅延利息）を課す時点でXYZ銀行が適用する基準金利より2%高い支払い利息（遅延利息）が付くものとする。

B

Basel〔Basle〕 バーゼル（スイス北西部バーゼル・シュタット準州の州都。国際決済銀行（BIS）の本部がある）

Basel Accord of 1988 1988年のバーゼル合意, 1988年のバーゼル協定

Basel Agreement バーゼル協定, BIS規制, BIS基準

Basel Capital Accord BIS自己資本比率規制, BIS規制

Basel Committee on Banking Regulation and Supervision 銀行規制監督に関するバーゼル委員会

Basel Committee on Banking Supervision バーゼル銀行監督委員会
◆The challenge of the Basel Committee on Banking Supervision is to develop a regulatory framework while fending off a recurrence of financial strife. バーゼル銀行監督委員会の課題は、金融危機の再発防止と規制の枠組みの策定だ。

Basel 3 バーゼル3（国際的に銀行業務を展開している銀行の経営の健全性を保持するための新自己資本規制のことで、2010年9月にバーゼル銀行監督委員会が公表）
◆Japan's three megabanks must increase their core capital as soon as possible, in accordance with the new rules known as Basel 3. 日本の3大メガバンクは、バーゼル3と呼ばれる新規則に従って、早期に中核資本を増強する必要がある。

basic agreement 基本的合意, 基本合意, 大筋合意, 基本合意書, 基本契約, 基本契約書
◆The Japanese, Iranian and Qatari governments have reached a basic agreement to allow a Japanese consortium and multinational companies to develop natural gas resources in Iran's Pars South and Qatar's North Field. 日本政府とイラン、カタール両国政府は、イランの南パルス・ガス田とカタールのノースフィールド・ガス田の天然ガス資源開発を、日本の企業連合体と多国籍企業が手がけることで基本的合意に達した（大筋合意した）。

basic balance of payments 基礎収支（総合収支－短期資本収支＝基礎収支）

basis （名）方針, 基準, 根本原理, 主義, 方式, 基礎, 根拠, 論拠, 土台, 主成分, ベース
as a basis for ～の根拠として
C&F Singapore 運賃込みシンガポール条件で
customs basis 通関ベース
market price basis 時価主義
on a consolidated basis 連結ベースで, 一括して
on a dollar denominated basis ドル表示で

on a full year basis 通年で, 通期で
on a group basis 連結ベースで（＝on a consolidated basis）
on a like-for-like basis 同一条件で, 同一条件下で, 既存店ベースで
on a nominal basis 名目で
on a priority basis 優先的に
on a regular basis 定期的に, 恒常的に
on a same-store basis 既存店ベースで
on a seasonally adjusted basis 季節調整済みで
on a temporary basis 一時的に
on a trial basis 試験的に, 実験的に
on an all-store basis 全店舗ベースで
on an annualized basis 年率換算で, 年換算で
on an FOB Tokyo basis 東京本船渡し条件で
on an optional basis 選択制で
on the basis of CIF Beyrouth〔Beirut〕 CIFベイルート条件で
on the basis of IMF formula IMF方式で
tax basis 課税標準, 税法基準 （＝tax base）
◆Banks participating in direct yen-yuan trading in the Tokyo interbank foreign exchange market will trade the yen and the yuan at an exchange rate calculated on the basis of actual supply and demand. 東京外国為替市場で円・人民元の直接取引に参加する銀行は、実際の需給などをもとに算出した取引レートで、円と人民元を銀行間で取引する。
◆Nursing-care robots produced on a trial basis by some Japanese companies cost as much as 20 million yen per unit, but the government hopes to promote the robots priced at about 100,000 yen for widespread use across the nation. 一部の日本企業が試験的に生産している介護ロボットは1台2,000万円と高額だが、政府は1台10万円程度の介護ロボットを全国に普及させたい考えだ。◆We may place a substantial order with you on a regular basis if your prices are competitive. 貴社の製品価格が他社より安ければ、定期的に大口の注文を出すことができます。

bear （動）義務・責任を負う, 費用などを負担する, ～を持つ, 有する, 利子などを生む, 商標などを付す
bear and pay for expenses necessary to ～するために必要な費用を負担し、支払う
bear liability jointly and severally 連帯責任を負う, 連帯債務を負う
bear the manufacturer's trademark メーカーの商標を付す
bear witness to ～を証明する
licensed products bearing the Trademarks 本商標を付した許諾品
◆ABC shall bear and pay for expenditures necessary to promote and advertise the products in accordance with the marketing and advertisement

plan of ABC approved by XYZ. ABCは、XYZが承認したABCのマーケティング・宣伝計画に従って本商品の宣伝・広告を行うのに必要な費用を負担し、支払うものとする。

become effective 効力を発する, 効力を生じる, 発効する
◆A separate individual sales and purchase contract shall become effective and binding upon the parties at the time when an order placed by XYZ is accepted by ABC by issuing sales confirmation in XYZ's standard form of sales contract in use. 個別の売買契約は、XYZが出した注文を、ABCがXYZの使用している売買契約標準書式の販売確認書を発行して受諾したときに発効し、当事者を拘束するものとする。

beef exporter 牛肉輸出業者, 牛肉輸出企業, 牛肉輸出国
◆Major beef exporters such as the United States have already threatened to impose some punitive action against Japan if it introduces an emergency tariff on imported beef. 日本が輸入牛肉に対して緊急関税を導入［発動］した場合、米国など牛肉の主な対日輸出国は、すでに日本に対して制裁措置を取る動きを示している。

beef exports 牛肉輸出
◆Japanese deluxe wagyu beef has started to hit the market in Europe due to the lifting of a ban on beef exports from Japan to the European Union. 日本からEU（欧州連合）への牛肉輸出の解禁で、日本の高級和牛が欧州の市場に出回り始めた。

beef products 牛肉製品
◆Japan has temporarily halted imports of beef products from the United States after the first U.S. case of mad cow disease was found. 米国で初めて狂牛病（BSE）の感染例が見つかったことを受けて、日本は米国からの牛肉製品の輸入を一時的に停止した。

belong to 所属する, 帰属する
◆In case actions are instituted by ABC without such discussion with or agreement of XYZ, all the expenses incurred for such action shall be borne by ABC, and all the damages recovered therefrom shall belong to ABC. ABCがXYZとの当該協議またはXYZの同意なしで訴訟を起こした場合、その訴訟費用はすべてABCが負担し、その訴訟により回収した損害賠償金もすべてABCに帰属するものとする。

benchmark （名）基準, 尺度, 目安, 基準値, 測定基準, 基準指数, 基準銘柄, 指標, 指標銘柄, 政策金利（benchmark interest rate）, ベンチマーク
benchmark corporate lending 基準法人貸出金利
benchmark five-year U.S. Treasury bonds 指標となる5年物財務省証券
benchmark interest rate 基準金利, 指標金利, 政策金利（=benchmark rate）
benchmark issue 指標銘柄

benchmark Nikkei Stock Average 日経平均株価
benchmark price 基準価格
benchmark short-term interest rate 短期金利の誘導目標, 短期金利の指標
benchmark year 基準年
benchmark yield 指標銘柄利回り, 指標利回り
international benchmark 国際指標
seasonal benchmark 季節調整の基準
◆In the crude oil contract market of the New York Mercantile Exchange（NYMEX）, the price of January WTI, the benchmark U.S. crude oil, fell below $60 a barrel for the first time since June 2009 on December 11, 2014 due to the forecast of rising global oil production. 2014年12月11日のニューヨーク・マーカンタイル取引所の原油先物市場では、指標となる米国産原油WTI（テキサス産軽質油）の1月渡し価格が、世界的な石油増産見通しから、2009年7月以来5年5か月ぶりに1バレル＝60ドルを割り込んだ。◆The international benchmark New York crude oil futures price started to decline after the price peaked at about $147 per barrel on July 11, 2008. 国際指標であるニューヨーク市場の原油先物価格は、2008年7月11日に1バレル＝147ドル前後の最高値を付けたあと、下落を始めた。◆The yield on the benchmark 10-year U.S. government bonds has been closing below 3 percent recently. 長期金利の指標となる10年物米国債の利回りは最近、3％を割り込んで［3％割れで］取引を終えている。

benchmark (interest) rate 基準金利, 指標金利, 政策金利
◆Libor, widely used globally as a benchmark rate for financial transactions, has been revealed to have been distorted by false submissions from Barclays which is one of Britain's top banking groups. 金融取引の基準金利として世界で幅広く使われているライボー（ロンドン銀行間取引金利）が、英国の大手金融グループ「バークレイズ」の虚偽申告で歪（ゆが）められていたことが、発覚した。

beneficial owner 実質上の所有者・株主, 受益権所有者, 受益株主, 受益権上の保有者
◆ABC is the legal, record and beneficial owner of the Shares free and clear of any liens, charges or other encumbrances. ABCは、先取特権、担保権その他の制限（負担・障害）がない本株式の法律上、登録上、実質上の所有者である。

beneficiary （名）受益者, 実質的権利者, 年金などの受取人, 商業信用状の名宛人

benefit （動）利益を与える, 〜の利益になる, 〜のプラスになる, 〜に貢献する, 利益を得る, 恩恵を受ける, 利益が発生する
a weak yen benefits the export industries 円安は輸出産業には追い風だ
benefit both companies 両社にメリットがある

benefit existing shareholders　株主の利益に
なる
　◆A weak yen benefits the export industries such
as automobiles and home appliances, but excessive depreciation of the yen could have the negative effect on the Japanese economy. 円安は自
動車や家電など輸出産業には追い風だが、過度の
円安は日本経済に悪影響を及ぼす可能性もある。
　◆If agricultural imports become cheaper due to
the lowered tariffs, consumers will greatly benefit. 関税の引下げで輸入農産品が安くなれば、消費
者の利点も大きい。

benefit　(名)利益, 利得, 便益, 給付, 給付金,
年金, 手当て
　◆Aeon and Ito-Yokado started discount sales of
foods imported from the United States to pass
along to consumers the benefits of the yen's
sharp climb against the dollar. イオンとイトー
ヨーカ堂は、急激な円高・ドル安による円高差益
を消費者に還元するため、米国から輸入した食料
品の値下げセールを開始した。◆The seller shall
nevertheless provide with the purchaser the benefit obtained by the seller under the guarantee（if
any）which the seller may have received from
the supplier of such products in respect of quality or fitness. 上記にかかわらず、売り主は、品
質または適合性について当該製品の供給者から売
り主が受けている保証（保証がある場合）に基づい
て売り主が得た利益を、買い主に提供するものと
する。◆This agreement is not intended to confer
any benefits upon or create any rights in favor of,
any person other than the parties hereto. 本契約
は、本契約当事者以外の者に利益を付与すること、
または当事者以外の者のために権利を創出するこ
とを意図したものではない。

benefit from　〜から利益を得る、〜の恩恵を
受ける、〜のメリットを受ける、〜を享受す
る、〜が追い風になる、〜の効果がある
benefit from a boom in exports　輸出好調の恩
恵を受ける
benefit from a fall in（interest）rates　金利の
低下から利益を得る、金利低下のメリット
を受ける、金利低下が追い風になる
benefit from higher commodity prices　市況商
品価格の上昇が追い風になる
benefit from the economic recovery　景気回復
の恩恵を受ける
benefit from the weak［weaker］yen　円安が
追い風になる、円安の恩恵を受ける、円安効
果がある
　◆As many domestic manufacturers have moved
their production sites from Japan to Asian nations and elsewhere, the Japanese economy benefits less and less from the weak yen which lowers export costs. 国内製造業の多くが生産拠点を日
本からアジアなどに移しているため、日本経済は、
輸出コストが下がる円安メリットを享受しにくく
なっている。◆Benefiting from the yen's depre-

ciation which resulted from Abenomics, the Abe
administration's economic policies, the earnings
environment for export-oriented companies has
greatly improved. 安倍政権の経済政策「アベノミ
クス」による円安効果で、輸出企業の収益環境が
大幅に改善した。

**benefits of falling［declining］crude oil
prices**　原油下落［原油安］の恩恵, 原油下落
のメリット
　◆Despite declining prices of crude oil, the weak
yen pushes up the cost of imports, partly offsetting the benefits of falling crude oil prices. 原油
価格は下落しているが、円安で輸入価格が押し上
げられ、原油安［原油下落］の恩恵が一部打ち消さ
れる面もある。

benefits of the strong yen　円高差益
　◆The prices of Audi's all-new Q5 sport-utility
vehicle range from ￥5.79 million to ￥6.37 mil-
lion（consumption tax included）, and it passed
the benefits of the strong yen on to consumers
by making high-grade aluminum wheels and car
navigation systems standard features. 独アウディ
の全面改良したスポーツ用多目的車（SUV）「Q5」の
価格は、579万〜637万円（消費税込み）で、高級ア
ルミホイールや高性能カーナビゲーションを標準
装備して、円高差益を消費者に還元した。

best　(名)最高のもの, 最高の状態, 名士, 〜に
よろしくとの挨拶　(形)最も良い, 最も［と
くに］望ましい, 最適の, 最高の, 絶好調の, 大
部分の, 大半の　(副)最もよく［うまく］, 最
も, 一番に, ひどく, とくに　(動)〜を負かす,
〜に勝る, 〜を出し抜く
best bid　最も有利な条件のオファー
best bid and offer quote　気配値段
best cooperation　最大限の協力
best effort clause　契約履行努力条項
best execution　最善の執行, 最良執行（顧客に
とってとくに有利な条件での売買）, 最良執
行義務
best execution duty　最良執行義務
（=best execution obligation）
our best prices for our best products　当社の極
上品に対する最低価格
　◆The quotations above are the best we could
make at the moment, so we could not reduce the
prices any further. 上記価格は、現在のところ当
社精一杯のもので、これ以上価格を下げることは
できません。◆We will do our best to speed up
delivery if you accept the counter offer. このカウ
ンター・オファーを受けていただければ、全力を
挙げて配送を急がせます。

best attention　最善の注意
　◆We will execute the order with best attention
upon receipt of your L/C. 貴社の信用状を受け取
り次第、当社は最善の注意を払って注文を履行し
ます。

best efforts　最大限の努力（best endeavor）,

最大努力, 最善の努力, 委託募集, 取扱い引
受け

best efforts issue　売出発行

◆You may count on our best efforts so long as
you can maintain moderate prices. 手頃な価格
[格安料金]を維持できるかぎり, 当社は最大限の
努力を貴社にお約束します。

best interests　最上の利益

◆The parties hereto believe it to be their best interests and the best interests of the New Company as defined in Article 1, that they provide for
certain rights, duties, and restrictions as among
themselves and others who may become shareholders of the New Company, all as provided in
this agreement. 本契約当事者は, すべて本契約に
規定するとおり, 両当事者と第1条に規定する新会
社の株主になる他の者との間で一定の権利, 義務
と制約について定めることが, 両当事者にとって
最上の利益となり, 新会社にとっても最上の利益
となる, と考えている。

best price　(売りの場合の)最高値(best
quotation), (買いの場合の)最低値(lowest
price, rockbottom price), 最低価格, 最低取引
価格, 勉強値段, 勉強値

our best prices for our best products　当社の極
　上品に対する最低価格

our best prices for our supplies　当社供給品の
　最低価格[勉強値]

◆The following price list shows our best prices
and rate of quantity discount for our supplies. 以
下の価格表は, 当社供給品の最低価格[勉強値]と
数量割引率を示しています。

best quotation　最低価格, 最低の見積り価
格, 建て値　(=the lowest quotation)

◆Please give us your best quotations in U.S. dollars for immediate shipment and proforma invoices. 直(じき)積みでドル建ての貴社の建て値
と試算送り状を, お送りください。

beyond　(前)〜の向こう(側)に, 〜を過ぎて,
〜以降の, 〜を越えて, 〜を超える, 〜以上に,
〜を除いて, 〜の他に, 〜以外に　(副)向こ
うに, その先に, 〜より後も, 以降に

a success beyond our expectations　予想外の
　大成功

be beyond the reach of　〜には手が届かない

be well beyond the average　平均をはるかに
　上回る

beyond all question　まったく疑問の余地な
　く, 無論のこと

beyond comparison [compare]　比較になら
　ない

beyond comprehension　理解できない

beyond one's control　〜の手に負えない, 〜
　の統御できない, 〜の支配が及ばない

beyond the control of　〜の支配できない, 〜
　の支配が及ばない

beyond the mark　的を外れて, 度を越えて, 過
　度に

beyond the time limit　制限時間を越えて

from beyond the sea(s)　海外から

go beyond　〜を超える, 〜を[〜の領域を]越
　える, 〜の領域を出る

in circumstances beyond the seller's control
　売り主の統御[支配]できない事情で

◆The best exchange rate for the Japanese economy might be near ￥90 to the dollar. Depreciation of the yen beyond ￥100 is harmful to the
economy. 日本経済に一番良い円相場は, 1ドル＝90
円近くではないだろうか。100円を超える円安は,
日本経済にはマイナス要素がある。◆The first of-
ficial ministerial-level talks between China and
Taiwan, at odds more than six decades since the
1949 creation of the People's Republic of China,
mark a big step toward expanding cross-strait dialogue beyond economic and trade issues. 1949
年の中華人民共和国の樹立[建国]以来60年以上も
対立している中国と台湾が初めて行った公式の閣
僚級会談(2014年2月11日)は, 経済や貿易問題を
超えた両岸対話拡大への大きな一歩を踏み出すも
のだ。

bidder　(名)入札者, 入札業者, 入札行, 競り
手, 参加などの申込み国

◆If golden shares held by a friendly company are
transferred to another party, such shares could be
transferred again to a hostile bidder. 友好的な企
業が保有する黄金株を第三者に譲渡した場合, そ
の黄金株はまた敵対的買収者に譲渡される可能性
もある。

bidding　(名)入札, 競り, 申込み
　(=bid, tendering)

bidding among designated companies　指名競
　争入札

bidding price　入札価格

collusive bidding　馴れ合い入札

competitive bidding　競争入札

designated bidding　指名競争入札

e-bidding　電子入札　(=Net bidding)

Net bidding　ネット入札, 電子入札

noncompetitive bidding　非競争入札

open bidding　公開入札, 一般競争入札

public bidding　一般競争入札

unsolicited bidding　直接入札

◆It is an entrenched bidding structure that allows
irregularities such as influence-wielding, bid-
rigging and subcontracting entire public works
contracts. 口利きや談合, 公共事業の丸投げなどの
不正行為を許しているのは, 旧態依然とした入札
の構造だ。◆Public bidding is the best way to secure transparency. 一般競争入札は, 透明性の確保
には最善の方法である。◆Two investment funds
are expected to join the second round of bidding

to choose a company to support the corporate rehabilitation of chipmaker Elpida Memory Inc. 半導体メーカーのエルピーダメモリの企業再建を支援する企業選びの二次入札に、投資ファンド2社が参加する［入札する］見通しだ。◆Under the e-bidding system, the whole procedure—from inviting tenders to giving notification of the results—will be conducted over the Internet. 電子入札制度では、入札に関する事前説明から結果の通知まで、手続きはすべてインターネット上で行われる。

bidding offer　入札申込み，入札の申込み
◆No material commitments, bids or bidding offers will be entered into by the Company in any case in excess of $10,000 whether or not in the ordinary course of business, except with the prior written consent of Purchaser. 買い主の書面による事前の同意がある場合を除いて、対象会社は、通常の業務過程であるか否かを問わずどんな場合にも1万ドルを超える重要な約束、入札、入札の申込みは行わないものとする。

bid-fixing　（名）談合行為
◆Cartels and bid-fixing can ruin economic activities. カルテルや談合行為は、経済活動を損なう可能性がある。

bid-rigging　（名）談合
◆Cartels and bid-fixing can ruin economic activities. カルテルや談合行為は、経済活動を損なう可能性がある。◆It is an entrenched bidding structure that allows irregularities such as influence-wielding, bid-rigging and subcontracting entire public works contracts. 口利きや談合、公共事業の丸投げなどの不正行為を許しているのは、旧態依然とした入札の構造だ。

big data　ビッグ・データ［ビッグデータ］（通常のデータベース管理システムでは記録や保管・解析が困難なほど巨大なデータの集まりのこと）
◆As the value of using big data, a sales practice prevailing in the mail-order business sector is to analyze purchase records of customers and then recommend products based on their tastes and preferences. ビッグ・データの利用価値として、通販業界で広がっている販売手法は、顧客の購入履歴を分析して、顧客の好みに合う商品を薦める方法だ。

bilateral　（形）相互の，双方の，両者の，両国の，相対の，二者の，二者間の，二国間の，左右相称の，両側性の，双務的な，相互に義務を負う，当事者双方が義務を負う，当事者間の
bilateral contract　双務契約，双方的契約（片務契約＝unilateral contract）
bilateral deal　二国間取引
bilateral deals　（石油の）直接取引（=bilateral oil purchase deals）
bilateral double taxation treaty　二国間の二重課税防止条約
bilateral line　相対取引，相対ベース
bilateral loan　相対ローン，相対ベースの融資

bilateral master agreement　当事者間の標準契約
bilateral monopoly　双方独占
bilateral oligopoly　双方寡占
bilateral settlement　双務決済
bilateral trade　二国間貿易，双務貿易
bilateral trade agreement　二国間通商協定
bilateral trade friction　二国間の貿易摩擦
bilateral transaction　二国間取引，双務取引，双方の取引，直接相対取引
negotiations on bilateral lines　相対ベースの交渉
on a bilateral basis　相対ベースで，相対契約で

bilateral agreement　双務協定，二国間協定，二国間の合意，双方の合意
◆Akira Amari, minister in charge of TPP negotiations, and U.S. Trade Representative Michael Froman started with around 30 minutes of one-on-one talks, with the aim of reaching a broad bilateral agreement before a Japan-U.S. summit meeting held on April 24, 2014. 甘利TPP担当相と米通商代表部のフロマン代表は、日米首脳会談（2014年4月24日）前に二国間の大筋合意を得るため、約30分の1対1の会談から始めた。

bilateral transaction　二国間取引，双方的取引，双務取引
◆In order to cut off funds to North Korea's nuclear weapons development program, the government will tighten controls on illegal bilateral transactions, including exports of materials for making missiles and smuggling of narcotics and counterfeit bank notes into the country. 北朝鮮の核兵器開発計画の資金源を断つため、政府はミサイル製造の関連物資の輸出や麻薬・偽造紙幣の密輸など、日朝間の不正取引の取締りを強化する方針だ。

bill　（名）手形，証券，証書，紙幣，札（さつ），料金，代金，請求金額，勘定書，クレジット・カードなどの利用明細書，明細書，請求書，法案
a huge bill is due next week　多額の請求書の期限が到来する
a set of bills　組手形
accept a bill　手形を引き受ける，手形の支払いを引き受ける
acceptance of bill（of exchange）　手形引受け（=acceptance bill）
accommodation bill［note］　融通手形
agency bill　代理手形
back a bill　手形の裏書きをする（=endorse a bill）
bank bill　銀行券，銀行手形，銀行引受手形（=bank note）
banker's acceptance bill　銀行引受手形，BA手形
banker's bill　銀行手形

BILL

bill accepted　引受手形

bill accompanied by warehouse receipts　倉庫証券付き手形

bill advice　手形満期通知状, 手形延期通知状

bill as collateral　担保手形

bill bearer　手形支持人

bill broker　手形仲買人

bill clearings　手形交換, 手形交換高

bill collection　集金

bill collector　手形取立人, 集金人

bill discount [discounted]　割引手形

bill discounted deposit　歩積 (ぶづ) み, 歩積み預金 (金融機関が手形を割り引く際、割引額の一部を強制的に預金させること)

bill discounter　手形割引業者

bill for acceptance　引受 (請求) 手形

bill for collection　取立て手形, 代金取立て手形, B/C

bill for premature delivery　早受手形

bill for term　定期払い手形

bill holder　手形所持人

bill in blank　白地手形 (=blank bill)

bill in foreign currency [money]　外貨手形

bill instructions　船荷証券作成

bill of adventure　積送品危険証券

bill of clearance　出港証書

bill of credit　支払い証券, 信用状

bill of date　確定日付け手形

bill of debt　約束手形, 債務証書

bill of dishonor　不渡り手形 (=dishonored bill)

bill of entry　通関申告書, 税関申告書, 入港証書

bill of expenditures　支出明細書

bill of materials　資材明細表, 資材購入表, 材料仕様書, BOM

bill of parcels　納品書, 積み荷明細書, 送り状

bill of quantities　建築見積り書

bill of quantity　数量表, 数量書

bill of sale　売渡し証, 売買証書

bill of sight　仮陸揚げ許可証, 仮陸揚げ申告書

bill of store　関税免除状

bill of sufferance　出港免許証

bill on demand　要求払い (為替) 手形 (=demand bill)

bill on presentation　提示 [呈示] 払い手形, 一覧手形 (=presentation bill)

bill rediscounted　再割引手形

bill rendered　債務明細書

bill validated by a government corporation　認証手形

bill with collateral security　担保付き手形

bills bought　買取り手形, 買取り輸出手形

bills discounted diary　割引手形期日

blank bill　白紙の請求書, (受取人) 無記名手形, 白地手形

charge a hefty bill　高額の代金を請求する

check a bill　請求書を確認する

clean bill　裸手形

clean bill of health　完全健康証明書

clear a bill　手形を交換する, 手形を清算する

collect a bill　集金する

commercial bill　商業手形, 為替手形

create a bill from a work order　作業発注書から請求書を起こす

customer's bill　顧客の利用明細書

demand bill　要求払い手形

discount a bill　手形を割り引く

dishonor a bill　手形の支払いを拒否する, 手形を不渡りにする

documentary bill　荷為替手形

domestic bill　内国為替 (=home bill, inland bill)

domiciled bill　他所払い手形

double name bill　複名手形 (=double named bill)

draw a bill on　〜に手形を振り出す

due bill　借用証書

duplicate bill　副為替手形, 手形の副本, 手形の第2券 (手形の正本・第1券 = original bill)

exchequer bill　英大蔵省証券

export bill　輸出手形

fail to honor a bill　手形の支払いをしない, 不渡り手形を出す, 不渡りを出す

fictitious bill　空 (から) 手形

finance bill　融通手形, 米国の金融手形

first class bill　一流手形 (=gilt-edged bill)

fit [fill] the bill　要求 [条件] を満たす, 申し分ない, ぴったりだ

foot the bill　勘定をする, 合計する

foot the bill for　〜の勘定をする, 〜の勘定を払う, 〜の費用を負担する, 〜の経費を持つ, 〜を合計する

foreign bill　外国為替手形

foul bill　故障手形

government bills　短期国債

honor a bill　手形を引き受ける, 手形を引き受けて (期日に) 支払う, 手形の支払いをする

huge bill　巨額の請求書

import settlement bill　輸入決済手形

interest bill　利付き手形

kite a bill　融通手形を振り出す

long bill 長期手形
(=long sighted bill, long term bill)

make out a bill to ～宛に請求書を出す

negotiable bill 流通手形

negotiate a bill 手形を買い取る, 手形を売買する

new $100 bill 新100ドル紙幣

original bill 原手形

outstanding bill 未払い請求書

pay a bill 手形を支払う
(=honor［meet, take up］a bill)

pay one's bills 請求書の支払いをする

pay the bill for ～の勘定を払う, ～の付けを払う

phone bill 電話料金, 電話料金請求書

presentation bill 一覧払い手形, 呈示払い手形

receive a bill for ～の請求書を受け取る

renew a bill 手形を書き換える

renewal bill 書換え手形

security bill 証券担保為替手形

set bill 組手形 (⇒bill of exchange, tenor)

settle a bill 請求を支払う, 請求書を決済する

short bill （30日払い以下の）短期手形
(=short sighted bill, short term bill)

sight bill 一覧払い手形

single name bill 単名手形 (=single named bill)

sola bill 単独手形, 単独為替手形 (=sole bill)

submit a bill 請求書を出す

take up a bill 手形を支払う, 手形の支払いを引き受けて支払う, 手形を引き受ける
(=honor a bill)

tax bill 納税通知書

time bill 期限付き手形, 期限付き為替手形

trade bill 商業手形

treasury bill 米財務省短期証券, 英大蔵省証券, 政府短期証券, 短期国債, Tビル

two-name bill 複名手形

unpaid bill 不渡り手形, 未払いの請求書, 代金の踏み倒し, 未払い代金, 代金の未払い

usance bill 期限付き手形

utility bills 光熱費

value bill 荷為替手形

way-bill 貨物引換証

write out a bill 請求書を作成する

◆The firm has gone effectively bankrupt after banks suspended transactions with it on its second failure to honor a bill. 同社が2回目の不渡りを出して銀行取引停止となり, 事実上倒産した。◆ Unpaid bills have emerged as a major structural problem in Chinese business. 中国との取引では, 代金の踏み倒しが大きな構造的問題として浮上している。

bill at sight 一覧払い手形

bill at maturity 満期手形

bill at 30 days' sight 一覧後30日払い手形, 30日払い手形
◆We have drawn a bill at 30 days' sight on you through the bank for $1,000. 当社は, 同行経由で1,000ドルの一覧後30日払い手形を貴社宛に振り出した。

bill of exchange 為替手形, B/E (=draft: 紛失防止策として通常、2通1組の組手形で振り出される)

accept a bill of exchange 為替手形を引き受ける

draw a bill of exchange 為替手形を振り出す

endorse a bill of exchange 為替手形に裏書きをする

bill of lading 船荷証券, 積み荷証券, 貨物引換証, 運送証券, 積み荷証, B/L (⇒B/L)

Bill of Lading Act 船荷証券法

bill of lading clause 船荷証券約款

minimum bill of lading 最低船荷証券

◆A full set of negotiable bills of lading made out to order must be endorsed by shipper. 指図人式で作成された譲渡可能な船荷証券一式には, 荷送人の裏書が必要である。◆Bills of lading shall be made out to order and marked notify party. 船荷証券は, 指図人式で作成し, 通知先を記入しなければならない。◆Payment for each delivery of the Products shall be by the purchaser in United States Dollars by means of telegraphic transfer remittance to such bank account in the City of San Francisco, as the seller may designate from time to time, no later than 30 days after the date of the bill of lading for each such delivery. 本製品の引渡しに対する支払いは, 当該引渡しにかかわる船荷証券の日付から30日以内に, 売り主が随時指定するサンフランシスコ市内の銀行口座に買い主が米ドルで電信為替で送金して行うものとする。◆ The date of the bill of lading shall be conclusive evidence of the date of the delivery. 船荷証券の日付は, 引渡し日の最終的な証拠とする。

bill payable 支払い手形

bill payable account 自動引落し口座

bill payable at a fixed date 確定日払い手形

bill payable at a fixed period after sight 一覧後定期払い手形

bill payable at sight 一覧払い手形

bill payable at sight a fixed period 定期後一覧払い手形

bill payable in foreign currency 外貨支払い手形

bill payable to bearer 持参人払い手形

bill payable to order 指図人払い手形

bill receivable 受取手形

  bill receivable discounted　割引手形

  bill receivable in foreign currency　外貨受取手形

billing （名）請求書作成, 請求書送付, 工事見積書作成, 船荷証券や送り状の作成, 出荷手配, （一定期間内の）取引額, 広告, 宣伝

  billing adjustment　請求書の訂正

  billing cycle　請求期間

  billing error　請求書上の間違い

  billing instructions　出荷指図, 船荷証券作成指図

  billing machine　請求書作成機

  billing statement　請求書

binary machine-readable or printed form　機械読取り可能なバイナリー形式または印刷された形態

  ◆ "Software" means all computer programs and related materials in binary machine-readable or printed form, and all Software Upgrades thereto. 「本ソフトウエア」とは, 機械読取り可能なバイナリー形式または印刷された形態のあらゆるコンピュータ・プログラムおよび関連資料と, そのソフトウエア・アップグレード版のことをいう。

bind　（動）法的に拘束する, 義務づける, 強制する, 契約を結ぶ, 拘束力がある

  bind a bargain with earnest　手付け金で売買を決めておく

  bind one's contract　契約を取り決める

  bind the parties　両当事者を拘束する

  ◆Any translation in any other language shall be for reference only and shall not bind the parties. 他の言語による翻訳はすべて参照（参考）のためにすぎず, 当事者を拘束するものではない。◆The assignor shall first obtain the execution by its assignee of an agreement whereby the assignee binds itself to the non-assigning party to observe and perform all the obligations and agreements of its assignor. 譲渡人は先ず譲受人による同意書への署名を得［譲渡人は先ず譲受人に同意書に署名させ］, それにより譲渡人のすべての義務と同意事項を遵守・履行する非譲渡当事者に対して約束させるものとする。

binder　（名）契約仮引受証

binding　（形）法律的に拘束力のある［法的拘束力のある］, 拘束力のある, 拘束性のある, 法的に拘束する, 義務付ける, 締めつける

  binding agreement　法律的に拘束力のある合意［契約］

  binding contract　拘束力のある契約

  binding effect of Agreement　契約の拘束力

  binding force　拘束力

  binding hours　（労働の）拘束時間

  binding materials　接着剤, 結合剤

  binding on［upon］　〜を拘束する

  binding power　拘束力

  binding underwriting agreement　拘束力のある引受参加契約

  legally binding optout　法的拘束力のある適用除外

  legally binding solution　法的拘束力のある解決策

  ◆Any and all disputes arising from or in connection with this Agreement or a transaction conducted under this Agreement shall be settled by arbitration in Tokyo in accordance with the Commercial Arbitration Rules of the Japan Commercial Arbitration Association. The award of the arbitration shall be final and binding upon the parties. 本契約もしくは本契約に基づいて行われる取引から生じる, またはこれに関連して生じる紛争は, すべて日本商事仲裁協会の商事仲裁規則にしたがって東京での仲裁により解決する。仲裁の判断は, 最終的なもので当事者を拘束［法的に拘束］するものとする。

binding arbitration　法律的に拘束力のある仲裁, 拘束力のある仲裁

  ◆If the parties are unable to settle the matter within 30 calendar days after their first meeting, then upon the demand of either party, the matter shall be submitted to binding arbitration. 当事者が最初の会談から30暦日以内に当該事項を解決できないときは, いずれか一方の当事者の要求により, 当該事項は法律的に拘束力のある仲裁に付託するものとする。

binding obligation　法的に拘束力のある義務, 拘束力のある義務

  ◆The execution and performance of this agreement by Seller constitute legal, valid and binding obligations of Seller, enforceable in accordance with the terms hereof. 売り主による本契約の締結と履行は, 本契約の条件に従って強制することができる法的, 有効かつ拘束力のある売り主の義務を構成する。

BIOS　基本入出力システム, バイオス（Basic Input/Output Systemの略）

  ◆LICENSOR may audit, at its own expense, the books of LICENSEE in which information relating to the quantities of LICENSEE's BIOS shipped, distributed transferred, or otherwise disposed of by LICENSEE is recorded, and LICENSEE's records supporting its entries in those books. ライセンサーは, その自己負担で, ライセンシーが出荷, 販売, 譲渡したまたはその他の方法で処分したライセンシーのBIOS（バイオス）の数量に関する情報が記載されているライセンシーの帳簿と, この帳簿の記入項目を立証するライセンシーの記録を監査することができる。

bitcoin［Bitcoin, BitCoin］　（名）（仮想通貨の）ビットコイン, BTC（インターネット上だけで流通する仮想通貨。通貨単位はBTC。「取引所」に口座を開設して, ドルや円などの通貨で購入できる。送金手数料は, ゼロに

近い。最大の取引所はMt.Gox（マウント・ゴックス）で日本に本社がある）
◆Bitcoin, a virtual currency circulated on the Internet, is traded in units of BTC. The value of bitcoin fluctuates excessively, but bitcoin has hovered at about $800 per BTC lately. ネット上で流通している仮想通貨「ビットコイン」は、BTCの単位で取引されている。ビットコインの相場は乱高下があまりにも激しいが、最近は1BTC=800ドル前後で推移している。◆Bitcoin, an online currency, is illegal in Thailand and financial services involving bitcoin are banned in China, but the virtual currency has been spreading around the world online. ネット通貨のビットコインはタイでは違法で、ビットコイン関連の金融サービス［ビットコインを使った金融サービス］は中国では禁止されているが、この仮想通貨はネット上で世界に拡散している。◆Bitcoin circulated only on the Internet is not under the control of central banks unlike regular currencies. インターネット上だけで流通しているビットコインは、通常の通貨と違って、中央銀行の統制を受けていない。◆Bitcoin traded in units of BTC currently stays outside the framework of financial regulations, so the risk management of the virtual currency is difficult. BTCの単位で取引されているビットコインは現在、金融規制の枠外にあるため、仮想通貨「ビットコイン」のリスク管理は難しい。

bitcoin exchange ビットコイン取引所
◆To seek information on cyber attacks, U.S. Attorney Preet Bharara has sent subpoenas to bitcoin exchanges including Mt.Gox and businesses that deal in bitcoin. サイバー攻撃に関する情報を得るため、プリート・バララ米連邦検事は、マウントゴックス社などビットコイン（仮想通貨）の取引所やビットコインの取扱い業者に対して、召喚状を送った。

B/L 船荷証券, 積み荷証券, ビーエル（bill of ladingの略。⇒bill of lading）
◆In case payment by the purchaser for the delivery of the products is delayed later than 35 days after B/L date, the purchaser shall pay to the seller on demand the amount due together with interest from the due date until paid at the annual rate equal to the prime rate plus 5 percent per year on any overdue amount. 買い主による本製品の引渡しに対する支払いが船荷証券の日付から35日を超えて遅延した場合、買い主は請求のあり次第売り主に対して期限到来債務の支払うとともに、延滞金については支払い期日から支払い日までプライム・レートに年率5%を加えた年間利率で利息を支払うものとする。

| 解説 | 船荷証券の種類 |

air B/L 空輸証券（=aircraft B/L）
charter party B/L 用船契約船荷証券
claused B/L 条項付き船荷証券
clean B/L 無故障船荷証券
custody B/L 保管付き船荷証券
Customs B/L 税関用船荷証券
domestic B/L 国内輸送証券
export B/L 輸出品船荷証券
foul B/L 故障付き船荷証券
negotiable B/L 流通性船荷証券 流通船荷証券 譲渡可能船荷証券
negotiable electronic B/L 電子式譲渡可能船荷証券
ocean B/L 海洋船荷証券（=marine B/L）
on board B/L 船積み船荷証券 船積み式船荷証券（=shipped B/L）
on-carriage B/L 貨車輸送証券
order B/L 指図式船荷証券 指図人式船荷証券
original B/L 船荷証券原本
overseas B/L 海外船荷証券
port B/L 積出港船荷証券
prepaid B/L 運賃前払い船荷証券
railroad B/L 鉄道貨物引換証
received B/L 受取船荷証券 受取式船荷証券
received-for-shipment B/L 船積み式船荷証券
red B/L 赤字船荷証券
shipped B/L 船積み船荷証券 船積み式船荷証券
short form B/L 略式船荷証券
stale B/L 時期経過船荷証券
straight B/L （荷受人）指名直送船荷証券 記名式船荷証券
sub-D/L 口別船荷証券
summary B/L 積荷明細表
through B/L 通し船荷証券
transshipment B/L 積替え船荷証券
truck B/L 自動貨車積送証券

blame （動）（人）のせいにする, 責任を～に負わせる, ～に責任があるという, 非難する（名）責め, 責任, 罪, 非難
both to blame 双方過失（他船と自船双方の過失による船舶の衝突）
neither to blame 無過失衝突（船舶の無過失による衝突）
one to blame 一方過失（他船または自船の過失による衝突）

blank （形）白紙の, 余白の, 白地（しらじ）式の, 無記名の, 無表情な, 生気のない, まったくの, 徹底的な （名）余白, 空欄, 書式
blank application 白紙の申込み書
blank bill 白紙の請求書, (受取人)無記名手形, 白地手形
blank check [cheque] 白地式小切手, 白紙委任
blank endorsement 白地裏書, 白地式裏書（=indorsement [endorsement] in blank）
blank order form 白紙の注文書

draw a blank　失敗に終わる

give A a blank check　Aに完全な自由裁量権を与える, Aに完全に任せる

order blank　注文用紙, 注文書式

blank receipt　白紙領収書
◆Some utilities companies have even started to issue blank receipts to their customers due to the bank's computer troubles. 同行のコンピュータのトラブルで, 顧客に白紙の領収書発行を開始した公益企業もある。

blanket　(形)一括の, 包括的な, 一斉の, 全面的な, 例外なしの

blanket ballot　連記等投票用紙

blanket clause　総括条項

blanket clearance　包括出入港許可, 総括出入港許可

blanket endorsement　無差別承認

blanket policy　(保険の)包括契約, 包括保険証券

blanket rate　総括保険料率

blanket rule　包括的規則

blanket ban on　〜の全面禁止, 〜についての全面禁止, 〜に対する全面禁止[規制, 禁止令]
◆The Agriculture, Forestry and Fisheries Ministry finally imposed a blanket ban on the use of meat and bone meal (MBM) feed, which is believed to be the source of infection of mad cow disease. 農水省は, 狂牛病の感染源とされる肉骨粉飼料の全面使用禁止に踏み切った。

block　(名)市街の一区画, 区域, 塊, スランプ, 一時的な思考の停止, 相手を妨げる行為, ブロック　(形)大口の, 大量の, 一括の, 包括的
a block of shares　1取引単位の株式

block booking　(券などの)一括購入, (映画などの)一括配給契約

block exemption　一括免除

block grants　包括補助金, 定額交付金, 定額助成金, ブロック交付金

block insurance　包括保険(各種輸送手段で積送される物品の危険をすべてカバーする保険)

block investor　大口投資家　(=bloc investor)

block offer　一括売出し, ブロック・オファー

block purchase　ブロック買い

block sale　ブロック売り

block sales　大量販売, 大量売却, 大量取引, 大量売付け

block trade　大口取引, 大量取引

place a block order　大口注文を出す

blue print　青写真

board of directors　会社の取締役会, 役員会, 重役会, 財団などの理事会, BOD
a board of directors meeting　取締役会の会議, 取締役会

a regular meeting of the board of directors　取締役会の定例会議
◆Khazanah National which owns 69 percent of Malaysia Airlines has proposed to buy out minority shareholders to the carrier's board of directors. マレーシア航空株の69%を保有するカザナ・ナショナル社(政府系投資会社)は, 少数株主の株を買い取ることを, 同航空の取締役会に提案した。
◆Nissan Motor Co.'s board of directors gave its approval for exploratory talks on a proposal for struggling U.S. auto giant General Motors Corp. 日産自動車の取締役会は, 経営再建中の米自動車大手ゼネラル・モーターズ(GM)に対する提携案の事前協議を承認した。

board of directors meeting　取締役会
◆A quorum for the board of directors meeting shall require the presence of four directors. 取締役会の定足数は, 取締役4名の出席を必要とする。

board structure　取締役会制度
◆Under the revised Commercial Code, only large companies with capital of more than ¥500 million would be qualified to adopt the U.S.-style board structure. 今回の商法改正では, 資本金5億円以上の大企業だけが米国型の取締役会制度を導入することができる。

body clauses　本文約款

bogus pharmaceutical product　偽造医薬品
◆About 70 websites which sold bogus pharmaceutical products on the Internet were forcibly shut down from April to September 2014 by the health ministry. インターネット上で偽造医薬品を販売していた約70サイトを, 厚生労働省が, 2014年4〜9月に強制的に閉鎖した。

bogus subscription　架空の加入契約

bona fide　善意の, 誠実な, 真実の, 正直な, 真正な, 善意で(in good faith)(反対語はmala fideで「悪意の, 不誠実な」という意味)

bona fide consultation　誠意ある協議(=consultation in good faith)

bona fide cost sharing arrangement　真正な原価負担契約

bona fide debt　真正な債権

bona fide hedge　純粋なヘッジ

bona fide holder　善意の所持人(=holder in due course: 手形や小切手などの正当な所持人), (契約品などの)善意の保管者

bona fide purchaser　善意の買い主, 善意の買い手, 善意の取得者

bona fide third party　善意の第三者

bona fide written offer　善意の書面による申込み, 誠意ある書面での申込み

bona fides　善意, 誠実, 真実

bona fide discussions　善意の話し合い(=discussions in good faith)

◆The parties hereto will enter into bona fide discussions in an attempt to solve any issues or dispute which may arise from the interpretation or performance of this agreement. 本契約当事者は、本契約の解釈または履行から生じる一切の問題または紛争を解決するための試みとして、善意の話し合いを行うものとする。

bona fide holder of Products 契約品［本製品］の善意の保管者
◆ABC shall take care of keeping its quality without any harm whatsoever as bona fide holder of Products on behalf of XYZ. ABCは、XYZを代理する契約品［本製品］の善意の保管者として、契約品［本製品］の品質保持上、どんな損害も生じないよう注意を払うものとする。

bona fide offer 善意の申込み、誠意ある申込み
◆In the event that, as a result of such offering, the party desiring to transfer receives a bona fide offer which it considers acceptable to purchase the rejected shares, it shall, before transferring such shares to such person, re-offer or cause such shares to be re-offered to other parties who rejected them, up in the terms of such offer to purchase. 当該オファーを行った結果、譲渡を希望する当事者が、拒絶された株式の購入受諾と考えられる善意の申込みを受けた場合、当該当事者は、当該株式をその者に譲渡する前に、株式を拒絶した他の当事者に対して購入申込み条件で再オファーする、または再オファーさせる。

bond （名）債券、社債、公社債、債務証書、借用証書、保証証書、支払い保証契約、保証、保証金、保釈金、契約、約定、保税貨物輸出証（動）保税倉庫に入れる、抵当に入れる、借入金を債券に振り替える
bid bond 入札保証、入札保証証券
bond insurance ボンド保険
bond note 保税品輸出許可証
enter into a bond with 〜と契約を結ぶ
go a person's bond 人の保証人に立つ
in bond 保税渡し、保税中の、保税倉庫［保税工場］にある
performance bond 契約履行保証、履行保証証券
refundment bond 前受金返還保証（=refund［advance payment］bond）
take out of bond 保税倉庫［保税工場］から出す

bonded （形）保税入庫中の、保税中の、保証付きの
bonded area 保税地域、BA
bonded carman 保税貨物運搬人
bonded display area 保税展示場、BDA（=bonded exhibiting area）
bonded factory［mill］ 保税工場
bonded goods 保税品

bonded manufacturing warehouse 保税工場、BMW
bonded shed 保税上屋、B/S
bonded transportation 保税運送
bonded value clause 保税品単独海損条項
bonded warehouse 保税倉庫、B/W
designated bonded area 指定保税地域、DBA

BOO 建設・運営・所有、BOO方式（build-operate-own:build, operate and own（建設・運営・所有する）の略）

BOO scheme BOO方式、建設・運営・所有方式（=BOO formula）

book （動）予約する、（資産を）積み増す
book property assets 不動産関連資産を積み増す
book shipping space （本船の）船腹を予約する
◆If delivery is made under the terms of FOB, the Buyer shall book shipping space in accordance with the time of delivery stipulated in this agreement. 引渡しがFOBの条件で行われる場合、買い主は、本契約で定める引渡し期限に従って（本船の）船腹を予約するものとする。

booking agent 集荷代理店
booking note 船腹申込み書
booking ship's space 船腹の予約
books and records 帳簿と記録、会計帳簿と会計記録、帳簿類（=records and books）
◆Licensee shall keep full, clear and accurate books and records of Products subject to the running royalty. ライセンシーは、ランニング・ロイヤルティの対象である［対象となる］本製品の完全、明瞭かつ正確な帳簿（会計帳簿）と記録を保持するものとする。

boost export competitiveness 輸出競争力を高める
◆In global currency wars, central banks effectively lower the value of their countries' currencies to boost their countries' export competitiveness. 世界の通貨安競争では、自国の輸出競争力を高めるため、中央銀行が自国通貨の価値を事実上切り下げる［自国通貨の為替相場を事実上安くする］。

boost exports 輸出を拡大する、輸出を伸ばす
◆In a currency war, countries intentionally devalue their currencies to boost exports. 通貨安戦争では、各国が輸出に追い風となるように自国通貨の為替レートを意図的に安く誘導する。

born and paid by 〜が負担し支払う（=borne and paid by）
◆Any tax arising out of the separate business activities conducted by XYZ and ABC pursuant to this agreement shall be born and paid by the party upon whom such tax is imposed by applicable law. 本契約に従ってXYZとABCが行う営業

活動から発生する税金は、適用法によりその税金が課される当事者が負担して支払うものとする。

borrow （動）借り入れる, 融資を受ける, 資金を調達する, 借金する

borrow massive amounts of money　巨額の借入れをする

borrow money from a bank　銀行から資金を借り入れる

borrowed capital　他人資本, 借入資本, 外部資本

borrowed money　借入金, 借金

borrowed security　借入有価証券

borrowed stock　借り株

◆In a global carry trade, hedge funds borrow low-interest yen funds to invest in dollar-denominated assets. グローバル・キャリー・トレード［グローバル・キャリー取引］では, ヘッジ・ファンドなどが, 低利の円資金を借りてドル建て資産に投資している。

borrower （名）借主［借り主］, 借り手, 資金の借り手, 貸付け先, 貸出先, 融資先, 融資先企業, 債務者, 発行体, 手形の振出人, ボロワー（⇒grace period）

AAA rated borrower　トリプルA格の発行体

borrower of record　契約上の借入人

creditworthy borrower　信用力［信用度］が高い借り手, 優良貸出先

large-scale borrowers　大口融資先

prime borrower　大口貸出先, 大口貸付け先, 大口融資先, 優良発行体, 優良な借入人

problematic borrowers　問題融資先

sovereign borrower　ソブリン発行体

subprime borrower　信用力の低い［劣る］借り手

top-notch borrower　超優良発行体

◆For Value Received, the undersigned ("Borrower") promises to pay to ABC Co., Ltd. , a Japanese corporation ("Holder"), or order, in lawful money of the United States, the principal sum of Five million Eight hundred Fifty thousand dollars ($5,850,000), with interest on the principal balance remaining unpaid from the date hereof until paid, at the following rates. 「対価の受領」については, 末尾署名者（以下「振出人」という）が, 元本585万ドル（$5,850,000）と本手形の振出日から決済日まで残存する元本の未払い残高利息を, 日本法人のABC株式会社（以下「所持人」という）にまたはその指図人に, 米国の法定通貨と以下の金利で支払うことを約束する。◆In case the borrower fails to pay any principal or interest payable under this agreement on the due date therefor, the borrower shall pay to the lender overdue interest on such overdue amount for each day for the period from and including the due date therefor up to and including the day immediately preceding the actual payment date.

借主が本契約に基づいて元本または支払い利息の支払い期日に元本の返済または支払い利息の支払いを怠った場合, 借主は, その支払い期日から実際の払込み日までの期間の各日数について, その支払い遅延金額の遅延利息を貸主に支払うものとする。◆The loan shall be advanced by the lender to the borrower wholly or partially in an amount of ten million Japanese Yen（￥10,000,000）or its integral multiple upon request by the borrower. 貸付け金は, 貸主の要請に基づき, 貸主が借主に対してその全額または一部を1千万円またはその倍数の金額で提供する。

BOT　建設・運営・譲渡, BOT方式（=BOT formula, build-operate-transfer:build, operate and transfer（建設・運営・譲渡する）の略）（=BOT formula, build-operate-transfer）

BOT project　BOT方式プロジェクト

BOT scheme　BOT方式, 建設・運営・譲渡方式　（=BOT formula）

both parties hereto　本契約の両当事者, 本契約両当事者

◆This agreement shall become effective on the date when both parties hereto affix their duly authenticated seals. 本契約は, 本契約の両当事者が正当に認証された社印を捺印した日に発効する。

bound by　～に拘束される

◆ABC hereby consents to such assignment and agrees for the benefit of XYZ to be bound by such terms and provisions. ABCは, ここに当該譲渡に同意し, XYZの利益のためにこのような条件と規定に拘束されることに同意する。

boycott against Japanese goods　日本製品の不買運動

◆Both the Japanese economy and Chinese businesses have been impacted by the boycott against Japanese goods being staged in protest of Japan's nationalization of the Senkakus. 日本の尖閣諸島国有化に反発［抗議］して行われている日本製品の不買運動で, 日本経済も中国企業も打撃を受けている。

brand　（名）商標, 銘柄, 特定の銘柄品, ブランド, ブランド品, ブランド商品, ブランド店

brand awareness　ブランド認知

brand-beef cattle　ブランド牛

brand identity　商標の存在価値, 商品の独自性, ブランド・アイデンティティ, BI

brand loyalty　商標忠実性, 銘柄忠実度, 商標信頼度, ブランドに対するこだわり, ブランド・ロイヤルティ

brand-named item　銘柄品, メーカー品

brand-new and state-of-the-art　最新技術の粋を集めた新製品

brand portfolio　有価証券一覧表, ブランド・ポートフォリオ

brand preference　商標選好, ブランド選好

brand recognition　ブランド認知

brand strength　ブランド競争力

brand switching　商標変更, ブランド遷移, ブランド・スイッチング

character brand　キャラクター・ブランド（大手メーカーの個性や特徴を強く打ち出した製品）

control brand　コントロール・ブランド（=double chip: メーカー名と流通業者名を併記したブランドのこと）

designer's brand　デザイナーズ・ブランド, デザイナーズ・ブランド（デザイナーの名を付した商標）

factory brand　生産工場独自の商標, ファクトリー・ブランド

family brand　統一ブランド, 代表商標, 共通ブランド, ファミリー・ブランド

foreign brand shops　海外のブランド店

generic brand　非銘柄商品, 無印商品, ジェネリック・ブランド（ノーブランド, ジェネリック・ラベルとも言う）

multibrand strategy　マルチブランド戦略, 複数ブランド戦略

national brand　全国ブランド, 製造元商標, ナショナル・ブランド

no-brand goods　ノーブランド商品（=no name goods, generic goods, generics）

own-brand goods　自主企画商品

private brand　自家商標, 商業者商標, プライベート・ブランド

store brand　自社ブランド, 自店独自のブランド, ストア・ブランド　（=private brand）

◆Chinese home appliance giant Haier Group Co. plans to actively add new washing machines to the high-end Aqua brand sold in Japan. 中国の家電大手・海爾集団（ハイアール）は, 日本で販売している高価格帯の「アクア」ブランドに, 洗濯機の新商品を積極的に投入する構えだ。◆The Customs Tariff Law bans imports that infringe on patent, design and commercial brand rights. 関税定率法で, 特許, 意匠権, 商標権などの侵害品の輸入は禁止されている。

brand name　ブランド名, ブランド力

◆Chinese companies are looking to enhance the value of their products in the market by acquiring Japan's state-of-the-art technology and brand names. 中国企業は, 日本の先端技術やブランド力を得て, 市場での自社製品の価値を高めようとしている。

breach　（名）違反, 侵害, 義務の不履行, 違反行為　（動）契約などを破る, 違反する, 侵害する

breach a contract　契約に違反する

breach of any agreement　契約違反

breach of contract　契約違反

commit a breach of any obligation under this agreement　本契約上の義務に違反する

constitute a breach of this agreement　本契約違反となる

cure such breach　当該違反を是正する, 当該違反を改める

in the event of a breach or threatened breach of this agreement　本契約の違反または違反の恐れがある場合

party in breach　違反している当事者

party not in breach　違反していない当事者

◆If I breach Article VI, ABC shall be entitled, in addition to all other remedies it may have, to injunctive or other appropriate relief to restrain any such breach without showing or proving any actual damages to ABC. 私が第6条に違反した場合, ABCが有する他のあらゆる救済手段のほかに, ABCは, ABCの実際の損害を証明または立証することなく, 当該違反を禁止するために差止めまたは他の適切な救済措置を受けられるものとする。◆ In the event of a breach or threatened breach by ABC of this agreement, XYZ will have no adequate remedy at law. ABCによる本契約の違反または違反の恐れがある場合, XYZは, コモン・ロー上の十分な救済を受けられない。

breach of this agreement　本契約の違反

◆Any failure, whether willful, through neglect or otherwise, of either party to perform or fulfill any of its duties, obligations or covenants in this agreement shall constitute a breach of this agreement. 故意であれ, 怠慢またはその他によるものであれ, 本契約における各当事者の責務, 義務または約束ごとを各当事者が履行または達成できない場合, これは本契約の違反を構成するものとする。◆In the event of the breach of this agreement by the seller, the limit of the seller's liability shall be for the actual damages directly sustained by the purchaser from such breach. 売り主が本契約に違反した場合, 売り主の責任限度は, 買い主が当該違反から直接被った実損額とする。

breach of warranty　保証違反, 保証義務違反, 保証の違反

◆ABC shall indemnify and hold XYZ harmless against all actions, claims, damages, costs and expenses resulting from any breach of ABC's warranty as referred to in Article III. ABCは, 第3条に規定するABCの保証の違反から生じるすべての訴訟, 請求, 損害, 経費については, XYZにこれを補償しその責任を免除する。

breakdown　（名）内訳, 交渉などの決裂, 中絶, 崩壊, 倒壊, 故障

breakdown of public common carrier　公共交通手段の故障

bribery　（名）贈収賄, 贈収賄行為, 賄賂の授受, 贈賄, 収賄, 汚職

◆To ensure fair international commercial trade, the law against unfair competition stipulates that both individuals involved in bribery and the corporations they belong to should be punished. 公

正な国際商取引を確保するため、不正競争防止法には、贈賄（外国公務員への贈賄）に関与した個人と法人を罰する規定（両罰規定）がある。

BRICS 有力新興国, ブリクス（高い経済成長を続けるBrazil（ブラジル）、Russia（ロシア）、India（インド）、China（中国）と南アフリカ（South Africa）の頭文字による造語）
◆Financial exchanges between the BRICs group, Indonesia and South Korea will move toward a tri-reserve-currency regime by losing a dependency on the U.S. dollar. BRICsグループ（ブラジル、ロシア、インド、中国）とインドネシア、韓国の新興6か国間の金融取引は今後、米ドルに依存しなくなるため、3準備通貨体制に移行するものと思われる。

British Bankers Association Interest Settlement Rate 英国銀行協会金利決済レート （⇒LIBOR）

broad agreement 大筋合意, 大筋一致, 基本合意
◆The APEC forum leaders were committed to reaching a broad agreement in the trade liberalization talks next month. アジア太平洋経済協力会議（APEC）の首脳は、来月予定されている貿易自由化交渉での大筋合意の達成を誓約した。

broadcast and exhibit 放映・上映する
◆In this agreement, the performance rights include the rights to broadcast and exhibit the picture in the media licensed herein. 本契約で、放映権には、本契約で許諾されたメディアで本映画を放映・上映する権利が含まれる。

bug （名）バグ, 故障, 不良・欠陥箇所（コンピュータのプログラムやシステムの誤り）
◆ABC requests that XYZ inform ABC of any suggestions for change or correction of bug. ABCは、XYZが変更またはバグの修正に関する提案をABCに通知するよう求めている。

bunker （名）（船舶の）燃料庫, 燃料置き場, 保管場所, 障害物, バンカー （動）燃料を積み込む

  bunker adjustment factor バンカー課徴金, BAF （=bunker surcharge: 燃料費割増料）

  bunker capacity 燃料庫容量

  bunker oil バンカー油

  bunkering station 燃料積込み地

burden （名）責任, 負担

  burden of going forward 証拠提出責任 （=burden of going forward with the evidence, burden of producing evidence）

  burden of persuasion 説得責任

  burden of producing evidence 証拠提出責任 （=burden of going forward）

  burden of proof 証明責任, 立証責任, 挙証責任
◆The burden of proving the facts set forth in subparagraphs (3) (a) through (d) shall rest with the licensee. 第三項(a)から(d)までに明記した事

実の立証責任は、ライセンシーが負うものとする。
◆The metropolitan government's bank tax lacks balance to an excessive degree when compared with the burden of other existing taxes. 東京都の銀行税は、従来の税負担に比べて著しく均衡を欠いている。

busiest season 書き入れ時
◆In the beer industry, a single day's shipment volume during the busiest season from June to August influences the annual performances of beer companies. ビール業界では、6〜8月の書き入れ時の1日の出荷量が、ビール各社の年間業績を左右する。

business （名）事業, 商売, 商業, 取引, 営業, 業務, 業容, 職務, 職業, 実務, 実業, 実業界, 産業界, 会社, 企業, 経営, 業績, 景気, 議事日程, 議題, ビジネス （⇒abroad）

  affairs of the business 会社の業務

  attract business 客を増やす, 売上増につなげる

  be away on business 出張中である

  be driven out of business 廃業に追い込まれる

  be in business 商売をしている, ビジネスに携わる

  build up this business この取引を成約［成立］させる

  business administration 経営管理体制 （⇒business improvement order）

  business background 業歴

  business climate 事業環境, 企業環境, 経営環境, 企業風土, 経営風土, 企業の体質, 景況, 商況, 景気 （=business environment）

  business continuity plan 業務継続計画, BCP （大災害や大規模テロ, 感染症流行などの非常時に、限られた人員や設備で緊急に必要な業務を続け、早期に事業を立て直せるように業務の優先順位や手順を取り決める計画

  business day 取引日, 営業日, 銀行営業日, 業務日 （⇒in the form of）

  business department 営業部

  business failure 企業倒産

  Business Industry Advisory Committee 経済産業諮問委員会, BIAC （OECDの民間諮問機関）

  business integration 事業統合, 経営統合 （=integration of business, merger）

  business relationship 取引関係

  business terms 取引条件

  future business 今後の取引
◆The three pillars of the Abe administration's growth strategy are restoring the nation's industries, strategically creating new markets and helping Japan's businesses expand abroad. 安倍政権の成長戦略の3本の柱は、日本産業の再興、戦略市場の創造と日本企業の国際展開である。◆We

hope that this trial order will lead to future business. この試験注文は、今後の取引につながるものと思います。◆We would assure you of our best cooperation in realizing business if you can secure these articles. これらの商品をすべて確保できれば、当社は成約に最大限の協力を致します。

business affairs　営業上の問題, 業務上の問題, 企業事象
◆The parties hereto shall keep in strict confidence from any third party any and all important matters concerning the business affairs and transactions covered by this agreement. 本契約当事者は、本契約の対象である営業上の問題や取引に関するすべての重要事項については、どんな第三者に対しても一切極秘にする。

business client　法人顧客
◆In the circular sales transactions, Katokichi's affiliates and business clients recorded the repeated sale and purchase of products only on paper receipts. 循環取引で、加卜吉の関連会社と法人顧客は、繰り返し行われた商品の売買を架空の売上だけに計上していた。

business combination　企業結合
◆A business combination is a significant economic event that results from bargaining between independent parties. 企業結合は、独立した当事者間の取引から生じるひとつの重要な経済事象である。

business environment　経営環境, 企業環境, 事業環境, 景気　(=business climate)
◆Alarmed by the likelihood that the business environment will become even more severe, the two companies had little leeway in concluding the merger agreement. 経営環境がさらに厳しくなるとの見通しから危機感を強め、両社は合併合意を急がなければならなかった。

business expansion　事業拡大, 事業拡張, 業容拡大
◆The company plans to focus more on merger and acquisition-based business expansion if it fails to reach the target of its medium-term business plan. 中期経営計画の目標を達成できない場合、同社はM&A(企業の合併・買収)による事業拡大を強化する方針だ。

business image　企業イメージ
◆Japanese companies can hedge exchange risks and improve their business image abroad through external bond financing. 日本企業は、外債発行による資金調達で、為替リスクを回避するとともに海外での企業イメージアップを図ることができる。

business improvement order　業務改善命令
◆The Financial Services Agency issued a business improvement order to the bank on the Banking Law and demanded it implement a fundamental review of compliance and business administration. 金融庁は、同行に対して銀行法に基づく業務改善命令を出し、法令順守と経営管理

体制を抜本的に見直すことを求めた。

business operator　事業者
◆Under the Consumer Contract Law, contracts that excessively protect the interests of the business operator can be canceled. 消費者契約法では、事業者側の利益を過剰に保護する契約は取り消すことができる。

Business Organization law　会社法
◆Companies are allowed to use poison pill defense tactics more easily by the Business Organization Law, which went into effect in fiscal 2006. 2006年度から施行された「会社法」で、企業はポイズン・ビル(毒薬条項)防衛策を以前より容易に行使できるようになった。

business partner　取引先企業, 取引先, 業務提携先
◆Mazda is expected to seek a new business partner in order to expand operations in emerging countries. 新興国での事業を拡大するため、マツダは今後、新たな業務提携先を模索するものと見られる。

business performance　営業成績, 業績, 経営状況, 経営　(=business results)
◆The business performance of Japanese exporting companies is deteriorating fast due to the simultaneous slowdown of the global economy. 世界同時不況で、日本の輸出企業の業績は急速に悪化している。

business practice　商慣習, 商慣行, 企業慣行, 取引慣行, 取引方法, 営業手法, 業務
◆The company maintained a long-standing business practice of receiving kickbacks from trade connections. 同社は、取引業者からリベートを取る以前からの商慣行を守り続けた。◆The FSA has ordered Mizuho Bank to rectify its business practices on the Banking Law as the bank had extended a total of ¥200 million in loans to members of crime syndicates. 金融庁は、みずほ銀行が暴力団員らに計2億円を融資していたため、みずほ銀行に対して銀行法に基づく業務改善命令を出した。

business processing service　事務処理サービス
◆In the Philippines, tertiary industries such as call center, financial, legal and other business processing services outsourced by foreign companies are also thriving. フィリピンでは、海外企業が業務委託するコールセンターや金融、法律業務の事務処理サービスなどのサービス産業も伸びている。

business reform　事業改革
◆The three electronics makers implemented business reforms, mainly streamlining of TV production businesses which had been the main cause of their losses. 家電メーカー3社は、赤字の元凶となってきたテレビ生産事業の合理化を中心に、事業改革を実施した。

business strategy　経営戦略, 事業戦略, 企業戦略, ビジネス戦略

◆If a company takes a delayed response in its business strategy, it is bound to hit a wall no matter how excellent the company is. 経営戦略が後手に回ると、どんな優良企業でも、壁にぶつかることになる。

business trip 出張
◆In case ABC Personnel makes business trips for the performance of the services, costs and expenses for such trips, including, inter alia, fares and allowances shall be born and paid or reimbursed by XYZ. 本サービスを提供するためにABC人員が出張する場合、当該出張の諸費用（とりわけ旅費と出張手当てを含む）は、XYZが負担して支払うかXYZがその補償をするものとする。

business year 事業年度
◆Toyota revised upward its consolidated operating profit estimates for the business year ending March 31, 2013, largely due to improved profitability in its exports from a weakening of the yen in response to "Abenomics," the economic policy of the Abe administration. トヨタは2013年3月期決算［2013年3月31日終了事業年度］の連結営業利益予想［連結業績予想］を上方修正するが、これは主に安倍政権の経済政策「アベノミクス」を好感しての円安で、輸出の採算が向上しているためだ。

buy （動）買う（purchase）、購入する、仕入れる、取得する（acquire）、買い取る、買収する、株などを引き受ける、〜に相当する［値する］、〜を買える
buy assets　資産を積み上げる、資産を購入する
buy at the bottom　底値で買いを入れる
buy at the top（of the market）　高値づかみになる、高値づかみする
buy bonds　債券を購入する、債券に投資する
buy direct from a maker［manufacturer］　製造元から直接仕入れる
buy dollars on speculation　思惑でドルを買う
buy in　買い込む、買いだめする、（競売品を）買い戻す［買い取る］（buy-in＝処分買い）
buy in at the bottom of the US dollars　米ドルを底値で拾う
buy in bulk　大量に仕入れる
buy into　〜に投資する、金を出して〜を手に入れる、（株を買って）株主になる、（考えなどを）信じ込む
buy low and sell high　安く買い高く売る、安く買って高く売る
buy off　（人を）買収する、（人を）抱き込む、（問題などを）金で処理する
buy on credit　クレジットで買う
buy over　買収する
buy the loan　ローンを買い取る
buy up　買い占める、買い取る

buy wholesale　卸値で買う［仕入れる］
◆Intercontinental Exchange（ICE）, an exchange that deals in investing contracts known as futures, is buying the NYSE for about $8 billion. 米インターコンチネンタル取引所（ICE: 先物と呼ばれる投資契約を扱う取引所）が、ニューヨーク証券取引所を約80億ドルで買収する。

Buy American 米製品の優先購入, 米製品の優先買付け［優先買付け政策］, バイ・アメリカン
Buy American Act　米製品優先購入法, 米商品優先購入法, バイ・アメリカン法（大恐慌下の1933年に制定された。米政府が橋や道路建設などの公共事業の契約を企業と結ぶときは、原則として米国製品を使うよう義務付けている）

buy American and ship American policy 自国貨自国船主義
◆Khazanah National which owns 69 percent of Malaysia Airlines has proposed to buy out minority shareholders to the carrier's board of directors. マレーシア航空株の69%を保有するカザナ・ナショナル社（政府系投資会社）は、少数株主の株を買い取ることを、同航空の取締役会に提案した。

Buy American provision バイ・アメリカン条項
◆The U.S. "Buy American" provision requires any public projects funded by stimulus money to use only U.S.-made products. 米国のバイ・アメリカン条項は、経済対策資金で賄われる公共工事に米国製品の使用を義務付けている。

buy out 買い取る、買い占める、買い上げる、買収する、乗っ取る、（株を買い上げて）営業権を得る

buyer （名）買い主, 買い手, 購入者, 仕入担当者, 海外の輸入者, バイヤー
buyer's credit　バイヤーズ・クレジット（輸出国の金融機関が海外の法人に輸入資金を貸し付けることをいう）
buyer's market　買い手市場
buyer's monopoly　買い手独占
buyer's option　買い手の選択, 買い主の選択（売り主の選択＝seller's option）
buyer's policy　買い主保険
buyer's sample　買い手見本
institutional buyer　機関投資家
premier buyer　最大の買い手
prospective buyer　見込みがありそうな買い主, 見込み客
◆After the delivery of the Goods, any taxes, customs duties, export or import surcharges or other governmental charges shall be for the account of the Buyer. 本商品の引渡し後、税金、関税、輸出・輸入税、その他政府が賦課する費用は、買い主の負担とする。◆Commencing on the date of

this agreement until the Closing, Buyer shall be permitted to perform such due diligence investigation related to the transactions contemplated by this agreement as Buyer deems necessary and appropriate in its discretion. 本契約締結日からクロージングまで、買い主は、本契約で意図されている取引に関して買い主が買い主の判断で必要かつ適切と考えるデュー・ディリジェンス調査を行うことができるものとする。◆If delivery is made under the terms of CFR or CIF, the Seller shall inform the Buyer of the name, nationality, age and other details of the carrying vessel by Fax or E-mail not later than fourteen (14) days before the time of delivery. 引渡しがCFR (運賃込み) またはCIF (運賃保険料込み) の条件で行われる場合、売り主は、引渡し期限の14日前までにファクスかEメールで本船の船名、船籍、船齢その他の詳細を買い主に通知するものとする。

buyer's premium バイヤーズ・プレミアム (競売会社に支払われる売買手数料)
◆The hammer price of Edvard Munch's painting "The Scream" was $107 million, and about $120 million with the buyer's premium. ノルウェーの画家エドバルド・ムンクの絵画「叫び」の競売落札価格は1億700万ドルで、バイヤーズ・プレミアム (競売会社に支払われる売買手数料) 込みでは約1億2,000万ドルだった。

buying (名) 買い, 買付け, 購入, 購買, 仕入れ
buying agent 買付け代理人
buying behavior 購買行動
buying branch 買付け事務所
buying budget 仕入予算
buying commission 買付け手数料
buying contract 買い予約, 輸出予約
buying exchange 買い為替
buying offer 買い申込み, 買いオファー
buying opportunity 買い場
buying out 買取り, 買占め, 買収, 営業権の取得 (=buyout)
buying period 仕入期間, 調達期間
buying power 購買力
buying preferences 消費者の好み
buying price 購入価格, 買付け価格, 買い値, 買価, 仕入値段, 仕入価格
buying rate 買い相場
buying up 買収, 買占め
central buying 集中仕入れ
consumer buying 個人消費支出
cooperative buying 共同仕入れ
foreign investor buying 外国人買い, 外国人の買い (=foreign buy)
historical buying price 購入価格
quantity buying 大量仕入れ, 多量仕入れ (=large-lot buying)

selective buying 物色買い
◆In the takeover bid system, the buying prices and the number of stocks a company wants to purchase are announced. 株式公開買付け制度では、企業が取得する株式の買付け価格と株数などが公表される。◆The buying force in the Tokyo stock market is overseas institutional investors. 東京株式市場での買いの主役は、海外の機関投資家だ。

by proxy 議決権委任状により, 代理人を立てて, 代理人により, 代理人が, 代理で
◆A shareholder may exercise its vote by proxy. 株主は、代理人により議決権を行使できる。◆Each party hereto shall have one vote for each share of which it is the holder and may be present at any meeting of shareholders either in person or by proxy. 本契約の各当事者は、自ら所有する1株につき1票の議決権を持ち、本人またはその代理人が株主総会に出席することができる。

by written notice 書面で通知して, 書面で通告して
◆Distributor or Supplier may terminate this agreement at will, at any time during the term of this agreement, with or without cause, by written notice given to the other party not less than 30 days prior to the effective date of such termination. 販売店または供給者は、この契約終了の効力発生日の30日以上前に相手方に書面で通知して、本契約中いつでも理由の有無を問わず自由に本契約を解除することができる。

bylaws (名) 会社の付属定款, 通常定款, 内規, 準則, 付則, 細則, 規則, 業務規則, 規約, 地方自治体の条例, 地方法 (=by-laws, byelaws)
◆The officers of the corporation shall consist of a President, one or more Vice-President as may be prescribed by the Bylaws, a Secretary, a Treasurer, and such other officers as may be prescribed by the Bylaws. 会社の役員は、社長、付属定款で定める1名以上の副社長、秘書役、会計役と、付属定款で定めるその他の役員とで構成するものとする。

Byrd Amendment 米バード修正法, バード法, 米国の反ダンピング (不当廉売) 関税分配法, 反ダンピング・相殺関税分配法 (米政府がダンピング (不当廉売) と認定した輸入製品に対して課す関税の収入を、ダンピング被害を申し立てた企業に救済金として分配することを定めた法律。正式名称はContinued Dumping and Subsidy Offset Actで、2000年10月に成立)
◆The Byrd Amendment requires antidumping and countervailing duties collected by customs authorities to be turned over to U.S. companies claiming damages for what they deem as dumping by overseas manufacturers. バード法では、税関当局が徴収したダンピング関税と相殺関税は、海外メーカーによるダンピング (不当廉売) と認定されたものに対して損害賠償を請求した米国企業に分配しなければならない。

C

C & F 運賃込み渡し, 運賃込み渡し条件 (cost and freightの略)

  C&F landed　陸揚げ費込みC&F

  C&F Singapore　運賃込みシンガポール条件で

C & I 保険料込み渡し, 保険料込み渡し条件, 保険料込み本船渡し (coast and insuranceの略)

CAF 通貨変動課徴金 (currency adjustment factorの略でcurrency surchargeとも呼ばれる)

calendar day 暦日 (真夜中から翌日の真夜中まで)

  ◆This letter of credit shall be opened not less than 30 calendar days before the first scheduled shipping date for each order and shall be 90 days beyond the anticipated final shipping date. この信用状は, 各注文の最初の出荷予定日から30暦日以上前に開設するものとし, 最終出荷予定日から90日を超えて有効でなければならない。

calendar quarter period 暦四半期, 四半期

  ◆The royalty shall be computed every calendar quarter period of each year. ロイヤルティは, 各年の四半期 (暦四半期) ごとに計算するものとする。

calendar year 暦年 (1月1日から12月31日までの1年)

  ◆At the beginning of each calendar year, ABC shall make a report to XYZ on the sales of the Product during the previous year and general market conditions. 各暦年の初めに, ABCは, XYZに対して前年度の契約品の販売 (実績) と市況全般について報告するものとする。

call (名)支払い要求, 払込み請求, 債券の繰上げ償還, (資本の) 導入, コール資金, 催告, コール (「コール資金」は, 金融機関同士が貸借する非常に短期の資金のこと)

  call account　未払い勘定

  call date　繰上げ償還日

  call deposit　通知預金 (=deposit at call)

  call letter　払込み請求書

  call on the market　市場での調達

  call price　繰上げ償還価格, 任意償還価格, 期前償還価格, 買入れ価格, 買戻し価格, コール価格

  call privilege　任意償還, 任意償還権

  call rate　コール・レート (コール取引による短期資金の貸借に適用される金利で, 年利建て (%表示) となっている)

  call redemption price　繰上げ償還価格

  call report　金融当局宛の業務報告書, 米連邦準備制度加盟銀行の報告書

  cash call　増資, 株主割当て発行増資

  deposit at call　通知預金

  half-day call　半日物

  long call　コールの買い, ロング・コール

call market 短期市場, 短期資金市場, コール市場 (=call money market)

  解説 **コール市場とは**: 金融機関や証券会社相互間の短期資金の貸借を行う場が「コール市場」で, 資金の貸し手から見た場合をコール・ローン, 資金の借り手から見た場合をコール・マネーという。コール取引には当日中に資金決済される半日物, 翌日決済の無条件物と, 翌々日決済の2日物から7日物までの期日物がある。

call money コール借入金, 銀行相互間の当座借入金, 短期融資, 短資, コール・マネー (=money at call, money on call)

  call money and discount markets　短期金融市場, 短資市場, コール・手形割引市場

  call money market　短資市場, コール市場 (=call market)

  day-to-day and unconditional call money　翌日物と無条件物のコール・マネー

call option 買付け選択権, 買取り特権, 買う権利, 買いオプション, 債券の任意償還, 繰上げ償還, コール・オプション (「コール・オプション」は, 金融商品を権利行使期間に権利行使価格で買う権利のこと。⇒put option)

  call option buyer　コール・オプションの買い手

  call option dealing　コール・オプション取引

  call option price　コール・オプション価格

  call option seller　コール・オプションの売り手

campaign to boycott Japanese products 日本製品の不買運動

  ◆The Chinese government allowed people to stage a campaign to boycott Japanese products following anti-Japan demonstrations. 中国政府は, 反日デモに続いて, 中国人の日本製品の不買運動をも容認した。

cancel (動)取り消す, 破棄する, 抹消する, 契約を終結させる, 契約を解除する, 解約する, 無効にする (⇒cooling-off period)

  cancel the agreement　本契約を解除する

  cancel the shipment　船積みを取り消す

  ◆The Seller may withhold delivery or cancel the Agreement if the Buyer fails to establish the letter of credit by the date stipulated in this Agreement. 買い主が本契約で定める期限までに信用状を開設することができない場合, 売り主は, 引渡しを保留するか契約を解除することができる。

cancellation (名)契約の解除, 解約, 取消し, 破棄, 抹消, 株式の消却

  cancellation agreement　解除契約 (=termination agreement)

  cancellation before maturity　中途解約

  cancellation charges　解除料, 解約手数料

  cancellation decree　除権判決

CAP   72

C

cancellation money　解約金

cancellation notice　解約通知

cancellation of a contract　契約の解除, 解約

cancellation of stocks　株式消却

make a cancellation　解約する, 取り消す,
キャンセルする

markdown cancellation　値下げ取消し高

markup cancellation　値上げ取消し高

◆In case the quality of Products shipped to Distributor turns out not to meet the above quality requirements, Distributor can claim a replacement against those inferior Products or cancellation of the individual contract. 販売店に発送した本製品の品質が上記品質基準に適合しないことが判明した場合, 販売店は, これら品質の劣る本製品の交換［これら粗悪品の交換］またはその個別契約［個々の契約］の解除を請求することができる。◆Notwithstanding termination of this agreement by cancellation, or its termination by expiration, the parties, except as otherwise provided, shall complete performance on any orders accepted prior to the effective date of such termination. 解除による本契約の終了または満了による本契約の終了にもかかわらず, 当事者は, 別途規定がないかぎり, 当該終了の効力発生日前に承諾した注文の履行を完了する。

cap and trade　キャップ・アンド・トレード
（温室効果ガスの排出権取引の手法の一つ。政府が企業ごとに温室効果ガスの排出量枠（キャップ［排出量の上限］）を割り当て, 排出量枠を超えた企業は枠を余らせた企業から超過分の排出権を買わなければならない仕組みのこと）

capacity　（名）能力, 資本, 資金, 設備, 生産能力, 操業度, 発電容量, 収容力, 地位, 資格, 立場, キャパシティ　（形）満員の, 場内一杯の

capacity building　人材開発

capacity utilization（rate）　設備稼働率, 操業度, 稼働率

capital capacity　資本生産能力

cargo capacity　載貨容積（measurement capacity）, 貨物積載力

displacement capacity　（船舶の）排水量

electrical capacity　発電容量

equipment capacity　設備能力

expand capacity　設備を拡張する, 生産能力を拡大する

export capacity　輸出余力, 輸出能力（=capacity to export）

factory capacity　工場の生産能力, 生産設備能力

increase production capacity　生産能力を拡大する

installed capacity　稼働発電能力

manufacturing capacity　生産能力, 製造能力, 生産設備　（=production capacity）

operate at full capacity　フル稼働状態にある, フル稼働を維持する, フル操業する

output capacity　生産能力

productive capacity　生産能力, 生産設備能力

shipbuilding capacity　造船能力, 建造量

◆As the demand for domestic steel has been increasing in China and among domestic appliance manufacturers, the nation's steel manufacturers are producing at full capacity. 中国向けや家電メーカー用の国内鉄鋼需要が増えているため, 国内鉄鋼各社はフル生産体制を取っている。◆The steelworks will have a blast furnace with an annual capacity of 3 million tons in operation by 2015. 同製鉄所の高炉1基は, 年産300万トンで, 2015年には稼動する。◆We have on hand such a rush of orders for this item that our output capacity cannot keep up with the demand. 本品に対しては多くの注文が入っているため, 当社の生産能力が需要に追いつかない状況で

capital　（名）資本, 資本金, 元金, 出資金, 保険会社の基金（株式会社の資本金に相当）, 正味財産, 純資産, 資本家階級, 資本家側

borrowed capital　他人資本, 借入資本, 外部資本

capital and interest　元金と利子, 元利

demand for capital　資金需要, 資本需要

enlarged capital　増資後の資本金

equity capital　自己資本, 株主資本

initial capital　創業資金

international capital　国際資本

operating capital　経営資本, 運転資本

private capital　民間資本

reduction of［in］capital　減資

share capital　株式資本, 株式資本金

Western capital　欧米資本

working capital　運転資金, 運転資本

◆In the joint venture with an Indian investment bank, Tokyo Marine Holdings Inc. put up about 26%, the maximum a foreign investor is allowed in an Indian company, of the new firm's capital. インドの投資銀行との合弁事業で, 東京海上ホールディングスは, 新会社の資本金の約26%（外資の持ち分比率の上限）を出資した。

capital account　資本収支（国際収支表の資本取引に伴う収支勘定）, 資本金勘定

balance of capital account　資本収支, 資本勘定収支, 資本勘定残高

capital account liberalization　対内投資の自由化

contributed capital accounts　払込み資本勘定

deficit in［of］capital account　資本収支の赤字

surplus in capital account　資本収支の黒字

capital base　資本基盤, 自己資本, 資本金
◆To strengthen its capital base ahead of the merger, the company will raise ¥30 billion through the allotment of new shares to DDI by the end of September. 合併に先立って資本基盤を強化するため、同社は、DDIへの新株割当てにより9月末までに300億円の資本を調達する。

capital flight　資本逃避, 他国への資本の流出, 資本の国外移転　(=flight of capital)
◆The decline in long-term interest rates since May is due to continued capital flight from high-risk assets such as stocks triggered by the debt crisis in Europe. 5月以降、長期金利が低下しているのは、欧州の財政危機をきっかけに株式などリスク［損失リスク］の高い資産からの資金逃避が続いたためだ。

capital flow　資本の流れ, 資金の流れ, 資本移動 (capital flows), 資金フロー
◆Developing Asia's capital markets have not shown excessive volatility, but the risk of rapid reversals in capital flows to the region is a concern. アジア途上国の資本市場に過度の変動は見られないが、資本移動の同地域への急激な逆転［反転］リスクが懸念される。◆The liberalization of capital flows in the globalized world economy is the core principle for ensuring the international financial system operated efficiently. グローバル化した世界経済における資本移動の自由化は、効率的な国際金融システムの運営確保の中核をなす原理である。

capital increase　増資, 資本増強, 保険会社の基金の積み増し・増額, 基金増資　(=capital expansion, capital increment, capital injection, increase of capital)
◆According to a probe conducted by the Tokyo Stock Exchange, there was a series of questionable stock deals in which trading volume surged just after the capital increase announcements by listed companies. 東京証券取引所の調査によると、上場企業が増資［公募増資］を公表した直後に（その銘柄の）売買高が急増する不自然な株取引が、相次いでいた。

capital inflow　資本流入, 資本の流れ, 資本移動, 資金の流入, 資本輸入, 流入資金, 買い越し　(=the inflow of capital)
　capital inflow figures　資本流入額, 資本収支上の流入額
　foreign capital inflows　外資流入, 外国からの資金流入, 外貨の流動性　(=foreign inflows)
　restrict capital inflow　資本流入を規制する
◆Such capital inflows have offset U.S. fiscal and trade deficits and boosted stock prices to record highs. これらの流入資金が、米国の財政や貿易の赤字を埋め合わせ、空前の株高を演出した。◆The latest rise in interest rates pushed up the exchange rates by attracting capital inflows. 今回の利上げが、資本流入を誘って、為替レートを押し上げた。

capital market　資本市場, 長期金融市場, キャピタル・マーケット
　capital market interest rates　資本市場の金利
　capital market transaction　資本市場取引
　tap the capital markets　資本市場で資金調達する
◆Developing Asia's capital markets have not shown excessive volatility, but the risk of rapid reversals in capital flows to the region is a concern. アジア途上国の資本市場に過度の変動は見られないが、資本移動の同地域への急激な逆転［反転］リスクが懸念される。

解説 資本市場とは：一般的には、株式・債券の発行市場（primary market: 新規発行の株式や債券が、発行者から投資家に売り渡される市場）と流通市場（secondary market: すでに発行された株式や債券が投資家間で売買される市場）を含めた証券市場とほぼ同義。ただし、広い意味では、金融機関の長期貸出資金をも含めた長期金融市場のこと。短期金融市場はmoney marketという。

capital market liberalization　資本市場の自由化
◆Albeit not free from risk, the benefits of capital market liberalization were considered to outweigh costs. リスクがないわけではないが［リスクはあるが］、資本市場自由化の便益は、そのコストを上回ると考えられた。

capital needs　資金需要, 資金のニーズ, 必要資本, 必要資本量, 資本必要額
◆Large firms such as trading and steel companies are taking out short-term loans to meet working capital needs. 商社や鉄鋼などの大企業は、運転資金のニーズを満たすため、短期ローンを組んでいる［短期借入れを行っている］。

capital outflow　資本流出, 対外投融資　(=the outflow of capital)
◆Direct investment and portfolio are included in capital outflow. 資本流出には、直接投資や証券投資が含まれる。

capital requirements　資本要件
◆The new company will pay dividends at such times and in such amounts as its board of directors determines are appropriate in the light of its earnings, cash flow and capital requirements. 新会社は、新会社の収益、キャッシュ・フローと資本要件に照らして新会社の取締役会が適切と決定する時期と金額により配当を支払う予定だ。

care　(名) 注意, 注意義務, 配慮, 保護, 看護, 介護, 世話, 面倒, 医療, 医療保険, 関心事, ケア
　no less than reasonable care　相当以上の注意
　take care of　〜に気をつける, 〜を処理する, 〜を引き受ける, （料金を）払う
　take care of the check　勘定を払う
　use the same degree of care as　〜と同程度の

注意を払う

with all one's care and attention　十分注意して，十分配慮して

◆ABC shall take care of keeping its quality without any harm whatsoever as bona fide holder of Products on behalf of XYZ. ABCは，XYZを代理する契約品［本製品］の善意の保管者として，契約品［本製品］の品質保持上，どんな損害も生じない注意を払うものとする。

cargo　（名）貨物，荷物，積み荷

accept［engage］cargo　貨物を引き受ける

air cargo system　航空物流システム

air cargo terminal　航空貨物ターミナル

assorted cargo　仕分け済み貨物

be loaded with a cargo　貨物を積んでいる

bonded cargo　保税貨物

break out the cargo　積み荷を解く

bulky cargo　ばら荷　（=cargo in bulk）

cargo afloat　未着船荷

cargo and passenger boat　貨客船

cargo arrival　着荷，貨物の到着

cargo arrival notice　着荷通知

cargo boat［ship, vessel］　貨物船

cargo boat note　船卸し票

cargo boat notice　揚荷証明書，揚荷明細書

cargo book　積み荷控帳

cargo booking　集荷

cargo broker　船腹仲介人［仲立人］

cargo capacity　載貨容積（measurement capacity），貨物積載力

cargo clause　貨物条項

cargo demurrage　留置料

cargo expenses　貨物費

cargo handling　荷役

cargo handling costs　荷役費，貨物費

cargo handling gear　荷役装置

cargo in dispute　詮議貨物

cargo insurance　積み荷保険，貨物保険，貨物海上保険

cargo liner　定期貨物船，貨物定期船

cargo manifest　積み荷目録

cargo movement　荷動き

cargo open　自由貨物

cargo owner　荷主

cargo passengers ship　貨客船

cargo plan　積み荷積付け図

cargo plane　貨物輸送機，貨物機

cargo policy　積み荷保険証券，積み荷海上保険証券，貨物保険証券

cargo preference　（貨物の）自国船優先制

cargo sharing　自国海運業優先策，積取比率

cargo space　全積載容積，カーゴ・スペース

cargo superintendent　積み荷監督

cargo sweat　貨物の汗濡れ，汗濡れ貨物

cargo to abandon　委付貨物

cargo worthiness　耐荷能力

conference cargo　同盟貨物

damaged cargo　損傷貨物

dangerous cargo　危険荷物，危険貨物

deadweight［heavy］cargo　重量貨物

deck cargo　甲板積み貨物

discharge the cargo　積み荷を降ろす（=unload the cargo）

domestic cargo transport　国内貨物輸送

exceptional cargo　（契約対象から外された）除外貨物

full cargo　満載積み荷

general cargo　一般貨物，普通貨物

homeward cargo　帰り荷　（=return cargo）

institute cargo clauses　保険協会貨物約款

insured cargo　付保貨物，保険付き貨物

light cargo　軽量貨物

liquid cargo　液体貨物

load cargo　貨物を船積みする　（=ship load）

marine cargo insurance　貨物海上保険

measurement cargo　才量貨物

mixed cargo　混合貨物

New Institute Cargo Clauses　新協会貨物約款

optional cargo　揚地選択貨物

outward cargo　往き荷

overstowed cargo　下積み貨物

part cargo　混載貨物の小口貨物，半端積み荷，パート・カーゴ

shut out（a part of）the cargo　貨物を積み残す，貨物の一部を積み残す

sort cargo　貨物を口分けする

take in［on］cargo　貨物を積み込む

through cargo arbitrary　通し貨物割増運賃

underdeck cargo　船室積み貨物

uniform cargo　単装貨物

unmanifested cargo　無表示貨物

unpack the cargo　積み荷を解装する，積み荷の包装を解く

valuable cargo　高価品貨物

◆The purchaser shall effect, at its own expense, marine insurance on each cargo of the products from the point where such cargo passes the rail of the vessel of the port of the shipment. 買い主は，買い主の自己費用で，本製品の各貨物が船積み港の本船の舷側欄干を越える時点から，当該貨

物に海上保険を付けるものとする。

carload （名）貨車1両分の貨物, 貸切り扱いの最少重量

carload lot　貸切り扱い荷物量

carload rate　貸切り扱い運賃率

carriage （名）運送, 運賃, 運送費, 4輪馬車, 乳母車, 振る舞い, 身のこなし, 姿勢

carriage by charter-party　用船運送

carriage forward　運賃着払い, 受取人払いで

carriage free　運賃元払い, 運賃不要で, 運送費無料

Carriage of Goods by Sea Act　国際海上物品運送法

carriage paid　運送費前払いで, 運賃先払い［元払い］で

carriage trade　商売の上客［上等の客］, 金持ちの得意客, 金持ち, 富裕階級の人々, 富裕階層

carrier （名）運送人, 運送業者, 航空・バス・トラック・鉄道会社, 持参人, 保険会社, 保険業者, 保険者, 通信業者, 電気通信事業者, 病原菌媒介体, 保菌者, キャリア

bulk carrier　ばら積み貨物船

carrier bag　買い物袋

flag［flagship］carrier　国を代表する航空会社, 国の代表的な航空会社

international carrier　国際通信事業者

low cost carrier　格安航空会社, LCC

straddle carrier　ストラドル・キャリア（重量貨物やコンテナを積み下ろして運搬できる構造のトラック）

◆Irrevocable letter of credit provides for payment upon presentation of Supplier's invoices and shipping documents evidencing delivery of the invoiced Products to the carrier or freight forwarder. 取消不能信用状は, 供給者の請求書と, 請求書に記載した本製品を運送人または海貨業者に引き渡したことを証明する船積み書類を提示して支払いを受けるものだ。◆Japan and the United States will sign the open skies agreement, and carriers in both countries will be able to apply for U.S. antitrust immunity. 日米両政府がオープンスカイ協定を締結することによって, 両国の航空会社は米国独占禁止法の適用除外申請が可能になる。◆The company is the world's largest mobile carrier. 同社は, 世界最大の携帯電話会社［携帯電話事業者］だ。

carrying vessel　本船

◆If delivery is made under the terms of CFR or CIF, the Seller shall inform the Buyer of the name, nationality, age and other details of the carrying vessel by Fax or E-mail not later than fourteen （14）days before the time of delivery. 引渡しがCFR（運賃込み）またはCIF（運賃保険料込み）の条件で行われる場合, 売り主は, 引渡し期限の14日前までにファクスかEメールで本船の船名,

船籍, 船齢その他の詳細を買い主に通知するものとする。

cartel （名）企業連合, 党派連合, 密売組織, カルテル（カルテルは, 価格形成やマーケット・シェア, 生産水準など競争を排除するために結ばれる協定や協定に基づく結合。⇒bid-fixing, price cartel）

anti-depression cartel　不況防止カルテル

anti-recession cartel　不況カルテル

cartel operation　カルテル活動

cartel tariff　カルテル関税

coercive cartel　強制的カルテル

conditional cartel　条件［生産条件］付きカルテル

depression［depressed］cartel　不況カルテル

export cartel　輸出カルテル

form［run］an international cartel　国際カルテルを結ぶ

import cartel　輸入カルテル

international petroleum cartel　国際石油カルテル

price fixing cartel　価格カルテル, 価格協定（=pricing cartel）

producers' cartel　生産国カルテル

profit-sharing cartel　利益配当カルテル

quantity cartel　生産数量カルテル

quotas cartel　割当カルテル

regional cartel　地域カルテル

trade cartel　貿易カルテル

◆Cartels and bid-fixing can ruin economic activities. カルテルや談合行為は, 経済活動を損なう可能性がある。◆The Fair Trade Commission plans to punish five manufacturers in Japan, Britain, France and Italy as these firms formed an international cartel. 公正取引委員会は, 国際カルテルを結んでいたとして, 日英仏伊のメーカー5社を処分する方針だ。◆Three steelmakers have formed a price cartel on galvanized steel sheets. 鉄鋼3社が, メッキ鋼鈑の価格カルテルを結んでいた。

cash against documents　書類引換現金渡し, 書類引換渡し

◆For a minimum of 6 months following the execution of this agreement, it is XYZ's established policy that all payments by ABC to XYZ for the XYZ Products or Services shall be made through irrevocable letter of credit, cash against documents, cash on delivery, or through full payment. 本契約の締結後最低6か月間, XYZの製品またはサービスに対するABCによるXYZへのすべての支払いは, 取消不能信用状, 書類引換現金渡し, 現金引換渡しにより, または全額払いにより行うのが, XYZの確立した方針である。

cash-in-advance　現金先払い　（⇒COD）

cash on delivery　現金引換渡し, 引渡し時現金払い, COD

CASH 76

cash tender offer 現金公開買付け, 現金による株式公開買付け, キャッシュ・テンダー・オファー（買収先の会社の株式を現金で公開買付けする方法）
◆Mitsubishi UFJ Financial Group Inc. will begin a cash tender offer to acquire about 35 percent of UnionBancal shares. 三菱UFJフィナンシャル・グループは、米金融持ち株会社ユニオンバンカルの株式の約35%を取得するため、現金による株式公開買付け (TOB) を開始する。

catalog [catalogue] （名）目録, 商品カタログ, カタログ
catalog buying カタログ仕入れ, カタログ購入, カタログ買付け
catalog order カタログ注文
catalog price カタログ価格, 表示価格
catalog retailing カタログ販売小売業, カタログ小売業
catalog sales [selling] カタログ販売, カタログ通販
catalog subscription カタログ販売
current catalog 最新カタログ
general catalog 総カタログ
priced catalog 定価表
selling by catalog カタログ販売
trade catalog 商品カタログ, カタログ
◆IKEA has come under criticism in its home market Sweden as it airbrushed women out of its latest catalog in Saudi Arabia. 家具小売業のイケアが、サウジアラビア版の最新商品カタログで女性モデルを画像処理で消したため、国内市場のスウェーデンで批判を浴びている。

Catch-all or End-use Controls キャッチオール規制, 補完的輸出規制 （=catch-all regulations）
◆The Catch-all or End-use Controls ban the exports of certain non-contraband goods. キャッチオール規制は、一部の輸出入非禁制品の輸出を禁止している。

catch-all regulations キャッチオール規制, 補完的輸出規制（リスト規制品目以外のものでも、大量破壊兵器などの開発に用いられる恐れがある場合や、通常兵器の開発・製造・使用に利用される恐れがある場合には、貨物の輸出や技術の提供に経済産業省大臣の許可が必要とする制度。⇒list control [rules]）
◆In April 2002, the government enforced so-called catch-all regulations aimed at controlling exports of goods and technology linked to weapons development. 2002年4月から政府は、兵器開発関連の機器と技術の輸出を取り締まるため、いわゆる「キャッチオール規制」を施行した。

cause （動）～を…させる, ～を引き起こす, ～の原因となる（cause以外に、使役動詞としてhaveも用いられる）
cause this agreement to be executed by 本契約書を～に（by以下に）作成させる、～により（by以下により）本契約を締結する
cause to be kept 保管させる, 維持させる, 保持させる
cause to be manufactured 製造させる, 制作させる （=have manufactured）
incorporate or cause to be incorporated 設立するまたは設立させる
pay or cause to be paid 支払うまたは支払わせる
◆IN WITNESS WHEREOF, the parties hereto have caused this agreement to be executed by duly authorized representatives of both parties on _____, 2015. 以上の証として、本契約当事者は、（両当事者の）正当な権限をもつ代表者により2015年 月 日、本契約を締結した。◆Throughout this agreement, Warrantee shall attempt to maintain an insurance policy to cover any claim, demand, liability, suit, damage or expense caused by Warrantee negligence. 本契約期間を通じて、被保証人は、被保証人の過失により生じるクレーム、要求、責任、訴訟、損害または費用を担保する保険証券の維持に努めるものとする。

cause （名）理由, 動機, 事由, 事件, 原因, 正当な理由, もっともな理由, 訴訟原因, 申立て, 信条, 目的, 論点 （⇒replacement）
any cause (whether arising from natural causes, human agency or otherwise) 事由（自然による事由か人間の行為による事由かその他の事由かを問わない）
from any cause or causes beyond the reasonable control of ～の合理的な支配が及ばない事由により、～が合理的に制御できない事由により

cease and terminate 終了する
◆In the event any such assignment or transfer is attempted without the prior written consent, this agreement and all the rights conferred hereunder shall, at the option of the other party, immediately cease and terminate. 当該譲渡または移転が書面による事前の承諾を得ないで企てられた場合、本契約と本契約に基づいて付与されたすべての権利は、相手方の選択で直ちに終了するものとする。

cede （動）（敗戦などで権利を）譲渡する, （領土を）割譲する, 引き渡す, 譲歩する, 委ねる, （再保険で元受保険者が引き受けたリスクを再保険者に）転嫁する, 再保険に出す, 出再する （名）（権利などの）譲渡, 出再保険
cede back 再再保険, シード・バック
cede premiums 出再保険料, 再保険料
cede to the reinsurer 再保険会社に出再する
ceded insurance 出再保険
ceded reinsurance 出再保険, 売再保険
policy ceded under this agreement 本協定により再保険される契約
◆The Company agrees to cede to the Rein-

surer such shares of all insurances covered by this Agreement as are set forth in the annexes（Schedule and any Addenda）to this Agreement. 元受会社は、本協定対象の全保険のうち、本協定の補遺（特別条項や追加条項）に明記した部分を再保険会社に出再することに合意する。

central bank 中央銀行（日本の場合は日本銀行（日銀）を指す）
◆An executive of the Bank of England, Britain's central bank, is suspected to have pressured Barclays to engage in the Libor rate manipulation. 英中央銀行のイングランド銀行幹部が、英金融大手バークレイズにライボー（ロンドン銀行間取引金利）の金利操作を促していた疑いが持たれている。◆In global currency wars, central banks effectively lower the value of their countries' currencies to boost their countries' export competitiveness. 世界の通貨安競争では、自国の輸出競争力を高めるため、中央銀行が自国通貨の価値を事実上切り下げる［自国通貨の為替相場を事実上安くする］。◆In the case of a negative interest rate which the ECB has introduced, commercial banks have to pay interest at this rate, which is like a handling fee, to place funds at the central bank. 欧州中央銀行（ECB）が導入したマイナス金利の場合、民間銀行は、手数料のようにマイナス金利の金利を払って、ECBに資金を預けることになる。◆Stock prices rose and the yen fell as markets reacted positively to LDP President Shinzo Abe's recent remarks on the central bank's unlimited monetary easing measures. 日銀の無制限の金融緩和についての自民党の安倍総裁の今回の発言に好感して、株高・円安が進んだ。◆The Chinese central bank's recent interest rate hikes is an important move to cool the overheating Chinese economy and guide it toward a soft landing. 中国の中央銀行である人民銀行（People's Bank of China）の今回の利上げ（貸出金利の引上げ）は、景気の過熱［中国経済の過熱］を鎮め、中国経済を安定成長に軟着陸させるための重要な動きである。◆The U.S. central bank will buy mortgage-backed securities（MBS）guaranteed by the government-controlled home loan giants Fannie Mae, Freddie Mac and Ginnie Mae. 米連邦準備制度理事会（FRB）は、米政府系住宅ローン大手のファニー・メイ（米連邦住宅貸付公社）、フレディ・マック（米連邦住宅抵当金庫）とジニー・メイ（米政府系住宅金融公庫）が保証した住宅ローン担保証券（MBS）を買い取ることになった。

解説アメリカの中央銀行について：アメリカには単一の中央銀行が存在せず、連邦準備制度（Federal Reserve System）のもと連邦準備区（Federal Reserve district）に設置された全米12の連邦準備銀行（Federal Reserve Bank）が実際の中央銀行業務をしている。ただし、the U.S. central bankといえば米連邦準備制度理事会（FRB）を指す）

certificate （名）証明書, 証書, 証券, 株券, 免状, 免許状, 認証, 認可証 （⇒stock

certificate）
audit certificate 監査証明書
beneficiary's certificate 受益者証明書
certificate and list of measurement and/or weight 容積重量証明書
certificate of incorporation 米国の会社設立定款, 英国の会社設立証明書
certificate of incumbency 在職証明
certificate of insurance 保険証明書, 保険承認状
certificate of one's seal impression 印鑑証明
certificate of origin 原産地証明
certificate of quality inspection 検査証明書
flag certificate 船籍証明書, 船齢証明書
fumigation certificate 燻蒸証明書
health certificate 検疫（けんえき）証明書
import certificate 輸入証明書
inspection certificate 検査証明書
insurance certificate 保険引受証, 保険承認状
official certificate 公式の証明書
routing certificate 不寄港証明書
tax certificate 納税証明書
◆The seller shall send a certificate issued by such surveyor of the quality and quantity of the products to the purchaser without delay. 売り主は、本製品の品質と数量について当該検査人が発行した証明書を遅滞なく買い主に送付するものとする。

certificate of inspection 検査証明書
◆The purchaser shall forward full particulars of such claim, accompanied by an authorized surveyor's certificate of inspection of quality and quantity of the products delivered in dispute, to the seller by registered airmail within 30 days after such notification. 買い主は、当該通知後30日以内に、引き渡された問題の製品の品質と数量に関する公認鑑定人の検査証明書を添付して、当該クレームの詳細を記載した書面を書留航空便で売り主に送付するものとする。

certified airmail 配達証明付き航空郵便
certified mail, return receipt required 受領通知付き配達証明郵便
CFR 運賃込み, 運賃込み条件（cost and freightの略）
◆If delivery is made under the terms of CFR or CIF, the Seller shall inform the Buyer of the name, nationality, age and other details of the carrying vessel by Fax or E-mail not later than fourteen（14）days before the time of delivery. 引渡しがCFR（運賃込み）またはCIF（運賃保険料込み）の条件で行われる場合、売り主は、引渡し期限の14日前までにファクスかE-メールで本船の船名、船籍、船齢その他の詳細を買い主に通知するものとする。

challenge （動）〜に挑戦する, （〜と）競う, 争う, （勝負などを）挑（いど）む, （正当性を）

疑う, 正当性を問う, 当然のこととして要求する, 異議を唱える, 疑問を提出する, 問いただす, 疑惑を感じる, ～の技能や能力を試す, (陪審員を)忌避する, 促す, 招く, 喚起(かんき)する, 刺激する, (投票が)無効であると主張する, 投票人の無資格を主張する
◆The United States, the EU and Mexico challenged China's export restrictions on raw materials and launched WTO legal cases in 2009. 米国, 欧州連合(EU)とメキシコが中国の原材料(鉱物資源)輸出規制は世界貿易機関(WTO)の協定違反に当たるとして, 2009年にWTOに提訴した。

chamber of commerce 商業会議所, 商工会議所
American Chamber of Commerce 米国商工会議所
International Chamber of Commerce 国際商業会議所, ICC
Japan Chamber of Commerce 日本商工会議所
Japan Chamber of Commerce and Industry 日本商工会議所

change (動)変える, 変更する, 転換する, 変化させる, 改める, 改造する, 替える, 交換する, 交替する, 両替する, 現金に換える, くずす(break) (自動)変わる, 変化する, 交代する, 移行する
◆If a quoted company with a one-share trading unit changes its trading unit to 100 shares without changing the price of individual shares, the amount required for investment would rise 100-fold. 売買単位が1株の上場企業が, 1株当たりの価格を変更しないで売買単位を100株に変更すると, 投資(株の売買)に必要な金額は100倍になってしまう。◆This in no way changes the validity of this Article. これは, 決して本条の効力を変更するものではない。

changes in exchange rates 為替相場の変動
◆Changes in exchange rates are a result of multiple factors, including the balance of international payments and market supply and demand. 為替相場の変動は, 国際収支や市場の需給など複数要因によるものだ。

channel (名)経路, チャネル
distribution channel 流通経路, 流通チャネル
marketing channel 販売チャネル, 販売経路, 流通チャネル, マーケティング・チャネル (ある商品・サービスがメーカーから最終消費者に渡るまでの取引の流れの経路。主に, メーカーの営業所, 卸売り業者, 小売業者, 配送業者などによって構成される)

chapter (名)章, 一区切り, 重要な時期, 一時期, 一時期を画するような出来事, 一連の出来事, (組織の)支部, 地方支部, 分会, 総会, 集会
Chapter 7 of the National Bankruptcy Act 米連邦破産法第7章, 米破産法7章(破たんした企業を再生させずに清算する手続きを定

めた法律)
Chapter 10 of the National Bankruptcy Act 米連邦破産法第10章, 米破産法10章
Chapter 11 米連邦改正破産法第11章, 米連邦破産法11章, チャプター・イレブン, 会社更生手続き(日本の会社更生法に相当)
Chapter 11 of the federal bankruptcy code 米連邦破産法第11章
Chapter 11 of the U.S. Bankruptcy Code 米連邦破産法11章
Chapter 11 bankruptcy 米連邦改正破産法(第)11章, 米連邦破産法11章, チャプター・イレブン, 会社更生手続き (=Chapter 11 of the U.S. Bankruptcy Reform Act)
◆Chapter 11 bankruptcy provides for a business to continue operations while formulating a plan to repay its creditors. 米連邦改正破産法11章の破産の規定では, 企業は事業を継続する一方, 債権者への債務返済計画を策定することができる。◆Enron Corp. filed for Chapter 11 bankruptcy under the U.S. Bankruptcy Reform Act. 米エネルギー大手のエンロンが, 米連邦破産改正法11章の破産法適用を申請した。

character merchandising 商品化権ライセンス, キャラクター・マーチャンダイジング

charge (動)請求する, 課する, 要求する, 支払わせる, 負担させる, 借方に記入する, 借記する, 計上する, クレジット・カードで買う, 責める, 非難する, 咎(とが)める, ～のせいにする, (罪などを)負わせる, 指令する, 命じる, 説諭する, 訓示する, 説明する, 告訴する, 告発する, 摘発する, 提訴する, 充電する, 充満させる, 満たす, 詰める
◆The federal funds rate is the interest that banks charge each other on overnight loans. フェデラル・ファンド(FF)金利は, 米国の民間銀行が翌日決済で相互に資金を貸し借りするときに適用する金利のことをいう。◆The U.S. Commodity Futures Trading Commission charged one investment fund with gaining illicit profits from manipulating crude oil and other markets. 米国の商品先物取引委員会は, 原油市場などで不正な利益を上げたとして, 投資ファンドの一つを摘発した。

charge (名)費用, 料金, 税金, 課税金, 手数料, 代価, 代金, 請求金額, 借方記入, 借記, 負債, 借金, 責任, 義務, 任務, 担保, 担保権, 管理, 監督, 保管, 運営, 処理, 告発, 提訴, 陪審に対する裁判官の説示, 起訴事実, 罪, 容疑, 嫌疑, 疑惑, 突撃, 攻撃, 充電, チャージ
burden charge 負担金
charge card クレジット・カード (=credit card)
export charges 輸出手数料
free of charge 無料で
in charge of ～を担う, ～を担当する, ～の世話[管理, 監督, 担任, 係]をする
incur late charges 延滞金がかかる

loading charge 積込み費

power charges 電力料金

take charge of 〜を担当［世話、監督］する，〜を引き受ける，〜を預かる，〜を担任する，〜を担（にな）う
◆After the delivery of the Goods, any taxes, customs duties, export or import surcharges or other governmental charges shall be for the account of the Buyer. 本商品の引渡し後、税金、関税、輸出・輸入税、その他政府が賦課する費用は、買い主の負担とする。◆Gasoline prices rose 6.4 percent in June, while city gas climbed 4.7 percent and electricity charges increased 9.8 percent, as the yen's depreciation pushed up import prices of crude oil and liquefied natural gas. 円安で原油や液化天然ガス（LNG）の輸入価格が上昇したため、6月はガソリン価格が6.4%上昇したのに対して、都市ガスは4.7%、電力料金が9.8%それぞれ上昇した。◆Late payment shall incur an interest charge of 2 percent over the base rate current in XYZ Bank at the time the charge is levied from the due date to the date of payment in full. 支払いが遅延した場合、支払い期日から全額支払い日まで、支払い利息（遅延利息）を課す時点でXYZ銀行が適用する基準金利より2%高い支払い利息（遅延利息）が付くものとする。

charter （名）用船，用船契約，会社の基本定款，特許状，設立認可証，証書，憲章，チャーター

　　charter contract 用船契約

　　charter documents 設立書類

　　charter party 用船契約

cheap （形）安い，安価な，廉価（れんか）な，割安の，割安感がある，低コストの，低金利の，低利の，購買力が低下した

cheap imports 安い輸入品
◆The European Union's head office formally adopted tariffs of up to 26 percent on steel to prevent a feared flood of cheap imports from countries hit by U.S. protective measures. EU（欧州連合）の欧州委員会は、米国の保護措置で打撃を受けた国から安い輸入鉄鋼製品が流入する恐れがあるのを防ぐため、鉄鋼製品に対して最高26%の関税をかけることを正式採択した。

cheaper dollar ドル安
◆A cheaper dollar does definitely serve to make U.S. producers more cost-competitive in international export markets. 国際輸出市場で米国の生産者の価格競争力を高めるには、間違いなくドル安のほうがよい。

cheaper labor 低賃金，低コストの労働力
◆As labor costs in China are expected to continue rising, labor-intensive industries such as fashion and electronics will keep relocating their manufacturing bases to Southeast Asia and other regions with cheaper labor. 中国の人件費上昇は今後も続く見通しなので、アパレルや家電などの労働集約型産業では、生産拠点を中国より低賃金の

東南アジアなどに移す流れが続くものと思われる。

cheaper labor costs 安い人件費，低賃金，安い賃金
◆The development of cross-border infrastructure in the Greater Mekong Subregion（GMS）has prompted a number of multinational corporations to transfer some of their manufacturing processes to Laos, Cambodia and Myanmar to take advantage of cheaper labor costs. 大メコン圏での国境を越えたインフラ整備に伴い、多くの多国籍企業が、安い人件費［低賃金］の利点を生かして生産工程の一部をラオスやカンボジア、ミャンマーに移転している。

cheaper product 低価格品
◆The firm will prepare for quick development of stores to respond to consumer demand for cheaper products. 同社は、消費者の低価格志向に対応する店舗の開発を急ぐ構えだ。

cheaper yen 円安
◆A cheaper yen increases import costs, but if the yen-dollar exchange rate is within the range of ¥95-105, it would be possible for companies to maintain competitiveness in exports. 円安で輸入コストは増えるが、円の対ドル為替相場が1ドル＝95〜105円の範囲内なら、企業は輸出競争力を維持できるだろう。

check （名）小切手

　　bounced check 不渡り小切手

　　check writer 小切手振出人
◆At the closing, ABC will deliver to XYZ share certificates, representing the number of the Shares sold under this agreement, affixing proper endorsement duly executed by ABC on the back of the certificates, against the payment of the purchase price therefor, by check payable to ABC or wire transfer per ABC's instructions. クロージングにおいてABCは、本契約に基づいて売り渡す本株式の株数に相当し、株券の裏面にABCが正式に署名して適切に裏書きした株券を、ABC宛の小切手またはABCの指示による電信送金による購入代金の支払いと引換えに、XYZに対して引き渡すものとする。◆The buyer shall deliver to the seller a check in the amount of U.S. $100,000. 買い主は、10万ドルの金額の小切手を売り主に引き渡すものとする。

chemical product 化学製品 （=chemical goods）
◆Shipments of raw materials, such as steel and chemical products, as well as construction equipment have been growing. 鉄鋼や化学製品などの素材のほか、建設機械などの輸出も伸びている。

China risks 中国リスク （⇒Chinese yuan）
◆To avert China risks such as the stronger Chinese yuan, surging labor costs and anti-Japan riots, some firms have shifted production lines to other countries in Southeast Asia and other regions with cheaper labor. 中国人民元高や人件費

高騰、反日暴動などの中国リスクを回避するため、一部の企業は、中国より低賃金の東南アジアなどの地域に生産ラインの移管［分散化］を進めている。

Chinese economy　中国経済
◆Partly due to a slowdown in the Chinese economy in the wake of the European financial crisis, Japan's exports and production have been on the decline. 欧州の金融危機による中国の景気減速もあって、日本の輸出や生産活動は落ち込んでいる。

Chinese food products　中国産食品
◆Concerns over the safety of Chinese food products are rising in Japan, but the percentage of safety violations involving food imports from China fell below the overall average for all imported foods in fiscal 2012. 日本では中国産食品の安全性への懸念が強まっているが、中国からの輸入食品のうち安全面での違反件数の割合は、2012年度は輸入食品全体の総平均を下回った。

Chinese yuan　中国の人民元, 中国人民元
（⇒China risks）
◆Japanese-affiliated companies operating in China will have to be aware of "China risks" such as rising production costs as well as the stronger Chinese yuan and anti-Japan riots. 中国に進出している日系企業は今後、生産コストの上昇のほか、人民元高や反日暴動などのような「中国リスク」を意識せざるを得ない。

Chinese yuan rate　中国人民元相場, 中国人民元レート, 中国の元レート（中国人民銀行（People's Bank of China）は2008年7月以降、対ドル人民元レートを1ドル＝6.83元付近で固定している）

choice of law　準拠法の選択, 適用法の選択, 法の選択, 法律選択

choice of (law) rules　準拠法選択のルール, 適用法選択のルール, 法の選択のルール, 法律選択のルール, 抵触法のルール
◆This agreement shall be governed by and construed in accordance with the laws of England without reference to its choice of law rules. 本契約は、適用法選択のルールに関わりなくイングランド法に準拠し、同法に従って解釈する。

CIF　運賃保険料込み, 運賃保険料込み値段, 運賃保険料込み条件, シフ（cost, insurance and freightの略。⇒trade terms）

　　CIF & C　運賃保険料手数料込み値段（cost, insurance, freight and commissionの略）

　　CIF & CI　運賃保険料手数料利息込み値段（CI＝commissionとinterest）

　　CIF & E　運賃保険料為替費用込み値段（cost, insurance, freight and exchangeの略）

　　CIF & I　運賃保険料利子込み値段（cost, insurance, freight and interestの略）

　　CIF cleared　通関費込みシフ, 通関費込みCIF値段（条件）

　　CIF duty landed　関税込みシフ（売り主が運賃、保険料と輸入関税を負担する条件）

　　CIF landed　陸揚げ費込みシフ（売り主が運賃、保険料と輸入港での陸揚げ費用を負担する条件）

　　CIF net　口銭なしシフ, 正味のCIF

　　on the basis of CIF Los Angeles　CIFロサンゼルス港条件で, ロサンゼルスを仕向け地とするCIF条件で

　　the trade term CIF［C.I.F.］　貿易条件のCIF, 貿易用語のCIF
◆If delivery is made under the terms of CFR or CIF, the Seller shall inform the Buyer of the name, nationality, age and other details of the carrying vessel by Fax or E-mail not later than fourteen（14）days before the time of delivery. 引渡しがCFR（運賃込み）またはCIF（運賃保険料込み）の条件で行われる場合、売り主は、引渡し期限の14日前までにファクスかEメールで本船の船名、船籍、船齢その他の詳細を買い主に通知するものとする。◆Kindly quote us your lowest prices on the basis of CIF Yokohama for your items. CIF横浜港条件で、貴社商品の最低値［建て値］を出していただきたい。◆The price for the products payable by the purchaser for the first year shall be U.S. $38.00 per set CIF San Francisco, U.S.A. 買い主が初年度に支払う本商品の価格は、CIFサンフランシスコ（米国）条件で1セット当たり38.00米ドルとする。◆Unless otherwise expressly provided for in this agreement, the price and trade term "C. I.F." shall be interpreted in accordance with Incoterms 2000. 本契約に特に明示の規定がないかぎり（本契約で別段に明確に規定しないかぎり）、価格と貿易条件のCIFは、2000年版インコタームズに従って解釈する。

CIF basis　CIF条件

　　on a CIF basis　CIF条件で

　　on a CIF New York Port basis　CIFニューヨーク港条件で
◆In case of individual contracts on a CIF basis, marine insurance covering All Risks shall be effected by the seller on behalf of and in the name of the purchaser, in respect of the products purchased by it under an individual contract unless the parties agree in writing to the contrary. CIF条件での個別契約の場合、両当事者が書面で別途合意しないかぎり、買い主が個別契約で購入した製品については、売り主が買い主に代わって買い主の名前で全危険担保条件による海上保険をかけるものとする。

CIF contract　CIF契約
◆In case of a CIF contract, the seller shall, at its own expenses, arrange for ocean freight of the products from the port of shipment stated in this agreement to the port of destination of the products. CIF契約の場合、売り主は、本契約に定める船積み港から本商品の仕向け港までの本商品の海上輸送の手配を、自己負担でするものとする。

CIF value　CIF価格（CIF価格は、FOB価格に輸入港までの海上運賃、海上保険料を加算

81 **CIVI**

the amount of CIF value of the products plus 10
percent　本製品のCIF価格プラス10パーセ
ントの保険金額, 本製品のCIF価格の110
パーセントの保険金額

the amount of 110 percent of CIF value of the
shipments of the products　本製品船送品の
CIF価格の110％の保険金額

◆ABC shall effect all risk (Institute Cargo
Clauses) marine insurance with underwriters
or insurance companies of good repute in an
amount of one hundred and ten (110) percent of
CIF value of the shipments of the products. ABC
は, 本製品積送品のCIF価格の110％の保険金額で,
評判の良い保険引受業者または保険会社と全危険
担保条件(協会貨物約款)の海上保険の保険契約を
するものとする。◆The seller shall, for its own
account, effect marine insurance only free from
particular average (FPA Institute Cargo Clause)
for the amount of CIF value of the products plus
10 percent. 売り主は, 売り主の自己負担で, 本商
品のCIF価格プラス10％の保険金額により単独海損
[分損]不担保条件(FPA協会貨物保険約款)の海上
保険を付けるものとする。

CIP　輸送費保険料込み, 輸送料保険料込み値
段(条件)(carriage and insurance paid toの略)

circa　(前)約, およそ, 概算で　(=about)

circles　(名)団体, グループ, 〜界, 〜社会,
サークル

business circles　経済界, 産業界, 実業界, 業
界　(=business community [world])

economic circles　経済界, 財界

financial circles [sector]　金融界, 財界

official circles　官界

political and business circles　政財界

security circles　公安関係者

trading circles　貿易業界

circular sales transaction　循環取引(複数
の企業間で商品を売買したように装い, 架空
の売上を計上する不正取引)

◆In the circular sales transactions, Katokichi's
affiliates and business clients recorded the repeated sale and purchase of products only on paper receipts. 循環取引で, 加ト吉の関連会社と法
人顧客は, 繰り返し行われた商品の売買を架空の
売上だけに計上していた。

circumstance　(名)事情, 情状, 状況, 環境, 動
向, 情勢, 状態, 事態, 場合, 出来事, 境遇, 暮ら
し向き, 身の上, 運命, 詳細, 詳しさ, ものもの
しさ, 仰々しさ

according to circumstances　事情により, 場合
により, 事情次第で

as circumstances stand　現状では, 現在の状況
では, 状況が示すとおり
(=as it stands, as [the way] things stand)

as far as circumstances permit　事情の許すか

ぎり

be not a circumstance to　〜とは比較になら
ない

be not acceptable under any circumstances　ど
んな事情があっても受け入れられない

business circumstances　事業環境

depend on circumstances　事情による, 事情次
第である

economic circumstances　経済環境, 経済状況,
景気動向

extraordinary circumstances　異常な事態

in circumstances beyond the seller's control
売り主の統御[支配]できない事情で

internal circumstances　内部事情

much regret the circumstances　その事情を大
いに[ひじょうに]遺憾に思う

price circumstances　物価動向, インフレ動向

the force of circumstances　やむを得ない事
情, 周囲のやむを得ない事情

under [in] any circumstances　どんな場合
でも

under certain circumstances　ある場合には

under [in] no circumstances　決して〜ない,
どんな事情[どんなこと]があっても〜な
い　(=not under any circumstances)

under [in, given] the circumstances　そうい
う状況では, こんな事情では, そういう事情
なので, こんな事情なので[だから]

under the existing circumstances　現状では

◆Business circumstances have changed though
we have made large-scale investment in liquid-
crystal displays. 当社は液晶ディスプレー(LCD)
に大型投資をしてきたが, 事業環境が変化した。

CITES　ワシントン条約, サイテス
(⇒CITIES)

CITIES　絶滅の恐れのある動植物の国際取引
に関する条約, ワシントン条約(Convention
on International Trade in Endangered Species
(of Wild Fauna and Flora)の略で, ワシント
ン条約の正式名称)

civil commotion　市民騒動, 動乱, 内乱
(⇒act [Act] of God)

civil penalty　民事罰, 制裁金, 過料, 民事制
裁金

Civil Monetary Penalties Act　民事制裁金法
(「民事制裁金」は, 米国で法律や規則の違
反に対して, 国や州などが科す金銭による
制裁)

◆Citigroup Inc. will pay $50 million each
in civil penalties to New York State and the
North American Securities Administrators Association. 米金融機関最大手のシティグループは,
ニューヨーク州と北米証券行政官協会にそれぞれ
5,000万ドルの制裁金を支払うことになった。

civil rehabilitation law　民事再生法

C

◆Soshisha Publishing Co. filed an application with the Tokyo District Court for protection from creditors under the Civil Rehabilitation Law. 草思社は、民事再生法に基づく資産保全[民事再生法の適用]を東京地裁に申請した。

claim （動）権利を要求する、請求する、権利や事実を主張する、訴える、責任などを認める

claim an allowance of 10 % for ～に対して[～を理由に]10%の値引きを要求する
◆In case the quality of Products shipped to Distributor turns out not to meet the above quality requirements, Distributor can claim a replacement against those inferior Products or cancellation of the individual contract. 販売店に発送した本製品の品質が上記品質基準に適合しないことが判明した場合、販売店は、これら品質の劣る本製品の交換[これら粗悪品の交換]またはその個別契約[個々の契約]の解除を請求することができる。
◆We claim $50,000 of damages for the nondelivery of the goods. 当社は、約定品の引渡し不履行に対して5万ドルの弁償金を請求する。◆Within 10 days of receipt of the shipment, Distributor shall notify Supplier in writing of any shortages, defects or damage which Distributor claims existed at the time of delivery. 引渡しの時点で存在したと販売店が主張する（認める）不足、瑕疵または損傷については、積み荷を受け取ってから10日以内に、販売店が書面で供給者に通知しなければならない。

claim （名）権利、権利の主張、申立て、請求、要求、請求権、請求事項、特許請求の範囲、債権、債権の届出、クレーム （⇒amount of such claim, free of any rightful claim for, motion, port of destination）

abandon one's claim 債権を放棄する、請求権を放棄する
accept our claim 当方の弁償要求[権利の主張、請求]を承諾する
amount of claim 請求額
any rightful claim of any third party for infringement of any patent 特許が侵害されたとする第三者の正当な申立て
assign a claim 債権を譲渡する、請求権を譲渡する
average claim 海損賠償要求
average general claim 共同海損賠償要求
claim agent 損害賠償要求代理人
claim clause クレーム約款（仲裁に関する規定が中心なので仲裁条項（arbitration clause）とも言う）
claim department 損害担当部署、損害事件部
claim, dispute or controversy 請求、紛争または論争、クレーム、紛争または論争
claim for compensation 損害賠償請求、賠償請求
claim for damages 損害賠償請求

claim for income tax credit 所得税控除の申請
claim for inferior quality 不良品損害賠償要求
claim for priority 特許の優先権主張
claim for reimbursement 手形金額償還請求
claim for relief 救済の申立て
claim for short delivery 不足品損害賠償要求
claim, if any, payable at/in 保険金の支払い地
claim in bankruptcy 破産債権
claim merchant クレーム商人、悪徳商人
claim note 保険金請求書、損害賠償請求書
claim notice 事故通知書（貨物の異常を通知する書類）、損害通知書
claim notice clause 損害通知約款
claim of patent 特許請求の範囲
claim on assets 資産に対する請求権
claim settling agent 損害査定代理店、クレーム精算代理店（保険会社の代理店）
claims adjuster 損害調査人
claims adjustment 損害査定
claims, demands, losses, suits, damages, liability and expenses 請求、要求、損失、訴訟、損害賠償[損害]、責任[債務]と経費
claims for damages 損害賠償請求、求償権
claims for shortage 数量不足に対するクレーム
claims on assets 資産に対する請求権
claims paid 保険金
claims-paying ability 保険金支払い能力
claims process 保険金支払いプロセス
claims, suits, losses, liabilities, costs or expenses and damages 請求、訴訟、損失、債務[責任]、経費と損害
claims survey 損害調査
collect claims 債権を回収する
collect the claims from the underwriters 保険会社から保険金を取る
contingent claim 条件付き請求権
defend such claim 当該申立ての防御をする
file a claim on ～について請求を起こす、～について請求権を申し立てる
for the purpose of any claim under the guarantee 本保証に基づく請求の目的上
formal claim 本クレーム
have a secondary claim on ～に対して二次的請求権を持つ
have a senior claim on ～に対して優先権を持つ
if any claim shall be asserted or brought about against ～に対して請求がなされるか起こされる場合
information concerning customer claims 顧客からのクレーム情報

insurance claims 保険金, 未収保険金, 保険請求, 保険請求権, 保険金請求, 保険金請求権

junior claim 劣後請求権

lay claim to ～に対する権利［所有権］を主張する, ～を自分のものと主張する

legal claim 法的請求権

lodge your claim with the insurance company at your end 貴地の保険会社に損害賠償請求を提起する

make a claim for damage 損害請求をする

make a claim on a person for compensation 人に賠償を要求する

make an insurance claim 保険金を請求する

money claim 金銭債権

nonpersonal injury claims 物件損害請求

owner's claims 株主の請求権

policy claims 保険金請求, 保険金

preliminary claim 予備クレーム

priority claim 優先弁済請求

put in a claim 保険金を請求する

put in ［make］a claim for expenses かかった費用を請求する

receive a claim for the infringement 侵害の申立てを受ける

refund claim 還付申請書

refuse a claim 請求を拒む

reimbursement claim 還付請求

reject our claim 当方の請求を拒絶する

secured claim 担保付き請求権

senior claim 上位請求権

settle claims 申立てを解決する

settle ［adjust］the pending claim 懸案のクレームを解決する

settled claim 確定した保険請求

take losses on one's claims 損失として負担する

the scope of claims 特許請求の範囲

trade claim 営業上の債権, 貿易クレーム（貿易クレームは、business claimとも言い、品質不良（inferior quality）や品質相違（different quality）など貿易取引で生じる損害賠償の請求のこと。これには運送クレームや保険クレームも含まれる）

transfer of claims 権利の移転

transportation claim 運送クレーム

unasserted claim 未請求のクレーム

unsecured claim 無担保請求権

waive a claim 債権を放棄する, 請求権を放棄する

warranty claim 品質保証に基づくクレーム

◆Distributor shall indemnify Company against all costs and damages whatsoever arising out of claim by third parties caused by the acts or defaults of Distributor, its employees, representatives or sub-distributors. 代理店、代理店の従業員、代理人または再代理店の行為または過失を原因とする第三者によるクレームから生じた経費や損害賠償金についてはすべてどんなものでも、代理店が会社に弁償するものとする。◆If the purchaser fails to comply with the above stipulation, the purchaser shall be deemed to have waived such claim. 買い主が上記規定に従わない場合、買い主は当該クレームを放棄したものと見なされるものとする。◆If the purchaser receives a claim from any third party for the infringement, the purchaser shall notify the seller promptly in writing of the claim and give the seller information, assistance and the authority to evaluate, defend and settle such claim. 買い主が第三者から侵害の申立てを受けた場合、買い主は当該申立てを速やかに書面で売り主に通知し、当該申立てを評価、防御して解決するための情報、援助と権限を売り主に与えるものとする。◆Seller shall waive any claim against Buyer under the Uniform Commercial Code or otherwise, with respect to a claim asserted against Seller or Buyer for patent, trademark or copyright infringement or the like. 売り主は、特許・商標・著作権の侵害等について売り主または買い主に対してなされる請求に関しては、買い主に対する米国統一商事法典その他に基づく請求権をすべて放棄する。

claim for infringement of the intellectual property 知的所有権侵害の申立て, 知的所有権侵害のクレーム
◆The Corporation has not received any claim for infringement of the intellectual property in connection with the operations of the Corporation. 当社は、当社の事業に関して知的所有権侵害のクレームは受けていない。

claim liquidated damages 損害賠償予定額を請求する
◆In case there is delay in delivery of all or any part of the Goods on the time as stipulated in this agreement, the buyer is entitled to claim liquidated damages at the rate of one-half of one percent（0.5％）of the amount of the delayed Goods for each complete week of delay. 本契約で定める期限に本商品の全部または一部に引渡し遅延が生じた場合、買い主は、遅延対象の各1週間につき引渡し遅延商品の代金の0.5％を損害賠償予定額として請求することができるものとする。

claim of infringement 侵害の請求, 権利侵害のクレーム
◆Supplier shall be responsible for any claim of infringement or alleged infringement of patents, designs, trademarks, copyrights or other rights brought by a third party in relation to Products. 本製品に関して第三者が提起する特許、意匠、商標、著作権またはその他の権利の侵害または申し立てられた侵害の請求については、供給者がすべて責任を負う。

claim or dispute 請求または紛争

◆The seller shall indemnify and hold the purchaser harmless against any claim or dispute which may arise in connection with infringement of patents, trademarks or any other intellectual property rights in connection with the products, whether in the seller's country or the country of destination indicated in this agreement. 売り主は、本製品に関連する特許、商標またはその他の知的財産権の侵害に関して生じる請求または紛争については、売り主の国内で生じたものであっても本契約に定める仕向け地で生じたものであっても、買い主に補償し免責するものとする。

claim or suit brought against 〜に対して起こされた請求または訴訟

◆Subject to the provisions of Paragraphs 5 and 6 of this Article, the licensor agrees to indemnify and hold the licensee harmless from and against any and all losses, damages and liabilities arising from or as a result of any claim or suit brought against the licensee. 本条第5項と6項の規定に従って、ライセンサーは、ライセンシーに対して起こされた請求または訴訟から生じるまたはその結果生じる一切の損失、損害と責任については、ライセンシーに補償しライセンシーを免責することに同意する。

claimant （名）権利の請求者, 要求者, 主張者, 申立て人, 原告

◆The other party（the "Respondent"）shall appoint its arbitrator within sixty（60）calendar days of receipt of the Demand and shall notify the Claimant of such appointment in writing. 相手方（「被申立て人」）は、仲裁申立て書の受領後60暦日以内にその仲裁人を指名し、その指名を書面で申立て人に通知するものとする。

class （名）クラス（同種類の証券, オプション）. ⇒director）

Class A common stock　Aクラス普通株式, A種普通株式

Class E common stock　Eクラス普通株式, E種普通株式

◆The holders of the new company's Class A common stock and Class B common stock shall be each entitled to nominate and elect ＿＿directors respectively. 新会社のAクラス普通株式とBクラス普通株式の各保有者は、それぞれ取締役＿＿名を指名して選任することができる。

classified documents 機密書類

classified information 機密情報

clause （名）（法律や契約などの）条項, 規定, 約款, 箇条, 項, 事項, 文言,（文法の）節

abandonment clause　（保険証券の）委付条項

all risk clause　オール・リスク（全危険）担保約款

choice of law clause　準拠法指定条項

consideration clause　対価条項

contractual clause　契約条項

entire agreement clause　完全合意条項

escape clause　免責条項, 例外規定

force majeure clause　不可抗力条項

incontestable clause　不可争条項

insurance clause　保険約款

interest clause　利息条項

negative clause　担保留保条項

negligence clause　免責条項

penal clause　罰則

red important clause　重要約款

saving clause　留保条項, 但し書き

severability clause　可分性条項

special clause　特別約款

standard clause　標準約款

unknown clause　不知条項

waiver clause　免責条項, 放棄約款

◆Such letter of credit shall be transferable and having the clause of definite undertaking by the issuing bank for unconditional payment against a draft at sight. この信用状は、一覧払い手形に対する無条件支払いに関して発行銀行が明確に約束した文言が入っているものとする。◆The contractual clause is a violation of the Antimonopoly Law. この契約条項は、独占禁止法違反である。◆The remedies under this clause shall be the sole compensation for the damages caused by such delay. 本条項に基づく補償は、当該遅延で生じた損害の唯一の補償とする。◆There is a contractual clause stipulating that Japanese PC makers will take no legal action even if Microsoft Corp.'s technologies are deemed to violate their patents. マイクロソフト社の技術が日本のパソコン・メーカーの特許侵害であると判断されても、日本のパソコン・メーカーは法的措置を一切取らない［訴訟を起こさない］、と定めた契約条項がある。

clear （動）許可する, 承認する, 税関を通過する, 通関［出港、出国］手続きを済ませる,（借金を）支払う［返済する、清算する］,（在庫品を）蔵払いする, 取り除く, 撤去する

clear customs and quarantine　税関と検疫を通過する

clear out excessive inventories　過剰在庫を一掃する

clear the goods　約定品の通関を済ます

clear the stringent emission standards　排ガス規制基準に合格する

clear your shipments from bonded warehouse　貴積み荷を保税倉庫から倉出しする

clearance （名）通関, 通関手続き, 出港許可証, 手形交換, 蔵払い, 在庫一掃セール

clearance certificates　入出港証明書

clearance fee　出港手数料, 出港料

clearance from customs　通関

clearance goods　棚卸し品

clearance inwards 入港手続き
clearance notice 出港通知書, 輸入貨物通関手続き
clearance order 建造物撤去命令
clearance outwards 出港手続き, 輸出貨物通関手続き
clearance papers 出港書類
clearance permit 出港許可書
clearance sale 見切り売り, 蔵払い, 在庫一掃セール, 在庫一掃大売出し
import clearance 輸入通関
the clearance of goods through the customs and their delivery 貨物の通関と貨物の受渡し
◆Please make prompt arrangements for a speedy clearance. 早急に通関するため、至急手はずを整えてください。

clearing agreement 清算協定

click wrap agreement クリック・ラップ・アグリーメント
|解説|クリック・ラップ・アグリーメントとは：ウェブ・サイト上でのライセンス契約には、コンピュータ・ソフトをダウンロードしようとするとディスプレー（表示端末装置）上の契約条件に応答しなければならない方式と、コンピュータ・ソフトのダウンロードは契約しないでできるが、フォーマットが圧縮されているため、これを開くにはユーザーに契約条件が提示される方式がある。この方式をclick wrap agreementという。

client （名）顧客, お得意, 得意先, 得意客, 取引先, 依頼人, 依頼者, 監査依頼会社, 被監査会社, クライアント （=customer）
accommodate a client 顧客の要望に応える
attract clients 顧客を引きつける, 顧客を開拓する
attract new clients 新規顧客を開拓する
attract our clients 当社顧客の関心をそそる
business clients 法人顧客
cater to clients 顧客にサービスを提供する
client company 取引先, 顧客企業
client management 顧客管理
client mandate 運用委託契約, 運用委託の条件, 運用委託上の指示事項
client order form 委託注文書
client roster 顧客名簿, 顧客リスト
client service 顧客サービス
client state [country] 貿易相手国
entertain a client 顧客を接待する
gain a client 顧客を獲得する
high net worth clients 富裕層の顧客
lure new clients 新規顧客を獲得する,
new corporate clients 新規顧客企業
prospective client 潜在顧客, 見込み客

(=prospective buyer)
solicitation of clients 顧客の勧誘
win clients 顧客を獲得する, 顧客を開拓する
◆Banks are allowed to sell insurance policies to clients. 銀行は、顧客に保険を販売することができる。◆Nonlife insurance companies used to disperse the risk of large contracts with new corporate clients through reinsurance contracts with other insurance or reinsurance companies. 損保各社は従来、他の保険会社もしくは再保険会社と再保険契約を結んで、新規顧客企業と大型契約を結ぶリスクを分散してきた。

client account 顧客口座
◆Mitsubishi UFJ Financial Group Inc. agreed to pay $8.6 million to the Treasury Department's Office of Foreign Assets Control to settle alleged U.S. sanction violations related to the transfer of funds to client accounts in Myanmar, Iran and Cuba. 三菱UFJフィナンシャル・グループは、ミャンマーやイラン、キューバなどの顧客口座に行った送金に関して、米国の経済制裁規制に違反した疑いで、米財務省外国資産管理局に860万ドルの和解金を支払うことで合意した。

climate （名）気候, 風土, 条件, 環境, 状況, 情勢, 傾向, 風潮, 思潮, 雰囲気, 空気, 地方, 地帯
deflationary climate デフレ傾向, デフレ環境, デフレ的雰囲気
difficult climate conditions 厳しい気候条件
financial climate 金融環境, 金融情勢
investment climate 投資環境
management climate 経営環境
organizational climate 組織風土, 組織環境, 経営風土
political climate 政治情勢, 政治状況, 政治環境, 政治的風土
regulatory climate 規制環境
◆Foreign investors, including Japanese firms, regard Thailand's political climate with its repeated coups as a risk factor for investing in the country. 日本企業など外国資本は、クーデターが繰り返されるタイの政治風土を、対タイ投資のリスク要因と見なしている。◆Indonesian President Yudhoyono has put the country's economy back on a growth track, but he has done little to go beyond macroeconomic stability and to reform the regulatory regime, improve the investment climate and promote manufacturing. インドネシアのユドヨノ大統領は、同国経済を成長軌道に乗せたが、マクロ経済の領域を出ることはなく、規制構造改革や投資環境の整備、産業促進などの政策はほとんど実施してこなかった。

Climate Change Levy 気候変動税
◆Britain's Climate Change Levy was introduced in April 2002 as a tax on overall energy consumption, including natural gas, in addition to the existing tax on gasoline. 英国の気候変動税は、既存のガソリン税に加え、天然ガスなどを含

むエネルギー消費全般に対する課税として2002年4月から導入された。

clinch a deal 取引・商談をまとめる, 取引にかたをつける

◆Argentina clinched a debt rollover deal with the IMF after a year of tortuous negotiations. アルゼンチンは, 1年にわたる難交渉の末, 国際通貨基金 (IMF) との債務返済繰延べ取引をまとめた。

close a bank account 銀行口座を解約する

closing (名)正式契約書の調印式[作成・署名], クロージング, 不動産売買の最終手続き, 株式の譲渡手続きと代金の払込み手続きの同時履行[株式のクロージング], 取引完了, 決済, 期末, 決算, 締切り, 休会, 結語 (⇒common stock)

after the closing クロージング後に

at the closing クロージングにおいて, クロージング時に

legal closing リーガル・クロージング (不動産取引で, 当事者が所定の書類を作成し, 代金を提供することによって取引対象の権利が移転すること)

prior to the closing クロージング以前に

◆ "Closing" means the completion of the sale and purchase of the Shares pursuant to Section 3 hereof. 「クロージング」とは, 本契約第3条に基づく本株式の売買完了を意味する。◆Commencing on the date of this agreement until the Closing, Buyer shall be permitted to perform such due diligence investigation related to the transactions contemplated by this agreement as Buyer deems necessary and appropriate in its discretion. 本契約締結日からクロージングまで, 買い主は, 本契約で意図されている取引に関して買い主が買い主の判断で必要かつ適切と考えるデュー・ディリジェンス調査を行うことができるものとする。◆In consideration for the Shares, ABC shall pay to XYZ at the closing, subject to the terms and conditions of the share purchase agreement, the amount of U.S. 500,000. 本株式の対価として, ABCは, 株式譲渡契約の条項に服することを条件として, クロージング時にXYZに50万米ドルを支払うものとする。

closing date 実行日, 払込み期日, 決算日, クロージング期日, クロージング日

◆On the Closing Date, the Buyer shall pay the Purchase Price. クロージング日に, 買い主は買取り価格を支払うものとする。◆The obligations of Purchaser to effect the transactions contemplated hereby shall be, at the option of Purchaser, subject to the fulfillment, at or prior to the closing date, of the following additional conditions: 本契約で企図されている取引を実行する買い主の義務は, 買い主の裁量で, クロージング日以前に以下の追加条件を達成することを条件とする。

CMI 万国海洋会 (Comité Maritime Internationalの略)

CMI Uniform Rules for Sea Waybills
海上運送状に関するCMI統一規則

COD 代金引換渡し, 代金引換払い (cash on delivery, collect on deliveryの略)

◆Deliveries will be available only on a COD, cash-in-advance, or irrevocable letter of credit basis. 引渡しは, 代金引換払い, 現金先払い, または取消不能信用状だけで行う。

collateral agreement 付随的契約, 担保約定

collateral agreement form 担保約定書

collect (動)(代金や債権などを)取り立てる, 回収する

◆The Byrd Amendment requires antidumping and countervailing duties collected by customs authorities to be turned over to U.S. companies claiming damages for what they deem as dumping by overseas manufacturers. バード法では, 税関当局が徴収したダンピング関税と相殺関税は, 海外メーカーによるダンピング(不当廉売)と認定されたものに対して損害賠償を請求した米国企業に分配しなければならない。

collection (名)代金取立, 代金回収, 集金, 債権取立, 債権回収

bill for collection 取立手形, 代金取立手形, B/C (=collection bill)

collection of bill 代金回収

collection of money 代金の回収

collection order 取立指図書

debt collection 債権回収

import bill for collection 輸入B/C

Uniform Rules for Collections 取立統一規則

collection experience 回収経験

◆To the best knowledge of Seller, based on its prior collection experience, such accounts receivable are collectible in full. 過去の回収経験に基づいて売り主が知るかぎり, この売掛金は全額回収可能である。

collectively (副)連帯して, 全体として, ひとまとめにして, 総称して, 総称して~という, 集合的に

collectively referred to as 総称して~という, 総称して~と呼ぶ

◆ABC Inc. and XYZ Kabushiki Kaisha may be referred to herein individually as a "Party" or, collectively, as the "Parties." ABC Inc.とXYZ株式会社は, 本契約ではそれぞれ各社を個別に指して「当事者」, 両者を総称して「両当事者」と呼ぶことができる。

come effective 発効する, 効力を発する

◆In consideration of the right and license granted under this agreement, Licensee shall pay to Company the fixed amount of ten million (10,000,000) Japanese Yen within 10 days after this agreement comes effective. 本契約に基づいて付与される権利とライセンス(実施許諾・実施権)の対価として, ライセンシーは, 本契約発効後10日以内に1,000万円の固定額を会社に支払わなければならない。

Comex (**in New York**) ニューヨーク商品取引所
◆Gold extended its rally to a record above $1,900 an ounce amid increased uncertainties over the U.S. and European economic outlook on the Comex in New York. ニューヨーク商品取引所では、米欧景気見通しへの懸念［米欧経済の先行き不透明感］の高まりを受け［懸念の高まりから］、金価格が急騰して、1トロイ・オンス＝1,900ドルを史上初めて突破した。

commencement （名）開始、着工、申立て、頭書
◆The price of the products for any subsequent year commencing on the annual anniversary of this agreement shall be such as may be negotiated and agreed upon between the parties not later than 30 days prior to the commencement of such year. 本契約から1年後の応答日に始まる次年度の本商品価格は、当該年度が始まる30日前までに当事者間で交渉して合意する価格とする。

commencing on the date of this agreement 本契約日［本契約締結日］から、本契約日に始まる
◆Commencing on the date of this agreement until the Closing, Buyer shall be permitted to perform such due diligence investigation related to the transactions contemplated by this agreement as Buyer deems necessary and appropriate in its discretion. 本契約締結日からクロージングまで、買い主は、本契約で意図されている取引に関して買い主が買い主の判断でお必要かつ適切と考えるデュー・ディリジェンス調査を行うことができるものとする。

commencing on the effective date and continuing throughout the term of this agreement 本契約の発効日から開始して本契約の有効期間中を通して、本契約の発効日から有効期間まで

commend （動）委（ゆだ）ねる、託す、推奨する、推挙する、賞賛する、ほめる
commend a thing to a person's care 人に〜を託す
commend itself to 〜に（好感を持って）受け入れられる
commend me to 〜によろしく
commend oneself to 〜の気に入る、〜に受け入れられる、〜に良い印象［感じ］を与える
commend our signature to your (kind) protection （手形振出人が名宛て人に対して言う）何とぞこの手形をお引き受けください、この手形の支払いをよろしくお願いします （＝recommend our signature to your protection）
have much to commend it 〜が受け入れられる、満足のいく
◆We negotiated our draft through the bank above-mentioned under L/C No. 5000 established by the ABC Bank, New York, and com-

mend our signature to your protection. 当社は、ABC銀行（ニューヨーク）発行の信用状5000号に従って上記銀行で手形を買い取ってもらいましたので、この手形の支払いをよろしくお願いします。

commerce （名）商取引、商業、通商、貿易、コマース

active commerce 自主貿易
agreement on commerce 通商協定
American Chamber of Commerce in Japan 在日米国商工会議所
census of commerce 商業統計
chamber of commerce 商業会議所
chamber of commerce and industry 商工会議所 （＝commerce and industry association）
commerce and industry 商工業、商工
commerce and industry association 商工会議所、商工組合
Commerce and Industry Association of New York 米ニューヨーク商工組合
commerce clause 通商条項
commerce court 商事裁判所
commerce finance 商業金融
commerce proper （商品売買だけの）固有商業
commerce system 商業体系、重商主義 （＝system of commerce）
commerce yearbook 通商年鑑
domestic commerce 国内商業、国内通商
foreign commerce 外国貿易
House Energy and Commerce Committee 米下院エネルギー・通商問題調査委員会
illicit commerce 密貿易
indirect commerce 間接貿易
inland commerce 国内通商
intermediary commerce 仲介貿易
internal commerce 国内商業、国内通商 （＝domestic commerce）
international commerce 国際商業、国際通商、国際貿易、国際商事
international commerce arbitration 国際商事仲裁
International Commerce Commission 国際商業委員会
interstate commerce 米州際商業、米州際通商、米州際貿易、米州内通商
Interstate Commerce Act 米州際商業法
Interstate Commerce Commission 米州際商業委員会、ICC
passive commerce 受動貿易
private foreign commerce 民間外国貿易、民間貿易
seaborne commerce 海上通商、海上貿易
special commerce 特殊貿易

COMM
88

system of commerce　商業体系

treaty of commerce　通商条約

treaty of commerce and navigation　通商航海条約（貨物や船舶の往来、個人の居住や営業の自由、財産の取得、関税、裁判権などが含まれる）

waterborne commerce　海上貿易, 海上通商

White Paper on Commerce　通商白書

world commerce　世界貿易, 国際貿易

◆Under the multilayered trade policy, Japan should strengthen bilateral and multilateral cooperation in commerce and help stimulate trade and investment to ensure the economic revival of the East Asian region. 重層的な通商政策のもとに、日本は東アジア地域の経済再生のため、通商面で二国間および多国間の連携を強化して、貿易と投資を促進していかなければならない。

Commerce Department　米商務省

◆The U.S. Commerce Department set dumping penalty margins of 115.22 percent each for the two Japanese steelmakers. 米商務省は、日本の鉄鋼メーカー2社に対してそれぞれ115.22％のダンピング率を認定した。

commercial　（形）商業の, 商業上の, 商業的な, 商業ベースの, 通商の, 営利の, 民間の, 民放の, 大量生産型の, 量産型の, 市販の, 消費者向けの　（名）宣伝, 広告放送, コマーシャル

commercial abbreviation　商用略語（CIF, FOBなどの略語）

commercial advertising　商業広告

commercial affairs　商務

commercial agency　信用調査機関, 商業興信所,（商業）代理店

commercial agent　（商業）代理人, 代理店, 商務官

commercial and industrial association　商工組合

commercial and industrial bond　商工債券

commercial arbitration　商事仲裁

commercial arbitration rules　商事仲裁規則

commercial area　商業地区, 商業地域（＝commercial district）

commercial attaché　（大公使館の）商務官（＝commercial counselor）

commercial auction　競売

commercial balance　商業取引上のバランス, 取引のバランス

commercial bank　商業銀行, 普通銀行, 市中銀行, 都市銀行

commercial bill　商業手形, 為替手形

commercial bill eligible for rediscount　再割引適格商業手形

commercial bill of exchange　商業為替手形

commercial blanket bond　商業包括保証, 営業包括保証保険

commercial block insurance　商業一括保険

commercial broker　営業用不動産仲介業者

commercial business　商業, 商用, 営利事業

commercial call　商用通信

commercial capital　商業資本

commercial carrier　商業運送業者

commercial casualty insurance　商業事故保険

commercial center　商業中心地

commercial channel　商業経路

commercial circuit　商業循環

commercial clean L/C　商業クリーン信用状, 無担保信用状

commercial company　商事会社, 営利会社

commercial correspondence　商業通信文, 商用文, 貿易通信文, コレポン

commercial counsellor　商業カウンセラー, 商業顧問

commercial country　商業国

commercial court　商事裁判所

commercial credit institution　商業信用機関

commercial credit insurance　商業信用保険

commercial custom　商慣習

commercial depression　（商業）不況, 不景気, 商業不振

commercial directory　商業人名簿

commercial discount　商業割引

commercial dispute　商事紛争

commercial distribution center　商品流通センター

commercial documentary credit　商業荷為替信用状

commercial draft　商業手形

commercial English　商業英語（＝business English, business writing）

commercial enterprise　営利事業, 営利企業

commercial expenses　営業費, 商業費

commercial fault　商業過失

commercial fertilizer　人工肥料, 化学肥料

commercial finance　商業金融

commercial forgery policy　偽造文書営業保険

commercial form　商用書式

commercial goods　商品

commercial grade　商業用等級

commercial impracticability　商業上の実行困難性

commercial instrument　商業証券

commercial insurance　商業保険, 営利保険

commercial intercourse　通商, 通商関係

commercial invoice　商業送り状, 商業インボイス,（関税法で）仕入書

commercial law　商事法, 商法

commercial lender　営利的貸し手
commercial letter of credit　商業信用状
　(=commercial credit)
commercial loan　商業貸付け, 営利貸付け, 商
業手形
commercial manufacture　商業ベースの生産
commercial marketing　商業マーケティング
commercial mission　実業視察団
commercial modus vivendi　暫定通商協定
commercial monopoly　商業独占
commercial morality　商業道徳
commercial operation　商業活動
commercial package　商業包装
commercial par　商業平価, 実際平価
commercial policy　商業政策, 通商政策, 貿易
政策
commercial port　商港, 商業港
commercial position　営業状態
commercial practices　商慣習, 商慣行, 商習慣
commercial printing　商業印刷物
commercial production　商業生産
commercial products　商品
commercial profit　商業利潤, 利益, 採算
commercial property　商業資産, 営利資産
commercial property policy　営利損害保険
commercial protection　商業保護
commercial pursuits　商業, 商事
commercial quantity　採算数量
commercial reference　同業者信用照会先
commercial register　商業登記簿
commercial registration　商業登記
commercial relations　商取引関係
commercial research　商業調査, 市場調査
　(=market research)
commercial right　商権
commercial risk　商業危険, 事業リスク
commercial route　商路
commercial service　商業サービス
commercial set　貿易用書類一式, 貿易書類
一式
commercial share　貿易株　(=commercial
stock)
commercial sign　商用符号 ($などの符号)
commercial spirit　商売気質
commercial standards　商業規格, CS
commercial statistics　商業統計
commercial stocks　流通在庫
commercial term　商用語
commercial terms　取引条件, 取引条項
commercial tour　商況視察旅行, 商業視察

旅行
commercial town　商業都市
commercial transaction　商取引, 商業取引, 営
業取引, 商行為
commercial traveler　巡回外交員 (commercial
salesman), 巡回販売者, 商用旅行者, 旅商
commercial treaty　通商協定, 通商条約
　(=trade agreement)
commercial usage　商習慣
commercial value　商品価値
commercial vehicle　商用車
commercial venture　商取引
commercial warehouse　営業倉庫, 商業倉庫
commercial warehouse industry　商業倉庫業
commercial work　商業労働
commercial year　営業年度

commercial activity　商業活動
　◆Diplomats are prohibited from engaging in
commercial activities for the purpose of their
personal profits under the Vienna Convention's
Article 42. ウイーン条約42条で, 外交官は個人の
利得を目的とした商業活動を禁止されている。

Commercial Arbitration Rules　商事仲裁
規則
　◆Any and all disputes arising from or in connection with this Agreement or a transaction
conducted under this Agreement shall be settled by arbitration in Tokyo in accordance with
the Commercial Arbitration Rules of the Japan
Commercial Arbitration Association. The award
of the arbitration shall be final and binding upon
the parties. 本契約もしくは本契約に基づいて行わ
れる取引から生じる, またはこれに関連して生じ
る紛争は, すべて日本商事仲裁協会の商事仲裁規
則にしたがって東京での仲裁による[と]解決する。仲
裁の判断は, 最終的なもので当事者を拘束[法的に
拘束]するものとする。

commercial brand right　商標権
　◆Imports of pirated designer goods violate commercial brand rights. 偽ブランド品の輸入は, 商
標権の侵害に当たる。◆The Customs Tariff Law
bans imports that infringe on patent, design and
commercial brand rights. 関税定率法で, 特許,
意匠, 商標権などの侵害品の輸入は禁止されて
いる。

Commercial Code　商法
　◆Sony is the first company to announce a reform
of its board under the revised Commercial Code,
a move that may influence other companies. 改
正商法に従って取締役会の改革を発表した会社は
ソニーが初めてで, この動きは他の企業にも影響
を与えそうだ。◆Under the revised Commercial
Code, only large companies with capital of more
than ￥500 million would be qualified to adopt
the U.S.-style board structure. 今回の商法改正で
は, 資本金5億円以上の大企業だけが米国型の取締

役会制度を導入することができる。

commercial launches of foreign satellites
外国の衛星の商用打上げ
◆Mitsubishi Heavy Industries Ltd. aims to win orders for commercial launches of foreign satellites with a current lineup of its core H-2A and H-2B rockets. 三菱重工業は、現在の主力ロケットH2AとH2Bロケットの二本柱で、外国の衛星の商用打上げ受注を目指している。

commercial paper 商業証券、商業手形、コマーシャル・ペーパー, CP

asset-backed commercial paper 資産担保CP

commercial paper and similar obligations 商業手形他

commercial paper market 手形市場
◆Asset-backed commercial paper refers to commercial paper whose creditworthiness is guaranteed by sales credit that the corporate issuer has with its debtors. 資産担保CPとは、企業発行体がその債務者に対して保有する売掛金によって信用度が保証されるコマーシャル・ペーパーを指す。

commercial production 商業生産
◆The government will make final judgments whether to go ahead with the commercial production of methane hydrate and seafloor hydrothermal deposits in fiscal 2018, based on the results of test drilling and investigation of the resources. メタンハイドレートと海底熱水鉱床の試掘や調査の結果を踏まえて、政府は、両資源の商業生産推進の可否について2018年度に最終判断する。

commercial real estate 商業用不動産

commercial real estate exposure［lending, loan］ 商業用不動産融資

commercial real estate market 商業用不動産市場

vacancy rate of commercial real estate 商業用不動産の空室率

commercial trade 商取引
◆To ensure fair international commercial trade, the law against unfair competition stipulates that both individuals involved in bribery and the corporations they belong to should be punished. 公正な国際商取引を確保するため、不正競争防止法には、贈賄（外国公務員への贈賄）に関与した個人と法人を罰する規定（両罰規定）がある。

commercially applied by 〜が商業的に応用する

commercially unreasonable 営業上、不合理な

commission （名）手数料, 報酬, 委任, 委任状, 委託, 代理業務, 授与, 授権, 任命, 任命書, 委員会, 任務, 権限, 職権, 過失, 作為, 犯罪, 犯行, 犯罪などの実行
◆Affiliates can earn a 10% commission on every item sold through their websites. アフィリエイトのウェブサイトを通じて販売した商品については、アフィリエイトはすべて10%のコミッションを

受け取ることができます。◆Nothing contained in this agreement shall be construed so as to require the commission of any act contrary to statute or law. 本契約に定めるいずれの規定も、制定法または法律に反する行為の実行を要求するものとは解釈しないものとする。

commit any breach of this agreement 本契約違反を犯す
◆In the event that either party fails to perform any obligation hereunder or otherwise commits any breach of this agreement, the other party may terminate this agreement by giving to the party in default a written notice. いずれか一方の当事者が本契約に基づく義務の履行を怠った場合、または別に本契約違反を犯した場合、相手方当事者は、不履行当事者に書面による通知を行って本契約を解除することができる。

commitment （名）参加, 取組, 関与, 献身, 社会貢献, 約束, 言質（げんち）, 確約, 約定, 公約, 誓約, 委任, 委託,（法案などの）委員会付託, 立場の明確な表明, 協調融資団への参加意思表示, 融資参加の意向表明, 銀行の融資承認, 融資先, 売買約定, 売買契約, 取引契約, 契約債務, 契約義務, 未履行債務,（お金や時間などを特定の目的に）利用する［使う］こと, コミットメント

capital commitments 資本参加, 出資

commitment clause 融資約定

commitment fee 契約手数料, 約定手数料, 約定料

financial commitment 資金協力

labor commitment 労働協約

lease commitment 貸借契約

letter of commitment 支払い引受書, LC

make substantial commitments to 〜に本格的に進出する

new loan commitment 新規融資契約, 新規ローンの確約

offset a firm commitment 成約済みの取引を相殺する

sales commitment 販売契約

strong commitment to the environment 環境保護の重視

underwriting commitment 引受額

commitment line 融資枠, コミットメント・ライン （=credit limit, credit line, line of credit）
解説 コミットメント・ラインとは：銀行から一定の範囲で自由に借入れができる融資枠の設定のこと。コミットメント・ラインを設定すると、金融機関は安定した手数料収入が得られるほか、優良企業との取引拡大を期待できる。また、企業にとっては、手数料を払う代わりに金利ゼロで融資を受けられるメリットがある。緊急の資金需要に備えられるほか、資金効率の改善効果もある。最近は、経営不振の企業が、信用不安を解消するため主力取

引銀行とコミットメント・ライン契約を結ぶことが多い。

committee of creditors 債権者委員会

commodity （名）商品, 市況商品, 市況品, 日用品, 製品, 産品, 物品, 生産物, 財貨, 財
commodities in general　市況商品
commodity agreement　国際商品協定
commodity assistance　商品援助
commodity bill　商品手形
commodity broker　商品仲買人, 商品ブローカー
commodity character　商品特性
commodity chemicals　基礎化学品
commodity classification　商品分類
commodity composition　商品構成
commodity contract　商品契約
commodity derivative　市況商品の派性商品
commodity excise　物品税
commodity firm　商品取引企業
commodity fund　商品ファンド
commodity import　商品輸入
commodity in general　財一般
commodity index futures　商品指数先物
commodity market　商品市場, 生産物市場, 財貨市場（⇒crude futures）
commodity paper　（船荷証券や倉庫商品の）商品手形
commodity products　汎用品
commodity speculation　商品投機
commodity supply　商品供給
commodity tax　物品税
commodity terms of trade　商品交易条件
commodity trading　商品取引
commodity transaction　商品取引
composite commodity　複合商品, 合成財
consumption commodity　消費商品
daily commodities　日用品
Dow-Jones Commodity Index　ダウ・ジョーンズ商品指数［相場指数］
exchange rate sensitive commodity　為替レートの動きに敏感な商品
household commodities　家庭用品
industrial commodity producer　素材メーカー
international commodity　国際商品, 国際市況商品
labor power commodity　労働力商品
listed commodity　上場商品
major commodity　主要商品, 主要産品
marketable commodity　市場性のある商品, 売れ行きの良い商品, 売買可能な商品

marketed commodity　市販品, 市販商品, 市場性商品
net commodity terms of trade　純商品交易条件
Nikkei Commodity Index（42 items）　日経商品指数（42種）
nonmarketed commodity　非市場性商品
perishable commodity　消耗財
prices of commodities　物価
primary commodities　一次産品
production of commodity　商品生産
seasonal commodity　季節商品
standard commodity　標準商品, 価値基準財, 価値尺度財
staple commodities　重要商品, 主要商品
taxed commodity　課税商品, 課税品
traffic in the bulk commodities　バルク輸送
◆All quantities of the Product manufactured by you shall be held by you to your order and we shall insure all quantities on your premises of the Commodity and the Product. 貴社が製造した契約品の数量はすべて当社の指図があるまで貴社が保管し, 当社は貴社の構内にある商品と契約品の全数量に保険を付けるものとする。◆Indonesia has enjoyed decent economic growth since the global financial crisis of 2008 due to the U.S. FRB's quantitative easing and higher prices of primary commodities such as coal and palm oil as the country's major exports. インドネシアは、2008年の世界金融危機以降、米連邦準備制度理事会（FRB）の量的金融緩和とインドネシアの主要輸出品である石炭、パーム油など一次産品の高値に支えられた、高い経済成長を享受している。

commodity exchange 商品取引, 商品取引所
Association of Commodity Exchange Firms　商品取引所会員協会
Commodities Exchange Commission　商品取引所委員会
Commodity Exchange　ニューヨーク商品取引所, COMEX
Commodity Exchange Act　商品取引法, 商品取引所法
Commodity Exchange Authority　商品取引所監督局
Commodity Exchange Law　商品取引所法
Commodity Exchanges Center　商品取引所センター
Kuala Lumpur Commodity Exchange　クアラルンプール商品取引所
London Commodity Exchange　ロンドン商品取引所
Tokyo Commodity Exchange for Industry　東京工業品取引所

U.S. Commodity Exchange Act 米国商品取引法, 米商品取引所法
◆Recently, a sizable amount of speculative funds have been flowing into New York's commodities exchanges. このところ、ニューヨークの商品取引所には、大量の投機資金が流入している。

commodity futures market 商品先物市場
◆Foreign players also are expected to enter the commodity futures market in line with the improvement in investment conditions. 投資の環境改善で、外資［海外企業］の商品先物市場への参入も見込まれる。

commodity futures trading 商品先物取引
◆Commodity futures trading is based on contracts to buy or sell a specified quantity of an underlying asset, such as gold, at a particular time in the future and at a price agreed when the contract was executed. 商品先物取引は、取引契約を結ぶ時点で、一定量の金などの対象資産を将来の特定の時期に合意した値段で売買する契約に基づいて行われる。◆In commodity futures trading, prices are decided when buyers and sellers make deals. So they can execute trades at promised prices even if the value of goods has changed drastically in the meantime. 商品先物取引では、売り手と買い手が取引契約をする時点で価格を決める。そのため、契約期間中に相場が大きく変動しても、売り手と買い手は約束した値段で取引を執行できる。

Commodity Futures Trading Commission 米商品先物取引委員会, CFTC
◆The U.S. Commodity Futures Trading Commission charged one investment fund with gaining illicit profits by manipulating crude oil and other markets. 米国の商品先物取引委員会は、原油市場などで不正な利益を上げたとして、投資ファンドの一つを摘発した。

commodity loans 商品借款
◆Commodity loans are used to import commodities such as industrial machinery, industrial raw materials, fertilizer, agricultural chemicals and machinery, and other various kinds of machinery, which are agreed upon beforehand between the Japanese and recipient governments. 商品借款は、日本政府と借入国政府が前もって合意した商品（工業資本財［工業用機械］、工業用原材料、肥料・農薬、農機具、各種機械など）の輸入のために使用される。

common stock 普通株式, 普通株
　common stock equivalent 準普通株式
　common stock in treasury 自己普通株式, 自己株式
　common stock share equity 普通株式
　common stock with a par value of 1株当たり額面〜の普通株式
◆Subject to the terms and conditions herein set forth, XYZ and ABC agree that at the closing, XYZ shall sell to ABC, and ABC shall purchase from XYZ, one hundred（100）shares of the common stock with no par value of the Company owned by XYZ at the purchase price of U.S. \$1,000,000. 本契約に定める条件に従って、XYZとABCは、クロージングにおいて、XYZが保有する本会社の無額面普通株式100株を、100万米ドルの購入価格［譲渡価格］で、XYZがABCに売り渡し、ABCがXYZから買い受けることに合意する。

communicate （動）伝達する, 通知する, 連絡を取る, 交信する
◆Such information was rightfully communicated to the receiving party free of any obligation of confidence subsequent to the time it was communicated to the receiving party by the disclosing party. 当該情報は、開示当事者が受領当事者に通知した時点以後に、秘密保持義務なしに受領当事者に合法的に通知された。◆This information was in the public domain at the time it was communicated to the receiving party by the disclosing party. この情報は、開示当事者が受領当事者に通知した時点で公知であった。

communication （名）通信, 伝達, 通知, 交信, 意思疎通, 意思表示, 相互理解, やり取り, 協議, 連絡, 連絡事項, 手紙, コミュニケーション
　all notices and other communications すべての通知と他の通信
　communication between the parties 当事者間の通信, 当事者間の連絡・交信
◆All notices and other communications hereunder shall be in writing. 本契約に基づく通知と他の通信は、すべて書面で行うものとする。

company name 社名

company's guide 会社案内

comparable （形）類似の, 似通った, 似たような, 同等の, 同様の, 比較可能な, 匹敵する, 相当する （名）類似物, 類似物件, 比較
　comparable basis 比較ベース, 継続事業ベース
　comparable legend それに［これに］相当する文言, それに相当する記載
　comparable to 〜に匹敵する, 〜に相当する, 〜と比べてもひけをとらない
　comparable with 〜と比較できる, 〜と同等の, 〜と同じと見られる
　comparables 類似物件
　international comparables 国際比較
　on a comparable structure and exchange rates 継続事業・為替調整ベースで
　other comparable companies 同業他社
　since comparable data became available in 1985 統計を比較できる1985年以降, 比較できるデータが入手できる1985年以降
◆Japan's customs-cleared trade deficit in April-September 2014 came to ￥5.43 trillion, up 8.6 percent from a year before and the largest for any

fiscal first-half period since comparable data became available in fiscal 1979. 日本の2014年度上半期（4〜9月）の通関ベースでの貿易収支の赤字額は、前年同期比8.6%増の5兆4,300億円となり、統計を比較できる1979年度以降で上半期としては最大だった。

comparative advantage　比較優位, 比較優位性　(=relative advantage; ⇒R & D)
◆Due to the IT revolution and trade liberalization, product specialization now is determined by comparative advantages not in finished products but in work unique to each country or region in the context of global value chains. 情報通信技術（IT）革命と貿易自由化で、製品の特化は、「最終財」の比較優位ではなく、国際的価値連鎖との関連で国・地域にそれぞれ特有の「仕事」の比較優位で決まるようになった。

compensate　(動)補償する, 賠償する, 補塡する, 償う, 埋め合わせる
◆Loss and damages sustained thereby shall be compensated by defaulting party responsible for the breach. それにより発生した損失および損害は、その違反の責めを負う不履行当事者が賠償しなければならない。

compensation　(名)報酬, 対価, 給与, 手当て, 報償, 補償, 賠償, 代償, 相殺, 報償金, 補償金, 賠償金, 慰謝料, 補うもの, 埋め合わせ(になるもの), 補塡, 慰め, 代償作用
as compensation for　〜に対する補償［賠償］として、〜の対価として　(=in compensation for)
ask for A in compensation　補償としてAを求める
be entitled to compensation for　〜の補償を受ける権利がある
claim compensation from　〜に賠償金を請求する、〜に補償を請求する
compensation duties　相殺関税
compensation for consequential damage　二次補償, 派生的損害の補償
compensation for principal loss　元本補塡
compensation for technical services　技術サービスの対価
compensation to dispossessed owners　所有者の立ち退きに対する補償
compensation trade　補償貿易, 求償貿易
demand compensation　報酬を要求する, 補償を要求する
financial compensation　賠償金
in compensation for　〜の補償［賠償］として、〜の損害賠償として、〜の対価として、〜の代償として、〜の償いとして　(=as compensation for)
launch［file］a compensation claim against　〜に対して賠償請求を行う

loss compensation　損失補塡, 損害の代償
monetary compensation　金銭賠償
net compensation amount　差額決済金額
right of demanding compensation　求償権
seek compensation for　〜に対する補償を求める
seek compensation from　〜に補償を求める、〜に賠償請求する　(=claim compensation from)
sue for compensation　補償を求めて訴えを起こす
◆In consideration of the license granted and the products delivered by XYZ, ABC shall, upon the delivery of the products, pay a royalty in the amount listed in Exhibit C as the exclusive method of compensation under this agreement. XYZが許諾するライセンスとXYZが引渡す本製品の対価として、ABCは、本製品の引渡し時に、本契約に基づく対価の唯一の支払い方法として付属書類Cに記載する額のロイヤルティを支払うものとする。◆The remedies under this clause shall be the sole compensation for the damages caused by such delay. 本条項に基づく補償は、当該遅延で生じた損害の唯一の補償とする。◆We are giving your order priority, but a slight delay in the shipment of yours will be unavoidable. 貴社の注文を優先的に扱っていますが、ご注文の船積みが少々遅れることは避けられません。

compete　(動)競争する, 競う, 争う, 張り合う, 渡り合う, 競合する, 対抗する, 参加する, 出場する
compete against　〜と競合する、〜と競争する
compete effectively　競争に勝つ
compete for market share　市場シェアを争う, シェアを争う, 市場シェアをめぐって争う, 市場シェア獲得競争をする
compete in the global marketplace　世界市場［国際市場］で競争する
compete on price with　〜と価格で競う、〜と価格で競合する
compete with other businesses on　〜で他社と競争する
◆There has been a rising tide of protectionism among U.S. businesses and labor unions that want Washington to restrict imports that compete with domestic products. 米国の業界や労組の間には、国産品と競合する輸入品の規制を政府に要請する保護主義的な動きが高まっている。

competent authority　所轄官庁, 監督官庁

competent jurisdiction　正当な管轄権
◆If any provision of this agreement is held by a court of competent jurisdiction to be illegal or invalid, the remainder of this agreement shall remain in effect. 本契約の条項のいずれかが、正当な管轄権のある裁判所によって違法または無効であると判断された場合でも、本契約のその他の条項は

依然として有効である。◆The arbitral award shall be final and judgment thereon may be entered in any court of competent jurisdiction. 仲裁判断は最終的なものとし、それに基づく判決は正当な管轄権のあるいずれの裁判所でも受けることができるものとする［正当な管轄権のある裁判所の記録に正式に登録することができる］。

competent substitute 適格交代人員
◆ABC reserves the right to replace on its own reasons any ABC Personnel so assigned with a competent substitute by giving XYZ a notice in advance. ABCは、XYZに事前通知を行って、派遣したABC人員を自社の都合で適格交替人員と交替させる権利を持つ。

competing （形）競争する，競合する，相容れない，相反する，対立している

competing demand 競争的需要

competing firms 競合他社

competing interests 利害の対立，相反する利害

competing price 競争価格，競合価格

competing product 競合品，競合商品，競合する商品［製品］ （=competing goods, competitive product）

competing representations 競業禁止

import-competing goods 輸入品と競合する商品［製品］

competing jet aircraft 競合ジェット機
◆As the MRJ uses highly fuel-efficient engine, the fuel consumption is at least 20 percent better than other competing jet aircraft. MRJ（三菱リージョナルジェット）は定燃費エンジンを採用しているので、燃費性能は、他の競合ジェット機より少なくとも2割以上は優れている。

competition （名）競争，競技，競技会，試合，（音楽や絵画などの）コンクール，コンテスト，競合，競業，競争相手，同業他社，ライバル，競合製品 （⇒preferential treatment）

Act Against Unfair Competition 不正競争防止法

be sheltered from A's competition Aとの競争にさらされていない

be subject to intense competition 激しい競争［競争の激化］にさらされる

beat the competition 競争相手を打ち負かす，競争［ライバル企業］に勝つ

competition in the market 市場での競争

competition law 競争法，独占禁止法，反トラスト法 （=antitrust law）

competition strategy 競争戦略

cope with competition 競争に取り組む

deregulation induced competition 規制緩和による競争激化

enhance [increase] competition 競争を高める

excess [excessive] competition 過当競争

fair competition 公正競争

fierce competition 熾烈な競争

foreign competition 国際競争，外国勢との競争

global competition 国際競争 （=international competition）

heightened [growing, increased, intensified] competition 競争激化

in competition with ～と競い合って

indirect competition 間接的な競争

industrial competition 製造分野での競争

limited competition 制限的競争

lose to A's competition Aとの競争に負ける

low-price competition 低価格競争，安値競争

marketing competition 販売競争

monopolistic competition 独占的な競争

open competition 自由競争，公開競争

promoting competition 競争促進

quality competition 品質競争

restricting competition 競争制限

sales competition 販売競争

set A apart from the competition Aで競争相手と差をつける

slip against the competition 競争［競争相手］に後れを取る

spur competition 競争を促す，競争を促進する

tough [toughening] competition 熾烈な競争

unfair competition 不正競争 （⇒fair international commercial trade）

vigorous competition 活発な競争
◆Japanese electronics makers are needed to shrug off the adversity of economic slowdowns overseas, a strongly appreciating yen, and ever-intensifying competition with foreign rivals by wielding their latent power. 日本の電機製造業各社は、底力を発揮して、海外経済の減速、超円高、海外勢との競争激化などの逆境を跳ね返す必要がある。

competition with foreign rivals 海外のライバル［ライバル企業］との競争，海外勢との競争
◆Domestic manufacturers have been exposed to the adverse winds of economic slowdowns overseas, a strongly appreciating yen and ever-intensifying competition with foreign rivals. 国内製造業各社は、海外経済の減速や超円高、海外勢との競争激化などの逆風にさらされている。

competitive （形）競争の，競い合う，張り合う，競争心旺盛な，競争心が強い，競争の激しい，競争力のある，競争的な，競争上の，（価格などが）他社に負けない，他より安い，安い，低

コストの （⇒cost-competitive）

at competitive prices　他より安い価格で, 他より安く

be overly competitive　過当競争になる

become more competitive　競争力を高める

competitive ability　競争力

competitive adaptive strategy　競争適合戦略

competitive advertising　競争広告

competitive auction [bid, bidding, tender]　競争入札

competitive bid [bidding, tender]　競争入札

competitive commission　競争手数料

competitive commodity demand　競争的商品需要

competitive conditions　競争状態

competitive cost position　コスト競争力

competitive demand　競争的需要

competitive depreciation　切下げ競争

competitive devaluation　平価切下げ競争, 競争的平価切下げ

competitive differentiation　競争的差別化

competitive environment　競争環境
　（=competitive dynamics [landscape]）

competitive financing　低コストの資金調達（手段）

competitive firm　競争的企業

competitive forces [mechanism]　競争原理

competitive goods　競争品, 競争商品, 競争財

competitive import　競争輸入

competitive industry　競争的産業（業界全体が完全競争の状況にある産業）

competitive level of prices　競争的価格水準

competitive lump sum contract　入札による一括受託契約

competitive margin　きつい金利条件

competitive market　競争的な市場, 競争市場

competitive mistakes　戦略上の誤り

competitive moves　競争力

competitive opportunities　競争の機会

competitive order　競争秩序

competitive posture　競争上のポジション

competitive power　競争力

competitive pressure [threat]　競争圧力

competitive price　競争価格, 競争力のある価格, 競争値段, 低価格, 安い価格 [値段]

competitive pricing　競争価格設定

competitive pricing strategy　競争力のある価格戦略

competitive product　競合品

competitive restriction　競争制限

competitive risks　競争上のリスク, 競争激化のリスク

competitive sale [selling]　競売, 競争的販売

competitive strategy　競争戦略

competitive strength　競争力
　（=competitive power [setting]）

competitive supply　競争的供給

competitive tariff　競争関税, 競争税率

competitive winners　競争での勝ち組, 競争での勝ち組企業

competitive yields　魅力的な利回り

feel competitive with　〜に対抗意識を持つ

invite competitive bids　競争入札を実施する

price-competitive　価格競争力がある

remain competitive　競争力を維持する, 競争力を保つ（=stay competitive）

weigh the competitive risks　競争上のリスクを検討する

◆By removing the tariffs on textile products, the three nations are expected to increase their exports to Japan of such low-priced products as underwear, silk and polo shirts in competition with price-competitive Chinese products. 繊維製品の関税撤廃で, これら3国は, 価格競争力の高い中国製品に対抗して, 下着類やシルク, ポロシャツなど安価な製品の対日輸出の増加が見込める。◆We may place a substantial order with you on a regular basis if your prices are competitive. 貴社の製品価格が他社より安ければ, 定期的に大口の注文を出すことができます。

competitive advantage　競争上の優位, 競争上の優位性, 競争力, 比較優位, 比較優位性, 競争有利性

build a competitive advantage　競争上の優位性を確立する, 競争力をつける [高める]

gain a competitive advantage　競争上の優位性を獲得する, 競争上の優位に立つ

hold a competitive advantage　競争上の優位を保つ

increase one's competitive advantage　〜の競争力 [競争上の優位性] を高める, 〜の競争上の優位を強化する

lose competitive advantage　競争上の優位性を失う, 競争力を失う

sustain competitive advantage　競争力を維持する

◆U.S. agricultural products have gained a greater competitive advantage in the Japanese market due to mounting concern toward the safety of food. 米国製農産物は, 食の安全に対する不安の高まりから, 日本市場での競争力が拡大している。

competitive edge　競争力, 競争上の優位 [優位性], 競争力での優位

◆The competitive edge of Japanese exporters vying with U.S. firms is affected by the yen-dollar rate and the price levels in the two countries. 米企業と競合している日本の輸出企業の競争力は、円・ドルレートや日本と米国の物価水準の影響をも受ける。

competitive factors in the market　市場での競争要因
◆Other competitive factors in the market for the products are service, delivery, technological capability, and product quality and performance. 市場での製品の競争要因としては、サービスや納入、技術活用能力［技術力］、品質、性能なども挙げられる。

competitive manufacturer　競争力の高い製造業者
◆Japanese people are becoming difficult to find jobs and maintain their quality of life in the absence of competitive manufacturers at home. 競争力の高い製造業者が国内から消えたため、日本人は雇用を求め、生活の質を維持するのが困難になっている。

competitive with　～と競合する，～に対抗する
any product similar to and competitive with the products　本製品に類似する競合品
◆No party hereto shall engage or be interested in the business of manufacturing, selling, or otherwise dealing with any product similar to and competitive with the products in the territory during the term of this agreement except with the consent of the other parties hereto. いずれの当事者も、他の本契約当事者の同意を得た場合を除いて、本契約の期間中、契約地域で本製品に類似する競合品を製造、販売その他の方法で取引する事業に従事または関与しないものとする。

competitiveness　（名）競争力
◆Japan must strengthen the competitiveness of its manufacturing industry which will lead to increasing exports in order to rebuild its status as a trading country. 貿易立国としての地位を立て直すには、日本は、輸出拡大につながる製造業の競争力強化が必要である。◆Many Japanese manufacturers have been prompted to review their production in China with labor costs surging in China and domestic production recovering competitiveness thanks to the weaker yen. 中国で人件費が高騰しているのに加え、円安進行で国内生産の競争力が回復しているため、日本メーカーの多くは中国での生産（体制）を見直す動きが加速している。◆The company needs to enhance its development strength for such products as hybrid cars to maintain the competitiveness of its vehicles and auto parts domestically manufactured, in addition to improving export-driven profits. 同社の場合、輸出主導の収益改善にとどまらず、国内生産の車両や自動車部品の競争力を維持するには、ハイブリッド車などの製品の開発力を強化する必要がある。

competitiveness in exports　輸出競争力

◆A cheaper yen increases import costs, but if the yen-dollar exchange rate is within the range of ￥95-105, it would be possible for companies to maintain competitiveness in exports. 円安で輸入コストは増えるが、円の対ドル為替相場が1ドル＝95〜105円の範囲内なら、企業は輸出競争力を維持できるだろう。◆If the yen-dollar exchange rate stayed around ￥100 to the dollar, give or take about ￥5, it would be possible for domestic companies to maintain competitiveness in exports. 円とドルの為替相場が1ドル＝100円プラス・マイナス5円程度で安定すれば、国内企業は輸出競争力を保てるだろう。

competitor　（名）競争相手, 競合他社, 同業者, ライバル企業, ライバル
a chief competitor　最大の競争相手, 最大のライバル
a competitor nation　競争相手国, 競争国
acquisition of one's competitor　競争相手の買収
beat a competitor　ライバル企業に勝つ, 競合他社を打ち負かす
competitor's price　競争者価格, 競争相手の価格
form an alliance with one's competitor　ライバル企業と提携する
head off competitors　ライバルの機先を制する, ライバルに対して先手を打つ
international competitors　世界の競争相手, 海外の競争相手, 外資系企業
lag one's major competitors　主な競争相手に遅れをとる
large-scale competitors　大手の競争相手
local competitors　国内の競争相手
one's main competitor　主要な競争相手, 最大のライバル, 最大の競争相手
outdo competitors　ライバルを追い抜く, ライバル企業の上を行く
potential competitor　潜在的競争相手, 潜在的ライバル
powerful competitor　強力な競争相手, 強力なライバル
smaller competitors　中小の競合他社
strategic competitors　強力な競争相手
the nearest competitor　僅差（きんさ）で争っているライバル企業
weaker competitors　弱小の競争相手
◆Comparative advantage in this new global market depends not only on superior R&D, but also on speed in making management decisions, finding unique applications for research advances and delivering them to customers ahead of competitors. この新しいグローバル市場で比較優位性を確立できるかどうかは、高度な研究開発だけでなく、経営の意思決定を迅速に行えるかどうかと、

研究を進めるうえで独創的な適用範囲［用途］を素早く確認して、それを競合他社に先駆けて製品化できるかどうかにかかっている。

complaint （名）苦情, 苦情の申立て, 不平, 不満, 抗議, 相談, クレーム, 告訴, 病気, 疾患

file a complaint with ～に提訴する, ～に告訴する

file a criminal complaint with ～に刑事告発する

lay a complaint 告訴する

◆The Fair Trade Commission filed criminal complaints with the public prosecutor general against three steelmakers on suspicion of violating the Antimonopoly Law. 公正取引委員会は、独占禁止法違反容疑で、鉄鋼メーカー3社を検事総長に刑事告発した。◆The NHTSA received 163 complaints from Corolla users about their cars' power steering system. トヨタ・カローラのユーザーから、米高速道路交通安全局（NHTSA）に、電動パワー・ステアリングに関する苦情が163件寄せられた。

complete （動）完成させる, 仕上げる, 完全なものにする, 全部揃える, 完結する, 完璧にする, 修了する, 達成する, 成し遂げる, 成就する, 完了する, 終える, 作成する, (書類に)書き込む

◆Delivery of the software products to the buyer shall be completed when shipped, FOB Seller's plant in New York. ソフトウエア製品の買い主への引渡しは、ニューヨークの売り主の工場でFOB条件で出荷された時点で完了するものとする。

complete （形）完全な, 全部揃っている, 欠けていない, 全体の, 完了した, 終了した, 徹底した, まったくの, この上ない, 熟達した, 極めた, まぎれもない, ～付きの, ～の, 備わっている

complete agreement 完全な合意, 完全な合意事項

complete checking 完全照合

complete discharge 完全な免責

complete liquidation 完全な清算

complete survey 全数調査

complete and accurate 完全かつ正確な, 完全で正確な

◆All insurance policies possessed or owned by the Company together with brief statements of the interest insured are complete and accurate. 本会社が所有または保有しているすべての保険証券とその被保険利益についての簡単な説明は、完全で正確である。

completion of the sale and purchase of ～の売買完了

◆ "Closing" means the completion of the sale and purchase of the Shares pursuant to Section 3 hereof. 「クロージング」とは、本契約第3条に基づく本株式の売買完了を意味する。

compliance （名）承諾, 受諾, 遵守（じゅんしゅ）［順守］, 法令遵守［順守］, 準拠性, 適合,
服従, コンプライアンス

compliance with laws 法の遵守, 法律の遵守, 法令の遵守

compliance with laws, regulations or orders 法律、規則、命令の遵守

◆All goods were produced in compliance with the applicable requirements of the Fair Labor Standards Act. 商品は、すべて米国の公正労働基準法の適用要件に従って生産された。◆The Financial Services Agency issued a business improvement order to the bank on the Banking Law and demanded it implement a fundamental review of compliance and business administration. 金融庁は、同行に対して銀行法に基づく業務改善命令を出し、法令順守と経営管理体制を抜本的に見直すことを求めた。

comply with ～に従う, ～を遵守（じゅんしゅ）する, ～に応じる, ～に同意する, ～に適合する, ～を承諾する

◆Guidelines, instructions and manuals provided under this agreement shall be complied with in full. 本契約に基づいて提供された要領、指示とマニュアルは、全面的に遵守するものとする。◆If the purchaser fails to comply with the above stipulation, the purchaser shall be deemed to have waived such claim. 買い主が上記規定に従わない場合、買い主は当該クレームを放棄したものと見なされるものとする。◆When Washington refuses to comply with the WTO's ruling, the EU will impose retaliatory tariffs on U.S. products. 米国が世界貿易機関（WTO）の決定に従わなかった場合、欧州連合（EU）は米国製品に報復関税を発動する方針だ。

component parts 構成部品

component parts, parts and materials 構成部品、部品と材料

comprehensive partnership agreement 包括的連携協定

◆By starting talks on a comprehensive partnership agreement, the EU and the United States will take the first step toward creating a giant free trade zone that would account for about 50 percent of the world's gross domestic product. 包括的連携協定の交渉を開始することで、欧州連合（EU）と米国は、世界のGDP（国内総生産）の5割近くを占める巨大な自由貿易圏の創設に一歩踏み出すことになる。

compromise （名）和解, 妥協 （動）和解する, 妥協する, 和解で解決する

◆The licensor may, without the licensee's consent, settle or compromise any claim against or consent to the entry of any judgment if such settlement, compromise or judgment involves only the payment of money by the licensor or provides for unconditional release by the claimant or the plaintiff of the licensee from all liability in respect of such claim and does not impose injunctive relief against the licensee. 当該解決、和解または判決がライセンサーによる金員の支払い

だけを伴う場合、または請求人または原告により当該請求に関するすべての責任からライセンシーが無条件で解放されライセンシーに対する差止め命令が下されない場合、ライセンサーは、ライセンシーの同意を得ないで当該請求の解決、和解と判決の執行に同意することができる。

compromise fee 和解金

computer security コンピュータの機密保持, コンピュータの安全性・信頼性の確保, コンピュータ・セキュリティ
◆Calling computer security one of the top problems in the United States, the government is forming special units to prosecute hacking and copyright violation. コンピュータのセキュリティを米国の最重要問題のひとつとして、米政府は現在、ハッキング(不正アクセス)や著作権侵害などを摘発する特別専門班を設置している。

computer software program コンピュータ・ソフトウエア・プログラム
◆ABC has developed, markets and licenses on a worldwide basis and owns all copyrights and other proprietary rights to or has the right to license the computer software programs. ABCは世界市場に向けてコンピュータ・ソフトウエア・プログラムをすでに開発してその販売と使用許諾をしており、このプログラムの著作権その他の所有権をすべて保有するとともに、このプログラムの使用を許諾する権利をもっている。

concerned (形)関係している, 関係のある, 当該の, 心配している, 案じている
◆Under the World Trade Organization rules, emergency import limits, or safeguard, are permitted as a temporary measure if the volume of imports of a certain product drastically increases, causing serious damages to industries concerned in the country. 世界貿易機関(WTO)のルールでは、緊急輸入制限措置(セーフガード)は、特定製品の輸入量が増加して、国内の関係業界に大きな被害が出ている場合には、一時的な措置として認められる。◆We are concerned about the trend of private businesses having difficulties in raising capital. 懸念されるのは、民間企業の資金繰りが悪化していることだ。

concerned provisions of Contract 本契約の関連規定
◆Pursuant to concerned provisions of Contract, all risks of loss or damage to Machines shall be directly transferred from Supplier to Customer. 本契約の関連規定に従って、本機械に関する損失または損害の全危険は、サプライヤーから顧客へ直接移転するものとする。

concession (名)権利, 特権, 免許, 許可, 認可, 譲歩, 割引, 割引料金, 減価, (デパートや映画館などの)売り場, 売店, 販売権, 営業権, 営業スペース, 利権, 権益
a liberal concession 大幅な譲歩
concession contract コンセッション・コントラクト

concession of business 営業免許
concession of tariff 関税譲許
concession shop [stand] 売店
duty [tariff] concession 関税譲許, 関税譲歩 (=concession of tariff)
forest concession 伐採権
make a concession to ～に譲歩する
make some concessions to ～に対していくらか[いくつか、一部]譲歩する
mining concession 鉱山採掘権
offer concessions to ～に割引料金を提供する
oil concession 石油採掘権
oil field concessions 油田の権益
policy concessions 政策面での歩み寄り
price concession 価格の下落
pricing concession 値下げ
production concessions 減産
reciprocal concession 相互互恵
selling concession 販売手数料
tax concession 租税譲許, 税制優遇措置, 減税, 税金の軽減
win major concessions from ～から大きな譲歩を引き出す
◆Our quotations do not allow us any concession. 当社の建て値には、値引きの余地がまったくありません。◆To date, the company's strategy has mainly been to obtain new oil field concessions and then embark on drilling and exploring before commercial production. これまで同社は戦略として、新規油田の権益を取得し、炭鉱・試掘などを経て商業生産することが多かった。

conciliation (名)調停, 斡旋(あっせん), 和解
accept the conciliation plan 斡旋案を受け入れる[受諾する]
conciliation committee of executives representing both parties 両当事者を代表する執行者の調停委員会

conclude (動)(契約や条約を)締結する[結ぶ], 結論を下す, 結論づける, 判断する, 断定する, 推論する, (会議などを)終える, 締めくくる, 完成させる, まとめる
conclude a contract 契約を結ぶ, 契約を締結する
conclude an interim agreement 暫定協定を結ぶ
◆Alarmed by the likelihood that the business environment will become even more severe, the two companies had little leeway in concluding the merger agreement. 経営環境がさらに厳しくなるとの見通しから危機感を強め、両社は合併合意を急がなければならなかった。◆The U.S. Federal Trade Commission (FTC) concluded there was not enough evidence that a Sony-BMG merger would violate U.S. antitrust laws. 米連邦取引委

員会（FTC）は、ソニーとBMG（独複合メディア大手ベルテルスマンの音楽事業部門）の統合が米国の独占禁止法に違反することを示す十分な証拠はない、との結論を下した。

conclude a basic agreement　基本契約を結ぶ，基本契約を締結する，基本合意する
◆Egypt's Morsi administration has concluded a basic agreement with the IMF on loans totaling $4.8 billion, with strings attached, in an effort to avert a default on debts. エジプトのモルシ政権は、債務不履行を回避するため、付帯条件付きで、国際通貨基金（IMF）との間で総額48億ドルの融資を受けることで基本合意した。

conclude a price fixing agreement　価格維持協定を結ぶ
◆France's Competition Commission has ordered Sony, Matsushita and Philips to pay fines for allegedly concluding price-fixing agreements on retail goods with their local distributors. フランスの競争評議会は、国内販売店と小売電気製品の価格維持協定を結んだとして、ソニー、松下電器産業とフィリップスに罰金の支払いを命じた。

conclusion　（名）締結，取決め，結論，決定，調査結果，推論，推断，終わり，終了，結末，終結，決着
a foregone conclusion　必然的結末，必然的結果，既定の結果，予測できる結末，初めから予想することができた結論，確実なこと
bring A to conclusion　Aを終える，Aを終結させる
bring about a speedy conclusion of the case　裁判を迅速に終わらせる
come to [arrive at, reach] the conclusion that　〜という結論に達する
in conclusion　結論として，終わりに，終わりに臨んで，最後に，結論的には
◆Both bilateral and multilateral talks regarding China's merchandise trade are now close to conclusion. 現在、中国のモノの貿易に関しては、二国間交渉も多国間交渉もほぼ終了している。

conclusive evidence　最終的な証拠
◆The date of the bill of lading shall be conclusive evidence of the date of the delivery. 船荷証券の日付は、引渡し日の最終的な証拠とする。

concurrently with　〜と同時に，〜時に
◆Concurrently with the statements required under Article 10, Licensee shall pay to Company the total amount of the running royalty. 第10条に基づいて要求される計算書［報告書］と同時に、ライセンシーは、会社にランニング・ロイヤルティを総額支払わねばならない。◆Licensee shall, concurrently with the royalty payment under subparagraph d) of Article 5, furnish Licensor quarterly with an auditor's statement of the royalty due hereunder for the preceding calendar quarter. ライセンシーは、第5条d）項に基づくロイヤルティの支払いと同時に、直前の暦四半期（四半期）に関して本契約に基づき支払い義務のあるロイ

ヤルティについての監査人の報告書を、四半期ごとにライセンサーに提供する。

condition　（名）条件，制約，前提条件，必要条件，契約条項，規定，状況，状態
condition to the closing　クロージングの条件
conditions of insurance　保険条件
in apparent good order and condition　外見上［外観上］良好な状態で
only on condition that　〜する場合にかぎって
◆The seller expressly disclaims any warranty of conditions, fitness for use or merchantability. 売り主は、状態、用途適合性または商品性の保証を明確に否認する。

conditional upon [on]　〜を条件とする，〜を前提条件とする，〜次第である
（=conditional on）
◆The foregoing warranties are conditional upon the Products being received, unloaded, installed, tested and maintained and operated by ABC in a proper manner. 上記の保証は、本製品をABCが適正な方法で受領、荷揚げ、設置し、試験、維持して運転することを前提条件とする。

conditionally　（形）条件付きで，制限付きで
◆Washington and Brussels will conditionally accept an abolition of subsidies to farmers in the United States and the EU who grow agricultural products for export. 米国や欧州連合（EU）は、それぞれ国内の輸出用農産物栽培農家に対する補助金の撤廃を条件付きで受け入れる方針だ。

conditioned upon　〜を条件とする
（=conditional upon）
◆Payment is not conditioned upon Products meeting any acceptance testing procedures Distributor may have. 支払いは、販売店が行う受入れ検査手続きに本製品が適合することを条件とするものではない。

conduct　（名）行為，行動，遂行，処理
business conduct　事業遂行，業務遂行，業務，営業上の指針
code of conduct　行動規範
conduct of business　事業の遂行，業務遂行
conduct of business rule　業務遂行基準
（=standards of business conduct）
market conduct examination　市場行動検査
◆In the event of any such violation of this Article, the party whose conduct does not violate this Article may, at its sole option, terminate this agreement. このような本条違反の場合、本条に違反していない行為の当事者（本契約に違反する行為をしていない当事者）は、その単独の裁量で本契約を解除することができる。

confer　（動）与える，付与する，授与する，授（さず）ける，協議する，会談する，会議を開く，相談する
confer any rights or remedies upon　〜に権利または救済方法を付与する
confer the benefit of the right upon　〜にこの

権利の利益を付与する

the rights conferred hereunder　本契約に基づいて付与された

◆In the event any such assignment or transfer is attempted without the prior written consent, this agreement and all the rights conferred hereunder shall, at the option of the other party, immediately cease and terminate. 当該譲渡または移転が書面による事前の承諾を得ないで企てられた場合、本契約と本契約に基づいて付与されたすべての権利は、相手方の選択で直ちに終了するものとする。

conference　（名）同盟, 海運同盟, 協議, 会議, 相談, 協議会

conference agreement　同盟規約, 海運規約（海運同盟の基本的事項（同盟の名称・管轄区域、運送対象貨物、同盟の運営方式など）を規定したもの）

conference cargo　同盟貨物

conference line　加盟船会社

conference member　同盟員, 加盟会社

conference member ship　同盟船

conference rate　同盟賃率, 協定運賃率

conference rules and regulations　同盟ルール

conference tariff　同盟運賃表

International Trade Conference　国際貿易会議

non-conference cargo　非同盟貨物

shipping conference　海運同盟, 運賃同盟

confidential disclosure agreement　秘密開示契約（書）, 信頼に基づく開示契約書, 秘密保持協定書

confidential information　秘密情報, 機密情報　（⇒act or failure to act）

obtain confidential information　秘密情報を得る

◆Recipient shall not transfer any confidential information received hereunder or any product made using such confidential information, to any country prohibited from obtaining such data or product by the U.S. Department of Commerce Export Administration Regulations without first obtaining a validated export license. 受領者は、本契約に従って受領した秘密情報またはこの秘密情報を使用して製造した製品を、米国商務省の輸出管理規則により当該データまたは製品の提供が禁止されている国に対して、最初に輸出承認の許可を得ないで譲渡することはないものとする。

confidentiality　秘密保持, 秘密遵守（じゅんしゅ）, 守秘義務, 秘密性

confidentiality agreement　秘密保持契約, 守秘義務合意書

confidentiality contract　秘密保持契約

◆Each party shall take all reasonable steps to ensure the confidentiality of all the confidential information. 各当事者は、すべての秘密情報を維持するため、あらゆる合理的な措置を取るものとする。

confirm　（動）確認する, 確かめる, 認める,

（正式に）承認する, （条約などを）批准する, （決意などを）固める［強める］, 裏づける

be confirmed as　〜として承認される

change or confirm ratings　格付けの変更または確認をする

confirm a renewal　更新を認可する

confirm the reservation　予約を確認する

confirmed credit［L/C］　確認信用状

◆The letter of credit shall be confirmed by and payable at the following bank: 信用状は、下記の銀行が確認して、下記の銀行が支払うものとする。◆The two companies will hold extraordinary shareholders meetings to confirm the takeover. 両社は今後、それぞれ臨時株主総会を開いて、買収案を正式に承認する。◆We are glad to accept your buying offer of March 15. To confirm this business, we are sending our Sales Note No. 120. 貴社の3月15日付け買いオファーを受諾します。この成約を確認するため、当社の売約書第120号をお送りします。◆We confirm our agreement to the contents of the above-written letter. 上記レターの内容に対する当方の同意を確認します。

confirm the order　本注文を確認する, この注文を確認する

◆If you find the terms of payment acceptable, please confirm the order subject to the modifications above. この支払い条件がのめるなら、上記の変更を条件として本注文の確認をお願いします。

confirmation　（名）確認, 承認, 確定, 確証, 裏づけ, 保証, 確認書, 確認状, 注文請け書

confirmation fee　確認料

confirmation note［sheet］　確認書, 確認通知書

confirmation of balance　残高承認, 預金残高承認状

confirmation of L/C　信用状の確認

confirmation of order　注文確認書

confirmation of purchase　買約書

confirmation of sale（s）　売約書

confirmation order　確認指図書

confirmation procedure　確認手続き

confirmation request　確認請求

letter of confirmation　取引確認書, 確認書

subject to confirmation　要確認

trade confirmation　売買確認

◆We accept your offer subject to immediate confirmation by letter. 書簡での至急確認を条件として、貴社のオファーを引き受けます。

confirmed and irrevocable letter of credit　確認済み取消不能信用状

◆Any payment for sale under this agreement shall be made by and under a confirmed and irrevocable letter of credit established through a first class bank who adopts Uniform Customs and Practice for Documentary Credits made by the International Chamber of Commerce. 本契約

に基づく売買に対する支払いは、すべて国際商業会議所が作成した荷為替信用状統一規則を採択している一流銀行が開設する確認済み取消不能信用状で行うものとする。

confiscate （動）押収する、没収する、（財産を）差し押さえる
◆By the instruction of the China Food and Drug Administration, the Shanghai city government suspended operations of Shanghai Husi Food and confiscated raw materials and products at the firm which had sold expired meat products. 中国の国家食品薬品監督管理総局の指示で、上海市は、品質保持期限切れの肉製品を販売していた上海福喜食品の営業を停止し、同社の原料と商品を差し押さえた。

confiscation （名）没収、押収、（財産の）差し押さえ

conflict （名）利害・意見などの衝突、争い、争議、論争、紛争、戦い、戦闘、対立、矛盾、不一致、抵触、葛藤、板ばさみ
conflict field　利害対立分野
conflict of interest［interests］　利害の対立、利害の不一致、利害の抵触、利害の衝突、利益相反、利益相反行為
debt conflicts　債権問題
industrial conflicts　労使紛争、労使闘争
regional conflicts　地域紛争
trade conflict　貿易摩擦、通商摩擦、貿易紛争
without regard to principles of conflicts of laws　法の抵触のルールに関係なく、衝突法に関わりなく
◆Regional conflicts stemming from religious or ethnic animosity, as well as the proliferation of weapons of mass destruction, pose a serious threat to the international community. 宗教や民族の対立が原因の地域紛争や、大量破壊兵器の拡散は、国際社会にとって大きな脅威となっている。

conflict of laws　抵触法、国際私法、州際私法、法の抵触、衝突法
◆This agreement shall be construed in accordance with and governed by the laws of the State of California without reference to principles of conflicts of laws. 本契約は、法の抵触のルールを排除してカリフォルニア州法に従って解釈し、同法に準拠するものとする。

conform to ［with］　～に従う、～に適合する、～に一致する、～に合致する
◆The consolidated financial statements conform in all material respects with International Financial Reporting Standards (IFRSs). 連結財務書類［連結財務諸表］の重要事項は、すべて国際財務報告基準に適合している。

confusingly similar　混同するほど類似している

connection （名）関係、関連、つながり、脈絡、前後関係、縁故、親戚、縁故者、人脈、コネ、取引先、取引業者、接続、連絡、密輸組織、秘密犯罪

組織、麻薬密売人
business connection　取引関係
causal connection　因果関係
economic connections　経済関係
government-business connection　官民一体
have a strong connection with　～と強いコネを持っている
in connection with　～に関連して、～と連携して
international connections　国際的な取引先
personal connections　人脈
trade connections　取引業者
◆The company maintained a long-standing business practice of receiving kickbacks from trade connections. 同社は、取引業者からリベートを取る以前からの商慣行を守り続けた。◆The investment advisory company exploited personal connections with the former bureaucrats to win clients. この投資顧問会社は、顧客開拓に官僚OBの人脈を利用していた。

consecutive （形）連続した (straight)、通しの、論理の一貫した
for a second consecutive year　2年連続で、2年連続の、2年連続
for three consecutive fiscal years　3期連続（=for three straight fiscal years）
for two consecutive quarters　2四半期連続
for two consecutive years　2年連続
◆The said term of this agreement shall be automatically extended for additional consecutive periods of three years each, unless terminated by either party hereto by giving the other party a written notice to that effect at least three months prior to the end of original term of this agreement or any extended term thereof. 本契約の上記期間は、少なくとも本契約の当初期間またはその延長期間が満了する3カ月前までに、本契約の当事者の一方が相手方に対して本契約を終了させる旨の書面による通知をして本契約を終了させないかぎり、さらに引き続き3年間ずつ自動的に延長するものとする。

consensus （名）合意、総意、同意、一致した意見、意見の一致、大多数の意見、コンセンサス
consensus document　合意文書
reach a consensus　合意に達する、合意を得る
◆The World Trade Organization has a long way to go before it can reach a consensus on a new set of rules governing free trade. 世界貿易機関（WTO）が貿易自由化の新ルールに関して合意が得られるまでの道のりは、まだまだ遠い。◆Tokyo, Taipei and Washington failed to reach a consensus about how to resolve the dispute over the EU's high tariffs on IT equipment imports. EUの情報技術 (IT) 機器輸入に対する高関税をめぐる紛争の解決法に関して、日本、台湾と米国は合意に達しなかった。

consent （動）同意する，承諾する，承認する

consent （名）同意，承諾，承認，合意，意見の一致，許可，同意書

with prior written consent of　～の書面による事前の承諾を得て，～の書面による事前の同意を得た上で

◆The nonassigning party's consent shall not be unreasonably withheld. 非譲渡人の同意は，不当に保留してはならない。◆This agreement may be terminated at any time upon written consent of all of the Parties hereto. 本契約は，本契約当事者全員の書面による合意が得られたときはいつでも解除することができる。

consent to　～に同意する，～を承諾する

consent to and confer nonexclusive jurisdiction 非専属管轄権に服する，非専属裁判管轄に服する

（=submit to nonexclusive jurisdiction）

◆ABC hereby consents to such assignment and agrees for the benefit of XYZ to be bound by such terms and provisions. ABCは，ここに当該譲渡に同意し，XYZの利益のためにこのような条件と規定に拘束されることに同意する。

consents, approvals, authorizations and other requirements　同意・承認・許可とその他の要件，同意・承認・許可その他の要求事項

◆All consents, approvals, authorizations and other requirements prescribed by any law, rule or regulation which must be obtained or satisfied by Purchaser in order to permit the consummation of the transactions contemplated by this agreement have been, or will have been as of the Closing Date, obtained and satisfied. 本契約により企図された取引を完了させるため，買い主が得なければならない同意，承認，許可と買い主が満たさなければならない法律や法令，法規で定められているその他の要件は，すべて取得済みで満たされているか，クロージング日までに取得するか満たされていなければならない。

consequential （形）結果として起こる

（consequent），当然の，必然的な，重要な，重大な，間接的な，間接の

consequential damage　間接的の損害，間接損害

consequential import　誘発的の輸入

（=induced import）

consequential loss　（生産を妨害されたための）間接的損害，間接的の損害

consequential loss insurance　間接（的）損害保険

consequential or indirect loss　間接損害

◆The seller shall not be liable for any indirect or consequential damages. 売り主は，間接的の損害の責任は一切負わないものとする。

consideration （名）約因，対価，報酬，代金，条件，要件，考慮　（⇒in consideration for）

as consideration for the services rendered

pursuant to this agreement　本契約に従って提供されたサービスの対価として

good consideration　有効な約因

money consideration　金銭上の約因

sufficient consideration　十分な約因，有効な約因

without consideration　無償で

◆NOW, THEREFORE, in consideration of the promises herein contained and other good consideration, the parties hereto do hereby agree as follows: そこで，本契約に定める約束ごとと他の有効な約因を対価として，両当事者はここに以下のとおり合意する。◆The seller shall not be liable in respect of any warranty or consideration as to quality or fitness which would arise by implication of law. 売り主は，法律の運用により生じる品質または適合性に関する保証または条件については，責任を負わないものとする。

consignee （名）荷受け人，受託販売者，受託者

◆It is necessary to write the name of notify party on the order B/L as it does not contain the name of consignee. 指図人式船荷証券には，荷受け人名が記載されていないので，通知先名を書かなければならない。

consignment （名）委託，委託販売，委託販売品，託送，託送貨物，積送品，運送品，委託品，注文の品，積み荷

air consignment note　航空運送状

consignment agreement　委託販売契約

consignment buying　委託購入，委託仕入れ

consignment deal　委託販売貿易

consignment distributor　委託販売業者

consignment fee　委託手数料

consignment flotation　委託募集

consignment goods　委託販売品，委託品，積送品　（=goods on consignment）

consignment guarantee money　委託保証金，委託証拠金

consignment import　委託輸入

consignment-in　受託販売

consignment inventories　積送品

consignment invoice　委託品送り状，委託販売送り状［インボイス］

consignment inward　受託品，販売受託，受託販売

consignment note　（鉄道の）出荷通知書，委託貨物運送状，航空運送状（air consignment note），受託書

consignment outward　積送品

consignment purchase　委託買付け，買付け委託

consignment sale(s)　委託販売

（=consignment selling［trade］, sale on

consignment）

consignment sheet　貨物引換え証

consignment with limit　制限委託品

consignments in　受託品

consignments out　委託品

export on consignment　委託販売輸出

foreign trade on a consignment basis　委託販売貿易

goods on consignment　積送品

goods on consignment-in　受託品

goods on consignment-out　委託品

limited consignment　指し値付き委託販売品

on consignment　委託販売（契約）で
　（=on a consignment basis）

products on consignment　委託品

reciprocal consignment　相互委託販売

sale on consignment　委託販売
　（=consignment sale, selling on a
　consignment basis）

sell on consignment through　〜を通して委託販売する

◆This consignment had to be shortshipped as part of it was badly damaged.　この積み荷に積み残しが出たのは、積み荷の一部がひどく破損したからです。

consist of　〜で構成される、〜から成る

consolidated　(形)整理統合した、統合した、一本化した、一元化した、連結対象の、連結した、連結ベースの、連結決算の

consolidated accounts　連結決算
　（consolidated accounting period figures），連結財務書類（consolidated financial statements, group accounts），連結財務諸表

consolidated accounts for the business year to March 31　3月期の連結決算

consolidated accounts for the six-month period through March next year　下半期（10月〜来年3月）の連結決算

◆The revision of the firm's assumed exchange rate will translate into an additional ¥150 billion loss in its consolidated accounts for the six-month period through March 2015.　同社の想定為替レートの修正に伴って、同社の2014年度下半期（2014年10月〜2015年3月）の連結決算では、追加で1,500億円の為替差損が生じることになる。

consolidated financial statements　連結財務書類、連結財務諸表、連結決算

◆Olympus Corp. inflated the goodwill value of its British subsidiary by 33.4 billion in the consolidated financial statements.　オリンパスは、英子会社の「のれん代」を連結決算で334億円水増ししていた。◆The consolidated financial statements conform in all material respects with International Financial Reporting Standards（IFRSs）.

連結財務書類［連結財務諸表］の重要事項は、すべて国際財務報告基準に適合している。

consolidated operating profit estimates　連結営業利益予想

◆Toyota revised upward its consolidated operating profit estimates for the business year ending March 31, 2013, largely due to improved profitability in its exports from a weakening of the yen in response to "Abenomics," the economic policy of the Abe administration.　トヨタは2013年3月期決算［2013年3月31日終了事業年度］の連結営業利益予想［連結業績予想］を上方修正したが、これは主に安倍政権の経済政策「アベノミクス」を好感しての円安で、輸出の採算が向上しているためだ。・

consolidated revenues　連結売上高、連結収益（親会社と子会社とで構成されている連結企業グループ全体としての売上高［収益］のこと）

◆The greater part of the consolidated revenues and assets of the company is denominated in U.S. dollars.　同社の連結売上高と連結資産の大半は、米ドル建てとなっている。

consolidated settlement of accounts　連結決算　（=consolidated results）

◆On the back of increased demand for travel, East Japan Railway Co.　posted a record high profit in its consolidated settlement of accounts for the business year ending March 2014.　旅行需要の増大を背景に、JR東日本は、2014年3月期連結決算で過去最高益となった。

constitute　(動)構成する、〜の構成要素となる（make up），（部分が集まって）〜になる、〜に等しい、〜に当たる、設立する、設置する、制定する、（役職に）任命する

◆At least sixty days prior to the requested delivery date, the buyer shall provide the seller with a written estimate of its requirements of the product, which shall constitute a firm order.　希望渡し日から少なくとも60日前に、買い主は、本製品の需要予測書［需要見積り書］を売り主に提出し、これを確定注文とするものとする。◆The execution and performance of this agreement by Seller constitute legal, valid and binding obligations of Seller, enforceable in accordance with the terms hereof.　売り主による本契約の締結と履行は、本契約の条件に従って強制することができる法的、有効かつ拘束力のある売り主の義務を構成する。

constitute a breach of this agreement　本契約違反となる、本契約の違反を構成する

◆Any failure, whether willful, through neglect or otherwise, of either party to perform or fulfill any of its duties, obligations or covenants in this agreement shall constitute a breach of this agreement.　故意であれ、怠慢またはその他によるものであれ、本契約における各当事者の責務、義務または約束ごとを各当事者が履行または達成できない場合、これは本契約の違反を構成するものとする。

constitute a continuing waiver of　〜に関

する継続的権利放棄となる, 〜に関する継続的権利放棄を構成する
◆No waiver by either party, whether expressed or implied, of any provision of this agreement, or of any breach or default, shall constitute a continuing waiver of such breach or default of such provision of this agreement. 明示・黙示を問わず本契約の規定または契約違反もしくは債務不履行に関する一方の当事者の権利放棄は、当該契約違反または本契約の当該規定の債務不履行に関する継続的権利放棄を構成しないものとする。

constitute a default of this agreement　本契約違反となる
◆Failure by Distributor to sell the minimum quota for any given period set forth in Exhibit B will constitute a default of this agreement by Distributor. 販売店が付属書類Bに記載する一定期間の最低割当量を販売できなかった場合には、販売店による本契約違反となる。

constitute a material breach　重大な違反に当たる, 重大違反になる
◆These are material omissions which in our view constitute another material breach. これらは重大な遺漏で、われわれの考えでは、もう一つの重大な違反に当たる。

constitute an event of default　不履行事由となる
◆It shall constitute an event of default if either party is the subject of any proceeding relating its liquidation or insolvency which is not dismissed within 30 days. いずれかの当事者が清算または支払い不能手続きの対象となり、当該手続きが30日以内に取り下げられないときは、不履行事由となる。

construction　(名)建設, 建築, 建造, 建設工事, 工事, 構造, 構文, 構成, 組立て, 建造物, 構築物, (契約や条項の)解釈, 意味(「解釈」の意味の動詞はconstrue。⇒construe)
advance on construction　建設工事前渡し金
construction and erection contract　建設・据え付け契約
construction and performance　解釈と履行
Construction Business Law　建設業法
construction contract　建設契約, 建設工事請負契約, 請負工事契約, 工事契約
construction in progress　建設仮勘定, 未成工事支出金　(=construction in process)
construction loan　建設借入金, 建設融資, 建設ローン
construction material supplier　建材メーカー
construction of completion　完成工事高
construction of cost　原価構成
construction or interpretation　解釈
construction project　建設工事
construction revenue　工事収益
　(=construction in progress)

construction-type contract　請負工事契約
construction work account receivable　建設工事未収金
estimated cost of construction work　見積り工事原価
public construction　公共工事
put a different construction on　〜を別の[異なった]意味で解釈する
put a good construction on　〜を善意に解釈する
◆At some of the petrochemical factories which are under construction, ethylene and other materials will be produced from natural gas. 現在建設中の石油化学(関連)工場の一部では、天然ガスからエチレンなどを生産することになっている。
◆The Bank of Tokyo-Mitsubishi UFJ will work together with foreign banks to extend 117 million Canadian dollars in joint loans to a mega solar power plant construction. 三菱東京UFJ銀行は、外銀数行の主幹事銀行として、カナダの大型太陽光発電所(メガソーラー)建設事業に1億1,700万カナダ・ドルを協調融資する。◆This agreement shall not be construed for or against any party based on any rule of construction who prepared the agreement. 本契約は、どちらの当事者が本契約書の起草をしたかによる解釈のルールに基づいて、一方の当事者に有利に解釈したり不利に解釈したりしないものとする。

construction and performance　解釈と履行
◆The construction and performance of this agreement shall be governed by the laws of Japan. 本契約の解釈と履行は、日本の法律に準拠する(本契約の解釈と履行には、日本法が適用される)。

construe　(動)解釈する　(=interpret)
be construed for or against　〜に有利に解釈されたり不利に解釈されたりする　(⇒construction)
be construed in accordance with　〜に従って解釈する
◆Nothing contained in this agreement shall be construed so as to require the commission of any act contrary to statute or law. 本契約に定めるいずれの規定も、制定法または法律に反する行為の実行を要求するものとは解釈しないものとする。◆This agreement shall be construed in accordance with and governed by the laws of the State of California without reference to principles of conflicts of laws. 本契約は、法の抵触のルールを排除してカリフォルニア州法に従って解釈し、同法に準拠するものとする。

consular　(形)領事の, 領事職の, 執政の, 執政官の, コンシュラー
consular agent　領事代理
consular fee　領事査証料, 領事手数料
consular invoice　領事送り状, 領事証明送り

状, コンシュラー・インボイス

consulting agreement コンサルティング契約

consumer (名)消費者, (車などの)ユーザー, コンシューマー
- consumer administration 消費者行政
- consumer (advice) center 消費者センター
- consumer awareness 消費者認知度
- consumer boom 消費ブーム (=consumption boom)
- consumer boycott 消費者不買運動, 不買運動
- Consumer Contract Law 消費者契約法
- consumer demand 消費需要, 個人消費
- consumer industry 消費財産業
- consumer movement 消費者運動
- consumer preference 消費者選好
- consumer price survey 消費者物価調査
- consumer product 消費者製品, 消費財, 民生用製品, 民生機器
- Consumer Product Safety Act 消費者製品安全法
- Consumer Product Safety Commission 消費者製品安全委員会, CPSA
- Consumer Protection Act 消費者保護法
- consumer purchases research 消費者購買調査
- consumer research 消費者需要調査, 消費者調査
- consumer resistance 消費者の購買拒否, 消費者拒否, 消費者不買運動 (=sales resistance)
- consumer rights 消費者の権利
- consumer safety 消費者の安全
- consumer satisfaction 消費者の満足
- consumer society 消費社会, 消費者中心社会
- consumer sovereignty 消費者主権
- consumer spending 消費者支出, 個人消費
- consumer staples 生活用品, 生活必需品
- consumer traffic 来店者数
- consumer trend 消費動向
- consumers' attitude 消費者意識
- consumer's choice 消費者選択
- Consumers Union 全米消費者同盟
- U.S. Consumer Financial Protection Bureau 米消費者金融保護局

◆Sharp Corp. intends to augment its home electronics business in Middle Eastern and African countries by introducing a series of luxury products to cater to increased demand from wealthy consumers. シャープは、高級家電を相次いで投入して、中東・アフリカ諸国の家電事業を強化し、増加する富裕層の需要に応える方針だ。◆The new tariff on beef imports favors producers rather than consumers. 牛肉の輸入に対する新関税は、消費

者ではなく生産者寄りの対応だ。◆To inflate the number of Facebook "Likes" and Twitter followers is the same as stealth marketing which misleads consumers. フェイスブック (FB) の「いいね！」やツイッターのフォロワー (閲覧者) の数の水増しは、消費者を誤認させるステルス・マーケティングと同じである。

Consumer affairs Agency 消費者庁
◆As stealth marketing by postings is problematic, the Consumer Affairs Agency has revised its guidelines for online transactions under the Law for the Prevention of Unreasonable Premiums and Misrepresentations concerning Products and Services. 書き込みによるステルス・マーケティングには問題があるので、消費者庁は、「景品表示法 (不当景品類及び不当表示防止法)」のネット取引に関する指針を改正した。

consumer loan 消費者金融, 消費者ローン
◆Many of the investors took out consumer loans to pay contract fees. 出資者の多くは、消費者金融から金を借りて契約料を支払った。

consumer market 消費者市場, 消費市場
◆Mexico with a population of more than 100 million represents a huge consumer market. 人口が1億人を超すメキシコは、巨大な消費市場だ。

consumer protection 消費者保護
◆The U.S. Federal Trade Commission exercises jurisdiction over matters including consumer protection issues in the United States. 米連邦取引委員会 (FTC) は、米国消費者保護などの問題を管轄している。

consummate the transactions 取引を完了する
◆Purchaser has all requisite corporate powers and authority to enter into this agreement and to consummate the transactions contemplated hereby. 買い主は、本契約を締結する上で必要な会社法上の権能・権限と、本契約により企図されている取引を完了するのに必要な権能・権限をすべて持っている。

consummation of the transactions 取引の完了, 取引の実行
◆The execution of this agreement and the consummation of the transactions contemplated hereby will not result in a breach of any of the terms or provisions of, or constitute a default under, any agreement, or other instrument to which Purchaser is a party or by which it is bound. 本契約の締結 (本契約書の作成) と本契約により企図されている取引の完了は、買い主が当事者となっているまたは当事者が拘束される契約書その他の証書のいかなる条項にも違反せず、またその不履行にもならないものとする。

consumption (名)消費, 個人消費, 消費量, 消費高, 消費額, 消費支出, 消耗, 減耗, 肺結核

consumption tax 消費税
◆The prices of Audi's all-new Q5 sport-utility vehicle range from ￥5.79 million to ￥6.37 mil-

lion〔consumption tax included〕, and it passed
the benefits of the strong yen on to consumers
by making high-grade aluminum wheels and car
navigation systems standard features. 独アウディ
の全面改良したスポーツ用多目的車（SUV）「Q5」の
価格は、579万〜637万円（消費税込み）で、高級ア
ルミホイールや高性能カーナビゲーションを標準
装備して、円高差益を消費者に還元した。

contact （名）接触, 交流, 連絡, つて, コネ, 関
係, 協議

business contact 取引関係, 仕事上つながり
のある相手

come into〔in〕contact with ～と触れる、～
と接触する、～に触れる

contact a person under separate cover 別途連
絡する

contact employee 得意先係

contact information 連絡先の情報

contact name 担当者名

contact number 連絡先の番号

contact person 窓口, 担当者

contact person responsible for inquiries お問
い合わせの窓口

contact with oil and other cargo 油、他貨物と
の接触損害, COOC

get in contact with ～と連絡を取る

high-level contacts 高官級協議

human contact 人的交流

◆Major financial groups do not have regular
business contacts with small and medium-sized
auto parts makers. 大手金融機関は、中小の自動
車部品メーカーと通常の取引関係がない。

contain （動）抑える, 抑え込む, 抑制する, 阻
止する, 封じ込める, 歯止めをかける, 削減す
る, 含む, 盛り込む, 取り込む, 書き込む, 記載
する, 収容する, ～に等しい

contain costs 経費を削減する

contain inflation インフレを抑える

contain margin erosion 利益率の低下に歯止
めをかける

contain the debt crisis in Greece ギリシャの
債務危機を封じ込める〔抑え込む〕

contain the financial crisis 金融危機を封じ込
める

contain upward price pressures 物価上昇圧力
を抑える

contained herein 本契約に定める, 本契約書
に規定する, 本契約書に記載する, 本契約に
含む

◆It is necessary to write the name of notify party
on the order B/L as it does not contain the name
of consignee. 指図人式船荷証券には、荷受け人名が
記載されていないので、通知先名を書かなければな
らない。◆Japan, the United States and emerging
countries are upping their pressure on Europe to
contain the Greek-triggered sovereign debt crisis. 日米と新興国は、欧州に対して、ギリシャに
端を発したソブリン危機（政府債務危機）封じ込め
の圧力を強めている。◆NOW, THEREFORE, in
consideration of the promises herein contained
and other good consideration, the parties hereto
do hereby agree as follows: そこで、本契約に定
める約束ごとと他の有効な約因として、両
当事者はここに以下のとおり合意する。

container （名）容器, コンテナ〔コンテナー〕

a container load of コンテナ1個分の～

bulk container ばら積み用コンテナ, バルク・
コンテナ

Container and Packaging Recycling Law 包
装・容器リサイクル法

container base コンテナ・ベース（混載貨物
の取扱いや通関業務を行うためのターミナ
ル）

container B/L コンテナ船荷証券
（＝container bill of lading）

container car コンテナ積載用貨車, コンテナ
車（＝container train）

container certificate コンテナ詰め報告書

container crane コンテナ起重機

container depot コンテナ集積所, コンテナ置
き場, コンテナ倉庫

container freight station コンテナ・フレー
ト・ステーション, コンテナ詰め貨物荷捌
（さば）き所, CFS

container handling charge コンテナ取扱い料

container insurance コンテナ保険

container interchange agreement コンテナ相
互交換協定

container lease system コンテナ賃貸制度, コ
ンテナ・リース制度

container liner 定期コンテナ船

container list 積卸しコンテナ一覧表

container load cargo コンテナ貨物, CL貨物

container load plan コンテナ内積付け書,
CLP

container loading list コンテナ船積み表

container on flat car コンテナ・オン・フラッ
ト・カー（鉄道台車にフォークリフトなど
でコンテナを積み込んで輸送する方式）

container operator コンテナ・オペレーター

container port コンテナ港

container rules コンテナ輸送規則

container seal コンテナ・シール

container service charge コンテナ・サービ
ス・チャージ

container ship コンテナ船

container shipping コンテナ輸送

container system コンテナ輸送方式

container terminal コンテナ・ターミナル

container trade terms　コンテナ貿易条件

container traffic　コンテナ輸送

container unloading list　コンテナ陸揚げ表

container yard　コンテナ・ヤード, コンテナ集積埠頭, CY

convertible container ship　コンテナ兼用船

dry cargo container　乾貨物用コンテナ

empty container　空コンテナ

flat rack container　フラット・ラック・コンテナ

flexible freight container　フレキシブル・フレート・コンテナ

folding container　折りたたみ式コンテナ

freight container　海上コンテナ

full container ship［vessel］　コンテナ専用船

gross weight of container　海上コンテナの陸送重量

insulated container　断熱コンテナ

insulated produce container　保冷コンテナ

large size container　大型コンテナ

less than container load cargo　小口混載貨物, 1コンテナに満たないLCL貨物, コンテナ未満貨物

liquid bulk container　液体用バルク・コンテナ

marine container　海上コンテナ

pallet in container　パレット・イン・コンテナ

reefer container　冷凍・冷蔵コンテナ

refrigerated container　冷凍コンテナ

solid bulk container　粉体用バルク・コンテナ

tank container　液体用コンテナ

ventilated container　通風コンテナ

containerizable cargo　コンテナ貨物

containerization　(名)コンテナ化, コンテナリゼーション

contemplate　(動)企図する, 意図する
◆Commencing on the date of this agreement until the Closing, Buyer shall be permitted to perform such due diligence investigation related to the transactions contemplated by this agreement as Buyer deems necessary and appropriate in its discretion. 本契約締結日からクロージングまで, 買い主は, 本契約で意図されている取引に関して買い主が買い主の判断で必要かつ適切と考えるデュー・ディリジェンス調査を行うことができるものとする。◆The closing of the transactions contemplated in this agreement shall be held at 10:00 a. m. at the office of ABC Law Firm on August 1, 2003. 本契約で企図している取引のクロージングは, 2003年8月1日, ABC法律事務所の事務所で午前10時から開催する。

contemplated hereby　本契約により企図［意図］されている, 本契約で意図している,

本契約の目的である
◆Purchaser has all requisite corporate powers and authority to enter into this agreement and to consummate the transactions contemplated hereby. 買い主は, 本契約を締結する上で必要な会社法上の権能・権限と, 本契約により企図されている取引を完了するのに必要な権能・権限をすべて持っている。

content　(名)情報・情報サービスの内容, 情報の中身, 情報, 趣旨, 要旨, 著作物, ラジオやテレビの番組, 番組の内容, 事業, 収入源, 含有量, 容量, 容積, 体積, 面積, 広さ, 産出量, 満足, コンテンツ　(⇒local content)

content partnership　コンテンツ提携

content production　コンテンツ作成, コンテンツの制作　(=production of content)

content provider　出店企業, コンテンツ・プロバイダー

contents note　包装の内容一覧表

contents unknown clause　内容不知条項

domestic content　国内部品調達比率, ドメスティック・コンテント

export content　輸出含有量

import content　輸入含有量

multimedia contents　マルチメディア・コンテンツ

popular content　有力なコンテンツ(情報の内容)

regulation of illegal and harmful contents　違法有害コンテンツ規制

resource content　資源含有量

service contents　サービス・コンテンツ

streaming contents　ストリーミング・コンテンツ

Web contents　ウェブ上の著作物, ウェブ・コンテンツ　(=Web content)

Web page content　ホームページの情報内容, ホームページの内容　(=home page content)
◆We confirm our agreement to the contents of the above-written letter. 上記レターの内容に対する当方の同意を確認します。

content industry　コンテンツ(情報の内容)産業
◆The cornerstone of the Cool Japan initiative aimed at promoting the exports of Japanese pop culture is the content industry which produces anime, video games and movies. 日本独自の文化産業の輸出促進を目指すクール・ジャパン構想の核は, アニメやビデオ・ゲーム, 映画などの製作にかかわるコンテンツ産業だ。

contest　(名)競争, 争い, 論争, 闘争, 抗争, 係争　(動)反論する, 異議を申し立てる, 無効であると主張する, 争う, 競争する, 論争する
◆Licensee agrees not to contest, nor to aid others in contesting, directly or indirectly, during the

context （名）文脈, 前後関係

◆In this Agreement, the following words and expressions shall, unless the context otherwise requires, have the following meanings. 本契約で、次の語句と表現は、文脈上、別段の意味を必要としないかぎり、次の意味を持つものとする。

contingency fee 成功報酬 （=contingent fee）

◆After new medicines are put on the market, Takeda will pay contingency fees to Kirin depending on worldwide sales. 新薬が市場に出された後（製品化された後）、武田は全世界での売上高に応じてキリンに対して成功報酬を支払うことになっている。

contingency fee system 成功報酬制（米国法律事務所の弁護士報酬基準のひとつ）

continuation of the Agreement 本契約の継続

◆As one of the main conditions prerequisite to the continuation of the Agreement, Distributor agrees to purchase the Products from Exporter in the quantity not less than 500 units for any contract year throughout the effective term of this Agreement. 本契約の継続に不可欠な主要条件の一つとして、販売店は、本契約の有効期間中、契約年に500台以上の数量の本製品を輸出者から購入することに同意する。

continue in effect for a period of 〜の間有効とする

◆The term of this agreement shall continue in effect for a period of seven years to and including March 31, 2020. 本契約の有効期間は、2020年3月31日までの7年間とする。

continue to and through 〜まで存続する

◆This agreement shall continue to and through April 30, 2018. 本契約は、2018年4月30日まで存続する。

continuing waiver 継続的権利放棄
（⇒constitute a continuing waiver of）

contraband （形）密輸による, 輸出入禁止の （名）禁制品

contraband goods 密輸品, 輸出入禁制品

contraband of import 輸入禁制品

non-contraband goods 輸出入非禁制品

◆The Catch-all or End-use Controls ban the exports of certain non-contraband goods. キャッチオール規制は、一部の輸出入非禁制品の輸出を禁止している。

contract （動）契約する, 契約などを結ぶ, 請け負う, 感染する

◆We contract interest rate swap contracts to manage our exposure to changes in interest rates and lower our overall costs of financing. 当社は、金利変動リスクに対処する目的と当社全体の資金調達コストを低減する目的で、金利スワップ契約を結んでいます。

contract （名）契約, 契約書, 規約, 協定, 協定書, 請負, 契約商品, 契約品, 約定品

accumulated contract costs incurred 契約原価発生累積額

agency contract 代理店契約

annul a contract 契約を無効とする, 契約を取り消す

assignment of contract 契約の譲渡

balance of buying contract 買い予約残高

be under contract 契約を結んでいる

bilateral contract 双務契約, 双方的契約（片務契約 = unilateral contract）

bilateral technology supply contract 技術交換契約

building contract 建築請負

business cooperation contract 提携契約

business tie-up contract 業務提携契約

buyer-seller contract 売買契約

buying contract 買い予約, 輸出予約

collective contract 労働協約

commodity contract 商品契約

completed contract method 工事完成基準

conclude a contract 契約を結ぶ, 契約を締結する

construction contract 建設契約, 建設工事請負契約, 請負工事契約, 工事契約

constructive contract 法定契約, 準契約

contract at completion 完成時契約

contract basis 契約条件

contract cancellation 契約の解除, 解約

contract charge 契約手数料

contract commencement date 契約開始日

contract document 契約書

contract for consignment of credits guaranty 保証委託契約

contract for the supply of a service サービス提供契約, 役務提供契約

contract in 正式に参加の契約をする, 参加契約する

contract manufacturing 契約製造, 委託製造

contract not fulfilled 契約不履行

contract of affreightment 個別運送契約

contract of continuous buying and selling 継続的売買契約

contract of granting credit 信用供与契約

contract of guarantee 保証契約

contract out　正式に不参加を表明する，契約や協約などから脱退する，下請に仕事を出す
contract-out　契約破棄，適用除外，拠出免除
contract policy　契約保険証券
contract production　委託生産
contract rate system　契約運賃制
contract renewal　契約更新
contract sheet　売買契約書，契約書
contract shipper　契約荷主
contract size　取引単位
contract supplies　契約供給品
contract termination　契約終了
contract to sell　売買契約
contract with a user　利用者契約
contract/confirmation note　売買報告書
correspondent contract　コルレス契約
covering contract　買戻し契約
deed of contract　契約書
deferred payment contract　延払い契約
enter into a contract with　～と契約する
exclusive dealing contract　排他的取引契約
execute a contract　契約を履行する，契約を実行する
export contract　輸出契約
export contract sheet　輸出契約書
fiduciary contract　信用契約
firm contract　確定契約
form a contract　契約を結ぶ，契約を締結する
formal contract　正式契約
forward contract　先物契約，先物予約，延べ取引
forward exchange contract　為替予約
forward supply contract　先物注文契約
freight contract　貨物運送契約，運送契約
futures contract　先物為替予約，先物契約
group insurance contract　団体保険契約
hire-purchase contract　割賦払い契約
import contract　輸入契約
life insurance contract　生命保険契約
loan contract　融資契約，貸付け契約
long term contract　長期請負契約，長期工事契約
　　(=long-term contract work in progress)
make a contract with　～と契約する
marine insurance contract　海上保険契約
master contract　基本契約
new contract　新規契約
open account　暫定契約，先渡し契約，清算勘定 (2国間協定貿易の決済方法)，当座預金，当座勘定，与信取引勘定，与信取引先
plant export contract　プラント輸出契約
price contract　価格契約
reinsurance contract　再保険契約
renew a contract　契約を更新する
sales contract　売買契約，売り契約書
supply contract　供給契約
system contract　システム契約
temporary contract　仮契約　(=provisional contract)
uncompleted contract　未成工事
win a contract　契約を取る，契約を獲得する，受注する
◆Domestic nonlife insurance companies usually renew contracts with most of their corporate clients each April. 国内の損保各社は通常，毎年4月に大半の顧客企業と(保険)契約の更新を行っている。◆Each individual contract for the sale of Products formed by Distributor's submission of orders to Supplier shall be subject to this agreement. 販売店が供給者に注文書を提出することによって締結される本製品の個別の販売契約は，それぞれ本契約に従うものとする。◆It is an entrenched bidding structure that allows irregularities such as influence-wielding, bid-rigging and subcontracting entire public works contracts. 口利きや談合，公共事業の丸投げなどの不正行為を許しているのは，旧態依然とした入札の構造だ。◆It is unlikely that any contracts will be executed. 契約が実行される見通しはない。◆Sharp Corp. aims to get contracts to provide large number of IGZO liquid-crystal panels for such products as Apple Inc.'s iPhone and ultrathin PCs developed under the initiative of Intel Corp. シャープは，米アップル社のスマートフォン(高機能携帯電話)「アイフォン(iPhone)」や，米半導体大手インテルの主導で開発される超薄型パソコンなどの製品への液晶パネル「イグゾー」の大量供給契約の獲得を目指している。◆The L/C shall be available for at least fifteen days after the latest date for shipment stipulated in the contract. 信用状は，本契約指定の積み期の後，少なくとも15日間は有効とする。

contract fee　契約料
◆Many of the investors took out consumer loans to pay contract fees. 出資者の多くは，消費者金融から金を借りて契約料を支払った。

contract in process　未成工事
◆Contracts in process are stated at costs incurred plus estimated profit less amounts billed to customers and advances and progress payments received. 未成工事は，発生原価と見積り利益の合計から得意先への請求額と前受金および契約工事の出来高に応じた入金額を控除して表示されています。

contract number　契約番号
◆The Buyer shall notify the Seller of the name of the carrying vessel, the estimated date of loading

and the contract number for the Seller to effect delivery, at least seven (7) days before the estimated date of arrival of the vessel at the port of shipment. 買い主は、少なくとも本船の船積み港への到着予定日の7日前までに、本船の船名、船積み予定日と売り主が引渡しを行う契約番号を、売り主に通知するものとする。

C **contract winner** 元請業者, 契約獲得企業, 受注者
◆The governor is believed to have instructed a contract winner of a public works project to include a firm that had offered him bribes among its subcontractors. この知事は、贈賄業者を公共事業の元請業者の下請け業者に入れるよう元請業者に指示したとされている。

contract worker 契約社員
◆Under the company's new policy, all full-time employees in managerial posts aged 45 and above were forced to become contract workers. 会社の新方針で、45歳以上の管理職の正社員は全員、契約社員にさせられた。

contract year 契約年, 契約年度, 契約期間
◆As one of the main conditions prerequisite to the continuation of the Agreement, Distributor agrees to purchase the Products from Exporter in the quantity not less than 500 units for any contract year throughout the effective term of this Agreement. 本契約の継続に不可欠な主要条件の一つとして、販売店は、本契約の有効期間中、契約年に500台以上の数量の本製品を輸出者から購入することに同意する。

contracted quantity 契約数量
◆Quantity is subject to a variation of 5% more or less than the contracted quantity at Seller's option unless otherwise specified. 数量は、他にとくに明記しないかぎり、売り主の裁量で契約数量より5%増減の変動が生じることがある。

contracted time limit 契約期限
◆Company shall maintain sufficient stocks of Products so that Company can ship within the contracted time limit of shipment whenever an order for Products is obtained from Distributor. 代理店から本製品[契約品]の注文を受けたときはいつでも、会社が船積みの契約期限内に船積みできるよう、会社は本製品(契約品)の在庫を十分保持しておくものとする。

contractor (名)契約当事者, 契約者, 契約荷主, 工事請負人, 請負人, 請負業者, コントラクター
◆The Contractor hereby guarantees that all materials and equipment furnished by and workmanship performed by the Contractor, its subcontractors and vendors shall be of first quality for the grades specified and free from defects or faults, and suitable for the respective uses intended. If any failures to conform to the foregoing guarantees are found within a period of twelve (12) months from the date on which the Take-Over Test is successfully completed (excepting, however, the results of ordinary wear, corrosion and erosion, or improper operation after the Owner takes over the Plant), the Owner shall promptly notify the Contractor thereof in writing, and the Contractor shall thereupon make all alterations, adjustments, repairs, and, if necessary, replacements to make the Plant and all materials, equipment and workmanship therein conform to the guarantees herein specified. [訳例]工事請負業者[工事請負人、契約者]は、本契約により、工事請負業者とその下請業者、機材納入業者が供給するすべての資材[材料]、設備と施工の仕上がりは、規定の等級に関して最高品質のもので、瑕疵(かし)・欠陥もなく、発注者[施主]が計画・意図したそれぞれの用途に適合することを保証する。「引渡し検査」が無事[首尾よく]完了した日から12か月間以内に当該保証に適合しないものが確認された[見つかった、判明した、発見された]場合(ただし、発注者[施主]が本プラントの引渡しを受けてから通常の磨耗、腐食、浸食作用や不適切な操作の結果として生じたものは除く)、発注者[施主]は即時に書面で工事請負業者にその旨を通知することとし、工事請負業者はそれに関する改変、調整、補修をすべて行うほか、必要に応じて取替えを実施して、本プラントとその資材・設備および仕上がりがすべて本契約書に定める保証事項に適合するようにするものとする。

contractual (形)契約の, 契約上の, 請負上の, 契約で取り決めた, 契約で保証された
contractual agreement 契約上の取決め, 契約上の規定, 契約上の責務
contractual interest rate 約定金利
contractual lending commitment 貸出予約, 契約に基づく貸出義務
contractual life 契約期間
contractual obligation 契約上の義務, 契約義務
contractual payment 債務の返済
contractual price 契約価格
contractual provision 契約条項
contractual rate 約定金利
contractual relationship 契約関係
contractual transfer 契約移転
contractual-type investment trust 契約型投資信託, 契約型投信
contractual vertical marketing system 契約型垂直的マーケティング・システム
contractual wage 契約賃金, 契約給
expected contractual income 期待契約所得
general contractual conditions 約款

contractual clause 契約条項
◆The contractual clause is a violation of the Antimonopoly Law. この契約条項は、独占禁止法違反である。◆There is a contractual clause stipulating that Japanese PC makers will take no legal action even if Microsoft Corp.'s technologies are

deemed to violate their patents. マイクロソフト社の技術が日本のパソコン・メーカーの特許侵害にあたるとしても、日本のパソコン・メーカーは法的措置を一切取らない［訴訟を起こさない］、と定めた契約条項がある。

contrary to 〜に反する、〜に反して
◆Whenever there is any conflict between any provisions of this agreement and any statute or law, contrary to which the parties have no legal right to contract, the latter shall prevail. 本契約の規定と、当事者がそれに反して契約する法的権利のない制定法または法律との間に矛盾がある場合には、いつも後者が優先するものとする。

control （動）支配する、掌握する、管理する、規制する、抑制する、抑える、鎮静化する、操作する
◆Japan and Russia inked a treaty on measures to control poaching and smuggling of crabs and other marine products in the Okhotsk Sea. 日本とロシアは、オホーツク海のカニなど水産物の密漁・密輸入対策に関する協定に署名した。◆Sharp's early investments in LCD propelled to control almost half the LCD television market. 液晶ディスプレーへの早期投資で、シャープは液晶テレビ市場のほぼ半分を支配することができた。◆The BOJ has traditionally controlled the quantity of money in circulation by guiding interest rate levels. This is based on the idea that there are fewer people who wish to borrow money when interest rates rise, while it will be easier to borrow money if interest rates fall. 日銀は伝統的に、金利水準を誘導して［動かして］市場に出回るお金の量を調節してきた。これは、金利が上がるとお金を借りたいと思う人が少なくなり、金利が下がるとお金が借りやすくなるという考えからだ。◆The firm controls its exposure to credit risk through credit approvals, credit limits and monitoring procedures. 同社は、信用供与承認や信用限度、監視手続きを通じて信用リスクを管理している。

control （名）支配、統制、管理、経営支配権、経営権、規制、抑制、制御、制御［操縦］装置 (controls)、整備点検地点、検査所、検査官、管制係、コントロール　（⇒force majeure clause, import control)
assume control of 〜の実権を握る、〜を支配する
be under state control 国の管理下にある、国有化されている
beyond one's control 〜の手に負えない、〜が統御できない、〜の支配が及ばない
bring A under state control Aを国有化する
buy control of 〜の経営権［経営支配権］を取得する、〜の経営権を買い取る
capital control 資本規制、資本取引規制
control chart 品質管理図、管理図表
control experiment 対象実験
control of ownership 経営権

control stock 支配株式
corporate control 企業経営
electronic controls 電子制御装置
fiscal control 財政調整
government controls 政府規制、政府による種々の統制
production control 生産管理、工程管理
quality control 品質管理、QC
sanitary controls 衛生管理
spin out of control 収拾がつかなくなる、歯止めがなくなる
stock control 在庫管理、在庫調整
take [gain] control of 〜を掌握する、〜の支配権を握る、〜を取り込む、〜の経営権を握る、〜の経営権を掌握する、〜の経営権を支配する、〜の主導権を握る
take full control of 〜の全権を掌握する、〜の経営権を完全に掌握する、〜を完全子会社化する
tighten controls on futures trading 先物取引の規制を強化する
◆After the Islamic militants known as ISIS advanced across northern Iraq and Iraqi security forces melted away, Kurdish fighters seized full control of the regional oil hub. 「イラクとシリアのイスラム国」と呼ばれるイスラム過激派がイラク北部に侵攻し、イラクの治安部隊が次第に姿を消した後、クルド人兵らが、域内の石油拠点を完全に掌握した。◆After the poisoned frozen gyoza incident, Japanese companies were spurred to tighten quality controls on Chinese food products at their factories in China. 冷凍ギョウザの中毒事件を機に、日系企業は、中国国内工場での中国産食品の品質管理強化を行うようになった。◆Bitcoin circulated only on the Internet is not under the control of central banks unlike regular currencies. インターネット上だけで流通しているビットコインは、通常の通貨と違って、中央銀行の統制を受けていない。◆In order to cut off funds to North Korea's nuclear weapons development program, the government will tighten controls on illegal bilateral transactions, including exports of materials for making missiles and smuggling of narcotics and counterfeit bank notes into the country. 北朝鮮の核兵器開発計画の資金源を断つため、政府はミサイル製造の関連物資の輸出や麻薬・偽造紙幣の密輸など、日朝間の不正取引の取締りを強化する方針だ。◆Mitsubishi UFJ Financial Group Inc. agreed to pay $8.6 million to the Treasury Department's Office of Foreign Assets Control to settle alleged U.S. sanction violations related to the transfer of funds to client accounts in Myanmar, Iran and Cuba. 三菱UFJフィナンシャル・グループは、ミャンマーやイラン、キューバなどの顧客口座に行った送金に関して、米国の経済制裁規制に違反した疑いで、米財務省外国資産管理局に860万ドルの和解金を支払うことで合意

した。◆Royal Dutch Shell and the two Japanese companies opposed Gazprom's taking control of the Sakhalin-2 project. ロイヤル・ダッチ・シェルと日本企業2社は、ガスプロムに「サハリン2」事業の主導権を握られることに反発した。

control exports of goods and technology 機器と技術の輸出を取り締まる
◆In April 2002, the government enforced so-called catch-all regulations aimed at controlling exports of goods and technology linked to weapons development. 2002年4月から政府は、兵器開発関連の機器と技術の輸出を取り締まるため、いわゆる「キャッチオール規制」を施行した。

controlling (形)支配的, 優先的
controlling influence　支配的影響力, 支配力
controlling text　正本, 正文, 文書の本文
◆Both parties agree that the English version shall be controlling. 両当事者は、英語版を優先することに合意する。

controls on futures trading　先物取引の規制, 先物取引に関する規制
◆Bills to tighten controls on futures trading have been submitted to Congress. 先物取引の規制を強化する法案が、米議会に提出された。

controls on steel imports　鉄鋼輸入の規制, 鉄鋼輸入に関する規制
◆The U.S. government has announced an action plan aimed at stepping up controls on steel imports from Japan and other nations. 米政府は、日本などからの鉄鋼輸入に関する規制を強化する行動計画を発表した。

controversy, claim or dispute　論争・請求または紛争, 論争・クレームまたは紛争

convene (動)招集する, 召集する
◆This Section shall not be deemed to prevent or prohibit the New Company from convening meetings of its shareholders or Board of Directors outside the territory. 本項は、新会社が地域外（許諾地域外）で株主総会または取締役会を招集するのを妨げるまたは禁止するもの、と解釈しないものとする。

convenience (名)便利, 便利さ, 好都合, 利便, 利便性, 便宜, 利益, 便益, 打算, コンビニエンス
as a matter of convenience　都合により（according to one' convenience), 便宜上
at your convenience　都合のよいときに, 都合のよい所で
at your earliest convenience　できるだけ早く［早急に], なるべく早く, 都合のつき次第　(=as soon as you can)
await a person's convenience　人の都合を待つ
consult［follow］one's own convenience　～の都合のよいようにする
convenience foods　インスタント食品, 調理済み食品, コンビニエンス・フード
convenience goods　最寄り品(消費者が小売

店で少量ずつ買う商品), 便宜品, 手近品, 日用雑貨食料品(日用雑貨品、タバコ、菓子類、雑誌などを指す)
flag-of-convenience ship　便宜置籍船
for convenience［convenience's] sake　便宜上, 便宜のために　(=for the sake of convenience)
if it suits［if it is to] your convenience　都合がよろしければ
◆May we expect your reply at your earliest convenience？ 早急にご返事をいただけるものと［賜るものと]、期待しております。

convention (名)大会, 定期大会, 党大会, 集会, 会議, 総会, 約束事, 申し合わせ, 協定, 協約, 条約, 伝統的な手法[型], 決まり, しきたり, 慣例, 慣行, コンベンション
Convention Concerning the Protection of the World Cultural and Natural Heritage　世界の文化遺産及び自然遺産の保護に関する条約, 世界遺産
Convention on Facilitation of International Maritime Traffic　国際海上交通簡素化条約, FAL条約(国際航海の入港・停泊・出港時の船舶、乗客、乗員、手荷物、貨物に適用する手続きや検疫手続きのほか、関連申請書類を簡素化、標準化することにより、国際海上輸送の円滑化を図るのが目的)
Convention on International Trade in Endangered Species of Wild Fauna and Flora　絶滅のおそれのある野生動植物の国際取引に関する条約, CITES［CITIES]
Convention on the Prior Informed Consent Procedure for Certain Hazardous Chemicals and Pesticides in International Trade　有害化学物質・農薬貿易の事前合意手続きに関する条約
convention, treaty or other agreement　協定, 条約またはその他の取決め
Geneva Convention　ジュネーブ協定
international convention　国際大会, 国際会議
market convention　市場慣行
Ramsar Convention　ラムサール条約, 国際湿地条約, 水鳥湿地保全条約
rounding convention　四捨五入方法
tax［taxation] convention　租税条約

Convention on Biological Diversity　生物多様性条約
◆At the 10th Conference of the Parties to the Convention on Biological Diversity (COP10), a protocol on access and benefit-sharing (ABS) of genetic resources was adopted. 生物多様性条約第10回締約国会議(COP10)で、生物遺伝資源の利用と利益配分に関する議定書が採択された。

Convention on the Law of the Seas　海洋法条約
◆The United Nations adopted its Convention on the Law of the Seas in 1982. 国連は、1982年に海

COPY

洋法条約を採択した。

convert （動）転換する, 変える, 公債などを切り替える, 換算する, 両替する
  convert bonds into shares 社債を株式に転換する
  convert securities into cash 有価証券を現金化する
  convert to a market economy 市場経済に移行する
  ◆As the yen's decline inflated the values of overseas earnings when converted into yen, the income account surplus in July 2013 hit a record high for July. 円安で円換算したときの海外収益額が膨らんだため, 2013年7月の所得収支の黒字額は, 7月としては過去最大だった。◆These subscription warrants could be converted into shares at a ratio of two new shares to one existing share if hostile acquirer obtains a stake of 20 percent or more. この新株予約権は, 敵対的買収者が株式を20%以上取得した場合に, 既存の株式1株に対して新株2株の割合で株式に転換できる。

convertible into ～に転換できる
  ◆Without first obtaining the written consent of other parties hereto, no party, nor its successors or assignees, shall sell, assign, transfer, pledge, encumber or otherwise dispose of, whether by operation of law or otherwise, any shares of voting of the new company or instruments convertible into such shares. 他の本契約当事者の書面による同意を最初に得ないで, いずれの当事者も, その承継人または譲受人も, 法律の運用によるかその他の方法によるかを問わず, 新会社の議決権付き株式またはこのような株式に転換できる証書を売却, 譲渡, 移転, 質入れ, 担保差入れ, その他の方法で処分することはしないものとする。

convey （動）譲渡する, 移転する, 付与する, 伝達する, 知らせる, 輸送する
  ◆Neither party shall assign, sell, pledge, encumber or otherwise convey any of its rights and interests in this agreement without the prior written consent of the other party. いずれの当事者も, 本契約上の一切の権利と権益を, 相手方の書面による事前の同意を得ないで譲渡, 売却, 入質, 担保設定したり, その他の方法で移転したりしないものとする。

Cool Japan initiative クール・ジャパン構想
  ◆The cornerstone of the Cool Japan initiative aimed at promoting the exports of Japanese pop culture is the content industry which produces anime, video games and movies. 日本独自の文化産業の輸出促進を目指すクール・ジャパン構想の核は, アニメやビデオ・ゲーム, 映画などの製作にかかわるコンテンツ産業だ。

cool money インターネット取引で動く投資資金, クール・マネー
  ◆Cool money flew away from low-interest America toward the higher interest euro-zone. ネット取引で動く投資資金は, 金利の低いアメリカ

から金利の高いユーロ圏に流れた。

cooling-off period クーリング・オフ期間
  ◆We can cancel a contract unconditionally within a cooling-off period even if it is signed with an unethical trader. 仮に悪質業者と契約を結んだ場合でも, クーリング・オフ期間内なら, 無条件で契約を解除できる。

cooperative advertising 協力宣伝

cooperative relationship 協力関係
  ◆GM and Toyota reaffirmed that they would reinforce cooperative relationship. GMとトヨタは, 両社の協力関係を強化する方針を改めて確認した。

copy （名）写し, 副本, 謄本, 抄本, ～部, ～通, ～冊, コピー （動）複写する, 複製する, 模倣する
  a duplicate copy 副本
  an original copy 正本
  certified copy 証明済み写し
  copy not negotiable 禁譲渡
  foul [rough] copy 下書き, 草稿
  negotiable copy （手形やB/Lなどの）流通写し
  non-negotiable copy 譲渡不能写し
  sample copy 見本版
  the duplicate copies of the shipping documents 船積み書類の副本
  true copy 正本
  ◆Enclosed are the copies of the shipping documents covering this order as follows: 本注文の船積み書類の写しは, 次のとおり同封してあります。◆Establishing original edition rights would enable publishing companies to file lawsuits demanding the deletion of data if pirated copies are found to be sold on the Internet. 出版物［書籍］原版権の創設によって出版社は, 海賊版がインターネット上で販売されていることが判明した場合に, データの削除を求める訴訟を起こすことができる。◆Music and images may not, in principle, be copied or used without the artists' prior permission. 音楽や映像は, 原則として著作者の事前許可なしに複製・利用することはできない。

copyright （動）著作権を取得する, 版権を取得する, ～の著作権を保護する
  copyrighted material 著作権のある著作物, 版権のある著作物, 著作権のある曲
  copyrighted music 著作権のある音楽
  copyrighted works 著作権のある著作物
  ◆Copyrighted materials can be used freely under the U.S. law as long as it is considered "fair use." 著作権のある著作物は, 「公正な利用」であれば, 米国の法律では自由に利用することができる。◆The program and related documentation are copyrighted. このプログラムと関連ドキュメンテーションには, 版権がある。

copyright （名）著作権, 版権 （形）著作権所

有の, 版権所有の

assign copyright　著作権を譲渡する

copyright and trademark protection　著作権と商標の保護

copyright-fee management contract　著作権料管理契約

copyright on a song　曲の著作権

copyright protection　著作権保護

copyright protection-market　著作権保護市場

copyright-related rights　著作隣接権

copyright royalty　著作権料

copyright violation　著作権侵害
　（=copyright infringement, copyright piracy）

infringe the copyright　著作権を侵害する, 版権を侵害する

out of copyright　著作権期限が切れた, 版権の期限が切れた

◆ABC shall promptly notify XYZ of any infringement or attempted infringement or misappropriation of any copyrights, trademarks or trade secrets of XYZ to the licensed products. ABCは、許諾製品に対するXYZの著作権、商標または営業秘密が侵害された場合や侵害される恐れがある場合、不正使用されている場合には、XYZに直ちにそれを通知するものとする。◆The execution of this agreement shall in no way constitute an admission of infringement by ABC of the Copyrights or its liability. 本契約の締結は、どんな意味でも、ABCによる本著作権の侵害またはその責任を認めることにはならないものとする。

copyright holder　著作権所有者, 版権所有者, 著作者
◆CD rental stores pay about ¥10 billion a year in royalties to copyright holders. CDレンタル店は、著作権所有者に年間100億円の許諾料を支払っている。

copyright infringement　著作権侵害
　（=copyright violation）
◆Seller shall waive any claim against Buyer under the Uniform Commercial Code or otherwise, with respect to a claim asserted against Seller or Buyer for patent, trademark or copyright infringement or the like. 売り主は、特許・商標・著作権の侵害等について売り主または買い主に対してなされる請求に関しては、買い主に対する米国統一商事法典その他に基づく請求権をすべて放棄する。

copyrighted　（形）著作権のある, 版権のある

copyrighted material　著作権のある著作物, 版権のある著作物, 著作権のある曲

copyrighted music　著作権のある音楽

copyrighted works　著作権のある著作物

◆Copyrighted materials can be used freely under the U.S. law as long as it is considered "fair use." 著作権のある著作物は、「公正な利用」であれば、米国の法律では自由に利用することができる。

corporate　（形）企業の, 会社の, 法人の, コーポレート

corporate authority　会社権限, 会社法上の権限, 会社の行為能力

corporate name　社名

corporate structure　企業構造

corporate acquirer　企業買収者, 買収企業, 取得企業
◆Many of listed companies are set to adopt measures to counter corporate acquirers, such as increasing their authorized capital or reducing the quorum of directors. 授権資本（株式発行可能枠）の拡大や取締役の定数削減など、買収防衛策を導入する上場企業も多い。

corporate identity　法人格
◆For the purpose of this agreement, any change of corporate identity of one of the parties, such as by amalgamation, reorganization, or merger or consolidation, has not been agreed to by the other party. 本契約の目的上、合併、会社更生または吸収合併や新設合併といった当事者の一方の法人格の変更については、相手方当事者が同意していない。

corporate income　法人所得
◆Delaware reportedly does not tax corporate income gained from overseas operations. 米デラウエア州では、国外での営業活動で得た法人所得には課税しないという。

corporate merger　企業の合併
◆A corporate merger plan is subject to legal screening by the Fair Trade Commission of Japan. 企業の合併計画は、公正取引委員会の法定審査を受けなければならない。◆The Fair Trade Commission of Japan is required to consider global economic trends when it screens corporate merger requests in light of the Antimonopoly Law. 公正取引委員会は、独占禁止法に照らして企業合併の申請を審査するにあたって、グローバル経済の潮流も検討する必要がある。

corporate performance　企業業績, 会社業績, 業績, 決算
◆At present, export industries including home appliances and automobiles are raising their expectations for improved corporate performance under the weak yen, which has also driven up stock prices. 現在、家電や自動車などの輸出産業は、円安で業績改善の期待を高めており、円安はまた株価も押し上げた。◆Rapidly increasing prices of primary commodities have had a positive influence on corporate performance with the yen's appreciation against the dollar. 円高・ドル安で、これまでのところ一次産品（原油や石炭など）の急騰が、企業の業績に好影響をもたらしている。

corporate powers and authority　会社法上の能力と権限, 会社法上の権能と権限
◆Purchaser has all requisite corporate powers and authority to enter into this agreement and

to consummate the transactions contemplated hereby. 買い主は、本契約を締結する上で必要な会社法上の権能・権限と、本契約により企図されている取引を完了するのに必要な権能・権限をすべて持っている。

Corporate Rehabilitation Law 会社更生法
◆Chipmaker Elpida Memory Inc. filed for protection under the Corporate Rehabilitation Law. 半導体メーカーのエルピーダメモリが、会社更生手続きを申請した。

corporate takeover 企業買収
◆Margin trading was used in a corporate takeover by exploiting legal shortcomings. 法の不備を利用して、企業買収に信用取引が使われた。

corporate value 企業価値
◆In order to forestall hostile takeover bids, companies should raise their corporate value. 敵対的TOB（株式公開買付けによる企業買収）を未然に防ぐには、企業が企業価値を高めなければならない。

corporation （名）会社、企業、法人、団体、コーポレーション
a corporation duly organized and existing under the laws of 〜の法律に基づいて正式に設立され存続する法人、〜法に基づいて適法に設立され存在する法人
Edge Act Corporation エッジ法会社、エッジ法法人
Financing Corporation 米連邦調達公社
foreign corporation 州外法人、国外法人、外国企業
giant [great] corporations 巨大企業
government corporation 公社
Model Business Corporation Act 米国の模範事業会社法、MBCA
multinational corporation 多国籍企業（=transnational corporation）
nonmanufacturing corporations 非製造業
public-interest corporation 公益法人
quasi-public corporation 第三セクター
special public corporation 特殊法人
surviving corporation 存続会社
◆The term "Subsidiary" shall mean a corporation, more than fifty percent (50％) of whose outstanding shares representing the right to vote for the election of directors, are, now or hereafter, owned or controlled, directly or indirectly, by a party hereto. 「子会社」という語は、取締役選任のための議決権を表す発行済み株式の50％超が、本契約の一当事者によって直接・間接的に現在または今後所有されるか支配される法人を意味する。

correspondence （名）一致、調和、符号、類似、類似点、通信、通信文、通信教育、文通、手紙、書簡
be in correspondence with 〜と取引してい

る、〜と文通している
business correspondence 商業通信文
commercial correspondence 商業通信文、商用文、貿易通信文、コレポン
correspondence card 取引状
enter into correspondence with 〜と取引を始める、〜と通信を始める

correspondent （名）特派員、通信員、記者、取引先、文通者、コルレス先、為替取組先
correspondent accounts 他店勘定、コルレス勘定
correspondent arrangement [agreement] コルレス契約（国外銀行に支店の役目をしてもらうこと）
correspondent bank 取引先銀行、コルレス銀行、コルレス先（為替取引契約をしている銀行）
foreign correspondent 海外特派員

corresponding （形）〜に対応する、一致する、相当する、類似する、（前に述べたことの）結果として起こる
compared with the corresponding month of last year 前年同月比で
corresponding period 対応する期間、同期間、同期
the corresponding amounts 前期の比較対応数値、対応数値
the corresponding period of last year 前年同期
◆Nonmonetary balance sheet items and corresponding income statement items are translated at rates in effect at the time of acquisition. 貸借対照表の非貨幣性項目とこれに対応する損益計算書項目は、取得日の為替レートで換算されています。◆We may not have to add that we do not hold ourselves responsible for the corresponding delay in shipment if your actions should not be taken in time. 言うまでもなく［申すまでもなく］、貴社の打つ手が遅れたら、それに伴って生じる船積みの遅延に対して、当社は責任を負いません。◆We shall not hold ourselves responsible for the corresponding delay in shipment if the credit should fail to arrive in time. 万一信用状が間に合わない場合、その結果として起こる［それに伴って生じる］船積みの遅延に対して、当社は責任を負わないものとする。

corresponding to 〜に対応する
◆"Products" as herein used shall mean the following products described below corresponding to Trademarks described in (a) above of this Article. 本契約で使用する「本製品」は、本条の上記(a)に定める本商標に対応する以下の製品を意味する。

corresponding value of an order 注文相当額
◆Our terms of payment are to value at 30 d/s un-

der an irrevocable letter of credit to be opened in our favor for the corresponding value of an order. 当社の決済条件は、注文相当額につき、当社を受益者として開設された取消不能信用状に基づいて一覧後30日払いの手形を振り出すことです。

cost (名)費用, 原価, 原価法, コスト (⇒labor costs, production cost)

borrowing cost 借入コスト, 資金調達コスト (=cost of borrowing)

cost and insurance 保険料込み価格

cost competitiveness コスト競争力

cost cutting コスト削減

cost of stowage 積付け費用

cost-plus contract 実費精算契約書

costs and expenses 費用, 諸費用, 経費, 諸経費 (⇒breach of warranty)

funding cost 資金調達コスト (=fundraising cost)

import cost 輸入費用

ingredient costs 原料コスト

insurance costs 保険費用

interest cost 利息費用, 金利コスト

land transportation costs 陸上輸送コスト

logistics cost 物流費, 物流コスト

market research cost 市場調査費

marketing cost 営業費

material cost 材料費

order-filling cost 注文履行費

packing costs 梱包費, 包装費

physical distribution cost 物流コスト

raw material import cost 原材料輸入コスト

raw material procurement cost 原材料調達コスト

transport costs 運送費

◆All costs for such inspection by the purchaser shall be borne by the purchaser. 買い主によるこの検査費用は、すべて買い主の負担とする。◆The Japanese economy is losing momentum with the burdens of a strong yen and high labor costs as well as higher electric power output costs. 日本経済は、円高や人件費高に電力生産コストの上昇などの負担が加わって失速している。◆The price of regular gas has gone up for six weeks because oil wholesalers have added their import costs, which have been going up due to the weak yen since the end of last year, to the retail price. レギュラー・ガソリンの価格は、昨年末からの円安で上昇している輸入費用の増加分を元売り各社が小売価格に転嫁しているため、6週間連続で上昇した。

cost-competitive (形)価格競争力がある, 価格競争力が高い, コスト競争力がある

◆A cheaper dollar does definitely serve to make U.S. producers more cost-competitive in international export markets. 国際輸出市場で米国の生産

者の価格競争力を高めるには、間違いなくドル安のほうがよい。

cost of domestic thermal power generation 国内火力発電のコスト

◆If reasonably priced oil and gas are exported to Japan by the U.S. "shale revolution," the cost of domestic thermal power generation would decrease. 米国の「シェール革命」で、安価な原油やガスが日本に輸出されれば、国内火力発電のコストは下がることになる。

cost of imports 輸入費用, 輸入コスト, 輸入価格, 輸入物価 (⇒import cost, yen's exchange rate)

◆Despite declining prices of crude oil, the weak yen pushes up the cost of imports, partly offsetting the benefits of falling crude oil prices. 原油価格は下落しているが、円安で輸入価格が押し上げられ、原油安[原油下落]の恩恵が一部打ち消される面もある。

COTIF 国際鉄道運送条約 (Convention concerning International Carriage of Goods by Railの略)

count on [upon] ～を当てにする, ～を当て込む, 期待する, 信頼する, (人に)～を約束する

◆Belarus is counting on striking a low-interest loan deal with the International Monetary Fund. ベラルーシは、国際通貨基金(IMF)から低利融資を受けるのを期待している。◆You may count on our best efforts so long as you can maintain moderate prices. 手頃な価格[格安料金]を維持できるかぎり、当社は最大限の努力を貴社にお約束します。

counter (動)対抗する, ～に反対する, 逆襲する, 反撃する, 阻止する, 排除する, 抑制する, 対応する, 反論する, 反証をあげる

◆Companies should obtain shareholder approval when introducing methods to counter hostile takeover attempts. 敵対的買収への対抗策を導入する場合、企業は株主の承認を得なければならない。◆The United States is under pressure to make some difficult monetary policy decisions to cool down the overheating economy by countering the inflationary pressure stemming from higher import prices due to the weaker dollar. 米国は現在、ドル安での輸入価格の高騰によるインフレ圧力を抑えて、過熱気味の景気を鎮めるための難しい金融政策の決断を迫られている。

counter (形)逆の, 反対の, 片方の, 副の, 対の (副)逆に, 反対に

counter acceptance (手形の)相互引受け

counter approval 追承認

counter argument 反対の議論, 反論

counter bid 逆指し値

counter check 相小切手, 預金払い戻し票

counter claim 反訴

counter-cycle policy 景気対策

counter cyclical policy 景気安定化政策

(=countercyclical policy)

counter mark 副マーク, 合荷印, 添え荷印 (=manufacturer's mark, sub-mark)

counter marketing 有害食品の追放運動, カウンター・マーケティング

counter mart 報復捕獲免許状

counter order 反対注文

counter proposal 逆提案

counter purchase 見返り輸入（交換買付けの条件を付けた輸入契約のこと）

counter remittance 戻し金送金

counter sample 対（たい）見本, 反対見本

counter security 逆担保

counter-signed B/L 副署付き船荷証券

counter store 対面販売店

counter tariff 対抗関税

counter trade カウンター・トレード（輸出と輸入を均衡させることを目的とした貿易形態）

counter value 対価

run [go, hunt] counter to 〜に反する, 〜に違反する, 〜に背く
◆China's retaliatory tariffs on Japanese cars, cellular phones and air conditioners clearly ran counter to WTO rules. 日本の自動車, 携帯電話とエアコンに課した中国の報復関税は, 明らかにWTOルールに違反していた。

counter offer 反対申込み, 逆申込み, 反対提案, 代案の提起, 代案, カウンター・オファー
accept the counter offer カウンター・オファーを受ける
make a counter offer カウンター・オファーを出す
venture on a counter offer 思い切ってカウンター・オファーを出す
◆We refrained from making a counter offer as the price you offered is about seven percent higher than the level workable to us. 貴社がオファーされた価格は, 当社の採算にのる水準よりも7%ほど高いので, カウンター・オファーを出すことを思いとどまりました。◆We will do our best to speed up delivery if you accept the counter offer. このカウンター・オファーを受けていただければ, 全力を挙げて配送を急がせます。

counterfeit （名）偽造品, 模造品, 偽物
◆ABC shall forthwith upon coming to its knowledge notify the licensor of any infringement or threatened infringement or counterfeit of the Trademarks. 本商標が侵害されたり, 侵害されそうになったり, 偽物が作られていることをABCが知った場合, ABCは直ちにこれをライセンサーに知らせるものとする。

counterfeit brand product 偽ブランド品 (=fake branded goods)
◆Counterfeit brand products are suspected to

have been sold at the special venue areas of five department stores which dealt with the same general merchandise sales company. 偽ブランド品が, 同じ雑貨販売業者と取引をしていた5百貨店の特設売り場で, 販売された疑いがある。

counterfeiting （名）偽造, 模造, 変造
◆Since electronic money requires safeguards against unauthorized use and counterfeiting, encryption technology, on the software side, and IC cards, on the hardware side, represent essential technologies. 電子マネーには不正使用や変造を防ぐ技術が必要で, ソフト面では暗号化技術, ハード面ではICカードが, その代表的な技術とされている。
◆The U.S. government froze the assets of four individuals and eight entities that were involved in illicit activities such as money laundering, currency counterfeiting and narcotics trafficking. 米政府は, 資金洗浄（マネー・ロンダリング）や通貨偽造, 麻薬取引などの違法行為に関与している4個人, 8団体の資産を凍結した。

counterparty （名）当事者, カウンターパーティー
◆The process of termination requires the agreement of both counterparties. 解約するには, 両当事者の合意が必要である。

countervailing duties 相殺関税
◆The Byrd Amendment requires antidumping and countervailing duties collected by customs authorities to be turned over to U.S. companies claiming damages for what they deem as dumping by overseas manufacturers. バード法では, 税関当局が徴収したダンピング関税と相殺関税は, 海外メーカーによるダンピング（不当廉売）と認定されたものに対して損害賠償を請求した米国企業に分配しなければならない。

countervailing tariff 相殺関税 (=countervailing duty: 外国政府の輸出補助金や奨励金を受けた製品が, 不当に低い価格で輸入された場合に, 国内産業保護のためその報復措置としてかける関税)
◆The government decided to decrease the rate of a countervailing tariff by 18.1 percentage points, as the WTO recommend. 政府は, 世界貿易機関（WTO）の勧告を踏まえて, 相殺関税の税率を18.1%引き下げる方針を固めた。

country of destination 仕向け国, 仕向け地
◆The seller shall indemnify and hold the purchaser harmless against any claim or dispute which may arise in connection with infringement of patents, trademarks or any other intellectual property rights in connection with the products, whether in the seller's country or the country of destination indicated in this agreement. 売り主は, 本製品に関連する特許, 商標またはその他の知的財産権の侵害に関して生じる請求または紛争については, 売り主の国内で生じたものであっても本契約に定める仕向け地で生じたものであっても, 買い主に補償し免責するものとする。

country of origin 原産地, 原産国, 国籍

COUN 118

(=nation of origin)

◆Access to genetic resources requires prior informed consent of the country of origin. 生物遺伝資源を利用する場合は、資源原産国の文書による事前の同意・承認を得なければならない。

country risk 国別信用度, カントリー・リスク (=sovereign risk)

coup (名)武力政変(coup d'état), クーデター, 大当たり, 大成功, 素晴らしい出来事[行動], とっさの行動, 予期しないこと

◆Foreign investors, including Japanese firms, regard Thailand's political climate with its repeated coups as a risk factor for investing in the country. 日本企業など外国資本は、クーデターが繰り返されるタイの政治風土を、対タイ投資のリスク要因と見なしている。

courier service 宅配便, 国際宅配便サービス, クーリエ・サービス

◆An internationally recognized courier service including DHL and Federal Express provides a delivery receipt. DHLやフェデラル・エクスプレスなど国際的に認知されたクーリエ・サービスは、配達証を発行している。

course of action 対抗措置

◆In case of any infringement or counterfeiting as referred to above, the parties hereto shall immediately mutually consult on the course of action to be taken. 上記の侵害または偽造が発生した場合、両当事者は、直ちに取るべき対抗措置について協議するものとする。

court (名)裁判所, 法廷, 公判, 裁判, 裁判官, 判事, 役員会, 重役会, 委員会, 役員, 重役幹部, 王室, 宮殿, 宮廷, 御前会議, 宮中会議, 陳列場の一区画, ご機嫌とり, モーテル, コート

bankruptcy court 破産裁判所, 破産審査裁判所

be taken to court 裁判にかけられる

bring A before the court Aを裁判沙汰にする, Aを訴える

civil court 民事法廷

Claims Court 請求裁判所

court action 訴訟 (=suit)

court actions 裁判

court case 法廷訴訟

court hearing 法廷審理

court of bankruptcy 破産裁判所

court of first instance 第一審裁判所, (EUの)初審裁判所

court proceedings 訴訟, 訴訟手続き, 裁判手続き

court protection from creditors 資産保全

court ruling 裁判所の裁定, 裁判所の判断, 裁判所の判決 (=court's ruling)

court trial 裁判

go through the courts 法的処理をする, 法的

処理を行う

go to court 訴訟を起こす, 裁判沙汰にする

hold (a) court 開廷する, 裁判を開く, 裁判を行う

in court 裁判で, 法廷で

local court 地方裁判所

lower court 下級裁判所

maritime court 海事裁判所

out of court 法廷外で, 示談で, 審理なしで

out-of-court negotiations 示談交渉

settle out of court 示談にする, 示談で解決する

settle the case out of court 事件を示談で解決する

summary court 簡易裁判所

superior court 上位裁判所

take A to an arbitration court Aを仲裁裁判所に提訴する

take A to court Aを訴える, Aを裁判所[法廷]に訴える, Aを裁判沙汰にする

territorial court 米準州裁判所, 連邦統治領裁判所

the Court of Admiralty (英国の)海事裁判所

the Court of Appeal (英国の)控訴院

the Court of Appeals (米国の)控訴裁判所 (=the federal appeals court)

the International Court of Justice 国際司法裁判所

the Supreme Court 最高裁判所

◆A federal appeals court in New York approved the sale of Chrysler assets to Fiat. ニューヨークの米連邦控訴裁判所は、クライスラー資産のフィアットへの売却を承認した。◆The guarantor hereby waives, and agrees not to assert by way of motion as a defence or otherwise, in a suit, action or proceeding pursuant to this guarantee, any claim that this guarantee or the subject matter hereof may not be enforced in or by such courts. 保証人は、本保証書に従う訴訟、裁判または手続き[訴訟または訴訟手続き]で、抗弁として申し立てることによりまたは他の方法により、本保証書またはその主題を上記裁判所でまたはその裁判所が強制することはできないとの主張をここに放棄し、これを主張しないことに同意する。

court of competent jurisdiction 正当な管轄権を有する裁判所, 正当な管轄権のある裁判所, 管轄裁判所 (⇒competent jurisdiction)

court order 裁判所命令, 法廷命令

◆The confidential information shall not include information which is required to be disclosed by court order or law. この秘密情報は、裁判所命令または法律によって開示を要求された情報を含まないものとする。

covenant (名)捺印(なついん)契約(捺印証

書による契約), 捺印証書, 契約, 約款, 約定,
誓約, 約束　**(動)** 誓約する, 約束する

covenant and agree that　～することを誓約し
［約束し］合意する, ～に対して誓約し合意
する

covenant of warranty　担保約款

covenants not to compete　競合禁止規定

covenant and agree with　～に対して誓約
し合意する, ～に対して約束し合意する
◆Seller covenants and agrees with Purchaser as
follows: 売り主は, 買い主に対して以下のとおり
約束し合意する。

**covenants, representations and
warranties**　誓約, 表明と保証, 約束, 表明
とその保証
◆The Purchaser, in reliance upon the covenants,
representations and warranties of the Seller contained in this agreement, is willing to purchase
from the Seller said shares of the Company.
買い主は, 本契約に定める売り主の約束, 表明と
その保証を信頼して, 売り主から本会社の当該株
式を買い受けることを希望している。

cover　**(動)** 代品購入をする, ～を含む, ～を対
象とする, 表示する, 範囲が及ぶ, 保険をかけ
る, 費用などを賄う, 損害額などを償う, 損
失・貸倒れを穴埋めする, 保証する, 保護する,
～を引き受ける, 取り扱う, ～を十分支払え
る, 相殺する, ～を抵当とする, ～を担保に入
れる, カバーする　**(名)** 代品購入, 代品入手,
担保, 保証金, 封筒, 表紙, 包装紙　(⇒SRCC)

automatic cover　自動再保険

cover, embrace, and include　包含する

the licensed products covered by the trademark
license agreement　本商標ライセンス契約
の対象となる許諾製品
◆All shipments shall be covered for 110% of
invoice value. 積み荷には, すべて送り状金額
の10%増し (110%) で保険を付けるものとする。◆
Any amounts exceeding the limits of automatic
cover shall be offered to the Reinsurer for facultative acceptance. 自動再保険の適用限度を超える
額は, 任意受再のために再保険会社に申し出るも
のとする。◆In case of individual contracts on a
CIF basis, marine insurance covering All Risks
shall be effected by the seller on behalf of and in
the name of the purchaser, in respect of the products purchased by it under an individual contract
unless the parties agree in writing to the contrary.
CIF条件での個別契約の場合, 両当事者が書面で別
途合意しないかぎり, 買い主が個別契約で購入した
製品については, 売り主が買い主に代わって買い主
の名前で全危険担保条件による海上保険をかけるも
のとする。◆Marine insurance policy shall cover
all risks and be endorsed in blank. 海上保険証券
は, 全危険担保条件を付保し, 無記名裏書き［白地
裏書き］するものとする。◆The Company agrees
to cede to the Reinsurer such shares of all insurances covered by this Agreement as are set forth

in the annexes（Schedule and any Addenda）to
this Agreement. 元受会社は, 本協定対象の全保険
のうち, 本協定の補遺（特別条項や追加条項）に明
記した部分を再保険会社に出再することに合意す
る。◆The Landlord shall effect insurance by itself or have other tenants effect insurance against
such accidents as aforementioned and indemnify
the Tenant within the extent covered by the insurance.「貸主」は, 前記の事故などに対して自ら保険
を付けるか他のテナントに保険を付けさせ, その保
険でカバーされる範囲内で「借主」に損害の補償を
するものとする。◆The parties hereto shall keep in
strict confidence from any third party any and all
important matters concerning the business affairs
and transactions covered by this agreement. 本契
約当事者は, 本契約の対象である営業上の問題や
取引に関するすべての重要事項については, どんな
第三者に対しても一切極秘にする。◆The trade in-
surance of Nippon Export and Investment Insurance previously only covered direct exports by
domestic firms. 独立行政法人・日本貿易保険の貿
易保険はこれまで, 国内企業の直接輸出だけが対象
だった。◆Throughout this agreement, Warrantee
shall attempt to maintain an insurance policy to
cover any claim, demand, liability, suit, damage
or expense caused by Warrantee negligence. 本
契約期間を通じて, 被保証人は, 被保証人の過失に
よって生じるクレーム, 要求, 責任, 訴訟, 損害ま
たは費用を担保する保険証券の維持に努めるものと
する。◆To cover this shipment, we have drawn
upon you at sight for the invoice amount under
the L/C opened by ABC Bank. この船積みに対し
て, 当社はABC銀行発行の信用状に基づいて, 一
覧払い送り状額面金額の手形を貴社宛に振り出
しました。◆We enclose the shipping documents
covering the goods and expect your remittance
in due course. 契約品の船積み書類を同封し, 期
日どおりのご送金を期待しております。◆We have
to inform you that the credit to cover your order
does not seem to have reached us yet. 貴社注文
［貴注文］に対する信用状が未着であることを, お
知らせしなければなりません。

cover up　隠ぺいする, 隠匿（いんとく）する,
隠す, もみ消す
◆The food firm covered up its labeling of imported beef as domestic beef. この食品メーカー
は, 輸入牛肉を国産牛肉と偽装表示［偽装工作］し
ていた。

cover-up　**(名)** もみ消し, もみ消し工作, 隠ぺ
い［隠蔽］, 隠ぺい工作, 隠ぺい行為, 隠し立て,
～隠し

a huge loss cover-up scandal　巨額損失隠し
事件

a systematic cover-up　組織的な隠ぺい

beef labeling cover-up　牛肉偽装工作隠し

the cover-up of vehicle defects　自動車の欠陥
隠し

the cover-up operations of bad loans　不良債権

の隠ぺい工作

the large-scale cover-up of defects　大規模な欠陥隠し

the systematic cover-up of a recall of vehicles　欠陥車両の組織的なリコール（無料回収・修理）隠し、組織的なリコール隠し

◆The company has punished 29 employees over the cover-up of vehicle defects.　同社は、自動車の欠陥隠し問題で社員29人を処分した。

coverage　（名）保険の担保、保険の填補（てんぽ）、担保範囲、付保範囲、適用範囲、範囲、限度、負担能力、正貨準備［準備金］、報道（reporting）、報道記事、取材、取材範囲、放送、カバレッジ

asset coverage　資産担保率

benefit coverage　給付内容

building coverage ratio　建ぺい率

catastrophic coverage　高額医療費保険

coverage amount range　保証額の範囲

coverage in the mass media　マスコミの取材

coverage limit　付保限度

coverage ratio　損失負担能力、長期支払い能力比率

credit- risk coverage ratio　信用リスク・カバレッジ比率

debt coverage　返済余力

duration of coverage　保険期間

earning coverage　収益カバレッジ

extended coverage　拡張担保、拡張危険担保

full coverage　全額保証

insurance coverage　保険の適用［対象］、保険担保、保険の付保、保険の担保範囲

life insurance coverage　保険金額、保険契約金額、生命保険給付

loan loss coverage　債権損失カバレッジ

make a blanket coverage　一括して引き受ける

make a regular coverage call　担当顧客に（電話で）定期連絡をする

news coverage　取材、新聞報道、報道

press coverage　新聞報道、マスコミ報道

protection against own-injury coverage　自損事故保険

renew one's coverage　担保範囲を更新する

sales coverage　販売可能範囲、販売対象範囲、販売活動範囲、セールス・カバレッジ

stop loss coverage　超過損害担保、ストップ・ロス保険

terrorism coverage exemption clauses　テロ免責条項

time insurance coverage　定期保険保障

◆Any additional premium for insurance coverage in excess of the value mentioned above, if so required by ABC, shall be borne by ABC.　ABCの要請により、上記価額を超えて付保する場合の追加保険料は、ABCが負担するものとする。◆ During the period when Products are in the custody of ABC, ABC shall keep Products insured at ABC's account for the benefit of XYZ against loss or damage by fire, theft or otherwise with extended coverage.　本製品［契約品］をABCが保管している期間中、火災、盗難、その他による滅失や損害を拡張担保するため、ABCはその勘定で、XYZを保険受取人として本製品に付保するものとする。

covering letter　荷為替手形買取り依頼書

CPI　消費者物価指数（consumer price indexの略）

◆The increase in the CPI in June 2013 is mainly attributed to a rise in gasoline prices and electricity charges as import prices of crude oil and liquefied natural gas were pushed up by the yen's depreciation.　2013年6月の消費者物価指数の上昇は、円安の影響による原油や液化天然ガス（LNG）の輸入価格上昇で、ガソリン価格や電気料金などが上昇したのが主因だ。

create a free trade zone　自由貿易圏を創設する

◆By starting talks on a comprehensive partnership agreement, the EU and the United States will take the first step toward creating a giant free trade zone that would account for about 50 percent of the world's gross domestic product.　包括的連携協定の交渉を開始することで、欧州連合（EU）と米国は、世界のGDP（国内総生産）の5割近くを占める巨大な自由貿易圏の創設に一歩踏み出すことになる。

credit　（動）貸方に記入する、計上する、差し引く、控除する

credit A against B　AをBから差し引く、AをBに充当する、AとBを相殺する

credit to　～に計上する、～に貸記する、～に入金する、～に充当する

◆The amount of the minimum royalty paid by ABC to Licensor will be credited against the payment of running royalty accruing under this agreement.　ABCがライセンサーに支払ったミニマム・ロイヤルティは、本契約により生じるランニング・ロイヤルティの支払い金と相殺されるものとする。

credit　（名）信用、与信、債権、貸方、貸金、預金、信用状、支払い猶予期間、税額控除、クレジット（映画やテレビ関係で「クレジット」というと、映画の提供者、製作者、原作、脚本、監督、音楽、俳優など、映画の製作に貢献、協力した人たちの名前を指す。⇒letter of credit）

additional credit　新規融資、追加融資

banker's credit　銀行信用状
　（=bank credit, banker's letter of credit）

be denied credit　融資を断られる

CRED

credit accommodation　信用供与
　(=credit extension)

credit activities　与信業務

credit administration　与信審査

credit agency　信用格付け機関（credit rating agency, rating agency）, 格付け会社, 信用調査機関, 興信所

credit agreement　融資契約［契約書］, 与信契約（書）

credit appraisal　信用度評価, 信用格付け
　(=credit rating)

credit association　信用組合

credit availability　未使用借入枠, 借入れ能力

credit balance of payments　国際収支の黒字

credit beneficiary　信用受益者

credit bureau　興信所

credit business　与信業務, 信用事業

credit ceiling　貸出限度, 信用供与限度, 貸出限度額

credit check［checking］　信用調査, 信用情報の確認

credit concerns　信用リスクに対する懸念, 信用リスク懸念

credit condition　信用状態, 信用状況, 信用供与状況

credit criteria　与信基準

credit customer　掛売り得意先

credit decision　与信判断, 融資判断, 信用判断, 与信決定

credit decline［deterioration］　信用の質の低下, 信用力の低下

credit exposure　信用リスク, 与信リスク

credit facility agreement　融資枠契約

credit information　信用情報

credit inquiry　信用照会

credit insurance　信用保険

credit investigation　信用調査

credit loan　信用貸付け

credit market　信用市場, 金融市場, 発行市場, 債券市場, クレジット市場

credit maximum　与信限度

credit on Products returned　返品された本製品の代金額

credit record　信用履歴, 信用情報, 与信記録

credit reference　信用照会先

credit report　信用調査報告書, 信用調書

credit reporting agency　興信所

credit research agency　信用調査機関

credit standards　与信基準

credit standing　信用状態

credit to current account　当座振込み

credit transaction　信用取引

credit worthiness　信用度

credits allowed for the returned licensed products　返品された許諾製品について認めた返金額, 返品された許諾製品の代金控除額, 許諾製品の返品分の代金控除額

deny credit　与信を断る

do business on a credit basis　信用状ベースで取引する

documentary（letter of）credit　荷為替信用状

draw from a credit facility　融資枠から資金を引き出す, 融資枠を利用する

export credit　輸出信用

extend credit　信用を供与する, 融資する

extended credit　長期貸付け

foreign tax credit　外国税額控除, 税額控除

grant credit　与信を認める, クレジットの利用を認める　(=give credit)

have credit　クレジットの残高がある

irrevocable（letter of）credit　取消不能信用状

line of credit　信用供与限度　(⇒credit line)

long-term credit　長期貸付け, 長期信用

negotiation（letter of）credit　買取信用状, 外国為替取組み信用状

on credit　掛けで, 付けで

open credit　信用貸し, 無条件信用状, 手形買取銀行無指定信用状, オープン・クレジット

outstanding credits　融資残高

provide a credit facility of $10 billion to　～に対して100億ドルの融資枠を設定する, provide credit, 信用を供与する, 融資する　(=extend credit)

raise credit　資金を調達する

relaxation of credit　金融緩和

revolving credit facility　回転融資枠, 回転信用ファシリティ

secured credit　有担保貸付け

security credit　証券金融

sell goods on credit　掛売りをする

short-term credit　短期信用

standby credit　スタンドバイ信用状（外国銀行に対して発行する銀行の債務保証額）

standby credit commitment　融資枠の設定額

standby letter of credit　スタンドバイ信用状

standby letter of credit facility　スタンドバイL/Cファシリティ

the quantitative relaxation of credit　量的金融緩和, 量的金融緩和策

the terms of a credit　信用状条件

tightening in the credit policy　金融引締め

trade credit　企業間信用, 企業信用, 輸出・輸入延払い

CRED 122

troubled credits 不良債権

under the credit 信用状に基づいて, L/Cに基づいて (=in accordance with the credit [L/C])

unsecured credit 無担保貸付け, 無担保債権

◆The credit reads that partial shipments are permitted. 信用状には, 「分割積み許可」とあります. ◆We have to inform you that the credit to cover your order does not seem to have reached us yet. 貴社注文[貴注文]に対する信用状が未着であることを, お知らせしなければなりません. ◆We shall not hold ourselves responsible for the corresponding delay in shipment if the credit should fail to arrive in time. 万一信用状が間に合わない場合, その結果として起こる[それに伴って生じる]船積みの遅延に対して, 当社は責任を負わないものとする.

credit advice 入金通知, 入金通知書

◆We have not received your credit advice of this item. 当社は, 本件についての貴社の入金通知(書)を受け取っていません.

credit approval 与信承認, 与信の決裁, 信用供与承認

◆The firm controls its exposure to credit risk through credit approvals, credit limits and monitoring procedures. 同社は, 信用供与承認や信用限度, 監視手続きを通じて信用リスクを管理している.

credit limit 与信限度, 貸出限度額, 信用供与限度額 (=credit line)

◆If ABC fails to meet XYZ's credit terms or exceeds its credit limit, ABC agrees to either: ABCがXYZの与信条件を満たさない場合, またはその与信限度額を超える場合, ABCは次のいずれかを行うことに同意する.

credit line 貸出限度(額), 貸付け限度(額), 与信限度(額), 信用限度, 信用保証枠, 信用供与限度, 信用供与枠, 融資枠, 融資限度額, 利用限度額, クレジット・ライン (=credit ceiling, commitment line, credit limit, line of credit)

◆U.S. and European banks gradually reduced their credit lines to Japanese banks. 欧米の銀行は, 邦銀に対するクレジット・ライン(貸出限度)を次第に引き下げた.

credit rating agency 格付け機関, 信用格付け機関

(=credit agency, credit rater, rating agency)

◆S&P credit-rating agency now rates debt issued by Spain BBB-, its lowest investment-grade status. 米格付け機関のスタンダード・アンド・プアーズ(S&P)は現在, スペイン発行国債の格付けを, 投資適格基準で最低の「BBB(トリプルB)マイナス」にしている.

credit risk 信用リスク, 与信リスク, 貸倒れリスク

◆The firm controls its exposure to credit risk through credit approvals, credit limits and mon-

itoring procedures. 同社は, 信用供与承認や信用限度, 監視手続きを通じて信用リスクを管理している.

credit terms 支払い条件, 与信条件, 融資条件, 信用期間 (⇒credit limit)

◆Shipments may be made on such credit terms as Supplier elects to extend to Distributor at the time an order is accepted. 出荷は, 注文を引き受けたときに供給者が販売店に供与することにした与信条件で行うことができる.

crime syndicate [gang] 暴力団, 組織暴力団

◆The FSA has ordered Mizuho Bank to rectify its business practices on the Banking Law as the bank had extended a total of ￥200 million in loans to members of crime syndicates. 金融庁は, みずほ銀行が暴力団員らに計2億円を融資していたため, みずほ銀行に対して銀行法に基づく業務改善命令を出した.

cross-border infrastructure 国境を越えたインフラ(社会基盤)

◆The development of cross-border infrastructure in the Greater Mekong Subregion (GMS) has prompted a number of multinational corporations to transfer some of their manufacturing processes to Laos, Cambodia and Myanmar to take advantage of cheaper labor costs. 大メコン圏での国境を越えたインフラ整備に伴い, 多くの多国籍企業が, 安い人件費[低賃金]の利点を生かして生産工程の一部をラオスやカンボジア, ミャンマーに移転している.

cross licensing agreement クロス・ライセンス契約, 交互実施許諾契約

◆The cross licensing agreement will allow the two firms to save time and costs for developing digital consumer electronics. クロス・ライセンス契約で, 両社はデジタル家電製品の開発期間とコストを削減することができる.

cross-shareholding ties among companies 企業間の株式持ち合い関係

◆Hostile mergers and acquisitions have been increasing rapidly as the dissolution of cross-shareholding ties among companies accelerates. 企業間の株式持ち合い関係の解消が加速するにつれ, 敵対的M&A(企業の合併・買収)の件数は急増している.

crude (名)原油 (=crude oil, crude petroleum)

Brent crude ブレント原油

Dubai crude ドバイ原油

heavy crude 重質原油

light crude 軽質原油

marker crude 基準原油

◆October Brent crude fell 6 cents to settle at $97.58 a barrel. 10月物のブレント原油が6セント値下りして, 終値は1バレル=97.58ドルとなった. ◆U.S. light crude hit $42.45 a barrel, the highest since futures were launched in New York in

1983. 米国の軽質原油は1バレル＝42.45ドルで、1983年にニューヨークで先物取引を開始して以来の最高値となった。

crude （形）天然の，天然のままの，精製［加工］していない，処理されていない，補正されていない，粗雑な，粗末な，粗い，大雑把な，洗練されていない，未熟な，みだらな

crude goods prices　原材料価格

crude markets　原油相場

crude materials　原材料

crude ore　粗鉱

crude palm oil　パーム原油

crude prices　原油価格

crude production　原油生産

crude productivity　粗生産性

crude quantity　素材数量

crude rubber　天然ゴム，生ゴム
◆The U.S. crude inventory declined by 27.1 million barrels over the last three weeks, the Energy Department said. 米エネルギー省によると，米国の原油在庫は，過去3週間で2,710万バレル減少した。

crude futures　原油先物，原油先物価格
◆Crude futures soared to $135 per barrel on the New York market. ニューヨーク市場の原油先物価格が，1バレル＝135ドルに急騰した［1バレル＝135ドルの高値を付けた］。◆The commodity market of crude futures has become increasingly speculative. 原油先物の商品市場は，次第に投機色を強めている。

crude oil　原油　（⇒light crude）

crude light oil　粗軽油

light-gravity crude oil　軽質原油

light sweet crude oil　低硫黄軽質油
◆These surplus funds are moving into crude oil and grain markets in search of profitable investments. これらの余剰資金が，有利な運用先を求めて原油や穀物市場に向かっている。

crude oil contract market　原油先物市場　（=crude oil futures market）
◆In the crude oil contract market of the New York Mercantile Exchange （NYMEX）, the price of January WTI, the benchmark U.S. crude oil, fell below $60 a barrel for the first time since June 2009 on December 11, 2014 due to the forecast of rising global oil production. 2014年12月11日のニューヨーク・マーカンタイル取引所の原油先物市場では，指標となる米国産原油WTI（テキサス産軽質油）の1月渡し価格が，世界的な石油増産見通しから，2009年7月以来5か月ぶりに1バレル＝60ドルを割り込んだ。

crude oil futures　原油先物
◆On the New York Mercantile Exchange, crude oil futures for October delivery rose 31 cents to settle at $101.18 a barrel. ニューヨーク商業取引所では，10月渡しの原油先物が前日比で0.31ドル値上がりして，終値は1バレル＝101.8ドルとなった。

crude oil futures trading　原油先物取引
◆Service charges or tax on crude oil futures trading should be raised to curb the inflow of speculative money not related to actual demand. 実需に関係ない投機マネーの流入を抑えるため，原油先物取引の手数料の引上げや課税強化をすべきだ。

crude oil imports　原油輸入
◆Washington will not ask Japan to ban crude oil imports from Iran. 米政府は，イランからの原油輸入禁止を求めない方針だ。

crude oil price movements　原油価格の変動，原油価格の動き，原油価格の動向
◆Export and import trends are influenced by various factors, including economic situations in and outside of the country, currency exchange rates and crude oil price movements. 輸出入動向は，国内外の景気や為替相場，原油価格の変動などの各種要因に左右される。

crude oil prices　原油価格
◆Crude oil prices have exceeded $70 a barrel in London and New York, setting all-time highs on these markets. ニューヨークとロンドン市場で原油価格が1バレル＝70ドルを上回って，両市場最高値を記録した。◆Despite declining prices of crude oil, the weak yen pushes up the cost of imports, partly offsetting the benefits of falling crude oil prices. 原油価格は下落しているが，円安で輸入価格が押し上げられ，原油安［原油下落］の恩恵が一部打ち消される面もある。◆The sharp rise in crude oil prices has caused increases in prices of other fuels and grains, triggering inflation in many parts of the world. 原油価格の高騰は，他の燃料価格や穀物価格の上昇を招き，国際的なインフレを引き起こしている。

currency　（名）通貨　（⇒depreciation of the dollar, dominant, monetary easing, original currency）

currency restrictions　通貨制限

eligible currency　国際送金通貨

functional currency　機能通貨

key currency　基軸通貨，国際通貨

local currency　現地通貨（建て），国内通貨（建て），自国通貨（建て）

regular currencies　通常の通貨
◆Bitcoin circulated only on the Internet is not under the control of central banks unlike regular currencies. インターネット上だけで流通しているビットコインは，通常の通貨と違って，中央銀行の統制を受けていない。◆In foreign exchange margin trading, investors repeatedly trade U.S. dollars, euros and other currencies, aiming to profit from fluctuations in exchange rates. 外国為替証拠金取引では，為替の変動による利益を狙って，投資家が米ドルやユーロなどの外貨を繰り返し売買する。◆The currency in which the borrower shall make all payments hereunder shall be U.S. Dollars. 借主が本契約に基づいて支払いを行う通貨は，すべ

て米ドルとする。◆The U.S. dollar has dropped sharply in value not only against the yen, but also against the euro, the South Korean won, the Thai baht and other currencies. 米ドル［米ドル相場］は、円に対してだけでなく、ユーロや韓国ウォン、タイ・バーツなどに対しても、急落している。

currency control 通貨規制
◆All payments shall be made in Japanese Yen, free of any currency control or other restrictions. 支払いは、すべて通貨規制その他の制限のない日本円で行うものとする。

currency exchange loss 為替差損
◆The firm plans to make up for some of the currency exchange loss by transferring some of its domestic production operations overseas. 同社は、一部の国内生産拠点を海外に移して、為替差損の一部を穴埋めする方針だ。

currency exchange rate 為替相場, 為替レート （=exchange rate）
◆Export and import trends are influenced by various factors, including economic situations in and outside of the country, currency exchange rates and crude oil price movements. 輸出入動向は、国内外の景気や為替相場、原油価格の変動などの各種要因に左右される。

currency market 為替市場, 外国為替市場, 通貨市場, 為替相場 （=foreign exchange market）
◆Losses from fluctuations of the currency market due to the yen's steep appreciation have added to Toyota's plight. 急激な円高による為替差損で、トヨタの経営状況が深刻化した。

currency swap 通貨スワップ（異なる通貨間の固定金利と固定金利を交換する取引。通貨スワップは、金利スワップと違って交換する通貨が異なるので、金利だけでなく元本交換をも伴う）
currency swap agreement 通貨スワップ協定, 通貨交換協定, 通貨スワップ契約
（=currency swap arrangement: 通貨スワップ協定は、資金繰りが行き詰まった国に対して、外貨準備を活用して短期に米ドルなどの外貨を融通しあう取決めのこと）
currency swap ceiling 通貨スワップ（交換）の枠
multilateral currency swap agreement 多国間通貨交換［スワップ］協定

currency swap arrangement 通貨交換協定, 通貨スワップ協定, 通貨スワップ（交換）協定
◆Japan's FX reserves have also been used to expand the financial base of the Chiang Mai Initiative, a multinational currency swap arrangement involving Japan, China and South Korea plus the ASEAN. 日本の外貨準備は、チェンマイ・イニシアチブ（日中韓＋東南アジア諸国連合（ASEAN）の多国間通貨交換［スワップ］協定）の資金枠拡大にも活用されている。

currency swap deal 通貨［外貨］交換取引, 通貨交換（スワップ）協定, 通貨スワップ取引, 通貨スワップ取引枠
◆As countermeasures against South Korean President Lee's words and deeds, Japan may scale down a credit line Japan was prepared to set for a bilateral currency swap deal designed for the transfer of foreign currencies to one of the two countries in time of a monetary crisis. 李韓国大統領の言動への対抗措置として、日本は、金融危機時に外貨を融通し合うための日韓［二国間］通貨交換（スワップ）協定のために日本が設定する予定だった融資枠を、縮小する可能性がある。

currency war 通貨安戦争
（⇒global currency wars）
◆Currency wars will cause turmoil in global markets and adversely impact the world economy if the wars become common practice. 通貨安戦争［通貨安競争］が広がれば、世界の市場の混乱を招き、世界経済に悪影響を及ぼすことになる。◆In a currency war, countries intentionally devalue their currencies to boost exports. 通貨安戦争では、各国が輸出に追い風となるように自国通貨の為替レートを意図的に安く誘導する。◆In global currency wars, central banks effectively lower the value of their countries' currencies to boost their countries' export competitiveness. 世界の通貨安競争では、自国の輸出競争力を高めるため、中央銀行が自国通貨の価値を事実上切り下げる［自国通貨の為替相場を事実上安くする］。

current （形）現在の, 今［今日、今週、今月、今年］の, 目下の, 最新の, 一般に使用されている［受け入れられている、通用している、流通している］, ～で適用されている
◆Late payment shall incur an interest charge of 2 percent over the base rate current in XYZ Bank at the time the charge is levied from the due date to the date of payment in full. 支払いが遅延した場合、支払い期日から全額支払い日まで、支払い利息（遅延利息）を課す時点でXYZ銀行が適用する基準金利より2%高い支払い利息（遅延利息）が付くものとする。◆Mitsubishi Heavy Industries Ltd. aims to win orders for commercial launches of foreign satellites with a current lineup of its core H-2A and H-2B rockets. 三菱重工業は、現在の主力ロケットH2AとH2Bロケットの二本柱で、外国の衛星の商用打上げ受注を目指している。

current account 経常収支（current balance）, 経常勘定, 当座預金（current accounts on deposit）（経常収支は、海外とのあらゆる経済取引の収支を示す）
current account imbalances 経常収支の不均衡
current account problems 経常赤字
Japan's current account 日本の経常収支
the outstanding balance of current accounts 当座預金の残高
◆Japan's current account posted its biggest

deficit in January since comparable data began in 1985, plunging ￥1.34 trillion on a year earlier. 日本の1月の経常収支は、前年同月比で1兆3,400億円減少し、比較可能なデータの発表を開始した1985年以来最大の赤字額となった。

current account [accounts] balance 経常収支 (モノの輸出入による「貿易収支」、旅行や輸送などモノ以外の「サービス収支」と、外国の子会社への投資・配当や外国債券の利子などの「第一次所得収支」、無償の経済協力などの「第二次所得収支」の4項目からなる) ◆Current account balance includes dividends and interest from overseas investment. 経常収支には、海外への投資による配当や利子の受取りなどが含まれる。◆In countries that are based on a genuine market economy model, current account balances are just the results of imports and exports freely carried out by the private sector. 純粋な市場経済モデルに立つ国では、経常収支は、民間が行う自由な輸出・輸入活動の結果に過ぎない。◆Japan's current account balance logged a record ￥173 billion deficit in January 2009. 日本の2009年1月の経常収支は、過去最高の1,730億円の赤字になった。

current account deficit 経常赤字, 経常収支の赤字, 経常収支の赤字額
cumulative current account deficit 経常赤字累計額
finance the current account deficit with long-term capital inflow 長期資本流入で経常赤字を補填する
reduce the current account deficit 経常赤字を削減する
significant reduction in the current account deficit 経常赤字の大幅減
◆China accounts for the largest portion of U.S. current account deficits. 中国は、米国の経常収支赤字額の最大部分を占めている。◆If Japan posts a current account deficit, it has to sell yen to buy U.S. dollars as the greenback remains the world's dominant currency for settling trade. 日本が経常収支の赤字を計上した場合、米ドルがまだ世界の貿易決済の主要通貨なので、米ドルを買うために円を売らなければならない。◆In the January-June period of 2014, Japan posted a current account deficit of ￥461.6 billion, the second consecutive half-year deficit. 2014年上期 (1～6月) で、日本は4,616億円の経常収支の赤字を計上し、前年下期に続く2期連続の赤字となった。

current account surplus 経常黒字, 経常収支の黒字, 経常収支の黒字額
an economy with a current account surplus 経常黒字国
chronic [persistent] current account surplus 慢性的な経常黒字, 経常黒字の慢性的な黒字, 経常黒字体質
correct current account surpluses or deficits 経常収支の黒字や赤字を是正する

dramatic rise of current account surpluses 経常黒字の急増
huge current account surplus 巨額の経常黒字
Japan's current account surplus 日本の経常収支の黒字額
narrowing in current account surplus 経常黒字の縮小
record a current account surplus of ～の経常黒字を計上する
seasonally adjusted current account surplus 季節調整済み経常黒字
widening [rise] in current account surplus 経常黒字の拡大, 経常黒字幅の拡大
◆Japan's current account surplus in July 2013 fell 12.9 percent from a year earlier to ￥577.3 billion, chiefly reflecting a wider gap in goods trade as imports of LNG for thermal power generation swelled due in part to an increase in electricity demand amid the hot summer. 2013年7月の日本の経常収支の黒字幅は、前年同月より12.9％減少して5,773億円となったが、これは主に猛暑で電力需要が増えたこともあって火力発電用の液化天然ガスの輸入が大幅に増加したため、モノの貿易での輸入超過[モノの貿易赤字]が拡大したことを反映している。◆The slowdown in exports has also drastically cut into Japan's current account surplus. 輸出の鈍化で、日本の経常黒字も激減している。

current state 現在の状況, 現在の情勢, 現状
◆The attack on a Panasonic Corp. factory which has played a pioneering role in expanding its operations in China by a violent mob of anti-Japan demonstrators symbolizes the current bleak state of Japan-China relations. 中国進出で先駆的役割を果たしてきたパナソニックの工場が、反日デモ隊の暴徒に襲われた事件は、日中関係の寒々しい現状を象徴している。

current trade structure 現在の貿易構造, 現状の貿易構造
◆A counselor to the Japan Research Institute warned that under the current trade structure, the yen's depreciation might apply downward pressure on the Japanese economy. 現状の貿易構造では、円安で日本の景気が押し下げられる懸念がある、と日本総研の理事が警告した。

current year 当期, 今期, 現年

currently (副)現在, その時点で, 広く, 一般に

custody (名)管理, 保管, 保護, 裁判所への拘引, 警察への拘留
◆During the period when Products are in the custody of ABC, ABC shall keep Products insured at ABC's account for the benefit of XYZ against loss or damage by fire, theft or otherwise with extended coverage. 本製品[契約品]をABCが保管している期間中、火災、盗難、その他による減失や損害を拡張担保するため、ABCはその勘定で、

XYZを保険受取人として本製品に付保するものとする。

customary trade discounts 通常の卸売り割引, 通常の卸売り割引額, 通常の卸売り値引き額

customer （名）顧客, 得意先, 得意客, 取引先, 需要家, 加入者, ユーザー

　attract customers　顧客を引きつける
　be customer focused　顧客を重視する, 顧客重視の姿勢をとる
　be good to customers　顧客を大切にする
　business customers　企業の顧客, 法人顧客, 企業のユーザー, 法人需要家
　corporate customer　法人顧客
　customer acquisition　顧客獲得
　customer buying history　顧客購買履歴
　customer complaint　顧客からの苦情, 顧客からのクレーム
　customer confirmation　取引確認書
　customer data　顧客情報
　customer-delighting product　客受けの良い製品
　customer enquiry　顧客からの問い合わせ
　customer-first　顧客本位の, 顧客志向の, 顧客重視の　(=customer-focused)
　customer information　顧客情報
　customer loyalty　顧客ロイヤルティ, 顧客の忠誠度, 顧客の忠誠心
　customer orientation　顧客志向, 顧客本位の姿勢
　customer reaction　顧客の反応
　customer relations　顧客関係, 顧客窓口, 苦情処理係, 顧客係
　customer relationship　顧客関係, 顧客との良好な取引関係
　customer retention　顧客維持, 顧客維持率
　customer safety　顧客の安全
　customer satisfaction　顧客の満足, 顧客満足度, CS
　customer strategy　顧客戦略
　customer support　顧客支援
　customer transaction　対顧客取引
　customers' trust　顧客の信頼
　deal with a customer　客の相手をする, 客と接する
　defecting customer　離れていく顧客, 顧客離れ
　develop customers　顧客を開拓する
　entertain a customer　客を接待する
　existing customers　既存顧客
　favored customer　得意客
　franchise customers　営業地域内の顧客

　get a customer　客をつかむ
　institutional customer　大口需要家
　Know Your Customer rule　顧客熟知規則
　loan customer　融資先
　look the customer ahead　顧客動向を先取りする
　lose a customer　顧客を失う
　major customer　主要顧客, 大口客
　make customers happy　顧客を満足させる
　potential customer　見込み客, 見込み顧客
　prospective customer　見込み客
　regular customer　常連客, 得意客　(=repeat customer)
　retain customers　顧客を引きとめる[つなぎとめる], 顧客離れを防ぐ
　serve a customer　客のニーズに応える
　wary customers　財布のヒモを引き締めている顧客
　win a customer　顧客を獲得する
◆Comparative advantage in this new global market depends not only on superior R&D, but also on speed in making management decisions, finding unique applications for research advances and delivering them to customers ahead of competitors. この新しいグローバル市場で比較優位性を確立できるかどうかは, 高度な研究開発だけでなく, 経営の意思決定を迅速に行えるかどうかと, 研究を進めるうえで独創的な適用範囲[用途]を素早く確認して, それを競合他社に先駆けて製品化できるかどうかにかかっている。◆Net Wholesale Price referred to in this agreement is defined as the amount of the gross sales by ABC of the licensed products to ABC's customers in the territory, less customary trade discounts, insurance premiums, transportation and delivery charges, taxes（VAT）and duties. 本契約書に記載される「純卸売り販売額」とは, ABCの顧客に対する契約地域内でのABCの許諾製品の総売上高（総販売額）から, 通常の卸売り割引額, 保険料, 運送・引渡し費用, 税金（付加価値税）と関税を差し引いた額のことをいう。◆Pursuant to concerned provisions of Contract, all risks of loss or damage to Machines shall be directly transferred from Supplier to Customer. 本契約の関連規定に従って, 本機械に関する損失または損害の全危険は, サプライヤーから顧客へ直接移転するものとする。

customs （名）関税, 税関, 通関手続き

　a Customs Declaration Form　税関申告書
　be cleared through the customs　～が通関を済ませる
　be in customs　通関手続き中である
　be searched by customs　税関で検査される
　be seized by customs　税関で押収される
　be stopped by customs　税関で引っかかる, 税関で止められる

be waved through customs　税関で止められずに済む

clear A through customs　Aを通関させる

clear customs　税関を通る, 通関する, 通関手続きを済ます

complete customs formalities　通関手続きを済ます

customs agent　税関代行者

Customs and Tariff Bureau　関税局

customs appraisement　関税評価, 税関賦課

customs autonomy　関税自主権

customs barrier　関税障壁

customs basis　通関ベース

customs bond　関税支払い保証書

customs broker　通関業者, 通関代行業者, 税関貨物取扱い業者　(=customs house broker)

customs bureau　関税局

customs certificate　税関証明書

customs classification　関税分類

customs clearance　通関, 通関手続き, 税関通過

Customs Clearance of Cargo aboard Ship　本船扱い

customs clearance system for import　輸入通関制度

customs clearing　通関

customs clearing [clearance] procedure　通関手続き

customs collection　関税徴収

customs convention on container　コンテナ通関条約

Customs Cooperation Council Nomenclature　関税協力理事会品目表, 税関番号

customs debenture　関税払い戻し証明書

customs declaration　税関申告, 税関申告書, 税関告知書

customs drawback　関税払い戻し, 関税払い戻し書

customs entry　通関手続き, 通関申告

customs examination　関税審査

customs formalities　通関手続き

customs house　税関　(=customhouse)

customs inspection　税関検査

Customs Inspection area　税関検査所

customs invoice　税関送り状, 税関インボイス

customs line　関税線

customs official [agent, inspector, officer]　税関職員, 税関吏

customs post　税関

customs procedure　通関手続き

customs regulation　関税規制, 税関規制

customs release　通関許可

customs schedule　税率表

customs service　税関業務

customs shed　税関上屋(うわや)

customs specification　通関明細書

customs statistics　通関統計

customs tariff　関税, 関税率, 関税定率

customs tariff table　関税率表

customs territory　関税領域

customs trade report　通関統計

customs union　関税同盟

customs valuation　関税評価

customs value　関税評価額

customs wall　関税障壁

customs warehouse　保税倉庫

declare A to customs　Aを税関に申告する

engage a customs broker　通関業者に頼む

ex customs compound　通関渡し条件

fill out a custom form　通関書類に記入する

go through customs　税関を通る, 税関検査を受ける

go through customs formalities　通関手続きをする

handle customs clearing　通関手続きの処理をする

surveyor of customs　税関検査官, 税関鑑定官, 税関倉庫管理人

(the) Customs and Excise　(英国の)関税消費税庁

the U.S. Customs Service　米国税関

Tokyo Customs　東京税関
◆Two drug detection dogs were introduced from the United States in 1979 by Tokyo Customs to fight illegal drug smuggling. 麻薬探知犬は、違法薬物の密輸入を阻止するため、東京税関が1979年に米国から2頭を導入した。◆Your order will be cleared through the customs tomorrow morning. 貴注文は明朝、通関を済ませます。

customs authorities　関税当局
◆The Byrd Amendment requires antidumping and countervailing duties collected by customs authorities to be turned over to U.S. companies claiming damages for what they deem as dumping by overseas manufacturers. バード法では、税関当局が徴収したダンピング関税と相殺関税は、海外メーカーによるダンピング(不当廉売)と認定されたものに対して損害賠償を請求した米国企業に分配しなければならない。

customs-cleared　(形)通関の, 通関ベースの

customs-cleared trade figure [report]　通関ベース貿易統計

customs-cleared trade result for　〜の通関ベースの貿易統計

customs-cleared trade surplus　通関ベース貿

易黒字, 通関ベースでの貿易収支の黒字
dollar-based customs-cleared trade surplus　ドル表示の通関ベース貿易黒字

customs-cleared trade deficit　通関ベース貿易赤字, 通関ベースの貿易収支の赤字
◆According to the Finance Ministry, Japan logged a customs-cleared trade deficit of ¥580 billion in July 1-20, 2012. 財務省によると、日本の2012年7月上中旬（1〜20日）の通関ベース貿易赤字は、5,800億円だった。◆Japan's customs-cleared trade deficit in April-September 2014 came to ¥5.43 trillion, up 8.6 percent from a year before and the largest for any fiscal first-half period since comparable data became available in fiscal 1979. 日本の2014年度上半期（4〜9月）の通関ベースでの貿易収支の赤字額は、前年同期比8.6%増の5兆4,300億円となり、統計を比較できる1979年度以降で上半期としては最大だった。

customs duty [duties]　関税
◆After the delivery of the Goods, any taxes, customs duties, export or import surcharges or other governmental charges shall be for the account of the Buyer. 本商品の引渡し後、税金、関税、輸出・輸入税、その他政府が賦課する費用は、買い主の負担とする。

Customs Tariff Law　関税定率法
◆The Customs Tariff Law bans imports that infringe on patent, design and commercial brand rights. 関税定率法で、特許、意匠権、商標権などの侵害品の輸入は禁止されている。

cutting-edge　（形）最前線の, 最先端の, 最新式の, 一歩先を行く, 他より抜きんでている
◆Besides a delay in the development of smartphones and cutting-edge displays, a tenaciously high yen hovering around ¥80 per dollar also contributed to the troubles of domestic electronics manufacturers. スマートフォン（高機能携帯電話）や最先端ディスプレーの開発の遅れのほか、1ドル＝80円前後の円高水準がずっと続いていることも、国内家電の不振につながっている。

cyber attack　サイバー攻撃
◆At the fifth round of the U.S.-China Strategic and Economic Dialogue, China was condemned for its actions of illicitly obtaining information of U.S. companies through cyber attacks. 第5回米中戦略・経済対話で、中国は、サイバー攻撃で米企業の情報を不正入手する中国の行為が激しく非難された。◆To seek information on cyber attacks, U.S. Attorney Preet Bharara has sent subpoenas to bitcoin exchanges including Mt.Gox and businesses that deal in bitcoin. サイバー攻撃に関する情報を得るため、プリート・バララ米連邦検事は、マウントゴックス社などビットコイン（仮想通貨）の取引所やビットコインの取扱い業者に対して、召喚状を送った。◆Washington is staying silent whether it launched a cyber attack in retaliation for the hacking attack against Sony Pictures Entertainment though North Korea's Internet was

on the fritz. 北朝鮮のインターネットが接続不能となったが、米国は、ソニー・ピクチャーズ・エンタテインメントへのハッキング攻撃に対する報復として米国がサイバー攻撃を行ったかどうかについては、沈黙を守っている。

D

daily allowance　日当　（=absence fee）
◆Licensee shall bear the daily allowance of thirty thousand（30,000）Japanese Yen. ライセンシーは、3万円の日当を負担しなければならない。

daily necessities　日用品, 生活必需品, 生活物資　（=daily commodities）
◆In Britain, the value added tax, a form of consumption tax, is set at 20 percent, but the rate for daily necessities such as groceries and newspapers is zero. 英国では、消費税にあたる付加価値税の税率は20%だが、食品や新聞など生活必需品の税率は0%だ。

damage　（動）損害を与える, 損傷を与える, 損なう, 傷つける
◆Insider trading, which is banned under the Financial Instruments and Exchange Law, harms ordinary investors and significantly damages stock market credibility. 金融商品取引法で禁じられているインサイダー取引は、一般の投資家が不利益を被（こうむ）り、証券市場の信頼性を大きく損なう。◆Japanese agricultural and marine products have been seriously damaged by harmful rumors. 日本の農産品や海産物［日本の農水産物］は、風評被害で大きな打撃を受けている。◆Protectionist moves could damage the global economy. 保護主義的な動きは、世界経済に打撃を与えかねない。◆This consignment had to be shortshipped as part of it was badly damaged. この積み荷に積み残しが出たのは、積み荷の一部がひどく破損したからです。

damage　（名）損害, 損害賠償, 被害, （悪）影響, 弊害　（複数形には「損害賠償金, 損害賠償額, 損害額, 被害額」の意味もある。⇒consequential）
actual damages　現実的損害賠償（金）, 実損
claim [demand] damages　損害賠償を求める
compensation for damages　損害賠償
consequential damages　間接的損害, 間接損害
consolation damages　精神的損害賠償
damage assessment　損害査定
demand damage compensation　損害賠償を請求する
financial damage　金銭的損害, 金銭的被害
incidental damages　付随的損害, 付随的損害賠償, 偶発的損害
money damages　金銭による損害賠償
passive damages　逸失利益
seek damages　損害賠償を請求する, 損害賠

償を求める
the amounts of damages from illegal withdrawals with bogus cards 偽造カードを使った不正な預金引出しによる被害額
the cost of damages caused by the massive earthquake and tsunami 東日本大震災の被害額
◆By supporting open trade, Pacific Rim leaders pledged to fend off the deepening damage from the European crisis. 開かれた貿易を後押しすることで、環太平洋地域の首脳は、深刻化する欧州危機の影響を回避することを誓った。◆California's Attorney General Bill Lockyer has sued the six largest U.S. and Japanese automakers for damages related to greenhouse gas emissions. 米カリフォルニア州のビル・ロッキャー司法長官は、自動車が排出する温室効果ガスについて日米の大手自動車メーカー6社に損害賠償を求める訴訟を起こした。◆Japanese factories in Thailand are unlikely to fully recover from the flood damage until the middle of next year. タイの日本工場は、来年前半まで洪水の被害から本格復旧しそうにない。◆The Chinese economy will become anemic and the world economy could suffer immense damage if China is faced with an unabated flight of capital due to speculative investments that its economic bubble has lured from abroad. 中国で、中国のバブル景気で海外から流入した投機マネーが大量に流出したら、中国経済は活気を失い、世界経済は甚大なダメージを受けることになろう。◆Under the World Trade Organization rules, emergency import limits, or safeguard, are permitted as a temporary measure if the volume of imports of a certain product drastically increases, causing serious damages to industries concerned in the country. 世界貿易機関（WTO）のルールでは、緊急輸入制限措置（セーフガード）は、特定製品の輸入量が増加して、国内の関係業界に大きな被害が出ている場合には、一時的な措置として認められる。

damages lawsuit 損害賠償請求訴訟, 損害賠償を求める訴訟, 損害賠償訴訟
◆Bereaved family members filed a damages lawsuit against the government and the importer and seller of the lung cancer drug Iressa, claiming that patients died from side effects of the drug. 患者が肺がん治療薬「イレッサ」の副作用で死亡したとして、患者の遺族が、国とイレッサの輸入販売元に損害賠償を求める訴訟を起こした。

dangerous （形）危険な, 危ない, 危害を及ぼす, 物騒な
dangerous article 危険物
dangerous cargo 危険荷物, 危険貨物
dangerous cargo list 危険物積み荷一覧表
dangerous drugs clause 危険薬品約款
dangerous goods 危険貨物, 危険物, 危険品
dangerous goods handling fee 危険貨物取扱い手数料

dangerous goods regulations 危険物規則書, DGR
dangerous, inflammable, and explosive goods 危険・引火・爆発性貨物
dangerous object 危険物
dangerous structure 危険構造物
International Maritime Dangerous Goods Code 国際海上危険物規程, IMDコード
shipper's declaration for dangerous goods （荷主の）危険物申告書

data （名）情報, 文書, 資料, 指標, 統計, データ
basic data 基礎資料, 基礎データ
big data ビッグ・データ［ビッグデータ］（通常のデータベース管理システムでは記録や保管・解析が困難なほど巨大なデータの集まりのこと）
consumer data 消費指標
data capture データの取り込み, 情報収集
data mining データ・マイニング
　（=knowledge discovery in database）
data on file 保管文書
data retrieval 情報検索, データ検索
economic data 景気指標, 経済指標, 経済データ
employment data 雇用統計
　（=job data, labor data, labor market data）
final data 確定値
fire and explosion hazard data 火災・爆発危険性データ
foreign trade data 貿易統計
housing data 住宅統計
industrial production data 鉱工業生産指数
key economic data 主要景気指標
labor market data 労働統計, 雇用統計
money supply data マネー・サプライ統計
official data 政府の統計, 政府の指標
positive data 好材料
preliminary balance of payments data 国際収支の速報値
real GDP data 実質GDP成長率
retail prices data 小売物価指数

date （名）日付, 日時, 期限 （動）日付を記入する
accounting date 決算日　（=terminal date）
acquisition date 取得日　（=balance sheet date）
contract date 契約実行日
date and time of execution 約定日時
date ended 終了日
date of acceptance 引受日, 受託日
date of airway bill 航空貨物運送状の日付
date of B/L 船荷証券の日付

DATE 130

(=the date of the bill of lading; ⇒bill of lading)

date of issuance　発行日

date of issue　（手形）振出日, 作成日, 発行日

date of loading　船積み日

date of maturity　満期日　（=maturity date）

date of repayment　返済期日

date of scheduled shipment　船積み予定日

date of the delivery　引渡し日

date permitted for shipment　船積み期日

date started　開始日

delivery date　引渡し日, 受渡し日, 納期

due date　支払い期日, 返済期日, 期日, 満期

effective date　効力発生日

expiry date　有効期限, 権利行使期限

extend the shipping and expiry dates in L/C respectively　信用状の船積み日と有効日をそれぞれ延長する

fall due at the date named　（手形などが）記載日に満期になる

for a period of three years from date　本日から3年間

out of date check　失効小切手, 期限経過小切手

record date　基準日

repayment date　返済期日

settlement date　決済日

start-up date　取引開始日

transaction date　取引日

◆The Seller may withhold delivery or cancel the Agreement if the Buyer fails to establish the letter of credit by the date stipulated in this Agreement. 買い主が本契約で定める期限までに信用状を開設することができない場合、売り主は、引渡しを保留するか契約を解除することができる。

date for shipment　船積み日　（=date of shipment）

the latest date for shipment　最終船積み日, 積み期　（=the latest shipping date）

◆The L/C shall be available for at least fifteen days after the latest date for shipment stipulated in the contract. 信用状は、本契約指定の積み期の後、少なくとも15日間は有効とする。

date of maturity of the loan　借入金の返済期日, 借入金の支払い期日

◆The interest rate to be paid by the borrower to the lender on the loan hereunder shall be five percent（5%）per annum on the balance of the loan from time to time outstanding calculated from each respective advance date to and including the date of maturity of the loan on the basis of a 365-day year, for the actual days elapsed. 本契約に基づいて借主が貸主に対して支払う借入金の金利は、1年を365日として各借入日から借入金の返済期日

まで実際に経過した日数についてそのつど計算した未決済の借入金残高について、年5%とする。

date of receipt　受領日

◆Notice shall be deemed given on the earlier of the date of receipt or ten（10）days after dispatch if sent by mail. 通知は、郵便で送付した場合には、受領日または発送した日から10日後のうちいずれか早いほうの日に行われたものと見なす。

date of shipment　船積み日, 船積み日付, 船積み期日, 出荷日, 出荷日付, 発送日, 船会社への貨物の引渡し日

date of the bill of lading　船荷証券日

◆The warranty set forth above in this Article shall apply to any part of the products which, if properly installed, used and maintained by the purchaser, proves to be defective in material or workmanship within nine months from the date of the bill of lading. 本条の上記保証は、買い主が適正に設置、使用し、維持している本製品のいずれかの部分が船荷証券日から9カ月以内に原料または仕上がりの面で瑕疵（かし）のあることが判明した場合に、当該部分に適用される。

dated　（形）〜日付の, 〜日付, 旧式の, 期限付き〜

dated as of the date hereof　本契約日付の

dated date　発行日

dated debt　期限付き債

long-dated bill　長期手形

long-dated paper　長期債

post-dated check　先日付（さきひづけ）小切手

ultra long-dated issuance　超長期債

day　（名）日, 1日, 期日, 期限, デイ

〜 days after date　（手形の）日付後〜日払い

〜 days after sight　一覧後〜日払い

account day　決済日, 勘定日

banking day　銀行の営業日

business day　取引日, 営業日, 銀行営業日, 業務日　（=working day）

calendar day　暦日

closing day　払込み日

current days　休日・祭日込みの連続日数　（=running days）

prompt day　競売の受渡し日, 受渡し最終日, 支払い期日

settlement day　決済日, 勘定日, 決算日, 受渡し日, 期日

trade day　取引日

without day　無期限に

de minimis potentially responsible party　小事象について潜在的に責任ある当事者, 小事象についての潜在責任当事者

deadlock　（名）デッドロック（両当事者の考え方が相容れず、合弁会社の運営が行き詰

まった状況のこと）

deadlock provision デッドロック規定

deal （名）取引, 取決め, 協定, 協約, 労使協約, 契約, 協議, 交渉, 提携, 政策, 重大事件, 案件 （⇒currency swap deal, financial deal, share swap deal）

a big deal 一大事, 重大事件, 大したこと, 非常に重要なこと, 大きな取引, 大物

a breakthrough deal 画期的な合意［協議］, 協議の飛躍的な［大幅な］進展

agree a deal 取決めをまとめる

blockbuster deal 大型債

budget deal 予算交渉

bullet deal 満期一括償還債

cash deal 現金取引

close the deal 取引をまとめる

cold deal 人気のない銘柄

compensation deal 補償取引

conclude a secret deal 裏取引を結ぶ

cut a deal 協定を結ぶ

deal terms 取引条件書

do［make］a deal with ～と取引する

drop out of the deal 案件から手を引く

emergency deal 緊急対策
　　（=emergency package）

exchange deal 為替取引, ジョイント買い, ジョイント売り

finalize a deal 最終調整に入る

finalize a deal for ～の最終調整をする, ～の最終協議をする

financial deal 金融取引

fund deal 資金取引

package deal 一括取引, 一括購入, 包括的合意, パッケージ・ディール

seal a deal 契約を結ぶ, 取引契約に調印する

secret deal 裏取引

secure a deal 合意を実現する, 合意を達成する

share swap deal 株式交換取引

sign a deal 契約を結ぶ, 案件に調印する, 提携する

sign a deal on ～の協定書［合意書］に署名する, ～の協定書に調印する, ～の協定を結ぶ

stock deal 株取引, 株式の売買

strike a deal with ～と取引する, ～と合意する, ～と合意に達する

structured deal 仕組み取引, 仕組み債

swap deal スワップ取引, スワップ協定

tentative deal 暫定的な取決め

terminate business deals with ～との取引を打ち切る

the number of M&A deals M&A（企業の合併・買収）取引件数

trust deal 信託契約

◆In commodity futures trading, prices are decided when buyers and sellers make deals. So they can execute trades at promised prices even if the value of goods has changed drastically in the meantime. 商品先物取引では, 売り手と買い手が取引契約をする時点で価格を決める。そのため, 契約期間中に相場が大きく変動しても, 売り手と買い手は約束した値段で取引を執行できる。◆In his State of the Union address delivered on February 12, 2013, U.S. President Barack Obama threw his weight behind a deal that would encompass half the world's economic output by calling for talks on a far-reaching free trade agreement with the EU. 2013年2月12日に行った一般教書演説で, オバマ米大統領は, 欧州連合（EU）との広範な自由貿易協定の交渉を呼びかけて, 世界の経済生産高の半分を含むことになる協定を後押しした。◆The survival of entire industries hung in the balance in the Andean region as a deal that let some businesses trade duty-free with the United States expired. 一部の企業と米国との取引を無関税と定めた協定が失効したため, アンデス地域（諸国）の産業全体の先行きが不透明な状態になった。

deal a blow to ～に打撃を加える, ～に打撃を与える, ～に難問を抱えさせる

deal a double blow to ～に二重の打撃を与える

deal a painful blow to ～に耐え難いほどの打撃を与える

◆After a Chinese fishing boat collided with Japan Coast Guard's patrol vessels near the Senkakus in 2010, China suspended rare earth exports to Japan and dealt a blow to Japanese manufacturers. 2010年に中国漁船が尖閣諸島近海で海上保安庁の巡視船に衝突した事件の後, 中国はレア・アースの対日輸出を停止し, 日本の製造業が打撃を受けた。◆The economic slowdown in Europe due to the sovereign debt crisis and slackening growth of China as a major exporter to Europe have dealt a painful blow to Japan's exports and production. 債務危機に伴う欧州経済の減速と, 欧州向け輸出の多い中国の成長鈍化が, 日本の輸出と生産に耐え難いほどの打撃を与えている。◆The rapid surge in the yen's value could deal a blow to Japan's export drive and export-related businesses. 急激な円高は, 日本の輸出競争力の低下や輸出関連企業の業績悪化をもたらす［日本の輸出競争力と輸出関連企業に打撃を与える］可能性がある。

deal with ～を処理［処置］する, 解決する, 取り扱う, 扱う, ～と取引する, 取引関係にある, 商う, 商売をする, ～と密約を結ぶ, ～と付き合う, ～と会談する, ～と折衝する, ～に対処する, ～に対応する

deal directly with ～と直接取引する

deal generally with 全般的に取引する

DEBI 132

deal well with　～を優遇する

deal with a crisis　危機に対処する, 難局に対処する

deal with the problem　問題に対処する, 問題に対応する, 問題を解決する

◆A higher capital adequacy ratio means that a bank has a greater capability to deal with risk. 自己資本比率が高いほど, 銀行のリスクへの対応力が高くなる。◆Each party is fully authorized to deal generally with and to make this agreement respecting the subject matter hereof. 各当事者は, 本契約の主題について全般的に取引し, 本契約を締結する権限を全面的に与えられている。◆No party hereto shall engage or be interested in the business of manufacturing, selling, or otherwise dealing with any product similar to and competitive with the products in the territory during the term of this agreement except with the consent of the other parties hereto. いずれの当事者も, 他の本契約当事者の同意を得た場合を除いて, 本契約の期間中, 契約地域で本製品に類似する競合品を製造, 販売その他の方法で取引する事業に従事または関与しないものとする。

debit　(名)借方(かりかた), 負債, 引落し, デビット　(=debtor:「借方」は, 勘定の左側)

automatic debit　自動引落し (=direct debit)

be paid by automatic direct debit　自動引き落としで支払われる

debit and credit　借方と貸方, 借方・貸方

debit balance　借方残高, 貸付け残高, 差引融資残高

debit card　銀行口座即時決済, デビット・カード(金融機関が発行するキャッシュ・カードを利用して, 買い物などの支払いができる即時決済方法)

debit equity ratio　負債持ち分比率, 他人資本比率

debit note　借方票, 借方伝票, 債務覚書, 代金請求書, デビット・ノート
(=debit memo, debit slip, debit ticket)

direct debit　自動引落し, 直接引落し, 口座引落し

Net-debit service　ネット決済サービス, インターネット即時決済サービス

online debit service　インターネット即時決済サービス, オンライン即時決済サービス

reverse your debit entry　貴行の借記を取り消す

◆The life insurer introduced a system that allows customers to pay their first insurance premiums by direct debit from their bank accounts. 同保険会社は, 顧客の銀行口座からの自動引落しで(契約時の)初回保険料を顧客が支払うことができるシステムを導入した。

debt　(名)債務, 負債, 借入れ, 借金, 債権, 借入金, 借入債務, 債務証券, 債券, 金銭債務, 金銭債務訴訟, 金融債務, デット

accrue debt　負債を抱え込む

accumulated debt　累積債務, 国債残高

bad debt　不良債権

clear debts　借金を返済する, 負債の返済に充てる

collect a debt　債権を回収する

cover debts　赤字を補塡する

debt adjustment　債務整理

debt capital　借入資本

debt for borrowed money　借入債務, 借入金に対する債務　(⇒grace period)

external debt　対外債務
(=foreign debt, overseas debt)

forgive debt　債務を免除する, 債権を放棄する

government debt　国債, 政府債, 財政赤字

in debt　赤字の

incur a debt　債務を負担する

massive debts　巨額の債務, 巨額の借金, 過剰債務

new debt　新発債

outstanding debt　既発債, 借入金残高

provision for doubtful debts　貸倒れ引当金

reduce debts　債務を削減する

repayment of one's debts　債務返済

restructuring of debt　債務の再編

retirement of debt　債務の返済

Spain's debt　スペインの国債

unrecoverable debts　不良債権　(=bad debts, nonperforming loans, uncollectible loans)

◆If the borrower shall fail to pay any debt for borrowed money or other similar obligation of the borrower, or interest thereon, when due, and such failure continues after the applicable grace period specified in the agreement relating to such indebtedness, the lender may in its discretion declare the entire unpaid principal amount of the loan, accrued interest thereon and all other sums payable under this agreement to be immediately due and payable. 借主が借主の借入債務(借入金に対する債務)や他の同様の債務またはその利息を支払い期日に支払うことを怠り, このような不履行が本契約に定める当該債務に関する適用猶予期間後も継続する場合, 貸主はその裁量で, 借入金の未返還元本全額, その発生利息と本契約に基づいて支払わなければならない他の未払い金の全額即時支払い[即時返済]を宣言することができる。

debt default　債務不履行

◆In the nick of time, the U.S. Congress passed legislation to end the partial government shutdown and avert a U.S. debt default. 間一髪で米議会は, 政府の一部閉鎖を解き, 債務不履行を回避する法案を可決した。

debt rollover deal　債務返済繰り延べ取引

DECL

◆Argentina clinched a debt rollover deal with the IMF after a year of tortuous negotiations. アルゼンチンは、1年にわたる難交渉の末、国際通貨基金（IMF）との債務返済繰延べ取引をまとめた。

debtor （名）債務者
◆The guarantor shall be liable under this guarantee as if it were the sole principal obligor and debtor and not merely a surety. 保証人は、保証人が単なる保証人ではなく唯一の主債務者であるかのように本保証書上の責任を負うものとする。

debtor's relief law 債務者救済法

decision or award of the arbitrator 仲裁人の決定または判断
◆Any decision or award of the arbitrator shall be final and conclusive on the parties to this agreement. 仲裁人の決定または判断は、最終的なもので、本契約の当事者を拘束するものとする。

declaration （名）宣言, 布告, 声明, 公表, 発表, 告白,（原告の）供述［訴答、請求申立て］,（証人の）非宣誓供述, 申告, 宣告, 決議, 宣言書, 布告文, 声明書, 声明文, 申告書
air-mail declaration 航空郵便申告
cargo declaration 貨物申告書
crew's effect declaration 乗組員携帯品申告書
declaration before carrying in bonded area 搬入前申告
declaration clause 通知約款
declaration date 配当宣言日
declaration for clearance （貨物を税関から出したときの）出関申告書
declaration for dangerous goods 危険物申告書
declaration for entry （貨物を税関に入れたときの）入関申告書
declaration for export 輸出申告書
declaration for import 輸入申告書
declaration for land transportation 陸運申告書
declaration for reshipment 積戻し申告書
declaration for sea transportation 海運申告者
declaration for transshipment 転送申告書
declaration for warehousing 倉入申告書
declaration forms 課税申告書, 収入申告書
declaration of bankruptcy 破産宣告
declaration of dangerous goods 危険物明細書
declaration of dividend 配当宣言
declaration of import 輸入申告
declaration of income 所得申告
declaration of intention 意思表示
declaration policy 申告（保険）証券, 確定保険証券
declaration required by international health regulations 検疫明書書
declaration required under the Universal Postal Convention 万国郵便条約に基づいて要求

される書類
duty of declaration 通知義務, 告知義務（主な告知内容は、積み荷の明細、保険金額、損害填補の範囲、船名、出港日、航路、保険金の支払い地、支払い通貨など）
export declaration 輸出申告,（銀行交認証用）輸出申告書, E/D
general declaration 一般申告書
import declaration system 輸入届け出制
joint declaration 共同宣言
ship's store declaration 船用品申告書
simplified declaration procedure （輸入通関を簡易化する）簡易申告制度

declare （動）発表する, 公表する, 宣言する, 申告する, 告知する
◆If the borrower shall default in the performance of any other term or agreement contained in this agreement, the lender may declare its commitment and its obligation to be null and void. 借主が本契約に定める他の条件または合意事項を履行しない場合、貸主は、貸主の約束と義務は無効であると宣言することができる。

decline （名）減少, 低下, 下降, 下落, 悪化, 低迷, 後退, 衰退, 縮小, 落ち込み
◆Partly due to a slowdown in the Chinese economy in the wake of the European financial crisis, Japan's exports and production have been on the decline. 欧州の金融危機による中国の景気減速もあって、日本の輸出や生産活動は落ち込んでいる。

decline in exports 輸出の減少, 輸出減
◆The record trade deficit in 2012 was caused by a decline in exports due to the European financial crisis and deceleration of the Chinese economy, together with a sharp increase in imports of liquefied natural gas and the rapid hollowing-out of the domestic manufacturing industry. 2012年の過去最大の貿易赤字の要因としては、欧州の金融危機や中国経済の減速などで輸出が減少する一方、液化天然ガス（LNG）の輸入が急増し、国内製造業の空洞化が加速していることも挙げられる。

decline in shipments 輸出の減少, 輸出減
◆Exports are decreasing moderately recently due to the decline in shipments to Europe and China. 輸出は、欧州や中国への輸出減で、このところ緩やかに減少している。

decline in stock prices 株価下落, 株価低迷, 株安, 株式相場の下落 （=decline in share prices）
◆Amid the strengthening of the yen and declines in stock prices, the stock and financial markets appear to be wooing the BOJ to come up with additional financial measures to stabilize the markets. 円高・株安を受けて、株式や金融市場は、市場安定化に向けて日銀に追加の金融緩和策を打ち出すよう催促するような相場展開である。

declining export profits 輸出の採算悪化
◆Sony has suffered from declining export profits

due to the yen's sharp appreciation. ソニーは、急激な円高で、輸出の採算悪化に見舞われている。

decrease （動）減少させる，引き下げる，低下させる，軽減する （自動）減少する，目減りする，低下する （名）減少，縮小，低下，下落

decreased demand　需要減

decreased dividend　減配，配当引下げ

decreased margin　利益率の低下

decreased profitability　収益力の低下，収益性の低下

◆Exports are decreasing moderately recently due to the decline in shipments to Europe and China. 輸出は、欧州や中国への輸出減で、このところ緩やかに減少している。◆If reasonably priced oil and gas are exported to Japan by the U.S. "shale revolution," the cost of domestic thermal power generation would decrease. 米国の「シェール革命」で、安価な原油やガスが日本に輸出されれば、国内火力発電のコストは下がることになる。◆In the case of Toyota, if the yen falls by ￥1 in relation to the dollar, its consolidated operating profit will decrease by about ￥30 billion on an annual basis. トヨタの場合、円がドルに対して1円下落すれば［ドルに対して1円円高が進めば］、同社の連結営業利益は年間で約300億円目減りする。

decrease in exports　輸出の減少

◆The huge decline in business sentiment among large manufacturers has mainly been attributed to the global economic slowdown, a decrease in exports due to a recent flare-up in tensions between Japan and China, and a slump in domestic auto sales. 大企業・製造業の景況感の大幅悪化は、主に世界経済の減速や最近の日中間の緊張激化に伴う輸出の減少、国内の自動車販売の鈍化によるものだ。

decreasing exports　輸出の減少

◆Decreasing exports due to the global economic slowdown are cooling business sentiment mainly among manufacturers. 世界経済の減速に伴う輸出の減少で、製造業を中心に企業マインドが冷え込んでいる。

deduct （動）差し引く，控除する

◆Licensee shall pay to Licensor the following guaranteed annual minimum royalties which shall be regarded as part of, and deducted from the running royalties set forth herein above. ライセンシーは、ライセンサーに次の年間保証ミニマム・ロイヤルティを支払うものとする。このミニマム・ロイヤルティは、本契約に定める上記ランニング・ロイヤルティの一部と見なされ、当該ランニング・ロイヤルティから差し引くものとする。

deduction （名）差引き，控除，差引額，控除額

deduction or withholding　控除または源泉徴収

tax deduction　税額控除

◆Distributor agrees to pay for Products as invoiced without deductions unless previously authorized by Supplier in writing. 供給者の書面に

よる事前の許諾を得ないかぎり、販売店は請求されたとおりに差引きなしで本製品の代金を支払うことに同意する。

deem （動）〜と考える，〜と見なす，〜と解釈する

◆Commencing on the date of this agreement until the Closing, Buyer shall be permitted to perform such due diligence investigation related to the transactions contemplated by this agreement as Buyer deems necessary and appropriate in its discretion. 本契約締結日からクロージングまで、買い主が買い主の判断で必要かつ適切と考えるデュー・ディリジェンス調査を行うことができるものとする。

default （動）履行しない，実行しない，出場しない，欠場する，欠席する，裁判に欠席する，欠席裁判を受ける，デフォルトになる，デフォルトに陥る，デフォルトを起こす

default on　〜を怠る，〜を履行しない，〜を実行しない

default on debt payments　債務返済でデフォルトを起こす，債務返済でデフォルトに陥る，債務返済を実行しない

default on one's obligations　〜の義務を履行しない，〜の義務を実行しない

default on the debt　債務を履行しない，債務が不履行になる，債務がデフォルトになる

defaulted corporate bonds　デフォルト社債

◆According to Moody's Investors Service, Egypt is likely to default on about 10 percent of its outstanding external debt in 2014 and fail to honor as much as 40 percent within five years. ムーディーズによると、エジプトは2014年には対外債務残高の約10%が不履行となり、5年以内に債務の40%が不履行になる見込みだ。

default （名）債務不履行，貸倒れ，支払い停止，滞納，欠場，不出場，法定への欠席，コンピュータの既定値，省略値，デフォルト値，デフォルト （=default of obligations）

after receipt of a written notice specifying the default　（債務・契約の）当該不履行を明記した書面による通知を受領した後，（債務・契約の）不履行を明記した通知書の受領後

be deemed in default of this agreement　本契約の不履行と見なされる

constitute a default　不履行となる，違反となる

default hereunder　本契約上の債務不履行，本契約上の義務不履行

default interest　遅延利息，遅延損害金

delay, failure or default in performance of any obligations hereunder　本契約上の義務の履行遅延，不履行または違反

in default　義務不履行で，不履行で

in default of　〜がない場合には

incident of default　債務不履行の発生

payment of interest upon default　不履行に基づく利子の支払い

remedy the default　当該不履行を是正する

threat of default　債務不履行の恐れ

upon default by the other party　相手方による不履行があったときは

◆Egypt's Morsi administration has concluded a basic agreement with the IMF on loans totaling $4.8 billion, with strings attached, in an effort to avert a default on debts. エジプトのモルシ政権は、債務不履行を回避するため、付帯条件付きで、国際通貨基金 (IMF) との間で総額48億ドルの融資を受けることで基本合意した。◆Greece must avert a crippling debt default by securing billions of dollars in emergency loans from European countries and the IMF. ギリシャは、欧州諸国 [ユーロ圏] と国際通貨基金 (IMF) による緊急融資で巨額の資金を確保して、壊滅的な債務不履行を回避しなければならない。◆The bank shall have the right, as the obligations become due, or in the event of their default, to offset cash deposits against such obligations due to the bank. 債務の期限が到来したとき、または債務不履行の場合、銀行はその債務とその預金を相殺する権利を持つものとする。

default in the performance of　〜を履行しない、〜の履行を怠る

◆If the borrower shall default in the performance of any other term or agreement contained in this agreement, the lender may declare its commitment and its obligation to be null and void. 借主が本契約に定める他の条件または合意事項を履行しない場合、貸主は、貸主の約束と義務は無効であると宣言することができる。

default of this agreement　本契約違反

◆In the event of such a default of this agreement Supplier may terminate this agreement immediately by providing written notice to Distributor. このような本契約違反が発生した場合には、供給者は、販売店に書面で通知することにより本契約を直ちに解除することができる。

defect　(名) 瑕疵 (かし), 欠陥　(⇒latent defect)

assembly defect rates　製品不良率

design defect　設計上の欠陥

latent defect　隠れた瑕疵 (かし)

manufacturer's defects　製造業者の過失

manufacturing defect　製造上の欠陥 (=production defect)

warning defect　警告状の欠陥

warranty for latent defect　瑕疵担保

◆The seller warrants that the Goods will be free from defects in material and workmanship for a period as specified in this agreement. 売り主は、本契約で定める期間、本商品が材料と仕上げの面で欠陥がないことを保証する。◆We couldn't foresee such defects in the preliminary study. 事前調査で、このような瑕疵 (かし) [欠陥] は予見できな

かった。

defence [defense]　(名) 防衛, 防御, 答弁, 抗弁, 弁護, 弁明, 正当防衛　(⇒assume the defence thereof)

assume the defence of such claim　当該請求の防御を引き受ける

by way of motion as a defence or otherwise　抗弁として申し立てることによりまたは他の方法により

Defence Export Services Organization　英国の防衛機器輸出局

defence of property　財産防衛

undertake the defence of the claim　請求の防御を引き受ける

◆The guarantor hereby waives, and agrees not to assert by way of motion as a defence or otherwise, in a suit, action or proceeding pursuant to this guarantee, any claim that this guarantee or the subject matter hereof may not be enforced in or by such courts. 保証人は、本保証書に従う訴訟、裁判または手続き [訴訟の手続き [訴訟手続き]] で、抗弁として申し立てることによりまたは他の方法により、本保証書またはその主題を上記裁判所でまたはその裁判所が強制することはできないとの主張をここに放棄し、これを主張しないことに同意する。

defence lawyers　弁護団

◆Tokyo metropolitan government made the proposal on a settlement to the banks through defence lawyers. 東京都は、弁護団を通じて銀行側に和解の申し入れをした。

deficit　(名) 損失, 欠損金, 損失金, 営業損失, 赤字, 不足, 不足額, 債務超過

a country having deficits in capital transactions　資本輸出国

a customs-cleared trade deficit　通関ベースの貿易赤字

current account deficit　経常赤字

external deficit　国際収支の赤字, 対外債務

financial surplus or deficit　資金の過不足

merchandise trade deficit　貿易赤字

services deficit (in the current account)　貿易外収支の赤字

services trade deficit　サービス収支の赤字

trade deficit　貿易赤字　(=foreign trade deficit)

◆According to the Finance Ministry, Japan logged a customs-cleared trade deficit of ¥580 billion in July 1-20, 2012. 財務省によると、日本の2012年7月上中旬 (1〜20日) の通関ベース貿易赤字は、5,800億円だった。◆Japan saw its goods trade deficit in January-June 2012 balloon to about ¥2.5 trillion from ¥495.7 billion a year before. 日本の2012年上半期 (1〜6月) のモノの取引を示す貿易収支の赤字額は、前年同期の4,957億円から約2兆5,000億円に急増した。◆Japan's services trade deficit in July 2013 was reduced by about 40 percent to ¥196.5 billion thanks to an increase in the number of visitors to Japan due to the weaker yen and a rise in patent royalty revenues. 2013年7月の日本のサービス収支の赤字は、円安で日本を訪れる外国人旅行者が増えたことや特許権使用料の収入が増えたため、約4割縮小して1,965億円となった。◆Japan's 2012 trading balance, or exports minus imports, ran up a record deficit of ¥6.9 trillion, 2.7 times more than the 2011 figure, the first trade deficit in 31 years due to the negative effects of the Great East Japan Earthquake. 輸出額から輸入額を差し引いた日本の2012年の貿易収支は、過去最大の6.9兆円の赤字で、東日本大震災の悪影響で31年ぶりに貿易赤字に転落した2011年と比べて2.7倍に増えた。

deficit in goods trade モノの取引を示す貿易収支の赤字 （=goods trade deficit）
◆The deficit in goods trade in the first half of 2012 expanded sharply due to a surge in imports of fuel for thermal power generation following the suspensions of nuclear power plants. 2012年上半期のモノの取引を示す貿易収支の赤字は、原発停止に伴う火力発電用燃料輸入の急増で、急速に膨らんだ。

deficit in trade モノの取引を示す貿易収支の赤字［赤字額］, モノの貿易赤字
◆According to the preliminary balance of payments data, the deficit in trade in July 2013 was ¥943.3 billion, 2.5 times the level a year earlier and marking the highest level for July since 1985. 国際収支の速報値によると、2013年7月のモノの取引を示す貿易収支（モノの輸出額から輸入額を差し引いた貿易収支）の赤字額は、9,433億円で前年同月の水準の2.5倍、7月としては1985年以降最大の水準となった。

define （動）定義する, 明らかにする, 明確にする, 限定する, 定める, 規定する
as defined below 以下に定義する, 以下に定める, 以下に定めるとおり
as defined in this agreement 本契約で定義する, 本契約で規定するとおり
◆Unless otherwise agreed, invoices will be mailed upon delivery of the Products, as defined in Article VIII hereof, or at the end of the month in which the Services are performed in accordance with this agreement. 別途合意しないかぎり、請求書は、本契約第8条に規定するとおり本商品の引渡しが行われたときに、または本契約に従ってサービスを提供した月の末日に郵送するものとする。

defined sales territory 指定販売地域
◆The Exporter grants the Distributor and the Distributor accepts to be the exclusive distributor for the sale and distribution of the products of the Exporter in the defined sales territory. 輸出者は、販売店が指定販売地域内で輸出者の製品販売の総代理店となることを認め、販売店はこれに同意する。

definite （形）明確な, 確定的な, 限定的な, 一定の
definite answer［reply］ 確答
definite declaration 確定保険申込み
definite insurance 確定保険, 確定保険証券, 確定海上保険証券
definite invoice 確定送り状
definite order 確定注文
definite policy 確定海上保険証券, 確定保険証券
definite time delivery 確定期受渡し

definition （名）定義, 限定, 明確にすること
◆For the purpose of this definition, the term "control" of a Person means the possession, direct or indirect, of the power to direct or cause the direction of the management and policies of such Person, whether by contract or otherwise. 本定義の目的上、人の「支配」という用語は、契約によるかその他によるかを問わず、当該人物の経営や方針などを指図するまたは指図させる権限を直接間接に持つことを意味する。

deflation （名）通貨収縮, 物価下落, 収縮, 下落, デフレ, デフレーション
◆Japan suffered from a strong yen and depression under deflation for many years. 日本は、円高とデフレ不況に長期にわたって苦しんだ。◆The fall in import prices that accompanies a strong yen could further prolong Japan's deflation. 円高に伴う輸入価格の下落で、日本のデフレがさらに長期化する可能性がある。

delay （動）遅らせる, 邪魔する, 延期する, 先送りする （自動）遅れる, 遅滞する, 道草を食う
◆If a company takes a delayed response in its business strategy it is bound to hit a wall no matter how excellent the company is. 経営戦略が後手に回ると、どんな優良企業でも、壁にぶつかることになる。◆In case payment by the purchaser for the delivery of the products is delayed later than 35 days after B/L date, the purchaser shall pay to the seller on demand the amount due together with interest from the due date until paid at the annual rate equal to the prime rate plus 5 percent per year on any overdue amount. 買い主による本製品の引渡しに対する支払いが船荷証券の日付から35日を超えて遅延した場合、買い主は請求のあり次第売り主に対して期限到来債務を支払うとともに、延滞金については支払い期日から支払い日までプライム・レートに年率5%を加えた年間利率で利息を支払うものとする。◆The unemployment of the United States hovers at a high level and its economic recovery has been delayed while the U.S. fiscal deficit has topped $1 trillion for four consecutive years. 米国の失業率は高止まりして景気回復も遅れている一方、財政赤字は4年連続で1兆ドルを超えている。

delay （名）遅れ, 遅延, 遅滞, 延期, 猶予 (ゆうよ)

a probable delay　遅れが出る恐れ

delay, failure or default in performance of any obligations　義務の履行遅延、不履行または違反

delay in collection　回収の遅れ

delay in [of] payment　支払いの遅れ, 支払い遅延, 代金支払い遅延

permissible delay　引渡し遅延容認期間

without delay　直ちに, 即刻, すぐに

◆A probable delay may be caused in the execution of your Order due to a strike. ストのため、貴社注文の執行[履行]に遅れが出る可能性があります。

delay in delivery　引渡し遅延　(=late delivery)

◆In case there is delay in delivery of all or any part of the Goods on the time as stipulated in this agreement, the buyer is entitled to claim liquidated damages at the rate of one-half of one percent (0.5%) of the amount of the delayed Goods for each complete week of delay. 本契約で定める期限に本商品の全部または一部に引渡し遅延が生じた場合、買い主は、遅延対象の各1週間につき引渡し遅延商品の代金の0.5%を損害賠償予定額として請求することができるものとする。

delay in shipment　船積みの遅れ, 船積み遅延　(=delayed shipment)

◆We are giving your order priority, but a slight delay in the shipment of yours will be unavoidable. 貴社の注文を優先的に扱っていますが、ご注文の船積みが少々遅れることは避けられません。◆We may not have to add that we do not hold ourselves responsible for the corresponding delay in shipment if your actions should not be taken in time. 言うまでもなく[申すまでもなく]、貴社の打つ手が遅れたら、それに伴って生じる船積みの遅延に対して、当社は責任を負いません。◆We shall not hold ourselves responsible for the corresponding delay in shipment if the credit should fail to arrive in time. 万一信用状が間に合わない場合、その結果として起こる[それに伴って生じる]船積みの遅延に対して、当社は責任を負わないものとする。

delay in the development of　～の開発の遅れ

◆Besides a delay in the development of smartphones and cutting-edge displays, a tenaciously high yen hovering around ¥80 per dollar also contributed to the troubles of domestic electronics manufacturers. スマートフォン（高機能携帯電話）や最先端ディスプレーの開発の遅れのほか、1ドル＝80円前後の円高水準がずっと続いていることも、国内家電の不振につながっている。

delay in the execution of your order　貴社注文[貴注文]履行の遅れ

◆We are very sorry to have to advise you of a delay in the execution of your order. 貴社注文の履行が遅れたことを、お知らせしなければなりません。

delay or omission　遅滞または不作為

◆No delay or omission in exercising any right or remedy hereunder shall operate as a waiver thereof or of any other right or remedy. 本契約に基づく権利または救済の行使の遅滞または不作為は、その権利放棄、その他の権利の放棄、または救済の権利放棄としては作用しないものとする。

delayed　(形)遅らせた, 延ばした, 延期された, 遅延した

delayed arrival　延着

delayed delivery　特約日受渡し

delayed interest　遅延利息, 延滞利息, 遅延金利

delayed payment　延納

delayed settlement　特約日決済

delayed settlement transaction　着地取引（将来の一定期日に一定の条件で債券を売買することを前もって約束しておく取引）

delayed shipment　積み遅れ, 船積み遅延

delayed goods　遅延商品

◆In case there is delay in delivery of all or any part of the Goods on the time as stipulated in this agreement, the buyer is entitled to claim liquidated damages at the rate of one-half of one percent (0.5%) of the amount of the delayed Goods for each complete week of delay. 本契約で定める期限に本商品の全部または一部に引渡し遅延が生じた場合、買い主は、遅延対象の各1週間につき引渡し遅延商品の代金の0.5%を損害賠償予定額として請求することができるものとする。

delegation　(名)権限の委任, 委譲, 義務履行の委託, 債務の転付, 代理権の授与, 下請け, 代表団

◆In the event of such assignment or delegation, the assigning party or delegating shall remain liable to the other party. かかる譲渡を行う場合または下請けに出す場合、譲渡する当事者または下請けに出す当事者が引き続き相手方に対して責任を負うものとする。

delete　(動)削除する, 抹消する, 消去する, 排除する

◆In exercising these rights, Distributor may not alter or delete any credit, logo, copyright notice or trademark notice appearing on the Picture. これらの権利を行使するにあたって、輸入代理店は、本映画に現われるクレジット、ロゴ、著作権表示または商標表示を変更または削除することはできない。

deletion　(名)削除, 抹消, 消去, 排除, 削除箇所

delinquent amounts　延滞金額, 延滞金

◆Interest shall accrue on any delinquent amounts owed by Distributor for Products at the lesser of 18% per annum, or the maximum rate permitted by applicable usury law. 利息は、販売店が負っている本製品の延滞金について発生し、年18%の利率と適用される利息制限法で認められる最高利率

のうちいずれか低いほうの利率によるものとする。

deliver （動）引き渡す, 渡す, 交付する, 送達する, 納入する （⇒assume, R & D）
deliver the shipments to the order of shippers 荷送人の指図人に積み荷を渡す
delivered at dock 波止場［岸壁］渡し
delivered at frontier 国境渡し, 国境持ち込み渡し条件, DAF
delivered at station 駅渡し
delivered cost 引渡し値段
delivered（duty paid） 仕向け地持ち込み渡し（関税込み）条件, DDP
delivered（duty unpaid） 仕向け地持ち込み渡し（関税抜き）条件, DDU
delivered ex quay 埠頭持ち込み渡し条件, DEQ
delivered ex ship 本船持ち込み渡し条件, DES
delivered price 引渡し値段
delivered sale 運賃込み販売
delivered terms 持ち込み渡し条件
delivered to order 指図人渡し
delivered weight 引渡し重量 （=delivery weight）
◆Provided Licensor delivers the software without any bug, by no later than the delivery dates, Licensee shall pay Licensor a minimum guarantee of royalties of one million U.S. dollars （$1,000,000）. ライセンサーがバグのないソフトウエアを引渡し日以前に引き渡した場合, ライセンシーは, ロイヤルティの最低保証料としてライセンサーに100万米ドルを支払うものとする。◆The seller shall sell and deliver the products and the buyer shall purchase and take delivery thereof. 売り主は本商品を販売して引き渡すものとし, 買い主は本商品を買い取ってその引渡しを受けるものとする。

deliver personally 手渡す, 手交する
◆Any such notice shall be deemed given when delivered personally or, if sent by registered mail, five business days after being sent. 当該通知は, 手渡しした時点に, または書留郵便で送付した場合には送付後5営業日目に行ったものと見なされる。

delivery （名）交付, 引渡し, 送達, 配送, 納品, 納入, 意見の発表, 陳述
agreed place of delivery 合意引渡し場所, 納品場所
alongside delivery 船側渡し, 自家取り
basket delivery バスケット方式
cash on delivery sale 代金引換え販売 （=collect on delivery sale）
collect on delivery 代金引換え渡し
collect on delivery sale 代金引換え販売
constructive delivery 推定引渡し

cut off delivery 配送を中止する
delay in delivery 引渡し遅延, 納品の遅れ
delivery against letter of guarantee 保証状荷渡し
delivery against payment 支払い渡し
delivery area 配送区域, 配達区域 （=delivery zone）
delivery arrangement 配送手配, 配達手配
delivery at a fixed future time 確定日渡し
delivery basis 出荷基準, 納入基準
delivery bill 引渡し証券
delivery by hand 直接手渡し, 手渡し, 手交 （=personal delivery）
delivery by installments 割賦引渡し （=installment delivery）
delivery confirmation 配達証明 （=delivery certificate）
delivery cost 運送費, 配送コスト
delivery deadline 納期
delivery distance 配送距離, 配達距離
delivery ex-warehouse 倉渡し, 総揚げ
delivery free 配達無料
delivery hose 引渡し用ホース
delivery in bond 保税渡し
delivery in full 全荷渡し （=full delivery）
delivery in lighter はしけ渡し
delivery in tank 油槽船渡し
delivery in truck 貨物自動車渡し
delivery inspection 出荷検査
delivery mechanism 受渡し方法
delivery month 限月（げんげつ）, 受渡し限月 （=contract month）
delivery note 納品書, 物品受領証, 貨物引渡し通知書, 配達証明書
delivery notice 受渡し通知, 納品書
delivery of exchange contract 為替予約の実行
delivery of goods 荷渡し, 商品の出荷
delivery of master tape マスター・テープの引渡し
delivery of public notice 公示送達
delivery of shares 株の受渡し
delivery on a fixed date 確定日渡し
delivery on arrival 到着渡し, 着荷渡し
delivery on rail 鉄道貨車渡し, 貨車積込み渡し
delivery on term 定期渡し
delivery on the depository 置場渡し
delivery order 荷渡し指図書, 積み荷渡し指図書, 蔵出し指図書, 出荷指示

delivery period 納期

delivery permit 引渡し許可書

delivery platform 荷渡し場

delivery price 受渡し値段

delivery receipt 受渡し品, 配達品受取証, 受取証

delivery record 貨物受渡し書類

delivery schedule 納品予定, 納品日程, 納期

delivery specification 受渡し明細

delivery system 配送システム

delivery tax 蔵出し税

delivery terms 引渡し条件, 受渡し条件 (=terms of delivery)

delivery time 納期, 引渡し期限, 配送に要する時間

delivery verification 通関証明書

delivery versus payment 証券と資金の同時決済, 支払い渡し

delivery weight 引渡し重量

delivery window 受渡し期間

direct delivery 直接引渡し

do delivery 引渡しを行う, 納品する, 配送する

export deliveries 輸出出荷

express delivery 急送, 速達

extension of delivery 荷渡し延期

final place of delivery 最終納品先

forward delivery 先渡し

full delivery 全荷渡し (=complete delivery)

future delivery 先渡し, 先限

home delivery service 宅配便

immediate delivery 直(じき)渡し (=prompt delivery)

industrial delivery 鉱工業製品出荷

international parcel delivery service 国際宅配便

joint delivery 共同配送

late delivery 引渡し遅延 (=delay in delivery)

make delivery 引渡しを行う, 納品する, 納品を行う

next-day delivery 翌日配送

non-delivery 引渡し不履行, 不着

offer same-day delivery 当日配送をする

on delivery 配送時に, 納品時に

overnight delivery 翌日渡し

pay on delivery 引渡し同時払い

payment after delivery 受渡し後払い

payment on delivery 受渡し払い, 引換え払い

personal delivery 手渡し

physical delivery 現物受渡し

port of delivery 貨物引渡し港, 引渡し港, 荷下ろし港

receive delivery 納品を受ける

refuse delivery 納品を拒否する

regular delivery 定期渡し

shipside delivery 自家取り

short delivery 不足配達, 受渡し品不足, 個数不足, 揚げ荷不足

special delivery 速達

spot delivery 現場渡し, 現物渡し

spread delivery 延べ渡し

take delivery 購入し引き取る, 買い取って引渡しを受ける

take delivery of shipment 納入された荷を受け取る

take in delivery 納品を受ける, 納品を受け取る

terms of delivery 引渡し条件

the delivery of the Goods 本商品の引渡し

the place of delivery 引渡し場所

the time of delivery 引渡し期限, 納期

timely delivery 期限どおりの納品

upon the delivery of the products 本商品の引渡しが行われ次第, 本商品の引渡し時に

withhold delivery 引渡しを保留する

wrong delivery 誤送配達

◆After the delivery of the Goods, any taxes, customs duties, export or import surcharges or other governmental charges shall be for the account of the Buyer. 本商品の引渡し後、税金、関税、輸出・輸入税、その他政府が賦課する費用は、買い主の負担とする。◆Delivery of the software products to the buyer shall be completed when shipped, FOB Seller's plant in New York. ソフトウエア製品の買い主への引渡しは、ニューヨークの売り主の工場でFOB条件で出荷された時点で完了するものとする。◆If delivery is made under the terms of CFR or CIF, the Seller shall inform the Buyer of the name, nationality, age and other details of the carrying vessel by Fax or E-mail not later than fourteen (14) days before the time of delivery. 引渡しがCFR (運賃込み)またはCIF (運賃保険料込み)の条件で行われる場合、売り主は、引渡し期限の14日前までにファクスかEメールで本船の船名、船籍、船齢その他の詳細を買い主に通知するものとする。◆If delivery is made under the terms of FOB, the Buyer shall book shipping space in accordance with the time of delivery stipulated in this agreement. 引渡しがFOBの条件で行われる場合、買い主は、本契約で定める引渡し期限に従って(本船の)船腹を予約するものとする。◆In case there is delay in delivery of all or any part of the Goods on the time as stipulated in this agreement, the buyer is entitled to claim liquidated damages at the rate of one-half of one percent（0.5％）of the amount of the delayed Goods for each complete week of delay. 本契約で定める期限に本商品の全部または一部に引渡し遅延が生じた場合、買い主は、遅延対象の各1週間につき引渡し遅延商品の代金の0.5％を損害賠償予定額として請求することができるものとする。◆Other competitive factors in the market for the products are service, delivery, technological capability, and product quality and performance. 市場での製品の競争要因としては、サービスや納入、技術活用能力［技術力］、品質、性能なども挙げられる。◆The irrevocable letter of credit shall not expire until fifteen（15）days after the last day of time of delivery specified in this Agreement. この取消不能信用状は、本契約で定める引渡し期限の最終日から15日までは失効しないものとする。◆The Seller may withhold delivery or cancel the Agreement if the Buyer fails to establish the letter of credit by the date stipulated in this Agreement. 買い主が本契約で定める期限までに信用状を開設することができない場合、売り主は、引渡しを保留するか契約を解除することができる。◆We will do our best to speed up delivery if you accept the counter offer. このカウンター・オファーを受けていただければ、全力を挙げて配送を急がせます。

delivery charge 配送料金, 運送・引渡し費用, 配達料
◆Net Wholesale Price referred to in this agreement is defined as the amount of the gross sales by ABC of the licensed products to ABC's customers in the territory, less customary trade discounts, insurance premiums, transportation and delivery charges, taxes（VAT）and duties. 本契約書に記載される「純卸売り販売額」とは、ABCの顧客に対する契約地域内でのABCの許諾製品の総売上高（総販売額）から、通常の卸売り割引額、保険料、運送・引渡し費用、税金（付加価値税）と関税を差し引いた額のことをいう。

delivery date 引渡し日, 受渡し日, 配送日, 納期
◆At least sixty days prior to the requested delivery date, the buyer shall provide the seller with a written estimate of its requirements of the product, which shall constitute a firm order. 希望渡し日から少なくとも60日前に、買い主は、本製品の需要予測書［需要見積り書］を売り主に提出し、これを確定注文とするものとする。

delivery of the products 本製品の引渡し
◆In case payment by the purchaser for the delivery of the products is delayed later than 35 days after B/L date, the purchaser shall pay to the seller on demand the amount due together with interest from the due date until paid at the annual rate equal to the prime rate plus 5 percent per year on any overdue amount. 買い主による本

製品の引渡しに対する支払いが船荷証券の日付から35日を超えて遅延した場合、買い主は請求のあり次第売り主に対して期限到来債務を支払うとともに、延滞金については支払い期日から支払い日までプライム・レートに年率5%を加えた年間利率で利息を支払うものとする。

delivery, use or performance of the licensed program 許諾プログラムの引渡し, 使用または履行
◆The express warranty stated above is in lieu of all liabilities or obligations of ABC for damages arising from or in connection with the delivery, use or performance of the licensed program. 上記の明示保証は、許諾プログラムの引渡し、使用または履行から生じる損害、またはこれに関連して発生する損害に対するABCの債務または責任に代わるものである。

demand （名）要求, 請求, 催促, 申立て書, 需要
be payable on demand 一覧払い
demand for arbitration 仲裁の請求, 仲裁申立て書
on demand 請求あり次第, 要求あり次第, 一覧払いの
◆As there is a limit to our output at present, we have some difficulty in meeting the demand. 現在のところ、当社の生産には限界があり、需要に応じるのがかなり困難です。◆In emerging countries, demand for infrastructure to improve the quality of life and promote industry is expected to grow fast. 新興国では、生活向上や産業振興のためのインフラ需要が高まると見られる。◆Japan's trade deficit in April-September 2014 hit a record high due to increased demand for liquefied natural gas for thermal power generation and a rise in overall import prices stemming from the yen's depreciation. 日本の2014年度上半期（4〜9月）の貿易赤字は、火力発電所向け液化天然ガス（LNG）の需要増加と円安による輸入物価全体の上昇で、過去最大となった。◆Sharp Corp. intends to augment its home electronics business in Middle Eastern and African countries by introducing a series of luxury products to cater to increased demand from wealthy consumers. シャープは、高級家電を相次いで投入して、中東・アフリカ諸国の家電事業を強化し、増加する富裕層の需要に応える方針だ。◆We have on hand such a rush of orders for this item that our output capacity cannot keep up with the demand. 本品に対しては多くの注文が入っているため、当社の生産能力が需要に追いつかない状況です。◆We regret to inform you that we may not be able to ship all of your requirements due to the unforeseen increase in the demand for the goods. 本品に対する需要が思いもかけず増大したため、遺憾ながらご入用の品全部の船積みは不可能になるかと思います。

demonstration （名）デモ, デモ行進, 集団意思表示, 示威運動, 実物宣伝, 実演, 実演宣伝, 実演販売, 実証実験, 実証, 表示, 表明, 明示, 立

証, 証明, 論証, 証拠, 例証, 実例, 陽動作戦, デモンストレーション

anti-Japan demonstration 反日デモ

citizen demonstration 市民デモ

demonstration against the government 反政府デモ

demonstration expenses 実演宣伝費

demonstration model 展示車

demonstration parade［march］ デモ行進

demonstration sales 実演販売, デモンストレーション・セールス

give a demonstration of a new product 新製品の実演販売をする

protest demonstration 抗議デモ

street demonstration 街頭デモ

◆The Chinese government allowed people to stage a campaign to boycott Japanese products following anti-Japan demonstrations. 中国政府は, 反日デモに続いて, 中国人の日本製品の不買運動をも容認した。

demonstrator （名）デモ参加者, デモ隊, 示威運動参加者, 実演販売員, 実演者, 実物宣伝用商品, 実地教授者, 立証者［証明者, 論証者］, 証拠となるもの

◆Some Japanese-affiliated companies and Japanese restaurants have been forced to suspend their factory operations or close their outlets due to the acts of destruction by Chinese demonstrators. 一部の日系企業や日本料理店は, 中国のデモ隊による破壊行為で, 工場の操業停止や店舗の休業に追い込まれている。◆The attack on a Panasonic Corp. factory which has played a pioneering role in expanding its operations in China by a violent mob of anti-Japan demonstrators symbolizes the current bleak state of Japan-China relations. 中国進出で先駆的役割を果たしてきたパナソニックの工場が, 反日デモ隊の暴徒に襲われた事件は, 日中関係の寒々しい現状を象徴している。◆This reckless violence by Chinese anti-Japan demonstrators followed vandalism against Japanese-affiliated companies in a number of places in China. 中国の反日デモ隊によるこうした狼藉は, 中国各地で起きた日系企業への破壊行為に続いて発生した。

-denominated （形）〜建ての, 〜表示の, 〜ベースの

dollar-denominated deal ドル建て案件

dollar-denominated instrument ドル建て商品

dollar-denominated new issuance ドル建て起債総額

dollar-denominated receivables ドル建て債権

foreign currency-denominated bonds 外貨建て債券

foreign currency-denominated securities 外貨建て債

in dollar-denominated terms ドル建てで, ドル表示で

yen-denominated amounts 円ベースの総額

yen-denominated bond 円建て債, 円債

yen-denominated exports 円建て輸出

◆The greater part of the consolidated revenues and assets of the company is denominated in U.S. dollars. 同社の連結売上高と連結資産の大半は, 米ドル建てとなっている。

Department of Commerce 米国商務省, 米商務省, DOC

Bureau of Export Administration 輸出管理局

Deputy Secretary of Commerce 商務副長官

Export Promotion Services 輸出促進部

International Trade Administration 国際貿易局

Office of Export Enforcement 輸出統制法執行法課

Office of Export Licensing 輸出免許課

Patent and Trademark Office 特許・商標局

Secretary of Commerce 商務長官

U.S. and Foreign Commercial Service 米国・外国商業促進サービス局

departure （名）出発, 出発地, 発車, 便, 出国, 逸脱, 離脱, 離反, 違反, 背反, 脱却, 決別, 変更, 転換, 辞職, 辞任, 発展, 新機軸, 新しい試み, 新方針

a departure from the normal 常軌を逸したもの

a new departure 新方針, 新しい試み, 新機軸, 新案

a point of departure 出発点

arrival and departure 発着

departure flight 出発便

departure from a time-honored management style 伝統的な経営手法からの脱却

departure gate 出発ゲート

departure lounge 出発ロビー, 乗客用待合室

departure time 出発時刻

departures board 出発時刻表示板

estimated time of departure 出港予定日, 出航予定日, 出発予定時刻［日時］, ETD

make a new departure in 〜に新機軸を生み出す

◆The move will make departure from Matsushita's time-honored management style, under which group companies have been given considerable discretionary powers. この動きは, グループ企業にかなりの自由裁量権を与えてきた松下電器の伝統的な経営手法からの脱却を目指すものだ。◆To correct unfairness in the industry caused by the government's bailout of JAL, the Land, Infrastructure, Transport and Tourism Ministry will allocate 11 arrival and departure slots for international flights, scheduled to be added to Haneda Airport in late March 2014, to ANA Holdings inc. and only five to Japan Airlines. 日航への公的支援により生じた業界格差［同業他社との格差］を是正するため、国土交通省は、2014年末から拡充する羽田空港の国際線発着枠について、ANAホールディングスに11便、日本航空には5便だけを割り当てる方針だ。

depend on [upon] ～による、～に依存する、～に頼る、～を信頼する、～次第である、～にかかっている、～を当てにする

◆As long as Japan depends on thermal power generation as an alternative electricity source, LNG imports will continue to increase and the nation's wealth will flow to countries rich in natural resources. 日本が代替電源として火力発電に依存するかぎり、天然液化ガス（LNG）の輸入額は増え続け、国富は天然資源の豊富な国に流出する。 ◆Comparative advantage in this new global market depends not only on superior R&D, but also on speed in making management decisions, finding unique applications for research advances and delivering them to customers ahead of competitors. この新しいグローバル市場で比較優位性を確立できるかどうかは、高度な研究開発だけでなく、経営の意思決定を迅速に行えるかどうかと、研究を進めるうえで独創的な適用範囲［用途］を素早く確認して、それを競合他社に先駆けて製品化できるかどうかにかかっている。 ◆Depending on moves in foreign exchange markets, there is a risk we may lose initial investments in foreign currency deposits. 為替相場の動き次第で、外貨預金では初期投資額を割り込むリスクがある。 ◆Japan depends on the Middle East for about 80 percent of its crude oil imports. 日本は、原油輸入の約8割を中東に依存している。

dependence （名）依存、依存状態、依存体質、依存度、依存症、依存関係、常用癖、信頼、信用、左右されること

dependence on imports　輸入依存 (=import dependence)

dependence on specific market segments　特定市場への依存［依存度］

economic dependence　経済的依存

external dependence　対外依存

trade dependence　貿易依存、貿易への依存度 (=dependence on trade)

trade dependence rate　貿易依存率

◆Japanese export companies must end their excessive dependence on North America. 日本の輸出企業は、過度の北米依存を止めなければならない。

dependency （名）依存、依存度、依存状態、依存物、保護領、属国

dependency on public bonds　公債依存度

oil dependency　石油［原油］依存度

◆Financial exchanges between the BRICs group,

Indonesia and South Korea will move toward a tri-reserve-currency regime by losing a dependency on the U.S. dollar. BRICsグループ（ブラジル、ロシア、インド、中国）とインドネシア、韓国の新興6か国間の金融取引は今後、米ドルに依存しなくなるため、3準備通貨体制に移行するものと思われる。

depreciate （動）通貨を切り下げる、減価償却する、償却する　（自動）低下する、下落する、価値が下がる、軟化する

(⇒depreciation of the dollar)

depreciate over time　長期的に下落する

depreciate the currency　通貨を切り下げる

◆All fixed assets are depreciated on the straight line basis. 固定資産は、すべて定額法で減価償却されている。 ◆In the case of Tokyo Electric Power Co., its fuel costs will increase by ￥33 billion per year if the yen is depreciated by ￥1 to the dollar for one year from the estimated exchange rate. 東京電力の場合、想定為替レートからドルに対して1ドル＝1円の円安が1年間続いた場合、同社の燃料費は1年間で330億円増える。

depreciation of the dollar　ドル安

◆A depreciation of the dollar may stimulate external demand and ignite an export-driven economic upturn. ドル安は、外需を喚起して、輸出主導の景気回復につながる可能性がある。 ◆The effects of the recent depreciation of the dollar have not been seen yet, but if the U.S. currency depreciates further, it may lead to an increase in imported commodity prices, which in turn may become an inflationary factor. 最近のドル安の影響はまだ見られないが、米ドルがさらに下落すれば、輸入品価格の上昇を招き、これがまた逆にインフレ要因になる恐れがある。

depreciation of the greenback　ドル安

◆The depreciation of the greenback will result in exchange losses on assets held in dollars. ドル安が進むと、保有するドル建て資産に為替差損が生じる。

depreciation of the yen　円安

◆A weak yen benefits the export industries such as automobiles and home appliances, but excessive depreciation of the yen could have the negative effect on the Japanese economy. 円安は自動車や家電など輸出産業には追い風だが、過度の円安は日本経済に悪影響を及ぼす可能性もある。 ◆The weaker yen helps exporters, but close attention must be paid to the fact that the excessive depreciation of the yen will further increase the prices of imports of LNG and other foreign products. 円安は輸出企業にはプラスだが、円安が行き過ぎると、天然液化ガス（LNG）など海外製品の輸入額が一段と増えることにも、警戒が必要である。

derangement （名）故障、混乱、無秩序、（精神）錯乱

a temporary derangement of machine　機械の一時的故障

DESI

deregulate （動）規制を緩和する, 規制を撤廃する, 自由化する, 市場開放する
◆Bank sales of insurance products were deregulated in April 2001. 保険商品の銀行窓口での販売は、2001年4月に自由化された。

deregulation （名）規制緩和, 規制撤廃, 自由化, 市場開放 （⇒regulation）
financial deregulation　金融の規制緩和 （=deregulation of finance）
increasing competition due to deregulation　規制緩和による競争の激化
interest rate deregulation　金利の自由化
◆Although there has been a gradual increase in passengers, airfares are dropping because of deregulation and fierce competition from foreign airlines. 旅客は少しずつ増えてはいるが、規制緩和と外国航空会社との熾烈な競争で、航空運賃が下がり続けている。◆As deregulation, the Abe administration's growth strategy includes a plan to lift a ban on the online sales of nonprescription drugs. 規制緩和として、安倍政権の成長戦略には、市販薬のネット販売解禁案が盛り込まれている。

derivative （名）派生商品, 金融派生商品, 派製品, 派生物, 二次著作物, デリバティブ （=derivative product）
currency derivatives　為替デリバティブ（銀行と顧客が、あらかじめ決めた価格で外貨を売買する契約を結ぶ商品。円安になると輸入コストが大きくなるが、一定の価格で外貨を売買する契約を結んでおけば、円安が進んでも実際のレートより安く外貨を調達できるので、輸入品の購入が有利となる。毎月一定額の外貨を購入する商品が中心で、途中解約すれば、違約金として銀行から数千万から数億円を求められるケースもある）
derivative product　派生商品, 金融派生商品, デリバティブ （=derivative）
◆ "Derivatives" are products manufactured by processing biological resources.「派生物」とは、生物資源を加工して製造した商品のことである。◆Gross foreign assets held by Japanese in the form of direct investment, securities investment, financial derivatives, loans and export credits, deposits, other investments and official foreign reserves came to ¥379.78 trillion. 直接投資、証券投資、金融派生商品、貸付け金や輸出信用、預金その他の投資と政府の外貨準備高の形で日本の政府や企業、個人が保有する海外資産の総額（対外資産残高）は、379兆7,800億円に達した。◆Investment advisory company AIJ started investing in financial derivatives through funds based in the Cayman Islands, a tax haven, since 2002. 投資顧問会社のAIJは、2002年から、租税回避地の英領ケイマン諸島を営業基盤とするファンドを通じて金融派生商品への投資を始めた。

解説 デリバティブとは：通貨や株式の現物取引でなく、相場の変動を予測して行う先物取引や異なる通貨や金利を交換するスワップ取引、株式や債券を売買する権利を取引するオプション取引など、特殊な取引を組み合わせた金融派生商品。

derivative contracts　金融派生商品
◆Libor is widely used as a benchmark for rates of corporate loans, derivatives contracts and many other financial deals. ライボー（ロンドン銀行間取引金利）は、企業向け融資や金融派生商品などの金融取引の金利の指標に幅広く使われている。

derivative transaction　デリバティブ取引
◆The credit union was engaged in derivative transactions with Lehman Brothers' branch office in Tokyo. 同信用組合は、米証券大手のリーマン・ブラザーズ証券東京支店とデリバティブ取引を行っていた。

describe （動）記載する, 記述する, 説明する, 解説する, 表示する
◆Licensor warrants that its products will conform to descriptions described in Exhibit C attached hereto. ライセンサーは、その製品が本契約書に添付する付属書類Cに記載した仕様に一致することを保証する。

description （名）記載, 記述, 説明, 解説, 表示, 明細, 明細書, 記載事項, 記載内容, 説明書, 解説書, 種類, 種目, 銘柄, 品名, 職業
any goods of the same description as the products　本製品と同じ種類の商品
description of goods　（契約上の）商品名
◆The Products to be delivered under this agreement shall conform to the samples to be supplied by the seller to the purchaser before the shipment in accordance with the provisions of Article V in regard to description, quality, color and conditions. 本契約に基づき引き渡す商品は、品目、品質、色と状態に関して、第5条の規定に従って船積み前に売り主が買い主に提供する見本と一致するものとする。◆The seller warrants and represents that the products will conform to their descriptions set forth in Exhibit D. 売り主は、本製品が付属書類Dに記載する本製品の明細に合致することを保証し、表明する。

design （名）意匠, 意匠権, 設計, 計画, 構想, デザイン （⇒intellectual property）
alternative design　代替設計
application for design registration　意匠登録出願
design examination　意匠審査
design registration　意匠登録
design right　意匠権 （=registered design right）
designs, specifications and drawings　設計図、仕様書と図面
identicalness of design　意匠の同一（物品や物品の形態が同一であること）

143

D

one application for one design　一意匠一出願

owner of a（registered）design right　意匠権者

similarity of design　意匠の類似

the Design Law　意匠法

◆The seller shall be responsible to the purchaser for such infringement in the seller's country, if the patent, utility model, design, trademark, copyright, trade secret or any other intellectual property right is not designated, selected or provided by the purchaser. 売り主は、売り主の国内での当該侵害については、その特許、実用新案、意匠、商標、著作権、トレード・シークレットまたはその他の知的財産権を買い主が指定、選定または提供した場合を除いて、買い主に対して責任を負うものとする。

designate　（動）示す, 明示する, 指示する, 指名する, 任命する, 指定する, 称する（⇒bill of lading, design）

designated goods　指定商品

◆ABC agrees to pay in cash the annual royalty set forth above, within 20 days after XYZ's approval of the samples of any item of the designated goods, or on or before the first day of April of each year, whichever comes first. ABCは、指定商品の品目の見本についてXYZの承諾を得てから20日以内と毎年4月1日のうち、いずれか早いうの日に、前項で定める年間ロイヤルティを現金で支払うことに同意する。

designated representative　指定代理人

destination　（名）仕向け地, 目的地

the country of destination　仕向け国, 仕向け地

the delivery at the final destination　最終目的地での引渡し

the final destination　最終目的地

◆Such inspection shall not, in any way, prejudice the purchaser's right of inspection of the products after the delivery at the final destination or rejection of the defective products. この検査は、最終目的地での引渡し後に本製品を検査する買い主の権利、または瑕疵（かし）ある製品を拒絶する買い主の権利をいかなる意味でも損なわないものとする。

destruction of data　データの破壊

detail　（名）詳細, 細部, 細目, 細かい点, 明細, 特派部隊（員）, 選抜隊（員）, 特別任務　（動）詳細に［詳しく］述べる, こまごまと記述する, ～するよう命令する

attention to detail　細部への気配り

detail account　明細清算書

detail checking　精査

details　詳細, 詳細な記述

for further details on　～についてさらに詳しいことは

for more details　詳細については, 詳しいことは

give full details of　～の詳細を伝える

go into detail　細部にわたる, 詳しく述べる

in detail　細部にわたって, 詳細に, 項目ごとに

rich detail　豊富なデータ

◆The period, time, method, and reasonable details of such visits shall be determined separately through mutual consultation between the parties. このような訪問［視察］の期間、時期、方法と合理的な詳細は、当事者間の相互協議により別途決定するものとする。◆The TSE does not plan to release details on names of stock issues or methods of short selling. 東証は、空売りの対象の個別銘柄や空売りの手口などの詳細については、公表しない方針だ。

detailed　（形）詳細な, 精密な, 細目の, 細かい

a more detailed account　より詳細な説明

a pamphlet giving detailed information on　～の詳細を示すパンフレット

detailed instructions　細かい指示

detailed statement　明細書

detention　（名）延滞料金

determine　（動）決定する, 判断する, 解決する, 裁定する, 裁決する, ～に判決を下す, ～を終結させる

◆The rights and liability of the parties shall be determined in accordance with the laws of Japan. 当事者の権利と義務は、日本の法律に従って判断するものとする。

devalue　（動）為替レートや通貨などを引き下げる, 平価を切り下げる, 価値を減じる, 通貨安になる　（=devaluate）

devalue the currency　通貨を切り下げる, 通貨を安くする

devalue the pound　ポンドを切り下げる

◆In a currency war, countries intentionally devalue their currencies to boost exports. 通貨安戦争では、各国が輸出に追い風となるように自国通貨の為替レートを意図的に安く誘導する。◆Rectifying trade imbalances mainly with China by devaluing the dollar is the top priority in Washington. ドル安により主に中国との貿易不均衡を是正するのが、米国の最優先課題だ。

devanning　（名）デバンニング（コンテナから貨物を取り出す作業のこと）

develop　（動）開発する, 開拓する, 整備する, 構築する, 策定する, 改善する, 改良する, 発展させる, 進展させる, 育成する, 土地などを造成する, 展開する, 現像する, （病気などに）かかる, ～を発病する, 引き起こす, （習慣などが）つく　（自動）発達する, 発展する, 成長する, 伸びる, 拡大する, 広がる, 深刻化する, 生じる, 改善する

develop a presence through mergers　合併で事業を拡大する

develop customers　顧客を開拓する

develop from　～から生じる

develop human resources　人材を開発する, 人材を育成する

develop line extensions　製品ラインの拡大を図る

develop the largest possible market　可能な最大の市場を開拓する

jointly develop　共同開発する

◆ABC has developed, markets and licenses on a worldwide basis and owns all copyrights and other proprietary rights to or has the right to license the computer software programs. ABCは世界市場に向けてコンピュータ・ソフトウエア・プログラムをすでに開発してその販売と使用許諾をしており, このプログラムの著作権その他の所有権をすべて保有するとともに, このプログラムの使用を許諾する権利をもっている。◆Sumitomo Corp. agreed to jointly develop rare earths and import the metals with Kazakhstan's state-owned resource firm Kazatomprom. 住友商事は, カザフスタンの国営資源企業「カザトムプロム」と, レア・アースを共同開発して輸入することで合意した。

develop a competitive product　競争力のある商品を開発する

◆The key to the success of a business hinges on how well it can cultivate a new market by capturing consumer needs before anyone else to develop competitive products. 企業成功のカギは, 消費者ニーズを先取りし, 競争力のある商品を開発して, いかに新市場を開拓できるかにある。

develop a technology　技術を開発する

◆Kirin has developed and holds a patent on a technology through which human antibodies can be created using a particular type of mice. キリンは, 特殊なマウスを使ってヒト抗体を作ることができる技術を開発して, その特許を持っている。

develop an attractive product　魅力的な商品を開発する

◆To increase exports, Japanese manufacturers must develop attractive products of high added value and find ways to capitalize on growing markets in the emerging economies of Asia and other regions. 輸出を拡大するには, 日本の製造業各社が, 付加価値の高い魅力的な商品を開発して, アジアなどの地域の新興国の成長市場を積極的に取り込む方法を見つける必要がある。

develop the market　市場を開拓する

◆Distributor shall use its best efforts to distribute the Products and fully develop the market within the Territory. 販売店は, 最善を尽くして販売地域内で本製品を販売し, 市場を十分に開拓する。

developing Asia　開発途上のアジア, アジアの開発途上国, アジアの途上国

◆Developing Asia's capital markets have not shown excessive volatility, but the risk of rapid reversals in capital flows to the region is a concern. アジア途上国の資本市場に過度の変動は見られないが, 資本移動の同地域への急激な逆転[反

転]リスクが懸念される。

developing country　発展途上国, 開発途上国, 途上国

◆The company supports the transfer of technology and knowhow that the developing countries need. 同社は, 開発途上国が必要としている技術やノウハウの移転を支援している。

development　（名）開発, 整備, 振興, 構築, 教育, 発展, 進歩, 進展, 展開, 推移, 動き, 情勢

application development system　アプリケーション開発システム

business development　ビジネス開発, ビジネスの展開, 業務展開

development block　開発拠点

development capital　開発資金

development cost　開発費

development finance　開発金融

development fund　開発基金, 開発資金

development loan　開発融資, 開発借款

development order　開発指図書

development project　開発プロジェクト

development risks　開発リスク

development scale　開発規模

development strategy　開発戦略

development work　開発作業

economic development　経済開発, 経済発展, 経済成長, 景気動向, 景気の動き

full-scale development　本格開発

industrial development　産業開発, 工業化

infrastructure development　インフラ開発, インフラ整備

initial development　初期開発

interest rate developments　金利動向

joint development　共同開発

market developments　市場の動き, 市場動向　(=market trends)

new-product development　新製品開発

ocean development　海洋開発

product development　製品開発

regional development　地域開発

research and development　研究開発, R&D

skills development　スキル開発

software development support　ソフトウエア開発支援

system development planning　システム開発設計

technical [technology] development　技術開発

◆The interest rate for long-term government bonds fluctuates depending on market developments. 長期国債の金利は, 市場の動き次第で大き

く変動する。

development bank 開発銀行
◆The leaders of the BRICS' five rising economies agreed to move toward creating a new development bank to help developing world. ブラジル、ロシア、インド、中国、南アフリカ（BRICS）の新興5か国首脳は、発展途上国を支援するため、BRICS開発銀行の新設を検討することで合意した。

development of a new drug 新薬の開発，創薬
◆If STAP cells using human cells can be created, this new method can be applied to medical treatment and the development of new drugs. 人間の細胞を使ってSTAP細胞を作ることができれば、この新手法は、医療や創薬への応用が可能となる。

development of cross-border infrastructure 国境を越えたインフラ整備
◆The development of cross-border infrastructure in the Greater Mekong Subregion（GMS）has prompted a number of multinational corporations to transfer some of their manufacturing processes to Laos, Cambodia and Myanmar to take advantage of cheaper labor costs. 大メコン圏での国境を越えたインフラ整備に伴い、多くの多国籍企業が、安い人件費［低賃金］の利点を生かして生産工程の一部をラオスやカンボジア、ミャンマーに移転している。

development program 開発計画，（選手などの）育成計画［プログラム］
◆In order to cut off funds to North Korea's nuclear weapons development program, the government will tighten controls on illegal bilateral transactions, including exports of materials for making missiles and smuggling of narcotics and counterfeit bank notes into the country. 北朝鮮の核兵器開発計画の資金源を断つため、政府はミサイル製造の関連物資の輸出や麻薬・偽造紙幣の密輸など、日朝間の不正取引の取締りを強化する方針だ。

development strength 開発力
◆The company needs to enhance its development strength for such products as hybrid cars to maintain the competitiveness of its vehicles and auto parts domestically manufactured, in addition to improving export-driven profits. 同社の場合、輸出主導の収益改善にとどまらず、国内生産の車両や自動車部品の競争力を維持するには、ハイブリッド車などの製品の開発力を強化する必要がある。

device （名）装置，周辺機器，電気部品，素子，道具，手段，方策，工夫，考案，操作，計画，図案，模様，意匠，デバイス
accounting device　会計上の操作
anti-inflationary device　インフレ抑制の手段
device lag　デバイス・ラグ（医療機器の開発から承認までにかかる時間の差）
devices such as personal computers and mobile phones　パソコンや携帯電話などの機器

electronic device　電子装置，電子機器
input device　入力装置
magnetic memory device　磁気記憶装置
mobile devices　携帯機器，携帯情報端末，携帯端末
mobile devices with internet capabilities　インターネット機能付き携帯情報端末，インターネット機能付き携帯端末
output device　出力装置
peripheral device　周辺装置，周辺機器
portable device　移動端末
silicon on insulator device　SOI素子
◆Because of the domestic lengthy process of approving production and sales of medical devices, some domestic medical device makers have been applying for product approval in Europe and the United States first.　国内での医療機器の製造販売承認手続きの遅れから、国内医療機器メーカーの一部は、製品の承認申請を欧米で先に行っている。◆Rare earths are indispensable for making parts for energy-saving household appliances and other devices. レア・アース（希土類）は、省エネ家電やその他の製品・機器の部品製造に欠かせないものだ。

DGR 危険物規則書（dangerous goods regulationsの略）

difference （名）差，差異，違い，区別，意見の違い［食い違い］，意見の不一致，意見の対立，不和，紛争，格差，差額，不足分，重大な変化［影響］
difference between winners and losers　勝ち組と負け組の差
share the difference on a 50-50 basis　差額を折半する
◆Even within the same electrical machinery sector, the difference between winners and losers has become more apparent. 同じ電機業界でも、勝ち組と負け組の差が鮮明になっている。

difference in quality 品質の差，品質差
◆The company offered a 10 percent discount to make up for the difference in quality. 品質差の埋め合わせのため、同社は10%値引きした。

difference or dispute 意見の相違または紛争，見解の相違または紛争
◆Any difference or dispute between the parties concerning the interpretation or validity of this agreement or the rights and liability of the parties shall be settled by arbitration in Tokyo, Japan. 本契約の解釈または有効性、または当事者の権利と責任に関して当事者間に意見の相違または紛争が生じた場合には、すべて日本国東京で仲裁により解決する。

digital consumer electronics デジタル家電，デジタル家電製品（=digital home appliances）
◆The cross licensing agreement will allow the

two firms to save time and costs for developing digital consumer electronics. クロス・ライセンス契約で、両社は、デジタル家電製品の開発期間とコストを削減することができる。

diligence （名）注意, 注意義務 （⇒due diligence）

dilute （動）薄める, 希薄化する, 希釈する, 減少する

dilute a trademark　商標を希薄化する, 商標の希薄化を招く

diluted common share　希薄化された普通株式

diluted earnings per share　希薄化後1株当たり利益　（=diluted EPS）

diluted earnings per share of common stock　希薄化後普通株式1株当たり純利益

fully diluted earnings per common shares　完全希薄化[完全希釈化]による普通株式1株当たり利益, 潜在株式調整後1株当たり利益

on a diluted basis　希薄化ベースで, 希釈化ベースで

on a fully diluted basis　完全希釈化ベースで, 完全希釈化ベースで

primary and fully diluted earnings per share　単純希薄化と完全希薄化による1株当たり利益

◆At December 2014, the investment in the firm represented an interest of approximately 30 % on a fully diluted basis. 2014年12月現在、同社に対する投資額は、完全希薄化ベースで約30%の持ち分を占めています。

direct export　直接輸出

◆The trade insurance of Nippon Export and Investment Insurance previously only covered direct exports by domestic firms. 独立行政法人・日本貿易保険の貿易保険はこれまで、国内企業の直接輸出だけが対象だった。

direct investment　直接投資 （⇒foreign direct investment）

direct overseas investment　海外直接投資

external direct investment　対外直接投資

foreign direct investment　海外からの直接投資, 対外直接投資

inward direct investment　対内直接投資

vertical direct investment　垂直的直接投資

◆All the numerical targets of private capital investment, infrastructure exports and direct investment to Japan Prime Minister Abe has revealed are ambitious and lofty goals, but these goals are meaningless if they end up as empty promises. 安倍首相が示した民間投資、インフラ輸出、対日直接投資の数値目標は、すべて野心的な高い目標ではあるが、これらの目標も最終的に空手形では意味がない。◆Japanese companies' direct investment in Southeast Asia in the first half of 2013 posted a fourfold year-on-year jump to about ￥1 trillion, which is twice as high as China-bound investment. 2013年上半期の日本企業の東南アジア向け直接投資は、前年同期比4倍増の約1兆円で、中国向け投資の2倍となっている。

direct yen-yuan trading　円と人民元の直接取引

◆Banks participating in direct yen-yuan trading in the Tokyo interbank foreign exchange market will trade the yen and the yuan at an exchange rate calculated on the basis of actual supply and demand. 東京外国為替市場で円・人民元の直接取引に参加する銀行は、実際の需給などをもとに算出した取引レートで、円と人民元を銀行間で取引する。◆Direct yen-yuan trading started on the interbank foreign exchange markets in Tokyo and Shanghai on June 1, 2012. 円と中国の通貨・人民元の直接取引が、東京、上海の銀行間外国為替市場で2012年6月1日から始まった。

director　（名）取締役（取締役会のメンバーであるが、日本と違って英米法ではかならずしも役員ではない）

the appointment of directors　取締役の指名 （=the nomination of directors）

the board of directors　取締役会

the death, resignation or other removal of a director　取締役の死亡、辞任または他の理由による退任

the election of directors　取締役の選任

the initial directors of the new company　新会社の最初の取締役

the term of office of a director　取締役の任期

◆JVOC shall have five （5）directors. JVOC（合弁会社）の取締役は、5名とする。◆The directors of the new company shall be elected at a general meeting of the shareholders. 新会社の取締役は、定時株主総会で選任される。◆The holders of New Company's Class A Common Stock and Class B Common Stock, by the affirmative vote of a majority of each class Common Stock, shall elect ____Special Class Directors and may increase or decrease the number of Special Class Directors. 新会社のAクラス普通株式とBクラス普通株式の各保有者は、各クラスの普通株式の過半数の賛成投票により、特別クラスの取締役を____名選任し、特別クラスの取締役の員数を増減することができる。

disburse　（動）支払う, 支出する, 貸し付ける, 貸し出す, 融資する　（=advance）

◆The Lender will disburse the loan to ABC in accordance with the Disbursement Schedule and Procedures attached hereto as Exhibit C. 貸主は、付属書類Cとして本契約書に添付する「貸付け予定表と手続き」に従って、ABCに融資金を貸し付けるものとする。

disbursement　（名）支払い, 支出, 立替え, 支払い金, 支出金, 立替え金, 費用, 歳出

disbursement schedule and procedures　融資予定表と手続き, 貸付け予定表と手続き （⇒disburse）

time and schedule for disbursement　融資実行時期

discharge （動）契約などを解除する、免除する、免責する、解消する、解雇する、解任する、取り消す、放免する、釈放する、借金を返済する、義務などを遂行する、義務・契約などを履行する
◆The guarantor shall not be discharged, nor shall its liability be affected by any time, indulgence, waiver, or consent at any time given to ABC by you. 保証人は、いつであれ貴社がABCに与えた時間、猶予、放棄または同意によって免責されないものとし、保証人の責任もこれによって影響を受けることはないものとする。

disclaim （名）責任を否認する、責任を負わない、拒否する、拒絶する、放棄する、排除する
◆The seller expressly disclaims any warranty of conditions, fitness for use or merchantability. 売り主は、状態、用途適合性または商品性の保証を明確に否認する。◆The seller makes no other warranties or representations with respect to the products and disclaims all warranties, including but not limited to implied warranties of merchantability, fitness for a particular purpose and noninfringement. 売り主は、本製品に関する他の保証または表明は行わず、商品性、特定目的への適合性および非侵害の黙示の保証などを含めてすべての保証を否認する。

disclaimer （名）責任の否認［放棄、排除］、責任免除、（監査意見の）意見差し控え、免責条項、免責事項、免責規定、権利の放棄、権利放棄条項
disclaimer of liability　責任の否認［放棄、排除］
disclaimer of opinion　意見差し控え
disclaimer of warranty　保証の否認、担保責任（warranty）を負わないこと
◆The use of this site is governed by our Disclaimer. このサイトの利用には、当社の「免責規定」が適用されます。

disclose （動）開示する、発表する、明示する
◆The Licensee shall furnish regular written report specified by the Licensor to Licensor in order to disclose in full detail pertinent information and data in connection with the sale of the Product. ライセンシーは、契約品の販売に関する関連情報とデータを十分詳細に開示するため、ライセンサーが指定する定期報告書をライセンサーに提出するものとする。

disclosure （名）企業内示の開示、企業経営内容の公開、情報の開示、情報の公開事実の開示、発明の開示、内容の特定、告知
access rights for disclosure　開示請求権
adequate disclosure　適切な開示、適正な開示
corporate disclosure　企業による情報開示
differential disclosure　差別的開示
disclosure letter　開示書
disclosure of technical information　技術情報の開示

disclosure statement　不動産物件賃貸借契約の際の重要事項説明書
financial disclosure　財務内容の開示
footnote disclosure　脚注による開示
full disclosure　完全開示
informative disclosure　情報開示
integrated disclosure system　総合開示制度
pro forma disclosure　見積りによる開示、仮定計算開示
risk disclosure　リスク開示
◆The licensee's obligation under this Article with respect to the confidential information shall not apply to information which is part of the public domain at the time of disclosure by the licensor, or thereafter becomes part of the public domain without fault on the part of the licensee. 本条に基づく秘密情報に関するライセンシーの義務は、ライセンサーによる開示の時点で公知であるか、その後ライセンシー側の過失なしに公知となる情報には適用されないものとする。

disclosure of the confidential information　秘密情報の開示
◆Each party shall not make any disclosure of the confidential information to anyone without the express written consent of the other party, except to employees, affiliate（s）or consultant（s）to whom disclosure is necessary for the performance of this agreement. 各当事者は、本契約履行のために開示が必要な従業員、関連会社またはコンサルタントに対して開示する場合を除いて、相手方の明示の書面による同意を得ないで誰に対しても秘密情報を開示しないものとする。

discontinuation of business　事業の中止
（=discontinuance of business）

discount （動）割り引く、割引する、割り引いて売る［買う］、織り込む、調整する
◆The stock price has already discounted recovery prospects. 株価は、すでに業績回復を織り込んでいる。◆The supermarket is planning to reduce the prices of more than 2,000 items including food and daily necessities this fiscal year though the company discounted about 230 items last year. このスーパーは昨年、約230品目の安売りを行ったが、今年度はさらに食料品や日用品などで2,000品目以上の値下げを計画している。

discount （名）割引、値引（き）、割引率、割引額、割引料、ディスカウント
cash discount　現金割引
discount battle　値引き競争
discount period　割引期間、割引対象期間
discount schedule　割引表
discount terms　値引き条件
offer［give］a 10% discount for large orders　大口注文には10%の割引［値引き］をする
official discount rate　公定歩合
（=discount rate）

purchase discount　仕入割引

quantity discount　数量割引

sales（cash）discount　売上割引

subdistributor discount　二次代理店割引

trade discount　卸売り割引, 仲間割引

volume discount　大口割引, 数量割引, 回数割引

◆Larger discounts are available due to the additional expense of handling trade-ins. 下取り品を扱うのに追加費用がかかるため、大幅な割引率が適用される。◆Please inform us what discount you will allow us for quantities. 大口取引に対してどれだけの値引きを認められるか、お知らせください。◆The company offered a 10 percent discount to make up for the difference in quality. 品質差の埋め合わせのため、同社は10%値引きした。◆The following price list shows our best prices and rate of quantity discount for our supplies. 以下の価格表は、当社供給品の最低価格［勉強値］と数量割引率を示しています。◆There is a discount available for a large order. 大量注文には、割引の恩典があります［値引も適用されます］。◆We hope that you will allow us an extra discount of 5 percent as the margin on this order is rather small. この注文の利益率はごく薄いので、とくに5%の値引きを認めていただきたい。

discount sales［sale, selling］　値下げセール, 割引販売, 割引売出し, ディスカウント・セール

◆Aeon and Ito-Yokado started discount sales of foods imported from the United States to pass along to consumers the benefits of the yen's sharp climb against the dollar. イオンとイトーヨーカ堂は、急激な円高・ドル安による円高差益を消費者に還元するため、米国から輸入した食品の値下げセールを開始した。

discounting　（名）割引

discounting of bill　手形割引

discounting process　割引過程

◆Excessive discounting would add to a deflationary spiral. 値引き［安売り］が行き過ぎると、デフレ・スパイラル（デフレの悪循環）につながることになる。

discovery　（名）開示, 事前開示, 証拠開示, 開示手続き

◆The arbitrators shall have the authority to order such discovery and production of documents, including the depositions of party witnesses, and to make such orders for interim relief, including injunctive relief, as they may deem just and equitable. 仲裁人は、当事者の証人の宣誓証言［証言録取書］を含めて文書の開示と提出を命じる権限と、差止救済を含めて仲裁人が正義かつ衡平と見なす暫定的救済を命じる権限を持つものとする。

discrepancy　（名）不一致, 相違, 食い違い, 信用状条件違反［ディスクレ］（=Discre: 船積書類が信用状条件と相違すること）

◆We found some discrepancies upon investiga-

tion of your letter of credit. 貴信用状を調べたところ、相違点が若干あることが判明しました。

discretion　（名）自由裁量, 裁量, 裁量権, 判断, 決定, 決定権

in one's sole discretion　～の単独の裁量で、～の単独の判断で、～のみの判断で

◆If some or all of the goods have not been received by the buyer on the termination of this contract, the buyer shall, in its sole discretion, cease to take delivery of the remaining goods and the seller shall return to the buyer any amounts paid in advance in respect of such goods. 本契約解除時に商品の一部または全部を買い主が受領していない場合、買い主は、買い主単独の選択で、残存商品［未引渡し商品］の引取りを中止し、売り主は当該商品に関して前払いで受領した代金を買い主に返還するものとする。

discuss and review in good faith　誠意をもって協議して見直す

◆If there should be a severe change in market condition or a drastic change in exchange rate during the term of this agreement, then both parties shall, at the request of either party, in good faith discuss and review the price of the Products set forth above. 本契約期間中に市況が激変した場合または為替レートが大幅に変動した場合、両当事者は、いずれか一方の要請に基づき誠意をもって上記商品の価格を協議し、その見直しをするものとする。

discussion　（名）協議, 話し合い

（⇒belong to, bona fide discussions）

◆Failure to conduct such discussions, and failure to agree upon the terms of an extension or renewal shall in no way constitute a breach of this agreement. 当該協議ができないとしても、また延長や更新の条件についての合意ができないとしても、本契約違反には決してならないものとする。

dishonor　（動）（銀行などが）手形などの支払い［引受け］を拒絶する, ～を不渡りにする（名）不渡り（nonpayment）, 不名誉, 不面目, 屈辱, 恥辱（ちじょく）

ask A for acceptance for honor if our bill has been dishonored　当社手形不渡りの場合はAに手形の参加引受けを依頼する

be dishonored　（手形が）不渡りになる

bill of dishonor　不渡り手形

dishonor a bill［check］　不渡りを出す

dishonor of bill　手形不渡り

notice of dishonor　手形不渡り通知, 不渡り通知

◆The company dishonored a bill for the first time on December 15. 同社は、12月15日に最初の不渡りを出した。

dishonored　（形）不渡りの, 不渡りになった, 不名誉な

dishonored bill　不渡り手形　（=bill of dishonor）

dishonored check　不渡り小切手

DISM 150

(=bad check, rubbed check）
note dishonored　不渡り手形
（=dishonored note）
pass a dishonored draft　不渡り手形を振り出す

dismiss　（動）解雇する，解散する，解任する，却下する，棄却する，取り下げる
◆It shall constitute an event of default if either party is the subject of any proceeding relating its liquidation or insolvency which is not dismissed within 30 days. いずれかの当事者が清算または支払い不能手続きの対象となり，当該手続きが30日以内に取り下げられないときは，不履行事由となる。

dispatch　（動）（文書などを）発送する，発信する，送信する，派遣する，動員する，配車する
◆We fear we have to advise you that we may not be able to dispatch in full your order due to the shortage of shipping space. 不本意ながら，船腹不足のため，貴社の注文が一部積み残しになる可能性があることをお伝えしなければなりません。

dispatch [dispatch]　（名）発送，発信，送信，派遣，迅速，至急便，速達便，運送店
advise the dispatch of your sample　貴社見本の発送を伝える
dispatch money　早出料
foreign dispatch　外電
with all possible dispatch　大至急
with dispatch　至急，てきぱきと
◆Notices, demands and communications mentioned above shall be deemed to be received ten（10）days after their dispatch. 上記の通知，要求，通信は，発信の10日後に受領したものと見なされる。

dispensation　（名）適用免除

disperse　（動）分散させる，解散させる，拡散させる，分散配置する，広める
disperse the risk　リスクを分散する
widely dispersed creditors　幅広く分散した債権者［債権保有者，資金供与者］
widely dispersed markets　幅広く分散した市場
◆Nonlife insurance companies used to disperse the risk of large contracts with new corporate clients through reinsurance contracts with other insurance or reinsurance companies. 損保各社は従来，他の保険会社もしくは再保険会社と再保険契約を結んで，新規顧客企業と大型契約を結ぶリスクを分散してきた。

displacement tonnage　排水トン数

display　（名）陳列，展示，展示会，〜大会，〜ショー，（能力や創造性の）発揮，表現，（感情の）現れ，（弱点などの）露呈，見せびらかし，誇示（こじ），（鳥や動物の）求愛行動，画面表示，表示装置，表示端末装置，ディスプレー
a display case　陳列ケース

be put［placed］on public display　一般に公開される
color liquid crystal display　カラー液晶ディスプレー
display ad　大型広告
display board　（電光）掲示板
display item　展示物
display panel　表示パネル
go on display　陳列展示される，一般に公開される
graphic display unit　図形表示装置
high quality display　高解像度ディスプレー　（=high resolution display）
liquid-crystal display　液晶ディスプレー，LCD
on display　陳列されて，展示されて
put A on display　Aを展示する，Aを陳列する
screen display　画面表示
visual display unit　ディスプレー装置，表示端末装置，VDU
◆A real-size cabin mock-up of the Mitsubishi Regional Jet（MRJ）was put on display at Japan International Aerospace Exhibition 2012. MRJ（三菱リージョナルジェット機）の実物大の客室模型が，2012年国際航空宇宙展で展示された。

display, advertising and use of　〜の陳列、宣伝と使用
◆Upon expiration or termination of this agreement, Distributor will immediately cease all display, advertising and use of all of Supplier's names, trademarks and logos. 本契約が満了または終了したときは，販売店は，直ちに供給者の一切の名称，商標とロゴの陳列，宣伝と使用をすべて止める。

display, demonstration and distribution　展示、宣伝と販売
◆For the purpose of display, demonstration and distribution, Distributor shall maintain at its own expense a stock of the Products. 展示，宣伝と販売のため，販売店は，本製品の在庫を自己費用で［自己負担で］維持するものとする。

disposable income　可処分所得
◆The consumer tendency of spending more than consumer's disposable income resulted in a worsening of the massive trade deficit of the United States. 支出が消費者の可処分所得を上回る消費者性向が，結果として膨大な米国の貿易赤字の拡大を生み出していた。

dispose of　〜を処分する　（⇒convertible into）
◆LICENSOR may audit, at its own expense, the books of LICENSEE in which information relating to the quantities of LICENSEE's BIOS shipped, distributed transferred, or otherwise disposed of by LICENSEE is recorded, and LICENSEE's records supporting its entries in those

books. ライセンサーは、その自己負担で、ライセンシーが出荷、販売、譲渡したまたはその他の方法で処分したライセンシーのBIOS（バイオス）の数量に関する情報が記載されているライセンシーの帳簿と、この帳簿の記入項目を立証するライセンシーの記録を監査することができる。

disposition （名）処分, 処理, 処置, 譲渡, 取扱い, 配置, 配列

dispute （動）議論する, 討論する, 〜に反対する, 〜に異を唱える, 争う

◆Distributor recognizes that all trademarks, designs, patents and other industrial property rights used or embodied in Products remain to be sole properties of Company, and shall not in any way dispute them. 代理店は、本製品（契約品）に使用または具体的に表示されているすべての商標、デザイン、特許その他の工業所有権が依然として会社単独の所有物であることを認め、これについてはどんな方法でも争わないものとする。

dispute （名）紛争, 争い, 意見の相違, 論争

all disputes under this agreement　本契約に基づくすべての紛争

alternative dispute resolution　代替的紛争処理（制度）

dispute resolution　紛争解決

dispute settlement　紛争の解決

dispute settlement body　紛争解決機関, DSB

in case of any dispute or claim　紛争または請求が生じた場合

in dispute　論争中の, 問題の

legal dispute　法的紛争

the settlement of disputes　紛争解決

◆In case any dispute arises in connection with the above right, the seller reserves the right to terminate unconditionally this agreement or any further performance of this agreement at the seller's discretion. 上記権利に関して紛争が生じた場合、売り主はその裁量で、本契約または本契約のその後の履行を無条件で終了させる権利を留保する。

◆The purchaser shall forward full particulars of such claim, accompanied by an authorized surveyor's certificate of inspection of quality and quantity of the products delivered in dispute, to the seller by registered airmail within 30 days after such notification. 買い主は、当該通知後30日以内に、引き渡された問題の製品の品質と数量に関する公認鑑定人の検査証明書を添付して、当該クレームの詳細を記載した書面を書留航空便で売り主に送付するものとする。

◆Tokyo, Taipei and Washington failed to reach a consensus about how to resolve the dispute over the EU's high tariffs on IT equipment imports. EUの情報技術（IT）機器輸入に対する高関税をめぐる紛争の解決法に関して、日本、台湾と米国は合意に達しなかった。

disputed claims　係争中のクレーム

◆The above-mentioned payment is in compromise of disputed claims. 上記の支払いは、係争中のクレームを和解で解決するためのものである。

disrepute （名）不評, 悪評

bring 〜 into disrepute　〜の名誉を傷つける

dissolution （名）解散, 契約の解除, 解消, 取消し, 解体, 廃棄

◆In the event of bankruptcy, insolvency, dissolution, modification, amalgamation, receivership proceedings effecting the operation of its business or discontinuation of business for any reason and/or reorganization by the third party in the other party, either of the parties hereto shall have the absolute right to terminate this agreement without any notice whatsoever to the other party. 本契約のいずれか一方の当事者は、相手方の破産、支払い不能、解散、改組、合併、事業運営に影響を及ぼす清算手続き、または何らかの理由による事業中止および/または第三者による会社整理の場合には、相手方に何ら一切の通知をしないで本契約を終了する絶対的な権利を持つものとする。

dissolve and liquidate　解散し清算する

distribute （動）販売する, 配布する, 配給する, 供給する, 分配する, 頒布する

◆Distributor shall not distribute any products in Territory competing with Products during the term of this agreement or any extensions thereof. 販売店は、本契約期間またはその延長期間中、本販売地域で本製品と競合する製品を一切販売してはならない。

distribution （名）流通, 物流, 配給, 配布, 配分, 供給, 頒布（はんぷ）, 販売, 分売, 分配, 配当, 配信, 分布, 分類, 区別, ディストリビューション

an exclusive distribution on the line　本商品の一手販売

distribution agreement　販売代理店契約書

◆Following the poisoned gyoza incident, the distribution of powdered milk mixed with a toxic chemical and cadmium-contaminated rice came to light in China. ギョウザ中毒事件後も、中国では、有害化学物質の混入した粉ミルクやカドミウム汚染米の流通が表面化した[発覚した]。◆Shareholders agree to cause JVCO to distribute to Shareholders not less than fifty percent（50%）of profits available for distribution by way of dividends in respect of each financial year. 株主は、各年度につき、配当として分配可能な利益の50%以上を株主に対して[株主に対する配当として]JVCO（合弁会社）に分配させることに合意する。

distribution cost　流通コスト

◆Higher gasoline prices will deal a direct blow to household budgets and domestic distribution costs. ガソリン価格の高騰は、家計や国内の流通コストを直撃する。

distribution of the products　本製品の販売

◆ABC possesses certain technology for the design, manufacture, use, and distribution of the products and certain intellectual property pertaining thereto. ABCは、本製品の設計、製造、使用および販売のための特定の技術と、それに関する知的財産権を所有している。

distributor （名）販売店, 販売代理店, 代理店, 輸入代理店, 総輸入元, 流通業者, 流通業, 問屋, 卸売り業者, 配達人, ディストリビュータ （⇒grant）

distributor agreement　販売総代理店契約（書）, 販売店契約, 販売店［輸入代理店］契約

distributor discount　業者間割引

distributor's brand　商業者商標

distributors' demand　仮需要

distributor's stock　流通在庫（=distributor's inventory）

exclusive distributor　独占販売業者, 独占販売店, 一手販売店　（=sole distributor）

general distributor　元引受人

industrial distributor　工業用品流通業者

nonexclusive distributor　非独占販売業者, 非独占販売店

◆As one of the main conditions prerequisite to the continuation of the Agreement, Distributor agrees to purchase the Products from Exporter in the quantity not less than 500 units for any contract year throughout the effective term of this Agreement. 本契約の継続に不可欠な主要条件の一つとして、販売店は、本契約の有効期間中、契約年に500台以上の数量の本製品を輸出者から購入することに同意する。◆France's Competition Commission has ordered Sony, Matsushita and Philips to pay fines for allegedly concluding price-fixing agreements on retail goods with their local distributors. フランスの競争評議会は、国内販売店と海外電気製品の価格維持協定を結んだとして、ソニー、松下電器産業とフィリップスに罰金の支払いを命じた。◆Subdistributor discount means the amount below the prices set forth in the price list, at which the subdistributor may purchase the products from Distributor. 「二次代理店割引」とは、価格表に記載する価格より低い金額のことで、二次代理店はこの金額で代理店から本製品を購入することができる。

distributorship （名）販売店, 販売代理店, 販売特約店, 販売権, 販売代理店制, 一手販売代理店制

distributorship agreement　販売代理店契約, 販売店契約, 販売特約店契約

exclusive distributorship　独占的販売権

nonexclusive distributorship　非独占的販売権

diversification （名）多様化, 多角化, 多角経営, 経営多角化, 分散, 分散化, 分散投資, 変化

business diversification　事業の多角化（=diversification of business）

commodity diversification　商品の多様化

diversification investment　分散投資

diversification of the portfolios　ポートフォリオの分散, ポートフォリオの分散投資, ポートフォリオの多様化　（=portfolio diversification）

diversification of the product mix　製品構成の多様化, 製品構成の多角化

market diversification　市場多様化

product diversification policy　製品多様化政策

risk diversification　危険の分散［分散化］

the diversification of suppliers　調達先の多角化

◆Through the diversification of rare earth suppliers, Japan will lessen the diplomatic pressure China is able to exert as it exclusively possesses heavy rare earth deposits. レア・アース調達先の多角化により、日本は、重レア・アース鉱床の独占を武器にした中国の外交圧力をかわす方針だ。

diversify （動）多角化する, 多様化する, リスク, 市場などを分散する, 拡大する

diversified business　多角的事業

diversified chemicals　総合化学

diversified holding company　多角化を推進している持ち株会社

diversify earnings sources　事業多角化を推進する

diversify into new areas　新規分野への多角化を推進する

diversify investment sites　投資先を分散する　（=diversify one's portfolio）

diversify one's product lines　製品ラインを多角化する

diversify products　製品［商品］を多様化する

diversify risks　リスクを分散する

international diversified investment　国際分散投資

well-diversified assets　十分に分散化された資産

◆As a result of the tie-up, the firm hopes to diversify its products. 業務提携により、同社は商品の多様化を見込んでいる。◆The industrial sector welcomes the government's latest move to diversify rare earth suppliers as it will lead to stable rare earth supplies. レア・アース調達先の多角化については、レア・アース（希土類）の安定供給につながるとして、産業界は政府の今回の動きを歓迎している。

dividend （名）配当, 利益配当, 配当金, 分配金

◆Current account balance includes dividends and interest from overseas investment. 経常収支には、海外への投資による配当や利子の受取りなどが含まれる。◆Dividends are declared at a general meeting within the scope of such sum as is permitted under applicable law. 配当は、適用法

により許される金額の範囲内で、株主総会で宣言
される。

dividend income 配当所得, 配当収入, 受取
配当金 (=dividend revenue)
◆The surplus in the income account that includes
dividend income from overseas subsidiaries narrowed to about ￥7.15 trillion in January-June
2012 from ￥7.28 trillion a year before. 2012年
上半期（1〜6月）の所得収支（海外子会社からの配
当収入［配当受取金］などを示す）の黒字額は、前
年同期の7兆2,800億円から約7兆1,500億円に縮小
した。

division （名）事業部, 事業部門, 部門, 部・課,
分野, 分割, 分配, （意見の）不一致［相違］, 不
和, 対立, 分裂, 亀裂, ねじれ
　accounting division　経理部, 経理課
　business division　事業部門, 事業分野
　division contract　分割発注契約
　division manager　部長
　division of duties　職務の分担, 事務分掌
　division organization［system］　事業部制
　domestic sales division　国内営業部門
　electronics division　エレクトロニクス事業
　　部, エレクトロニクス事業部門
　engineering division　技術部
　financial division　金融部門
　general affairs division　総務部
　manufacturing division　製造部門
　material handling division　搬送機器部門
　operating division　事業部門
　operational administration division　業務本部
　perfect division of labor　完全分業
　planning division　企画部
　plant construction division　プラント建設部門
　property division　不動産部門
　sales promotion division　販売促進部
　shipping division　出荷部
　TV division　テレビ事業部門
◆Sony will focus on developing next generation
4K TVs as its new TV division strategy, but it
will refrain from waging a price war with its rivals in the 4K market, giving priority to enhancing its profitability mainly through luxury models. ソニーは今後、テレビ事業部門の新戦略として
次世代4Kテレビの開発に注力するが、4K市場でラ
イバルとの安売り競争には走らず、主に高級品に軸
足を置いて収益性を高める方針だ。◆The business
tie-up does not include the firms' sales divisions
or the abandonment and consolidation of refineries. 今回の業務提携に、両社の製油所の統廃合や
販売部門は含まれていない。◆The company re-
lies on its financial division, rather than its core
online division, for profits. 同社の収益は、同社の
本業のネット部門ではなく、金融部門に依存して
いる。

division of labor 分業
◆Japan and China have established a system of
international division of labor in which China
imports industrial parts from Japan to assemble into finished products in China and these are
marketed domestically or exported to the U.S.,
Europe and elsewhere. 日本と中国は、中国が日
本から工業部品を輸入して中国で最終製品に組み
立て、中国国内で販売したり欧米などに輸出した
りする国際分業体制を築いてきた。

divulge （名）（秘密などの情報を）漏（も）ら
す, 漏（ろ）えいする, 曝露する, 打ち明ける,
明かす, 明らかにする, 公表する, 開示する
（⇒generally known or publicly available）
　be in the middle of a divorce　離婚手続き中で
　　ある　(=be going through a divorce)
　divulge information such as　〜などの情報を
　　漏らす
　divulge research data to　研究データを〜に漏
　　えいする
　divulge that　〜ということを暴（あば）く
◆An engineer held on suspicion of illegally di-
vulging Toshiba research data on flash memory
to Hynix, a South Korean firm, may have been
rewarded with a large sum of money in return.
東芝のフラッシュ・メモリーの研究データを、韓
国企業のSKハイニックスに不正漏えいした容疑で
逮捕された技術者は、見返りに巨額の報酬を得て
いた可能性がある。

dock receipt 本船貨物受取書, D/R
（=mate's receipt)

document （名）文書, 書類, 船積み書類, 資
料, 文献, 記録, ドキュメント
　acceptance against document　船積み書類渡し
　　手形引受け
　accompanying document　添付書類
　accounting documents　経理書類, 会計書類
　　(=financial documents)
　aircrafts documents　空輸明細書類
　application document　申請書類
　auditor-submitted documents　監査人提出書類
　classified document　機密文書
　combined transport document　複合一貫運送
　　書類, 複合運送書類
　commercial document　商業書類
　delivery of document　書類の引渡し
　destroy document　文書を廃棄する
　disclose documents　文書を公開する
　document bill　荷為替手形
　document credit　荷為替信用状
　　(=documentary credit)
　document executed　同封書類, 署名捺印済み
　　書類
　document of contract　契約証書

document of obligation　借用証書, 債権証書

document of permission　設立認可証書

document on payment of draft　書類支払い渡し

document retention schedule　文書保存期間

document signed　署名書類

document to bearer　持参人渡し証券

document to order　指図人渡し証券

documents against acceptance　手形引受渡し, 手形引受書類渡し, 引受渡し, 引受渡し条件, D/A

documents against acceptance bill　引受渡し手形, 引受譲渡為替手形

documents against direction of collecting bank　取立銀行指図渡し

documents against payment　代金引替え書類渡し, 手形支払い（書類）渡し, 支払い渡し, 支払い渡し条件, D/P

documents against payment bill　支払い渡し手形, 支払い渡し荷為替手形

documents against trust receipt　書類貸渡し

documents attached　添付書類

documents of title　権利証書

documents required　所要書類, 必要書類

export documents　輸出書類

import document　輸入書類

internal document　内部文書

issue of document　書類の交付

loan document　借入証書

marine document　船積み書類, 船用書類

maritime document　海事書類

material document　重要書類, 重要文書

negotiable documents　譲渡可能書類, 流通書類

nonnegotiable documents　譲渡不能書類, 非流通書類

notarial document　公正証書

operative documents　営業書類

original document　正本, 原本

payment against documents　書類引換え払い

related documents　関連資料

shipping documents　船積み書類（=documents of shipping）

sign a document　文書に署名する

supporting document　付属書類

title document　権利証書

transport document　輸送書類（=transporting document）

trust document　信託証書

◆The Antimonopoly Law stipulates that documents submitted to FTC hearings may be disclosed to certain concerned parties upon their request. 独占禁止法は、「公正取引委員会の審判に提出された書類［記録］は特定の利害関係人の請求に基づいて利害関係人に開示することができる」と定めている。◆The letter of credit set forth above shall be negotiable against a draft at sight signed by the seller upon the presentation of the following documents: 上記の信用状は、次の船積み書類の提示がある場合には、売り主が振り出した一覧払い手形と引換えに買い取られるものとする。

document or otherwise prove　文書その他で証明する

◆ABCD's obligations under Article 5 shall terminate when the party seeking to avoid its obligations under such Articles can document or otherwise prove that: 第5条に基づくABCDの義務は、当該条項に基づくその義務の回避を求める当事者が以下を文書その他で証明できる場合には、終了するものとする。

documentary　（形）文書の, 記録の, 記録による

commercial documentary credit　商業荷為替信用状

documentary acceptance credit　荷為替引受け, 引受手形

documentary bill for acceptance　荷為替引受手形

documentary clean bill　荷落ち為替手形, 裸荷為替手形（=documentary clean credit）

documentary clean (letter of) credit　荷落ち為替信用状

documentary commercial bill　荷為替信用状

documentary credit　荷為替信用状

documentary draft　荷為替手形, 荷為替書類付き手形

documentary draft under［with］L/C　信用状付き荷為替手形（=documentary bill）

documentary evidence　書証, 文書的証拠

documentary evidence bond　証拠証書, 証書

documentary exchange　荷為替

documentary export bill　輸出荷為替（手形）

documentary foreign bill (of exchange)　荷付き外国為替手形

documentary import bill　輸入荷為替（手形）

documentary instruction　書類処理通知書

documentary letter of credit　荷為替信用状（=documentary credit）

documentary material　証拠書類

documentary paper　荷為替手形, 荷為替

documentary rate　荷為替相場

documentary stamp　印紙, 印紙税

Uniform Customs and Practice for Commercial Documentary Credits　商業荷為替信用状に関する統一規則および慣例, UCP（1933年

に国際商業会議所が制定。1994年1月1日に発行された「1993年版」が最新の改訂版)

documentary bill 荷為替手形, 荷為替
(=documentary bill of exchange)
◆We have drawn upon you a documentary bill at 60 d/s through ABC Bank for the invoice amount, which we hope you will kindly honor on presentation. 送り状金額に対して、ABC銀行を通じて60日払い荷為替手形を貴社宛てに振り出しましたので、提示[呈示]のあり次第お引き受け下さい。

documentation (名)文書, 書類, 証拠書類, 契約書[文書], 契約書作成, 文書の利用, 文書の提供, 文書作成, 文書化, 書面化, 情報管理, ドキュメンテーション
BBA documentation BBA(英国銀行協会)の標準契約書
bilateral documentation 相対取引の契約書
documentation bank 契約文書作成行
documentation meeting 文書作成会議, 証券発行関係文書作成会議
documentation of decisions 決定事項の文書化[書面化]
ISDA documentation ISDA契約書
multilateral documentation 標準取引契約書
shelf documentation 一括契約書
standard documentation 標準契約書
(=standardised documentation)
swap documentation スワップ取引契約書, スワップ契約書, スワップ取引の契約書作成
terms and documentation 取引条件と契約書
◆ "Documentation" means the printed or electronic instructions, manuals and diagrams pertaining to the use and installation of Products. 「ドキュメンテーション」とは、本商品の使用とインストレーションに関する印刷されたまたは電子式の説明書、取扱い説明書と図表を意味する。

documented discount notes 信用状付き商業手形

Doha Round of multilateral trade talks 世界貿易機関(WTO)の新ラウンド(新多角的貿易交渉), ドーハ・ラウンド
◆The G-8 agreed to aim for the early completion of the Doha Round of multilateral trade talks. 主要8か国は、世界貿易機関(WTO)の新多角的貿易交渉(ドーハ・ラウンド)の早期妥結を目指すことで一致した。

doing business 営業活動, 営業行為, 商行為

dollar (名)ドル
◆Aeon and Ito-Yokado started discount sales of foods imported from the United States to pass along to consumers the benefits of the yen's sharp climb against the dollar. イオンとイトーヨーカ堂は、急激な円高・ドル安による円高差益を消費者に還元するため、米国から輸入した食料品の値下げセールを開始した。

dollar-denominated assets ドル建て資産

◆In a global carry trade, hedge funds borrow low-interest yen funds to invest in dollar-denominated assets. グローバル・キャリー・トレード[グローバル・キャリー取引]では、ヘッジ・ファンドなどが、低利の円資金を借りてドル建て資産に投資している。

domestic consumption 国内消費, 国内の個人消費
◆A recovery will be export-driven, dependent on U.S. growth and the yen's depreciation, instead of being led by increased domestic consumption and capital investment. 今後の景気回復は、アメリカ経済の好転や円安を背景にした輸出主導型の回復で、国内の個人消費や設備投資の伸びがその牽引役となるわけではない。

domestic exporter 国内輸出企業, 国内輸出業者
◆A recent plunge in the yen due to the economic and monetary policies of Prime Minister Shinzo Abe is a boon for domestic exporters. 安倍晋三首相の経済・金融政策による最近の円安は、国内の輸出企業にとっては追い風[恩恵]だ。

domestic manufacturing industry 国内製造業
◆The record trade deficit in 2012 was caused by a decline in exports due to the European financial crisis and deceleration of the Chinese economy, together with a sharp increase in imports of liquefied natural gas and the rapid hollowing-out of the domestic manufacturing industry. 2012年の過去最大の貿易赤字の要因としては、欧州の金融危機や中国経済の減速などで輸出が減少する一方、液化天然ガス(LNG)の輸入が急増し、国内製造業の空洞化が加速していることも挙げられる。

domestic product 国内製品, 国産品
◆Food self-sufficiency ratio indicates the proportion of domestic products in consumed food. 食料自給率は、消費する食料のうち国産品が占める割合を示す。◆Under the food self-sufficiency rate on a calorie basis, even beef and pork from animals raised in Japan are not considered domestic products if they consumed imported feed. カロリー・ベースの食料自給率では、国内で育てた家畜の牛肉や豚肉[国内で育てた]牛や豚の肉)でも、餌が輸入品の場合は国産品と見なされない。

domestic production 国内生産
◆Many Japanese manufacturers have been prompted to review their production in China with labor costs surging in China and domestic production recovering competitiveness thanks to the weaker yen. 中国で人件費が高騰しているのに加え、円安進行で国内生産の競争力が回復しているため、日本メーカーの多くは中国での生産(体制)を見直す動きが加速している。

domestic trunk route 国内幹線ルート, 幹線
◆Since the deregulation of the civil aviation industry, two airlines entered the market on domestic trunk routes. 空の規制緩和[航空自由化]以来、

航空会社2社が、国内幹線市場に参入した。

domestic yield　国内利回り

◆Domestic yields are low relative to those in other nations, causing Japanese money to go overseas. 他国の利回りに比べて国内利回りが低いため、日本の資金が外国に流れている。

dominant　(形)支配的な, 優勢な, 有力な, 最有力の, 最大の, 圧倒的な, 顕著な, 目立つ, 主要な, 中心的な

dominant company [firm]　支配的な企業

dominant currency　支配的通貨, 基軸通貨 (key currency), 主要通貨

dominant driving force　大きな原動力

dominant factor　支配的要因

dominant force　優勢な力, 最有力者

dominant growth rate　支配的成長率, 際立った伸び率

dominant market share　圧倒的な市場シェア, 圧倒的なシェア

dominant patent　基本特許

dominant position　支配的な地位, 優越的地位

dominant theme　最大のテーマ

◆If Japan posts a current account deficit, it has to sell yen to buy U.S. dollars as the greenback remains the world's dominant currency for settling trade. 日本が経常収支の赤字を計上した場合、米ドルがまだ世界の貿易決済の主要通貨なので、米ドルを買うために円を売らなければならない。

dotted line　署名欄, 点線

sign on the dotted line　署名欄に署名する

draft　(名)為替手形(bill of exchange:commercial paper (商業証券) や negotiable instrument (流通証券) の一種), 手形, 契約書案, 草案, 原案, 起案, 起草, 草稿, 起案書, 設計図, ドラフト

a draft at sight　一覧払い手形

a draft at 30 d/s　一覧後30日払いの手形 (=30 days after sight)

demand draft　送金小切手, 送金為替手形, 要求払い為替手形

draw a draft at 30 day's sight on you　貴社宛てに一覧後30日払い手形を振り出す

draw a draft for the invoice amount　送り状金額に対して手形を振り出す

◆Draft on you falls due at the date named. 貴社宛の手形は、記載日に満期になる。◆Drafts shall be negotiated not later than May 10, 2015. 為替手形は、2015年5月10日以前に買い取るものとする。◆For reimbursement, we have drawn upon you through ABC Bank a draft at 90 d/s for $50,000 against your order No. 50. 代金回収のため、当社は貴社注文第50号に対しABC銀行を通じて50,000ドルの一覧後90日払い為替手形を貴社宛てに振り出しました。◆The letter of credit set forth above shall be negotiable against a draft at sight signed

by the seller upon the presentation of the following documents: 上記の信用状は、次の船積み書類の提示がある場合には、売り主が振り出した一覧払い手形と引換えに買い取られるものとする。◆We have valued upon you today for the amount specified above, at sight, and ask you to accord our draft your due protection. 当社は本日、貴社宛てに上記金額に対する一覧払い手形を振り出しましたので、この手形のお引受けをお願い致します。◆We hope you will kindly protect the draft on presentation. 手形提示の節は、何とぞお引受け下さい。◆We negotiated our draft through the bank abovementioned under L/C No. 5000 established by the ABC Bank, New York, and commend our signature to your protection. 当社は、ABC銀行 (ニューヨーク) 発行の信用状5000号に従って上記銀行で手形を買い取ってもらいましたので、この手形の支払いをよろしくお願いします。

draft at sight signed by　～が振り出す一覧払い手形, ～が振り出した一覧払い手形

◆The letter of credit set forth above shall be negotiable against a draft at sight signed by the seller upon the presentation of the following documents: 上記の信用状は、次の船積み書類の提示がある場合には、売り主が振り出した一覧払い手形と引換えに買い取られるものとする。

draw　(動)文書を作成する, 小切手・手形を振り出す, 預貯金を引き出す, 為替を取り組む

draw a daft on　～宛てに手形を振り出す

◆Against our shipments we have drawn a draft for 100% of invoice value. 当社の積み荷に対して、当社は送り状金額と同額の手形を振り出した。◆For reimbursement, we have drawn upon you through ABC Bank a draft at 90 d/s for $50,000 against your order No. 50. 代金回収のため、当社は貴社注文第50号に対しABC銀行を通じて50,000ドルの一覧後90日払い為替手形を貴社宛てに振り出しました。◆To cover this shipment, we have drawn upon you at sight for the invoice amount under the L/C opened by ABC Bank. この船積みに対して、当社はABC銀行発行の信用状に基づいて、一覧払い送り状面金額の手形を貴社宛てに振り出しました。◆To cover this shipment, we have drawn upon you at 60 d/s, in the amount $50,000, in favor of ABC Bank, and recommend our signature to your protection. この船積みに対して、一覧後60日払い、ABC銀行を受取人とする額面5万ドルの手形を貴社宛てに振り出しましたので、何とぞこの手形をお引受けください。◆We have drawn a draft at 30 day's sight on you through ABC Bank for $1,000. ABC銀行経由で1,000ドルの一覧後30日払い手形を、貴社宛に振り出しました。

drawing　(名)図面, 製図, デッサン, 線画, (小切手や手形の)振り出し, (金銭の)引出し

a driving force behind　～の原動力, ～の牽引役

detailed engineering drawing　詳細な工事図面

drawing bank　振出銀行

drawing in blank　（手形の）白地振出し

drawing of bill　手形振出し

drawing right　（IMFの）引出権

driving force　原動力, 推進力, 牽引役, 牽引車, 主因　（=driver, locomotive engine）

go back to the drawing board　最初からやり直す, 一から出直す

machine drawing　機械製図, 機械図

notice of drawing　借入れ通知書

on the drawing board（s）　立案中で

outline drawing　略図

place of drawing　振出地

sectional drawing　断面図

Special Drawing Rights　（IMFの）特別引出権

technical drawings　技術用製図

working drawing　運転図, 設計図, 工作図

◆If the driving forces for the Japanese economy, namely capital investment and exports, lose steam, the economy inevitably will slow down further. 設備投資と輸出という日本経済の牽引役［日本経済の牽引役である設備投資と輸出］に勢いがなくなれば, 景気の一段の減速は避けられないだろう。

drug smuggling　麻薬密輸

◆The United States, Japan and South Korea agreed to take tough action against alleged illegal activities by North Korea, including drug smuggling and money counterfeiting. 米国, 日本と韓国は, 北朝鮮によるとされる麻薬密輸や通貨偽造などの非合法活動に断固対処することで合意した。

d/s［**D/S, d.s.**］　一覧後〜日払い, 〜日払い（days after sightの略）

◆For reimbursement, we have drawn upon you through ABC Bank a draft at 90 d/s for $50,000 against your order No. 50. 代金回収のため, 当社は貴社注文第50号に対しABC銀行を通じて50,000ドルの一覧後90日払い為替手形を貴社宛てに振り出しました。◆Our terms of payment are to value at 30 d/s under an irrevocable letter of credit to be opened in our favor for the corresponding value of an order. 当社の決済条件は, 注文相当額につき, 当社を受益者として開設された取消不能信用状に基づいて一覧後30日払いの手形を振り出すことです。◆We have drawn upon you a documentary bill at 60 d/s through ABC Bank for the invoice amount, which we hope you will kindly honor on presentation. 送り状金額に対して, ABC銀行を通じて60日払い荷為替手形を貴社宛てに振り出しましたので, 提示［呈示］のあり次第お引受け下さい。

dual　（形）二重の, 両用の, 二元的な

dual aspect concept　貸借一致の原則（資産＝負債＋純資産の関係が成り立つことを言う）

dual capacity　（株式仲買いと株式自己売買の）2業務兼営, 兼任, 兼務

dual circulation period　二重流通期間, 移行期間

dual exchange market　二重為替市場, 二重為替市場制

dual exchange rates（the official and swap rates）　中国の二重相場制（公定レートと外貨調整センター・レート）

dual fund　デュアル・ファンド（=dual-purpose fund: 値上がり益と利子配当収入を目的とするもののいずれかを選択できる投資信託）

dual interest policy　二重金利政策

dual price of gold　金の二重価格

dual pricing　二重価格制, 二重価格表示

dual-purpose fund　二重目的ファンド（=dual fund）

dual rate system　二重運賃制, 二重為替相場制（dual exchange rate system）

dual tariff　複関税, 二重関税

dual taxation　二重課税

dual trading　二重取引, 二重勘定取引, 二者取引

dual vendor system　2社購買

on a dual currency basis　二重通貨建ての

due　（形）正当な, 正式の, 適切な, 適正な, 適法の, 合法の, 十分な, 相当の, 合理的な, 支払い義務のある, 履行義務のある, 満期のすぎた, 支払い期日のきた, 当然支払われるべき, 予定されている　（⇒when due）

a huge bill is due　巨額の請求書の期限が到来する

any royalty or other payments due under this agreement　本契約により支払うべきロイヤルティまたはその他の支払い

become due　支払い期日のきた, 支払わなければならなくなる

due performance of obligations hereunder　本契約上の債務を期日に履行すること, 本契約上の期日履行

payment of any sums which may become due　支払い期日のきた金額の支払い

payment when due　期日どおりの支払い, 期日どおりに支払うこと

the date on which it is due　支払い期日

when due　期日に, 支払い期日に, 満期が過ぎたとき

whether due or to become due　弁済期が到来しているか否かを問わず

◆Shipments will reach you in due course time. 積み荷は, やがて到着します。◆Simultaneously with making each report, Licensor shall compute the running royalty due and make payment thereof to Licensor. 各報告を行うと同時に, ライ

センシーは、支払い義務のあるランニング・ロイヤルティを計算し、ライセンサーに対してその支払いをしなければならない。◆The bank shall have the right, as the obligations become due, or in the event of their default, to offset cash deposits against such obligations due to the bank. 債務の期限が到来したとき、または債務不履行の場合、銀行はその債務とその預金を相殺する権利を持つものとする。◆We have valued upon you today for the amount specified above, at sight, and ask you to accord our draft your due protection. 当社は本日、貴社宛てに上記金額に対する一覧払い手形を振り出しましたので、この手形のお引受けをお願い致します。

due and payable　支払い義務のある、支払い期限にある、支払い期限が到来した、支払わなければならない、支払期限が到来して支払う義務がある　（⇒withholding）

due and payable no later than　～までに支払う
◆Upon expiration of the term of this agreement, all exclusive rights granted to Licensee herein shall revert to Licensor, provided that Licensee shall continue to pay all royalties which become due and payable. 本契約期間の満了と同時に、ライセンシーに付与した独占的権利はすべてライセンサーに復帰する。ただし、ライセンシーは、支払う義務のあるロイヤルティをすべて継続して支払わなければならない。

due and punctual performance　適正な期限どおりの履行
◆Guarantors hereby guarantee jointly and severally as and for its own obligation, until full payment and performance are effected by ABC in accordance with the terms and conditions of the agreement, the due and punctual performance by or on behalf of ABC, of all obligations under the agreement. 保証人は、契約の条件に従ってABCが当該支払いと履行を完全に行うまで、ABCによるまたはABCに代わる契約上のすべての債務の適正かつ期限どおりの履行を、自己の義務（債務）としてここに各自連帯して保証する。

due date　満期日、支払い期日、履行期日
◆If the buyer fails to pay any amount under this agreement when due, the buyer shall be liable to pay to the seller overdue interest on such unpaid amount from the due date until the actual payment date at the rate of 15% per annum. 買い主が支払い期日に本契約に基づく代金の支払いを怠った場合、買い主は、支払い期日から実際の払込み日までの当該未払い金額に対する年率15%の遅延金利を、売り主に支払わなければならない。

due diligence　相当の注意、正当な努力、監査手続き　（契約締結前、契約交渉中または契約締結後クロージング前に監査法人や法律事務所によって行われる財務調査と法的な監査手続き）、デュー・ディリジェンス　（=due diligence investigation）

due diligence investigation　事業買収前のデュー・ディリジェンス調査、事前精査、資産査定, 財務調査（「デューディリジェンス調査」は、事業買収希望者が譲渡側の協力を得て行う専門家による買収対象会社の資産、債務、財務内容や営業内容、従業員などに関する調査。買収額や増資の際に引き受ける株式の価格を判断する基準となる）
◆Commencing on the date of this agreement until the Closing, Buyer shall be permitted to perform such due diligence investigation related to the transactions contemplated by this agreement as Buyer deems necessary and appropriate in its discretion. 本契約締結日からクロージングまで、買い主は、本契約で意図されている取引に関して買い主が買い主の判断で必要かつ適切と考えるデュー・ディリジェンス調査を行うことができるものとする。

due hereunder　本契約に基づき支払い義務のある
◆Licensee shall, concurrently with the royalty payment under subparagraph d) of Article 5, furnish Licensor quarterly with an auditor's statement of the royalty due hereunder for the preceding calendar quarter. ライセンシーは、第5条d)項に基づくロイヤルティの支払いと同時に、直前の暦四半期（四半期）に関して本契約に基づき支払い義務のあるロイヤルティについての監査人の報告書を、四半期ごとにライセンサーに提供する。

due to　～により、～が原因で、～のため、～で
due to (the) said causes　上記の事由により
◆The Chinese economy will become anemic and the world economy could suffer immense damage if China is faced with an unabated flight of capital due to speculative investments that its economic bubble has lured from abroad. 中国で、中国のバブル景気で海外から流入した投機マネーが大量に流出したら、中国経済は活気を失い、世界経済は甚大なダメージを受けることになろう。◆We fear we have to advise you that we may not be able to dispatch in full your order due to the shortage of shipping space. 不本意ながら、船腹不足のため、貴社の注文が一部積み残しになる可能性があることをお伝えしなければなりません。

duly　（副）正当に、正式に、十分に、適切に、適法に、期日どおりに、遅滞（ちたい）なく
duly authorized officer　正当に権限を与えられた［付与された］役員, 正当な権限を持つ役員
duly signed by　～が正式に署名する

duly authorized representative　正当に権限を付与された代表［代表者・代理人］, 正式に権限を与えられた代表, 正式に授権された代表, 正当な権限を持つ代表
◆IN WITNESS WHEREOF, the parties hereto have caused this instrument to be executed by their duly authorized representatives, as of the date and year first above written. 上記の証として、本契約の両当事者は、冒頭に記載した日付で正式に権限を与えられた代表者に本契約書［本証書］を作成させた。◆The licensee shall make its

records and accounts available for inspection by the licensor or its duly authorized representatives upon reasonable advance notice. ライセンシーは、(ライセンサーから)合理的な事前の通知を受けたときは、ライセンサーまたはその正当な権限を持つ代理人の検査のためにライセンシーの記録と帳簿を提供するものとする。

duly executed by　〜が正当に作成した
◆This agreement may be amended, modified, altered or changed only by a written instrument duly executed by the authorized representatives of both parties. 本契約は、両当事者の権限のある代表者が正当に作成した証書によってのみ、訂正、修正、改変または変更することができる。

dumping　(名)投げ売り, 不当廉売(れんばい), 乱売, たたき売り, ゴミなどの投げ捨て, 廃棄物の投棄, ダンピング

antidumping　反ダンピング, ダンピング防止, アンチダンピング

antidumping duties　反ダンピング関税, ダンピング防止関税, ダンピング関税

antidumping law　反ダンピング法, ダンピング防止法, 不当廉売防止法, アンチダンピング法

antidumping tariff　反ダンピング関税, ダンピング防止関税

commercial dumping　商業ダンピング

concealed dumping　隠ぺいダンピング

continued dumping　持続的ダンピング

continuing dumping　継続的ダンピング

credit dumping　信用ダンピング

dumping code　ダンピング綱領

dumping export　ダンピング輸出

dumping field　投げ売り市場, 廉売市場, ダンピング市場　(=dumping market)

dumping margin　ダンピング率 (=dumping penalty margin)

dumping of toxic chemicals　有毒化学薬品の投棄

dumping petition　ダンピング提訴

exchange dumping　為替ダンピング(輸出品の競争力を高めるため自国通貨の為替相場を不当に切り下げること)

file a dumping complaint against　〜をダンピング提訴する, 〜をダンピングで提訴する

genuine dumping　真のダンピング

illegal dumping　不法投棄

intermittent dumping　断続的ダンピング

monopoly dumping　独占廉売, 独占ダンピング

ocean dumping　海洋投棄

predatory dumping　略奪的ダンピング

reversal dumping　逆ダンピング

sporadic dumping　一時的ダンピング

spurious dumping　疑似ダンピング

systematic dumping　組織的ダンピング

try dumping　投げ売りする, ダンピングする
◆Domestic industries harmed by dumping require urgent protection. ダンピングによる損害を受けている国内産業は、緊急保護を必要としている。◆Dumping may force rival companies out of business and lead to a market oligopoly. 不当廉売は、同業他社を廃絶に追い込み、市場の寡占(かせん)につながる可能性がある。◆In the United States, a provisional ruling on dumping is usually issued about six months after launching antidumping probes. 米国では、ダンピング(不当廉売)の仮決定をするのは通例、反ダンピング調査の開始から半年程度である。

dumping penalty margin　ダンピング率
◆The U.S. Commerce Department set dumping penalty margins of 115.22 percent each for the two Japanese steelmakers. 米商務省は、日本の鉄鋼メーカー2社に対してそれぞれ115.22%のダンピング率を認定した。

duplicate　(名)副本, 写し, 謄本, 複写, 複製 (形)同文の, 複製の, 写しの, 副の, 現物どおりの, まったく同様の, 対の, 重複の, 重複する (動)2倍にする, 2通作成する, 複写する

be made in duplicate　正副2通作成される

draw up the document in duplicate　書類を2通作成する

duplicate bill　副為替手形, 手形の副本, 手形の第2券　(手形の正本・第1券＝original bill)

duplicate bill of exchange　副為替手形 (=duplicate draft)

duplicate bill of lading　船荷証券副本

duplicate copy　副本, 複製品, 写し

duplicate invoice　副本送り状, 送り状副書[副本], 連写式の請求書

duplicate letter　書簡控え

duplicate receipt　受取証副本, 領収書控え, 複写式領収書

duplicate sample　控え見本 (=file sample, keep sample)

duplicate taxation　二重課税

duplicate the last shipment　前回の荷口を(同品、同量、同条件で)再度出荷する

execute in duplicate　正副2通作成する, 正副2部一式として署名する

in duplicate　正副2通の, 正副2通に

insurance policy in duplicate　保険証書[保険証券]2通

make out in duplicate　正副2通作成する
◆IN WITNESS WHEREOF, each of the parties hereto has caused this agreement to be executed

in duplicate by its duly authorized officers or representatives as of the date first above written. 上記の証として、本契約の各当事者は、正式に権限を与えられたその役員または代表者により、冒頭に記載した日付で本契約書を2通作成させた。◆This letter is addressed to you in duplicate original. 貴社宛に本レターを2部送付します。◆We have forwarded to you the invoice in duplicate. 送り状2通は、貴社宛発送済みです。

D duration (名)継続, 始終, 長さ, 満期, 期間, 有効期間, 継続期間, 持続期間, 存続期間, 航続期間, 通話時間, デュレーション(債券価格の金利変動に対する敏感度)
  duration of risk clause 保険期間約款, 危険期間条項
  short duration instrument 短期商品
  the duration of a portfolio ポートフォリオのデュレーション
  the duration of carrier's liability 運送人の責任の始終
  the duration of coverage 保険期間 (=the duration of insurance)
  the duration of life 生存期間
  the duration of New Company 新会社の存続期間
  the duration of possible sunshine 可照時間
  the duration of prescription 時効
  the duration of risk 危険期間, 危険付保期間, 危険負担期間
  the duration of sunshine 日照時間
  the duration of the policy 保険契約期間
  the duration of treaty 再保険特約期間
  yields on short-duration bonds 短期物の利回り
  ◆The duration of the New Company shall be indefinite. 新会社の存続期間は、無期限とする。

during (前)~の間, ~の間中, ~の時期に
  during the period from … through ~から…までの期間中
  during the term of this agreement or any extensions thereof 本契約の期間またはその延長期間中, 本契約期間またはその更新期間中

during the term of this agreement [Agreement] 本契約期間中
  ◆Licensee agrees to pay to Licensor during the term of this agreement the minimum royalty for each contract year as set forth below. ライセンシーは、本契約期間中、以下に定める各契約年度のミニマム・ロイヤリティをライセンサーに支払うことに同意する。

duty (名)義務, 責任, 任務, 職務, 仕事, 職責, 勤務, 税, 関税 (⇒tariff)
  ad valorem duties 従価税
  alternative duties 選択関税, 選択税

anti-discrimination duties 差別待遇対抗税
anti-dumping duties 不当廉売対抗税, ダンピング防止関税
as in duty bound 義務上
compensating duties 相殺関税 (=compensation duties)
compensatory duties 補正関税
compound duties (従価と従量との)複合関税, 複合税 (=mixed duties)
consumption duties 消費税
countervailing duties 相殺関税
customs duties 関税
dead duties 相続税 (=death duties)
differential duties 差別関税 (=discriminant [discriminating, discriminative] duties)
division of duties 職務の分担, 事務分掌
do [discharge, fulfill] one's duties 職務を果たす
duty appraiser 関税審査官
duty classification 関税分類, 任務分類
duty clause 輸入税特別約款, 輸入税担保約款
duty concession 関税譲許
duty contingency 未必輸入税
duty cost 関税込みコスト
duty drawback 関税戻し税, 戻し税
duty exemption 免税
duty forward 関税先払い
duty insurance 輸入税保険
duty of averting [minimizing] losses 損害防止義務
duty of confidentiality 守秘義務
duty of declaration 通知義務, 告知義務(主な告知内容は、積み荷の明細、保険金額、損害填補の範囲、船名、出港日、航路、保険金の支払い地、支払い通貨など)
duty of disclosure 告知義務 (=duty to disclose: 保険締結時に、被保険者が保険者に保険料算定などの判断に影響を及ぼす情報を正確に知らせる義務)
duty of noncompetition 競争制限義務, 競業避止(ひし)義務
duty paid 納税済み, 通関渡し
duty-paid 関税支払い済みの, 関税売り手負担の, 通関渡し条件の
duty-paid price 輸入手続き済み値段(輸入貨物の陸揚げ値段＋関税、通関費用)
duty-paid value 関税込み価格, 関税込み値段 (=duty price)
duty rate 関税率
duty unpaid 関税未払い, 関税買い持ち, 輸入手続き未済

entertainment duties　娯楽税, 興行税

ex quay（duty paid）　埠頭渡し（輸入税込み［関税込み、関税支払い済み］）

ex quay（duty unpaid）　埠頭渡し（輸入税含まず［関税未払い］）

excise duties　消費税, 物品税

existing preferential duties　既存特恵関税

export duties　輸出関税, 輸出税

export preferential duties　輸出優遇関税

fail in［neglect］one's duties　職務を怠る

fiduciary duty　受託者の義務

financial duties　財源関税

free of duties　免税の

free of duty entry　無税品通関

general preferential duties　一般特恵関税

gross weight duties　総掛輸入税

import duties　輸入税

import preferential duties　輸入優遇関税

inland duty　内国税

lay a duty on　～に課税する

luxury duties　奢侈（しゃし）税

mixed duties　混合税（=compound duties）

mutual preferential duties　相互特恵関税

nonpreferential duties　非特恵関税

one-sided preferential duties　一方的特恵関税

port duties　入港税, 港税

preferential duties　特恵関税

preserving duties　維持関税

primary duty　輸入付加税

probate duties　検証税

prohibitive［prohibition］duties　禁止関税, 禁止的輸入税

protective duties　保護関税

public duties　公務

reciprocal duties　互恵関税

refund of duties　戻し税

regional preferential duties　地域特恵関税

retaliatory duties　報復関税

revenue duties　収入関税

safeguarding duties　産業保護税, 保護輸入税

social duties　社会義務

special tonnage duties　特別トン税

specific duties　従量税（コメや石油税など、商品の重量や体積を単位として税額を算定。為替変動の影響は受けない）

stamp duty　印紙税

tonnage duties　トン税

transfer duty　証券譲渡税

transit duties　通過税

◆Net Wholesale Price referred to in this agreement is defined as the amount of the gross sales by ABC of the licensed products to ABC's customers in the territory, less customary trade discounts, insurance premiums, transportation and delivery charges, taxes（VAT）and duties. 本契約書に記載する「純卸売り販売額」とは、ABCの顧客に対する契約地域内でのABCの許諾製品の総売上高（総販売額）から、通常の卸売り割引額、保険料、運送・引渡し費用、税金（付加価値税）と関税を差し引いた額のことをいう。◆The Patent Law stipulates that patents obtained as a result of duties performed by a corporate employee belong to the employee. 日本の特許法では、企業の従業員が企業の職務の一環として得た特許権は、その従業員に帰属する、としている。

duty free　免税

duty-free　（形）免税の, 無税の, 無関税の

duty-free allowance　免税限度

duty-free cargo　関税なしの積み荷, 免税貨物

duty-free entry　無税参入

duty-free goods　免税品, 無税品

duty-free imported goods　輸入免税品

duty free imports　免税輸入品

duty-free item　免税品

duty-free shop　免税店

E

e-commerce　（名）電子商取引, ネット商取引, ネット取引, Eコマース, EC　（=e-business, E-commerce, electronic commerce, Internet-based commerce: インターネットやパソコン通信サービスを利用した商取引）

e-commerce page　電子商取引のページ

e-commerce service　eコマース・サービス

the e-commerce industry　電子商取引業界

◆As e-commerce requires little investment in premises or facilities, many company workers, housekeepers and students take part in Internet-based auction. ネット取引は店舗や設備への投資が不要のため、サラリーマンや主婦、学生の多くがネット・オークションなどに参加している。

e-commerce site　電子商取引サイト

◆TBS plans to launch a new e-commerce site. TBSは、新たな電子商取引サイトの開設を計画している。

EAR　米国輸出規則（Export Administration Regulationsの略）

earlier of A or B　AかBのうちいずれか早いほう, AとBのうちいずれか早いほう

◆Any notice served by registered mail or by telex as aforesaid shall be deemed served on the earlier of actual receipt or the expiry of 120 hours after posting. 上記のとおり書留郵便またはテレックスで送達された通知は、実際の受領日と

投函から120時間後のうちいずれか早いほうの日に送達されたものと見なすものとする。

earn （動）稼ぐ, 稼得（かとく）する, 利益を上げる, 報酬などを得る, 獲得する, 生む, もたらす, ～に値する
earn a profit　利益を上げる
earn a reputation as　～として評判を得る
earn a reputation for　～で評判になる
earn above-average returns　市場平均を上回る利益を上げる
earn interest　利息が付く
earn no interest　利息が付かない
◆Tokyo will likely earn profits even with exports of cars manufactured in Japan thanks to the decline of the yen. 円安効果で, トヨタは今後, 日本国内で生産した車を輸出しても, 利益が見込めるように［利益を上げられるように］なっている。

ECB　欧州中央銀行　（⇒European Central Bank）
◆It's pointed out that the ECB's introduction of a negative deposit rate will increase the burden on commercial banks and worsen their finances, leading to a minimization of new loans and higher lending rates. 欧州中央銀行（ECB）のマイナス金利［マイナス中銀預入金利］の導入については, 民間銀行の負担が増し, 銀行の財務が悪化して, 新規融資の抑制や貸出金利の上昇につながる, と指摘されている。◆The ECB's introduction of a negative deposit rate also aims to lower interest rate levels in general and redress the strong euro. ECB（欧州中央銀行）のマイナス（中銀預入）金利導入には, 金利水準全体の引下げとユーロ高是正の狙いもある。

economic activities　経済活動
◆Cartels and bid-fixing can ruin economic activities. カルテルや談合行為は, 経済活動を損なう可能性がある。

economic and monetary policies　経済・金融政策, 経済政策と金融政策
◆A recent plunge in the yen due to the economic and monetary policies of Prime Minister Shinzo Abe is a boon for domestic exporters. 安倍晋三首相の経済・金融政策による最近の円安は, 国内の輸出企業にとっては追い風［恩恵］だ。

economic assessment　景気判断, 景気の基調判断　（=assessment of the economy）
◆As a basis for its economic assessment, the report referred to increases in exports, progress in inventory adjustment and the bottoming out of industrial production. 景気判断の根拠として, 同報告書は輸出が増加し, 在庫調整が進展して, 鉱工業生産も底を打ったことを挙げている。

economic cooperation agreement　経済協力協定, 経済連携協定
◆The domestic market has been shrinking due to an aging population and declining birthrate, so Japan must expand its economic cooperation agreements with other countries to have overseas markets act as quasi-domestic markets where there are no barriers to entry for Japanese companies. 少子高齢化で国内市場が縮小しているので, 日本は他国との経済連携協定を拡大して, 海外市場を日本企業が垣根なしで参入できる準国内市場にする必要がある。

economic event　経済事象, 経済の動き, 経済動向
◆A business combination is a significant economic event that results from bargaining between independent parties. 企業結合は, 独立した当事者間の取引から生じるひとつの重要な経済事象である。

economic growth　経済成長
◆Japan's economic growth is driven by exports, but it will have to vie for export markets with emerging economies. 日本の経済成長の原動力は輸出だが, 今後は新興国と輸出市場の争奪戦になろう。

economic growth of emerging economies　新興国の経済成長
◆The positive effects of the yen's depreciation have not yet fully appeared, but sluggish increases in exports in the future due to a slowdown in the economic growth of emerging economies are worried about by some economists. 円安のプラス効果はまだ本格的に現われていないが, 新興国の経済成長の鈍化で, 今後の輸出の伸び悩みをエコノミストは懸念している。

economic partnership agreement　経済連携協定, EPA（人と資本の交流を含む協定）（⇒EPA）
◆Japan has signed economic partnership agreements with 11 economies, including Mexico and Singapore. 日本のEPA（経済連携協定）署名国は, メキシコやシンガポールなど11か国だ。◆The government will compile a basic policy on economic partnership agreements, including the TPP. 政府は, TPP（環太平洋経済連携協定）を含めて, 経済連携協定（EPA）の基本方針をまとめる。

economic policy　経済政策
◆Toyota revised upward its consolidated operating profit estimates for the business year ending March 31, 2013, largely due to improved profitability in its exports from a weakening of the yen in response to "Abenomics," the economic policy of the Abe administration. トヨタは2013年3月期決算［2013年3月31日終了事業年度］の連結営業利益予想［連結業績予想］を上方修正したが, これは主に安倍政権の経済政策「アベノミクス」を好感しての円安で, 輸出の採算が向上しているためだ。

economic recovery　景気回復
◆The growth in exports is due to economic recovery in the United States. この輸出の伸びは, 米国の景気回復によるものだ。◆With the economic recovery gaining momentum, U.S. companies have begun investing in the Japanese stock mar-

ket again, giving a lift to stock prices. 景気回復
が力強さを増していることから、米国企業が日本
の株式市場に再び投資するようになり、株価を押
し上げている。

economic situation 景気全般, 景気, 経済状
況, 経済情勢
◆Export and import trends are influenced by various factors, including economic situations in
and outside of the country, currency exchange
rates and crude oil price movements. 輸出入動
向は、国内外の景気や為替相場、原油価格の変動
などの各種要因に左右される。

economic slowdown 経済の減速, 景気減速
◆The economic slowdown in Europe due to the
sovereign debt crisis and slackening growth of
China as a major exporter to Europe have dealt a
painful blow to Japan's exports and production.
債務危機に伴う欧州経済の減速と、欧州向け輸出
の多い中国の成長鈍化が、日本の輸出と生産に耐
え難いほどの打撃を与えている。

economic turmoil 経済の混乱, 経済の混迷,
経済不安, 経済危機
◆Exporting firms are working all out to secure
profits under the current economic turmoil. 現在
の経済混乱の状況下で、輸出企業各社は収益の確
保に躍起となっている。

economic upswing 景気回復
◆The export-led economic growth could falter
if the U.S. economic upswing slows down or if
there is a rapid surge in the value of the yen. 輸
出主導の経済成長は、米国の景気回復にブレーキ
がかかるか、急激な円高が進めば、大きくつまず
く可能性がある。

economic upturn 景気回復 （=economic
upswing）
the current economic upturn led by exports 現
在の輸出主導の景気回復
the latest change in tone of the economic upturn
今回の景気回復の変調
◆A depreciation of the dollar may stimulate external demand and ignite an export-driven economic upturn. ドル安は、外需を喚起して、輸出
主導の景気回復につながる可能性がある。

economies of scale 規模の経済, 規模の経済
性, 規模の拡大, 規模の利益, スケール・メ
リット, 数量効果, エコノミー・オブ・スケー
ル （=economy of scale, scale merit: 少品種大
量生産の経済効率を意味する。⇒strategic
location）
economies of scale strategy 数量効果を追求
する戦略
maintain economies of scale 規模の経済を維
持する, スケール・メリットを維持する
pursue economies of scale 規模の経済を追求
する, 規模の拡大を追及する
◆Mergers and acquisitions to pursue economies
of scale will be carried out worldwide. 規模の経
済［規模の拡大］を追求するためのM&A（企業の合

併・買収）は今後、国際的規模で実施される見込
みだ。

economy （名）経済, 経済性, 景気, 節約, 倹約,
効率的使用［利用］, 経済機構, 経済組織, 経済
国, 社会, 経済成長率, 成長率, エコノミー
（⇒global economy）
◆A counselor to the Japan Research Institute
warned that under the current trade structure, the
yen's depreciation might apply downward pressure on the Japanese economy. 現状の貿易構造
では、円安で日本の景気が押し下げられる懸念が
ある、と日本総研の理事が警告した。◆Both the
Japanese economy and Chinese businesses have
been impacted by the boycott against Japanese
goods being staged in protest of Japan's nationalization of the Senkakus. 日本の尖閣諸島国有
化に反発［抗議］して行われている日本製品の不買
運動で、日本経済も中国企業も打撃を受けている。
◆Japan's economy is vulnerable to foreign exchange fluctuations as Japanese firms depend so
heavily on foreign demand. 日本企業は外需に大
きく依存しているため、日本経済は為替相場の変動
の影響を受けやすい。◆Japan's exports and production have been reduced because of the slowdown of foreign economies and the worsening
of relations with China. 海外経済の減速と日中関
係の悪化で、日本の輸出や生産は低迷している。◆
The Abe administration faces several major challenges such as lifting the economy out of deflation, reconstruction from the Great East Japan
Earthquake and the TPP negotiations. 安倍政権
は、デフレ脱却、震災復興やTPP（環太平洋経済連
携協定）交渉など、大きな課題にいくつか直面して
いる。◆The economy of Japan depends a great
deal on exports to the United States. 日本経済の
対米輸出への依存度は、極めて高い。

EDI 電子データ交換（electronic data
interchangeの略）

effect （動）行う, 実施する, 実行する, 手配す
る, 成就する, 成し遂げる,（目的などを）達成
する,（結果を）もたらす, 発効させる, 保険を
付ける, 保険をかける, ～に影響を及ぼす
effect a policy 契約を完了して保険証書を受
け取る
effect a sale 売却する
effect a sale for 〜の需要をもたらす
effect drastic reforms 抜本的改革を行う, 徹
底的改革を行う
effect payment 支払いを行う, 納付する
◆All reinsurances shall be effected in the original currency. 再保険は、すべて元受通貨で行う
ものとする。◆The undersigned （"Guarantor"),
hereby unconditionally guarantees as and for its
obligations, until full performance is effected by
or on behalf of ABC in accordance with the
terms and conditions of the license agreement
between XYZ and ABC, a copy of which is attached hereto; 下記署名者（「保証人」）は、XYZと

ABC間のライセンス契約（その写しを本保証状に添付する）の条件に従ってABCによりまたはABCに代わり完全な履行が行われるまで、その義務としてここに以下を無条件に保証する。

effect （名）影響, 影響額, 発効, 施行, 効力, 効果, 効用, 効能, 効き目, 現象, 印象, 雰囲気, 趣旨, 意味, 個人の資産, 所持品（effects）
（⇒immediate effect, remain in full force and effect）

adverse effect 逆効果, 不利な影響, 悪影響, マイナス影響, 弊害, 悪材料, 逆境

come into effect 施行される, 効力を発する, 発効する （=take effect）

competitiveness effort 競争力効果

continue in effect for a period of 〜の間効力が存続する, 〜の間有効である

currency effects 為替の影響

cyclical effects 景気循環要因

exchange rate effect 為替換算の効果

expansionary effect 景気刺激効果

give effect to 〜を発効させる, 実施する, 施行する, 実行に移す, 〜に影響を及ぼす

go into effect 発効する, 実施される, 施行される

harmful effect 弊害

have effect 効力をもつ, 効力を生じる, 発効する, 実施される

immediate effect 即時効力, 即時発効

leverage effect 他人資本効果, テコの効果, 梃率（ていりつ）効果, レバレッジ効果

liquidity effect 流動性効果

lose effect 失効する

price effect 価格効果

productivity effect 生産力効果

pump-priming effect 呼び水効果

put into effect 施行する, 実施する

remain in effect 依然として有効である, 有効に存続する, 〜の間有効である, 〜まで効力が存続する

restraint effect 抑止効果

ripple effect 波及効果
（=repercussion effect, spin-off effect）

side effect 副作用

take effect 実施される, 施行される, 発効する, 効く, 効果が出る［現れる］

take full effect 完全実施される

tax effect 税効果

while this Agreement remains in effect 本契約が有効に存続する間, 本契約有効期間中

◆A stronger yen has the favorable effect of stemming rises in import prices. 円高には, 輸入物価の高騰を抑えるプラス面もある。◆A weak yen benefits the export industries such as automobiles and home appliances, but excessive depreciation of the yen could have the negative effect on the Japanese economy. 円安は自動車や家電など輸出産業には追い風だが, 過度の円安は日本経済に悪影響を及ぼす可能性もある。◆The effects of the recent depreciation of the dollar have not been seen yet, but if the U.S. currency depreciates further, it may lead to an increase in imported commodity prices, which in turn may become an inflationary factor. 最近のドル安の影響はまだ見られないが, 米ドルがさらに下落すれば, 輸入品価格の上昇を招き, これがまた逆にインフレ要因になる恐れがある。◆The term of this agreement shall continue in effect for a period of seven years to and including March 31, 2020. 本契約の有効期間は, 2020年3月31日までの7年間とする。◆This agreement shall have effect as from January 1, 2015. 本契約は, 2015年1月1日から発効する。

effect all risk marine insurance with （保険会社と）全危険担保条件の海上保険の保険契約をする
◆ABC shall effect all risk（Institute Cargo Clauses）marine insurance with underwriters or insurance companies of good repute in an amount of one hundred and ten（110）percent of CIF value of the shipments of the products. ABCは, 本製品積送品のCIF価格の110％の保険金額で, 評判の良い保険引受業者または保険会社と全危険担保条件（協会貨物約款）の海上保険の保険契約をするものとする。

effect（an）insurance 保険を付ける, 付保する, 保険をかける, 保険の手配をする
◆The Landlord shall effect insurance by itself or have other tenants effect insurance against such accidents as aforementioned and indemnify the Tenant within the extent covered by the insurance. 「貸主」は, 前記の事故などに対して自ら保険を付けるか他のテナントに保険を付けさせ, その保険でカバーされる範囲内で「借主」に損害の補償をするものとする。

effect delivery 引渡しを行う
◆The Buyer shall notify the Seller of the name of the carrying vessel, the estimated date of loading and the contract number for the Seller to effect delivery, at least seven（7）days before the estimated date of arrival of the vessel at the port of shipment. 買い主は, 少なくとも本船の船積み港への到着予定日の7日前までに, 本船の船名, 船積み予定日と売り主が引渡しを行う契約番号を, 売り主に通知するものとする。

effect delivery of the products 本商品の引渡しを行う
◆Delivery of the products shall be effected at Yokohama Port, Japan on or before the December 20, 2003, on a C.I.F. New York Port basis. 本商品の引渡しは, CIFニューヨーク港条件で, 2003年12月20日までに横浜港（日本）で行うものとする。

effect marine insurance 海上保険を付ける［かける］, 海上保険の手配をする, 〜と保険

契約する （⇒vessel）
◆In case of individual contracts on a CIF basis, marine insurance covering All Risks shall be effected by the seller on behalf of and in the name of the purchaser, in respect of the products purchased by it under an individual contract unless the parties agree in writing to the contrary. CIF 条件での個別契約の場合、両当事者が書面で別途合意しないかぎり、買い主が個別契約で購入した製品については、売り主が買い主に代わって買い主の名前で全危険担保条件による海上保険をかけるものとする。

effect the operation of one's business ～ の事業運営に影響を及ぼす
◆In the event of bankruptcy, insolvency, dissolution, modification, amalgamation, receivership proceedings effecting the operation of its business or discontinuation of business for any reason and/or reorganization by the third party in the other party, either of the parties hereto shall have the absolute right to terminate this agreement without any notice whatsoever to the other party. 本契約のいずれか一方の当事者は、相手方の破産、支払い不能、解散、改組、合併、事業運営に影響を及ぼす清算手続き、または何らかの理由による事業中止および/または第三者による会社整理の場合には、相手方に何ら一切の通知をしないで本契約を終了する絶対的な権利を持つものとする。

effective （形）有効な, 効果的な, 効率的な, 実施されている, 実施中の, 効力をもつ, 実効の, 実効性のある, 事実上の, 実際の, 実働の
　cost-effective　コスト効率がよい, 費用効率がよい, 費用効果が高い
　effective competition　有効競争
　effective date of termination or expiration　終了または満了の効力発生日
　effective demand　有効需要
　effective devaluation　実効為替切下げ
　effective immediately upon sending　送付後直ちに発効する
　effective tariff　実効関税
　real effective exchange rate　実質実効為替レート

effective as of ～の日付で発効する, ～日付けで発効する
　effective as of the date first set forth above　頭書の日付で発効する, 頭書の日付で発効した
◆This letter sets forth our Agreement with you, effective as of May 1, 2015. このレターは、2015年5月1日付けで発効する当社の貴社との合意事項を明示する（確認する）ためのものです。

effective corporate tax rate 法人税の実効税率
◆The government will lower the effective corporate tax rate to boost the international competitiveness of Japanese companies and at the same time to attract greater foreign investment to Japan. 日本企業の国際競争力強化と対日投資拡大に向けて、政府は法人税の実効税率を引き下げる方針だ。

effective date 契約の発効日, 法令の施行日, 効力発生日, 有効日
◆Distributor or Supplier may terminate this agreement at will, at any time during the term of this agreement, with or without cause, by written notice given to the other party not less than 30 days prior to the effective date of such termination. 販売店または供給者は、この契約終了の効力発生日の30日以上前に相手方に書面で通知して、本契約中いつでも理由の有無を問わず自由に本契約を解除することができる。

effective term of this Agreement 本契約の有効期間
◆As one of the main conditions prerequisite to the continuation of the Agreement, Distributor agrees to purchase the Products from Exporter in the quantity not less than 500 units for any contract year throughout the effective term of this Agreement. 本契約の継続に不可欠な主要条件の一つとして、販売店は、本契約の有効期間中、契約年に500台以上の数量の本製品を輸出者から購入することに同意する。

effectuate （動）実施する、～を発効させる, 遂行する, 達成する
◆Application may be made to such court for confirmation of such decision or award of the arbitrator, or for an order of enforcement, and for any other legal remedies that may be necessary to effectuate such decision or award. 当該裁判所に対しては、この仲裁人の決定または判断の確認、執行命令や、当該決定または判断を実施するために必要なその他の法的救済を申請することができる。

effectuation （名）法律などの実施, 発効, 遂行

effort （名）努力, 尽力
　diligent efforts　不断の努力
　do one's utmost efforts to　～するために最大限の努力をする
　exercise all reasonable efforts　合理的なあらゆる努力をする
　exercise one's best efforts　最大限の努力をする
　make every reasonable effort　合理的なあらゆる努力をする
　make one's best efforts to　～するために最善の努力をする
　reasonable commercial efforts　合理的な営業努力
　use one's best efforts　最善の努力をする, 最善をつくす
◆In terms of trade volume, South Korea is currently among the top 10 countries partly due to its efforts to promote free trade agreements with

the United States, the European Union and others. 貿易額で、韓国は現在、米国や欧州連合（EU）などとの自由貿易協定（FTA）推進策を軸に、世界トップ10入りを果たしている。

either party （名）各当事者, 契約当事者, 当事者の一方, 当事者のいずれか一方, いずれか一方の当事者, いずれかの当事者, いずれの当事者も （⇒election）
◆Any failure, whether willful, through neglect or otherwise, of either party to perform or fulfill any of its duties, obligations or covenants in this agreement shall constitute a breach of this agreement. 故意であれ、怠慢またはその他によるものであれ、本契約における各当事者の責務、義務または約束ごとを各当事者が履行または達成できない場合、これは本契約の違反を構成するものとする。

elapse （名）（時の）経過, 休止期間 （動）経過する,（時が）経つ, 過ぎ去る
◆Unless other party cures such breach within 30 days after the receipt of such written notice of breach and intention of termination, this agreement shall be automatically terminated on the elapse of such 30-day period. 相手方が契約の違反と契約解除の意思に関する書面での通知を受けてから30日以内に当該違反を改めないかぎり、本契約は、この30日の期間が経過した時点で自動的に解除されるものとする。

election （名）選択, 選択権, 選択義務, 選任, 選挙
◆Failure of either party to exercise any of said provisions, rights, or elections shall not preclude or prejudice such party from later enforcing or exercising the same or any other provisions, rights, or elections which it may have under this agreement. いずれか一方の当事者が上記条項、権利または選択権を行使しない場合でも、その当事者が本契約に基づいて保有できる同一または他の条項、権利、または選択権を強制・行使することを後で妨げられることや、不利益を被ることはないものとする。

election of directors 取締役の選任
◆The term "Subsidiary" shall mean a corporation, more than fifty percent （50%）of whose outstanding shares representing the right to vote for the election of directors, are, now or hereafter, owned or controlled, directly or indirectly, by a party hereto. 「子会社」という語は、取締役選任のための議決権を表す発行済み株式の50%超が、本契約の一当事者によって直接・間接的に現在または今後所有されるか支配される法人を意味する。

electronic （形）電子の, 電子工学の, コンピュータ化された, エレクトロニック
electronic application 電子出願
electronic authentication 電子認証
electronic certification 電子認証
electronic component 電子部品, エレクトロニクス部品

electronic data processing system 電子データ処理システム, 電子情報処理システム, 電子情報処理方式
electronic equipment 電子機器, 電子設備
electronic funds transfer 電子資金振替え, 電信送金, 電子資金取引, 電子資金移動取引, EFT
electronic gadget 電子機器
electronic goods 電子製品, エレクトロニクス製品
electronic intelligence 電子情報
electronic transfer of shipping documents 貿易書類の電子化
electronic traveller's check 電子旅行小切手

electronic instructions 電子式の説明書
◆"Documentation" means the printed or electronic instructions, manuals and diagrams pertaining to the use and installation of Products.「ドキュメンテーション」とは、本商品の使用とインストレーションに関する印刷されたまたは電子式の説明書、取扱い説明書と図表を意味する。

electronic money 電子マネー
◆Since electronic money requires safeguards against unauthorized use and counterfeiting, encryption technology, on the software side, and IC cards, on the hardware side, represent essential technologies. 電子マネーには不正使用や変造を防ぐ技術が必要で、ソフト面では暗号化技術、ハード面ではICカードが、その代表的な技術とされている。

electronic settlement ネット・ショッピングなどの電子決済
◆In addition to offering electronic settlement for online shoppers, Rakuten Inc. plans to offer loans for retail and corporate clients. ネット・ショッパー［オンライン・ショッパー］向けの電子決済業務のほかに、楽天は個人と企業向けの融資も手がける計画だ。

electronic trading 電子取引, 電子商取引, 電子売買, コンピュータ取引, 電子トレーディング, システム売買 （=e-commerce, e-trading, electronic dealings through internet）
◆The U.S. light crude front month contract rose a further 36 cents a barrel in after-hours electronic trading to top $50. 米国の軽質原油の翌月渡し価格は、時間外の電子取引で1バレル当たり36セント上伸して、1バレル＝50ドルを突破した。

eligible currency 国際送金通貨, 送金通貨, 送金通貨条項

eliminate （動）排除する, 削除する, 除去する, 取り除く, 廃止する, 廃棄する
◆In the event a final judgment is determined in favor of the licensee and eliminates such claim or suit, all expenses and fees shall be born by the licensee. 最終判決でライセンシー勝訴の判決が下され、当該請求または訴訟が排除された場合、費用と報酬はすべてライセンシーの負担とする。

elimination of nontariff barriers 非関税障壁の撤廃
◆The framework of a Free Trade Area of the Asia-Pacific is aimed at liberalizing trade and investment as well as the elimination of nontariff barriers, regulatory reform and smoother logistics. アジア太平洋自由貿易地域（FTAAP）の枠組みは、貿易や投資の自由化のほか、非関税障壁の撤廃、規制改革、物流の円滑化などを目指している。

embargo （名）通商禁止［停止］, 通商禁止命令, 出入港停止命令, 通商停止, 輸出［輸入］禁止, 禁輸, 禁輸政策, 貿易制限, 貿易禁止, 制限, 禁止, 禁止措置, 制裁
  be under an embargo　貿易が禁止されている, 輸出禁止になっている, 出入港禁止になっている, 出港禁止中である, 停止されている
  ease the embargo　禁輸政策を緩和する
  embargo goods　禁輸品
  embargo of imports　輸入禁止
  gold embargo　金輸出禁止　（=embargo on gold）
  impose［lay, place, put］an oil embargo against ～に対して石油［原油］輸出禁止を課す, ～に対する石油輸出を禁止［停止］する
  lift the embargo　制裁を解除する
  lift［raise, remove, take off］the embargo on arms to ～に対する武器輸出禁止を解除する, ～に対する武器輸出禁止を解く
  oil embargo on Iran　対イラン石油全面禁輸措置
  U.N. embargo　国連経済制裁
◆Trading of North Korea's weapons and other products of North Korea are subject to the U.N. embargo. 北朝鮮の武器などの取引は、国連の経済制裁の対象になっている。

emergence （名）出現, 発生, 誕生, 浮上, 開始, 台頭, 激化,（危機などからの）脱出, 脱却
◆The emergence of a global trade dispute could hamper smooth transactions in services and goods. 世界的な貿易摩擦が激化すれば、モノとサービスの円滑な取引が阻害されかねない。

emergency and first aid procedures 緊急処置方法

emergency import limits 緊急輸入制限措置　（=safeguard）
◆Under the World Trade Organization rules, emergency import limits, or safeguard, are permitted as a temporary measure if the volume of imports of a certain product drastically increases, causing serious damages to industries concerned in the country. 世界貿易機関（WTO）のルールでは、緊急輸入制限措置（セーフガード）は、特定製品の輸入量が増加して、国内の関係業界に大きな被害が出ている場合には、一時的な措置として認められる。

emergency import restrictions 緊急輸入制限, 緊急輸入制限措置（セーフガード）（=emergency import limits, emergency "safeguard" import restriction, safeguard）
◆The United States defended emergency import restrictions taken to protect domestic steelmakers. アメリカは、鉄鋼産業を保護するために取った緊急輸入制限措置（セーフガード）を正当化［弁護］した。

emergency loan 緊急融資, 救援融資, つなぎ融資
◆Two domestic carriers have been given a total of ¥85 billion in emergency loans by the governmental Development Bank of Japan to overcome losses caused by a downturn in airline passengers as a result of the Iraq war and SARS outbreak. イラク戦争や新型肺炎（SARS）による利用客の減少で発生した損失を補填するため、国内航空会社2社が、政府系金融機関の日本政策投資銀行から計850億円の緊急融資を受けた。

emergency tariff 緊急関税
◆Japan filed a complaint with the World Trade Organization over U.S. emergency tariffs on steel imports. 輸入鉄鋼製品についてのアメリカの緊急関税に対して、日本は世界貿易機関（WTO）に提訴した。◆Major beef exporters such as the United States have already threatened to impose some punitive action against Japan if it introduces an emergency tariff on imported beef. 日本が輸入牛肉に対して緊急関税を導入［発動］した場合、米国など牛肉の主な対日輸出国は、すでに日本に対して制裁措置を取る動きを示している。

emerging economies 新興国
◆Before the G-20 meeting, representatives from emerging economies expressed concern that the Abe administration's economic policy dubbed as Abenomics, which involves bold monetary easing and an active fiscal stimulus package, is aimed at the depreciation of the yen. G20（主要20か国・地域）会議前に、新興国の代表らは、「大胆な金融緩和や積極的な財政出動を含む安倍政権の経済政策『アベノミクス』は、円安誘導ではないか」との懸念を表明していた。◆Japan's economic growth is driven by exports, but it will have to vie for export markets with emerging economies. 日本の経済成長の原動力は輸出だが、今後は新興国と輸出市場の争奪戦になろう。◆To increase exports, Japanese manufacturers must develop attractive products of high added value and find ways to capitalize on growing markets in the emerging economies of Asia and other regions. 輸出を拡大するには、日本の製造業各社が、付加価値の高い魅力的な商品を開発して、アジアなどの地域の新興国の成長市場を積極的に取り込む方法を見つける必要がある。

emerging markets 新興国市場
◆Fast-growing emerging markets are becoming a key battlefield for automakers around the world. 急成長の新興国市場が、世界の自動車各社が狙う主戦場になっている。

emission credit trading system　排出量取引制度
◆The Environment Ministry is examining the domestic emission credit trading system to determine how to reduce greenhouse gas emissions more efficiently. 環境省は現在、温室効果ガス（排出量）削減の効率化を図る方法を決めるため、国内排出量取引制度を検討している。

emission credits　排出枠, 排出量, 排出権
（=emission permits, emission rights）
◆To reduce greenhouse gas emissions more efficiently, the 10 percentage of 25 percent cut may be covered by purchasing emission credits from other nations.　温室効果ガスの排出量を一段と効率的に削減するには、（日本の2020年までの目標の）25%削減のうち10%を海外からの排出枠購入で賄うことも考えられる。

emission [emissions] trading　排出量取引
（温暖化ガスの排出削減が進んで余裕が出た国と、逆に増加して温暖化ガス削減目標の達成が難しい国との間で、「排出枠」を売買する方式）
emission quota trading　排出量取引, 排出権取引
emission trading system　排出量取引制度
◆Under the emission trading system created by the government, businesses can trade carbon dioxide emissions on a newly established market at home. 政府が創設した排出量取引制度では、国内に新設される市場で、企業が二酸化炭素の排出量を売買することができる。

emissions of greenhouse gases　温室効果ガスの排出量
◆The Kyoto Protocol requires industrial nations to reduce emissions of greenhouse gases, including carbon dioxide. 京都議定書は、先進各国に二酸化炭素など温室効果ガスの排出量削減を義務付けている。

employee　（名）従業員, 社員, 職員, 被雇用者, 雇い人, 使用人
◆Japanese employees of JGC Corp., a major plant manufacturing firm, were caught up in the hostage-taking incident launched by an armed Islamist group in Algeria.　大手プラント・メーカー「日揮」の邦人従業員が、アルジェリアでイスラム武装勢力が引き起こした人質事件に巻き込まれた。◆The Patent Law stipulates that patents obtained as a result of duties performed by a corporate employee belong to the employee. 日本の特許法では、企業の従業員が企業の職務の一環として得た特許権は、その従業員に帰属する、としている。

enact　（動）法律を制定する, 立法化する
◆A revised Foreign Exchange and Foreign Trade Control Law has been enacted to enable the swift freezing of funds belonging to terrorist organizations. テロ組織の資金［資産］凍結を迅速に行うための改正外為法は、すでに成立して［制定されて］いる。◆The Trademark Law was enacted to protect a trademark by giving a monopoly such as an exclusive right and a prohibitive right to an owner of a trademark right. 商標法は、商標権者に専用権や禁止権などの独占権を与えて商標を保護するために制定された。

enclose　（動）同封する
◆Enclosed are the copies of the shipping documents covering this order as follows: 本注文の船積み書類の写しは、次のとおり同封してあります。◆We enclose a few samples of our product and should be obliged if you would send us samples of the nearest quality you could offer from stock. 当社製品の見本を数点同封しますので、在庫から提供できるほぼ同品質の見本を送っていただけるとありがたいのですが［ほぼ同品質の見本があれば送っていただけないでしょうか］。◆We enclose the shipping documents covering the goods and expect your remittance in due course. 契約品の船積み書類を同封し、期日どおりのご送金を期待しております。

enclosed　（形）同封の, 同封された
a model as per the enclosed specifications　同封仕様書どおりの機種
the enclosed catalogue　同封カタログ

enclosed copy　同封の副本
◆If you accept the terms and conditions stated in this letter, please date, sign, and return the enclosed copy. このレター記載の条件に同意いただける場合には、同封の副本に日付を記入し、署名の上、ご返送ください。

enclosed price list　同封の価格表
◆The prices and other particulars inquired for are shown in the enclosed price list. お問い合わせの価格その他の明細は、同封の価格表に示してあります。

encryption technology　暗号化技術
◆Since electronic money requires safeguards against unauthorized use and counterfeiting, encryption technology, on the software side, and IC cards, on the hardware side, represent essential technologies. 電子マネーには不正使用や変造を防ぐ技術が必要で、ソフト面では暗号化技術、ハード面ではICカードが、その代表的な技術とされている。

encumber　（動）担保・抵当に入れる, 担保を設定する, 抵当権・担保権を設定する, 債務を負わせる, 〜を課す
encumber a property with a mortgage　土地に抵当権を設定する
encumbered with　〜を抱えている, 〜を背負っている

encumbrance　（名）妨害物, 抵当権, 担保権, 負担, 債務, 制限

end use　最終使用, 最終利用, 一般使用, 最終用途

end user　最終使用者, 最終利用者, 最終顧客, 最終投資家, 一般使用者, 端末利用者, エン

ド・ユーザー

end user certificate　規制用途に使用しない誓約書

end user charge　最終利用者料金

end user development　エンド・ユーザー開発、EUD

end user license　エンド・ユーザーに対するライセンス

endangered species　絶滅危惧種
◆Eel farmers and eel restaurants have been shaken by the Environment Ministry's designation of the Japanese eel as an endangered species. 環境省が日本ウナギを絶滅危惧種に指定したことで、ウナギの養殖業者やウナギ料理店には動揺が広がっている。

endorse　(動)手形・証券などに裏書きする、証書に署名する、裏面に記載する、手形などの記載金額を裏書譲渡する、～を保証する（=indorse）

endorse a document with a signature　文書に署名する、文書に裏書きする

endorse generally　無記名裏書きする

endorse in blank　無記名裏書き［白地裏書き］する、宛先ブランクで裏書きする

endorse in full　記名裏書きする

endorse off　額面金額の一部領収を証する

endorse over to　～に裏書譲渡する

endorse specially　記名裏書きする（=endorse in full）
◆A full set of negotiable bills of lading made out to order must be endorsed by shipper. 指図人式で作成された譲渡可能な船荷証券一式には、荷送人の裏書が必要である。◆Marine insurance policy shall cover all risks and be endorsed in blank. 海上保険証券は、全危険担保条件を付保し、無記名裏書き［白地裏書き］するものとする。

endorsee　(名)被裏書人、譲受人

endorsement　(名)裏書、裏書署名、海上保険の追約書、保証、是認

accommodation endorsement　融通裏書

bank endorsement　銀行裏書

bear the endorsement of　～の裏書がある

blank endorsement　白地裏書、白地式裏書（=endorsement in blank）

endorsement for transfer　譲渡裏書

full endorsement　記名裏書

general endorsement　無記名式裏書、無記名裏書

joint endorsement　共同裏書

partial endorsement　一部裏書

special endorsement　記名式裏書、記名裏書（=endorsement in full）

successive endorsement　連続裏書
◆At the closing, ABC will deliver to XYZ share certificates, representing the number of the Shares sold under this agreement, affixing proper endorsement duly executed by ABC on the back of the certificates, against the payment of the purchase price therefor, by check payable to ABC or wire transfer per ABC's instructions. クロージングにおいてABCは、本契約に基づいて売り渡す本株式の株式数に相当し、ABCが正式に署名して適切に裏書きした株券を、ABC宛の小切手またはABCの指示による電信送金による購入代金の支払いと引換えに、XYZに対して引き渡すものとする。◆Russia opposes the enforcement of anti-Syria sanctions because Syria is an important importer of weapons from Russia, and Syria provides the Russian Navy with supply bases. シリアはロシアにとって重要な武器輸出先であると同時に、ロシア海軍に補給拠点も提供しているため、ロシアは対シリア制裁の実施に反対している。◆The enforcement of the revised Mining Law enables the government to take the lead in specifying candidate sites for extracting seafloor resources and selecting developers. 改正鉱業法施行で、政府は、政府主導で海底資源の鉱区候補地の指定と開発業者の選定が可能になった。

endorser　(名)裏書人、譲渡人、保証人、推薦人

blank endorser　白地式裏書人

endorser for accommodation　融通裏書人

endorser for value　有償裏書人

qualified endorser　条件付き裏書人

restrictive endorser　限定裏書人

special endorser　記名式裏書人、記名裏書人

enforce　(動)施行する、実施する、履行する、権利を行使する、執行する、強制する、強行する、実現する
◆The guarantor hereby waives, and agrees not to assert by way of motion as a defence or otherwise, in a suit, action or proceeding pursuant to this guarantee, any claim that this guarantee or the subject matter hereof may not be enforced in or by such courts. 保証人は、本保証書に従う訴訟、裁判または手続き［訴訟または訴訟手続き］で、抗弁として申し立てることによりまたは他の方法により、本保証書またはその主題を上記裁判所ではたはその裁判所が強制することはできないとの主張をここに放棄し、これを主張しないことに同意する。◆This agreement, and all matters relating hereto, including any matter or dispute arising out of this agreement, shall be interpreted, governed, and enforced according to the laws of the State of New York, U.S.A. 本契約と、本契約から生じる一切の事項または紛争を含めて本契約に関連するすべての事項は、米国のニューヨーク州法に従って解釈し、同法に準拠し、同法に従って履行する［権利行使を行う］ものとする。

enforceability　(名)実行可能性、強制執行性、強制可能性、強行可能性、施行可能性

enforceability of the remaining provisions hereof　本契約の残存規定の強

制可能性

◆In case any one or more of the provisions of this agreement are held invalid, illegal or unenforceable in any respect, the validity, legality and enforceability of the remaining provisions hereof shall not be in any way affected or impaired thereby, except to the extent that giving effect to the remaining provisions would be unjust or inequitable. 本契約の一つ以上の規定がいずれかの点で無効、違法または強制不能と判断された場合、残存規定の実施が不公正または不均衡となる範囲を除いて、本契約の残存規定の有効性、合法性と強制可能性はその影響を受けることはなく、またそれによって損なわれることはないものとする。

enforceable （形）実行可能な、強制執行できる、施行可能な、強制可能な
◆Any orders or debts which exist as of the date of this agreement shall be enforceable in accordance with the terms thereof. 本契約の締結日時点で存在する注文や債務は、その条件に従って強制執行できるものとする。

enforcement （名）施行、実施、実行、権利行使、強制、強要、強行、執行、判決の強制執行
early enforcement of tariff cuts　関税引下げの繰上げ実施
enforcement or the absence of enforcement of this agreement　本契約の履行の強要または強要がないこと
law enforcement　法の執行、～を強制する法的権利
order of enforcement　執行命令
rights of enforcement　強制権
◆ABC National Corporation hereby waives and agrees to waive in any proceedings for the enforcement of this agreement, any and all privileges or sovereign immunity, including the privilege of sovereign immunity from suit or immunity of the property from attachment or execution, to which it may be entitled under international or domestic laws, as a procedural defense or otherwise. ABC国営会社は、本契約を実施するための一切の手続きにおいて、手続き上の抗弁その他として当該国営企業が国際法または国内法により有する一切の特権または主権免除（国家主権に基づく裁判からの免除特権や財産の差し押さえまたは強制執行からの免除を含む）を本契約により放棄するとともに、その放棄に同意する。

engaged in the business of　～の事業に携わる、～の事業を営む
◆Licensee is engaged in the business of manufacturing, distributing, and selling software devices as defined below. ライセンシーは、以下に定義するソフトウエアの記憶媒体の製造・流通および販売業務に従事している。

engagement （名）合意、約束、確約、取決め、協約、契約、監査契約、雇用、雇用期間、従事、活動、業務、負債、債務

audit engagement　監査契約
be under an engagement　契約がある
break off an engagement　解約する、破談にする
business engagement　仕事の取決め
cargo engagement　船荷契約
compilation engagement　財務諸表の調製契約
consulting engagements　コンサルティング業務
engagement letter　契約書、（法律事務所や会計事務所などの）委任契約書、監査報告書
engagement sheet　船腹予約書
forward engagement　先物契約
letter of audit engagement　監査契約書
letter of engagement　契約書、契約時の取り交わし文書　（＝engagement letter）
make an engagement　契約する、約束する
make no binding engagement with　～との契約を控える
meet one's engagements　債務を果たす
previous [prior] engagement　先約
review engagement　レビュー契約
We offer you without engagement A　Aを不確定オファーする
without engagement　（売買申込みや値段を）確約なしで[確約しないで]
◆The prices are without engagement and subject to change with or without notice. 価格は確約なしで、予告の有無にかかわらず変更することがある。

engineering, design or manufacture　エンジニアリング、設計または製造
engineering, procurement and construction　設計・調達・建設、EPC
on the engineering, procurement and construction basis　設計・調達・建設契約で　（＝on the EPC basis）
enhancements and modifications　改訂と変更、拡張と変更、拡張版と変更版
enhancements, modifications and improvements　拡張、変更と改良、拡張、変更および改良版
enquire　⇒inquire
ensure fair international commercial trade　公正な国際商取引を確保する
◆To ensure fair international commercial trade, the law against unfair competition stipulates that both individuals involved in bribery and the corporations they belong to should be punished. 公正な国際商取引を確保するため、不正競争防止法には、贈賄（外国公務員への贈賄）に関与した個人と法人を罰する規定（両罰規定）がある。
enter （動）市場などに参入する、団体などに加入する、加盟する、入会する、参加する、参加登録する、入る、記入する、記載する、提起す

る, 提出する, 申請する, 申し出る, 申し込む, 正式に記録にのせる, (判決などを) 正式に登録する, 契約を結ぶ, (コンピュータにデータなどを) 入力する, 立ち上げる, 〜にログインする, 土地に立ち入る, 占取する

enter A as evidence 証拠品としてAを提出する

enter a complaint 告訴の申立てを行う

enter a new stage 新しい段階に入る, 新しい段階を迎える

enter a protest 異議を申し立てる

enter a recession 景気後退局面入りする

enter an action against 〜に対する訴状を提出する, 〜を告訴する

enter an offer 提議の申立てを行う

enter an opposition 異議の申立てを行う

enter judgment 判決を裁判所の記録に正式に記録する

enter new markets abroad 海外の新市場に進出する

enter the bond market 債券を発行する

enter the data into a computer データ［情報］をコンピュータに入力する

enter the debt market 起債する

enter up (支払いなどを) きちんと記入する, 〜を正式に記録する, (裁判を) 記録に残す
◆A new firm to be formed in October from the merging of Mitsubishi Pharma Corp. and Tanabe Seiyaku Co. will enter the generic drug market as an all-round producer of pharmaceuticals. 三菱ウェルファーマと田辺製薬の合併で10月に設立される新会社は, 総合医薬品メーカーとして後発医薬品［ジェネリック医薬品］市場に参入する。

enter a sell order 売り注文を入力する, 売り注文を出す
◆A Mizuho Securities employee entered a sell order from a client as "sell 610,000 shares at ¥ 1 each" though the client's actual order was "sell one share at ¥610,000." 顧客の実際の注文は「61万円で1株の売り」であったが, みずほ証券の社員は「1株1円で61万株の売り」と入力して顧客の売り注文を出してしまった。

enter full-scale negotiations 本格交渉に入る
◆Japan has yet to enter full-scale TPP negotiations, but the LDP has not presented concrete measures to prepare for the liberalization of trade, including steps to bolster competitiveness in the agricultural sector. 日本が環太平洋経済連携協定(TPP)の本格交渉に入るのはこれからだが, 自民党は, 農業分野での競争力強化策など, 貿易自由化に備えた具体策をまだ示していない。

enter into a code-sharing arrangement 共同運航協定を結ぶ
◆The two airlines have agreed to enter into a code-sharing arrangement on international routes. 両航空会社は, 国際線の共同運航協定を結ぶことで合意した。

enter into a contract 契約を結ぶ, 契約を締結する (=make a contract)
◆Yahoo stopped entering into new contracts for banner advertisements for adult merchandise. ヤフーは, 成人向け商品のバナー広告の新規契約を中止した。

enter into a patent license agreement 特許ライセンス契約を結ぶ
◆Nokia Corp. of Finland has settled a series of patent disputes over mobile phones products with Kyocera Corp. by entering into a patent license agreement. フィンランドのノキアは, 携帯電話の製品をめぐる京セラとの一連の特許紛争で, 特許ライセンス契約を結ぶことで和解した。

enter into an agreement 契約を結ぶ, 契約を締結する (=enter into a contract, make a contract, make an agreement, make and enter into an agreement; ⇒made and entered into)

enter into force 効力を生じる, 発効する
◆An international treaty to ban the use, development, production, stockpiling and transfer of cluster bombs entered into force on August 1, 2010. クラスター(集束)爆弾の使用, 開発, 製造, 保有と移転を禁止する国際条約が, 2010年8月1日に発効した。

enter the market 市場に参入する
◆Since the deregulation of the civil aviation industry, two airlines entered the market on domestic trunk routes. 空の規制緩和［航空自由化］以来, 航空会社2社が, 国内幹線市場に参入した。

enter the mobile phone business 携帯電話事業に新規参入する
◆The firm is preparing to enter the mobile phone business in Japan. 同社は, 日本での携帯電話事業への新規参入を目指している。

entire understanding and agreement 完全な了解と合意, 完全な了解と合意事項
◆This agreement sets forth the entire understanding and agreement between the parties as to the matters covered herein. 本契約は, 本契約に含まれる事項に関する両当事者間の完全な了解と合意を規定するものである。

entirely and completely 完全に

entitle (動) 〜する権利を与える, 〜する資格を与える, (本に) 表題を付ける

be entitled to 〜の権利がある, 〜を持つ［もらう］権利がある, 〜の権利を持つ, 〜の資格がある, 〜を受ける資格がある, 〜できる

be entitled to claim liquidated damages 損害賠償予定額を請求することができる

be entitled to terminate the contract 契約を解除する権利がある
◆By the revised Labor Contract Law, researchers are now entitled to maintain job contracts until the mandatory retirement age, provided their length of service has exceeded five years. 労働契

約法の改正により、研究者は現在、勤続期間が5年を過ぎた場合には、定年まで雇用契約を継続できるようになった。◆Except as otherwise expressly provided for in this agreement, ABC shall not be entitled to set off or withhold any amount owing to ABC under this agreement, against any payment to XYZ for the performance by XYZ of this agreement. 本契約に別に明文の規定がないかぎり、ABCには、本契約に基づきABCに支払われる金額を、XYZによる本契約の履行に対するXYZへの支払い金と相殺する権利はなく、またその支払いを保留する権利もないものとする。

entrust (動)託す, 任せる, 預ける, 委託する, 委任する, ～の管理を任せる
◆The Tokyo metropolitan government entrusted the bids for the construction project to the company. 東京都は、この建設工事の入札業務を同社に委託した。

entry (名)記入, 記載, 記帳, 記録, 登録, 登記, 記載項目, 記載事項, 参加, 参入, 加盟, 入会, 入場, 入国, 参加者, 出品物, 土地への立ち入り, 通関手続き, 通関申告, 入力
  age at entry 保険年齢, 契約年齢
  book entry 帳簿記入
  correct an entry 記載事項を訂正する
  data entry データ入力
  entry and operation of foreign capital 外資の流入と活動
  entry barriers 参入障壁
    (=barriers to entry, entry problems)
  entry market 参入市場
  entry of any judgment 判決登録(判決を裁判所の記録に登録する行為), 判決の執行
  entry of such order of divestiture 剥奪命令の言い渡し
  EU entry EU加盟
  export entry 輸出手続き
  import entry 輸入手続き
  make a false entry 虚偽記載をする
  make an entry 記入する, 記載する, 記帳する
  market entry 市場参入, 市場への参入
  order entry 受注, 注文処理
  stock exchange entries 証券取引所[株式市場]への新規上場
◆Domestic stock exchange entries continue to languish, reflecting the tough conditions faced by emerging firms wanting to publicly list their shares. 国内株式市場への新規上場は、株式上場を目指す新興企業が直面している厳しい状況を反映して、低迷が続いている。

environment (名)環境, 情勢, 動向, 局面, 展開
  business environment 経営環境, 企業環境, 事業環境, 景気 (=business climate)
  the earnings environment for export-oriented

companies 輸出企業の収益環境
◆Benefiting from the yen's depreciation which resulted from Abenomics, the Abe administration's economic policies, the earnings environment for export-oriented companies has greatly improved. 安倍政権の経済政策「アベノミクス」による円安効果で、輸出企業の収益環境が大幅に改善した。◆European countries and China have various kinds of bubbles and/or swollen monetary environments. 欧州や中国は、バブルや金融膨張などの市場環境を抱えている。

envisaged international safety standards 国際安全基準案
◆Nursing-care robots under the envisaged international safety standards of the ISO stop or go around such hazards as objects or bumps. 国際標準化機構(ISO)の国際安全基準案に基づく介護ロボットは、障害物や凹凸などの危険があれば、止まったり避けたりする。

EPA 経済連携協定
(⇒economic partnership agreement)
◆EPAs are better known, in general, as free trade agreements. EPAは、一般的には、自由貿易協定としてよく知られている。

EPA 米環境保護局(Environmental Protection Agencyの略)

EPC agreement 設計・調達・建設契約, EPC契約 (=engineering, procurement and construction agreement)

equal to ～に相当する
  an amount equal to the multiple of five times of the net profits per share 1株当たり純利益の5倍に相当する金額
  at a price which shall be equal to ～と同額の価格で

equally (副)均等に
◆All expenses, including attorney's fees shall be borne and paid by the licensor and the licensee equally. 弁護士報酬を含めて、費用はすべてライセンサーとライセンシーが均等に負担して支払うものとする。

equipment (名)機器, 設備
  equipment dispatch order コンテナ機器引渡し指図書, EDO
  equipment interchange receipt 機器受渡し証, EIR

equipment, materials, and processes 設備, 原料と製法
◆The licensee shall use and practice substantially similar equipment, materials, and processes as the licensor does in its plant. ライセンシーは、ライセンサーがその工場で使用し、実施しているのと実質的に同じ設備、原料と製法を使用し、実施するものとする。

equitable (形)公平な, 公正な, 正当な, 衡平法上の, エクイティ上の
  equitable action 衡平法上の訴訟, エクイティ

上の訴訟
equitable charge　エクイティ上の担保
equitable consolidation　一体併合
equitable interest　衡平法上の権利,衡平法上の財産権
equitable lien　衡平法上のリーエン
equitable obligation　衡平法上の債務
equitable power　衡平法上の権限
equitable remedy　衡平法上の救済[救済手段],エクイティ上の救済
equitable title　衡平法上の権原[所有権]
◆The arbitrators shall have the authority to order such discovery and production of documents, including the depositions of party witnesses, and to make such orders for interim relief, including injunctive relief, as they may deem just and equitable. 仲裁人は、当事者の証人の宣誓証言[証言録取書]を含めて文書の開示と提出を命じる権限と、差止救済を含めて仲裁人が正義かつ衡平とみなす暫定的救済を命じる権限を持つものとする。
equitable relief　エクイティ上の救済,エクイティ上の救済手段,エクイティ上の救済方法,衡平法上の救済,衡平法上の救済手段 (=equitable remedy)
◆In the event of a breach or threatened breach by ABC of this agreement, XYZ shall be entitled to injunctive and other equitable relief against such breach or threatened breach in addition to any remedy it might have at law or in equity. ABCによる本契約の違反または違反の恐れがある場合、XYZは、コモン・ロー上または衡平法上有する救済手段のほかに、当該違反または違反の恐れに対して差止命令その他衡平法上の救済を受ける権利を持つものとする。
equity fund　投資ファンド,株式ファンド
◆The firm envisioned negotiations with the U.S. equity fund over financing for restructuring in a reconstruction plan it formulated in June. 同社は、経営合理化の資金調達に関しては、6月に策定した再建計画でこの米国の投資ファンドとの交渉を見込んでいた。
equity participation　資本参加
◆By gaining Intel's equity participation, NEC and Hitachi aim to make Elpida one of top three makers of multipurpose DRAM (dynamic random access memory) chips in the world, rivaling Samsung Electronics Co. of South Korea and Micron Technology Inc. of the United States. インテルの資本参加を得ることにより[インテルの出資により]、NECと日立は、汎用(はんよう)DRAM(記憶保持動作が必要な随時書き込み読み出しメモリ)の製造で、エルピーダ(NECと日立が折半出資する合弁会社)を韓国のサムスン電子、米国のマイクロン・テクノロジー社と並ぶ世界3強の一角に押し上げる戦略だ。
eroding　(形)減少する,低下する,悪化する,~の減少[低下、下落、悪化]

eroding export profitability　輸出の採算性の悪化,輸出の採算悪化
eroding international competitiveness　国際競争力の悪化
◆There was a time when the more we exported, the more money we lost, by eroding export profitability due to the excessive rise in the value of the yen. 超円高による輸出の採算悪化で、輸出するほど赤字になる時もあった。
error　(名)間違い,誤り,ミス,失策,思い違い,考え違い,誤った信念,過ち,悪行,誤差,誤審,コンピュータのエラー,故障,障害,エラー
◆Errors in computing systems at financial institutions could lead to problems in making international fund transactions. 金融機関のコンピュータ・システムのエラーは、国際的な資金取引上、トラブルが生じる可能性がある。
escape clause　免責条項,責任免除条項,責任回避条項,緊急輸入制限条項,エスケープ・クローズ (=safeguard clause)
escrow　(名)第三者預託,寄託,条件付き捺印(なついん)証書,条件付き譲渡証書,エスクロ勘定,エスクロ[エスクロー]
escrow account　寄託勘定,預託勘定,エスクロ勘定
escrow agent　不動産取引代行業者,第三者
escrow agreement　条件付き譲渡契約,停止条件付き払戻し預託金契約,エスクロ契約,エスクロ取引
escrow credit　寄託信用状,預託信用状 (=escrow letter of credit)
escrow holder　エスクロ所持人
escrow instructions　エスクロ指図書
escrow number　エスクロ番号
general escrow provisions　一般エスクロ規定
hold A in escrow until　~までAをエスクロ勘定で管理する
the opening of escrow　エスクロの開設
establish　(動)設立する,設置する,創設する,信用状を開設する・発行する,確立する,制定する,定める,規定する,担保権などを設定する
establish a letter of credit　信用状を開設する (=establish an L/C)
◆On orders over U.S. $50,000, payment shall be made through a medium of a Letter of Credit to be established by ABC at its expense. 5万米ドルを超える注文の場合、支払いは、ABCがその費用で開設する費用で信用状で行うものとする。◆The Buyer shall establish in favor of the Seller an irrevocable letter of credit issued by a first-class international bank acceptable to the Seller. 買主は、売り主のために、売り主が承諾できる[同意できる]第一級の国際銀行が発行する取消不能の信用状を開設するものとする。◆The Seller may withhold delivery or cancel the Agreement if the

ESTA

Buyer fails to establish the letter of credit by the date stipulated in this Agreement. 買い主が本契約で定める期限までに信用状を開設することができない場合、売り主は、引渡しを保留するか契約を解除することができる。◆We have already arranged with our bankers for an L/C to be established by the end of this month. 今月末までに信用状を開設する件については、当社が当社の取引銀行にすでに手配してあります。

establishing bank （信用状の）発行銀行, 開設銀行 （=issuing bank, opening bank: 一般に、信用状の発行依頼者である輸入者の取引銀行）

establishment of JVCO 合弁会社の設立

estimate （動）見積もる, 試算する, 推定する, 推計する, 評価する

estimate （名）見積り, 推定, 推計, 予想, 予測, 見通し, 目安, 概算, 試算, 推定値, 推定量, 評価, 判断, 見積り, 見積り書, 概算書 （⇒consolidated operating profit estimates）
　growth estimate　経済成長率見通し, 成長率見通し, 成長率予測
　initial estimate　当初の予想, 当初予想
　market consensus estimate　市場のコンセンサス予想
　market estimates　市場予想
　preliminary estimate　暫定推定値, 仮見積り
　profit estimate　利益予想, 損益予想, 業績予想 （=profit forecast）
　◆Please give us an estimate as soon as possible as it doesn't have to be very exact. 大ざっぱ[アバウト]で結構ですので、当社に至急[すぐに]見積りを出して下さい。

estimated （形）見積りの, 推定の, 推測の, 想定される, 予定の, 大体の, 概算の, およその
　estimated balance sheet　見積り貸借対照表
　estimated charges　見積り費用
　estimated date of loading　船積み予定日
　estimated expense　見積り費用
　estimated financial statements　見積り財務諸表, 見積り財務書類
　estimated liabilities　見積り負債[債務]
　estimated loss　見積り損失額, 損失見積り額
　estimated premium　概算保険料
　estimated price　予想価格
　estimated purchase　見積り購入額
　estimated reserves　推定埋蔵量
　estimated sum　見積り高, 見積り額
　estimated tare　見積り風袋, 推定風袋
　estimated time of arrival　到着予定日, ETA
　estimated time of clearance　（荷役作業や輸入通関の）作業完了予定日, ETC
　estimated time of departure　出港予定日, 出航予定日, 出発予定時刻[日時], ETD

estimated value　見積り額
estimated weight　見積り重量, 推定重量
◆Suntory Holdings Ltd. is expected to use about ￥500 billion in estimated proceeds from the listing of its beverage and food unit to finance mergers and acquisitions abroad. サントリーホールディングスは、清涼飲料・食品子会社の上場により推定で5,000億円程度の資金を調達して、海外企業の買収に充てる見込みだ。

estimated costs 見積り費用, 見積り原価, 費用見積り（cost estimate）, 原価見積り
◆The estimated costs of ￥600 million will be defrayed by medical device manufacturers and financial institutions. 6億円の見積り費用は、医療機器メーカーと金融機関が負担することになっている。

estimated date of arrival of the (carrying) vessel 本船の到着予定日
◆The Buyer shall notify the Seller of the name of the carrying vessel, the estimated date of loading and the contract number for the Seller to effect delivery, at least seven （7）days before the estimated date of arrival of the vessel at the port of shipment. 買い主は、少なくとも本船の船積み港への到着予定日の7日前までに、本船の船名、船積み予定日と売り主が引渡しを行う契約番号を、売り主に通知するものとする。

estimated exchange rate 想定為替レート （=assumed exchange rate, projected exchange rate）
◆In the case of Tokyo Electric Power Co., its fuel costs will increase by ￥33 billion per year if the yen is depreciated by ￥1 to the dollar for one year from the estimated exchange rate. 東京電力の場合、想定為替レートからドルに対して1ドル＝1円の円安が1年間続いた場合、同社の燃料費は1年間で330億円増える。

estimated time of arrival 到着予定時刻[日時], 到着予定日, ETA
　estimated time of departure　出港予定日, 出航予定日, 出発予定時刻[日時], ETD
◆As soon as practicable after ocean freight is secured by the purchaser, the purchaser will notify the seller of the name of the vessel and the estimated time of arrival （ETA）of the vessel at the port of shipment. 買い主による海上輸送の手配ができ次第、買い主は、本船の名前と本船の船積み港への到着予定日（ETA）を売り主に通知するものとする。

EU 欧州連合 （⇒European Union）
◆By starting talks on a comprehensive partnership agreement, the EU and the United States will take the first step toward creating a giant free trade zone that would account for about 50 percent of the world's gross domestic product. 包括的連携協定の交渉を開始することで、欧州連合（EU）と米国は、世界のGDP（国内総生産）の5割近くを占める巨大な自由貿易圏の創設に一歩踏み

出すことになる。◆Washington and Brussels will conditionally accept an abolition of subsidies to farmers in the United States and the EU who grow agricultural products for export. 米国や欧州連合 (EU) は、それぞれ国内の輸出用農産物栽培農家に対する補助金の撤廃を条件付きで受け入れる方針だ。

Euribor ユーロ銀行間取引金利, ユーロ銀行間貸し手金利, ユーライボー (Euro inter-bank offered rateの略。欧州銀行協会が公表するユーロ建て取引に関するレートのこと。⇒LIBOR)

euro （名）ユーロ (=Euro: 欧州単一通貨)。1991年1月1日に導入された。独仏伊など11か国でスタートしたユーロ導入国は、2009年1月から16か国に拡大して、基軸通貨ドルに次ぐ「第二の通貨」としての存在感が高まっている。）
◆As European authorities failed to take swift action, the yields of Italian and Spanish government bonds rose, and there were violent fluctuations in the value of the euro. 欧州当局が迅速に対応しなかったので、イタリアやスペインの国債流通利回りが上昇し、ユーロの為替相場が乱高下した。◆In foreign exchange margin trading, investors repeatedly trade U.S. dollars, euros and other currencies, aiming to profit from fluctuations in exchange rates. 外国為替証拠金取引では、為替の変動による利益を狙って、投資家が米ドルやユーロなどの外貨を繰り返し売買する。◆Nominal foreign exchange rates are quoted at ¥110 to the U.S. dollar or ¥135 to the euro as we see in the media. 名目為替レートは、新聞や雑誌で見られるように、1ドル＝110円とか、1ユーロ＝135円と表示される。◆The U.S. dollar has dropped sharply in value not only against the yen, but also against the euro, the South Korean won, the Thai baht and other currencies. 米ドル［米ドル相場］は、円に対してだけでなく、ユーロや韓国ウォン、タイ・バーツなどに対しても、急落している。

Europe （名）欧州, ヨーロッパ, ヨーロッパ連合
◆The economic slowdown in Europe due to the sovereign debt crisis and slackening growth of China as a major exporter to Europe have dealt a painful blow to Japan's exports and production. 債務危機に伴う欧州経済の減速と、欧州向け輸出の多い中国の成長鈍化が、日本の輸出と生産に耐え難いほどの打撃を与えている。

European Central Bank 欧州中央銀行, 欧州中銀, ECB
◆Finance ministers from the European Union's 27 countries agreed to give the European Central Bank the authority to supervise eurozone banks from March 2014. 欧州連合 (EU) 27か国の財務相は、2014年3月から、欧州中央銀行 (ECB) にユーロ圏の銀行を監督する権限を与えることで合意した。

European Commission 欧州委員会, 欧州委
◆A European Commission trade commissioner

said at the European Parliament's International Trade Committee meeting that the EU and the United States could sign a comprehensive partnership agreement as early as the end of 2014. 欧州委員会の通商担当委員は、欧州議会の国際貿易委員会で、EU (欧州連合) と米国は2014年中に包括的連携協定を結ぶことも可能だと述べた。

European financial crisis 欧州の金融危機
◆Partly due to a slowdown in the Chinese economy in the wake of the European financial crisis, Japan's exports and production have been on the decline. 欧州の金融危機による中国の景気減速もあって、日本の輸出や生産活動は落ち込んでいる。

European Patent Convention 欧州特許条約

European Union 欧州連合, EU
◆Canada and the European Union have already decided to impose tit-for-tat tariffs on U.S. products. カナダと欧州連合 (EU) は、米国の製品に報復関税をかけることをすでに決めている。◆In terms of trade volume, South Korea is currently among the top 10 countries partly due to its efforts to promote free trade agreements with the United States, the European Union and others. 貿易額で、韓国は現在、米国や欧州連合 (EU) などとの自由貿易協定 (FTA) 推進策を軸に、世界トップ10入りを果たしている。◆Japanese deluxe wagyu beef has started to hit the market in Europe due to the lifting of a ban on beef exports from Japan to the European Union. 日本からEU (欧州連合) への牛肉輸出の解禁で、日本の高級和牛が欧州の市場に出回り始めた。◆The European Union and the United States agreed at a summit meeting in November 2011 to establish a framework to encourage trade and investment. 欧州連合 (EU) と米国は、2011年11月の首脳会議で、貿易や投資を促進させる枠組みの構築で合意した。◆The European Union's head office formally adopted tariffs of up to 26 percent on steel to prevent a feared flood of cheap imports from countries hit by U.S. protective measures. EU (欧州連合) の欧州委員会は、米国の保護措置で打撃を受けた国から安い輸入鉄鋼製品が流入する恐れがあるのを防ぐため、鉄鋼製品に対して最高26％の関税をかけることを正式採択した。

EU's tariff policy EUの関税政策
◆The EU's tariff policy toward IT equipment imports violates a WTO agreement. 情報技術 (IT) 機器の輸入品に対するEUの関税政策は、WTO (世界貿易機関) 協定に違反している。

event （名）出来事, 事件, 事項, 事象, 事態, 事由, 結果, 成り行き
event or condition 事態または状態
events constituting a default 不履行を構成する事由
if any of the following events shall occur 次の事態のいずれかが発生した場合
the nature of the event 事態の種類

the party claiming an event of force majeure 不可抗力事態を申し立てる当事者

◆Either party shall have the right to terminate this agreement on the occurrence of any of the following events by giving a written notice to the other party of such breach and intention of termination. 契約当事者は、次の事態のいずれかが生じた場合には、当該違反と契約解除の意思を相手方に書面で通知して、本契約を解除する権利を持つものとする。

events of defaults 不履行事由, 不履行事態, 期限の利益喪失事由, 債務不履行事由, デフォルト事由, 契約違反行為

◆Events of default shall include the failure by a party to perform a material obligation under this agreement. 不履行事由には、当事者による本契約上の重大な義務の不履行が含まれる。◆It shall constitute an event of default if either party is the subject of any proceeding relating its liquidation or insolvency which is not dismissed within 30 days. いずれかの当事者が清算または支払い不能手続きの対象となり、当該手続きが30日以内に取り下げられないときは、不履行事由となる。

evidence （動）示す, 明示する, 表示する, 立証する, 証明する, 〜の証拠となる

◆Irrevocable letter of credit provides for payment upon presentation of Supplier's invoices and shipping documents evidencing delivery of the invoiced Products to the carrier or freight forwarder. 取消不能信用状は、供給者の請求書と、請求書に記載した本製品を運送人または海貨業者に引き渡したことを証明する船積み書類を提示して支払いを受けるものだ。

evidence （名）証拠, 根拠, 証拠資料, 押収資料, 資料, 証拠物件 (evidential matter), 証言, 証人, 指標, 兆候, 兆し, 形跡

evidence of a pick-up in economic activity 景気回復の兆候, 景気が上向いていることを示す指標

evidence of bottoming inflation インフレが底を打った兆し

evidence to the contrary 反対の証拠, 反証

give evidence 証言する, 事情 [状況] を説明する

hard evidence 物的証拠

◆Date of marine bill of lading shall be proof of the date of shipment in the absence of the evidence to the contrary. 海上船荷証券の日付は、反対の証拠がない場合、船積み日の証拠となる。◆The U.S. Federal Trade Commission （FTC） concluded there was not enough evidence that a Sony-BMG merger would violate U.S. antitrust laws. 米連邦取引委員会 (FTC) は、ソニーとBMG（独複合メディア大手ベルテルスマンの音楽事業部門）の統合が米国の独占禁止法に違反することを示す十分な証拠はない、との結論を下した。

examine （動）調査する, 試験する, 検査する, 検証する, 監査する, 診断する, 審査する, 尋問

する （⇒independent accountant）

exceed （動）越える [超える], 上回る, 〜以上である, 〜に勝る

◆Crude oil prices have exceeded $70 a barrel in London and New York, setting all-time highs on these markets. ニューヨークとロンドン市場で原油価格が1バレル＝70ドルを上回って、両市場最高値を記録した。◆The working hours of Engineer shall not exceed seven （7） hours a day and shall include not less than one hour's rest. 技術者の労働時間は1日7時間を超えないものとし、1時間以上の休憩を含むものとする。

exceeding （形）〜を超える, 〜超の（〜の数量・程度を含まない）

（⇒irrevocable documentary letter of credit）

except （前・接）〜の場合を除いて, 〜でないかぎり （=unless）

except by the mutual express consent in writing 書面で相互に明示的に同意しないかぎり, 書面で明示的に合意しないかぎり, 書面で明示的に合意する場合を除いて

except in the case where 〜の場合を除いて, 〜する場合を除いて

except provided by this Article below 本条の下記の規定による場合を除いて

except the prior written consent of 〜の書面による事前の同意がないかぎり, 〜の書面による事前の同意がある場合を除いて

except as 〜しないかぎり, 〜する場合を除いて, 〜するものを除いて

（=except when, if not, unless）

◆All payments to the licensor under this agreement, except as otherwise herein set forth, shall be remitted in United States dollars by telegraphic transfer to the account of the licensor at a bank in the city of San Francisco designated by the licensor. 本契約に基づくライセンサーへのすべての支払いは、本契約で別途規定する場合を除いて、ライセンサーが指定するサンフランシスコ市にある銀行のライセンサーの口座に電信送金により米ドルで送金して（振り込んで）行うものとする。

except as and to the extent 〜しないかぎり、また〜した場合にかぎって、〜するものを除いて、また〜するかぎりにおいて

◆Except as and to the extent specifically reflected in the March 31, 2003 balance sheet included in Schedule 6, the Company does not have any liabilities or financial obligations of any nature. 付属書類6に記載した2003年3月31日付け貸借対照表に特に示されているものを除いて、また同表に特に示されているかぎり、対象会社はいかなる性質の債務も金銭的債務も有していない。

except as herein expressly provided 本契約で明文がある場合を除いて, 本契約に明文の規定がないかぎり, 本契約書で明示されている場合を除き

◆Distributor will not have, and will not represent that it has, any power, right or authority to bind

Supplier, or to assume or create any obligation or responsibility, express or implied, on behalf of Supplier or in Supplier's name, except as herein expressly provided. 本契約に明文の規定がある場合を除いて、販売店は供給者を拘束する権能、権利または権限も、また明示・黙示を問わず供給者のためにまたは供給者の名義で債務・責任を負担するまたは負担させる権能、権利または権限も有しておらず、これらを有する旨表明することもしない。

except as otherwise expressly provided for in 〜に別に明文の規定がある場合は除いて、〜にとくに明文の規定がないかぎり、〜で別段に明確に取り決めないかぎり
◆Except as otherwise expressly provided for in this agreement, ABC shall not be entitled to set off or withhold any amount owing to ABC under this agreement, against any payment to XYZ for the performance by XYZ of this agreement. 本契約に別に明文の規定がないかぎり、ABCには、本契約に基づきABCに支払われる金額を、XYZによる本契約の履行に対するXYZへの支払い金と相殺する権利はなく、またその支払いを保留する権利もないものとする。

except for 〜を除いて
except for information otherwise publicly available　他の公知・公用の情報を除いて
except for the purpose of　〜の目的を除いて、〜の目的以外は
◆Any claim by the purchaser, except for latent defects, shall be made in writing as soon as reasonably practicable after the arrival, unpacking and inspection of the products, whether by the purchaser or any subsequent purchaser of the products. 買い主によるクレームは、隠れた瑕疵（かし）を除いて、買い主によるか本製品のその後の購入者によるかを問わず本製品の到着、開梱および検査後、合理的に実行可能なかぎり速やかに書面で行うものとする。

except insofar as 〜の場合を除いて
◆During the life of this agreement and thereafter Distributor shall not divulge any confidential information which it may acquire in connection with Products, this agreement or performance thereunder, except insofar as such information is or becomes generally known or publicly available at the time of disclosure under this agreement or subsequent thereto. 本契約期間中とその後も、代理店は、本契約に基づく開示時点とその後に公知または公用となる場合を除いて、本製品（契約品）、本契約または本契約に基づく履行に関連して取得することができる一切の秘密情報を漏洩しないものとする。

except pursuant to 〜による場合を除いて
◆This lease shall not be subject to termination by the Lessor, except pursuant to Article 6. hereof, nor by the Lessee, for any reason whatsoever. 本リースは、本契約第6条による場合を除いて貸主により解除されないものとし、また理由のいかんを問わず借主により解除されないものとする。

except to the extent that 〜の範囲を除いて、〜の限度を除いて
◆In case any one or more of the provisions of this agreement are held invalid, illegal or unenforceable in any respect, the validity, legality and enforceability of the remaining provisions hereof shall not be in any way affected or impaired thereby, except to the extent that giving effect to the remaining provisions would be unjust or inequitable. 本契約の一つ以上の規定がいずれかの点で無効、違法または強制不能と判断された場合、残存規定の実施が不公正または不均衡となる範囲を除いて、本契約の残存規定の有効性、合法性と強制可能性はその影響を受けることはなく、またそれによって損なわれることはないものとする。

except with the prior written consent of 〜の書面による事前の同意がある場合を除いて、〜の書面による同意がないかぎり
◆No material commitments, bids or bidding offers will be entered into by the Company in any case in excess of $10,000 whether or not in the ordinary course of business, except with the prior written consent of Purchaser. 買い主の書面による事前の同意がある場合を除いて、対象会社は、通常の業務過程であるか否かを問わずどんな場合でも1万ドルを超える重要な約束、入札、入札の申込みは行わないものとする。

excessive appreciation of the yen 過度の円高　(=the yen's excessive appreciation)
◆Excessive appreciation of the yen will harm business performance, especially for exporters. 過度の円高で、輸出企業を中心に業績の悪化が見込まれる。

excessive changes in the exchange rate 為替相場の過度な変動
◆The government will stem any excessive changes in the exchange rate. 政府は、為替相場の過度な変動を抑制する方針だ。

excessive depreciation of the yen 過度の円安
◆A weak yen benefits the export industries such as automobiles and home appliances, but excessive depreciation of the yen could have the negative effect on the Japanese economy. 円安は自動車や家電など輸出産業には追い風だが、過度の円安は日本経済に悪影響を及ぼす可能性もある。◆The weaker yen helps exporters, but close attention must be paid to the fact that the excessive depreciation of the yen will further increase the prices of imports of LNG and other foreign products. 円安は輸出企業にはプラスだが、円安が行き過ぎると、天然液化ガス（LNG）など海外製品の輸入額が一段と増えることにも、警戒が必要である。

excessive movements [moves] of foreign exchange rates 行き過ぎた為替相場［為替レート、外国為替相場］の動き
◆Excessive movements of foreign exchange

rates are not desirable. 行き過ぎた為替相場の動きは、好ましくない。

excessive rise in the value of the yen 行き過ぎた円相場の上昇, 超円高, 過度の円高
◆There was a time when the more we exported, the more money we lost, by eroding export profitability due to the excessive rise in the value of the yen. 超円高による輸出の採算悪化で、輸出すればするほど赤字になる時もあった。

excessive volatility in exchange rates 為替変動の過度な変動
◆By being vigilant against excessive volatility in exchange rates, the G-20 will reduce the risk of speculative money causing appreciation of currencies and inflation in emerging countries. 為替相場の過度な変動を監視して、世界[主要]20か国・地域（G20）は、投機マネーが新興国の通貨高やインフレを招くリスクを軽減する方針だ。

exchange （名）交流, 交換, やりとり, 意見交換, 会話, 議論, 両替, 為替, 為替相場, 証券や商品の取引所, 取引, 交易, 電話交換所, 職業安定所

arbitration of exchange 為替裁定取引

commodity exchange 商品取引所

cultural exchange between the two countries 両国間[二国間]の文化交流

currency exchange office 両替所

economic exchange 経済交流

exchange contract 為替予約

exchange contract slip 為替予約票

exchange control 為替管理

exchange dealing 為替ディーリング

exchange depreciation 為替の切下げ, 為替価値の下落[減少]

exchange dumping 為替ダンピング（輸出品の競争力を高めるため自国通貨の為替相場を不当に切り下げること）

exchange gains 為替差益

exchange gains from a [the] strong yen 円高差益

exchange-listed company [firm] 証券取引所上場企業, 上場企業

exchange losses from a [the] strong yen 円高による為替差損

exchange parity 為替平価

exchange position （為替銀行の）為替の持ち高, 為替ポジション

exchange speculation 為替投機

first of exchange 為替手形の第一券, 第一手形

flexible exchange policy 為替政策

floating exchange 変動相場

foreign exchange 外国為替

forward exchange 先物為替

second of exchange 為替手形の第二券
◆Intercontinental Exchange (ICE), an exchange that deals in investing contracts known as futures, is buying the NYSE for about $8 billion. 米インターコンチネンタル取引所（ICE: 先物と呼ばれる投資契約を扱う取引所）が、ニューヨーク証券取引所を約80億ドルで買収する。

exchange fluctuations 為替変動
◆The yen's stable rate at about ¥110 against the dollar serves as a stabilizing factor for importers, exporters and others doing business susceptible to exchange fluctuations. 円の対ドル為替相場が110円台（前後）で安定していることは、輸出入業者など為替変動に左右されやすい仕事をしている者にとって安定要因となる。

exchange loss 為替差損
（為替差益＝exchange gain）
◆The depreciation of the greenback will result in exchange losses on assets held in dollars. ドル安が進むと、保有するドル建て資産に為替差損が生じる。

exchange rate 為替相場, 為替レート, 為替, 交換レート, 交換比率, 取引レート （=rate of exchange; ⇒foreign exchange rate, yen's exchange rate）

according to the exchange rate 為替相場に応じて

applicable exchange rate 適用される為替レート, 為替レートの適用

assumed exchange rate 想定為替レート（=estimated exchange rate, projected exchange rate）

average exchange rates prevailing during the year 期中の実勢平均為替レート

control exchange rates 為替相場をコントロールする

current exchange rate 現行為替レート

effective exchange rate 実効為替レート

engage in exchange rate speculation 為替投機を行う

exchange rate allocation 外貨割当て

exchange rate appreciation 為替レートの切上げ

exchange rate band 為替変動幅

exchange rate control 為替管理

exchange rate depreciation 為替レートの切下げ

exchange rate flexibility 為替レートの伸縮性

exchange rate for the dollar ドルの為替レート

exchange rate overvaluation 為替レートの過大評価

exchange rate parity 為替交換比率

exchange rate policy 為替政策

exchange rate realignment　為替相場の再編成

exchange rate rigidity　為替レートの硬直性

exchange (rate) risk　為替リスク

favorable exchange rate　有利な為替レート

fixed exchange rate　固定相場, 固定相場制

floating exchange rate policy　変動相場政策

forward exchange rate　先物レート

in-house exchange rate　社内為替レート
(=in-house rate of exchange)

lock in an exchange rate　為替レートを予め確
定する

push down the exchange rate　為替レートを押
し下げる

push up the exchange rate　為替レートを押し
上げる

real effective exchange rate　実質実効為替
レート

real exchange rate　実質為替レート

realistic exchange rate　現実的為替レート

stock-for-stock exchange rate　株式交換の交
換比率

the dollar's exchange rate against the Japanese
yen　円に対するドル相場, 円・ドル相場

the exchange rates for US dollars　米ドルの為
替レート

the prevailing exchange rate　実勢為替レート

the yen-dollar exchange rate　円とドルの為替
レート, 円・ドルレート, 円の対ドル相場

the yen's exchange rate against the dollar　ドル
に対する円相場

unfavorable exchange rate　不利な為替レート,
不利な為替相場

◆A cheaper yen increases import costs, but if the
yen-dollar exchange rate is within the range of
￥95-105, it would be possible for companies to
maintain competitiveness in exports. 円安で輸
入コストは増えるが, 円の対ドル為替相場が1ド
ル＝95〜105円の範囲内なら, 企業は輸出競争力
を維持できるだろう。◆Banks participating in direct yen-yuan trading in the Tokyo interbank foreign exchange market will trade the yen and the
yuan at an exchange rate calculated on the basis of actual supply and demand. 東京外国為替
市場で円・人民元の直接取引に参加する銀行は,
実際の需給などをもとに算出した取引レートで,
円と人民元を銀行間で取引する。◆Erratic fluctu-
ations of both stock prices and exchange rates
have continued, reflecting the turbulent moves of
speculative money on world markets. 世界的な投
機マネーの激しい動きを反映して, 株価と為替相
場の乱高下が止まらない。◆Every three months,
McDonald's Japan revises the price of the beef
it imports from Australia according to the exchange rate. 3か月ごとに, 日本マクドナルドは, 為

替相場に応じてオーストラリアから輸入している牛
肉の価格を見直している。◆If the exchange rate
remains around ￥90 to the dollar for the next
12 months, income equivalent to 0.6 percent of
Japan's GDP will flow overseas mainly due to
higher fuel imports stemming from the suspension of nuclear power reactors. 為替相場が今後1
年間, 1ドル＝90円程度の水準が続いた場合に, 主に
原子力発電所の運転停止に伴う燃料輸入の増加に
より, 日本の国内総生産 (GDP) の0.6%相当の所得
が海外に流出する。◆If the yen-dollar exchange
rate stayed around ￥100 to the dollar, give or
take about ￥5, it would be possible for domestic companies to maintain competitiveness in exports. 円とドルの為替相場が1ドル＝100円プラス・
マイナス5円程度で安定すれば, 国内企業は輸出競争
力を保てるだろう。◆In foreign exchange margin
trading, investors repeatedly trade U.S. dollars,
euros and other currencies, aiming to profit from
fluctuations in exchange rates. 外国為替証拠金取
引では, 為替の変動による利益を狙って, 投資家
が米ドルやユーロなどの外貨を繰り返し売買する。

exchange rate fluctuations　為替変動
◆Yen-denominated trade frees domestic companies from the risk of exchange rate fluctuations.
円建て貿易は, 国内企業にとって為替変動のリス
クがない。

exchange rate of the yen　円の為替相場,
円の為替レート, 円相場
◆Japan Chamber of Commerce and Industry
Chairman Tadashi Okamura thinks that the appropriate exchange rate of the yen is between ￥
85 and ￥90 to the dollar. 日本商工会議所の岡村
正会頭は, 1ドル＝85円〜90円が円相場の適正水準
であると考えている。

exchange risk　為替変動リスク, 為替リスク,
為替危険

exchange risk insurance　為替変動保険, 為替
変動リスク保険
◆Japanese companies can hedge exchange
risks and improve their business image abroad
through external bond financing. 日本企業は, 外
債発行による資金調達で, 為替リスクを回避する
とともに海外での企業イメージアップを図ること
ができる。

excise　**(名)** 消費税, 物品税, 免許税
Board of Customs and Excise　英国の間接税
税務局 (現在は2005年4月の合併でHM
Revenue & Customs (歳入関税庁) となって
いる)

commodity excise　物品税

Customs and Excise　間接物品税庁

excise allowance [drawback]　消費税の戻
しель

excise duty　消費税, 物品税

excise license　間接税免許

excise on liquor　酒税

EXCL

excise permit 消費税支払い証明書

excise tax 消費税, 物品税

federal excise tax 連邦物品税

gasoline excise ガソリン税

general excise tax 一般消費税

exclusive (形)独占的, 排他的, 専属の, 専有の

appoint you as our exclusive selling representatives 貴社を当社の一手販売代理店に指名する

exclusive agency agreement 総代理店契約

exclusive agent 一手販売店, 専属特約店, 専売代理店, 総代理店

exclusive and nontransferable right 独占的で譲渡不可能な権利 (⇒have manufactured)

exclusive bargaining 単一交渉権

exclusive buying agent 一手買付け代理人

exclusive contract 排他の契約

exclusive dealing 排他的取引

exclusive dealing contract 排他的取引契約

exclusive exporter's selling agent 輸入総代理店

exclusive import agent 輸入総代理店

exclusive importer's buying agent 輸入総代理店

exclusive industrial district 専用工業地域

exclusive line 専売品

exclusive listing arrangements 独占上場取決め

exclusive of 〜を除いて

exclusive outlet selling agent 一手販売代理店, 特約一手販売店

exclusive possession 独占, 占有

exclusive privilege 独占権

exclusive residential district 専用住宅地域, 高級住宅地域

exclusive sales agreement 独占販売協定

exclusive sales territory 独占的販売地域

exclusive selling 特約一手販売

exclusive selling agent〔agency〕 一手販売代理店

exclusive trade 排他的条件付き取引

exclusive transaction 排他的取引

mutually exclusive events 排反事象

on an exclusive basis 独占的に, 排他的に, 一手販売で

sole and exclusive right 唯一の排他的な権利, 唯一かつ絶対的な権利, 独占の権利

◆The express warranties set forth in this Article are exclusive. 本条に定める明示の保証は, 排他的である。

exclusive distribution 一手販売, 独占販売

exclusive distribution channel 限定的販売経路, 独占販売経路

exclusive distribution right 独占販売権

exclusive distribution vehicle 独占販売契約企業

exclusive distributor 独占的代理店, 総代理店, 独占的販売店, 一手販売店, 独占販売業者

◆The Exporter grants the Distributor and the Distributor accepts to be the exclusive distributor for the sale and distribution of the products of the Exporter in the defined sales territory. 輸出者は, 販売店が指定販売地域内で輸出者の製品販売の総代理店となることを認め, 販売店はこれに同意する。

exclusive distributorship 一手販売権, 独占的販売権, 総販売代理店, 総販売特約店

exclusive distributorship agreement 一手販売契約(書), 一手販売店契約, 独占販売契約, 独占的販売店契約, 総代理店契約

exclusive territorial distributorship 排他的地域販売権

exclusive economic zone 排他的経済水域, EEZ(国連海洋法条約により, 沿岸国は200カイリ(約370キロ・メートル)まで排他的経済水域を設定することができ, この水域で沿岸国は海洋, 海底とその下で天然資源の開発, 探査, 管理や経済活動に関して主権的権利を持つとされる)

◆Fishermen catching tuna in the exclusive economic zone of foreign countries are required to pay fishing fees. マグロ漁船が他国の200カイリ排他的経済水域(EEZ)内で操業する場合, マグロ漁船は入漁料を支払わなければならない。

exclusive jurisdiction 専属的裁判管轄, 専属管轄, 専属的裁判管轄権, 専属管轄権

be subject to the exclusive jurisdiction of 〜の専属管轄権に服する

◆Any dispute arising out of this agreement or any individual contract hereunder shall be subject to the exclusive jurisdiction of the Tokyo District Court. 本契約または本契約に基づく個別契約から生じる紛争は, すべて東京地方裁判所の専属管轄権に服するものとする。◆The parties hereto consent to the exclusive jurisdiction of the federal court in the City of New York for the resolution of any dispute arising out of this agreement. 本契約当事者は, 本契約から生じる一切の紛争を解決するためにニューヨーク市の連邦裁判所の専属管轄権に服することに同意する。◆The Tokyo District Court shall have the exclusive jurisdiction in relation to any dispute arising under this agreement. 東京地方裁判所は, 本契約から発生する紛争に関して専属管轄権を持つ。

exclusive license 独占的ライセンス, 排他的ライセンス, 独占的実施許諾, 排他的実施許諾, 独占的実施権, 商標などの独占的使用権(=exclusive license)

exclusive license agreement 独占的ライセン

ス契約

obtain an exclusive license　独占的ライセンスを取得する

exclusive method of compensation　対価の唯一の支払い方法として，唯一の支払い方法
◆In consideration of the license granted and the products delivered by XYZ, ABC shall, upon the delivery of the products, pay a royalty in the amount listed in Exhibit C as the exclusive method of compensation under this agreement. XYZが許諾するライセンスとXYZが引渡す本製品の対価として，ABCは，本製品の引渡し時に，本契約に基づく対価の唯一の支払い方法として付属書類Cに記載する額のロイヤルティを支払うものとする。

exclusive, nonassignable and nontransferable license　譲渡不能，移転不能の独占的ライセンス，譲渡不能，移転不能の独占的実施権，商標の譲渡不能，移転不能の独占的使用権
◆Licensor hereby grants during the term of this agreement to Licensee an exclusive, nonassignable and nontransferable license to use Trademarks in Territory on Products under the terms and conditions of this agreement. ライセンサーは，本契約期間中，本契約の条件に基づき本製品について契約地域で本商標を使用する譲渡不能，移転不能の独占的権利を，本契約によりライセンシーに付与する。

exclusive right　独占的権利，独占権，占有権

exclusive right to sell　独占的販売権

exclusive rights to list　独占状条件

the exclusive right herein granted　本契約で付与される独占的権利

the exclusive right to a patent　特許独占権
◆Bic Camera will have the exclusive right to buy more than 50 percent of Kojima in Kojima's private placement of new shares in June 2012. コジマが2012年6月に実施する第三者割当増資で，ビックカメラは，コジマの株式の50%超を引き受ける独占権を持つことになっている。◆The Trademark Law was enacted to protect a trademark by giving a monopoly such as an exclusive right and a prohibitive right to an owner of a trademark right. 商標法は，商標権者に専用権や禁止権などの独占権を与えて商標を保護するために制定された。

exclusively　（副）もっぱら，まったく〜のみ，排他的に，独占的に，専門的に，相容れずに

exclusively authoritative　唯一の正文の

exclusively for one's use　〜の専用の

exclusively possess　占有する，独占する
◆The original and copies of the licensor's Program, in whole or in part and however modified, which are made by the licensee, as between the licensor and the licensee shall be the property exclusively of the licensor. ライセンシーが作成する

ライセンサーのコンピュータ・プログラムのオリジナルとコピー（複製）は，その全部であれ一部であれ，またどんな変更が加えられたとしても，ライセンサーとライセンシーの間では排他的にライセンサーの財産とする。◆Through diversifying rare earth suppliers, Japan will lessen the diplomatic pressure China is able to exert as it exclusively possesses heavy rare earth deposits. レア・アース調達先の多角化により，日本は，重レア・アース鉱床の独占を武器にした中国の外交圧力をかわす方針だ。

exclusivity clause　除外条項

exculpatory clause　免責条項

excuse　（動）免責する，免除する，許す，解除する　（名）免責

excused performance　不可抗力による免責

execute　（動）契約書などを作成する，署名する，調印する，完成する，履行する，執行する，実行する，実施する，遂行する

execute a large trade　大口取引を執行する

execute a share split　株式分割を実施する

execute a strategy　戦略を実施する，戦略を実行する
◆Commodity futures trading is based on contracts to buy or sell a specified quantity of an underlying asset, such as gold, at a particular time in the future and at a price agreed when the contract was executed. 商品先物取引は，取引契約を結ぶ時点で，一定量の金などの対象資産を将来の特定の時期に合意した値段で売買する契約に基づいて行われる。

execute an agreement　契約書を作成する，契約書に署名する［調印する］，契約を結ぶ［締結する］　(=execute a contract)
◆IN WITNESS WHEREOF, the parties have executed this agreement as of the date first above written. 以上の証として［本契約の証として］，両当事者は，冒頭に記載した日をもって本契約書に署名した。◆This agreement may be executed in counterparts, each of which shall be deemed an original. 本契約は複数の副本で作成することができ［本契約は複数の副本で締結することができ］，その副本をそれぞれ原本と見なすものとする。

execute and sign　作成して署名する，作成・署名する
◆This agreement is executed and signed in the English version, and all correspondence between the parties shall be in English. 本契約書は英語版を作成して署名し，当事者間の通信はすべて英語で行うものとする。

execute the order　注文を執行する，注文を履行する
◆We will execute the order with best attention upon receipt of your L/C. 貴社の信用状を受け取り次第，当社は最善の注意を払って注文を履行します。

execute trades　取引を執行する

◆In commodity futures trading, prices are decided when buyers and sellers make deals. So they can execute trades at promised prices even if the value of goods has changed drastically in the meantime. 商品先物取引では、売り手と買い手が取引契約をする時点で価格を決める。そのため、契約期間中に相場が大きく変動しても、売り手と買い手は約束した値段で取引を執行できる。

executed （形）作成された、履行済みの、既履行の、執行済みの、完成した

executed consideration 既行約因、履行済み約因

executed contract 履行済み契約、既履行契約、既行契約

executed contract of sale 完成売買契約

executed in duplicate 正副2通作成した

executed trust 完成信託

fully executed contract 完全履行済み契約

execution （名）作成、署名、調印、締結、履行、遂行、実行、実施、施行、執行（証券会社などが取引を実行すること）、強制執行、達成、成立、業務

daily execution 日常業務

execution capability 売買執行能力

execution creditor 執行債権者

execution date of this agreement 本契約締結日

execution debtor 執行債務者

execution of loan ローンの実行

execution of right 権利の行使

execution of stock warrants ワラント（株式ワラント、新株引受権）の権利行使

execution of the budget 予算の執行

execution price 執行価格、約定価格

execution report 約定報告

execution sale 強制売買

order execution 注文執行、注文処理 (=execution of order)

skill in trade execution 取引執行力

term of execution 履行期限

the execution of your order 貴社注文［貴注文］の履行、貴注文の執行

◆On the closing date, ABC shall transfer the Shares to XYZ through the execution by the parties of the deed of transfer. クロージングの日に、ABCは、譲渡証書に両当事者が調印することにより、本株式をXYZに譲渡するものとする。 ◆The assignor shall first obtain the execution by its assignee of an agreement whereby the assignee binds itself to the non-assigning party to observe and perform all the obligations and agreements of its assignor. 譲渡人は先ず譲受人による同意書への署名を得［譲渡人は先ず譲受人に同意書に署名させ］、それにより譲渡人のすべての義務と同意事項を遵守・履行する非譲渡当事者に対して約束さ

せるものとする。

execution and performance of this agreement 本契約の締結と履行、本契約書の作成と本契約の履行

◆The execution and performance of this agreement by Seller constitute legal, valid and binding obligations of Seller, enforceable in accordance with the terms hereof. 売り主による本契約の締結と履行は、本契約の条件に従って強制することができる法的、有効かつ拘束力のある売り主の義務を構成する。

execution of this agreement 本契約の締結、本契約の成立、本契約の履行

◆For a minimum of 6 months following the execution of this agreement, it is XYZ's established policy that all payments by ABC to XYZ for the XYZ Products or Services shall be made through irrevocable letter of credit, cash against documents, cash on delivery, or through full payment. 本契約の締結後最低6か月間、XYZの製品またはサービスに対するABCによるXYZへのすべての支払いは、取消不能信用状、書類引換現金渡し、現金引換渡しにより、または全額払いにより行うのが、XYZの確立した方針である。

execution of your order 貴社注文の履行、貴注文の履行

◆We are very sorry indeed to have to advise you of a delay in the execution of your order. 貴社注文の履行が遅れたことを、お知らせしなければなりません。

executive （名）経営者、管理職、重役、会社役員、役職員、執行役員、執行部、執行機関、行政部 (executive department)、行政官、エグゼクティブ

chief executive 企業などのトップ、最高経営責任者（CEO）、理事長

company executive 会社経営者、企業経営者、経営者 (=corporate executive)

executive managing director 代表取締役

executive vice president 代表取締役副社長

incumbent executives 現経営陣、現職の経営陣

subordinate executive 従属役員、（副社長などの）副業務執行役員

top executive 最高経営者、最高執行部、最高経営幹部、経営首脳、経営者

exercise （名）権利などの行使 （動）権利などを行使する、指導力などを発揮する、影響・圧力などを及ぼす

◆In exercising these rights, Distributor may not alter or delete any credit, logo, copyright notice or trademark notice appearing on the Picture. これらの権利を行使するにあたって、輸入代理店は、本映画に現われるクレジット、ロゴ、著作権表示または商標表示を変更または削除することはできない。 ◆Such late charge shall be paid without prejudice to the right of Holder to collect any other amounts due or to declare a default under this

Note or the Deed of Trust or to exercise any other rights and remedies of Holder. 当該遅延料は、手形所持人の他の未払い金をすべて取り立てる権利や本手形または信託証書に基づいて債務不履行を宣言する権利、または手形所持人の他のあらゆる権利と救済手段を行使する権利を損なわないで支払うものとする。

exert one's utmost efforts 最善の努力をする，最善をつくす（=use one's best efforts）
◆For the purpose of maintaining and enhancing Licensee's sale of Products in Territory, Licensee shall exert its utmost efforts to manufacture, sell and adequately advertise Products under this agreement, with full respect for Licensor's Trademarks. ライセンシーの契約地域での本製品の販売を維持・促進するため、ライセンシーはライセンサーの本商標を十分尊重して、本契約に基づく本製品の製造・販売と十分な宣伝広告に最善をつくさなければならない。

exhibit （動）陳列する，展示する，上映する，放映する

exhibit （名）付属書類，添付書類，付属の図表，別添，別紙，証拠物件，物証，書証
◆Exhibit D sets forth a complete and accurate list of all claims, suits, actions, arbitrations, legal or other proceedings or governmental investigations to which the Company is a party or which is, to the knowledge of ABC, threatened against the Company. 付属書類Dには、本会社が当事者である、またはABCが知るかぎり本会社が当事者になる恐れのある［本会社に対して提起される恐れがある］すべての請求、訴訟、仲裁、法的手続きもしくはその他の手続き、または政府調査の完全かつ正確なリストが記載されている。◆The particulars of the services and assistance are set forth in Exhibit A hereto. サービスと指導の詳細は、本契約書の付属書類Aに定める。

exhibition （名）展示，表示，陳列，展覧，一般公開，展示［陳列］品，展示［展覧，博覧］会，品評会，講演会，公開演技，実演，練習試合，（才能などの）発揮，露呈，奨学金

competitive exhibition 品評会，共進会
exhibition clause 展示約款
exhibition export 展覧会出品輸出
exhibition gallery 展覧会場，博覧会場
exhibition hall 展示会場
exhibition insurance 展覧展示保険
exhibition room 陳列室，展示室
exhibition stand 展示ブース
industrial exhibition 産業博覧会
industrial parts and materials exhibition and procurement negotiation fair 工業部品・素材展示調達商談会
international exhibition 万国博覧会
◆A real-size cabin mock-up of the Mitsubishi Regional Jet（MRJ）was put on display at Japan International Aerospace Exhibition 2012. MRJ

（三菱リージョナルジェット機）の実物大の客室模型が、2012年国際航空宇宙展で展示された。◆About ten major Japanese automakers are scheduled to take part in an industrial parts and materials exhibition and procurement negotiation fair in Seoul. 韓国・ソウルで開かれる工業部品・素材展示商談会には、日本の自動車メーカー約10社が参加する予定だ。

exhibitor （名）出品者，出展企業

Exim Bank［Eximbank］ 米国輸出入銀行（Export-Import Bank of the United Statesの略）

Eximbank-backed financing 米輸銀保証付き融資案件
US Eximbank 米国輸銀

existing （形）存在する，現存する，存続している，現行の，既存の，実績ベースの

call the existing bonds 既発債を任意償還する
existing agreement 現存協定
existing assets 既存資産
existing condition of business 現在の業務業況，現在の業況
existing conditions 現状
existing contract 現存契約
existing contracts 既存の商品
existing deals 既発債（=existing bonds, existing issues）
existing debt 既存の債務
existing goods 現物
existing homes 中古住宅
existing inflation 実績ベースのインフレ率
existing law 現行法
existing lines 現在の取扱い製品
existing operations 既存の事業，従来の事業，現地企業
existing preferential duties 既存特恵関税
existing reserves 埋蔵資源
existing shareholder 現株主
existing tax rates 現行の税率，現行税率
existing treaty 現存条約，既存の条約
refinance existing debt 既存の債務を借り換える
terminate existing joint venture 合弁事業から撤退する

Exon-Florio provision of the 1988 trade law 1988年通商法のエクソン・フロリオ条項（米国の安全保障を損なう企業買収の禁止）
◆In the United States, the Exon-Florio provision of the 1988 trade law can prevent takeover bids that are deemed a threat to national security. 米国では、1988年通商法のエクソン・フロリオ条項で、国家の安全保障上、脅威と考えられる企業買

収を阻止することができる。

expect （動）期待する，望む，見込む，予想する，見積もる，推定する，〜するつもりである，〜するだろうと思う，〜と思う，要求する，求める

be expected to　〜することが予想［期待］される，〜するものと考えられる，〜と見込まれる，〜になりそうだ，〜する見込みである，〜する見通しである，〜する方向だ
◆If Washington's permission to import natural gas produced in the United Stated is granted, the LNG production of Mitsui & Co. and Mitsubishi Corp. at the Cameron Parish facility is expected to start as early as 2017. 米国で生産した天然ガスの輸入を米政府が許可した場合、米ルイジアナ州のキャメロン郡にあるLNG基地での三井物産と三菱商事のLNG生産は、早ければ2017年からスタートする予定だ。◆May we expect your reply at your earliest convenience？ 早急にご返事をいただけるものと［賜るものと］、期待しております。◆Two investment funds are expected to join the second round of bidding to choose a company to support the corporate rehabilitation of chipmaker Elpida Memory Inc. 半導体メーカーのエルピーダメモリの企業再建を支援する企業選びの二次入札に、投資ファンド2社が参加する［入札する］見通しだ。◆You may expect a large order from us very soon. 早速、貴社に大口の注文を差し上げます。

expected （形）期待される［期待した］、見込まれる、予想される、見積もられる、推定される、要求される、求められる、〜の期待［予想、見通し］、期待［予想］〜

expected amount of losses　予想される損失額

expected contractual income　期待契約所得

expected inflation（figures）　期待インフレ率、予想インフレ率

expected profit　期待利益、予想利益、期待利潤

expected profitability　期待利益率、予想利益率

expected return　期待収益、予想収益、期待収益率

expected value　期待値

expected number of shares　予想株式数
◆Based on the expected number of Facebook shares after its initial public offering of stock, the Facebook's IPO values the firm at $76 billion to $95 billion. フェイスブックの新規株式公開（IPO）後の予想株式数に基づいて計算すると、新規株式公開で、同社の企業価値は760億ドル〜950億ドルとなる。

expected shipping date　船積み予定日、出荷予定日
◆ABC shall give firm orders for the products at least 6 weeks in advance of expected shipping date from San Francisco, California. ABCは、カリフォルニア州サンフランシスコからの船積み予

定日の少なくとも6週間前に、本製品の確定注文を出すものとする。

expeditiously and amicably　迅速かつ友好的に

expenses　（名）経費、費用、支出
◆All expenses, including attorney's fees shall be borne and paid by the licensor and the licensee equally. 弁護士報酬を含めて、費用はすべてライセンサーとライセンシーが均等に負担して支払うものとする。

expenses, costs and fees　経費、費用と報酬

experimental fishing　調査漁獲
◆The Hamburg-based International Tribunal for the Law of the Sea issued an interim injunction on Japan's experimental fishing for southern bluefin tuna. 国際海洋法裁判所（ドイツ・ハンブルク）は、日本が行っているミナミマグロの調査漁獲に暫定的な命令を下した。

expiration　（名）契約期間の満了、満了、失効、終了、消滅

expiration date hereof　本契約の終了日

expiration of the initial term or any renewed term hereof　本契約の当初期間または更新期間の満了

expiration of the original term or any such extended term of this agreement　本契約の当初期間またはその延長期間の満了

expiration of one's term　〜の任期満了
◆In case of the death, resignation or other removal of a director prior to the expiration of his term, the parties hereto agree to cast their votes as shareholders, so as to appoint as his replacement a director nominated by the party hereto who has nominated the director whose death, resignation or other removal was the cause of such vacancy. 取締役の任期満了前に取締役が死亡、辞任またはその他の理由で退任した場合、本契約当事者は、その死亡、辞任その他の理由による退任で当該欠員を生じさせた取締役を指名した本契約当事者が後任取締役を指名できるように、株主としてその議決権を行使することに合意する。

expiration or termination of this agreement　本契約の満了もしくは終了
◆Article 10 shall survive the expiration or termination of this agreement for any reason. 第10条は、どんな理由であれ、本契約の満了もしくは終了後も存続するものとする。

expire　（動）（期間が）満了する、終了する、満期になる、（期限が）切れる、（時効が）成立する、失効する、（権利が）消滅する
◆The irrevocable letter of credit shall not expire until fifteen（15）days after the last day of the time of delivery specified in this Agreement. この取消不能信用状は、本契約で定める引渡し期限の最終日から15日までは失効しないものとする。◆This U.S. patent for iPS cells will expire in December in 2026. このiPS細胞の米国特許の有効期限は、2026年12月となっている。

EXPO

expired （形）期限が切れた，期間が満了した，終了した，満期となった，失効した
  expired agreement 満期になった契約，契約の満了
  expired card 期限切れのカード
  expired meat product 品質保持期限切れの肉［食肉］製品
  expired utility 経過効用
  ◆By the instruction of the China Food and Drug Administration, the Shanghai city government suspended operations of Shanghai Husi Food and confiscated raw materials and products at the firm which had sold expired meat products. 中国の国家食品薬品監督管理総局の指示で，上海市は，品質保持期限切れの肉製品を販売していた上海福喜食品の営業を停止し，同社の原料と商品を差し押さえた。

expiry （名）期間の満了（expiration），終了，満期
  ◆Any notice served by registered mail or by telex as aforesaid shall be deemed served on the earlier of actual receipt or the expiry of 120 hours after posting. 上記のとおり書留郵便またはテレックスで送達された通知は，実際の受領日と投函から120時間後のうちいずれか早いほうの日に送達されたものと見なすものとする。
expiry date set forth in this agreement 本契約に定める満了日
expiry or termination of this agreement 本契約の満了または終了
  ◆The obligation under this Article shall continue for five years after the expiry or termination of this agreement. 本条に基づく義務は，本契約の満了または終了から5年間存続するものとする。

explosion of the factory 工場の爆発

export （動）輸出する，移出する（他のデータ処理システム用に変換して取り出すこと）
  ◆A slight increase in exports led by automobiles was more than offset by a sharp rise in imports of liquefied natural gas and crude oil for thermal power generation. 自動車を中心に輸出は若干伸びたものの，これは火力発電用の液化天然ガス（LNG）や原油などの輸入急増でかなり相殺された。
  ◆If reasonably priced oil and gas are exported to Japan by the U.S. "shale revolution," the cost of domestic thermal power generation would decrease. 米国の「シェール革命」で，安価な原油やガスが日本に輸出されれば，国内火力発電のコストは下がることになる。◆Japanese deluxe wagyu beef has started to hit the market in Europe due to the lifting of a ban on beef exports from Japan to the European Union. 日本からEU（欧州連合）への牛肉輸出の解禁で，日本の高級和牛が欧州の市場に出回り始めた。

export （名）輸出，輸出品，輸出製品，輸出額（exports），供給
  export acceptance bill 輸出引受手形
  Export Administration Act 米国の輸出管理法

Export Administration Regulations 米国輸出規則，EAR
export advance 輸出前貸金融，輸出前貸し［前貸金］
export advertising 輸出広告
export agent 輸出代理店
export and import transaction law 輸出入取引法
export association 輸出組合
export bill 輸出手形
export bill insurance 輸出手形保険
export bond insurance 輸出保証保険
export bonus 輸出補助金
export bounty 輸出奨励金
export broker 輸出仲買人
export by turn-key system ターンキー方式輸出
export catalog（ue） 輸出カタログ
export clearing 輸出通関
export commission house 輸出問屋
Export Credits Guarantee Department 英国の輸出信用保証庁，ECGD
export customs clearance 輸出通関
export declaration 輸出申告，（銀行認証用）輸出申告書，E/D
export destination 輸出先
export discount 輸出割引
export documents 輸出書類
export drive 輸出ドライブ
export duties 輸出関税，輸出税
export financing［finance］ 輸出金融，輸出信用（「輸出信用」は，政府・政府系金融機関が，民間企業の海外プロジェクトや輸出に融資したり，これらを保証したり，貿易保険を引き受けたりすること）
export FOB insurance 輸出FOB保険
export freight 輸出運賃
export-import credit company 輸出入金融会社
export incentive system 輸出奨励制
export indemnity 輸出損害補償
export inspection 輸出検査
export insurance 輸出保険
export invoice 輸出送り状
export laws 輸出管理法
export letter of credit 輸出信用状
export license 輸出許可，輸出承認，輸出承認証
export market 輸出市場
export marketing 輸出マーケティング

E

export merchant 輸出商

export of technique 技術輸出

export order 輸出注文

export outlet 輸出販路

export packing 輸出包装

export point of gold 正貨現送点

export price 輸出代金

export priority 輸出優先権, 輸出優先順位

export proceeds insurance 輸出代金保険

export profitability 輸出採算

export promotion 輸出促進, 輸出振興

export quota 輸出割当て

export quotation 輸出相場, 輸出相場申入れ

export ratio 輸出比率

export report 輸出報告書

export sales contract 輸出売買契約

export sample 輸出見本

export shipper 輸出出荷人

export standard エクスポート・スタンダード

export with exchange 有為替輸出

export without exchange 無為替輸出

export/import statistical schedule 輸出入統計品目表

net exports 純輸出 (輸出から輸入を差し引いた正味の輸出額)

offer export credit facility 輸出信用を供与する

strengthen export competitiveness 輸出競争力を高める

use export credit 輸出信用を利用する

◆In a currency war, countries intentionally devalue their currencies to boost exports. 通貨安戦争では, 各国が輸出に追い風となるように自国通貨の為替レートを意図的に安く誘導する。◆In April 2002, the government enforced so-called catch-all regulations aimed at controlling exports of goods and technology linked to weapons development. 2002年4月から政府は, 兵器開発関連の機器と技術の輸出を取り締まるため, いわゆる「キャッチオール規制」を施行した。◆Japan's exports and production have been reduced because of the slowdown of foreign economies and the worsening of relations with China. 海外経済の減速と日中関係の悪化で, 日本の輸出や生産は低迷している。◆Partly due to a slowdown in the Chinese economy in the wake of the European financial crisis, Japan's exports and production have been on the decline. 欧州の金融危機による中国の景気減速もあって, 日本の輸出や生産活動は落ち込んでいる。◆The yen's appreciation will not only reduce the volume of exports but also harm a wide variety of other areas. 円高は輸出の減少だけでなく, その弊害は広範に及ぶ。

Export Administration Regulations 米輸出管理規則, 米輸出管理規制

◆Recipient shall not transfer any confidential information received hereunder or any product made using such confidential information, to any country prohibited from obtaining such data or product by the U.S. Department of Commerce Export Administration Regulations without first obtaining a validated export license. 受領者は, 本契約に従って受領した秘密情報またはこの秘密情報を使用して製造した製品を, 米国商務省の輸出管理規則により当該データまたは製品の提供が禁止されている国に対して, 最初に輸出承認の許可を得ないで譲渡することはないものとする。

export and import trends 輸出入動向

◆Export and import trends are influenced by various factors, including economic situations in and outside of the country, currency exchange rates and crude oil price movements. 輸出入動向は, 国内外の景気や為替相場, 原油価格の変動などの各種要因に左右される。

export ban 輸出禁止

◆The three principles on arms exports add up to a de facto arms export ban. 武器輸出3原則とは, 要するに事実上の武器輸出禁止を意味する。

export business 輸出事業, 輸出企業, 輸出ビジネス

◆It will be impossible for Japan to advance the nuclear reactor export business if Japan moves toward no nuclear power. 日本が原発ゼロに向かえば, 原発輸出ビジネスの展開はできなくなる。

export competitiveness 輸出競争力

◆In global currency wars, central banks effectively lower the value of their countries' currencies to boost their countries' export competitiveness. 世界の通貨安競争では, 自国の輸出競争力を高めるため, 中央銀行が自国通貨の価値を事実上切り下げる [自国通貨の為替相場を事実上安くする]。

export cost 輸出コスト

◆As many domestic manufacturers have moved their production sites from Japan to Asian nations and elsewhere, the Japanese economy benefits less and less from the weak yen which lowers export costs. 国内製造業の多くが生産拠点を日本からアジアなどに移しているため, 日本経済は, 輸出コストが下がる円安メリットを享受しにくくなっている。

export credit 輸出金融 (export financing), 輸出信用, 輸出信用状 (export letter of credit)

export credit agency 輸出信用機関

export credit financing 輸出信用ファイナンス

export credit guarantee 輸出信用保証

export credit insurance 輸出信用保険

Export Credits Guarantee Department 英輸出信用保証庁

offer export credit facility　輸出信用を供与する

use export credit　輸出信用を利用する

◆Gross foreign assets held by Japanese in the form of direct investment, securities investment, financial derivatives, loans and export credits, deposits, other investments and official foreign reserves came to ¥379.78 trillion. 直接投資、証券投資、金融派生商品、貸付け金や輸出信用、預金その他の投資と政府の外貨準備高の形で日本の政府や企業、個人が保有する海外資産の総額（対外資産残高）は、379兆7,800億円に達した。

export-dependent economy　輸出依存国
◆A slump in global demand weighs on Asian region's powerhouses China and India and on its export-dependent economies. 世界的な需要の低迷が、アジア地域の牽引役である中国とインドや輸出依存国の足を引っ張っている。

export drive　輸出ドライブ, 輸出攻勢, 輸出拡大圧力, 輸出競争力
◆China has been viewed as a nation whose export drive derives from its inexpensive products. これまで中国は、安値の製品で輸出攻勢をかける国と見られてきた。

export-driven　(形)輸出主導の, 輸出主導型の　(=export-led)

export-driven economic recovery　輸出主導の景気回復

export-driven growth　輸出主導の成長, 輸出主導型［先行型］成長, 輸出リード型成長
◆A recovery will be export-driven, dependent on U.S. growth and the yen's depreciation, instead of being led by increased domestic consumption and capital investment. 今後の景気回復は、アメリカ経済の好転や円安を背景にした輸出主導型の回復で、国内の個人消費や設備投資の伸びがその牽引役となるわけではない。◆The company needs to enhance its development strength for such products as hybrid cars to maintain the competitiveness of its vehicles and auto parts domestically manufactured, in addition to improving export-driven profits. 同社の場合、輸出主導の収益改善にとどまらず、国内生産の車両や自動車部品の競争力を維持するには、ハイブリッド車などの製品の開発力を強化する必要がある。

export-driven economic upturn　輸出主導の景気回復
◆A depreciation of the dollar may stimulate external demand and ignite an export-driven economic upturn. ドル安は、外需を喚起して、輸出主導の景気回復につながる可能性がある。

export-driven profits　輸出主導の収益
◆The company needs to enhance its development strength for such products as hybrid cars to maintain the competitiveness of its vehicles and auto parts domestically manufactured, in addition to improving export-driven profits. 同社の場合、輸出主導の収益改善にとどまらず、国内生産

の車両や自動車部品の競争力を維持するには、ハイブリッド車などの製品の開発力を強化する必要がある。

export firm　輸出企業
◆Exporting firms are working all out to secure profits under the current economic turmoil. 現在の経済混乱の状況下で、輸出企業各社は収益の確保に躍起となっている。

export growth　輸出の伸び
◆Export growth has slowed due to the high value of the yen and the weakness of economies overseas. 円高と海外経済の減速で、輸出の伸びが鈍った。

export industry　輸出産業
◆A weak yen benefits the export industries such as automobiles and home appliances, but excessive depreciation of the yen could have the negative effect on the Japanese economy. 円安は自動車や家電など輸出産業には追い風だが、過度の円安は日本経済に悪影響を及ぼす可能性もある。◆At present, export industries including home appliances and automobiles are raising their expectations for improved corporate performance under the weak yen, which has also driven up stock prices. 現在、家電や自動車などの輸出産業は、円安で業績改善の期待を高めており、円安はまた株価も押し上げた。

export item　輸出品目, 輸出品, 輸出製品
◆While Japan's mainstay export item to the U.S. market is vehicles, the shipments to China are mainly electronic parts for assembly. 日本の米市場向け輸出の主力製品は自動車なのに対して、中国向け輸出製品は組立用電子部品が中心だ。

export market　輸出市場
◆Japan's economic growth is driven by exports, but it will have to vie for export markets with emerging economies. 日本の経済成長の原動力は輸出だが、今後は新興国と輸出市場の争奪戦になろう。

export-oriented company　輸出企業
◆Benefiting from the yen's depreciation which resulted from Abenomics, the Abe administration's economic policies, the earnings environment for export-oriented companies has greatly improved. 安倍政権の経済政策「アベノミクス」による円安効果で、輸出企業の収益環境が大幅に改善した。

export-oriented industrialization　輸出志向型工業化
◆An important role of the NIEs is to act as a nucleus or center in the promotion of export-oriented industrialization in the Asian-Pacific region. 新興工業経済地域（NIEs）のひとつの重要な役割は、アジア太平洋地域における輸出志向型工業化の中核あるいはセンターとして機能することにある。

export-oriented industry　輸出企業
◆The recent yen's appreciation is not so painful

as to deal a heavy blow to export-oriented industries. 最近の円高は、輸出企業に大きな打撃を与えるほどの痛手［大きな打撃を与える水準］ではない。

export-oriented manufacturer 輸出企業
◆The strengthening of the yen would force Japanese export-oriented manufacturers to globalize themselves further. 円高で、日本の輸出企業はさらなるグローバル化を強いられることになろう。

export permit 輸出許可, 輸出許可書
apply for an export permit 輸出許可を申請する
issue an export permit 輸出許可を発給する

export profitability 輸出の採算性, 輸出の採算
◆There was a time when the more we exported, the more money we lost, by eroding export profitability due to the excessive rise in the value of the yen. 超円高による輸出の採算悪化で、輸出すればするほど赤字になる時もあった。

export-related businesses 輸出関連企業, 輸出関連業界
◆The rapid surge in the yen's value could deal a blow to Japan's export drive and export-related businesses. 急激な円高は、日本の輸出競争力の低下や輸出関連企業の業績悪化をもたらす［日本の輸出競争力と輸出関連企業に打撃を与える］可能性がある。

export restriction 輸出規制, 輸出制限（=export restraint）
◆China lost an appeal at the WTO in a case about its export restrictions on raw materials including bauxite, magnesium and zinc. 中国によるボーキサイトやマグネシウム、亜鉛などの鉱物資源［原材料］輸出規制に関する問題で、中国は世界貿易機関（WTO）で敗訴した。◆The United States, the EU and Mexico challenged China's export restrictions on raw materials and launched WTO legal cases in 2009. 米国、欧州連合（EU）とメキシコが中国の原材料（鉱物資源）輸出規制は世界貿易機関（WTO）の協定違反に当たるとして、2009年にWTOに提訴した。

export terms 輸出条件, 輸出取引条件
◆We should be glad to have particulars of your export terms as we take keen interest in your products. 貴社製品がとても気に入ったので、貴社の輸出取引条件の詳細をお知らせいただければありがたい。

export trade 輸出業, 輸出貿易, 輸出貿易業, 輸出取引
Export Trade Act 輸出貿易法, 輸出取引法
export trade bill 輸出貿易手形
export trade control 輸出管理
export trade control laws 輸出管理法令

exporter （名）輸出業者, 輸出企業, 輸出産業, 輸出国
an exporter of oil 原油輸出国

incentives for exporters 輸出振興策
Japanese exporters 日本の輸出企業, 日本の輸出産業
◆A recent plunge in the yen due to the economic and monetary policies of Prime Minister Shinzo Abe is a boon for domestic exporters. 安倍晋三首相の経済・金融政策による最近の円安は、国内の輸出企業にとっては追い風［恩恵］だ。◆In the agricultural negotiations at the World Trade Organization, Japan has been under strong pressure from rice exporters to lower import tariffs on rice and to expand access for foreign rice. 世界貿易機関（WTO）の農業交渉で日本は、コメ輸出国から、コメの輸入関税率引下げや外国産米の輸入枠拡大への強い圧力を受けている。◆New trade partnerships with Europe and the Asia-Pacific will help exporters create more jobs. 欧州やアジア太平洋地域との新自由貿易協定は、輸出企業の雇用創出拡大につながる。◆Since the launch of the second Abe administration in late 2012, business performances of major companies, especially exporters, have picked up, and employment conditions also have improved. 2012年末に第二次安倍政権が発足してから、大企業、とくに輸出企業の業績は好転し、雇用情勢も改善した。◆The competitive edge of Japanese exporters vying with U.S. firms is affected by the yen-dollar rate and the price levels in the two countries. 米企業と競合している日本の輸出企業の競争力は、円・ドルレートや日本と米国の物価水準の影響をも受ける。◆The economic slowdown in Europe due to the sovereign debt crisis and slackening growth of China as a major exporter to Europe have dealt a painful blow to Japan's exports and production. 債務危機に伴う欧州経済の減速と、欧州向け輸出の多い中国の成長鈍化が、日本の輸出と生産に耐え難いほどの打撃を与えている。◆The weaker yen helps exporters, but close attention must be paid to the fact that the excessive depreciation of the yen will further increase the prices of imports of LNG and other foreign products. 円安は輸出企業にはプラスだが、円安が行き過ぎると、天然液化ガス（LNG）など海外製品の輸入額が一段と増えることにも、警戒が必要である。

exporting company 輸出企業
◆The business performance of Japanese exporting companies is deteriorating fast due to the simultaneous slowdown of the global economy. 世界同時不況で、日本の輸出企業の業績は急速に悪化している。

exporting firm 輸出企業
◆Japanese exporting firms have been enjoying positive earnings, benefiting from thriving markets in the United States and the weak yen. 日本の輸出企業は、米国の好調な市場と円安を追い風に、好業績が続いている。

exports of Japanese pop culture 日本独自の文化産業の輸出
◆The cornerstone of the Cool Japan initiative

aimed at promoting the exports of Japanese pop culture is the content industry which produces anime, video games and movies. 日本独自の文化産業の輸出促進を目指すクール・ジャパン構想の核は、アニメやビデオ・ゲーム、映画などの製作にかかわるコンテンツ産業だ。

exports to the United States 対米輸出
◆The economy of Japan depends a great deal on exports to the United States. 日本経済の対米輸出への依存度は、極めて高い。

expose (動)(危険に)さらす、むき出しにする、暴露する、正体をあばく、浮き彫りにする、公然と売り出す、陳列する、展示する、摘発する、すっぱ抜く、経験[体験]させる、触れさせる、直面させる、(作用や影響を)受けさせる、世[世の中]の物笑いにする、世の中の非難の的にする、(子どもなどを)捨てる、遺棄する、露出する、感光させる
  be exposed to credit risk 信用リスクを負う、与信リスクを負う、信用リスクにさらされる
  be exposed to interest rate risk 金利リスクにさらされる
  be exposed to losses 損失を被る
  be exposed to new influences 新しい影響を受ける
  expose goods for sale in a sore 店頭に販売商品を陳列する、店頭に販売品を展示する
◆Domestic manufacturers have been exposed to the adverse winds of economic slowdowns overseas, a strongly appreciating yen and ever-intensifying competition with foreign rivals. 国内製造業各社は、海外経済の減速や超円高、海外勢との競争激化などの逆風にさらされている。◆The FSA inspections exposed the bank's illegal activities. 金融庁の検査で、同行の違法行為が暴かれた。

exposition (名)(詳細な)説明、解説、論評、解説的論文、提示、開陳、展示、陳列、展覧会、博覧会、遺棄、捨てること
  brief exposition 簡単な説明
  world exposition 万国博覧会

exposure (名)危険などにさらされること、影響されること、損失の危機に瀕していること、暴露、摘発、発覚、露顕、露出、(商品の)陳列、(テレビや新聞に)取り上げられること、リスク、危険度、投資、融資、リスク資産総額、融資総額、与信残高、債権、債権額、エクスポージャー
  credit exposure 与信リスク、信用リスク
  economic exposure 経済リスク
  Exposure Draft 米財務会計基準審議会 (FASB)などの討議資料、公開草案、ED
  exposure to highly leveraged transactions 負債比率の高い取引(HLT)への融資、HLT融資
  exposure to property developers 不動産開発

業者向け融資
  external exposure 対外債権残高
  financial exposure 資金負担、金融リスク
  have a large exposure to ～の運用比率が高い、～リスクが高い
  investment exposure 投資リスク、投資
  real estate exposure 不動産投資、不動産融資
  reduce exposure to the risk of loss 損失リスクを減らす、損失リスクを軽減する
  risk exposure リスク、リスク・エクスポージャー

exposure to credit risk 信用リスク
◆The firm controls its exposure to credit risk through credit approvals, credit limits and monitoring procedures. 同社は、信用供与承認や信用限度、監視手続きを通じて信用リスクを管理している。

exposure to variable rate debt 変動金利負債に係わるリスク
◆The Company has entered into several transactions which reduce financing costs and exposure to variable rate debt. 最近実施した数件の取引で、当社の資金調達コストと変動円負債に係わるリスクは軽減されています。

express (形)明示の、明示的、明確な、直接の、実際の
  express, implied or statutory 明示、黙示もしくは法律上の、明示の、黙示の、または法律上当然に認められた
  express or implied 明示または黙示の、明示的なものであれ黙示的なものであれ
  express or implied warranty 明示または黙示の保証、明示・黙示の保証

express warranty 明示的保証、明示の保証、明示的担保
◆ABC agrees to XYZ's disclaimer of all warranties except for the express warranty set forth in Article III of this agreement. ABCは、本契約の第3条に定める明示の保証を除いて、すべての保証をXYZが否認することに同意する。

express written consent of the other party 相手方の書面による明白な同意、相手方の明示の書面による同意
◆Each party shall not make any disclosure of the confidential information to anyone without the express written consent of the other party, except to employees, affiliate (s) or consultant (s) to whom disclosure is necessary for the performance of this agreement. 各当事者は、本契約履行のために開示が必要な従業員、関連会社またはコンサルタントに対して開示する場合を除いて、相手方の明示の書面による同意を得ないで誰に対しても秘密情報を開示しないものとする。

expressions (名)表現、表示
◆In this Agreement, the following words and expressions shall, unless the context otherwise re-

quires, have the following meanings. 本契約で、次の語句と表現は、文脈上、別段の意味を必要としないかぎり、次の意味を持つものとする。

expressly （副）とくに、明確に、明白に、明示的に
expressly consent　明示的に同意する、明示的に合意する
expressly or impliedly　明示ないし黙示に
◆Except as otherwise expressly provided for in this agreement, ABC shall not be entitled to set off or withhold any amount owing to ABC under this agreement, against any payment to XYZ for the performance by XYZ of this agreement.　本契約に別に明文の規定がないかぎり、ABCには、本契約に基づきABCに支払われる金額を、XYZによる本契約の履行に対するXYZへの支払い金と相殺する権利はなく、またその支払いを保留する権利もないものとする。◆The seller expressly disclaims any warranty of conditions, fitness for use or merchantability. 売り主は、状態、用途適合性または商品性の保証を明確に否認する。

extend （動）与える、供与する、提供する、行う、延長する、更新する、述べる
◆Shipments may be made on such credit terms as Supplier elects to extend to Distributor at the time an order is accepted. 出荷は、注文を引き受けたときに供給者が販売店に供与することにした与信条件で行うことができる。◆Supplier agrees to extend to Distributor the lowest price on Products given to any distributor or purchaser for resale, notwithstanding the provisions of this agreement or the agreement of the parties. 本契約の規定または当事者の合意にもかかわらず、供給者は、再販売のために販売業者や買い主に提供している本製品の最低価格を、販売店にも提供することに同意する。

extended coverage　拡張担保、拡張危険担保、担保範囲の拡張
◆During the period when Products are in the custody of ABC, ABC shall keep Products insured at ABC's account for the benefit of XYZ against loss or damage by fire, theft or otherwise with extended coverage. 本製品［契約品］をABCが保管している期間中、火災、盗難、その他による滅失や損害を拡張担保するため、ABCはその勘定で、XYZを保険受取人として本製品に付保するものとする。

extension agreement　延長契約
extension or renewal of this agreement　本契約の延長または更新
◆It is agreed that not less than three months prior to the normal expiration date hereof, the parties shall discuss an extension or renewal of this agreement. 通常の本契約終了日の3カ月前までに、両当事者は本契約の延長または更新について協議することで合意している。

extent （名）程度、範囲、限度、限界、差し押さえ令状
◆The Landlord shall effect insurance by itself or

have other tenants effect insurance against such accidents as aforementioned and indemnify the Tenant within the extent covered by the insurance. 「貸主」は、前記の事故などに対して自ら保険を付けるか他のテナントに保険を付けさせ、その保険でカバーされる範囲内で「借主」に損害の補償をするものとする。

external （形）外部の、対外的な、国外の
external assets　対外資産、対外資産残高（日本の政府や企業、個人が海外に持っている資産）
external borrowing　対外借入れ
external deficit　国際収支の赤字、対外債務
external equilibrium　対外均衡
external financing　外部調達資金、外部資金の調達、外部金融（=external funding）
external funds　外部資金、外部調達資金（銀行などからの借入れ、株式や社債、手形債務などにより外部から調達する資金）
external position　対外収支
external pressure　外圧
external surplus　国際収支の黒字、貿易収支の黒字、経常海外余剰
external trade　対外貿易、貿易収支
external transaction　外部取引

external balance of payments　対外収支
◆Due to the turmoil that followed the regime change, Egypt's external balance of payments deteriorated and foreign reserves dropped sharply. 政変による混乱で、エジプトの対外収支が悪化し、外貨準備は激減した。

external bond financing　外債発行による資金調達
◆Japanese companies can hedge exchange risks and improve their business image abroad through external bond financing. 日本企業は、外債発行による資金調達で、為替リスクを回避するとともに海外での企業イメージアップを図ることができる。

external debt　対外債務
◆According to Moody's Investors Service, Egypt is likely to default on about 10 percent of its outstanding external debt in 2014 and fail to honor as much as 40 percent within five years. ムーディーズによると、エジプトでは2014年には対外債務残高の約10%が不履行となり、5年以内に債務の40%が不履行になる見込みだ。

external demand　外需、純輸出、海外需要
◆A depreciation of the dollar may stimulate external demand and ignite an export-driven economic upturn. ドル安は、外需を喚起して、輸出主導の景気回復につながる可能性がある。

F

facilitate （動）助長する、促進する、進める、

円滑に進める, 容易にする, 後押しする, 楽にする, ～の手助けをする, ～を手伝う

◆The headings to the Articles of this agreement are to facilitate reference only, do not form a part of this agreement and shall not in any way affect the interpretation of this agreement. 本契約条項の見出しは, 参照の便宜だけの目的のもので, 本契約の一部を構成するものではなく, いかなる場合でも本契約の解釈に影響を与えないものとする。

facilitate the financing of small and midsize companies 中小企業の資金調達を容易にする

◆This legal amendment is designed to facilitate the financing of small and midsize companies through the injection of public funds into financial institutions. この法改正の狙いは, 金融機関への公的資金注入により中小企業の資金調達を容易にすることにある。

facilitate trades 取引を容易にする, 売買をしやすくする

◆The firm will split each share held by investors who are stockholders on September 30, 2013 into two shares, aiming to increase investors and facilitate trades through the firm's stock split. 同社は, 2013年9月30日時点の株主の投資家が保有する株式1株を2株に分割するが, これは株式分割を通じて投資家を増やすと同時に売買を成立しやすくするのが狙いだ。

fact (名)事実, 真実, 現実, 犯行

cause-in fact 物理的因果関係

proximate fact 法律的因果関係

factor (名)要素, 要因, 原因, 因子, 遺伝子, 遺伝因子, 材料, 原動力, 金融業者, 金融会社, 金融機関, ファクタリング業者, 債権買取り業者, 代理店, 問屋, 土地管理人, ～率, 係数, 指数, ファクター

a factor causing disarray in the foreign exchange markets 為替混乱の原因

a risk factor リスク要因

a stabilizing factor 安定要因

an inflationary factor インフレ要因

buying factor 買い材料

critical factor 決定的な要素, 決定的な役割

demographic factors 人口動態

major factor 主な要因, 大きな要因, 主因, 最大の要因

market factor 市場要因, 市場因子, 市場要素

multiple factors 複数の要因

negative factor マイナス要因, 悪材料, 売り材料 (=unfavorable factor)

one-off factor 一時的要因

political-economic factors 政治経済要因, 政治経済的要因

positive factor プラス要因, 好材料, 買い材料 (=favorable factor)

risk factor 危険因子, リスク要因

seasonal factor 季節要因

special factor 特殊要因

technical factors テクニカル要因, 市場内部要因

temporary factor 一時的要因

various factors 各種要因 (⇒export and import trends)

◆Changes in exchange rates are a result of multiple factors, including the balance of international payments and market supply and demand. 為替相場の変動は, 国際収支や市場の需給など複数要因によるものだ。◆Foreign investors, including Japanese firms, regard Thailand's political climate with its repeated coups as a risk factor for investing in the country. 日本企業など外国資本は, クーデターが繰り返されるタイの政治風土を, 対タイ投資のリスク要因と見なしている。◆Other competitive factors in the market for the products are service, delivery, technological capability, and product quality and performance. 市場での製品の競争要因としては, サービスや納入, 技術活用能力［技術力］, 品質, 性能なども挙げられる。◆The Bank of Japan pointed to risk factors, including unstable global financial markets and the economic slowdown in the United States, Japan's main export market. 日本銀行は, 世界の不安定な金融市場や日本の主要輸出市場である米国の景気減速などのリスク要因も指摘した。◆The effects of the recent depreciation of the dollar have not been seen yet, but if the U.S. currency depreciates further, it may lead to an increase in imported commodity prices, which in turn may become an inflationary factor. 最近のドル安の影響はまだ見られないが, 米ドルがさらに下落すれば, 輸入品価格の上昇を招き, これがまた逆にインフレ要因になる恐れがある。◆The yen's stable rate at about ¥110 against the dollar serves as a stabilizing factor for importers, exporters and others doing business susceptible to exchange fluctuations. 円の対ドル為替相場が110円台（前後）で安定していることは, 輸出入業者など為替変動に左右されやすい仕事をしている者にとって安定要因となる。

factoring (名)売掛債権の買取り, 売掛債権売却, (売掛債権の)債権買取業, 取立て代理業, ファクタリング

debt factoring 債権買取り

factoring charge ファクタリング手数料

factoring company 債権買取会社, ファクタリング会社

factoring facility ファクタリング・ファシリティ

factoring program 手形割引

factorization (名)債権差し押さえ通告

factory (名)工場, 生産設備, 製造業, メーカー, 在外［海外］代理店

assembly factory 組立工場

factory capacity　工場の生産能力, 生産設備能力

factory closing　工場閉鎖　(=factory closure)

factory demand　製造業新規受注高

factory inventories　製造業在庫

factory management　工場管理

factory operation　工場の操業

factory output　製造業生産高, 製造業の生産

factory shipment　工場出荷

machine factory　機械工場

pilot factory　実験工場

subcontracting factory　下請工場

◆No significant improvement in air pollution in China has been seen as many factories have ignored government regulations, putting short-term profits ahead of environmental issues. 多くの工場が環境問題よりも目先の利益を優先し、政府の規制を無視してきたので、中国の大気汚染の大きな改善は見られない。◆People on the factory floor study computer-aided design, robotics and customized manufacturing. 工場の従業員は、コンピュータ支援設計、ロボット工学や特注化製造について研究をしている。◆Several factories were shut down during a major strike by employees. 社員による大規模ストライキで、工場が数か所、閉鎖された。◆The attack on a Panasonic Corp. factory which has played a pioneering role in expanding its operations in China by a violent mob of anti-Japan demonstrators symbolizes the current bleak state of Japan-China relations. 中国進出で先駆的役割を果たしてきたパナソニックの工場が、反日デモ隊の暴徒に襲われた事件は、日中関係の寒々しい現状を象徴している。

factory operations　工場の操業
◆Some Japanese-affiliated companies and Japanese restaurants have been forced to suspend their factory operations or close their outlets due to the acts of destruction by Chinese demonstrators. 一部の日系企業や日本料理店は、中国のデモ隊による破壊行為で、工場の操業停止や店舗の休業に追い込まれている。

facultative acceptance　任意受再
◆Any amounts exceeding the limits of automatic cover shall be offered to the Reinsurer for facultative acceptance. 自動再保険の適用限度を超える額は、任意受再のために再保険会社に申し出るものとする。

fail to　～できない, ～しない, ～することを怠る

fail to fulfill any of one's material obligations hereunder　本契約上の重大な義務の履行を怠る, 本契約に基づく重大な義務の履行を怠る

fail to pay　～の支払いを怠る, ～を支払わない

◆If the buyer fails to pay any amount under this agreement when due, the buyer shall be liable to pay to the seller overdue interest on such unpaid amount from the due date until the actual payment date at the rate of 15% per annum. 買い主が支払い期日に本契約に基づく代金の支払いを怠った場合、買い主は、支払い期日から実際の払込み日までの当該未払い金額に対する年率15%の遅延金利を、売り主に支払わなければならない。◆The Seller may withhold delivery or cancel the Agreement if the Buyer fails to establish the letter of credit by the date stipulated in this Agreement. 買い主が本契約で定める期限までに信用状を開設することができない場合、売り主は、引渡しを保留するか契約を解除することができる。

failure　(名)倒産, 破産, 債務の不履行, 不履行, 欠落, 不成就, 不成立

failure to establish L/C　信用状の開設遅延, 信用状発行遅延

failure to perform　不履行

failure to perform part or whole of this agreement　本契約の一部または全部の不履行

◆If the borrower shall fail to pay any debt for borrowed money or other similar obligation of the borrower, or interest thereon, when due, and such failure continues after the applicable grace period specified in the agreement relating to such indebtedness, the lender may in its discretion declare the entire unpaid principal amount of the loan, accrued interest thereon and all other sums payable under this agreement to be immediately due and payable. 借主が借主の借入債務(借入金に対する債務)や他の同様の債務またはその利息を支払い期日に支払うことを怠り、このような不履行が本契約に定める当該債務に関する適用猶予期間後も継続する場合、貸主はその裁量で、借入金の未返還元本全額、その発生利息と本契約に基づいて支払わなければならない他の未払い金の全額即時支払い[即時返済]を宣言することができる。

failure or breach　不履行または違反
◆The failure or breach shall be corrected within said 10 days period. この不履行または違反は、その10日の期間内に是正しなければならない。

fair　(名)見本市, 展示会, 博覧会, 定期市, 慈善市, 市, バザー, 共進会, 品評会, フェア

floating fair　巡航見本市

international trade fair　国際見本市

job fair　会社説明会　(=career fair)

parts and materials fair　部品素材見本市

state fair　州共進会, 州農産物共進会

summer fair　夏の市

trade fair　見本市

world's fair　万国博覧会, 国際見本市

◆About ten major Japanese automakers are scheduled to take part in an industrial parts and materials exhibition and procurement negotiation fair in Seoul. 韓国・ソウルで開かれる工業部品・素材展示調達商談会には、日本の自動車メーカー約10社が参加する予定だ。

fair （形）公正な, 公平な, 平等な, 差別をしない, 妥当な, 適正な, 正しい, 美しい, 魅力的な, 汚れのない, フェア
assume one's fair share of responsibility for ～に応分の責任を負う［取る］
fair average quality 標準品, FAQ
Fair Credit Reporting Act 公正信用報告法, 公正消費者信用報告法
Fair Employment Practices Committee 米公正雇用慣行委員会, FEPC
fair market value 公正市場価格, 適正市場価格, 公正市場価値, 公正市価, 時価
fair play 公正な取扱い, 公明正大な処置, 平等な行動, フェア・プレー
fair presentation 適正表示, 公正表示
fair price 適正価格
fair trial 公正な裁判
fair use 公正使用
Rules of Fair Practice 公正慣習規則, 公正慣行ルール（全米証券業協会の業界規則）

fair competition 公正競争, 公正な競争
◆In Egypt, military-related business groups receive preferential treatment, so fair competition has been impeded. エジプトでは、軍関連の企業グループが優遇されるので、公正な競争が妨げられてきた。◆NTT's monopolization of subscribers' lines connecting NTT telephone stations and households has impeded fair competition among telecommunications companies. NTTの電話局と各戸を結ぶ加入者回線のNTTによる独占が、通信事業者間の公正な競争を阻害している。

fair competition law 公正競争法, 不正競争防止法

fair international commercial trade 公正な国際商取引
◆To ensure fair international commercial trade, the law against unfair competition stipulates that both individuals involved in bribery and the corporations they belong to should be punished. 公正な国際商取引を確保するため、不正競争防止法には、贈賄（外国公務員への贈賄）に関与した個人と法人を罰する規定（両罰規定）がある。

Fair Labor Standards Act （米国の）公正労働基準法, FLSA
◆All goods were produced in compliance with the applicable requirements of the Fair Labor Standards Act. 商品は、すべて米国の公正労働基準法の適用要件に従って生産された。

fair trade 公正取引, 適正取引, 公正な貿易, 互恵貿易, フェアトレード［フェア・トレード］（途上国の生産者の暮らしを考えて、農産物などを適正な価格で購入する仕組みのことも、「フェアトレード」と言う）

a fair-trade organization フェアトレード認証機関
a fair-trade premium フェアトレード・プレミアム（途上国の生産者の生活向上のために支出される上乗せ金）
a fair-trade product フェアトレード商品［製品］
fair-trade certification フェアトレード認証
fair trade items 公正取引商品
fair-trade mark フェアトレード認証マーク
fair trade price 公正取引価格, 適正取引価格
the fair trade movement フェアトレード運動

Fair Trade Commission 日本の公正取引委員会, FTC
◆The Fair Trade Commission approved a local Web-search partnership between Yahoo-Japan Corp. and Google inc. 公正取引委員会は、ヤフーとグーグルのインターネット検索の国内提携を承認した。◆The Fair Trade Commission probed about a dozen industrial gas providers over price cartel suspicions. 公正取引委員会は、価格カルテルの疑いで産業用ガス・メーカー十数社を立ち入り検査した。

Fair Trade Commission of Japan 公正取引委員会 （⇒corporate merger, FTC）
◆A corporate merger plan is subject to legal screening by the Fair Trade Commission of Japan. 企業の合併計画は、公正取引委員会の法定審査を受けなければならない。

fair trade law 公正取引法
◆The FTC's warnings to the three major beer wholesalers are a kind of administrative guidance if violations of fair trade laws are suspected. この大手ビール卸売り3社に対する公正取引委員会（FTC）の警告は、公正取引法違反の疑いがある場合に出される行政指導に当たる。

fair use 公正な利用, フェア・ユース
the introduction of U.S.-type provisions on fair use 米国型フェア・ユース規定の導入
the U.S. fair use system of copyrighted materials 著作権のある著作物についての米国のフェア・ユース制度
◆Copyrighted materials can be used freely under the U.S. law as long as it is considered "fair use." 著作権のある著作物は、「公正な利用」であれば、米国の法律では自由に利用することができる。

fair use system フェア・ユース制度
◆The U.S. fair use system of copyrighted materials is disadvantageous to their copyright holders. 著作権のある著作物についての米国のフェア・ユース制度は、著作権所有者には不利な制度である。

fall behind ～に［～より、～］遅れる, ～に後れを取る, ～から落伍（らくご）する, ～に先行される, ～を滞納する （=get behind, lag behind）
fall behind in global competitiveness 国際競争に遅れる, 国際競争から落伍する

fall behind in parts shipments 部品の出荷が予定より遅れる, 部品の出荷が予定に追いつかない

fall behind in tax payments 納税が遅れる, 税金を滞納する, 税金が支払えない

fall behind in the development of ～の開発で後れを取る

fall behind with one's payments 支払いが遅れる, 決済が遅れる
◆In the markets of flat-screen televisions, mobile phones and others, Japanese electrical appliance makers have fallen behind their South Korean rivals. 薄型テレビや携帯電話などの市場で, 日本の電機業界は, 韓国などのライバル企業に出遅れた。

fall behind one's rivals ライバルに後れを取る, ライバル企業に後れを取る
◆In the development of smartphones and cutting-edge displays, domestic electronics companies have fallen behind their U.S. and South Korean rivals. スマートフォン（高機能携帯電話）や最先端ディスプレーの開発で, 国内家電各社は米国や韓国のライバル企業に後れを取っている。

fall behind schedule 予定より遅れる
◆The big U.S. semiconductor maker Qualcomm put Japanese firms on low priority when it fell behind schedule in parts shipments this summer. 米半導体大手のクアルコムは今夏, 部品の出荷が予定より遅れた際, 日本企業への出荷を後回しにした［日本企業への出荷の優先順位を低くした］。

fall below ～を割り込む, ～を割る, ～を下回る
◆Concerns over the safety of Chinese food products are rising in Japan, but the percentage of safety violations involving food imports from China fell below the overall average for all imported foods in fiscal 2012. 日本では中国産食品の安全性への懸念が強まっているが, 中国からの輸入食品のうち安全面での違反件数の割合は, 2012年度は輸入食品全体の総平均を下回った。◆In the crude oil contract market of the New York Mercantile Exchange（NYMEX）, the price of January WTI, the benchmark U.S. crude oil, fell below $60 a barrel for the first time since June 2009 on December 11, 2014 due to the forecast of rising global oil production. 2014年12月11日のニューヨーク・マーカンタイル取引所の原油先物取引では, 指標となる米国産原油WTI（テキサス産軽質油）の1月渡し価格が, 世界的な石油増産見通しから, 2009年7月以来5年5か月ぶりに1バレル＝60ドルを割り込んだ。

fall in import prices 輸入価格の下落
◆The fall in import prices that accompanies a strong yen could further prolong Japan's deflation. 円高に伴う輸入価格の下落で, 日本のデフレがさらに長期化する可能性がある。

false reporting 虚偽申告
◆The false reporting by Barclays is a clear betrayal of investors' trust. 英金融大手バークレイ

ズの虚偽申告は, 明らかに投資家の信頼を裏切る行為だ。

false submission 虚偽申告
◆Barclays, one of Britain's top banking groups, has paid a huge fine over its false Libor submission. 英大手銀行・金融グループのバークレイズは, ライボー（ロンドン銀行間取引金利）の虚偽申告で, 巨額の罰金を支払った。

fast-growing emerging markets 急成長の新興国市場
◆Fast-growing emerging markets are becoming a key battlefield for automakers around the world. 急成長の新興国市場が, 世界の自動車各社が狙う主戦場になっている。

FATCA （米国の）外国口座税務コンプライアンス法
（⇒Foreign Account Tax Compliance Act）

fault （名）過失, 過誤, 過失・過誤の責任, 欠陥, 瑕疵（かし）, 不完全
◆The licensee's obligation under this Article with respect to the confidential information shall not apply to information which is part of the public domain at the time of disclosure by the licensor, or thereafter becomes part of the public domain without fault on the part of the licensee. 本条に基づく秘密情報に関するライセンシーの義務は, ライセンサーによる開示の時点で公知であるか, その後ライセンシー側の過失なしに公知となる情報には適用されないものとする。

fault or negligence 過失, 帰責事由や過失
（帰責事由＝法的に責任を負わせる理由）
◆Neither party shall be in default hereunder by reason of any failure or delay in the performance of any obligation under this agreement where such failure or delay arises without the fault or negligence of such party. 本契約に基づく義務の不履行または遅滞が当事者の過失がないのに発生した場合, いずれの当事者も, 義務の不履行または遅滞を理由として本契約上の債務不履行があったものと見なさないものとする。

favor［favour］ （動）～を好む, ～に好意を示す, ～を歓迎する, ～に賛成する, ～を支持する, ～をえこひいきする, ～に有利になる, ～に味方する, ～を助ける, ～を促進する, ～を大事に扱う, ～をいたわる, ～に似る

be favored with ～に恵まれる

favor A over B BよりAを優先する, AをBより高く評価する

favor A with B AにBをしてあげる, AにBを与える

favored customer 得意客

favored treatment 優遇措置

most-favored nation treatment 最恵国待遇
◆Please favor us with an immediate reply［answer］. 至急ご返答願います。◆The new tariff on beef imports favors producers rather than consumers. 牛肉の輸入に対する新関税は, 消費者ではなく生産者寄りの対応だ。◆We ask you to

kindly favor us with a large allowance. 大幅［多額の］値引きを、お願いします。

favor［favour］（名）好意, 引き立て, 利益, 便宜供与, 支持

dollar's favor　ドル高

establish an L/C in our favor　当社を受益者として信用状を開設する

in favor of　～宛ての, ～を受取人として, ～を（信用状の）受益者として　（＝in one's favor）

in our favor　当社宛てに, 当社を受益者として

◆Our terms of payment are to value at 30 d/s under an irrevocable letter of credit to be opened in our favor for the corresponding value of an order. 当社の決済条件は、注文相当額につき、当社を受益者として開設された取消不能信用状に基づいて一覧後30日払いの手形を振り出すことです。◆The APEC's special statement came out in favor of the promotion of free trade. アジア太平洋経済協力会議（APEC）の特別声明は、自由貿易推進を打ち出した。◆We have issued an irrevocable letter of credit in your favor. 貴社を受益者として、取消不能信用状を発行しました。

favorable［favourable］（形）有利な, 有望な, 好都合の, 好ましい, 良好な, 順調な, 好調な, 明るい, 追い風になる　（⇒unfavorable）

a favorable answer［reply］　色よい返事

a favorable comment　好評

a favorable opportunity　好機会

be favorable to　～に有利である

favorable balance of payments　国際収支の黒字

favorable balance of trade　貿易収支の黒字, 輸出超過

favorable economic and political environments　良好な政治・経済環境

favorable factor　好材料

favorable inflation outlook　明るいインフレ見通し

favorable winds　順風

on favorable terms　有利な条件で

receive a favorable view　好評を博する

times take a favorable turn　事情が好転する

favorable effect　プラス面, プラス効果, 好ましい影響

◆A stronger yen has the favorable effect of stemming rises in import prices. 円高には、輸入物価の高騰を抑えるプラス面もある。

favorable steel exports　好調な鉄鋼輸出, 鉄鋼輸出の好調

◆This increase in recurring profits is largely due to an expansion in domestic demand for steel sheets used to produce automobiles and favorable steel exports to the Chinese market. この経常利益の増加は、主に自動車生産用鋼板の内需拡大と中国向け鉄鋼輸出の好調によるものだ。

favorable treatment to foreign companies　外資優遇, 外資優遇策

◆China is reviewing its policy of giving favorable treatment to foreign companies. 中国は、外資優遇策を見直している。

FAZ　輸入促進地域（foreign access zoneの略）

FC & S　捕獲拿捕（だほ）不担保

FCA　運送人渡し（買い主が指定した輸出地の運送人の管理下に貨物を引き渡すまでが、売り主の負担となる）

FCL　フル・コンテナ・ロード（コンテナ単位でフルに積載された貨物。full container loadの略）

FCSRCC　捕獲・拿捕・騒擾（そうじょう）・内乱不担保（free from［of］capture, seizure, riots and civil commotionsの略）

feasibility study　実行可能性調査, 実現可能性調査, 実行可能性研究, 企業化調査, 企業化可能性調査, 準備調査, 採算性調査, フィージビリティ・スタディ

◆Wal-Mart, Sumitomo and Seiyu set up a working committee to conduct a feasibility study of Wal-Mart's entry into Japan. ウォルマート、住友、西友の3社は、作業委員会を設けて、ウォルマートの日本進出についてのフィージビリティ・スタディを進めている。

federal funds rate　フェデラル・ファンド（FF）金利

◆The federal funds rate is the interest that banks charge each other on overnight loans. フェデラル・ファンド（FF）金利は、米国の民間銀行が翌日決済で相互に資金を貸し借りするときに適用する金利のことをいう。

Federal Trade Commission　米連邦取引委員会, FTC　（⇒FTC）

◆The U.S. Federal Trade Commission exercises jurisdiction over matters including consumer protection issues in the United States. 米連邦取引委員会（FTC）は、米国消費者保護などの問題を管轄している。◆The U.S. Federal Trade Commission (FTC) concluded there was not enough evidence that a Sony-BMG merger would violate U.S. antitrust laws. 米連邦取引委員会（FTC）は、ソニーとBMG（独複合メディア大手ベルテルスマンの音楽事業部門）の統合が米国の独占禁止法に違反することを示す十分な証拠はない、との結論を下した。

fee（名）料金, 入会金, 入場料, 納付金, 会費, 手数料, 使用料, 報酬, 謝礼, 実施料, 対価, フィー, 所有権, 相続財産権　（⇒contingency fee）

absence fee　不在補償費, 派遣技術指導者などの日当

after fee　手数料込みで　（＝at full fees）

agency fee　代理店料

application fee　出願手数料

attorney's fee　弁護士料, 弁護士報酬, 弁護士費用, 顧問料　(=attorney fee)

audit fee　監査報酬

before fee　手数料差引き前で

brokerage fee　仲介手数料, 委託手数料

charge a fee　料金を徴収する

clearance fee　出港手数料, 出港料

commitment fee　契約手数料, 約定手数料, 約定料

consulting fee　顧問料

contingent fee system　成功報酬制

credit fee　信用状手数料

custodial fee　保管業務の手数料, 保管料

custody fee　保管料

custom fee　通関手数料

fees and commissions　手数料

fixed filing fee　定額登録料

flat fee　定額　(=fixed fee)

legal fee　弁護士費用, 弁護士報酬

license fee　実施料, 特許権使用料, ライセンス料

listing fee　上場手数料

management fee　運用報酬, 幹事手数料, 経営報酬

merchant fee　加盟店手数料

official fee　印紙料

paid-up license fee　一括払いのライセンス料

patent fee　特許料, 特許権使用料

pay a fee　料金を支払う

professional fee　専門家報酬

publication fee　公告料

quote a fee for　～の料金を見積もる

redemption fee　解約手数料

registration fee　登録料, 登記料

renewal fee　更新料, 更新手数料, 書換え手数料

retaining fee　弁護士依頼料, 弁護士報酬, 弁護士顧問料

scale fee　基準手数料

sealing fee　調印料

service fee　サービス手数料

transfer fee　振替料, 振替料金

trust fee　信託手数料

underwriting fee　引受手数料

◆All other costs, including counsel and witness fees, shall be borne by the party incurring them. 弁護士料や証人の費用などその他の費用は, すべて当該費用を発生させた当事者が負担するものとする。◆Fishermen catching tuna in the exclusive economic zone of foreign countries are required to pay fishing fees. マグロ漁船が他国の

200カイリ排他的経済水域 (EEZ) 内で操業する場合、マグロ漁船は入漁料を支払わなければならない。◆The amount of fees for the services shall be U.S. $ _____ per month. サービスの対価は、月額_____米ドルとする。

fertilizer　(名)化学肥料, 肥料, 肥沃[豊か]にする物・人, 受精媒介者
◆Commodity loans are used to import commodities such as industrial machinery, industrial raw materials, fertilizer, agricultural chemicals and machinery, and other various kinds of machinery, which are agreed upon beforehand between the Japanese and recipient governments. 商品借款は、日本政府と借入国政府が前もって合意した商品 (工業資本財[工業用機械]、工業用原材料、肥料・農薬、農機具、各種機械など) の輸入のために使用される。

file　(動)書類を提出する, 訴訟を提起する, 登録する
file a lawsuit against A with B　Aを相手どってBに提訴する, Aを相手どってBに訴訟を起こす
　(=file a suit against A with B)
file a petition in bankruptcy against　～に対する破産申請書を提出する, ～に対する破産申請をする, 第三者が破産申請書を提出する
file a request for asset protection　財産の保全処分を申し立てる, 財産保全申請をする
file a complaint with　～に提訴する, ～に告訴する, ～に告発する, ～に告訴状を提出する
file a complaint with prosecutors　検察に告発する
file a complaint with [make a complaint to] **the FTC**　公正取引委員会に苦情を申し立てる
file a complaint with the WTO over　～に対して世界貿易機関 (WTO) に提訴する
◆South Korea filed a complaint with the World Trade Organization over Japan's restrictions on imports of laver or nori seaweed. 韓国が、日本の食用のり輸入制限に対して世界貿易機関 (WTO) に提訴した。
file a declaration of bankruptcy and a request for asset protection with　～に破産宣告と財産保全の処分を申請する, ～に破産宣告と財産保全の処分を申し立てる
◆The financial authorities filed a declaration of bankruptcy and a request for asset protection with the Tokyo District Court for the brokerage firm. 金融当局は、同証券会社の破産宣告と財産保全処分を東京地裁に申し立てた。
file a lawsuit against　～を相手どって提訴する, ～を提訴する, 告訴する, 訴訟を起こす
◆Since sellers of fake products tend to disappear overnight after quickly selling their bogus goods, it is impossible to file lawsuits against them. 偽ブランド商品[コピー商品]の販売業者は、手早くコピー商品を売り尽くすとすぐに行方をくらます

ため、訴訟を起こすこともできない。

file a petition in bankruptcy 破産申請する、破産申請書を提出する
◆In the event that either party files a petition in bankruptcy or a petition in bankruptcy is filed against it, or either party becomes insolvent or bankrupt, or goes into liquidation or receivership. いずれかの当事者が破産申請をするか、第三者により破産申請書を提出された場合、またはいずれかの当事者が支払い不能もしくは破産状態になった場合、またはいずれかの当事者が清算手続きに入るか、管財人による財産管理が開始された場合。

file a suit against A for B AをBで提訴する、AをBで訴える
◆The U.S. Securities and Exchange Commission began taking actions, filing suits against companies for window-dressing their accounting records. 米証券取引委員会 (SEC) は、会計記録の粉飾 (粉飾決算) で企業を提訴するなどの行動をとり始めた (米証券取引委員会は粉飾決算企業を提訴するなどの行動をとり始めた)。

file a suit at 〜に提訴する、〜に訴えを起こす (=file a lawsuit)
◆The construction company filed a suit at the Osaka District Court, demanding the contract be renewed. この建築会社は、契約更新を求めて大阪地裁に提訴した。

file an administrative lawsuit 行政訴訟を起こす
◆Dissatisfied with the FTC's decision, the companies filed an administrative lawsuit demanding that the FTC reverse its decision. 公正取引委員会の決定を不服として、企業側は同委員会の決定取消しを求める行政訴訟を起こした。

file for 〜を申請する、〜を申し込む、〜の申告を出す、〜に提訴する、〜を求めて訴えを起こす
file for bankruptcy 破産を申し立てる、破産申請する、破産法を申請する、再生法を申請する
file for protection from creditors 会社更生手続きを申請する、破綻 (はたん) 申請する、資産保全を申請する (=apply for protection from creditors, file for court protection from creditors)
file for protection from creditors under the Civil Rehabilitation Law 民事再生法の適用を申請する (=file for protection from creditors under the bankruptcy reform law)

file for court protection from creditors 会社更生手続きを申請する、破綻 (はたん) 申請する、資産保全を申請する (=file for protection from creditors)
◆Nippon Shokuhin Co. filed for court protection from creditors under the civil rehabilitation law with liabilities of about ¥22 billion in the wake of a beef false-labeling scandal. 牛肉の偽装表示

事件の結果、約220億円の負債を抱えて、日本食品が民事再生法の適用を申請した。

file for insolvency proceedings with 〜に破産手続きをする、〜に破綻 (はたん) 処理手続きをする
◆Ishikawa Bank filed for insolvency proceedings with the Financial Services Agency under the Deposit Insurance Law. 石川銀行は、預金保険法に基づき金融庁に対して破綻処理手続きを申請した。

file for protection from creditors under the bankruptcy reform law 民事再生法の適用を申請する
◆Aoki Corp. filed for protection from creditors under the bankruptcy reform law at the Tokyo District Court. 青木建設が、東京地裁に民事再生法の適用を申請した。

file for protection from creditors under the Corporate Rehabilitation Law 会社更生法の適用を申請する、会社更生法を申請する
◆The midsize general contractor affiliated with collapsed major retailer Mycal Corp. filed with the Tokyo District Court for protection from creditors under the Corporate Rehabilitation Law. 経営破綻した大手スーパー、マイカル系の中堅ゼネコンは、会社更生法の適用を東京地裁に申請した。

file for protection under Chapter 11 of the U.S. Bankruptcy Code 米連邦破産法11章の適用を申請する
◆WorldCom Inc. filed for protection under Chapter 11 of the U.S. Bankruptcy Code nearly four weeks after it disclosed that it had concealed almost 4 billion dollars in expenses through deceptive accounting. 米通信大手のワールドコムは、虚偽の会計処理 (粉飾決算) で費用 (経費) 約40億ドルを隠蔽 (いんぺい) していたことを公表してから4週間後に、米連邦破産法11章の適用を申請した。

final and binding 最終的なもので法的拘束力がある
◆The award in such arbitration shall be final and binding in any court of competent jurisdiction. この仲裁での裁定は、最終的なもので正当な管轄権のあるいずれの裁判所でも法的拘束力がある。

final and binding upon 最終的なもので〜を拘束する
◆The award rendered by arbitrator (s) shall be final and binding upon parties. 仲裁人が行った仲裁判断は、最終的なもので、両当事者を拘束する。

final and conclusive 最終的で確定的な、最終の、終局の
◆Any decision or award of the arbitrator shall be final and conclusive on the parties to this agreement. 本契約の当事者に関しては、仲裁人の決定または判断を最終的で確定的なものとする。

final and entire agreement 完全な最終合意、最終的かつ完全な合意
◆This agreement constitutes the final and entire

FINA   198

agreement between the parties with respect to
any and all subjects and shall supersede all previous negotiations, understandings and agreements
between the parties relating thereto. 本契約は、あ
らゆる事項に関する両当事者間の完全な最終合意
を構成し、それに関する両当事者間の事前の協議、
了解、合意事項に代わるものとする。

final destination　最終目的地
◆Such inspection shall not, in any way, prejudice
the purchaser's right of inspection of the products after the delivery at the final destination or
rejection of the defective products. この検査は、
最終目的地での引渡し後に本製品を検査する買い
主の権利、または瑕疵（かし）ある製品を拒絶する
買い主の権利をいかなる意味でも損なわないもの
とする。

finance　（動）融資する、貸し付ける、出資す
る、資金を出す、資金を供給する、資金を調達
する、赤字などを埋め合わせる、補填する
◆Suntory Holdings Ltd. is expected to use about
¥500 billion in estimated proceeds from the listing of its beverage and food unit to finance mergers and acquisitions abroad. サントリーホール
ディングスは、清涼飲料・食品子会社の上場によ
り推定で5,000億円程度の資金を調達して、海外企
業の買収に充てる見込みだ。

finance lease　金融性リース、ファイナンス・
リース　（=financial lease; ⇒operating lease)
解説ファイナンス・リース契約の特徴：機器
のリースはファイナンス・リースとオペレー
ティング・リースの二つに分けられる。この
うちファイナンス・リース契約の特徴として
は、契約期間が長期であること、原則として契
約の中途解約が不能であること、不可抗力に
よるリース物件の滅失、損傷は借主が負担す
ること、保険も借主がかけることを挙げる
ことができる。ただし、リース物件の補修費
用やサービス費用は、オペレーティング・リー
ス契約の場合と違って貸主の負担ではない。

financial assistance　金融支援
◆As financial assistance to the cash-strapped
chipmaker Renesas, its three shareholders and
founders are to provide about ¥50 billion, while
lines of credit established by its main banks will
make up the rest of ¥50 billion. 資金繰りが悪化
している半導体メーカーのルネサスへの金融支援
として、同社の株主で設立母体の3社が約500億円
を調達するほか、同社の主力取引銀行が設定した
融資枠で、残りの500億円を賄（まかな）う。

financial condition　財政状態、財政状況、財
務状態、財務内容、財務基盤、金融情勢
（=financial position, financial state)
◆Financial conditions of major companies have
improved substantially. 大手企業の財務状況は、
大幅に改善した。

financial crisis in Europe　欧州の金融危機、
欧州の財政・金融危機（European fiscal and
financial crisis)

◆If the financial crisis in Europe worsens, exports from China and other emerging economies
to Europe will slow down. 欧州の財政・金融危
機が拡大すれば、中国など新興国の対欧輸出は鈍
化するだろう。◆Partly due to a slowdown in the
Chinese economy in the wake of the European
financial crisis, Japan's exports and production
have been on the decline. 欧州の金融危機による
中国の景気減速もあって、日本の輸出や生産活動
は落ち込んでいる。

financial deal　金融取引
◆Libor is widely used as a benchmark for rates
of corporate loans, derivatives contracts and
many other financial deals. ライボー（ロンドン
銀行間取引金利）は、企業向け融資や金融派生商
品などの金融取引の金利の指標に幅広く使われて
いる。

financial deficit　経営赤字

financial derivatives　金融派生商品
◆Investment advisory company AIJ started investing in financial derivatives through funds
based in the Cayman Islands, a tax haven, since
2002. 投資顧問会社のAIJは、2002年から、租税回
避地の英領ケイマン諸島を営業基盤とするファン
ドを通じて金融派生商品への投資を始めた。

financial exchange　金融取引
◆Financial exchanges between the BRICs group,
Indonesia and South Korea will move toward a
tri-reserve-currency regime by losing a dependency on the U.S. dollar. BRICsグループ（ブラ
ジル、ロシア、インド、中国）とインドネシア、韓
国の新興6か国間の金融取引は今後、米ドルに依存
しなくなるため、3準備通貨体制に移行するものと
思われる。

**Financial Instruments and Exchange
Law**　金融商品取引法
◆According to the Financial Instruments and Exchange Law, penalties for making false securities reports are tightened from up to five years in
prison to up to 10 years in prison. 金融取引法に
よれば、有価証券報告書の虚偽記載の刑罰は、懲役5
年以下から懲役10年以下に引き上げられている。◆
Insider trading, which is banned under the Financial Instruments and Exchange Law, harms ordinary investors and significantly damages stock
market credibility. 金融商品取引法で禁じられて
いるインサイダー取引は、一般の投資家が不利益を
被（こうむ）り、証券市場の信頼性を大きく損なう。

financial obligations　金銭的義務、金銭債務
◆Except as and to the extent specifically reflected in the March 31, 2003 balance sheet included in Schedule 6, the Company does not
have any liabilities or financial obligations of any
nature. 付属書類6に記載した2003年3月31日付け
貸借対照表に特に示されているものを除いて、ま
た同表に特に示されているかぎり、対象会社はい
かなる性質の債務も金銭的債務も有していない。

financial position　財政状態、財務状況、財務
状態、財務体質　（=financial condition)

◆The annual financial statements for the financial year ending on December 31, 2015 present a true and fair view of the financial position as of the date thereof. 2015年12月31日に終了する事業年度［会計年度］の年次財務書類は、同日現在の財政状態について真実かつ公正な見方を提示している。

financial regulation　金融規制
◆Bitcoin traded in units of BTC currently stays outside the framework of financial regulations, so the risk management of the virtual currency is difficult. BTCの単位で取引されているビットコインは現在、金融規制の枠外にあるため、仮想通貨「ビットコイン」のリスク管理は難しい。

financial report　財務報告, 財務報告書, 業績報告, 有価証券報告書
◆Japanese companies listed on the London Stock Exchange will submit financial reports based on the IAS or the U.S. GAAP. ロンドン証券取引所に上場している日本企業は今後、国際会計基準か米国会計基準に基づく［に準拠した］財務報告書を提出することになる。

financial service(s)　金融事業, 金融サービス, 金融, 投資情報サービス機関
◆Singapore serves as ASEAN's hub for logistics and financial services. シンガポールは、アセアンの物流と金融サービスのハブ（拠点）となっている。

Financial Stability Board　金融安定化理事会, 金融安定理事会, FSB（金融監督に関する国際基準を制定する機関の金融安定化フォーラム（FSF）に代わる新機関）
◆The Financial Stability Board set up by the Group of 20 major economies（G20）unveiled a list of 28 global systematically important banks including the three Japanese megabanks of Mitsubishi UFJ Financial Group Inc., Sumitomo Mitsui Financial Group Inc. and Mizuho Financial Group Inc. 主要20か国・地域（G20）が設けた金融安定化理事会（FSB）は、国際金融システムへの影響が大きい金融機関（G-SIFIs）28行のリストを発表したが、これには日本の3大銀行グループの三菱UFJフィナンシャル・グループ、三井住友フィナンシャルグループとみずほフィナンシャルグループが含まれている。

financial statements　財務諸表, 財務書類, 決算報告書（財政状態や経営成績に関する報告書で、損益計算書や貸借対照表などの総称）
◆All such financial statements have been prepared in accordance with generally accepted accounting principles consistently applied throughout the periods indicated. これらの財務書類は、当該期間中に一貫して適用した一般に公正妥当と認められた会計原則（会計基準）に従って作成されている。◆The annual financial statements for the financial year ending on December 31, 2015 present a true and fair view of the financial position as of the date thereof. 2015年12月31日に終了する事業年度［会計年度］の年次財務

書類は、同日現在の財政状態について真実かつ公正な見方を提示している。

financial stress test　金融のストレス・テスト（特別検査）（⇒stress test）
米政府が、金融機関の不良資産問題を抜本的に解決するため、経済がさらに落ち込んだ場合やブラック・マンデー、アジア通貨危機など通常ではあまり考えられないケースを「負荷」として織り込んで、2009年2月25日から大手19行に対して「ストレス・テスト」を行った。このテストで、資本不足と認定された金融機関には、市場からの資金調達を促す。市場で資金調達できなかった場合は、政府が優先株を引き受ける形で公的資金を注入する。金融機関の経営がさらに悪化した場合は、政府が優先株を普通株に転換して、金融機関が事実上、国有化される可能性もある。

financial year　会計年度, 事業年度, 営業年度, 会計期間（=business year, fiscal year, financial position）

financing　（名）資金調達, 資本調達, 金融, 融資, 借入れ, ローン, 財務, 資金, ファイナンス
debt financing　借入れによる資金調達, 債券発行による資金調達
equity financing　株式発行による資金調達
external bond financing　外債発行による資金調達
financing activities　財務活動, 資金調達活動, 金融活動, 資金調達と返済に関する活動
financing deal　資金調達取引
financing document　融資契約書類
financing transaction　資本取引
get financing　資金を調達する, 資金を確保する
private equity financing　未上場株の交付による資金調達
provide short-term financing　短期融資をする
◆Japanese companies can hedge exchange risks and improve their business image abroad through external bond financing. 日本企業は、外債発行による資金調達で、為替リスクを回避するとともに海外での企業イメージアップを図ることができる。◆The firm envisioned negotiations with the U.S. equity fund over financing for restructuring in a reconstruction plan it formulated in June. 同社は、経営合理化の資金調達に関しては、6月に策定した再建計画でこの米国の投資ファンドとの交渉を見込んでいた。

financing operations　金融活動, 融資活動, 金融事業, 市場からの資金調達, 財務活動, 財務
◆This struggling auto producer is considering setting up a joint venture with an American major securities firm to engage in North American financing operations. 経営再建中のこの自動車メーカーは現在、米証券大手と北米で金融事業［販

FIND

売金融事業]を手がける合弁会社の設立を検討している。

finder's fee　仲介料, 紹介手数料

fine　(名)罰金, 違約金, 制裁金, 課徴金, 手数料, 許可料

be subject to a fine　罰金の対象となる, 罰金が科される

civil fines　民事制裁金, 民事の罰金

impose a fine　罰金を科す

large fines　巨額の罰金　(=huge fines)

◆Barclays, one of Britain's top banking groups, has paid a huge fine over its false Libor submission. 英大手銀行・金融グループのバークレイズは, ライボー(ロンドン銀行間取引金利)の虚偽申告で, 巨額の罰金を支払った。◆The TSE will consider taking punitive measures, such as revoking trading licenses, restricting business or imposing fines if any violations of the law or TSE rules are found in the inspections of major securities firms. 主要証券会社への立ち入り調査で法令違反や東証ルール違反があった場合, 東証は, 取引免許の取消しや売買の制限, 過怠金(罰金)の課徴などの厳しい措置を取る[厳しい処分をする]方針だ。

finish　(動)終える, 終了する, 済ます, 言い終える, 締めくくる, (学業や課程を)修了する, 卒業する, やり終える, 取引を終える, 完成させる, 仕上げる, (物を)使いきる, 負かす, やっつける, 〜にとどめを刺す, (事が)〜の命取りになる　(自動)終わる, 済む, おしまいにする, 〜位[着]でゴールする[ゴールインする], 決勝点に入る

finish and complete　完了する

◆Nasdaq composite index finished at levels not seen since October. ナスダック店頭市場の総合指数は, 10月以来の水準で取引を終えた。◆The broader TOPIX index of all First Section issues finished down 11.71 points at 706.08. 一部上場全銘柄の総合東証株価指数は, 11.71ポイント安の706.8で終了した。◆Tokyo stocks extended their winning streak to a third day with the key Nikkei index finishing above the 9,000 line. 東京の株価[東京株式市場の株価]は, 3日連続で値上がりし, 日経平均株価(225種)の終値は9,000円台を上回った。

finish　(名)仕上げ, 仕上がり, 出来栄え, 磨き, 終り, 終了, 最後, 結末, 結果, ゴール, ゴールイン, 破滅, 滅亡, 洗練, 垢(あか)抜け

a delicate finish　上品な仕上げ

an artistic finish　芸術的仕上げ

finish coating　上塗り

finish cut [machining]　仕上げ削り

finish forging　仕上げ打ち

finish mark　仕上げ記号

finish schedule　仕上げ表

◆The prices will vary slightly according to the finish you prefer. 価格は, お好みの仕上げによっ

て多少変わります。

finished goods　製品, 完成品, 加工品　(=finished product)

finished goods inventory　製品在庫

finished goods prices　生産者物価指数

finished goods stock [on hand]　製品在庫

partly finished goods　半製品

semi-finished goods　半製品

◆The cost of finished goods and work in process comprise material, labor, and manufacturing overhead. 製品と仕掛品の原価は, 材料費と労務費と製造間接費から成っています。

finished product　最終製品, 最終財
(⇒international division of labor)

◆Due to the IT revolution and trade liberalization, product specialization now is determined by comparative advantages not in finished products but in work unique to each country or region in the context of global value chains. 情報通信技術(IT)革命と貿易自由化で, 製品の特化は, 「最終財」の比較優位ではなく, 国際的価値連鎖との関連で国・地域にそれぞれ特有の「仕事」の比較優位で決まるようになった。

firm belief　確信

firm offer　確約申込み, 確定申込み, (承諾)回答期限付きオファー, ファーム・オファー

◆Unless otherwise stipulated, firm offers shall remain in force for five days. 別段の定めがないかぎり, ファーム・オファーは5日間有効とする。

firm order　確定注文, ファーム・オーダー

◆At least sixty days prior to the requested delivery date, the buyer shall provide the seller with a written estimate of its requirements of the product, which shall constitute a firm order. 希望渡し日から少なくとも60日前に, 買い主は, 本製品の需要予測書[需要見積り書]を売り主に提出し, これを確定注文とするものとする。

first　(形)第一の, 最初の, 第一位の, 最上の

first and second unpaid　第一, 第二手形不払いの節　(3通1組の為替手形の第三手形に書き入れる文句)

first and third unpaid　第一, 第三手形不払いの節

first beneficiary　原受益者(信用状を最初に受理した輸出者)

first clearing　手形の第一交換, 第一手形交換

first excess of loss cover　第一次超過損害再保険特約

first exchange　手形の第一交換, 第一手形交換　(=first clearing)

first hand　直買品

first hand goods　直仕入品

first loss insurance　第一次損害保険

first mortgage　第一抵当, 1番抵当

first of exchange　為替手形の第一券, 第一

手形

first offer 株式の先売権, 株式の先買権者へ
の提供（第一優先権者に株式を買い取らせ
る機会を与えること）

first option 株式譲渡の先買権, 第一優先権
（株式を譲渡する者があるとき, 会社また
は他の株主がその株を第一優先順位で買い
取る権利のこと）

first payment 第一回払込み金

first premium 第一回保険料

first refusal 株式の優先先買権, 先買権, 先買
権行使の拒絶（refusalは「優先権, 選択権」
という意味で, optionと同義。株式の譲渡
に先買権の制約がある場合, 株式の先買権
行使の拒絶があってはじめて第三者に株式
を売却できるようになる）

first supply 初物

first via （為替組手形の）第一通

first above referred to 冒頭に記載した, 頭
書の
◆All notices, demands and communications
mentioned above shall be addressed to the parties at each party's respective office first above
referred to, except that either party may change
such office by notice in accordance with this Article. 上記の通知, 要求, 通信の宛先は, 冒頭に記
載した各当事者のそれぞれの営業所に所在する当
事者とする。ただし, いずれの当事者も, 本条に
従って通知を行って当該営業所を変更することが
できる。

first above written 冒頭に記載した
◆This agreement shall come into force on the
date first above written. 本契約は, 冒頭に記載
した日付に発効する。

first instance 第一審
◆Each party hereby agrees that the Tokyo District Court shall have exclusive jurisdiction for
the first instance over any lawsuit in connection
with this agreement. 本契約に関する訴訟はすべ
て東京地方裁判所を第一審の専属管轄とすること
に, 各当事者は本契約により同意する。

first right 優先権, 第一優先権
◆The purchaser shall have the first right to purchase all of such quantities or any part thereof
under the same terms and conditions of this
agreement. 買い主は, 当該数量の全部または一
部を本契約と同じ条件で優先的に購入する権利を
もつものとする。

fiscal year 事業年度, 会計年度, 営業年度, 会
計期間
after the end of each fiscal year 各会計年度の
終了後
fiscal year then ended 当該日に終了した事業
年度

fit and suitable 適当な, 適切な, 適合する

fitness （名）適合, 適合性, 適格, 健康, 健康

状態
◆The seller shall not be liable in respect of any
warranty or consideration as to quality or fitness
which would arise by implication of law. 売り主
は, 法律の運用により生じる品質または適合性に
関する保証または条件については, 責任を負わな
いものとする。

fitness for a particular purpose 特定目的
適合性, 特定目的への適合性
◆The seller makes no other warranties or representations with respect to the products and disclaims all warranties, including but not limited
to implied warranties of merchantability, fitness
for a particular purpose and noninfringement. 売
り主は, 本製品に関する他の保証または表明は行
わず, 商品性, 特定目的への適合性および非侵害の
黙示の保証などを含めてすべての保証を否認する。

fitness for use 用途適合性
◆The seller expressly disclaims any warranty of
conditions, fitness for use or merchantability. 売
り主は, 状態, 用途適合性または商品性の保証を
明確に否認する。

fix （動）固定する, 確定する, 日取りなどを決
める
fixed amount 固定額, 定額
fixed annual payment 定額年間支払い
fixed or contingent 確定的または偶発的なも
のであれ
◆Unless otherwise expressly agreed by the parties hereto in writing, the prices stated in this
agreement are fixed during the term of this agreement. 本契約当事者の書面による別段の明確な合
意がないかぎり, 本契約書に記載した価格は, 本
契約期間中, 固定価格とする。

fixture note 船腹確約書

flag （名）旗, 国旗, 旗艦旗, 標識
flag additional premium 国籍割増し （=flag
AP）
flag discrimination 船籍差別待遇, 国旗差別
主義
flag-of- convenience vessel 便宜置籍船
flag of necessity 便宜国旗
house flag 社旗

flagship （名）主力商品, 主力製品, 目玉商品,
最重要製品, 目玉, 最も代表的なもの, 最も重
要なもの, 旗艦, 最高級船, 最大の船・航空機,
最上位機種, 主力機種
flagship carrier 代表的な航空会社
flagship film camera フイルム・カメラの最
上位機種
flagship operation 主力事業
flagship store 旗艦店, 母店, 主力店, 主力店舗

flagship product 主力製品, 主力商品, 目玉
商品
◆Sony's liquid-crystal display TV is one of the
company's flagship products. ソニーの液晶テレ

ビは、同社の主力製品の一つだ。

flange connection フランジ接続点
◆Risk of and title to the products shall pass from the seller to the purchaser when the products pass the flange connection between the delivery hose and the vessel's intake. 本製品の危険負担と所有権は、本製品が引渡し用ホースと本船の貨物受入口とのフランジ接続点を通過した時点で、売り主から買い主に移転する。

flight of capital 資本逃避, 資金逃避, 資金の流出, 他国への資本の流出, 資本の国外移転 (=capital flight)
◆The Chinese economy will become anemic and the world economy could suffer immense damage if China is faced with an unabated flight of capital due to speculative investments that its economic bubble has lured from abroad. 中国で、中国のバブル景気で海外から流入した投機マネーが大量に流出したら、中国経済は活気を失い、世界経済は甚大なダメージを受けることになろう。

floating rate 変動金利 (=floating interest rate)
◆The borrower shall pay to the lender an interest on the loan for each interest payment period applicable to the loan at the floating rate of the LIBOR (British Bankers Association Interest Settlement Rate in U.S. Dollars) plus 1.625 percent per annum, calculated on the basis of actual number of days elapsed and a year of 360 days. 借主は、1年を360日として実際に経過した日数に基づいて計算した、ロンドン銀行間取引金利(米ドルでの英国銀行協会金利決済レート)に年1.625%を加算した変動金利で、この借入れに適用される各利払い期間の借入金の利息を貸主に対して支払うものとする。

fluctuation (名)変動, 変化, 上がり下がり, 乱高下, 騰落, 動き
business fluctuation 景気変動
currency fluctuation 為替変動, 為替レートの変動
demand fluctuation 需要変動
dollar fluctuation ドル価の変動
exchange (rate) fluctuation 為替変動, 為替相場の変動, 為替の騰落 (=fluctuation in foreign exchange rate, foreign exchange fluctuation)
fluctuations in interest rates 金利の変動 (=interest rate fluctuations)
fluctuations in stock prices and credit ratings 株価や信用格付けの動き
fluctuations of the currency market 為替相場の変動
foreign exchange rate fluctuations 為替相場の変動, 外国為替相場の変動
losses from fluctuations of the currency market 為替差損
market fluctuations 市場変動, 市況の変動

price fluctuation 価格の変動, 物価の変動, 価格騰落, 株価の乱高下 (=fluctuation in price)
rapid fluctuations in exchange markets 為替相場の急激な変動
seasonal fluctuation 季節変動
trade fluctuation 景気変動
wild fluctuations in oil prices 原油価格の乱高下
◆Erratic fluctuations of both stock prices and exchange rates have continued, reflecting the turbulent moves of speculative money on world markets. 世界的な投機マネーの激しい動きを反映して、株価と為替相場の乱高下が止まらない。◆Losses from fluctuations of the currency market due to the yen's steep appreciation have added to Toyota's plight. 急激な円高による為替差損で、トヨタの経営状況が深刻化した。

fluctuations in exchange rates 為替の変動
◆In foreign exchange margin trading, investors repeatedly trade U.S. dollars, euros and other currencies, aiming to profit from fluctuations in exchange rates. 外国為替証拠金取引では、為替の変動による利益を狙って、投資家が米ドルやユーロなどの外貨を繰り返し売買する。

fluctuations in the value of the euro ユーロの為替相場の変動
◆As European authorities failed to take swift action, the yields of Italian and Spanish government bonds rose, and there were violent fluctuations in the value of the euro. 欧州当局が迅速に対応しなかったので、イタリアやスペインの国債流通利回りが上昇し、ユーロの為替相場が乱高下した。

FOB [f.o.b.] 本船渡し, 本船渡し条件 (free on boardの略。⇒internal laws)
FOB & I 保険料込み(FOB価格に海上保険料を含めた価格)
FOB airport 空港渡し, 航空FOB
FOB airport price 指定出発空港渡し値段, 空港渡し値段
FOB attachment clause FOBアタッチメント約款
FOB contract 本船渡し契約
FOB destination 着荷地渡し, 到着港本船渡し条件
FOB exporter's factory 輸出者工場渡し値段
FOB Japanese ports 日本港本船渡し
FOB mill price 工場渡し価格
FOB price 指定地渡し価格, 本船渡し価格
FOB pricing 指定地渡し価格の決定
FOB shipping point 出荷地渡し, 積出し港本船渡し値段
FOB trade surplus 貿易黒字(FOBベース), FOBベースの貿易黒字

FOOD

FOB vessel at port of shipment　輸出港本船渡し値段

heavy fuel oil FOB delivery　重燃料油先物

◆All deliveries of Products sold by Supplier to Distributor pursuant to this agreement shall be made FOB Yokohama, Japan. 本契約に従って供給者が販売店に販売した本製品の引渡しは、すべてFOB条件により日本国横浜港で行う。◆All prices are FOB Yokohama, Japan. 価格は、すべてFOB横浜港（日本）条件とする。◆Delivery of the software products to the buyer shall be completed when shipped, FOB Seller's plant in New York. ソフトウエア製品の買い主への引渡しは、ニューヨークの売り主の工場でFOB条件で出荷された時点で完了するものとする。◆If delivery is made under the terms of FOB, the Buyer shall book shipping space in accordance with the time of delivery stipulated in this agreement. 引渡しがFOBの条件で行われる場合、買い主は、本契約で定める引渡し期限に従って（本船の）船腹を予約するものとする。◆The Seller shall ship the product to the place designated by the Buyer from New Jersey, U.S.A. on the basis of FOB Yokohama, Japan. 売り主は、買い手が指定する場所に、米国ニュージャージーから日本国横浜港条件で本製品を出荷する。◆Trade terms for each sale under this agreement shall be in principle, FOB（ ）Port. 本契約に基づく各売買の貿易条件は、原則としてFOB（ ）港渡しとする。

FOC［**f.o.c.**］　無料で（free of chargeの略）

following expiration of the warranty period　保証期間の満了後

food　(名)食品, 食料, 食物, 食べ物, フード

additive-free food　無添加食品

dairy foods　乳製品

ensure the safety of Chinese food products　中国産食材の安全性を確保する

fermented food　発酵食品

food & beverage control　食材・飲料管理, FBコントロール

food additives　食品添加物

food allergy　食品アレルギー, 食物アレルギー（=food intolerance）

Food and Agriculture Organization　国連食糧農業機関, FAO

Food and Drug Administration　米食品医薬品局, FDA

food basket　穀倉地帯, 食糧生産地帯

food contamination　食品汚染

food defense　食品防御, フード・ディフェンス

food distribution center　食品流通センター, 食品集配センター

food irradiation　食品照射

food labeling　食品表示

food maker　食品メーカー

food mileage　フード・マイレージ（=food miles）

food miles　食品の輸送距離

food prices　食品価格

food processing　食品加工

Food Recycling Law　食品リサイクル法

food service industry　外食産業, 外食業界

food supply　食糧供給

food to go　お持ち帰り食品

food traceability　食品トレーサビリティ

food value　栄養価, 食品栄養価

fresh food　生鮮食品

frozen food　冷凍食品

functional food　栄養機能食品

health［healthy］foods　健康食品

iron-rich food　鉄分の豊富な食品

natural food　自然食品

processed food　加工食品

◆By the instruction of the China Food and Drug Administration, the Shanghai city government suspended operations of Shanghai Husi Food and confiscated raw materials and products at the firm which had sold expired meat products. 中国の国家食品薬品監督管理総局の指示で、上海市は、品質保持期限切れの肉製品を販売していた上海福喜食品の営業を停止し、同社の原料と商品を差し押さえた。

food imports　食品の輸入, 食品の輸入量

◆Food imports from China declined sharply after the poisoned frozen gyoza incident, but now the figure has almost returned to the levels recorded prior to the incident. 冷凍ギョウザの中毒事件後、中国からの食品の輸入量は大きく落ち込んだが、今は事件前の水準にほぼ回復している。

food market　食料市場

◆Itochu Corp. formed a tie-up with Chinese food firm to strengthen bargaining power in the global food market. 伊藤忠商事は、世界の食料市場での交渉力［買付け交渉力］を強化するため、中国の食料企業と提携した。

food product　食品, 食料品, 食材

Chinese food products　中国産食品, 中国製食材

special health food products　特定保健用商品, 特保

◆After the poisoned frozen gyoza incident, Japanese companies were spurred to tighten quality controls on Chinese food products at their factories in China. 冷凍ギョウザの中毒事件を機に、日系企業は、中国国内工場での中国産食品の品質管理強化を行うようになった。◆Supermarkets, convenience stores and other retailers throughout the country were busy removing from their shelves food products containing the banned chemicals. 全国のスーパーやコンビになどの小売店は、無認可の化学薬品を使用した食品の棚からの撤去作業に追われた。

Food Sanitation Law 食品衛生法
◆Mister Donuts outlets sold imported nikuman (Chinese steamed meat buns) that contained an antioxidant banned under the Food Sanitation Law. ミスタードーナッツのチェーン店が、食品衛生法で禁止されている酸化防止剤を使った輸入肉まんを販売していた。

food self-sufficiency rate [ratio] on a calorie basis カロリー・ベースの食料自給率
◆Under the food self-sufficiency rate on a calorie basis, even beef and pork from animals raised in Japan are not considered domestic products if they consumed imported feed. カロリー・ベースの食料自給率では、国内で育てた家畜の牛肉や豚肉[国内で育てた]牛や豚の肉]でも、餌が輸入品の場合は国産品と見なされない。

food shortage 食糧不足
◆The establishment of the regulations would hinder not only free trade, but also development of biotechnology that could alleviate food shortages in poor countries. 規制を設ければ、自由貿易を阻害するだけでなく、貧困国の食糧不足の改善につながるバイオテクノロジーの発展も妨げることになる。

for （前）～を求めて、～の目的で、～のために、～に対して、～に備えて、～に関して、～に賛成して、～を支持して、～の間
for a reasonable time 合理的な期間、相当の期間、相当の期限 （=for a reasonable period）
for an initial period 当初期間
for and during the period of ～の期間、～の期間中、～の間
for and during the term of ～の期間、～の期間中、～の間
For and on behalf of: 契約当事者名
for any cause 理由を問わず、理由のいかんを問わず （=for any reason）
for any cause whatever 理由が何であれ
for any length of time 一定期間
for any reason 理由のいかんを問わず、どんな理由であれ （=for any cause）
for intended use by ～が使用予定の
for one's own benefit 自己の利益のために
for one's own use 自己使用のため、自己使用を目的として
For the attention: ～様
for the entire term of this agreement 本契約の全期間中
for the term of this agreement 本契約の期間中, 本契約の有効期間中
（=during the term of this agreement）

for value received 受領した価値あるものを約因として、価値あるものを受領した見返りに

for any purpose どんな目的にも、どんな目的においても、どんな目的であれ
◆Distributor is an independent contractor and is not the legal representative or agent of Supplier for any purpose. 販売店は独立した契約当事者であり、どんな目的であれ供給者の法律上の代表者または代理人ではない。

for convenience 便宜上、便宜上のもの
for convenience and reference only 単に便宜と参照のため、便宜上のものと参照のためにすぎない
for one's convenience 便宜上、自己の都合のよいように、自由裁量により

for convenience of reference 参照の便宜上、参考の便宜のため、参照の便のため
◆The headings used herein are for convenience of reference only and do not constitute a part of this agreement. 本契約書で使用する見出しは、参照の便宜上にすぎず、本契約の一部を構成するものではない。

for convenience only 単に便宜上のもの
◆Headings in this agreement are for convenience only and shall not affect the interpretation hereof. 本契約の見出し語は、単に便宜上のもので、本契約の解釈に影響を与えないものとする。

for normal use 通常の使用のため、通常の用途に
◆Company warrants that Products shall be fit and suitable for normal use in Territory. 会社は、本製品[契約品]が契約地域での通常の用途に適合することを保証する。

for one's account ～の勘定で、～の負担で
◆Any additional insurance required by the purchaser shall be for the purchaser's account. 買い主が要求する追加の保険は、すべて買い主の負担とする。

for one's own account ～の自己負担で、～の自己勘定で、自己の勘定負担で
◆The seller shall, for its own account, effect marine insurance only free from particular average （FPA Institute Cargo Clause）for the amount of CIF value of the products plus 10 percent. 売り主は、売り主の自己負担で、本商品のCIF価格プラス10%の保険金額により単独海損[分損]不担保条件（FPA協会貨物保険約款）の海上保険を付けるものとする。

for or against ～に有利または不利に
◆This agreement shall not be construed for or against any party based on any rule of construction who prepared the agreement. 本契約は、どちらの当事者が本契約書の起草をしたかによる解釈のルールに基づいて、一方の当事者に有利に解釈したり不利に解釈したりしないものとする。

for tax purposes 税務上
◆Payment by ABC to XYZ of the royalties shall

be subject to a withholding by ABC for Japanese tax purposes of ten percent of the aggregate royalties actually due and payable to XYZ. XYZに対するABCのロイヤルティの支払いについては、日本の税務上、実際にXYZに支払わなければならないロイヤルティ総額の10%がABCによる源泉徴収の対象となるものとする。

for the account of 〜の勘定で, 〜の負担で, 〜の勘定とする, 〜の負担とする
◆After the delivery of the Goods, any taxes, customs duties, export or import surcharges or other governmental charges shall be for the account of the Buyer. 本商品の引渡し後、税金、関税、輸出・輸入税、その他政府が賦課する費用は、買い主の負担とする。◆All taxes in respect of payments under this agreement shall be for the account of the licensee. 本契約上の支払いにかかわる税金は、すべてライセンシーの勘定とする。

for the benefit of 〜のために, 〜の利益のために, 〜を受益者として, 〜を受取人として
◆During the period when Products are in the custody of ABC, ABC shall keep Products insured at ABC's account for the benefit of XYZ against loss or damage by fire, theft or otherwise with extended coverage. 本製品［契約品］をABCが保管している期間中、火災、盗難、その他による滅失や損害を拡張担保するため、ABCはその勘定で、XYZを保険受取人として本製品に付保するものとする。◆Each payment under the Note shall be credited first to any expense reimbursements due under the Note and the Deed of Trust of even date herewith securing this Note and executed by Borrower, as Trustor, for the benefit of Holder (the "Deed of Trust"), then to any late charges, then to accrued and unpaid interest, and the remainder to principal. 本手形に基づく各払い込み金は、先ず本手形と、信託設定者としての振出人が手形所持人を受益者として作成して本手形を保証するこれと同日付の信託証書（以下「信託証書」という）とに基づいて支払う義務がある経費の弁済に充当し、次いで遅延料に、その後は未払いの経過利息に充当し、残金は元本に充当するものとする。

for the convenience of the parties 当事者の便宜のため, 当事者の便宜上
◆Any translation into any other language shall be solely for the convenience of the parties. 他の言語への翻訳は、当事者の便宜のためだけである。

for the purpose of 〜の目的上、〜のため、〜する目的のために, 〜の解釈上　（⇒have manufactured）
for the purpose of this clause　本条項の目的上, 本条項の解釈上
for the purpose of this definition　本定義の目的上

for the purpose of this agreement 本契約の目的上
◆For the purpose of this agreement, any change of corporate identity of one of the parties, such as by amalgamation, reorganization, or merger or consolidation, has not been agreed to by the other party. 本契約の目的上、合併、会社更生または吸収合併や新設合併といった当事者の一方の法人格の変更については、相手方当事者が同意していない。◆For the purpose of this agreement, the prime rate shall mean that rate announced by the principal bank of the seller as its prime commercial lending rate from time to time. 本契約の目的上、プライム・レートとは、売り主の主要取引銀行が最優遇商業貸出金利として随時発表する利率を意味する。

force majeure 不可抗力, 天災
any event of force majeure　不可抗力の事態
constitute events or conditions of force majeure 不可抗力の事態または状態を構成する
in the event of force majeure　不可抗力の場合には, 不可抗力が発生した場合
on the occurrence of any event of Force Majeure 不可抗力の事態が発生した場合

force majeure clause 不可抗力条項, 天災条項　（⇒act［Act］of God）
◆In the event of prohibition of export, refusal to issue export license, acts of God, war, blockade, embargoes, insurrection, mobilization or any other actions of Government authorities, riots, civil commotions, war-like conditions, strikes, lockout, shortage or control of power supply, plague or other epidemics, quarantine, fire, flood, tidal waves, typhoon, hurricane, cyclone, earthquake, lightning, explosion, or any other causes beyond the control of Seller, Seller shall not be liable for any delay in shipment or delivery, non-delivery, or destruction or deterioration, of all or any part of Products, or for any default in performance of this Agreement arising therefrom. 輸出禁止や輸出ライセンスの発行拒否、天災、戦争、封鎖、通商停止、反乱、動員その他政府当局の決定［処分・措置］、暴動、騒乱、戦争状態、ストライキ、ロックアウト、電力供給の不足・制限、疫病その他の伝染病、検疫、火災、洪水、洪浸、台風、ハリケーン、サイクロン、地震、落雷、爆発、その他売主が支配できない事由が生じた場合、売主は本商品の全部または一部の船積み・引渡しの遅延や不着、損壊・劣化に対して一切責任を負わないし、これから生じる本契約の不履行に対しても一切責任を負わないものとする。

forecast of rising global oil production 世界的な石油増産見通し
◆In the crude oil contract market of the New York Mercantile Exchange （NYMEX）, the price of January WTI, the benchmark U.S. crude oil, fell below $60 a barrel for the first time since June 2009 on December 11, 2014 due to the forecast of rising global oil production. 2014年12月11日のニューヨーク・マーカンタイル取引所の原油先物市場では、指標となる米国産原油WTI（テキサス産軽質油）の1月渡し価格が、世界的な石油増産見通しから、2009年7月以来5年5か月ぶりに1バレル＝60ドルを割り込んだ。

Foreign Account Tax Compliance Act
(米国の)外国口座税務コンプライアンス法,
FATCA（米政府が、外国の金融機関に対し
て、米国人が保有する口座の情報を求める法
律。米国人が海外口座を使って脱税するのを
阻止する一方、税収を増やすのが狙いで、
2010年に成立し2014年7月1日に施行された。
協力する外国の金融機関は、内国歳入庁
（IRS）に、米国人や米企業の口座情報を提供
する。協力しない金融機関に対しては、米政
府が米国の債券や株式の利息・配当などから
30%の源泉徴収を行う）

foreign assets 海外資産, 外国資産, 対外資
産, 海外資産勘定 （⇒net foreign assets）
◆Gross foreign assets held by Japanese in the
form of direct investment, securities investment,
financial derivatives, loans and export credits,
deposits, other investments and official foreign
reserves came to ￥379.78 trillion. 直接投資、証
券投資、金融派生商品、貸付け金や輸出信用、預
金その他の投資と政府の外貨準備高の形で日本の
政府や企業、個人が保有する海外資産の総額（対外
資産残高）は、379兆7,800億円に達した。

foreign branded product 海外ブランド品
◆In addition to rampant piracy of foreign
branded products, the issue of customers failing
to pay their bills has become a serious problem.
海外ブランド品の模倣品が大量に出回っているほ
か、最近は支払いの踏み倒しが重大問題化している。

foreign capital inflows 外資流入, 外国から
の資金流入, 外貨の流動性 （=foreign
inflows）
◆The shortage of foreign capital inflows saw
Mexico on the verge of default and bankruptcy
in early 1995. 外貨の流動性不足から、メキシコ
は1995年の初めには債務不履行と倒産の危機に見
舞われた。

foreign-capitalized company 外資系企業
◆Both foreign-capitalized and Japanese companies are forced to relocate their headquarters
functions overseas. 外資系企業も日本企業も、本
社機能を海外に移さざるを得なくなっている。

foreign demand 外需, 海外需要
◆Japan's economy is vulnerable to foreign exchange fluctuations as Japanese firms depend so
heavily on foreign demand. 日本企業は外需に大
きく依存しているため、日本経済は為替相場の変
動の影響を受けやすい。

foreign direct investment 海外からの直接
投資, 対外直接投資
◆Philippine President Benigno Aquino III has
pressed ahead with fiscal reforms and reinforced
the development of infrastructure, which have
led to increased foreign direct investment. フィ
リピンのベニグノ・アキノ3世大統領が、財政改革
を推し進め、インフラ整備を強化した結果、海外
からの直接投資も伸びた。

foreign economies 海外経済

◆Japan's exports and production have been reduced because of the slowdown of foreign
economies and the worsening of relations with
China. 海外経済の減速と日中関係の悪化で、日本
の輸出や生産は低迷している。

foreign exchange 外国為替, 外国為替取引,
為替差損益, 外貨 （=forex）
Foreign Exchange and Foreign Trade Law　外
国為替及び外国貿易法, 外為法
foreign exchange bill　外国為替手形
foreign exchange contract　外国為替予約
foreign exchange control　外国為替管理, 為替
制限（foreign exchange restriction）
foreign exchange earnings　外貨収入
foreign exchange gain　為替差益
foreign exchange position　外国為替持ち高
foreign exchange restriction［control］　為替
制限
Foreign Exchange Sale［Purchase］Ticket　外
国為替取引メモ
foreign exchange trader　外国為替トレーダー
foreign exchange trading［dealing］　外国為替
取引
**Foreign Exchange and Foreign Trade
Control Law** 外為法
◆A revised Foreign Exchange and Foreign Trade
Control Law has been enacted to enable the swift
freezing of funds belonging to terrorist organizations. テロ組織の資金［資産］凍結を迅速に行うた
めの改正外為法は、すでに成立して［制定されて］
いる。

**Foreign Exchange and Foreign Trade
Law** 外国為替及び外国貿易法
◆The revised Foreign Exchange and Foreign
Trade Law allows Japan to suspend or limit remittances and trade with North Korea. 改正外国
為替及び外国貿易法によると、北朝鮮に関して日
本は送金や貿易を停止・制限することができる。

foreign exchange bank 外国為替銀行, 貿易
決済銀行
◆The Bank of China, one of the country's
biggest state-owned lenders, has shut the account
of the Foreign Trade Bank of North Korea, the
country's main foreign-exchange bank. 中国国有
銀行最大手の中国銀行が、北朝鮮の主要外国為替
銀行［貿易決済銀行］の「朝鮮貿易銀行」の口座を
閉鎖した。

foreign exchange fluctuations 為替変動,
為替相場の変動 （=foreign currency
fluctuations）
◆Japan's economy is vulnerable to foreign exchange fluctuations as Japanese firms depend so
heavily on foreign demand. 日本企業は外需に大
きく依存しているため、日本経済は為替相場の変
動の影響を受けやすい。

foreign exchange loss 為替差損

◆The exporting companies are attempting to avoid further foreign exchange losses arising from the yen's appreciation by buying forward contracts. 輸出企業は、買い為替予約（買い予約）で円高による為替差損を避けようとしている。

foreign exchange margin trading　外国為替証拠金取引
◆In foreign exchange margin trading, investors repeatedly trade U.S. dollars, euros and other currencies, aiming to profit from fluctuations in exchange rates. 外国為替証拠金取引では、為替の変動による利益を狙って、投資家が米ドルやユーロなどの外貨を繰り返し売買する。

foreign exchange market　外国為替市場, 為替市場, 為替相場
◆Banks participating in direct yen-yuan trading in the Tokyo interbank foreign exchange market will trade the yen and the yuan at an exchange rate calculated on the basis of actual supply and demand. 東京外国為替市場で円・人民元の直接取引に参加する銀行は、実際の需給などをもとに算出した取引レートで、円と人民元を銀行間で取引する。◆Interbank trading between the U.S. dollar and the Chinese currency yuan accounts for 99. 3 percent of the Shanghai foreign exchange market. 米ドルと中国の通貨・人民元の銀行間取引［銀行間為替取引］が、上海外国為替市場の99.3％を占めている。◆On foreign exchange markets, the excessively strong yen has been corrected and the weaker yen is becoming the norm. 為替市場では、超円高が是正され、円安が定着してきた。

foreign exchange rate　外国為替レート, 外国為替相場, 為替相場, 為替レート, 外貨交換比率［交換率］
fluctuations in foreign exchange rates　為替相場の変動
forward foreign exchange rate　先物予約レート
nominal (foreign) exchange rate　名目為替レート
the realignment of foreign exchange rates　為替レートの調整
◆Nominal foreign exchange rates are quoted at ￥110 to the U.S. dollar or ￥135 to the euro as we see in the media. 名目為替レートは、新聞や雑誌で見られるように、1ドル＝110円とか、1ユーロ＝135円と表示される。◆The Egyptian currency's foreign exchange rate plunged by 20 percent between January 2011 and July 2013. エジプトの通貨の外貨交換率は、2011年1月から2013年7月にかけて、20％も急落した。

foreign exchange trading　外国為替取引
◆The Diet enacted laws to impose restrictions on foreign exchange trading with low margin requirements. 少ない証拠金での外国為替取引［外国為替証拠金取引］を規制する法律が、国会で成立した。

foreign financial institution　海外の金融機関
◆Amid the ongoing European financial crisis, concern is mounting in South Korea that the value of its won currency may steeply decline if foreign financial institutions and investors withdraw funds from the country. 今回の欧州金融危機の影響で、韓国では、海外の金融機関や投資家が同国から資金を引き揚げたら、韓国の通貨ウォンの相場が急落しかねない、との懸念［危機感］が強まっている。

foreign investment　外国・海外からの投資, 外国資本の投資, 対内投資, 対外投資

foreign investment to Japan　海外からの対日投資, 対日投資
◆Bold corporate tax cuts and deregulation to realize economic revitalization can also be expected to help lure foreign investment to Japan. 大胆な企業減税［法人税減税］と経済活性化を実現するための規制緩和は、海外からの対日投資を呼び込む効果も期待される。

foreign investor　外国人投資家, 海外投資家, 外国投資企業, 外国資本, 外資
foreign investor buying　外国人買い, 外国人の買い
foreign investor interest　外国からの資本
foreign investor shareholding limit　海外投資家の株式保有限度額
◆Foreign investors, including Japanese firms, regard Thailand's political climate with its repeated coups as a risk factor for investing in the country. 日本企業など外国資本は、クーデターが繰り返されるタイの政治風土を、対タイ投資のリスク要因と見なしている。◆In the joint venture with an Indian investment bank, Tokyo Marine Holdings Inc. put up about 26%, the maximum a foreign investor is allowed in an Indian company, of the new firm's capital. インドの投資銀行との合弁事業で、東京海上ホールディングスは、新会社の資本金の約26％（外資の持ち分比率の上限）を出資した。◆One factor considered responsible for the recent stock market plunge is that foreign investors who purchased Japanese stocks in large quantities have started to sell their shareholdings. 今回の株安を招いたと思われる要因の一つは、日本株を大量に買った海外投資家［外国人投資家］が、保有株を売りに転じたことだ。

foreign product　海外製品, 外国製品
◆The weaker yen helps exporters, but close attention must be paid to the fact that the excessive depreciation of the yen will further increase the prices of imports of LNG and other foreign products. 円安は輸出企業にはプラスだが、円安が行き過ぎると、天然液化ガス（LNG）など海外製品の輸入額が一段と増えることにも、警戒が必要である。

foreign production　海外生産
rate of foreign production　海外生産比率

foreign trade　外国貿易, 外国取引, 貿易取引,

貿易

American foreign trade definitions　アメリカ貿易定義

conduct foreign trade　貿易取引を行う

degree of dependence on ［upon］foreign trade　貿易依存度

dependence on ［upon］foreign trade　貿易依存,貿易依存度

engage in foreign trade　貿易に従事する

foreign trade accelerator　外国貿易加速度因子

foreign trade activity　貿易活動

Foreign Trade Bank of Russia　ロシア外国取引銀行

foreign trade business　貿易業

foreign trade by country　国別外国貿易

foreign trade by region　地域別外国貿易

foreign trade control　貿易管理

foreign trade credits　貿易信用

foreign trade data　貿易統計

foreign trade deficit　貿易赤字

foreign trade definition　外国貿易条件定義

foreign trade elasticity　貿易弾力性,外国貿易弾力性

foreign trade finance　貿易金融

foreign trade index　貿易指数
　（=index of foreign trade）

foreign trade marketing　貿易マーケティング

foreign trade multiplier　貿易乗数,外国貿易乗数

foreign trade on consignment basis　委託販売貿易

foreign trade payments certificate　外国貿易支払い票

foreign trade policy　貿易政策,外国貿易政策

foreign trade quotation　外国貿易相場表

foreign trade ratio　外国貿易比率

foreign trade statistics　貿易統計

foreign trade unit value index　貿易単価［価格］指数　（=unit value indexes of foreign trade）

foreign trade zone　外国貿易地帯

gains from foreign trade　貿易利益

private foreign trade　民間外国貿易,民間貿易

quantity index of foreign trade　貿易数量指数

unfavorable balance in foreign trade　輸入超過,外国貿易の逆調

Foreign Trade Bank of North Korea　朝鮮貿易銀行
　◆The Bank of China, one of the country's biggest state-owned lenders, has shut the account of the Foreign Trade Bank of North Korea, the country's main foreign-exchange bank. 中国国有銀行最大手の中国銀行が,北朝鮮の主要外国為替銀行［貿易決済銀行］の「朝鮮貿易銀行」の口座を閉鎖した。

forex　（名）為替,外国為替,為替相場（forex rate）,フォレックス,FX　（⇒foreign exchange）

average forex rate　平均為替レート

forex business　為替取引
　（=foreign exchange transaction, forex trading）

forex gains　為替差益

forex intervention　為替介入

forex losses　為替差損

forex moves　為替相場の動き

forex rate　為替相場,為替レート

forex risk　為替リスク

forex reserves　外貨準備高,外貨準備
　（=foreign currency reserves, foreign exchange reserves, foreign reserves）
　◆Japan's forex reserves topped the $1 trillion mark for the first time in four months at the end of November, supported by sharp gains in market prices of U.S. Treasury bonds. 日本の11月末の外貨準備高は,米国債の時価評価額の大幅増に支えられて,4か月ぶりに1兆ドル台を超えた。

form　（名）書式,様式,形式,用紙,申込み書,法律文書などの決まり文句,慣用句,フォーム

a computer readable form　コンピュータで読み取れる書式

in the form attached to this agreement as Exhibit A　付属書類Aとして本契約書に添付する書式で

in the form of　〜の形式で,〜の様式で,〜の形で

MAR form policy　MARフォーム（英国で1982年に制定された英文貨物海上保険証券の種類）

S.G. form policy　S.G.フォーム（英文貨物海上保険証券の種類で,英国式の古いフォーム）
　◆A copy of such standard form in use as of the date of this agreement is attached hereto as Exhibit C. 本契約締結日に使用されている当該標準書式の写しは,付属書類Cとして本契約書に添付してある。

form a part of this agreement　本契約の一部を構成する
　◆The headings to the Articles of this agreement are to facilitate reference only, do not form a part of this agreement and shall not in any way affect the interpretation of this agreement. 本契約条項の見出しは,参照の便宜だけの目的のもので,本契約の一部を構成するものではなく,いかなる場合でも本契約の解釈に影響を与えないものとする。

form a tie-up with　〜と提携する

◆Itochu Corp. formed a tie-up with Chinese food firm to strengthen bargaining power in the global food market. 伊藤忠商事は、世界の食料市場での交渉力［買付け交渉力］を強化するため、中国の食料企業と提携した。

formal （形）形式的な、形式ばった、形の、形態［形式、外形］上の、うわべだけの、実質を伴わない、堅苦しい、堅い、公式の、正式の、本式の、格式の高い、儀礼的な、秩序だった、整然とした、調和［釣り合い］のとれた、規則正しい、理論的な、系統立った、組織的な、正規の、伝統的な、因習的な、慣例による、フォーマル

formal announcement　公式発表

formal arrangement　正式の取決め

formal authorization　正式の認可、公認

formal claim　本クレーム

formal lawsuit　本訴

formal party　形式的当事者

formal proposal　正式提案、正式見積り書

formal status　法律上の分類

formal agreement　正式契約、正式合意
◆Economy, Trade and Industry Minister Takeo Hiranuma will reach a formal agreement on the natural gas development projects in the meeting with Iranian Oil Minister Bijan Namdar-Zangeneh and Qatari Energy and Industry Minister Abdullah Bin Hamad al-Attiyah. この天然ガス事業については、平沼経済産業相がイランのザンギャネ石油相、カタールのアティーヤ・エネルギー工業相と会談して正式に合意する。

formal contract　正式契約, 方式契約, 要式契約
◆A formal contract is expected to be concluded later this year. 正式契約は、今年末に締結される見通しだ。◆After signing a memorandum of understanding in April, a formal contract has yet to be finalized and negotiations are likely to drag on for longer than expected. 4月に基本合意書に署名してから正式契約の最終調整は済んでおらず、交渉は予想以上に長引きそうだ。

formal investigation　本格調査
◆The NHTSA is set to launch a formal investigation into the power steering glitch in Toyota's Corolla subcompact. 米高速道路交通安全局（NHTSA）は、トヨタの小型乗用車カローラの電動パワー・ステアリングの不具合の本格調査を開始する方針だ。

formation, acquisition or sale of any subsidiary　子会社の設立、買取または売却

formation and performance of this agreement　本契約の成立と履行

formation, validity, construction, and performance of this agreement　本契約の成立、有効性、解釈と履行

formulate　（動）策定する、形成する、立案する、案出する、方針などを打ち出す、（計画・提案などを）まとめる、明確に述べる、体系化する、公式化［定式化］する、（製法に基づいて）製造する、製剤化する
◆Chapter 11 bankruptcy provides for a business to continue operations while formulating a plan to repay its creditors. 米連邦改正破産法11章の破産の規定では、企業は事業を継続する一方、債権者への債務返済計画を策定することができる。

formulation　（名）策定、形成、立案、案出、まとめ、体系化、公式化、表現の仕方、（薬などの）調合、成分、薬剤、化粧品

forthwith　（副）直ちに、至急

forthwith on request　要求のあり次第直ちに

forthwith upon the execution of this agreement　本契約の締結後直ちに

forthwith upon termination of this agreement　本契約の終了後直ちに
◆Forthwith upon termination of this agreement for any reason, ABC shall immediately pay all amounts payable under this agreement. 理由のいかんを問わず本契約の終了後直ちに、ABCは、本契約に基づいて期限が到来したすべての金額を直ちに支払うものとする。

forum　（名）裁判所、裁判地、法廷地
◆The suit, action or proceedings the guarantor brought is an inconvenient forum. 保証人が提起した訴訟または訴訟手続きは、不便な法廷地である。

forward　（名）先渡し契約、先渡取引、先物予約　（動）出荷する、発送する、積み出す、送付する、送達する、転送する、促進する　（形）先物の、先払いの

charges forward　諸掛着払い

forward a call　電話を転送する

forward business　先物取引

forward currency contract　為替先物, 為替予約

forward delivery　先渡し

forward earnings　予想利益

forward linkage effect　前方連関効果

forward margin　先物マージン, 直先差（直物為替と先物為替との開き）

forward order　先物注文

forward position　先物持ち高

forward premium　先物プレミアム（先物為替相場が直物為替相場より高いこと）

forward price　先物価格, 先物値段

forward pricing　先物価格

forward quotations［rate］　先物相場

forward rate agreement　金利先渡し契約, FRA

forward sales　先物販売

forward shipment　先積み

forward spread　フォワード・スプレッド（直物相場と先物相場の開き）

forward stock　店頭在庫

forward supply contract　先物注文契約

forward transaction 先物取引
（=forward operation）
◆The purchaser shall forward full particulars of such claim, accompanied by an authorized surveyor's certificate of inspection of quality and quantity of the products delivered in dispute, to the seller by registered airmail within 30 days after such notification. 買い主は、当該通知後30日以内に、引き渡された問題の製品の品質と数量に関する公認鑑定人の検査証明書を添付して、当該クレームの詳細を記載した書面を書留航空便で売り主に送付するものとする。◆We have forwarded to you the invoice in duplicate. 送り状2通は、貴社宛発送済みです。

forward contract 先物契約, 先物取引, 先渡し取引, フォワード
　forward contracts on securities　有価証券先渡し取引
　have a long position in a forward contract　先渡し取引でロングポジションを取る, 買い持ちとなる
　have a short position in a forward contract　先渡し取引でショートポジションを取る, 売り持ちとなる

forward exchange 先物為替
　foreign exchange dealing　先物為替取引
　foreign exchange dealing rate　先物為替取引相場
　foreign exchange operation　先物為替操作
　forward exchange market　先物為替市場
　forward exchange policy　先物為替政策
　forward (exchange) rate　先物為替相場
　forward exchange transaction　先物為替取引

forward exchange contract 先物為替の予約, 為替予約
　◆We acquired a 60-day forward exchange contract for US $1,000,000, in anticipation of an increase in the spot rates for US dollars. 当社は、米ドルの直物レートが上がるのを期待して100万米ドル、60日後の先物為替予約を取得した。

forwarder （名）運送代理人, 貨物運送取扱い業者
（=forwarding agent, freight forwarder）
　forwarder's cargo receipt　フォワーダー・カーゴ・レシート（運送代理人が荷主に発行する受取証）
　freight forwarder　運送業者, 運送会社, 小口運送業, 海運業者, 乙仲

forwarding （名）発送, 出荷, 輸送, 転送, 促進, 推進
　forwarding address　転送先
　forwarding agency　運送業者, 運送会社, 乙仲（おつなか）
　forwarding agent　運送業者, 運送取扱い人, 運送代行業者

forwarding business　運送業
forwarding by mail［post］　郵送
forwarding charges　輸送費
forwarding charges clause　輸送費用約款, 継搬費用条項
forwarding clause　輸送約款
forwarding commission　運送手数料
forwarding instructions　運送指図書
forwarding merchant　運送取扱い人
forwarding order　貨物託送状
forwarding station　発送駅

fossil fuels 化石燃料
　◆Japan has to import most of its fossil fuels from the Middle East in which supplies and prices remain unstable. 日本は、化石燃料の大半を、供給量も価格も不安定な中東からの輸入に頼っている。
　◆Japan lost more than ¥3 trillion of national wealth in 2011 to import fossil fuels as a result of the power scarcity due to the suspension of all nuclear power reactors. 全原発の停止による電力不足の結果、日本は化石燃料を輸入するため、2011年度は3兆円以上の国富を流出させた。

FPA 単独海損不担保, 分損不担保（free from particular averageの略）
　◆Notwithstanding the above, the seller may, if the seller deems it necessary, insure for an amount in excess of the amount set forth above or risks other than FPA for the purchaser's account. 上記の規定にかかわらず、売り主が必要と見なした場合、売り主は上記の金額を超える金額の保険を付ける、またはFPA以外の危険に対して買い主の負担で保険を付けることができるものとする。

FPA Institute Cargo Clause FPA協会貨物保険約款
　◆The seller shall, for its own account, effect marine insurance only free from particular average（FPA Institute Cargo Clause）for the amount of CIF value of the products plus 10 percent. 売り主は、売り主の自己負担で、本商品のCIF価格プラス10％の保険金額により単独海損［分損］不担保条件（FPA協会貨物保険約款）の海上保険を付けるものとする。

France's Competition Commission フランスの競争評議会
　◆France's Competition Commission has ordered Sony, Matsushita and Philips to pay fines for allegedly concluding price-fixing agreements on retail goods with their local distributors. フランスの競争評議会は、国内販売店と小売電気製品の価格維持協定を結んだとして、ソニー、松下電器産業とフィリップスに罰金の支払いを命じた。

franchise （動）営業免許を与える, 独占販売権を与える （名）事業免許, 営業免許, 営業権, 独占販売権, 一手販売権, 加盟権, 特許, 特権, 営業網, 営業地域, 事業上のウェイト, フラ

ンチャイズ

business franchise　営業基盤 (operating franchise), 事業基盤, 市場支配力

continuing franchise fee　継続フランチャイズ料

franchise agent　フランチャイジー

franchise chain system　フランチャイズ制

franchise risk　顧客リスク (顧客とのトラブルで企業の社会的信用を失うリスク)

franchise tax　事業免許税, 営業税, 法人税

franchises　営業網, 営業権

grant the franchise and license　フランチャイズとライセンスを許諾する

nationwide franchises　全国的な販売網

state franchise tax　州法人税

franchise agreement　フランチャイズ契約, フランチャイズ契約書
◆The guarantor waives any and all notices of nonpayment or nonperformance or demand for payment or performance of such obligations under the franchise agreement. 保証人は、フランチャイズ契約に基づく当該債務の不払いまたは不履行について一切の通知を受ける権利と、当該債務の支払いまたは履行について一切の催告通知を受ける権利を放棄する。

fraudulent business　不正取引, ダーク・ビジネス
◆The revision of the Nationality Law may be abused as part of a fraudulent business by means of fabricating parental ties. 国籍法の改正は、親子関係の偽装認知などでダーク・ビジネスに悪用される可能性がある。

fraudulent business tactics　詐欺商法
◆We must take caution against fraudulent business tactics that prey on people's interest in the 2020 Tokyo Olympics. 2020年東京オリンピックへの関心につけ込んだ詐欺商法には、注意する必要がある。

fraudulent gains　不当利得

FRB　米連邦準備制度理事会 (Federal Reserve Board の略)
◆Indonesia has enjoyed decent economic growth since the global financial crisis of 2008 due to the U.S. FRB's quantitative easing and higher prices of primary commodities such as coal and palm oil as the country's major exports. インドネシアは、2008年の世界金融危機以降、米連邦準備制度理事会 (FRB) の量的金融緩和とインドネシアの主要輸出品である石炭、パーム油など一次産品の高値に支えられ、高い経済成長を享受している。

free　(形)自由な, 自由主義の, 制約[制限]を受けない, 解放された, 釈放された, ひまな, 無料の, ただの, 気前の良い, 物惜しみをしない, 率直な, オープンな

for free　ただで, 無料で, 無償で, ～だけはハッキリ (言っておく)

free alongside ship [vessel]　船側渡し

free and fair trade　自由で公正な貿易

free enterprise　自由企業

free hand　自由裁量, 行動の自由, 決定の自由

free laborer　非組合労働者, 日雇い労働者

free market　自由市場

free on board　積み込み渡し (で), 本船渡し (の), FOB [f.o.b.]

free on rail　貨車渡し, 貨車渡しの[で], FOR [f.o.r.]

free port　自由港, 無関税港

on an f.o.b [free on board] basis　本船渡し価格で

free and clear of　～がまったくない, ～の制約がない, ～の制約を受けることがない, ～を一切負担しない, 担保権などが付いていない, 担保権などが付いていない状態で, 担保権などの対象でない
◆The Company has good and marketable title to each item of personal property used by it in the business of the Company, free and clear of all liens or security interests. 対象会社は、対象会社の事業で対象会社が使用している各動産 (担保権は一切付いていない) を売買できる正当な権原をもっている。

free from　～から自由の, ～のない, ～を負担しない

free from all average　全損のみ担保 FAA (=total loss only)

free from capture and seizure clause　捕獲拿捕 (だほ) 不担保約款, F.C.& S.

free from liability for　～に対する責任を負わないで, ～に対する責任の負担なしで

free from defects　瑕疵 (かし) がない, 欠陥がない (=free of defects)
◆The seller warrants that the Goods will be free from defects in material and workmanship for a period as specified in this agreement. 売り主は、本契約で定める期間、本商品が材料と仕上げの面で欠陥がないことを保証する。◆The seller warrants that the Product shall be free from defects in title. 売り主は、本製品の所有権に瑕疵がないことを保証する。

free from particular average　単独海損不担保, 分損不担保, FPA (free fromは「～を負担しない」という意味)
◆The seller shall, for its own account, effect marine insurance only free from particular average (FPA Institute Cargo Clause) for the amount of CIF value of the products plus 10 percent. 売り主は、売り主の自己負担で、本商品のCIF価格プラス10％の保険金額により単独海損[分損]不担保条件 (FPA協会貨物保険約款) の海上保険を付けるものとする。

free of　～がない, ～を受けない

free of any claim or suit by　～による請求ま

たは提訴を受けないで, 〜による請求また
は提訴を受けることなしに
free of any claims of infringement of a third
party's rights　第三者の権利侵害の申立て
を受けない, 第三者の権利侵害の申立てが
ない状態で
free of defects　欠陥がない, 瑕疵 (かし) がな
い (=free from defects)
free of any obligation of confidence　秘密
保持義務なしに
◆Such information was rightfully communicated
to the receiving party free of any obligation of
confidence subsequent to the time it was communicated to the receiving party by the disclosing party. 当該情報は, 開示当事者が受領当事者
に通知した時点以後に, 秘密保持義務なしに受領
当事者に合法的に通知された。
free of any rightful claim for　〜の正当な
申立てのない状態で
◆The seller warrants that the products shall be
sold and delivered free of any rightful claim of
any third party for infringement of any patent,
trademark or other industrial rights by virtue
of the use of the products by the purchaser or
end-users indicated in this agreement in the purchaser's country. 売り主は, 買い主の国内の買い
主または本契約に定めるエンド・ユーザーが本製
品を使用することによって特許, 商標またはその
他の財産権 (工業所有権) が侵害されたとする第三
者の正当な申立てのない状態で, 本製品を販売し,
引き渡すことを保証する。
free of charge　無料で, 無償で
◆Licensor shall furnish Licensee with technical
documents stated in Paragraph 3 of this Article
free of charge. ライセンサーは, ライセンシーに
対して本条3項に明示する技術書類を無償で提供す
る。◆We will supply you with our samples free
of charge. 当方見本は, 無料で差し上げます。
free trade　自由貿易, 自由貿易主義
ASEAN Free Trade Area　アセアン自由貿易
地域, AFTA (1993年に発足したアセアンの
自由貿易協定のこと)
ASEAN Free Trade Arrangement　アセアン
(ASEAN) 自由貿易地域
barriers to free trade　自由貿易への障壁 [障
害]
European Free Trade Association　欧州自由貿
易連合
free international trade　自由貿易
free trade accord　自由貿易協定
Free Trade Area of the Asia-Pacific　アジア太
平洋自由貿易地域
free trade association　自由貿易連合
free trade group　自由貿易派
free trade movement　自由貿易運動, 自由貿易
主義, 自由貿易化
free trade pact　自由貿易協定

free trade policy　自由貿易政策
free trade sector　自由貿易部門
free trade system　自由貿易体制
free trade tariff　自由貿易関税
gains from foreign trade　貿易利益
Latin America Free Trade Association　ラテン
アメリカ自由貿易連合, ラフタ, LAFTA
(1981年にLatin American Integration
Association (ラテンアメリカ統合連合) に
改組)
North American Free Trade Agreement　北米
自由貿易協定, ナフタ, NAFTA
North American free-trade area　北米自由貿
易圏
regional free-trade area　地域的自由貿易圏
U.S.-Canada Free Trade Agreement　米加自由
貿易協定
◆If it is not certain five agricultural items, including rice and wheat, will be treated as exceptions to free trade, the government will not hesitate to pull out from the TPP negotiations. コメ
や麦など農産品5項目を自由貿易の聖域として確保
できなければ, 政府はTPP (環太平洋経済連携協定)
交渉からの脱退も辞さない方針だ。◆The APEC's
special statement came out in favor of the promotion of free trade. アジア太平洋経済協力会議
(APEC) の特別声明は, 自由貿易推進を打ち出し
た。◆The World Trade Organization has a long
way to go before it can reach a consensus on a
new set of rules governing free trade. 世界貿易機
関 (WTO) が貿易自由化の新ルールに関して合意が
得られるまでの道のりは, まだまだ遠い。
free trade agreement　自由貿易協定, FTA
◆A free trade agreement is a treaty between two
or more nations and territories seeking to reduce
or abolish tariffs on industrial, agricultural and
other products. 自由貿易協定 (FTA) は, 鉱工業
品や農産品 [農産物] の関税の引下げや撤廃を求め
る2か国以上の国や地域間の協定だ。◆In his State
of the Union address delivered on February 12,
2013, U.S. President Barack Obama threw his
weight behind a deal that would encompass half
the world's economic output by calling for talks
on a far-reaching free trade agreement with the
EU. 2013年2月12日に行った一般教書演説で, オバ
マ米大統領は, 欧州連合 (EU) との広範な自由貿易
協定の交渉を呼びかけて, 世界の経済生産高の半
分を含むことになる協定を後押しした。◆In terms
of trade volume, South Korea is currently among
the top 10 countries partly due to its efforts to
promote free trade agreements with the United
States, the European Union and others. 貿易額
で, 韓国は現在, 米国や欧州連合 (EU) などとの
自由貿易協定 (FTA) 推進策を軸に, 世界トップ10
入りを果たしている。◆Japan lags behind other
countries in terms of bilateral free trade agreements. 日本は, 二国間の自由貿易協定 (FTA) で他

国に後れをとっている。◆The APEC forum leaders agreed to the importance of promoting free trade. アジア太平洋経済協力会議（APEC）の首脳は、自由貿易の推進が重要であるとの認識で合意した。

free trade area 自由貿易地域, 自由貿易圏
◆The currency strategies of China and the Unites States also seem to affect the issue of a free trade area. 中国と米国の通貨戦略も、自由貿易圏の問題に影響を及ぼしているようだ。

Free Trade Area of the Asia-Pacific アジア太平洋自由貿易地域, アジア太平洋自由貿易圏, FTAAP（APEC域内での自由貿易圏構想。⇒FTAAP）
◆The framework of a Free Trade Area of the Asia-Pacific is aimed at liberalizing trade and investment as well as the elimination of nontariff barriers, regulatory reform and smoother logistics. アジア太平洋自由貿易地域（FTAAP）の枠組みは、貿易や投資の自由化のほか、非関税障壁の撤廃、規制改革、物流の円滑化などを目指している。

free trade negotiations 自由貿易交渉
（=free trade talks）
◆It seems inevitable that the TPP free trade negotiations will drag on for a protracted period. TPP（環太平洋経済連携協定）の自由貿易交渉が今後、長期間にわたって続くことは避けられないようだ。

free trade talks 自由貿易交渉
（=free trade negotiations）
◆Japan, which is being pushed to further open its agricultural markets, is taking a wait-and-see attitude toward the free trade talks. 農業分野での一層の市場開放を迫られる日本は、自由貿易交渉については様子見の構えだ。◆The Doha Round of WTO free trade talks broke down over conflicting opinions between the United States and Europe and between industrialized and developing countries. 世界貿易機関（WTO）の新多角的貿易交渉（ドーハ・ラウンド）は、米国と欧州、先進国と途上国の間の主張対立で決裂した。

free trade zone 自由貿易圏, 自由貿易地域, 保税地域 （=free trade bloc）
◆By starting talks on a comprehensive partnership agreement, the EU and the United States will take the first step toward creating a giant free trade zone that would account for about 50 percent of the world's gross domestic product. 包括的連携協定の交渉を開始することで、欧州連合（EU）と米国は、世界のGDP（国内総生産）の5割近くを占める巨大な自由貿易圏の創設に一歩踏み出すことになる。

free trading 自由貿易
Agreement on ASEAN Preferential Trading Arrangements アセアン特恵貿易協定
claim to be free trading 自由貿易を表看板にする
free trading bloc 自由貿易地域, 自由貿易圏

freedom of navigation at sea 航海の自由
◆Japan-ASEAN ties are meaningful in ensuring regional security, particularly freedom of navigation at sea. 日本とアセアン（東南アジア諸国連合）との関係は、地域の安全保障、とりわけ航海の自由を確保するうえで重要である。

freeze （動）凍結する, 据え置く, 中止する, 停止する
◆The U.S. government froze the assets of four individuals and eight entities that were involved in illicit activities such as money laundering, currency counterfeiting and narcotics trafficking. 米政府は、資金洗浄（マネー・ロンダリング）や通貨偽造、麻薬取引などの違法行為に関与している4個人、8団体の資産を凍結した。

freezing of funds 資金の凍結, 資産凍結
◆A revised Foreign Exchange and Foreign Trade Control Law has been enacted to enable the swift freezing of funds belonging to terrorist organizations. テロ組織の資金[資産]凍結を迅速に行うための改正外為法は、すでに成立して[制定されて]いる。

freight （名）運賃, 運送料, 貨物運送, 運送貨物
additional freight 追加運賃
freight absorption 運賃込み
freight account 運賃明細書
freight agent ［agency］ 貨物取扱い業者, 貨物取扱い人
freight agreement 貨物協定, 運賃協定
freight all kinds rate 品目無差別運賃, FAK
freight and carriage 運賃
freight and demurrage 運賃と滞船料
freight as arranged 運賃契約どおり
freight basis 運賃建て
freight bill 運賃請求書
freight broker 貨物仲立人
freight by measurement 容積貨物
freight by weight 重量貨物
freight cargo 重量荷物
freight clause 運賃収得約款
freight collect 運賃着払い, 荷受人払い運賃
freight conference 海運同盟, 運賃同盟
（=liner conference, shipping conference）
freight contract 運送契約, 貨物運送契約
（=freight engagement）
freight dumping 運賃ダンピング
freight expenses 運送費
freight forward 運賃先払い
freight free 運賃無料
freight house 貨物置き場
freight in ［inward］ 引取り運賃, 仕入運賃
freight index 運賃指数

FREI 214

freight insurance　運賃保険

freight is payable at destination　運賃は仕向け地で支払うこと

freight list　積み荷目録, 積み荷明細録, 運賃表

freight market　不定期船市場

freight note　運賃請求書

freight on delivery　運賃引換え払い

freight or carriage paid to　運送手配済み

freight out [outward]　販売運賃

freight out and home　往復運賃

freight paid　運賃支い済み

freight paid in advance　運賃前払い

freight payable at destination　運賃先払い

freight payable on outturn weight　運賃揚高払い

freight pick-up　貨物引揚げ

freight prepaid　運賃前払い

freight rate　貨物運賃, 運賃率

freight rebate　運賃割戻し

freight space　船腹

freight to collect　運賃後払い

freight ton　容積トン, 運賃トン

freight traffic　貨物運送

freight vessel　貨物船

freight/carriage and insurance paid to　運送・保険手配済み

freight/carriage paid to　運送手配済み

◆The insurance premium and freight are payable by you. 保険料と運賃の支払いは, 貴社負担です。

freight forwarder　小口運送業, 海運業者, 海貨業者(海運貨物取扱い業者でforeign freight forwarder, forwarding agentともいう), 乙仲

◆Irrevocable letter of credit provides for payment upon presentation of Supplier's invoices and shipping documents evidencing delivery of the invoiced Products to the carrier or freight forwarder. 取消不能信用状は, 供給者の請求書と, 請求書に記載した本製品を運送人または海貨業者に引き渡したことを証明する船積み書類を提示して支払いを受けるものだ。

fresh water damage　淡水濡れ損害

friendly　(形)友好的な, 好意的な, 親しい, 親善的な, 交戦状態にない, 敵対関係にない

friendly acquirer　友好的買収者

◆A "white knight" is a friendly acquirer sought by the target of an unfriendly takeover. 「ホワイト・ナイト」とは, 非友好的買収の標的の企業が探し求める友好的買収者をいう。

friendly company　友好的な企業, 友好的な企業

◆If golden shares held by a friendly company are transferred to another party, such shares could be transferred again to a hostile bidder. 友好的な企業が保有する黄金株を第三者に譲渡した場合, その黄金株はまた敵対的買収者に譲渡される可能性もある。

friendly offer　友好的買取　(=friendly acquisition, friendly takeover, friendly takeover bid)

◆White knight is a company that saves another firm threatened by a hostile takeover by making a friendly offer. ホワイト・ナイトは, 友好的な買収により, 敵対的買収の脅威にさらされている他企業を救済する企業のことだ。

from　(前)〜から, 〜で, 〜に対して

from and including　〜日から(同日を含む)

from and including 〜 up to and including　〜日から〜日まで

from the date of this agreement until the closing date　本契約締結日からクロージング日まで, 本契約日からクロージング日までの間

from the due date to date of payment in full　支払い期日から全額支払い日まで

from the due date until paid　支払い期日から支払い日まで, 支払い期日から支払い日までの期間

from time to time　随時, 適宜(てきぎ), そのつど

from time to time whenever necessary　必要な場合にはいつでも適宜(てきぎ), 必要に応じて随時

◆As used in this agreement, Licensed Products means the software products listed on Schedule B attached hereto together with all enhancements and modifications thereto as may from time to time be made by the licensor. 「使用許諾製品」とは, 本契約で使用する場合には, 本契約書に添付する付属書類Bに記載したソフトウエア製品と, ライセンサーが随時行うその改訂および変更をすべて意味する。◆For the purpose of this agreement, the prime rate shall mean that rate announced by the principal bank of the seller as its prime commercial lending rate from time to time. 本契約の目的上, プライム・レートとは, 売り主の主要取引銀行が最優遇商業貸出金利として随時発表する利率を意味する。

from year to year for one year term　1年単位で年毎に, 1年毎に1年間

◆This agreement shall be automatically renewed from year to year for one year term hence expiration of the initial term of this agreement. 本契約は, 本契約の当初の期間満了後は, 1年単位で年毎に自動更新されるものとする。

front month　直近の月, 期近物　(front monthは一番手前の月, 直近の月, つまり翌月を指す。期近物は, 石油先物取引では翌月から9か月の先物商品を指す)

◆The U.S. light crude front month contract rose a further 36 cents a barrel in after-hours electronic trading to top $50. 米国の軽質原油の翌月渡し価格は、時間外の電子取引で1バレル当たり36セント上伸して、1バレル＝50ドルを突破した。

frozen food product 冷凍食品
◆Following the discovery of frozen food products tainted with a pesticide known as malathion, Maruha Nichiro Holdings Inc. announced a voluntary recall of the products made by its subsidiary Aqli Foods. マラチオンと呼ばれる農薬（殺虫剤）が混入した冷凍食品が検出されたのを受けて、マルハニチロホールディングス（HD）は、子会社のアクリフーズ社が生産［製造］した冷凍食品を自主回収すると発表した。

FSB 金融安定化理事会、金融安定理事会
（⇒Financial Stability Board）
◆The 28 global big banks were divided into four groups by the FSB, in which Mitsubishi UFJ Financial Group Inc. is in the group with a targeted 1.5 percent capital surcharge. 世界の大手銀行28行が金融安定化理事会（FSB）で4グループに分けられたが、このうち三菱UFJフィナンシャル・グループは、1.5%の自己資本上積みを目標とするグループに入っている。

FTA 自由貿易協定 （⇒free trade agreement）
◆An expanded FTA is a key to bolstering growth in the EU indispensable to overcome its fiscal and financial crises. 自由貿易協定（FTA）の拡大は、EU（欧州連合）の財政・金融危機を克服するうえで欠かせないEUの経済成長促進のカギである。◆FTAs are a regime under which import tariffs are eliminated bilaterally or regionally. 自由貿易協定（FTA）は、2国間で、または地域で輸入関税を撤廃する制度である。◆Mexico has already signed FTAs with several countries, leading to mutually abolished tariffs. メキシコは、複数の国々、地域とFTA（自由貿易協定）をすでに締結して、相互に関税を撤廃している。

FTAAP アジア太平洋自由貿易地域、アジア太平洋自由貿易圏, エフタープ（APEC域内での自由貿易圏構想。⇒Free Trade Area of the Asia-Pacific）
◆In a joint statement released after the two-day APEC Summit in Beijing, the leaders of the 21 APEC member economies said that they would aim to realize a Free Trade Area of the Asia-Pacific (FTAAP) at the earliest possible time. 北京で行われた2日間のアジア太平洋経済協力会議（APEC）の首脳会談後に発表された共同声明で、加盟21か国・地域の首脳は、できるだけ早期に「アジア太平洋自由貿易圏（FTAAP）」構想の実現を目指すと述べた。

FTC 日本の公正取引委員会（Fair Trade Commissionの略。⇒Fair Trade Commission of Japan）
◆Dissatisfied with the FTC's decision, the companies filed an administrative lawsuit demanding that the FTC reverse its decision. 公正取引委員会の決定を不服として、企業側は同委員会の決定取消しを求める行政訴訟を起こした。◆The An-

timonopoly Law stipulates that documents submitted to FTC hearings may be disclosed to certain concerned parties upon their request. 独占禁止法は、「公正取引委員会の審判に提出された書類［記録］は特定の利害関係人の請求に基づいて利害関係人に開示することができる」と定めている。

FTC 米連邦取引委員会
（⇒Federal Trade Commissionの略）
◆The U.S. Federal Trade Commission (FTC) concluded there was not enough evidence that a Sony-BMG merger would violate U.S. antitrust laws. 米連邦取引委員会（FTC）は、ソニーとBMG（独複合メディア大手ベルテルスマンの音楽事業部門）の統合が米国の独占禁止法に違反することを示す十分な証拠はない、との結論を下した。

FTC hearings 米公正取引委員会（FTC）の審判
◆The Antimonopoly Law stipulates that documents submitted to FTC hearings may be disclosed to certain concerned parties upon their request. 独占禁止法は、「公正取引委員会の審判に提出された書類［記録］は特定の利害関係人の請求に基づいて利害関係人に開示することができる」と定めている。

fuel （動）給油する、燃料を補給［供給］する、活気づかせる、勢いづかせる、激化させる、加速する、拍車をかける、悪化させる、あおる、あおり立てる、刺激する、支持する、～を支える要因となる

be fueled by ～で動く、～で勢いづく［拍車がかかる、高まる、激化する、加速する］、～が原動力となる、～に支えられる

fuel domestic demand 国内需要を拡大する、国内需要を喚起する［刺激する］

fuel inflation インフレを加速させる、インフレ再燃をもたらす

fuel the economic bubble バブルをあおる、バブルに拍車をかける

fuel the yen's rise 円高に拍車をかける
◆A strong yen lowers the prices of imported goods and fuels deflation. 円高は輸入品の価格を下げ、デフレに拍車をかける。◆Japan's imports are also climbing because the economic recovery is fueling domestic demand. 景気回復で国内需要が拡大しているため、日本の輸入も伸びている。

fuel （名）燃料、核燃料、エネルギー、エネルギー源
◆As an abnormal situation, imports of liquefied natural gas, the fuel needed for operating power companies' thermal power stations, have increased to a massive ¥6 trillion a year after the operations of nuclear reactors were suspended around the country. 異常事態として、原子力発電所の運転が全国で停止した後、電力各社の火力発電の稼働に必要な液化天然ガス（LNG）の輸入額が、年間で6兆円もの巨額に達している。◆The deficit in goods trade in the first half of 2012 expanded sharply due to a surge in imports of fuel for ther-

mal power generation following the suspensions of nuclear power plants. 2012年上半期のモノの取引を示す貿易収支の赤字は、原発停止に伴う火力発電用燃料輸入の急増で、急速に膨らんだ。

fuel imports 燃料輸入 （=imports of fuel)
◆If the exchange rate remains around ￥90 to the dollar for the next 12 months, income equivalent to 0.6 percent of Japan's GDP will flow overseas mainly due to higher fuel imports stemming from the suspension of nuclear power reactors. 為替相場が今後1年間、1ドル＝90円程度の水準が続いた場合、主に原子力発電所の運転停止に伴う燃料輸入の増加により、日本の国内総生産（GDP）の0.6%相当の所得が海外に流出する。

fulfill [fulfil] （動）（義務や約束などを）果たす，実現する，達成する，（可能性を）最大限に実現する，（目的などに）かなう，（命令や指示に）従う
◆Any failure, whether willful, through neglect or otherwise, of either party to perform or fulfill any of its duties, obligations or covenants in this agreement shall constitute a breach of this agreement. 故意であれ、怠慢またはその他によるものであれ、本契約における各当事者の責務、義務または約束ごとを各当事者が履行または達成できない場合、これは本契約の違反を構成するものとする。

full （形)完全な，全部の，十分な，全面的，正式の，正規の，詳しい，充実した，総額の （副)完全に，十分に，たっぷり，全面的に，正式に，詳しく （名)全部，十分，真っ盛り，絶頂期

full amount 全額，満額

full and accurate 完全、正確な、詳細かつ正確な

full and complete 完全な, 詳細かつ完全な

full and effective assignment, conveyance and transfer 完全かつ効力のある譲渡, full and proper books and records, 完全かつ適正な帳簿と記録

full force and effect 全面的に有効な, 完全に有効な

full payment, performance and observance 完全な支払い、履行と遵守

full performance 完全な履行

full service 完全なサービス

full set of 〜一式

full, clear and accurate books and records 完全、明瞭かつ正確な帳簿と記録
◆Licensee shall keep full, clear and accurate books and records of Products subject to the running royalty. ライセンシーは、ランニング・ロイヤルティの対象である［対象となる］本製品の完全、明瞭かつ正確な帳簿（会計帳簿）と記録を保持するものとする。

full responsibility 全責任，一切の責任
◆Licensee shall, during Engineer's stay in New York, undertakes the full responsibility for Engineer's health, life, body, property, etc. ライセン

シーは、技術者のニューヨーク滞在中、技術者の健康、生命、身体、財産等に対して全責任を負うものとする。

full-scale negotiations 本格交渉
◆Japan has yet to enter full-scale TPP negotiations, but the LDP has not presented concrete measures to prepare for the liberalization of trade, including steps to bolster competitiveness in the agricultural sector. 日本が環太平洋経済連携協定（TPP）の本格交渉に入るのはこれからだが、自民党は、農業分野での競争力強化策など、貿易自由化に備えた具体策をまだ示していない。

full-scale operation 本格稼働、フル稼働
◆The plant, constructed as the joint venture of Sumitomo Corp. and Kazakhstan's state-owned resource firm to extract rare earths by refining soil left in a uranium mine, is scheduled to start full-scale operations in the nation in November 2012. 住友商事とカザフスタンの国営資源企業の合弁事業として、ウラン鉱山で採掘された残土を精錬してレア・アースを抽出するために建設された同工場は、2012年11月からカザフスタンで本格稼働に入る。

full written notice of 〜を詳細に記載した通知書、〜を詳細に記載した書面による通知
◆Full written notice of the purchaser's claim accompanied by a licensed surveyor's report when the quality or quantity of the products is in dispute shall be sent by registered airmail by the purchaser to the seller within 20 days after the above notification. 本製品の品質または数量について争いがある場合、買い主は、上記通知後20日以内に、買い主のクレームを詳細に記載した通知書に公定鑑定人の報告書を添付して、書留航空郵便で売り主に送付するものとする。

fully authorized to 全面的に〜する権限を与えられている
◆Each party is fully authorized to deal generally with and to make this agreement respecting the subject matter hereof. 各当事者は、本契約の主題について全般的に取引し、本契約を締結する権限を全面的に与えられている。

fully bound by 〜に全面的に拘束される
◆A party hereto may sell all or any portion of the shares of the new company then owned by it to a third party only on condition that such purchaser agrees in writing, concurrently with such sale, to be fully bound by the terms and conditions of this agreement. 本契約当事者は、当該当事者がその時点で保有する新会社の株式の全部または一部を第三者に売却することができる。ただし、これは、当該購入者が売買時に本契約の条件に全面的に拘束されることに書面で同意した場合にかぎる。

fully furnished living accommodations 一切が備わった住居、完備した住居
◆Licensee shall arrange fully furnished living accommodations for Engineer. ライセンシーは、技術者のために完備した住居の手配をするものとする。

fully paid 全額払込み済みの, 全額払込み方式の, 全額払込み済みで
◆All such issued and outstanding shares are validly issued, fully paid and nonassessable. 当該発行済み社外株式は, すべて有効に発行され, 全額払込み済みで, 追加払込みの請求はないものとする。

fully paid-up license 全額払込み済みライセンス

functional currency 機能通貨
◆Local currencies are generally considered the functional currencies outside the United States. 米国外では, 一般に現地通貨を機能通貨と見なしています。

fund (動)資金を調達する, 積み立てる, 資金を賄(まか)う, 資金を提供する, 拠出する, 出資する, 赤字などを補填(ほてん)する
amounts funded 積立額
be fully funded 十分積み立ててある
fund large public expenditures 巨額の財政赤字を賄う
fund through issuance of debt 債券の発行で資金を調達する
◆A petrochemical plant funded equally by BASF and Chinese government-owned China Petroleum & Chemical Corporation started full operation in the suburbs of Nanjing. ドイツの大手化学メーカーBASFと中国国有の中国石油化工集団(SINOPEC)が折半出資した石油化学プラントが, 南京市郊外で本格稼動した。◆The U.S. "Buy American" provision requires any public projects funded by stimulus money to use only U.S.-made products. 米国のバイ・アメリカン条項は, 経済対策資金で賄われる公共工事に米国製製品の使用を義務付けている。

fund (名)資金, 基金, 積立金, ファンド
additional funds 追加資金
Asian Development Fund アジア開発基金
buyout fund 買収ファンド
development fund 開発基金, 開発資金
fund management 資金運用, 資金管理, 資金運用管理, 投資運用, 投資管理, 投資顧問
fund manager 資金運用担当者
fund raising 資金調達, 資本調達
growth fund グロース・ファンド
investment fund 投資信託
quick fund 当座資金
set up a fund 基金を設立する
supply of funds 資金の供給
trust fund 信託基金
◆A stock split is a measure designed to enable investors, including those with only limited funds, to invest in a company by reducing the share purchase unit. 株式分割は, 株式の購入単位を小口化して, 少額の資金しかない投資家でも企業に投資できるようにするための手段[資本政策]だ。◆Cerberus Capital Management LP, the U.S. fund, proposed eight director candidates of its own at the shareholders meeting of Seibu Holdings Inc., but it failed to gain majority approval for its proposal. 米ファンドのサーベラス・キャピタル・マネジメントは, 西部ホールディングスの株主総会で独自の取締役候補8人を提案したが, この提案に対して多数の承認は得られなかった。◆Investment advisory company AIJ started investing in financial derivatives through funds based in the Cayman Islands, a tax haven, since 2002. 投資顧問会社のAIJは, 2002年から, 租税回避地の英領ケイマン諸島を営業基盤とするファンドを通じて金融派生商品への投資を始めた。

fund transaction 資金取引
◆Errors in computing systems at financial institutions could lead to problems in making international fund transactions. 金融機関のコンピュータ・システムのエラーは, 国際的な資金取引上, トラブルが生じる可能性がある。

fundamentals (名)基本, 原理, 根本原理, 基礎, 基礎的条件, 基本的指標(国の成長率, インフレ率, 財政収支, 金融情勢, 為替レート, 経常・貿易収支の六つ), 基調, 体質, ファンダメンタルズ
economic fundamentals 経済のファンダメンタルズ, 経済の基礎的条件, 景気のファンダメンタルズ, 経済の体質, 経済の実態 (=fundamentals of the economy)
financial fundamentals 財務面のファンダメンタルズ, 財務体質
supply fundamentals 供給のファンダメンタルズ
◆Exchange rates should reflect economic fundamentals. 為替レートは, 経済のファンダメンタルズ(経済の基礎的条件)を反映しなければならない。◆If we look at the yen's current exchange rate in terms of its real effective exchange rate, it is basically within a range consistent with the mid-and long-term fundamentals of the economy. 今の円相場[円の為替相場]は, 実質実効為替レートで見ると, 基本的には中長期的な経済のファンダメンタルズ(基礎的条件)と整合的な範囲内にある。

furnish (動)提供する, 供給する, 提出する, 取り付ける
furnish and supply 供給する, 提供する
◆ABC shall furnish XYZ within sixty days of the end of each term of license of this agreement with all documentation as shall be necessary to establish the amount of taxes actually paid. ABCは, 本契約の各ライセンス期間終了後60日以内に, 実際に納付した税額を立証するのに必要な書類をすべてXYZに提供するものとする。◆Company shall further furnish Licensee with the following technical information relating to the machinery of the plant free of charge: 会社は, プラントの機械類に関してさらに次の技術情報をライセンシーに無償で提供する。◆The Licensee shall furnish reg-

FURN 218

ular written report specified by the Licensor to Licensor in order to disclose in full detail pertinent information and data in connection with the sale of the Product. ライセンシーは、契約品の販売に関する関連情報とデータを十分詳細に開示するため、ライセンサーが指定する定期報告書をライセンサーに提出するものとする。

furnishing （名）造作

further instruments of assignment, conveyance and transfer 追加の譲渡証書
◆After the closing, Seller, upon request of Purchaser, shall take such action and execute and deliver such further instruments of assignment, conveyance and transfer as may be necessary to assure, complete and evidence the full and effective assignment, conveyance and transfer to Purchaser of the Shares. クロージング後、買い主の要求に基づいて売り主は、本株式の買い主に対する完全かつ効力ある譲渡を保証、実行し、証明するのに必要な行動を取り、追加の譲渡証書を作成して交付するものとする。

further performance of this agreement 本契約のその後の履行
◆In case any dispute arises in connection with the above right, the seller reserves the right to terminate unconditionally this agreement or any further performance of this agreement at the seller's discretion. 上記権利に関して紛争が生じた場合、売り主はその裁量で、本契約または本契約のその後の履行を無条件で終了させる権利を留保する。

furthermore （副）さらに

futures （名）先物，先物取引，先物契約，先物為替 （⇒crude futures, light crude)
bond futures 債券先物，債券先物取引
commodity futures 商品先物
crude futures 原油先物
financial futures 金融先物，金融先物取引
(foreign) currency futures 通貨先物
futures exchange 先物取引所
futures instrument 先物商品
futures market 先物市場
futures purchases and sales 先物売買
futures trading [transaction] 先物取引
gold futures 金先物
grain futures 穀物先物
interest rate futures 金利先物，金利先物取引
livestock futures 畜類先物
managed fund futures 商品ファンド
New York Futures Exchange ニューヨーク先物取引所
oil futures 原油先物
option on futures 先物オプション
property futures 不動産先物

stock futures 株式先物
stock index futures 株価指数先物
synthetic futures 合成先物
wood products futures 林産品先物
◆Crude futures were launched on the New York Mercantile Exchange in 1983. 原油先物の取引は、1983年からニューヨーク・マーカンタイル取引所で開始された。◆Gold futures for December delivery closed at \$1,891.90 an ounce at 2:05 p.m. on the Comex in New York. ニューヨーク商品取引所では、12月渡しの金先物価格が、午後2時5分の時点でトロイ・オンス（約31グラム)=1,891.90ドルに達した。◆Intercontinental Exchange (ICE), an exchange that deals in investing contracts known as futures, is buying the NYSE for about \$8 billion. 米インターコンチネンタル取引所(ICE: 先物と呼ばれる投資契約を扱う取引所)が、ニューヨーク証券取引所を約80億ドルで買収する。

FX margin trading 外国為替証拠金取引
◆In FX margin trading, investors can trade around the clock via the Internet. 外国為替証拠金取引の場合、投資家はインターネットで24時間取引できる。

G

GAAP 一般に認められた会計原則［会計基準]，一般に公正妥当と認められた会計原則，一般会計基準［会計原則]，会計基準，ジー・エイ・エイ・ピー，ギャップ （⇒generally accepted accounting principles)
Canadian GAAP カナダの会計基準，カナダのGAAP
follow GAAP 一般に認められた会計基準［会計原則]を順守する
German GAAP ドイツの会計基準，ドイツのGAAP
United States ［U.S.] GAAP 米国会計基準，米国のGAAP （⇒IAS)
◆According to the earnings report, the firm's consolidated sales dropped 4 percent from the previous year for the business year ended in December 2015, based on U.S. GAAP. 決算報告によると、同社の2015年12月期［2015年度]の連結売上高（米国会計基準)は、前期比で4%減少した。

gap in goods trade モノの貿易赤字，モノの貿易での輸入超過
◆Japan's current account surplus in July 2013 fell 12.9 percent from a year earlier to ￥577.3 billion, chiefly reflecting a wider gap in goods trade as imports of LNG for thermal power generation swelled due in part to an increase in electricity demand amid the hot summer. 2013年7月の日本の経常収支の黒字幅は、前年同月より12.9%減少して5,773億円となったが、これは主に猛暑で電力需要が増えたこともあって火力発電用の液化天然ガスの輸入が大幅に増加したため、モノの貿易での輸入超過［モノの貿易赤字]が拡大したこ

とを反映している。

gasoline prices ガソリン価格
◆Gasoline prices rose 6.4 percent in June, while city gas climbed 4.7 percent and electricity charges increased 9.8 percent, as the yen's depreciation pushed up import prices of crude oil and liquefied natural gas. 円安で原油や液化天然ガス（LNG）の輸入価格が上昇したため、6月はガソリン価格が6.4％上昇したのに対して、都市ガスは4.7％、電気料金は9.8％それぞれ上昇した。

GATT 関税と貿易に関する一般協定, 関税・貿易一般協定, ガット （⇒General Agreement on Tariffs and Trade）

GDP deflator GDPデフレーター（物価動向の主要指数）
◆The GDP deflator shows the level of prices of all new, domestically produced final goods and services in an economy. GDPデフレータは、一国の国内で生産されたすべての新製品とサービスの価格水準を示す。

解説 GDPデフレーターとは：消費者物価指数が店頭価格の動向を示すのに対して、GDPデフレーターは、消費のほか投資なども含めた経済全体の物価動向を示す。物価変動を反映する名目GDPを、物価変動の影響を除く実質GDPで割って産出する。

general （形）一般の, 一般的な, 全般的な, 総合的, 多岐にわたる, 概略的な, 概略の, 通常の, 総〜
General Accounting Office 米議会会計検査院, GAO
general administration 全般的な管理
general agency 総代理店
General Agreement to Borrow 国際通貨基金（IMF）の一般借入取決め, GAB
general balance sheet 一般貸借対照表, 総貸借対照表
general bond 総括輸入宣誓書
general cargo 一般貨物, 普通貨物
general catalogue 総目録, 総カタログ
general closing 通常決算
general conditions of marine and/or transport insurance 貨物保険普通保険約款
general contract 元請, 一括発注契約, 主契約
general contractor 一般請負人, 総建築請負業者, 元請業者, 元請工事業者 （=prime contractor）
general contractual conditions 約款
general council 通常理事会
General Council of British Shipping 英国海運評議会
general dealer 雑貨商
general drawing 基本設計図, 一般図, 全体図
general endorsement 無記名式裏書, 無記名裏書

general exclusion clause 一般免責条項
general export insurance 普通輸出保険
general freight agent 一般貨物運送店
general immunities clause 一般免責約款
general importers and exporters 総合輸出入商
general L/C 手形買取銀行無指定信用状, ジェネラル信用状 （=circular negotiation L/C, open L/C）
general letter of hypothecation 外国向荷為替手形約定書（輸出手形の買取りに関する約定書）
general liability insurance 一般賠償責任保険
general merchandize 雑貨
general object of the new company 新会社の全般的な事業目的
general order 保税倉庫収容命令
general partnership 合名会社
general planning 全般的な計画立案
general power of attorney 全権委任状
general preferential duties 一般特恵関税
general provisions 総則, 通則
general rate increase 運賃の一括引上げ
general rate of duty 基本税率
general remarks 一般摘要
general reserve 別途積立金
general restriction 一般制限
general sales agent 総販売代理店
General Services Administration 米調達局
general ship 一般貨物船, 共同船
general shortage of materials 原材料の総体的不足
general statutory tariff （一般）固定税率
general store 雑貨店
general strike ゼネスト, 総同盟罷業, 総罷業
general tariff 一般税率, 固定関税
general terms and conditions 一般取引条項, 一般取引条件, 一般条項, 一般条件
general terms and conditions of business 一般取引条件, 一般的取引条件
general trading company 総合貿易商社, 総合商社 （=general trade company）
general transire 総括沿岸航行許可書
general view 全体図
general warrant 共通（倉荷）預証券
General Agreement on Tariffs and Trade ガット（関税・貿易一般協定）
◆The WTO was inaugurated in 1995, as an outgrowth of the General Agreement on Tariffs and Trade, with the aim of promoting a framework

for multilateral free trade toward 21st century. 世界貿易機関（WTO）は、21世紀に向けた多角的な自由貿易体制の推進を目的に、ガット（関税・貿易一般協定）を発展改組して1995年に発足した。

general average 共同海損, G.A.

general average adjustment 共同海損清算

general average bond 共同海損契約書

general average clause 共同海損約款

general average contribution 共同海損分担額

general average deposit 共同海損供託金

general average disbursements insurance 共同海損費用保険

general average expenditure 共同海損費用

general average sacrifice 共同海損犠牲

general average settlement 共同海損決済

general market conditions 一般市況, 一般的な市場状況［市況］, 市況全般, 全般的な市場環境
◆At the beginning of each calendar year, ABC shall make a report to XYZ on the sales of the Product during the previous year and general market conditions. 各暦年の初めに、ABCは、XYZに対して前年度の契約品の販売（実績）と市況全般について報告するものとする。

general or special meetings of shareholders 定時株主総会または臨時株主総会
◆The president of the new company shall act as chairman at general or special meetings of shareholders. 定時株主総会または臨時株主総会では、新会社の社長が議長を務める。

general public 一般公衆
◆ABC's obligation under this Article shall not apply to any information relating to the licensed products that is or becomes available without restriction to the general public by acts not attributable to ABC or its employees. 本条に基づくABCの義務は、ABCまたはその従業員が引き起こしたと考えることができない行為によって一般公衆に制限なく知られている、または知られるようになった許諾製品に関する情報には適用されないものとする。

generalized system of preferences 一般特恵関税制度, GSP

generally accepted accounting practices 一般に認められた会計慣行, 一般に認められた会計実務, 一般に認められた会計処理

generally accepted accounting principles 一般に（公正妥当と）認められた会計原則, 一般に認められた会計基準, GAAP
（=generally accepted accounting practices）
be based on U.S. Generally Accepted Accounting Principles 米国の会計基準をベースにしている
in accordance with generally accepted accounting principles 一般に（公正妥当と）

認められた会計基準［会計原則］に従って
present fairly in conformity with generally accepted accounting principles 一般に認められた会計基準に準拠して［会計原則に従って］適正に表示している
under generally accepted accounting principles 一般に認められた会計基準に従って［会計基準に基づいて、会計基準により］, 一般に認められた会計基準では
◆All such financial statements have been prepared in accordance with generally accepted accounting principles consistently applied throughout the periods indicated. これらの財務書類は、当該期間中に一貫して適用した一般に公正妥当と認められた会計原則（会計基準）に従って作成されている。◆The firm's business performance is based on U.S. Generally Accepted Accounting Principles. 同社の業績は、米国の会計基準［米国の一般に認められた会計基準］をベースにしている。

generally known or available 公知公用の, 公知であるか一般に入手することができる
◆The confidential information shall not include information which is or becomes generally known or available through no act or failure to act by ABC. この秘密情報は、公知であるか一般に入手することができる情報、またはABCの作為または不作為によらずに公知となるか一般に入手することができる情報を含まないものとする。

generally known or publicly available 公知または公用の, 公知であるか一般に入手することができる
◆During the life of this agreement and thereafter Distributor shall not divulge any confidential information which it may acquire in connection with Products, this agreement or performance thereunder, except insofar as such information is or becomes generally known or publicly available at the time of disclosure under this agreement or subsequent thereto. 本契約期間中とその後も、代理店は、本契約に基づく開示時点とその後に公知または公用となる場合を除いて、本製品（契約品）、本契約または本契約に基づく履行に関連して取得することができる一切の秘密情報を漏洩しないものとする。

genetic resource 遺伝資源, 生物遺伝資源
◆Access to genetic resources requires prior informed consent of the country of origin. 生物遺伝資源を利用する場合は、資源原産国の文書による事前の同意・承認を得なければならない。

genetically modified [engineered] food 遺伝子組換え食品 （=genetically altered food, GM food）
◆Japan requires labeling of 30 genetically modified food items from 2001. 日本は、2001年から遺伝子組換え食品30品目について表示を義務付けている。

genetically modified organism 遺伝子組換え生物, 遺伝子組換え作物, 遺伝子組換え農

産物, GMO
(=living modified organism)
◆In the next round of negotiations, labeling and trade rules for food produced with genetically modified organisms (GMOs) are expected to be discussed. 次期交渉では、遺伝子組換え食品（遺伝子組換え作物を使って生産される食品）の表示問題や貿易ルールづくりが話し合われる見通しだ。

geographical area　地域

G-G trade　政府間貿易（government-to-government tradeの略）

give and grant　与える, 付与する
(give=grant)
◆Company hereby gives and grants to Licensee, and Licensee accepts, on the terms and conditions set forth herein on the date of this agreement: 本契約により会社は、本契約に定める条件で本契約日に以下をライセンシーに与え、ライセンシーはこれを受諾する。

give, devise and bequeath　遺贈する

give effect to　〜を発効させる, 実施する, 施行する, 実行に移す, 〜に影響を及ぼす
◆In case any one or more of the provisions of this agreement are held invalid, illegal or unenforceable in any respect, the validity, legality and enforceability of the remaining provisions hereof shall not be in any way affected or impaired thereby, except to the extent that giving effect to the remaining provisions would be unjust or inequitable. 本契約の一つ以上の規定がいずれかの点で無効、違法または強制不能と判断された場合、残存規定の実施が不公正または不均衡となる範囲を除いて、本契約の残存規定の有効性、合法性と強制可能性はその影響を受けることはなく、またそれによって損なわれることはないものとする。

given　(形)一定の, 規定の, 特定の　(名)当然のこと　(接)〜と仮定すると, 〜を考慮に入れると, 〜を考慮して, 〜があるとすると, 〜した以上
◆Failure by Distributor to sell the minimum quota for any given period set forth in Exhibit B will constitute a default of this agreement by Distributor. 販売店が付属書類Bに記載する一定期間の最低割当量を販売できなかった場合には、販売店による本契約違反となる。

global　(形)全世界の, 世界の, 世界の規模の, 国際的な, 地球規模の, 地球全体の, 包括的, グローバルな, 広範囲の, 全体的な, 全面的な, 総合的な, 包括的な
global budget　グローバル予算

global carry trade　グローバル・キャリー取引, グローバル・キャリー・トレード
◆In a global carry trade, hedge funds borrow low-interest yen funds to invest in dollar-denominated assets. グローバル・キャリー・トレード［グローバル・キャリー取引］では、ヘッジ・ファンドなどが、低利の円資金を借りてドル建て資産に投資している。

global currency wars　世界の通貨安戦争
◆In global currency wars, central banks effectively lower the value of their countries' currencies to boost their countries' export competitiveness. 世界の通貨安競争では、自国の輸出競争力を高めるため、中央銀行が自国通貨の価値を事実上切り下げる［自国通貨の為替相場を事実上安くする］。

global economy　世界経済, 世界の景気, 地球規模の経済　(=world economy)
◆G-20 countries would not tolerate a rapid decline of the yen that could destabilize the global economy though some of them expect the yen to fall further in Japan's fight against deflation. 日本がデフレ脱却の過程で円安がさらに進むとG20参加国の一部は見ているが、G20各国は、世界経済が不安定化するほどの急激な円安を容認することはないと思われる。

global financial crisis　世界的な金融危機, 世界の金融危機, 世界金融危機
◆Indonesia has enjoyed decent economic growth since the global financial crisis of 2008 due to the U.S. FRB's quantitative easing and higher prices of primary commodities such as coal and palm oil as the country's major exports. インドネシアは、2008年の世界金融危機以降、米連邦準備制度理事会（FRB）の量的金融緩和とインドネシアの主要輸出品である石炭、パーム油など一次産品の高値に支えられ、高い経済成長を享受している。

global financial market　世界の金融市場
◆The Bank of Japan pointed to risk factors, including unstable global financial markets and the economic slowdown in the United States, Japan's main export market. 日本銀行は、世界の不安定な金融市場や日本の主要輸出市場である米国の景気減速などのリスク要因も指摘した。

global market　グローバル市場, 世界市場, 国際市場, グローバル・マーケット
(=global marketplace, international market)
◆Comparative advantage in this new global market depends not only on superior R&D, but also on speed in making management decisions, finding unique applications for research advances and delivering them to customers ahead of competitors. この新しいグローバル市場で比較優位性を確立できるかどうかは、高度な研究開発だけでなく、経営の意思決定を迅速に行えるかどうかと、研究を進めるうえで独創的な適用範囲［用途］を素早く確認して、それを競合他社に先駆けて製品化できるかどうかにかかっている。◆The company holds a leading position in global markets in the area of multimedia application development. 同社は、マルチメディア・アプリケーション開発の分野では、グローバル市場で主導的な地位を堅持している。

global market share　世界シェア（占有率）, 世界市場でのシェア, 世界全体でのシェア
◆South Korea came to grips with fostering its

shipbuilding industry and increased the global market share of the country's shipbuilders. 韓国は、造船業の育成に取り組んで、造船各社の世界シェア（占有率）を高めた。

global oil prices 国際原油価格
◆Upward pressure on global oil prices is feared due to increased tensions in the Middle East and political turmoil in Venezuela. 中東情勢の緊迫化やベネズエラの政局混乱のため、国際原油価格の上昇懸念が強まっている。

global strategy 世界戦略
◆Japan's major automakers are capitalizing on improved quality at production plants overseas as part of their global strategies. 日本の大手自動車メーカーは、自動車各社の世界戦略の一環として、海外生産拠点での品質向上を活用している。

global systemically important financial institutions 金融システム上重要な国際金融機関, G-SIFIs
◆According to a list of 28 global systemically important financial institutions published by the Financial Stability Board, Citigroup, Deutsche Bank and HSBC Holdings will be targeted for a capital surcharge of 2.5 percent. 金融安定化理事会（FSB）が発表した金融システム上重要な国際金融機関（G-SIFIs）28行のリストによると、米シティグループやドイツ銀行、英金融大手のHSBCなどが、2.5%の自己資本上積みの対象となる。

global trade dispute 世界的な貿易摩擦
◆The emergence of a global trade dispute could hamper smooth transactions in services and goods. 世界的な貿易摩擦が激化すれば、モノとサービスの円滑な取引が阻害されかねない。

global value chains 国際的な価値連鎖
◆Due to the IT revolution and trade liberalization, product specialization now is determined by comparative advantages not in finished products but in work unique to each country or region in the context of global value chains. 情報通信技術（IT）革命と貿易自由化で、製品の特化は、「最終財」ではなく、国際的価値連鎖との関連で国・地域にそれぞれ特有の「仕事」の比較優位で決まるようになった。

globalize （動）世界化する, 国際化する, 地球的規模にする, グローバル化する
◆The strengthening of the yen would force Japanese export-oriented manufacturers to globalize themselves further. 円高で、日本の輸出企業はさらなるグローバル化を強いられることになろう。

GMQ 適商品質条件（good merchantable quality termsの略）

GMS 大メコン圏 （⇒Greater Mekong Subregion）

go into liquidation 清算手続きに入る, 清算を開始する
◆In the event that either party files a petition in bankruptcy or a petition in bankruptcy is filed

against it, or either party becomes insolvent or bankrupt, or goes into liquidation or receivership. いずれかの当事者が破産申請をするか、第三者により破産申請書を提出された場合、またはいずれかの当事者が支払い不能もしくは破産状態になった場合、またはいずれかの当事者が清算手続きに入るか、管財人による財産管理が開始された場合。

go into receivership 管財人による財産管理を開始する

gold （名）金, 金貨, 金メダル, ゴールド
（形）金の, 金製の
（⇒commodity futures trading）

gold and foreign currency reserve 外貨準備高

gold clause 金約款

gold exchange standard 金為替本位制
◆Gold is still becoming the safe haven as people fear recession in the U.S. and the eurozone debt problems. 米国の景気後退やユーロ圏の債務危機問題への懸念から、まだ金が安全な投資先［資金の逃避先］となっている。◆In the case of hyper-inflation, investors put their assets in hard assets like real estate and gold. 超インフレの場合、投資家は、保有資産を不動産や金などの有形資産［有価資産］に投資する。

gold standard 金本位制
◆At the time of the Great Depression of 1930s, foreign exchange rates were fixed by the gold standard, preventing Japan from devaluing its currency. 1930年代の世界恐慌当時、為替相場は金本位制で固定されていたため、日本は自国通貨の切り下げができなかった。

golden share 黄金株, 特権株 （「黄金株」は、株主総会での合併などの提案に拒否権を発動できる「拒否権付き株式（種類株式）」のこと）

the expiry of the golden share 黄金株の期限切れ

the transfer of golden shares 黄金株の譲渡
◆A company is allowed to set restrictions on the transfer of golden shares. 企業は、黄金株（拒否権付き種類株式）に譲渡制限を付けることができる［黄金株の譲渡に制限を設けることができる］。◆If golden shares held by a friendly company are transferred to another party, such shares could be transferred again to a hostile bidder. 友好的な企業が保有する黄金株を第三者に譲渡した場合、その黄金株はまた敵対的買収者に譲渡される可能性もある。

good and marketable title 売買できる有効な権原, 売買できる正当な権原, 有効かつ売買可能な （⇒free and clear of）
◆Except as indicated in Schedule 5, the Company has good and marketable title to each item of personal property used by it in the business of the Company, free and clear of all liens or security interests. 別紙5に表示するものを除いて、対象会社は、対象会社がその事業で利用している各動

産のうち担保権の対象になっていない動産については、それを売買できる正当な権限を持っている。

good buy 掘り出し物, お買い得
◆We are certain that you will find it to be a very good buy. 御社にとってこれは大変お買い得と思われる、と確信します。

good cause 十分な理由, 正当な理由, 正当な事由

good consideration 有効な約因, 十分な約因 (=sufficient consideration, valuable consideration:「無効な約因」という意味もある)
◆NOW, THEREFORE, in consideration of the promises herein contained and other good consideration, the parties hereto do hereby agree as follows: そこで、本契約に定める約束ごとと他の有効な約因を対価として、両当事者はここに以下のとおり合意する。

good title 優良権原, 有効権原, 良権原, 瑕疵なき権原, 正当な権原
◆Seller has good and marketable title to the Shares, free and clear of any and all covenants, conditions, restrictions, liens, options and adverse claims or rights. 売り主は、一切の約束、条件、制約、議決権信託契約、担保権、選択権、不利益を及ぼすクレームや権利をまったく負担しない本株式を売買できる正当な権原を持っている。

goods (名) 物品, 商品, 製品, 財貨, 財産, 財, 貨物, 動産, 有体動産
basic goods 生活必需品
branded goods ブランド商品
brown goods テレビ、ビデオ、オーディオなどの電子製品
capital goods 資本財
character goods キャラクター商品
competitive goods 競争品, 競争商品, 競争財
consumer durable goods 耐久消費財 (=durable consumer goods)
consumer goods 消費財
consumer nondurable goods 非耐久消費財
convenience goods 最寄り品 (消費者が小売店で少量ずつ買う商品), 便宜品, 手近品, 日用雑貨食料品 (日用雑貨品、タバコ、菓子類、雑誌などを指す)
cost of goods and services 売上原価
custom-made [made-to-order, tailored] goods オーダーメード商品
delayed goods 遅延商品
electrical goods 電化製品
exported goods 輸出品
final goods 最終財, 製品
finished goods 製品, 完成品, 加工品, 最終財
goods in bond 保税貨物 (=bonded goods)

goods in transit 未着品, 輸送品
goods-oriented economy ハード社会
household goods 家庭用品, 家具什器 (じゅうき)
imports of final goods 製品輸入
impulse goods 衝動買い商品, 衝動購買商品, 衝動品
industrial goods 生産財, 産業財, 工業品
information-related goods 情報関連財
investment goods 投資財
natural goods 天然財
nondurable goods 非耐久財
public goods 公共財
semimanufactured [semi-processed] goods 半製品 (=semifinished goods)
shopping goods 買い回り品 (ファッション間連や耐久消費財などの商品)
sporting goods スポーツ用品
substitute goods 代替財
the goods 契約品, 約定品, 当該商品 [製品]
white goods 冷蔵庫や洗濯機などの大型家電製品, タオルやシーツなどの家庭用リンネル製品
◆After the delivery of the Goods, any taxes, customs duties, export or import surcharges or other governmental charges shall be for the account of the Buyer. 本商品の引渡し後、税金、関税、輸出・輸入税、その他政府が賦課する費用は、買い主の負担とする。 ◆France's Competition Commission has ordered Sony, Matsushita and Philips to pay fines for allegedly concluding price-fixing agreements on retail goods with their local distributors. フランスの競争評議会は、国内販売店と小売電気製品の価格維持協定を結んだとして、ソニー、松下電器産業とフィリップスに罰金の支払いを命じた。 ◆In case there is delay in delivery of all or any part of the Goods on the time as stipulated in this agreement, the buyer is entitled to claim liquidated damages at the rate of one-half of one percent (0.5%) of the amount of the delayed Goods for each complete week of delay. 本契約で定める期限に本商品の全部または一部に引渡し遅延が生じた場合、買い主は、遅延対象の各1週間につき引渡し遅延商品の代金の0.5%を損害賠償予定額として請求することができるものとする。 ◆In processing trade, imported raw materials are manufactured into goods that are then sold to other countries. 加工貿易では、輸入された原材料が製品に仕上げられた後、製品は海外に販売される。 ◆The goods are to be insured for 25% over the invoice value. 約定品には、送り状金額の125%で付保することになっている。 ◆The payment for the Goods shall be made by a letter of credit. 「商品」の支払いは、信用状で行うものとする。 ◆We enclose the shipping documents cover-

GOOD　224

ing the goods and expect your remittance in due course. 契約品の船積み書類を同封し、期日どおりのご送金を期待しております。◆We trust that the goods will open up to your entire satisfaction. 契約品［約定品］は、開装の上、十分ご満足いただけるものと思います。

goods and service trade　モノとサービスの取引［貿易］, モノとサービスの取引を示す貿易・サービス収支, 貿易・サービス収支
◆The deficit in goods and service trade combined in January-June 2012 expanded to a record high of about ¥3.42 trillion from ¥1.08 trillion a year before. 2012年上半期（1〜6月）のモノとサービスの取引を示す貿易・サービス収支の赤字幅は、前年同期の1兆800億円から過去最大の約3兆4,200億円に拡大した。

goods and services　モノとサービス
◆The balance of trade in goods and services logged a surplus of ¥3.43 trillion in the April-September period. 4〜9月期のモノとサービスの貿易収支は、3兆4,300億円の黒字を記録した。

goods trade　モノの取引, モノ［財］の貿易, モノの取引を示す貿易収支, 物品貿易
◆Japan's current account surplus in July 2013 fell 12.9 percent from a year earlier to ¥577.3 billion, chiefly reflecting a wider gap in goods trade as imports of LNG for thermal power generation swelled due in part to an increase in electricity demand amid the hot summer. 2013年7月の日本の経常収支の黒字幅は、前年同月より12.9％減少して5,773億円となったが、これは主に猛暑で電力需要が増えこったため火力発電用の液化天然ガスの輸入が大幅に増加したため、モノの貿易での輸入超過［モノの貿易赤字］が拡大したことを反映している。

goods trade deficit　財の貿易赤字, モノの貿易赤字, モノの取引を示す貿易収支の赤字［赤字額］, 貿易赤字
◆Japan saw its goods trade deficit in January-June 2012 balloon to about ¥2.5 trillion from ¥495.7 billion a year before. 日本の2012年上半期（1〜6月）のモノの取引を示す貿易収支の赤字額は、前年同期の4,957億円から約2兆5,000億円に急増した。

goods trade surplus　財の貿易黒字, モノの貿易黒字, モノの取引を示す貿易収支の黒字［黒字額］, 貿易黒字　(=merchandise trade surplus)
◆Japan's goods trade surplus stood at ¥6.05 trillion, down 7.9 percent from the corresponding period of last year. 日本の貿易黒字は、6兆500億円で、前年同期より7.9％減少した。

goodwill　(名)のれん, 営業権, 得意先, 信用, 善意, 好意, 親善, 快諾
purchased goodwill　取得営業権
substantial goodwill and reputation　多大な信用と営業上の名声, 大きな信用と高い評判
◆Licensor is the owner of the well-known trade-

mark and of the substantial goodwill and reputation associated with it. ライセンサーは、有名な商標の所有者であり、それに付随する多大な信用と営業上の名声の所有者でもある。

goodwill value　のれん代　(=intangible value)
◆Olympus Corp. inflated the goodwill value of its British subsidiary by 33.4 billion in the consolidated financial statements. オリンパスは、英子会社の「のれん代」を連結決算で334億円水増ししていた。

govern　(動)支配する, 統治する, 治める, 管理する, 運営する, 管理運営する, 取り締まる, 制御する, 規定する, 決定する, 左右する, 〜に適用される, 〜の決定基準［原則］となる
◆The laws of Japan shall govern as to matters involving the governance of the new company. 新会社の管理・運営に関する事項については、日本法が適用される。◆The use of this site is governed by our Disclaimer. このサイトの利用には、当社の「免責規定」が適用されます。◆The World Trade Organization has a long way to go before it can reach a consensus on a new set of rules governing free trade. 世界貿易機関（WTO）が貿易自由化の新ルールに関して合意が得られるまでの道のりは、まだまだ遠い。◆This agreement shall be governed in all respects by the laws of Japan. 本契約は、すべての点で日本法に準拠するものとする。

governance　(名)会社の管理・運営, 管理法, 統治, 支配, ガバナンス
◆This agreement shall be governed by the laws of the State of New York, provided that the laws of _____ shall govern as to matters involving the governance of the new joint venture company. 本契約は、ニューヨーク州法に準拠するものとする。ただし、新合弁会社の運営に関する事項については、_____の法律（新会社設立地の会社法）が適用されるものとする。

governing language　支配する言語, 支配言語, 準拠言語, 適用言語, 基準となる言語, 基準言語
◆The governing language of this agreement shall be English. 本契約の基準言語は、英語とする。

governing law　準拠法, 適用法
governing law and interpretation　準拠法と解釈
governing law and venue　準拠法と裁判地
◆Governing Law: This Agreement shall be governed by and interpreted［construed］in accordance with the laws of Japan. 準拠法：本契約は、日本の法律［日本法］に準拠し、日本の法律［同法］に従って解釈するものとする［本契約には日本の法律が適用され、また本契約は同法に従って解釈するものとする］。

government　(名)政府, 政治, 政権, 内閣, 行政
government procurement　政府調達

government-backed trade insurance　政

府保証付き貿易保険
◆The METI has decided to expand the scope of government-backed trade insurance for overseas social infrastructure projects. 経済産業省は、海外の社会基盤（インフラ）事業に対する政府保証付き貿易保険の対象を拡大することを決めた。

government bond　国債
◆LDP President Abe said that he will ask the BOJ to buy construction bonds, or the government bonds issued for public works projects, through open market operations, which is a typical monetary control measure conducted by the central bank. 自民党の安倍総裁は、日銀が買い取る通常の金融調節手法である公開市場操作［買いオペ］で、建設国債（公共事業のために発行する国債）の買取りを日銀に求めると述べた。

government regulations　政府規制, 政府の規制
◆No significant improvement in air pollution in China has been seen as many factories have ignored government regulations, putting short-term profits ahead of environmental issues. 多くの工場が環境問題よりも目先の利益を優先し、政府の規制を無視してきたので、中国の大気汚染の大きな改善は見られない。

governmental　(形)政府の, 政府間の, 政府関連の, 政府系の, 国家統治の, 政府出資の, 国営の
governmental actions　政府の行為
governmental authorities　政府諸機関, 政府機関, 政府当局
governmental or regulatory authorities　政府当局または監督官庁, 政府機関または監督機関
governmental regulations or orders　政令・規制, 政令または規則

governmental charges　政府が賦課する費用
◆After the delivery of the Goods, any taxes, customs duties, export or import surcharges or other governmental charges shall be for the account of the Buyer. 本商品の引渡し後、税金、関税、輸出・輸入税、その他政府が賦課する費用は、買い主の負担とする。

grace period　猶予期間, 据え置き期間, 払込み猶予期間　（=days of grace）
◆If the borrower shall fail to pay any debt for borrowed money or other similar obligation of the borrower, or interest thereon, when due, and such failure continues after the applicable grace period specified in the agreement relating to such indebtedness, the lender may in its discretion declare the entire unpaid principal amount of the loan, accrued interest thereon and all other sums payable under this agreement to be immediately due and payable. 借主が借主の借入債務（借入金に対する債務）や他の同様の債務またはその利息を支払い期日に支払うことを怠り、このような不履行が本契約に定める当該債務に関する適用猶予期

間後も継続する場合、貸主はその裁量で、借入金の未返還元本全額、その発生利息と本契約に基づいて支払わなければならない他の未払い金の全額即時支払い［即時返済］を宣言することができる。

grain　(名)穀物, 穀類, 粒, 粒子, (木材の)木目, (人の)気質, 性質, 少量, 微量, ほんの少し
a cargo of grain　穀物の船荷
grain elevator　（円筒形の）穀物倉庫
grain embargo　穀物輸出禁止
grain tonnage　散荷（ばらに）容積トン数
◆The sharp rise in crude oil prices has caused increases in prices of other fuels and grains, triggering inflation in many parts of the world. 原油価格の高騰は、他の燃料価格や穀物価格の上昇を招き、国際的なインフレを引き起こしている。

grain export　穀物輸出
◆Russia has temporarily banned grain exports after a severe drought. ロシアは、大干ばつを受けて、穀物輸出を一時停止した。

grain market　穀物市場
◆These surplus funds are moving into crude oil and grain markets in search of profitable investments. これらの余剰資金が、有利な運用先を求めて原油や穀物市場に向かっている。

grant　(名)権利の付与, 財産の移転, 譲渡, 譲与, 実施許諾, 補助金, 交付金　(動)与える, 付与する, 許諾する, 許可する, 承諾する, 認める, 譲渡する, 移転する　(⇒have manufactured)
grant a license　実施権を許諾する, 実施権を付与する, 使用権を与える, 使用許諾を与える
grant and license the use of　～の使用を許可し許諾する, ～の使用を許諾する
grant back　使用許諾, 戻し特許, グラント・バック, グラント・バック条項（ライセンシーによる改良技術のライセンサーに対する使用許諾）
grant of license　実施権の許諾, 実施権の付与, 使用許諾, 商標使用許諾, ライセンスの付与
grant permission　許可を与える
granted under this agreement　本契約に基づいて付与される, 本契約に基づいて与えられる
the right to grant a license to customers　顧客に対して使用許諾を行う権利
◆If Washington's permission to import natural gas produced in the United Stated is granted, the LNG production of Mitsui & Co. and Mitsubishi Corp. at the Cameron Parish facility is expected to start as early as 2017. 米国で生産した天然ガスの輸入を米政府が許可した場合、米ルイジアナ州のキャメロン郡にあるLNG基地での三井物産と三菱商事のLNG生産は、早ければ2017年からスタートする予定だ。◆The Exporter grants the Distributor and the Distributor accepts to be

the exclusive distributor for the sale and distribution of the products of the Exporter in the defined sales territory. 輸出者は、販売店が指定販売地域内で輸出者の製品販売の総代理店となることを認め、販売店はこれに同意する。

grantor （名）譲渡人, 譲与人, 許諾者, ライセンス許諾者, 特許権など知的財産権の使用許諾者, 不動産権設定者
◆Subject to the provisions of Article V of this agreement, each party, as Grantor, on behalf of itself and its Subsidiaries, grants to the other party, as Grantee, a worldwide and nonexclusive license under the Grantor's licensed products and copyrights; 本契約第5条の規定に従って、ライセンス許諾者としての各当事者は、自社とその子会社を代表して、ライセンス許諾者の許諾特許と著作権に基づく世界を対象とした非独占的なライセンスを、被許諾者としての相手方に許諾する。

great rotation グレート・ローテーション（大転換）
◆Great rotation refers to the shift of investment money from low-risk assets such as U.S. Treasuries and the yen into riskier assets such as stocks. 「グレート・ローテーション（大転換）」とは、投資資金を米国債や円などの低リスク資産[安全資産]から株式などリスクの高い資産に移すことを言う。

Greater Mekong Subregion 大メコン圏, GMS
◆The development of cross-border infrastructure in the Greater Mekong Subregion（GMS）has prompted a number of multinational corporations to transfer some of their manufacturing processes to Laos, Cambodia and Myanmar to take advantage of cheaper labor costs. 大メコン圏での国境を越えたインフラ整備に伴い、多くの多国籍企業が、安い人件費[低賃金]の利点を生かして生産工程の一部をラオスやカンボジア、ミャンマーに移転している。

greenback （名）米ドル, 米ドル紙幣（米ドル紙幣の裏面がすべてグリーンなのでこう呼ばれている）
◆If Japan posts a current account deficit, it has to sell yen to buy U.S. dollars as the greenback remains the world's dominant currency for settling trade. 日本が経常収支の赤字を計上した場合、米ドルがまだ世界の貿易決済の主要通貨なので、米ドルを買うために円を売らなければならない。◆The depreciation of the greenback will result in exchange losses on assets held in dollars. ドル安が進むと、保有するドル建て資産に為替差損が生じる。

greenhouse gas 温室効果ガス, 温暖化ガス
◆California's Attorney General Bill Lockyer has sued the six largest U.S. and Japanese automakers for damages related to greenhouse gas emissions. 米カリフォルニア州のビル・ロッキャー司法長官は、自動車が排出する温室効果ガスについて日米の大手自動車メーカー6社に損害賠償を求め

る訴訟を起こした。

greenhouse gas emission target 温室効果ガス排出（削減）目標
◆As a new greenhouse gas reduction framework to replace the Kyoto Protocol is to be implemented in 2020, the participating countries agreed to present their voluntary greenhouse gas emission targets for the years beyond 2020 in 2015. 京都議定書に代わる温室効果ガス削減の新たな枠組みが2020年に発効する予定なので、(国連気候変動枠組み条約の) 締約国会議への参加各国は、2020年以降の自主的な温室効果ガス排出削減目標を、2015年に提示することで合意した。

gross domestic product 国内総生産, GDP
◆By starting talks on a comprehensive partnership agreement, the EU and the United States will take the first step toward creating a giant free trade zone that would account for about 50 percent of the world's gross domestic product. 包括的連携協定の交渉を開始することで、欧州連合（EU）と米国は、世界のGDP（国内総生産）の5割近くを占める巨大な自由貿易圏の創設に一歩踏み出すことになる。

gross sales 総売上高, 総売上, 総収益, 総販売額

gross selling price 総販売価格, 総販売額
◆For the purpose of this agreement, Net selling Price means the gross selling price of the licensed products as invoiced by ABC, less the following items to the extent they are included in gross sales in accordance with generally accepted accounting principles. 本契約の解釈上、「純販売額」とは、ABCが請求した許諾製品の総販売額から一般に公正妥当と認められた会計基準に従って総販売額に含まれる範囲内で次の費用項目を差し引いた金額を意味する。

gross up グロスアップ（グロスアップとは純額を控除前の金額に戻すことで、源泉徴収による差引きがなかった場合と同じ金額を税引き後で受け取れるように、契約金額を増額すること）

Group of 20 major economies 主要20か国・地域（G20）（⇒Financial Stability Board）

growing market 成長市場
◆To increase exports, Japanese manufacturers must develop attractive products of high added value and find ways to capitalize on growing markets in the emerging economies of Asia and other regions. 輸出を拡大するには、日本の製造業各社が、付加価値の高い魅力的な商品を開発して、アジアなどの地域の新興成長市場を積極的に取り込む方法を見つける必要がある。

growth （名）成長, 成長率, 経済成長, 伸び, 伸び率, 増加, 増大, 景気（⇒sales growth）
◆An expanded FTA is a key to bolstering growth in the EU indispensable to overcome its fiscal and financial crises. 自由貿易協定（FTA）の拡大

は、EU（欧州連合）の財政・金融危機を克服するうえで欠かせないEUの経済成長促進のカギである。◆Pacific Rim leaders pledged to revive flagging growth in the region by supporting open trade. 環太平洋地域の首脳は、開かれた貿易を後押しして、低迷する環太平洋地域の成長を回復させることを誓った。◆The economic slowdown in Europe due to the sovereign debt crisis and slackening growth of China as a major exporter to Europe have dealt a painful blow to Japan's exports and production. 債務危機に伴う欧州経済の減速と、欧州向け輸出の多い中国の成長鈍化が、日本の輸出と生産に耐え難いほどの打撃を与えている。

growth strategy 成長戦略
◆In the Abe administration, infrastructure exports including nuclear reactors and high-speed railway systems are considered a major pillar of Japan's growth strategy. 安倍政権では、原発や高速鉄道などのインフラ（社会基盤）輸出は、日本の成長戦略の柱［大きな柱］と考えられている。◆The three pillars of the Abe administration's growth strategy are restoring the nation's industries, strategically creating new markets and helping Japan's businesses expand abroad. 安倍政権の成長戦略の3本の柱は、日本産業の再興、戦略市場の創造と日本企業の国際展開である。

G-SIFIs 金融システム上重要な国際金融機関 （⇒global systemically important financial institutions）

GSP 一般特恵関税制度 （generalized system of preferenceの略）

guarantee （動）保証する, 請けあう
◆We are prepared to place a prompt trial order if you can guarantee supply of products strictly in accordance with our specifications. 貴社が当社の仕様書どおりの商品の供給［納入］を保証するなら、早速、試験注文を出します。

guarantee （名）保証, 保証人, 引受人, 保証額, 保証契約, 保証書, 保証状, 担保, 抵当, 担保物
◆Notwithstanding any other provision in this guarantee to the contrary, the guarantor's liability to ABC under the guarantee shall not exceed the liability of XYZ pursuant to the agreement. 本保証書のこれと異なる他の条項にかかわらず、保証書に基づく保証人のABCに対する責任は、当該契約によるXYZの責任を超えないものとする。◆The guarantor hereby waives, and agrees not to assert by way of motion as a defence or otherwise, in a suit, action or proceeding pursuant to this guarantee, any claim that this guarantee or the subject matter hereof may not be enforced in or by such courts. 保証人は、本保証書に従う訴訟、裁判または手続き［訴訟または訴訟手続き］で、抗弁として申し立てることによりまたは他の方法により、本保証書またはその主題を上記裁判所でまたはその裁判所が強制することはできないとの主張をここに放棄し、これを主張しないことに同意する。◆The guarantor shall be liable under this guarantee as if it were the sole principal obligor

and debtor and not merely a surety. 保証人は、保証人が単なる保証人ではなく唯一の主債務者であるかのように本保証書上の責任を負うものとする。

guaranteed minimum royalty 最低ロイヤルティ保証額, 保証された最低ロイヤルティ, 最低ロイヤルティの保証, 保証ミニマム・ロイヤルティ
◆The amount of the guaranteed minimum annual royalty for each year shall be paid in advance by ABC to Licensor by remittance to the bank account as designated by Licensor on or before the 22nd day of December of the year in question. 各年度の年間最低ロイヤルティ保証額は、前払いで、ライセンサーが指定する銀行口座に当該年の12月22日までにABCが振り込むことによって支払うものとする。

guarantor （名）保証人
◆Guarantor hereby waives any right it may have of first requiring ABC to pursue its legal remedies against XYZ. 保証人は、保証人が持てる権利にして、まずXYZに対して法的救済を求めることをABCに要求する権利を、ここに放棄する。

guaranty （名）保証 (guarantee), 権利保証, 権利の保護, 保証契約, 保証書, 保証人, 担保, 担保物, 担保物件（商品やサービスの保証というより、借入金の保証などの場合に使う）

contract of guaranty 保証契約

financial guaranty insurance policy 信用保証保険証券

guaranty bond 保証書

guaranty money 保証金

guaranty of indebtedness 債務保証

guaranty of liabilities 信用保証

liability on guaranty 保証債務
◆The guarantor shall not be released from the obligations under this guaranty by reason of any modification, amendment or supplement of the franchise agreement. 保証人は、フランチャイズ契約の変更、修正または補足を理由として、本保証に基づく義務から解放されないものとする。

guidelines, instructions and manuals 要領, 指示とマニュアル
◆Guidelines, instructions and manuals provided under this agreement shall be complied with in full. 本契約に基づいて提供された要領、指示とマニュアルは、全面的に遵守するものとする。

H

hacking attack ハッキング攻撃
◆Washington is staying silent whether it launched a cyber attack in retaliation for the hacking attack against Sony Pictures Entertainment though North Korea's Internet was on the fritz. 北朝鮮のインターネットが接続不能となったが、米国は、ソニー・ピクチャーズ・エンタテインメントへのハッキング攻撃に対する報復とし

て米国がサイバー攻撃を行ったかどうかについて
は、沈黙を守っている。

halt imports 輸入を停止する
◆Japan has temporarily halted imports of beef
products from the United States after the first
U.S. case of mad cow disease was found. 米国
で初めて狂牛病（BSE）の感染例が見つかったこと
を受けて、日本は米国からの牛肉製品の輸入を一
時的に停止した。

hammer price 競売落札価格、落札価格、ハ
ンマー・プライス［ハンマープライス］
◆The hammer price of Edvard Munch's painting
"The Scream" was $107 million, and about $120
million with the buyer's premium. ノルウェーの
画家エドバルド・ムンクの絵画「叫び」の競売落
札価格は1億700万ドルで、バイヤーズ・プレミア
ム（競売会社に支払われる売買手数料）込みでは約
1億2,000万ドルだった。

hand （名）手、手中、所有、保護、管理、支配、世
話、技量、腕前、手腕、人、職人、働き手、人手、
誓約
cash on [in] hand 手元現金
（=funds on [in] hand）
change hands 所有者［持ち主］が変わる、株
主が変わる、人手に渡る、（一定の金額で）
商品が売れる、政権を交替する、更迭する
gain [get, have] the upper hand of [over] ～
に勝つ、～より優勢になる、～より優位に立
つ、～より有利な立場を得る、～を支配す
る、～を掌握する、～を出し抜く （=gain
the whip hand of [over]）
goods on hand 在庫品 （=stock in hand）
hand delivery 手渡し
join hands with ～と提携する［提携を結ぶ］、
～と手を組む、～と両手を取り合う、～と結
婚する、夫婦になる
on hand 手持ちの［で］、所有して、持ち合わ
せて、（時間などを）持て余じて、間近に、目
前に、近くに居合わせて、待機して、出迎え
に出て、出席して
quantity on hand 手持ち数量
stock on hand 手持ち在庫
strike hands with ～と契約を交わす［取り決
める］、～と契約する、～と協力を約束する、
～と手を握り合う
the upper hand 優勢、優位、優越、支配
units on hand 手持ち有り高
with what is left on hand 手持ちの商品で
◆Golden shares could fall into the hands of a
hostile takeover bidder. 黄金株は、敵対的買収
者の手に渡る場合もある。◆In the case of a lack
of liquidity, either bridge lending or debt defer-
ment can save the borrower as there is no cash
on hand. 流動性不足の場合は、手元に現金がな
いので、つなぎ資金を貸す［つなぎ融資］か債務返
済の延長で借り手は助かる。◆We were unable to

meet their wishes with what was left on hand. 当
社は、手持ちの商品で先方［同社］の要望に応える
ことができなかった。

handle （動）取り扱う、扱う、さばく、処理す
る、対処する、対応する、操作する
◆An increase in transactions that brokerages
handle has accompanied the brisk stock market
business. 証券会社が扱う取引の増加は、そのま
ま株式相場の盛況と重なる。◆Following the integration of the TSE and OSE, the two exchanges
may be reorganized by function, with one entity
to handle spot trading and another derivatives. 東
証と大証の統合後、両取引所は機能別に再編され、
それぞれ現物取引とデリバティブを扱うようになる
可能性がある。◆This research and development
center established in Kyoto will mainly handle
product design and function improvements for
new washing machines. 京都に新設されたこの
研究開発（R&D）センターは、主に洗濯機の新製品
の製品設計や機能向上などを担当する。

handling （名）取扱い、操作、操縦、処理、対応、
運用、運営、手法、荷役、運搬、（商品の）出荷、
盗品の取引、ハンドリング
careful h handling 慎重な扱い［操作、対応］
careless handling 不注意な扱い、取扱いの
不注意
cargo handling costs 荷役費、貨物費
direct handling 直扱い
ground handling 地上業務
handling allowance 荷役手当て、出荷手当て
handling charges 貨物取扱い費、取扱い手数
料、手形買入れ手数料
handling cost 荷役費
handling customer complaint 顧客苦情処理
handling expenses 取扱い手数料、荷役費
handling fee 取扱い手数料
handling instructions 貨物取扱い指示
handling of goods 商品の取扱い、商品荷役、
貨物取扱い
handling time 荷役時間、手作業時間
lighter aboard ship handling vessel ラッ
シュ船
material handling 荷役、荷役運搬、資材運搬、
運搬管理、原材料取扱い、マテリアル・ハン
ドリング、マテハン
poor handling of the situation 状況に対する
対応のまずさ
safe handling and storage 安全取扱いと保
管法
sensitive handling 慎重な扱い［取扱い］、慎
重な対応
◆In the event that Supplier is requested to assist
Distributor in arranging for transportation, Distributor shall reimburse Supplier for all costs relating to such arrangements, including, without

limitation, insurance, transportation, loading and unloading, handling and storage following their delivery to Distributor. 供給者が販売店から運送手配の支援を要請された場合、販売店は、供給者が（本製品を）販売店へ引き渡した後の保険、運送、積み下ろし、貨物取扱い、保管料などの関連費用を、すべて供給者に償還するものとする。◆This damage is due to the careless handling of our goods. この破損は、当社商品の取扱いが慎重でなかったことによるものです。

hardship （名)困難, 履行困難な状況, 履行困難な事態, ハードシップ
◆If there should be a material change in market conditions or other circumstances, or a substantial change in exchange rate, which would impose hardship on either party in performing its obligations under this agreement, then both parties hereto shall, at the request of either party, meet, discuss and review in good faith, the terms and conditions of this agreement as that it may be revised to resolve and overcome such hardship for the mutual benefit of both parties and the maintenance of good relationship. 市況やその他の状況に重大な変化が生じてまたは為替レートに著しい変動が生じて、本契約に基づく一方の当事者の義務履行が困難になると、両当事者は、一方の当事者の要請に応じて、両当事者の相互利益と良好な関係維持のためその履行困難な事態の解決と克服に向けて本契約を修正できるよう誠意をもって会合、協議し、本契約条項を見直すものとする。

harm （動)害する, 傷つける, 痛める, 損なう, 危害を加える
harm economic growth 経済成長にマイナスになる
harm the economy ～で経済が打撃を受ける
◆Domestic industries harmed by dumping require urgent protection. ダンピングによる損害を受けている国内産業は、緊急保護を必要としている。◆The yen's appreciation will not only reduce the volume of exports but also harm a wide variety of other areas. 円高は輸出の減少だけでなく、その弊害は広範に及ぶ。

harm （名)損害, 害, 弊害, 危害, 悪意, 悪気, 不都合, 差し支え
do harm to ～に危害[損害]を与える
financial harm 金銭的被害
irreparable harm 回復不能の損害
physical harm 物的損害
◆ABC shall take care of keeping its quality without any harm whatsoever as bona fide holder of Products on behalf of XYZ. ABCは、XYZを代理する契約品[本製品]の善意の保管者として、契約品[本製品]の品質保持上、どんな損害も生じないよう注意を払うものとする。

harmful rumors 風評被害
◆Japanese agricultural and marine products have been seriously damaged by harmful rumors. 日本の農産品や海産物[日本の農水産物]は、風評被害で大きな打撃を受けている。

harmless （形)無害の, 害を及ぼさない, 悪意のない, 損害・損傷を受けない, 責任を受けない （⇒hold harmless)

harmonized commodity description and coding system 商品名の名称・分類についての統一システム

have （動)所有する, 保有する, 置く（have＋目的語＋動詞の原形、過去分詞のhaveは、次の文例に示すように「～させる、～してもらう」という意味)
have and hold [obtain] 保有する, 所有する
Have Made Clause ハブ・メイド条項, 下請生産条項（第三者に発注して製造させる「委託生産」に関する条項のこと。⇒have manufactured)
◆Licensee shall not register or have any other party register any intellectual property right with respect to Know-How or other technical information in any country, without a prior written consent of Company. ライセンシーは、会社の書面による事前の承諾を得ないで、本ノウハウまたはその他の技術情報に関する知的財産権[知的所有権]をいずれの国においても登録せず、他のいかなる関係者にも登録させないものとする。◆The Landlord shall effect insurance by itself or have other tenants effect insurance against such accidents as aforementioned and indemnify the Tenant within the extent covered by the insurance. 「貸主」は、前記の事故などに対して自ら保険を付けるか他のテナントに保険を付けさせ、その保険でカバーされる範囲内で「借主」に損害の補償をするものとする。

have manufactured （第三者に)製造させる, 下請生産させる
◆ABC hereby grants to XYZ during the term of this agreement, an exclusive and nontransferable right and license, with the right to grant a sublicense, to use the information and the proprietary rights, for the purpose of manufacturing, having manufactured, using and developing and the application or the improvement of the licensed products at one or more plants located in the territory. 本契約期間中ABCは、契約地域に所在する一つまたは複数の工場で許諾製品を製造させるおよび製造させる目的と使用、開発および利用・改良する目的のために、本情報と財産権を使用する独占的で譲渡不可能な権利とライセンスを、サブライセンスを付与する権利とともに、本契約によりXYZに付与する。

hazard （名)危険, 危険性, 危険要因, 危険なもの, 危険を引き起こすもの, 障害, 障害物, 混乱, 危機, 妨げる要因, 偶然, 運, ハザード
economic hazards 経済的混乱, 経済の混乱
environmental hazards 環境汚染
explosion hazard 爆発の危険, 爆発危険性
external hazard 外的危険

health hazards　健康危害

inherent hazard　固有の危険, 固有危険, 内部危険

investment hazards　投資の障害

loading hazards　積付け危険

moral hazard　倫理の欠如, 道徳的危険, モラル・ハザード

natural hazard　自然現象に由来する危険

occupational hazard　業務上の危険, 職業上の危険

physical hazard　物理的危険, 物的危険, フィジカル・ハザード

hazardous　(形) 危険な, 危険を及ぼす, 危険の多い, 有害な, 冒険的な, 運任 (まか) せの

hazardous chemicals　危険な化学薬品 (=hazchem)

hazardous goods　危険貨物

hazardous material [substance]　危険物質

hazardous risk　危険物件

hazardous waste　有害廃棄物

hazardous waste removal　有害廃棄物除去

heading　(名) 見出し, 見出し語, 表題
◆The Section headings set forth in this agreement are for convenience only and shall not be considered for any purpose in interpreting or construing this agreement. 本契約書に記載する各条項の見出し語は, 単に便宜上のもので, どんな目的であれ本契約の解釈の際には考慮しないものとする。

headings to the Articles of this agreement　本契約条項の見出し
◆The headings to the Articles of this agreement are to facilitate reference only, do not form a part of this agreement and shall not in any way affect the interpretation of this agreement. 本契約条項の見出しは, 参照の便宜だけの目的のもので, 本契約の一部を構成するものではなく, いかなる場合でも本契約の解釈に影響を与えないものとする。

headquarters function　本社機能
◆Both foreign-capitalized and Japanese companies are forced to relocate their headquarters functions overseas. 外資系企業も日本企業も, 本社機能を海外に移さざるを得なくなっている。

hearing　(名) 聴力, 音の聞こえる範囲, 意見聴取, 公聴会, 聴聞 (ちょうもん) 会, 裁判所の審理, 公判, 審問, 委員会などの尋問・審理

a congressional [Congressional] hearing　米連邦議会の公聴会, 米議会の聴聞会

a Senate Banking Committee hearing　米上院銀行委員会の公聴会

FTC hearings　公正取引委員会 (FTC) の審判

grand bench hearings　大法廷聴聞会

hold a public hearing　公聴会を開く

open hearing　公聴会

preliminary hearing　事前審理, 予備審問, 予審

private hearing　非公開の聴聞会

public hearing　公聴会, 公判

Senate hearing　米上院公聴会
◆Many of the U.S. media slammed Akio Toyoda, president of Toyota Motor Corp., who announced that he will not attend a Toyota-related U.S. congressional hearing. トヨタ関連の問題に関する米議会の公聴会への出席を見合わせる意向を表明したトヨタ自動車の豊田章男社長に対して, 米メディアの多くが厳しく批判した。◆The Antimonopoly Law stipulates that documents submitted to FTC hearings may be disclosed to certain concerned parties upon their request. 独占禁止法は,「公正取引委員会の審判に提出された書類 [記録] は特定の利害関係人の請求に基づいて利害関係人に開示することができる」と定めている。

hedge　(動) 損失予防策をとる, 未然に防ぐ, 売り (買い) つなぎして損失を防ぐ, 分散投資して損失リスクを少なくする, 掛けつなぎする, 掛けつなぐ, リスクを回避する

hedge against currency risk　為替リスク [為替変動リスク] に対してヘッジする, 為替リスクをヘッジする

hedge against inflation　インフレに対してヘッジする

hedge business exposure　事業リスクをヘッジする

hedge interest rate risk　金利 (変動) リスクをヘッジする

hedge one's bets　損失の危険を減らす, 損失リスクを回避する

hedge the price risk of a stock　株式の価格リスクをヘッジする
◆We can hedge exchange risk through forward markets. 為替予約で, 為替リスクをヘッジすることができる。

hedge　(名) 備え, 損失予防手段, 防護策, 掛けつなぎ売買, 保険つなぎ, 為替リスクの防止・軽減, ヘッジ　(=hedging)

as a hedge against　～に備えて, ～に対する防壁として, ～に対するつなぎとして

as a hedge against inflation　インフレ・ヘッジとして

as a hedge against losses　損失に対するつなぎとして

futures hedge　先物ヘッジ

hedge-buying　買いつなぎ　(=buying hedge)

hedge operation　ヘッジ操作, 為替ヘッジ取引

hedge-selling　売りつなぎ　(=selling hedge)

hedge transaction　ヘッジ取引 (=hedging transaction)

hedged asset [property]　ヘッジ対象資産, ヘッジする資産

hedges of existing assets or liabilities　既存の資産または債務のヘッジ

inflationary hedge インフレ・ヘッジ
（=inflation hedge）

lift a hedge ヘッジを外（はず）す

long hedge 買いヘッジ

rebalance the hedge ヘッジを見直す

risk hedge リスク・ヘッジ

short hedge 売りヘッジ
◆Gains and losses on hedges of existing assets or liabilities are marked to market on a monthly basis. 既存の資産または債務のヘッジに関する損益は毎月、評価替えされている。

hedge exchange risks 為替リスク［為替変動］を回避する，為替リスクをヘッジする
◆Japanese companies can hedge exchange risks and improve their business image abroad through external bond financing. 日本企業は、外債発行による資金調達で、為替リスクを回避するとともに海外での企業イメージアップを図ることができる。

hedge fund ヘッジ・ファンド，短期投資資金（「ヘッジ・ファンド」は、株式や債券、通貨、原油など幅広い市場で、巨額の資金を運用して投機性の高い取引を行う機関投資家）

a high-profile hedge fund 著名なヘッジ・ファンド

short-term speculative hedge funds 投機性の高い短期投資資金
◆In a global carry trade, hedge funds borrow low-interest yen funds to invest in dollar-denominated assets. グローバル・キャリー・トレード［グローバル・キャリー取引］では、ヘッジ・ファンドなどが、低利の円資金を借りてドル建て資産に投資している。◆Japanese nonbanks blamed for fueling the economic bubble and hedge funds responsible for triggering the collapse of Lehman Brothers in 2008 can be broadly defined as China's shadow banks. 日本のバブルをあおった原因のノンバンクや2008年のリーマン・ブラザーズ経営破たん（リーマン・ショック）の引き金になったヘッジ・ファンドは、広い意味で中国の「影の銀行」と言える。◆The underdeveloped state of financial systems in East Asian countries allowed a massive influx and exodus of short-term speculative hedge funds from abroad. 東アジア諸国の金融システムの未整備が、海外からの投機性の高い短期投資資金の大量流入と流出を許した。

hence expiration of 〜の満了後
◆This agreement shall be automatically renewed from year to year for one year term hence expiration of the initial term of this agreement. 本契約は、本契約の当初の期間満了後は、1年単位で年毎に自動更新されるものとする。

hereby （副）これにより（by this），本契約により（by this agreement），本契約書により，本状の規定により，ここに　（=by the provisions of this Article）

hereby accept 本契約により受諾する，本契約により承諾する，本契約により承認する

hereby agree 本契約により合意する［同意する］

hereby agree as follows 本契約により以下のとおり合意する

hereby appoint 本契約により指名する

hereby grant 本契約により付与する
◆Guarantor hereby waives any right it may have of first requiring ABC to pursue its legal remedies against XYZ. 保証人は、保証人が持てる権利にして、まずXYZに対して法的救済を求めることをABCに要求する権利を、ここに放棄する。◆Now IT IS HEREBY AGREED AS FOLLOWS: そこで、本契約により次のとおり合意する。

hereby waive ここに放棄する
◆The guarantor hereby waives any right it may have as surety which may be at any time inconsistent with any of the provisions of this guarantee. 保証人は、本保証書［保証状］の条項にどんな時でも矛盾する可能性のある、保証人が保証人として持つことができる一切の権利をここに放棄する。

herein （副）本契約で，本契約書に，本条で，本条に，本文で，本文に　（hereは、this agreement, this article, this sentenceなどを表わす）

herein set forth 本契約［本契約書］に定める，本契約に規定する，本契約に明記する

hereinafter referred to as 以下〜という，本契約書で以下〜という

hereinafter referred to as the "Products" 以下「本製品」という，本契約書で以下「本製品」という

herein contained 本契約書に記載する，本契約に明記する，本契約に定める
◆NOW, THEREFORE, in consideration of the promises herein contained and other good consideration, the parties hereto do hereby agree as follows: そこで、本契約に定める約束ごとと他の有効な約因を対価として、両当事者はここに以下のとおり合意する。

hereof （副・形）これに関して，この契約書の，本契約書の，本文書の

hereto （副・形）本契約の，本契約書の，これに関して　（regarding this agreement）
◆Neither party hereto shall, by virtue of its being a party to this agreement, so hold itself out by advertising or otherwise. 本契約当事者のいずれも、本契約の当事者であることによって、広告その他によりその旨名乗らないものとする。◆The particulars of the services and assistance are set forth in Exhibit A hereto. サービスと指導の詳細は、本契約書の付属書類Aに定める。

heretofore delivered to これまで〜に引き渡した　（heretofore=before this）
◆The balance sheet, operation statement and profit and loss statement and the statement of changes in the fiscal position of the Company as

at December 31, 2014 prepared by the Company, heretofore delivered to the Buyer, are in accordance with the books, records and accounts of the Company. 本会社が作成してこれまで買い主に引き渡した2014年12月31日現在の本会社の貸借対照表、営業報告書と損益計算書および財務状態変動表は、本会社の会計帳簿、記録と勘定に従って作成されている。

hereunto （副）本契約までに
（=up to the date of this agreement）

hidden dangerous goods 目に見えない危険物

high-quality （形）良質の, 質の高い
◆A prerequisite for the continued existence of industry in Japan is an affordable and stable supply of high-quality electricity. 日本の産業が生き残るための必要条件として、良質の電力の安価で安定した供給が挙げられる。

high tariffs 高関税
◆Despite strong criticism from Washington's trading partners against high tariffs on steel imports to rescue the ailing U.S. steel industry, the USTR stressed the legitimacy of such safeguard measures. 不況の米鉄鋼業界を救済するための輸入鉄鋼製品に対する高関税について、米国の貿易相手国から強い批判がなされているにもかかわらず、米国通商代表はこの緊急輸入制限（セーフガード）措置の正当性を強調した。◆Tokyo, Taipei and Washington failed to reach a consensus about how to resolve the dispute over the EU's high tariffs on IT equipment imports. EUの情報技術（IT）機器輸入に対する高関税をめぐる紛争の解決法に関して、日本、台湾と米国は合意に達しなかった。

high value of the yen 円高
◆Export growth has slowed due to the high value of the yen and the weakness of economies overseas. 円高と海外経済の減速で、輸出の伸びが鈍った。

high yen 円高
◆Besides a delay in the development of smartphones and cutting-edge displays, a tenaciously high yen hovering around ¥80 per dollar also contributed to the troubles of domestic electronics manufacturers. スマートフォン（高機能携帯電話）や最先端ディスプレーの開発の遅れのほか、1ドル＝80円前後の円高水準がずっと続いていることも、国内家電の不振につながっている。

higher electric power output costs 電力生産コストの上昇
◆The Japanese economy is losing momentum with the burdens of a strong yen and high labor costs as well as higher electric power output costs. 日本経済は、円高や人件費高に電力生産コストの上昇などの負担が加わって失速している。

higher fuel imports 燃料輸入の増加
◆If the exchange rate remains around ¥90 to the dollar for the next 12 months, income equivalent to 0.6 percent of Japan's GDP will flow over-

seas mainly due to higher fuel imports stemming from the suspension of nuclear power reactors. 為替相場が今後1年間、1ドル＝90円程度の水準が続いた場合、主に原子力発電所の運転停止に伴う燃料輸入の増加により、日本の国内総生産（GDP）の0.6％相当の所得が海外に流出する。

higher import prices 輸入価格の上昇, 輸入価格の高騰
◆The United States is under pressure to make some difficult monetary policy decisions to cool down the overheating economy by countering the inflationary pressure stemming from higher import prices due to the weaker dollar. 米国は現在、ドル安での輸入価格の高騰によるインフレ圧力を抑えて、過熱気味の景気を鎮めるための難しい金融政策の決断を迫られている。

higher lending rates 貸出金利の引上げ, 貸出金利の上昇
◆It's pointed out that the ECB's introduction of a negative deposit rate will increase the burden on commercial banks and worsen their finances, leading to a minimization of new loans and higher lending rates. 欧州中央銀行（ECB）のマイナス金利［マイナス中銀預入金利］の導入については、民間銀行の負担が増し、銀行の財務が悪化して、新規融資の抑制や貸出金利の上昇につながる、と指摘されている。

higher prices 値上がり, 価格引上げ, 高値
◆Indonesia has enjoyed decent economic growth since the global financial crisis of 2008 due to the U.S. FRB's quantitative easing and higher prices of primary commodities such as coal and palm oil as the country's major exports. インドネシアは、2008年の世界金融危機以降、米連邦準備制度理事会（FRB）の量的金融緩和とインドネシアの主要輸出品である石炭、パーム油など一次産品の高値に支えられ、高い経済成長を享受している。

hijacking （名）ハイジャック

hit the market 市場に登場する, 市場に出回る
◆Japanese deluxe wagyu beef has started to hit the market in Europe due to the lifting of a ban on beef exports from Japan to the European Union. 日本からEU（欧州連合）への牛肉輸出の解禁で、日本の高級和牛が欧州の市場に出回り始めた。

hold （動）保有する, 所有する, 保持する, 所持する, 保管する, 判断する, 判決する, 拘束する, 義務付ける, 主張する, 証明する, 遂行する
hold and keep 保持する, 維持する
hold in confidence 秘密に保持する, 機密に保持する （=maintain in confidence）
hold oneself out as ～と広告する, ～として広告する
hold oneself out to be ～と称する, ～と名乗る
hold over 延期する, 保有期間満了後も占有する
◆All quantities of the Product manufactured by

you shall be held by you to our order and we shall insure all quantities on your premises of the Commodity and the Product. 貴社が製造した契約品の数量はすべて当社の指図があるまで貴社が保管し、当社は貴社の構内にある商品と契約品の全数量に保険を付けるものとする。◆If any provision or any portion of any provision of this agreement shall be held to be void or unenforceable, the remaining provisions of this agreement and the remaining portion of any provision held void or unenforceable in part shall continue in full force and effect. 本契約の規定またはその一部が無効または実施不能と判断された場合、本契約の残りの規定と、一部が無効または実施不能と判断された規定の残りの部分は、すべて有効に存続するものとする。◆In case any one or more of the provisions of this agreement are held invalid, illegal or unenforceable in any respect, the validity, legality and enforceability of the remaining provisions hereof shall not be in any way affected or impaired thereby, except to the extent that giving effect to the remaining provisions would be unjust or inequitable. 本契約の一つ以上の規定がいずれかの点で無効、違法または強制不能と判断された場合、残存規定の実施が不公正または不均衡となる範囲を除いて、本契約の残存規定の有効性、合法性と強制可能性はその影響を受けることはなく、またそれによって損なわれることはないものとする。◆Licensee hereby agrees to hold in the strictest secrecy Know-How and other technical information disclosed by Company pursuant to the terms hereof. ライセンシーは、本契約により、本契約の条件に従って会社が開示したノウハウとその他の技術情報を特に厳格に秘密にしておくことに同意する。

hold （名）船倉, 倉内

  break out the hold　積み荷を降ろし始める

  hold capacity　倉内容積

  hold cargo　船倉貨物

  hold clearing　倉内清掃

  stow the hold　船倉に貨物を積み込む

hold harmless　補償する, 損失・不利益にならないようにする, 損害を与えない, 責任を免除する

  hold harmless clause　免責条項

  ◆The seller indemnify and hold the buyer and the Company harmless up to an aggregate maximum of U.S. $ _____, against any loss and damages caused to the buyer or to the Company by any misrepresentation, breach of warranty or breach of any agreement on the part of the seller in this agreement. 本契約上の売り主側の不実表明、保証違反または契約違反により買い主と本会社に生じたすべての損失と損害については、合計最高額 _____ 米ドルまで、売り主が買い主と本会社に補償し、損害・損失を与えないものとする。

hold oneself responsible for　～に対して責任を負う

◆We may not have to add that we do not hold ourselves responsible for the corresponding delay in shipment if your actions should not be taken in time. 言うまでもなく［申すまでもなく］、貴社の打つ手が遅れたら、それに伴って生じる船積みの遅延に対して、当社は責任を負いません。◆We shall not hold ourselves responsible for the corresponding delay in shipment if the credit should fail to arrive in time. 万一信用状が間に合わない場合、その結果として起こる［それに伴って生じる］船積みの遅延に対して、当社は責任を負わないものとする。

hold oneself so [so hold oneself]　その旨名乗る

◆Neither party hereto shall, by virtue of its being a party to this agreement, hold itself out by advertising or otherwise. 本契約当事者のいずれも、本契約の当事者であることによって、広告その他によりその旨名乗らないものとする。

holder　（名）所有者, 保有者, (手形や小切手の)所持人, 占有者, (貨物の)荷主

  asset holder　資産の保有者

  bill holder　手形所持人

  bona fide holder　善意の所持人 (=holder in due course: 手形や小切手などの正当な所持人), (契約品などの)善意の保管者

  bond holder　社債権者, 債券所有者, 債券所持人

  check holder　小切手振出人

  debenture holder　債券保有者

  debt holder　債券保有者

  draft holder　手形所持人

  equity holder　持ち分証券保有者

  gold holder　金保有者

  holder for value　(手形の)有償所持人

  holder in bad faith　悪意の第三者

  holder in due course　正当な所持人, 正当所持人

  holder in good faith　善意有償所持人

  holder of a preferential right　先取特権保有者

  holder of record　名簿上の株主

  holder on good faith　善意の第三者, 善意取得者

  land holder　土地所有者, 借地人

  loan holder　債権者

  option holder　オプション保有者, オプションの買い手

  policy holder　保険証券保持者, 保険契約者, 保険加入者

  portfolio holder　金融資産保有者

  real asset holder　実物資産保有者

  real estate holder　不動産所有者

  security holder　証券所有者, 証券保有者

  share [stock] holder　株式保有者, 株主

speculative holder　投機的な保有者

wealth holder　資産所有者［保有者］

◆For Value Received, the undersigned ("Borrower") promises to pay to ABC Co., Ltd. , a Japanese corporation ("Holder"), or order, in lawful money of the United States, the principal sum of Five million Eight hundred Fifty thousand dollars（$5,850,000）, with interest on the principal balance remaining unpaid from the date hereof until paid, at the following rates. 「対価の受領」については、末尾署名者（以下「振出人」という）が、元本585万ドル（$5,850,000）と本手形の振出日から決済日まで残存する元本の未払い残高利息を、日本法人のABC株式会社（以下「所持人」という）にまたはその指図人に、米国の法定通貨と以下の金利で支払うことを約束する。

hollowing-out　（名）空洞化
（=hollowing, hollowing out, hollowization）
◆Introducing renewable energy sources instead of nuclear power plants may lead to the hollowing-out of the domestic industrial sector in the face of increased production costs, and bankruptcies of small and midsized businesses. 原発の代わりに再生可能エネルギーを導入すると、生産コストの上昇による国内産業の空洞化や中小企業の倒産を招く可能性がある。

hollowing-out of industry　産業空洞化
◆The government's policy of ending reliance on nuclear power generation will accelerate the hollowing-out of industry and hamper nuclear power plant exports. 政府の原発ゼロ方針［原発への依存度をゼロにする政府方針］は、産業空洞化を加速し、原発輸出を妨げることになる。

hollowing-out of Japanese industry　日本の産業空洞化
◆Improvement of industrial technology in China and other Asian countries leads to the hollowing-out of Japanese industry. 中国を始めとするアジア地域の工業技術水準の向上が、日本の産業空洞化を招いている。

hollowing-out of the domestic manufacturing industry　国内製造業の空洞化
◆The record trade deficit in 2012 was caused by a decline in exports due to the European financial crisis and deceleration of the Chinese economy, together with a sharp increase in imports of liquefied natural gas and the rapid hollowing-out of the domestic manufacturing industry. 2012年の過去最大の貿易赤字の要因としては、欧州の金融危機や中国経済の減速などで輸出が減少する一方、液化天然ガス（LNG）の輸入が急増し、国内製造業の空洞化が加速していることも挙げられる。◆To avoid the high costs of operating domestically, Japanese companies are moving their production overseas. And this leads to the rapid hollowing-out of the domestic manufacturing industry. 国内操業のコスト高を回避するため、日本企業が生産拠点を海外に移転しており、これが国内製造業の

急速な空洞化を招いている。

home appliance　家電, 家電製品, 家庭用電気器具, 白物　（=home electrical appliance, household appliance）
◆At present, export industries including home appliances and automobiles are raising their expectations for improved corporate performance under the weak yen, which has also driven up stock prices. 現在、家電や自動車などの輸出産業は、円安で業績改善の期待を高めており、円安はまた株価も押し上げた。

home market　国内市場
◆IKEA has come under criticism in its home market Sweden as it airbrushed women out of its latest catalog in Saudi Arabia. 家具小売業のイケアが、サウジアラビア版の最新商品カタログで女性モデルを画像処理で消したため、国内市場のスウェーデンで批判を浴びている。

honor　（動）〜に敬意を払う［表する］、〜を尊敬する［敬う］,（メダルなどを）授与する, 栄誉を与える, 表彰する, 〜に賞状を与える, 祀（まつ）る,（約束や契約を）履行する, 遵守［順守］する,（参加引受けする,（小切手や手形などを）引き受ける, 期日に支払う, 債務を返済する, 債務を履行する　（⇒dishonor）

be deeply honored to do　〜することを大変光栄に思う, 〜できることを大変光栄に思う, 〜できて大変光栄に思う

honor a bill　手形を引き受ける, 手形を引き受けて（期日に）支払う, 手形の支払いをする

honor a contract　契約金額を（期日に）支払う

honor a draft　手形を引き受ける
（=honor a bill）

honor debt guarantee　債務保証を引き受ける

honor foreign currency obligations　外貨建てローンを返済する

honor one's agreement　〜の取決めを守る

honor one's checks　〜の振り出した小切手を引き受ける, 〜の振り出した小切手の支払いをする

honor the claims　債務を返済する, 債務を履行する

honor your draft on presentation　手形の提示［呈示］あり次第, 貴社の手形の支払いをする

refuse to honor one's cheque　（銀行が）〜の小切手引受けを拒む
◆According to Moody's Investors Service, Egypt is likely to default on about 10 percent of its outstanding external debt in 2014 and fail to honor as much as 40 percent within five years. ムーディーズによると、エジプトは2014年には対外債務残高の約10％が不履行となり、5年以内に債務の40％が不履行になる見込みだ。◆The company plans to honor debt guarantee on a total of ¥86.8 billion. 同社は、総額868億円の債務保証を引き受ける方針だ。◆The firm has gone effec-

tively bankrupt after banks suspended transactions with it on its second failure to honor a bill. 同社が2回目の不渡りを出して銀行取引停止となり、事実上倒産した。◆The solvency margin ratio indicates the ability of insurers to honor insurance claims and other payments. ソルベンシー・マージン比率は、保険会社の保険金その他の支払い金の支払い能力を示す。◆We have drawn upon you a documentary bill at 60 d/s through ABC Bank for the invoice amount, which we hope you will kindly honor on presentation. 送り状金額に対して、ABC銀行を通じて60日払い荷為替手形を貴社宛てに振り出しましたので、提示[呈示]のあり次第お引受け下さい。

honor (名)(手形の)引受け[支払い]、尊敬、敬意、名誉、誉(ほま)れ、栄誉、光栄、特権、信義、自尊心、道義心、名声、信用、叙勲、表彰、褒章(ほうしょう)、優等
a debt of honor　信用借り、無証書借金
acceptance for honor　(手形の)参加引受け
acceptance for the honor of a drawer　振出人に対する信用上の手形引受け
ask A for acceptance for honor　Aに手形の参加引受けを依頼する
business [commercial] honor　商業上の信用
count it an honor to　～できることを光栄に思う
do honor to A　Aに敬意を表する[敬意を払う]、Aの名誉となる　(=do A honor)
for (the) honor of　～の信用上
have the honor of　光栄にも～をする、～をする光栄に浴する
honor agreement [contract]　名誉(保険)契約
honor policy　名誉保険証券、栄誉保険証券

honorarium (名)弁護士報酬、謝礼

hostage-taking incident　人質事件
◆Japanese employees of JGC Corp., a major plant manufacturing firm, were caught up in the hostage-taking incident launched by an armed Islamist group in Algeria. 大手プラント・メーカー「日揮」の邦人従業員が、アルジェリアでイスラム武装勢力が引き起こした人質事件に巻き込まれた。

hostile bidder　敵対的買収者
◆If golden shares held by a friendly company are transferred to another party, such shares could be transferred again to a hostile bidder. 友好的な企業が保有する黄金株を第三者に譲渡した場合、その黄金株はまた敵対的買収者に譲渡される可能性もある。

hostile mergers and acquisitions　敵対的M&A(企業の合併・買収)
◆Hostile mergers and acquisitions have been increasing rapidly as the dissolution of cross-shareholding ties among companies accelerates. 企業間の株式持ち合い関係の解消が加速するにつ

れ、敵対的M&A(企業の合併・買収)の件数は急増している。

hostile takeover　敵対的買収、乗っ取り、非友好的経営権買収、敵対的M&A　(=hostile acquisition, unsolicited takeover; ⇒white knight)
◆About 15 percent of the leading companies are studying the possibility of using a poison pill to counter a hostile takeover by using the issue of warrants. 主要企業の約15％は、新株予約権の発行などで敵対的買収に対抗するポイズン・ピル(毒薬)の導入可能性を検討している。◆Companies should obtain shareholder approval when introducing methods to counter hostile takeover attempts. 敵対的買収への対抗策を導入する場合、企業は株主の承認を得なければならない。

hostile takeover bid　敵対的TOB
◆In order to forestall hostile takeover bids, companies should raise their corporate value. 敵対的TOB(株式公開買付けによる企業買収)を未然に防ぐには、企業が企業価値を高めなければならない。◆Nireco Corp. has scrapped its plan to invoke the nation's first poison pill scheme to ward off hostile takeover bids. ニレコは、敵対的TOB(株式公開買付けによる企業買収)を防ぐための日本で最初のポイズン・ピル防衛策の実施計画を白紙撤回した。

hostile takeover bidder　敵対的買収者
◆Golden shares could fall into the hands of a hostile takeover bidder. 黄金株は、敵対的買収者の手に渡る場合もある。

hostilities (名)敵対行為、戦闘、戦争、戦争状態、交戦

HS　関税率表(Harmonized Commodity Description and Coding Systemの略)

human resources　人的資源、人材、人事部、人事[人材]管理部門、労務管理部門
◆The Trans-Pacific Partnership framework to promote free trade among member countries is expected to invigorate the movement of human resources. 加盟国間の自由貿易化を進めるための環太平洋経済連携協定(TPP)で、人材の移動も盛んになることが予想される。

human resources development program　人材開発プログラム
◆Corporations must work on job training for those people who will lead future industries, through improved technical training and other human resources development programs. 企業は、技術訓練の強化や他の人材開発プログラムなどで、これからの産業の担い手の職業訓練に取り組まなければならない。

hyper-appreciation of yen　超円高
◆The hyper-appreciation of yen that had afflicted the Japanese economy was corrected after the launch of the Abe Cabinet. 日本経済を苦しめてきた超円高は、安倍内閣の発足後、是正された。

I

IAIS 保険監督者国際機構（International Association of Insurance Supervisorsの略）

IAS 国際会計基準（International Accounting Standardsの略）
◆Japanese companies listed on the London Stock Exchange will submit financial reports based on the IAS or the U.S. GAAP. ロンドン証券取引所に上場している日本企業は今後、国際会計基準か米国会計基準に基づく［に準拠した］財務報告書を提出することになる。

ICAO 国際民間航空機関、イカオ（International Civil Aviation Organizationの略）

ICC 国際商業会議所（International Chamber of Commerceの略）

ICC model international sale contract ICC（国際商業会議所）標準売買契約書式

ICE 米インターコンチネンタル取引所（⇒Intercontinental Exchange）

ICJ 国際司法裁判所
◆Japan will abide by the ruling of the ICJ as a nation that attaches great importance to the rule of law, the director of the International Affairs Division at the Fisheries Agency said about Japan's research whaling. 日本は法の支配を重視する国家として国際司法裁判所（ICJ）の判決に従う、と水産庁の国際課長は日本の調査捕鯨について述べた。

identify （動）特定する、認定する、確認する、識別する、見分ける、表示する
be identified as an order 注文書として表示される
identified in Schedule A attached hereto 本契約書に添付する付属書類Aで特定する
◆Each order for Products issued by Distributor to Supplier under this agreement shall be in writing and identified as an order. 本契約に基づき販売店が供給者に発行する個別の注文書は、書面で行って、注文書と表示しなければならない。

identity （名）住所・氏名、身元、正体、素性、身分証明、本人、同一、同一性、独自性、本質、アイデンティティ
◆A party hereto proposing to effect a sale of any shares of the new company（the Offerer）shall give a written notice to the other parties hereto, or their assignee, who are then shareholders of the new company（the Offerees）, of the Offerer's intention, the identity of the prospective third party purchaser, and the terms and conditions of the proposed sale. 新会社の株式の売却を申し出る本契約当事者（「申込み者」）は、他の当事者またはその時点で新会社の株主である譲受人（「被申込み者」）に対して、申込み者の売却意思、予定される第三者購入者の住所・氏名と申し出をした売却の条件を、書面で通知するものとする。
◆For the purpose of this agreement, any change

of corporate identity of one of the parties, such as by amalgamation, reorganization, or merger or consolidation, has not been agreed to by the other party. 本契約の目的上、合併、会社更生または吸収合併や新設合併といった当事者の一方の法人格の変更については、相手方当事者が同意していない。

if （接）もし～ならば、～なら、～の場合は、たとえ～だとしても
if and to the extent ～する場合または～する場合にかぎって、～する場合または限度［範囲］内で、～ならその限度内で、～する場合にかぎって
if any いくらかでもあれば、もしあれば、もしあるとすれば、たとえあるとしても
if decided adversely 不利益な決定が下されても
if otherwise agreed 別段の合意があれば
if so requested 要求に応じて
If to XYZ, to it at: XYZ宛ての場合は、下記住所の同社宛て：

IFC 国際金融公社（International Finance Corporationの略）

IFRS 国際財務報告基準（International Financial Reporting Standardsの略。2004年まで「国際会計基準（International Accounting Standards（IAS）」と呼ばれていた。⇒International Financial Reporting Standards）
◆The Financial Services Agency gave up its initial goal to make the introduction of the IFRS mandatory in around 2015. 金融庁は、2015年にもIFRS（国際財務報告基準）の導入を義務化するという当初の目標を断念した。

illegal （形）違法な、非合法な、不法な
illegal or invalid 違法または無効の（=invalid or illegal）
per se illegal 当然違法

illegal act 不法行為、違法行為
◆According to the Finance Ministry's Customs and Tariff Bureau, 127 drug detection dogs uncovered 46 cases of drug smuggling and other illegal act last fiscal year. 財務省関税局によると、昨年度は、127頭の麻薬犬が麻薬密輸などの違法行為を46件摘発した。

illegal activity 不法行為、違法行為
◆The FSA inspections exposed the the bank's illegal activities. 金融庁の検査で、同行の違法行為が暴かれた。◆The United States, Japan and South Korea agreed to take tough action against alleged illegal activities by North Korea, including drug smuggling and money counterfeiting. 米国、日本と韓国は、北朝鮮によるとされる麻薬密輸や通貨偽造などの非合法活動に断固対処することで合意した。

illegal bid 不正入札
◆The firm was investigated in connection with

an alleged illegal bid for a construction bid. 建設工事をめぐる不正入札事件の関連先として、同社は捜索を受けた。

illegal drug sales 麻薬の不正販売
◆Money laundering is the practice of legitimizing money gained through illegal drug and gun sales or other crimes by putting it through bank accounts. マネー・ロンダリングは、麻薬や銃器の不正販売やその他の犯罪で得た資金を、銀行口座を経由させて合法的に見せる行為だ。

illegal drug smuggling 違法薬物［麻薬］の密輸入
◆Two drug detection dogs were introduced from the United States in 1979 by Tokyo Customs to fight illegal drug smuggling. 麻薬探知犬は、違法薬物の密輸入を阻止するため、東京税関が1979年に米国から2頭を導入した。

illegal export 不正輸出, 違法輸出
(=unlawful export)
◆It is difficult to regulate illegal exports through a third country. 第三国を迂回した不正輸出を取り締まるのは難しい。◆The statute of limitations on this illegal export has already expired. この不正輸出の時効は、すでに迎えている。

illegal image 違法画像
◆Companies operating Internet auction sites prohibit pornographic and other illegal images from being auctioned. ネット競売サイトの運営会社は、ポルノなどの違法画像のオークションへの出品を禁止している。

illegal trading 不正取引
◆The Financial Services Agency will tighten regulations over insider trading, following a series of illegal trading incidents involving the leakage of companies' internal information by major securities firms. 金融庁は、大手証券会社による企業の内部情報漏えいに伴う一連の不正取引事件を受けて、インサイダー取引に関する規制を強化する方針だ。

illegal transaction 不正取引, 違法取引, 違法行為
◆In order to cut off funds to North Korea's nuclear weapons development program, the government will tighten controls on illegal bilateral transactions, including exports of materials for making missiles and smuggling of narcotics and counterfeit bank notes into the country. 北朝鮮の核兵器開発計画の資金源を断つため、政府はミサイル製造の関連物資の輸出や麻薬・偽造紙幣の密輸など、日朝間の不正取引の取締りを強化する方針だ。

illegally export 不正輸出する
◆A car dealer tried to illegally export a tractor through China to North Korea. 自動車販売会社が、トラクター(牽引車)を中国経由で北朝鮮に不正輸出しようとしていた。

illicit activity 違法行為
◆The U.S. government froze the assets of four

individuals and eight entities that were involved in illicit activities such as money laundering, currency counterfeiting and narcotics trafficking. 米政府は、資金洗浄(マネー・ロンダリング)や通貨偽造、麻薬取引などの違法行為に関与している4個人、8団体の資産を凍結した。

IMDG Code 国際海上危険物規程, IMDGコード (IMDGはInternational Maritime Dangerous Goodsの略)

IMF 国際通貨基金 (International Monetary Fundの略)
◆Egypt's Morsi administration has concluded a basic agreement with the IMF on loans totaling $4.8 billion, with strings attached, in an effort to avert a default on debts. エジプトのモルシ政権は、債務不履行を回避するため、付帯条件付きで、国際通貨基金(IMF)との間で総額48億ドルの融資を受けることで基本合意した。

immediate confirmation 至急確認
◆We accept your offer subject to immediate confirmation by letter. 書簡での至急確認を条件として、貴社のオファーを引き受けます。

immediate effect 即時発効, 即時効力
◆ABC may terminate this agreement with immediate effect by sending a written notice to XYZ within 30 days after expiry of the relevant period. ABCは、当該期間の満了後30日以内にXYZに通知書を送付して、即時発効で本契約を解除することができる。

immediate shipment 直(じき)積み
◆Please give us your best quotations in U.S. dollars for immediate shipment and proforma invoices. 直(じき)積みでドル建ての貴社の建て値と試算送り状を、お送りください。◆This article is available for immediate shipment. 本品は、直積み可能です。

immunity (名)免除, 除外, 免責, 免除特権, 免責特権, 免税, 非課税
immunity bath 起訴免除
immunity from prosecution 訴追の免除
immunity from taxation 課税免除
immunity of witness 証言義務の免除特権
leave the goods in bond till immunity is obtained 免税あるまで倉出ししない
sovereign immunity 主権免除, 主権免除特権
tax immunity 免税, 課税免除
(=immunity from taxation)
waiver of sovereign immunity 主権免除特権の放棄
◆Japan and the United States will sign the open skies agreement, and carriers in both countries will be able to apply for U.S. antitrust immunity. 日米両政府がオープンスカイ協定を締結することによって、両国の航空会社は米国独占禁止法の適用除外申請が可能になる。

immunity of the property from attachment 財産の差し押さえからの免

除　(⇒sovereign immunity)

IMO　国際海事機関（International Maritime Organizationの略。1958年に設立された国連の専門機関で、政府間海洋協議機関（IMCO）の名称を1982年5月から改称）

impair　（動）損なう，損ねる，害する，減損する，責任などを縮減する

impair the obligation of contracts　契約上の債権債務関係を害する

impair the right Licensor to Trademarks　本商標に対するライセンサーの権利を損なう

◆In case any one or more of the provisions of this agreement are held invalid, illegal or unenforceable in any respect, the validity, legality and enforceability of the remaining provisions hereof shall not be in any way affected or impaired thereby, except to the extent that giving effect to the remaining provisions would be unjust or inequitable. 本契約の一つ以上の規定がいずれかの点で無効，違法または強制不能と判断された場合，残存規定の実施が不公正または不均衡となる範囲を除いて，本契約の残存規定の有効性，合法性と強制可能性はその影響を受けることはなく，またそれによって損なわれることはないものとする。◆The guarantor hereby agrees that no such modification, amendment or supplement shall release, affect or impair its liability under this guarantee. 保証人はここに，このような変更，修正または補足が本保証書に基づく保証人の責任を免除せず，またその責任に影響を与えず，その責任を縮減するものでもないことに同意する。

impair or prejudice　損なうまたは侵害する，損なう

◆Any termination of this agreement shall not impair or prejudice any right of such party not in default or insolvency accrued up to the date of such termination. 本契約のいかなる解除も，その解除日までに違反や支払い不能に陥っていない当事者の権利を損なわないものとする。

implement　（動）履行する，遂行する，実行する，実施する，施行する，供給する，提供する

implement a contract　契約を実行する

implement an aggressive capital investment　設備投資を積極的に進める

implement an international business strategy　国際企業戦略［経営戦略］を実行する，国際企業戦略をとる

◆The Abe administration will have to show the world that its economic policies do not depend solely on the yen's depreciation by steadily implementing the so-called three arrows of "Abenomics," or bold monetary easing, flexible fiscal spending and a growth strategy, in a balanced way. 安倍政権は今後，同政権が掲げる「アベノミクス」のいわゆる3本の矢（大胆な金融緩和，財政出動と成長戦略）をバランスよく着実に実行［実践］して，安倍政権の経済政策が単なる円安頼みではないことを，世界に示す必要がある。

implement a business reform　事業改革を実施する

◆The three electronics makers implemented business reforms, mainly streamlining of TV production businesses which had been the main cause of their losses. 家電メーカー3社は、赤字の元凶となってきたテレビ生産事業の合理化を中心に、事業改革を実施した。

implement structural reforms　構造改革を実施する，構造改革を進める

◆Among major electronics makers, Toshiba and Hitachi downsized their TV and mobile phone production businesses by quickly implementing structural reforms after recording huge losses. 電機大手のうち東芝や日立製作所は、巨額赤字を計上した後、素早く構造改革を進めてテレビや携帯電話の生産事業を縮小した。

implication of law　法律の運用

◆The seller shall not be liable in respect of any warranty or consideration as to quality or fitness which would arise by implication of law. 売り主は、法律の運用により生じる品質または適合性に関する保証または条件については、責任を負わないものとする。

implied warranties of merchantability, fitness for a particular purpose and noninfringement　商品性、特定目的への適合性および非侵害の黙示の保証

◆The seller makes no other warranties or representations with respect to the products and disclaims all warranties, including but not limited to implied warranties of merchantability, fitness for a particular purpose and noninfringement. 売り主は、本製品に関する他の保証または表明は行わず、商品性、特定目的への適合性および非侵害の黙示の保証などを含めてすべての保証を否認する。

implied warranty of merchantability　商品性の黙示保証

import　（動）輸入する、導入する、データなどを転送する、移動する、取り込む、持ち込む、発生させる

◆As long as Japan depends on thermal power generation as an alternative electricity source, LNG imports will continue to increase and the nation's wealth will flow to countries rich in natural resources. 日本が代替電源として火力発電に依存するかぎり、天然液化ガス（LNG）の輸入額は増え続け、国富は天然資源の豊富な国に流出する。◆Every three months, McDonald's Japan revises the price of the beef it imports from Australia according to the exchange rate. 3か月ごとに、日本マクドナルドは、為替相場に応じてオーストラリアから輸入している牛肉の価格を見直している。◆In Japan, ensuring a stable supply of the fuel for thermal power generation and importing the gas from a wide array of countries have become important issues since the accident at the Fukushima No. 1 nuclear power plant. 日本では、福島第一原発事故以来、火力発電用燃料

の安定供給確保［安定調達］とガス輸入先の多様化が重要な課題となっている。◆Japan and China have established a system of international division of labor in which China imports industrial parts from Japan to assemble into finished products in China and these are marketed domestically or exported to the U.S., Europe and elsewhere. 日本と中国は、中国が日本から工業部品を輸入して中国で最終製品に組み立て、中国国内で販売したり欧米などに輸出したりする国際分業体制を築いてきた。◆Japan has to import most of its fossil fuels from the Middle East in which supplies and prices remain unstable. 日本は、化石燃料の大半を、供給量も価格も不安定な中東からの輸入に頼っている。◆MMC's Outlander sport-utility vehicles produced in the Netherlands are currently assembled at its Dutch plant with parts imported from Japan. オランダで生産されている三菱自動車の多目的スポーツ車「アウトランダー」は現在、部品を日本から輸入してオランダの自社工場で組み立てている。◆Nissan Motor Co. and Mitsubishi Motor Co. have been importing and selling small cars they made in Thailand. 日産自動車や三菱自動車工業は、タイで生産した小型車を輸入、販売している。◆Sumitomo Corp. agreed to jointly develop rare earths and import the metals with Kazakhstan's state-owned resource firm Kazatomprom. 住友商事は、カザフスタンの国営資源企業「カザトムプロム」と、レア・アースを共同開発して輸入することで合意した。◆The new tariff on beef imports favors producers rather than consumers. 牛肉の輸入に対する新関税は、消費者ではなく生産者寄りの対応だ。

import （名）輸入, 輸入品 (imports), 輸入製品, 輸入量, 輸入額 (imports), 導入, 重要性, 重大, 意味, 趣意, 趣旨, インポート

a matter of great import　重大なこと

development import　開発輸入

direct imports　直輸入品

entire import of oral argument　口頭弁論の全趣旨

export-import cartel　輸出入カルテル

have a very grave import　極めて重い意味を持っている

import agent　輸入代理店

import demand　輸入品に対する需要, 輸入品需要, 輸入需要

import growth　輸入の伸び

import inflow　輸入拡大

import levy　輸入課税, 輸入課徴金

import liberalization　輸入自由化

import license　輸入許可, 輸入承認

import license bond rate　輸入担保率（=import deposit rate)

import of final goods　製品輸入

import of foreign capital　外資導入

import payment　輸入代金支払い, 輸入支払い

import promotion　輸入促進

import promotion activities　輸入促進事業

import quota system　輸入割当制度（⇒protect)

import replacement industry　輸入代替産業

import saving　輸入節約

import settlement　輸入決済

import stability　輸入安定

import subsidy　輸入補助金, 輸入奨励金

import substitution　輸入代替

import supply　輸入供給

import surcharge　輸入課徴金, 輸入税（=import surtax)

import surplus　輸入超過, 貿易収支赤字, 貿易赤字

import usance　輸入代金の延べ払い, 輸入ユーザンス

import usance financing method　輸入ユーザンス金融方式

import without (foreign) exchange　無為替輸入

import WPI　輸入物価指数

increased import　輸入の増加

invisible export and import　貿易外収支

iron ore import　鉄鉱石輸入

parallel import　並行輸入

product import　製品輸入

put a curb on imports　輸入制限措置（セーフガード)を発動する

put emergency curbs on imports　暫定輸入制限措置を発動する

reverse imports　逆輸入品

rise in import prices　輸入物価の上昇

rise in imports　輸入の伸び［増加］

◆As long as Japan depends on thermal power generation as an alternative electricity source, LNG imports will continue to increase and the nation's wealth will flow to countries rich in natural resources. 日本が代替電源として火力発電に依存するかぎり、天然液化ガス（LNG）の輸入額は増え続け、国富は天然資源の豊富な国に流出する。◆Despite strong criticism from Washington's trading partners against high tariffs on steel imports to rescue the ailing U.S. steel industry, the USTR stressed the legitimacy of such safeguard measures. 不況の米鉄鋼業界を救済するための輸入鉄鋼製品に対する高関税について、米国の貿易相手国から強い批判がなされているにもかかわらず、米国通商代表はこの緊急輸入制限（セーフガード）措置の正当性を強調した。◆Food imports from China declined sharply after the poisoned frozen gyoza incident, but now the figure has almost returned to the levels recorded prior to the incident. 冷凍ギョウザの中毒事件後、中国からの食品の輸入量は大きく落ち込んだが、今は事件前の水準にほぼ回復している。◆If agricultural imports become cheaper due to the lowered tariffs, consumers will greatly benefit. 関税の引下げで輸入農産品が安くなれば、消費者の利点も大きい。◆If we consider a good balance of exports and imports, a desirable exchange rate between the yen and the U.S. dollar would be ¥95-¥105 to the dollar. 輸出と輸入の妥当なバランスを考えるなら、円とドルの望ましい為替相場は、1ドル=95〜105円程度だろう。◆Imports in July 1-20, 2012 were up 4.7 percent at ¥3.92 trillion reflecting increases in imports of communications equipment as well as LNG. 2012年7月上中旬（1〜20日）の輸入額は、通信機器と液化天然ガス（LNG）の輸入増を反映して、（前年同期比）4.7%増の3兆9,200億円だった。◆Japan depends on the Middle East for about 80 percent of its crude oil imports. 日本は、原油輸入の約8割を中東に依存している。◆Japan has an about ¥3 trillion a year excess in imports in the growing markets of medicine and medical equipment. 医薬・医療機器の成長市場で、日本は年約3兆円の輸入超過になっている。◆Japan's current account surplus in July 2013 fell 12.9 percent from a year earlier to ¥577.3 billion, chiefly reflecting a wider gap in goods trade as imports of LNG for thermal power generation swelled due in part to an increase in electricity demand amid the hot summer. 2013年7月の日本の経常収支の黒字幅は、前年同月より12.9%減少して5,773億円となったが、これは主に猛暑で電力需要が増えたこともあって火力発電用の液化天然ガスの輸入が大幅に増加したため、モノの貿易での輸入超過［モノの貿易赤字］が拡大したことを反映している。◆Japan's overall exports in April-September 2014 increased 1.7 percent from a year earlier to ¥35.9 trillion, while imports grew at a faster pace of 2.5 percent to ¥41.32 trillion. 日本の2014年度上半期（4〜9月）の輸出総額は、前年同期比1.7%増の35兆9,000億円だったのに対して、輸入額は2.5%増の41兆3,200億円で大幅に増えた。◆Japan's 2012 trading balance, or exports minus imports, ran up a record deficit of ¥6.9 trillion, 2.7 times more than the 2011 figure, the first trade deficit in 31 years due to the negative effects of the Great East Japan Earthquake. 輸出額から輸入額を差し引いた日本の2012年の貿易収支は、過去最大の6.9兆円の赤字で、東日本大震災の悪影響で31年ぶりに貿易赤字に転落した2011年と比べて2.7倍に増えた。◆The Customs Tariff Law bans imports that infringe on patent, design and commercial brand rights. 関税定率法で、特許、意匠権、商標権などの侵害品の輸入は禁止されている。◆The government imposes a countervailing tariff on the imports of South Korean DRAM chips. 政府は、韓国製DRAMチップの輸入

に対して相殺関税を課している。◆The U.S. government has announced an action plan aimed at stepping up controls on steel imports from Japan and other nations. 米政府は、日本などからの鉄鋼輸入に関する規制を強化する行動計画を発表した。◆The value of imports decreased by 31.7 percent to ¥4.13 trillion. 輸入額は、31.7%減の4兆1,300億円だった。◆The weaker yen helps exporters, but close attention must be paid to the fact that the excessive depreciation of the yen will further increase the prices of imports of LNG and other foreign products. 円安は輸出企業にはプラスだが、円安が行き過ぎると、天然液化ガス（LNG）など海外製品の輸入額が一段と増えることにも、警戒が必要である。

import agency 輸入代行業者
◆The woman bought the diet aid through an import agency. この女性は、輸入代行業者を通じてダイエット食品を購入した。

import ban 輸入禁止
◆The safety of U.S. beef must be confirmed before lifting the import ban. 輸入禁止を解く前に、米国産牛肉の安全性を確認する必要がある。

import barriers 輸入障壁
combat import barriers 輸入規制に対応する （=overcome import barriers）
erect import barriers 輸入障壁を設ける［築く］ （=create import barriers）
fall in import barriers 輸入障壁がなくなること
heavy import barriers 高い輸入障壁
liberalize import barriers 輸入障壁を撤廃する
reduce import barriers 輸入障壁を軽減する、輸入障壁を引き下げる［低める］
remove import barriers 輸入障壁を撤廃する、輸入障壁を取り除く

import commodities 商品を輸入する
◆Commodity loans are used to import commodities such as industrial machinery, industrial raw materials, fertilizer, agricultural chemicals and machinery, and other various kinds of machinery, which are agreed upon beforehand between the Japanese and recipient governments. 商品借款は、日本政府と借入国政府が前もって合意した商品（工業資本財［工業用機械］、工業用原材料、肥料・農薬、農機具、各種機械など）の輸入のために使用される。

import control 輸入制限, 輸入規制, 輸入統制, 輸入貿易管理
a safeguard emergency import control measure 緊急輸入制限（セーフガード）措置
import control policy 輸入統制政策
◆The government plans to raise its tariff on imported beef from August as a safeguard emergency import control measure in the wake of a

steep year-on-year increase in imports of beef. 牛肉の輸入量が前年に比べて急増していることから、政府は8月から緊急輸入制限（セーフガード）措置として輸入牛肉の関税を引き上げる方針だ。

import cost 輸入費用，輸入コスト，輸入物価（輸入品の購入価格にマージンを加えて販売するまでのコスト。⇒cost of imports）
◆A cheaper yen increases import costs, but if the yen-dollar exchange rate is within the range of ¥95-105, it would be possible for companies to maintain competitiveness in exports. 円安で輸入コストは増えるが、円の対ドル為替相場が1ドル＝95〜105円の範囲内なら、企業は輸出競争力を維持できるだろう。◆The price of regular gas has gone up for six weeks because oil wholesalers have added their import costs, which have been going up due to the weak yen since the end of last year, to the retail price. レギュラー・ガソリンの価格は、昨年末からの円安で上昇している輸入費用の増加分を元売り各社が小売価格に転嫁しているため、6週間連続で上昇した。

import duties 輸入関税
impose import duties 輸入関税を課す，輸入関税をかける
lift import duties 輸入関税を撤廃する
◆Japanese agricultural products such as rice have been protected by high import duties. 日本のコメなどの農産物は、高い輸入関税で保護されている。

import fossil fuels 化石燃料を輸入する
◆Japan lost more than ¥3 trillion of national wealth in 2011 to import fossil fuels as a result of the power scarcity due to the suspension of all nuclear power reactors. 全原発の停止による電力不足の結果、日本は化石燃料を輸入するため、2011年度は3兆円以上の国富を流出させた。

import growth 輸入の伸び，輸入の増加
◆Import growth outpaced export growth, thus producing the trade imbalance. 輸入の伸びが輸出の伸びを上回ったため、貿易の不均衡が生じた。

import of agricultural products 輸入農産品，農産品の輸入
◆Japan's protectionist policies impose high tariffs on imports of agricultural products. 日本の保護政策は、輸入農産品に高率の関税をかけている。

import of fuel 燃料輸入
◆The deficit in goods trade in the first half of 2012 expanded sharply due to a surge in imports of fuel for thermal power generation following the suspensions of nuclear power plants. 2012年上半期のモノの取引を示す貿易収支の赤字は、原発停止に伴う火力発電用燃料輸入の急増で、急速に膨らんだ。

import of liquefied natural gas 液化天然ガス（LNG）の輸入［輸入量］
imports of liquefied natural gas 液化天然ガス（LNG）の輸入額
◆A slight increase in exports led by automobiles was more than offset by a sharp rise in imports of liquefied natural gas and crude oil for thermal power generation. 自動車を中心に輸出は若干伸びたものの、これは火力発電用の液化天然ガス（LNG）や原油などの輸入急増でかなり相殺された。◆As an abnormal situation, imports of liquefied natural gas, the fuel needed for operating power companies' thermal power stations, have increased to a massive ¥6 trillion a year after the operations of nuclear reactors were suspended around the country. 異常事態として、原子力発電所の運転が全国で停止した後、電力各社の火力発電の稼働に必要な液化天然ガス（LNG）の輸入額が、年間で6兆円もの巨額に達している。

import prices 輸入物価，輸入価格（⇒thermal power generation）
◆A stronger yen has the favorable effect of stemming rises in import prices. 円高には、輸入物価の高騰を抑えるプラス面もある。◆Gasoline prices rose 6.4 percent in June, while city gas climbed 4.7 percent and electricity charges increased 9.8 percent, as the yen's depreciation pushed up import prices of crude oil and liquefied natural gas. 円安で原油や液化天然ガス（LNG）の輸入価格が上昇したため、6月はガソリン価格が6.4%上昇したのに対して、都市ガスは4.7%、電気料金は9.8%それぞれ上昇した。◆Japan's current account surplus in July 2013 fell 12.9 percent from a year earlier to ¥577.3 billion, chiefly reflecting a wider gap in goods trade as imports of LNG for thermal power generation swelled due in part to an increase in electricity demand amid the hot summer. 2013年7月の日本の経常収支の黒字幅は、前年同月より12.9%減少して5,773億円となったが、これは主に猛暑で電力需要が増したこともあって火力発電用の液化天然ガスの輸入が大幅に増加したため、モノの貿易での輸入超過［モノの貿易赤字］が拡大したことを反映している。◆The fall in import prices that accompanies a strong yen could further prolong Japan's deflation. 円高に伴う輸入価格の下落で、日本のデフレがさらに長期化する可能性がある。◆The import prices of crude oil and grains have surged, causing spikes in the prices of food products and daily necessities that have dampened household spending. 原油や穀物の輸入価格高騰で、食品や日用品の価格が上昇し、個人消費も冷え込んでいる［個人消費の低迷を招いている］。◆The United States is under pressure to make some difficult monetary policy decisions to cool down the overheating economy by countering the inflationary pressure stemming from higher import prices due to the weaker dollar. 米国は現在、ドル安での輸入価格の高騰によるインフレ圧力を抑えて、過熱気味の景気を鎮めるための難しい金融政策の決断を迫られている。

import restrictions [restraints] 輸入規制，輸入制限
be subject to import restrictions 輸入規制の対象となっている

IMPO 242

invoke provisional import restraints on 〜に暫定輸入制限措置を発動する
◆Due to concern about radioactive contamination, a number of Japanese agricultural and industrial products have been subject to import restrictions. 放射能汚染への懸念から、日本の農業・工業品の多くは輸入規制の対象となっている。

import tariff 輸入関税
◆FTAs are a regime under which import tariffs are eliminated bilaterally or regionally. 自由貿易協定（FTA）は、2国間で、または地域で輸入関税を撤廃する制度だ。◆In the agricultural negotiations at the World Trade Organization, Japan has been under strong pressure from rice exporters to lower import tariffs on rice and to expand access for foreign rice. 世界貿易機関（WTO）の農業交渉で日本は、コメ輸出国から、コメの輸入関税率引下げや外国産米の輸入枠拡大への強い圧力を受けている。

import vaccine ワクチンを輸入する
◆To cover the shortfall in domestically produced vaccine, the government plans to import vaccine against the new Type A/H1N1 strain of influenza from two European makers. 国産ワクチンの不足分をカバーするため、政府は、欧州メーカー2社から新型インフルエンザ（A型/H1N1）のワクチンを輸入する計画だ。

important matter 重要事項
◆The parties hereto shall keep in strict confidence from any third party any and all important matters concerning the business affairs and transactions covered by this agreement. 本契約当事者は、本契約の対象である営業上の問題や取引に関するすべての重要事項については、どんな第三者に対しても一切極秘にする。

importation （名）輸入、輸入品、海外からの導入、海外から導入されたもの
certificate of importation 輸入証明書
　（＝importation certificate）
foreign capital importation 外資導入
　（＝importation［introduction］of foreign capital）
importation of refined petroleum products 石油精製品の輸入
parallel importation 並行輸入
port of importation 輸入港
speculative importation 見越し輸入

imported （形）輸入される［輸入された］、導入される、〜の輸入、〜の導入
imported capital 資本の導入
imported goods price 輸入物価
　（＝price of imported goods）
imported inflation 輸入インフレ［インフレーション］　（＝import inflation）
imported input content 輸入投入含有量
imported items 輸入品目、輸入財

imported items in local currency terms 自国通貨建て輸入財
imported oil dependency 輸入原油への依存度
imported technology 輸入技術、導入技術、技術輸入、技術の導入　（＝borrowed technology）
price of imported goods 輸入物価
◆Under the food self-sufficiency rate on a calorie basis, even beef and pork from animals raised in Japan are not considered domestic products if they consumed imported feed. カロリー・ベースの食料自給率では、国内で育てた家畜の牛肉や豚肉［国内で育てた］牛や豚の肉）でも、餌が輸入品の場合は国産品と見なされない。

imported beef 輸入牛肉
◆Major beef exporters such as the United States have already threatened to impose some punitive action against Japan if it introduces an emergency tariff on imported beef. 日本が輸入牛肉に対して緊急措置を導入［発動］した場合、米国など牛肉の主な対日輸出国は、すでに日本に対して制裁措置を取る動きを示している。◆The food firm covered up its labeling of imported beef as domestic beef. この食品メーカーは、輸入牛肉を国産牛肉と表示したことを隠していた。

imported car 輸入車
◆Following the collapse of Lehman Brothers, people who switched to Japanese cars are back to purchasing imported cars. リーマン・ブラザーズの破たん後［リーマン・ショック後］、日本車に乗り換えた人が、再び輸入車を購入するようになった。◆Imported cars are generally more expensive than Japanese vehicles. 輸入車のほうが、一般に日本車より高価だ。◆Sales of imported cars have continued to grow even after domestic automakers recovered most of their domestic production in autumn. 国内自動車メーカー各社の国内生産がほぼ復旧した秋以降も、輸入車販売の伸びは続いている。

imported car sales 輸入車販売、輸入車販売台数
◆Imported car sales soared by 22.9 percent to 295,149 units in 2011 from the previous year. 2011年度の輸入車販売台数は29万5,149台と、前年度に比べて22.9%の大幅増となった。

imported commodity prices 輸入品価格
◆The effects of the recent depreciation of the dollar have not been seen yet, but if the U.S. currency depreciates further, it may lead to an increase in imported commodity prices, which in turn may become an inflationary factor. 最近のドル安の影響はまだ見られないが、米ドルがさらに下落すると、輸入品価格の上昇を招き、これがまた逆にインフレ要因になる恐れがある。

imported foods 輸入食品
◆Concerns over the safety of Chinese food products are rising in Japan, but the percentage of

safety violations involving food imports from China fell below the overall average for all imported foods in fiscal 2012. 日本では中国産食品の安全性への懸念が強まっているが、中国からの輸入食品のうち安全面での違反件数の割合は、2012年度は輸入食品全体の総平均を下回った。

imported goods 輸入品
◆One good point of the rise in the yen is that we can buy imported goods at low prices. 円高のメリットの一つは、輸入品を安く買えることだ。

imported materials 輸入材
◆Domestic lumber has lost international competitiveness year after year, hit by inexpensive imported materials. 国産材は、価格が安い輸入材に押されて年々、国際競争力を失っている。

imported new-flu vaccine 輸入した新型インフルエンザのワクチン
◆Domestic vaccine makers are expressing dissatisfaction with a legislative bill aimed at helping only the victims of side effects caused by imported new-flu vaccine. 国内ワクチン・メーカーは、輸入した新型インフルエンザのワクチン接種による副作用の被害者だけを救済する特別措置法案に不満を表明している。

imported raw materials 輸入された原材料, 輸入原材料, 輸入原料, 原材料の輸入
◆In processing trade, imported raw materials are manufactured into goods that are then sold to other countries. 加工貿易では、輸入された原材料が製品に仕上げられた後、製品は海外に販売される。◆Japanese small and midsize businesses have been tormented by the rise in prices of imported raw materials due to the weakened yen. 日本の中小企業は、円安による輸入原材料価格の上昇で、苦しんでいる。

importer (名)輸入者, 輸入商, 輸入業者, 輸入国
capital importer　資本輸入国, 資本導入国
cooperative importer　協同輸入業者
direct importer　直輸入者, 直輸入業者
exclusive importer's buying agent　輸入総代理店
huge importer of goods　製品の輸入大国
importers' association　輸入組合
independent importer　独立輸入業者
net capital importer　入超の資本収支
net importer　純輸入国, 輸入超過国
resource importer　資源輸入国
◆A major bone of contention in the trial of the lung cancer drug Iressa case was whether the importer and seller's provision of information on Iressa's side effects to medical institutions was sufficient. 肺がん治療薬「イレッサ」訴訟の裁判の大きな争点は、輸入販売元による医療機関への イレッサの副作用に関する情報の提供が十分だったか、という点だ。◆Japan is the world's largest LNG importer and its total LNG imports totaled

¥6 trillion in 2012. 日本は世界最大のLNG輸入国で、2012年の日本のLNG総輸入額は6兆円に達する。
◆Russia opposes the enforcement of anti-Syria sanctions because Syria is an important importer of weapons from Russia, and Syria provides the Russian Navy with supply bases. シリアはロシアにとって重要な武器輸出先であると同時に、ロシア海軍に補給拠点も提供しているため、ロシアは対シリア制裁の実施に反対している。◆Syria is a major importer of Russian weapons. シリアは、ロシア製武器の主要輸入国だ。◆The yen's stable rate at about ¥110 against the dollar serves as a stabilizing factor for importers, exporters and others doing business susceptible to exchange fluctuations. 円の対ドル為替相場が110円台（前後）で安定していることは、輸出入業者など為替変動に左右されやすい仕事をしている者にとって安定要因となる。

importer and seller 輸入販売元
◆Bereaved family members filed a damages lawsuit against the government and the importer and seller of the lung cancer drug Iressa, claiming that patients died from side effects of the drug. 患者が肺がん治療薬「イレッサ」の副作用で死亡したとして、患者の遺族が、国とイレッサの輸入販売元に損害賠償を求める訴訟を起こした。

impose (動)課税をする, 税金などを課する, 義務などを負わせる, 危険などを与える, 条件などを設ける, 売りつける, 押し付ける, 強いる
impose a tax on　～に課税する, ～に税をかける
impose conditions on　～に条件を付ける, ～に条件を設ける
impose economic sanctions　経済制裁に踏み切る, 経済制裁を科する
impose high tariffs on　～に高率の関税をかける　（⇒import of agricultural products）
impose restrictions on　～を規制する, ～を制限する
impose some manner of limitations on　～に一定の歯止めをかける
the obligations imposed by this agreement　本契約により課される義務
◆An additional taxation of about ¥500 million was imposed on the group. 同グループに、約5億円の追徴課税が課された。◆The EU has imposed a 14 percent tariff on imported LCD monitors for computers. 欧州連合（EU）は、パソコン用液晶モニターに14％の関税を課している。

impose a countervailing tariff on ～に［に対して］相殺関税を課す
◆The government imposes a countervailing tariff on the imports of South Korean DRAM chips. 政府は、韓国製DRAMチップの輸入に対して相殺関税を課している。

impose retaliatory tariffs on ～に報復関

税を発動する

◆When Washington refuses to comply with the WTO's ruling, the EU will impose retaliatory tariffs on U.S. products. 米国が世界貿易機関（WTO）の決定に従わなかった場合、欧州連合（EU）は米国製品に報復関税を発動する方針だ。

improve export-driven profits 輸出主導の収益を改善する

◆The company needs to enhance its development strength for such products as hybrid cars to maintain the competitiveness of its vehicles and auto parts domestically manufactured, in addition to improving export-driven profits. 同社の場合、輸出主導の収益改善にとどまらず、国内生産の車両や自動車部品の競争力を維持するには、ハイブリッド車などの製品の開発力を強化する必要がある。

improve international competitiveness 国際競争力を高める，国際競争力を向上させる

◆To liberalize trade further, it is imperative to arrest a decline in Japan's agriculture sector and improve its international competitiveness. 一層の貿易自由化に向けて、日本の農業衰退に歯止めをかけ、農業の国際競争力を高めるのが急務だ。

improved quality 品質向上，品質改善

◆Japan's major automakers are capitalizing on improved quality at production plants overseas as part of their global strategies. 日本の大手自動車メーカー各社が、自動車品質の世界戦略の一環として、海外生産拠点での品質向上を活用している。

improvements （名）改良，改良技術，改良技術の問題，改良工事，造作，改良費，改良情報改良版

◆Licensee hereby agrees to promptly disclose to Licensor any improvements owned, acquired, or controlled by Licensee during the life of this agreement. ライセンシーは、本契約期間中ライセンシーが所有、取得または支配する改良技術はすべてライセンサーに速やかに開示することに、本契約により同意する。

in accordance with 〜に従って，〜に基づき，〜により

◆For invoices for orders exceeding U.S. dollars 50,000, XYZ may require ABC to open for XYZ an irrevocable documentary letter of credit, in the form satisfactory to XYZ for an amount at least equal to 100% of the order value payable in accordance with the provisions of Section（5）of this Article above. 5万米ドルを超える注文に対する請求書については、XYZは、XYZのために、上記本条第5項の規定に従って支払われる注文金額の少なくとも100%に相当する金額の取消不能の荷為替信用状をXYZが満足するフォームで開設するようABCに対して要求することができる。

in addition to 〜のほかに，〜に加えて

◆In addition to the payment under the preceding paragraph, Licensee shall further pay to Company a running royalty equal to 10 percent of Net Selling Price of Products manufactured and sold by Licensee during the life of this agreement. 前項に基づく支払いについて、ライセンシーはさらに、本契約期間中ライセンシーが製造・販売する本製品［契約品］の正味販売価格の10%に等しい継続実施料（ランニング・ロイヤリティ）を会社に対して支払うものとする。

in advance of 〜に先立って，〜の前に（=ahead of, before）

◆The licensee shall deliver twice a year in advance of the each Season to the licensor free of charge samples of each item of the licensed products currently being manufactured by the licensee or its sublicensees, including labels and packages in order to exercise the licensor's rights of quality control. ライセンシーは年2度、各シーズン前に、ライセンサーの品質管理権を行使するため、ラベルと包装を含めてライセンシーまたはそのサブライセンシーがその時点で製造している許諾製品の各品目の見本を無料でライセンサーに送達するものとする。

in case 〜の場合には（=in case that; ⇒legality）

in case of the occurrence of any of the following events 次のいずれかの事態が発生した場合

in case that 〜の場合には （=in case）

◆In case the borrower fails to pay any principal or interest payable under this agreement on the due date therefor, the borrower shall pay to the lender overdue interest on such overdue amount for each day for the period from and including the due date therefor up to and including the day immediately preceding the actual payment date. 借主が本契約に基づいて元本または支払い利息の支払い期日に元本の返済または支払い利息の支払いを怠った場合、借主は、その支払い期日から実際の払込み日の前日までの期間の各日数について、その支払い遅延金額の遅延利息を貸主に支払うものとする。

in case there is delay in delivery 引渡し遅延が生じた場合

◆In case there is delay in delivery of all or any part of the Goods on the time as stipulated in this agreement, the buyer is entitled to claim liquidated damages at the rate of one-half of one percent（0.5%）of the amount of the delayed Goods for each complete week of delay. 本契約で定める期限に本商品の全部または一部に引渡し遅延が生じた場合、買い主は、遅延対象の各1週間につき引渡し遅延商品の代金の0.5%を損害賠償予定額として請求することができるものとする。

in competition with 〜と競合する，〜と競争関係にある

◆For a period of 5 years from the Closing date, Seller shall not engage or be interested, whether directly or indirectly, in any business in any place in which the Company now transact its business that would be in competition with business as now transacted by the Company. クロージング日から5年間、売り主は、対象会社が現在その事業を行っている場所で、対象会社が現在行っている事業と競合する事業に直接間接を問わず従事せず、また係らないものとする。

in compliance with 〜に準拠して、〜に従って (=in accordance with, in conformity with)
◆All goods were produced in compliance with the applicable requirements of the Fair Labor Standards Act. 商品は、すべて米国の公正労働基準法の適用要件に従って生産された。

in complying with 〜に応じて、〜に従って
◆Distributor shall bear any reasonable expenses incurred by Supplier in complying with such modified procedures. 販売店は、供給者のこの手続き変更に応じて生じる合理的な費用を負担しなければならない。

in connection with 〜に関する、〜に関して、〜に関連して (=concerning)
in connection with the sales, use or delivery of the products 本製品の販売、使用または引渡しに関連して
◆The express warranty stated above is in lieu of all liabilities or obligations of ABC for damages arising from or in connection with the delivery, use or performance of the licensed program. 上記の明示保証は、許諾プログラムの引渡し、使用または履行から生じる損害、またはこれに関連して発生する損害に対するABCの債務または責任に代わるものである。

in consideration for 〜の対価として
◆In consideration for the license of the trademark and the technical information granted under this agreement, Licensee shall pay to Licensor the minimum royalty for each contract year as set forth below: 本契約で付与する商標と技術情報の使用許諾の対価として、ライセンシーは、下記の各契約年度のミニマム・ロイヤリティをライセンサーに支払うものとする。

in consideration of 〜を約因として、〜の対価として、〜を考慮して、〜に鑑（かんが）みて（「約因」とは、契約を成立させるための理由・主要要因）

in consideration of the license granted by 〜が許諾するライセンスの対価として
◆In consideration of the license granted and the products delivered by XYZ, ABC shall, upon the delivery of the products, pay a royalty in the amount listed in Exhibit C as the exclusive method of compensation under this agreement. XYZが許諾するライセンスとXYZが引渡す本製品の対価として、ABCは、本製品の引渡し時に、本契約に基づく対価の唯一の支払い方法として付属書類Cに記載する額のロイヤリティを支払うものとする。

in consideration of the promises herein contained and other good consideration 本契約に定める約束ごとと他の有効な約因を対価として
◆NOW, THEREFORE, in consideration of the promises herein contained and other good consideration, the parties hereto do hereby agree as follows: そこで、本契約に定める約束ごとと他の有効な約因を対価として、両当事者はここに以下のとおり合意する。

in due course 期日どおり、期限どおり
◆We enclose the shipping documents covering the goods and expect your remittance in due course. 契約品の船積み書類を同封し、期日どおりのご送金を期待しております。

in due course time やがて、期日どおりに
◆Shipments will reach you in due course time. 積み荷は、やがて到着します。

in duplicate 2通、正副2通
◆IN WITNESS WHEREOF, each of the parties hereto has caused this agreement to be executed in duplicate by its duly authorized officers or representatives as of the date first above written. 以上の証として、本契約当事者は、その正当な権限をもつ役員または代表者により、冒頭に記載した日付で本契約書を2通作成させた。

in effect 事実上、実際、実質的に、有効な、効力をもつ、実施されている
in effect as of the date of this agreement 本契約日現在で有効な、本契約日の時点で有効な
in effect at the time of acquisition 取得日の時点で有効な
in effect on the date hereof 本契約日に効力をもっている、本契約締結日に効力を有する
◆Nonmonetary balance sheet items and corresponding income statement items are translated at rates in effect at the time of acquisition. 貸借対照表の非貨幣性項目とこれに対応する損益計算書項目は、取得日の為替レートで換算されています。

in favor [favour] of 〜を受益者として、〜を受取人として、〜宛の、〜を支持して、〜に賛成して、〜の利益になるように (=in one's favor)
◆All letters of credit shall be in favor of and acceptable to ABC. 信用状は、すべてABCを受益者としてABCが受諾できるものとする。◆The APEC's special statement came out in favor of the promotion of free trade. アジア太平洋経済協力会議（APEC）の特別声明は、自由貿易推進を打ち出した。◆The Buyer shall establish in favor of the Seller an irrevocable letter of credit issued by a first-class international bank acceptable to the Seller. 買い主は、売り主のために、売り主が承諾できる［回収できる］第一級の国際銀行が発行する取消不能の信用状を開設するものとする。

in full 全部、全額、値引きしないで、省略しないで、省略なしで、詳細に、全面的に、完全に
◆We fear we have to advise you that we may not be able to dispatch in full your order due to the shortage of shipping space. 不意ながら、船腹

不足のため、貴社の注文が一部積み残しになる可能性があることをお伝えしなければなりません。

in full detail 十分詳細に, 詳細に
◆The Licensee shall furnish regular written report specified by the Licensor to Licensor in order to disclose in full detail pertinent information and data in connection with the sale of the Product. ライセンシーは, 契約品の販売に関する関連情報とデータを十分詳細に開示するため, ライセンサーが指定する定期報告書をライセンサーに提出するものとする。

in good faith 善意で, 善意の, 誠実に, 誠意をもって　(=bona fide)
◆The parties hereto agree to use their best efforts to resolve any dispute arising out of or in connection with this agreement through consultation in good faith. 本契約当事者は, 本契約からまたは本契約に関連して生じる紛争を誠意ある協議で解決するため最善の努力を払うことに合意する。

in good standing 完全な法的地位にある, グッド・スタンディングな状態にある
◆The Company is a corporation duly organized, validly existing and in good standing under the laws of the State of Delaware. 契約対象の会社は, デラウエア州法の法律に基づいて正式に設立され, 有効に現存し, 完全な法的地位にある法人（会社）である。

in material and workmanship 材料と仕上げ[仕上がり]の面で
◆The seller warrants that the Goods will be free from defects in material and workmanship for a period as specified in this agreement. 売り主は, 本契約で定める期間, 本商品が材料と仕上げの面で欠陥がないことを保証する。

in no instance どんな場合でも〜しない
◆In no instance shall either party be liable to the other for special, consequential or indirect damages arising out of breach. どんな場合でも, 当事者はいずれも, 契約違反から生じる特別, 派生的または間接的損害については相手方に責任を負わないものとする。

in no way 決して〜しない, 少しも〜しない
◆The execution of this agreement shall in no way constitute an admission of infringement by ABC of the Copyrights or its liability. 本契約の締結は, どんな意味でも, ABCによる本著作権の侵害またはその責任を認めることにはならないものとする。
◆This in no way changes the validity of this Article. これは, 決して本条の効力を変更するものではない。

in one's discretion 〜の判断で, 〜の裁量で, 〜の決定権で
◆Commencing on the date of this agreement until the Closing, Buyer shall be permitted to perform such due diligence investigation related to the transactions contemplated by this agreement as Buyer deems necessary and appropriate in its discretion. 本契約締結日からクロージングまで, 買い主は, 本契約で意図されている取引に関して

買い主が買い主の判断で必要かつ適切と考えるデュー・ディリジェンス調査を行うことができるものとする。

in one's favor [favour] 〜を受益者として, 〜を受取人として, 〜のため, 〜を支持して, 〜に賛成して, 〜の利益になるように　(=in favor of, in one's favour of)
◆Each payment shall be made by Distributor by an irrevocable letter of credit with 60 days' sight to be opened in Supplier's favor. 販売店が行う各支払いは, 供給者を受取人[受益者]として開設される一覧後60日払い取消不能信用状によって行うものとする。◆Our terms of payment are to value at 30 d/s under an irrevocable letter of credit to be opened in our favor for the corresponding value of an order. 当社の決済条件は, 注文相当額につき, 当社を受益者として開設された取消不能信用状に基づいて一覧後30日払いの手形を振り出すことです。

in one's sole discretion 〜のみの判断で, 〜の単独の判断で
◆If some or all of the goods have not been received by the buyer on the termination of this contract, the buyer shall, in its sole discretion, cease to take delivery of the remaining goods and the seller shall return to the buyer any amounts paid in advance in respect of such goods. 本契約解除時に商品の一部または全部を買い主が受領していない場合, 買い主は, 買い主単独の選択で, 残存商品[未引渡し商品]の引取りを中止し, 売り主は当該商品に関して前払いで受領した代金を買い主に返還するものとする。

in question 当該の, 当の, 問題の, 問題になっている, 論争中の
the party in question　当該当事者
the shares in question of the new company　新会社の当該株式
the year in question　当該年
◆The amount of the guaranteed minimum annual royalty for each year shall be paid in advance by ABC to Licensor by remittance to the bank account as designated by Licensor on or before the 22nd day of December of the year in question. 各年度の年間最低ロイヤルティ保証額は, 前払いで, ライセンサーが指定する銀行口座に当該年の12月22日までにABCが振り込むことによって支払うものとする。

in respect of 〜に関する, 〜に関して, 〜について, 〜にかかわる　(=in respect to)
◆The seller shall not be liable in respect of any warranty or consideration as to quality or fitness which would arise by implication of law. 売り主は, 法律の運用により生じる品質または適合性に関する保証または条件については, 責任を負わないものとする。

in terms of 〜では, 〜の点で, 〜に関して, 〜について, 〜の見地から
◆In terms of price competitiveness, Japan is

weaker than China and South Korea. 価格競争力の点で、日本は中国や韓国より弱い。◆JAL stock was the most actively traded Tokyo Stock Exchange's First Section issue in terms of trading value. 日航株は、売買高では東証1部の銘柄でとくに活発に取引された。

in the absence of　〜がない場合には
　in the absence of default by　〜による不履行がない場合には
　in the absence of the proof to the contrary　反証がない場合には
　◆Date of marine bill of lading shall be proof of the date of shipment in the absence of the evidence to the contrary. 海上船荷証券の日付は、反対の証拠がない場合、船積み日の証拠となる。

in the event of　〜の場合、〜の場合には、〜が生じた場合、〜がある場合　(=in case of)
　◆The bank shall have the right, as the obligations become due, or in the event of their default, to offset cash deposits against such obligations due to the bank. 債務の期限が到来したとき、または債務不履行の場合、銀行はその債務とその預金を相殺する権利を持つものとする。

in the form of　〜の様式で、〜の形式で
　in the form attached hereto as　〜として本契約書に添付した様式［形式］で
　in the form attached to this agreement　本契約書に添付する［添付した］書式で
　◆Such request shall be made by the borrower to the lender within 10 years from the date first above written by giving to the lender the request for advance in the form attached to this agreement as Exhibit B, five business days prior to the respective advance date. この要請は、本契約締結日から10年以内に、付属書類Bとして本契約書に添付する書式で借入れの要請を各借入日の5営業日前に貸主に通知して、借主が貸主に対して行うものとする。

in the ordinary course of business　通常の業務過程で、通常の事業の過程で、業務の通常の過程で、事業の通常の過程で、通常の事業活動で
　◆The outstanding accounts receivable of the Company have arisen out of the sales of inventory or services in the ordinary course of business. 対象会社の売掛金債権は、通常の業務過程で在庫品の販売またはサービスの提供によって生じたものである。

in the possession of　〜の保有下にある、〜が保有している

in whole or in part　全部または一部, 全部か一部かを問わず, 全部であれ一部であれ
　◆The original and copies of the licensor's Program, in whole or in part and however modified, which are made by the licensee, as between the licensor and the licensee shall be the property exclusively of the licensor. ライセンシーが作成するライセンサーのコンピュータ・プログラムのオリ

ジナルとコピー（複製）は、その全部であれ一部であれ、またどんな変更が加えられたとしても、ライセンサーとライセンシーの間では排他的にライセンサーの財産とする。

IN WITNESS　上記を証するため

IN WITNESS WHEREOF　以上の証として, 本契約の証として, 上記の証として, 上記の証拠として, 上記を証するため
　◆IN WITNESS WHEREOF, the parties have executed this agreement as of the date first above written. 以上の証として［本契約の証として］、両当事者は、冒頭に記載した日をもって本契約書に署名した。

incidental　(形) 付随的(な), 偶発的, 付帯的, 臨時の, 〜に付随する (incidental to)

incidental, consequential or tort damages　付随的, 派生的または不法行為による損害
　◆In no event shall XYZ be liable for incidental, consequential or tort damages of any kind, including damages resulting from any loss of profits, loss of use or loss of data, even if XYZ is advised of the possibility of such damages. 逸失利益、使用の喪失またはデータの喪失により生じる損害を含めて、あらゆる種類の付随的、派生的または不法行為による損害については、たとえXYZがその損害の可能性を知らされていても、XYZは一切責任を負わないものとする。

incidental damages　付随的損害, 偶発的損害, 付随的損害賠償, 付随的損害賠償金
　◆In no event will either party be liable for incidental, consequential, or special damages, even if the other party is notified of the possibility of such damages. どんな場合でも各当事者は、付随的、派生的または特別損害の可能性を知らされているとしても、それに対する責任は負わないものとする。

include　(動) 含む, 記載する, 定める, 表示する, 算入する, 計上する, 処理する
　◆ABC acknowledges the assignment and other terms and provisions included in the assignment agreement. ABCは、この譲渡契約に定められた譲渡とその他の条件および規定を確認する。

including, but not limited to　〜を含むがこれには限定しないで, 〜などを含めて (=including but not limited to)
　◆The seller makes no other warranties or representations with respect to the products and disclaims all warranties, including but not limited to implied warranties of merchantability, fitness for a particular purpose and noninfringement. 売り主は、本製品に関する他の保証または表明は行わず、商品性、特定目的への適合性および非侵害の黙示の保証などを含めてすべての保証を否認する。

inclusive　(形) 〜を含む
　for the period between January 1 (inclusive) and March 31 (inclusive)　1月1日（同日を含む）から3月31日（同日を含む）まで

INCO 248

from January 1 to March 31, both inclusive 1月1日から3月31日まで（いずれも同日を含む）

inclusive of ～を含めて、～を算入して

income account 所得収支
◆The surplus in the income account that includes dividend income from overseas subsidiaries narrowed to about ¥7.15 trillion in January-June 2012 from ¥7.28 trillion a year before. 2012年上半期（1～6月）の所得収支（海外子会社からの配当収入［配当受取金］などを示す）の黒字額は、前年同期の7兆2,800億円から約7兆1,500億円に縮小した。

income account surplus 所得収支の黒字［黒字額］, 所得黒字 （=income surplus）
◆As the yen's decline inflated the values of overseas earnings when converted into yen, the income account surplus in July 2013 hit a record high for July. 円安で円換算したときの海外収益額が膨らんだため、2013年7月の所得収支の黒字額は、7月としては過去最大だった。

income statement 損益計算書
◆Nonmonetary balance sheet items and corresponding income statement items are translated at rates in effect at the time of acquisition. 貸借対照表の非貨幣性項目とこれに対応する損益計算書項目は、取得日の為替レートで換算されています。

income surplus 所得収支の黒字［黒字額］ （=income account surplus）
◆The income surplus fell 24.5 percent, to about ¥1.1 trillion on a year-to-year basis, on the back of declining interest rates on foreign bonds. 所得収支の黒字額は、外債の金利低下の影響で（利子収入が減ったため）、前年同月比で24.5％減の約1兆1,000億円だった。

income tax 所得税
◆All Japanese income taxes, if any, levied on the royalties to be paid by ABC to XYZ shall be born by XYZ and withheld by ABC in accordance with the tax laws of Japan. ABCがXYZに支払うロイヤルティに対して課税される日本国の所得税があれば、これはすべてXYZが負担するものとし、日本の税法に従ってABCが源泉徴収するものとする。

inconsistent with ～と矛盾する、～に抵触しない、～と相容れない、両立しない （=incompatible with）
◆The guarantor hereby waives any right it may have as surety which may be at any time inconsistent with any of the provisions of this guarantee. 保証人は、本保証書［保証状］の条項にどんな時でも矛盾する可能性のある、保証人が保証人として持つことができる一切の権利をここに放棄する。

incorporate （動）設立する、会社組織にする、組み込む、組み入れる、合併する、契約の一部とする
a company incorporated and existing under the laws of ～の法律に基づいて［法律に準拠

して］設立され現存する会社、～法のもとで設立され存続している会社

incorporated and existing 設立され現存する

incorporated by reference 参照により組み込んだ, 参照により組み込まれる
◆The parties concerned have not entered into this agreement on the basis of any representations that are not expressly incorporated into this agreement. 両当事者は、本契約に明示的に組み込んでいない表明・説明に基づいて本契約を締結したものではない。

incorporation （名）会社の設立, 法人格の付与, 法人組織, 会社, 合併, 編入, 組込み （⇒articles of incorporation）

Incoterms インコタームズ（International Commercial Termsの略。国際商業会議所が1936年に制定した「貿易条件の解釈に関する国際規則（International Rules for the Interpretation of Trade Terms）」の通称で、改訂された2000年版インコタームズではCIF（運賃保険料込み条件）やFOB（本船渡し条件）などを含めて13種類の貿易条件が定義されている。なお、インコタームズ2010では、terms（条件）がrules（規則）に置き換えられている。⇒as amended, trade terms）
◆Unless otherwise expressly provided for in this agreement, the price and trade term "C.I.F." shall be interpreted in accordance with Incoterms 2010. 本契約に特に明示の規定がないかぎり（本契約で別段に明確に規定しないかぎり）、価格と貿易条件のCIFは、2010年版インコタームズに従って解釈する。

increase （名）増加, 増大, 拡大, 伸び, 上昇, 高騰, 向上, 高まり, 激化, 引上げ

increase in consumer confidence 消費意欲の向上

increase in cost コストの増大

increase in demand for ～需要の増加

increase in (interest) rates 金利の上昇

increase in oil prices 原油価格の上昇［高騰］

increase in productivity 生産性の伸び

increase in the discount rate 公定歩合の引上げ

increase of capital 増資
◆We regret to inform you that we may not be able to ship all of your requirements due to the unforeseen increase in the demand for the goods. 本品に対する需要が思いもかけず増大したため、遺憾ながらご入用の品全部の船積みは不可能になるかと思います。

increase exports 輸出を拡大する
◆To increase exports, Japanese manufacturers must develop attractive products of high added value and find ways to capitalize on growing markets in the emerging economies of Asia and other regions. 輸出を拡大するには、日本の製造業各社が、付加価値の高い魅力的な商品を開発し

て、アジアなどの地域の新興国の成長市場を積極的に取り込む方法を見つける必要がある。

increase in imported commodity prices　輸入品価格の上昇

◆The effects of the recent depreciation of the dollar have not been seen yet, but if the U.S. currency depreciates further, it may lead to an increase in imported commodity prices, which in turn may become an inflationary factor. 最近のドル安の影響はまだ見られないが、米ドルがさらに下落すれば、輸入品価格の上昇を招き、これがまた逆にインフレ要因になる恐れがある。

increase in imports of beef　牛肉輸入量の増加，牛肉輸入の増加

◆The government plans to raise its tariff on imported beef from August as a safeguard emergency import control measure in the wake of a steep year-on-year increase in imports of beef. 牛肉の輸入量が前年に比べて急増していることから、政府は8月から緊急輸入制限（セーフガード）措置として輸入牛肉の関税を引き上げる方針だ。

increase in overseas sales　海外販売の増加，海外での販売増

◆A large increase in overseas sales made up for the ￥180 billion earmarked for settlements and other costs for the company's large-scale recalls in the United States. 海外での販売の大幅増で、同社が米国での大規模なリコール（回収・無償修理）訴訟の和解などの費用として計上した1,800億円が補填された。

indebtedness　（名）負債，債務，負債額

◆If the borrower shall fail to pay any debt for borrowed money or other similar obligation of the borrower, or interest thereon, when due, and such failure continues after the applicable grace period specified in the agreement relating to such indebtedness, the lender may in its discretion declare the entire unpaid principal amount of the loan, accrued interest thereon and all other sums payable under this agreement to be immediately due and payable. 借主が借主の借入債務（借入金に対する債務）や他の同様の債務またはその利息を支払い期日に支払うことを怠り、このような不履行が本契約に定める当該債務に関連する適用猶予期間後も継続する場合、貸主はその裁量で、借入金の未返還元本全額、その発生利息と本契約に基づいて支払わなければならない他の未払い金の全額即時支払い［即時返済］を宣言することができる。

indemnify　（動）損失・損害を補償する、賠償・弁償する、保護する、責任を免除する

◆The Landlord shall effect insurance by itself or have other tenants effect insurance against such accidents as aforementioned and indemnify the Tenant within the extent covered by the insurance. 「貸主」は、前記の事故などに対して自ら保険を付けるか他のテナントに保険を付けさせ、その保険でカバーされる範囲内で「借主」に損害の補償をするものとする。

indemnify and hold ～ harmless from

(and against)　（from（and against）以下のものについて）補償するとともに～に損害・損失を与えない、（against以下のものについては）～の責任を免除する、（from（and against）以下のものについては）～に補償し～を免責する

◆Subject to the provisions of Paragraphs 5 and 6 of this Article, the licensor agrees to indemnify and hold the licensee harmless from and against any and all losses, damages and liabilities arising from or as a result of any claim or suit brought against the licensee. 本条第5項と6項の規定に従って、ライセンサーは、ライセンシーに対して起こされた請求または訴訟から生じるまたはその結果生じる一切の損失、損害と責任については、ライセンシーに補償しライセンシーを免責することに同意する。

◆The seller indemnify and hold the buyer and the Company harmless up to an aggregate maximum of U.S. $ ＿＿＿, against any loss and damages caused to the buyer or to the Company by any misrepresentation, breach of warranty or breach of any agreement on the part of the seller in this agreement. 本契約上の売り主側の不実表明、保証違反または契約違反により買い主と本会社に生じたすべての損失と損害については、合計最高額＿＿＿米ドルまで、売り主が買い主と本会社に補償し、損害・損失を与えないものとする。

◆The seller shall indemnify and hold the buyer harmless from, and reimburse the buyer for, any damages, loss or expenses resulting from the inaccuracy as of the date hereof of any representation or warranty of the seller which is contained in or made pursuant to this agreement. 売り主は、本契約書に明記するまたは本契約に従って明記された売り主の表明または保証が本契約現在で不正確であったことから生じた損害、損失または費用については、すべて買い主に補償し、買い主を免責し、買い主に弁償するものとする。

indemnify, defend and hold harmless ～ from (and against)　（from（and against）以下のものについて）～の責任を免除し、～を守るとともに、～に損害を与えない、（from（and against）以下のものについては）～に補償し、～を守るとともに、～の責任を免除する

◆Each party hereto shall indemnify, defend and hold harmless ABC from and against any and all claims, damages, losses, demands, costs or expenses including reasonable attorneys' fees, judgments, liabilities, or settlement amounts resulting directly or indirectly from the gross negligence or willful misconduct of the indemnifying party in connection with its business. 損失補償当事者の取引に関してその重大な過失または故意の違反行為により直接間接的に発生した支払い請求額、損害額、損失額、支払い要求額、妥当な弁護士費用などの費用、判決に伴う支払い額、賠償責任額または和解金については、本契約の各当事者がABCに補償し、ABCを守るとともにその責

任を免除する。

indemnity （名）補償, 損失補償, 損害塡補, 損失補償契約, 補償金
◆The foregoing indemnity shall not apply to the products or any part thereof manufactured in compliance with the purchaser's specification or design, pattern, trademark or any other intellectual property designated or provided by the purchaser. 上記の補償は, 買い主の仕様または買い主が指定または提供したデザイン, パターン, 商標またはその他の知的財産権に従って製造した本製品またはその部品には適用されないものとする。

indemnity obligations 免責義務
◆The indemnity obligations set forth in this agreement shall survive the termination of this agreement. 本契約に定める免責義務は, 本契約の終了後も存続する。

independent accountant 独立した会計士, 独立の会計士, 独立会計士（一般に公認会計士をいう）

independent certified public accountant 独立した公認会計士, 独立の公認会計士, 独立公認会計士

independent contractor 独立契約者, 独立の契約者, 請負人, 請負業者
◆Distributor is an independent contractor and is not the legal representative or agent of Supplier for any purpose. 販売店は独立した契約当事者であり, どんな目的であれ供給者の法律上の代表者または代理人ではない。

independent distributor 独立した販売店, 独立販売店
◆Distributor desires to act as an independent distributor of Products under the terms and conditions set forth herein. 販売店は, 本契約書に記載する条件に従って本製品［契約品］の独立した販売店になることを希望している。

independent party 独立した当事者
◆A business combination is a significant economic event that results from bargaining between independent parties. 企業結合は, 独立した当事者間の取引から生じるひとつの重要な経済事象である。

indication （名）表示, 指示
◆Licensee shall not change the manner of use of Trademarks or combine Trademarks with any other letters, names, trademarks, marks or other indications. ライセンシーは, 本商標の使用方法を変更せず, 本商標に他の文字, 名称, 商標, 標章や他の表示を結合することも一切しないものとする。

indulgence （名）猶予（ゆうよ）, 履行猶予, 支払い猶予

industrial （形）産業の, 工業の, 鉱工業の, 工業の発達した, 工業生産の, 産業［工業］用の, インダストリアル
industrial action 労働争議, 争議行為, 順法闘争, 抗議行動, ストライキ （=job action）

industrial disturbances 労働争議

industrial espionage 産業スパイ
（=economic espionage, industrial spy）
◆Information about advanced technologies is sold to overseas rivals in industrial espionage, which has become a common threat for Japanese manufacturers. 産業スパイでは先端技術情報が海外のライバル企業に売り渡されるので, 日本のメーカーにとって産業スパイは, 共通の脅威となっている。

industrial machinery 工業用機械, 工業資本財
◆Commodity loans are used to import commodities such as industrial machinery, industrial raw materials, fertilizer, agricultural chemicals and machinery, and other various kinds of machinery, which are agreed upon beforehand between the Japanese and recipient governments. 商品借款は, 日本政府と借入国政府が前もって合意した商品（工業資本財［工業用機械］、工業用原材料、肥料・農薬、農機具、各種機械など）の輸入のために使用される。

industrial parts 工業部品
◆Japan and China have established a system of international division of labor in which China imports industrial parts from Japan to assemble into finished products in China and these are marketed domestically or exported to the U.S., Europe and elsewhere. 日本と中国は, 中国が日本から工業部品を輸入して中国で最終製品に組み立て, 中国国内で販売したり欧米などに輸出したりする国際分業体制を築いてきた。

industrial product 工業製品
◆Due to the massive floods in central Thailand, the supply chains of parts for industrial products were disrupted, forcing factories in Thailand and neighboring countries to suspend production. タイ中部の大規模洪水で, 工業製品のサプライ・チェーン（部品供給網）が寸断され, タイや周辺国の工場が生産停止を余儀なくされた。◆The ISO, a private organization that sets international standards for industrial products, will adopt Japan-led global safety criteria for nursing-care robots. 工業製品の国際規格を定める民間組織の「国際標準化機構（ISO）」は, 日本政府が主導する介護ロボットの国際安全基準を採用する方針だ。

industrial property right 工業所有権
◆Distributor recognizes that all trademarks, designs, patents and other industrial property rights used or embodied in Products remain to be sole properties of Company, and shall not in any way dispute them. 代理店は, 本製品（契約品）に使用または具体的に表示されているすべての商標, デザイン, 特許その他の工業所有権が依然として会社単独の所有物であることを認め, これについてはどんな方法でも争わないものとする。

industrialization （名）工業化, 産業化
export-led industrialization 輸出主導型工業

化, 輸出リード型工業化

export-oriented industrialization 輸出志向型工業化

import-substituting industrialization 輸入代替工業化

regional industrialization 地域工業化

◆An important role of the NIEs is to act as a nucleus or center in the promotion of export-oriented industrialization in the Asian-Pacific region. 新興工業経済地域（NIEs）のひとつの重要な役割は、アジア太平洋地域における輸出志向型工業化の中核あるいはセンターとして機能することにある。

industries concerned 関係業界

◆Under the World Trade Organization rules, emergency import limits, or safeguard, are permitted as a temporary measure if the volume of imports of a certain product drastically increases, causing serious damages to industries concerned in the country. 世界貿易機関（WTO）のルールでは、緊急輸入制限措置（セーフガード）は、特定製品の輸入量が増加して、国内の関係業界に大きな被害が出ている場合には、一時的な措置として認められる。

industry （名）産業, 工業, 産業界, 工業会, 業界, 〜業, 企業, メーカー

aviation industry 航空業界

basic material industry 素材産業

cattle industry 畜牛産業, 畜牛業界

competitive industry 競争的産業（業界全体が完全競争の状況にある産業）

content industry コンテンツ（情報の内容）産業

distribution industry 流通産業, 流通業, 流通業界

downstream industry 川下産業

emerging industry 先端産業

financial industry 金融業界, 金融界, 金融産業

food service industry 外食産業, 外食業界

industry-government alliance 官民協力, 官民共同

information technology industry IT産業（=IT industry）

key industry 基幹産業, 基礎産業, 重要産業

leading industries 主導［先導］産業, 主力産業

mining and manufacturing industries 鉱工業

network industry ネットワーク産業

new industries 新規産業

nuclear power industry 原子力産業

passenger ship industry 旅客船業界

promote industry 産業を振興する

reproductive industry 再生産業

service industry サービス産業, サービス業,

サービス業界

steel industry 鉄鋼産業

sunrise industry 成長産業, サンライズ産業

sunset industry 斜陽産業, 衰退産業, サンセット産業

supporting industry 裾野（すその）産業

telecommunications and information industry 情報通信産業

tertiary industry 第三次産業, 三次産業（サービス産業とほぼ同じで、商業、運輸・通信業、金融業、公務・自由業、有給の家事サービス業などのこと）

the hollowing out of (Japanese) industry 産業空洞化 （=deindustrialization）

trigger industry トリガー産業（景気回復や革新の牽引役を果たす産業のこと）

U.S. industries 米国産業, 米国企業

warehousing industry 倉庫業

◆A prerequisite for the continued existence of industry in Japan is an affordable and stable supply of high-quality electricity. 日本の産業が生き残るための必要条件として、良質な電力の安価で安定した供給が挙げられる。◆A weak yen benefits the export industries such as automobiles and home appliances, but excessive depreciation of the yen could have the negative effect on the Japanese economy. 円安は自動車や家電など輸出産業には追い風だが、過度の円安は日本経済に悪影響を及ぼす可能性もある。◆As labor costs in China are expected to continue rising, labor-intensive industries such as fashion and electronics will keep relocating their manufacturing bases to Southeast Asia and other regions with cheaper labor. 中国の人件費上昇は今後も続く見通しなので、アパレルや家電などの労働集約型産業では、生産拠点を中国より低賃金の東南アジアなどに移す流れが続くものと思われる。◆To seek information on cyber attacks, U.S. Attorney Preet Bharara has sent subpoenas to bitcoin exchanges including Mt.Gox and businesses that deal in bitcoin. サイバー攻撃に関する情報を得るため、プリート・バララ米国連邦検事は、マウントゴックス社などビットコイン（仮想通貨）の取引所やビットコインの取扱い業者に対して、召喚状を送った。

inequitable （形）不均衡な, 不衡平な, 不公正な, 不公平な

◆In case any one or more of the provisions of this agreement are held invalid, illegal or unenforceable in any respect, the validity, legality and enforceability of the remaining provisions hereof shall not be in any way affected or impaired thereby, except to the extent that giving effect to the remaining provisions would be unjust or inequitable. 本契約の一つ以上の規定がいずれかの点で無効、違法または強制不能と判断された場合、残存規定の実施が不公正または不均衡となる範囲を除いて、本契約の残存規定の有効性、

合法性と強制可能性はその影響を受けることはなく、またそれによって損なわれることはないものとする。

inexpensive （形）費用［金］のかからない, 価格が安い, 安い, 安価な, 低コストの, 高価でない, 値段の割に価値がある

inexpensive goods　安い商品, 値段の安い商品

inexpensive imported materials　価格が安い輸入材, 安い輸入材

inexpensive labor　安い労働力

inexpensive products　安値の製品, 安い製品

◆China has been viewed as a nation whose export drive derives from its inexpensive products. これまで中国は, 安値の製品で輸出攻勢をかける国と見られてきた。◆Domestic lumber has lost international competitiveness year after year, hit by inexpensive imported materials. 国産材は, 価格が安い輸入材に押されて年々, 国際競争力を失っている。

inferior （形）劣っている, 粗悪な, 劣等の, 二流の, 二級の, 下位の, 下級の, 平均以下の

an inferior court of law　下級裁判所

an inferior grade of wine　二流のワイン

inferior assets　劣等資産

inferior claim　不良債権

inferior description　劣等品, 劣等財, 下級財（＝inferior goods）

inferior goods　下級財, 下級品, 劣等財（＝inferior commodity）

inferior item　粗悪品, 劣悪品（＝inferior product）

products of an inferior quality　粗悪品, 粗悪な製品

inferior Products　品質の劣る本製品

◆In case the quality of Products shipped to Distributor turns out not to meet the above quality requirements, Distributor can claim a replacement against those inferior Products or cancellation of the individual contract. 販売店に発送した本製品の品質が上記品質基準に適合しないことが判明した場合, 販売店は, これら品質の劣る本製品の交換［これら粗悪品の交換］またはその個別契約［個々の契約］の解除を請求することができる。

inferior quality　品質不良, 劣等品質, 下等品質

◆Licensee shall not sell any Products, bearing Trademarks, of such an inferior quality that may jeopardize the reputation and goodwill of Licensor's products. ライセンシーは, ライセンサーの製品の評判とのれんに傷をつけるような品質不良の本製品に, 本商標を付して販売してはならない。

inflation （名）物価上昇, 物価上昇率, 物価高騰, 通貨膨張, インフレ, インフレ率, インフレーション（モノやサービスの全体の価格レベル（物価）が, ある期間に持続的に上昇する経済環境の現象）

◆The sharp rise in crude oil prices has caused increases in prices of other fuels and grains, triggering inflation in many parts of the world. 原油価格の高騰は, 他の燃料価格や穀物価格の上昇を招き, 国際的なインフレを引き起こしている。

influence-wielding （名）口利き

◆It is an entrenched bidding structure that allows irregularities such as influence-wielding, bid-rigging and subcontracting entire public works contracts. 口利きや談合, 公共事業の丸投げなどの不正行為を許しているのは, 旧態依然とした入札の構造だ。

inform （動）知らせる, 通知する

◆Company agrees to inform Licensee of improvements which Company conceives or acquires subsequent to the execution of this agreement and during the life of this agreement. 本契約の締結後と本契約期間中に会社が考案または取得した改良については, 会社がライセンシーに通知することに同意する。◆Please inform us what discount you will allow us for quantities. 大口取引に対してどれだけの値引きを認められるか, お知らせください。◆We have to inform you that the credit to cover your order does not seem to have reached us yet. 貴社注文［貴注文］に対する信用状が未着であることを, お知らせしなければなりません。◆We regret to inform you that we may not be able to ship all of your requirements due to the unforeseen increase in the demand for the goods. 本品に対する需要が思いもかけず増大したため, 遺憾ながらご入用の品全部の船積みは不可能になるかと思います。

informal documents　非公式の書面

◆For such purpose the minutes of meetings or other informal documents shall not constitute a waiver made in writing. 当該目的上, 会議の議事録またはその他の非公式の書面は, 書面による権利放棄とはならないものとする。

information （名）情報, データ, 資料, 消息, 報告, ニュース, 知識, 電話番号案内, 案内業務, 案内係, 受付け, 略式起訴, 告訴状, 告発状, インフォメーション（⇒personal information, pertinent information, technical information）

accounting information　会計情報

classified information　機密情報, 極秘情報

confidential information　秘密情報, 機密情報

confidentiality of personal information　個人情報の秘密遵守

equipment information　設備情報

financial information　財務情報, 金融情報

for your information　ご参考のために

information appliances　情報機器

information consumers　情報消費者

information governance　情報統治, 情報ガバナンス

inside information　内部情報, インサイダー情報, 未公開の重要情報, インサイド情報

（=insider information）

insurance information　保険情報, 保険に関する情報

internal information　内部情報, investigative information, 捜査情報

market information　市場情報

marketing information　マーケティング情報

nonpublic information　非公開情報

primary information　一次情報

public information　公開情報, 情報公開, 広報

supplementary information　補足情報

technical information　技術情報

technological information　技術情報, 専門情報, ノウハウ

trade information　貿易情報, 通商情報

trading information　取引情報

travel information by Ministry of Foreign Affairs　（外務省の）海外危険情報
◆According to the U.S. Energy Information Administration, recoverable U.S. shale gas resources are projected to be 862 trillion cubic feet （about 24 trillion square meters）, the world's second-largest after China. 米エネルギー情報局によると、採掘可能な米国のシェール・ガス資源量［埋蔵量］は、862兆立方フィート（約24兆平方メートル）と推定され、中国に次いで世界2位となっている。◆At the fifth round of the U.S.-China Strategic and Economic Dialogue, China was condemned for its actions of illicitly obtaining information of U.S. companies through cyber attacks. 第5回米中戦略・経済対話で、中国は、サイバー攻撃で米企業の情報を不正入手する中国の行為が激しく非難された。◆Information about advanced technologies is sold to overseas rivals in industrial espionage, which has become a common threat for Japanese manufacturers. 産業スパイでは先端技術情報が海外のライバル企業に売り渡されるので、日本のメーカーにとって産業スパイは、共通の脅威となっている。◆Such information was rightfully communicated to the receiving party free of any obligation of confidence subsequent to the time it was communicated to the receiving party by the disclosing party. 当該情報は、開示当事者が受領当事者に通知した時点以後に、秘密保持義務なしに受領当事者に合法的に通知された。◆The other party shall not disclose such confidential information to any third party. 他方当事者は、この秘密情報を第三者に開示してはならない。◆The Tokyo Stock Exchange Group, Inc. will inspect major securities companies in response to a series of illegal stock transactions using information leaked by major securities firms. 大手証券会社の情報漏れによる株の不正取引が相次いだことを受けて、東京証券取引所グループは、主要証券会社に立ち入り検査を行う方針だ。

information disclosure　情報開示, 情報公開
◆Financial institutions have no time to lose in enhancing their profitability, streamlining and information disclosure. 金融機関の場合、収益力の向上や一層の合理化、情報開示は待ったなしだ。◆It is important to enhance information disclosure to ensure general investors are not disadvantaged. 一般投資家が不利な立場にならないよう、徹底した情報公開を進めることが重要だ。

Information Technology Agreement　情報技術協定, ITA　（デジタル製品の関税撤廃を目指してWTO加盟の国・地域が参加する協定で、2014年現在、日本や米国、EU、韓国、台湾、中国、インド、アセアン（ASEAN）諸国など78か国・地域が参加）

infrastructure　（名）経済・社会・産業の基盤, 社会的生産基盤, 基本施設・設備, 社会資本, 企業・組織の下部組織, 下部構造, インフラ整備, インフラ, インフラストラクチャー

build infrastructure　インフラを整備する

business infrastructure　営業基盤

economic infrastructure　経済的下部構造

global information infrastructure　世界情報基盤, グローバル情報基盤

information infrastructure　情報通信基盤, 情報インフラ

infrastructure facilities　基礎的施設

infrastructure for the Internet　インターネットのインフラ

infrastructure program　インフラ整備計画

oil infrastructure　原油関連設備

public infrastructure　社会資本, 社会インフラ

social infrastructure　社会的経済基盤, 社会資本, 社会資本整備, 社会的生産基盤, 社会基盤, 社会のインフラ

the development of infrastructure　インフラ整備

urban infrastructure　都市インフラ
◆In emerging countries, demand for infrastructure to improve the quality of life and promote industry is expected to grow fast. 新興国では、生活向上や産業振興のためのインフラ需要が高まると見られる。◆The development of cross-border infrastructure in the Greater Mekong Subregion （GMS） has prompted a number of multinational corporations to transfer some of their manufacturing processes to Laos, Cambodia and Myanmar to take advantage of cheaper labor costs. 大メコン圏での国境を越えたインフラ整備に伴い、多くの多国籍企業が、安い人件費［低賃金］の利点を生かして生産工程の一部をラオスやカンボジア、ミャンマーに移転している。◆The METI has decided to expand the scope of government-backed trade insurance for overseas social infrastructure projects. 経済産業省は、海外の社会基盤（インフラ）事業に対する政府保証付き貿易保険の対象を拡大することを決めた。

infrastructure exports　インフラ輸出
◆In the Abe administration, infrastructure ex-

ports including nuclear reactors and high-speed railway systems are considered a major pillar of Japan's growth strategy. 安倍政権では、原発や高速鉄道などのインフラ（社会基盤）輸出は、日本の成長戦略の柱［大きな柱］と考えられている。◆ The Japan Bank for International Cooperation is using dollar-denominated FX reserves to help finance Japanese firms' infrastructure exports. 国際協力銀行は、外貨準備のドル建て資金［ドル資金］を使って、日本企業のインフラ輸出の金融支援をしている。

infrastructure risks　インフラ面でのリスク
◆In expanding into India's market, Japanese companies must work out a strategy that includes possible infrastructure risks. インド市場に進出するにあたって、日本企業は、想定されるインフラ面でのリスクを念頭に置いた戦略を練る必要がある。

infringe on　〜を侵害する
◆The Customs Tariff Law bans imports that infringe on patent, design and commercial brand rights. 関税定率法で、特許、意匠権、商標権などの侵害品の輸入は禁止されている。

infringement　(名)権利の侵害, 契約違反 (⇒alleged infringement)
constitute an infringement on　〜の侵害にあたる
in case of any infringement or counterfeiting　侵害や偽造が発生した場合
infringement, misappropriation or other unauthorized use of　侵害, 不正流用やその他の不正使用, 侵害、不正流用などの不正使用
infringement of copyright　著作権侵害
infringement or counterfeiting　侵害または偽造
infringement or threatened infringement　侵害または侵害の恐れ, 侵害されたり侵害されそうになったりすること　(⇒knowledge)
infringement remedy　権利侵害に対する救済
third party infringement of　第三者による〜の侵害
threatened infringement　侵害の恐れ
◆Seller shall waive any claim against Buyer under the Uniform Commercial Code or otherwise, with respect to a claim asserted against Seller or Buyer for patent, trademark or copyright infringement or the like. 売り主は、特許・商標・著作権の侵害等について売り主または買い主に対してなされる請求に関しては、買い主に対する米国統一商事法典その他に基づく請求権をすべて放棄する。

infringement or attempted infringement　侵害または侵害の恐れ
◆ABC shall promptly notify XYZ of any infringement or attempted infringement or misappropriation of any copyrights, trademarks or trade secrets of XYZ to the licensed products.

ABCは、許諾製品に対するXYZの著作権、商標または営業秘密が侵害された場合や侵害される恐れがある場合、不正使用されている場合には、XYZに直ちにそれを通知するものとする。

inherent　(形)固有の, 特有の, 生まれつきの, 本来備わっている, 本来の, 持ち前の, 切り離せない, 内在する, 構造的な
inherent cost　固有の費用
inherent delay　固有の遅れ
inherent hazard　固有の危険, 固有危険, 内部危険
inherent hazards insurance (policy)　内部危険担保保険 (証券)
inherent limitations　固有の限界, 取り除くことができない制約
inherent overcapacity　構造的な過剰生産能力
inherent power　固有権
inherent rights　生得権
inherent risk　固有のリスク
inherent stability　固有安定性
inherent vice　(保険)固有の瑕疵 (かし) (外力がかからなくても自然変質や自然損傷をもたらす貨物・財産の性質)
inherent vice or nature　貨物固有の瑕疵 (かし)もしくは性質
uncertainties inherent in　〜に内在する不確実性, 〜にはつきものの不確実性

initial articles of incorporation　原始定款

initial license fee　イニシャル・ライセンス・フィー

initial ownership (interest)　会社設立時の出資比率, 設立時の所有比率, 当初の出資比率
◆Pursuant to the terms of the articles of association of the Joint Venture Company, ABC will have an initial ownership interest of forty percent of the voting shares of the Joint Venture Company. 合弁会社の定款の規定に従って、ABCの当初の出資比率は、合弁会社の議決権付き株式の40%とする。

initial public offering　株式公開, 新規株式公開, 新規株式公募, 新規公募, 公開公募, 株式公募, 上場直前の公募, 第一回株式公募, 株式の公開公募, IPO　(=debut)
◆The firm appointed Deutsche Bank AG and Daiwa Securities SMBC to arrange an initial public offering to raise about ¥100 billion. 同社は、約1,000億円を調達するため、ドイツ銀行と大和証券SMBCを株式公募の取りまとめ役に指名した。

initial royalty　イニシャル・ロイヤルティ (一種の契約金)

initial sum　頭金
◆Licensee shall pay an initial sum of ten million (10,000,000) Japanese yen within 10 days after the execution of this agreement. ライセンシーは、

本契約締結後10日以内に1,000万円の頭金を支払わなければならない。

injunctive relief　差止救済, 差止命令による救済

injury　(名)傷害, 負傷, けが, 損害, 損傷, 苦痛, 侮辱, 無礼, 権利侵害
　industrial injuries　労働災害
　injury compensation　損害補償, 傷害補償
　material injury　実質的な損害
　nonpersonal injury claims　物件損害請求
　serious injury　重大な損害

ink a treaty　協定[協約]に署名する, 条約に署名する
　◆Japan and Russia inked a treaty on measures to control poaching and smuggling of crabs and other marine products in the Okhotsk Sea. 日本とロシアは, オホーツク海のカニなど水産物の密漁・密輸入対策に関する協定に署名した。

inquire　(動)尋ねる, 聞く, 問いただす
　inquire for　(〜について)問い合わせる, 〜に面会を求める
　inquire into　〜について調査する, 〜について取り調べる
　◆The prices and other particulars inquired for are shown in the enclosed price list. お問い合わせの価格その他の明細は, 同封の価格表に示してあります。◆We would like to inquire whether you are interested in our products. 当社製品に関心がおありか, 伺いたい。

inquiry　(名)問い合わせ, 相談, 引合い, 照会, 引合書, 照会状, 調査, 審査(「引合い」は, 買い主・買い手(buyer)から売り主・売り手(seller)への問い合わせ)
　answer customer inquiries　顧客の問い合わせに答える
　balance inquiry　残高照会
　confidential inquiry　信用問い合わせ, 秘密調査
　handle customer inquiries　顧客からの問い合わせに対応する[応じる]
　have an inquiry for　〜の引合いを受ける
　inquiry agency　信用調査機関
　inquiry and order　引合いと注文
　inquiry frequency　照会件数
　inquiry of credit data　信用照会
　　(=inquiry of credit profile)
　inquiry received　引合い受取り
　letter of inquiry　照会状, 問い合わせ状
　make inquiries about　〜について問い合わせる
　product inquiry　製品照会
　receive inquiries about our products from　〜から当社製品の引合いを受ける

refer to your inquiry about　〜についての貴社の問い合わせについて申し述べる
respond to your inquiry about　〜についての問い合わせに答える
write you an inquiry about　御社に〜についての問い合わせをする
　◆In reply to your inquiry of March 5, we are pleased to quote you our prices as follows: 貴社の3月5日付け引合いに対して, 下記のとおり当社の価格見積りについてご回答申し上げます。◆Supplier shall refer to Distributor any and all inquiries or orders for Products which Supplier may receive from any party in Territory. 供給者が販売地域の一切の関係者から受けた本製品についての引合いまたは注文は, 供給者が販売店に取り次ぐものとする。◆They did not write to us against our inquiry. 同社は, 当方の照会状に返事をよこさなかった。◆We should be glad to have your inquiries for our products when you are in the market again. 再びご入用の際は, 当社製品に対してお引合いをいただければと思います。

insider trading　インサイダー取引
　◆Insider trading, which is banned under the Financial Instruments and Exchange Law, harms ordinary investors and significantly damages stock market credibility. 金融商品取引法で禁じられているインサイダー取引は, 一般の投資家が不利益を被(こうむ)り, 証券市場の信頼性を大きく損なう。

insolvency　(名)支払い不能, 債務超過, 倒産, 破たん
　cross-border insolvency　多国間の倒産
　insolvency law　破産法
　insolvency or bankruptcy　支払い不能または破産
　insolvency practitioner　破産管財人
　insolvency proceeding　破産手続き
　insolvency, receivership or bankruptcy　支払い不能, 財産管理または破産
　take advantage of insolvency laws　支払い不能に関する法律の恩典を受ける
　◆In the event that any proceeding for insolvency or bankruptcy is instituted by or against either party or a receiver is appointed for such party, the other party may forthwith terminate this agreement. いずれかの当事者により, またはいずれかの当事者に対して支払い不能または破産手続きが開始された場合, またはその当事者のために財産管理人が選任された場合, 相手方当事者は直ちに本契約を解除することができる。

insolvent　(形)支払い不能の, 返済不能の, 債務超過の, 倒産した, 破たんした　(名)支払い不能者, 破産者
　be declared insolvent　破産[経営破たん, 支払い不能]の宣告を受ける, 支払い不能と判断される[認定される]
　be [become] insolvent　支払い不能[債務超

過]に陥る, 支払い不能になる, 破たんする

insolvent borrower　支払い不能[返済不能]の借り手, 債務返済不能の発行体

insolvent liquidation　支払い不能による清算
◆Under civil law, a preferential right is applied to cases such as employees' salaries when their companies become insolvent. 民法では, 先取特権は会社が破産したときの社員の給料などについて適用される。

inspect　(動)調べる, 点検する, 検査する, 視察する, 監査する　(⇒warehouse)

inspection　(名)物品の検査, 帳簿の閲覧, 財産の検分, 実査, 査閲

inspection tour　視察旅行

pre-shipment inspection　船積み前検査, PSI
◆Any claim by the purchaser, except for latent defects, shall be made in writing as soon as reasonably practicable after the arrival, unpacking and inspection of the products, whether by the purchaser or any subsequent purchaser of the products. 買い主によるクレームは, 隠れた瑕疵(かし)を除いて, 買い主によるか本製品のその後の購入者によるかを問わず本製品の到着, 開梱および検査後, 合理的に実行可能なかぎり速やかに書面で行うものとする。

inspection and acceptance　検収
◆The seller shall be liable for latent defects of the products at any time after delivery to the purchaser of the products or any subsequent purchaser, notwithstanding the inspection and acceptance of the products by the purchaser or any subsequent purchaser. 売り主は, 本製品の隠れた瑕疵(かし)については, 買い主またはその後の購入者による本製品の検収にかかわらず, 本製品の買い主またはその後の購入者への引渡し後, いつでも責任を負うものとする。

installment　(名)割賦払い, 分割払い, 分割引渡し, 分割積み　(=instalment)

in equal annual installments　毎年均等払いで, 毎年均等割りの分割払いで

in twelve equal monthly installments　12回の毎月均等払いで

in two installments　2回の分割払いで, 2回の分割積みで
◆This payment may be made in five installments. この支払いは, 5回の分割払いで行うことができる。

institute　(動)開始する, 創設する, 設立する, 設ける, 訴訟を起こす

institute a suit against　〜を相手どって訴訟を起こす
◆In case actions are instituted by ABC without such discussion with or agreement of XYZ, all the expenses incurred for such action shall be borne by ABC, and all the damages recovered therefrom shall belong to ABC. ABCがXYZとの当該協議またはXYZの同意なしで訴訟を起こした場合, その訴訟費用はすべてABCが負担し, その訴

訟により回収した損害賠償金もすべてABCに帰属するものとする。◆In the event that any proceeding for insolvency or bankruptcy is instituted by or against either party or a receiver is appointed for such party, the other party may forthwith terminate this agreement. いずれかの当事者により, またはいずれかの当事者に対して支払い不能または破産手続きが開始された場合, またはその当事者のために財産管理人が選任された場合, 相手方当事者は直ちに本契約を解除することができる。

institute　(名)協会

Institute Clauses　協会約款

Institute of Marine Underwriters　海上保険協会

Institute Strikes, Riots and Civil Commotion Clause　協会ストライキ、暴動、騒乱危険担保約款　(⇒SRCC)

Institute Cargo Clauses　協会貨物約款, ICC
◆ABC shall effect all risk (Institute Cargo Clauses) marine insurance with underwriters or insurance companies of good repute in an amount of one hundred and ten (110) percent of CIF value of the shipments of the products. ABCは, 本製品積送品のCIF価格の110%の保険金額で, 評判の良い保険引受業者または保険会社と全危険担保条件(協会貨物約款)の海上保険の保険契約をするものとする。

institutional investor　機関投資家
(=institutional lender: 資産運用を専門とする銀行や保険会社、年金、投資顧問、各種団体・組合などの投資家の総称)
◆Nissay, the largest private institutional investor in Japan, has invested in about 1,800 companies listed on Japanese stock exchanges. 日本国内最大の民間機関投資家の日本生命保険は, 日本の証券取引所に上場している企業約1,800社に出資している。

instruction　(名)指示, 通達, 指示書き, 指図(さしず)書, (機器の)取扱い説明[説明書], 指令, 命令, 教授, 訓練, 教育, 研修, 知識, 教訓, 学問, インストラクション

at the instruction of　〜の支持を受けて, 〜の指示で

corrective instructions　是正指導

follow the instructions　指示[指図]に従う, 指示書きの手順に従う

in strict accordance with your instructions　貴社の指図どおり

instruction manual　取扱い説明書

instructions for use　使用上の指示, 取扱い説明

issue instructions　指示を出す, 通達を出す

letter of instruction　指図書, 信用指図書, 手形買取り指図書

on the instructions of　〜の指示に基づいて

remittance instruction　送金通知書[案内書]

INSU

shipping instruction 船積み指図, 船積み指図書, 船積み依頼書
◆By the instruction of the China Food and Drug Administration, the Shanghai city government suspended operations of Shanghai Husi Food and confiscated raw materials and products at the firm which had sold expired meat products. 中国の国家食品薬品監督管理総局の指示で、上海市は、品質保持期限切れの肉製品を販売していた上海福喜食品の営業を停止し、同社の原料と商品を差し押さえた。◆ "Documentation" means the printed or electronic instructions, manuals and diagrams pertaining to the use and installation of Products. 「ドキュメンテーション」とは、本商品の使用とインストレーションに関する印刷されたまたは電子式の説明書、取扱い説明書と図表を意味する。◆Guidelines, instructions and manuals provided under this agreement shall be complied with in full. 本契約に基づいて提供された要領、指示とマニュアルは、全面的に遵守するものとする。

instrument （名）文書, 書面, 法律文書, 証拠文書, 証書, 契約書, 証券, 書証, 手段
◆Such counterparts shall together constitute only one instrument. これらの副本は、全部合わせて一つの法律証書を構成するものとする。

instrument of indebtedness 債務証書

insufficient packing 梱包不良

insurable interest 被保険利益

insurable value 保険価額

insurance （名）保険, 保険契約, 保険金額, 保険料, 保険条件
cargo insurance 積み荷保険, 貨物保険, 貨物海上保険
certificate of insurance 保険証明書, 保険承認状
claim for ～ on one's insurance ～について保険金支払いを求める, ～の保険金を請求する
deck cargo insurance 甲板積貨物保険
deviation insurance 航路変更保険
effect the insurance on ～に保険を付ける, 保険をかける, 付保する, ～の保険の手配をする, ～の保険契約をする
exchange risk insurance 為替変動保険, 為替変動リスク保険
export bill insurance 輸出手形保険
export credit insurance 輸出信用保険
freight insurance 運賃保険 (=insurance on freight)
goods awaiting shipment insurance 積込み滞貨物保険
indemnity insurance 損害保険
insurance against nonperformance 契約不履行保険
insurance against sweating （貨物）発汗保険

insurance against wave 潮害保険
insurance agent 保険代理人, 保険代理店
insurance agreement［contract］ 保険契約
insurance application 保険申込み書
insurance broker 保険仲介人
insurance certificate 保険引受証, 保険承認状 (＝certificate of insurance)
insurance clauses or conditions 保険約款
insurance costs if insured 付保した場合の保険費用
insurance covers 保険で～が補償される, ～を保険でカバーする
insurance for piracy damage 海賊保険
insurance liabilities 保険契約準備金
insurance of charter hire 用船料保険
insurance on shipments to customers 顧客への輸送にかかわる保険料
insurance slip 保険申込み書
insurance underwriter 保険業者
International Union of Marine Insurance 国際海上保険連合
internet insurance exchange インターネット保険取引所
jettison insurance 投荷保険
liquidated damages insurance ペナルティ偶発費用保険
marine insurance 海上保険
Marine Insurance Act 英国海上保険法
nonlife insurance 損害保険, 損保
overseas investment insurance 海外投資保険
port risks insurance 係船保険
product liability insurance 製造物責任保険, 製造物賠償責任保険, PL保険
purchase an insurance policy 保険をかける
purchase insurance 保険に入る, 保険に加入する (=buy insurance)
re-insurance 再保険
recall insurance リコール保険
repairing risks insurance 船舶修繕保険
take out insurance 保険に入る, 保険に加入する, 保険をかける
technical cooperation insurance 技術提供等保険
trade insurance 貿易保険
transport insurance 運送保険
transportation insurance 輸送保険
under insurance 一部保険
voyage risks insurance 航海保険
◆The Company agrees to cede to the Reinsurer such shares of all insurances covered by this Agreement as are set forth in the annexes (Schedule and any Addenda) to this Agree-

ment. 元受会社は、本協定対象の全保険のうち、本協定の補償（特別条項や追加条項）に明記した部分を再保険会社に出再することに合意する。◆The Landlord shall effect insurance by itself or have other tenants effect insurance against such accidents as aforementioned and indemnify the Tenant within the extent covered by the insurance. 「貸主」は、前記の事故などに対して自ら保険を付けるか他のテナントに保険を付けさせ、その保険でカバーされる範囲内で「借主」に損害の補償をするものとする。

insurance claim 保険クレーム, 保険請求権, 保険金

insurance claims 保険金, 未収保険金, 保険請求, 保険請求権, 保険金請求, 保険金請求権

insurance claims unsettled 未決済保険金

◆The solvency margin ratio indicates the ability of insurers to honor insurance claims and other payments. ソルベンシー・マージン比率は、保険会社の保険金その他の支払い金の支払い能力を示す。

insurance company 保険会社

◆ABC shall effect all risk（Institute Cargo Clauses）marine insurance with underwriters or insurance companies of good repute in an amount of one hundred and ten（110）percent of CIF value of the shipments of the products. ABCは、本製品積送品のCIF価格の110％の保険金額で、評判の良い保険引受業者または保険会社と全危険担保条件（協会貨物約款）の海上保険の保険契約をするものとする。

insurance coverage 保険担保, 保険担保範囲, 保険の補償範囲, 保険填補（てんぽ）範囲, 付保危険

◆Any additional premium for insurance coverage in excess of the value mentioned above, if so required by ABC, shall be borne by ABC. ABCの要請により、上記価額を超えて付保する場合の追加保険料は、ABCが負担するものとする。

insurance policy 保険証券, 保険証書, 保険契約

marine insurance application 外航貨物海上保険申込み書

marine insurance policy 海上保険証券

take out an insurance policy 保険を付ける, 保険に入る

◆All insurance policies possessed or owned by the Company together with brief statements of the interest insured are complete and accurate. 本会社が所有または保有しているすべての保険証券とその被保険利益についての簡単な説明は、完全で正確である。◆Throughout this agreement, Warrantee shall attempt to maintain an insurance policy to cover any claim, demand, liability, suit, damage or expense caused by Warrantee negligence. 本契約期間を通じて、被保証人は、被保証人の過失によって生じるクレーム、要求、責任、訴訟、損害または費用を担保する保険証券の維持に努めるものとする。

insurance premium 保険料

◆The insurance premium and freight are payable by you. 保険料と運賃の支払いは、貴社負担です。

insurance service 保険サービス, 保険サービス業, 保険業務, 保険事業

◆Nippon Export and Investment Insurance（NEXI）was established in 2001 to provide foreign trade and investment insurance services. 独立行政法人の日本貿易保険は、貿易保険事業と対外投資保険事業を提供するため、2001年に設立された。

insure（動）（加入者が〜に）保険をかける, 保険を付ける, 付保する,（保険業者が〜について）保険契約を結ぶ, 保険契約する, 保険を引き受ける, 保険証券を発行する, 保証する, 請合う, 確保する

insure a person against death 〜に（人）に生命保険をかける

insure against all risks オールリスク保険をかける, 全危険担保の条件で保険契約を結ぶ

insure one's life for $300,000 30万ドルの生命保険に入る

insure one's life with the company 同社と生命保険契約を結ぶ

insure one's property against fire 〜の財産に火災保険をかける

insure one's property for $500,000 〜の財産に50万ドルの保険をかける

◆All quantities of the Product manufactured by you shall be held by you to our order and we shall insure all quantities on your premises of the Commodity and the Product. 貴社が製造した契約品の数量はすべて当社の指図があるまで貴社が保管し、当社は貴社の構内にある商品と契約品の全数量に保険を付けるものとする。◆During the period when Products are in the custody of ABC, ABC shall keep Products insured at ABC's account for the benefit of XYZ against loss or damage by fire, theft or otherwise with extended coverage. 本製品［契約品］をABCが保管している期間中、火災、盗難、その他による減失や損害を拡529担保するため、ABCはその勘定で、XYZを保険受取人として本製品に付保するものとする。◆The goods are to be insured for 25% over the invoice value. 約定品には、送り状金額の125％で付保することになっている。◆The term "Net Selling Price" shall mean the invoiced price on a sale of Products by Licensee in the Territory defined hereinafter, less sales taxes, packing costs, transport costs, insurance costs if insured, credit on Products returned, and the usual trade discounts. 「正味販売価格」という用語は、以下に定義する契約地域でライセンシーが本製品を販売する際のインボイス価格から、売上税（物品売買税）、梱包費、運送費、付保した場合の保険費用、本製品の返品分の代金と通常の取引割引を差し引いたものを意味する。

insured（形）保険がかかっている, 〜に対して保険がかけられている, 〜に対して保険が

きく［保険に入っている］, 保険付きの, 付保された, 被保険〜　（名）被保険者, 保険契約者

insured account　付保勘定, 保険付き勘定, （預金保険）保険口座

insured amount　保険金額, 保険契約金額 （=assured amount）

insured article　被保険物

insured bank　被保険銀行, 預金保険加入銀行 （米連邦預金保険制度に加入している銀行）

insured B/L　保険付き船荷証券

insured cargo　付保貨物, 保険付き貨物

insured cause　保険事故

insured credit exposure　付保された信用リスク

insured event　保険事故, 保険事象

insured firm　被保険企業（保険をかけている企業）

insured invoice　ノン・ポリ（輸出者が保険会社と包括保険契約を結んでいる場合, 商業送り状（commercial invoice）の空欄に「当該貨物は付保済みである」旨の文言を記入したものをいう）

insured ledger　信用状発行元帳

insured loan　保険付きローン

insured loss index　保険損失指数

insured object　被保険物

insured par　付保総額

insured period　加入期間

insured person　被保険者

insured plan　保険付き制度

insured portfolio　保険付きポートフォリオ

insured property　被保険物

insured value　保険価額

insured value of vessel　船舶保険価額

perils insured against　担保危険

the insured　被保険者, 保険契約者

the sum insured　保険金額

◆All insurance policies possessed or owned by the Company together with brief statements of the interest insured are complete and accurate. 本会社が所有または保有しているすべての保険証券とその被保険利益についての簡単な説明は, 完全で正確である。◆The nonlife insurance industry wants all kinds of buildings and other properties not insured for terrorist attacks. 損害保険業界は, すべての物件をテロ免責にしたいと考えている。

insurer　（名）保険会社, 保険業者, 保険者, 保証人　（=insurance company, insurance enterprise, insurance firm）

◆The solvency margin ratio indicates the ability of insurers to honor insurance claims and other payments. ソルベンシー・マージン比率は, 保険会社の保険金その他の支払い金の支払い能力を示す。

intaken weight final　船積み数量条件

（intaken weight=shipped weight）

integral multiple　整数倍, 倍数

◆The loan shall be advanced by the lender to the borrower wholly or partially in an amount of ten million Japanese Yen （￥10,000,000） or its integral multiple upon request by the borrower. 貸付け金は, 借主の要請に基づき, 貸主が借主に対してその全額または一部を1千万円またはその倍数の金額で提供する。

integral part　不可分の一体, 構成部分, 構成要素

◆All the terms and conditions set forth on the reverse side hereof are confirmed to be an integral part of this agreement. 裏面に記載する条件は, すべて本契約の不可分の一部であることを確認する。

intellectual asset　知的資産（「知的資産」には, 特許や著作権などの知的財産のほかに, 企業のノウハウやブランドなどが含まれる）

◆Businesses in Japan and other industrial nations need to make more active use of patents, copyrights, brands and other intellectual assets to keep up with changes in the global economy. 日本などの先進国企業は, 世界経済の変革に対応するため, 特許や著作権, ブランドなどの知的資産を一段と積極的に活用する必要がある。

intellectual or industrial property rights 知的財産権ないし工業所有権

◆To the best of Seller's knowledge, the Company has not and is not infringing the intellectual or industrial property rights of any third party. 売り主の知るかぎり, 対象会社は第三者の知的財産権ないし工業所有権を過去においても現在においても侵害していない。

intellectual property　知的所有権, 知的財産権　（=intellectual property right: 特許 （patent）、商標（trademark）、実用新案 （utility model）、意匠（design）、著作権 （copyright）、トレード・シークレット（trade secret）などの総称）

Agreement on Trade-Related Aspect of Intellectual Property Rights　知的財産権の貿易的側面に関する協定, TRIP

claim for infringement of the intellectual property　知的所有権侵害の申立て, 知的所有権侵害のクレーム

infringement of intellectual property vs. imports 知的財産権侵害物品と輸入

intellectual property infringement　知的所有権侵害, 知的財産権侵害

the United Nations' World Intellectual Property Organization　国連の世界知的所有権機関, WIPO

◆ABC possesses certain technology for the design, manufacture, use, and distribution of the products and certain intellectual property pertaining thereto. ABCは, 本製品の設計、製造、使用および販売のための特定の技術と, それに関する知的財産権を所有している。◆The most advanced technologies are often at stake in lawsuits over intellectual property. 知的財産を巡る訴訟では、最先端技術が争点になることが多い。

Intellectual Property High Court　知的財産高等裁判所
◆The Intellectual Property High Court specializes in lawsuits over intellectual property, such as the infringement of patents. 知的財産高等裁判所は、特許権侵害など知的財産を巡る訴訟を専門に手がける。

intellectual property right　知的所有権, 知的財産権 (=intellectual property)
◆Sharp has accused manufacturers in Taiwan of infringing on its intellectual property rights. シャープは、同社の知的財産権侵害で台湾メーカーを訴えた。◆The seller shall not be responsible for any infringement with regard to patents, utility models, designs, trademarks, copyrights, trade secrets or any other intellectual property rights in any country, except for the seller's country, in connection with the sales, use or delivery of the products. 売り主は、本製品の販売、使用と引渡しに関連する特許、実用新案、意匠、商標、著作権、トレード・シークレットまたはその他の知的財産権に関する侵害に対しては、売り主の国を除いていずれの国においても責任を負わないものとする。

intended to　〜することを意図した、〜を目的とする (=meant to)
◆Unless specifically set forth herein, nothing in this agreement is intended to confer any rights or remedies upon any persons other than the parties and their respective successors and assigns. 本契約書に特に明記しないかぎり、本契約の規定は、契約当事者とその各承継人および譲受人以外の者に権利または救済方法を付与することを意図したものではない。

intent　(名)意思, 目的, 意図, 計画, 決意, 趣旨, 意味
prior understanding, statement of intent or memorandum of understanding　従前の(契約締結前の)了解事項、意図の表明または了解覚書
◆This agreement supersedes and replaces any prior understanding, agreement, statement of intent or memorandum of understanding, written or oral. 本契約は、書面または口頭による従前の一切の了解、合意、意図の表明または了解覚書に優先するもので、これらに代わるものである。◆This Memorandum of Agreement is intended to be a non-binding expression of the intent of the parties. この合意覚書は、両当事者の意図に法的拘束力がないことを表明することを意図している。

intention　(名)意思, 目的, 意図, 計画, 故障, 概念, 観念, 意味, 趣旨
have the intention to extend this agreement　本契約を更新する意思がある
intention of termination　解除の意思
◆A party hereto proposing to effect a sale of any

shares of the new company (the Offerer) shall give a written notice to the other parties hereto, or their assignee, who are then shareholders of the new company (the Offerees), of the Offerer's intention, the identity of the prospective third party purchaser, and the terms and conditions of the proposed sale. 新会社の株式の売却を申し出る本契約当事者(「申込み者」)は、他の当事者またはその時点で新会社の株主である譲受人(「被申込み者」)に対して、申込み者の売却意思、予定される第三者購入者の住所・氏名と申し出をした売却の条件を、書面で通知するものとする。

intentional torts　故意の不法行為

inter alia　とくに, とりわけ, 〜その他, 〜などと (=above all, among other things)
◆In case ABC Personnel makes business trips for the performance of the services, costs and expenses for such trips, including, inter alia, fares and allowances shall be born and paid or reimbursed by XYZ. 本サービスを提供するためにABC人員が出張する場合、当該出張の諸費用(とりわけ旅費と出張手当てを含む)は、XYZが負担して支払うかXYZがその補償をするものとする。

interbank trading　銀行間取引
◆Interbank trading between the U.S. dollar and the Chinese currency yuan accounts for 99.3 percent of the Shanghai foreign exchange market. 米ドルと中国の通貨・人民元の銀行間取引[銀行間為替取引]が、上海外国為替市場の99.3%を占めている。

Intercontinental Exchange　(名)米インターコンチネンタル取引所, ICE
◆Intercontinental Exchange (ICE), an exchange that deals in investing contracts known as futures, is buying the NYSE for about $8 billion. 米インターコンチネンタル取引所(ICE: 先物と呼ばれる投資契約を扱う取引所)が、ニューヨーク証券取引所を約80億ドルで買収する。

interest　(名)利権, 利害関係, 利益, 権利, 権益, 利息, 株, 関心, 興味, 重要性, 〜側, 関係者
any interest in such Stock　当該株式の権利
bear interest　利息を負担する, 利息を支払う, 利息が生じる, 利息が付く
bear interest at 8 % p.a.　年8%の利息が付く[利息が生じる]
create a security interest　担保権を設定する
delayed interest　遅延利息, 延滞利息, 遅延金利
earn interest　利息が付く
earn no interest　利息が付かない
interest arbitration　金利裁定取引
interest bill　利付き手形
interest clause　利息条項
interest policy　金利政策, 利益者保険証券, 被保険利益所有者保険証券
overdue interest　遅延金利, 遅延利息

pay interest　利息を支払う, 利払いがある

receive interest on　〜の利息を受け取る

◆For Value Received, the undersigned ("Borrower") promises to pay to ABC Co., Ltd. , a Japanese corporation ("Holder"), or order, in lawful money of the United States, the principal sum of Five million Eight hundred Fifty thousand dollars ($5,850,000), with interest on the principal balance remaining unpaid from the date hereof until paid, at the following rates. 「対価の受領」については, 末尾署名者 (以下「振出人」という) が, 元本585万ドル ($5,850,000) と本手形の振出日から決済日まで残存する元本の未払い残高利息を, 日本法人のABC株式会社 (以下「所持人」という) にまたはその指図人に, 米国の法定通貨と以下の金利で支払うことを約束する。

interest charge　支払い利息

◆Late payment shall incur an interest charge of 2 percent over the base rate current in XYZ Bank at the time the charge is levied from the due date to the date of payment in full. 支払いが遅延した場合, 支払い期日から全額支払い日まで, 支払い利息 (遅延利息) を課す時点でXYZ銀行が適用する基準金利より2%高い支払い利息 (遅延利息) が付くものとする。

interest insured　被保険利益

◆All insurance policies possessed or owned by the Company together with brief statements of the interest insured are complete and accurate. 本会社が所有または保有しているすべての保険証券とその被保険利益についての簡単な説明は, 完全で正確である。

interest payable　支払い利息

◆In case the borrower fails to pay any principal or interest payable under this agreement on the due date therefor, the borrower shall pay to the lender overdue interest on such overdue amount for each day for the period from and including the due date therefor up to and including the day immediately preceding the actual payment date. 借主が本契約に基づいて元本または支払い利息の支払い期日に元本の返済または支払い利息の支払いを怠った場合, 借主は, その支払い期日から実際の払込み日の前日までの期間の各日数について, その支払い遅延金額の遅延利息を貸主に支払うものとする。

interest payment period　利払い期間

◆The borrower shall pay to the lender an interest on the loan for each interest payment period applicable to the loan at the floating rate of the LIBOR (British Bankers Association Interest Settlement Rate in U.S. Dollars) plus 1.625 percent per annum, calculated on the basis of actual number of days elapsed and a year of 360 days. 借主は, 1年を360日として実際に経過した日数に基づいて計算した, ロンドン銀行間取引金利 (米ドルでの英国銀行協会金利決済レート) に年1.625%を加算した変動金利で, この借入れに適用される各

利払い期間の借入金の利息を貸主に対して支払うものとする。

interest rate　利率, 金利, 利子率　(⇒annul)

◆In the case of a negative interest rate which the ECB has introduced, commercial banks have to pay interest at this rate, which is like a handling fee, to place funds at the central bank. 欧州中央銀行 (ECB) が導入したマイナス金利の場合, 民間銀行は, 手数料のようにマイナス金利の金利を払って, ECBに資金を預けることになる。◆The ECB's introduction of a negative deposit rate also aims to lower interest rate levels in general and redress the strong euro. ECB (欧州中央銀行) のマイナス (中銀預入) 金利導入には, 金利水準全体の引下げとユーロ高是正の狙いもある。

interim agreement　仮契約

intermediary　(形) 中間の, 仲介の, 媒介の (名) 仲介者, 仲介人, 仲介機関, 仲裁人, 仲裁者, 仲裁機関, 調停者, 媒介, 媒介の手段, 媒介物

financial intermediary　金融仲介機関

intermediary bank　仲介銀行

intermediary business　仲介業

intermediary commerce　仲介貿易

intermediary goods　中間財

intermediary improvement trade　中継加工貿易

intermediary trade　通過貿易, 仲介貿易, 3国間貿易 (日本企業が日本以外の二国間貿易の取引を採り結ぶ場合を「仲介貿易」という)

market intermediary　証券会社

risk intermediary　リスク仲介機関

◆Alternative dispute resolution (ADR) for the revitalization of a business is a procedure that uses an intermediary from the private sector. 事業再生ADR (裁判外紛争解決手続き) は, 民間の仲介機関 [第三者機関] を活用する再建手続きだ。◆As we save intermediary costs, we can make the clothes much cheaper than other products of the same quality. 中間コストを省いているため, 衣類は同じ品質の他の製品よりずっと安く製造できます。

intermediate　(形) 中間の, 中級の, 中型の, 介在する

intermediate commodity　中間財 (=intermediate goods)

intermediate consumption　中間消費

intermediate demand　中間需要

intermediate goods trade　中間財貿易

intermediate improvement trade　中継加工貿易

intermediate product　中間生産物

intermediate stock　中間在庫品

intermediate-term loan　中期ローン

intermediate trade　中継貿易 : 仲介貿易

INTE 262

intermodal （形）協同一貫輸送の, インター
モーダル （=multimodal）

intermodal B/L　インターモーダル船荷証券

intermodal carrier　協同一貫運送人

Intermodal Surface Transportation Efficiency
Act　陸上一貫輸送効率化法

intermodal transportation　複合一貫輸送, 協同
一貫輸送

internal documentation　内部文書

internal laws　州内法
◆The term "FOB" shall be interpreted in accordance with the internal laws of California, including the Uniform Commercial Code. 用語の
「FOB」は, 米国統一商事法典を含めて, カリフォ
ルニア州内法に従って解釈するものとする。

Internal Revenue Service　米国の内国歳入
庁, IRS　（日本の国税庁に相当）

international （形）国際的, 国際間の, 国際上
の, 国際社会の, インターナショナル

international access number　国際アクセス
番号

international accounts　国際収支

international agreement　国際協定, 国際合意

International Air Transport Association　国際
航空運送協会, IATA

International Air Transportation Competition
Act of 1979　国際航空輸送競争法

international airfares　国際航空運賃

international application　特許の国際出願

international authority　国際機関

international bank transfer　国際送金

international banking day　海外送金取扱い日,
外国為替/国際金融業務取扱い日

international banking facilities　国際金融機関

international carriage　国際運送

international cartel　国際カルテル

International Chamber of Commerce　国際商
業会議所, ICC

international combined transport　国際複合輸
送　(=international intermodal
［multimodal］transport）

International Commercial Terms　国際貿易条
件基準, インコタームズ　(=Incoterms,
INCOTERMS）

international commodities　国際商品

International Convention for the Unification of
Certain Rules relating to Bills of Lading　統
一船荷証券条約

international currency　国際通貨

international customs transit　国際保税運送

international deal　国債取引

international demand　国際的需要, 海外需要

international division of manufacturing　国際
分業　(⇒shipment）

International Institute for Management
Development　国際経営開発研究所

International Labor Organization　国際労働機
関, ILO

International Law Association　国際法協会

international liquidity　国際流動性

International Maritime Organization　国際海事
機関, IMO（1958年に設立された国連の専
門機関で, 政府間海洋協議機関（IMCO）の
名称を1982年5月から改称した）

international marketing　国際マーケティング

International money order　国際為替

international oil majors　国際石油資本

international operation　国際業務, 海外業務,
海外事業活動, 国際的事業

International Organization for Standardization
国際標準化機構, ISO

international parcel delivery service　国際宅
配便

international policies　対外政策

international portfolio diversification　国際分
散投資

international portfolio investment　国際証券
投資

international preliminary examination　国際予
備審査

international procurement　国際的調達, 海外
調達　(=international sourcing）

international publication　特許の国際公開

International Rules for the Interpretation of
Trade Terms　貿易条件の解釈に関する国
際規則, インコタームズ　(=Incoterms）

international sales　海外販売, 海外売上, 海外
営業, 国際販売部門

international search［searching］　国際調査

international settlement　国際決済

international sourcing　海外調達, 国際的調
達　(=international procurement）

International Standard Book Number　国際標
準図書番号, ISBN

International System（of Units）　国際単位系

International Trade Organization　国際貿易機
構, ITO

international transfer　国際送金

international waters　公海　(=high seas）

International Whaling Commission　国際捕鯨
委員会

Law on International Carriage of Goods by Sea
国際海上物品運送法

UN Convention on Contracts for the
International Sales of Good　国連国際動産
売買条約

United Nations Convention on International

Carriage of Goods by Sea　国連国際海上物品運送条約

International Accounting Standards
（国際会計基準審議会（IASB）が作成している）国際会計基準, IAS（2005年1月1日から新しい呼び名として「国際財務報告基準（International Financial Reporting Standards）」に改められた。⇒IFRS）

International Accounting Standards Board　国際会計基準理事会, IASB

International Accounting Standards Committee　国際会計基準委員会, IASC

international accounting standards　国際会計基準
◆The SEC proposed a plan to allow public companies to using international accounting standards for reporting financial results. 米証券取引委員会（SEC）は、株式公開企業［上場企業］に対して（2014年をめどに）決算報告に国際会計基準の導入［採用］を認める計画を提案した。

international balance of payments　国際収支　（⇒balance of payments）
解説 国際収支関連用語：
basic balance　基礎収支
capital balance　資本収支
current account balance　経常収支（＝current balance）
foreign reserves　外貨準備
goods & services balance　貿易・サービス収支
income balance　所得収支
investment balance　投資収支
invisible balance　貿易外収支
long-term capital balance　長期資本収支
overall balance　総合収支
services balance　サービス収支
short-term capital balance　短期資本収支
trade balance　貿易収支
transfer balance　移転収支

international bank　国際銀行
◆The Buyer shall establish in favor of the Seller an irrevocable letter of credit issued by a first-class international bank acceptable to the Seller. 買い主は、売り主のために、売り主が承諾できる［同意できる］第一級の国際銀行が発行する取消不能の信用状を開設するものとする。

International Bank for Reconstruction Development　国際復興開発銀行, IBRD

international business　国際経営, 国際ビジネス, 国際事業, 国際企業, 世界企業, 多国籍企業
international business activities　国際事業活動, 国際ビジネス
international business management　国際経営管理
international business planning　国際事業計画, 国際企業の事業計画
international business policy　国際経営政策
international business strategy　国際事業戦略, 国際企業戦略, グローバル戦略（＝global business strategy）

international capital markets　国際資本市場
◆In the second half of the 1980s, the IMF began supporting the liberalization of international capital markets. 1980年代後半から、国際通貨基金（IMF）は国際資本市場の自由化を支持するようになった。

international commercial trade　国際商取引
◆To ensure fair international commercial trade, the law against unfair competition stipulates that both individuals involved in bribery and the corporations they belong to should be punished. 公正な国際商取引を確保するため、不正競争防止法には、贈賄（外国公務員への贈賄）に関与した個人と法人を罰する規定（両罰規定）がある。

international competitiveness　国際競争力
◆The government will lower the effective corporate tax rate to boost the international competitiveness of Japanese companies and at the same time to attract greater foreign investment to Japan. 日本企業の国際競争力強化と対日投資拡大に向けて、政府は法人税の実効税率を引き下げる方針だ。◆The international competitiveness of companies and a country's balance of trade with the rest of the world are affected not by nominal exchange rates but by real exchange rates, so we need to follow real exchange rates. 企業の国際競争力や国の他国との貿易収支などの動きは、名目為替レートではなく、実質為替レートの影響を受けるので、われわれは実質為替レートの動きを見る必要がある。◆To liberalize trade further, it is imperative to arrest a decline in Japan's agriculture sector and improve its international competitiveness. 一層の貿易自由化に向けて、日本の農業衰退に歯止めをかけ、農業の国際競争力を高めるのが急務だ。

international division of labor　国際分業
◆Japan and China have established a system of international division of labor in which China imports industrial parts from Japan to assemble into finished products in China and these are marketed domestically or exported to the U.S., Europe and elsewhere. 日本と中国は、中国が日本から工業部品を輸入して中国で最終製品に組み立て、中国国内で販売したり欧米などに輸出したりする国際分業体制を築いてきた。

international exchanges　国際為替市場, 国際取引所
◆The value of the renminbi（yuan）is rising on international exchanges. 国際為替市場で、中国の人民元の価値が上昇している。

INTE 264

international export markets 国際輸出
市場
◆A cheaper dollar does definitely serve to make
U.S. producers more cost-competitive in international export markets. 国際輸出市場で米国の生産
者の価格競争力を高めるには、間違いなくドル安
のほうがよい。

International Finance Corporation 国際
金融公社, IFC （世界銀行グループ（World
Bank Group）の一つで発展途上国のための金
融機関）
◆The World Bank will issue the yuan-based
bonds through the International Finance Corporation. 世界銀行は、国際金融公社を通じて人民元
建て債を発行する。

**International Financial Reporting
Standards** 国際財務報告基準, IFRS
［IFRSs］（国際財務報告規準（IFRS）は、国
際会計基準審議会（IASB）が設定するIAS
（International Accounting Standards: 国際会計
基準）の新しい呼び名で、2005年1月1日に採
択された。⇒IFRS）
◆The consolidated financial statements conform
in all material respects with International Financial Reporting Standards（IFRSs）. 連結財務書
類［連結財務諸表］の重要事項は、すべて国際財務
報告基準に適合している。

international financial system 国際金融
システム
◆The liberalization of capital flows in the globalized world economy is the core principle for
ensuring the international financial system operated efficiently. グローバル化した世界経済におけ
る資本移動の自由化は、効率的な国際金融システ
ムの運営確保の中核をなす原理である。

international fund transaction 国際的な
資金取引, 国際資金取引
◆Errors in computing systems at financial institutions could lead to problems in making international fund transactions. 金融機関のコンピュー
タ・システムのエラーは、国際的な資金取引上、ト
ラブルが生じる可能性がある。

international market 国際市場
◆The market share of the newly merged firm is
expected to be relatively low in the international
market. 合併新会社の市場シェアは、国際市場で
は比較的低いと思われる［予想される］。

International Monetary Fund 国際通貨
基金, IMF
◆Belarus is counting on striking a low-interest
loan deal with the International Monetary Fund.
ベラルーシは、国際通貨基金（IMF）から低利融資
を受けるのを期待している。◆The International
Monetary Fund warned of growing Japanese
government bond risk in Japanese banks. 国際
通貨基金（IMF）は、邦銀の日本国債保有リスクの
高まりに警鐘を鳴らした。

international payment 国際支払い, 国際
送金

international payment balance 国際収支尻, 国
際収支

international payment currency 国際決済通貨

international payments position 国際収支

the balance of international payments 国際
収支
◆Changes in exchange rates are a result of multiple factors, including the balance of international
payments and market supply and demand. 為替
相場の変動は、国際収支や市場の需給など複数要
因によるものだ。

international quality standard 国際品質
基準
◆This manufacturing facility was registered for
international quality standard ISO 9001. この製
造施設［製造工場］は、国際品質基準「ISO 9001」
の認定を受けた。

international ratings agency 国際格付け
機関
◆In new sovereign debt ratings by Germany's
Bertelsmann Foundation, Japan earned a score
of 6 on a scale of one to ten, equivalent to A
minus on the rating scales adopted by major international ratings agencies. ドイツのベルテルス
マン財団の新国債格付けで、日本は1～10の格付け
段階のうち6の評価を得たが、これは主要国際格付
け機関が採用している格付け基準で「Aマイナス」
に相当する。

international requirement 国際規制
◆The global 28 megabanks will be subject to
the FSB's new international requirement to absorb losses and reduce the moral hazard posed
by these banks. 世界のメガ銀行28行が、これらの
巨大銀行による損失の吸収とモラル・ハザード抑
制に向けての金融安定化理事会（FSB）の新国際金
融規制の対象になる見込みだ。

international route 国際線
◆The two airlines have agreed to enter into
a code-sharing arrangement on international
routes. 両航空会社は、国際線の共同運航協定を
結ぶことで合意した。

international rules 国際基準, 国際ルール
**International Rules for the Interpretation of
Trade Terms** 貿易条件の解釈に関する国
際規則, インコタームズ （=Incoterms）
◆Twenty-eight banks of the world will face capital surcharges of 1 percent to 2.5 percent by the
application of international rules in too-
big-to-fail lenders. 大きすぎて破たんさせられな
い銀行［金融機関］を規制する国際基準が適用され
ると、世界の28行が、1～2.5%の資本［自己資本］
上積みの対象となる。

international safety standards 国際安全
基準 （=global safety standards［criteria］）
◆Nursing-care robots under the envisaged international safety standards of the ISO stop or go
around such hazards as objects or bumps. 国際標
準化機構（ISO）の国際安全基準案に基づく介護ロ

ボットは、障害物や凹凸などの危険があれば、止まったり避けたりする。

international standard 国際規格
◆The ISO, a private organization that sets international standards for industrial products, will adopt Japan-led global safety criteria for nursing-care robots. 工業製品の国際規格を定める民間組織の「国際標準化機構（ISO）」は、日本政府が主導する介護ロボットの国際安全基準を採用する方針だ。

international trade 国際貿易, 国際商取引
Charter for an International Trade Organization 国際貿易憲章, ハバナ憲章
Commission on International Commodity Trade 国際商品貿易［取引］委員会
horizontal international trade 水平貿易
International Trade and Development Act of 1989 1989年国際貿易開発法
International Trade Charter 国際貿易憲章
International Trade Fair 国際見本市, ITF
international trade friction 貿易摩擦
International Trade Law 国際商取引法
international trade multiplier 外国貿易乗数
International Trade Organization 国際貿易機構, ITO
international trade policy 国際貿易政策, 通商政策
international trade relations 国際貿易関係, 通商関係
primary international trade framework 国際貿易の中心的枠組み
Standard International Trade Classification 標準国際貿易分類, SITC
UN Commission on International Trade Law 国連国際商取引法委員会

International Trade Commission 米国際貿易委員会, ITC
◆U.S. electronic equipment maker asked the International Trade Commission to determine whether Nintendo has infringed on the maker's patents to make Wii video game console. 米国の電子機器メーカーは、米国際貿易委員会（ITC）に対して、任天堂が同社の特許を侵害して任天堂のビデオ・ゲーム機「Wii（ウィー）」を製造しているか否かの裁定を求めた。

International Trade Committee （欧州議会の）国際貿易委員会
◆A European Commission trade commissioner said at the European Parliament's International Trade Committee meeting that the EU and the United States could sign a comprehensive partnership agreement as early as the end of 2014. 欧州委員会の通商担当委員は、欧州議会の国際貿易委員会で、EU（欧州連合）と米国は2014年中に包括的連携協定を結ぶことも可能と述べた。

international trade imbalances 国際貿易不均衡, 貿易の不均衡
◆The two oil crises in the 1970s increased international trade imbalances worldwide and stepped up the international flow of funds. 1970年代の2度の石油危機で、世界的な貿易不均衡が激化し、国際的資金の流れが拡大した。

international treaty 国際条約
◆An international treaty to ban the use, development, production, stockpiling and transfer of cluster bombs entered into force on August 1, 2010. クラスター（集束）爆弾の使用、開発、製造、保有と移転を禁止する国際条約が、2010年8月1日に発効した。

International Tribunal for the Law of the Sea 国際海洋法裁判所
◆The Hamburg-based International Tribunal for the Law of the Sea issued an interim injunction on Japan's experimental fishing for southern bluefin tuna. 国際海洋法裁判所（ドイツ・ハンブルク）は、日本が行っているミナミマグロの調査漁獲に暫定的な命令を下した。

internationally recognized 国際的に認知された
◆An internationally recognized courier service including DHL and Federal Express provides a delivery receipt. DHLやフェデラル・エクスプレスなど国際的に認知されたクーリエ・サービスは、配達証を発行している。

Internet （名）インターネット, ネット
（＝internet, INET, Net:internetworkの略）
◆Bitcoin circulated only on the Internet is not under the control of central banks unlike regular currencies. インターネット上だけで流通しているビットコインは、通常の通貨と違って、中央銀行の統制を受けていない。◆Establishing original edition rights would enable publishing companies to file lawsuits demanding the deletion of data if pirated copies are found to be sold on the Internet. 出版物［書籍］原版権の創設によって出版社は、海賊版がインターネット上で販売されていることが判明した場合に、データの削除を求める訴訟を起こすことができる。◆In FX margin trading, investors can trade around the clock via the Internet. 外国為替証拠金取引の場合、投資家はインターネットで24時間取引できる。◆Washington is staying silent whether it launched a cyber attack in retaliation for the hacking attack against Sony Pictures Entertainment though North Korea's Internet was on the fritz. 北朝鮮のインターネット接続不能となったが、米国は、ソニー・ピクチャーズ・エンタテインメントへのハッキング攻撃に対する報復として米国がサイバー攻撃を行ったかどうかについては、沈黙を守っている。

Internet shopping mall インターネット上の仮想商店街
◆A major Internet shopping mall program which began in March 2000 allows payments to be made immediately through the bank accounts of users. 2000年3月にスタートした大規模なインター

ネット上の仮想商店街プログラムは、利用者の銀行口座から即時決済できる。

Internet trading インターネット取引, ネット取引, インターネット販売, ネット・トレーディング, インターネットによる売買, ネット販売 (=Net trading, online trade, online trading)
◆By embarking on Internet trading, the medium-sized brokerage house aims to offer greater convenience for existing customers. ネット取引に参入して、この準大手の証券会社は、既存の顧客の利便性向上を図ることを目指している。

interpret (動)解釈する
interpret or construe 解釈する
◆Unless otherwise expressly provided for in this agreement, the price and trade term "C.I.F." shall be interpreted in accordance with Incoterms 2000. 本契約に特に明示の規定がないかぎり（本契約で別段に明確に規定しないかぎり）、価格と貿易条件のCIFは、2000年版インコタームズに従って解釈する。

interpretation (名)解釈
interpretation or validity of this agreement 本契約の解釈または有効性
the construction or interpretation of this agreement 本契約の解釈
the interpretation and performance of this agreement 本契約の解釈と履行
◆The headings to the Articles of this agreement are to facilitate reference only, do not form a part of this agreement and shall not in any way affect the interpretation of this agreement. 本契約条項の見出しは、参照の便宜だけの目的のもので、本契約の一部を構成するものではなく、いかなる場合でも本契約の解釈に影響を与えないものとする。

interpretation hereof 本契約の解釈
◆Headings of the Articles used in this agreement are inserted for convenience of reference only and shall in no way affect the interpretation hereof. 本契約書で使用する条項の見出しは、参照の便宜のために挿入するにすぎず、本契約の解釈に一切影響を与えないものとする。

interpretation or performance of this agreement 本契約の解釈または履行
◆The parties hereto will enter into bona fide discussions in an attempt to solve any issues or dispute which may arise from the interpretation or performance of this agreement. 本契約当事者は、本契約の解釈または履行から生じる一切の問題または紛争を解決するための試みとして、善意の話し合いを行うものとする。

interrupt (動)妨げる, 妨害する, 邪魔をする, さえぎる, 中断する
interrupt the economic recovery 景気回復の腰を折る
◆Should the Fed misjudge the timing or level of its next rate hike, it may interrupt the economic recovery and even bring about rapid inflation. 米

連邦準備制度理事会(FRB)が追加利上げの幅やタイミングを誤ると、景気回復の腰を折り、急激なインフレを招く可能性もある。

interruption (名)妨害, 邪魔, 中断, 中止, 停止
interruption of business 営業妨害, 業務妨害
interruption of electric supply [current, service] 停電
interruption of power 電力の中断
without interruption 連続で

Interstate Commerce Commission 米州際交通委員会

introduce (動)導入する, 持ち込む, 投入する, 使用を開始する, 始める, 着手する, 踏み切る, 発売する, 売り出す, 公開する, 上場する, 法案を議会に提出する, 紹介する, 〜の始まりとなる
introduce a new open market operation 新型の公開市場操作(オペ)を導入する
introduce a new product 新製品[新商品]を発売する
introduce an early retirement scheme 早期退職制度を導入する
introduce various regulation measures 各種の規制措置を導入する
introduced a market economy 市場経済を導入する
introduced capital 出資金 (=capital introduced)
introduced stock [share] 公開株
◆Sharp Corp. intends to augment its home electronics business in Middle Eastern and African countries by introducing a series of luxury products to cater to increased demand from wealthy consumers. シャープは、高級家電を相次いで投入して、中東・アフリカ諸国の家電事業を強化し、増する富裕層の需要に応える方針だ。

introduce an emergency tariff on 〜に対して緊急関税を導入する[発動する]
◆Major beef exporters such as the United States have already threatened to impose some punitive action against Japan if it introduces an emergency tariff on imported beef. 日本が輸入牛肉に対して緊急関税を導入[発動]した場合、米国など牛肉の主な対日輸出国は、すでに日本に対して制裁措置を取る動きを示している。

introduce renewable energy sources 再生可能エネルギーを導入する
◆Introducing renewable energy sources instead of nuclear power plants may lead to the hollowing-out of the domestic industrial sector in the face of increased production costs, and bankruptcies of small and midsized businesses. 原発の代わりに再生可能エネルギーを導入すると、生産コストの上昇による国内産業の空洞化や中小企業の倒産を招く可能性がある。

introduction （名）紹介, 導入, 実施, 新規導入, 新規導入品, 使用開始, 輸入, 伝来, 伝来品, 発売, 公開, 上場, 核兵器などの持ち込み, 注入, 挿入, 紹介, 序論, 序説, 概論, 入門書
◆Abe advertised Japan at the New York Stock Exchange by explaining that introduction of a high-speed railway system using Japan's superconducting magnetic levitation technology could connect New York and Washington in less than an hour. 安倍首相は、ニューヨーク証券取引所で、「日本の超電導リニア技術を用いた高速鉄道を導入すれば、ニューヨークとワシントンは1時間足らずで結ばれる」と説明して、日本を売り込んだ。

introduction of a negative （bank) deposit rate マイナス中銀預入金利の導入, マイナス金利の導入
◆The ECB's introduction of a negative deposit rate also aims to lower interest rate levels in general and redress the strong euro. ECB（欧州中央銀行）のマイナス（中銀預入）金利導入には、金利水準全体の引下げとユーロ高是正の狙いもある。

introduction of new models 新型車の導入
◆Mitsubishi Motors Corp. expects to be profitable for the first time in four years with the introduction of new models. 三菱自動車は、新型車の導入で、4年ぶりの黒字転換を見込んでいる。

introduction of the IFRS 国際財務報告基準（IFRS）の導入
◆The Financial Services Agency gave up its initial goal to make the introduction of the IFRS mandatory in around 2015. 金融庁は、2015年にもIFRS（国際財務報告基準）の導入を義務化するという当初の目標を断念した。

inure to 効力を生じる, 有効となる, 〜に適用される, 〜の利益になる, 〜に役立つ
◆Upon any permitted assignment, this agreement shall inure to the benefit of and be binding upon the successors and assigns of both parties. 譲渡の許諾を受けると同時に、本契約は両当事者の承継人と譲受人に適用され、承継人と譲受人を拘束するものとする。

invalid, illegal or unenforceable 無効、違法または強制不能の
◆In case any one or more of the provisions of this agreement are held invalid, illegal or unenforceable in any respect, the validity, legality and enforceability of the remaining provisions hereof shall not be in any way affected or impaired thereby, except to the extent that giving effect to the remaining provisions would be unjust or inequitable. 本契約の一つ以上の規定がいずれかの点で無効、違法または強制不能と判断された場合、残存規定の実施が不公正または不均衡となる範囲を除いて、本契約の残存規定の有効性、合法性と強制可能性はその影響を受けることはなく、またそれによって損なわれることはないものとする。

invalidity or unenforceability 無効または実施不能, 無効または強制不能

invention （名）発明, 発明品, 発明力, 発明の才（inventiveness）, 考案, 新案, 創作, 創案, 新案品, 創作品, 創案品, 作り話, でっち上げ, ねつ造

finding ［identifying］ of a claimed invention 発明の認定
invention in service 職務発明
invention of process 方法の発明
joint invention 共同発明
protection of inventions 発明の保護
purpose of the invention 発明の目的
scope of an invention 発明の範囲
sole invention 単独発明
title of the invention 発明の名称
utilization of inventions 発明の利用
◆The belief that inventions by employees belong to their employers is deep-rooted in the Japanese corporate culture. 日本の企業風土では、社員の発明は会社の財産という考え方が根強い［確立している］。

invest in 〜に投資する, 出資する, 投じる, 投入する
invest in a joint venture 合弁会社に投資する
invest in common stocks 普通株式に投資する
invest in dollar-denominated assets ドル建て資産に投資する
invest in financial assets 金融資産に投資する
invest in R&D 研究開発に投資する
invest in the stock 株式に投資する（⇒IPO roadshow）
invest in the stock market 株式市場に投資する
◆Foreign investors, including Japanese firms, regard Thailand's political climate with its repeated coups as a risk factor for investing in the country. 日本企業など外国資本は、クーデターが繰り返されるタイの政治風土を、対タイ投資のリスク要因と見なしている。◆In a global carry trade, hedge funds borrow low-interest yen funds to invest in dollar-denominated assets. グローバル・キャリー・トレード［グローバル・キャリー取引］では、ヘッジ・ファンドなどが、低利の円資金を借りてドル建て資産に投資している。◆Nissay, the largest private institutional investor in Japan, has invested in about 1,800 companies listed on Japanese stock exchanges. 日本国内最大の民間機関投資家の日本生命保険は、日本の証券取引所に上場している企業約1,800社に出資している。◆With the economic recovery gaining momentum, U.S. companies have begun investing in the Japanese stock market again, giving a lift to stock prices. 景気回復が力強さを増していることから、米国企業が日本の株式市場に再び投資するようになり、株価を押し上げている。

investigation （名）調査, 検査, 審査, 監査, 査察, 研究, 究明, 取調べ, 捜査, 調査［研究］報告,

調書, 調査書, 研究論文
◆The government will make final judgments whether to go ahead with the commercial production of methane hydrate and seafloor hydrothermal deposits in fiscal 2018, based on the results of test drilling and investigation of the resources. メタンハイドレートと海底熱水鉱床の試掘や調査の結果を踏まえて, 政府は, 両資源の商業生産推進の可否について2018年度に最終判断する。◆The Health, Labor and Welfare Ministry will embark on on-site investigations of black companies and make public the names of firms whose labor practices are deemed especially vicious. 厚生労働省は, ブラック企業の立入り調査を開始し, 労働慣行がとくに悪質と思われる企業については社名を公表する方針だ。◆The Securities and Exchange Surveillance Commission has embarked on a full-fledged investigation of AIJ on suspicion the investment advisory company violated the Financial Instruments and Exchange Law. 証券取引等監視委員会は, 投資顧問会社のAIJについて, 金融取引法違反の容疑で本格調査に着手した。

investing contract　投資契約
　◆Intercontinental Exchange (ICE), an exchange that deals in investing contracts known as futures, is buying the NYSE for about $8 billion. 米インターコンチネンタル取引所 (ICE: 先物と呼ばれる投資契約を扱う取引所) が, ニューヨーク証券取引所を約80億ドルで買収する。

investment　(名)投資, 出資, 運用, 投資額, 投資物, 投資事業, 投資資産, 投資勘定, 資金投下, 証券, インベストメント　(＝investing)
　discretionary investment contract　一任勘定の運用契約, 運用委託契約
　diversified investment　分散投資
　equipment investment　設備投資
　equity investment　株式投資
　international investment　国際投資
　investment decision　投資判断, 投資の意思決定, 投資決定
　investment-grade securities　投資適格債
　investment law　出資法
　investment opportunity　投資機会, 投資対象, 運用先
　investment performance　運用実績, 投資実績, 投資成績
　investment portfolio　投資ポートフォリオ, 投資資産, 投資資本構成, 投資の内容
　investment trust　投資信託, 投信 (一般投資家から資金を集め, 集めた金を専門家が株や債券などに投資して, その運用益を投資家に還元する金融商品)
　large-scale investment　大型投資
　new investment　新規投資
　overseas investment　海外投資, 対外投資
　portfolio investment　証券投資, 株式・債券投資, ポートフォリオ投資
◆Gross foreign assets held by Japanese in the form of direct investment, securities investment, financial derivatives, loans and export credits, deposits, other investments and official foreign reserves came to ¥379.78 trillion. 直接投資, 証券投資, 金融派生商品, 貸付け金や輸出信用, 預金その他の投資と政府の外貨準備高の形で日本の政府や企業, 個人が保有する海外資産の総額 (対外資産残高) は, 379兆7,800億円に達した。◆If a quoted company with a one-share trading unit changes its trading unit to 100 shares without changing the price of individual shares, the amount required for investment would rise 100-fold. 売買単位が1株の上場企業が, 1株当たりの価格を変更しないで売買単位を100株に変更すると, 投資 (株の売買) に必要な金額は100倍になってしまう。◆Investment advisory company AIJ started investing in financial derivatives through funds based in the Cayman Islands, a tax haven, since 2002. 投資顧問会社のAIJは, 2002年から, 租税回避地の英領ケイマン諸島を営業基盤とするファンドを通じて金融派生商品への投資を始めた。◆Japanese companies' direct investment in Southeast Asia in the first half of 2013 posted a fourfold year-on-year jump to about ¥1 trillion, which is twice as high as China-bound investment. 2013年上半期の日本企業の東南アジア向け直接投資は, 前年同期比4倍増の約1兆円で, 中国向け投資の2倍となっている。◆Sumitomo Corp., a Japanese major trading house, lost $2.2 billion in investments, including Texas shale oil and Australian coal mining. 日本の大手商社の住友商事は, 米テキサス州でのシェール・オイルの開発や豪州での炭鉱事業などへの投資で, 22億ドルの損失を出した。◆The Chinese economy will become anemic and the world economy could suffer immense damage if China is faced with an unabated flight of capital due to speculative investments that its economic bubble has lured from abroad. 中国で, 中国のバブル景気で海外から流入した投機マネーが大量に流出したら, 中国経済は活気を失い, 世界経済は甚大なダメージを受けることになろう。◆These surplus funds are moving into crude oil and grain markets in search of profitable investments. これらの余剰資金が, 有利な運用先を求めて原油や穀物市場に向かっている。

investment climate　投資環境
　(＝investment environment [conditions])
　◆As a member country of the WTO, Moscow should first improve Russia's investment climate, including the abolition of trade barriers. 世界貿易機関 (WTO) 加盟国として, ロシアはまず貿易障壁の撤廃など投資環境を改善する必要がある。

investment conditions　投資環境
　(＝investment climate [environment])
　◆Foreign players also are expected to enter the commodity futures market in line with the improvement in investment conditions. 投資の環境

改善で, 外資 [海外企業] の商品先物市場への参入も見込まれる。

investment fund 投資資金, 投資ファンド, 投資信託 (「投資ファンド」は, 機関投資家などから資金を集めて, 不良債権の売買や企業買収などを行う組織)
◆Investment funds have driven up crude oil prices. 投資ファンドが, 原油価格の高騰を演出してきた。

investment money 投資資金
◆Great rotation refers to the shift of investment money from low-risk assets such as U.S. Treasuries and the yen into riskier assets such as stocks. 「グレート・ローテーション (大転換)」とは, 投資資金を米国債や円などの低リスク資産 [安全資産] から株式などリスクの高い資産に移すことを言う。

investor (名) 投資家, 投資者, 投資会社, 出資者, 出資企業, 資本主, 投資側, 投資国, 権利などの授与者, インベスター
bloc investor 大口投資家
bond investor 債券投資家
debt investor 債券投資家, 債券保有者
equity investor 株式投資家
fixed income investor 債券投資家
foreign investors 外国人投資家, 海外投資家, 外資 (=overseas investors)
individual investor 個人投資家
institutional investor 機関投資家
international investor 国際投資家
major investor 大手の投資家
private investor 個人投資家, 民間投資家
professional investor 機関投資家
retail investor 小口投資家, 個人投資家, 最終投資家, 一般投資家
small investor 個人投資家, 小口投資家
wholesale investor 機関投資家
Yen-based investor 円ベースの投資家
◆Amid the ongoing European financial crisis, concern is mounting in South Korea that the value of its won currency may steeply decline if foreign financial institutions and investors withdraw funds from the country. 今回の欧州金融危機の影響で, 韓国では, 海外の金融機関や投資家が同国から資金を引き揚げたら, 韓国の通貨ウォンの相場が急落しかねない, との懸念 [危機感] が強まっている。◆Insider trading, which is banned under the Financial Instruments and Exchange Law, harms ordinary investors and significantly damages stock market credibility. 金融商品取引法で禁じられているインサイダー取引は, 一般の投資家が不利益を被 (こうむ) り, 証券市場の信頼性を大きく損なう。◆Investors were generally adopting a wait-and-see stance on mainstay issues. 主力銘柄については, 投資家は全般に模様眺めのスタンスを取った [模様眺めの展開となった]。

invisible (形) 目に見えない, 無形の, 隠れた, 貿易外の (⇒visible)
invisible balance 貿易外収支 (=invisible account, balance of [on] invisible trade, invisible trade balance)
invisible capital 無形資本
invisible current item 貿易外経常項目
invisible current transaction 貿易外経常取引
invisible earnings 貿易外収入
invisible exports and imports 貿易外輸出入, 無形の輸出入, 貿易外収支
invisible goods 無形財
invisible hand 見えざる手
invisible payment 貿易外支払い
invisible supply 市場外供給, 未出荷高
invisible trade 貿易外取引, 無形貿易 (目に見えないサービス、海上運賃、海上保険料、観光、特許料、代理店手数料などの取引)
invisible trade balance 貿易外収支
invisible trade deficit 貿易外取引の赤字
invisible trade surplus 貿易外取引の黒字

invitation to offer 申込みの誘引 (=引合い)

invoice (名) 送り状, 仕入書, 請求書, 納品書, インボイス (動) 送り状を作成する, 支払いを請求する, インボイスを送付する (「インボイス」は、企業や商店などが取引ごとに取引金額や消費税率、税額などを記す書類)
after (the) receipt of invoice 請求書を受領後
amounts of invoices 請求金額, 請求書の金額, 送り状金額, 送り状額面金額
certify an invoice 送り状を (領事が) 査証する
CIF invoice 仕向け地までの運賃・保険料込みで仕切った送り状
commercial invoice 商業送り状, 商業インボイス, (関税法で) 仕入書
consignment invoice 委託品送り状, 委託販売送り状 [インボイス]
consular invoice 領事送り状, 領事証明送り状, コンシュラー・インボイス
customer invoice 得意先への請求書
customs invoice 税関送り状
duplicate invoice 副本送り状, 送り状副書 [副本], 連写式の請求書
FOB invoice 本船渡しで仕切った送り状
franco invoice 輸入地持ち込みまでの費用を含めて仕切った送り状, 持ち込み売約送り状 (franco (持ち込み渡し) =free delivered)
gross invoice price 総送り状価格
in settlement of an invoice 請求書の支払いのため
indent invoice 委託買付け品用インボイス

INVO 270

invoice copying-book 送り状控え帳

invoice cost 送り状価格, 送り状原価

invoice date 請求書の日付

invoice for the shipment この船積みに対する
送り状

invoice guard-book 送り状整理帳

invoice manipulation 請求書の操作

invoice price 本体価格, 直接原価, 送り状値
段, 仕切り値段, 決済価格, 請求書価格, イン
ボイス価格

invoice quantity 送り状数量

invoice register 送り状記入帳

invoices for orders 注文に対する請求書

issuance of the invoice 請求書の発行, 送り状
の発行

issue an invoice 送り状を発行する, 請求書を
発行する

make out an invoice 送り状を作成する, 請求
書を作成する

net invoice price 正味請求書価格

number of invoice 送り状番号
（=invoice number）

official invoice 公用送り状（税関送り状と領
事送り状のこと）

outstanding invoice 未払いの請求書

paid invoice 支払い済み請求書

pay an invoice 請求額を支払う

payment of one's invoice 請求額の支払い

pro forma invoice 仮請求書, 試算送り状

process an invoice 請求書を処理する

purchase invoice 仕入れ請求書

raise an invoice 請求書を起こす

sales invoice 売買用送り状

sales invoices 販売請求書

sample invoice 見本用インボイス

settle an invoice（amount） 送り状［送り状金
額］を決済する, 請求書の支払いをする

shipping invoice 船積み送り状, 船積みイン
ボイス

submit an invoice 請求書を出す

swear an invoice before a consul 領事の面前
で送り状の記載内容を宣誓する

verify an invoice 送り状内容を照合する

◆Irrevocable letter of credit provides for payment upon presentation of Supplier's invoices
and shipping documents evidencing delivery of
the invoiced Products to the carrier or freight forwarder. 取消不能信用状は, 供給者の請求書と, 請
求書に記載した本製品を運送人または海貨業者に
引き渡したことを証明する船積み書類を提示して
支払いを受けるものだ。◆The invoice is to be issued upon shipment. 請求書は, 発送と同時に発行
される。◆We have forwarded to you the invoice

in duplicate. 送り状2通は, 貴社宛発送済みです。

invoice amount 送り状価額［価格］, 送り状
金額, 送り状額面金額
◆To cover this shipment, we have drawn upon
you at sight for the invoice amount under the L/C
opened by ABC Bank. この船積みに対して, 当
社はABC銀行発行の信用状に基づいて, 一覧払い
送り状額面金額の手形を貴社宛てに振り出しまし
た。◆We have drawn upon you a documentary
bill at 60 d/s through ABC Bank for the invoice
amount, which we hope you will kindly honor
on presentation. 送り状金額に対して, ABC銀行
を通じて60日払い荷為替手形を貴社宛てに振り出
しましたので, 提示［呈示］のあり次第お引受け下
さい。

invoice value 送り状価額, 送り状金額, 送り
状額面金額, 請求金額

be covered for 110% of invoice value 送り状
金額の10%増しで保険が付けられている

draw a draft for 100% of invoice value 送り状
金額と同額の手形を振り出す

marine insurance policy endorsed in blank for
110 per cent of the invoice value 送り状金
額の110%をカバーする金額で付保した無
記名裏書の海上保険証券

◆The goods are to be insured for 25% over the
invoice value. 約定品には, 送り状金額の125%で
付保することになっている。◆To cover this shipment, we have drawn upon you at sight for the
invoice amount under the L/C opened by ABC
Bank. この船積みに対して, 当社はABC銀行発行
の信用状に基づいて, 一覧払い送り状額面金額の
手形を貴社宛てに振り出しました。

invoices for orders 注文に対する請求書
◆For invoices for orders exceeding U.S. dollars
50,000, XYZ may require ABC to open for XYZ
an irrevocable documentary letter of credit, in
the form satisfactory to XYZ for an amount at
least equal to 100% of the order value payable in
accordance with the provisions of Section（5）
of this Article above. 5万米ドルを超える注文に
対する請求書については, XYZは, XYZのために,
上記本条第5項の規定に従って支払われる注文金額
の少なくとも100%に相当する金額の取消不能の荷
為替信用状をXYZが満足するフォームで開設する
ようABCに対して要求することができる。

involve （動）含む, 包含する, 伴う, 絡ませる,
意味する

be involved in 〜に関与する

matters involving the governance of the new
company 新会社の管理・運営に関する
事項

the formation of any partnership or joint venture
involving the new company 新会社を参加
者とするパートナーシップまたは合弁会社
の設立

involving （形）〜を含む, 〜を伴う, 〜に関す
る, 〜に関連する

inward [**inwards**] （形）内部に向かう, 内部の, 対内的な, 輸入の, 入港の
　freight [carriage] inwards　戻り運賃
　invoice inward　仕入れ書
　inward B/L [b/l]　輸入船荷証券
　inward cargo　輸入貨物
　inward charges　入港書諸掛かり
　inward correspondence　受信（書類）
　inward entry　輸入申告書
　inward foreign manifest　輸入品目録
　inward freight　引取り運賃
　inward indent　受入れ買付け委託
　inward investment　対内投資
　inward packing　内装
　inward pilotage　入港水先料
　inward reinsurance（contract）　受け再保険（契約）
　return inward　戻り品

IPCC　気候変動に関する政府間パネル（Intergovernmental Panel on Climate Changeの略。1988年, 世界気象機関（WMO）と国連環境計画（UNEP）が母体となって設立され, 参加国は2013年現在195か国。事務局はスイス）

IPE　ロンドン国際石油取引所（International Petroleum Exchangeの略）

IPO　株式公開, 新規株式公開, 新規株式公募, 公開公募, 新規公募, 上場（initial public offeringの略。会社が一般投資家に株式を初めて売り出すこと）
　IPO business　株式公開業務
　IPO deal　IPO取引, IPO案件
　IPO paperwork　新規株式公開の書類, 株式新規公開の書類
　IPO price　公開価格, 公募価格
　IPO shares　新規公開株
　IPO stocks'trading　新規株式公開（IPO）銘柄の取引

IPO price range　新規株式公開（IPO）の価格帯 [公募価格帯], 公募価格帯
　◆Facebook disclosed its IPO price range of $28 to $35 per share in the paperwork filed with the SEC. フェイスブックは, 米証券取引委員会（SEC）に提出した書類で, 新規株式公開（IPO）に伴う [IPOの際の] 株式の売出価格を1株当たり28〜35ドルに設定することを明らかにした。

IPO roadshow　新規株式公開（IPO）の募集説明会, IPOの投資家説明会
　◆In an IPO roadshow, corporate executives talk to potential investors about why they should invest in the stock. 新規株式公開（IPO）の募集説明会 [投資家説明会] では, 会社経営者が, 新規上場銘柄に投資するメリットについて潜在的投資家に説明する。

irregularity　（名）不正行為, 不法行為, 不正, 乱脈経営, 乱脈融資, 不祥事, 不品行, 不規則性, 変則, 誤記, 手違い
　accounting irregularities　不正経理
　irregularities such as influence-wielding, bid-rigging and subcontracting entire public works contracts　口利きや談合, 公共事業の丸投げなどの不正行為
　owing to some irregularity　ちょっとした手違いのため
　trading irregularities　不正取引
　◆It is an entrenched bidding structure that allows irregularities such as influence-wielding, bid-rigging and subcontracting entire public works contracts. 口利きや談合, 公共事業の丸投げなどの不正行為を許しているのは, 旧態依然とした入札の構造だ。◆Your Order No. 50 was shut out of the steamer for which it had been scheduled due to some irregularity in Yokohama. 横浜でのちょっとした手違いで, 貴注文第50号は手配した [予定していた] 船に積めませんでした。

irreparable harm [**injury**]　回復できない損害, 回復不能の損害

irrevocable　（形）取消不能の, 撤回不能の
　irrevocable agreement　取消不能契約, 撤回不能契約
　irrevocable and confirmed letter of credit　取消不能の確認信用状, 撤回不能の確認信用状
　irrevocable guarantee　取消不能の保証

irrevocable documentary letter of credit　取消不能の荷為替信用状
　◆For invoices for orders exceeding U.S. dollars 50,000, XYZ may require ABC to open for XYZ an irrevocable documentary letter of credit, in the form satisfactory to XYZ for an amount at least equal to 100% of the order value payable in accordance with the provisions of Section（5）of this Article above. 5万米ドルを超える注文に対する請求書については, XYZは, XYZのために, 上記本条第5項の規定に従って支払われる注文金額の少なくとも100％に相当する金額の取消不能の荷為替信用状をXYZが満足するフォームで開設するようABCに対して要求することができる。

irrevocable letter of credit　取消不能信用状, 撤回不能信用状
　◆Irrevocable letter of credit provides for payment upon presentation of Supplier's invoices and shipping documents evidencing delivery of the invoiced Products to the carrier or freight forwarder. 取消不能信用状は, 供給者の請求書と, 請求書に記載した本製品を運送人または海貨業者に引き渡したことを証明する船積み書類を提示して支払いを受けるものだ。◆Our terms of payment are to value at 30 d/s under an irrevocable letter of credit to be opened in our favor for the corresponding value of an order. 当社の決済条件は, 注文相当額につき, 当社を受益者として開設された取消不能信用状に基づいて一覧後30日払いの手形を振り出すことです。◆The Buyer shall establish in

favor of the Seller an irrevocable letter of credit issued by a first-class international bank acceptable to the Seller. 買い主が、売り主のために、売り主が承諾できる[同意できる]第一級の国際銀行が発行する取消不能の信用状を開設するものとする。
◆The irrevocable letter of credit shall not expire until fifteen (15) days after the last day of the time of delivery specified in this Agreement. この取消不能信用状は、本契約で定める引渡し期限の最終日から15日までは失効しないものとする。

irrevocably （副）撤回不能条件で、取消不能条件で

ISBP 国際標準銀行実務（International Standard Banking Practiceの略）

ISO 国際標準化機構（International Standards Organizationの略。International Organization for Standardizationともいう）
ISO certification ISOの認定
ISO 14000 環境管理システムと環境監査に関するISOの国際規格
ISO 9000 品質管理と品質保証に関するISOの国際規格
◆ISO 9001 is the highest quality certification of the International Organization for Standardization. ISO 9001は、国際標準化機構（ISO）の最高の品質基準である。◆Nursing-care robots under the envisaged international safety standards of the ISO stop or go around such hazards as objects or bumps. 国際標準化機構（ISO）の国際安全基準案に基づく介護ロボットは、障害物や凹凸などの危険があれば、止まったり避けたりする。◆The ISO, a private organization that sets international standards for industrial products, will adopt Japan-led global safety criteria for nursing-care robots. 工業製品の国際規格を定める民間組織の「国際標準化機構（ISO）」は、日本政府が主導する介護ロボットの国際安全基準を採用する方針だ。◆This manufacturing facility was registered for international quality standard ISO 9001. この製造施設[製造工場]は、国際品質基準「ISO 9001」の認定を受けた。

issuance of an irrevocable letter of credit 取消不能信用状の発行、取消不能信用状の開設 （=the establishment of an irrevocable letter of credit）
◆If ABC fails to meet XYZ's credit terms, ABC agrees to secure the issuance of an irrevocable letter of credit strictly in accordance with XYZ's instructions for the total amount of the XYZ Products ordered. ABCがXYZの与信条件を満たさない場合、ABCは、発注したXYZ製品の総額について、XYZの指図に厳格に従って取消不能信用状を確実に開設することに同意する。

issuance of new shares 新株の発行
◆Issuance of new shares shall be approved by the resolution of the board of directors of JVCO. 新株の発行は、合弁会社（JVCO）の取締役会の決議による承認を得るものとする。

issuance, sale or repurchase of the shares of 〜の株式の発行、売却または買戻し

issue （名）発行、起債、振出、債券、刊行、発給 （動）発行する、起債する、配当などを行う、出版する、支給する、配給する、命令などを出す
issue and allot 発行し割り当てる
issued and outstanding capital stock 発行済み社外株式
issued and outstanding stocks 発行済み社外株式 （=issued and outstanding shares）
issued capital 発行済み資本金、発行済み株式、発行株式
◆The payment of the remuneration for Services shall be made by ABC within ten business days after the receipt of the invoice issued by XYZ. サービスに対する報酬の支払いは、XYZが発行した請求書の受領後10営業日以内に、ABCが支払うものとする。

issue a business improvement order 業務改善命令を出す
◆The Financial Services Agency issued a business improvement order to the bank on the Banking Law and demanded it implement a fundamental review of compliance and business administration. 金融庁は、同行に対して銀行法に基づく業務改善命令を出し、法令順守と経営管理体制を抜本的に見直すことを求めた。

issue of warrants 新株予約権の発行
◆About 15 percent of the leading companies are studying the possibility of using a poison pill to counter a hostile takeover by using the issue of warrants. 主要企業の約15%は、新株予約権の発行などで敵対的買収に対抗するポイズン・ピル（毒薬）の導入可能性を検討している。

issued and outstanding shares 発行済み社外株式、外部発行済み株式、発行済み社外流通株式 （=shares issued and outstanding）
◆The Seller is the owner of all of the issued and outstanding shares of ABCD Inc. 売り主は、ABCD社の外部発行済み株式を全株所有している。

issuing bank 信用状の発行銀行、開設銀行
◆Such letter of credit shall be transferable and having the clause of definite undertaking by the issuing bank for unconditional payment against a draft at sight. この信用状は、譲渡可能で、一覧払い手形に対する無条件支払いに関して発行銀行が明確に約束した文言が入っているものとする。

IT equipment imports 情報技術（IT）機器の輸入
◆Tokyo, Taipei and Washington failed to reach a consensus on how to resolve the dispute over the EU's high tariffs on IT equipment imports. EUの情報技術（IT）機器輸入に対する高関税をめぐる紛争の解決法に関して、日本、台湾と米国は合意に達しなかった。

IT revolution 情報技術革命, IT（情報通信技術）革命
◆Due to the IT revolution and trade liberalization, product specialization now is determined by comparative advantages not in finished products but in work unique to each country or region in the context of global value chains. 情報通信技術（IT）革命と貿易自由化で、製品の特化は、「最終財」の比較優位ではなく、国際的価値連鎖との関連で国・地域にそれぞれ特有の「仕事」の比較優位で決まるようになった。

ITA 情報技術協定
（⇒Information Technology Agreement）

ITC 米国際貿易委員会（International Trade Commissionの略）

item （名）条, 条項, 項目, 品目, 費用項目, 種目, 細目, 内訳, 事項, 商品, 用品, 品物, 物品, 単品, 単一機器, 機器, アイテム
（⇒abolish tariffs, U.S. Trade Representative）

balance sheet item 貸借対照表項目

balancing item 調整項目

basic item 定番商品, ベーシック商品

big item 目玉商品

big-ticket item 高額商品, 高価な商品

brand-named item 銘柄品, メーカー品

corporate items 本社事項

fungible items 汎用品

gift item 贈答品

hot item ヒット商品 （=big hit, big hit product, winning product）

infrequent item 突発事項

must-have item どうしても欲しい商品

operating item 営業項目, 営業品目

popular item 売れ筋商品, 売れ筋, 人気商品 （=hot item）

sensitive item 輸入要注意品目, センシティブ品目

winter item 冬物商品
◆If it is not certain five agricultural items, including rice and wheat, will be treated as exceptions to free trade, the government will not hesitate to pull out from the TPP negotiations. コメや麦など農産品5項目を自由貿易の聖域として確保できなければ、政府はTPP（環太平洋経済連携協定）交渉からの脱退も辞さない方針だ。◆Nonmonetary balance sheet items and corresponding income statement items are translated at rates in effect at the time of acquisition. 貸借対照表の非貨幣性項目とこれに対応する損益計算書項目は、取得日の為替レートで換算されています。◆Promptly upon the receipt of a shipment of Products, Distributor shall examine the Products to determine whether any item or items to be included in the shipment are missing, defective, or damaged. 本製品の荷受けをしたら速やかに、販売店は、本製品を検査

して積み荷中の目的物が不足（紛失）しているかどうか、瑕疵（かし）があるかどうか、または損傷しているかどうかを判断しなければならない。◆We have on hand such a rush of orders for this item that our output capacity cannot keep up with the demand. 本品に対しては多くの注文が入っているため、当社の生産能力が需要に追いつかない状況です。◆While Japan's mainstay export item to the U.S. market is vehicles, the shipments to China are mainly electronic parts for assembly. 日本の米市場向け輸出の主力製品は自動車なのに対して、中国向け輸出製品は組立用電子部品が中心だ。

J

Japan Bank for International Cooperation 国際協力銀行
◆The Japan Bank for International Cooperation is using dollar-denominated FX reserves to help finance Japanese firms' infrastructure exports. 国際協力銀行は、外貨準備のドル建て資金［ドル資金］を使って、日本企業のインフラ輸出の金融支援をしている。

Japan Chamber of Commerce and Industry 日本商工会議所
◆Japan Chamber of Commerce and Industry Chairman Tadashi Okamura thinks that the appropriate exchange rate of the yen is between ￥85 and ￥90 to the dollar. 日本商工会議所の岡村正会頭は、1ドル＝85円〜90円が円相場の適正水準であると考えている。

Japan Exchange Group Inc. 株式会社日本取引所グループ, JPX（2013年1月1日、東京証券取引所と大阪証券取引所が経営統合。この統合で、現物市場、デリバティブ市場、自主規制機関（東京証券取引所自主規制法人）と清算・決済機関（日本証券クリアリング機構）をあわせ持つ取引所グループが誕生）
◆Through the integration of the Osaka Securities Exchange's cash equity market into that of the TSE, Japan Exchange Group Inc. debuted the world's third-largest stock exchange. 大阪証券取引所の株式市場を東京証券取引所に一本化して、日本取引所グループ（JPX）は、（上場企業数で）世界第3位の証券取引所に浮上した。

Japan External Trade Organization 日本貿易振興機構（ジェトロ）
◆Local labor costs of Japanese companies operating in China rose by about 60 percent over the past three years since 2010, according to the Japan External Trade Organization. 日本貿易振興機構（ジェトロ）によると、中国に進出している日本企業の現地での人件費は、2010年以来ここ3年間で1.6倍に上昇している。

Japanese Agricultural Standards Law 日本の農林規格（JAS）法
◆The Japanese Agricultural Standard（JAS）Law specifies standards on the labeling of food. 日本の農林規格（JAS）法は、食品の表示（品質表

JAPA 274

示）基準を定めている。

Japanese goods 日本製品
◆Both the Japanese economy and Chinese businesses have been impacted by the boycott against Japanese goods being staged in protest of Japan's nationalization of the Senkakus. 日本の尖閣諸島国有化に反発［抗議］して行われている日本製品の不買運動で、日本経済も中国企業も打撃を受けている。

Japan's exports and production 日本の輸出と生産
◆Japan's exports and production have been reduced because of the slowdown of foreign economies and the worsening of relations with China. 海外経済の減速や日中関係の悪化で、日本の輸出や生産は低迷している。◆The economic slowdown in Europe due to the sovereign debt crisis and slackening growth of China as a major exporter to Europe have dealt a painful blow to Japan's exports and production. 債務危機に伴う欧州経済の減速と、欧州向け輸出の多い中国の成長鈍化が、日本の輸出と生産に耐え難いほどの打撃を与えている。

Japan's three principles on arms export restrictions 日本の武器輸出規制3原則, 日本の武器輸出3原則
◆Japan once provided patrol vessels to Indonesia as an exception to Japan's three principles on arms export restrictions. かつて日本は、日本の武器輸出規制［武器輸出］3原則の例外として、インドネシアに巡視船を供与したことがある。

Japan's trading balance 日本の貿易収支
◆Japan's 2012 trading balance, or exports minus imports, ran up a record deficit of ¥6.9 trillion, 2.7 times more than the 2011 figure, the first trade deficit in 31 years due to the negative effects of the Great East Japan Earthquake. 輸出額から輸入額を差し引いた日本の2012年の貿易収支は、過去最大の6.9兆円の赤字で、東日本大震災の悪影響で31年ぶりに貿易赤字に転落した2011年と比べて2.7倍に増えた。

job contract 雇用契約
◆By the revised Labor Contract Law, researchers are now entitled to maintain job contracts until the mandatory retirement age, provided their length of service has exceeded five years. 労働契約法の改正により、研究者は現在、勤続期間が5年を過ぎた場合には、定年まで雇用契約を継続できるようになった。

joint （形）共同の, 合同の, 連帯の, 連合の, 合弁の, 共有の, 共通の, ジョイント
　joint branch　共同店舗
　joint company　合弁会社
　joint consultation　労使協議
　joint debt　連帯債務
　joint decision　共同決定, 共同決定事項
　joint efforts　一致した努力, 協力

　joint enterprise　合弁企業, 合弁事業
　Joint FAO/WHO　FAO/WHO合同食品規格委員会
　joint fare　共同運賃
　joint float　共同変動相場制, 変動相場制への共同移行
　joint holding company　共同持ち株会社（=joint holding firm）
　joint international services with Japan Airlines　日航との国際線の共同運航
　joint management　共同経営（joint operation）, 共同管理
　joint owners　共有者, 共同所有者
　joint product　結合生産物, 連産品
　joint product development　製品［商品］の共同開発
　joint production　共同生産
　joint project［enterprise］　共同［合同］事業, 共同プロジェクト
　joint property　共有財産
　joint purchase　共同購入, 共同仕入れ
　joint responsibility［liability］　共同責任, 連帯責任, 連座制
　joint signature　連署, 副署（=countersignature）
　joint stake　共同出資, 共同出資比率

joint action 協調行動, 共同行為
◆As joint actions, major industrial nations have taken such measures as further interest rate reductions, quantitative monetary relaxation to increase the money supply, the injection of public funds and increased public spending. 協調行動として、主要先進諸国は、さらなる金利の引下げ、通貨供給量を増やすための量的金融緩和や公的資金の注入、財政出動［公共支出の拡大］などの措置を取った。

joint intervention 協調介入, 協調市場介入（=coordinated intervention, joint market intervention）
◆Japan and the United States began joint interventions in New York. ニューヨークで、日米の協調介入が実施された。

解説 協調介入：複数の国の通貨当局が、協力して特定の通貨を売買し、為替相場水準の修正を図ること。1か国が単独で行う介入（単独介入）より、効果はずっと大きいとされる。1995年に円相場が1ドル＝79円75銭の史上最高値を付けた際、日銀は約5兆円の介入資金で米欧の通貨当局と円売り・ドル買いの協調介入を行って、円高を是正した。

joint loan 協調融資
◆The Bank of Tokyo-Mitsubishi UFJ will work together with foreign banks to extend 117 million Canadian dollars in joint loans to a mega solar power plant construction. 三菱東京UFJ銀行

は、外銀数行の主幹事銀行として、カナダの大型太陽光発電所（メガソーラー）建設事業に1億1,700万カナダ・ドルを協調融資する。

joint venture 合弁会社, 合弁事業, 合弁, 共同企業, 共同企業体, 共同事業, 共同事業体, 共同出資会社, ジョイント・ベンチャー, JV
◆In the joint venture with an Indian investment bank, Tokyo Marine Holdings Inc. put up about 26%, the maximum a foreign investor is allowed in an Indian company, of the new firm's capital. インドの投資銀行との合弁事業で、東京海上ホールディングスは、新会社の資本金の約26%（外資の持ち分比率の上限）を出資した。◆The plant, constructed as the joint venture of Sumitomo Corp. and Kazakhstan's state-owned resource firm to extract rare earths by refining soil left in a uranium mine, is scheduled to start full-scale operations in the nation in November 2012. 住友商事とカザフスタンの国営資源企業の合弁事業として、ウラン鉱山で採掘された残土を精錬してレア・アースを抽出するために建設された同工場は、2012年11月からカザフスタンで本格稼働に入る。◆This struggling auto producer is considering setting up a joint venture with an American major securities firm to engage in North American financing operations. 経営再建中のこの自動車メーカーは現在、米証券大手と北米で金融事業［販売金融事業］を手がける合弁会社の設立を検討している。

joint venture company 合弁会社
◆Pursuant to the terms of the articles of association of the Joint Venture Company, ABC will have an initial ownership interest of forty percent of the voting shares of the Joint Venture Company. 合弁会社の定款の規定に従って、ABCの当初の出資比率は、合弁会社の議決権付き株式の40%とする。

joint venturer JV参加者

jointly （副）共同で, 合同で, 共に, 連合して, 連帯して, 連隊で, 連帯的に
jointly and separately 連帯して, 各自連帯して （=jointly and severally）
jointly own 共同所有する, 共同保有する
jointly set up a new company 共同出資で新会社を設立する
jointly use 共用する

jointly and severally 連帯して, 各自連帯して （=jointly and separately）
bear liability jointly and severally 連帯責任を負う, 連帯債務を負う
guarantee jointly and severally 連帯して保証する, 連帯保証する
◆Guarantors hereby guarantee jointly and severally as and for its own obligation, until full payment and performance are effected by ABC in accordance with the terms and conditions of the agreement, the due and punctual performance by

or on behalf of ABC, of all obligations under the agreement. 保証人は、契約の条件に従ってABCが当該支払いと履行を完全に行うまで、ABCによるまたはABCに代わる契約上のすべての債務の適正かつ期限どおりの履行を、自己の義務（債務）としてここに各自連帯して保証する。

jointly and severally assume the obligation of 連帯して〜の義務を負う
◆KEPCO and Kyushu Electric Power Co. have signed a one-year contract with a U.S. firm to jointly buy a total of 1 million tons of U.S. coal in the one year. 関西電力と九州電力は、米国産の石炭を1年間で計100万トン共同購入［共同調達］する1年契約を、米国の企業と結んだ。

jointly buy 共同購入する, 共同調達する
◆KEPCO and Kyushu Electric Power Co. have signed a one-year contract with a U.S. firm to jointly buy a total of 1 million tons of U.S. coal in the one year. 関西電力と九州電力は、米国産の石炭を1年間で計100万トン共同購入［共同調達］する1年契約を、米国の企業と結んだ。

judgment ［judgement］ （名）判断, 判定, 判決, 裁判, 審判, 意見, 考え, 見解, 見識, 思慮分別, 判断力, 非難, 批判, 天罰, 神罰, 報い
◆Judgment upon such award may be entered in any court having jurisdiction thereof. この仲裁判断に基づく判決は、その管轄権のある裁判所で受けることができる（その管轄権のある裁判所の記録に正式に登録することができる）。◆The government will make final judgments whether to go ahead with the commercial production of methane hydrate and seafloor hydrothermal deposits in fiscal 2018, based on the results of test drilling and investigation of the resources. メタンハイドレートと海底熱水鉱床の試掘や調査の結果を踏まえて、政府は、両資源の商業生産推進の可否について2018年度に最終判断する。

judgment thereon それに基づく判決
◆The arbitral award shall be final and judgment thereon may be entered in any court of competent jurisdiction. 仲裁判断は最終的なものとし、それに基づく判決は正当な管轄権のあるいずれの裁判所でも受けることができるものとする［正当な管轄権のある裁判所の記録に正式に登録することができる］。

judgment upon the award 仲裁判断に基づく判決, 仲裁裁定の執行判決
◆Judgment upon the award rendered by the arbitrator（s）may be entered in any court having jurisdiction thereof. 仲裁人が行った仲裁判断に基づく判決は、その管轄権のある裁判所の記録に正式に登録することができる［仲裁人による仲裁裁定の執行判決は、その管轄権のあるいずれの裁判所でも受けることができる］。

judicial process 司法手続き
◆Neither this agreement nor any of the rights conferred hereby shall be assigned or transferred, by judicial process or otherwise, to any person, firm or corporation without the prior

written consent of the other party. 本契約と本契約により付与された権利は、司法手続きその他により、相手方の書面による事前の承諾を得ないでいかなる個人、企業または法人にも譲渡・移転しないものとする。

jurisdiction （名）裁判管轄, 裁判管轄権, 裁判権, 管轄権, 管轄区域, 法域, 権限, 司法権, 司法行政, 司法権, 行政権や徴税権などを行使できる国家や地方自治体

competent jurisdiction　正当な管轄権

court of competent jurisdiction　正当な管轄権のある裁判所, 管轄裁判所

exclusive jurisdiction　専属的裁判管轄, 専属管轄

nonexclusive jurisdiction　非専属的裁判管轄, 非専属管轄

null and void with respect to the jurisdiction of any court of competent jurisdiction　管轄裁判所の管轄地域に関して無効

personal jurisdiction　対人管轄権

personally subject to the jurisdiction of the courts of　～の裁判所の管轄に人的に服する

subject matter jurisdiction　事物管轄権

◆If a provision of this agreement becomes invalid, illegal or unenforceable in any jurisdiction, that shall not affect; 本契約の一規定がいずれかの法域で無効, 違法または強制不能となった場合でも, それは次の事項に影響を及ぼさないものとする。◆The arbitral award shall be final and judgment thereon may be entered in any court of competent jurisdiction. 仲裁判断は最終的なものとし, それに基づく判決は正当な管轄権のあるいずれの裁判所でも受けることができるものとする [正当な管轄権のある裁判所の記録に正式に登録することができる]。◆The licensee shall have the right to employ one separate counsel per jurisdiction in any of the foregoing claims and to participate in the defense thereof. ライセンシーは, 上記請求で法域あたり別の弁護士を1名雇用して, その防御に参加する権利を持つものとする。◆The U.S. Federal Trade Commission exercises jurisdiction over matters including consumer protection issues in the United States. 米連邦取引委員会（FTC）は, 米国消費者保護などの問題を管轄している。

just and equitable　正義かつ衡平な

◆The arbitral award may grant any relief deemed by the arbitrators to be just and equitable, including, without limitation, specific performance. 仲裁判断は, 特定履行などを含めて, 仲裁人が正義かつ衡平と見なす救済を認めることができる。

K

keep　（動）保持する, 保管する, 帳簿などをつける

keep and maintain　維持する, 保持する

keep or cause to be kept　保管するか保管させる, 保持するか保持させる

keep the books and records of Products　本製品の帳簿と記録を保持する

◆ABC shall take care of keeping its quality without any harm whatsoever as bona fide holder of Products on behalf of XYZ. ABCは, XYZを代理する契約品 [本製品] の善意の保管者として, 契約品 [本製品] の品質保持上, どんな損害も生じないよう注意を払うものとする。◆During the period when Products are in the custody of ABC, ABC shall keep Products insured at ABC's account for the benefit of XYZ against loss or damage by fire, theft or otherwise with extended coverage. 本製品 [契約品] をABCが保管している期間中, 火災, 盗難, その他による滅失や損害を拡張担保するため, ABCはその勘定で, XYZを保険受取人として本製品に付保するものとする。◆Licensee shall keep full, clear and accurate books and records of Products subject to the running royalty. ライセンシーは, ランニング・ロイヤルティの対象である [対象となる] 本製品の完全, 明瞭かつ正確な帳簿 (会計帳簿) と記録を保持するものとする。

keep up　続ける, 維持する, 保つ, ～と接触 [連絡, 音信] を続ける, ～の手入れ [管理, 整備] をする, (病気や悲しみに) 屈しない, 遅れずについて行く, 続く, なり続く, 降り続く

◆Major electronics makers such as NEC and Fujitsu are not keeping up in the race to develop products for the global market and this trouble makes it difficult to regain footing. NECや富士通などの家電大手は, 世界市場向けの商品開発競争に遅れており, これによる業績不振で, 挽回が厳しくなっている。

Kelly's Directory　ケリーの商工人名録

kind and character　性質

kind and nature　性質, 種類

knockdown　（形）格安の, 廉価な, 特価の, 最低の, 組立方式 [組立式] の, 現地組立方式の, 折りたたみ式の, 圧倒的な, 強烈な, ノックダウン方式の, ノックダウン

knockdown blow　大打撃, 必殺打

knockdown export　現地組立輸出, ノックダウン輸出 (部品を輸出して現地で組み立ててから販売する方法)

knockdown import　国内組立輸入, ノックダウン輸入

knockdown plan　組立 [現地] 方式, ノックダウン方式　（=knockdown system）

knockdown price　最低価格, 最安値, 格安値, 底値

knockdown table　組立式 [折りたたみ式] のテーブル

knockoff　（名）にせブランド品 [商品], 模造品, イミテーション

knowhow [know-how] （名）ノウハウ, 技術情報, 技術知識, 専門知識, 専門技術, 製造技術, 技術秘密, 技術秘訣, 手法, 秘伝, 奥義, コツ （=expertise）

business knowhow　経営手法, 商売の秘訣, 商売のコツ

computer knowhow　コンピュータ技術

confidential knowhow　秘密ノウハウ

management knowhow　経営ノウハウ, 経営専門知識

technical knowhow　技術的専門知識

◆Knowhow shall mean technical information and data useful for manufacturing Products. ノウハウとは, 契約品製造のために有用な技術情報とデータを意味する。◆Such knowhow shall consist of designs, specifications and drawings of Products, assembling drawings, and other information and data agreed between the parties in writing. このノウハウは, 契約品の設計図・仕様書・図面, 組立て図面と, 当事者が書面で合意するその他の情報およびデータから成る。◆The company supports the transfer of technology and knowhow that the developing countries need. 同社は, 開発途上国が必要としている技術やノウハウの移転を支援している。

knowledge （名）認識, 理解, 承知, 知識, 精通, 熟知, 知りうる範囲, ナレッジ

at the time it comes into one's knowledge　〜が知るに至った時点で

common knowledge　周知の事実

prior knowledge　予備知識

public knowledge　公知

to the knowledge of　〜が知るかぎり

upon coming to one's knowledge of　〜を知った場合には, 〜を知ったときは

◆ABC shall forthwith upon coming to its knowledge notify the licensor of any infringement or threatened infringement or counterfeit of the Trademarks. 本商標が侵害されたり, 侵害されそうになったり, 偽物が作られていることをABCが知った場合, ABCは直ちにこれをライセンサーに知らせるものとする。

known （形）既知の, 周知の, 公知の, 〜と呼ばれる

known and described as　〜と呼ばれる

known misstatement　既知の虚偽表示

known or suspected infringement of　〜の侵害を知るかその恐れが疑われること

known or unknown　既知のまたは未知の, 既知であれ未知であれ, 知っているものでも知らないものでも

known outstanding claims or license or other encumbrances　既知の継続中の請求や実施権やその他の抵当権

known programming　公知のプログラミング

little-known name　無名の銘柄

well known name　なじみの銘柄

◆Distributor agrees to notify Supplier of any known or suspected infringement of Supplier's intellectual property rights that comes to Distributor's attention. 販売店の注意に止まって供給者の知的所有権（知的財産権）の侵害を知るかその恐れがある場合, 販売店はこのことを供給者に通告することに同意する。

known to the public　公知の

◆The foregoing restrictions on disclosure and use will not apply to information which becomes known to the public other than by a disclosure prohibited by this Article. 開示上に関する上記の制限は, 本条が禁止する開示以外の方法で公知となった情報には適用しないものとする。

L

labeling （名）表示, 分類, ラベル表示, ラベルの貼付（てんぷ）, ラベリング （=label）

best before date labeling　賞味期限の表示

descriptive labeling　品質表示

false labeling of beef products　牛肉の偽装表示, 牛肉偽装

false labeling of food　食品の偽装表示, 食品偽装

food labeling　食品表示

food labeling system　食品表示制度

grade labeling　等級ラベル表示

ingredient labeling　成分表示

mandatory labeling　義務表示

mislabeling　虚偽表示, 不当表示, 不正表示

◆In the next round of negotiations, labeling and trade rules for food produced with genetically modified organisms（GMOs）are expected to be discussed. 次期交渉では, 遺伝子組換え食品（遺伝子組換え作物を使って生産される食品）の表示問題や貿易ルールづくりが話し合われる見通しだ。◆Japan requires labeling of 30 genetically modified food items from 2001. 日本は, 2001年から遺伝子組換え食品30品目について表示を義務付けている。◆The food firm covered up its labeling of imported beef as domestic beef. この食品メーカーは, 輸入牛肉を国産牛肉と表示したことを隠していた。◆The Japanese Agricultural Standard（JAS）Law specifies standards on the labeling of food. 日本の農林規格（JAS）法は, 食品の表示（品質表示）基準を定めている。

labor [labour] （名）労働, 労務, 労働力, 労働者, 労働者側, 仕事, 骨折り, 苦心, 苦しみ, 苦悩, 陣痛, 産みの苦しみ, 分娩（ぶんべん）

collective labor agreement　労働協約 （=labor agreement）

dispute between capital and labor　労使間紛争

International Labor [Labour] Organization　国

際労働機関, ILO

labor arbitration　労働仲裁

labor conditions　労働条件

Labor Department　米労働省

labor dispute　労働争議

labor leader　組合の幹部

labor organization　労働組織, 労働団体, 労働
機関

labor productivity　労働生産性

labor saving investment　省力化投資

labor turnover　労働力の移動, 雇用・解雇に
よる労働者の動き

labor unrest　労働不安

seasonal labor　季節的労働

spring labor offensive　春闘
（=spring offensive）

supporting industry　裾野（すその）産業

trigger industry　トリガー産業（景気回復や
革新の牽引役を果たす産業のこと）

union labor　組合労働, 組合労働者

wage labor　賃金労働

◆As labor costs in China are expected to continue rising, labor-intensive industries such as fashion and electronics will keep relocating their manufacturing bases to Southeast Asia and other regions with cheaper labor. 中国の人件費上昇は今後も続く見通しなので, アパレルや家電などの労働集約型産業では, 生産拠点を中国より低賃金の東南アジアなどに移す流れが続くものと思われる。

Labor Contract Law　労働契約法
◆By the revised Labor Contract Law, researchers are now entitled to maintain job contracts until the mandatory retirement age, provided their length of service has exceeded five years. 労働契約法の改正により, 研究者は現在, 勤続期間が5年を過ぎた場合には, 定年まで雇用契約を継続できるようになった。

labor costs　人件費, 労働費, 労働コスト, 労務費（⇒labor-intensive industry）
◆Many Japanese manufacturers have been prompted to review their production in China with labor costs surging in China and domestic production recovering competitiveness thanks to the weaker yen. 中国で人件費が高騰しているのに加え, 円安進行で国内生産の競争力が回復しているため, 日本メーカーの多くは中国での生産（体制）を見直す動きが加速している。◆ The development of cross-border infrastructure in the Greater Mekong Subregion（GMS）has prompted a number of multinational corporations to transfer some of their manufacturing processes to Laos, Cambodia and Myanmar to take advantage of cheaper labor costs. 大メコン圏での国境を越えたインフラ整備に伴い, 多くの多国籍企業が, 安い人件費［低賃金］の利点を生かして生産工程の一部をラオスやカンボジア, ミャン

マーに移転している。◆To avert China risks such as the stronger Chinese yuan, surging labor costs and anti-Japan riots, some firms have shifted production lines to other countries in Southeast Asia and other regions with cheaper labor. 中国人民元高や人件費高騰, 反日暴動などの中国リスクを回避するため, 一部の企業は, 中国より低賃金の東南アジアなどの地域に生産ラインの移管［分散化］を進めている。

labor-intensive industry　労働集約型産業
◆As labor costs in China are expected to continue rising, labor-intensive industries such as fashion and electronics will keep relocating their manufacturing bases to Southeast Asia and other regions with cheaper labor. 中国の人件費上昇は今後も続く見通しなので, アパレルや家電などの労働集約型産業では, 生産拠点を中国より低賃金の東南アジアなどに移す流れが続くものと思われる。

labor movement　労働者組織, 労働組合, 労働支持団体, 労働運動

flexible labor movement　労働移動の柔軟性

global labor movement　グローバル労働運動

independent labor movement　自主管理労働
運動

international labor movement　国際労働運動

land　（名）土地, 用地, 農地, 農耕地, 陸, 陸地, 地帯, 場所, 所有地, 国土, 国民, ランド

land acquisition cost　土地取得価格

land agency　土地斡旋（あっせん）業, 土地斡旋所, 土地管理人

land agent　土地売買周旋業者, 不動産業者, 土地管理人

land bank　不動産銀行, 土地抵当貸し銀行

land-borne trade　陸上貿易

land bridge transport　（コスト節減のための）海陸一貫輸送, ランド・ブリッジ運送

land broker　土地ブローカー

land carriage　陸上運送

land deal　土地取引

land dealer　土地取引業者, 土地仲買人

land developer　土地開発業者, 土地開発企業

land development　土地開発

land freeze　土地売買凍結, 土地譲渡凍結

land grab　（政府などによる）土地の収奪

land grant　無償土地払い下げ

land holder　土地所有者, 借地人

land holding tax　地価税　（=land price tax）

land holdings　保有地

land inspection　陸上検疫

land jobber　土地売買業者, 土地取引業者

land-lease payments　土地使用料

land owner　地主

land purchase　土地購入

land registry　土地登記所

land rent　地代

land risk　陸上危険

land selling　土地売却

land shark　地上げ屋

land sharking　地上げ, 地上げ行為

land speculation　土地投機

land steward　地所管理人

land survey　陸地測量

land tenure　土地保有権, 土地保有

land transaction　土地取引

land transfer　土地所有権移転, 土地譲渡

land transfer tax　土地譲渡益課税, 土地上と税

land transportation　陸上輸送, 陸上運送

land use planning　土地利用計画

land value　地価, 土地価格

land value tax　地価税

land waiter　荷揚げ監視人, 輸出品監視人

private land　私有地

land price　土地価格, 地価

falling land prices　地価の下落
（=decreasing land price）

the average land price for commercial areas　商業地の全国平均の地価

the average land price for residential areas　住宅地の全国平均の地価

◆In many cases, the complicated property tax system results in increased taxes despite decreasing land prices. 多くの場合、固定資産税の仕組みが複雑で、地価が下落しても税額が増える結果になっている。◆The prolonged slump in the real estate market is maintaining the decline in land prices. 不動産取引市場の長期低迷が、引き続き地価の下落を招いている。

landed　（形）土地を持っている, 土地の, 陸揚げした, 陸揚げされる, 困難に陥った

a landed estate　不動産, 土地不動産, 地所

landed cost　陸揚げ費込み原価

landed interests　地主側

landed price　陸揚げ費込み値段

landed property　不動産, 地所, 所有地

landed proprietor　土地所有者, 地主

landed quality terms　陸揚げ時品質条件, 陸揚げ品質条件　（=landing quality terms）

landed security　土地の担保

landed terms　陸揚げ条件, 陸揚げ渡し条件

landed weight final　陸揚げ数量条件

landed weight terms　陸揚げ重量条件, 陸揚げ数量条件　（=landing weight terms）

landing　（名）陸揚げ, 荷揚げ, 荷卸し［荷下ろし］(discharging), 上陸, 着陸

landing accommodation　陸揚げ設備

landing agent　陸揚げ代理人, 陸揚げ代行業者

landing book　陸揚げ明細書

landing bridge　桟橋（さんばし）　（=landing pier）

landing cargo　揚げ荷

landing certificate　陸揚げ証明書

landing charges　陸揚げ費, 陸揚げ費用

landing fee　着陸料

landing harbor　陸揚げ港　（=landing post）

landing order　陸揚げ指図書

landing pier　陸揚げ桟橋（さんばし）

landing place　陸揚げ場所

landing quantity terms　陸揚げ数量条件（=landed weight final, outturn weight final）

landing report　陸揚げ報告［報告書］, 陸揚げ故障報告

landing waiter　陸揚げ監視人

landing weight　陸揚げ重量

landlord　（名）地主, 家主, 賃貸人, 不動産貸主, 土地所有者
◆The Landlord shall effect insurance by itself or have other tenants effect insurance against such accidents as aforementioned and indemnify the Tenant within the extent covered by the insurance. 「貸主」は、前記の事故などに対して自ら保険を付けるか他のテナントに保険を付けさせ、その保険でカバーされる範囲内で「借主」に損害の補償をするものとする。

large contract　大型契約
◆Nonlife insurance companies used to disperse the risk of large contracts with new corporate clients through reinsurance contracts with other insurance or reinsurance companies. 損保各社は従来、他の保険会社もしくは再保険会社と再保険契約を結んで、新規顧客企業と大型契約を結ぶリスクを分散してきた。

large order　大量注文, 大口注文
◆There is a discount available for a large order. 大量注文には、割引の恩典があります［値引も適用されます］。◆You may expect a large order from us very soon. 早速、貴社に大口の注文を差し上げます。

large-scale investment　大型投資
◆In Thailand, budget compilation and the approval of large-scale investments have been hindered by the government's failure to function effectively due to the political imbroglio. タイでは、政治の混迷で政府機能が十分に働かず、予算編成や大型投資の認可に弊害が出ている。

late payment　期日に遅れた支払い, 支払い遅延
◆Late payment shall incur an interest charge of 2 percent over the base rate current in XYZ Bank at the time the charge is levied from the due date to the date of payment in full. 支払いが遅延した

場合、支払い期日から全額支払い日まで、支払い利息（遅延利息）を課す時点でXYZ銀行が適用する基準金利より2％高い支払い利息（遅延利息）が付くものとする。

latent defect 隠れた欠陥, 隠れた瑕疵（かし）
◆Any claim by the purchaser, except for latent defects, shall be made in writing as soon as reasonably practicable after the arrival, unpacking and inspection of the products, whether by the purchaser or any subsequent purchaser of the products. 買い主によるクレームは、隠れた瑕疵（かし）を除いて、買い主によるか本製品のその後の購入者によるかを問わず本製品の到着、開梱および検査後、合理的に実行可能なかぎり速やかに書面で行うものとする。

Latin American Integration Association ラテンアメリカ自由貿易連合（南米10か国＋メキシコで構成。）

latter（the） （名）後者, 後の方（前者＝the former）
◆If there is any inconsistency between any provisions of this agreement and that of the joint venture agreement, the latter shall prevail. 本契約の規定と合弁会社の規定との間に矛盾がある場合は、後者（合弁会社の規定）が優先するものとする。

law （名）法律, 法, コモン・ロー, 規範
administrative law　行政法
anti-dumping law　反ダンピング法, ダンピング防止法, 不当廉売防止法, アンチダンピング法
Antimonopoly Law　独占禁止法
antitrust law　独占禁止法
Big Retailer Law　大規模小売店舗法
choice of law　準拠法の指定
civil law　民法
commercial law　商事法, 商法 （＝business law）
Commodity Exchange Law　商品取引所法
competition Law　競争法, 独占禁止法, 反トラスト法
conflict of laws　抵触法, 国際私法, 州際私法, 法の抵触
constitutional law　憲法
consumer protection law　消費者保護法
contract law　契約法
copyright law　著作権法
customary commercial law　商慣習法
customs law　関税法
Customs Tariff Law　関税定率法
design law　意匠法
economic law　経済法
foreign exchange control law　外為法
governing law　準拠法
intellectual property law　知的財産法

international economic law　国際経済法
international private law　国際私法
Law on Foreign Trade　貿易法
law-related services　法律関連業務
laws and acts　法律
laws of England　英国法
laws of the state of New York　ニューヨーク州法
laws, ordinances, regulations　法律、法令、法規
local law　地域的個別法律, 実質法, 地域法, 現地法
private international law　国際私法（＝conflict of laws）
private law　私法, 個別法律
product liability law　製造物責任法, PL法
proper law　準拠法
public law　公法
special law　個別法律
the internal laws of the State of New York　ニューヨーク州の州内部の法律、ニューヨーク州法
the laws of England　イングランド法, 英国法
the substantive laws of the State of California, U.S.A.　米国カリフォルニア州の実体法
Trademark Law Treaty　商標法条約
usury law　利息制限法, 高利制限法
◆As stealth marketing by postings is problematic, the Consumer Affairs Agency has revised its guidelines for online transactions under the Law for the Prevention of Unreasonable Premiums and Misrepresentations concerning Products and Services. 書き込みによるステルス・マーケティングには問題があるので、消費者庁は、「景品表示法（不当景品類及び不当表示防止法）」のネット取引に関する指針を改正した。◆The FTC's warnings to the three major beer wholesalers are a kind of administrative guidance if violations of fair trade laws are suspected. この大手ビール卸売り3社に対する公正取引委員会（FTC）の警告は、公正取引法違反の疑いがある場合に出される行政指導に当たる。◆The seller shall not be liable in respect of any warranty or consideration as to quality or fitness which would arise by implication of law. 売り主は、法律の運用により生じる品質または適合性に関する保証または条件については、責任を負わないものとする。

law against unfair competition 不正競争防止法
◆To ensure fair international commercial trade, the law against unfair competition stipulates that both individuals involved in bribery and the corporations they belong to should be punished. 公正な国際商取引を確保するため、不正競争防止法には、贈賄（外国公務員への贈賄）に関与した個人と法人を罰する規定（両罰規定）がある。

lawful currency 法定通貨
(=lawful money, legal currency)

lawful money 法定通貨

lawfully (副)合法的に, 適法に, 法に反することなく
◆Any withholding tax lawfully levied by the Japanese tax authorities on any amount due to XYZ under this agreement shall be born by XYZ. 本契約に基づくXYZへの支払い金に対して日本の税務当局が合法的に課す源泉徴収税は, すべてXYZが負担するものとする。

lawsuit (名)訴訟, 民事訴訟 (=suit)
civil lawsuit [suit] 民事訴訟
class action lawsuit 集団代表訴訟
collective lawsuit 集団訴訟
derivative lawsuit 株主代表訴訟
enter [bring in] a lawsuit against ～に対して訴訟を起こす
file a lawsuit with ～に提訴する
formal [plenary] lawsuit 本訴
lawsuit claims 訴訟による請求権
pending lawsuit 係争中の訴訟
pollution-related lawsuit 公害訴訟
settle a lawsuit 訴訟で和解する
withdraw a lawsuit against ～に対する訴訟を取り下げる
◆Establishing original edition rights would enable publishing companies to file lawsuits demanding the deletion of data if pirated copies are found to be sold on the Internet. 出版物[書籍]原版権の創設によって出版社は, 海賊版がインターネット上で販売されていることが判明した場合に, データの削除を求める訴訟を起こすことができる。◆In lawsuits over patent rights, courts have increasingly awarded inventors compensation for the transfer of patent rights. 特許権をめぐる訴訟で, 裁判所は裁定で発明者に特許権移転の対価[報酬]を認めるケースが増えている。◆ In the lawsuits against big banks over the sales of risky investments, the U.S. government wants to be compensated for lost principal and interest payments. 高リスク証券の販売をめぐっての大手金融機関に対する訴訟で, 米政府は, 元本と利払い分の損失補償を求めている。◆The most advanced technologies are often at stake in lawsuits over intellectual property. 知的財産を巡る訴訟では, 最先端技術が争点になることが多い。

layout of the machinery 機械類の配置

laytime (名)停泊期間, 停泊日数(laydays)

L/C [1/c] 信用状(letter of creditの略。複数形はL/C's, L/Cs。銀行が取引先の依頼に応じて, その信用を補強するために発行する証書。⇒letter of credit)
amend the L/C 信用状を修正する
an extension of the L/C 信用状の延長

anticipational L/C 輸出前払い信用状

application for amendment L/C 信用状変更依頼書

back-to-back L/C 同時発行信用状

bankers' [bank] L/C 銀行信用状

blank L/C 白地式信用状

cash L/C キャッシュ・クレジット

circular L/C 巡回信用状

clean L/C 無担保信用状

commercial clean L/C 商業クリーン信用状, 無担保信用状

commercial L/C 商業信用状

confirmed L/C 確認信用状

delay in establishment of L/C 信用状開設[発行]の遅延

direct L/C 直接信用状

documentary clean L/C ドキュメンタリー・クリーン信用状

documentary L/C 荷為替信用状

doing business on an L/C basis 信用状取引

domestic L/C 国内信用状

escrow L/C エスクロウ信用状

escrow L/C barter trade エスクロウ・バーター貿易

establish an irrevocable L/C for $5,000 in your favor with XYZ Bank 御社宛に5,000ドルの取消不能信用状をXYZ銀行で開設する

export L/C 輸出信用状

extend the shipping and expiry dates in L/C respectively 信用状の船積み日と有効日をそれぞれ延長する

failure to establish L/C 信用状開設遅延, 信用状発行遅延

fixed L/C 定額信用状

funding against a L/C facility L/Cファシリティを裏付けとする資金供与

general L/C 手形買取銀行無指定信用状, ジェネラル信用状 (=circular negotiation L/C, open L/C)

import L/C 輸入信用状

impound L/C インバウンド信用状

irrevocable L/C 取消不能信用状

issue an L/C to cover this order 本注文に対する信用状を発行する[開く]

issue an L/C without delay 信用状を直ちに発行する

L/C advising [notifying, transmitting] bank 信用状通知銀行, 信用状取次銀行

L/C applicant 信用状発行依頼人 (=L/C opener)

L/C basis L/Cベース

L/C beneficiary 信用状受益者

L/C confirming bank　信用状確認銀行

L/C confirming charge　信用状確認手数料

L/C establishing bank　信用状発行銀行, 信用状開設銀行 (=L/C issuing bank, L/C opening bank)

L/C issued account　信用状発行勘定

L/C issuing [opening] bank　信用状発行銀行, 信用状開設銀行 (一般に買い主の取引銀行)

L/C margin money　信用状開設保証金

L/C number　信用状番号

L/C opener　信用状発行依頼人 (=L/C applicant)

L/C opening charge　信用状発行手数料

L/C original　信用状原本

L/C parties　L/C当事者

L/C received register　信用状通知受入帳

L/C with guarantee　保証状付き信用状

local L/C　国内信用状, ローカル・クレジット, ローカルL/C

negotiation L/C　買取信用状, ネゴシエイション信用状

open an L/C as soon as practicable　早急に信用状を開設する[開く, 発行する]

open L/C　買取り銀行無指定信用状, 買取り銀行無指定L/C

open the L/C covering your orders　貴社注文 [貴注文] に対する信用状を開設する

packing L/C　前貸付き信用状 (=red clause L/C)

payment on receipt L/C　受領証払い信用状

reciprocal L/C　同時開設信用状

red clause L/C　レッド・クローズ付き信用状

restricted L/C　買取銀行指定信用状

revocable L/C　取消可能信用状

revolving L/C　循環信用状, 回転信用状

sight L/C　一覧払い信用状, サイト・クレジット

special L/C　スペシャル・クレジット

straight L/C　特定人割引信用状, ストレート信用状

the amount of the L/C　信用状金額

the country of L/C issuing bank　L/C発行銀行の所在国

the L/C is available valid] until　信用状は～まで有効である

the total value of the L/C　信用状の総額

transferable L/C　譲渡可能信用状

traveler's [traveller's] L/C　旅行者信用状, 旅行信用状

unconfirmed L/C　無確認信用状

usance L/C　引受条件付き信用状

without L/C payment　信用状を伴わない手形決済

Within two weeks after receipt of L/C　L/C受領後2週間以内

without recourse L/C　償還請求権を伴わない信用状, 無償還請求権信用状

◆For reimbursement, we have applied to our bankers for an L/C to be opened.（本注文に対する）代金支払いのため, 当社は銀行に信用状の発行を申請しました。◆The L/C shall be available for at least fifteen days after the latest date for shipment stipulated in the contract. 信用状は, 本契約指定の積み期の後, 少なくとも15日間は有効とする。◆To cover this shipment, we have drawn upon you at sight for the invoice amount under the L/C opened by ABC Bank. この船積みに対して, 当社はABC銀行発行の信用状に基づいて, 一覧払い送り状額面金額の手形を貴社宛てに振り出しました。◆We have already arranged with our bankers for an L/C to be established by the end of this month. 今月末までに信用状を開設する件については, 当社が当社の取引銀行にすでに手配してあります。◆We negotiated our draft through the bank above-mentioned under L/C No. 5000 established by the ABC Bank, New York, and commend our signature to your protection. 当社は, ABC銀行（ニューヨーク）発行の信用状5000号に従って上記銀行で手形を買い取ってもらいましたので, この手形の支払いをよろしくお願いします。◆We opened an L/C for $50,000 in your favor with XY bank. 貴社を受益者として, 5万ドルの信用状をXY銀行で発行しました。◆We shall be responsible for any consequences arising out of your opening L/C. 当社 (L/Cの開設依頼人) は, 貴行 (L/Cの開設銀行) がL/Cを開設することによって生じるいかなる事態にも責任を負うものとする。◆We will execute the order with best attention upon receipt of your L/C. 貴社の信用状を受け取り次第, 当社は最善の注意を払って注文を履行します。

lease　（動）賃貸しする, 賃借りする, 借り上げる

◆The government has concluded a contract to lease three of the five Senkaku islands in Okinawa Prefecture for a total of about ￥22 million a year. 日本政府は, 沖縄・尖閣諸島の五つの島のうち3島を年間約2,200万円で借り上げる契約を結んだ。

lease　（名）賃貸借, 賃貸借契約 (書), 賃貸契約 (書), リース契約, リース

finance lease　金融性リース, ファイナンス・リース

finance lease agreement　ファイナンス・リース契約

operating lease　営業型リース, 賃貸性リース, オペレーティング・リース

operating lease agreement　オペレーティン

グ・リース契約

◆This lease shall not be subject to termination by the Lessor, except pursuant to Article 6. hereof, nor by the Lessee, for any reason whatsoever. 本リースは, 本契約第6条による場合を除いて貸主により解除されないものとし, また理由のいかんを問わず借主により解除されないものとする。

leasehold interest 不動産賃借権, 定期不動産権 (=interest)

◆The Company's only interest in real estate is a leasehold interest relating to the Company's office. 対象会社の唯一の不動産の権利は, 対象会社の事務所に関する不動産賃借権である。

leaseholder (名)賃借人, 借地人, 賃貸借による土地保有権者, 借地権者

◆The owner did not agree to register the lease, so the government's right as leaseholder has not been registered. 所有者が賃借権の登記に同意しなかったため, 政府の賃借権はまだ設定されていない。

leasing (名)賃貸借, リース

◆The leasing contract was signed because the agreement with U.S. forces was still valid. 米軍との合意事項がまだ失効していないため, この賃貸借契約が締結された。

legal (形)法律の, 法律上の, 法定の, 法的な, 合法的な, 適法の, 司法の場での, リーガル

international legal department 国際法務部

legal act 合法的行為

legal adviser 法律顧問, 顧問弁護士 (=legal counsel)

legal agent or representative 法定代理人または法律上の代理者

legal capital 法定資本

legal closing リーガル・クロージング(不動産取引で, 当事者が所定の書類を作成し, 代金を提供することによって取引対象の権利が移転すること)

legal condition 法的状況, 法務的状況

legal consultation 訴訟協議

legal counsel 顧問弁護士, 法律顧問

legal department 法務部, 法務部門

legal description 土地表示

legal detriment 法的不利益

legal duty 法的義務

legal estate コモン・ロー上の不動産権

legal expert 法律専門家

legal fee 弁護士費用, 弁護士報酬

legal framework for the contract 取引の法的枠組み

legal interest 法定利息, 法定利子, コモン・ロー上の財産権, コモン・ロー上の権利, 適法な権利

legal obligation 法的義務

legal procedures for international bankruptcy 国際倒産法制

legal proceedings 法的手続き, 法律上の手続き, 訴訟手続き, 裁判手続き, 法的手段

legal process 法的手続き, 合法的手続き

legal rate 法定利率

legal representative or agent 法律上の代表者または代理人, 法律上の代理人

legal restrictions 法的規制

legal risk 法的リスク, 法務上のリスク, 法務リスク

legal services 法律サービス

legal value 法定価格, 法的価値

legal action 法的措置, 法律上の訴え, 訴訟

◆There is a contractual clause stipulating that Japanese PC makers will take no legal action even if Microsoft Corp.'s technologies are deemed to violate their patents. マイクロソフト社の技術が日本のパソコン・メーカーの特許侵害にあたるとしても, 日本のパソコン・メーカーは法的措置を一切取らない[訴訟を起こさない], と定めた契約条項がある。

legal opinion 法律意見書

◆Seller shall submit a legal opinion of Seller's Counsel in the form attached hereto as Exhibit 5. 売り主は, 付属書類5として本契約書に添付した様式で, 売り主の弁護士の法律意見書を提出するものとする。

legal remedy コモン・ロー上の救済手段, 法的救済

◆Guarantor hereby waives any right it may have of first requiring ABC to pursue its legal remedies against XYZ. 保証人は, 保証人が持てる権利にして, まずXYZに対して法的救済を求めることをABCに要求する権利を, ここに放棄する。

legal requirements 法律要件

◆In such event, the provisions of this agreement affected shall be curtailed and limited only to the extent necessary to bring it within the legal requirements. この場合, その影響を受けた本契約の規定は, 当該規定を法律要件の限度内に収めるために必要な範囲にかぎって削除し, 当該規定を制限するものとする。

legal screening 法定審査

◆A corporate merger plan is subject to legal screening by the Fair Trade Commission of Japan. 企業の合併計画は, 公正取引委員会の法定審査を受けなければならない。

legal shortcoming 法の不備

◆Margin trading was used in a corporate takeover by exploiting legal shortcomings. 法の不備を利用して, 企業買収に信用取引が使われた。

legal tax avoidance 合法的課税逃れ

◆In a report released by the U.S. Senate Permanent Subcommittee on Investigations, Apple was held up as an example of legal tax avoidance. 米

上院行政監察小委員会が公表した報告書で、米アップル社は、合法的課税逃れの典型例と指摘された。

legal, valid and binding obligations 法的, 有効かつ拘束力のある義務
◆The execution and performance of this agreement by Seller constitute legal, valid and binding obligations of Seller, enforceable in accordance with the terms hereof. 売り主による本契約の締結と履行は, 本契約の条件に従って強制することができる法的, 有効かつ拘束力のある売り主の義務を構成する。

legality (名)適法, 合法, 適法性, 合法性

legally binding 法的拘束力をもつ, 法的拘束力がある

legend (名)表示, 貨幣などの題銘, 銘, 表題, 記号の一覧表, 説明表, 説明文, 文言, 記載
bear the following legend 次の文言を付す, 以下の説明文を付す
comparable legend それに[これに]相当する文言, それに相当する記載

legible and clearly visible 読みやすくてはっきりと目に見える
◆Such legend shall be legible and clearly visible to purchasers. この説明文は, 購入者にとって読みやすく, しかもはっきりと目に見えるものにしなければならない。

lender (名)貸主, 貸し手, 貸金業者, レンダー
◆In case the borrower fails to pay any principal or interest payable under this agreement on the due date therefor, the borrower shall pay to the lender overdue interest on such overdue amount for each day for the period from and including the due date therefor up to and including the day immediately preceding the actual payment date. 借主が本契約に基づいて元本または支払い利息の支払い期日に元本の返済または支払い利息の支払いを怠った場合, 借主は, その支払い期日から実際の払込み日の前日までの期間の各日数について, その支払い遅延金額の遅延利息を貸主に支払うものとする。

length of service 勤続期間, 在職期間
◆By the revised Labor Contract Law, researchers are now entitled to maintain job contracts until the mandatory retirement age, provided their length of service has exceeded five years. 労働契約法の改正により, 研究者は現在, 勤続期間が5年を過ぎた場合には, 定年まで雇用契約を継続できるようになった。

less (前)差し引いて, 差引で, 控除して (=minus, without)
◆Net Wholesale Price referred to in this agreement is defined as the amount of the gross sales by ABC of the licensed products to ABC's customers in the territory, less customary trade discounts, insurance premiums, transportation and delivery charges, taxes (VAT) and duties. 本契約書に記載する「純卸売り販売額」とは, ABCの顧客に対する契約地域内でのABCの許諾製品の総売上高 (総販売額) から, 通常の卸売り割引額, 保険料, 運送・引渡し費用, 税金 (付加価値税) と関税を差し引いた額のことをいう。

less than 〜未満 (=in short of)

lesser of (形)〜のうちいずれか低い[少ない, 小さい, 軽い]ほう
◆Interest shall accrue on any delinquent amounts owed by Distributor for Products at the lesser of 18% per annum, or the maximum rate permitted by applicable usury law. 利息は, 販売店が負っている本製品の延滞金について発生し, 年18%の利率と適用される利息制限法で認められる最高利率のうちいずれか低いほうの利率によるものとする。

letter (名)手紙, 書簡, 文字, 字体, 文学 (letters), レター
a business letter 商用文, 商業通信文, ビジネス・レター
a confirmation letter 確認状
a cover [covering] letter 添付の手紙, 添え状
a covering letter 添え状
a letter of apology 詫 (わ) び状, 謝罪の手紙, 謝罪文
a letter of complaint 苦情の手紙, 抗議文
a letter of credence (大使などの) 紹介状
a letter of credit (銀行発行の) 信用状, L/C
a letter of inquiry (売り主に対する) 引合い状
a letter of intent 同意書, 予備的合意書, 仮契約
a letter of recommendation 推薦状
a letter of reference (仕事の) 紹介状
a letter of sympathy 見舞い状
a letter of thanks 感謝状
a thank-you letter お礼状
an open letter 公開状
attorney letter 紹介状
collections letter 督促状
comfort letter 念書
deficiency letter 訂正指示書
incoming letter 受取郵便物
investment letter 投資確認書
letter agreement 書簡形式の契約書
letter of acceptance 承諾書, 注文請書
letter of acknowledgement 確認書
letter of advice 通知状, 荷送り通知書, 手形振出し通知書, 積み荷通知書
letter of agreement 合意書, 往復書簡形式の契約書
letter of application 申込み書
letter of approval 同意書, LOA
letter of attorney 委任状
letter of audit engagement 監査契約書

letter of authority　手形買入れ授権書

letter of authorization　授権書

letter of award　落札決定書

letter of commitment　支払い引受書, LC

letter of demand　催告状

letter of engagement　契約書, 契約時の取り交わし文書

letter of guarantee　保証状 (L/G), （輸入）荷物引取り保証書, 信用保証状

letter of indemnity　念書, 補償状, L/I

letter of inquiry　照会状, 問い合わせ状

letter of instruction　指図書, 信用指図書, 手形買取り指図書

letter of insurance　付保決定通知書

letter of intent　予備的合意書, 仮合意書, 仮契約書, 契約予備書面, 趣意書, 念書, 基本合意書, 意思表明状, 契約意図表明状, レター・オブ・インテント, L/I

letter of interest　基本合意書, 予備的合意書（=letter of intent）

letter of introduction　紹介状

letter of invitation　公募入札情報, 招聘（しょうへい）状

letter of license　支払い期日延期状, 債務履行猶予契約［契約書］

letter of proxy　委任状

letter of regret　遺憾状

letter of reminder　催告書

letter of representation　陳述書

letter of subrogation　権利移転書（=subrogation format）

letter ruling　書面回答

letter stock　非公開株

letter telegram　書信電報

letters patent　（政府・国王発行の）許可証, 特許証

opinion letter　意見書

outgoing letter　発送郵便物

remittance letter　送金通知状

rights letter　新株購入権通知状

testimonial letter　証明書

the letter agreement of acknowledgement　秘密保持確約書

the letter of the law　法律の文言

upon receipt of this letter　本状受取りの上

◆We accept your offer subject to immediate confirmation by letter. 書簡での至急確認を条件として、貴社のオファーを引き受けます。◆We confirm our agreement to the contents of the above-written letter. 上記レターの内容に対する当方の同意を確認します。◆We have received your letter of August 15, from which we note that you are in the market for our products. 8月15日付け貴状

を拝受しました。それによると貴社は当社製品をご入用とのこと、確かに承（うけたまわ）りました。

letter of credit　信用状, L/C　（⇒credit, L/C）

acceptance letter of credit　引受信用状

anticipated letter of credit　輸出前払い信用状

applicant of letter of credit　信用状開設依頼人

assignable letter of credit　譲渡可能信用状

back-to-back letter of credit　見返り信用状, 同時開設信用状

bank letter of credit　銀行信用状（=bankers' letter of credit）

be backed by a letter of credit　信用状で保証される

be partially supported by a bank letter of credit　銀行信用状による一部信用補強を付けている, 銀行信用状で一部信用補強されている

be secured by a letter of credit from　～の信用状で担保されている

blank letter of credit　白地式信用状

cash letter of credit　現金信用状

circular letter of credit　巡回信用状

clean letter of credit　クリーン信用状

commercial letter of credit (written)　商業信用状, 商業送り状

confirmed letter of credit　確認信用状

cumulative revolving letter of credit　累積回転信用状

deferred payment letter of credit　後日払い信用状

direct letter of credit　直接信用状

documentary clean letter of credit　荷落ち為替信用状

documentary draft under letter of credit　信用状付き荷為替手形

documentary letter of credit　荷為替信用状

domestic letter of credit　国内発行信用状

escrow letter of credit　寄託信用状

establish a letter of credit　信用状を開設する

export letter of credit　輸出信用状

first-loss letter of credit　一次免責を保証する信用状

fully-supported letter of credit　完全保証型信用状

guarantee through letters of credits　信用状などで保証を付ける

import letter of credit　輸入信用状

irrevocable letter of credit　取消不能信用状

issuance of a letter of credit　信用状の発行

letter of credit advising bank　信用状通知銀行

letter of credit applicant　信用状発行依頼人

letter of credit at sight　一覧払い信用状

L

letter-of-credit-backed CP　信用状を裏付けとするCP

letter of credit beneficiary　信用状受益者

letter of credit claimants　信用状に基づく求償権保有者

letter of credit confirming bank　信用状確認銀行

letter of credit confirming charge　信用状確認手数料

letter of credit issuing bank　信用状発行銀行

letter of credit margin money　信用状開設保証金

letter of credit opener　信用状発行依頼人

letter of credit opening bank　信用状発行銀行

local letter of credit　国内発行信用状

negotiation letter of credit　買取銀行［手形買取銀行］無指定信用状　(=general L/C, open L/C)

nontransferable letter of credit　譲渡不能信用状

open a letter of credit　信用状を開設する

original letter of credit　原信用状（=prime letter of credit）

packing letter of credit　輸出前貸し信用状

payment by letter of credit　信用状決済

prime letter of credit　原信用状

reciprocal letter of credit　抱き合わせ信用状, 相殺信用状, 同時開設信用状

red clause letter of credit　レッド・クローズ付き信用状

restricted letter of credit　買取銀行指定信用状　(=special letter of credit)

revocable letter of credit　取消可能信用状

revolving letter of credit　回転信用状

sight letter of credit　一覧払い手形信用状

special letter of credit　買取銀行指定信用状

standby letter of credit（written）　スタンドバイ信用状

straight letter of credit　特定割引信用状

trade without letter of credit　信用状なし取引　(=transaction without letter of credit)

transferable letter of credit　譲渡可能信用状

uncollateralized irrevocable letter of credit　担保が付かない取消不能信用状

unconfirmed letter of credit　不確認信用状

usance letter of credit　期限付き信用状, ユーザンス信用状

with recourse letter of credit　遡及義務不免除信用状, 償還請求権付き信用状

without recourse letter of credit　遡求義務免除信用状, 償還請求権なき信用状

◆All bank charges, commissions and other costs associated with a bank wire transfer or establishing and maintaining a letter of credit associated with payments under this agreement shall be for the account of ABC. 本契約に基づく支払いにかかわる銀行の電信送金または信用状の開設・維持にかかわる銀行費用、手数料、その他の費用は、すべてABCの負担とする。◆The letter of credit set forth above shall be negotiable against a draft at sight signed by the seller upon the presentation of the following documents: 上記の信用状は、次の船積み書類の提示がある場合には、売り主が振り出した一覧払い手形と引換えに買い取られるものとする。◆The payment for the Goods shall be made by a letter of credit. 「商品」の支払いは、信用状で行うものとする。◆The Seller may withhold delivery or cancel the Agreement if the Buyer fails to establish the letter of credit by the date stipulated in this Agreement. 買い主が本契約で定める期限までに信用状を開設することができない場合、売り主は、引渡しを保留するか契約を解除することができる。◆This letter of credit shall be opened not less than 30 calendar days before the first scheduled shipping date for each order and shall be 90 days beyond the anticipated final shipping date. この信用状は、各注文の最初の出荷予定日から30暦日以上前に開設するものとし、最終出荷予定日から90日を超えて有効でなければならない。

解説 信用状について：信用状は銀行が取引先（貿易取引の場合は輸入者）の依頼に応じてその信用を補強するために発行する証書で、主に売買商品の代金決済に用いられる。貿易取引の商品代金の決済に用いられる信用状を商業信用状（commercial letter of credit）という。一般に、発行銀行が手形の引受け、支払いを保証・確認する取消不能信用状（irrevocable L/C）となっている。

letter of intent　仮合意書［契約書］, 趣意書, 念書, 基本合意書, 意思表明状, L/I

level　(名) 水準, 標準, 程度, 度合い, 数値, 高さ, 段階, 面, 観点, 幅, 水位, ～台, レベル
◆According to the preliminary balance of payments data, the deficit in trade in July 2013 was ¥943.3 billion, 2.5 times the level a year earlier and marking the highest level for July since 1985. 国際収支の速報値によると、2013年7月のモノの取引を示す貿易収支（モノの輸出額から輸入額を差し引いた貿易収支）の赤字額は、9,433億円で前年同月の水準の2.5倍、7月としては1985年以降最大の水準となった。◆We refrained from making a counter offer as the price you offered is about seven percent higher than the level workable to us. 貴社がオファーされた価格は、当社の採算にのる水準よりも7%ほど高いので、カウンター・オファーを出すことを思いとどまりました。

levy　(動) 課する, 徴収する, 取り立てる
◆Late payment shall incur an interest charge of 2 percent over the base rate current in XYZ Bank at the time the charge is levied from the due date to the date of payment in full. 支払いが遅延した

場合、支払い期日から全額支払い日まで、支払い利息（遅延利息）を課す時点でXYZ銀行が適用する基準金利より2％高い支払い利息（遅延利息）が付くものとする。

L/G 保証状（letter of guaranteeの略）

L/I レター・オブ・インテント（letter of intentの略）

liability （名）責任, 義務, 債務, 負債, 借金, 賠償責任 （⇒impair, limit of the seller's liability）

absolute liability　絶対責任, 厳格責任, 無過失責任, 確定債務

accrued liability　未払い負債, 既発生債務

automobile liability insurance　自動車責任保険

civil liability　民事責任

contingent liability　偶発債務, 不確定責任, 未必責任

criminal liability　刑事責任

defect liability　欠陥責任

liabilities, debts, obligations or claims　責任, 負債, 債務またはクレーム

limited liability　有限責任

maximum liability　責任限度, 責任限度額

product liability insurance　製造物責任保険, 製造物賠償責任保険, PL保険

strict liability　厳格責任, 無過失責任

unlimited liability　無限責任

◆The execution of this agreement shall in no way constitute an admission of infringement by ABC of the Copyrights or its liability. 本契約の締結は、どんな意味でも、ABCによる本著作権の侵害またはその責任を認めることにはならないものとする。◆The express warranty stated above is in lieu of all liabilities or obligations of ABC for damages arising from or in connection with the delivery, use or performance of the licensed program. 上記の明示保証は、許諾プログラムの引渡し、使用または履行から生じる損害、またはこれに関連して発生する損害に対するABCの債務または責任に代わるものである。◆The purchaser shall assume all risks and liability for the damages or loss of third parties, lives or properties resulting from the use of the products which are delivered under this agreement. 買い主は、本契約に基づいて引き渡された製品の使用により生じる第三者, 生命または財産に対する損害または損失にかかわるすべての危険と責任を引き受けるものとする。

liable （形）法的責任がある, 責任がある, 責任を負う, ～する義務がある, ～しがちな, ～しやすい

◆The guarantor shall be liable under this guarantee as if it were the sole principal obligor and debtor and not merely a surety. 保証人は、保証人が単なる保証人ではなく唯一の主債務者であるか

のように本保証書上の責任を負うものとする。

liable for　～の責任がある, ～の責任を負う

liable for the debts　負債を払う責任がある, 債務を返済する責任がある

◆The seller shall not be liable for any indirect or consequential damages. 売り主は、間接的損害の責任は一切負わないものとする。

liable to　～する義務がある, ～する責任がある

liable to the law　法の適用を受ける, 法に服さなければならない

liable to the other（party）　相手方［他方当事者］に対して責任を負う

◆If the buyer fails to pay any amount under this agreement when due, the buyer shall be liable to pay to the seller overdue interest on such unpaid amount from the due date until the actual payment date at the rate of 15% per annum. 買い主が支払い期日に本契約に基づく代金の支払いを怠った場合、買い主は、支払い期日から実際の払込み日までの当該未払い金額に対する年率15％の遅延金利を、売り主に支払わなければならない。

liaison office　駐在員事務所（=representative office）

liberalization of brokerage commissions　委託手数料の自由化

◆The liberalization of brokerage commissions on commodity futures trading has paved the way to potentially dramatic realignment of the industry. 商品先物取引の委託手数料の自由化で、業界が劇的に再編される可能性が出てきた。

liberalization of capital flows　資本移動の自由化

◆The liberalization of capital flows in the globalized world economy is the core principle for ensuring the international financial system operated efficiently. グローバル化した世界経済における資本移動の自由化は、効率的な国際金融システムの運営確保の中核をなす原理である。

liberalization of international capital markets　国際資本市場の自由化

◆In the second half of the 1980s, the IMF began supporting the liberalization of international capital markets. 1980年代後半から、国際通貨基金（IMF）は国際資本市場の自由化を支持するようになった。

liberalization of trade　貿易自由化

◆Japan has yet to enter full-scale TPP negotiations, but the LDP has not presented concrete measures to prepare for the liberalization of trade, including steps to bolster competitiveness in the agricultural sector. 日本が環太平洋経済連携協定（TPP）の本格交渉に入るのはこれからだが、自民党は、農業分野での競争力強化策など、貿易自由化に備えた具体策をまだ示していない。

liberalize air traffic　航空を自由化する

◆Japan and United States agreed to liberalize air traffic under a so-called open skies agreement.

日米両政府は、いわゆるオープンスカイ協定に基づく航空自由化で合意した。

liberalize the yuan's exchange rate completely 人民元の為替レートを完全に自由化する
◆Keeping in mind transactions with China, which has yet to liberalize the yuan's exchange rate completely, G-20 participants included in the joint statement the necessity of swiftly shifting to exchange rate system determined by market. 人民元の為替レートをまだ完全に自由化していない中国との取引を念頭に、G20参加国は、市場で決められる為替レートの体制に速やかに移行する必要性を、共同声明に盛り込んだ。

liberalize trade 貿易を自由化する
◆The framework of a Free Trade Area of the Asia-Pacific is aimed at liberalizing trade and investment as well as the elimination of nontariff barriers, regulatory reform and smoother logistics. アジア太平洋自由貿易地域（FTAAP）の枠組みは、貿易や投資の自由化のほか、非関税障壁の撤廃、規制改革、物流の円滑化などを目指している。
◆To liberalize trade further, it is imperative to arrest a decline in Japan's agriculture sector and improve its international competitiveness. 一層の貿易自由化に向けて、日本の農業衰退に歯止めをかけ、農業の国際競争力を高めるのが急務だ。

LIBOR ロンドン銀行間取引金利, ロンドン銀行間出し手金利, ライボー（London interbank offered rateの略）
◆Libor is widely used as a benchmark for rates of corporate loans, derivatives contracts and many other financial deals. ライボー（ロンドン銀行間取引金利）は、企業向け融資や金融派生商品などの金融取引の金利の指標に幅広く使われている。◆The borrower shall pay to the lender an interest on the loan for each interest payment period applicable to the loan at the floating rate of the LIBOR（British Bankers Association Interest Settlement Rate in U.S. Dollars）plus 1.625 percent per annum, calculated on the basis of actual number of days elapsed and a year of 360 days. 借主は、1年を360日として実際に経過した日数に基づいて計算した、ロンドン銀行間取引金利（米ドルでの英国銀行協会金利決済レート）に年1.625％を加算した変動金利で、この借入れに適用される各利払い期間の借入金の利息を貸主に対して支払うものとする。

[解説] **LIBORとは**：ロンドンのユーロ市場で資金を貸し出す銀行側が提示するレートで、英国の中央銀行（イングランド銀行）が経済の安定のために設定する政策金利とは異なり、金融機関が資金調達するときの基準金利。一般的には、指定された複数の有力銀行（reference banks）から報告された毎営業日11:00時点のレートを指す。国際金融取引の指標として利用されているが、一般にユーロ建て取引はEuriborベース、米ドルなどユーロ以外の取引はLIBORベースを使用するケースが多い。2012

年6月末にLIBORをめぐる不正操作事件の発覚後、英政府は2013年4月にLIBORの監督部門を、業界団体の英銀行協会（BBA）から英金融行動監視機構（FCA）に移管した。また2014年早期から、運営主体も、BBAからニューヨーク証券取引所などを運営するNYSEユーロネクストに移すことになった。なお現在は、米アトランタに本部を置くインターコンチネンタル取引所（Intercontinental Exchange:ICE）が、LIBORの算出・運営を2014年2月1日から開始している。

licensable （形）許諾可能な, 許諾できる, 認可できる

license （名）許可, 認可, 許諾, 実施許諾, 商標やソフトウエアなどの使用許諾, 免許, 特許, 許可書, 免許状, 不動産の立入り権, 実施権, 使用権, 鉱業権, ライセンス （動）免許・認可・許可・特許を与える, 許諾する, 実施許諾する, 使用許諾する, 許可する, ライセンス供与する （=licence）

acquire a license　ライセンスを取得する

application for export license　輸出承認申請書

bank license　銀行免許

blanket license　包括許可

business license　営業免許
（=license of business）

compulsory license　強制実施

computer soft license　コンピュータ・ソフト・ライセンス

concurrent license　同時ライセンス

corporate license　コーポレート・ライセンス

cross license　クロス・ライセンス, 交互実施許諾

exclusive license　専用実施, 専用実施権, 独占的実施権, 商標やソフトウエアの独占的使用権

exclusive right and license　独占的権利と実施権

export license　輸出許可, 輸出承認, 輸出承認証

fully paid-up license　全額払い込み済みライセンス

grant of license　実施権の許諾, 実施権の付与, 使用許諾, 商標使用許諾, ライセンスの付与

import license　輸入許可, 輸入承認

import license bond rate　輸入担保率

import license statistics　輸入承認統計

letter of license　支払い期日延期状, 債務履行猶予契約［契約書］

license agreement　使用許諾契約, 実施権許諾契約, 特許権実施契約, 実施権契約, 技術援助契約, ライセンス契約

license application　免許申請

license business　ライセンス・ビジネス（ラ

イセンス契約で使用料（ロイヤルティ）を
払って傘やハンカチ、下着などにブランド
のロゴやデザインを使うビジネス）

license granted hereunder 本契約に基づき付
与されたライセンス

license server ライセンス・サーバー

license tax 免許税, 事業免許税, 特許税

noncommercial license 非商業用途の使用
許諾

nonexclusive license 通常実施, 通常実施権,
非独占的実施権, 非独占的使用権

patent license 特許ライセンス, 特許実施権

product development license 製品開発ライセ
ンス

revoke one's license 免許を取り消す

right to license 許諾権

single copy license シングル・コピー・ライ
センス（パソコン1台につき1ライセンスが
提供される契約形態）

site license サイト・ライセンス（複数の
ユーザーが一つのソフトウエアを特定の場
所で利用する権利）

software license agreement ソフトウエア使
用許諾契約, 使用許諾契約, ソフトウエア・
ライセンス契約（書）

software product license ソフトウエア使用許
諾契約, ソフトウエア・ライセンス契約

source license ソース・ライセンス（プログ
ラムのソースを含めた形でのソフトウエア
の提供）

technical license 技術実施権, 技術ライセン
ス, テクニカル・ライセンス

trademark license 商標使用許諾
◆Neither party shall acquire any licenses under
any other intellectual property rights of the other
party under this Agreement. いずれの当事者も、
本契約の他方当事者が所有する他の知的財産権に
基づくライセンスは一切取得しないものとする。

license fee 免許料, 免許手数料, 実施料, 特許
権使用料, 免許税, ライセンス料
◆The license fee shall be payable in two installments as follows: ライセンス料は、次のとおり2
回の分割払いとする。

解説 特許のライセンス料：特許利用の対価と
して、発明者などに支払われる特許権使用許
諾料のこと。基本的には、基本料のほかに、製
品の生産、販売量あるいは販売額に応じて算
定するロイヤルティが一般的。

license for the exclusive use of the
Trademarks 本商標を独占的に使用する
権利
◆Licensee shall have a license for the exclusive
use of the Trademarks on Products only in these
countries. ライセンシーは、本製品についてこれ
らの国々だけで本商標を独占的に使用する権利を
持つものとする。

license to use a trademark 商標使用の許
諾, 商標を使用する権利
◆Licensee desires to obtain a license to use
the Licensor's trademarks hereinafter defined in
connection with the distribution and sale of certain products in certain countries. ライセンシー
は、特定製品の特定国での頒布と販売に関して、本
契約の以下に定めるライセンサーの商標を使用す
る権利の取得を希望している。

licensed （形）実施許諾された, 許諾対象の,
実施対象の, ライセンス対象の, 契約対象の
licensed herein 本契約で許諾された
licensed patent 許諾特許, 許諾対象特許, 実
施許諾された特許, 実施許諾特許, 実施対象
特許

licensed product ライセンス製品, 実施許諾
製品, 商標やソフトウエアなどの使用許諾製
品, 許諾対象製品, 許諾製品, 契約対象製品
（⇒have manufactured）
◆ABC's obligation under this Article shall not
apply to any information relating to the licensed
products that is or becomes available without
restriction to the general public by acts not attributable to ABC or its employees. 本条に基づ
くABCの義務は、ABCまたはその従業員が引き起
こしたと考えることができない行為によって一般
公衆に制限なく知られている、または知られるよう
になった許諾製品に関する情報には適用されないも
のとする。◆As used in this agreement, Licensed
Products means the software products listed on
Schedule B attached hereto together with all enhancements and modifications thereto as may
from time to time be made by the licensor. 「使
用許諾製品」とは、本契約で使用する場合には、本
契約書に添付する付属書類Bに記載したソフトウ
エア製品と、ライセンサーが随時行うその改訂お
よび変更をすべて意味する。

licensed program 許諾プログラム
◆The express warranty stated above is in lieu of
all liabilities or obligations of ABC for damages
arising from or in connection with the delivery,
use or performance of the licensed program. 上
記の明示保証は、許諾プログラムの引渡し、使用
または履行から生じる損害、またはこれに関連し
て発生する損害に対するABCの債務または責任に
代わるものである。

licensed software 使用許諾ソフトウエア,
許諾対象ソフトウエア
◆Pursuant to the terms and conditions herein
contained, LICENSEE shall not grant to any
other party any right to copy, modify, duplicate,
manufacture or distribute the Licensed Software.
本契約書に定める条件に従って、ライセンシーは、
許諾対象ソフトウエアを複写、修正、複製、製造
または販売する一切の権利を他の当事者に付与し
てはならない。

licensed surveyor 公認鑑定人
◆Full written notice of the purchaser's claim accompanied by a licensed surveyor's report when

the quality or quantity of the products is in dispute shall be sent by registered airmail by the purchaser to the seller within 20 days after the above notification. 本製品の品質または数量について争いがある場合、買い主は、上記通知後20日以内に、買い主のクレームを詳細に記載した通知書に公定鑑定人の報告書を添付して、書留航空郵便で売り主に送付するものとする。

licensee （名）特許権などの実施権者, 商標権などの使用権者, 被許諾者, 被実施権者, 許可・認可・免許を受けた者, 免許保有者, 土地・建物への立ち入り権者

  limited exclusive and nontransferable license 制限付きの譲渡不可能な独占的ライセンス

  ◆Licensee shall have a license for the exclusive use of the Trademarks on Products only in these countries. ライセンシーは, 本製品についてこれらの国々だけで本商標を独占的に使用する権利を持つものとする。

licenser （名）実施権許諾者, ライセンサー
（=licensor）

licensing （名）実施許諾, 認可, 免許, 許認可, ライセンス供与, ライセンス契約, ライセンシング

  cross licensing クロス・ライセンス, 交互実施許諾, 特許権交換, 特許技術の交換, 相互特許使用権 （=cross license）

  director of patent licensing 特許許諾担当取締役

  licensing agreement ライセンス契約, ライセンス供与契約, 使用許諾契約, 実施権契約

  licensing of technology 技術供与

  licensing right 使用許諾権, 実施権
（⇒recitals）

  licensing rules ライセンス契約, 使用許可規約

  patent licensing 特許実施許諾

  technology licensing arrangements 技術のライセンス契約

licensor （名）ライセンサー, 実施権許諾者, 許諾者, 技術実施許諾者, ライセンス許諾者

lien （名）リーエン, 先取特権, 留置権, 物的担保, 担保権

  ◆ABC is the legal, record and beneficial owner of the Shares free and clear of any liens, charges or other encumbrances. ABCは, 先取特権, 担保権その他の制限（負担・障害）がない本株式の法律上, 登録上, 実質上の所有者である。

liens or security interests 担保権

  ◆The Company has good and marketable title to each item of personal property used by it in the business of the Company, free and clear of all liens or security interests. 対象会社は, 対象会社の事業で対象会社が使用している各動産（担保権は一切付いていない）を売買できる正当な権原をもっている。

lift the import ban 輸入禁止を解く, 輸入

を解禁する

  ◆The safety of U.S. beef must be confirmed before lifting the import ban. 輸入禁止を解く前に, 米国産牛肉の安全性を確認する必要がある。

lifting of the ［a］ ban on ～の解禁

  ◆Japanese deluxe wagyu beef has started to hit the market in Europe due to the lifting of a ban on beef exports from Japan to the European Union. 日本からEU（欧州連合）への牛肉輸出の解禁で, 日本の高級和牛が欧州の市場に出回り始めた。

light crude 軽質油, 軽質原油

  light crude contract 軽質油の先物

  light crude oil 軽質原油

  ◆The U.S. light crude front month contract rose a further 36 cents a barrel in after-hours electronic trading to top $50. 米国の軽質原油の翌月渡し価格は, 時間外の電子取引で1バレル当たり36セント上伸して, 1バレル＝50ドルを突破した。

  ◆U.S. light crude hit $42.45 a barrel, the highest since futures were launched in New York in 1983. 米国の軽質原油は1バレル＝42.45ドルで, 1983年にニューヨークで先物取引を開始して以来の最高値となった。

lightning and thunder 落雷

limit （動）制限する, 制限［限度］を設ける, 限定する, 規制する, 制約する, 抑える, 歯止めをかける

  limit competition 競争を制限する

  limit domestic demand 内需を抑える

  limit one's downside exposure to the currency 為替差損を最小限にとどめる

  ◆The revised Foreign Exchange and Foreign Trade Law allows Japan to suspend or limit remittances and trade with North Korea. 改正外国為替及び外国貿易法によると, 北朝鮮に関して日本は送金や貿易を停止・制限することができる。

limit （名）限度, 極度, 限界, 制限, 限度額, 規制値（ceiling）, 基準値, リミット

  be in limited supply 供給が限られている

  borrower limit 与信限度, 借入限度［限度額］

  coverage limit 付保限度

  credit limit 信用限度, 与信限度, 信用貸出限度

  daily（price）limit 値幅制限 （=price limit）

  debt limit 負債制限, 国債発行限度額

  export limit 輸出制限

  exposure limit 与信枠, エクスポージャー制限

  foreign stock-ownership limit 外国人保有比率の上限

  import limit 輸入制限

  impose import limits 輸入制限する

  lending limit 貸出限度

  liability limits 填補限度額

limit down　ストップ安

limit move　値幅制限

limit on banks' cross shareholdings　銀行の持ち合い株保有制限

limit price　指し値

limit pricing　独占企業による参入阻止価格

limit up　ストップ高

lower limit　値幅制限の下限, 下限

maximum limit system　最高発行額制限制度

oil output limits　原油生産枠

order without limit　成り行き注文

policyholder limits　保険契約者に対する与信限度

price limit　値幅制限, ストップ値段

purchase limit　購入限度額

purchase limit on bills bought　手形買取制限

set a time limit　期限を設ける

set limits to imports　輸入制限する

trading limit　取引制限, 取引枠, 取引限度, 値幅制限

upper limit money rate　上限金利

weight limit　重量制限, 制限重量

◆As there is a limit to our output at present, we have some difficulty in meeting the demand. 現在のところ, 当社の生産には限界があり, 需要に応じるのはかなり困難です。 ◆If ABC fails to meet XYZ's credit terms or exceeds its credit limit, ABC agrees to either: ABCがXYZの与信条件を満たさない場合, またはその与信限度額を超える場合, ABCは次のいずれかを行うことに同意する。 ◆The Reinsurer agrees to accept all reinsurance cessions automatically up to the limits shown in the annexes to this Agreement. 再保険者は, 本協定書の補遺に示す限度まですべての出再契約を自動的に引き受けることに同意する。

limit of the seller's liability　売り主の責任限度

◆In the event of the breach of this agreement by the seller, the limit of the seller's liability shall be for the actual damages directly sustained by the purchaser from such breach. 売り主が本契約に違反した場合, 売り主の責任限度は, 買い主が当該違反から直接被った実損額とする。

line　(名)商品の種類, 取扱い商品, 機種, 事業部門, 組立工程, 路線, 進路, 経路, 方向, 方針, 方法, 考え方, 政策, 主義, 姿勢, 手段, 対策, 損益計算書の経常利益または当期純利益, 電話線, 伝送路, 通信回線, 回線, 職業, 商売, 仕事, 職種, 家系, 血統, 境界線, 国境線, 境目, 限界, 限度, 列, 行列, 航路, 運送会社, 輸送会社, ライン

above the line　標準以上で, 経常費以上で

above the line profit　経常利益

assembly line　組立ライン, 流れ作業, アセン

ブリ・ライン

bank line　銀行与信枠

be in line with　～と一致する, ～と変わらぬ水準[同水準]にある, ～と連動する, ～に沿っている, ～を反映している

be in one's line　～の得意分野である

below the line　異常損益項目, 範囲外, 標準以下で, 経常費以下で

bottom line　利益, 収益性

common line of trade　商売仲間

full line　全機種, 全製品, 全品種, フルライン

general lines　一般方針

line of products　品揃え

line rate　(広告の)1行当たり料金

main lines　主要取扱い商品

merchandise line　取扱い商品, 商品構成, 商品ライン

New York line　ニューヨーク航路

prices not in line with the market　市況に添わない値段

product line　製品構成, 製品系列, 製品ライン

product line control　製品別管理

production line　生産ライン

the competition in this line　この種の商品の競争

this line of business　この種の取引

this line of goods　この種の商品, この商品, この取扱い品目

top of the line　最高機種

◆In an effort to secure the profitability of its loss-making electronics business lines, Sony will launch a massive business restructuring, spinning off its key TV operations into a wholly owned subsidiary. 不振の電機部門[赤字続きのエレクトロニクス事業]の採算性[収益性]を確保するため, ソニーは, 同社の看板だったテレビ事業を完全所有子会社に分社化するなど, 大規模なリストラに踏み切る。 ◆The Japanese maker of small and midsize liquid crystal displays plans to relocate part of its production lines in China to Japan. この中小型液晶パネルの日本メーカーは, 中国の生産ラインの一部を国内工場に移す計画だ。 ◆The primary factor behind the company's sizable loss is poor business performance in its main product lines such as flat-screen TVs and digital cameras. 同社の巨額赤字の主因は, 薄型テレビやデジタル・カメラなど同社の主要製品ライン[本業]の業績不振だ。 ◆We fear we may not supply exactly the same articles you want as they are not in our lines. 貴社お望みの商品は扱っていませんので, 当社としてはお望みの商品とまったく同じものを提供することはできないと思います。

line of credit　信用限度, 信用供与限度, 信用供与枠, 与信限度, 与信限度額, 与信限度枠, 融資限度, 融資枠, 融資限度額, 貸出[貸付け]限

LINE 292

度額, 借入限度額, 借入枠, 借入枠中未借入額,
クレジット・ライン
(=credit line)
◆As financial assistance to the cash-strapped
chipmaker Renesas, its three shareholders and
founders are to provide about ¥50 billion, while
lines of credit established by its main banks will
make up the rest of ¥50 billion. 資金繰りが悪化
している半導体メーカーのルネサスへの金融支援
として, 同社の株主で設立母体の3社が約500億円
を調達するほか, 同社の主力取引銀行が設定した
融資枠で, 残りの500億円を賄(まかな)う。

liner (名)定期船, 定期客船, 定期旅客機
liner conference　海運同盟
　(=shipping conference)
liner service　定期海運業者
liner shipping　定期船運送
regular liner　定期船
techno-super liner　超高速貨物船, TSL

lineup (名)顔ぶれ, 陣容, 編成, 布陣, 品揃え,
商品構成, 機種構成, 車種構成, 製品一覧表, 番
組編成, テレビ番組編成予定表, ラインアップ
management lineup　経営陣
product lineup　品揃え, 商品数
starting lineup　発足時の陣容
◆Mitsubishi Heavy Industries Ltd. aims to win
orders for commercial launches of foreign satellites with a current lineup of its core H-2A and
H-2B rockets. 三菱重工業は, 現在の主力ロケッ
トH2AとH2Bロケットの二本柱で, 外国の衛星の
商用打上げ受注を目指している。◆The company
has been strengthening its lineup of in-house
processed and prepared food items which have
higher profit rates. 同社は, 利益率の高い店内加
工食品の品揃えを強化している。

liquefied natural gas　液化天然ガス,
LNG　(=liquid natural gas)
◆As an abnormal situation, imports of liquefied natural gas, the fuel needed for operating
power companies' thermal power stations, have
increased to a massive ¥6 trillion a year after the
operations of nuclear reactors were suspended
around the country. 異常事態として, 原子力発
電所の運転が全国で停止した後, 電力各社の火力
発電の稼働に必要な液化天然ガス(LNG)の輸入額
が, 年間で6兆円もの巨額に達している。◆Busi-
nesses are wary of too-low yen as it would raise
the costs of crude oil and liquefied natural gas.
過度の円安で原油や液化天然ガス(LNG)などの燃
料費が高騰するので, 経済界は過度の円安を警戒
している。

liquidate (動)(借金や負債を)弁済する[返
済する, 支払う], 決済する, 清算する, 債務金
額を確定する, 処分する, 処理する, 整理する, 資
産(などを)売却[現金化]する, 在庫を削減す
る, 会社などを整理する, 解散する, 破産する
◆Citigroup agreed to make best efforts to liqui-

date by the end of next year all of the about $12
billion of auction rate securities it sold to institutional investors. 米シティグループは, 機関投
資家に販売した約120億ドル相当の金利入札証券
(ARS)すべての買戻し問題については, 来年末ま
での決着に向けて最大限の努力をすることで合意
した。

liquidate or dissolve　清算または解散する
◆This agreement terminates automatically if
Distributor is liquidated or dissolved. 本契約は,
販売店が清算または解散した場合には自動的に終
了する。

liquidated damages　損害賠償予定(額), 損
害賠償額の予定, 確定損害賠償額, 定額損害賠
償, 予定損害金
◆In case there is delay in delivery of all or any
part of the Goods on the time as stipulated in
this agreement, the buyer is entitled to claim liquidated damages at the rate of one-half of one
percent (0.5%) of the amount of the delayed
Goods for each complete week of delay. 本契
約で定める期限に本商品の全部または一部に引渡
し遅延が生じた場合, 買い主は, 遅延延延商品の各1週
間につき引渡し遅延商品の代金の0.5%を損害賠償
予定額として請求することができるものとする。

liquidation (名)流動性, 流動化, 決済, 清算,
処分, 処理, 整理, 解散, 破産, 売却, 現金化, 換
金(「流動化」は, 保有資産の支配権を第三者
に移転して資金調達すること)
asset liquidation　資産売却
compulsory liquidation　強制清算
corporate liquidation　会社整理
creditors' voluntary liquidation　和議
forced liquidation　強制破産
go into liquidation　破産する, 清算を開始す
　る, 清算する, 解散する
income at liquidation　清算所得
　(=liquidation income)
inventory liquidation　在庫削減, 在庫整理, 在
　庫取り崩し
involuntary liquidation　強制破産, 強制整理
　(=compulsory liquidation, forced
　liquidation)
legal liquidation　法的整理
liquidation dividend　清算配当
liquidation preference　残余財産分配優先権
liquidation risk　流動性リスク
liquidation value　清算価格, 清算価値
voluntary liquidation　任意清算, 任意整理, 自
　主解散, 自主精算

liquidation or insolvency　清算または支払
い不能
◆It shall constitute an event of default if either
party is the subject of any proceeding relating its
liquidation or insolvency which is not dismissed

within 30 days. いずれかの当事者が清算または支払い不能手続きの対象となり、当該手続きが30日以内に取り下げられないときは、不履行事由となる。

list （動）上場する, 上場される, 表示する, 表記する, 記載する, 掲載する, 記録する, 計上する, 名を挙げる, 指定する
◆As used in this agreement, Licensed Products means the software products listed on Schedule B attached hereto together with all enhancements and modifications thereto as may from time to time be made by the licensor. 「使用許諾製品」とは, 本契約で使用する場合には, 本契約書に添付する付属書類Bに記載したソフトウエア製品と, ライセンサーが随時行うその改訂および変更をすべて意味する。◆NEPRO IT Co., an Internet advertising firm, became the first Japanese company to be listed on South Korea's stock exchange in April 2009. 2009年4月に, ネット広告会社のネプロアイティが, 日本企業としては初めて韓国の証券取引所に上場した。

list （名）表, 名簿, 一覧表, 目録, 明細書, リスト
Commerce Control List　米国の（輸出）規制品目リスト
crew list　乗組員名簿
foreign buyers list　海外商社名簿
list of weight and measurement　重量・容積証明書
list price　定価, 表示価格　(=sticker price)
operation list　作業手順書
packing list　包装明細書, 梱包明細書, P/L
passenger list　旅客名簿
price list　価格表
stockholder list　株主名簿
　(=list of stockholders)
waiting list　キャンセル待ちの名簿, 補欠者名簿
watch list　監理ポスト
◆According to a list of 28 global systemically important financial institutions published by the Financial Stability Board, Citigroup, Deutsche Bank and HSBC Holdings will be targeted for a capital surcharge of 2.5 percent. 金融安定化理事会（FSB）が発表した金融システム上重要な国際金融機関（G-SIFIs）28行のリストによると, 米シティグループやドイツ銀行, 英金融大手のHSBCなどが, 2.5%の自己資本上積みの対象となる。

list control [rules]　リスト規制（武器や軍事転用の可能性がある品目をリスト化し, これに該当する貨物や技術を輸出・提供する場合は, 経済産業省への許可申請を義務付ける制度。⇒catch-all regulations）

litigation （名）訴訟, 論争, 紛争
as a result of a litigation which is initiated
　against　～に対して提起された訴訟の結果

として, ～に対して提起された訴訟の結果
litigation, proceeding or controversy　訴訟, 訴訟行為または紛争

living and other expenses　宿泊その他の費用, 滞在その他の費用

Lloyd's （名）ロイズ
Lloyd's agent　ロイズ代理人, ロイズ代理店
Lloyd's broker　ロイズ・ブローカー
Lloyd's form　ロイズ・フォーム（ロイズの保険証券の様式）
Lloyd's form of policy　ロイズ保険証券
Lloyd's Insurance Brokers' Association　ロイズ保険仲立人協会
Lloyd's list　海事日報, ロイズ日報, ロイズ・リスト
Lloyd's of London　ロイズ保険組合, ロイズ
Lloyd's policy　ロイズ保険証券
Lloyd's register　ロイズ船名録, ロイズ船舶登録簿
Lloyd's SG policy　ロイズ保険証券（SGはship and goodsの略）
Lloyd's surveyor　ロイズ［ロイド］鑑定人
Lloyd's Underwriters' Association　ロイズ保険業者協会
Names at Lloyd's of London　ロイズ会員
Society of Lloyd's Register of British and Foreign Shipping　ロイズ船級協会

LNG imports　LNGの輸入, LNGの輸入額（⇒gap in goods trade）
◆As long as Japan depends on thermal power generation as an alternative electricity source, LNG imports will continue to increase and the nation's wealth will flow to countries rich in natural resources. 日本が代替電源として火力発電に依存するかぎり, 天然液化ガス（LNG）の輸入額は増え続け, 国富は天然資源の豊富な国に流出する。

loading （名）積載, 積込み, 船積み, ローディング
◆Provided, however, that the purchaser shall have the right to inspect the products by an independent inspection company designated by the purchaser at the premises of the manufacturer of the products at such time as may be agreed upon by the seller and the purchaser prior to loading. ただし, 買い主は, 積込み前に売り主と買い主が合意する時期に, 本製品製造者の構内で, 買い主指定の独立した検査会社により本製品を検査する権利を持つものとする。◆The Buyer shall notify the Seller of the name of the carrying vessel, the estimated date of loading and the contract number for the Seller to effect delivery, at least seven (7) days before the estimated date of arrival of the vessel at the port of shipment. 買い主は, 少なくとも本船の船積み港への到着予定日の7日前までに, 本船の船名, 船積み予定日と売り主が引渡しを

LOAD 294

行う契約番号を、売り主に通知するものとする。◆The quality and quantity of the products shall be determined by a mutually acceptable surveyor at the expense of the seller prior to loading. 本製品の品質と数量は、売り主の費用で、相互に受諾できる検査人が積込み前に決定するものとする。

loading and unloading 積み下ろし
◆In the event that Supplier is requested to assist Distributor in arranging for transportation, Distributor shall reimburse Supplier for all costs relating to such arrangements, including, without limitation, insurance, transportation, loading and unloading, handling and storage following their delivery to Distributor. 供給者が販売店から運送手配の支援を要請された場合、販売店は、供給者が(本製品を)販売店へ引き渡した後の保険、運送、積み下ろし、貨物取扱い、保管料などの関連費用を、すべて供給者に償還するものとする。

loan (名)貸付け、融資、借入れ、債務、借款、債券発行、貸付け金、融資金、借入金、ローン
◆Large firms such as trading and steel companies are taking out short-term loans to meet working capital needs. 商社や鉄鋼などの大企業は、運転資金のニーズを満たすため、短期ローンを組んでいる[短期借入れを行っている]。◆The borrower shall pay to the lender an interest on the loan for each interest payment period applicable to the loan at the floating rate of the LIBOR (British Bankers Association Interest Settlement Rate in U.S. Dollars) plus 1.625 percent per annum, calculated on the basis of actual number of days elapsed and a year of 360 days. 借主は、1年を360日として実際に経過した日数に基づいて計算した、ロンドン銀行間取引金利(米ドルでの英国銀行協会金利決済レート)に年1.625%を加算した変動金利で、この借入れに適用される各利払い期間の借入金の利息を貸主に対して支払うものとする。◆The loan shall be advanced by the lender to the borrower wholly or partially in an amount of ten million Japanese Yen (¥10,000,000) or its integral multiple upon request by the borrower. 貸付け金は、借主の要請に基づき、貸主が借主に対してその全額または一部を1千万円またはその倍数の金額で提供する。

loan agreement 貸付け契約、融資契約、ローン契約、金銭消費貸借契約、融資契約書
◆If ABC defaults in the performance of any term, condition or agreement contained in this loan agreement, the Lender may by notice to ABC, declare the Loan together with all accrued interest to be forthwith due and payable. ABCが本融資契約に定めるいずれかの条項、条件または合意事項の履行を怠った場合、貸主は、ABCに通知して、本融資資金[貸付け金]とそのすべての発生利息について即時支払い[返済]義務を宣言することができる。

loan amount 貸付け金額、融資金額、融資額

loan facility 融資枠、融資金 (=credit facility)

◆The Lender will make available to ABC, on and subject to the terms and conditions of this agreement, a loan facility ("Loan") in U.S. Dollars in aggregate amount not exceeding U.S. $1,000,000. 貸主は、本契約の条件(条項と条件)に従って、総額100万米ドル以下の融資金(「貸し付け金」)を、米ドルでABCに貸し付けるものとする。

local company 地元企業、現地企業
◆Mitsui & Co. and Mitsubishi Corp. struck an agreement with a local company over the right to use the LNG facility in Cameron Parish, La. in April 2012. 三井物産と三菱商事は2012年4月、米ルイジアナ州キャメロン郡にあるLNG基地の使用権を得ることで地元企業と合意した。

local content 現地調達、現地調達率、国産化率、ローカル・コンテント
Local Content Act 自動車部品国内調達法、ローカル・コンテント法、現地調達率規制[条項]、ローカル・コンテント規制[条項]
local content rate 現地調達率、現地部品[現地物資]調達率、国産化率
local content requirements [provisions] 現地調達率規制[条項]、国産化率規制、ローカル・コンテント条項

local currency 現地通貨、国内通貨、自国通貨、現地[国内]通貨建て、ローカル・カレンシー
non-local currencies 非現地通貨
subsidiaries operating in a local currency environment 現地通貨を用いる経済環境で営業活動をしている子会社
◆Local currencies are generally considered the functional currencies outside the United States. 米国外では、一般に現地通貨を機能通貨と見なしています。

local labor costs 現地の人件費
◆Local labor costs of Japanese companies operating in China rose by about 60 percent over the past three years since 2010, according to the Japan External Trade Organization. 日本貿易振興機構(ジェトロ)によると、中国に進出している日本企業の現地での人件費は、2010年以来ここ3年間で1.6倍に上昇している。

local office 現地事務所
◆The firm transferred a large amount of funds to its local office under the guise of expenses to collect information. 同社は、情報収集経費を装って巨額の資金を現地事務所に送金していた。

located at ～に所在する、～所在の、～にある

location (名)位置、所在地、立地、拠点、ロケーション
comparative location advantages 比較立地優位
industrial location 産業立地、工業立地 (=location of industry)
location abroad 海外拠点、海外立地
location force 立地因子、立地要因

locations for operation　進出先

manufacturing location　工業立地, 産業立地

offshore locations　海外拠点

poor locations　不利な立地, 立地の悪さ

store location　商業立地

strategic location　地理的条件, 地理的に有利な条件

the location of the assets　資産の所在地

the location of the selling organization　販売組織の所在地

◆The point of origin（the location of the selling organization）of revenues and the location of the assets determine the geographic area. 地域別区分は、収益の源泉地（販売組織の所在地）と資産の所在地に基づいています。

lodging and living expenses　宿泊費と生活費

◆Licensee shall pay Company 30,000 Japanese Yen per day per person as remuneration for Engineer in which includes lodging expenses and living expenses. ライセンシーは、技術者の報酬として1人当たり1日3万円を会社に対して支払うが、これには宿泊費と生活費が含まれるものとする。

logistics　（名）事業の詳細な計画・実行, 後方業務, 後方支援技術, 物資の全般的管理［総合管理］法, 物流管理, トータル物流管理, 効率的物流システム, 物流, 兵站（へいたん）学, 兵站業務, ロジスティックス

business logistics　ビジネス・ロジスティックス（物資の総合管理に関する企業の研究, 手法, 戦略, システムなどのこと）

logistics activities　物流活動, 物流部門

logistics system　効率的物流システム, トータル物流システム, 物流システム

◆Singapore serves as ASEAN's hub for logistics and financial services. シンガポールは、アセアンの物流と金融サービスのハブ（拠点）となっている。◆The framework of a Free Trade Area of the Asia-Pacific is aimed at liberalizing trade and investment as well as the elimination of nontariff barriers, regulatory reform and smoother logistics. アジア太平洋自由貿易地域（FTAAP）の枠組みは、貿易や投資の自由化のほか、非関税障壁の撤廃、規制改革、物流の円滑化などを目指しています。

logo　（名）ロゴ, 成語活字, 表記社名, 意匠登録の商品名・会社名

◆ABC represents and warrants that it owns and possesses all rights, title, interest, in all of the Software Products, and any trademarks, logos, trade secrets and proprietary rights associated with the Software Products. ABCは本ソフトウエア製品の全部に対するすべての権利、権原、権益と、本ソフトウエア製品に関連する一切の商標、ロゴ、トレード・シークレットおよび財産権を所有していることを、ABCは表明しこれを保証する。◆The company uses the logo on its stationery, business cards, billboard signs and pamphlets. 同社はこの

ロゴを、同社の書類や名刺、看板、パンフレットなどに使用している。◆Upon expiration or termination of this agreement, Distributor will immediately cease all display, advertising and use of all of Supplier's names, trademarks and logos. 本契約が満了または終了したときは、販売店は、直ちに供給者の一切の名称、商標とロゴの陳列、宣伝と使用をすべて止める。

long arm statute　ロング・アーム法（米裁判所の管轄権の域外適用）

long term purchase sales agreement　長期売買契約

look forward to　～を楽しみにして待つ, ～を期待する

◆We have a large turnover in this line of goods, so we look forward to a favorable quotation from you. 本品は売上高が大きいので、好条件の建て値がいただけるのを心待ちにしております。◆We look forward to hearing from you soon. さっそくのご返事を、心待ちにしております。

lookout　（名）見張り, 警戒, 用心, 仕事, 関心事, 問題, 監視場所, 見晴らし, 眺望, 見込み, 形勢

a poor［bad］lookout　形勢が悪い, 暗い見通し［前途］

be on［up］the lookout for　～が入用である, ～に目を光らせている, ～を警戒［用心, 監視］している, ～を探している

◆We are on the lookout for the following items: Please quote us your keenest［best］export prices for them. 当社は、以下の商品が入用です［以下の商品を求めています］。これら商品の最低輸出価格の建て値をお知らせください。

lose　（動）赤字を出す, 損失を被（こうむ）る, 失う, 喪失する, 紛失する, なくす, 見失う, 聞きもらす, 混乱させる, （体重を）減らす, （競争などに）負ける, （賞などを）取り損なう, （乗り物に）乗り遅れる, （時間を）浪費する, （時計が）遅れる, （相手を）引き離す［振り切る］, （追っ手などを）まく　（自動）損をする, 失う, 負ける, 敗れる, （時計が）遅れる, 弱る, 衰える, 下落する

lose a lawsuit　訴訟に敗れる

lose both principal and interest　元も子もなくなる　（=lose everything, suffer a total loss）

lose competitiveness　競争力を失う　（=lose competitive edge）

lose heavily on the job　その仕事で大損をする

lose on a contract　契約で損をする

lose one's credit　信用を失う, 信用を損なう

lose out on　～で損をする, ～で損失を出す

◆Sumitomo Corp., a Japanese major trading house, lost $2.2 billion in investments, including Texas shale oil and Australian coal mining. 日本の大手商社の住友商事は、米テキサス州でのシェール・オイルの開発や豪州での炭鉱事業など

LOSE 296

への投資で、22億ドルの損失を出した。

lose effect 失効する, 効力を失う
◆The firm allows employees to set aside annual paid leaves, which lose effect after two years under the law. 同社は、法律上は2年で失効する年次有給休暇の積立てを、従業員に認めている。

lose ground 勢力を失う, 人気を失う, 衰える, 衰退する, 忘れられる, 値を下げる, 売られる
◆The yen lost ground against higher-yielding currencies. 円は、高金利通貨に対して値を下げた[高金利通貨に対して売られた]。

lose international competitiveness 国際競争力を失う
◆Domestic lumber has lost international competitiveness year after year, hit by inexpensive imported materials. 国産材は、価格が安い輸入材に押されて年々、国際競争力を失っている。

lose money 損失を出す, 赤字を出す, 損失を被る, 儲け損なう
◆There was a time when the more we exported, the more money we lost, by eroding export profitability due to the excessive rise in the value of the yen. 超円高による輸出の採算悪化で、輸出すればするほど赤字になる時もあった。

loss (名) 喪失, なくすこと, 減少, 低下, 削減, 損失, マイナス, 欠損, 欠損金, 赤字, 赤字額, 損害, 損害額, 減損, (時間や労力の) 浪費[無駄], 敗北, 負け, 失敗, 死, ロス

absorb losses 損失を吸収する

compensation for loss 損失補塡

conceal a loss 損失を隠す

cut one's losses (投機などから) 手を引く, 損切りをする, 損失を確定させる (=cut a loss)

exchange gain (s) or loss (es) 為替差損益

incur a loss 損失を被る

investors' exposure to losses 投資家の損失負担

loss adjuster (保険会社の) 賠償額査定係

loss adjustment 損害査定

loss due to stock outs 欠品による損失, 売り損ねによる損失

loss in the terms of trade 交易条件の悪化

loss leader 目玉商品, 特価品

loss-leading 出血大サービスの

loss maker 赤字部門, 赤字製品

loss of data データの喪失 (⇒loss of use)

loss of earnings 逸失利益

loss of machine or equipment 機械または装置の損失

loss of principal value 元本割れ

loss of production 生産の減少

loss of productivity claim 生産性喪失クレーム

loss of records or files 記録またはファイルの

損失

loss on contract 受注損失

loss or destruction 滅失または毀損 (きそん), 滅失毀損, 損失または損害, 損失・損傷 (=loss or damage)

losses of asset disposals 資産売却損

lossmaker 赤字続きの商売, 赤字部門, 赤字製品 (=loss maker)

market value losses 市場価格の下落

pay for losses 損失を補塡する

plunge into loss 赤字に転落する

post losses 赤字を計上する (=report losses)

reduced losses 赤字縮小 (=reduction in losses)

report a net loss 赤字決算になる

sell A at a loss 赤字でAを売る, Aを売って損をする

shortage loss 品切れ損失

suffer a loss 損失を被る (=take a loss)

trade at a loss 赤字営業を続ける

translation loss 為替差損
◆The revision of the firm's assumed exchange rate will translate into an additional ￥150 billion loss in its consolidated accounts for the six-month period through March 2015. 同社の想定為替レートの修正に伴って、同社の2014年度下半期 (2014年10月〜2015年3月) の連結決算では、追加で1,500億円の為替差損が生じることになる。 ◆Two domestic carriers have been given a total of ￥85 billion in emergency loans by the governmental Development Bank of Japan to overcome losses caused by a downturn in airline passengers as a result of the Iraq war and SARS outbreak. イラク戦争や新型肺炎 (SARS) による利用客の減少で発生した損失を補塡するため、国内航空会社2社が、政府系金融機関の日本政策投資銀行から計850億円の緊急融資を受けた。

loss of profits 利益の損失, 逸失利益 (⇒loss of use)

loss of use 使用の損失, 使用の喪失, 使用不能損失
◆In no event shall XYZ be liable for incidental, consequential or tort damages of any kind, including damages resulting from any loss of profits, loss of use or loss of data, even if XYZ is advised of the possibility of such damages. 逸失利益、使用の喪失またはデータの喪失により生じる損害を含めて、あらゆる種類の付随的、派生的または不法行為による損害については、たとえXYZがその損害の可能性を知らされていても、XYZは一切責任を負わないものとする。

loss or damage 滅失毀損 (きそん), 損失[滅失]または損害, 損失・損傷 (=loss or destruction)
◆During the period when Products are in the cus-

tody of ABC, ABC shall keep Products insured at ABC's account for the benefit of XYZ against loss or damage by fire, theft or otherwise with extended coverage. 本製品[契約品]をABCが保管している期間中、火災、盗難、その他による滅失や損害を拡張担保するため、ABCはその勘定で、XYZを保険受取人として本製品に付保するものとする。
◆Pursuant to concerned provisions of Contract, all risks of loss or damage to Machines shall be directly transferred from Supplier to Customer. 本契約の関連規定に従って、本機械に関する損失または損害の全危険は、サプライヤーから顧客へ直接移転するものとする。

losses, damages and liabilities 損失、損害と責任
◆Subject to the provisions of Paragraphs 5 and 6 of this Article, the licensor agrees to indemnify and hold the licensee harmless from and against any and all losses, damages and liabilities arising from or as a result of any claim or suit brought against the licensee. 本条第5項と6項の規定に従って、ライセンサーは、ライセンシーに対して起こされた請求または訴訟から生じるまたはその結果生じる一切の損失、損害と責任については、ライセンシーに補償しライセンシーを免責することに同意する。

losses from fluctuations of the currency market 為替差損
◆Losses from fluctuations of the currency market due to the yen's steep appreciation have added to Toyota's plight. 急激な円高による為替差損で、トヨタの経営状況が深刻化した。

lost profit 逸失利益, 失われた収益
(=loss of profits)
◆ABC shall not be liable for any lost profit or for indirect, special, incidental or consequential damages, or for any claim against XYZ by any third party, except for patent or copyright infringement as expressly set forth in this agreement. ABCは、逸失利益に対しても、また間接損害、特別損害、付随的損害または派生的損害に対しても、また本契約に明確に規定する特許権、著作権侵害の場合を除いて、XYZに対する第三者によるクレームに対しても、一切責任を負わないものとする。

low-interest yen fund 低利の円資金
◆In a global carry trade, hedge funds borrow low-interest yen funds to invest in dollar-denominated assets. グローバル・キャリー・トレード[グローバル・キャリー取引]では、ヘッジ・ファンドなどが、低利の円資金を借りてドル建て資産に投資している。

lump sum contract ランプサム契約, 定額請負契約, 固定価格契約, 一括払い契約(プラント契約で、プラント完成まで一定金額で請け負う方式)

lump sum fixed price 一定金額, 固定金額

M

M & A 企業の吸収合併, 合併・買収, 企業取得と合併(merger and acquisition 〔mergers and acquisitions〕の略。acquisitionは企業の株式や資産の取得を意味し、M&Aには会社の株式の譲渡(売買)と会社の資産の譲渡(売買)がある。⇒mergers and acquisitions)

financial M&A 財務的M&A(財務上の利益を上げることが目的のM&A)

M&A advisory firm M&A(企業の合併・買収)助言会社

M&A bid 企業の合併・買収提案, M&Aの提案

M&A deal M&A取引, M&A案件 (=M&A transaction)

M&A market M&A市場
◆The recent M&A is a strategy with an eye on Asia, which has a great potential for sales growth. 今回のM&Aは、販売が伸びる可能性が大きいアジアを視野に入れた戦略です。◆The survey found about 68 percent of M&As were aimed at strengthening the foundations of existing businesses, followed by 15 percent for investment purposes. 調査の結果、M&A(企業の合併・買収)の目的は約68%が既存事業の基盤強化で、次いで15%が投資目的であった。

machine (名)機械, コンピュータ, パソコン
machine readable works 機械読取り可能な著作物

machine tools 工作機械
◆Pursuant to concerned provisions of Contract, all risks of loss or damage to Machines shall be directly transferred from Supplier to Customer. 本契約の関連規定に従って、本機械に関する損失または損害の全危険は、サプライヤーから顧客へ直接移転するものとする。◆The modified program shall be used by the licensee only on the machine designated by this agreement, and for its internal use of the licensee. 変更プログラムは、本契約で指定された機械(コンピュータ)上でだけ、またライセンシーの社内での使用にだけ、ライセンシーが使用するものとする。

machine readable form 機械読取り可能な形, コンピュータで解読できる形
◆Licensee may, for its own use, modify or improve the licensed program in machine readable form. ライセンシーは、その自己使用のため、許諾プログラムを機械読取り可能な形で変更または改良することができる。

machinery (名)機械, 機械類, 機械装置, 機器, 機構, 組織, 機構, 機関, 体制, 勢力, 分子
◆Commodity loans are used to import commodities such as industrial machinery, industrial raw materials, fertilizer, agricultural chemicals and machinery, and other various kinds of machinery, which are agreed upon beforehand between

the Japanese and recipient governments. 商品借款は、日本政府と借入国政府が前もって合意した商品（工業資本財［工業用機械］、工業用原材料、肥料・農薬、農機具、各種機械など）の輸入のために使用される。

made and entered into　締結した、調印した、作成した
◆This AGREEMENT, made and entered into this day of July 15, 2015 by and between ABC and XYZ, WITNESSETH THAT. 本契約は、2015年7月15日にABCとXYZが締結したもので、以下を証する。

made out to order　指図人式で作成された
◆A full set of negotiable bills of lading made out to order must be endorsed by shipper. 指図人式で作成された譲渡可能な船荷証券一式には、荷送人の裏書が必要である。

mail transfer　郵便送金、郵便為替

main bank　主要取引銀行、主力取引銀行、主力行、メインバンク
◆As financial assistance to the cash-strapped chipmaker Renesas, its three shareholders and founders are to provide about ¥50 billion, while lines of credit established by its main banks will make up the rest of ¥50 billion. 資金繰りが悪化している半導体メーカーのルネサスへの金融支援として、同社の株主で設立母体の3社が約500億円を調達するほか、同社の主力取引銀行が設定した融資枠で、残りの500億円を賄（まかな）う。

main export market　主要輸出市場
◆The Bank of Japan pointed to risk factors, including unstable global financial markets and the economic slowdown in the United States, Japan's main export market. 日本銀行は、世界の不安定な金融市場や日本の主要輸出市場である米国の景気減速などのリスク要因も指摘した。

main line of merchandise　主要取扱い品目

mainstay　（名）主力, 主力商品, 支え, 支柱, 大黒柱, 頼みの綱, 拠（よ）り所
mainstay business　主力事業（=core business, main business, main operation）

mainstay issues　主力銘柄

mainstay export item　輸出の主力製品［商品、品目］
◆While Japan's mainstay export item to the U.S. market is vehicles, the shipments to China are mainly electronic parts for assembly. 日本の米市場向け輸出の主力製品は自動車なのに対して、中国向け輸出製品は組立用電子部品が中心だ。

maintain　（動）保つ, 維持する, 持続する, 続ける, 貫く, 進める, 据え置く, 整備する, 保守する, 保全する, 手入れをする, （家族などを）養う, 支える, 支持する, 主張する
maintain a steady hand　金融政策を据え置く

maintain a tight monetary policy stance　金融引締めのスタンスを維持する

maintain diversification　多角化を進める

maintain good relations with　～と良好な関係を保つ

maintain international price competitiveness　国際価格競争力を維持する
◆Citibank Japan Ltd. is arranging to sell its retail banking business by the end of March 2015 if it can obtain approval from the Financial Services Agency, while it will maintain its corporate banking business. 米金融大手シティグループの日本法人「シティバンク銀行」は、金融庁の承認が得られれば、2015年3月末までに個人向けの小口取引銀行業務の売却を打診しているが、企業との取引を行うコーポレート銀行業務は続ける方針だ。
◆Japanese people are becoming difficult to find jobs and maintain their quality of life in the absence of competitive manufacturers at home. 競争力の高い製造業者が国内から消えたため、日本人は雇用を求め、生活の質を維持するのが困難になっている。

maintain competitiveness in exports　輸出競争力を維持する, 輸出競争力を保つ
◆If the yen-dollar exchange rate stayed around ¥100 to the dollar, give or take about ¥5, it would be possible for domestic companies to maintain competitiveness in exports. 円とドルの為替相場が1ドル＝100円プラス・マイナス5円程度で安定すれば、国内企業は輸出競争力を保てるだろう。

maintain the competitiveness of　～の競争力を維持する
◆The company needs to enhance its development strength for such products as hybrid cars to maintain the competitiveness of its vehicles and auto parts domestically manufactured, in addition to improving export-driven profits. 同社の場合、輸出主導の収益改善にとどまらず、国内生産の車両や自動車部品の競争力を維持するには、ハイブリッド車などの製品の開発力を強化する必要がある。

maintenance agreement　保守契約

major contract　大口契約, 主要契約

major export　主要輸出品
◆Indonesia has enjoyed decent economic growth since the global financial crisis of 2008 due to the U.S. FRB's quantitative easing and higher prices of primary commodities such as coal and palm oil as the country's major exports. インドネシアは、2008年の世界金融危機以降、米連邦準備制度理事会（FRB）の量的金融緩和とインドネシアの主要輸出品である石炭、パーム油など一次産品の高値に支えられ、高い経済成長を享受している。

major exporter　輸出大国, 主要輸出国, 輸出の多い国, 主要輸出企業［業者］
◆The economic slowdown in Europe due to the sovereign debt crisis and slackening growth of China as a major exporter to Europe have dealt a painful blow to Japan's exports and production. 債務危機に伴う欧州経済の減速と、欧州向け輸出

の多い中国の成長鈍化が、日本の輸出と生産に耐え難いほどの打撃を与えている。

major importer 輸入大国, 主要輸入国, 輸入の多い国, 主要輸入企業 [業者]
◆Japan should make its arguments for its position as a major importer of farm products. 日本は、農産物の輸入大国としての日本の立場を主張すべきだ。

make （動）作る, 製作 [制作] する, 作成する, 創作する, 創造する, 製造する, 生産する, 準備する, 用意する, 引き起こす, 完成させる, 成功させる, 得る, 儲ける, 〜させる
◆Following the discovery of frozen food products tainted with a pesticide known as malathion, Maruha Nichiro Holdings Inc. announced a voluntary recall of the products made by its subsidiary Aqli Foods. マラチオンと呼ばれる農薬 (殺虫剤) が混入した冷凍食品が検出されたのを受けて、マルハニチロホールディングス (HD) は、子会社のアクリフーズ社が生産 [製造] した冷凍食品を自主回収すると発表した。◆In order to cut off funds to North Korea's nuclear weapons development program, the government will tighten controls on illegal bilateral transactions, including exports of materials for making missiles and smuggling of narcotics and counterfeit bank notes into the country. 北朝鮮の核兵器開発計画の資金源を断つため、政府はミサイル製造の関連物資の輸出や麻薬・偽造紙幣の密輸など、日朝間の不正取引の取締りを強化する方針だ。◆Nissan Motor Co. and Mitsubishi Motor Co. have been importing and selling small cars they made in Thailand. 日産自動車や三菱自動車工業は、タイで生産した小型車を輸入、販売している。

make （名）製作, 製造, 製造元, (物の) 作り [型], 〜製, 〜型, 銘柄 (brand), 生産高, 種類, モデル, 気質, 体質, 性格
be in the make 生産 [製造] 中である, 制作中である, 進行中である
be our own make 自社製である
be out of make 生産 [製造] 中止になっている
◆The model you have in mind has been out of make for the moment, and we could not tell exactly when our supply might be made. 貴社ご要望の機種はここ当分、生産中止になっており、供給可能の時期は目下不明です。

make a transaction with 〜と取引をする
◆In its guidelines for banking supervision, the Financial Services Agency calls on banks not to make transactions with crime-affiliated forces. 銀行に対する監督指針で、金融庁は、反社会的勢力との取引をしないよう銀行に求めている。

make an agreement 契約を結ぶ, 契約を締結する
（=enter into an agreement, make a contract）
◆This agreement is made pursuant to and shall be governed by, and construed in accordance with the laws of France. 本契約はフランス法に

従って締結するもので、同法に準拠し、同法に従って解釈するものとする。

make and enter into 締結する
（=make and conclude）
◆This agreement is made and entered into this first day of September 1, 2003 between ABC and XYZ. 本契約は、ABCとXYZが2003年9月1日に締結した。

make available to 〜に提供する, 〜に利用させる, 〜に貸し付ける
◆The lender agrees to make available to the borrower, on and subject to the terms and conditions of this agreement, a loan facility in Japanese Yen in an aggregate amount not exceeding ¥ 500,000,000 or its equivalents. 貸主は、本契約の条件に従って、借主に対して日本円で合計額が5億円またはその相当額を超えない融資枠を設定することに同意する。

make out （書類を）作成する, 書く, 記載する, 認める, 判読する, 見分ける, 聞き分ける, 理解する, 分かる, 上手くやって行く
◆A full set of negotiable bills of lading made out to order must be endorsed by shipper. 指図人式で作成された譲渡可能な船荷証券一式には、荷送人の裏書が必要である。◆Bills of lading shall be made out to order and marked notify party. 船荷証券は、指図人式で作成し、通知先を記入しなければならない。

make payments 支払いをする
◆The epoch-making service features "multimedia banking" that permits access to financial services from a personal computer in a corporate network and "multimedia shopping," in which users can order goods and make payments. この画期的なサービスの特色は、企業ネットワーク内のパソコンから金融サービスにアクセスできる「マルチメディア・バンキング」と、利用者が商品の注文とその支払いができる「マルチメディア・ショッピング」である。

make up 構成する, 形成する, (比率などを) 占める, 〜に達する, 作り上げる, でっちあげる, かさ上げする, 埋め合わせる, 負担する, (資金などを) 調達する, (薬を) 調合する
◆As financial assistance to the cash-strapped chipmaker Renesas, its three shareholders and founders are to provide about ¥ 50 billion, while lines of credit established by its main banks will make up the rest of ¥ 50 billion. 資金繰りが悪化している半導体メーカーのルネサスへの金融支援として、同社の株主で設立母体の3社が約500億円を調達するほか、同社の主力取引銀行が設定した融資枠で、残りの500億円を賄 (まかな) う。

manage （動）運営する, 運用する, 管理する, 経営する, うまく処理する
managed assets 管理資産
managed currency 管理通貨
managed float system 管理フロート制
managed floating (rate) system 管理フロー

MANA 300

ト制

managed futures trade　商品ファンド業

managed money　商品ファンド

◆The new company shall be managed under the provisions of this agreement, the articles of incorporation and the applicable laws and regulations of Japan. 新会社は、本契約の規定、定款と日本の適用法令に従って運営する。

managed trade　管理貿易
◆Numerical targets may lead to managed trade which runs counter to the principle of free trade. 数値目標は、自由貿易の原則に反する「管理貿易」につながりかねない。

management agreement　業務運営契約, 業務運営契約書, 経営委託契約, マネジメント契約（書）

management and direction　経営と指揮, 運営と指揮, 運営と監督
◆Responsibility for the management and direction of the new company shall be vested in the board of directors of the new company. 新会社の経営と指揮に対する責任は、新会社の取締役会に帰属する。

management decision　経営の意思決定, 経営者の意思決定, 経営判断
◆Comparative advantage in this new global market depends not only on superior R&D, but also on speed in making management decisions, finding unique applications for research advances and delivering them to customers ahead of competitors. この新しいグローバル市場で比較優位性を確立できるかどうかは、高度な研究開発だけでなく、経営の意思決定を迅速に行えるかどうかと、研究を進めるうえで独創的な適用範囲［用途］を素早く確認して、それを競合他社に先駆けて製品化できるかどうかにかかっている。

management right　経営権
◆Fashion apparel maker Onward Kashiyama acquired the management rights of Italian shoemaker Iris. ファッション・アパレル・メーカーのオンワード樫山が、イタリアの靴メーカー「イリス社」の経営権を獲得した。

man-day　(名)人日（にんび）, 延べ日数, 工数, 1人1日（人員を日数で掛け合わせて算定する）
◆The total period of such technical assistance and services shall not exceed 90 man-days. この技術指導とサービスの総期間（延べ日数）は、90人日（にんび）を超えないものとする。

manifest　(名)積み荷目録(M/F), 公知の事実

a corrected manifest　訂正（積み荷）目録

cargo manifest　積み荷目録

import manifest　輸入積み荷目録

inward manifest　輸入税用積み荷目録

manifest measures　積み荷目録面容積

manifest weight　積み荷目録重量

ship's manifest　積み荷明細書

man-month　(名)人月, 延べ月数, マン・マンス（人員と期間を掛け合わせて算定する）
◆Such visits for training shall be conducted one time only and the training period shall not exceed 6 man-months. 訓練のための当該訪問は1回限りとし、訓練期間は6人月を超えないものとする。

manner　(名)方法, やり方, 様式, 形式, 種類
◆The foregoing warranties are conditional upon the Products being received, unloaded, installed, tested and maintained and operated by ABC in a proper manner. 上記の保証は、本製品をABCが適正な方法で受領、荷揚げ、設置し、試験、維持して運転することを前提条件とする。

manual　(名)手引書, 入門書, 参考書, 案内, 便覧, 作業手順書, 仕様説明書, 取扱い説明書, 解説書, 業務規定, マニュアル

instruction manual　取扱い説明書

operating manual　業務マニュアル, 業務便覧, 操作マニュアル, 使用マニュアル

operation manual　操作マニュアル, 運転マニュアル, オペレーション・マニュアル

operations manual　作業マニュアル

procedures manual　手続きマニュアル, 業務マニュアル

reference manual　リファレンス・マニュアル（ソフトの機能の解説書）

setup manual　セットアップ・マニュアル（ソフトをセットアップするための説明書）

system［organization］manual　組織便覧

system overall manual　システム概要説明書

user's manual　取扱い説明書, ユーザー・マニュアル

◆ "Documentation" means the printed or electronic instructions, manuals and diagrams pertaining to the use and installation of Products. 「ドキュメンテーション」とは、本商品の使用とインストレーションに関する印刷されたまたは電子式の説明書、取扱い説明書と図表を意味する。

manufacture　(動)製造する, 生産する, 製作する, 作る, 作り出す, ねつ造する, でっち上げる　(⇒have manufactured)

manufacture, copy and distribute　製造、複製、販売する
◆In processing trade, imported raw materials are manufactured into goods that are then sold to other countries. 加工貿易では、輸入された原材料が製品に仕上げられた後、製品は海外に販売される。◆The company needs to enhance its development strength for such products as hybrid cars to maintain the competitiveness of its vehicles and auto parts domestically manufactured, in addition to improving export-driven profits. 同社の場合、輸出主導の収益改善にとどまらず、国内生産の車両や自動車部品の競争力を維持するには、ハイブリッド車などの製品の開発力を強化する必要がある。

manufacture （名）製造, 生産, 製作, 製品
ceramic manufacture　窯業（ようぎょう）製品
certificate of manufacture　製作証明書
craft manufacture　工芸製品
domestic manufacture　国産品, 国内製品
export manufacture　輸出製品
foreign manufacture　外国製品, 外国品
leather manufacture　皮革製品
local manufacture　現地生産
（=local manufacturing）
manufacture and sales of products　製品の製造販売
manufacture and supplier of　〜の製造・供給者
manufacture, assembly and/or sale of　〜の製造、組立ておよび/または販売, 〜の製造、組立てや販売
manufacture order　製造指図書
manufacture, sale and use　製造、販売と使用
nondurable manufactures　非耐久財製造
outside manufacture　外注製品
process of manufacture　製造工程, 製法, 製造方法
semi-manufacture　半製品
trade and manufacture　商工業
◆Mazda Motor Corp. has asked Toyota Motor Corp. to provide core parts for the manufacture of a hybrid car. マツダが、トヨタにハイブリッド車製造のための基幹部品供給を要請した。

manufacture and marketing　製造［生産］と販売, 製造とマーケティング
◆The parties hereto desire to establish a stock corporation under the laws of Japan to undertake and accomplish the manufacture and marketing of the products in the territory as described in Article 1. 本契約当事者は、第1条に定める地域で本製品の製造とマーケティングを引き受け、実行するために、日本法のもとに株式会社を設立することを望んでいる。

manufacture, use and sell　製造、使用、販売する, 製造・使用および販売する
◆Licensor hereby grants to Licensee during the life of this agreement an exclusive license to manufacture, use and sell Products under Patents now owned or controlled by Licensor in Territory. 本契約によりライセンサーは、本契約の有効期間中、契約地域でライセンサーが現在所有または支配している本特許に基づいて本製品を製造、使用、販売する独占的実施権をライセンシーに付与する。

manufactured　（形）製造された［製造される］, 生産された, 製作された, ねつ造された, 自製の, 〜の製造［生産、製作］
cost of goods manufactured　製造原価
manufactured exports　製品輸出, 工業製品輸出, 輸出工業製品
manufactured-goods import ratio　製品輸入比率
manufactured imports　製品輸入, 工業製品輸入, 輸入工業製品
manufactured material　自製材料
manufactured parts　自製部品
semi-manufactured goods　半製品
total manufactured product　製造業生産高
◆All quantities of the Product manufactured by you shall be held by you to our order and we shall insure all quantities on your premises of the Commodity and the Product. 貴社が製造した契約品の数量はすべて当社の指図があるまで貴社が保管し、当社は貴社の構内にある商品と契約品の全数量に保険を付けるものとする。

manufactured goods　工業製品, 工業品, 加工品　（=manufactured product）
◆The trade surplus in manufactured goods stood at a record high ￥16.04 trillion, up 17.7 percent from the previous year. 工業製品の貿易収支の黒字額は、前年度より17.7％増の16兆400億円で、過去最高となった。

manufacturer　（名）製造業者, 製造会社, 製造企業, 製造者, 製造元, 製作者, メーカー, 工場主　（=maker）
chemicals manufacturer　化学品メーカー
computer manufacturer　コンピュータ・メーカー
export manufacturer　輸出メーカー
headline business conditions diffusion index of manufacturers　製造業の業況判断DI
index reading for manufacturers' sentiment　製造業の景況感
integrated manufacturer　一貫メーカー
major manufacturers of home appliances　大手家電メーカー
manufacturer-owned chain　メーカー［製造業者］直営チェーン店
manufacturers　製造業各社, 製造業, 製造業界
manufacturer's inventories　製造業在庫
manufacturers' suggested retail prices　メーカー希望小売価格
non-manufacturers　非製造業
◆After a Chinese fishing boat collided with Japan Coast Guard's patrol vessels near the Senkakus in 2010, China suspended rare earth exports to Japan and dealt a blow to Japanese manufacturers. 2010年に中国漁船が尖閣諸島近海で海上保安庁の巡視船に衝突した事件の後、中国はレア・アースの対日輸出を停止し、日本の製造業が打撃を受けた。◆As many domestic manufacturers have moved their production sites from Japan to Asian nations and elsewhere, the Japanese economy benefits less and less from the weak yen

which lowers export costs. 国内製造業の多くが生産拠点を日本からアジアなどに移しているため、日本経済は、輸出コストが下がる円安メリットを享受しにくくなっている。◆Information about advanced technologies is sold to overseas rivals in industrial espionage, which has become a common threat for Japanese manufacturers. 産業スパイでは先端技術情報が海外のライバル企業に売り渡されるので、日本のメーカーにとって産業スパイは、共通の脅威となっている。◆Many Japanese manufacturers have been prompted to review their production in China with labor costs surging in China and domestic production recovering competitiveness thanks to the weaker yen. 中国で人件費が高騰しているのに加え、円安進行で国内生産の競争力が回復しているため、日本メーカーの多くは中国での生産（体制）を見直す動きが加速している。◆To increase exports, Japanese manufacturers must develop attractive products of high added value and find ways to capitalize on growing markets in the emerging economies of Asia and other regions. 輸出を拡大するには、日本の製造業各社が、付加価値の高い魅力的な商品を開発して、アジアなどの地域の新興国の成長市場を積極的に取り込む方法を見つける必要がある。

manufacturing （名）製造、生産、加工、製作、モノづくり（craftsmanship）、生産拠点、産業、マニュファクチュアリング

computer-aided manufacturing　コンピュータ支援［援用］製造

customized manufacturing　特注化製造

flexible manufacturing system　フレキシブル生産システム

full scale manufacturing　一貫製造　（=integrated manufacturing）

labor-intensive manufacturing　労働集約型製造業, 労働集約型産業

large scale manufacturing　大規模製造

mass manufacturing　大量生産

original equipment manufacturing　相手方ブランド製造業者, 相手先商標製品［製造］, OEM

set up manufacturing　生産拠点を設ける

shift manufacturing offshore　海外に生産拠点を移す

manufacturing （形）製造の, 生産の, 製造過程の, 製造業の

manufacturing capacity　生産能力, 製造能力, 生産設備

manufacturing consignment agreement　製造委託契約, 製造物委託契約

manufacturing cost　製造費, 製造原価, 製造コスト, 生産コスト

manufacturing date　製造年月日

manufacturing department　製造部門

manufacturing expertise　製造技術

manufacturing improvement　生産効率の改善

manufacturing industry product　工業製品

manufacturing inventory　生産者在庫

manufacturing lead time　製造期間　（=production lead time）

manufacturing location　工業立地, 産業立地

manufacturing management　生産管理

manufacturing order　製造指図書

manufacturing output［production］　製造業の生産, 工業生産, 製造業生産高

manufacturing specification　製造仕様書

manufacturing base　生産拠点, 製造拠点
◆As labor costs in China are expected to continue rising, labor-intensive industries such as fashion and electronics will keep relocating their manufacturing bases to Southeast Asia and other regions with cheaper labor. 中国の人件費上昇は今後も続く見通しなので、アパレルや家電などの労働集約型産業では、生産拠点を中国より低賃金の東南アジアなどに移す流れが続くものと思われる。

manufacturing facility　生産拠点, 製造拠点, 生産設備　（=production facility）
◆This manufacturing facility was registered for international quality standard ISO 9001. この製造施設［製造工場］は、国際品質基準「ISO 9001」の認定を受けた。

manufacturing industry　製造業, 製造工業, 製造業界　（=manufacturing companies）
◆Japan must strengthen the competitiveness of its manufacturing industry which will lead to increasing exports in order to rebuild its status as a trading country. 貿易立国としての地位を立て直すには、日本は、輸出拡大につながる製造業の競争力強化が必要である。◆The Japanese manufacturing industry is expected to benefit from the weak yen. 日本の製造業は、円安でメリットが期待される。

manufacturing process　生産工程, 製造工程, 生産［製造］過程, 生産［製造］部門　（=production process）
◆The development of cross-border infrastructure in the Greater Mekong Subregion（GMS）has prompted a number of multinational corporations to transfer some of their manufacturing processes to Laos, Cambodia and Myanmar to take advantage of cheaper labor costs. 大メコン圏での国境を越えたインフラ整備に伴い、多くの多国籍企業が、安い人件費［低賃金］の利点を生かして生産工程の一部をラオスやカンボジア、ミャンマーに移転している。

manufacturing technology　製造技術

margin （名）開き, 幅, 差, 票差, 得点差, 余裕, 余地, 売上総利益, 利益率, 利ざや, 証拠金, 委託証拠金, 委託保証金, 担保金, 手付け金, マージン

a large margin 大きな利ざや

a narrow margin 小さな利ざや

after-tax margin 税引き後利益率

buying on margin 思惑買い

by a wide margin 大差で, 大幅に

gross margin 売上総利益, 売上利益率, 粗利益率 (=gross margin percentage)

margin buying 株式のカラ買い, 信用買い

margin calls 追加証拠金

margin improvement 利益率改善

margin of fluctuation 変動幅

margin percentage 利益率

margin requirement 証拠金, 証拠金率

margin stock 信用銘柄

margin trader 信用取引者

margins around the parity 為替変動幅

narrow margin of profit 薄利

net margin 純販売利益, 純売買差益, 純利益

net profit margin 売上高利益率

operating income margin 営業利益率 (=operating margin)

product margins 製品利益率

profit margin on sales 売上高利益率

retail margins 小売マージン

◆In foreign exchange margin trading, investors repeatedly trade U.S. dollars, euros and other currencies, aiming to profit from fluctuations in exchange rates. 外国為替証拠金取引では、為替の変動による利益を狙って、投資家が米ドルやユーロなどの外貨を繰り返し売買する。◆We hope that you will allow us an extra discount of 5 percent as the margin on this order is rather small. この注文の利益率はごく薄いので、とくに5%の値引きを認めていただきたい。

margin of profit 利ざや, 採算, 売上高営業利益率 (=profit margin)

◆As our margin of profit is so small, it might not pay for us to make any better offer. 当社の(建て値の)利ざやはひじょうに薄いので、これ以下の値段を出すことはできません。◆The firm is doing business on a narrow margin of profit. 同社は、薄利で営業している。

margin trading 信用取引

◆In margin trading, stocks can be purchased on credit. 信用取引では、掛けで[購入代金を借りて]株を買うことができる。◆Margin trading was used in a corporate takeover by exploiting legal shortcomings. 法の不備を利用して、企業買収に信用取引が使われた。

marine (形)海の, 海に住む, 海産の, 船舶の, 海運の, 海軍の, 航海の (名)(一国の)全船舶, 海上勢力, 海兵, 米海兵隊員

fire and marine insurance rating 損害保険料

率の算定

fire and usual marine risks 海上保険

marine accidents 海難 (=marine casualty, marine perils)

Marine Accidents Inquiry Agency 海難審判庁

marine barometer 船用晴雨計

marine bill of lading 海上船荷証券

◆Date of marine bill of lading shall be proof of the date of shipment in the absence of the evidence to the contrary. 海上船荷証券の日付は、反対の証拠がない場合、船積み日の日付の証拠となる。

marine insurance 海上保険

◆The purchaser shall effect, at its own expense, marine insurance on each cargo of the products from the point where such cargo passes the rail of the vessel of the port of the shipment. 買い主は、買い主の自己費用で、本製品の各貨物が船積み港の本船の舷側欄干を越える時点から、当該貨物に海上保険を付けるものとする。◆The seller shall, for its own account, effect marine insurance only free from particular average (FPA Institute Cargo Clause) for the amount of CIF value of the products plus 10 percent. 売り主は、売り主の自己負担で、本商品のCIF価格プラス10%の保険金額により単独海損[分損]不担保条件(FPA協会貨物保険約款)の海上保険を付けるものとする。

解説 海上保険の種類:

cargo insurance 貨物保険 積み荷保険

freight insurance 貨物保険

hull insurance 船体保険

profit insurance 希望利益保険

marine insurance policy 海上保険証券

◆Marine insurance policy shall cover all risks and be endorsed in blank. 海上保険証券は、全危険担保条件を付保し、無記名裏書き[白地裏書き]するものとする。

marine product 海産物, 水産物 (=aquatic product)

◆Japan and Russia inked a treaty on measures to control poaching and smuggling of crabs and other marine products in the Okhotsk Sea. 日本とロシアは、オホーツク海のカニなど水産物の密漁・密輸入対策に関する協定に署名した。◆Japanese agricultural and marine products have been seriously damaged by harmful rumors. 日本の農産品や海産物[日本の農水産物]は、風評被害で大きな打撃を受けている。

marine transportation 海上輸送

◆Japan relies on marine transportation for imports of 90 percent of its energy and 60 percent of its food. 日本は、エネルギー輸入の9割、食糧輸入の6割を、海上輸送に依存している。

maritime (形)沿海の, 臨海の, 海の, 海洋の, 海上の, 海事の, 海に関する, 海の近くに住む, 船員特有の

boosting one's maritime security capability　海上保安能力の向上

Convention on Facilitation of International Maritime Traffic　国際海上交通簡素化条約, FAL条約（国際航海の入港・停泊・出港時の船舶, 乗客, 乗員, 手荷物, 貨物に適用する手続きや検疫手続きのほか, 関連申請書類を簡素化, 標準化することにより, 国際海上輸送の円滑化を図るのが目的）

Federal Maritime Administration　連邦海事局

International Maritime Organization　国際海事機関, IMO

maritime affairs　海事

maritime bonds　海事債

maritime border　海上境界線

maritime insurance　海上保険

maritime law　海事法

maritime lien　船舶先取特権, 海事リーエン

maritime perils　海上危険

maritime pollution　海洋汚染

maritime protection and indemnity insurance　船主責任保険, PI保険

maritime traffic　海上交通

maritime security capability　海上保安能力

◆Enhancing the Philippines' maritime security capability is conductive to beefing up piracy and terrorism countermeasures in the South China Sea and to securing vital shipping lanes to Japan. フィリピンの海上保安能力の向上は, 南シナ海の海賊・テロ対策の強化と, 日本にとって極めて重要な海上交通路（シーレーン）の安全確保に役立つ。

mark　（動）〜に印をつける, 〜を表す, 記入する, 〜の位置を示す, を示す, 物語る, 特徴づける, 目立たせる, 際立たせる, 記念する, 祝う, 記録する, 点数[評価]をつける, 採点する, 〜に注意を払う

marked with a confidential, proprietary or other similar notice　秘密, 専有または他の同様の表示を付して

◆Bills of lading shall be made out to order and marked notify party. 船荷証券は, 指図人式で作成し, 通知先を記入しなければならない。

mark　（名）水準, 標準, 〜台, 〜の大台, 記号, 符号, 標識, 標的, 目標, 成績, 評価, マーク

解説 主な荷印：

care mark　注意マーク

caution mark　取扱い注意マーク

counter mark　副マーク（荷送人を示す）

country of origin mark　原産地国マーク

main mark　主印 主マーク（荷受人を示す）

port mark　仕向け港マーク

quality mark　品質マーク

running case number　連続荷番号

shipping mark　荷印

mark to market　（動）（金融商品について）評価替えをする, 〜を時価で評価替えする, 時価で評価する, 時価評価する, 値洗いする, 洗い替えを行う

be marked to market　評価替えされている, 時価で評価替えされる, 時価評価されている

mark assets and liabilities to market　資産と負債を時価評価する

◆Gains and losses on hedges of existing assets or liabilities are marked to market on a monthly basis. 既存の資産または債務のヘッジに関する損益は毎月, 評価替えされている。

market　（動）市場で売買する, 市場に出す, 市場で売りさばく, 販売する

◆Japan and China have established a system of international division of labor in which China imports industrial parts from Japan to assemble into finished products in China and these are marketed domestically or exported to the U.S., Europe and elsewhere. 日本と中国は, 中国が日本から工業部品を輸入して中国で最終製品に組み立て, 中国国内で販売したり欧米などに輸出したりする国際分業体制を築いてきた。

market　（名）市場, 市（いち）, 食料品店, 日用雑貨店, 株式市場, 市中, 相場, 市況, 売買, 販路, 需要, 購買者層, マーケット
（＝marketplace, mart：⇒tap the market）

a brisk market　活発な市況

a bull market　強気市場, 上げ相場, 買い相場, 上向きの市況

a buyer's market　買い手市場

a drop in the market　相場の下落

a dull market　不振の市況, 鈍調な市況

a quiet market　閑散とした市況

a seller's market　売り手市場

a steady market　手堅い市況

active market　活況市場

aftermarket　販売後市場, 有価証券の流通市場, 補修部品市場, 関連ハードウエア/ソフトウエア/周辺装置の市場, アフター・マーケット　（＝after market, aftermath market）

appear on the market　上場する

at the market　市価で, 時価で, いちばん良い値で, 成り行きで

be in the market for　〜を買おうと思っている, 〜を購入したいと考えている

be not available on the open market　市販では手に入らない

bear market　弱気市場, 下げ相場, 売り相場

bring new goods to market　新商品を売り出す

capture the market　シェアを獲得する

come on [into, onto] the market　市場に出る, 市場に現われる, 市販される

corner the market in　〜の市場を買い占める, 〜の市場を独占する, 〜を買い占める

MARK

credit market　信用市場, 金融市場, 発行市場, 債券市場, クレジット市場

enter the market　市場に参入する, 市場に進出する, 市場を利用する, 市場に加わる

exchange market　為替市場

exploit the market　市場を開拓する

find a market　販路が見つかる, 買い手がつく, 売りさばける

find a market for goods　商品の買い手がつく

go badly to market　買い損をする, 売り損をする, 損な取引をする

go to (the) market　市場に行く, 市場に買い物に行く, 試みる, やってみる

govern the market　市価を左右する

hit the market　市場に登場する, 市場に出回る

hold the market　市場を左右する

hyper market　ハイパー・マーケット
(=hypermarket, superstore: 都市郊外に広大な売場もち, ワン・フロアの倉庫式店舗で, 食料品, 非食料品 (衣料品, 電気器具, 家具, 家庭用品, 園芸用品, 建材など) を幅広く品揃えし, 可能なかぎりの安売りを売り物にしてセルフサービス方式を採用した大型スーパー)

in the market for　〜を求めて, 〜を買いたいと望んで, 〜を買おうとして, 〜が入用で, 売りに出されて (on the market)

intervene in the market　市場に介入する, 市場介入に踏み切る

issue market　発行市場　(=investment market)

lose one's market　商機を逃がす

maintain the share of the market　市場のシェアを維持する

make a market　マーケット・メークを行う, 市場を形成する, 値付け業務を行う, マーケット・メーキング, (株式・市場の) 人気をあおる, 空 (から) 景気をつける (=market making)

make a [one's] market of　〜から利益を得る, 〜を利用する, 〜を食いものにする

make inroads in the market　市場に参入する　(=enter the market)

mar one's market　取引を台なしにする

market access　市場への参入 [接近], 市場アクセス

market analysis　市場分析

market crash　暴落　(=crash)

market development　市場開発

market downfall　市場急落

market growth　市場の拡大, 市場の伸び, 市場の成長　(=market expansion)

market interest rate　市中金利
(=open market rate)

market leader　商品購入決定者, 商品購入影響者, 消費者, 主力株, 主導株, 先導株, 業界トップ, マーケット・リーダー

market maker　市場開拓者, 市場を形成する消費者, 証券業者, 証券ディーラー, 値付け業者, 仕手, 最大手企業, 売れ筋商品, マーケット・メーカー (「値付け業者」は, 株や債券などの流通市場で, 価格形成を行う証券業者のこと)

market opportunity　市場機会, ビジネス機会, 事業機会

market order　成り行き注文

market outlook　市場見通し

market overt　公開市場

market quotes　市場相場価額

market research firm　市場調査会社

market researcher　市場調査員

market trends　市場の動向, 市場動向

mend one's market　取引を有利にする

on [into, onto] the market　売りに出されている, 売りに出ている, 市販されている

on the open market　市販されている

one's market　商機, 売買の機会

play the market　株の投機をする, 株式に投機する, 商品に投機する, 相場をやる

price (oneself) out of the market　(相場を無視した) 無謀な値を付ける, 無茶な値段を付ける

primary market for securities　証券の発行市場

put 〜 on the market　〜を売りに出す, 〜を市場に出す, 〜を発売する, 〜を市販する

real estate market　不動産市場

secondary market　流通市場

security market　証券市場

seek a new market　新販路を求める

sensitive market　不安定市場, 不安定相場, 不安市況

shares on the market　流通している株式

stock and bond markets　株式・債券市場

stock market　株式市場

strong market　強気市場, 強気市況

tap the market　市場に登場する

time the market　市場の好機を選ぶ, 市場のタイミングをとらえる, 市場のタイミングを判断する, 市場のタイミングに合わせる, 市場のタイミングを図る

trading market　流通市場, 売買市場, トレーディング・マーケット

weak market　軟弱市況, 軟調市況　(=soft market)

withdraw from the Japanese market　日本市場から撤退する

◆Amid the strengthening of the yen and declines

M

in stock prices, the stock and financial markets appear to be wooing the BOJ to come up with additional financial measures to stabilize the markets. 円高・株安を受けて、株式や金融市場は、市場安定化に向けて日銀に追加の金融緩和策を打ち出すよう催促するような相場展開である。◆Crude oil prices have exceeded $70 a barrel in London and New York, setting all-time highs on these markets. ニューヨークとロンドン市場で原油価格が1バレル＝70ドルを上回って、両市場最高値を記録した。◆In expanding into India's market, Japanese companies must work out a strategy that includes possible infrastructure risks. インド市場に進出するにあたって、日本企業は、想定されるインフラ面でのリスクを念頭に置いた戦略を練る必要がある。◆Japanese deluxe wagyu beef has started to hit the market in Europe due to the lifting of a ban on beef exports from Japan to the European Union. 日本からEU（欧州連合）への牛肉輸出の解禁で、日本の高級和牛が欧州の市場に出回り始めた。◆We have received your letter of August 15, from which we note that you are in the market for our products. 8月15日付け貴状を拝受しました。それによると貴社は当社製品をご入用とのこと、確かに承（うけたまわ）りました。◆We should be glad to have your inquiries for our products when you are in the market again. 再びご入用の際は、当社製品に対してお引合いをいただければと思います。

M

market access barrier 市場参入障壁
◆The United States will continue to actively address anticompetitive activity, market access barriers, and or market-distorting trade practices. アメリカは、非競争的行為や市場参入障壁、市場を歪める商慣行に引き続き取り組んで行く方針だ。

market and sell 市場に出して販売する, 販売する
◆Supplier and Distributor recognize that in order to market and sell Products effectively in the territory described in Exhibit A, it is necessary that they be marketed and sold through Distributor. 別紙Aに記載する契約地域で本製品を効果的に販売するためには、販売店を通じて販売する必要があることを、供給者と販売店は認識している。

market condition 市況, 市場の状況, 市場環境
◆At the beginning of each calendar year, ABC shall make a report to XYZ on the sales of the Product during the previous year and general market conditions. 各暦年の初めに、ABCは、XYZに対して前年度の契約品の販売（実績）と市況全般について報告するものとする。

market-distorting trade practices 市場を歪める商慣行
◆The United States will continue to actively address anticompetitive activity, market access barriers, and or market-distorting trade practices. アメリカは、非競争的行為や市場参入障壁、市場を歪める商慣行に引き続き取り組んで行く方針だ。

market economy 市場経済, 市場型経済
capitalist market economy 資本主義市場経済
emerging market economies 新興市場国, 急成長市場国
move to a market economy 市場経済への移行
open market economies 自由市場経済, 市場経済
socialist market economy 社会主義市場経済
◆The most advanced market economies of Japan and the Unites States, if bound together, would put a powerful brake on protectionism. もっとも高度に進化した市場経済の日本と米国が手を結べば、保護貿易主義化に強力な歯止めをかけることになろう。

market economy model 市場経済モデル
◆In countries that are based on a genuine market economy model, current account balances are just the results of imports and exports freely carried out by the private sector. 純粋な市場経済モデルに立つ国では、経常収支は、民間が行う自由な輸出・輸入活動の結果に過ぎない。

market for startups 新興企業向け市場
◆Japan Exchange Group Inc. reorganized the group's cash equity markets into the TSE's First and Second sections, Jasdaq and Mothers markets for startups, and the Tokyo Pro Market. 日本取引所グループは、同グループの株式市場を、東証一部・二部、新興企業向け市場のジャスダック、マザーズと、東京プロマーケット（プロ投資家向け市場）に再編した。

market oligopoly 市場の寡占（かせん）
◆Dumping may force rival companies out of business and lead to a market oligopoly. 不当廉売は、同業他社を廃業に追い込み、市場の寡占（かせん）につながる可能性がある。

market opening 市場開放
◆The United States urged Japan to redouble its market opening efforts in key sectors such as telecommunications, agriculture and automobiles. アメリカは、日本に対して、通信や農業、自動車などの主要分野で市場開放努力を一段と進めるよう強く迫った。

market plunge 市場の低迷, 相場の下落, 株安（stock market plunge）
◆Two factors responsible for the recent market plunge are speculative moves intended to drive down stock prices and high-speed, automated transactions. 最近の株安を招いた二つの要因は、売り崩し（大量の売りを出して相場を崩すこと）を狙う投機筋の動きと、（瞬時に売買が成立する）コンピュータでの高速の自動取引である。

market potential 市場潜在力, 市場潜在性, 市場の可能性

market research 市場調査, マーケット・リサーチ
◆East Japan Railway Co. sold records of the use of its Suica cards, prepaid e-money cards, at rail-

ways and subways, to business firms that analyze them for market research, without prior consent of the users. JR東日本は、カード利用者の事前の同意［承諾］を得ないで、プリペイド式電子マネー・カード「スイカ」の使用による鉄道や地下鉄での乗降履歴を、分析して市場調査などに使う企業に売却していた。

market share 市場占拠率, 市場占有率, 市場シェア, マーケット・シェア, シェア
(=share; ⇒global market share)

acquire market share シェアを獲得する, シェアを確保する

build up market share シェアを確保する, シェアを拡大する

carve［capture］market share シェアを奪う, シェアを獲得する

command market share シェアを支配する, 圧倒的なシェアを握る

compete for market share 市場シェアを争う, シェアを争う, 市場シェアをめぐって争う, 市場シェア獲得競争をする

declining market share 市場シェアの低下

dominant market share 圧倒的な市場シェア, 圧倒的なシェア

dwindling market share 先細りのシェア, シェアの減少, シェアの先細り

expand one's market share シェアを拡大する, シェアを高める

expansion of market share 市場シェアの拡大

gain market share シェアを獲得する, シェアを拡大させる［拡大する］, シェアを奪う

gains in market share 市場シェアの拡大, 市場シェアの伸び

grab market share シェアを奪う

have a 20 percent market share 20％のシェアがある

hold market share シェアを占める, シェアを守る

improve market share シェアを拡大する, シェアを高める

increase market share シェアを拡大する, シェアを高める

keep hold of market share シェアを維持する

large market share 高いシェア

leading market share 業界トップのシェア

lose market share シェアを失う, シェアを奪われる

maintain market share シェアを維持する, 市場シェアを維持する (=keep hold of market share)

make market share gains シェアを伸ばす

market share erosion 市場占有率［市場シェア］の低下, シェアの低下

market share expansion シェア拡大

market share gain 市場占有率［市場シェア］の拡大, シェアの拡大

market share loss 市場シェア低下

preserve one's market share シェアを守る (=protect market share)

race for market share シェア拡大戦争

recovering market share シェアの回復

rising market share シェアの拡大

slipping［falling］market share シェアの低下

soaring market share シェアの急拡大

take market share シェアを伸ばす

vulnerable market share 浸食されやすいシェア, シェアの流動性

win back market share from 〜からシェアを奪い返す［奪い取る］

world market share 世界市場でのシェア, 世界シェア（占有率）
(=global［international］market share)

◆Apple and other foreign electronics companies are able to obtain high-tech parts at low prices as they hold large market shares in the area of smartphones. アップルなどの海外家電メーカーは、スマートフォンの分野で高いマーケット・シェア（市場占有率）を占めているので、高性能部品を安く仕入れることができる。◆The market share of the newly merged firm is expected to be relatively low in the international market. 合併新会社の市場シェアは、国際市場では比較的低いと思われる［予想される］。

market supply and demand 市場の需給
◆Changes in exchange rates are a result of multiple factors, including the balance of international payments and market supply and demand. 為替相場の変動は、国際収支や市場の需給など複数要因によるものだ。

marketability （名）市場性

marketable （形）売買可能な, 売買できる, 市販可能な, 市場性のある, 市場向きの, よく売れる, 売り物になる

marketable area 販売区域

marketable assets 市場性のある資産

marketable commodity 市場性のある商品, 売れ行きの良い商品, 売買可能な商品

marketable debt 市場性証券

marketable equity securities 市場性のある持ち分証券, 市場性ある株式

marketable goods 市販可能財

marketable price 市場価格

marketable product 商品, 市場性ある生産物

marketable quality 市販可能財

marketable securities 市場性証券, 市場性のある有価証券

marketable skill 売り物になる技術

marketable surplus 市場向け余剰

marketable Treasury financing　米国債発行

marketable value　市場価値, 市価

non-marketable debt［issues］　非市場性証券

non-marketable securities　非市場性証券, 市場性のない有価証券

marketable title　瑕疵（かし）なき権原, 売買できる権原
◆Seller has good and marketable title to the Shares, free and clear of any and all covenants, conditions, restrictions, voting trust arrangements, liens, options and adverse claims or rights. 売り主は, 一切の約束, 条件, 制約, 議決権信託契約, 担保権, 選択権, 不利益を及ぼすクレームや権利をまったく負担しない本株式を売買できる正当な権原を持っている。

marketing　（名）市場取引, 市販, 販売, 売買, 流通, 配給, 分配, 公開, マーケティング（「マーケティング」は, 優れた製品を適正な価格で, 最適な販売チャネルを通じて消費者に提供するための活動のこと。⇒stealth marketing）

direct marketing　直接販売

global marketing　世界規模のマーケティング

marketing agreement　マーケティング契約

marketing campaign　販促キャンペーン

marketing channel　販売チャネル, 販売経路, 流通チャネル, マーケティング・チャネル（ある商品・サービスがメーカーから最終消費者に渡るまでの取引の流れの経路。主に, メーカーの営業所, 卸売り業者, 小売業者, 配送業者などによって構成される）

marketing clout　営業力

marketing environment　市場環境

marketing goal　マーケティング目標

marketing plan　営業計画, マーケティング計画

marketing strategy　マーケティング戦略（マーケティング目標を達成するための活動で, 具体的にはターゲットを設定し, それに向けて最も効果的なマーケティング・ミックス（商品, 価格, プロモーション・チャネルなど）を構築すること）

niche marketing　ニッチ・マーケティング（未開発のすき間市場・ニッチ市場への適応をめざすマーケティング）

social marketing　ソーシャル・マーケティング（企業の社会的責任を果たすために行う企業の市場活動）

test marketing　試験販売

transaction marketing　取引志向マーケティング

◆The parties hereto desire to establish a stock corporation under the laws of Japan to undertake and accomplish the manufacture and marketing of the products in the territory as described in Article 1. 本契約当事者は, 第1条に定める地域で本製品の製造とマーケティングを引き受け, 実行するために, 日本法のもとに株式会社を設立することを望んでいる。

marking　（名）荷印の刷り込み

CE marking　CEマーキング（CEはConformité Européenne（ヨーロッパの安全規格に一致している）の略）

mask work right　マスクワーク権（知的所有権・知的財産権の一つで, 日本法の半導体集積回路の「回路配置利用権」に相当）

master　（形）最重要な, 主要な, 中心の, 基本の, コピー元の, 元になる

master agreement　標準契約, 基本協約, 基準協定, マスター契約

master file　基本ファイル

master franchise agreement　マスター・フランチャイズ契約

master licensee　マスター・ライセンシー

master plan　基本計画, 総合基本計画

master production schedule　基準清算計画, MPS

material　（名）材料, 材質, 原料, 資料, 素材, 物質, 構成物質, 服地

presentation materials　プレゼンテーション用資料

promotional materials　販促資料

related materials　関連資料
◆Copyrighted materials can be used freely under the U.S. law as long as it is considered "fair use." 著作権のある著作物は, 「公正な利用」であれば, 米国の法律では自由に利用することができる。◆Domestic lumber has lost international competitiveness year after year, hit by inexpensive imported materials. 国産材が安い輸入材に押されて年々, 国際競争力を失っている。◆Measures to tighten quality controls on Chinese food products, taken by many Japanese manufacturers in China, include more stringent tests on the amounts of agricultural chemicals used at Chinese farms and on the quality of processing materials used at Chinese factories. 中国の日系メーカーの多くが取っている中国産食品の品質管理強化策としては, 中国農場での農薬使用量の検査や中国の工場で使用している加工原料の品質チェックの強化などが挙げられる。◆The seller warrants that the Goods will be free from defects in material and workmanship for a period as specified in this agreement. 売り主は, 本契約で定める期間, 本商品が材料と仕上げの面で欠陥がないことを保証する。

material　（形）物質的な, 肉体の, 肉体的な, 官能的な, 物資の, 有形の, 具体的な, 世俗的な, 重要な, 重大な, 不可欠な, 欠かせない, 大きな影響力のある, 影響力の強い
◆The consolidated financial statements conform in all material respects with International Finan-

cial Reporting Standards（IFRSs）. 連結財務書類［連結財務諸表］の重要事項は，すべて国際財務報告基準に適合している。

material breach 重大な違反, 重大違反
◆Upon the occurrence of any material breach, the nondefaulting party may terminate this agreement by giving a written notice of termination specifying the nature of the material breach. 重大な違反が発生した場合，違反を行っていない当事者は，その重大な違反の性格を明記した書面による解除通知を行って本契約を解除することができる。

material obligation under this agreement 本契約上の重大な義務, 本契約に基づく重大な義務
◆In the event either party fails to fulfill its material obligations under this agreement, the parties hereto shall first make efforts to settle to their mutual satisfaction any matter causing such failure as expeditiously and amicably as possible. 当事者の一方が本契約上の重大な義務の履行を怠った場合、本契約当事者は、できるかぎり迅速かつ友好的に、当該不履行を引き起こした事項について先ず双方の満足の行くよう解決する努力をするものとする。

material omission 重大な遺漏（いろう）
◆These are material omissions which in our view constitute another material breach. これらは重大な遺漏で、われわれの考えでは、もう一つの重大な違反に当たる。

material violation 重大な違反

matter （名）問題, 主題, 対象, 内容, 事項, 議題, 事態, 事柄, 主要事実, 重要
all matters relating hereto 本契約に関連する一切の事項
as to matters involving ～に関する事項については
this agreement and all matters related thereto 本契約と本契約に関するすべての事項
◆This agreement, and all matters relating hereto, including any matter or dispute arising out of this agreement, shall be interpreted, governed, and enforced according to the laws of the State of New York, U.S.A. 本契約と、本契約から生じるすべての事項または紛争を含めて本契約に関連する一切の事項は、米国ニューヨーク州法に従って解釈し、同法を適用し、同法に従って権利を行使する。

matured obligation 期日到来債務

maximum （名）最高, 最高点, 最大, 最大量, 最大数, 最大限, 極大, 上限 （形）最高の, 最大の, 最大限の
be over the maximum 限度を越える
export maximum 輸出最大量
maximum capacity 最大生産能力
maximum hour legislation 最高就業時間規定
maximum interest rate 最高金利, 最高利子率,

最高利率
maximum level 最高水準, 最大水準
maximum liability 責任限度, 責任限度額, 責任の最高限度額, 賠償責任限度額
maximum limit 上限
maximum limits 発行枠, 発行限度, 最高限度, 最高限度額
maximum order quantity 最大発注量
maximum price 上限価格, 最高価格
maximum quantity 最大数量, 最大量, 最大在庫量
maximum rate of growth 最大成長率, 極大成長率
maximum scale［size］ 最大規模
maximum shelf life 品質保持期限
maximum stock 最高在庫, 最高在庫量
maximum sustainable yield 最大持続生産量
maximum tariff 最高税率
maximum turnover 最高回転率
◆In the joint venture with an Indian investment bank, Tokyo Marine Holdings Inc. put up about 26%, the maximum a foreign investor is allowed in an Indian company, of the new firm's capital. インドの投資銀行との合弁事業で、東京海上ホールディングスは、新会社の資本金の約26%（外資の持ち分比率の上限）を出資した。

maximum rate 最高利率
◆Interest shall accrue on any delinquent amounts owed by Distributor for Products at the lesser of 18% per annum, or the maximum rate permitted by applicable usury law. 利息は、販売店が負っている本製品の延滞金について発生し、年18%の利率と適用される利息制限法で認められる最高利率のうちいずれか低いほうの利率によるものとする。

may （助動）～することができる、～する権利がある（契約上の権利、許可を表す）、～してもよい、～かもしれない
◆May we expect your reply at your earliest convenience？ 早急にご返事をいただけるものと［賜るものと］、期待しております。◆The Seller may withhold delivery or cancel the Agreement if the Buyer fails to establish the letter of credit by the date stipulated in this Agreement. 買い主が本契約で定める期限までに信用状を開設することができない場合、売り主は、引渡しを保留するか契約を解除することができる。◆You may count on our best efforts so long as you can maintain moderate prices. 手頃な価格［格安料金］を維持できるかぎり、当社は最大限の努力を貴社にお約束します。◆You may expect a large order from us very soon. 早速、貴社に大口の注文を差し上げます。

may not ～してはならない（禁止を表わす）、～することはできない、～する権利はない、～でないかもしれない
◆We fear that we may not accept your order as the production of these products has been sus-

pended for some time. この製品の生産がしばら
く中止となっておりますので、貴社の注文はお受け
致しかねます。◆We fear we may not supply exactly the same articles you want as they are not
in our lines. 貴社お望みの商品は扱っていません
ので、当社としてはお望みの品とまったく同じもの
を提供することはできないと思います。◆We may
not have to add that we do not hold ourselves
responsible for the corresponding delay in shipment if your actions should not be taken in time.
言うまでもなく［申すまでもなく］、貴社の打つ手
が遅れたら、それに伴って生じる船積みの遅延に
対して、当社は責任を負いません。

MDP 異業種間共同事業（multidisciplinary
partnership［practice］の略。弁護士と公認会
計士やコンサルタント等が共同で法的サービ
スを提供すること）

mean （動）意味する、表す、意図する、〜する
つもりである、〜しようと思う、（ある目的
に）予定する、計画する、当てる、〜の重要性
［意味］を持つ、〜を本気で言う、〜する結果
になる、〜の前兆である
be meant to 〜しなければならない、〜する
ことになっている、（〜の）狙い［目的］は〜
にある
mean and include 〜を意味する
◆The life insurers' status as large shareholders
means that when the market dives, their portfolios also take a tumble. 大株主としての生命保険
会社の地位は、株価が大きく下がると資産内容も
急激に悪化することを意味する。

meaning （名）意味
◆In this Agreement, the following words and expressions shall, unless the context otherwise requires, have the following meanings. 本契約で、
次の語句と表現は、文脈上、別段の意味を必要と
しないかぎり、次の意味を持つものとする。

mediation （名）調停、仲裁、メディエー
ション

meet （動）要求・条件などを満たす、要求に
応じる、費用を支払う、債務を履行する、課題
などをうまく処理する
meet one's credit terms 与信条件を満たす
meet the demand 需要を満たす、需要に応
じる
◆All letters of credit shall be maintained in sufficient amounts and the period necessary to meet
all payment obligations. すべての信用状は、すべ
ての支払い債務を履行するに足る金額と支払い債
務の履行に必要な期間を維持するものとする。◆
As there is a limit to our output at present, we
have some difficulty in meeting the demand. 現
在のところ、当社の生産には限界があり、需要に
応じるのはかなり困難です。

megafloat （名）超大型浮体式海洋構造物、メ
ガフロート

memorandum for the tie-up 提携覚書

memorandum of agreement 合意覚書

memorandum of understanding 了解覚
書、了解事項覚書、基本合意書、意思表明状
（letter of intent）、予備的合意書
◆This agreement supersedes and replaces any
prior understanding, agreement, statement of intent or memorandum of understanding, written
or oral. 本契約は、書面または口頭による従前の
一切の了解、合意、意図の表明または了解覚書に
優先するもので、これらに代わるものである。

mentioned above 上記の、前記の
◆Notices, demands and communications mentioned above shall be deemed to be received ten
(10) days after their dispatch. 上記の通知、要
求、通信は、発信の10日後に受領したものと見な
される。

mentioned and referred to 記載した

mercantile （形）商業の、商人の、商売の、貿
易の、重商主義の、報酬目当ての、欲得ずくの
mercantile bill 商業手形
mercantile burglary insurance 商品盗難保険
mercantile capital 商業資本
mercantile credit 商業信用、企業間信用、商業
信用貸し
mercantile（credit）agency 商業興信所、興信
所、信用調査機関 （=commercial agency,
commercial enquiry office, credit bureau）
mercantile house 商社
mercantile law 商事法、商法
（=commercial law, law merchant）
mercantile marine 商船、商船隊、海運力
mercantile nation 貿易国
mercantile open stock burglary policy 商業財
盗難保険
mercantile paper 商業証券、商業手形、売買手
形、為替手形、約束手形
mercantile report 商業興信報告
mercantile risk 商業危険、商品危険、商品リ
スク
mercantile trade［trading, transaction］ 商
取引

mercantile exchange 商品取引所、商業取引
所、マーカンタイル取引所
Chicago Mercantile Exchange シカゴ・マー
カンタイル取引所、CME
New York Mercantile Exchange ニューヨー
ク商業取引所、NYMEX［Nymex］
◆Oil prices on the New York Mercantile Exchange soared to the $100 level a barrel for the
first time during the trading hours. ニューヨー
ク・マーカンタイル取引所の原油価格は、取引時
間中に初めて1バレル＝100ドル台まで上昇した。
◆On the New York Mercantile Exchange, crude
oil futures for October delivery rose 31 cents to
settle at $101.18 a barrel. ニューヨーク商業取引

所では、10月渡しの原油先物が前日比で0.31ドル値上りして、終値は1バレル＝101.8ドルとなった。

merchandise （名）商品, 物品, 品物, 製品, モノ

affordable and high-quality merchandise　手頃で高品質の商品

basic merchandise　基礎商品, 基本商品

carry merchandise　商品を取り揃える

display a merchandise　商品を展示する

examine the merchandise　商品を点検する

family-oriented merchandise　ファミリー向け商品

fashion merchandise　流行商品, ファッション商品

general merchandise　雑貨

general merchandise store　総合小売業, GMS

high-tech merchandise　ハイテク商品

international merchandise　一般商品

low-end ［lower-end］ merchandise　低価格品, 普及品

merchandise account　商品勘定

merchandise agent　商品販売代理店

merchandise allowance　商品値引き

merchandise and services　商品とサービス

merchandise assortment　品揃え

merchandise balance　商品取引収支, 貿易収支

merchandise bond　商品券

merchandise check　商品小切手, 商品券

merchandise declaration　出荷品明細書

merchandise display　商品展示, 商品ディスプレー

merchandise exports　商品輸出, 財の輸出額

merchandise freight　商品運送料［輸送料］, 商品運賃

merchandise handled　取扱い商品

merchandise insurance　商品保険

merchandise inventory　商品在庫, 商品棚卸し高, 繰越し商品

merchandise inventory turnover　商品在庫回転率

merchandise item　商品品目, 品目

merchandise line　取扱い商品, 商品構成, 商品ライン

merchandise management　商品管理

merchandise mark　登録商標, トレードマーク （=trademark）

merchandise market　商品市場, 製品市場

merchandise mix　商品構成, 品揃え

merchandise note　商品約束手形

merchandise plan　商品計画

merchandise procurement　商品調達

merchandise purchased　購入商品

merchandise receive　商品受領, 商品入荷

merchandise resources　仕入先

merchandise return　返品

merchandise sourcing capability　商品調達力

merchandise to arrive　未着品

merchandise transfer　商品移動

merchandise turnover （ratio）　商品回転率

original merchandise　オリジナル商品

purchase merchandise　商品を買う［購入する, 仕入れる］

range of merchandise　品揃え

rapidly selling merchandise　売れ筋商品

reorder merchandise　商品を補充する

return the merchandise　返品する

sales merchandise ratio　商品回転率

seasonal merchandise　季節商品

sell merchandise　商品を売る

staple merchandise　主力商品, 主要生産物

stock merchandise　商品の在庫を確保しておく

superior merchandise　優良商品

top-of-the-line merchandise　最高級品

upscale merchandise　高級品

merchandise trade　モノの貿易, モノの取引, 商品貿易, 財の輸出入, 貿易取引

merchandise trade balance　貿易収支

merchandise trade gap　モノの貿易赤字, 財の貿易赤字, 貿易収支の赤字額, 商品貿易の赤字, 貿易赤字　（=merchandise trade deficit）

merchandise trade surplus　モノの貿易黒字, 財の貿易黒字, 貿易収支の黒字額, 商品貿易の黒字, 貿易黒字

◆Both bilateral and multilateral talks regarding China's merchandise trade are now close to conclusion. 現在、中国のモノの貿易に関しては、二国間交渉も多国間交渉もほぼ終了している。◆The surplus in merchandise trade in August stood at ￥303.7 billion against a deficit of ￥141.2 billion a year earlier. 8月の（輸出額から輸入額を差し引いた）貿易収支は、前年同月の1,412億円の赤字に対して3,037億円の黒字となった。

merchantability （名）商品性, 市販可能性, 市販性, 市場性

◆No other warranties of any kind, whether statutory, written, oral, express or implied, including warranties of fitness for a particular purpose or merchantability shall apply. 特定目的への適合性または商品性の保証を含めて、法定か書面によるか口頭によるかを問わず、また明示・黙示を問わず、他のいかなる種類の保証も適用されないものとする。

◆The seller expressly disclaims any warranty of conditions, fitness for use or merchantability. 売り主は、状態、用途適合性または商品性の保証を明確に否認する。

merchantable quality 商品性, 適商品質

  good merchantable quality 適商品質, 適商品質条件

  of merchantable quality 商品性がある

merger （名）合併, 経営統合, 事業統合, 統合, 吸収合併, 併合 （⇒corporate merger）

  acquisitions and mergers 企業取得と合併

  agree to the proposed merger 合併案件に同意する

  announce a merger 合併を発表する

  approve a merger 合併を承認する

  arrange a merger 合併を仕組む, 合併の段取りをつける

  big merger 大型合併 （=large merger）

  block a merger 合併を阻(はば)む

  business merger 経営統合, 企業の合併 （=merger of businesses）

  conglomerate merger 複合的合併, 複合企業型合併, コングロマリット合併

  debt-financed merger 借入れによる合併

  defensive merger 防衛的合併

  downstream merger 逆吸収合併（子会社による親会社の吸収のこと）

  economics of a merger 合併の経済効果

  enter into a merger 合併契約を結ぶ[締結する]

  friendly merger 友好的買収

  giant merger 巨大合併

  horizontal merger 水平的合併, 同業他社との合併

  hostile merger 敵対的買収

  megamerger 超大型合併, 超巨大合併 （=mega-merger）

  merger of operations 事業部門の合併

  merger on an equal basis 対等合併 （=merger of equals）

  merger partner 合併相手

  merger ratio 合併比率

  mergers and realignments 統合や再編, 統合・再編

  multi-merger 多角的合併

  oppose a merger 合併に反対する

  outright merger 友好的合併

  regulatory-assisted merger 行政指導型合併

  seek a merger 合併を求める

  stock-for-stock merger 株式交換による合併

  the merger of the two firms' holding companies and banking divisions 両社の持ち株会社と銀行分野の統合

  vertical merger 垂直的合併

  withdraw from a merger 合併を見送る, 合併を中止する

  ◆The U.S. Federal Trade Commission（FTC）concluded there was not enough evidence that a Sony-BMG merger would violate U.S. antitrust laws. 米連邦取引委員会(FTC)は、ソニーとBMG（独複合メディア大手ベルテルスマンの音楽事業部門）の統合が米国の独占禁止法に違反することを示す十分な証拠はない、との結論を下した。◆To strengthen its capital base ahead of the merger, the company will raise ￥30 billion through the allotment of new shares to DDI by the end of September. 合併に先立って資本基盤を強化するため、同社は、DDIへの新株割当てにより9月末までに300億円の資本を調達する。

merger and acquisition deals M&A（合併・買収）取引, M&A案件

  ◆The recent increase in merger and acquisition deals will boost revenues and corporate value. 最近のM&A（合併・買収）取引の増加は、企業収益の増加や企業価値の向上につながる。

merger negotiations 合併交渉, 経営統合交渉 （=merger talks）

  ◆Kirin and Suntory, the nation's two largest food and beverage makers, have started merger negotiations. 国内最大手の食品・飲料メーカーのキリンとサントリーが、経営統合の交渉に入った。

merger or consolidation 吸収合併または新設合併

  ◆The action on any merger or consolidation with or into any other corporation or entity or any dissolution not otherwise in accordance with this agreement requires the unanimous written approval of all the shareholders of the new company. 他の法人もしくは事業体との吸収合併もしくは新設合併、または別段に本契約に従わない解散に関する決議は、新会社の株主全員の書面による全員一致の決議を必要とする。

mergers and acquisitions 企業の合併・買収, M&A （=merger and acquisition; ⇒hostile mergers and acquisitions）

  ◆Mergers and acquisitions to pursue economies of scale will be carried out worldwide. 規模の経済[規模の拡大]を追求するためのM&A（企業の合併・買収）は今後、国際的規模で実施される見込みだ。◆Suntory Holdings Ltd. is expected to use about ￥500 billion in estimated proceeds from the listing of its beverage and food unit to finance mergers and acquisitions abroad. サントリーホールディングスは、清涼飲料・食品子会社の上場により推定で5,000億円程度の資金を調達して、海外企業の買収に充てる見込みだ。

METI 経済産業省 （Ministry of Economy, Trade and Industryの略）

  ◆The METI has decided to expand the scope of government-backed trade insurance for overseas social infrastructure projects. 経済産業省は、海外の社会基盤（インフラ）事業に対する政府保証付

き貿易保険の対象を拡大することを決めた。

Middle East　中東
◆Japan has to import most of its fossil fuels from the Middle East in which supplies and prices remain unstable. 日本は、化石燃料の大半を、供給量も価格も不安定な中東からの輸入に頼っている。

middleman　（名）仲買人, 仲卸業者, 仲介者
◆A financial intermediary acts as a middleman between cash surplus units in the economy（savers）and deficit spending units（borrowers）. 金融仲介機関は、経済の資金余剰主体(貯蓄者)と資金不足主体(借り手)との間に立つ仲介者として機能している。

minimum　（名）最低, 最小, 最小限, 最小値, ミニマム　（形）最低の, 最小の, 最小限の
amount of minimum purchase　最低購入量
minimum access　最低輸入量, 最低輸入義務, 最低輸入枠, ミニマム・アクセス（義務としてのコメの最低輸入量）
minimum access quota　ミニマム・アクセス
minimum bid　最低入札価格
minimum capital　最低資本金, 最低自己資本
minimum freight　最低運賃
minimum net sales　最低純販売額
minimum price　最低価格
minimum quota　最低割当て, 最低割当量
minimum sales amount　最低販売金額
minimum sales quantity　最低販売数量

minimum amount　最低金額, 金額の下限
◆Hoping to attract individual investors by lowering the minimum amount needed to buy stock, more and more publicly listed companies are carrying out stock splits this year. But a stock split does not necessarily mean a company's stock price will rise. 株式を買うのに最低限必要な金額を引き下げて個人投資家を拡大する狙いから、今年は株式分割を実施する上場企業が増えている。しかし、株式を分割しても、企業の株価が必ずしも上がるわけではない。

minimum guarantee　最低保証, 最低保証料, 最低保証額
◆Provided Licensor delivers the software without any bug, by no later than the delivery dates, Licensee shall pay Licensor a minimum guarantee of royalties of one million U.S. dollars（$1,000,000）. ライセンサーがバグのないソフトウエアを引渡し日以前に引き渡した場合、ライセンシーは、ロイヤルティの最低保証料としてライセンサーに100万米ドルを支払うものとする。

minimum purchase　最低購入量
minimum purchase amount　最低購入金額, 最低購入額
minimum purchase guarantee　最低購入保証
minimum purchase obligation　最低購入義務
◆Minimum purchase for the successive conse-

quent year or years shall be decided upon by mutual negotiation before commencing such each year. その後に続く年度の最低購入量は、当該各年度の開始前に相互の協議により決定する。

minimum purchase quantity　最低購入量, 最低購入数量
◆After the second year of this agreement, the yearly minimum purchase quantity shall be decided by negotiation between the parties hereto. 本契約の2年目以降、年間最低購入量は、本契約当事者間の協議により決定する。

minimum quantity　最低引取り数量, 最低数量
minimum quantity acceptable　最小引受可能数量
◆For each one（1）year period commencing on the date hereof during this agreement, ABC shall purchase from XYZ not less than a minimum quantity of the products as set forth below. 本契約日から始まる本契約期間中の各1年間に、ABCは下記の最低数量以上の本製品をXYZから購入するものとする。

minimum quota　最低割当量
◆Failure by Distributor to sell the minimum quota for any given period set forth in Exhibit B will constitute a default of this agreement by Distributor. 販売店が付属書類Bに記載する一定期間の最低割当量を販売できなかった場合には、販売店による本契約違反となる。

minimum royalty　最低ロイヤルティ, 最低使用料, ミニマム・ロイヤルティ
◆Even if the royalty computed pursuant to the preceding subparagraph b）of this Article does not amount to five million（5,000,000）Japanese yen, Licensee guarantees to pay Licensor said sum as a minimum royalty. 本条の前記b）項に従って計算したロイヤルティの額が500万円に達しない場合でも、ライセンシーは、上記金額をミニマム・ロイヤルティとしてライセンサーに支払うことを保証する。

mining　（名）採鉱, 採炭業, 鉱業
coal mining　炭鉱業, 石炭採掘
mining and manufacturing production　鉱工業生産
mining damage　鉱害
mining industry　鉱業
mining lease　採鉱権, 租鉱権
mining right　鉱業権
mining tax　鉱業税

mining and manufacturing products　鉱工業製品
◆The list of issues to be negotiated under the new round runs the gamut from farm products to mining and manufacturing products. 新ラウンドでの交渉分野は、農業製品から鉱工業製品にいたるまで多岐にわたっている。

minority shareholder 少数株主
◆Khazanah National which owns 69 percent of Malaysia Airlines has proposed to buy out minority shareholders to the carrier's board of directors. マレーシア航空株の69%を保有するカザナ・ナショナル社（政府系投資会社）は、少数株主の株を買い取ることを、同航空の取締役会に提案した。

mirror image rule 鏡像の原則

misappropriation （名）流用, 不正流用, 不正使用, 不正目的使用, 窃盗, 悪用, 着服, 横領, 背任横領, 使い込み
　fund misappropriation　資金の流用, 資金の着服
　misappropriation of any copyrights, trademarks or trade secrets　著作権, 商標または営業秘密の不正使用
　misappropriation of company assets　会社資産の横領, 会社資産の流用
◆ABC shall promptly notify XYZ of any infringement or attempted infringement or misappropriation of any copyrights, trademarks or trade secrets of XYZ to the licensed products. ABCは、許諾製品に対するXYZの著作権、商標または営業秘密が侵害された場合や侵害される恐れがある場合、不正使用されている場合には、XYZに直ちにそれを通知するものとする。

miscellaneous （形）いろいろな種類の, 多種多様の, 種々雑多な, 多面的な, 多方面にわたる, 多方面の, 多才な, 雑則, その他
　miscellaneous expenses　雑費
　miscellaneous goods　雑貨

misconduct （名）不正行為, 違法行為, 職権乱用, ずさんな管理・運営, 不始末
◆According to the Japanese Bankers Association's investigation, banks in Japan have not committed any misconduct involving the Tokyo interbank offered rate. 全国銀行協会の調査によると、日本の銀行は、東京銀行間取引金利（TIBOR）に関する不正行為はしていなかった。◆The seller shall not be responsible for defects in material and workmanship in the event that such defects arise from proven negligence or misconduct on the part of the buyer, its employees or customers. 材料と仕上がりの欠陥が買い主、買い主の従業員または顧客の側の明確な過失または不始末に起因して生じた場合、売り主は当該欠陥の責任を負わないものとする。

mislabeling （名）不当表示, 不正表示, 偽装表示
　food mislabeling　食品の不当表示
　mislabeling fraud　偽装工作
　mislabeling of beef products　牛肉偽装表示
◆A series of recent mislabeling scandals show that this wicked practice is common among meat dealers. 最近の一連の偽装表示事件は、この悪質な行為が食肉販売業者の間では常態化しているこ

とを示している。◆In response to a series of false labeling cases at hotels, department stores and elsewhere, the Consumer Affairs Agency will introduce a system to impose administrative monetary penalties on those involved in food mislabeling. ホテルや百貨店などで相次いだ（食材や食品メニューの）偽装表示事件を受けて、消費者庁は、食品の不当表示に関与した業者に課徴金を科す制度を導入する方針だ。

misrepresentation （名）不実表明, 不実表示, 虚偽の表示, 不真正表示
◆As stealth marketing by postings is problematic, the Consumer Affairs Agency has revised its guidelines for online transactions under the Law for the Prevention of Unreasonable Premiums and Misrepresentations concerning Products and Services. 書き込みによるステルス・マーケティングには問題があるので、消費者庁は、「景品表示法（不当景品類及び不当表示防止法）」のネット取引に関する指針を改正した。

missile development ミサイル開発
◆Five executives of a Tokyo-based engineering machinery maker were arrested on suspicion of systematically and illegally exporting to Iran jet mills that could be used for missile development. 東京に本社のある工学機器メーカーの役員5人が、ミサイル開発に転用できる粉砕機「ジェットミル」をイランに組織ぐるみで不正輸出していた容疑で逮捕された。

Missile Technology Control Regime ミサイル関連技術輸出規制, ミサイル関連技術規制MTCR
◆Exports of such machines are regulated by the Missile Technology Control Regime. このような機器の輸出は、「ミサイル関連技術規制」で規制されている。

missing, defective, or damaged 不足している、瑕疵がある、または損傷している
◆Promptly upon the receipt of a shipment of Products, Distributor shall examine the Products to determine whether any item or items to be included in the shipment are missing, defective, or damaged. 本製品の荷受けをしたら速やかに、販売店は、本製品を検査して積み荷中の目的物が不足（紛失）しているかどうか、瑕疵（かし）があるかどうか、または損傷しているかどうかを判断しなければならない。

MJP 法域以外での弁護士の法律業務
（multijurisdictional practiceの略。弁護士資格を付与された法域（国、州、地域）以外で弁護士が法律業務を行うこと）

model （名）モデル, 模型, 型, 型式, 車種, 機種, 新案, 模範
　business model　ビジネス・モデル
　buying behavior model　購買行動モデル
　consumer behavior model　消費者行動モデル
　decision model　意思決定モデル
　existing models　現行機種

MONE

leading model　主力車種, 主力車

management model　経営モデル

market model　市場モデル

Model Business Corporation Act　米国の模範事業会社法, MBCA

model change　型式変更, モデル・チェンジ

model home　モデル・ハウス　(=show house)

new model　新車種, 新機種, 新型車, ニュー・モデル

performance model　業績モデル

popular model　人気車種, 人気機種, 人気モデル

pricing model　価格決定モデル

simulation model　シミュレーション・モデル

stock valuation model　株式評価モデル

successive model　後継機種

utility model　実用新案

valuation model　評価モデル

working model　実用モデル, 実用模型

◆The model you have in mind has been out of make for the moment, and we could not tell exactly when our supply might be made. 貴社ご要望の機種はここ当分, 生産中止になっており, 供給可能の時期は目下不明です。

moderate　(形) 手頃な, 適度の, 程よい, 適当な, 並みの, 格安の, 安価の, 普通の, 中程度の, 中くらいの, 僅かの (slight), 小幅な, 軽度な, 穏健な, 穏健派の, 穏和な, 穏やかな, 緩慢な

a moderate demand　需要薄, 控え目な要求

a moderate income　まあまあの収入

at a moderate price　手頃な価格 [値段] で, 格安料金 [値段] で

buy for a moderate sum　手頃な金額で買う

low or [and] moderate-income individuals or families　中低所得者層

moderate discount　緩やかな証券発行差金

moderate economic growth path　穏やかな成長軌道

moderate growth　緩やかな伸び [成長, 経済成長], 穏やかな景気拡大

moderate inflation　緩慢なインフレ, 軽度のインフレ, 穏やかなインフレ

moderate level　緩やかな水準, 中程度の水準

moderate reliance on debt　適度な借入れ依存

moderate supply　供給薄

◆You may count on our best efforts so long as you can maintain moderate prices. 手頃な価格 [格安料金] を維持できるかぎり, 当社は最大限の努力を貴社にお約束します。

modification　(名) 修正, 変更, 改訂, 改変, 改組

modification, change, or amendment of this

agreement　本契約の修正、変更、改訂

modification of licensed program　許諾プログラムの改変

◆If you find the terms of payment acceptable, please confirm the order subject to the modifications above. この支払い条件がのめるなら, 上記の変更を条件として本注文の確認をお願いします。

modified procedures　手続きの変更, 変更手続き

◆Distributor shall bear any reasonable expenses incurred by Supplier in complying with such modified procedures. 販売店は、供給者のこの手続き変更に応じて生じる合理的な費用を負担しなければならない。

modified program　変更プログラム

◆The modified program shall be used by the licensee only on the machine designated by this agreement, and for its internal use of the licensee. 変更プログラムは、本契約で指定された機械 (コンピュータ) 上でだけ、またライセンシーの社内での使用にだけ、ライセンシーが使用するものとする。

modify and change　変更する

modify or alter　修正または変更する, 修正または改変する, 変更する

◆Licensee shall not modify or alter Products without the prior written approval of Licensor. ライセンシーは、ライセンサーの書面による事前の承認を得ないで本製品を修正または改変してはならない。

monetary control measure　金融調節手法

◆LDP President Abe said that he will ask the BOJ to buy construction bonds, or the government bonds issued for public works projects, through open market operations, which is a typical monetary control measure conducted by the central bank. 自民党の安倍総裁は、日銀が買い取る通常の金融調節手法である公開市場操作 [買いオペ] で、建設国債 (公共事業のために発行する国債) の買取りを日銀に求めると述べた。

monetary easing　金融緩和

◆Speculative money has poured into emerging economies, causing an appreciation of their currencies and asset inflation because of drastic monetary easing by Japan, the United States and Europe. 日米欧の大胆な [大規模な] 金融緩和で、投機マネーが新興国に流れ込み、新興国の通貨高や資産インフレを招いている。

monetary policy　金融政策

◆The U.S. monetary policy has a major impact on global liquidity and capital flows. 米国の金融政策は、国際流動性と国際資本移動に大きな影響力を持つ。

money　(名) 金銭, 金員, 資金, 通貨, 金融, マネー

◆The Borrower wishes to borrow from the Lender certain amount of money for its ＿＿＿. 借主は、貸主から＿＿＿の資金として一定の金員を

M

MONE 316

借り受けることを希望している。

money laundering 不正資金の洗浄, 資金洗浄, マネー・ロンダリング （=money washing: 犯罪で得た資金の出所や所有者を隠す行為）
◆Bitcoin deals may be abused as they are highly anonymous and in the United States, a trader who gave bitcoin to an illegal drug dealer faced prosecution on charges of money laundering. ビットコインでの取引は, 匿名性が高いので悪用される可能性があり, 米国では, 違法な麻薬取引の当事者にビットコインを提供した業者が, マネー・ロンダリング（資金洗浄）の罪で刑事訴追された。
◆Money laundering is the practice of legitimizing money gained through illegal drug and gun sales or other crimes by putting it through bank accounts. マネー・ロンダリングは, 麻薬や銃器の不正販売やその他の犯罪で得た資金を, 銀行口座を経由させて合法的に見せる行為だ。◆The U.S. government froze the assets of four individuals and eight entities that were involved in illicit activities such as money laundering, currency counterfeiting and narcotics trafficking. 米政府は, 資金洗浄（マネー・ロンダリング）や通貨偽造, 麻薬取引などの違法行為に関与している4個人, 8団体の資産を凍結した。

monies due 支払い期限にある金銭

monopoly （名）独占, 独占権, 専売, 専売権, 専売商品, 独占商品
Antimonopoly Law 独占禁止法
buyer's monopoly 買い手独占
market monopoly 市場独占
monopoly price 独占価格
monopoly provider 独占企業
perfect monopoly 完全独占
regional monopoly 地域独占 （=local monopoly）
technology monopoly 技術独占
trade monopoly 貿易独占, 交易独占
◆The Trademark Law was enacted to protect a trademark by giving a monopoly such as an exclusive right and a prohibitive right to an owner of a trademark right. 商標法は, 商標権者に専用権や禁止権などの独占権を与えて商標を保護するために制定された。

monthly report 月次報告書

moral hazard 倫理観・責任感の欠如, 道徳的危険, モラル・ハザード
◆The global 28 megabanks will be subject to the FSB's new international requirement to absorb losses and reduce the moral hazard posed by these banks. 世界のメガ銀行28行が, これらの巨大銀行による損失の吸収とモラル・ハザード抑制に向けての金融安定化理事会（FSB）の新国際金融規制の対象になる見込みだ。

more or less than the contracted

quantity 契約数量より〜増減
◆Quantity is subject to a variation of 5% more or less than the contracted quantity at Seller's option unless otherwise specified. 数量は, 他にとくに明記しないかぎり, 売り主の裁量で契約数量より5%増減の変動が生じることがある。

more than 〜以上の（〜の数量を含まない。more than three people=4人以上）

mortgage agreement 抵当権設定契約

mortgage deed 抵当権設定契約, 譲渡抵当設定契約証書

most advanced technologies 最先端技術
◆The most advanced technologies are often at stake in lawsuits over intellectual property. 知的財産を巡る訴訟では, 最先端技術が争点になることが多い。

most favorable purchase terms and conditions 最も有利な購入条件
◆Supplier agrees to grant to Distributor the most favorable purchase terms and conditions given to any distributor or purchaser for resale of Products or similar products or equipment. 供給者は, 本製品または類似の製品, 装置の再販売の目的で販売業者や買い主に提供している最も有利な購入条件を, 販売店にも供与することに同意する。

most favored customer 最も優遇された契約条件を与えられる顧客

most favored nation 最恵国, MFN
◆Lawmakers voted 260-170 to continue for a year what is now called normal trade relations （NTR） and used to be called most favored nations（MFN） trade status. 議員が260対170で票決して, これまで最恵国待遇と呼ばれていた（中国に対する）正常通商関係を1年間継続することになった。

most favored nation treatment 最恵国待遇

motion （名）動議, 提案, 申立て, 異議申立て, 申請
◆The guarantor hereby waives, and agrees not to assert by way of motion as a defence or otherwise, in a suit, action or proceeding pursuant to this guarantee, any claim that this guarantee or the subject matter hereof may not be enforced in or by such courts. 保証人は, 本保証書に従う訴訟, 裁判または手続き［訴訟または訴訟手続き］で, 抗弁として申し立てることによりまたは他の方法により, 本保証書またはその主題を上記裁判所でまたはその裁判所が強制することはできないとの主張をここに放棄し, これを主張しないことに同意する。

motion to dismiss 訴え却下の申立て, 却下申立て

movement （名）動き, 行動, 活動, 運動, 移動, 動向, 流れ, 機運, 進展, 進行, 変化, 変動
capital movement 資本移動
cash and security movement 厳禁と証券の受

渡し
crude oil price movements　原油価格の変動

free trade movement　自由貿易運動, 自由貿易主義, 自由貿易化

interest rate movements　金利動向, 金利変動　(=movements in interest rates)

market movement　市場の動き, 相場の動き, 相場変動

merger movement　合併運動, 合併活動

price movement　価格変動, 物価動向

price movement restrictions　値幅制限

recession movement　景気後退の動き

seasonal movement　季節的変動

security price movement　証券の価格変動

stock price movement　株価変動, 株価動向

the movement of human resources　人材の移動

◆Export and import trends are influenced by various factors, including economic situations in and outside of the country, currency exchange rates and crude oil price movements. 輸出入動向は, 国内外の景気や為替相場, 原油価格の変動などの各種要因に左右される。◆The Trans-Pacific Partnership framework to promote free trade among member countries is expected to invigorate the movement of human resources. 加盟国間の自由貿易化を進めるための環太平洋経済連携協定 (TPP) で, 人材の移動も盛んになることが予想される。

m.s.　[MS, M/S]　機船 (motor shipの略。motor vesselともいう)
◆Your orders are arriving in Yokohama soon and will be transshipped on to m.s. "President Wilson" which is leaving Yokohama for your port on August 10. 貴注文は間もなく横浜に到着し, 貴地に向けて8月10日に横浜を出港予定のディーゼル船「プレジデント・ウイルソン」号に積み換える予定である。

MSDS　製品安全データシート (material safety data sheetsの略)

multidisciplinary partnership [practice]　異業種間共同事業, MDP (弁護士と公認会計士やコンサルタント等が共同で法的サービスを提供すること)

multijurisdictional practice　法域以外での弁護士の法律業務, MJP　(弁護士資格を付与された法域 (国, 州, 地域) 以外で弁護士が法律業務を行うこと)

multilateral　(形) 多国間の, 多国間主義の, 多国籍の, 多数国参加の, 多角的な, 多面的な, 多元的な, 多辺の

multilateral accord　多国間合意

multilateral agreement　多数当事者の合意, 多国間協定, 多辺的の協定, 多角協定

multilateral and nondiscriminatory world trade　多辺的の無差別貿易, 多辺的の無差別の世界貿易

multilateral trading system　国際貿易体制

multilateral treaty　多国間条約

new round of multilateral trade negotiations　新多角的の貿易交渉 (新ラウンド)

multilateral free trade　多角的の自由貿易, 多角的自由貿易体制
◆The WTO was inaugurated in 1995, as an outgrowth of the General Agreement on Tariffs and Trade, with the aim of promoting a framework for multilateral free trade toward 21st century. 世界貿易機関 (WTO) は, 21世紀に向けた多角的の自由貿易体制の推進を目的に, ガット (関税・貿易一般協定) を発展改組して1995年に発足した。

multilateral free trade system　多角的自由貿易体制
◆The WTO is trying to implement the full-fledged multilateral free trade system globally. 世界貿易機関 (WTO) は, 本格的な多角的の自由貿易体制を世界レベルで実施しようとしている。

multilateral talks　多国間協議, 多国間交渉
◆Both bilateral and multilateral talks regarding China's merchandise trade are now close to conclusion. 現在, 中国のモノの貿易に関しては, 二国間交渉も多国間交渉もほぼ終了している。

multilateral trade　多角貿易, 多角的の貿易, 多角的の通商, 多辺貿易, 求償貿易, バーター貿易

multilateral and non-discriminatory trade　多辺的[多角的]無差別の貿易

multilateral trade agreement　多角的貿易協定

multilateral trade negotiations　多角的の貿易交渉, 多角的の通商交渉, 多国間貿易交渉, MTN
◆The leaders of the Group of Eight major nations reconfirmed to ensure sustainable growth in the global economy and promote free trade through a new round of multilateral trade negotiations at the WTO. 主要8か国 (G8) 首脳は, 世界経済の持続的成長を図り, 世界貿易機関 (WTO) の次期多角的の貿易交渉 (新ラウンド) を通じて自由貿易を推進することを再確認した。

multilateral trade talks　多角的の貿易交渉, 多国間貿易交渉　(=multilateral trade negotiations)

Doha Round of multilateral trade talks　世界貿易機関 (WTO) の新ラウンド (新多角的貿易交渉), ドーハ・ラウンド
◆The G-8 agreed to aim for the early completion of the Doha Round of multilateral trade talks. 主要8か国は, 世界貿易機関 (WTO) の新多角的の貿易交渉 (ドーハ・ラウンド) の早期妥結を目指すことで一致した。

multilayered trade policy　重層的な通商政策
◆Under the multilayered trade policy, Japan should strengthen bilateral and multilateral cooperation in commerce and help stimulate trade and investment to ensure the economic revival of the East Asian region. 重層的な通商政策のもと

に、日本は東アジア地域の経済再生のため、通商面で二国間および多国間の連携を強化して、貿易と投資を促進していかなければならない。

multimedia shopping マルチメディア・ショッピング
◆The epoch-making service features "multimedia banking" that permits access to financial services from a personal computer in a corporate network and "multimedia shopping," in which users can order goods and make payments. この画期的なサービスの特色は、企業ネットワーク内のパソコンから金融サービスにアクセスできる「マルチメディア・バンキング」と、利用者が商品の注文とその支払いができる「マルチメディア・ショッピング」である。

multinational （形）多国籍の, 多国間の, 多角的 （名）多国籍企業
multinational bank 多国籍銀行, 国際投資銀行（consortium bank）
multinational banking 国際銀行業務
multinational currency alignment 多国間通貨調整
multinational rival 多国籍競走企業
multinational safeguard 多角的セーフガード, 多面的セーフガード

multinational corporation 多国籍企業（=multinational company［enterprise, firm］）
◆The development of cross-border infrastructure in the Greater Mekong Subregion（GMS）has prompted a number of multinational corporations to transfer some of their manufacturing processes to Laos, Cambodia and Myanmar to take advantage of cheaper labor costs. 大メコン圏での国境を越えたインフラ整備に伴い、多くの多国籍企業が、安い人件費［低賃金］の利点を生かして生産工程の一部をラオスやカンボジア、ミャンマーに移転している。

multinetting （名）（関連グループ企業を対象にした総合商社などの）多元的相殺決済, マルチネッティング
apply the law mutatis mutandis 法律を準用する
mutatis mutandis 必要な変更を加えて, 準用して（=with necessary changes）
mutatis mutandis application 準用規定
mutatis mutandis apply 〜が準用される
◆The provisions of Article V hereof shall apply mutatis mutandis. 本契約第5条の規定を準用するものとする。

mutual （形）相互の, 共通の, 共同の, 共有する, ミューチュアル
mutual assent 相互の同意, 合意
mutual consent of the parties hereto 本契約当事者の合意
mutual covenants and agreements herein contained 本契約に記載する相互の誓約と

合意事項を約因として
mutual interest contract 相互利益契約
mutual mistake 相互錯誤
mutual promise 相互約束
mutual recognition of standards/certification 基準・認証の相互承認

mutual agreement 合意, 相互の同意, 相互的同意
mutual agreement contained herein 本契約に定める相互の同意
mutual agreement of the both parties 両当事者の合意
mutual consultation between the parties 当事者間の相互協議

mutual negotiation 相互の協議, 相互交渉
◆Minimum purchase for the successive consequent year or years shall be decided upon by mutual negotiation before commencing such each year. その後に続く年度の最低購入量は、当該各年度の開始前に相互の協議により決定する。

N

NACCS 貨物通関情報処理システム（Nippon Automated Cargo Clearance Systemの略）

NAFTA 北米自由貿易協定（North American Free Trade Agreementの略）

name （動）指名する, 任命する, 選ぶ, 選出する, 指定する, 命名する, 〜の名前を挙げる, 公表する, 決める
fall due at the date named （手形などが）記載日に満期になる
◆Draft on you falls due at the date named. 貴社宛の手形は、記載日に満期になる。

name （名）名称, 氏名, 名前
Name of Company: 会社名
names, marks, emblems, trade names or trademarks 名称、標章、記章、商号または商標
names, trademarks and logos 名称、商標とロゴ（⇒logo）
under any fictitious or assumed name or name（s）of any shareholders 架空、仮想の名前または株主の名前で
◆It is necessary to write the name of notify party on the order B/L as it does not contain the name of consignee. 指図人式船荷証券には、荷受け人名が記載されていないので、通知先名を書かなければならない。◆The right to use or publish Licensor's name as well as any names or trademarks associated with or embodied in the licensed products. ライセンス製品に関連するまたはライセンス製品に具体化されている名称または商標と、ライセンサーの名前を使用、出版する権利。

narcotics trafficking 麻薬取引

◆The U.S. government froze the assets of four individuals and eight entities that were involved in illicit activities such as money laundering, currency counterfeiting and narcotics trafficking. 米政府は、資金洗浄（マネー・ロンダリング）や通貨偽造、麻薬取引などの違法行為に関与している4個人、8団体の資産を凍結した。

national strategic special deregulation zones 国家戦略特区, 規制緩和を推進する国家戦略特区
◆As the centerpiece of deregulation measures, the government plans to create "national strategic special deregulation zones" to attract companies and talented workers from all over the world by boldly relaxing regulations in the zones. 規制緩和策の目玉として、政府は「国家戦略特区」を創設し、特区内で大胆な規制緩和を断行して、世界中から企業や有能な人材を集める方針だ。

national wealth 国富
◆Japan lost more than ¥3 trillion of national wealth in 2011 to import fossil fuels as a result of the power scarcity due to the suspension of all nuclear power reactors. 全原発の停止による電力不足の結果、日本は化石燃料を輸入するため、2011年度は3兆円以上の国富を流出させた。

Nationality Law 国籍法
◆The revision of the Nationality Law may be abused as part of a fraudulent business by means of fabricating parental ties. 国籍法の改正は、親子関係の偽装認知などでダーク・ビジネスに悪用される可能性がある。

natural disaster 天災, 自然災害

natural resources 天然資源, 自然資源
◆Amid surging prices of crude oil and other resources, the sovereign wealth fund will invest mainly in solar power generation, fuel cells, and other new energy technologies and natural resources. 原油その他の資源価格の高騰を受け、同政府系投資ファンドは、太陽光や燃料電池などの新エネルギー技術や天然資源に投資の重点をおく方針だ。◆As long as Japan depends on thermal power generation as an alternative electricity source, LNG imports will continue to increase and the nation's wealth will flow to countries rich in natural resources. 日本が代替電源として火力発電に依存するかぎり、天然液化ガス（LNG）の輸入額は増え続け、国富は天然資源の豊富な国に流出する。

nature （名）性質, 性格, 内容, 種類, 自然
any damages or losses of whatsoever nature いかなる種類の損害または損失も
in nature 現実に, 現存して, まったく, この上なく
of any nature whatsoever あらゆる種類の, 性質のいかんにかかわらず
of like nature 同じ性質の, 類似の性質の
of whatsoever nature あらゆる種類の, 性質のいかんにかかわらず

proprietary nature of any information 情報の専有性
◆The technical information, knowhow, trade secrets and other information disclosed by the licensor is valuable, confidential and proprietary in nature. ライセンサーが開示する技術情報、ノウハウ、企業秘密その他の情報は、金銭的価値があるもので、機密であり、財産的価値がある。◆Upon the occurrence of any material breach, the nondefaulting party may terminate this agreement by giving a written notice of termination specifying the nature of the material breach. 重大な違反が発生した場合、違反を行っていない当事者は、その重大な違反の性格を明記した書面による解除通知を行って本契約を解除することができる。

navigation （名）航行, 航海, 航海術, 航空, 航空術, ナビゲーション
car navigation system カーナビ, 自動車経路誘導システム, カー・ナビゲーション・システム
freedom of navigation at sea 航海の自由
inland［internal］navigation 内陸航行
Navigation Acts 航海条例
◆Japan-ASEAN ties are meaningful in ensuring regional security, particularly freedom of navigation at sea. 日本とアセアン（東南アジア諸国連合）との関係は、地域の安全保障、とりわけ航海の自由を確保するうえで重要である。◆Pirates are threatening the safe navigation of oil tankers and other ships in Southeast Asian waters. 東南アジアの海域では、海賊が原油タンカーなどの船舶の安全な航行を脅かしている。

near futures（期近物（きじかもの）
◆Near futures may be had within a fortnight of receipt of an order. 期近物は、受注後半月以内に入手可能です。

needs of emerging markets 新興市場のニーズ
◆The keys to the revival of Japanese manufacturers are to discern the needs of emerging markets with strong growth potential and to develop strategically important products through originality and ingenuity. 日本の製造業各社復活のカギは、潜在成長力［成長率］が高い新興国市場のニーズの発掘と、創意工夫による重要な戦略的商品の開発である。

negative interest rate マイナス金利
◆In the case of a negative interest rate which the ECB has introduced, commercial banks have to pay interest at this rate, which is like a handling fee, to place funds at the central bank. 欧州中央銀行（ECB）が導入したマイナス金利の場合、民間銀行は、手数料のようにマイナス金利の金利を払って、ECBに資金を預けることになる。

neglect （名）義務・支払いなどを怠ること, 怠慢, 不注意, 懈怠（けたい・かいたい）, 不作為, 無視, 軽視
◆Any failure, whether willful, through neglect

or otherwise, of either party to perform or fulfill any of its duties, obligations or covenants in this agreement shall constitute a breach of this agreement. 故意であれ、怠慢またはその他によるものであれ、本契約における各当事者の責務、義務または約束ごとを各当事者が履行または達成できない場合、これは本契約の違反を構成するものとする。

negligence （名）過失, 怠慢, 不注意, 過失責任, 手抜かり, 手抜き

comparative negligence　比較過失, 過失相殺

concurrent negligence　過失の競合

contributory negligence　寄与過失

death by negligence　過失致死

gross negligence　重過失, 重大な過失

medical negligence　医療過失

negligence in contract　契約締結上の過失

negligence laws　過失責任法

negligence of duty　職務怠慢

negligence resulting in death　過失致死

negligence tax　過少申告加算税

ordinary negligence　通常過失

professional negligence　業務上過失

proven negligence　明確な過失

slight negligence　軽過失

◆Elevator manufacturers, inspection and maintenance companies and building management firms must bear in mind that their negligence could deprive elevator users of their lives. エレベータのメーカーや点検・保守業者、ビル管理者は、それぞれ過失がエレベータ利用者の命を奪う可能性があることを肝に銘じる必要がある。◆The seller shall not be responsible for defects in material and workmanship in the event that such defects arise from proven negligence or misconduct on the part of the buyer, its employees or customers. 材料と仕上がりの欠陥が買い主、買い主の従業員または顧客の側の明確な過失または不始末に起因して生じた場合、売り主は当該欠陥の責任を負わないものとする。

negotiable （形）流通可能の, 流通性のある, 手形などを譲渡できる, 譲渡可能な, 買い取ることができる

be negotiable against a draft at sight　一覧払い手形と引換えに買い取られる

negotiable clean on-board bill of lading　譲渡可能無故障船荷証券

◆The letter of credit set forth above shall be negotiable against a draft at sight signed by the seller upon the presentation of the following documents: 上記の信用状は、次の船積み書類の提示がある場合には、売り主が振り出した一覧払い手形と引換えに買い取られるものとする。

negotiable bill of lading　譲渡可能な船荷証券, 流通性船荷証券

◆A full set of negotiable bills of lading made out

to order must be endorsed by shipper. 指図人式で作成された譲渡可能な船荷証券一式には、荷送人の裏書が必要である。

negotiate （動）交渉する, 協議する, 商談する,（手形・証券・小切手などを）譲渡する, 手形を買い取る, 権利を移転する, 手形の買取り銀行に書類を提出する, 金に代える

be on a strong［good］negotiating position　交渉上有利な立場にある

negotiate a new deal with　～と新規契約を結ぶ

negotiated agreement　合意事項, 随意契約

negotiated contract　随意契約

negotiated market　顧客市場, 相対（あいたい）売買市場

negotiated price　協議価格, 交渉価格, 相対で決めた価格

negotiated transaction　（株の）相対売買, 交渉案件

negotiated underwriting　協議引受け（方式）

◆Drafts shall be negotiated not later than May 10, 2015. 為替手形は、2015年5月10日以前に買い取るものとする。◆Title with respect to each shipment of the products shall pass from the seller to purchaser when the seller negotiates relative documents and receives proceeds from the negotiating bank for such shipment with effect retrospect to the time of such shipment. 本製品の各船積みに関する所有権は、売り主が関連書類を手形買取り銀行に提出して本製品の代金を当該銀行から受領した時点で、当該船積み時に遡及して売り主から買い主に移転するものとする。◆We negotiated our draft through the bank above-mentioned under L/C No. 5000 established by the ABC Bank, New York, and commend our signature to your protection. 当社は、ABC銀行（ニューヨーク）発行の信用状5000号に従って上記銀行で手形を買い取ってもらいましたので、この手形の支払いをよろしくお願いします。

negotiating （形）交渉の, 協議の, 交渉に関する

negotiating bank　信用状の買取り銀行, 手形買取り銀行, 買取り銀行（外貨建ての荷為替手形を買い取る銀行）

negotiating leverage　交渉力

negotiating position　交渉力

negotiating right　交渉権

negotiating session　交渉の場

negotiating skills　交渉術, 交渉の手腕

negotiating table　交渉のテーブル, 交渉［協議］の場, 交渉の席

negotiation （名）交渉, 協議, 商談, 取引, 流通, 権利の移転, 譲渡, 輸出地の取引銀行による荷為替手形の買取り, ネゴシエーション

business negotiations　商談

conclude negotiations 交渉をまとめる

contract negotiation 契約交渉

enter into final negotiations with ～と最終調整に入る

first-round negotiations 初協議, 第一回協議

indirect negotiation 間接交渉

integrative negotiation 統合的交渉

management-labor negotiations 労使交渉

merger negotiations 経営統合交渉

multilateral negotiation 多国間交渉, 多角的交渉, 多国間協議

negotiation by draft 取立て為替, 逆為替

negotiation charge 手形買取手数料, 買取手数料 (手形取組み時に銀行が請求する手数料)

negotiation credit 手形買取銀行無指定信用状, 外国為替取組み信用状, 買取信用状, ネゴシエーション信用状

negotiation of export bill 輸出手形の買取り

negotiations fall through 交渉が決裂する

negotiations on the capital increase 増資交渉

new round of multilateral trade negotiations 新多角的貿易交渉, 新ラウンド

second-round negotiations 2回目の協議

sectoral negotiation 分野別交渉

tie-up negotiation 提携交渉

under negotiation 交渉中で

upcoming negotiations 今後の交渉

◆About ten major Japanese automakers are scheduled to take part in an industrial parts and materials exhibition and procurement negotiation fair in Seoul. 韓国・ソウルで開かれる工業部品・素材展示調達商談会には、日本の自動車メーカー約10社が参加する予定だ。◆Argentina clinched a debt rollover deal with the IMF after a year of tortuous negotiations. アルゼンチンは、1年にわたる難交渉の末、国際通貨基金 (IMF) との債務返済延べ取引をまとめた。◆If it is not certain five agricultural items, including rice and wheat, will be treated as exceptions to free trade, the government will not hesitate to pull out from the TPP negotiations. コメや麦など農産品5項目を自由貿易の聖域として確保できなければ、政府はTPP (環太平洋経済連携協定) 交渉からの脱退も辞さない方針だ。◆Japan has yet to enter full-scale TPP negotiations, but the LDP has not presented concrete measures to prepare for the liberalization of trade, including steps to bolster competitiveness in the agricultural sector. 日本が環太平洋経済連携協定 (TPP) の本格交渉に入るのはこれからだが、自民党は、農業分野での競争力強化策など、貿易自由化に備えた具体策をまだ示していない。◆Kirin and Suntory, the nation's two largest food and beverage makers, have started merger negotiations. 国内最大手の食品・飲料メーカーの

キリンとサントリーが、経営統合の交渉に入った。◆The firm envisioned negotiations with the U.S. equity fund over financing for restructuring in a reconstruction plan it formulated in June. 同社は、経営合理化の資金調達に関しては、6月に策定した再建計画でこの米国の投資ファンドとの交渉を見込んでいた。◆The upcoming negotiations will determine practical measures to strengthen ties, including the merger ratio, the name of the new group and the positions to be held by top executives. 今後の交渉で、統合比率や新グループの名称、首脳人事など提携強化の具体策を詰める。◆The WTO General Council manages the overall WTO negotiations. WTO一般理事会は、世界貿易機関 (WTO) の交渉全体を取りまとめる。

negotiation between the parties hereto 本契約当事者間の協議

◆After the second year of this agreement, the yearly minimum purchase quantity shall be decided by negotiation between the parties hereto. 本契約の2年目以降、年間最低購入量は、本契約当事者間の協議により決定する。

neither party shall いずれの当事者も～しないものとする, いずれの当事者も～してはならない

net (形) 基本的な, 最終的な, 結局の, 正味の, 掛け値のない, 純粋の, 税引き後の, 正味金額の, 純額の

net amount after deduction 控除後の純額

net credits against debits 債権と債務の差額

net current assets 運転資金

net exposure (カントリー・リスク保険の) 正味危険額

net invoice value 純送り状価格

net of ～控除後の

net asset value 純資産額, 正味資産額, 正味資産価額, 純資産

◆The price of the Shares is based on the net asset value of the Shares as of October 30, 2015, determined by ABC and reviewed and checked by XYZ accounting firm. 本株式の価格は、2015年10月30日現在の本株式の純資産額に基づいてABCが決定し、XYZ会計事務所が検討、チェックするものとする。

net exports 純輸出 (純輸出=輸出-輸入)

◆While external demand, or net exports, made a positive 0.3 percent contribution to the economic growth, domestic demand only added 0.2 percent. 外需、つまり純輸出の経済成長率への寄与度はプラス0.3%となった反面、内需の寄与度は0.2%にとどまったにすぎない。

net external assets 対外純資産 (対外純資産=日本の政府、企業、個人が海外に持つ資産 (対外資産:external assets) −海外の政府、企業、個人が日本に持つ資産 (対外負債:external debts, external liabilities)。net foreign assets ともいう)

◆The nation's net external assets stood at ￥172.

82 trillion, down 1.4 percent from a year. 日本の対外資産（対外資産の残高）は、前年比1.4%減の172兆8,200億円となった。

net foreign assets 対外純資産
◆Japan's net foreign assets, or the difference between assets and liabilities overseas, rose 16 percent from a year earlier to a record ¥250.2 trillion at the end of 2007. 2007年末の日本の対外純資産（日本の対外資産と対外負債との差額）は、前年末比16%増の250兆2,000億円で過去最高となった。

net selling price 正味販売価格, 純販売価格, 純販売額
◆Licensee shall pay a royalty at the rate of five (5) percent of the net selling price of Products. ライセンシーは、本製品の正味販売価格の5%の料率でロイヤリティを支払わなければならない。

net wholesale price 正味卸売り価格, 純卸売り価格, 純卸売り販売額
◆Net Wholesale Price referred to in this agreement is defined as the amount of the gross sales by ABC of the licensed products to ABC's customers in the territory, less customary trade discounts, insurance premiums, transportation and delivery charges, taxes（VAT）and duties. 本契約書に記載する「純卸売り販売額」とは、ABCの顧客に対する契約地域内でのABCの許諾製品の総売上高（総販売額）から、通常の卸売り割引額、保険料、運送・引渡し費用、税金（付加価値税）と関税を差し引いた額のことをいう。

new round 新ラウンド
◆The list of issues to be negotiated under the new round runs the gamut from farm products to mining and manufacturing products. 新ラウンドでの交渉分野は、農業製品から鉱工業製品にいたるまで多岐にわたっている。

new trade partnership 新貿易協定, 新自由貿易協定
◆New trade partnerships with Europe and the Asia-Pacific will help exporters create more jobs. 欧州やアジア太平洋地域との新自由貿易協定は、輸出企業の雇用創出拡大につながる。

New York market ニューヨーク市場
◆Crude futures soared to $135 per barrel on the New York market. ニューヨーク市場の原油先物価格が、1バレル＝135ドルに急騰した〔1バレル＝135ドルの高値を付けた〕。

New York Mercantile Exchange ニューヨーク商業取引所, ニューヨーク・マーカンタイル取引所, NYMEX〔Nymex〕
◆At the New York Mercantile Exchange on July 11, the benchmark indicator hit a record high of $147.27 per barrel. 7月11日のニューヨーク・マーカンタイル取引所では、指標となる原油が1バレル＝147.27ドルの史上最高値を記録した。◆In the crude oil contract market of the New York Mercantile Exchange（NYMEX）, the price of January WTI, the benchmark U.S. crude oil, fell below $60 a barrel for the first time since June

2009 on December 11, 2014 due to the forecast of rising global oil production. 2014年12月11日のニューヨーク・マーカンタイル取引所の原油先物市場では、指標となる米国産原油WTI（テキサス産軽質油）の1月渡し価格が、世界的な石油増産見通しから、2009年7月以来5年5か月ぶりに1バレル＝60ドルを割り込んだ。

New York Stock Exchange ニューヨーク証券取引所, NYSE （=Big Board）
◆Abe advertised Japan at the New York Stock Exchange by explaining that introduction of a high-speed railway system using Japan's superconducting magnetic levitation technology could connect New York and Washington in less than an hour. 安倍首相は、ニューヨーク証券取引所で、「日本の超電導リニア技術を用いた高速鉄道を導入すれば、ニューヨークとワシントンは1時間足らずで結ばれる」と説明して、日本を売り込んだ。◆The New York Stock Exchange is to be sold to ICE（Intercontinental Exchange）in Atlanta, which was established in May 2000, for about $8 billion. ニューヨーク証券取引所（NYSE）が、商品先物市場を運営するアトランタのインターコンチネンタル取引所（ICE:2000年5月設立）に、約80億ドルで身売りすることになった。◆ "Wall Street is always ahead of the curve, and so now is your chance." By saying so at the New York Stock Exchange, Prime Minister Abe called on investors to actively invest in Japan. 「ウォール街の皆さんは、つねに時代の先端を行く。今がチャンスです」と安倍首相がニューヨーク証券取引所で述べて、投資家に日本への積極的な投資を呼びかけた。

NHTSA 米全国高速道路交通安全局, 米全国高速道路安全局, 米高速道路交通安全局（National Highway Traffic Safety Administrationの略。⇒probe）
◆The NHTSA received 163 complaints from Corolla users about their cars' power steering system. トヨタ・カローラのユーザーから、米高速道路交通安全局（NHTSA）に、電動パワー・ステアリングに関する苦情が163件寄せられた。

NIEs〔NIES〕 新興工業経済地域, 新興工業経済群 （=NICs:newly industrializing〔industrialized〕economiesの略）
◆An important role of the NIEs is to act as a nucleus or center in the promotion of export-oriented industrialization in the Asian-Pacific region. 新興工業経済地域（NIEs）のひとつの重要な役割は、アジア太平洋地域における輸出志向型工業化の中核あるいはセンターとして機能することにある。◆The NIEs consist of Hong Kong, Korea, Singapore and Taiwan. 新興工業経済地域（NIEs）は、香港、韓国、シンガポールと台湾から成る。

Nippon Automated Cargo Clearance System 貨物通関情報処理システム, NACCS

Nippon Export and Investment Insurance 独立行政法人・日本貿易保険

◆The trade insurance of Nippon Export and Investment Insurance previously only covered direct exports by domestic firms. 独立行政法人・日本貿易保険の貿易保険はこれまで、国内企業の直接輸出だけが対象だった。

no （形）一つの～もない，決して～ではない，～禁止，～反対，～お断り

no agency or partnership　代理人またはパートナーシップの否定

no binding effect　法的拘束力がないこと

no bribery　贈賄禁止，贈賄禁止条項

no competition with　～との競争禁止

no undisclosed liabilities　隠された債務の不存在

No. ［no.］　番号，～番，第～号，～番地

Contract No.　契約番号

Order No.　注文番号

Package No.　梱包番号

no later than　～までに，～以前に，～以内に
◆Payment for each delivery of the Products shall be by the purchaser in United States Dollars by means of telegraphic transfer remittance to such bank account in the City of San Francisco, as the seller may designate from time to time, no later than 30 days after the date of the bill of lading for each such delivery. 本製品の引渡しに対する支払いは、当該引渡しにかかわる船荷証券の日付から30日以内に、売り主が随時指定するサンフランシスコ市内の銀行口座に買い主が米ドルで電信為替で送金して行うものとする。◆Provided Licensor delivers the software without any bug, by no later than the delivery dates, Licensee shall pay Licensor a minimum guarantee of royalties of one million U.S. dollars ($1,000,000). ライセンサーがバグのないソフトウエアを引渡し日以前に引き渡した場合、ライセンシーは、ロイヤルティの最低保証料としてライセンサーに100万米ドルを支払うものとする。

nominal exchange rate　名目為替レート
◆The international competitiveness of companies and a country's balance of trade with the rest of the world are affected not by nominal exchange rates but by real exchange rates, so we need to follow real exchange rates. 企業の国際競争力や国の他国との貿易収支などの動きは、名目為替レートではなく、実質為替レートの影響を受けるので、われわれは実質為替レートの動きを見る必要がある。

nominal foreign exchange rate　名目為替レート
◆Nominal foreign exchange rates are quoted at ￥110 to the U.S. dollar or ￥135 to the euro as we see in the media. 名目為替レートは、新聞や雑誌で見られるように、1ドル＝110円とか、1ユーロ＝135円と表示される。

Nominal Value for Customs Clearance Purpose Only　通関用の名目価格にすぎ

ない

nominate　（動）指名する，推薦する，推挙する，任命する
◆ABC shall have the right to nominate three directors. ABCは、3名の取締役を指名する権利を持つ。◆The holders of the new company's Class A common stock and Class B common stock shall be each entitled to nominate and elect ＿＿＿directors respectively. 新会社のAクラス普通株式とBクラス普通株式の各保有者は、それぞれ取締役＿＿＿名を指名して選任することができる。

nonassessable　（形）追加出資義務のない，追加払込み請求がない，追加払込み義務を負わない，追徴不能の
◆All such issued and outstanding shares are validly issued, fully paid and nonassessable. 当該発行済み社外株式は、すべて有効に発行され、全額払込み済みで、追加払込みの請求はないものとする。

nonassignable and nontransferable　譲渡不能・移転不能の

nonassigning party　非譲渡当事者，非譲渡人
◆The assignor shall remain in all respects responsible to the nonassigning party for the performance of the assignor's obligations set forth in this agreement. 譲渡人は、本契約に定める譲渡人の義務の履行について、引き続きすべての点で非譲渡当事者に対して責任を負うものとする。

nonbinding　（形）拘束力のない
◆Keidanren's charter on ethical recruitments, which stipulates job-hunting rules for member companies, is nonbinding and has no penalties for violators. 会員企業に向けて就職活動のルールを定めている経団連の倫理憲章（新卒者の採用選考に関する企業の倫理憲章）には、拘束力がないし、違反企業への罰則もない。

noncompetition agreement　競合禁止契約

nonconditional payment　無条件支払い
◆Such letter of credit shall be transferable and having the clause of definite undertaking by the issuing bank for unconditional payment against a draft at sight. この信用状は、譲渡可能で、一覧払い手形に対する無条件支払いに関して発行銀行が明確に約束した文言が入っているものとする。

nondefaulting party　不履行のない当事者，不履行に陥っていない当事者，違反を行っていない当事者

nondisclosure agreement　守秘契約，開示禁止契約，秘密保持契約（＝confidentiality agreement）

nondisclosure of information　情報の非開示

nonexclusive　（形）非独占的な，非専属的な
nonexclusive agency agreement　非独占的代理店契約

nonexclusive distributorship agreement　非独

占的販売店契約

nonexclusive jurisdiction 非専属管轄（権），非専属的裁判管轄（権）

nonexclusive right 非独占的な権利

nonexclusive license 非独占的実施権，非独占的ライセンス
◆Subject to the provisions of Article V of this agreement, each party, as Grantor, on behalf of itself and its Subsidiaries, grants to the other party, as Grantee, a worldwide and nonexclusive license under the Grantor's licensed products and copyrights; 本契約第5条の規定に従って，ライセンス許諾者としての各当事者は，自社とその子会社を代表して，ライセンス許諾者の許諾特許と著作権に基づく世界を対象とした非独占的なライセンスを，被許諾者としての相手方に許諾する。

noninfringement （名）非侵害

nonlife insurance company 損害保険会社
◆Nonlife insurance companies used to disperse the risk of large contracts with new corporate clients through reinsurance contracts with other insurance or reinsurance companies. 損保各社は従来，他の保険会社もしくは再保険会社と再保険契約を結んで，新規顧客企業と大型契約を結ぶリスクを分散してきた。

nonlife insurance industry 損害保険業界
◆The nonlife insurance industry wants all kinds of buildings and other properties not insured for terrorist attacks. 損害保険業界は，すべての物件をテロ免責にしたいと考えている。

nonpayment or nonperformance 不払いまたは不履行，支払い義務違反または不履行
◆The guarantor waives any and all notices of nonpayment or nonperformance or demand for payment or performance of such obligations under the franchise agreement. 保証人は，フランチャイズ契約に基づく当該債務の不払いまたは不履行について一切の通知を受ける権利と，当該債務の支払いまたは履行について一切の催告通知を受ける権利を放棄する。

nonperformance （名）不履行，不実行

nonperformance of this agreement 本契約の不履行
◆If performance of this agreement is interfered with, for any length of time, by an Act of God, war, civil commotion, epidemics and other similar occurrences which are beyond the control of either party, neither party shall be held liable for nonperformance of this agreement for such length of time. 本契約の履行が，天災、戦争、動乱（内乱）、流行病やいずれか一方の当事者の支配が及ばないその他の同種の事態により一定期間妨げられた場合，いずれの当事者も，当該期間の本契約不履行については責任を負わないものとする。

nonrefundable （形）返還不能の，払戻し不可の

nontariff barriers 非関税障壁
◆The framework of a Free Trade Area of the Asia-Pacific is aimed at liberalizing trade and investment as well as the elimination of nontariff barriers, regulatory reform and smoother logistics. アジア太平洋自由貿易地域（FTAAP）の枠組みは、貿易や投資の自由化のほか、非関税障壁の撤廃、規制改革、物流の円滑化などを目指している。

nontransferable, nonexclusive, perpetual license 譲渡不能、非独占的かつ永久的なライセンス

normal trade relations 正常通商関係
◆Lawmakers voted 260-170 to continue for a year what is now called normal trade relations（NTR）and used to be called most favored nations（MFN）trade status. 議員が260対170で票決して、これまで最恵国待遇と呼ばれていた（中国に対する）正常通商関係を1年間継続することになった。

not （副）～でない，～しない，～禁止，～不可

not less than ～以上，少なくとも～，～弱，～またはそれ以上

not less than all 全部でない場合は不可，一部は不可，一部の売却等は不可

not more than once 1回限り

not negotiable 流通禁止，譲渡禁止

not otherwise specified 別段の指定がないかぎり

not provided for 資金不足，N.P.F.

not responsible clause 船主免責条項

not sufficient fund 預金不足

not to be laid flat 平積み無用

not to insurance clause 保険利益不供与約款

not wanted 航海中不要（手荷物など船客荷物の表記用語）

not working days 荷役不能日

wanted on voyage 航海中入用品（手荷物など船客荷物の表記用語）

not later than ～までに，～以前に（～の日を含む）
◆Drafts shall be negotiated not later than May 10, 2015. 為替手形は、2015年5月10日以前に買い取るものとする。

not less than ～以上（～の数量・程度を含む）
◆This letter of credit shall be opened not less than 30 calendar days before the first scheduled shipping date for each order and shall be 90 days beyond the anticipated final shipping date. この信用状は、各注文の最初の出荷予定日から30暦日以上前に開設するものとし、最終出荷予定日から90日を超えて有効でなければならない。

notation （名）覚書，記録，注釈，表記法，表示法，記号法

chemical notation 化学記号表

on board notation 船積み証明，船積みの付記

radix notation 基数表記法

note （動）～に言及する，～と発言する，～と記

指摘する, ～を示す, ～に気づく, ～に注意[注目]する, ～を覚えておく, ～を書き留める, メモを取る

except as noted　別記のものを除いて

note down　～を書き留める

◆Note that mama and papa stores are now rapidly disappearing and that chain store drugstores are now becoming the major player in the retail sector. 注意すべき点として, 零細小売店は現在, 急速に姿を消しており, いまはチェーン店のドラッグストアが小売部門の主流になっている。◆The International Monetary Fund noted the current state of the Japanese economy has led to grave anxiety over deflation and capital investment. 日本経済の現状は, デフレと設備投資について重大な懸念が生じている, と国際通貨基金(IMF)が指摘した。◆We have received your letter of August 15, from which we note that you are in the market for our products. 8月15日付け貴状を拝受しました。それによると貴社は当社製品をご入用とのこと, 確かに承(うけたまわ)りました。

note　(名)手形, 約束手形, 証券, 債券, 債権表示証書, 紙幣, 通知書, 文書, 書類, 伝票, 覚書, 注釈, 注記, 解説, 注意, 注意事項, 注意書き, 但し書き, 原稿, 手記, 短信, 書き置き, 音符, 音色, 調子, 印象, 特徴, 特色, ノート(証券の「ノート」は一般に中期の債務証券を指すが, 米財務省証券に対して使うときは, 償還期限が1年超10年以内の中期証券のことをいう)

accommodation note　融通手形

advice note　通知書, 案内状, 発送通知書, 発送案内

auditing for note receivable　受取手形監査

cargo boat note　船卸し票

carriage note　貨物引換え証

carrier's note　運送目録

claim note　保険金請求書, 損害賠償請求書

consignment note　(鉄道の)出荷通知書, 委託貨物運送状, 航空運送状(air consignment note), 受託書

contract note　契約書, 売買契約書

delivery note　納品書, 物品受領証, 貨物引渡し通知書, 配達証明書

dispatch note　発送通知書

endorsed note　裏書手形

loan on note　手形貸付け

note discounted　割引手形

note payable　支払い手形

premium note　保険料支払い約束手形

private note　私募債

promissory note　約束手形, 手形

sales note　売約書

savings note　貯蓄債券

secured note　担保付き手形

sight note　一覧払い約束手形, 一覧払い手形

ten-year note auction　米国債10年物の入札

unpaid note　不渡り手形

warrant-attached note　ワラント債

nothing contained in this agreement shall　本契約のいかなる規定[条項]も～するものでない, 本契約に定めるいかなる条項も～しないものとする

◆Nothing contained in this agreement shall create relationship of partnership, joint venture, sales agency, franchise or principal and agent between the parties. 本契約のいかなる規定によっても, 両者間にパートナーシップ, 共同事業体, 販売代理店, フランチャイズまたは本人と代理人との関係は生じないものとする。

notice　(名)通知, 通知書, 通知方法, 通告, 通告書, 告知, 告知書, 予告, 広告, 公示, 告示, 表示, 認識　(⇒franchise agreement, full written notice of)

actual notice　現実の通知, 現実の認識

advance notice　事前通告, 予告

claim notice　事故通知書(貨物の異常を通知する書類), 損害通知書

constructive notice　擬制通知, 擬制認識

copyright notice　著作権表示

drawdown notice　借入金の引出し通知

give notice of　～について通知する, ～の通知をする

judicial notice　裁判所による確知

legal notice　適法な通知, 法定通知, 擬制通知, 擬制認識

notice of abandonment　委付の通知, 委付通知, 委付申込み書

notice of acceptance　(手形)引受通知

notice of arrival　着船通知書, 入港届け(=arrival notice)

notice of clearance　出航届け

notice of damage　留保通知

notice of dishonor　手形不渡り通知, 不渡り通知

notice of import [importation]　輸入申告

notice of loss or damage　事故通知

notice of protest　(手形)支払い拒絶通知

notice of readiness　荷役準備完了通知書

official notice　公式通知, 公知, 公知の証拠

post a notice　掲示する

prior notice　事前通知, 事前通告

public notice　公示, 広告, 告示

trademark notice　商標表示

upon notice to　～に通知することにより

with or without notice　通知の有無にかかわらず, 予告の有無にかかわらず

without notice　善意で, 通知なしで, 無断で

◆In the event of such a default of this agreement Supplier may terminate this agreement immediately by providing written notice to Distributor. このような本契約違反が発生した場合には、供給者は、販売店に書面で通知することにより本契約を直ちに解除することができる。◆The prices are without engagement and subject to change with or without notice. 価格は確約なしで、予告の有無にかかわらず変更することがある。

notice of nonpayment or nonperformance　不払いまたは不履行の通知
◆The guarantor waives any and all notices of nonpayment or nonperformance or demand for payment or performance of such obligations under the franchise agreement. 保証人は、フランチャイズ契約に基づく当該債務の不払いまたは不履行について一切の通知を受ける権利と、当該債務の支払いまたは履行について一切の催告通知を受ける権利を放棄する。

notification　(名)通知, 通告, 告示
　(⇒full written notice of)
◆The purchaser shall forward full particulars of such claim, accompanied by an authorized surveyor's certificate of inspection of quality and quantity of the products delivered in dispute, to the seller by registered airmail within 30 days after such notification. 買い主は、当該通知後30日以内に、引き渡された問題の製品の品質と数量に関する公認鑑定人の検査証明書を添付して、当該クレームの詳細を記載した書面を書留航空便で売り主に送付するものとする。

notify　(動)通知する, 通告する, 通報する
　(⇒accompanying by the satisfactory proof)
◆The Buyer shall notify the Seller of the name of the carrying vessel, the estimated date of loading and the contract number for the Seller to effect delivery, at least seven（7）days before the estimated date of arrival of the vessel at the port of shipment. 買い主は、少なくとも本船の船積み港への到着予定日の7日前までに、本船の船名、船積み予定日と売り主が引渡しを行う契約番号を、売り主に通知するものとする。

notify party　到着通知人, 通知先
◆Bills of lading shall be made out to order and marked notify party. 船荷証券は、指図人式で作成し、通知先を記入しなければならない。◆It is necessary to write the name of notify party on the order B/L as it does not contain the name of consignee. 指図人式船荷証券には、荷受け人名が記載されていないので、通知先名を書かなければならない。

notifying bank　通知銀行

notwithstanding　(前)～にもかかわらず, ～にかかわらず　(=in spite of)
notwithstanding any of the provisions of this agreement　本契約の規定のいかんにかかわらず, 本契約のいずれの規定にもかかわらず, 本契約の規定にかかわらず

notwithstanding any provision in this agreement　本契約中のいかなる規定にもかかわらず

notwithstanding any provision of this agreement to the contrary　本契約のこれと異なるいかなる規定にもかかわらず

notwithstanding anything herein　本契約中のいかなる規定にもかかわらず

notwithstanding anything herein to the contrary　本契約にこれと矛盾する規定があるにもかかわらず, 本契約にこれと異なる規定があるにもかかわらず, 本契約の他の別段の規定にかかわらず

notwithstanding the above provisions　上記の規定にかかわらず

notwithstanding the foregoing provisions of　前記の規定にかかわらず, 上記規定にかかわらず

notwithstanding the provisions of　～の規定にかかわらず

◆The seller shall be liable for latent defects of the products at any time after delivery to the purchaser of the products or any subsequent purchaser, notwithstanding the inspection and acceptance of the products by the purchaser or any subsequent purchaser. 売り主は、本製品の隠れた瑕疵（かし）については、買い主またはその後の購入者による本製品の検収にかかわらず、本製品の買い主またはその後の購入者への引渡し後、いつでも責任を負うものとする。

now or hereafter　現在または今後, 現在もしくは将来, 現在も将来も

now or hereafter in effect　現在もしくは将来効力を有する

NOW, THEREFORE　そこで, よって
NOW, THEREFORE, IT IS AGREED as follows:　そこで、以下のとおり合意する。
◆NOW, THEREFORE, in consideration of the premises and the mutual covenants, conditions and undertakings of the parties herein contained, the parties hereto do hereby agree as follows: そこで、ここに（本契約により）、前文と本契約書に記載する相互の誓約、条件および約束ごとを約因として、本契約当事者は次のとおり合意する。

nuclear power plant　原子力発電所, 原発
　(=nuclear power station)
nuclear power plant［station］　原子力発電所

nuclear power technology　原子力技術

resume［restart］nuclear power plant operations　原発を再稼働する

suspend the operation of a nuclear power plant　原子力発電所の運転を停止する

the restart of nuclear power plants　原発再稼働
◆After the release of radioactive substances from Fukushima No.1 nuclear power plant, two major food companies decided not to sign contracts this fiscal year with JA Zen-noh Fukushima which cultivates tomatoes. 福島第一原子力発電所から

の放射性物質の流出を受けて、大手食品メーカー2社が、トマト栽培をしているJA全農福島と今年度の栽培契約を結ばないことを決めた。

nuclear power plant arm 原発子会社
◆Toshiba will be given priority in negotiations for the right to acquire Westinghouse, British Nuclear Fuels PLC's U.S. nuclear power plant arm. 東芝に、ウェスチングハウス（英核燃料会社の米原発子会社）買収権獲得のための優先交渉権が与えられることになった。

nuclear power plant exports 原発輸出
◆The government's policy of ending reliance on nuclear power generation will accelerate the hollowing-out of industry and hamper nuclear power plant exports. 政府の原発ゼロ方針［原発への依存度をゼロにする政府方針］は、産業空洞化を加速し、原発輸出を妨げることになる。

nuclear power reactor 原子力発電所, 原発
◆If the exchange rate remains around ¥90 to the dollar for the next 12 months, income equivalent to 0.6 percent of Japan's GDP will flow overseas mainly due to higher fuel imports stemming from the suspension of nuclear power reactors. 為替相場が今後1年間、1ドル＝90円程度の水準が続いた場合、主に原子力発電所の運転停止に伴う燃料輸入の増加により、日本の国内総生産（GDP）の0.6%相当の所得が海外に流出する。
◆Japan lost more than ¥3 trillion of national wealth in 2011 to import fossil fuels as a result of the power scarcity due to the suspension of all nuclear power reactors. 全原発の停止による電力不足の結果、日本は化石燃料を輸入するため、2011年度は3兆円以上の国富を流出させた。

nuclear reactor export business 原発輸出ビジネス
◆It will be impossible for Japan to advance the nuclear reactor export business if Japan moves toward no nuclear power. 日本が原発ゼロに向かえば、原発輸出ビジネスの展開はできなくなる。

null and no effect [force, value] 無効の

null and void 無効の, 失効の, 取消しできる
◆Any assignment or transfer without such consent shall be null and void. このような同意を得ないで行われた譲渡は無効とする。◆If the borrower shall default in the performance of any other term or agreement contained in this agreement, the lender may declare its commitment and its obligation to be null and void. 借主が本契約に定める他の条件または合意事項を履行しない場合、貸主は、貸主の約束と義務は無効であると宣言することができる。

number of shares 株式数, 持ち株数

NVOCC 国際複合運送一貫業者, 国際複合運送業者 （non-vessel operating common carrierの略）

NYMEX ニューヨーク・マーカンタイル取引所 （⇒New York Mercantile Exchange）

NYSE ニューヨーク証券取引所

（=Big Board; ⇒New York Stock Exchange）
◆Intercontinental Exchange（ICE）, an exchange that deals in investing contracts known as futures, is buying the NYSE for about $8 billion. 米インターコンチネンタル取引所（ICE: 先物と呼ばれる投資契約を扱う取引所）が、ニューヨーク証券取引所を約80億ドルで買収する。

NYSE Group NYSEグループ
◆NYSE Group struck a deal to buy European bourse operator Euronext for $9.96 billion. （ニューヨーク証券取引所を運営する）NYSEグループは、欧州（パリやオランダなど）の証券取引所を運営する「ユーロネクスト」を99億6,000万ドルで買収する取引をした。

O

object code オブジェクト・コード, 機械語のコード （=object program: コンピュータが理解する2進級（バイナリー）の機械語で書かれたプログラムのこと）

objection （名）苦情, 反対, 異議, 抗議
make an objection to ～に対して異議を申し立てる
raise an objection to ～に対して異議を申し立てる
written objection 書面による抗議, 書面での抗議

obligation （名）義務, 債務, 約束, 金銭債務証書, 債権債務関係 （⇒avoid, debt）
all obligations under this agreement 本契約上のすべての義務, 本契約上のすべての債務
assume the obligation of ～の義務を負う
debt obligation 債務負担, 債務, 債務証書, 債務契約書
default of obligation 債務不履行, 義務不履行
expiration of obligation 債務消滅
guarantee of obligation 保証債務
joint and several obligation 連帯責任, 連帯債務, 共同債務
joint obligation 共同責任, 共同債務, 連帯責任
obligation of confidence 秘密保持義務 （=obligation of confidentiality）
obligation or responsibility 義務または責任, 債務または責任
obligation to secrecy 守秘義務
obligations to make payment when due 期日が到来した支払い債務, 期日が到来した金銭債務
payment obligation 支払い債務, 支払い義務
performance obligation 履行債務
repayment obligation 返済義務
rights and obligations 権利と義務

under the obligation of ～する義務がある, ～する義務を負う

waiver of obligation 債務免除

◆The execution and performance of this agreement by Seller constitute legal, valid and binding obligations of Seller, enforceable in accordance with the terms hereof. 売り主による本契約の締結と履行は, 本契約の条件に従って強制することができる法的, 有効かつ拘束力のある売り主の義務を構成する。◆The guarantor waives any and all notices of nonpayment or nonperformance or demand for payment or performance of such obligations under the franchise agreement. 保証人は, フランチャイズ契約に基づく当該債務の不払いまたは不履行について一切の通知を受ける権利と, 当該債務の支払いまたは履行について一切の催告通知を受ける権利を放棄する。

obligation of secrecy 秘密保持義務

◆The licensee's obligation under this Article with respect to confidential information shall not apply to information which may be acquired hereafter by the licensee from any third party without any obligation of secrecy. 本条に基づく秘密情報に関するライセンシーの義務は, 秘密保持義務なしに第三者からライセンシーが今後取得する情報には適用されないものとする。

oblige (動)強いる, 義務付ける, 義務を負わせる, ～をしてやる, (人を)喜ばせる, (人に)親切にする, 恩恵を施す (自動)手伝う, お役に立つ, 好意を示す, 喜ばせる

be much obliged for ～に深く感謝する

be obliged by ～に義務付けられる, ～に強制される

be obliged for ～に感謝する, ～していただいてありがとうございます

be obliged to ～しなければならない, ～せざるを得ない

I'd be obliged if you'd … ～していただけるとありがたいのですが

Will you oblige me by doing ～していただけませんか

◆We are obliged for your order. ご注文に感謝いたします。◆We enclose a few samples of our product and should be obliged if you would send us samples of the nearest quality you could offer from stock. 当社製品の見本を数点同封しますので, 在庫から提供できるほぼ同品質の見本を送っていただけるとありがたいのですが[ほぼ同品質の見本があれば送っていただけないでしょうか]。

obliged to ～する義務を負う

◆In the event that the purchaser does not wish to purchase all or any part of the products from the seller, the purchaser shall so advise the seller and shall not be obliged to purchase such quantities of the products. 買い主が売り主から本製品の全部または一部を購入することを希望しない場合, 買い主はその旨売り主に通知するものとし, 買い主

は本製品の当該数量を購入する義務は負わないものとする。

obligor (名)債務者

sole principal obligor 唯一の主債務者

◆The guarantor shall be liable under this guarantee as if it were the sole principal obligor and debtor and not merely a surety. 保証人は, 保証人が単なる保証人ではなく唯一の主債務者であるかのように本保証書上の責任を負うものとする。

obtain (動)取得する, 入手する, 獲得する, 得る

◆Proprietary Rights shall include such patent, design and trademark, and copyrights and trade secrets as may be obtained or acquired by Licensor during the term of this agreement. 所有権(知的財産権)は, 本契約期間中にライセンサーが取得または獲得する特許, 意匠, 商標と著作権およびトレード・シークレットを含むものとする。

ocean freight 海上輸送

◆In case of a CIF contract, the seller shall, at its own expenses, arrange for ocean freight of the products from the port of shipment stated in this agreement to the port of destination of the products. CIF契約の場合, 売り主は, 本契約に定める船積み港から本商品の仕向け港までの本商品の海上輸送の手配を, 自己負担でするものとする。

ODA 政府開発援助
(⇒official development assistance)

OEM 相手先ブランド製造業者, 相手先ブランドによる生産, 相手先ブランド販売, 相手先商標商品(製造), 委託生産方式 (⇒original equipment manufacturing [manufacturer])

OEM manufacturer OEM製造業者

of record or beneficially 登録株主としてまたは受益者(実質的な所有者)として

◆No director of the new company shall be required to own of record or beneficially any shares of the stock of the new company. 新会社の取締役は, 登録株主としてまたは株式の受益者として新会社の株式を保有することを要求されないものとする。

of the essence of this agreement 本契約の重要条件である, 本契約の絶対条件である

◆Time of shipment is of the essence of this agreement. 船積み時期は, 本契約の重要な条件である。

offer (動)申し込む, 申し出る, 提供する, 差し出す, 販売する, (金利などを)提示する, (買収などを)提案をする, ～しようとする, (株式などを)発行する, 株式を売り出す, (感謝の意や敬意などを)示す[表わす] (自動)申し出る, 提案する, 現われる, 到来する, 起こる

as soon as occasion [opportunity] offers 機会があり次第, 機会あるごとに

if opportunity offers 機会があったら, 機会が到来したら

offer a bid to ～に対して買収提案をする

offer a 5 percent discount　5%割り引く

offer customers the best value　顧客に最大の価値を提供する

offer shares for public subscription　株式を公開する

offer special thanks to　～に特別の感謝を表わす、～に特に感謝の意を表する

offer stocks for public subscription　株式を公募する

offer the stock at ¥250,000 a share in the initial public offering　新規株式公開で同株を1株25万円で売り出す

offer 24-hour service　24時間サービスを提供する

◆In addition to offering electronic settlement for online shoppers, Rakuten Inc. plans to offer loans for retail and corporate clients. ネット・ショッパー［オンライン・ショッパー］向けの電子決済業務のほかに、楽天は個人と企業向けの融資も手がける計画だ。◆The company offered a 10 percent discount to make up for the difference in quality. 品質差の埋め合わせのため、同社は10%値引きした。◆We are pleased to offer you as follows. 当方のオファーは、次のとおりです。◆We enclose a few samples of our product and should be obliged if you would send us samples of the nearest quality you could offer from stock. 当社製品の見本を数点同封しますので、在庫から提供できるほぼ同品質の見本を送っていただけるとありがたいのですが［ほぼ同品質の見本があれば送っていただけないでしょうか］。◆We refrained from making a counter offer as the price you offered is about seven percent higher than the level workable to us. 貴社がオファーされた価格は、当社の採算にのる水準よりも7%ほど高いので、カウンター・オファーを出すことを思いとどまりました。

offer　(名) 申込み、売り申込み、申し出、提案、提示、提示額、申請額、取引希望価格、付け値、売呼び値、割引、値引き、オファー（「オファー（申込み・売り申込み）」は、売り主・売り手 (seller) から買い主・買い手 (buyer) への売買条件の提示）

accept an offer　オファーを引き受ける［受ける、受諾する］、申込みを受諾する

accept this offer　このオファーを受ける［引き受ける、受諾する］、この申込みを受諾する

at the price on offer　提示価格で、大安売り中

be open to offers　値段交渉に応じる用意がある

be under offer　契約済みである、売約済みである

buying offer　買い申込み、買いオファー

buyout offer　買収の申込み、買収提案（=acquisiton offer）

counter offer　反対申込み、反対提案、代案の

提起、代案、カウンター・オファー

firm offer　回答期限付きオファー、ファーム・オファー

offer by tender　（株式の）入札発行

offer for sale　募集売出し、売出発行、売出し、間接発行

offer of credit　信用供与の申し入れ、与信枠の提供

offer price　募集価格、発行価額、売出価格、買付け価格、買取価格、提示価格、TOB（株式公開買付け）価格

offer sheet　見積書、オファー・シート

offer subject to our final confirmation　最終確認条件付きオファー

offer subject to prior sale　先売りご免条件付き売り申込み（=offer subject to being unsold）

offer subject to seller's final confirmation　売り主の最終確認条件付き売り申込み

offer without engagement　不確定売り申込み

offers to existing shareholders　割当て発行

on offer　申込み受付け中、募集中、販売中、売りに出されている、提供中

original offer　原申込み（売り主から買い主に最初に提示されたオファー）

revocation of offer　申込みの撤回

special offer　特別提供

◆We accept your offer subject to immediate confirmation by letter. 書簡での至急確認を条件として、貴社のオファーを引き受けます。◆We will accept your offer if you assure us of an order for at least 1,000 pieces per quarter for one year. 1年間、四半期ごとに最低1,000個の注文をご確約いただければ、貴社のオファーをお受けします。◆We will do our best to speed up delivery if you accept the counter offer. このカウンター・オファーを受けていただければ、全力を挙げて配送を急がせます。

offer, sell or export　販売申込み、販売または輸出をする

◆Supplier shall not directly or indirectly offer, sell or export Products to Territory through any other channel than Distributor. 供給者は、販売店以外の経路を通じて直接間接に契約地域に対して本製品の販売申込み、販売または輸出をしないものとする。

offered　(形) 提示された、申し込まれた、売り出された、提供された

bonds offered through private placement　私募債

continuously offered long-term securities　継続的に発行される［継続発行ベースの］長期債

employment offered　求人

offered market　買い手市場

offered price　付け値、呼び値、売り呼び値、申

込み価格［値段］

publicly-offered local government bonds　公募地方債

offeree　(名)申込み受人, 申込みの相手方, 被申込み者

◆A party hereto proposing to effect a sale of any shares of the new company (the Offerer) shall give a written notice to the other parties hereto, or their assignee, who are then shareholders of the new company (the Offerees), of the Offerer's intention, the identity of the prospective third party purchaser, and the terms and conditions of the proposed sale. 新会社の株式の売却を申し出る本契約当事者（「申込み者」）は, 他の当事者またはその時点で新会社の株主である譲受人（「被申込み者」）に対して, 申込み者の売却意思, 予定される第三者購入者の住所・氏名と申し出をした売却の条件を, 書面で通知するものとする。

offerer　(名)申込み人, 申込み者, 提案者, 提供者, TOBの買収会社　(=offeror)

offering　(名)申込み, 申し出, オファー, 提供, 発売, 株式売出し, 株式発行, 株式公開, 進物 (=offer; ⇒bona fide offer)

cross-border offering　国際的募集

equity offering　株式発行, 株式公開

initial public offering　新規公募

international offerings　国際公募

new share offering　新株発行

offering circular　公募募集案内書, 目論見書

offering date　申込み期日, 応募期日, 公募日, 割当日

offering day　募集取扱い日

offering memorandum　募集覚書, 目論見書

offering price　(株式の)売出価格, 発売価格, 公募価格, 募集価格, 申込み価格

offering size　入札総額

offering statement　発行目論見書, 募集届け出書

offerings to shareholders　株主割当て

private offering　私募

private offering exemption　私募免除

public offering　公募, 株式公開

public offering bond　公募債

public offering of bonds on fixed conditions　定率公募

rights offering　株主割当発行

shelf offering　一括募集

special offering　特別売出し

terms of the offering　発行条件

the line of product offerings　品揃え

underwrite the offering　売出しを引き受ける

official　(形)公の, 公的な, 公式の, 正式の, 公認の, 公示の, 公用の, 公務上の, 表向きの, 一般に公開されていない

file an official complaint　正式に苦情申立てをする

official barriers　法律上の制約, 法的な障壁

official certificate　公式の証明書

official exchange rate　公定レート

official interest rate　政策金利　(=official rate)

official invoice　公用送り状（税関送り状と領事送り状のこと）

official log book　航海日誌

official receiver　破産管財人

official report　正式な報告

official retail price　公定小売価格

Official Score Certificate　公式認定証

official state documents　公文書

official telecommunications equipment supplier　公認通信機器納入業者

official development assistance　政府開発援助, ODA

◆A Foreign Ministry panel has proposed the relaxation of the blanket ban on the military-related use of official development assistance. 外務省の有識者会議は, 政府開発援助（ODA）の軍事に絡む利用の全面禁止を緩和するよう提案した。

offset　(動)相殺をする, 埋め合わせをする, 帳消しにする, 吸収する, 吸い上げる, 解消する, 打ち消す, リスクなどをカバーする　(名)相殺, 相殺額, 差引勘定, 埋め合わせ

be partially offset by　〜で一部相殺される, 〜で部分的に相殺される

more than offset　十分相殺する, かなり相殺する

offset an account payable against an account receivable　買掛金を売掛金と相殺する

offset market risk　市場リスクを吸収する, 市場リスクを相殺する, 市場リスクをカバーする

offset the loss　損失の穴埋めをする, 損失をカバーする

◆A slight increase in exports led by automobiles was more than offset by a sharp rise in imports of liquefied natural gas and crude oil for thermal power generation. 自動車を中心に輸出は若干伸びたものの, これは火力発電用の液化天然ガス（LNG）や原油などの輸入急増でかなり相殺された。◆Despite declining prices of crude oil, the weak yen pushes up the cost of imports, partly offsetting the benefits of falling crude oil prices. 原油価格は下落しているが, 円安で輸入価格が押し上げられ, 原油安［原油下落］の恩恵が一部打ち消される面もある。◆The bank shall have the right, as the obligations become due, or in the event of their default, to offset cash deposits against such obligations due to the bank. 債務の期限が到来したと

き、または債務不履行の場合、銀行はその債務と
その預金を相殺する権利を持つものとする。

offshore [off-shore] （形）沖合の, 海上の,
海外の, 海外で取り決めた, オフショア
offshore assembly plant　海外組立工場
offshore asset　海外資産
offshore banking facility　オフショア市場, オ
　フショア金融センター
　（=offshore market, offshore banking center）
offshore borrowing　オフショア調達, 外貨借
　入れ
offshore center　オフショア市場
Offshore Control　オフショア・コントロール
　（有事の際, 米国が同盟国と協力して中国
　を海上封鎖すること）
offshore dealer　海外ディーラー
offshore drilling　海底石油掘削, 沖合掘削
offshore exploration　沖合調査, 沖合探査
offshore fund　海外投信（国際投資信託とし
　て海外に投資して税金を回避するもの）
offshore investment　海外投資
offshore loading and unloading　沖荷役
offshore market　オフショア市場
offshore oil and gas field　沖合石油ガス資源
offshore oil drilling　海底石油掘削
offshore operations　国外事業
offshore production　海外生産
offshore production area　経済特区
offshore purchase　域外調達, 域外買付け
offshore reserves of oil and gas　沖合石油ガス
　埋蔵
offshore oil field　海底油田
　◆Mitsui Oil Exploration Co. has a 10 percent
　stake in offshore oil fields in the oil spill in the
　Gulf of Mexico. 三井石油開発（三井物産の子会
　社）は, メキシコ湾の原油流出地域の海底油田に
　10%出資している。
OGL　包括輸入許可制（open general licenseの
　略）
oil crisis [crunch, shock]　石油危機, 石油
　ひっ迫, 石油ショック, オイル・ショック
　◆The record trade deficit of ¥6.9 trillion in 2012
　far exceeded ¥2.6 trillion in 1980 that immedi-
　ately followed the second oil crisis. 2012年の6.9
　兆円もの過去最大の貿易赤字は, 第二次石油危機直
　後の1980年に記録した2.6兆円を大きく上回った。
oil exploration　石油探査, 石油開発, 石油
　探鉱
oil exploration contract　石油探査契約
oil exploration cost　石油探査費
oil exploration subsidiary　石油開発子会社
　◆BP has asked an oil exploration subsidiary of
　Mitsui & Co. to pay $111 million to help cover

the expenses of a massive oil spill in the Gulf of
Mexico. 英国の国際石油資本BPは, 三井物産の石
油開発子会社（三井石油開発）に対して, メキシコ
湾の大量原油流出事故の処理費用として1億1,100
万ドルの負担を求めている。

oil output　石油生産量
　◆The actual oil outputs of Nigeria, Venezuela,
　Iran and other OPEC members have been below
　allocated country-by-country quotas. ナイジェリ
　アやベネズエラ, イランなどOPEC（石油輸出国機
　構）加盟国の実際の石油生産量は, OPECの国別生
　産枠を下回っている。
oil prices　原油価格
　◆Oil prices on the New York Mercantile Ex-
　change soared to the $100 level a barrel for the
　first time during the trading hours. ニューヨー
　ク・マーカンタイル取引所の原油価格は, 取引時
　間中に初めて1バレル＝100ドル台まで上昇した。
oil production　石油生産, 原油生産
　◆In the crude oil contract market of the New
　York Mercantile Exchange (NYMEX), the
　price of January WTI, the benchmark U.S. crude
　oil, fell below $60 a barrel for the first time since
　June 2009 on December 11, 2014 due to the fore-
　cast of rising global oil production. 2014年12月
　11日のニューヨーク・マーカンタイル取引所の原
　油先物取引では, 指標となる米国産原油WTI（テキ
　サス産軽質油）の1月渡し価格が, 世界的な石油増
　産見通しから, 2009年7月以来5年5か月ぶりに1バ
　レル＝60ドルを割り込んだ。
oil supply　原油供給
　◆Japan depends on imports for nearly 100 per-
　cent of its oil supply. 日本は, その原油供給のほ
　ぼ100%を輸入に依存している。
oil tanker　原油タンカー, 油送船, オイル・タ
　ンカー　（=oiler）
　◆Pirates are threatening the safe navigation of oil
　tankers and other ships in Southeast Asian wa-
　ters. 東南アジアの海域では, 海賊が原油タンカー
　などの船舶の安全な航行を脅かしている。
oil wholesaler　石油元売り, 石油元売り会社,
　元売り　（=oil refiner-distributor, oil wholesale
　company）
　◆The price of regular gas has gone up for six
　weeks because oil wholesalers have added their
　import costs, which have been going up due to
　the weak yen since the end of last year, to the re-
　tail price. レギュラー・ガソリンの価格は, 昨年末
　からの円安で上昇している輸入費用の増加分を元
　売り各社が小売価格に転嫁しているため, 6週間連
　続で上昇した。
omission　（名）脱落, 脱漏, 省略, 記載漏れ, 義
　務の怠慢, 懈怠（かいたい, けたい）, 不作為
　◆These are material omissions which in our view
　constitute another material breach. これらは重大
　な遺漏で, われわれの考えでは, もう一つの重大
　な違反に当たる。
**Omnibus Trade and Competitiveness
　Act of 1988**　1988年米包括通商・競争力法

ON　332

on　（前）〜の上に［で，の］，〜に，〜に基づいて，〜に関する，〜について，〜で，〜と同時に，〜次第

　on a CIF New York Port basis　CIFニューヨーク港条件で　（⇒effect delivery of the products）

　on a confidential basis　秘密裡に

　on a dollar denominated basis　ドル表示で

　on a full year basis　通年で，通期で

　on a limited time basis　限られた期間

　on a noncommitment basis　特定の義務なしで，特定の義務を負わないで　（=without commitment, without committing oneself）

　on a quarterly basis　四半期ごとに

　on a receipt basis　受領毎に，受領ベースで，受領した場合に

　on a semi-annual basis　半年ごとに

　on a worldwide basis　世界に向けて，世界市場に向けて

　on and after　〜以降　（=on or after）

　on and subject to the terms and conditions of this agreement　本契約の条件に従って，本契約の条項と条件に従って

　on any occasion　いずれかの機会に

　on arrival　到着次第

　on arrival terms　到着条件

　on conditions as advantageous as possible to　〜にできるかぎり有利な条件で

　on good terms with　〜と良好な関係にある

　on one's own responsibility　〜の自己の責任で

　on reasonable notice　合理的な通知の上（で）

　on reasonable terms　合理的な条件で

　on sale or return　承認売買，見計らい取引　（=sale on approval）

　on-site investigation［survey］　実地調査，立入検査

　on the conditions satisfactory to　〜が満足する条件で

　on the date hereof　本契約日に，本契約の締結日に　（=on the date of this agreement）

　on the date when　〜する日に

　on the due date therefor　その支払い期日に

　on the numbers of outstanding shares basis　発行済み株式数に基づいて

　on the part of　〜の側に

　on the terms and conditions set forth herein　本契約に定める条件で，本契約に規定する条件で

on a consolidated basis　連結ベースで
　◆The firm is expected to suffer more than ¥260 million in operating losses on a consolidated basis in the settlement term ending on March 31, 2016. 同社の2016年3月期の営業赤字は，連結ベースで2億6,000万円に達する見込みだ。

on a regular basis　定期的に
　◆We may place a substantial order with you on a regular basis if your prices are competitive. 貴社の製品価格が他社より安ければ，定期的に大口の注文を出すことができます。

on a trial basis　試験的に，実験的に
　◆Nursing-care robots produced on a trial basis by some Japanese companies cost as much as 20 million yen per unit, but the government hopes to promote the robots priced at about 100,000 yen for widespread use across the nation. 一部の日本企業が試験的に生産している介護ロボットは，1台2,000万円と高額だが，政府は1台10万円程度の介護ロボットを全国に普及させたい考えだ。

on a yearly basis　1年毎に，1年ずつ
　◆This agreement shall be automatically extended on a yearly basis until or unless terminated by either party giving to the other party ninety days prior notice by register mail. 本契約は，一方の当事者が相手方に対して書留郵便で90日間の事前通知をして終了させないかぎり，1年ずつ自動更新するものとする。

on an as is basis　現状有り姿ベースで，現状有り姿条件で，現状有り姿のままで，現状のままで　（=on an as is where is basis）
　◆ABC confirms and agrees that the Products are hereby licensed and supplied to ABC on an "as is" basis. 本製品が本契約により「現状有り姿」条件で使用許諾され，供給されることを，ABCは確認し，これに同意する。

on behalf of　〜に代わって，〜の代理として，〜を代表して，〜のために　（=in behalf of）
　on behalf of and in the name of　〜に代わり，〜の名前で
　on behalf of any of the other parties hereto　他の本契約当事者に代わり
　◆ABC shall take care of keeping its quality without any harm whatsoever as bona fide holder of Products on behalf of XYZ. ABCは，XYZを代理する契約品［本製品］の善意の保管者として，契約品［本製品］の品質保持上，どんな損害も生じないよう注意を払うものとする。

on board　積み込み
　on board B/L　船積み船荷証券，船積み式船荷証券　（=shipped B/L）
　on board endorsement　船積み裏書き　（=on board notation）
　on board only clause　本船のみ担保約款

on credit　信用貸しで，付けで，掛で，代金を借りて
　◆In margin trading, stocks can be purchased on credit. 信用取引では，掛けで［購入代金を借りて］株を買うことができる。

on deck　甲板積み

O

on deck cargo 甲板積み貨物

on deck clause 甲板積み約款
（＝on deck stowage clause）

on deck container 甲板積みコンテナ

on demand 請求と同時に，請求のあり次第，請求次第，要求払い，一覧払いの，参着為替（要求払い為替手形（demand draft［O/D］）のこと）
◆In case payment by the purchaser for the delivery of the products is delayed later than 35 days after B/L date, the purchaser shall pay to the seller on demand the amount due together with interest from the due date until paid at the annual rate equal to the prime rate plus 5 percent per year on any overdue amount. 買い主による本製品の引渡しに対する支払いが船荷証券の日付から35日を超えて遅延した場合，買い主は請求のあり次第売り主に対して期限到来債務を支払うとともに，延滞金については支払い期日から支払い日までプライム・レートに年率5%を加えた年間利率で利息を支払うものとする。

on hand 手持ちの［で］，手元の，手元に，所有して，持ち合わせて，（時間などを）持て余して，間近に，目前に，近くに居合わせて，待機して，出迎えに出て，出席して
◆We have on hand such a rush of orders for this item that our output capacity cannot keep up with the demand. 本品に対しては多くの注文が入っているため，当社の生産能力が需要に追いつかない状況です。

on one's own account 自己の費用で，自己の負担で，～の勘定で，自己の利益のために
◆Licensee shall, on its own account, purchase and send an economy class trip air ticket for each engineer ten days prior to his or her departure from Tokyo. ライセンシーは，自己負担で，各技術者のためのエコノミー・クラスの往復航空切符を購入し，東京から出発する10日前に送付する。

on one's own reasons ～の自己の都合で
◆ABC reserves the right to replace on its own reasons any ABC Personnel so assigned with a competent substitute by giving XYZ a notice in advance. ABCは，XYZに事前通知を行って，派遣したABC人員を自社の都合で適格交替人員と交替させる権利を持つ。

on presentation （手形の）提示［呈示］次第［提示のあり次第］，手形提示の節は，手形提示の折は
◆We have drawn upon you a documentary bill at 60 d/s through ABC Bank for the invoice amount, which we hope you will kindly honor on presentation. 送り状金額に対して，ABC銀行を通じて60日払い荷為替手形を貴社宛てに振り出しましたので，提示［呈示］のあり次第お引き受け下さい。◆We hope you will kindly protect the draft on presentation. 手形提示の節は，何とぞお引き受け下さい。

on the basis of ～に基づいて，～をもとに，

～を基礎として，～を標準として
◆Banks participating in direct yen-yuan trading in the Tokyo interbank foreign exchange market will trade the yen and the yuan at an exchange rate calculated on the basis of actual supply and demand. 東京外国為替市場で円・人民元の直接取引に参加する銀行は，実際の需給をもとに算出した取引レートで，円と人民元を銀行間で取引する。

on the basis of 360 days 1年を360日として（＝on the basis of a 360 day year; ⇒LIBOR）

on the due date 支払い期日に
◆If ABC is compelled by law to make payment subject to any tax and XYZ does not actually receive on the due date a net amount equal to the full amount provided for under this agreement, ABC shall pay all necessary additional amounts to ensure receipt by XYZ of the full amount so provided for. ABCが法律で税金の対象の支払いを強制され，XYZが本契約に規定する満額どおりの正味金額を支払い期日に実際に受領しない場合，XYZが契約の規定どおり満額を受領できるようにするために必要なすべての加算金を，ABCは支払うものとする。

on the elapse of ～が経過した時点で，～の経過により
◆Unless other party cures such breach within 30 days after the receipt of such written notice of breach and intention of termination, this agreement shall be automatically terminated on the elapse of such 30-day period. 相手方が契約の違反と契約解除の意思に関する書面での通知を受けてから30日以内に当該違反を改めないかぎり，本契約は，この30日の期間が経過した時点で自動的に解除されるものとする。

on the termination of this contract 本契約解除時に
◆If some or all of the goods have not been received by the buyer on the termination of this contract, the buyer shall, in its sole discretion, cease to take delivery of the remaining goods and the seller shall return to the buyer any amounts paid in advance in respect of such goods. 本契約解除時に商品の一部または全部を買い主が受領していない場合，買い主は，買い主単独の選択で，残存商品［未引渡し商品］の引取りを中止し，売り主は当該商品に関して前払いで受領した代金を買い主に返還するものとする。

on the time as stipulated in this agreement 本契約で定める期限
◆In case there is delay in delivery of all or any part of the Goods on the time as stipulated in this agreement, the buyer is entitled to claim liquidated damages at the rate of one-half of one percent（0.5%）of the amount of the delayed Goods for each complete week of delay. 本契約で定める期限に本商品の全部または一部に引渡し遅延が生じた場合，買い主は，遅延対象の各1週

ONCE 334

間につき引渡し遅延商品の代金の0.5％を損害賠償
予定額として請求することができるものとする。

once-land（名）仮陸揚げ

one（形）一つの, 1人の, 1個の, ある〜, 片方
の, 同じ　（名）一つ, 1人, 1個, 片方, 一方

one-day settlement　翌日決済

one-man business［operation］　個人事業

one-name paper　単名手形

one of the parties　両当事者の一方, 当事者の
一方

one-off bulk order　一括払いの大口注文

one-off charge　1回かぎりの費用, 一時的費
用, 特別損失

one-off payment　一時金

one shipment　1荷口　（=one lot）

one-side balance of exchange　片為替

one-side trade　片貿易　（=one-way trade）

one-sided market　売り一色, 買い一色

one-time royalty　1回限りのロイヤルティ, 1
回全額払いのロイヤルティ

one-time write-off　一括償却

one to blame　一方過失（他船または自船の
過失による衝突）

the one share/one vote principle　1株1議決権
の原則

one or more　1人以上の, 1個以上の, 1通また
は複数の
　◆In case any one or more of the provisions of
this agreement are held invalid, illegal or unenforceable in any respect, the validity, legality
and enforceability of the remaining provisions
hereof shall not be in any way affected or impaired thereby, except to the extent that giving
effect to the remaining provisions would be unjust or inequitable. 本契約の一つ以上の規定がい
ずれかの点で無効, 違法または強制不能と判断さ
れた場合, 残存規定の実施が不公正または不均衡
となる範囲を除いて, 本契約の残存規定の有効性,
合法性と強制可能性はその影響を受けることはな
く, またそれによって損なわれることはないもの
とする。

online trading system　電子取引システム,
オンライン取引システム
　◆The Proprietary Trading System and other online trading systems facilitate trading of stocks
outside stock exchanges.　私設取引システム
（PTS）などの電子取引システムは, 取引所外で株
の売買（注文）を成立させる。

online transaction　ネット取引
　◆As stealth marketing by postings is problematic, the Consumer Affairs Agency has revised
its guidelines for online transactions under the
Law for the Prevention of Unreasonable Premiums and Misrepresentations concerning Products and Services. 書き込みによるステルス・マー
ケティングには問題があるので, 消費者庁は,「景品

表示法（不当景品類及び不当表示防止法）」のネッ
ト取引に関する指針を改正した。

only to the extent necessary to　〜するの
に必要な範囲にかぎって, 〜するのに必要な
限度まで

only to the extent of　〜を限度として

OPEC　石油輸出国機構, オペック
　（Organization of Petroleum Exporting
Countriesの略）
　◆The actual oil outputs of Nigeria, Venezuela,
Iran and other OPEC members have been below
allocated country-by-country quotas. ナイジェ
リアやベネズエラ, イランなどOPEC（石油輸出国
機構）加盟国の実際の石油生産量は, OPECの国別
生産枠を下回っている。◆The OPEC talks broke
down in acrimony as Saudi Arabia failed to convince other member nations to raise production.
石油輸出国機構（OPEC）の協議は, サウジアラビ
アが増産［生産量の引上げ］について他の加盟国を
説得できなかったため, 険悪なムードのなかで決
裂した。

open（動）開く, 開ける, 開設する, 出店する,
開店する, 開業する, 営業を始める, 暴露する,
（市場などを）開放する, 初値を付ける, 始め
る, 開始する,（事件の）冒頭陳述をする,（再
審理のために判決などを）取り消す　（自動）
始まる, 開演する,（ファイルなどが）開く,
（道路などが）開通する, 開店する,（景色が）
開ける, 展開する,（映画などが）初公開され
る, 封切りになる, オープンする

open a bank account　銀行口座を開く

open a market　市場を開拓する

open an account with　〜に口座を開く, 〜に
口座を開設する, 〜と取引を開始する［始め
る］, 〜と取引関係を結ぶ（establish a
connection with）

open an irrevocable L/C in your favor　貴社を
受益者として取消不能信用状を開設する

open business　事業を起こす

open the domestic market　国内市場を開放
する

open the public debt markets　公募債市場を開
放する, 公募債市場を自由化する

open up to public ownership　株式を公開する
　◆This letter of credit shall be opened not less
than 30 calendar days before the first scheduled
shipping date for each order and shall be 90 days
beyond the anticipated final shipping date. この
信用状は, 各注文の最初の出荷予定日から30暦日
以上前に開設するものとし, 最終出荷予定日から
90日を超えて有効でなければならない。

open（形）開かれた, 開放的な, 制限のない,
自由な, 公開の, 周知の, 営業中の, 開会中の,
未決定の, 未解決の, 未決算の, 非武装の, 無防
備の, オープン

leave the matter open　問題を未解決のまま
残す

OPEN

open account 暫定契約, 先渡し契約, 清算勘
定(2国間協定貿易の決済方法), 当座預金,
当座勘定, 与信取引勘定, 与信取引先

open account contract 前貸生産契約

open accounts receivable 掛売り代金

open-air market 青空市場

open ballot 無記名投票

open bid 公開入札, 一般競争入札
(=open tendering)

open bidding system 公開入札制度

open buying 新規買い(株の信用取引でのカ
ラ買い)

open cargo 自由貨物, (契約対象外の)除外
貨物, オープン・カーゴ

open certificate policy 包括予定保険証券

open charter 予定用船契約, オープン・
チャーター(未確定事項については後で協
議する条件で締結する用船契約)

open check [cheque] 普通小切手

open competition 自由競争, 公開競争

open contract (先物売買の)未定契約, 暫定
契約, 包括予定保険

open corporation 公開会社

open cover 包括予定保険, 包括予定保険契約

open credit 信用貸し, 無条件信用状, 手形買
取り銀行無指定信用状, オープン・クレ
ジット

open dock 開放荷扱いドック

open dollar オープン・ドル(ドル表示の債
権や債務)

open-door policy 門戸開放政策

open economy 開放経済

open-end contract 未定数量売約, 不定契約

open-end policy 可変保険証券

open-end pricing オープンエンド契約(購入
数量を決めないで単価を決める購入契約)

open endorsement 無記名裏書き

open exclusive license 限定独占ライセンス

open futures position 先物の未決済玉(ぎょ
く)

open general license 包括輸入許可制

open house 工場参観日

open indent 仕入先無指定買付け委託, オー
プン・インデント(買付け委託の際, 買入
れ先を指定しないで受託者に任せる方式)

open interest 建玉(たてぎょく)

open L/C 買取銀行無指定信用状, 買取銀行
無指定L/C

open letter 公開状

open mortgage 一部抵当

open mortgage clause 単純抵当債権者払い

約款

open order (数量、価格を売り手の裁量に任
せる)見計らい注文, (取消しがあるまで有
効な)保留注文, 無条件注文, 市価注文

open period 公開期間

open policy 包括予定保険(証券), 予定保
険 (=open contract, open cover)

open port [harbor] 開港(関税法に基づいて
貿易のために開かれた港)

open position (為替の)オープン・ポジ
ション

open price 公開価格, オープン価格

open price agreement 販売価格公開契約

open price tag オープン価格

open question 未決問題, 自由応答

open rate 基本料金, 任意運賃率

open rate cargo オープン・レート・カー
ゴ (=free rate cargo: 運賃率について船会
社と自由に取り決めできる貨物)

open sea 公海, 外洋

open selling 新規売り(株の信用取引でのカ
ラ売り), 公開販売

open shed (税関の)戸外上屋

open slip 保険申込み書

open stock 店頭商品

open stock burglary policy 商品盗難保険証券

open tender (一般)入札

open to buy 購買余力, 発注残高

open-top container オープントップ・コン
テナ

open trading system 開放貿易体制

open-yard storage clause 野積み約款

**open an irrevocable documentary letter
of credit** 取消不能の荷為替信用状を開設
する

◆For invoices for orders exceeding U.S. dollars
50,000, XYZ may require ABC to open for XYZ
an irrevocable documentary letter of credit, in
the form satisfactory to XYZ for an amount at
least equal to 100% of the order value payable in
accordance with the provisions of Section (5)
of this Article above. 5万米ドルを超える注文に
対する請求書については, XYZは, XYZのために,
上記本条第5項の規定に従って支払われる注文金額
の少なくとも100%に相当する金額の取消不能の荷
為替信用状をXYZが満足するフォームで開設する
ようABCに対して要求することができる。

open an L/C 信用状を発行する, 信用状を開
設する (=establish an L/C)

◆For reimbursement, we have applied to our
bankers for an L/C to be opened. (本注文に対
する)代金支払いのため, 当社は銀行に信用状の
発行を申請しました。◆To cover this shipment,
we have drawn upon you at sight for the invoice

amount under the L/C opened by ABC Bank. この船積みに対して、当社はABC銀行発行の信用状に基づいて、一覧払い送り状額面金額の手形を貴社宛てに振り出しました。

open for business　営業している
◆The Business Day means any day on which the banks are open for business in both cities of Tokyo and London. 「営業日」とは、東京とロンドンの両市で銀行が営業している日を意味する。

open market　公開市場, 一般市場, 市中市場, 自由市場, 市場開放

open market（discount）rate　市中銀行割引歩合

open market economies　自由市場経済, 市場経済

open market forces　市場原理

open market mechanisms　自由市場原理

open market papers　市場流通手形, 一般市場商業手形

open market policy　公開市場政策, 市場開放政策　（=market opening policy）

open market quotations　市中相場, 通り相場

open market rates　短期市場金利, 市中金利

open market selling operation　売オペ

open market operation　公開市場操作, 金融調節（日銀などの中央銀行が公開市場で政府債券の売買を行って、通貨量の増減により利率や為替相場を調節すること）
◆LDP President Abe said that he will ask the BOJ to buy construction bonds, or the government bonds issued for public works projects, through open market operations, which is a typical monetary control measure conducted by the central bank. 自民党の安倍総裁は、日銀が買い取る通常の金融調節手法である公開市場操作［買いオペ］で、建設国債（公共事業のために発行する国債）の買取りを日銀に求めると述べた。

open one's [the] market　市場を開放する
◆Japan, which is being pushed to further open its agricultural markets, is taking a wait-and-see attitude toward the free trade talks. 農業分野での一層の市場開放を迫られる日本は、自由貿易交渉については様子見の構えだ。

open skies agreement　航空自由化協定, オープンスカイ協定　（⇒antitrust immunity）
◆Japan and United States agreed to liberalize air traffic under a so-called open skies agreement. 日米両政府は、いわゆるオープンスカイ協定に基づく航空自由化で合意した。◆The open skies agreement will allow Japanese and U.S. carriers to freely decide on the routes and numbers of flights between the countries in principle. オープンスカイ協定により、日米の航空会社は原則として両国間の路線と便数を自由に設定できるようになる。

open trade　開かれた貿易, 開放貿易, 未決済

取引, 新規売買
◆By supporting open trade, Pacific Rim leaders pledged to fend off the deepening damage from the European crisis. 開かれた貿易を後押しすることで、環太平洋地域の首脳は、深刻化する欧州危機の影響を回避することを誓った。

open up to one's satisfaction　開装してご満足いただける
◆We trust that the goods will open up to your entire satisfaction. 契約品［約定品］は、開装の上、十分ご満足いただけるものと思います。

opener　（名）（信用状）発行依頼者

opening bank　発行銀行, 信用状発行銀行

opening charge　信用状発行手数料

opening date　開店日

opening hours　営業時間

operating　（形）経営上の, 営業上の, 業務の

operating deficit　営業赤字　（=operating loss）

operating earnings［profit］　営業利益

operating expenses［costs］　営業費用, 営業費

operating fund［capital］　運転資金

operating performance　営業成績, 経営成績, 営業業績, 業績

operating real estate　事業用不動産

operating reports　事業報告

operating system　基本ソフトウエア, 基本ソフト, システム・ソフト, オペレーティング・システム, OS

operating technology　運転技術

◆The firm is expected to suffer more than ￥260 million in operating losses on a consolidated basis in the settlement term ending on March 31, 2016. 同社の2016年3月期の営業赤字は、連結ベースで2億6,000万円に達する見込みだ。

operating lease　オペレーティング・リース, 営業型リース, 賃貸性リース　（⇒finance lease）

解説 オペレーティング・リース契約の特徴：機器のリースには、オペレーティング・リースとファイナンス・リースの二つがある。このうちオペレーティング・リース契約の特徴としては、契約期間が短期であること、契約の中途解約が不能であること、不可抗力によるリース物件損失、損傷は貸主が負担すること、リース物件の補修費用、サービス費用は貸主が負担することなどを挙げることができる。

operation　（名）操業, 営業, 営業活動, 事業, 企業, 組織, 業務, 経営, 活動, 作業工程, 生産過程, （組織の）展開, （警察の）捜査活動, 操作, 運転, 運行, 運航, 稼動, 機能, （器官などの）働き, 作用, 影響, 公開市場操作, 介入操作, 投機売買, 思惑買い, 作戦, 軍事作戦, 軍事行動, 計画, 手術, （コンピュータの）演算, 演算処理, オペレーション

business operations audit　業務監査

combine operations　業務を統合する

core strategic operations　主力戦略事業

export operations　輸出業務, 輸出事業, 輸出部門

go into operation　操業を開始する, 業務を開始する　(=begin operations)

import operations　輸入業務, 輸入事業, 輸入部門

operation contract　運航委託契約

operation flow chart　工程図, 工程表

operation of hostility　敵対行為　(=act of hostility, hostilities)

overseas operations　海外事業, 海外業務

◆Mazda is expected to seek a new business partner in order to expand operations in emerging countries. 新興国での事業を拡大するため, マツダは今後, 新たな業務提携先を模索するものと見られる。◆Some Japanese-affiliated companies and Japanese restaurants have been forced to suspend their factory operations or close their outlets due to the acts of destruction by Chinese demonstrators. 一部の日系企業や日本料理店は, 中国のデモ隊による破壊行為で, 工場の操業停止や店舗の休業に追い込まれている。

operation of law　法律の運用
　◆Without first obtaining the written consent of other parties hereto, no party, nor its successors or assignees, shall sell, assign, transfer, pledge, encumber or otherwise dispose of, whether by operation of law or otherwise, any shares of voting of the new company or instruments convertible into such shares. 他の本契約当事者の書面による同意を最初に得ないで, いずれの当事者も, その承継人または譲受人も, 法律の運用によるかその他の方法によるかを問わず, 新会社の議決権付き株式またはこのような株式に転換できる証書を売却, 譲渡, 移転, 質入れ, 担保差入れ, その他の方法で処分することはしないものとする。

option　(名)選択, 取るべき道, 選ぶべき方法 [手段], 選択肢, 選択手段, 選択の余地, 選択科目, 選択権, 優先的選択権, 購入選択権, 売買選択権, 商品の有料付属品, 付加的機能, オプション取引, オプション

at one's option　〜の選択で

business tie-up options　業務提携策

call option　買付け選択権, 買う権利, コール・オプション

currency option　通貨オプション (将来の特定日にあらかじめ取り決めた価格 (striking price: 行使価格)で外国通貨を買う権利 (call option)または売る権利 (put option)を売買する取引)

equity option　株式オプション

exercise of option　オプションの行使

futures and options market　金融先物市場, 先物・オプション市場

index option　株価指数オプション, 指数オプション

option agreement　オプション契約

option deal　オプション取引 (買う権利をコール・オプション、売る権利をプット・オプションという)

option holder　オプション保有者, オプションの買い手

option price　オプション価格

option trading　オプション取引　(=option transaction: あらかじめ決められた期日に株を売買する権利 (オプション)を売買する取引)

option trading of individual stocks　個別株オプション取引

options exercisable　行使可能オプション

put option　売付け選択権, 売る権利, プット・オプション

spot option　現物オプション

stock option plan　株式購入選択権制度, 株式選択権制度

trade option　約定オプション, 上場オプション

◆The licensor shall have an option to terminate this agreement and the license granted by this agreement by giving a written notice of such termination to the licensee. ライセンサーは、ライセンシーに対して書面による終了通知を行って、本契約と本契約により付与するライセンスを終了させることができる。

or otherwise　またはその他で, またはその他の方法で, またはそれ以外の, または別段に, 〜にせよそうでないにせよ, またはその反対
　◆LICENSOR may audit, at its own expense, the books of LICENSEE in which information relating to the quantities of LICENSEE's BIOS shipped, distributed transferred, or otherwise disposed of by LICENSEE is recorded, and LICENSEE's records supporting its entries in those books. ライセンサーは、その自己負担で、ライセンシーが出荷、販売、譲渡したまたはその他の方法で処分したライセンシーのBIOS (バイオス)の数量に関する情報が記載されているライセンシーの帳簿と、この帳簿の記入項目を立証するライセンシーの記録を監査することができる。

oral　(形)口頭の, 口頭による

oral contract　口頭契約

oral evidence　口頭証拠

oral understanding　口頭による了解, 口頭による了解事項

order　(動)命じる, 命令を出す, 指示する, 指図する, 注文する, 発注する, 並べる, 陳列する

order goods　商品を注文する

order online　ネット（で）注文する

◆France's Competition Commission has ordered Sony, Matsushita and Philips to pay fines for allegedly concluding price-fixing agreements on retail goods with their local distributors. フランスの競争評議会は、国内販売店と小売電気製品の価格維持協定を結んだとして、ソニー、松下電器産業とフィリップスに罰金の支払いを命じた。◆ The arbitrators shall have the authority to order such discovery and production of documents, including the depositions of party witnesses, and to make such orders for interim relief, including injunctive relief, as they may deem just and equitable. 仲裁人は、当事者の証人の宣誓証言［証言録取書］を含めて文書の開示と提出を命じる権限と、差止救済を含めて仲裁人が正義かつ衡平と見なす暫定的救済を命じる権限を持つものとする。

order　（名）注文, 注文書, 注文品, 受注品, 受注高, 申込み書, 指図, 指図人, 命令, 規則, 秩序（⇒letter of credit）

　a large order　大口の注文, 大口注文, 大量注文

　a small order　小口の注文, 小口注文

　a trial order　試験的注文, 見本注文（order for samples）, 試買注文

　accept your order　貴社の注文を受ける［受諾する］, 貴注文を受ける

　administrative order　行政命令

　after receipt of order　受注後

　an order by mail ［letter, post］　書信注文

　an order sample　見本注文, 見本による注文

　assembly （production） order　組立指図書

　be made out to order　指図人式で作成される

　be on order　注文を出してある

　blanket order　一括注文

　cancel an order　注文を取り消す

　canvass for orders　注文取りに奔走する

　carte blanche order　白紙注文, 無条件注文

　complete your order　貴注文を履行する, 貴社注文［貴社の注文］を履行する

　confirm ［acknowledge］ an order　注文を確認・受諾する

　congestion of orders　注文の殺到

　Could you please acknowledge the order by return?　折り返し、注文請け書お願いできますか［折り返し、注文請け書をお送りいただけますでしょうか］。

　delivery order　荷渡し指図書, 積み荷渡し指図書, 蔵出し指図書, 出荷指示

　execute an order　注文を執行する, 納品する

　fill an order　注文を処理する, 注文を執行する, 注文に応える

　firm order　確定注文

　fixed order　固定注文

　get an order　注文を取り付ける

　goods against an order　注文品

　goods （made） to order　注文品, あつらえ品

　goods on order　注文中の品, 未達商品

　in good order and condition　無事に

　initial order　初注文

　issue an order　注文書を発行する, 発注する, 注文を出す

　lose an order　注文を逃す, 注文を取り損ねる

　main （production） order　主指図書

　make up ［out］ an order　注文書を作成する

　open order　（数量、価格を売り手の裁量に任せる）見計らい注文,（取消しがあるまで有効な）保留注文, 無条件注文, 市価注文

　order blank　注文用紙, 注文書式

　order form　注文書式

　order number　注文番号, 製造番号

　order of application of payment　支払いの充当の順序, 支払いの充当順位

　order of credit　債権の順位

　order of divestiture　剥奪命令, 集中排除命令, 排除措置命令

　order of enforcement　執行命令

　order policy　指図式保険証券

　order processing　注文処理

　order production　注文生産

　order rates　受注状況

　order sheet　注文書

　original order　原注文

　pass an order through　～を通じて発注する

　pay to ～, or order the sum of　合計金額…を～にまたはその指図により［その指図人に］支払う

　payment order　支払い指図, 支払い指図書

　place an order　注文を出す, 注文する, 注文書を作成する, 注文書を交付する

　place an order for　～を注文する, ～の注文を出す

　place an order with　～に注文する

　place regular orders　定期的に注文を出す

　postal money order　郵便為替

　process an order　注文を取り消す

　purchase order　売約書, 注文書

　receive an order　注文を受ける

　release order　航空貨物引渡し指図書

　repeat an order　再注文する

　sample order　見本的注文

　secure an order　注文を獲得する

　solicit orders　注文を求める, 注文を取る

　split order　分割注文

　supply an order　受注品を納入する

suspend an order　注文を見合わす
　　(=hold up an order)

take an order　注文を受ける, 受注する

telephone order　電話注文

the execution of your order　貴社注文[貴注文]の履行, 貴注文の執行

the giving of the order　発注

verbal order　口頭注文

win an order　受注する, 注文を獲得する

withdraw an order　注文を取り消す, 注文を撤回する

your order　貴社の注文, 貴社注文, 貴注文
◆A full set of negotiable bills of lading made out to order must be endorsed by shipper. 指図人式で作成された譲渡可能な船荷証券一式には, 荷送人の裏書が必要である. ◆All quantities of the Product manufactured by you shall be held by you to our order and we shall insure all quantities on your premises of the Commodity and the Product. 貴社が製造した契約品の数量はすべて当社の指図があるまで貴社が保管し, 当社は貴社の構内にある商品と契約品の全数量に保険を付けるものとする. ◆Bills of lading shall be made out to order and marked notify party. 船荷証券は, 指図人式で作成し, 通知先を記入しなければならない. ◆For reimbursement, we have drawn upon you through ABC Bank a draft at 90 d/s for $50,000 against your order No. 50. 代金回収のため, 当社は貴社注文第50号に対しABC銀行を通じて50,000ドルの一覧後90日払いの為替手形を貴社宛てに振り出しました. ◆Mitsubishi Heavy Industries Ltd. aims to win orders for commercial launches of foreign satellites with a current lineup of its core H-2A and H-2B rockets. 三菱重工業は, 現在の主力ロケットH2AとH2Bロケットの二本柱で, 外国の衛星の商用打上げ受注を目指している. ◆Our terms of payment are to value at 30 d/s under an irrevocable letter of credit to be opened in our favor for the corresponding value of an order. 当社の決済条件は, 注文相当額につき, 当社を受益者として開設された取消不能信用状に基づいて一覧後30日払いの手形を振り出すことです. ◆The shipment will be made late in March as our subcontractors are somewhat behind in completing your order. 貴社注文の履行に下請けが少々遅れを出しているため, 積み出しは3月末になる見込みです. ◆There is a discount available for a large order. 大量注文には, 割引の恩恵があります[値引も適用されます]. ◆We are giving your order priority, but a slight delay in the shipment of yours will be unavoidable. 貴社の注文を優先的に扱っていますが, ご注文の船積みが少々遅れることは避けられません. ◆We are obliged for your order. ご注文に感謝いたします. ◆We are very sorry indeed to have to advise you of a delay in the execution of your order. 貴社注文の履行が遅れたことを, お知らせしなければなりません. ◆We fear we have to advise you that we may not be able to dispatch in full your order due to the shortage of shipping space. 不本意ながら, 船腹不足のため, 貴社の注文が一部積み残しになる可能性があることをお伝えしなければなりません. ◆We have on hand such a rush of orders for this item that our output capacity cannot keep up with the demand. 本品に対しては多くの注文が入っているため, 当社の生産能力が需要に追いつかない状況です. ◆We have to inform you that the credit to cover your order does not seem to have reached us yet. 貴社注文[貴注文]に対する信用状が未着であることを, お知らせしなければなりません. ◆We may place a substantial order with you on a regular basis if your prices are competitive. 貴社の製品価格が他社より安ければ, 定期的に大口の注文を出すことができます. ◆We will accept your offer if you assure us of an order for at least 1,000 pieces per quarter for one year. 1年間, 四半期ごとに最低1,000個の注文をご確約いただければ, 貴社のオファーをお受けします. ◆We will execute the order with best attention upon receipt of your L/C. 貴社の信用状を受け取り次第, 当社は最善の注意を払って注文を履行します. ◆Your orders are arriving in Yokohama soon and will be transshipped on to m.s. "President Wilson" which is leaving Yokohama for your port on August 10. 貴注文は間もなく横浜に到着し, 貴地に向けて8月10日に横浜を出港予定のディーゼル船「プレジデント・ウイルソン」号に積み換える予定です.

order B/L[bill of lading]　指図人式船荷証券
◆It is necessary to write the name of notify party on the order B/L as it does not contain the name of consignee. 指図人式船荷証券には, 荷受け人名が記載されていないので, 通知先名を書かなければならない.

order value　注文金額
◆For invoices for orders exceeding U.S. dollars 50,000, XYZ may require ABC to open for XYZ an irrevocable documentary letter of credit, in the form satisfactory to XYZ for an amount at least equal to 100% of the order value payable in accordance with the provisions of Section (5) of this Article above. 5万米ドルを超える注文に対する請求書については, XYZは, XYZのために, 上記本条第5項の規定に従って支払われる注文金額の少なくとも100%に相当する金額の取消不能の荷為替信用状をXYZが満足するフォームで開設するようABCに対して要求することができる.

ordering forecast　注文見込み, 注文予測

ordinary business hours　通常の営業時間
◆The licensee, at the request and at the expense of the licensor, permit its personnel and/or an independent accountant designated by the licensor to have access to, examine and copy during ordinary business hours such records as may be necessary to verify or determine any royalties, paid or payable, under this agreement. ライセンシーは, ライセンサーの要請があるときはライセンサー

ORDI 340

の費用で、ライセンサーの人員および/またはライセンサーが指定する独立会計士が、本契約のもとに支払ったまたは支払うべきロイヤルティの額を確認、決定するために必要な記録を、ライセンシーの通常の営業時間中に閲覧、検証し、コピーすることを許可する。

ordinary conduct of the party's business 当事者の通常の事業行為

ordinary course of business 通常の業務過程
◆No material commitments, bids or bidding offers will be entered into by the Company in any case in excess of $10,000 whether or not in the ordinary course of business, except with the prior written consent of Purchaser. 買い主の書面による事前の同意がある場合を除いて、対象会社は、通常の業務過程であるか否かを問わずどんな場合でも1万ドルを超える重要な約束、入札、入札の申込みは行わないものとする。

ordinary general meeting 通常株主総会
◆The term of office of a director shall expire at the close of the second ordinary general meeting of shareholders to be held subsequent to this election. 取締役の任期は、その選任後に開催される2回目の通常株主総会の終了時に満了する。

organization and corporate authority 設立と会社法上の権限, 設立と行為能力

organized and existing under the laws of 〜の法律に基づいて設立され現存する, 〜法に基づいて設立され現存する

original （名）原本, 契約原本, 正本, 原文, 原作, オリジナル
◆This agreement may be executed simultaneously in one or more counterparts, each of which shall be deemed an original. 本契約書は1通またはそれ以上の副本で作成することができるが、これらの副本はそれぞれ原本と見なされるものとする。

original agreement 原契約, 当初の契約

original currency 元受通貨
◆All reinsurances shall be effected in the original currency. 再保険は、すべて元受通貨で行うものとする。

original edition rights 書籍原版権, 出版物原版権
◆Establishing original edition rights would enable publishing companies to file lawsuits demanding the deletion of data if pirated copies are found to be sold on the Internet. 出版物［書籍］原版権の創設によって出版社は、海賊版がインターネット上で販売されていることが判明した場合に、データの削除を求める訴訟を起こすことができる。

original equipment manufacturing [manufacturer] 相手先ブランド製造業者, 相手先ブランドによる生産, 相手先ブランド販売, 相手先商標商品（製造）, 委託生産方式, OEM
◆The two companies plan to market products that better meet the needs of each region through so-called original equipment manufacturing, in

which one company manufactures products that bear the trademark of the other. 両社は、相手先の商標を付した商品を生産するいわばOEMを通じて、各地域のニーズに一段と合った製品の提供を計画している。

original term of this agreement 本契約の当初期間, 当初の契約期間
◆The said term of this agreement shall be automatically extended for additional consecutive periods of three years each, unless terminated by either party hereto by giving the other party a written notice to that effect at least three months prior to the end of original term of this agreement or any extended term thereof. 本契約の上記期間は、少なくとも本契約の当初期間またはその延長期間が満了する3カ月前までに、本契約の当事者の一方が相手方に対して本契約を終了させる旨の書面による通知をして本契約を終了させないかぎり、さらに引き続き3年間ずつ自動的に延長するものとする。

other party 他方の当事者, 他方当事者, 他方, 相手方

other than as provided above in this Article 本条の上記規定以外に
◆The seller does not make and hereby disclaim any warranty in respect of the products other than as provided above in this Article, whether express or implied, including without limitation any implied warranty of merchantability or fitness for any purpose. 売り主は、商品性または特定目的への適合性の黙示保証などを含めて、本条の規定以外に明示・黙示を問わず本製品に関する保証を一切行わず、本製品に関する保証を本契約により否認する。

other than as security for indebtedness 借入れ担保とする場合を除いて, 借入れ担保として〜する場合を除いて

other than for force majeure 不可抗力以外の事由で, 不可抗力以外の事由により
◆Business of a Party is suspended for more than 60 days continuously other than for force majeure. 当事者の事業が、不可抗力以外の事由で継続して60日を超えて停止する。

other than pursuant to this agreement 本契約による以外に, 本契約によらないで

otherwise （形）他の, その他の, 別の, 別種の （副）別に, 別段に, 別途, 別のやり方で, 他の方法で, その他の手段で, 他の点では, もしそうでなければ （=if not）
except as otherwise expressly provided for in this agreement 本契約に別に明文の規定がないかぎり
or otherwise 〜にせよそうでないにせよ, またはその反対, またはそれ以外の, または別段に
unless otherwise specified 他にとくに明記［明示］しないかぎり, 別段の記載［定め］がないかぎり
◆Any failure, whether willful, through neglect

O

or otherwise, of either party to perform or fulfill any of its duties, obligations or covenants in this agreement shall constitute a breach of this agreement. 故意であれ、怠慢またはその他によるものであれ、本契約における各当事者の責務、義務または約束ごとを各当事者が履行または達成できない場合、これは本契約の違反を構成するものとする。
◆Except as otherwise expressly provided for in this agreement, ABC shall not be entitled to set off or withhold any amount owing to ABC under this agreement, against any payment to XYZ for the performance by XYZ of this agreement. 本契約に別に明文の規定がないかぎり、ABCには、本契約に基づきABCに支払われる金額を、XYZによる本契約の履行に対するXYZへの支払い金と相殺する権利はなく、またその支払いを保留する権利もないものとする。
◆Quantity is subject to a variation of 5% more or less than the contracted quantity at Seller's option unless otherwise specified. 数量は、他にとくに明記しないかぎり、売り主の裁量で契約数量より5%増減の変動が生じることがある。
◆Seller shall waive any claim against Buyer under the Uniform Commercial Code or otherwise, with respect to a claim asserted against Seller or Buyer for patent, trademark or copyright infringement or the like. 売り主は、特許・商標・著作権の侵害等について売り主または買い主に対してなされる請求に関しては、買い主に対する米国統一商事法典その他に基づく請求権をすべて放棄する。

ounce （名）オンス, 少量, わずか, oz.（重さの単位として28.3495g、貴金属や薬量の単位としては31.1035g）
◆Gold extended its rally to a record above $1,900 an ounce amid increased uncertainties over the U.S. and European economic outlook on the Comex in New York. ニューヨーク商品取引所では、米欧景気見通しへの懸念［米欧経済の先行き不透明感］の高まりを受け［懸念の高まりから］、金価格が急騰して、1トロイ・オンス＝1,900ドルを史上初めて突破した。

out of 〜の中から外へ, 〜から, 〜から離れて, 〜を脱して, 〜の外で, 〜の範囲外に, 〜を切らして, 〜がなくなって, 〜から脱して, 〜の中で, 〜のうち
be out of stock 在庫がない, 在庫が切れている, 在庫切れとなっている, 品切れだ
be out of the doldrums 底を脱する
be out of the woods 低迷を脱する
made out of 〜製の
out of action 動かない, 故障中の, 動けない, 活動できない,（電話などが）通じない
out of book asset 簿外資産
out of date check 失効小切手, 期限経過小切手 （＝outdated check）
out of debt 借金なしの
out of line （株価が）独立高の, 独立安の
out-of-pocket 現金払いの, 現金支出の, 一時

払いの, 立て替えの
out-of-pocket expense 当座払い費用, 実費, 現金支出, 従業員立替え金

out-of-court settlement 示談による和解, 示談, 和解
◆Six executives of Kobe Steel Ltd. agreed in an out-of-court settlement to pay back ￥310 million to the company. 神戸製鋼の幹部6人が、示談による和解で3億1,000万円を会社に返済することで合意した。

out of make 生産中止
◆The model you have in mind has been out of make for a few years. ご要望の機種はここ数年、生産中止となっております。

outbreak of a state of emergency 緊急事態の勃発

outlet （名）店舗, 〜店, 販路, 市場, 小売店, 出店, 特約店, 系列販売店, 工場直売店, 支店, 出口, 放送局, アウトレット
a profitable outlet for one's investment 有利な投資先
affiliated outlet 系列販売店
distribution outlet 販路
fast-food outlet ファースト・フード店, ファースト・フード販売店
investment outlet 投資先
lending outlet 融資先, 貸付け先
merchant outlet 加盟店店舗
network of outlets 店舗網
outlet mall アウトレット・モール
outlet store 系列販売店
retail outlet 小売店, 小売販売店
sales outlet 販売店
single outlet 単一店舗
◆According to a salesperson at the TV section of Bic Camera Inc.'s Yurakucho outlet, low-priced products are not selling well now. ビックカメラ有楽町店のテレビ売場の販売担当者によると、今は格安品［低価格品］の売れ行きはかんばしくない。◆Some Japanese-affiliated companies and Japanese restaurants have been forced to suspend their factory operations or close their outlets due to the acts of destruction by Chinese demonstrators. 一部の日系企業や日本料理店は、中国のデモ隊による破壊行為で、工場の操業停止や店舗の休業に追い込まれている。

output （名）生産, 生産量, 生産高, 製作, 産出量, 産出高,（電力などの）出力,（電気製品の）出力装置, 表現力, 生成された文, アウトプット
aggregate output 総生産高, 総生産量, 総産出高
crude steel output 粗鋼生産量
cutbacks in output 生産の削減
economic output 国内総生産

O

factory output　製造業生産高, 製造業の生産　(=manufacturing output)

industrial output　工業生産, 鉱工業生産, 工業生産高

natural gas output　天然ガスの産出

natural output　自然産出量

optimal〔optimum〕output　最適生産量

output cut　減産

output of consumer goods　消費財の生産高

output power　出力電力

output volume　生産量

potential output　潜在生産力

real output　実質生産高, 実質産出高, 実質GDP

◆As there is a limit to our output at present, we have some difficulty in meeting the demand. 現在のところ、当社の生産には限界があり、需要に応じるのはかなり困難です。◆Because of soaring labor costs, the Japanese maker of small and midsize televisions lowered its production ratio in China that previously accounted for 90 percent of its total output. 人件費が高騰しているため、中小型テレビを生産しているこの日本企業は、これまで総生産の9割を占めていた中国生産比率を引き下げた。◆G-7 finance ministers urged oil-producing countries to raise output to ensure the market is well supplied. 日米欧の先進7か国（G7）の財務相は、市場に石油が確実に十分供給されるよう、産油国に原油増産を要請した。

output capacity　生産能力
◆We have on hand such a rush of orders for this item that our output capacity cannot keep up with the demand. 本品に対しては多くの注文が入っているため、当社の生産能力が需要に追いつかない状況です。

output ceiling　生産枠
◆The OPEC's oil production in July stood at 27.11 million bpd, 1.11 million bpd more than the output ceiling set for August. 石油輸出国機構（OPEC）の7月の原油生産高は日量2,711万バレルで、8月の生産枠を111万バレル（日量）上回った。

output cost　製造原価, 生産コスト
◆The Japanese economy is losing momentum with the burdens of a strong yen and high labor costs as well as higher electric power output costs. 日本経済は、円高や人件費高に電力生産コストの上昇などの負担が加わって失速している。

outsource　（動）外部資源を活用する, 外部委託する, 外注する, 社外調達する, 業務委託する
◆In the Philippines, tertiary industries such as call center, financial, legal and other business processing services outsourced by foreign companies are also thriving. フィリピンでは、海外企業が業務委託するコールセンターや金融、法律業務の事務処理サービスなどのサービス産業も伸びている。

outsourcing　（名）外部資源の活用, 外部委託, 外注, 社外調達, 海外調達, 業務委託, アウトソーシング（企業が周辺業務を外部に委託すること）

outsourcing deal　業務委託契約

outsourcing of frozen food production　冷凍食品の生産委託

◆J.P. Morgan Chase & Co. is scrapping a $5 billion outsourcing deal with International Business Machines Corp. JPモルガン・チェース（米銀2位）は、IBMとの50億ドルの業務委託契約を打ち切ることになった。

outstanding　（形）継続している, 未決定の, 未解決の, 未処理の, 未履行の, 未決済の, 未払いの, 発行済み, すでに発生している, 傑出した

outstanding accounts receivable　未決済の売掛金, 売掛金債権

outstanding amount　残高

outstanding and issued capital　発行済み社外株式, 外部発行済み株式　(=issued and outstanding shares)

outstanding invoice　未払い請求書

outstanding payment　未払い金

◆The borrower shall repay the outstanding amount of the loan in Japanese Yen to the lender on the first day of August of 2015. 借主は、借入金の残高を日本円で貸主に2015年8月1日に返済する。◆The interest rate to be paid by the borrower to the lender on the loan hereunder shall be five percent（5%）per annum on the balance of the loan from time to time outstanding calculated from each respective advance date to and including the date of maturity of the loan on the basis of a 365-day year, for the actual days elapsed. 本契約に基づいて借主が貸主に対して支払う借入金の金利は、1年を365日として各借入日から借入金の返済期日まで実際に経過した日数についてそのつど計算した未決済の借入金残高について、年5%とする。

outstanding share　発行済み株式, 社外株式, 社外発行株式（発行済み株式から自己株式・金庫株（treasury stock）を除いたもの）
◆The term "Subsidiary" shall mean a corporation, more than fifty percent（50%）of whose outstanding shares representing the right to vote for the election of directors, are, now or hereafter, owned or controlled, directly or indirectly, by a party hereto. 「子会社」という語は、取締役選任のための議決権を表す発行済み株式の50%超が、本契約の一当事者によって直接・間接的に現在または今後所有されるか支配される法人を意味する。

outturn　（名）陸揚げ, 着荷, 結果, 実績, 生産高, 産出高

actual outturn　実際の数値

forecasts and outturns　予想と実績

outturn report　陸揚げ報告書

outturn sample　着荷見本

outturn weight　陸揚げ重量

outward [outwards]　(形)外に向かう、外への、外部の、対外的な、輸出の、表面上の、外見の、往路の、行きの

carriage [freight] outwards　戻し運賃

outward bound　往路の

outward check　銀行渡り小切手

outward correspondence　発送信書

outward entry　輸出申請書

outward freight　往路運賃

outward indent　買付け注文

outward investment　対外投資

outward invoice　発送送り状

outward packing　外装

outward reinsurance　売り再保険

outward voyage　往路

over　(前・副)〜を超える、〜を超えて、〜より高い(〜の数量・程度を含まない)
◆Late payment shall incur an interest charge of 2 percent over the base rate current in XYZ Bank at the time the charge is levied from the due date to the date of payment in full.　支払いが遅延した場合、支払い期日から全額支払い日まで、支払い利息(遅延利息)を課す時点でXYZ銀行が適用する基準金利より2%高い支払い利息(遅延利息)が付くものとする。◆On orders over U.S. $50,000, payment shall be made through a medium of a Letter of Credit to be established by ABC at its expense.　5万米ドルを超える注文の場合、支払いは、ABCがその費用で開設する費用で信用状で行うものとする。

overall balance of payments　総合収支(経常収支＋資本収支＝総合収支)
◆According to the preliminary balance of payments data, the deficit in trade in July 2013 was ¥943.3 billion, 2.5 times the level a year earlier and marking the highest level for July since 1985.　国際収支の速報値によると、2013年7月のモノの取引を示す貿易収支(モノの輸出額から輸入額を差し引いた貿易収支)の赤字額は、9,433億円で前年同月の水準の2.5倍、7月としては1985年以降最大の水準となった。

overall exports　総輸出額、輸出総額、輸出全体
◆Japan's overall exports in April-September 2014 increased 1.7 percent from a year earlier to ¥35.9 trillion, while imports grew at a faster pace of 2.5 percent to ¥41.32 trillion.　日本の2014年度上半期(4〜9月)の輸出総額は、前年同期比1.7%増の35兆9,000億円だったのに対して、輸入額は2.5%増の41兆3,200億円で大幅に増えた。

overall import prices　全体的な輸入価格

[輸入物価]、輸入物価全体
◆Japan's trade deficit in April-September 2014 hit a record high due to increased demand for liquefied natural gas for thermal power generation and a rise in overall import prices stemming from the yen's depreciation.　日本の2014年度上半期(4〜9月)の貿易赤字は、火力発電所向け液化天然ガス(LNG)の需要増加と円安による輸入物価全体の上昇で、過去最大となった。

overdue　(形)期限の経過した、満期の経過した、支払い遅延の、支払い期限の過ぎた、延滞の

overdue amount　支払い遅延金額
◆If any installment of interest under this Note shall not be received by Holder prior to the tenth (10th) day after the date on which it is due, Holder may at its option impose a late charge of three percent (3%) of the overdue amount.　本手形に基づく利息の割賦金を支払い期日の翌日から起算して10日目以前に手形所持人が受領しない場合、手形所持人は、その裁量で支払い遅延額の3パーセント(3%)の遅延料を課すことができる。

overdue interest　遅延利息、延滞利息、遅延金利
◆If the buyer fails to pay any amount under this agreement when due, the buyer shall be liable to pay to the seller overdue interest on such unpaid amount from the due date until the actual payment date at the rate of 15% per annum.　買い主が支払い期日に本契約に基づく代金の支払いを怠った場合、買い主は、支払い期日から実際の払込み日までの当該未払い金額に対する年率15%の遅延金利を、売り主に支払わなければならない。

overseas earnings　海外収益

boost overseas earnings　海外収益を押し上げる

the values of overseas values　海外収益の額
◆As the yen's decline inflated the values of overseas earnings when converted into yen, the income account surplus in July 2013 hit a record high for July.　円安で円換算したときの海外収益額が膨らんだため、2013年7月の所得収支の黒字額は、7月としては過去最大だった。

overseas investment　対外投資、海外への投資、海外からの投資
◆Current account balance includes dividends and interest from overseas investment.　経常収支には、海外への投資による配当や利子の受取りなどが含まれる。

overseas markets　海外市場
◆The domestic market has been shrinking due to an aging population and declining birthrate, so Japan must expand its economic cooperation agreements with other countries to have overseas markets act as quasi-domestic markets where there are no barriers to entry for Japanese companies.　少子高齢化で国内市場が縮小しているので、日本は他国との経済連携協定を拡大して、海

外市場を日本企業が垣根なしで参入できる準国内市場にする必要がある。

overseas operations 国外での営業活動, 海外事業
◆Delaware reportedly does not tax corporate income gained from overseas operations. 米デラウエア州では, 国外での営業活動で得た法人所得には課税しないという。

overseas rivals 海外のライバル, 海外のライバル企業
◆Information about advanced technologies is sold to overseas rivals in industrial espionage, which has become a common threat for Japanese manufacturers. 産業スパイでは先端技術情報が海外のライバル企業に売り渡されるので, 日本のメーカーにとって産業スパイは, 共通の脅威となっている。

overseas sourcing 海外調達
◆The recent surges in the yen's strength have made it imperative for Japanese carmakers to substantially bring down their parts procurement costs by overseas sourcing. 最近の円高で, 日本の自動車メーカー各社は, 海外調達による部品調達コストの大幅引下げが緊急課題となっている。

overseas subsidiary 海外子会社
◆The surplus in the income account that includes dividend income from overseas subsidiaries narrowed to about ￥7.15 trillion in January-June 2012 from ￥7.28 trillion a year before. 2012年上半期 (1〜6月) の所得収支 (海外子会社からの配当収入 [配当受取金] などを示す) の黒字額は, 前年同期の7兆2,800億円から約7兆1,500億円に縮小した。

overtime payments 残業代

owe (動) 支払う義務がある, 負担する
◆Except as otherwise expressly provided for in this agreement, ABC shall not be entitled to set off or withhold any amount owing to ABC under this agreement, against any payment to XYZ for the performance by XYZ of this agreement. 本契約に別に明文の規定がないかぎり, ABCには, 本契約に基づきABCに支払われる金額を, XYZによる本契約の履行に対するXYZへの支払い金と相殺する権利はなく, またその支払いを保留する権利もないものとする。

own and possess 所有する, 所有し保有する
◆ABC represents and warrants that it owns and possesses all rights, title, interest, and any trademarks, logos, trade secrets and proprietary rights associated with the Software Products. ABCは本ソフトウエア製品の全部に対するすべての権利, 権原, 権益と, 本ソフトウエア製品に関連する一切の商標, ロゴ, トレード・シークレットおよび財産権を所有していることを, ABCは表明しこれを保証する。

owner of a trademark right 商標権者
◆The Trademark Law was enacted to protect a trademark by giving a monopoly such as an ex-

clusive right and a prohibitive right to an owner of a trademark right. 商標法は, 商標権者に専用権や禁止権などの独占権を与えて商標を保護するために制定された。

ownership (名) 所有, 所有権, 領有権, 所有者, 保有株式, 所有比率, 出資比率, 持ち株比率, 経営権, オーナーシップ　(⇒initial ownership (interest))
　capital ownership　出資比率
　change of ownership　所有権の移転, 株式の譲渡
　control of ownership　経営権
　employee stock ownership　従業員持ち株制度
　equity ownership　持ち株比率
　foreign ownership　外国人持ち株比率, 外国人保有比率
　joint ownership　共有権
　ownership or control　所有権または経営支配権, 所有権または支配関係, 所有者または支配者
　public ownership　株式公開, 株式上場
　share ownership　持ち株数
　transfer of ownership　所有権の移転, 企業移転
◆The firm will have an initial ownership of forty percent of the voting shares of the joint venture company. 同社の当初の出資比率は, 合弁会社の議決権付き株式の40%とする方針だ。◆You agree that you neither own nor hereby acquire any claim or right of ownership to the program and documentation or to any related patents, copyrights, trademarks or other intellectual property. 貴社はこのプログラム, ドキュメンテーションと関連特許, 著作権, 商標権などの知的所有権を所有しておらず, 本契約によりこれらの請求権や所有権を取得しないことに, 貴社は同意する。

P

pack (動) 包装する
　be packed in　〜に包装されている
　be packed with the greatest care　慎重に包装される

package (名) 荷造り, 包装, 梱包, 荷物, パッケージ
　commercial package　商業包装
　industrial package　興行包装
　package contract　一括受注契約
　package deal　一括取引, 一括購入, 包括的合意, パッケージ・ディール
　package design　包装デザイン
　package enclosure　商品包装内封入
　package insurance　総合保険
　　(=blanket insurance, package policy)

PAR

  package limitation of liability　責任制限額
  psychological package　心理的包装
  shrink package　収縮包装
packaging　(名)内装
packing　(名)包装, 外装, 梱包
  bad packing　不良包装
  bale packing　俵包装
  case packing　木箱包装
  export bale packing　輸出用俵包装
  export packing　輸出包装
  inferior [inadequate] packing　不適当包装
  inner packing　内部包装
  insufficient packing　梱包不良, 荷造りの不十分
  outer packing　外装
  packing charge　包装費
  packing credit　前貸信用状, 輸出前貸付け信用状
  packing inspection　包装検査
  packing list　包装明細書, 梱包明細書, P/L
  packing note　包装指図書
  seaworthy packing　耐航包装
  waterproof packing　耐水包装
  ◆Supplier shall, at its expense, pack all Products in accordance with Supplier's standard packing procedure. 供給者は, 供給者の費用で, 供給者の標準梱包手続きに従って本製品をすべて梱包する。
pact　(名)(国際間の)協定, 条約, 協約, 契約, 取決め, 約束, 議定書　(=protocol, treaty; ⇒protocol)
  alliance pact　提携契約
  bilateral pact　二国間協定, 二国間条約
  commercial pact　通商条約
  economic partnership pact　経済連携協定　(=economic partnership agreement)
  form a new auto trade pact　新たな自動車貿易協定を結ぶ
  free trade pact　自由貿易協定
  nude pact　無償契約
  service trade pact　サービス貿易協定
  sign a pact　条約に調印する, 条約を締結する
  strategic alliance pact　戦略的提携契約
  trade pact　通商協定, 貿易協定
  Washington Pact　ワシントン条約
  ◆NEC Corp. and Hitachi Ltd. unveiled a broad alliance pact, including a possible joint venture to develop new DRAM chips. NECと日立製作所は, DRAMチップの新規開発の合弁事業をも視野に入れた包括的提携契約を発表した。◆Taiwan needs to pass a contentious service trade pact with China, Taiwan President Ma Ying-jeou said. 物議を醸(かも)している[世間の論議を引き起こしている]中国とのサービス貿易協定を, (立法院で)可決する必要がある, と台湾の馬英九総統は述べた。◆The pact, formally called the Kyoto Protocol to the U.N. Framework Convention on Climate Change, was adopted by an international conference in Kyoto in 1997. 気候変動枠組み条約京都議定書と呼ばれていたこの条約は, 1997年に京都で開かれた国際会議で採択された。◆U.S. trade organization the United Auto Workers (UAW) has urged the U.S. government to immediately begin talks with Japan to form a new auto trade pact as part of efforts to correct huge trade imbalance favoring Tokyo. 米国の同業者組織「全米自動車労組(UAW)」は, 日本の大幅貿易黒字の是正策の一環として, 日本と即時交渉を開始して新たな自動車貿易協定を結ぶよう米政府に要請した。

paper　(形)架空の, 名目上の, 書面の, 帳簿上の
  paper assets　金融資産
  paper audit　書面監査
  paper company　名目会社, 幽霊会社, ペーパー・カンパニー
  paper gain [profit]　含み益, 評価益, 架空利益
  paper gold　ペーパー・ゴールド(国際通貨基金(IMF)の特別引出権(special drawing rights)の通称)
  paper issuance　CP発行
  paper loss　含み損, 評価損, 架空損失
  paper manufacturers　製紙業界
  paper margin　帳簿上の利益
  paper marketing plan　ペーパー商法
  paper mill　製紙工場
  paper money　紙幣　(=paper currency)
  paper profit or loss　含み損益, 評価損益(証券類の取得価格と時価との差額)
paper receipt　架空の売上
  ◆In the circular sales transactions, Katokichi's affiliates and business clients recorded the repeated sale and purchase of products only on paper receipts. 循環取引で, 加卜吉の関連会社と法人顧客は, 繰り返し行われた商品の売買を架空の売上だけに計上していた。
paper work [paperwork]　(名)文書業務, 文書事務, 書類事務, 机上(きじょう)事務, 事務処理, 事務の仕事, 書類
  ◆Facebook disclosed its IPO price range of $28 to $35 per share in the paperwork filed with the SEC. フェイスブックは, 米証券取引委員会(SEC)に提出した書類で, 新規株式公開(IPO)に伴う[IPOの際の]株式の売出価格を1株当たり28〜35ドルに設定することを明らかにした。
par value　株式の額面価格, 為替平価
  no par value stock　無額面株式
  par value capital　額面株式

PARA 346

par value common voting stock　額面普通議決
権株式

par value stock　額面株式

stock［share］with no par value　無額面株式

◆ABC owns one hundred（100）shares of the
common stock, with no par value per share, of
the Company. ABCは、本会社の無額面普通株式
を100株保有している。

paragraph　（名）契約書の項・節、条項

◆Except as provided in Paragraph 3 of this Article, ABC appoints XYZ as its exclusive distributor of the products in the territory. 本条第3項に規
定する場合を除いて、ABCは、この販売地域にお
ける本商品のABCの独占的販売店としてXYZを指
定する。◆The payment to Company under Paragraph 1 of this Article shall be made in Japanese
Yen and remitted to such a bank account as Company shall have specified by written notice. 本条
第一項に基づく会社への支払いを、日本円で行い、
会社が書面通知で指定した銀鉱口座に送金するも
のとする。

pari　（形）(ラテン語で) 同等の、均等の、等し
い　（=equal）

be secured pari passu with　～と同順位である

be treated as being pari passu with　～と同等
の取扱いを受ける

pari delicto　同等の過失

pari material　同一事項に関する

pari passu　一様に、均等に、対等に、優先権な
く、公正に、同一速度で（with equal speed）、
同順位、パリパス条項（pari passu clause）、
パリパス

P

parol　（形）口頭の、口頭による　（=oral,
verbal）

parol agreement　口頭合意

parol contract　口頭契約、捺印証書によらな
い契約

parol evidence rule　口頭証拠排除の原則

part　（名）一部、部分、当事者、役割、部品

in the first part　一方の当事者として

in the second part　もう一方の当事者として

of the one part　一方の当事者、～を一方の当
事者として

of the other part　他方の当事者、～を他方の当
事者として

part cargo　混載貨物の小口貨物、半端積み荷、
パート・カーゴ

part carriage　部分運送

part of　～の一部［部分、一環］、～の面［点］、
～の一員［構成員］、多少　（=a part of）

part performance　一部履行

parts procurement　部品の調達、部品調達

parts shipment　部品の出荷

the first part　第一当事者

the second part　第二当事者

the third part　第三当事者

◆The big U.S. semiconductor maker Qualcomm
put Japanese firms on low priority when it fell
behind schedule in parts shipments this summer.
米半導体大手のクアルコムは今夏、部品の出荷が
予定より遅れた際、日本企業への出荷を後回しにし
た［日本企業への出荷の優先順位を低くした］。◆
The licensee's obligation under this Article with
respect to the confidential information shall not
apply to information which is part of the public
domain at the time of disclosure by the licensor,
or thereafter becomes part of the public domain
without fault on the part of the licensee. 本条に
基づく秘密情報に関するライセンシーの義務は、ラ
イセンサーによる開示の時点で公知であるか、その
後ライセンシー側の過失なしに公知となる情報に
は適用されないものとする。◆The recent surges
in the yen's strength have made it imperative for
Japanese carmakers to substantially bring down
their parts procurement costs by overseas sourcing. 最近の円高で、日本の自動車メーカー各社は、
海外調達による部品調達コストの大幅引下げが緊
急課題となっている。

partial　（形）部分的な、一部分の、不完全な、
片寄った、不公平な、とくに好きな

partial acceptance　（為替手形の）一部引受け

partial assignment　一部譲渡

partial charter　一部用船

partial delivery　一部受渡し

partial endorsement　一部裏書

partial insurance　一部保険

partial loss　（海上保険）分損

partial payment　一部支払い、部分返済、分割
払い、分割払込み、内払い、手形内入れ金

partial payment bond　分割払込み債

partial transfer　一部譲渡

partial shipment　一部船積み、分割船積み、
分割積み

◆The credit reads that partial shipments are permitted. 信用状には、「分割積み許可」とあります。

particular address　特別宛先

particular average　単独海損、特担分損

◆The seller shall, for its own account, effect marine insurance only free from particular average
（FPA Institute Cargo Clause）for the amount of
CIF value of the products plus 10 percent. 売り
主は、売り主の自己負担で、本商品のCIF価格プラ
ス10％の保険金額により単独海損［分損］不担保条
件（FPA協会貨物保険約款）の海上保険を付けるも
のとする。

particular charges　特別費用

◆The purchaser shall forward full particulars of
such claim, accompanied by an authorized sur-

veyor's certificate of inspection of quality and quantity of the products delivered in dispute, to the seller by registered airmail within 30 days after such notification. 買い主は、当該通知後30日以内に、引き渡された問題の製品の品質と数量に関する公認鑑定人の検査証明書を添付して、当該クレームの詳細を記載した書面を書留航空便で売り主に送付するものとする。

particulars （名）詳細, 明細
（⇒authorized surveyor）
bill of particulars　訴状上の請求明細書
relative particulars　関連事項
◆The particulars of the services and assistance are set forth in Exhibit A hereto. サービスと指導の詳細は、本契約書の付属書類Aに定める。◆ The prices and other particulars inquired for are shown in the enclosed price list. お問い合わせの価格その他の明細は、同封の価格表に示してある。

parties （名）両当事者, 契約当事者, 当事者
parties concerned　当事者, 利害関係者, 関係者
parties hereto　本契約当事者, 両当事者, 当事者
parties in interest　利害関係人
the both parties　両当事者
◆The parties are independent contractors. 両当事者は、独立した契約者である。

partner （名）パートナー, 共同経営者, 共同出資者, 共同所有者, 提携者, 提携先, 組合員, 社員, 相手国 （⇒prospective partner）
alliance partner　提携先, 提携相手
joint partner　共同出資者, 共同パートナー
trading partner　貿易相手国
◆Going out on a limb that may anger European partners, French President Sarkozy said it was time to stop the uncontrolled influx of cheap imports. 欧州の友邦国を怒らせる危険を冒して、サルコジ仏大統領は、安価な輸入品の野放図な流入を止める時だと述べた。◆Marubeni Corp. will soon enter into separate negotiations with Aeon Co. and Wal-Mart Stores Inc. to choose a partner to assist in the rehabilitation of Daiei. 丸紅は、ダイエー再建に協力する事業提携先として、イオン、米ウォルマート・ストアーズとそれぞれ近く交渉に入る。

partnership （名）共同出資, 共同所有, 共同経営, 提携, 連携, 協力, 組合, 合名会社, パートナー関係, パートナーシップ
agreement not to constitute a partnership　非パートナーシップ契約
business partnership　業務提携
equal partnership　折半出資, 対等提携, 対等な協力関係
equity and business partnership　資本業務提携
form a partnership　提携する, 提携を結ぶ

limited liability partnership　有限責任パートナーシップ
limited partnership　合資会社, 有限責任組合, リミテッド・パートナーシップ
partnership, agency or joint venture　パートナーシップ、代理関係またはジョイント・ベンチャー
partnership shares　パートナーシップの株式
strategic partnership　戦略的提携, 戦略的パートナーシップ
the new trade partnerships with Europe and the Asia-Pacific　欧州やアジア太平洋地域との新自由貿易協定
three-way partnership　3社共同契約
trading partnership　商事組合
Trans-Pacific Partnership　環太平洋経済連携協定, TPP
voluntary partnership　任意組合
◆New trade partnerships with Europe and the Asia-Pacific will help exporters create more jobs. 欧州やアジア太平洋地域との新自由貿易協定は、輸出企業の雇用創出拡大につながる。◆ The agreement paves the way for the company to fully enter the aviation business through the partnership with GE. この契約で同社は、ゼネラル・エレクトリック（GE）との提携により航空事業に本格的に参入することが可能になる。

partnership agreement　連携協定, 組合規約, 組合契約, 組合約款・定款（articles of partnership）
a comprehensive partnership agreement　包括的連携協定
an economic partnership agreement　経済連携協定, EPA
◆By starting talks on a comprehensive partnership agreement, the EU and the United States will take the first step toward creating a giant free trade zone that would account for about 50 percent of the world's gross domestic product. 包括的連携協定の交渉を開始することで、欧州連合（EU）と米国は、世界のGDP（国内総生産）の5割近くを占める巨大な自由貿易圏の創設に一歩踏み出すことになる。◆The government will compile a basic policy on economic partnership agreements, including the TPP. 政府は、TPP（環太平洋経済連携協定）を含めて、経済連携協定（EPA）の基本方針をまとめる。

party （名）当事者, 契約当事者, 関係者
any of the parties hereto　いずれかの本契約当事者, いずれかの当事者, 本契約の各当事者, 本契約のいずれの当事者も
any party to this agreement　本契約当事者
assigning party　譲渡する当事者, 譲渡人
both parties　両当事者
each party　各当事者

either of the parties hereto　本契約のいずれか一方の当事者

nonassigning party　非譲渡当事者, 非譲渡人

nonbreaching party　違反のない当事者

notifying party　通知を出す当事者

one of the parties　両当事者の一方, 当事者の一方

other party　他方の当事者, 相手方, 相手方当事者

party so affected　その影響を受けた当事者

relevant parties　当該当事者

respective parties　各当事者

the breaching party　違反当事者, 違反した当事者

the concerned parties　利害関係人

the defaulting parties　不履行当事者, 債務不履行当事者, 契約不履行当事者

the disclosing party　開示当事者, 開示した当事者

the objecting party　抗議した当事者

the parties　当事者, 両当事者, 契約当事者

the parties, and each party of them　全当事者および各当事者

the parties hereto　本契約当事者, 当事者, 両当事者

the party in breach　違反した当事者

the party in default　不履行当事者

the party in question　当該当事者

the party not in breach　違反をしていない当事者

the receiving party　受領当事者

the recipient party　開示を受けた当事者, 相手方

the two parties　両当事者, 当事者双方（=both parties）

transferring party　譲渡当事者

◆Exhibit D sets forth a complete and accurate list of all claims, suits, actions, arbitrations, legal or other proceedings or governmental investigations to which the Company is a party or which is, to the knowledge of ABC, threatened against the Company. 付属書類Dには, 本会社が当事者である, またはABCが知るかぎり本会社が当事者になる恐れのある［本会社に対して提起される恐れがある］すべての請求, 訴訟, 仲裁, 法的手続きもしくはその他の手続き, または政府調査の完全かつ正確なリストが記載されている。◆It is necessary to write the name of notify party on the order B/L as it does not contain the name of consignee. 指図人式船荷証券には, 荷受け人名が記載されていないので, 通知先名を書かなければならない。

passive improvement trade　受動的加工貿易

patent　（名）特許, 特許権, 特許物件, 特権, 権利, 公有地譲渡証書　（形）明白な, 公開の（⇒share patents）

annual fee for patent　特許料

application for patent　特許出願（=patent application）

apply for patent　特許出願する, 特許を申請する（=file a patent application）

BM patent　ビジネス・モデル特許, BM特許, ビジネス方法の特許

business method patent　ビジネス方法の特許, ビジネス・モデル特許

business model patent　ビジネス・モデル特許

certificate of patent　特許証

cessation of a patent　特許権の中止, 特許権の終了

cession of a patent　特許権の譲渡

confirmation patent　確認特許

decision to grant a patent　特許査定

dependent patent　従属特許

design patent　意匠特許

dominant patent　基本特許

grant a patent　特許を付与する

grant of a patent　特許付与

importation patent　輸入特許

improvement patent　改良特許

independent patent　独立特許

indication of existence of patent　特許表示

International application of the Patent and Related Matters　特許協力条約に基づく国際出願等

international patent　国際特許

invalidation of a patent　特許無効

invention for which a patent is sought　特許を受けようとする発明

issue of a patent　特許証の発行（=issuance of a patent）

litigious patent　係争特許

maintain the patent　特許を維持する

mechanical patent　機械特許

non-shared patent　相互利用の対象となっていない特許

opposition to the grant of a patent　特許異議申立て

patent administrator　特許管理人

patent and copyright indemnity　特許および著作権の補償

patent assignment agreement　特許権譲渡契約

patent attorney　弁理士,（米国の）特許弁護士

Patent Cooperation Treaty　特許協力条約

patent document　特許文献

patent fee　特許料, 特許権使用料

patent friction　特許摩擦

Patent Gazette　特許公報

patent information　特許情報

patent license agreement　特許ライセンス契約, 特許実施許諾契約, 特許発明実施許諾契約, 特許発明ライセンス契約, 特許ライセンス契約書　(⇒patent dispute)

patent litigation　特許訴訟　(=patent suit)

patent management　特許管理

patent on one-click technology　ワンクリック特許

patent pending　特許申請中

patent pool　特許プール

patent protection　特許保護

patent register　(特許庁の) 特許原簿

Patent Registration Order　特許登録令

patent revenue stamp　特許印紙

pending patent　係属特許

petty patent　小特許, 実用新案

plant patent　植物特許

pro-patent　特許重視, プロパテント

pro-patent policy　プロパテント政策

process patent　方法特許, 製法特許

product patent　製品特許

registered patent　公認特許

reissue of a patent　特許証の再発行

revalidation patent　再確認特許

revoke the patent　特許を取り消す

right to obtain a patent　特許を受ける権利

the offense of infringement of patent right　特許権侵害罪

the official gazette containing the patent　特許公報

trial for invalidation of a patent　特許無効審判

U.S. Patent and Trademark Office　米特許商標庁

U.S. patents covering the Products　本製品の米国特許

use of a patent　特許権の使用

working of a patent　特許権の実施

written opposition to the grant of a patent　特許異議申立て書

written supplement of grounds for opposition to the grant of a patent　特許異議申立て理由補充書

◆Kirin has developed and holds a patent on a technology through which human antibodies can be created using a particular type of mice. キリンは、特殊なマウスを使ってヒト抗体を作ることがで

きる技術を開発して、その特許を持っている。◆Licensor hereby grants to Licensee during the life of this agreement an exclusive license to manufacture, use and sell Products under Patents now owned or controlled by Licensor in Territory. 本契約によりライセンサーは、契約地域でライセンサーが現在保有または支配する特許に基づいて本製品を製造、使用および販売する独占的実施権を、本契約期間中、ライセンシーに付与する。◆The Customs Tariff Law bans imports that infringe on patent, design and commercial brand rights. 関税定率法で、特許、意匠権、商標権などの侵害品の輸入は禁止されている。◆The three steelmakers are considering preventing acquirers from using the acquired company's non-shared patents without the other two firms' permission. 鉄鋼3社は、他の2社の許可がなければ、相互利用の対象となっていない買収された会社の特許を買収者が使えないようにすることも検討している。◆There is a contractual clause stipulating that Japanese PC makers will take no legal action even if Microsoft Corp.'s technologies are deemed to violate their patents. マイクロソフト社の技術が日本のパソコン・メーカーの特許侵害にあたるとしても、日本のパソコン・メーカーは法的措置を一切取らない[訴訟を起こさない]、と定めた契約条項がある。

patent application　特許出願

complete patent application　完全特許明細書

patent application maintenance fees　特許申請維持費用

patent applications　特許出願件数
　(=the number of patent applications)

provisional patent application　仮特許明細書

patent dispute　特許紛争
　(=dispute on patent issues)
◆Nokia Corp. of Finland has settled a series of patent disputes over mobile phones products with Kyocera Corp. by entering into a patent license agreement. フィンランドのノキアは、携帯電話の製品をめぐる京セラとの一連の特許紛争で、特許ライセンス契約を結ぶことで和解した。

patent filing　特許出願　(⇒World Intellectual Property Organization)
◆Despite the sluggish economy, the number of global patent filings continued to grow, the United Nations' WIPO said. 国連の世界知的所有権機関(WIPO)の発表によると、景気は低迷しているものの、世界の特許出願件数の増加は続いている。

patent infringement　特許侵害, 特許権侵害, 特許抵触　(=patent violation)

allege patent infringement　特許侵害を主張する

patent infringement on　〜の特許権侵害
◆Sony has agreed to pay $40 million to Ampex Corp. to settle a lawsuit filed by the U.S. visual

information technology company over patent infringement on its digital camera-related technology. デジタル・カメラ関連技術の特許権侵害をめぐって米国の視覚情報技術会社のアンペックスが起こした訴訟を和解で解決するため、ソニーは、アンペックスに400万ドル支払うことに同意した。

Patent Law　特許法

　Patent Law Enforcement Order　特許法施行令

　Patent Law Treaty　特許法条約, PLT

　◆The Patent Law stipulates that patents obtained as a result of duties performed by a corporate employee belong to the employee. 日本の特許法では、企業の従業員が企業の職務の一環として得た特許権は、その従業員に帰属する、としている。

patent right　特許権

　extend the term of a patent right　特許権の存続期間を延長する, 特許期間を延長する

　the establishment of a patent right　特許権の設定

　the exhaustion of patent right　特許権消耗, 特許権用尽, 特許権消尽

　the extension of term of patent right　特許期間の延長

　the owner of a patent right　特許権者

　the registration of patent right　特許権の設定登録, 特許権登録

　trial for invalidation of a patent right　特許無効審判

　work the patent right into effect　特許権を実施する, 特許発明を実施する

　◆In lawsuits over patent rights, courts have increasingly awarded inventors compensation for the transfer of patent rights. 特許権をめぐる訴訟で、裁判所は裁定で発明者に特許権移転の対価［報酬］を認めるケースが増えている。◆Kyoto University has obtained U.S. iPS patent rights for the R&D of new medicines. 京都大は、新薬の研究開発も対象とするiPSの米国特許権を取得した。

patent royalty　特許権使用料

patent royalty revenues　特許権使用料の収入

　◆Japan's services trade deficit in July 2013 was reduced by about 40 percent to ￥196.5 billion thanks to an increase in the number of visitors to Japan due to the weaker yen and a rise in patent royalty revenues. 2013年7月の日本のサービス収支の赤字は、円安で日本を訪れる外国人旅行者が増えたことや特許権使用料の収入が増えたため、約4割縮小して1,965億円となった。

patentability　(名)特許性

　requirements for patentability　特許要件, 特許性要件　(=patentability requirement)

patented invention　特許発明, 特許を受けた発明

patentee　(名)特許権者

patents, designs, trademarks, copyrights or other rights　特許、意匠、商標、著作権またはその他の権利

　◆Supplier shall be responsible for any claim of infringement or alleged infringement of patents, designs, trademarks, copyrights or other rights brought by a third party in relation to Products. 本製品に関して第三者が提起する特許、意匠、商標、著作権またはその他の権利の侵害または申し立てられた侵害の請求については、供給者がすべて責任を負う。

pattern　(名)柄見本

pay　(動)支払う、払い込む、納付する、返済する、弁済する、負担する

　be paid out early　期限前に返済される

　pay dividends　配当金を支払う

　pay (down) debt　債務を返済する

　pay for losses　損失を補填する

　pay in cash　現金で支払う

　pay off　完済する, 返済する

　pay off the loan　ローンを返済する

　pay on application　請求払い

pay in advance　前払いする

　◆Royalty with respect to each of the licensed program shall be paid semiannually in advance on each April 1 and October 1, during the term of this agreement for the six-month period. 許諾された各プログラムについてのロイヤルティは毎年2回、本契約期間中の4月1日と10月1日にそれぞれ6カ月分を前払いするものとする。

pay in full　全額を払い込む, 全額支払う

　◆The parties hereto shall, upon allocation, pay in full in cash for the shares subscribed for pursuant to Section 5. hereof. 本契約当事者は、株式の割当てを受け次第、本条5項で引き受けた株式について現金で全額を払い込むものとする。

pay when due　期限どおりに支払う, 支払い期日どおりに支払う

　◆If the buyer fails to pay any amount under this agreement when due, the buyer shall be liable to pay to the seller overdue interest on such unpaid amount from the due date until the actual payment date at the rate of 15% per annum. 買い主が支払い期日に本契約に基づく代金の支払いを怠った場合、買い主は、支払い期日より実際の払込み日までの当該未払い金額に対する年率15%の遅延金利を、売り主に支払わなければならない。

payable　(形)支払うべき、支払い満期の、支払い期限に達した、支払い期日の到来した

　account payable　買掛金, 未払い金, 支払い債務

　amounts payable　支払期限の到来した金額

　(be) payable at destination　仕向け地支払い

　check payable to　～宛の小切手

　payable in one lump sum　一括支払い

payable on completion of discharge　運賃揚げ
高支払い

payable to　〜に支払うべき

the amount of royalties to be payable　支払う
べきロイヤルティ額, ロイヤルティ支払
い額

◆For invoices for orders exceeding U.S. dollars
50,000, XYZ may require ABC to open for XYZ
an irrevocable documentary letter of credit, in
the form satisfactory to XYZ for an amount at
least equal to 100% of the order value payable in
accordance with the provisions of Section（5）
of this Article above. 5万米ドルを超える注文に
対する請求書については、XYZは、XYZのために、
上記本条第5項の規定に従って支払われる注文金
額の少なくとも100%に相当する金額の取消不能
の荷為替信用状をXYZが満足するフォームで開設
するようABCに対して要求することができる。◆
In case the borrower fails to pay any principal
or interest payable under this agreement on the
due date therefor, the borrower shall pay to the
lender overdue interest on such overdue amount
for each day for the period from and including
the due date therefor up to and including the day
immediately preceding the actual payment date.
借主が本契約に基づいて元本または支払い利息の
支払い期日に元本の返済または支払い利息の支払
いを怠った場合、借主は、その支払い期日から実
際の払込み日の前日までの期間の各日数について、
その支払い遅延金額の遅延利息を貸主に支払うも
のとする。◆The insurance premium and freight
are payable by you. 保険料と運賃の支払いは、貴
社負担です。

payback period　返済期間

paying agency agreement　支払い代理契約

paying bank　支払い銀行

payment　（名）支払い, 払込み, 振込み, 決済,
納入, 返済, 弁済, 支払い金額, 債権

accept payment　支払いを受ける

advance payment　前払い, 前払い金
　（=advanced payment, payment in advance）

arrange for payment　支払いの手続きをする

balance of payments　国際収支, 支払い差額,
支払い残高, BOP

cash payment　現金支払い

commission payments　手数料収入

deferred payment　後払い（post payment）, 延
べ払い

deferred payment export　延べ払い輸出
　（=installment payment export）

delay of［in］payment　支払い遅延, 支払いの
遅れ

dividend payment　配当支払い

down payment　頭金, 手付け金

equal monthly payment　均等払い

export on a deferred payment basis　延べ払い
輸出

external debt payment　対外債務の返済

import payments　輸入総額

installment payment　割賦返済, 分割払い

interest and final payments　元利払い

interest payment　金利の支払い, 利払い, 支払
い利息

late payment　期限を過ぎた支払い

late payment penalty　延滞税

license payment　ライセンス料の支払い

monthly payment　月払い

non-payment　不渡り

one-off payment　一時金

partial payment　一部支払い, 部分返済, 分割
払い, 分割払込み, 内払い, 手形内入れ金

payment advice　支払い通知, 払い込み通知
書, 保険金支払い通知書

payment against documents　書類引換え払い

payment by letter of credit　信用状決済

payment by results　出来高払い, 業績給, 歩合
給, 能率給

payment commission　支払い手数料

payment for services reimbursement　サービス
の対価・報酬

payment in full　全額払い

payment instruction　支払い指図

payment of claim clause　保険金支払い約款

payment of premium clause　保険料支払い
約款

payment of royalties　ロイヤルティの支払い

payment on invoice　請求書払い

payment on receipt credit　受取証払い信用状

payment order　支払い指図, 支払い指図書

payment period　決済期間

payment pressures　返済負担

payment surplus　国際収支の黒字

payment system　決済手段, 支払い手段, 決済
システム

payment terms［conditions］　支払い条件, 決
済条件

payment when due　期日どおりの支払い, 期
日どおりに支払うこと

preferential payment　優先支払い

prompt payment　即時払い

sight payment　一覧払い

single payment　一括払い　（=lump-sum
payment）

suspend payment　支払いを停止する

tax payment　納税

temporary payment　仮払い金
　(=suspense payment)

terms of payment　支払い条件, 決済条件

the terms of payment　決済条件

transfer payment　移転支出, 移転所得

Uniform New Payment Code　統一支払い法典
◆A Japanese plastics maker in China did not receive payments for its products from a major Chinese electrical appliance maker after the date of payment. 中国に進出した日本のあるプラスチック・メーカーは, 中国の大手家電メーカーから, 期日を過ぎても納品の代金支払いがなかった。◆A major Internet shopping mall program which began in March 2000 allows payments to be made immediately through the bank accounts of users. 2000年3月にスタートした大規模なインターネット上の仮想商店街プログラムは, 利用者の銀行口座から即時決済できる。◆If you find the terms of payment acceptable, please confirm the order subject to the modifications above. この支払い条件がのめるなら, 上記の変更を条件として本注文の確認をお願いします。◆In case payment by the purchaser for the delivery of the products is delayed later than 35 days after B/L date, the purchaser shall pay to the seller on demand the amount due together with interest from the due date until paid at the annual rate equal to the prime rate plus 5 percent per year on any overdue amount. 買い主による本製品の引渡しに対する支払いが船荷証券の日付から35日を超えて遅延した場合, 買い主は請求のあり次第売り主に対して期日到来債務を支払うとともに, 延滞金については支払い期日から支払い日までプライム・レートに年率5%を加えた年間利率で利息を支払うものとする。◆Our terms of payment are to value at 30 d/s under an irrevocable letter of credit to be opened in our favor for the corresponding value of an order. 当社の決済条件は, 注文相当額につき, 当社を受益者として開設された取消不能信用状に基づいて一覧後30日払いの手形を振り出すことです。◆The payment for the Goods shall be made by a letter of credit. 「商品」の支払いは, 信用状で行うものとする。

payment date　払込み日, 払込み期日, 支払い日　(=date of payment; ⇒pay when due)
◆In case the borrower fails to pay any principal or interest payable under this agreement on the due date therefor, the borrower shall pay to the lender overdue interest on such overdue amount for each day for the period from and including the due date therefor up to and including the day immediately preceding the actual payment date. 借主が本契約に基づいて元本または支払い利息の支払い期日に元本の返済または支払い利息の支払いを怠った場合, 借主は, その支払い期日から実際の払込み日の前日までの期間の各日数について, その支払い遅延金額の遅延利息を貸主に支払うものとする。

payment for each delivery of the Products　本製品の引渡しに対する支払い
◆Payment for each delivery of the Products shall be by the purchaser in United States Dollars by means of telegraphic transfer remittance to such bank account in the City of San Francisco, as the seller may designate from time to time, no later than 30 days after the date of the bill of lading for each such delivery. 本製品の引渡しに対する支払いは, 当該引渡しにかかわる船荷証券の日付から30日以内に, 売り主が随時指定するサンフランシスコ市内の銀行口座に買い主が米ドルで電信為替で送金して行うものとする。

payment of money　金員の支払い
◆The licensor may, without the licensee's consent, settle or compromise any claim against or consent to the entry of any judgment if such settlement, compromise or judgment involves only the payment of money by the licensor or provides for unconditional release by the claimant or the plaintiff of the licensee from all liability in respect of such claim and does not impose injunctive relief against the licensee. 当該解決, 和解または判決がライセンサーによる金員の支払いだけを伴う場合, または請求人または原告により当該請求に関するすべての責任からライセンシーが無条件で解放されライセンシーに対する差止め命令が下されない場合, ライセンサーは, ライセンシーの同意を得ないで当該請求の解決, 和解と判決の執行に同意することができる。

payment(s) due　支払い期限, 満期の支払い, 満期支払い金, 満期支払い額
◆Payment due from ABC shall be made to XYZ in United States dollars and invoices shall be issued upon shipment of the Products with payment due by means of one of the following: ABCからの予定されている支払いは, 米ドルでXYZに対して行うものとし, 請求書は本商品の出荷時に発行し, 支払い期限に次のいずれかの方法で支払うものとする。

PCAOB　米上場企業会計監視委員会（Public Company Accounting Oversight Boardの略。民間の独立機関で, 2002年に制定された企業改革法に基づいて2003年に発足。米上場企業を扱う監査法人は, 国内外を問わずPCAOBへの登録を義務付けられている）

pecuniary　(形)金銭の, 金銭上の, 金銭に関する

pecuniary aid　財政援助

pecuniary consideration　金銭的約因

pecuniary damages　金銭的損害, 金銭的損害賠償額

pecuniary penalty　罰金刑

penalty　(名)処罰, 処分, 罰金, 違約金, 延滞金, 反則金, 制裁金, 制裁, 罰則, 刑罰, 罰, 報い, 不利なこと, ペナルティ
◆According to the Financial Instruments and Exchange Law, penalties for making false securi-

ties reports are tightened from up to five years in prison to up to 10 years in prison. 金融取引法によれば、有価証券報告書の虚偽記載の刑罰は、懲役5年以下から懲役10年以下に引き上げられている。◆In response to a series of false labeling cases at hotels, department stores and elsewhere, the Consumer Affairs Agency will introduce a system to impose administrative monetary penalties on those involved in food mislabeling. ホテルや百貨店などで相次いだ（食材や食品メニューの）偽装表示事件を受けて、消費者庁は、食品の不当表示に関与した業者に課徴金を科す制度を導入する方針だ。

pending （形）懸案の、未決の、係争中の、継続している
　pending action　係争中の事件［訴訟］
　pending lawsuit　係争中の訴訟
　pending or threatened　係争中の、または提起される恐れがある
　settle［adjust］the pending claim　懸案のクレームを解決する
　◆There is no action, suit or proceeding to which the Company is a party（either as a plaintiff or defendant）pending before any court or governmental agency. 対象会社が当事者（原告か被告かは問わない）となって、裁判所または行政機関で係争中の訴訟や法的手続きは存在しない。

per annum　1年につき、1年当たり、毎年
　◆If the buyer fails to pay any amount under this agreement when due, the buyer shall be liable to pay to the seller overdue interest on such unpaid amount from the due date until the actual payment date at the rate of 15% per annum. 買い主が支払い期日に本契約に基づく代金の支払いを怠った場合、買い主は、支払い期日から実際の払込み日までの当該未払い金額に対する年率15%の遅延金利を、売り主に支払わなければならない。

per quarter　四半期当たり、四半期ごとに
　◆We will accept your offer if you assure us of an order for at least 1,000 pieces per quarter for one year. 1年間、四半期ごとに最低1,000個の注文をご確約いただければ、貴社のオファーをお受けします。

per set　セット当たり、1セット当たり
　◆The price for the products payable by the purchaser for the first year shall be U.S. $38.00 per set CIF San Francisco, U.S.A. 買い主が初年度に支払う本商品の価格は、CIFサンフランシスコ（米国）条件で1セット当たり38.00米ドルとする。

perform （動）義務や債務を履行する、実行する、遂行する、実演する、上演する、演奏する
　perform and discharge　遂行する
　perform in accordance with　～に従って履行する
　◆ABC hereby accepts such assignment and delegation and agrees to assume and perform all of the obligations of XYZ under the original agree-

ment. ABCは、ここに、当該譲渡と委託を引き受け、原契約に基づくXYZのすべての義務を引き受けて履行することに同意する。◆Commencing on the date of this agreement until the Closing, Buyer shall be permitted to perform such due diligence investigation related to the transactions contemplated by this agreement as Buyer deems necessary and appropriate in its discretion. 本契約締結日からクロージングまで、買い主は、本契約で意図されている取引に関して買い主が買い主の判断で必要かつ適切と考えるデュー・ディリジェンス調査を行うことができるものとする。◆The parties hereto agree to abide by and perform in accordance with any award rendered by the arbitrator in such arbitration proceedings. 本契約当事者は、上記の仲裁手続きで仲裁人が下した判断を遵守し、その判断に従って履行することに同意する。

performance （名）実績、業績、（義務・債務の）履行、実行、遂行、実演、性能
　（⇒default in the performance of）
　any further performance of this agreement　本契約のその後の履行
　due and punctual performance　適正な期限どおりの履行
　impossibility of performance　履行不能
　part performance　一部履行
　performance of obligations　義務の履行、債務の履行
　performance rights of the picture　映画の放映権
　place of performance　履行地
　specific performance　特定履行
　until full performance is effected by　～により履行が完全になされるまで
　◆In the beer industry, a single day's shipment volume during the busiest season from June to August influences the annual performances of beer companies. ビール業界では、6～8月の書き入れ時の1日の出荷量が、ビール各社の年間業績を左右する。◆Other competitive factors in the market for the products are service, delivery, technological capability, and product quality and performance. 市場での製品の競争要因には、サービスや納入、技術活用能力［技術力］、品質、性能なども挙げられる。◆The undersigned（"Guarantor"）, hereby unconditionally guarantees as and for its obligations, until full performance is effected by or on behalf of ABC in accordance with the terms and conditions of the license agreement between XYZ and ABC, a copy of which is attached hereto; 下記署名者（「保証人」）は、XYZとABC間のライセンス契約（その写しを本保証状に添付する）の条件に従ってABCによりまたはABCに代わり完全な履行が行われるまで、その義務としてここに以下を無条件に保証する。

performance of the services　サービスの提供

◆Particulars of the number of ABC's personnel required to render the services under this agreement and the duration of his or their assignment for the performance of the services are set forth in Exhibit A. 本契約に基づくサービスを提供するために要求されるABCの人員の数と本サービス提供のための当該人員の派遣期間の詳細は、付属書類Aに定める。

performance of this agreement　本契約の履行　(⇒constitute)
◆In case any dispute arises in connection with the above right, the seller reserves the right to terminate unconditionally this agreement or any further performance of this agreement at the seller's discretion. 上記権利に関して紛争が生じた場合、売り主はその裁量で、本契約または本契約のその後の履行を無条件で終了させる権利を留保する。

perils of the seas　海難

period　(名)期間, 時期
　period of services　サービス期間, サービス提供期間
　period of stay　滞在期間
◆The seller warrants that the Goods will be free from defects in material and workmanship for a period as specified in this agreement. 売り主は、本契約で定める期間、本商品が材料と仕上げの面で欠陥がないことを保証する。

Permanent Normal Trade Relations　恒久的正常貿易関係, PNTR

permanent operating license　恒久操業許可

permission　(名)許可, 許し, 認可, 承認, 同意　(⇒prior permission)
◆If Washington's permission to import natural gas produced in the United Stated is granted, the LNG production of Mitsui & Co. and Mitsubishi Corp. at the Cameron Parish facility is expected to start as early as 2017. 米国で生産した天然ガスの輸入を米政府が許可した場合、米ルイジアナ州のキャメロン郡にあるLNG基地での三井物産と三菱商事のLNG生産は、早ければ2017年からスタートする予定だ。◆The three steelmakers are considering preventing acquirers from using the acquired company's non-shared patents without the other two firms' permission. 鉄鋼3社は、他の2社の許可がなければ、相互利用の対象となっていない買収された会社の特許を買収者が使えないようにすることも検討している。

permit　(名)許可, 認可, 許可書, 許可証, 免許, 免許証　(動)許可する, 認可する, 許す, 認める
　be permitted to　〜することができる
　import permit　輸入許可書
　permits and approvals　許認可
◆Commencing on the date of this agreement until the Closing, Buyer shall be permitted to per-

form such due diligence investigation related to the transactions contemplated by this agreement as Buyer deems necessary and appropriate in its discretion. 本契約締結日からクロージングまで、買い主は、本契約で意図されている取引に関して買い主が買い主の判断で必要かつ適切と考えるデュー・ディリジェンス調査を行うことができるものとする。◆Interest shall accrue on any delinquent amounts owed by Distributor for Products at the lesser of 18% per annum, or the maximum rate permitted by applicable usury law. 利息は、販売店が負っている本製品の延滞金について発生し、年18%の利率と適用される利息制限法で認められる最高利率のうちいずれか低いほうの利率によるものとする。◆The credit reads that partial shipments are permitted. 信用状には、「分割積み許可」とあります。

personal　(形)人的, 個人的, 個人に向けられた, 人身の, 身体の
　personal contract　人的財産 (personal property) に関する契約, 対人契約
　personal liability　人的責任
　personal security　身体の安全, 個人の安全

personal information　個人情報　(=personal data)
◆There are cases in which Google's Android smartphone users are asked to pay large bills after installing a virus-infected application that steals their personal information. 米グーグルのスマホ「アンドロイド」の利用者が、個人情報を抜き取るウイルス感染アプリ (応用ソフト) をインストールして、高額請求金額の支払いを求められるケースがある。

personal to　〜個人に向けられた, 〜に属する, 〜に限る
◆The license and all of ABC's rights hereunder are personal to ABC. 本契約に基づくライセンスとABCのすべての権利は、ABCに限るものである。

personnel　(名)要員, 人員, 職員, 従業員, 人事
　localization of personnel　現地採用
　personnel expenses [costs]　人件費
　personnel reduction　人員削減
　personnel transfer agreement　要員派遣契約
◆ABC shall select the personnel who shall be assigned as ABC Personnel to render the services under this agreement. ABCは、本契約に基づくサービスを提供するためABC人員として派遣する人員を選定するものとする。

pertaining to　〜に関する
◆ "Documentation" means the printed or electronic instructions, manuals and diagrams pertaining to the use and installation of Products. 「ドキュメンテーション」とは、本商品の使用とインストレーションに関する印刷されたまたは電子式の説明書、取扱い説明書と図表を意味する。

pertinent　(形)関係のある, 関連する, 〜に該

当する, 時宜にかなった, 適切な, 当を得た（to the point）, ぴったり当てはまる

be not pertinent to ～に関係がない, ～に関連性がない, ～には当てはまらない

pertinent advice 適切な助言

pertinent data 関連資料, 関連データ

pertinent details 関連項目

pertinent law 関連法, 関係法律

pertinent information 関連情報
◆The Licensee shall furnish regular written report specified by the Licensor to Licensor in order to disclose in full detail pertinent information and data in connection with the sale of the Product. ライセンシーは, 契約品の販売に関する関連情報とデータを十分詳細に開示するため, ライセンサーが指定する定期報告書をライセンサーに提出するものとする。

pirated copy 海賊版コピー
◆Establishing original edition rights would enable publishing companies to file lawsuits demanding the deletion of data if pirated copies are found to be sold on the Internet. 出版物［書籍］原版権の創設によって出版社は, 海賊版がインターネット上で販売されていることが判明した場合に, データの削除を求める訴訟を起こすことができる。

pirated designer goods 偽ブランド品
◆Imports of pirated designer goods violate commercial brand rights. 偽ブランド品の輸入は, 商標権の侵害に当たる。

pirates （名）ジャック（ハイジャックやカージャックなど）

place an order 注文を出す, 注文書を作成する, 注文書を交付する

place a substantial order 大口注文を出す

place an order for A with B BにAを発注する, BにAを注文する
◆We may place a substantial order with you on a regular basis if your prices are competitive. 貴社の製品価格が他社より安ければ, 定期的に大口の注文を出すことができます。

place of arbitration 仲裁地, 仲裁の場所, 仲裁の場
◆The place of arbitration shall be Tokyo, Japan, in case ABC is the respondent, and Paris, France, in case of XYZ is the respondent. 仲裁地は, ABCが被請求人のときは日本国東京とし, XYZが被請求人のときはフランス国のパリとする。

place of business 営業場所, 営業地, 営業所, 事業所
◆The seller's obligation under the warranty set forth above in this Article is limited to repairing or replacing at the seller's option, at the seller's place of business or such other place of the country of shipment as the case may be agreed by the seller and the purchaser. 本条の上記保証に基づく売り主の義務は, 売り主の選択で, 売り主の事業所または売り主と買い主が場合に応じて合意した

船積み国の他の場所での修理または交換に制限される。

place of origin 原産地
◆The Japanese Agricultural Standards（JAS）Law requires the producers of perishable foods to ensure that labels mention place of origin. 日本農林規格（JAS）法は, 生鮮食品の生産者に原産地表示を義務付けている。

place of the delivery 引渡し場所
◆Unless otherwise agreed between the parties, invoices will be issued and mailed by the seller to the purchaser upon the delivery of the Products at the place of the delivery set forth in this agreement. 当事者間で別途合意しないかぎり, 請求書は, 本契約に定める引渡し場所で本製品の引渡しが行われ次第, 売り主が買い主に発行し, 郵送するものとする。

planning （名）企画, 立案, 計画, 計画立案, 計画策定, プランニング

plant （名）工場, 生産設備, 工場設備, 施設, プラント, 植物

assembling plant 組立工場 （=assembly plant）

chemical plant 化学工場

idle plant 遊休設備, 遊休施設

industrial plant 工場設備, 工場

investment in plant and equipment 設備投資

new plant startup 新工場の稼動, 工場の操業開始

nuclear power plant 原子力発電所 （=atomic power station, nuclear power station）

petrochemical plant 石油化学プラント

pilot plant 試験工場, 実験工場, パイロット・プラント

plant and equipment 工場設備, 生産設備, 設備装置, 設備, 有形固定資産

plant closure 工場閉鎖

plant construction プラントの建設, プラント建設, プラント工事請負

plant construction contract プラント工事請負契約

plant design プラント設計

plant export プラント輸出

power plant 発電所 （=electric power plant）

processing plant 加工工場, 加工処理工場

producer's plant and equipment 生産設備

property, plant and equipment 有形固定資産
◆Japan's major automakers are capitalizing on improved quality at production plants overseas as part of their global strategies. 日本の大手自動車メーカーは, 自動車各社の世界戦略の一環として, 海外生産拠点での品質向上を活用している。
◆The plant, constructed as the joint venture of

Sumitomo Corp. and Kazakhstan's state-owned resource firm to extract rare earths by refining soil left in a uranium mine, is scheduled to start full-scale operations in the nation in November 2012. 住友商事とカザフスタンの国営資源企業の合弁事業として、ウラン鉱山で採掘された残土を精錬してレア・アースを抽出するために建設された同工場は、2012年11月からカザフスタンで本格稼働に入る。

plant manufacturing firm プラント・メーカー

◆Japanese employees of JGC Corp., a major plant manufacturing firm, were caught up in the hostage-taking incident launched by an armed Islamist group in Algeria. 大手プラント・メーカー「日揮」の邦人従業員が、アルジェリアでイスラム武装勢力が引き起こした人質事件に巻き込まれた。

plunge (名)市場の低迷、株価の急落、下落、激減、減少、急下降、落ち込み、突入

economic plunge 景気の急降下

plunge in demand 需要の落ち込み

register a record plunge 過去最大の下げを記録する

stock market [market's] plunge 株式市場の低迷、株安

the sharp plunge in the dollar's value 急激なドル安

plunge in the yen 円安

◆A recent plunge in the yen due to the economic and monetary policies of Prime Minister Shinzo Abe is a boon for domestic exporters. 安倍晋三首相の経済・金融政策による最近の円安は、国内の輸出企業にとっては追い風[恩恵]だ。

point of origin 源泉地

◆The point of origin (the location of the selling organization) of revenues and the location of the assets determine the geographic area. 地域別区分は、収益の源泉地(販売組織の所在地)と資産の所在地に基づいています。

poison pill 毒薬条項、敵対的買収に対する防衛手段、買収防衛策、ポイズン・ピル(敵対的買収に対する防衛策の一つ。「毒薬条項」は、既存株主に対して転換優先株式を株式配当の形で発行することを定めた条項を指す)

poison pill defense [defence] ポイズン・ピル防衛、毒薬条項防衛、毒入り避妊薬

poison pill defense tactics ポイズン・ピル(毒薬条項)防衛策

poison pill plan ポイズン・ピル方式(=poison pill scheme)

poison pill strategy ポイズン・ピル戦略

poison pill variant ポイズン・ピルの一種、毒薬条項の一種

◆About 15 percent of the leading companies are studying the possibility of using a poison pill to counter a hostile takeover by using the issue of warrants. 主要企業の約15%は、新株予約権の発行などで敵対的買収に対抗するポイズン・ピル(毒薬)の導入可能性を検討している。

poison pill defense tactics ポイズン・ピル(毒薬条項)防衛策

◆Companies are allowed to use poison pill defense tactics more easily by the Business Organization Law, which went into effect in fiscal 2006. 2006年度から施行された「会社法」で、企業はポイズン・ピル(毒薬条項)防衛策を以前より容易に行使できるようになった。

poison pill scheme ポイズン・ピル防衛策

◆Nireco Corp. has scrapped its plan to invoke the nation's first poison pill scheme to ward off hostile takeover bids. ニレコは、敵対的TOB(株式公開買付けによる企業買収)を防ぐための日本で最初のポイズン・ピル防衛策の実施計画を白紙撤回した。

policy (名)保険証書、保険証券、保険契約、政策、方針、方策、法の目的

cargo policy 積み荷保険証券、積み荷海上保険証券、貨物保険証券

definite policy 確定海上保険証券、確定保険証券

floating policy 船名未詳保険証券

hull policy 船舶保険証券

insurance policy 保険証券

MAR form policy MARフォーム(英国で1982年に制定された英文貨物海上保険証券の種類)

marine insurance policy 海上保険証券(⇒all risks)

mixed policy 混合保険証券

open policy 包括予定保険(証券)、予定保険

policy body 保険証券本文

policy clause [conditions] 保険約款

policy form 保険証券用紙

policy holder 保険証券保持者、保険契約者、保険加入者(=policyholder)

policy term 保険証券の期間[期限]

policy valuation 協定保険価額(=insured value)

policy value 保険価額、保険証券の価格、(保険証)券面価格

policy year 証券年度

provisional policy 予定保険証券

S.G. form policy S.G.フォーム(英文貨物海上保険証券の種類で、英国式の古いフォーム)

term policy 有期保険証券

time policy 船の期間保険証券、定期保険証券、定期保険

voyage policy 航海保険証券

◆In light of complaints from emerging economies that a glut of speculative funds due to monetary easing measures taken by advanced countries have caused the appreciation of their currencies and asset inflation, the G-20 participants agreed that they will monitor and minimize the negative ripple effects of their respective financial policies. 先進国の金融緩和策でだぶついた投機マネーが新興国の通貨高や資産インフレを招いているという新興国の不満に配慮して、G20参加国は、それぞれ金融政策の負の波及効果を監視し、最小化することで合意した。

policy rate （中央銀行の）政策金利（中央銀行が一般の銀行（市中銀行）に融資するときの金利。景気が良いときは高く設定され、景気が悪いときは低く設定される）
◆To prevent the European economy from falling into deflation, the ECB will cut its annual policy rate to a record low 0.15 percent and lower the overnight deposit rate, which is applied to funds commercial banks park at the ECB, to minus 0.1 percent from zero percent. 欧州経済がデフレに転落するのを阻止するため、欧州中央銀行（ECB）は、ECBの年間政策金利を過去最低の0.15％に引き下げ、民間銀行がECBに預ける資金に適用される翌日物の預金金利は0％からマイナス0.1％に下げることになった。

policyholder （名）保険契約者, 契約者, 保険加入者 （=insurance policyholder）
dividend to policyholders　契約者配当（=policyholder dividend）
meeting of representatives of policyholders　総代会
policyholder benefits　契約者給付金
policyholder claim　保険契約者の保険金請求
policyholder flight　保険契約者の逃避, 保険契約の解約
policyholder limit　保険契約者に対する与信限度
policyholders' representative meeting　総代会
senior policyholder　上位保険加入者
◆After the three-month period of full protection, the collapsed nonlife insurance firm will dissolve the contracts with their policyholders. （破綻後）3か月の全額保護期間が経過したら、破綻した損害保険会社は契約者との契約を打ち切る方針だ。◆The insurance premiums are determined by the age and other characteristics of policyholders. この保険料は、保険加入者の年齢などの特性に応じて決められる。

political climate　政治風土
◆Foreign investors, including Japanese firms, regard Thailand's political climate with its repeated coups as a risk factor for investing in the country. 日本企業など外国資本は、クーデターが繰り返されるタイの政治風土を、対タイ投資のリスク要因と見なしている。

political imbroglio　政治の混迷, 政治の混乱
◆In Thailand, budget compilation and the approval of large-scale investments have been hindered by the government's failure to function effectively due to the political imbroglio. タイでは、政治の混迷で政府機能が十分に働かず、予算編成や大型投資の認可に弊害が出ている。

pop culture　大衆文化, 流行文化, 文化商品, 文化産業, ポップ・カルチャー
◆Japan's pop culture, including its anime, games, food and fashion, is popular and being promoted under the name of "Cool Japan" in Asia, Europe and North America. アニメやゲーム、食品、ファッションなど日本のポップ・カルチャー（文化商品）は、アジアや欧米などで人気があり、「かっこいい日本」として売り込まれている。
◆Japan's pop culture, namely its anime, games, food, and fashion, has great potential for improving Japan's image and making its products more competitive internationally. アニメやゲーム、食、ファッションなど日本の文化商品は、日本のイメージ向上と日本製品の国際競争力アップにつながる可能性が大きい。

popularity　（名）人気, 評判, 支持, 普及
◆In step with the growing popularity of virtual engineering, the United States has launched a national strategy aimed at reinvigorating its manufacturing sector. バーチャル・エンジニアリング［仮想エンジニアリング］の普及とともに、米国は製造業の再活性化をめざした国家戦略を打ち出した。
◆The number of Twitter followers is used as a barometer of companies' popularity and reliability. ツイッターのフォロワー（閲覧者）の数は、企業の人気度や信頼度のバロメーターになっている。

port　（名）港, 港湾
cargo port　貨物港
commercial port　商業港, 商港
discharging port　陸揚げ港
entrepôt port　中継港
ex-quay port of arrival　着地払い運賃
free port　自由港, 無関税港
general cargo port　雑貨港
grain port　穀物港
home port　船籍港, 母港
industrial port　工業港
inland port　内陸港
junction port　中継接続港
landing port　船積み港
major port　重要港湾
open port　開港
picked port　選抜港
port area　港湾地域
port authority　港湾当局
port bill of lading　積出し港船荷証券

PORT 358

port call〔entry〕 寄港

port charges 入港税, 港税, 港湾料

port clearance 通関手続き, 出航手続き, 出港許可

port clearance fee 通関手数料, 出港手数料

port congestion 港湾滞貨

port despatch〔dispatch〕 仕出し港

port duties 入港税, 港税

port facilities 港湾施設

port management body 港湾管理者

port mark 揚げ地荷印

port of arrival 到着港

port of barge はしけ港

port of call 寄港地

port of debarkation 陸揚げ港

port of delivery 貨物引渡し港, 引渡し港, 荷下ろし港

port of discharge 荷揚げ港, 陸揚げ港

port of embarkation 船積み港, 船積み地, 出荷地

port of entry 通関手続き港, 輸入港, 通関港, 入国港

port of exit 輸出港, 仕出し港

port of exportation 輸出港

port of importation 輸入港

port of loading 船積み港, 積み荷港, 積出港

Port of London Authority ロンドン港管理部, PLA

port of refugee 避難港

port of registry 船籍港 (=port of register)

port of reshipment 積戻し港

port of transshipment 積換え港

port of unloading 陸揚げ港

port rates 入港税

port right 港湾使用権

port risks insurance 係船保険

port services 港湾業務

port transport industry 港湾運送事業, 港湾輸送事業

port warehouse 港湾倉庫

quarantine port 検疫港

quay port 荷下ろし港

safe port 安全港

sea port 海港

shipping port 積出し港

trade port 貿易港 (=trading port)

treaty port 条約港, 条約による貿易港

upriver port 上流港

way port 中間港

◆Your orders are arriving in Yokohama soon and will be transshipped on to m.s. "President Wilson" which is leaving Yokohama for your port on August 10. 貴注文は間もなく横浜に到着し, 貴地に向けて8月10日に横浜を出港予定のディーゼル船「プレジデント・ウイルソン」号に積み換える予定です。

port of destination 荷揚げ港, 陸揚げ港, (積荷が陸揚げされる) 輸入港, 仕向け港 (⇒port of shipment)

◆Any claim by the purchaser shall be made in writing and shall be received by the seller within 30 days after the arrival of the products at the port of destination. 買い主によるクレームは書面で行い, 本製品の仕向け港到着30日以内に売り主が受領するものとする。◆In case of a CIF contract, the seller shall, at its own expenses, arrange for ocean freight of the products from the port of shipment stated in this agreement to the port of destination of the products. CIF契約の場合, 売り主は, 本契約に定める船積み港から本商品の仕向け港までの本商品の海上輸送の手配を, 自己負担でするものとする。◆The port of destination of the products shall be Yokohama Port, Japan. 本商品の仕向け港は, 横浜港(日本)とする。

port of shipment 船積み港, 輸出港, 積出し港 (⇒port of destination)

◆In case of a FOB contract, the purchaser will, at its own expenses, arrange for ocean freight of the products from the port of shipment stated in this agreement to the port of destination of the products. FOB契約の場合, 買い主は, 本契約に定める船積み港から仕向け港までの本商品の海上輸送を, 自己の費用で手配するものとする。◆The Buyer shall notify the Seller of the name of the carrying vessel, the estimated date of loading and the contract number for the Seller to effect delivery, at least seven (7) days before the estimated date of arrival of the vessel at the port of shipment. 買い主は, 少なくとも本船の船積み港への到着予定日の7日前までに, 本船の船名, 船積み予定日と売り主が引渡しを行う契約番号を, 売り主に通知するものとする。

positive earnings 好業績, 好決算

◆Japanese export-oriented companies have been enjoying positive earnings for the last few years. 日本の輸出企業は, ここ数年, 好業績が続いた。

positive effect 正の効果, プラス効果

◆The positive effects of the yen's depreciation have not yet fully appeared, but sluggish increases in exports in the future due to a slowdown in the economic growth of emerging economies are worried about by some economists. 円安のプラス効果はまだ本格的に現われていないが, 新興国の経済成長の鈍化で, 今後の輸出の伸び悩みをエコノミストは懸念している。

possess or own 保有または所有する, 占有または所有する

possession (名)所有, 占有, 所有権

in one's possession 〜が所有する、〜が占有する

right of possession 占有権, 所有権

◆The licensee's obligation under this Article with respect to the confidential information shall not apply to information which is already in the possession of the licensee prior to the disclosure by the licensor and was not acquired by the licensee directly or indirectly from the licensor. 本条に基づく秘密情報に関するライセンシーの義務は、ライセンサーが開示する前にライセンシーがすでに保有していて、ライセンシーがライセンサーから直接または間接的に取得しなかった情報には適用されないものとする。

posting （名）立入り, 投函, 郵送, 発表, 公示, 提示, 掲示, 通知, 公告送達, 記録, 記帳, 記入, 書き込み, 登録, 更新, 転記, 仕訳, 達成, 計上, (担保などの) 差し入れ, 担保の設定, (人材などの) 配置, 配属, 任命, 派遣, 駐在, 保釈金の支払い

◆Any notice served by registered mail or by telex as aforesaid shall be deemed served on the earlier of actual receipt or the expiry of 120 hours after posting. 上記のとおり書留郵便またはテレックスで送達された通知は、実際の受領日と投函から120時間後のうちいずれか早いほうの日に送達されたものと見なすものとする。

posting （名）(ネットの) 書き込み, 書き込み情報, ニュースグループに送られるメッセージ, 発信, 投稿 （=online chat）

posting site 投稿サイト

postings on social network sites 交流サイト (SNS) 上の書き込み情報

stealth marketing by posting 書き込みによるステルス・マーケティング

◆As stealth marketing by postings is problematic, the Consumer Affairs Agency has revised its guidelines for online transactions under the Law for the Prevention of Unreasonable Premiums and Misrepresentations concerning Products and Services. 書き込みによるステルス・マーケティングには問題があるので、消費者庁は、「景品表示法 (不当景品類及び不当表示防止法)」のネット取引に関する指針を改正した。

potential （名）可能性, 将来性, 見込み, 恐れ, 潜在能力, 潜在力, (潜在的な) 力, 潜在成長率, 成長力, 余力, 余地, 才能, 能力, 素質, 資質, ポテンシャル

◆Exporting companies must strengthen structures to glean earnings in countries around the globe, including newly emerging markets with high growth potential. 輸出企業は、潜在成長力の高い新興市場を含めて、グローバルに収益を上げる [稼ぐ] 体制を強化する必要がある。◆The recent M&A is a strategy with an eye on Asia, which has a great potential for sales growth. 今回のM&Aは、販売が伸びる可能性が大きいアジアを視野に入れた戦略です。

power and authority 権能と権限, 権限

◆Licensee hereby represents and warranties that Licensee has the full power and authority to enter into this agreement, to perform its obligations, and is free to enter into this agreement. ライセンシーは本契約を締結し、本契約に基づくその義務を履行する全権能と権限をもっており、自由に本契約を締結できることを、ライセンシーは本契約により表明し、これを保証する。

power, right or authority 権能, 権利または権限

practice （名）実行, 実践, 実務, 営業, 開業, 業務, 慣行, 慣習, 習慣, 習慣, 手法, 仕組み, 法律事務, 訴訟実務, 訴訟手続き

backdoor practice 裏口操作

best practice 最善の手法, 最良の方法, 卓越した事例, 最善の実施例 [業務慣行], 最善の慣行

business practice 商慣習, 商慣行, 企業慣行, 取引慣行, 取引方法, 営業手法, 業務

collusive practices 談合

commercial practices 商慣習, 商慣行, 商習慣

evil practice 悪弊

fair practice 公正慣行, 公正慣習

financial practice 金融措置

Foreign Corrupt Practices Act 海外不正行為防止法

fraudulent practices 詐欺商法, 悪質商法

general practice 一般慣習

lending practice 融資慣行

malicious business practices 悪質商法, 悪徳商法

malicious sales practices 悪徳商法

management accounting practice 管理会計実務

market-distorting trade practices 市場を歪める商慣行

market practice 市場慣行

operating practice 経営手法 （=practice management）

practice improvement plan 業務改善計画

practice of law 法律業務

priority practice 優先交渉慣行

product development practice 製品開発戦略

restrictive labor practices 制限的労働慣行

Rules of Fair Practice 公正慣習規則, 公正慣行ルール (全米証券業協会の業界規則)

sales practice 販売手法

trade practices 貿易慣行, 取引慣行, 商慣行

unfair business practices 不公正取引慣行, 不公正商慣習

unfair practice 不正商慣行, 不正商慣習, 不公

正な取引方法, 不当営業行為, 不公正競争
uniform practice code　統一慣習規則
unlawful business practices　違法な営業手法

preceding paragraph　前項
under the preceding paragraph　前項に基づ
いて
◆In addition to the payment under the preceding
paragraph, Licensee shall further pay to Company a running royalty equal to 10 percent of Net
Selling Price of Products manufactured and sold
by Licensee during the life of this agreement. 前
項に基づく支払いのほかに, ライセンシーはさら
に, 本契約期間中ライセンシーが製造・販売する
本製品［契約品］の正味販売価格の10%に等しい継
続実施料（ランニング・ロイヤルティ）を会社に対
して支払うものとする。

preclude　(動)排除する, 妨げる
◆No single or partial exercise thereof shall preclude any other or further exercise thereof or the
exercise of any other right or remedy. その単独
または一部行使は, 他のもしくはそれ以上の行使,
またはその他の権利もしくは救済の行使を排除し
ないものとする。

predecessor　(名)前任者
◆The term of office of a director elected to fill a
vacancy shall be the same term with the remainder of the term of office of his predecessor. 欠員
補充のために選任された取締役の任期は, 前任者
の残りの任期と同じとする。

preemptive right　新株引受権, 株主の先買権
◆Shareholders of JVCO shall have preemptive
rights. JVCO（合弁会社）の株主は, 新株引受権を
持つものとする。

preferential treatment　優遇措置
◆In Egypt, military-related business groups receive preferential treatment, so fair competition
has been impeded. エジプトでは, 軍関連の企業グ
ループが優遇されるので, 公正な競争が妨げられて
きた。◆With competition between domestic and
foreign companies intensifying, criticism has increased over the preferential treatment given to
foreign firms in China. 内外企業の競争激化で,
中国では最近, 外資系企業優遇への批判が高まっ
ている。

prejudice　(名)不利益, 損なうこと, 害するこ
と, 侵害, 損害, 損傷　(動)損なう, 害する, 損
害を与える, 傷つける　(⇒without prejudice)
without prejudice to any other rights or
remedies　他の権利または救済手段を侵害
することなく, 他の権利または救済手段を
失うことなく
◆In case of any dispute or claim in connection
with such infringement, the purchaser may cancel this agreement or any part of this agreement
without prejudice to any other rights the purchaser may have under the applicable law or the
agreement. 当該侵害に関連して紛争または請求が
発生した場合, 買い主は, 適用法または本契約によ

り買い主が所有する他の権利を損なわないで本契
約または本契約の一部を解除することができる。◆
Such inspection shall not, in any way, prejudice
the purchaser's right of inspection of the products after the delivery at the final destination or
rejection of the defective products. この検査は,
最終目的地での引渡し後に本製品を検査する買い
主の権利, または瑕疵（かし）ある製品を拒絶する
買い主の権利をいかなる意味でも損なわないもの
とする。

preliminary　(形)前置きの, 予備の, 準備の
ための, 予備的な, 暫定的な, 仮の　(名)前置
き, 予備交渉, 予備的行為, 準備, 予備試験, 予
選, 前座試合
be still at a preliminary stage in the
conversations　まだ交渉の予備的段階に
ある
preliminary claim　予備クレーム
preliminary condition　予備的条件
preliminary contract　仮契約
preliminary data　速報値
preliminary estimate　暫定推定値, 仮見積り
preliminary examination［exam］　予備調査,
予備審査, 予備試験
preliminary exploration　予備調査
preliminary hearing　事前審理, 予備審問, 予審
preliminary injunction　暫定的差止め命令
preliminary inquiry　概算見積照会
preliminary negotiation　予備交渉
preliminary notice　予告
preliminary projections　暫定値
preliminary prospectus　仮目論見書
preliminary quotation　暫定見積り, 仮見積り
preliminary rating　予備格付け
preliminary research　予備調査, 予備的調査
preliminary review　予備調査, 予備審査
preliminary terms　基本条件
preliminary balance of payments data
国際収支の速報値
◆According to the preliminary balance of payments data, the deficit in trade in July 2013 was
¥943.3 billion, 2.5 times the level a year earlier and marking the highest level for July since
1985. 国際収支の速報値によると, 2013年7月のモ
ノの取引を示す貿易収支（モノの輸出額から輸入額
を差し引いた貿易収支）の赤字額は, 9,433億円で
前年同月の水準の2.5倍, 7月としては1985年以降
最大の水準となった。

preliminary inspection　予備検査, 予備的
検査
◆The products supplied under this agreement
shall be subject to preliminary inspection of the
seller at the seller's premises prior to the shipment. 本契約に基づき供給する本製品は, 出荷前

に売り主の構内で売り主の予備検査を受けるものとする。

preliminary study 予備調査, 事前調査
◆We couldn't foresee such defects in the preliminary study. 事前調査で, このような瑕疵(かし)[欠陥]は予見できなかった。

premises (名)契約の頭書, 前文(nonoperative part), 前記事項, 上記事項, 既述事項, 不動産, 土地, 建物, 施設, 構内, 敷地, 不動産物件, 物件, 賃貸物件, 根拠, 前提
◆All quantities of the Product manufactured by you shall be held by you to our order and we shall insure all quantities on your premises of the Commodity and the Product. 貴社が製造した契約品の数量はすべて当社の指図があるまで貴社が保管し, 当社は貴社の構内にある商品と契約品の全数量に保険を付けるものとする。◆Provided, however, that the purchaser shall have the right to inspect the products by an independent inspection company designated by the purchaser at the premises of the manufacturer of the products at such time as may be agreed upon by the seller and the purchaser prior to loading. ただし, 買い主は, 積込み前に売り主と買い主が合意する時期に, 本製品製造者の構内で, 買い主指定の独立した検査会社により本製品を検査する権利を持つものとする。

解説 **契約の頭書**: 契約の頭書とは, 契約書の冒頭部分のことで, 契約の締結日や契約当事者の会社の名称, 本社・本店の所在地, 会社設立の準拠法などが示される。(⇒made and entered into)

at the premises of 〜の構内で

be the main premise for 〜の大前提である

in consideration of the premises 前文を約因として 前記事項を約因として

on the premise of 〜という前提に基づいて 〜という根拠に基づいて

on the premise that… 〜という前提で

the demised premises 賃貸物件

the premises 敷地 構内 店内 施設

premium (名)保険料, 保険金, 額面超過額, 割増金, 手数料, 権利金, 賞金, 上乗せ, プレミアム (⇒buyer's premium)

extra premium 割増保険料

invest policyholders' premiums in stocks 保険契約者の保険料を株式に投資する

premium installments 保険料の分割部分

premium rate 保険料率, 再保険料率

premium schedules 元受保険料率表

renewal premium 更新保険料, 継続保険料

statement of premium 保険料明細書
◆As stealth marketing by postings is problematic, the Consumer Affairs Agency has revised its guidelines for online transactions under the Law for the Prevention of Unreasonable Premiums and Misrepresentations concerning Products and Services. 書き込みによるステルス・マーケティングには問題があるので, 消費者庁は,「景品表示法(不当景品類及び不当表示防止法)」のネット取引に関する指針を改正した。

prepare (動)文書を作成する, 準備する, 用意する, 計画する, 段取りを整える, 下調べをする, 整備する, 覚悟させる, 心の準備をさせる, (薬品などを)調製する, 調合する
◆These financial statements have been prepared in accordance with the U.S. GAAP consistently applied throughout the periods indicated. これらの財務書類は, 当該期間中に一貫して適用した米国の一般に公正妥当と認められた会計原則[米国の会計基準]に従って[準拠して]作成されています。
◆This agreement shall not be construed for or against any party based on any rule of construction who prepared the agreement. 本契約は, どちらの当事者が本契約書の起草をしたかによる解釈のルールに基づいて, 一方の当事者に有利に解釈したり不利に解釈したりしないものとする。

prepay (動)期限前に返済する, 期限前に繰上げ返済する, 満期前に支払う
◆The borrower may from time to time prepay the principal amount of the loan, in whole or part, together with accrued interest therefrom, if any, with the lender's prior written consent. 借主は, 貸主の書面による事前の承諾(同意)を得て, 随時, 借入金元金(借入額)の全部または一部を, 借入金の経過利息(もしあれば)とともに, 繰上げ返済することができる。

prepayment (名)前払い金, 前渡し金, 前払い費用, 期限前返済, 期限前の繰上げ返済, 満期前支払い
◆All payments, repayments, or prepayments to be made by the borrower under the agreement shall be made in Japanese Yen by telegraphic transfer to such bank account in Tokyo designated by the lender. 本契約に基づいて借主が行うすべての支払い, 返済, 繰上げ返済は, 貸主が指定する東京の銀行口座に対して電信送金により日本円で行うものとする。

prerequisite (名)前提条件, 必要条件, 先行条件, 要件 (形)〜に不可欠な, 〜に必須の (⇒high-quality)
◆A prerequisite to restoring the country's fiscal health is to promptly and boldly take effective pump priming measures and to overcome the economic crisis. 日本の財政健全化への前提条件は, 迅速, 果敢に効果的な景気浮揚策を実行して, 経済危機を克服することだ。◆Prime Minister Abe said that at a summit meeting with U.S. President Barack Obama, the two leaders confirmed abolishing tariffs on all items was not a prerequisite for joining the TPP negotiations. 安倍首相は,「オバマ大米統領との首脳会談で, 両首脳は全品目に対する関税の撤廃がTPP(環太平洋経済連携協定)交渉参加の前提条件ではないことを確認した」と語った。

PRES 362

presence （名）出席, 立入り, 存在
◆A quorum for the board of directors meeting shall require the presence of four（4）directors. 取締役会の定足数は, 4名の取締役の出席を必要とする。

presence of shareholders 株主の出席
◆A quorum for a meeting of Shareholders shall require the presence of shareholders（or their proxy）whose voting rights shall constitute sixty five（65）percent of the issued and outstanding stocks. 株主総会の定足数は, 発行済み社外株式（発行済み社外流通株式）の65％の議決権を有する株主の出席（または株主の委任状）を必要とする。

present （動）表示する, 提示する, 示す, 引き起こす, 〜に出席する, 〜に紹介する, 引き合わせる, 〜を司会する, 放映する, 上演する, 演奏する, 作成する, 提出する, 提供する, 与える, 贈呈する, 口頭で説明する, 陳述する, 申し立てる,（犯罪を）〜に告発する
fairly present 適正に表示する
（=present fairly）
present consolidated financial statements 連結財務書類［連結財務諸表］を作成する
◆As a new greenhouse gas reduction framework to replace the Kyoto Protocol is to be implemented in 2020, the participating countries agreed to present their voluntary greenhouse gas emission targets for the years beyond 2020 in 2015. 京都議定書に代わる温室効果ガス削減の新たな枠組みが2020年に発効する予定なので,（国連気候変動枠組み条約の）締約国会議への参加各国は, 2020年以降の自主的な温室効果ガス排出削減目標を, 2015年に提示することで合意した。◆Japan has yet to enter full-scale TPP negotiations, but the LDP has not presented concrete measures to prepare for the liberalization of trade, including steps to bolster competitiveness in the agricultural sector. 日本が環太平洋経済連携協定（TPP）の本格交渉に入るのはこれからだが, 自民党は, 農業分野での競争力強化策など, 貿易自由化に備えた具体策をまだ示していない。◆The annual financial statements for the financial year ending on December 31, 2015 present a true and fair view of the financial position as of the date thereof. 2015年12月31日に終了する事業年度［会計年度］の年次財務書類は, 同日現在の財政状態について真実かつ公正な見方を提示している。

presentation （名）提示, 提案, 提出, 手形の提示［呈示］, 公表, 発表, 公開, 表示, 表示方法, 説明, 説明会, 報告, 演説, 概要紹介, 上演, 贈呈, 進呈, 授与, プレゼンテーション
fair presentation 適正表示, 公正表示
financial statement presentation 財務諸表の表示, 財務書類の表示
misleading presentation 不当表示
on presentation （手形の）提示［呈示］次第［提示のあり次第］, 手形提示の節は, 手形

提示の折は
presentation bill 一覧払い手形, 呈示払い手形
presentation for acceptance 引受提示
presentation for payment 支払い要求提示
presentation of bill（of exchange） 為替手形の提示
presentation of documents 船積み書類の提示
presentation of draft 手形の提示［呈示］
presentation of seal 印鑑届け
presentation period 提示期間
（=time of presentation）
presentation ticket 商品券
◆Irrevocable letter of credit provides for payment upon presentation of Supplier's invoices and shipping documents evidencing delivery of the invoiced Products to the carrier or freight forwarder. 取消不能信用状は, 供給者の請求書と, 請求書に記載した本製品を運送人または海貨業者に引き渡したことを証明する船積み書類を提示して支払いを受けるものだ。◆The letter of credit set forth above shall be negotiable against a draft at sight signed by the seller upon the presentation of the following documents: 上記の信用状は, 次の船積み書類の提示がある場合には, 売り主が振り出した一覧払い手形と引換えに買い取られるものとする。◆We hope you will kindly protect the draft on presentation. 手形提示の節は, 何とぞお引受け下さい。

presentment （名）（手形や小切手などの）提示
presentment for acceptance 引受提示
presentment for payment 支払い提示
presentment warranty 提示保証

press release 新聞発表, プレス・リリース
（=news release）

prevail （動）優先する, 優先適用される, 勝訴する, 有力である, 支配的である, 規則・慣習などが行われる
◆Whenever there is any conflict between any provisions of this agreement and any statute or law, contrary to which the parties have no legal right to contract, the latter shall prevail. 本契約の規定と, 当事者がそれに反して契約する法的権利のない制定法または法律との間に矛盾がある場合には, いつも後者が優先するものとする。

prevail over 〜に優先する
◆In the event of any dispute, this English version of this agreement will prevail over any other language versions. 紛争が生じたときは, 本契約の英語版が他の言語版に優先するものとする。

prevailing （形）優勢な, 有力な, 卓越した, 優勢を占めている, 支配的な, 勢力がある, 広く受け入れられている, 広く行われている, 普及［流行］している, 実勢の, 現行の, ごく普通の, 世間一般の, 一般の
prevailing exchange rate 現在の為替レート

prevailing interest rate　現行金利［利子率］, 実勢金利, 金利の実勢

prevailing market yield　市場実勢利回り

prevailing opinion　支配的な意見

prevailing price　一般価格 時価

prevailing wages　現行賃金, 一般賃金
◆As the value of using big data, a sales practice prevailing in the mail-order business sector is to analyze purchase records of customers and then recommend products based on their tastes and preferences. ビッグ・データの利用価値として、通販業界で広がっている販売手法は、顧客の購入履歴を分析して、顧客の好みに合う商品を薦める方法だ。

prevailing rate　市場の実勢金利, 市場金利, 実勢相場, 中心相場, 中心レート, 一般賃金, 一般賃率
◆The prevailing rate of interest for a note payable of this type is 12%. この種の支払い手形の通常［現行］の利子率は、12%である。

price　（名）価格, 値段, 代金, 物価, プライス

best price　（売りの場合の）最高値（best quotation）,（買いの場合の）最低値（lowest price, rock-bottom price）, 最低価格, 最低取引価格, 勉強値段, 勉強値

maintain moderate prices　手頃な価格［格安料金］を維持する

price discrimination　価格差別
◆Every three months, McDonald's Japan revises the price of the beef it imports from Australia according to the exchange rate. 3か月ごとに、日本マクドナルドは、為替相場に応じてオーストラリアから輸入している牛肉の価格を見直している。◆Japan has to import most of its fossil fuels from the Middle East in which supplies and prices remain unstable. 日本は、化石燃料の大半を、供給量も価格も不安定な中東からの輸入に頼っている。◆We may place a substantial order with you on a regular basis if your prices are competitive. 貴社の製品価格が他社より安ければ、定期的に大口の注文を出すことができます。◆We refrained from making a counter offer as the price you offered is about seven percent higher than the level workable to us. 貴社がオファーされた価格は、当社の採算にのる水準よりも7%ほど高いので、カウンター・オファーを出すことを思いとどまりました。◆You may count on our best efforts so long as you can maintain moderate prices. 手頃な価格［格安料金］を維持できるかぎり、当社は最大限の努力を貴社にお約束します。

price cartel　価格カルテル, 価格協定
（=price agreement）
◆The Fair Trade Commission probed about a dozen industrial gas providers over price cartel suspicions. 公正取引委員会は、価格カルテルの疑いで産業用ガス・メーカー十数社を立ち入り検査した。◆The firm also was involved in the price

cartel. 同社も、価格カルテルに関与していた。

price competitiveness　価格競争力
◆In terms of price competitiveness, Japan is weaker than China and South Korea. 価格競争力の点で、日本は中国や韓国より弱い。

price-fixing agreement　価格維持協定, 価格カルテル, ヤミ価格協定
◆France's Competition Commission has ordered Sony, Matsushita and Philips to pay fines for allegedly concluding price-fixing agreements on retail goods with their local distributors. フランスの競争評議会は、国内販売店と小売電気製品の価格維持協定を結んだとして、ソニー、松下電器産業とフィリップスに罰金の支払いを命じた。

price fixing conspiracy　価格カルテル
◆Yazaki and Denso have agreed to pay about $548 million in criminal fines for a price fixing conspiracy in the sale of parts to U.S. automakers. 矢崎総業とデンソーが、米自動車メーカーへの部品販売で他社と共謀して価格カルテルを結んでいたため、計約5億4,800万ドルの罰金を支払うことで合意した。

price level　物価水準, 物価

price-level basis of accounting　物価変動会計基準

price-level change　物価変動

price-level policy　物価対策
◆Japan's economic growth is driven by exports, but it will have to vie for export markets with emerging economies. 日本の経済成長の原動力は輸出だが、今後は新興国と輸出市場の争奪戦になろう。◆The competitive edge of Japanese exporters vying with U.S. firms is affected by the yen-dollar rate and the price levels in the two countries. 米企業と競合している日本の輸出企業の競争力は、円・ドルレートや日本と米国の物価水準の影響をも受ける。

price list　価格表
◆Subdistributor discount means the amount below the prices set forth in the price list, at which the subdistributor may purchase the products from Distributor. 「二次代理店割引」とは、価格表に記載する価格より低い金額のことで、二次代理店はこの金額で代理店から本製品を購入することができる。◆The following price list shows our best prices and rate of quantity discount for our supplies. 以下の価格表は、当社供給品の最低価格［勉強値］と数量割引率を示しています。◆The prices and other particulars inquired for are shown in the enclosed price list. お問い合わせの価格その他の明細は、同封の価格表に示してあります。

price of regular gas [gasoline]　レギュラー・ガソリンの価格
◆The price of regular gas has gone up for six weeks because oil wholesalers have added their import costs, which have been going up due to the weak yen since the end of last year, to the re-

tail price. レギュラー・ガソリンの価格は、昨年末からの円安で上昇している輸入費用の増加分を元売り各社が小売価格に転嫁しているため、6週間連続で上昇した。

price of the product 本商品の価格
◆The price of the products for any subsequent year commencing on the annual anniversary of this agreement shall be such as may be negotiated and agreed upon between the parties not later than 30 days prior to the commencement of such year. 本契約から1年後の応答日に始まる次年度の本商品価格は、当該年度が始まる30日前までに当事者間で交渉して合意する価格とする。

price wars 価格競争
◆Home electrical appliances including TVs have been exposed to fierce price wars. テレビなどの家電製品は、激しい価格競争にさらされてきた。

prices of imported goods 輸入品の価格、輸入物価
◆If the euro should weaken further, the prices of imported goods will rise, raising hopes that the deflationary pressure will ease. ユーロ安がさらに進めば、輸入物価は上昇し、デフレ圧力の緩和が期待される。

prices of imports 輸入額
◆The weaker yen helps exporters, but close attention must be paid to the fact that the excessive depreciation of the yen will further increase the prices of imports of LNG and other foreign products. 円安は輸出企業にはプラスだが、円安が行き過ぎると、天然液化ガス（LNG）など海外製品の輸入額が一段と増えることにも、警戒が必要である。

prima facie evidence 一応の証拠、推定的証拠

primary （形）最初の、第一次の、一次的な、第一順位の、主要な、最も重要な、最大の、中心的な、有力な、本来の、根源的な、初歩の、初期の、初期段階の、基本的な、希薄化前の、プライマリー

primary activities 第一次産業活動、起債活動、発行活動

primary beneficiary 第一順位保険金受取人

primary benefit 主要便益

primary bond 新発債

primary capital 第一次資本、本源的資本、銀行の自己資本、プライマリー・キャピタル （=Tier 1 capital）

primary change in money （輸出入の超過による）通貨の一次増減

primary concern 最大の関心事

primary customers 中心顧客

primary data 一次的データ

primary dealer 米国の公認政府証券ディーラー、プライマリー・ディーラー

primary deficit 基礎的赤字、財政の基礎収支

の赤字

primary demand 基礎的需要、第一次需要、基本的需要

primary distribution 募集、第一次分売、第一次売出 （=primary offering）

primary duty 輸入付加税

primary earnings per share of common stock 普通株式1株当たり基本的利益

primary evidence 一次的証拠

primary export product 一次産品輸出生産物

primary export substitution 第一次輸出代替

primary exporting country 一次産品輸出国

primary exports 一次産品輸出

primary financial statements 主要財務諸表［財務書類］、基本財務諸表、基本財務書類、第一次財務諸表［財務書類］ （第二次財務諸表＝secondary financial statements）

primary goods 第一次産品 （=primary product［commodity］）

primary import substitution 第一次輸入代替

primary importing country 一次産品輸入国

primary imports 一次産品輸入

primary industry 第一次産業、一次産業（=primary sectors: 農業、林業、畜産、漁業、鉱業など）

primary issues 主要な問題

primary jurisdiction 第一次的管轄、第一次的管轄権

primary lender 最大の借入先、メインバンク

primary line 売り手段階

primary market 主要市場、新規取引市場、発行市場［新発債市場、プライマリー市場］

primary material 原材料

primary mineral 原成鉱物

primary objective 最大の目標

primary package 第一位包装

primary paper 新発債

primary party 手形振出人、為替手形引受人、小切手の支払い人［引受人］

primary point 原生品集産地

primary processed goods 主要加工品

primary processing 一次加工、川上部門

primary produce 一次産品

primary producer 第一次生産国、第一次産品国 （=primary producing country）

primary producing country 原料生産国

primary product line 主力製品

primary production 一次生産

primary products 一次産品、農産品、主要製品

primary reserve assets （IMFの）第一次準備

資産

primary resources 原産資源, 天然資源

primary sample 一次サンプル

primary sector 第一次産業

primary shipment 農産物出荷高, 農産物積み荷高

primary specialization 一次産品特化

primary trade 第一次産品貿易

primary trade specialization 第一次産品貿易特化

primary wholesaler 一次卸し

prime product industry 原料工業, 原産品産業

primary commodity 一次産品
◆Indonesia has enjoyed decent economic growth since the global financial crisis of 2008 due to the U.S. FRB's quantitative easing and higher prices of primary commodities such as coal and palm oil as the country's major exports. インドネシアは、2008年の世界金融危機以降、米連邦準備制度理事会（FRB）の量的金融緩和とインドネシアの主要輸出品である石炭、パーム油など一次産品の高値に支えられ、高い経済成長を享受している。◆Rapidly increasing prices of primary commodities have had a positive influence on corporate performance with the yen's appreciation against the dollar. 円高・ドル安で、これまでのところ一次産品（原油や石炭など）の急騰が、企業の業績に好影響をもたらしている。

primary commodity prices 一次産品の価格
◆Indonesia has chalked up large trade deficits due to the decline in primary commodity prices and the rupiah has weakened as much as 17 percent against the U.S. dollar as of September 2013. インドネシアは一次産品の価格の下落で大幅な貿易赤字を計上し、通貨ルピアは2013年9月現在、対ドルで17％安となっている。

primary informed consent 文書による事前の同意・承認
◆Access to genetic resources requires prior informed consent of the country of origin. 生物遺伝資源を利用する場合は、資源原産国の文書による事前の同意・承認を得なければいけない。

prime （形）主要な, 主な, 首位の, 最重要な, 優秀の, 優良な, 最優良な, 最高級の, 第一等の, 最上の, 最良の, 極上の, 信用等級が最高の, 短期貸出金利の, 素数の （名）全盛期, 最盛期, 盛り［男盛り、女盛り、血気盛り］, 絶頂期, 最上等, 最上部, 初期, 初期の段階, 初め, 夜明け, 春, 素数, プライム・レート

a cut in prime プライム・レートの切下げ

at prime プライム・レートで

float with prime プライム・レートに連動する

of prime importance 最も重要な

prime agent 主因, 主要因

prime bankers' acceptance 一流銀行引受手形

prime bill 優良手形, 一流手形

prime borrower 大口貸出先, 大口貸付け先, 大口融資先, 優良発行体, 優良な借入人

prime business 優良企業

prime cause 主因, 第一原因

prime commercial lending rate 最優遇商業貸出金利

prime commercial paper 一流商業手形

prime contract 主契約

prime contractor プライム・コントラクター, 元請工事業者, 元請業者 (=general contractor: 発注者から最初にプラント建設工事を請け負う契約者のこと)

prime corporate bonds 優良企業が発行する社債, 一流社債

prime cost 仕入れ値段, 原価, 主要費用

prime credit 原信用状 (=prime letter of credit)

prime customer 優良顧客, 優良取引先

prime debtor［issuer］有力借入先

prime endorsed acceptance 一流銀行裏書引受手形

prime entry 仮輸入手続き, (仕訳帳への) 第一次記入

prime factor 主要因

prime interest（rate）最優遇貸出利, プライム・レート (=prime rate)

prime loan 一流（顧客向け）貸出

prime loan rate 最優遇貸出金利, 一流企業向け貸出金利, プライム・レート

prime-location 立地条件の良い

prime maker 当初振出人

prime name 超一流企業, 一流手形, 優良銘柄

prime paper 一流手形

prime product 主製品

prime quality 最上品, 最良品

prime quantity 一流の質

prime rating 高格付け, プライム格付け

prime stock 主力株, 花形株

prime teller 関税収入票

prime warrant 全荷倉庫証券

Prime/LIBOR basis swap プライム・レートとライボー間のベーシス・スワップ

prime asset 優良資産
◆A new GM will inherit only the firm's prime assets, including profitable brands. 新GMは、収益が見込めるブランドなど、同社の優良資産だけを引き継ぐことになろう。

prime lending rate 一流企業向け最優遇貸出金利, プライム・レート (=prime rate)

◆The Fed decision means that commercial banks' prime lending rate will remain unchanged at 5 percent. 米連邦準備制度理事会（FRB）の今回の決定は、商業銀行のプライム・レートが現行の5%に据え置かれることを意味する。

prime rate（of interest） プライム・レート, 一流企業向け最優遇貸出金利, 標準金利
◆For the purpose of this agreement, the prime rate shall mean that rate announced by the principal bank of the seller as its prime commercial lending rate from time to time. 本契約の目的上、プライム・レートとは、売り主の主要取引銀行が最優遇商業貸出金利として随時発表する利率を意味する。

principal （名）本人, 主債務者, 元本, 元金, 基本財産, 株式の額面価額 （⇒relationship）

principal amount of the loan 借入金の元金, 借入金の元本金額, 借入額, 融資金の元本, 貸付け金の元本
◆If the borrower shall fail to pay any debt for borrowed money or other similar obligation of the borrower, or interest thereon, when due, and such failure continues after the applicable grace period specified in the agreement relating to such indebtedness, the lender may in its discretion declare the entire unpaid principal amount of the loan, accrued interest thereon and all other sums payable under this agreement to be immediately due and payable. 借主が借主の借入債務（借入金に対する債務）や他の同様の債務またはその利息を支払い期日に支払うことを怠り、このような不履行が本契約に定める当該債務に関する適用猶予期間後も継続する場合、貸主はその裁量で、借入金の未返還元本全額、その発生利息と本契約に基づいて支払わなければならない他の未払い金の全額即時支払い［即時返済］を宣言することができる。

principal balance remaining unpaid 残存する元本の未払い残高
◆For Value Received, the undersigned（"Borrower"）promises to pay to ABC Co., Ltd. , a Japanese corporation（"Holder"）, or order, in lawful money of the United States, the principal sum of Five million Eight hundred Fifty thousand dollars（$5,850,000）, with interest on the principal balance remaining unpaid from the date hereof until paid, at the following rates. 「対価の受領」については、末尾署名者（以下「振出人」という）が、元本585万ドル（$5,850,000）と本手形の振出日から決済日まで残存する元本の未払い残高利息を、日本法人のABC株式会社（以下「所持人」という）にまたはその指図人に、米国の法定通貨と以下の金利で支払うことを約束する。

principal obligor and debtor 主債務者
◆The guarantor shall be liable under this guarantee as if it were the sole principal obligor and debtor and not merely a surety. 保証人は、保証人が単なる保証人ではなく唯一の主債務者であるかのように本保証書上の責任を負うものとする。

principal office 主たる事務所, 本社事務所,

本店事務所, 本社, 本店, 本部
having its principal office at ～に主たる事務所を置く, ～に本社を置く, ～に本店を置く （=with its principal office at）
◆The principal office may be moved to any other place in _____ approved by all the parties hereto. 本店は、契約当事者全員が承認した他の _____ の場所に移転できる。

principal or interest payable 元本または支払い利息
◆In case the borrower fails to pay any principal or interest payable under this agreement on the due date therefor, the borrower shall pay to the lender overdue interest on such overdue amount for each day for the period from and including the due date therefor up to and including the day immediately preceding the actual payment date. 借主が本契約に基づいて元本または支払い利息の支払い期日に元本の返済または支払い利息の支払いを怠った場合、借主は、その支払い期日から実際の払込み日の前日までの期間の各日数について、その支払い遅延金額の遅延利息を貸主に支払うものとする。

principal place of business 主たる営業地, 営業の本拠地, 本社, 本店

principal terms 主要条件, 基本的条件, 基本条件（取引の主な契約内容のこと）

principle of free trade 自由貿易の原則
◆Numerical targets may lead to managed trade which runs counter to the principle of free trade. 数値目標は、自由貿易の原則に反する「管理貿易」につながりかねない。

Printed Name: 記名

prior （形）前の, 事前の, 先の
a prior engagement 先約
prior consent 事前の同意, 事前の承諾, 事前の承認 （⇒prior informed consent）
prior contact 事前の連絡
prior notice 事前通知, 事前通告
prior oral or written representations and agreements 口頭または書面による従前の表示事項と合意事項, 口頭または書面による事前の表示事項と合意事項
prior understanding, agreement, statement of intent or memorandum of understanding 事前の了解, 合意, 意図の表明または了解覚書
prior written or oral agreement 書面または口頭による事前の合意, 書面による事前許可, 契約締結前の書面または口頭による合意

prior approval 事前承認
◆Samples of all promotional materials or plans of advertisements referring to the Trademarks for intended use by the licensee shall be submitted by the licensee to the licensor for its prior approval before the commencement of the li-

censee's advertising campaigns to the public. ライセンシーが使用する予定の本商標にかかわるすべての販促用資料の見本または広告宣伝計画書は、ライセンシーが一般公衆に対する広告宣伝活動を開始する前にライセンサーに提出して、その事前承認を受けなければならない。

prior consultation　事前協議, 事前相談
（=preconsultation）
◆It takes a year or more for the FTC to complete the prior consultation on a corporate merger plan before the legal screening starts. 法定審査の開始前に, 公正取引委員会が企業の合併計画について事前相談を受けてから終了するまでに, 1年以上かかる。

prior informed consent　十分な説明［情報提供］に基づく事前の同意・承諾, 文書による同意・承諾
◆Access to genetic resources requires prior informed consent of the country of origin. 生物遺伝資源を利用する場合は, 資源原産国の文書による事前の同意・承諾を得なければならない。

prior permission　事前許可
◆Music and images may not, in principle, be copied or used without the artists' prior permission. 音楽や映像は, 原則として著作者の事前許可なしに複製・利用することはできない。

prior to　〜に先立って, 〜より前に, 〜の前に, 〜を前に（=before; ⇒constitute）
◆Food imports from China declined sharply after the poisoned frozen gyoza incident, but now the figure has almost returned to the levels recorded prior to the incident. 冷凍ギョウザの中毒事件後, 中国からの食品の輸入量は大きく落ち込んだが, 今は事件前の水準にほぼ回復している。

priority　（名）優先, 優先事項, 優先権, 優先順位, 優先度, 先取権
cost priority　コスト優先, コスト重視
creditor by priority　優先債権者
establish a first-priority lien position　第一順位先取特権を設定する
export priority　輸出優先権, 輸出優先順位
first priority　最優先, 最優先事項, 最優先順位
give priority in negotiations for　〜の優先交渉権を与える
give priority to　〜に優先権を与える, 〜を優先する, 〜を第一に考える, 〜を優先的に扱う, 〜に軸足を置く
have priority over　〜より優先する, 〜に優先する
high priority　高い優先順位
highest priority　最優先順位, 最優先すべきこと, 最優先事項, 最優先
investment priority　投資の優先順位
low priority　低い優先順位, 低い優先度
on a priority basis　優先的に

payment priorities　支払いの優先順位, 元本返済の優先順位
place priority on　〜を優先する, 優先して〜する
place top priority on　〜を最優先する
priority creditor　優先債権者
priority measures　優先課題, 優先策
priority of claim on assets　資産に対する上位の請求権
priority of creditors　債権者の優先順位
priority of payment　支払いの優先順位
priority of repayment　弁済順位
priority project　優先プロジェクト
priority rate of duty　実行関税率
priority subscription period　優先割当て期間
put priority on efficiency　効率を重視する
put top priority on　〜を第一に考える
take priority of　〜を先取する, 〜より上位を占める
take priority over　〜より優先する, 〜より優先権がある, 〜の優先権を得る
top priority　最優先課題, 最優先事項, 最優先, トップ
◆The big U.S. semiconductor maker Qualcomm put Japanese firms on low priority when it fell behind schedule in parts shipments this summer. 米半導体大手のクアルコムは今夏, 部品の出荷が予定より遅れた際, 日本企業への出荷を後回しにした［日本企業への出荷の優先順位を低くした］。◆Toshiba will be given priority in negotiations for the right to acquire Westinghouse, British Nuclear Fuels PLC's U.S. nuclear power plant arm. 東芝に, ウェスチングハウス（英核燃料会社の米原発子会社）買収権獲得のための優先交渉権が与えられることになった。◆We are giving your order priority, but a slight delay in the shipment of yours will be unavoidable. 貴社の注文を優先的に扱っていますが, ご注文の船積みが少々遅れることは避けられません。

priority in negotiations　優先交渉権
◆Toshiba will be given priority in negotiations for the right to acquire Westinghouse, British Nuclear Fuels PLC's U.S. nuclear power plant arm. 東芝に, ウェスチングハウス（英核燃料会社の米原発子会社）買収権獲得のための優先交渉権が与えられることになった。

private placement of new shares　新株の私募発行, 第三者割当増資
◆Bic Camera will have the exclusive right to buy more than 50 percent of Kojima in Kojima's private placement of new shares in June 2012. コジマが2012年6月に実施する第三者割当増資で, ビックカメラは, コジマの株式の50%超を引き受ける独占権を持つことになっている。

private sector　民間部門, 民間セクター, 民間

企業, 民間

◆In countries that are based on a genuine market economy model, current account balances are just the results of imports and exports freely carried out by the private sector. 純粋な市場経済モデルに立つ国では、経常収支は、民間が行う自由な輸出・輸入活動の結果に過ぎない。

privilege （名）特権, 特典, 特別免除, 特別認可, 基本的権利, 基本的人権, 株取引の売付け・買付け選択権

any and all privileges or sovereign immunity 一切の特権または主権免責

◆ABC National Corporation hereby waives and agrees to waive in any proceedings for the enforcement of this agreement, any and all privileges or sovereign immunity, including the privilege of sovereign immunity from suit or immunity of the property from attachment or execution, to which it may be entitled under international or domestic laws, as a procedural defense or otherwise. ABC国営会社は、本契約を実施するための一切の手続きにおいて、手続き上の抗弁その他として当該国営企業が国際法または国内法により有する一切の特権または主権免除（国家主権に基づく裁判からの免除特権や財産の差し押さえまたは強制執行からの免除を含む）を本契約により放棄するとともに、その放棄に同意する。

probe （動）徹底的に調べる (inspect), 調査する, 探る, 探り出す, 探査する, 探索する, 検査する, 立ち入り検査する

probe for some way　何か方法を探す

probe into　〜を徹底的に調べる、〜を精査する、〜を検査する

probe the case to the bottom　事件を徹底的に調査する

◆The Fair Trade Commission probed about a dozen industrial gas providers over price cartel suspicions. 公正取引委員会は、価格カルテルの疑いで産業用ガス・メーカー十数社を立ち入り検査した。

probe （名）厳密な調査, 徹底的な調査, 本格調査, 精査, 探査, 探索, （疑惑の）解明, 宇宙探査機, 探測機, 探査用ロケット, 宇宙探査機による調査, （医療器具の）探り針, プローブ

antidumping probes　反ダンピング調査

conduct a probe　調査を行う

in-depth probe　徹底調査, 本格的な調査

launch a probe into　〜に対する調査を開始する

the SEC probe　米証券取引委員会 (SEC) の調査

◆In the United States, a provisional ruling on dumping is usually issued about six months after launching antidumping probes. 米国では、ダンピング（不当廉売）の仮決定をするのは通例、反ダンピング調査の開始から半年程度である。◆The probe of the National Highway Traffic Safety Administration will target the 2009 and 2010 Corolla models manufactured in the United States. 米高速道路交通安全局 (NHTSA) の本格調査の対象は、米国で生産されたカローラの2009年と2010年のモデルだ。◆The SEC probe was focused on several transactions that had led to higher revenues at AOL Time Warner Inc. 米証券取引委員会 (SEC) の調査は、AOLタイム・ワーナーの売上高水増し（疑惑）につながった一部の取引を中心に行われた。

procedural defense　手続き上の抗弁 (=procedural defence; ⇒privilege)

procedures of cargo insurance contract by internet　貨物保険手続きの電子化

proceeding （名）行為, 行動, 手続き, 手順, 処置, 処分, 訴訟行為

a legal proceeding　合法的なやり方, 法的手続き, 裁判手続き

any proceeding for insolvency or bankruptcy 支払い不能または破産手続き

◆The guarantor hereby waives, and agrees not to assert by way of motion as a defence or otherwise, in a suit, action or proceeding pursuant to this guarantee, any claim that this guarantee or the subject matter hereof may not be enforced in or by such courts. 保証人は、本保証書に従う訴訟、裁判または手続き［訴訟または訴訟手続き］で、抗弁として申し立てることによりまたは他の方法により、本保証書またはその主題を上記裁判所でまたはその裁判所が強制することはできないとの主張をここに放棄し、これを主張しないことに同意する。◆This agreement shall terminate immediately and without any prior written notice if Licensee or Company becomes insolvent or bankrupt or enters into a similar proceeding. 本契約は、ライセンシーまたは会社が支払い不能となるか、破産するか、同様の手続きに入る場合、書面による事前の通知なしで直ちに終了するものとする。

proceedings （名）議事録, 決議録, 会議録, 会報, 訴訟手続き, 訴訟, 弁論 （⇒forum, privilege）

◆Exhibit D sets forth a complete and accurate list of all claims, suits, actions, arbitrations, legal or other proceedings or governmental investigations to which the Company is a party or which is, to the knowledge of ABC, threatened against the Company. 付属書類Dには、本会社が当事者である、またはABCが知るかぎり本会社が当事者になる恐れのある［本会社に対して提起される恐れがある］すべての請求、訴訟、仲裁、法的手続きもしくはその他の手続き、または政府調査の完全かつ正確なリストが記載されている。

proceeds （名）代金, 手取り金, 売上, 売上高, 所得, 収益, 純利益

◆Proceeds shall have the meaning given to such term in the Uniform Commercial Code as in effect in the State of California from time to time. 「売上高」は、カリフォルニア州で随時実施されている米統一商事法典 (UCC) の規定で用いられて

いる意味を持つものとする。◆Title with respect to each shipment of the products shall pass from the seller to purchaser when the seller negotiates relative documents and receives proceeds from the negotiating bank for such shipment with effect retrospect to the time of such shipment. 本製品の各船積みに関する所有権は、売り主が関連書類を手形買取り銀行に提出して本製品の代金を当該銀行から受領した時点で、当該船積み時に遡及して売り主から買い主に移転するものとする。

process (名)過程, 製法, 方法, 訴訟, 訴訟手続き, 訴訟手続き上の令状, 訴状, 被告召喚令状, プロセス

due process 適正過程

final process 執行令状

judicial process 司法判断形成過程

mesne process 中間令状

original process 始審令状

◆Because of the domestic lengthy process of approving production and sales of medical devices, some domestic medical device makers have been applying for product approval for Europe and the United States first. 国内での医療機器の製造販売承認手続きの遅れから、国内医療機器メーカーの一部は、製品の承認申請を欧米で先に行っている。

process server 訴状を届けるサービス, 送達実施人

processes (名)製法
◆The licensee shall use and practice substantially similar equipment, materials, and processes as the licensor does in its plant. ライセンシーは、ライセンサーがその工場で使用し、実施しているのと実質的に同じ設備、原料と製法を使用し、実施するものとする。

processing materials 加工原料
◆Measures to tighten quality controls on Chinese food products, taken by many Japanese manufacturers in China, include more stringent tests on the amounts of agricultural chemicals used at Chinese farms and on the quality of processing materials used at Chinese factories. 中国の日系メーカーの多くが取っている中国産食品の品質管理強化策としては、中国農場での農薬使用量の検査や中国の工場で使用している加工原料の品質チェックの強化などが挙げられる。

processing trade 加工貿易, 委託加工貿易
◆In processing trade, imported raw materials are manufactured into goods that are then sold to other countries. 加工貿易では、輸入された原材料が製品に仕上げられた後、製品は海外に販売される。

procure (動)調達する, 購入する, 仕入れる, 取得する, 入手する, 獲得する, 引き起こす, 招来する
◆The purchaser may at its option procure replacements or substitutes for the products for the seller's account from other sources at such price and time as the purchaser may deem reasonable.

買い主は、その裁量により、買い主が合理的と見なす価格と時期に、他の供給元から売り主の勘定で本製品の取替え品または代替品を調達できるものとする。

procure shares 株式を購入する, 株式を取得する, 株式を引き受ける
◆U.S. equity fund KKR is likely to procure shares to be issued by Renesas as an allocation to a third party to become the biggest shareholder, with an equity holding of more than 50 percent. 米投資ファンドのコールバーグ・クラビス・ロバーツ (KKR) は、半導体大手ルネサスが第三者割当て増資で発行する株式を引き受け、ルネサス株の50%超を得て、筆頭株主になる[経営権を握る]見通しだ。

procurement (名)調達, 購入, 仕入れ, 機器調達, 取得, 入手, 獲得, プロキュアメント

competitive procurement 一般競争による調達

e-procurement 電子調達, eプロキュアメント

full-scale procurement 本格調達

fund procurement 資金調達

Internet procurement インターネット調達, ネット調達

local procurement of components [parts] 部品の現地調達

overseas procurement 海外調達 (=overseas sourcing)

parts procurement 部品の調達, 部品調達

procurement cost 調達価格

procurement demand 調達要求書

procurement management 調達管理

procurement of funds 資金調達, 資本調達 (=fund procurement)

procurement of materials 材料の調達

special procurements 特需

◆Major Japanese automakers will begin full-scale procurement of low-cost auto parts from South Korean suppliers. 日本の自動車大手が、韓国の部品メーカーから割安な自動車部品の本格調達に乗り出すことになった。◆The recent surges in the yen's strength have made it imperative for Japanese carmakers to substantially bring down their parts procurement costs by overseas sourcing. 最近の円高で、日本の自動車メーカー各社は、海外調達による部品調達コストの大幅引下げが緊急課題となっている。

procurement negotiation fair 調達商談会
◆About ten major Japanese automakers are scheduled to take part in an industrial parts and materials exhibition and procurement negotiation fair in Seoul. 韓国・ソウルで開かれる工業部品・素材展示調達商談会には、日本の自動車メーカー約10社が参加する予定だ。

produce (動)生産する, 製造する, 創造する, 提出する, 提示する

PROD 370

produce a product 製品を製造［生産］する，商品を生産する
◆The Japanese Agricultural Standards（JAS）Law requires the producers of perishable foods to ensure that labels mention place of origin. 日本農林規格（JAS）法は、生鮮食品の生産者に原産地表示を義務付けている。◆The new tariff on beef imports favors producers rather than consumers. 牛肉の輸入に対する新関税は、消費者ではなく生産者寄りの対応だ。◆The universal standard is determined by a majority vote among nations producing the products. ユニバーサル・スタンダードは、製品生産国間の多数投票によって決められる。

producing evidence 証拠提出
◆A free trade agreement is a treaty between two or more nations and territories seeking to reduce or abolish tariffs on industrial, agricultural and other products. 自由貿易協定（FTA）は、鉱工業品や農産品［農産物］の関税の引下げや撤廃を求める2か国以上の国や地域間の協定だ。

product （名）製品，商品，生産品，生産物，産物，成果，生産高，契約品，約定品
（⇒free trade agreement, production）
◆At the beginning of each calendar year, ABC shall make a report to XYZ on the sales of the Product during the previous year and general market conditions.　各暦年の初めに、ABCは、XYZに対して前年度の契約品の販売（実績）と市況全般について報告するものとする。◆The U.S. "Buy American" provision requires any public projects funded by stimulus money to use only U.S.-made products. 米国の「バイ・アメリカン」条項は、経済対策資金で賄われる公共工事に米国製製品の使用を義務付けている。◆The weaker yen helps exporters, but close attention must be paid to the fact that the excessive depreciation of the yen will further increase the prices of imports of LNG and other foreign products. 円安は輸出企業にはプラスだが、円安が行き過ぎると、天然液化ガス（LNG）など海外製品の輸入額が一段と増えることにも、警戒が必要である。◆We are almost certain that these products will meet your requirements as the products have been enjoying a good reputation in EU markets. 本製品はこれまでEU市場で好評を博しており、かならずや貴社のご要望に沿うものと確信しております。

product approval 製品の承認
◆Because of the domestic lengthy process of approving production and sales of medical devices, some domestic medical device makers have been applying for product approval in Europe and the United States first. 国内での医療機器の製造販売承認手続きの遅れから、国内医療機器メーカーの一部は、製品の承認申請を欧米で先に行っている。

product quality 製品の品質，品質
◆Other competitive factors in the market for the products are service, delivery, technological capability, and product quality and performance. 市場での製品の競争要因としては、サービスや納入、技術活用能力［技術力］、品質、性能なども挙げられる。

product specialization 製品特化
◆Due to the IT revolution and trade liberalization, product specialization now is determined by comparative advantages not in finished products but in work unique to each country or region in the context of global value chains. 情報通信技術（IT）革命と貿易自由化で、製品の特化は、「最終財」の比較優位ではなく、国際的な価値連鎖との関連で国・地域にそれぞれ特有の「仕事」の比較優位で決まるようになった。

production （名）生産，製造，製作，生産高，（書類の）提出，プロダクション

production, application, use or sale 生産、応用、使用または販売

production burden 証拠提出責任
◆Because of the domestic lengthy process of approving production and sales of medical devices, some domestic medical device makers have been applying for product approval in Europe and the United States first.　国内での医療機器の製造販売承認手続きの遅れから、国内医療機器メーカーの一部は、製品の承認申請を欧米で先に行っている。◆Japan's exports and production have been reduced because of the slowdown of foreign economies and the worsening of relations with China. 海外経済の減速と日中関係の悪化で、日本の輸出や生産は低迷している。◆Partly due to a slowdown in the Chinese economy in the wake of the European financial crisis, Japan's exports and production have been on the decline. 欧州の金融危機による中国の景気減速もあって、日本の輸出や生産活動は落ち込んでいる。◆To avoid the high costs of operating domestically, Japanese companies are moving their production overseas. And this leads to the rapid hollowing-out of the domestic manufacturing industry. 国内操業のコスト高を回避するため、日本企業が生産拠点を海外に移転しており、これが国内製造業の急速な空洞化を招いている。◆We fear that we may not accept your order as the production of these products has been suspended for some time. この製品の生産がしばらく中止となっておりますので、貴社の注文はお受け致しかねます。

production cost 生産コスト，生産費，製造コスト，製造原価，製品原価
◆Introducing renewable energy sources instead of nuclear power plants may lead to the hollowing-out of the domestic industrial sector in the face of increased production costs, and bankruptcies of small and midsized businesses. 原発の代わりに再生可能エネルギーを導入すると、生産コストの上昇による国内産業の空洞化や中小企業の倒産を招く可能性がある。

production in China 中国での生産
◆Many Japanese manufacturers have been prompted to review their production in China with labor costs surging in China and domestic

production recovering competitiveness thanks to the weaker yen. 中国で人件費が高騰しているのに加え、円安進行で国内生産の競争力が回復しているため、日本メーカーの多くは中国での生産（体制）を見直す動きが加速している。

production line　生産ライン
◆To avert China risks such as the stronger Chinese yuan, surging labor costs and anti-Japan riots, some firms have shifted production lines to other countries in Southeast Asia and other regions with cheaper labor. 中国人民元高や人件費高騰、反日暴動などの中国リスクを回避するため、一部の企業は、中国より低賃金の東南アジアなどの地域に生産ラインの移管［分散化］を進めている。

production of documents　文書の提出, 証拠書類の提出
◆The arbitrators shall have the authority to order such discovery and production of documents, including the depositions of party witnesses, and to make such orders for interim relief, including injunctive relief, as they may deem just and equitable. 仲裁人は、当事者の証人の宣誓証言［証言録取書］を含めて文書の開示と提出を命じる権限と、差止救済を含めて仲裁人が正義かつ衡平と見なす暫定的救済を命じる権限を持つものとする。

production operations　生産拠点
◆The firm plans to make up for some of the currency exchange loss by transferring some of its domestic production operations overseas. 同社は、一部の国内生産拠点を海外に移して、為替差損の一部を穴埋めする方針だ。

production plants overseas　海外の生産拠点
◆Japan's major automakers are capitalizing on improved quality at production plants overseas as part of their global strategies. 日本の大手自動車メーカーは、自動車各社の世界戦略の一環として、海外生産拠点での品質向上を活用している。

production site　生産拠点
◆As many domestic manufacturers have moved their production sites from Japan to Asian nations and elsewhere, the Japanese economy benefits less and less from the weak yen which lowers export costs. 国内製造業の多くが生産拠点を日本からアジアなどに移しているため、日本経済は、輸出コストが下がる円安メリットを享受しにくくなっている。

profitability in exports　輸出の採算, 輸出の採算性
◆Toyota revised upward its consolidated operating profit estimates for the business year ending March 31, 2013, largely due to improved profitability in its exports from a weakening of the yen in response to "Abenomics," the economic policy of the Abe administration. トヨタは2013年3月期決算［2013年3月31日終了事業年度］の連結営業利益予想［連結業績予想］を上方修正したが、これは主に安倍政権の経済政策「アベノミクス」を好感しての円安で、輸出の採算が向上しているた

めだ。

profitable investments　有利な運用先
◆These surplus funds are moving into crude oil and grain markets in search of profitable investments. これらの余剰資金が、有利な運用先を求めて原油や穀物市場に向かっている。

proforma［pro forma］　（形）仮の, 試算用の
a proforma invoice　仮送り状, 試算用の送り状, 見積り送り状
proforma account of sale　見積り売上計算書, 試算用売上勘定書
proforma account of sheet　見積り貸借対照表
proforma balance sheet　見積り貸借対照表
proforma bill　見積り荷為替手形
proforma financial statements　見積り財務諸表, 見積り財務書類
◆Please give us your best quotations in U.S. dollars for immediate shipment and proforma invoices. 直（じき）積みでドル建ての貴社の建て値と試算送り状を、お送りください。

program　（名）計画, 予定, 制度, 番組, コンピュータ・プログラム, プログラム　（動）プログラムを作成する
◆The original and copies of the licensor's Program, in whole or in part and however modified, which are made by the licensee, as between the licensor and the licensee shall be the property exclusively of the licensor. ライセンシーが作成するライセンサーのコンピュータ・プログラムのオリジナルとコピー（複製）は、その全部であれ一部であれ、またどんな変更が加えられたものでも、ライセンサーとライセンシーの間では排他的にライセンサーの財産とする。◆The program and related documentation are copyrighted. このプログラムと関連ドキュメンテーションには、版権がある。

progress status report　進捗状況報告書

prohibit　（動）禁止する, 〜が〜するのを妨げる
◆Diplomats are prohibited from engaging in commercial activities for the purpose of their personal profits under the Vienna Convention's Article 42. ウイーン条約42条で、外交官は個人の利得を目的とした商業活動を禁止されている。◆In principle, any foodstuff with radioactive cesium exceeding the provisional limits has been prohibited from being put on the market. 原則として、暫定規制値を超える放射性セシウムを含んだ食品は、流通を禁じられている。◆Recipient shall not transfer any confidential information received hereunder or any product made using such confidential information, to any country prohibited from obtaining such data or product by the U.S. Department of Commerce Export Administration Regulations without first obtaining a validated export license. 受領者は、本契約に従って受領した秘密情報またはこの秘密情報を

使用して製造した製品を、米国商務省の輸出管理規則により当該データまたは製品の提供が禁止されている国に対して、最初に輸出承認の許可を得ないで譲渡することはないものとする。

prohibited competing business 競合禁止事業

prohibition （名）禁止, 禁制, 禁止法, 禁止令, 酒類製造販売禁止

a prohibition on drugs 麻薬禁止, 麻薬禁止法

export prohibition 輸出禁止

monopoly prohibition law 独占禁止法

prohibition of competitive transaction 競業禁止

the Act Concerning Prohibition of Private Monopoly and Maintenance of Fair Trade 独占禁止法

the prohibition of party-in-interest transactions 利害関係者取引の禁止

prohibitive （形）禁止する, 禁制の, （行為を）阻止するための, 差し止める, 手が出ないほど高い, 法外な

a prohibitive duty ［tariff］ 禁止関税, 高率輸入関税

a prohibitive right 禁止権

a prohibitive tax 禁止的重税, 高率輸入税

at a prohibitive price （手が出ないほどの）高値で, 法外な値段で

◆The Trademark Law was enacted to protect a trademark by giving a monopoly such as an exclusive right and a prohibitive right to an owner of a trademark right. 商標法は, 商標権者に専用権や禁止権などの独占権を与えて商標を保護するために制定された。

project （名）計画, 企画, もくろみ, 企て, 構想, 案, 考案, 工夫, 対策, 案件, 事業, 事業計画, 開発事業, 公共事業計画, 長期目標, 研究課題, 自主研究, プロジェクト

◆Sakharin-1 project is an international program for energy resource development off Russia's Sakharin Island. 「サハリン1」プロジェクトは, ロシア・サハリン島沖で行われているエネルギー資源開発の国際プログラムだ。◆The METI has decided to expand the scope of government-backed trade insurance for overseas social infrastructure projects. 経済産業省は, 海外の社会基盤（インフラ）事業に対する政府保証付き貿易保険の対象を拡大することを決めた。

prolonged failure or shortage of electric power 長期間にわたる電力不足

promise （名）約束, 約束ごと, 契約, 契約事項

◆NOW THEREFORE, in consideration of the promises and the mutual covenants, hereinafter contained, the parties hereto agree as follows: そこで, 本契約に定める［本契約書に記載する］約束ごとと相互の誓約を約因として, 本契約当事者は次のとおり合意する。

promising （形）前途有望な, 有望な, 有力な, 前途を嘱望（しょくぼう）された, 将来見込みある, 将来の見込める, 将来のある, 明るい, 期待の持てる, 幸先のよい, 好転しそうな

promising business area 期待できる事業分野

promising country for investment 有望な投資先

promising market 期待できる市場, 有望市場, 成長市場

promissory （形）約束の, 確約の, 確約的, 支払いを約束する, 見込みのある

inland promissory note 国内約束手形

issue promissory notes worth 〜相当の約束手形を発行する

pay with a promissory note 約束手形で支払う

promissory estoppel 約束的禁反言

promissory letter 誓約書

promissory note 約束手形, 手形

promissory note payable 金融手形債務

promissory warranty 約束的担保

short-term promissory note 短期約束手形

promote （動）促進する, 推進する, 振興する, 増進する, 助長する, 育成する, 発展させる, 奨励する, （製品などを）売り込む［宣伝する］, 販売を促進する, 主催する, （事業などを）発起する, 〜の発起人になる, 始める（launch）, 昇進させる, 昇格させる, 進級させる, 起用する, 登用する, （議案, 法案の）通過に努める, 支持する

promote a new company 新会社の発起人となる, 新会社を設立する

promote a new product 新製品の販売を促進する, 新製品を売り込む

promote competition 競争を促進する, 競争を促す

promote disorder 混乱を助長する

promote economic growth 経済成長を促進する

promote employment 雇用を促進する

promote-from-within policy 社内人材登用の方針

promote growth and jobs 成長と雇用を促進する

promote product segmentation 商品［製品］の差別化を進める

promote productivity 生産性を向上させる, 生産性の向上を図る

◆In terms of trade volume, South Korea is currently among the top 10 countries partly due to its efforts to promote free trade agreements with the United States, the European Union and others. 貿易額で, 韓国は現在, 米国や欧州連合（EU）などとの自由貿易協定（FTA）推進策を軸に, 世界ト

ップ10入りを果たしている。◆The cornerstone of the Cool Japan initiative aimed at promoting the exports of Japanese pop culture is the content industry which produces anime, video games and movies. 日本独自の文化産業の輸出促進を目指すクール・ジャパン構想の核は、アニメやビデオ・ゲーム、映画などの製作にかかわるコンテンツ産業だ。

promote free trade among member countries 加盟国間の自由貿易化を進める ◆The Trans-Pacific Partnership framework to promote free trade among member countries is expected to invigorate the movement of human resources. 加盟国間の自由貿易化を進めるための環太平洋経済連携協定 (TPP) で、人材の移動も盛んになることが予想される。

promote the sales of the products 本製品の販売を促進する ◆ABC accepts such appointment and undertakes to use its best efforts, at its own expenses, to promote the sales of the products throughout the territory at all times during the term of this agreement. ABCは当該指定を受諾し、本契約期間中つねに、その自己負担で、契約地域全域で本製品の販売を促進するため最善の努力をすることを約束する。

promotion (名)昇進, 昇級, 昇格, 昇任, 促進, 推進, 増進, 助長, 振興, 奨励, 販売促進, 販売促進活動, 創設, 創立, 設立, 発起, プロモーション

advertising and promotion 広告・宣伝

business promotion 起業, 興業

company promotion 会社設立, 会社創業

compete on the front line of promotion and sales 販促や販売の最前線で競い合う

employment promotion 雇用促進

export promotion 輸出振興, 輸出促進

export promotion scheme 輸出振興策

import promotion policy 輸入促進政策

productivity promotion 生産性向上

promotion by age 年功序列

promotion expense 販売促進費 (sales promotion cost), 創業費 (organization cost) 創立費, 設立費用

promotion shares 発起人株

sales promotion 販売促進, 販促, 販促活動, セールス・プロモーション

sales promotion activity 販売促進活動

the promotion of the disposal of nonperforming loans 不良債権処理の促進

trade promotion 貿易振興, 貿易促進, 貿易推進

promotion of free trade 自由貿易推進 ◆The APEC's special statement came out in favor of the promotion of free trade. アジア太平洋

経済協力会議 (APEC) の特別声明は、自由貿易推進を打ち出した。

promotional materials 販売促進用資料, 販促用資料, 宣伝用資料 ◆Samples of all promotional materials or plans of advertisements referring to the Trademarks for intended use by the licensee shall be submitted by the licensee to the licensor for its prior approval before the commencement of the licensee's advertising campaigns to the public. ライセンシーが使用する予定の本商標にかかわるすべての販売用資料の見本または広告宣伝計画書は、ライセンシーが一般公衆に対する広告宣伝活動を開始する前にライセンサーに提出して、その事前承認を受けなければならない。

promotional release 宣伝発表

prompt (形)即時の, 即座の, 迅速な, 素早い, 早期の, 機敏な, 即座払いの, 即時渡しの, 直 (じき) 渡しの

for prompt cash 即金で

prompt answer [reply] 速答

prompt attention to 〜に対する迅速な手配

prompt cash 即金払い, 即時払い (4,5日以内に支払う決済条件)

prompt cash discount 直払い割引

prompt day 競売の受渡し日, 受渡し最終日, 支払い期日

prompt delivery 直渡し

prompt exchange 直物為替

prompt note 買上票, 代金請求書, 支払い期日通知書, 即時払い手形

prompt payment 即時払い

prompt response 素早い対応, 素早い回答

prompt sale 延べ取引

prompt shipment 直 (じき) 積み, 早積み, 即時船積み, 即時船積み条件, 即時出荷 (=as soon as possible shipment, immediate shipment)

◆We are prepared to place a prompt trial order if you can guarantee supply of products strictly in accordance with our specifications. 貴社が当社の仕様書どおりの商品の供給 [納入] を保証するなら、早速、試験注文を出します。◆Your prompt reply would be highly appreciated. 早急にご返事いただければ、有り難い。

promptly (副)即座に, 即時に, 迅速に, 敏速に, 速やかに

promptly upon the receipt of 〜を受領したら即座に、〜を受領したら速やかに ◆Promptly upon the receipt of a shipment of Products, Distributor shall examine the Products to determine whether any item or items to be included in the shipment are missing, defective, or damaged. 本製品の荷受けをしたら速やかに、販売店は、本製品を検査して積み荷中の目的物が不

足（紛失）しているかどうか、瑕疵（かし）があるかどうか、または損傷しているかどうかを判断しなければならない。

proof （名）証明, 立証, 証拠
◆Provided that the purchaser notifies the seller of such defect, within 14 days from the date the purchaser finds such defects, in writing, accompanying by the satisfactory proof. ただし、買い主が当該瑕疵（かし）に気づいた日から14日以内に、買い主は満足できる証拠を添えて売り主に当該瑕疵の通知をするものとする。

proof of the date of shipment 船積み日の証拠
◆Date of marine bill of lading shall be proof of the date of shipment in the absence of the evidence to the contrary. 海上船荷証券の日付は、反対の証拠がない場合、船積み日の証拠となる。

properly （副）適正に, 適切に, 正確に, 正しく, 本式に, 正当に
◆The warranty set forth above in this Article shall apply to any part of the products which, if properly installed, used and maintained by the purchaser, proves to be defective in material or workmanship within nine months from the date of the bill of lading. 本条の上記保証は、買い主が適正に設置、使用し、維持している本製品のいずれかの部分が船荷証券日から9ヶ月以内に原料または仕上がりの面で瑕疵（かし）のあることが判明した場合に、当該部分に適用される。

properties and assets 資産
◆The Company is entitled to own, lease or operate the properties and assets it now owns, leases or operates. 契約対象会社は、現在所有、リース、利用している資産を所有、リースまたは利用することができる。

property （名）財産, 有体財産, 資産, 固定資産, 有形固定資産, 不動産, 土地, 建物, 所有, 所有権, 所有地, 所有物, 財産権, 特性, 属性, 物件
（「有体財産」には、営業用・製造業用の固定設備としての土地（land）、建物（buildings）、機械装置（machinery）および什器備品（furniture and fixtures）と、鉱山（mine）、山林（timber tract）、油井（oil well）などの天然資源が含まれる）
◆The nonlife insurance industry wants all kinds of buildings and other properties not insured for terrorist attacks. 損害保険業界は、すべての物件をテロ免責にしたいと考えている。◆The original and copies of the licensor's Program, in whole or in part and however modified, which are made by the licensee, as between the licensor and the licensee shall be the property exclusively of the licensor. ライセンシーが作成するライセンサーのコンピュータ・プログラムのオリジナルとコピー（複製）が、その全部であれ一部であれ、またどんな変更が加えられたとしても、ライセンサーとライセンシーの間では排他的にライセンサーの財産とする。

property right 所有権, 財産権, 財産所有権,

資産権利
◆The expanded application of the Copyright Law to the Net means the curtailment of the property right of copyright holders such as music producers, composers and singers. 著作権法のネットへの拡大適用は、音楽会社や作曲者、歌手など著作権者の所有権［知的所有権］の縮小を意味する。

proposal letter 提案書

propose （動）提案する, 提唱する, 企画する, 打ち出す, 申し出る, 提出する, 提示する, 指名する, 推薦（すいせん）する
◆Khazanah National which owns 69 percent of Malaysia Airlines has proposed to buy out minority shareholders to the carrier's board of directors. マレーシア航空株の69％を保有するカザナ・ナショナル社（政府系投資会社）は、少数株主の株を買い取ることを、同航空の取締役会に提案した。◆The SEC proposed a plan to allow public companies to using international accounting standards for reporting financial results. 米証券取引委員会（SEC）は、株式公開企業［上場企業］に対して（2014年をめどに）決算報告に国際会計基準の導入［採用］を認める計画を提案した。

proposition （名）提案, 提議, 申し出, 主張, 陳述, 説, 命題, 定理, （提案された）計画, 企画, 事柄, 問題, 仕事, 事業, 取引条件の提示, 提供品, 商品, 住民提案（米州の住民投票にかけるために州民から一定の署名を集めた住民投票の提案）, 建議案

proprietary （形）所有者の, 所有権者の, 独占の, 専有の, 専売の, 特許の, 財産的価値のある　（名）所有, 所有者, 所有権, 所有権者, 所有物, 不動産, 特許, 医薬品

proprietary brand 自社ブランド

proprietary material 財産の権利のある資産

proprietary trading 自己取引, 自己売買, 自己勘定取引, ディーリング業務

proprietary information 有価値情報, 専有情報, 財産たる情報, 財産価値のある情報
◆Provided that neither party shall assert such information as set forth in 1）through 6）above as its proprietary information. ただし、いずれの当事者も、上記1）号から6）号に定める情報を自己の専有情報と主張しないものとする。

proprietary right 所有権, 財産権, 知的所有権, 知的財産権, 財産価値のある権利
（⇒have manufactured）
◆Proprietary Rights shall include such patent, design and trademark, and copyrights and trade secrets as may be obtained or acquired by Licensor during the term of this agreement. 所有権（知的財産権）は、本契約期間中にライセンサーが取得または獲得する特許、意匠、商標と著作権およびトレード・シークレットを含むものとする。

prospect （名）眺め, 見込み, 見込み客, 予測, 見通し, 期待
be in prospect 〜が予想されている

call on three prospects 見込み客3人を訪問する

have a bright prospect in your market 貴市場で大いに見込みがある

in prospect of large profits 大きな利益を見込んで［予想して］

there is no prospect of ～の見込みはまったくない

◆This article has a bright prospect in your market. 本商品は、貴市場で大いに見込みがある。

prospective (形)未来の、将来の、今後の、予想される、予期される、期待される、見込みのある、～になる予定の

negotiate with several buyers 見込みがありそうな買い主数人と商談する

prospective buyer 見込みがありそうな買い主, 見込み客

prospective customer 見込み客（=prospective buyer）

prospective licensee 予定されるライセンシー, 顧客としてのライセンシー

prospective profits 予想収益, 収益見通し

prospective retirees 退職予定者, 予想される退職者

prospective site 候補地

prospective supplier 仕入先候補

prospective third party purchaser 予定される第三者購入者

prospective partner 提携する予定の会社, 提携企業の候補

◆The two prospective partners have extensive expertise in mergers and acquisitions, as well as the securitization of bad loans. 提携する予定の両社は、企業の合併・買収（M&A）や不良債権の証券化などに豊富なノウハウを持っている。

prospective third party purchaser 予定される第三者購入者

◆A party hereto proposing to effect a sale of any shares of the new company（the Offerer）shall give a written notice to the other parties hereto, or their assignee, who are then shareholders of the new company（the Offerees）, of the Offerer's intention, the identity of the prospective third party purchaser, and the terms and conditions of the proposed sale. 新会社の株式の売却を申し出る本契約当事者（「申込み者」）は、他の当事者またはその時点で新会社の株主である譲受人（「被申込み者」）に対して、申込み者の売却意思、予定される第三者購入者の住所・氏名と申し出をした売却の条件を、書面で通知するものとする。

protect (動)保護する、守る、防ぐ、保全する、保証する、補償する、確保する、（手形の）支払い資金を準備する、手形の支払いをする、手形を引き受ける（⇒emergency import restrictions）

be protected from ～から保護される、～から守られる、～を免（まぬが）れる

protect a bill［draft］ 手形を引き受ける, 手形の支払いをする, 手形が不払いにならないように保護する

protect a signature 署名人を保全する

protect asset returns 資産の利回りを確保する

protect investors from loses 投資家を損失から保護する

protected trade 保護貿易

◆Financial authorities should stiffen the penalties for illegal transactions to protect the financial system from rumors and speculative investment. 金融当局は違法取引（違法行為）に対する罰則を強化して、金融システムを風評や投機［投機的投資］から守らなければならない。◆Japan maintains an import quota system for nori to help protect domestic producers. 国内生産者の保護を支援するため、日本は依然、食用ノリの輸入割当制度を堅持している。◆Please let the drawees protect your draft as it was dishonored. 貴社の手形が不渡りとなったので、名宛て人に直ちに支払うようにしていただきたい。◆The Trademark Law was enacted to protect a trademark by giving a monopoly such as an exclusive right and a prohibitive right to an owner of a trademark right. 商標法は、商標権者に専用権や禁止権などの独占権を与えて商標を保護するために制定された。◆We hope you will kindly protect the draft on presentation. 手形提示の節は、何とぞお引受け下さい。

protectable inventions 保護可能な発明

protection (名)保護, 保全, 保証, 保障, 補償, 対策, 手形の支払い［引受け］

apply for protection from creditors 会社更生手続きを申請する, 資産保全を申請する

commend our signature to your（kind）protection （手形振出人が名宛て人に対して言う）何とぞこの手形をお引き受けください, この手形の支払いをよろしくお願いします（=recommend our signature to your protection）

Consumer Credit Protection Act 消費者信用保護法

data protection データ保護（=data protect）

debtholder［debt holder］protection 債権保有者保護

environmental protection 環境保護, 環境保全

import protection 輸入保護, 輸入制限

insurance protection 保険保障

intellectual property protection 知的所有権の保護

protection of password パスワード保護

protection of personal information 個人情報保護

provide against liquidity protection 流動性リ

スクをカバーする

provide protection against the risk of default
債務不履行リスクをカバーする［保証する］

secret protection　機密保持

Securities Investor Protection Act of 1970
1970年証券投資家保護法

tariff protection　関税による保護, 関税保護

trade protection　貿易保護

◆Domestic industries harmed by dumping require urgent protection. ダンピングによる損害を受けている国内産業は, 緊急保護を必要としている。◆To cover this shipment, we have drawn upon you at 60 d/s, in the amount $50,000, in favor of ABC Bank, and recommend our signature to your protection. この船積みに対して, 一覧後60日払い, ABC銀行を受取人とする額面5万ドルの手形を貴社宛てに振り出しましたので, 何とぞこの手形をお引受けください。◆We have valued upon you today for the amount specified above, at sight, and ask you to accord our draft your due protection. 当社は本日, 貴社宛てに上記金額に対する一覧払い手形を振り出しましたので, この手形のお引受けをお願い致します。

protection from creditors　資産保全, 会社更生手続き
◆Soshisha Publishing Co. filed an application with the Tokyo District Court for protection from creditors under the Civil Rehabilitation Law. 草思社は, 民事再生法に基づく資産保全［民事再生法の適用］を東京地裁に申請した。◆The firm filed for protection from its creditors in a Delaware court under Chapter 11 of the federal bankruptcy code. 同社は, 米連邦破産法の第11章に基づき, デラウェア州連邦地裁に資産保全を申請した。

protection of intellectual property　知的財産の保護
◆Washington sees the protection of intellectual property as one of its key policies in boosting the international competitiveness of its industry. 米国政府は, 知的財産の保護を, 米国産業の国際競争力強化の重要な政策の一つと見ている。

protection of the right　権利の保護
◆ABC agrees to assist the licensor in the procurement of any protection of the licensor's right pertaining to the Trademarks, at the licensor's request and expenses. ABCは, ライセンサーの要請と費用で, 本商標に関するライセンサーの権利の保護を取得するにあたり, ライセンサーを支援することに同意する。

protectionism　（名）保護主義, 保護貿易主義
◆In preventing the rise of protectionism and the worsening of the world economy, settling the Doha Round of free trade talks would be effective. 保護貿易主義の台頭を押さえ, 世界経済の悪化［不況深刻化］を防ぐには, 世界貿易機関（WTO）の新多角的貿易交渉（ドーハ・ラウンド）の決着が有効だ。◆The most advanced market economies of Japan and the Unites States, if bound together,

would put a powerful brake on protectionism. もっとも高度に進化した市場経済の日本と米国が手を結べば, 保護貿易主義化に強力な歯止めをかけることになろう。◆There has been a rising tide of protectionism among U.S. businesses and labor unions that want Washington to restrict imports that compete with domestic products. 米国の業界や労組の間には, 国産品と競合する輸入品の規制を政府に要請する保護主義的な動きが高まっている。

protectionist　（名）保護貿易論者, 保護貿易主義者, 保護主義者, 野生動物保護論者, プロテクショニスト

protectionist action　保護主義的行動

protectionist economic regionalism　保護主義者の経済的地域主義, 保護主義的な経済圏

protectionist forces　保護主義勢力

protectionist policy　保護主義的な政策, 保護主義政策, 保護政策, 保護貿易政策, 貿易保護政策　（⇒import of agricultural products）

protectionist regionalism　保護主義的な地域主義

protectionist trade barriers　保護主義的な貿易障壁, 保護貿易障壁

protectionist trade policy　保護貿易政策

restrictive protectionist tariffs　制限的な保護貿易主義的関税
◆Politicians ignorant of basic economics tend in every country to be protectionist by nature. 経済の基礎知識にうとい政治家は, どこの国でもおのずと保護主義者になる傾向がある。（ポール・A・サミュエルソン）

protectionist measures　保護主義的な措置
◆In addition to the United States, China and Russia also have adopted protectionist measures. 米国のほかに, 中国とロシアもすでに保護主義的な措置を取っている。

protectionist moves　保護主義的な動き, 保護政策　（⇒damage）
◆During the Great Depression of the 1930s, protectionist moves aggravated the economic malaise. 1930年代の世界恐慌では, 保護政策によって景気沈滞は深刻化した。

protectionist sentiment　保護主義, 保護主義の高まり
◆Increasing inflationary pressures stemming from high oil prices are pointed out as a risk factor that could hamper stable growth, in addition to protectionist sentiment and growing global imbalances. 安定成長を阻害する恐れがあるリスク要因として, 保護主義の高まりや世界的な不均衡の拡大のほかに, 原油高によるインフレ圧力の上昇が指摘されている。

protective　（形）保護する, 保護用の, 保護を与える, 保護貿易の, 保護主義の, 保護貿易主義に基づく

protective covenant　証券所有者保護条項, 所

有者保護条項

protective device　保護措置

protective foods　栄養食品

protective legislation　貿易保護法

protective policy　保護政策

protective substances　保護物質

protective system　保護貿易制度

protective tariff［duties］　保護関税

protective trade　保護貿易

protective trust　保護信託

protective measures　保護策, 保護対策, 保護政策, 保護措置, 防衛策, 対応策, 防御策
◆The European Union's head office formally adopted tariffs of up to 26 percent on steel to prevent a feared flood of cheap imports from countries hit by U.S. protective measures. EU（欧州連合）の欧州委員会は, 米国の保護措置で打撃を受けた国から安い輸入鉄鋼製品が流入する恐れがあるのを防ぐため, 鉄鋼製品に対して最高26%の関税をかけることを正式採択した。

protocol　(名)契約・条約などの原案・原本, 議定書, 条約議定書, 協定・条約の付随書, 国家間の補足協定, 国家間の協定・協約, 議事録, 外交上の儀礼書, 外交文書, 外交慣習, 通信規約, プロトコル
◆No protocol has yet been signed between KEDO and North Korea concerning North Korea's obligation to pay compensation for losses that may be incurred due to accidents during the project. KEDO（朝鮮半島エネルギー開発機構）と北朝鮮は, 工事中の事故により生じる損害賠償金の北朝鮮の支払い義務に関する議定書にまだ署名していない。

prove to be　～であることが判明する
◆The warranty set forth above in this Article shall apply to any part of the products which, if properly installed, used and maintained by the purchaser, proves to be defective in material or workmanship within nine months from the date of the bill of lading. 本条の上記保証は, 買い主が適正に設置, 使用し, 維持している本製品のいずれかの部分が船荷証券日から9カ月以内に原料または仕上がりの面で瑕疵（かし）のあることが判明した場合に, 当該部分に適用される。

provide　(動)提供する, 供給する, 与える, 付与する, 支給する, 拠出する, 販売する, 創出する, 調達する, 発生する, 設定する, 定める, 規定する, 算定する, 計上する, 発表する

provide A with　Aに～を提供する

provide goods or services　モノやサービスを販売する, モノやサービスを提供する

provide liquidity　流動性を提供する, 流動性を供給する

provide the required capital　必要資本を調達する
◆Sharp Corp. aims to get contracts to provide

large number of IGZO liquid-crystal panels for such products as Apple Inc.'s iPhone and ultra-thin PCs developed under the initiative of Intel Corp. シャープは, 米アップル社のスマートフォン（高機能携帯電話）「アイフォン（iPhone）」や, 米半導体大手インテルの主導で開発される超薄型パソコンなどの製品への液晶パネル「イグゾー」の大量供給契約の獲得を目指している。

provide for　規定する, 定める, 記載する, 許す
◆The parties hereto believe it to be their best interests and the best interests of the New Company as defined in Article 1, that they provide for certain rights, duties, and restrictions as among themselves and others who may become shareholders of the New Company, all as provided in this agreement. 本契約当事者は, すべて本契約に規定するとおり, 両当事者と第1条に規定する新会社の株主になる他の者との間で一定の権利, 義務と制約について定めることが, 両当事者にとって最上の利益となり, 新会社にとっても最上の利益となる, と考えている。

provide written notice to　～に書面で通知する
◆In the event of such a default of this agreement Supplier may terminate this agreement immediately by providing written notice to Distributor. このような本契約違反が発生した場合には, 供給者は, 販売店に書面で通知することにより本契約を直ちに解除することができる。

provided (that)　ただし～, ～の条件で, もし～ならば, ～する場合には　(=if, providing)

provided that:　ただし,　(=provided that, providing that)

provided that the same shall not apply to　ただし～についてはこの限りではない
◆By the revised Labor Contract Law, researchers are now entitled to maintain job contracts until the mandatory retirement age, provided their length of service has exceeded five years. 労働契約法の改正により, 研究者は現在, 勤続期間が5年を過ぎた場合には, 定年まで雇用契約を継続できるようになった。◆Provided Licensor delivers the software without any bug, by no later than the delivery dates, Licensee shall pay Licensor a minimum guarantee of royalties of one million U.S. dollars ($1,000,000). ライセンサーがバグのないソフトウエアを引渡し日以前に引き渡した場合に, ライセンシーは, ロイヤルティの最低保証料としてライセンサーに100万米ドルを支払うものとする。

provision　(名)提供, 供給, 供与, 支給, 用意, 準備, 備え, 蓄え, 貯蔵品, 準備金, 引当金, 引当金繰入額・充当額, 計上, 設備, 施設, 条項, 規定　(⇒concerned provisions of Contract)

provisions of this Article　本状の規定

provisions of this guarantee　本保証書の条項, 本保証状の条項

provisions or terms of this agreement　本契約の規定または条件

provisions, rights, or elections　条項、権利、または選択権

◆At TEPCO's shareholders meeting, the Tokyo metropolitan government as a major shareholder in the utility, proposed to include in the articles of incorporation a provision stipulating that putting customer service first is the company's mission. 東電の株主総会で、同社の大株主としての東京都が、「顧客サービス第一を会社の使命とする」との規定を定款に盛り込むよう提案した。

◆The U.S. "Buy American" provision requires any public projects funded by stimulus money to use only U.S.-made products. 米国のバイ・アメリカン条項は、経済対策資金で賄われる公共工事に米国製製品の使用を義務付けている。

provision of information　情報の提供, 情報提供

◆A major bone of contention in the trial of the lung cancer drug Iressa case was whether the importer and seller's provision of information on Iressa's side effects to medical institutions was sufficient. 肺がん治療薬「イレッサ」訴訟の裁判の大きな争点は、輸入販売元による医療機関へのイレッサの副作用に関する情報の提供が十分だったか、という点だ。

provisional　(形)臨時の, 一時的な, 仮の, 暫定的な, 予備の

apply for a provisional injunction　仮処分を申請する

provisional agreement　仮契約, 仮条約, 暫定協定

provisional attachment　仮差し押さえ

provisional disposition　仮処分

provisional fishery accord　暫定漁業協定

provisional insurance　予定保険

provisional license　仮免許

provisional rating　予備格付け

provisional registration　仮登録, 仮登記

provisional treaty　仮条約

provisional limit　暫定規制値（=provisional ceiling）

◆In principle, any foodstuff with radioactive cesium exceeding the provisional limits has been prohibited from being put on the market. 原則として、暫定規制値を超える放射性セシウムを含んだ食品は、流通を禁じられている。

provisional ruling　仮決定

◆In the United States, a provisional ruling on dumping is usually issued about six months after launching antidumping probes. 米国では、ダンピング（不当廉売）の仮決定をするのは通例、反ダンピング調査の開始から半年程度である。

provisions of this agreement　本契約の規定

◆The new company shall be managed under the provisions of this agreement, the articles of incorporation and the applicable laws and regulations of Japan. 新会社は、本契約の規定、定款と日本の適用法令に従って運営する。◆Whenever there is any conflict between any provisions of this agreement and any statute or law, contrary to which the parties have no legal right to contract, the latter shall prevail. 本契約の規定と、当事者がそれに反して契約する法的権利のない制定法または法律との間に矛盾がある場合には、いつも後者が優先するものとする。

proxy　(名)代理人, 代行者, 代理行為, 代理権, 委任状, 議決権行使委任状

in person or by proxy　本人自らまたは代理人を立てて, 本人または代理人が

proxy fight　委任状争奪戦, 委任状合戦, プロキシー・ファイト　(=proxy contest)

proxy solicitation　委任状勧誘

proxy statement　委任状, 委任状説明書, 代理勧誘状, 代理権勧誘状, 議決権代理行使勧誘状, プロクシー・ステートメント

◆Each party hereto shall have one vote for each share of which it is the holder and may be present at any meeting of shareholders either in person or by proxy. 本契約の各当事者は、自ら所有する1株につき1票の議決権を持ち、本人またはその代理人が株主総会に出席することができる。

PRP　潜在責任当事者（potentially responsible partyの略）

public announcement　公表, 発表

public company　株式公開企業, 上場企業

◆The SEC proposed a plan to allow public companies to using international accounting standards for reporting financial results. 米証券取引委員会（SEC）は、株式公開企業［上場企業］に対して（2014年をめどに）決算報告に国際会計基準の導入［採用］を認める計画を提案した。

public domain　公知, 公有, 公有地, 公有の著作物, 公的資産, 社会の共有財産, 公共領域, 権利の消滅状態

become part of the public domain　公知となる

enter the public domain　公知になる

◆The licensee's obligation under this Article with respect to the confidential information shall not apply to information which is part of the public domain at the time of disclosure by the licensor, or thereafter becomes part of the public domain without fault on the part of the licensee. 本条に基づく秘密情報に関するライセンシーの義務は、ライセンサーによる開示の時点で公知であるか、その後ライセンシー側の過失なしに公知となる情報には適用されないものとする。

public hearing　公聴会, 公判

◆At a public hearing at the U.S. Senate, many members of the chamber bitterly accused Takata Corp., the world's second-largest air bag supplier, and Honda of having possibly covered up the faults in the air bags manufactured by Takata. 米上院の公聴会で、上院議員の多くが、タカタ製エアバッグの欠陥を隠ぺいしているのではないかと、タカタ（世界第2位のエアバッグ・メーカー）とホンダを厳しく批判した。

publicly available 公用の, 公知の
◆During the life of this agreement and thereafter Distributor shall not divulge any confidential information which it may acquire in connection with Products, this agreement or performance thereunder, except insofar as such information is or becomes generally known or publicly available at the time of disclosure under this agreement or subsequent thereto. 本契約期間中とその後も、代理店は、本契約に基づく開示時点とその後に公知または公用となる場合を除いて、本製品（契約品）、本契約または本契約に基づく履行に関連して取得することができる一切の秘密情報を漏洩しないものとする。

publicly known 公知の （=generally known）
◆The foregoing restrictions will not apply to information that has become publicly known through no wrongful act of Distributor. 前記の制限は、販売店の不法行為によらないで公知になった情報には適用されない。

punctual （形）時間を厳守する, 時間に正確な, 正確な, 厳密な, 遅滞のない
punctual performance 期限どおりの履行, 正確な時間どおりの履行
◆We need to have the goods by the end of October at the latest, so punctual shipment is essential. 同品は遅くとも10月末には入手しなければならないので、積み期に遅れないことが肝要です。

punitive （形）刑罰の, 懲罰的な, 制裁の, 報復の (retaliatory), 報復的な, 因果応報の (retributive), 極めて厳しい, 過酷な
punitive damage award 懲罰的損害賠償金
punitive duties 報復関税
punitive regulation 懲罰的規制
take punitive measures [action, steps] against ～に対して制裁措置を取る

punitive action 制裁措置, 対抗措置, 処罰行為
◆Major beef exporters such as the United States have already threatened to impose some punitive action against Japan if it introduces an emergency tariff on imported beef. 日本が輸入牛肉に対して緊急関税を導入［発動］した場合、米国など牛肉の主な対日輸出国は、すでに日本に対して制裁措置を取る動きを示している。

punitive damages 懲罰的損害賠償, 懲罰的損害賠償金［賠償額］, 懲罰的賠償, 制裁的慰謝料
authority to award punitive damages 懲罰的損害賠償を命じる権限

punitive damage remedy 懲罰的損害賠償による救済
◆Punitive damages are aimed at preventing a recurrence of similar crimes and accidents by claiming an amount larger than the actual damages for defendants. 制裁的慰謝料の目的は、加害者［被告］に対して実際の損害以上の損害賠償額を請求することにより、同種の犯罪や事故の再発防止を図ることにある。

punitive surcharge 課徴金
◆Punitive surcharges to be imposed on the companies for rigging bids are expected to exceed ¥5 billion each. 入札談合でこれらの企業に課される課徴金は、1社当たり50億円を超えるものとみられる。

punitive tariff 制裁関税, 報復関税
remove a punitive tariff 報復関税を撤廃する
scrap punitive tariffs 報復関税を廃止する
◆Japan urged Beijing to scrap punitive tariffs slapped on imports from cars to mobile phones. 日本は、中国政府に対して、自動車から携帯電話にいたる輸入品に課した報復関税の廃止を求めた。

purchase （動）購入する, 仕入れる, 買い取る, 買い付ける
◆In margin trading, stocks can be purchased on credit. 信用取引では、掛けで［購入代金を借りて］株を買うことができる。 ◆On the closing date Seller shall sell, and Purchaser shall purchase, the Shares in accordance with the terms and conditions of this agreement. クロージング日に、本契約の条件に従って売り主は本株式を売却し、買い主は本株式を購入する。

purchase （名）買取り, 買付け, 買入れ, 購入, 購入品, 購買, 調達, 調達先, 引受け, 仕入れ, 買収, 取得, 獲得, パーチェス
amount of minimum purchase 最低購入量
bargain purchase 割引購入
cost of purchase 購入原価, 仕入原価
equity purchase 株式投資
gross purchases 総仕入高
lump-sum purchase 一括購入 （=bulk purchase）
margin purchase 信用買い
material purchase order 材料注文書
purchase allowance 仕入値引き
purchase discount 仕入割引
purchase of business 買収
purchase of materials 原料調達
purchase order 売約書, 注文書
purchase transaction 仕入取引
returned purchase 仕入戻し品
the purchase of Products 本製品の購入
◆The company considered switching purchases of chicken from Thailand to China following the

ban on imports of Thai chicken. 同社は、タイ産鶏肉の輸入停止で、鶏肉の調達先をタイから中国に切り替えることを検討した。◆The Federal Reserve will cut its monthly bond purchases starting in February 2014 by $10 billion to $65 billion. 米連邦準備制度理事会（FRB）は、2014年2月から、債券の月間購入額を100億ドル減らして650億ドルにする。◆The purchase of Sanyo Electric Co. by Panasonic Corp. turned out to be a miscalculation. パナソニックによる三洋電機の買収は、誤算に終わった。

purchase agreement　購入契約
asset purchase agreement　資産購入契約
share purchase agreement　株式購入契約

purchase and take delivery　購入して引き取る、買い取って引き取る
◆The seller shall sell and deliver the products and the buyer shall purchase and take delivery thereof. 売り主は本商品を販売して引き渡すものとし、買い主は本商品を買い取ってその引渡しを受けるものとする。

purchase price　購入価格、購入代金、買入れ価格、買取り価格、譲渡価格、仕入れ値段
◆Subject to the terms and conditions herein set forth, XYZ and ABC agree that at the closing, XYZ shall sell to ABC, and ABC shall purchase from XYZ, one hundred（100）shares of the common stock with no par value of the Company owned by XYZ at the purchase price of U.S. $1,000,000. 本契約に定める条件に従って、XYZとABCは、クロージングにおいて、XYZが保有する本会社の無額面普通株式100株を、100万米ドルの購入価格［譲渡価格］で、XYZがABCに売り渡し、ABCがXYZから買い受けることに合意する。

purchase records of customers　顧客の購入履歴
◆As the value of using big data, a sales practice prevailing in the mail-order business sector is to analyze purchase records of customers and then recommend products based on their tastes and preferences. ビッグ・データの利用価値として、通販業界で広がっている販売手法は、顧客の購入履歴を分析して、顧客の好みに合う商品を薦める方法だ。

purchase the product　本製品を購入する
◆Subdistributor discount means the amount below the prices set forth in the price list, at which the subdistributor may purchase the products from Distributor.　「二次代理店割引」とは、価格表に記載する価格より低い金額のことで、二次代理店はこの金額で代理店から本製品を購入することができる。

purchaser　（名）買い主、買い手、買取り人、購入者、購買者、得意先　（⇒obliged to）
◆If the purchaser fails to comply with the above stipulation, the purchaser shall be deemed to have waived such claim. 買い主が上記規定に従わない場合、買い主は当該クレームを放棄したも

のと見なされるものとする。

purpose　（名）目的、意図、決意、決心、〜上、用途、使途
all purpose card　汎用カード、多目的カード
business purpose　事業目的、経営目的（=purpose of business）
cash flow purpose　資金繰りの目的
charitable purpose　非営利目的
dual purpose　二重目的
for entry purposes　市場参入のため、市場参入の目的で
for financial statement and income tax reporting purposes　会計上および税務上
for general corporate purposes　全社的な目的で
for income tax purposes　税務会計上、税務上
for investment purposes　投資目的のため、投資目的で
for the purpose of this agreement　本契約の目的上、本契約の目的のために、本契約上、本契約の解釈上
general corporate purposes　一般事業目的
general purpose　一般目的
general-purpose lines of credit　使途を限定しない信用枠
government bond for the purpose of public works　建設国債
humanitarian purposes　民生用
mono-purpose credit　単一目的カード
multipurpose card　汎用カード
on purpose　故意に　（=intentionally）
purpose-built　特注の
purpose of loan　資金使途
special-purpose borrowings　特定目的借入金
special purpose company［corporation, entity］　特別目的会社
to no purpose　まったく効果がなく
to the purpose　適切な、有用な
◆Diplomats are prohibited from engaging in commercial activities for the purpose of their personal profits under the Vienna Convention's Article 42. ウイーン条約42条で、外交官は個人の利得を目的とした商業活動を禁止されている。◆For such purpose the minutes of meetings or other informal documents shall not constitute a waiver made in writing. 当該目的上、会議の議事録または本その他の非公式の書面は、書面による権利放棄とはならないものとする。◆The seller makes no other warranties or representations with respect to the products and disclaims all warranties, including but not limited to implied warranties of merchantability, fitness for a particular purpose and noninfringement. 売り主は、本製品に関する

他の保証または表明は行わず、商品性、特定目的への適合性および非侵害の黙示の保証などを含めてすべての保証を否認する。

put option　売付け選択権, 売る権利, 特権付き売り, プット・オプション

put up　掲示する, 掲げる, 出す, 売りに出す, 競売にする, 提出する, (資金を)融通する, 出資する, 寄付する, (価格を)上げる, (抵抗など)を示す, 〜を行う

put A up to the news　Aにそのニュースを知らせる

put up a candidate　候補者を立てる

put up a house for sale　家を売りに出す

put up a notice　掲示を出す

put up for auction　競売にかける

put up tough resistance　頑強な抵抗を示す

◆In the joint venture with an Indian investment bank, Tokyo Marine Holdings Inc. put up about 26%, the maximum a foreign investor is allowed in an Indian company, of the new firm's capital. インドの投資銀行との合弁事業で, 東京海上ホールディングスは, 新会社の資本金の約26% (外資の持ち分比率の上限)を出資した。

Q

qualified　(形) 適格の, 適任の, 有資格の, 一定の技能を有する, 権能を与えられた, 免許のある, 制限された, 限定された, 条件付きの, 修正・手直しした

◆The distributor shall, at all time during the term of this agreement, maintain adequate spare parts and adequately trained staff and qualified merchandise to provide qualified customers and repair service. 販売店は, 本契約の期間中つねに, 適格の顧客・修理サービスを提供するため, 十分なスペアパーツと十分に訓練されたスタッフおよび適切な商品を維持するものとする。

qualified merchandise　適切な商品

qualify　(動) 〜を制限する, 限定する, 〜を〜と見なす, 資格がある, 適任である

◆The headings set forth in this agreement are for convenience of reference only and do not qualify or affect in any way the meaning or interpretation of this agreement. 本契約に明記する見出し語は, 単に参照の便宜上のもので, 本契約の意味または解釈をなんら制限するものではなく, また影響を与えるものでもない。

quality　(名) 品質, 品位, 特質, 特性, 優良品 (⇒acceptable, high-quality, merchantable quality)

any warranty or condition in quality　品質に関する保証または条件

merchantable quality　商品性

the difference in quality　品質の差, 品質差

◆ABC shall take care of keeping its quality without any harm whatsoever as bona fide holder of Products on behalf of XYZ. ABCは, XYZを代理する契約品[本製品]の善意の保管者として, 契約品[本製品]の品質保持上, どんな損害も生じないよう注意を払うものとする。◆The company offered a 10 percent discount to make up for the difference in quality. 品質差の埋め合わせのため, 同社は10%値引きした。◆We enclose a few samples of our product and should be obliged if you would send us samples of the nearest quality you could offer from stock. 当社製品の見本を数点同封しますので, 在庫から提供できるほど同品質の見本を送っていただけるとありがたいのですが[ほぼ同品質の見本があれば送っていただけないでしょうか]。

quality and quantity　品質と数量

◆The inspection by the purchaser of quality and quantity of the products after the delivery at the final destination shall be final between the seller and the purchaser. 最終目的地での引渡し後に買い主が行う本製品の品質と数量の検査を, 売り主と買い主間では最終とする。

quality control　品質管理, QC

◆After the poisoned frozen gyoza incident, Japanese companies were spurred to tighten quality controls on Chinese food products at their factories in China. 冷凍ギョウザの中毒事件を機に, 日系企業は, 中国国内工場での中国産食品の品質管理強化を行うようになった。◆Measures to tighten quality controls on Chinese food products, taken by many Japanese manufacturers in China, include more stringent tests on the amounts of agricultural chemicals used at Chinese farms and on the quality of processing materials used at Chinese factories. 中国の日系メーカーの多くが取っている中国産食品の品質管理強化策としては, 中国農場での農薬使用量の検査や中国の工場で使用している加工原料の品質チェックの強化などが挙げられる。

quality requirements　品質条件

◆In case the quality of Products shipped to Distributor turns out not to meet the above quality requirements, Distributor can claim a replacement against those inferior Products or cancellation of the individual contract. 販売店に発送した本製品の品質が上記品質基準に適合しないことが判明した場合, 販売店は, これら品質の劣る本製品の交換[これら粗悪品の交換]またはその個別契約[個々の契約]の解除を請求することができる。

quality standard　品質基準, 品質標準, 品質規格

◆This manufacturing facility was registered for international quality standard ISO 9001. この製造施設[製造工場]は, 国際品質基準「ISO 9001」の認定を受けた。

quality terms　品質条件

landed quality terms　陸揚げ時品質条件, 陸揚げ品質条件

shipped quality terms　船積み時品質条件, 船

積み品質条件, 積出し品質条件

quantity （名）量, 数量, 総量, 多量, 購入量
（⇒acceptable, obliged to）

annual minimum sales quantity　年間最低販売数量

economic order quantity　経済的発注量

landed quantity terms　揚げ地数量条件

quantities　大口取引

quantity adjustment　数量調整

quantity afloat　積送中の数量

quantity available　手に入る数量

quantity buying　大量仕入れ, 多量仕入れ

quantity cartel　生産数量カルテル

quantity claim　数量クレーム

quantity delivered　受渡し数量

quantity in transit　運送中の数量

quantity on hand　手持ち数量

quantity order　多量注文, 大量注文

quantity production　大量生産, 量産

quantity quotation　数量建て相場

quantity rebate　大量買い割引

quantity shipped　積込み数量, 積送数量

quantity supplied　供給量

quantity terms　数量条件

quantity variance　数量差異

quantity variation　数量の相違

quarterly minimum quantity　四半期毎の最低購入量

rate of quantity discount　数量割引率

sales quantity　販売数量

◆All quantities of the Product manufactured by you shall be held by you to our order and we shall insure all quantities on your premises of the Commodity and the Product. 貴社が製造した契約品の数量はすべて当社の指図があるまで貴社が保管し、当社は貴社の構内にある商品と契約品の全数量に保険を付けるものとする。◆Please inform us what discount you will allow us for quantities. 大口取引に対してどれだけの値引きを認められるか、お知らせください。◆Quantity is subject to a variation of 5% more or less than the contracted quantity at Seller's option unless otherwise specified. 数量は、他にとくに明記しないかぎり、売り主の裁量で契約数量より5%増減の変動が生じることがある。◆The quantity of the Products to be delivered under this agreement shall be as follows: 本契約に基づいて引き渡す本商品の数量は、次のとおりとする。

quantity discount　数量割引
◆The following price list shows our best prices and rate of quantity discount for our supplies. 以下の価格表は、当社供給品の最低価格[勉強値]と数量割引率を示しています。

quarantine　（名）検疫, 検疫期間, 検疫停船期間, 検疫所, 隔離, 隔離期間, 隔離所, 孤立化, 追放, 排斥

animal quarantine　動物検疫所

in quarantine　隔離中に, 隔離して

plant quarantine　植物防疫所

quarantine anchorage　検疫停泊

quarantine certificate　検疫証明書

quarantine depot　検疫所

quarantine fee　検疫料

quarantine inspection　検疫検査

quarantine office　検疫所

quarantine officer　検疫官, 防疫官

quarantine port　検疫港

quarantine regulation　検疫規則

quarantine restrictions　検疫制限, 伝染病による隔離

quarantine station　検疫所

◆Quarantine officers must pick samples to make sure imported stock farm products have not been tampered with. 検疫官は、検体を抽出して、輸入畜産物に異物の混入[不正開封]などがないかどうかを確認する必要がある。

quarantining　（名）検査, 検疫
◆Quarantining of imported food was found inappropriate. 輸入食品の検査は、不十分であることが判明した。

quarter　（名）四半期（1年の4分の1、つまり3か月を指す。暦年の第1四半期は、1月1日から3月31日までの3か月のこと）, 4分の1, 25セント, (情報などの)筋, ある方面, 関係筋, 地区, 区域, 地域, 場所, 部屋, 住居, 宿舎　（形）4分の1の

for three consecutive quarters　3四半期連続して, 3四半期連続

quarter-on-quarter comparison　前期比

the accounts settlement for the first three quarters to September　1-9月期決算

the April-June quarter　4—6月期（日本の3月期決算企業の第1四半期にあたる）

the fifth straight quarter　5四半期連続, 五・四半期連続

the final [last] quarter　第4四半期, 第四・四半期　（=the fourth quarter）

the first quarter　第1四半期, 第一・四半期

the first two quarters　上半期の第1四半期と第2四半期

the preceding quarter　前期
（=the previous quarter）

the quarter ended Dec. 31　10—12月期
（=the October-December quarter）

the second two quarters　下半期の第3四半期と第4四半期

the third quarter 第3四半期, 第三・四半期
◆ANA was in the red to the amount of ¥27. 3 billion during the April-June quarter. 全日空(全日本空輸)は、4—6月期は273億円の赤字だった。 ◆Business sentiment among large companies worsened for two consecutive quarters. 大企業の景況感が、2四半期連続の悪化となった。◆Companies are becoming willing to make capital investments and growth in capital investment turned positive for the first time in six quarters. 企業の設備投資意欲は上向きつつあり、設備投資の伸びは、6四半期ぶりにプラスに転じた。◆Foreign electronics companies such as Apple inc. and Samsung Electronics Co. posted all-time sales records in the July-September quarter while Japanese rivals have been hit by major setbacks recently. 米アップル社や韓国のサムスン電子など海外の家電メーカーが7〜9月期決算の業績で売上高が過去最高だったのに対して、日本勢は最近の収益の大幅減で大きな痛手を負っている。◆We will accept your offer if you assure us of an order for at least 1,000 pieces per quarter for one year. 1年間、四半期ごとに最低1,000個の注文をご確約いただければ、貴社のオファーをお受けします。

quorum （名）定足数
　a quorum for a meeting of shareholders 株主総会の定足数
　achieve a quorum 定足数を満たす
　be short of the quorum 定足数を欠く
　constitute a quorum 定足数に達する, 定足数とする (=form [make] a quorum)
　fail to meet the quorum 定足数を欠く (=do not come up to the quorum)
　have a quorum 定足数を満たす
　lack of a quorum 定足数不足
　represent a quorum 定足数を満たす
　the quorum of directors 取締役の定数
　there is a quorum 定足数が満たされている
◆At each meeting of the board of directors, a majority of each of the Class A directors and Class B directors shall be necessary and sufficient to constitute a quorum for the transaction of business. 取締役会の各会議には、Aクラスの取締役とBクラス取締役の各過半数の出席が必要で、これを議事進行の十分な定足数とする。◆Many of listed companies are set to adopt measures to counter corporate acquirers, such as increasing their authorized capital or reducing the quorum of directors. 授権資本（株式発行可能枠）の拡大や取締役の定数削減など、買収防衛策を導入する上場企業も多い。◆The board of directors may act at a meeting at which a quorum is present by the affirmative vote of a majority of those present at such meeting. 取締役会は、定足数の取締役が出席した会議で、出席取締役の過半数の賛成投票により決議することができる。

quota （名）割当て, 割当数量, ノルマ, 持ち分, 分担, 分担割当額, クォータ
　abolish a quota 割当てを撤廃する
　allocated country-by-country quotas 国別生産枠
　be offered on a quota basis 比例配分ベースで行われる
　catch quotas 漁獲割当て
　consumption quota 消費割当て
　export quota 輸出割当て
　face import quotas 輸入割当ての対象になる
　fall short of a quota 割当量を下回る
　hiring quota 採用枠, 雇用枠
　IMF quota IMFクォータ
　import quota 輸入割当て
　import quota system 輸入割当制度
　marketing quota 販売割当て
　meet a quota 割当量に達する
　percentage quota 比例割当て
　production quota 生産割当て, 生産ノルマ
　quota performance ノルマ達成度
　quota restrictions 輸入割当制限
　quota share reinsurance 比例再保険
　set sales quota 販売割当て［販売ノルマ］を決める
　tariff quota 関税割当て
◆The actual oil outputs of Nigeria, Venezuela, Iran and other OPEC members have been below allocated country-by-country quotas. ナイジェリアやベネズエラ、イランなどOPEC（石油輸出国機構）加盟国の実際の石油生産量は、OPECの国別生産枠を下回っている。

quotation （名）相場, 相場づけ, 相場表, 時価, 見積り, 見積り価格, 見積り書, 引用
　ask for quotations on 〜の建て値を求める
　asked quotation 呼び値相場
　best quotation obtainable 成行き最高相場
　bid quotation 付け値相場
　black market quotation 闇相場
　bond price quotation 債券の建て値
　buying quotation （為替の）買い相場
　closing quotation 引け値, 大引け相場
　current quotation 現行相場, 時価
　exchange quotation 為替相場
　export quotation 輸出相場, 輸出相場申入れ
　flat quotation 裸相場
　forced quotation 人為相場
　forward quotation 先渡し相場, 先物相場
　futures quotation 先物相場
　giving quotation 支払い勘定建て相場

(=rate in home currency)

grey [gray] market quotation　黙認相場

have one's lowest quotation for the following items　下記商品に対する［下記商品の］最低相場を出す

in view of the quotation ruling in this market　市場の時価の観点からすると

indicative interest quotations　気配値

marine quotation　海上保険料率見積り書

market quotation　市場相場, 市場呼び値

nominal quotation　名目相場

official quotation　公定相場

open market quotations　市中相場, 通り相場

opening quotation　寄り付き相場

price quotation　建て値, 時価相場

public quotation　公定相場

quantity quotation　数量建て相場

quotation after the close　引けあと気配

quotation board　相場告知板

quotation in dollars　ドル建て相場

quotations advance [rise]　相場が上がる

quotations are given　相場が立つ

quotations decline [fall]　相場が下がる

receive a quotation　相場の提示を受ける

receiving quotation　受取相場, 受取勘定建て相場, 外貨建て相場　(=receiving quotation)

rising quotation　上げ相場, 上向き相場

selling quotation　(為替の)売り相場

split quotation　小刻み相場, 分割相場

spot quotation　現物相場, 現場渡し値段

stock exchange quotation　株式相場, 株式市況

stock market quotation　株式相場

stock quotation　株式相場, 株価　(=share quotation)

the best [lowest] quotation　最低価格, 最低の見積り価格, 建て値

two-way quotation　二重相場

volume quotation　外貨建て建て値

◆All quotations are subject to change without prior notice.　相場は, すべて事前の通知［予告］なしで変動することがあります。◆Our quotations do not allow us any concession.　当社の建て値には, 値引きの余地がまったくありません。◆Please give us your best quotations in U.S. dollars for immediate shipment and proforma invoices.　直（じき）積みでドル建ての貴社の建て値と試算送り状を, お送りください。◆The quotations above are the best we could make at the moment, so we could not reduce the prices any further.　上記価格は, 現在のところ当社精一杯のもので, これ以上価格を下げることはできません。◆Your prompt

quotation is awaited.　貴社の早急な見積りを, お待ちします。

quote (動) 示す, 表示する, 値を付ける, 価格を提示する, 値段［相場］を言う, (値段を) 見積もる, 上場する, 引用する

be quoted a reasonable price for　〜の手頃な値段を見積もってもらう

be quoted at　〜の値を付ける, 〜で取引される

be quoted in terms of interest rates　金利ベースで建て値される

premiums are quoted as　保険料は〜と見積もられる

quote a fee for　〜の料金を見積もる

quote lower prices　安値を呼ぶ

quote one's best [keenest, lowest, rockbottom] prices　〜の最低値を見積もる, 〜の建て値を出す

quote one's rock bottom [best] prices on CIF basis　CIFの条件で最低値を見積もる

quote the lowest rate against WPA (with particular average) on the goods　本製品について単独海損担保 (WPA) の条件で最低保険料率を見積もる

quote two-way prices　売り買い両方の気配値［取引価格］を提示する

◆In New York, the dollar was quoted at ¥111. 60-70 at 8:30 a.m.　ニューヨークの外国為替市場で, ドル相場は午前8時30分に1ドル＝111円60-70銭の値を付けた。◆In reply to your inquiry of March 5, we are pleased to quote you our prices as follows: 貴社の3月5日付け引かいに対して, 下記のとおり当社の価格見積りについてご回答申し上げます。◆Kindly quote us your lowest prices on the basis of CIF Yokohama for your items.　CIF横浜港条件で, 貴社商品の最低値［建て値］を出していただきたい。◆Nominal foreign exchange rates are quoted at ¥110 to the U.S. dollar or ¥135 to the euro as we see in the media.　名目為替レートは, 新聞や雑誌で見られるように, 1ドル＝110円とか, 1ユーロ＝135円と表示される。◆Shortly after issuance, the warrants were quoted on the market for $5 each.　発行直後, 引受権の時価は1口当たり5ドルとなった。◆We are in the market for the following items. Will you please quote us your best export prices for them？　当社は, 下記商品の購入を望んでいます。つきましては, これらの商品を輸出する場合の貴社の建て値をお知らせいただけないでしょうか。◆We are on the lookout for the following items: Please quote us your keenest [best] export prices for them. 当社は, 以下の商品が入用です［以下の商品を求めています］。これら商品の最低輸出価格の建て値をお知らせください。

quote (名) 見積り, 値付け, 相場, 建て値, 気配値, 呼び値, 引用

be quoted on the current indicative market quote 時価に基づく

best quote　最低価格の見積り
　　(=best price quote, lowest quote)

bond quote　債券相場, 債券価格　(=bond price)

calculate LIBOR component from quotes provided by group of reference banks　(相場の気配値を提供する) レファレンス・バンクが提示するレートを基準にLIBOR (ロンドン銀行間取引金利) を決定する

closing quote　終値 (おわりね)

direct quotes　直接呼び値

give the quote　(ディーラーが) 呼び値を出す

indirect quotes　間接呼び値

mandatory quote period　値付け義務時間

opening quote　始値 (はじめね)

price quote　見積り　(=quote)

quote in dollars　ドル建て

quote request　(価格の) 引合い

quotes　気配

render a quote　気配値を示す

stock quote　株価　(=stock price)

the current indicative market quote　時価

the highest quote　最高値

◆At 5 p.m., the dollar traded at ¥85.52-¥85.53, compared with Tuesday's 5 p.m. quotes of ¥85.98-¥86 in Tokyo. 東京の外国為替市場では、午後5時の時点で、ドル相場は火曜日 [前日] 午後5時の1ドル＝85円98～86銭に対して、1ドル＝85円52～53銭で取引された。

quoted　(形) 値の付いた, 相場の付いた, (相場、時価、値段が) 見積もられた, 取引される, 上場した

quoted investment　上場有価証券, 上場銘柄
　　(=listed investment)

quoted market price　時価, 市場 [市場の] 相場

quoted market value　市場価格

quoted price　相場, 市場相場価格, 最新取引価格

quoted share [stock]　上場株, 上場銘柄

quoted value　時価

quoted company　上場会社, 上場企業
　　(=listed company, publicly quoted company)
◆If a quoted company with a one-share trading unit changes its trading unit to 100 shares without changing the price of individual shares, the amount required for investment would rise 100-fold. 売買単位が1株の上場企業が、1株当たりの価格を変更しないで売買単位を100株に変更すると、投資 (株の売買) に必要な金額は100倍になってしまう。

R

R & D　研究開発 (research and development の略)
◆Comparative advantage in this new global market depends not only on superior R&D, but also on speed in making management decisions, finding unique applications for research advances and delivering them to customers ahead of competitors. この新しいグローバル市場で比較優位性を確立できるかどうかは、高度な研究開発だけでなく、経営の意思決定を迅速に行えるかどうかと、研究を進めるうえで独創的な適用範囲 [用途] を素早く確認して、それを競合他社に先駆けて製品化できるかどうかにかかっている。◆Kyoto University has obtained U.S. iPS patent rights for the R&D of new medicines. 京都大は、新薬の研究開発も対象とするiPSの米国特許権を取得した。

rail of the vessel　本船の舷側欄干, 本船の欄干　(⇒vessel)

raise　(動) (資金などを) 調達する, (料金や価格・資金などを) 引き上げる, 上げる, (旗などを) 揚げる, 上方修正する, 増やす, 増強する, (地位や名声を) 高める, 昇進させる, (子どもを) 育てる, 養育する, (家族などを) 養う, (家畜を) 飼う, 飼育する, (作物を) 栽培する, (問題などを) 提起する, 提出する, (封鎖などを) 解く, 解除する, (建物を) 建てる, (指名手配犯などを) 見つける
◆In an attempt to recapitalize itself, the bank raised ¥15 billion through a third-party share allotment. 資本再編のため、同行は第三者株式割当てで150億円を調達した。◆The firm appointed Deutsche Bank AG and Daiwa Securities SMBC to arrange an initial public offering to raise about ¥100 billion. 同社は、約1,000億円を調達するため、ドイツ銀行と大和証券SMBCを株式公募の取りまとめ役に指名した。

raise funds　資金を調達する
◆Except as otherwise set forth herein, the new company shall be responsible for raising the funds necessary to carry on the business of the new company. 本契約に別途定める場合を除いて、新会社の事業遂行に必要な資金を調達する責任を負うものとする。

rare earth　希土類, レア・アース [レアアース]
◆After a Chinese fishing boat collided with Japan Coast Guard's patrol vessels near the Senkakus in 2010, China suspended rare earth exports to Japan and dealt a blow to Japanese manufacturers. 2010年に中国漁船が尖閣諸島近海で海上保安庁の巡視船に衝突した事件の後、中国はレア・アースの対日輸出を停止し、日本の製造業が打撃を受けた。◆Rare earths are indispensable for making parts for energy-saving household appliances and other devices. レア・アース (希土類) は、省エネ家電やその他の製品・機器の部品製造

RATE 386

に欠かせないものだ。◆Sumitomo Corp. agreed to jointly develop rare earths and import the metals with Kazakhstan's state-owned resource firm Kazatomprom. 住友商事は、カザフスタンの国営資源企業「カザトムプロム」と、レア・アースを共同開発して輸入することで合意した。◆Through diversifying rare earth suppliers, Japan will lessen the diplomatic pressure China is able to exert as it exclusively possesses heavy rare earth deposits. レア・アース調達先の多角化により、日本は、重レア・アース鉱床の独占を武器にした中国の外交圧力をかわす方針だ。

解説 レア・アースとは：レアメタルに指定されているニッケルやリチウムなど47元素から構成される31の鉱物のうちの一つで、ネオジムやセリウムなど17種類の金属元素に分けられる。鉄鉱石やウランなど他の鉱石の副産物として採取され、採集量は鉱石1トンにつき100～200グラム程度、含有量は0.01～0.02%にすぎない。2009年の世界の生産量は、推定12万4,000トンで、中国がその97%を占める。世界の推定埋蔵量は9,900万トン、このうち中国が36%を占め世界最多。用途は自動車、家電製品、産業用機械や医療用機器など幅広く、主要材料の金属や合成樹脂などに添加剤として少量加えるだけで各種製品の性能が向上するため、「産業のビタミン」とも呼ばれている。

rate （名）割合、率、金利、歩合、料金、値段、運賃、相場、等級、速度、進度、程度、レート（⇒exchange rate, interest rate, prime lending rate）

bill discount rate　手形レート

buying rate　買い相場

commodity classification rate　品目分類賃率, CCR

contract rate　契約運賃,（為替の）予約相場

fixed rate　固定相場

flat rate　均一料金, 定額制

floating rate　自由変動相場

freight rate　貨物運賃, 運賃率

general cargo rate　一般貨物賃率, GCR

insurance premium rate　保険料率

insurance rate　保険料金

keep interest rates unchanged　金利を据え置く

lending rate　貸出金利

long rate　長期為替相場

market rate　市場金利, 市場相場, 市場レート, 銀行間相場

measured rate　従量制

money market rate　市中金利, 短期市場金利

official rate　公定歩合, 公定利率, 公定レート

open rate　基本料金, 任意運賃率

opening rate　始め値, 寄り付き

operating rate　操業率, 設備稼働率

postal rates　郵便料金

prevailing rate　市場の実勢金利, 市場金利, 中心相場

quote the lowest rate against WPA（with particular average）on the goods　本製品について単独海損担保（WPA）の条件で最低保険料率を見積もる

rate basis　運賃建て

rate cutting　料率引下げ, 賃率引下げ

rate hike　利上げ, 金利引上げ, 料金引上げ, 値上げ

rate in foreign money［currency］　外貨建て相場

rate in home money［currency］　邦貨建て相場

rate of duty　関税率

rate of economic expansion　経済成長率（=economic growth rate, pace of economic expansion, rate of business expansion）

rate of foreign exchange　為替相場, 為替レート（=rate of exchange）

rate of passage　船の運賃

rate of price increase　物価上昇率

rate of price inflation　物価インフレ率

rate of return on investment　投資収益率, 資本利益率, 投資の運用利回り

rate sheet　料金表

rate shopping　格付けの相見積り

rate war　値下げ競争, 料金戦

real rate　実勢レート, 実効金利

selling rate　売り相場

short rate　短期為替相場

specific commodity rate　特定品目賃率, SCR

tax rate　税率（=rate of taxation）

the yen-dollar rate　円・ドル［円ドル］相場, 円・ドルレート, 円・ドル為替レート, 円の対ドル・レート

the yen rate　円相場, 円レート, 円為替レート

through rate　通し運賃

U.S. rates　米国の金利（公定歩合とFF金利の誘導目標）

◆Nonmonetary balance sheet items and corresponding income statement items are translated at rates in effect at the time of acquisition. 貸借対照表の非貨幣性項目とこれに対応する損益計算書項目は、取得日の為替レートで換算されています。◆The competitive edge of Japanese exporters vying with U.S. firms is affected by the yen-dollar rate and the price levels in the two countries. 米企業と競合している日本の輸出企業の競争力は、円・ドルレートや日本と米国の物価水準の影響をも受ける。

ratify （動）（条約などを）批准する,（契約などを）追認する, 承認する, 裁可する

◆The United Auto Workers ratified a four-year contract with Mitsubishi Motor North America. 全米自動車労組は、北米三菱自動車との4年労使協約を承認した。

rating [ratings] agency　格付け機関, 信用格付け機関, 格付け会社　(=credit rating agency, rating company, rating firm, ratings service agency)

bond rating agency　債券格付け機関

credit rating agency　信用格付け機関, 格付け機関

independent rating agency　独立格付け機関

international rating(s) agencies　国際格付け機関

rating agency system　格付け制度 (=rating system)

recognized rating agency　一般に認められている格付け機関

◆S&P credit-rating agency now rates debt issued by Spain BBB-, its lowest investment-grade status. 米格付け機関のスタンダード・アンド・プアーズ(S&P)は現在、スペイン発行国債の格付けを、投資適格基準で最低の「BBB(トリプルB)マイナス」にしている。

rating scale　格付け段階

◆In new sovereign debt ratings by Germany's Bertelsmann Foundation, Japan earned a score of 6 on a scale of one to ten, equivalent to A minus on the rating scales adopted by major international ratings agencies. ドイツのベルテルスマン財団の新国債格付けで、日本は1～10の格付け段階のうち6の評価を得たが、これは主要国際格付け機関が採用している格付け基準で「Aマイナス」に相当する。

raw materials　原材料

◆By the instruction of the China Food and Drug Administration, the Shanghai city government suspended operations of Shanghai Husi Food and confiscated raw materials and products at the firm which had sold expired meat products. 中国の国家食品薬品監督管理総局の指示で、上海市は、品質保持期限切れの肉製品を販売していた上海福喜食品の営業を停止し、同社の原料と商品を差し押さえた。◆China lost an appeal at the WTO in a case about its export restrictions on raw materials including bauxite, magnesium and zinc. 中国によるボーキサイトやマグネシウム、亜鉛などの鉱物資源[原材料]輸出規制に関する問題で、中国は世界貿易機関(WTO)で敗訴した。◆In processing trade, imported raw materials are manufactured into goods that are then sold to other countries. 加工貿易では、輸入された原材料が製品に仕上げられた後、製品は海外に販売される。◆The United States, the EU and Mexico challenged China's export restrictions on raw materials and launched WTO legal cases in 2009. 米国、欧州連合(EU)とメキシコが中国の原材料(鉱物資源)輸出規制は世界貿易機関(WTO)の協定違反に当たるとして、

2009年にWTOに提訴した。

RCEP　東アジア地域16か国の包括的経済連携, 東アジア地域包括的経済連携, 域内包括的経済連携, アールセップ(Regional Comprehensive Economic Partnershipの略。東南アジア諸国連合(ASEAN)加盟10か国と日本、中国、韓国、インド、オーストラリア、ニュージーランドの計16か国による包括的経済連携)

R&D base　研究開発拠点

◆European and U.S. companies established R&D bases in China and put their energy into developing products for use by Chinese consumers. 欧米の企業は、中国に研究開発拠点を設けて、中国仕様の製品開発に力を注いだ。

real effective exchange rate　実質実効為替レート, REER

◆If we look at the yen's current exchange rate in terms of its real effective exchange rate, it is basically within a range consistent with the mid- and long-term fundamentals of the economy. 今の円相場[円の為替相場]は、実質実効為替レートで見ると、基本的には中長期的な経済のファンダメンタルズ(基礎的条件)と整合的な範囲内にある。

real estate market　不動産市場, 不動産取引市場, 不動産市況

◆The prolonged slump in the real estate market is maintaining the decline in land prices. 不動産取引市場の長期低迷が、引き続き地価の下落を招いている。

real exchange rate　実質為替レート

◆Real exchange rates are nominal rates adjusted for the different price levels in different countries. 実質為替レートは、名目為替レートを各国の異なる物価水準[物価の動き]で調整したものだ。◆The international competitiveness of companies and a country's balance of trade with the rest of the world are affected not by nominal exchange rates but by real exchange rates, so we need to follow real exchange rates. 企業の国際競争力や国の他国との貿易収支などの動きは、名目為替レートではなく、実質為替レートの影響を受けるので、われわれは実質為替レートの動きを見る必要がある。

real GDP　実質GDP(国内総生産)

◆The improvement in the real GDP was mainly due to a recovery in exports and policy initiatives under the government's stimulus packages. この実質GDP(国内総生産)の改善は、主に輸出回復と、政府の経済対策による政策効果によるものだ。

real money trade [trading]　リアル・マネー・トレード[トレーディング], 仮想通貨の現金化　(オンライン上のキャラクターやゲーム内の通貨(仮想通貨)などをインターネット上で売買し、現実世界の通貨などと取引すること)

reasonable　(形)妥当な, 相当な, 合理的な, 公正な, 適切な

reasonable amount　合理的な金額

reasonable assurance　合理的な保証

reasonable basis　合理的な基準

reasonable care　相当な注意

reasonable cause　正当事由, 相当な理由

reasonable commercial standards of fair dealing in the trade　取引上の信義則

reasonable definiteness　相当な確実性

reasonable diligence　相当の注意

reasonable out-of-pocket expenses　合理的な直接経費

reasonable price　適正価格

reasonable details　合理的な詳細
◆The period, time, method, and reasonable details of such visits shall be determined separately through mutual consultation between the parties. このような訪問［視察］の期間、時期、方法と合理的詳細は、当事者間の相互協議により別途決定するものとする。

reasonable step　適正措置, 合理的な措置
◆Each party shall take all reasonable steps to ensure the confidentiality of all the confidential information. 各当事者は、すべての秘密情報を維持するため、あらゆる合理的な措置を取るものとする。

reasonableness　(名)合理性, 妥当性, 適正なこと, 妥当性にかなっていること

reasonably　(副)合理的に, 公平に, 適切に, 満足できるくらい, 無理なく, かなり
reasonably priced oil and gas　安価な原油やガス

reasonably request　合理的に要求する

the requirement reasonably anticipated in the territory　合理的に予想される契約地域内の必要量
◆ABC shall, at all times during the term of this agreement, maintain an adequate stock of the products so as to enable it to meet the requirement and supply promptly all orders reasonably anticipated in the territory. ABCは、本契約の期間中つねに、合理的に予想される契約地域内の必要量をみたすことができるようにするため、またすべての注文品を迅速に供給できるようにするため、本製品の十分な在庫を維持するものとする。
◆If reasonably priced oil and gas are exported to Japan by the U.S. "shale revolution," the cost of domestic thermal power generation would decrease. 米国の「シェール革命」で、安価な原油やガスが日本に輸出されれば、国内火力発電のコストは下がることになる。

rebellion　(名)反乱, 暴動

recall　(動)リコール（無料回収・修理）する, 回収する, 撤回する, 取り消す, 召還する, 呼び戻す, 解任する, 思い出す, 回想する
◆Toyota is recalling 7.43 million vehicles globally for a faulty power window switch. トヨタが、パワー・ウインドーのスイッチ欠陥のため、全世界で743万台のリコール（回収・無償修理）を行っ

ている。

recall　(名)（欠陥車・欠陥品の）回収, リコール（無料回収・修理）, 撤回, 取消し, 召喚, 呼び戻し, 公職者の解任請求, 解任・解職権, 回想
◆The U.S. Congress is planning to pursue matters related to the recall of Toyota cars by holding hearings. 米議会は、公聴会を開いて、トヨタ車のリコール関連問題を追及する構えだ。

recall problem　リコール問題
◆Sony's battery recall problem hurts the company's reliability as a supplier. ソニーの充電回収問題は、同社のサプライヤーとしての信頼性を損ねている。

receipt　(名)受領, 受取り, 領収書, 受領書, 受領証, 売上, 収入, 売上金, レシート
acknowledge receipt of this letter　本状の受領を確認する

after the receipt of　～の受領後, ～を受領してから

be in receipt of　～を受け取る

call receipt　払込み領収書

cash receipt　現金収入, 現金出納

delivery receipt　受渡し品, 配達品受取証, 受取証

dock receipt　埠頭管理人貨物受取証, 本船貨物受取書, D/R　(=mate's receipt)

equipment interchange receipt　機器受渡し証, EIR

export receipt　輸出収入, 輸出受取高

foreign exchange receipts　外国為替収入, 外国為替受取高

freight receipts　運賃収入

in receipt of　～を受け取って, ～を受領して

invisible receipts　貿易外受取り

mate's receipt　本船貨物受取証, MR

negotiable warehouse receipt　指図式倉庫証券

net receipts (from overseas)　(海外からの)純所得

on (the) receipt of　～を受取り次第

parcel receipt　小口貨物受取証

payable on receipt　貨物引換え払い

provisional receipt　仮領収書

receipt in full　全額領収書

receipt note　貨物引換証

receipt slip　入金伝票

receipt stamp　受領印, 受取印

receipts of dividends　配当収入

report on bonded warehouse receipt　保税倉庫庫入申告書

shipping receipt　積み荷受取証

ship's receipt　本船受領書

so long as receipt is acknowledged　受領の確

認が取れるかぎり

stock receipt 株式譲渡証, 株券譲渡証

suspense receipt 仮受け金

temporary receipts 仮受け金, 仮領収書

trust receipt 輸入担保荷物〔貨物〕保管証, 荷為替担保荷物保管証

upon receipt of this order 本オファー受領と同時に, 本オファーを受取り次第

visible receipt 貿易受取り

warehouse keeper's receipt 倉荷証券, 倉庫証券

warehouse receipt 倉庫証券

wharfinger's receipt 波止場〔埠頭〕管理人貨物受取証

◆Any notice served by registered mail or by telex as aforesaid shall be deemed served on the earlier of actual receipt or the expiry of 120 hours after posting. 上記のとおり書留郵便またはテレックスで送達された通知は, 実際の受領日と投函から120時間後のうちいずれか早いほうの日に送達されたものと見なすものとする. ◆In the circular sales transactions, Katokichi's affiliates and business clients recorded the repeated sale and purchase of products only on paper receipts. 循環取引で, 加卜吉の関連会社と法人顧客は, 繰り返し行われた商品の売買を架空の売上だけに計上していた. ◆The payment of the remuneration for Services shall be made by ABC within ten business days after the receipt of the invoice issued by XYZ. サービスに対する報酬の支払いは, XYZが発行した請求書の受領後10営業日以内に, ABCが支払うものとする. ◆We are in receipt of your kind letter of March 5 regarding abovementioned goods. 上記商品に関する3月5日付け貴状を拝受.

receive (動)受領する, 受け取る, 受信する
◆If some or all of the goods have not been received by the buyer on the termination of this contract, the buyer shall, in its sole discretion, cease to take delivery of the remaining goods and the seller shall return to the buyer any amounts paid in advance in respect of such goods. 本契約解除時に商品の一部または全部を買い主が受領していない場合, 買い主は, 買い主単独の選択で, 残存商品〔未引渡し商品〕の引取りを中止し, 売り主は当該商品に関して前払いで受領した代金を買い主に返還するものとする. ◆We have received your letter of August 15, from which we note that you are in the market for our products. 8月15日付け貴状を拝受しました. それによると貴社は当社製品をご入用とのこと, 確かに承(うけたまわ)りました.

receiver (名)管財人, 財産保全管理人, 荷受人

receivership proceedings 清算手続き
◆In the event of bankruptcy, insolvency, dissolution, modification, amalgamation, receivership

proceedings effecting the operation of its business or discontinuation of business for any reason and/or reorganization by the third party in the other party, either of the parties hereto shall have the absolute right to terminate this agreement without any notice whatsoever to the other party. 本契約のいずれか一方の当事者は, 相手方の破産, 支払い不能, 解散, 改組, 合併, 事業運営に影響を及ぼす清算手続き, または何らかの理由による事業中止および/または第三者による会社整理の場合には, 相手方に何ら一切の通知をしないで本契約を終了する絶対的な権利を持つものとする.

receiving (名)受領, 受入れ, 受け取ること, 荷受け (形)受領の, 受け取る方の, 受信の, 受像の, 迎えるための, 歓迎の

be on the receiving end of 〜を受ける立場になる, 〜の対象となる, 〜で嫌な思いをする

receiving and inspection department 受入れ検査部門

receiving and storing department 受入れ保管部門

receiving bank 受取銀行

receiving book 収納帳

receiving cargo under L/G 保証状荷渡し

receiving clerk 荷受係, 受入れ係

receiving end 受益者

receiving inspection 受入れ検査

receiving merchandise 荷受品

receiving note 積み荷受取証, 積み荷貨物指図書, 積み荷受取貨物指図書

receiving office 荷受事務所

receiving order (破産した財産の)管理命令(書), (裁判所の)管財人任命書

receiving party 受領当事者 (⇒rightfully)

receiving process 検品手続き

receiving quotation 受取相場, 受取勘定建て相場, 外貨建て相場 (=rate in foreign currency, receiver quotation)

receiving record 荷受記録

receiving report 受入れ報告書

receiving room 荷受室

receiving set (テレビやラジオの)受信機, 受像機

receiving stamp 受領印

receiving teller 収納係

◆This information was in the public domain at the time it was communicated to the receiving party by the disclosing party. この情報は, 開示当事者が受領当事者に通知した時点で公知であった.

recipient (名)受領者, 受信者, 受領国, 被援助国, 受取人, 受賞者, 受給者, 情報開示を受けた者, 容器

aid recipient　援助受入れ国, 援助受入れ側, 援助を受ける側

ODA recipient　政府開発援助 (ODA) 受入れ国

recipient government　借入国政府

recipient of the assistance　支援先

recipient of the benefits　受益者

recipient of the secret information　秘密情報の開示を受けた者

recipient party　開示を受けた当事者, 相手方
◆Commodity loans are used to import commodities such as industrial machinery, industrial raw materials, fertilizer, agricultural chemicals and machinery, and other various kinds of machinery, which are agreed upon beforehand between the Japanese and recipient governments. 商品借款は, 日本政府と借入国政府が前もって合意した商品 (工業資本財 [工業用機械], 工業用原材料, 肥料・農薬, 農機具, 各種機械など) の輸入のために使用される。

reciprocal　(形)相互の, 相互間の, 双方に作用する, 相補的な, 互恵的な, お返しの, 返礼の, 仕返しの, 逆の, 相対応する　(名)相互的なもの, 相対物, 対になるもの, 逆, 反対, 逆数, 反数

reciprocal account　相互勘定, 対応勘定

reciprocal arrangement　相互協定

reciprocal business　互恵主義

reciprocal buying　相互購買

reciprocal concession　相互互恵

reciprocal consignment　相互委託販売

reciprocal contract　双務契約

reciprocal duties　互恵関税　(=reciprocal tariff)

reciprocal (letter of) credit　同時開設信用状, 相殺信用状, 抱き合わせ信用状

reciprocal recognition　相互承認

reciprocal share holding　株式の相互保有, 株式の持ち合い, 株式持ち合い

reciprocal supply　相互供給

reciprocal trade　相互貿易, 相互通商, 互恵通商

Reciprocal Trade Agreement Act　互恵通商協定法, 互恵通商法

strategically reciprocal relationship　戦略的互恵関係

reciprocity　(名)相互取引, 相互性, 相互関係, 相互主義, 互恵主義, 相互作用, 相互互恵, 相互利益, 相互依存の関係 [状態], 互恵関係

equal reciprocity　相互平等主義

Japan-China reciprocity　日中の互恵関係

reciprocity agreement　互恵協約

reciprocity bill　相互主義法案

reciprocity legislation　相互主義法案

reciprocity theorem　相互性定理

reciprocity treaty　互恵条約

recitals　(名)契約書の前文, 契約書の説明部分, 契約の経緯, 経緯, 事実の詳述, 証書の備考部分　(=preamble)

recognize　(動)正式に認める, 承認する, 認知する
◆Distributor recognizes that all trademarks, designs, patents and other industrial property rights used or embodied in Products remain to be sole properties of Company, and shall not in any way dispute them. 代理店は, 本製品 (契約品) に使用または具体的に表示されているすべての商標, デザイン, 特許その他の工業所有権が依然として会社単独の所有物であることを認め, これについてはどんな方法でも争わないものとする。

reconstruction plan　再建計画
◆The firm envisioned negotiations with the U.S. equity fund over financing for restructuring in a reconstruction plan it formulated in June. 同社は, 経営合理化の資金調達に関しては, 6月に策定した再建計画でこの米国の投資ファンドとの交渉を見込んでいた。

record　(名)記録, 登記, 登録, 経歴, 略歴, 成績, 最高記録　(動)記録する, 登記・登録する, 表示する, 示す

full and accurate records and accounts　完全, 正確な記録と帳簿

of record or beneficially　登録株主としてまたは受益者 (実質的な所有者) として

records and books　記録と帳簿, 帳簿類　(=books and records)
◆No director of the new company shall be required to own of record or beneficially any shares of the stock of the new company. 新会社の取締役は, 登録株主としてまたは株式の受益者として新会社の株式を保有することを要求されないものとする。

records and accounts　記録と帳簿
◆The licensee shall make its records and accounts available for inspection by the licensor or its duly authorized representatives upon reasonable advance notice. ライセンシーは, (ライセンサーから) 合理的な事前の通知を受けたときは, ライセンサーまたはその正当な権限を持つ代理人の検査のためにライセンシーの記録と帳簿を提供するものとする。

records and reports　記録と報告
◆The licensee shall keep full and accurate records and accounts relating to the manufacture and sales of the licensed products. ライセンシーは, 許諾製品の製造, 販売に関する完全, 正確な記録と帳簿を保持するものとする。

recourse　(名)遡求 (そきゅう), 償還請求, 償還請求権 (手形などの振出人または裏書人に支払いを請求する権利), 第二次的の請求, 依頼,

頼みの綱, 手段

endorsement without recourse 遡求に応じない裏書き

without recourse 償還請求に応ぜず（振出人, 裏書人が手形に書く文句）, 遡求に応じない

without recourse credit 償還請求権なき信用状

without recourse to 〜に頼らずに, 〜に訴えることなく
◆ABC shall have no recourse against XYZ for any obligations under the original agreement assigned pursuant to this assignment agreement. ABCは, この譲渡契約に従って譲渡された原契約上の債務については, XYZに履行の請求を一切求めないものとする。

recover （動）財産, 権利などを回復する, 取り戻す, 回収する

recover competitiveness 競争力を回復する
◆Many Japanese manufacturers have been prompted to review their production in China with labor costs surging in China and domestic production recovering competitiveness thanks to the weaker yen. 中国で人件費が高騰しているのに加え, 円安進行で国内生産の競争力が回復しているため, 日本メーカーの多くは中国での生産（体制）を見直す動きが加速している。

recovery （名）回復, 景気回復, 景気や市場の持ち直し, 相場の回復, 回収, 再建, 復興
◆A recovery will be export-driven, dependent on U.S. growth and the yen's depreciation, instead of being led by increased domestic consumption and capital investment. 今後の景気回復は, 米経済の好転や円安を背景にした輸出主導型の回復で, 国内の個人消費や設備投資の伸びがその牽引役となるわけではない。

recovery in exports 輸出の回復, 輸出回復
◆The improvement in the real GDP was mainly due to a recovery in exports and policy initiatives under the government's stimulus packages. この実質GDP（国内総生産）の改善は, 主に輸出回復と, 政府の経済対策による政策効果によるものだ。

rectify or remedy 是正または矯正する

rectify trade imbalances 貿易不均衡を是正する
◆Rectifying trade imbalances mainly with China by devaluing the dollar is the top priority in Washington. ドル安により主に中国との貿易不均衡を是正するのが, 米国の最優先課題だ。

redeem （動）買い戻す, 抵当物を受け戻す, 社債や株式を償還する, 株式などを現金と交換する, 現金化する, 債務を弁済する, 取り戻す, 約束を実行する, 履行する, 名誉などを回復する

redistribution （名）再販売, 再販
◆Distributor's dealers shall be prohibited from selling Products for redistribution outside of Territory except as explicitly provided by EC law. 販売店のディーラーは, EC法に明文の規定がないかぎり, 販売区域外での本製品の再販売は禁止される。

Ref. No. 参照番号, 照会番号
Our Ref. No. 当社参照番号
Your Ref. No. 貴社参照番号

refer to 参照する, 照会する, 取り次ぐ, 言及する, 触れる, 記載する, 〜と呼ぶ, 適用する, 示す, 指す, 〜に関係する, 〜に関連する, 調べる （⇒shift）
◆Supplier shall refer to Distributor any and all inquiries or orders for Products which Supplier may receive from any party in Territory. 供給者は, 供給者が販売区域内の一切の関係者から受けた本製品の引合いまたは注文を販売店に取り次ぐものとする。◆This letter of credit shall refer to this agreement by its number. この信用状は, その契約番号により本契約に言及するものとする。

referee （名）仲裁の裁定人

reference （名）参照, 参考, 照会, 信用照会先, 身元保証, 人物証明書, （仲裁人への）委託［付託］

bank reference 銀行照会, 銀行信用照会先
reference in case of need 予備支払い人指定
reference sample 参考見本
trade reference 同業照会, 同業者信用照会先, 信用照会先, 商業興信所 （=commercial reference）
◆The headings to the Articles of this agreement are to facilitate reference only, do not form a part of this agreement and shall not in any way affect the interpretation of this agreement. 本契約条項の見出しは, 参照の便宜だけの目的のもので, 本契約の一部を構成するものではなく, いかなる場合でも本契約の解釈に影響を与えないものとする。

referral （名）照会, 取り次ぎ

refund （動）払い戻す, 返済する, 還付する, 弁済する, 借り換える, 償還する
◆In case of any claim for which the seller is responsible, the seller has the option to either repair the defects on the seller's account or to replace the defective products or parts thereof or to refund the purchaser damages. 売り主が責任を負うべきクレームの場合, 売り主は, 売り主の勘定で瑕疵（かし）を修理するか, 瑕疵ある製品または部品を取り替えるか, 買い主に損害額を払い戻すかのいずれかの選択権を持つ。

refusal （名）拒絶, 拒否, 取捨選択権, 優先権, 先買権

first refusal 株式の優先先買権, 先買権, 先買権行使の拒絶（refusalは「優先権, 選択権」という意味で, optionと同義。株式の譲渡に先買権の制約がある場合, 株式の先買権行使の拒絶があってはじめて第三者に株式を売却できるようになる）
refusal to issue licenses 政府許可書の発行拒絶

refuse （動）断る, 拒否する, 拒絶する, 拒（こ
ば）む, 辞退する
◆The U.S. government refused to provide public
funds to keep Lehman Brothers afloat. 米政府は、
リーマン・ブラザーズの破たんを避けるための公
的資金の注入［投入］を拒んだ。◆When Washing-
ton refuses to comply with the WTO's ruling, the
EU will impose retaliatory tariffs on U.S. products. 米国が世界貿易機関（WTO）の決定に従わな
かった場合、欧州連合（EU）は米国製品に報復関税
を発動する方針だ。

regional conflicts　地域紛争
◆Regional conflicts stemming from religious or
ethnic animosity, as well as the proliferation
of weapons of mass destruction, pose a serious
threat to the international community. 宗教や民
族の対立が原因の地域紛争や、大量破壊兵器の拡
散は、国際社会にとって大きな脅威となっている。

regional economic partnership　地域経済
連携, 地域経済連携協定
◆Tokyo is to kick off preparatory talks with
members of the Association of Southeast Asian
Nations（ASEAN）to try to realize a regional
economic partnership with FTAs at its center. 日
本は、東南アジア諸国連合（ASEAN）とFTA（自由
貿易協定）を柱とする地域経済連携協定の実現をめ
ざして準備協議を始めることにしている。

regional free trade area　地域自由貿易圏
◆Leaders of the Asia-Pacific Economic Cooperation forum adopted a road map toward an envisioned regional free trade area which would
cover about 60 percent of the world economy.
アジア太平洋経済協力会議（APEC）の各国首脳は、
世界経済の6割をカバーする地域自由貿易圏構想の
工程表を採択した。

**regional integration and cooperation in
trade**　通商面での地域統合や地域連携
◆Until now, Japan has kept a low profile concerning such efforts as strengthening regional integration and cooperation in trade. これまで日本
は、通商面での地域統合や地域連携の強化策につ
いて目立った行動は控えてきた。

regional production network　地域的な生産
ネットワーク
◆As Indonesia had not been as deeply integrated
as Thailand and Malaysia in the regional production network, the impact of the global financial
crisis of 2008 on Indonesia was limited. インド
ネシアはタイやマレーシアほど地域的な生産ネット
ワークに深く組み込まれていなかったため、2008
年の世界金融危機の影響は少なかった。

regionally　（副）地域的に, 地域で, 地方で, 局
部的に
◆FTAs are a regime under which import tariffs
are eliminated bilaterally or regionally. 自由貿易
協定（FTA）は、2国間で、または地域で輸入関税を
撤廃する制度だ。

register　（動）登録する, 登記する, 正式に記
録する, 郵便物を書留にする, 〜を示す

◆The owner did not agree to register the lease,
so the government's right as leaseholder has not
been registered. 所有者が賃借権の登記に同意しな
かったため、政府の賃借権はまだ設定されていな
い。◆This manufacturing facility was registered
for international quality standard ISO 9001. この
製造施設［製造工場］は、国際品質基準「ISO 9001」
の認定を受けた。

register of shareholders　株主名簿
◆ABC undertakes to cause the Company to acknowledge the transfer of the Shares as of the
closing date and to register such transfer in its
register of shareholders on the closing date. ABC
は、クロージングの日に本株式を譲渡することを
本会社に確認させ、当該譲渡をクロージングの日
にその株主名簿に登録させることを約束する。

registered　（形）登録された, 登記された, 記
録された, 記名の, 書留扱いの, 公認の
registered name　登録名
registered number　登録番号
registered or not　登録の如何を問わず, 登録
の有無を問わず
registered owner　登録所有者, 登録済み商標
権者, 名義上の証券保有者

-registered　（連結形）〜船籍の, 〜登録の
a Japanese-registered vessel　日本国籍の船舶
a Panamanian freighter　パナマ船籍の貨物船
the SEC-registered US tranche　SEC登録の米
国トランシュ

registered airmail　書留航空郵便
（=registered airmail letter）
◆All notices, demands and other communications which shall or may be given under this
agreement shall be made by registered airmail,
postage prepaid, or cable. 本契約に基づいて行う
または行うことができる通知、要求、その他の通
信は、すべて料金前納［料金前払い］の書留航空郵
便か電信で行うものとする。

registration　（名）登録, 登記, 正式記録, 登録
事項, 記録事項, 登録物件, 名義書換え
date of registration and renewal　登録日と更
新日
registration of trademarks　商標登録
status of registration　登録の状況

regular　（形）一定の, 不変の, 規則正しい, 秩
序正しい, 正規の, 正式の, 本職の, 定期的な,
定期の, 定例の, 習慣的な, 常連の, 通常の, い
つもの, 一般の, 並みの, 普通の, 標準サイズ
の, 完全な, まぎれもない, 感じのいい, 均整の
とれた, 整った, （党の）公認の, レギュラー

regular general shareholders meeting
定時株主総会, 定例株主総会
（=regular general meeting of shareholders）
◆At the regular general shareholders meeting of
Tokyo Electric Power Co., de facto nationalization of TEPCO was approved. 東京電力の定時株

主総会で、同社の事実上の国有化が承認された。

regular written report　書面による定期報告, 書面による定期レポート, 定期報告書
◆The Licensee shall furnish regular written report specified by the Licensor to Licensor in order to disclose in full detail pertinent information and data in connection with the sale of the Product. ライセンシーは, 契約品の販売に関する関連情報とデータを十分詳細に開示するため, ライセンサーが指定する定期報告書をライセンサーに提出するものとする。

regulation　(名)規則, 規定, 規程, 規制, 統制, 統括, 取締り, 管理, 調節, 調整, 法規, 法令, 行政規則, 通達, レギュレーション
(⇒catch-all regulations, food shortage)
advertising regulation　広告規制
building regulations　建築規則
business regulations　業務規定, 業務規則
comprehensive regulation　包括規制
credit regulation　信用規制, 信用統制, 信用規則
customs regulation　関税規制, 税関規制
easing of regulations　規制緩和
economic regulation　経済的規制
Export Administration Regulations　米国輸出規則, EAR
financial regulations　金融規制
government regulation　政府の規制, 政府による規制, 政府規制
governmental regulations or orders　政令・規制, 政令または規則
in-house regulations　社内規定
international regulations　国際法
issuing regulations　発行規制
noise regulation　騒音規制
operating regulations　事務取扱い規則
organization regulation　組織規程
price regulation　価格規制, 価格調整
punitive regulation　懲罰的規制
regulation on total emissions　排ガスの総量規制
regulations on investment funds　投資ファンド規制
regulations on large-lot loans　大口融資規制
regulations on stock prices　株価規制
relaxed regulations　規制の緩和
(=relaxation of regulations)
rules and regulations　規約
safety regulations　安全規則
SEC regulations　SECの規制
self-regulation　自主規制
◆As the centerpiece of deregulation measures,

the government plans to create "national strategic special deregulation zones" to attract companies and talented workers from all over the world by boldly relaxing regulations in the zones. 規制緩和策の目玉として, 政府は「国家戦略特区」を創設し, 特区内で大胆な規制緩和を断行して, 世界中から企業や有能な人材を集める方針だ。◆The U.S. government finalized regulations that will force automakers to nearly double the average gas mileage of all new cars and trucks they sell in the United States by 2025. 米政府は, 2025年までに米国内で販売する新車 (乗用車とトラック) の燃料1ガロン当たりの平均走行距離を, すべて現行の約2倍とすることを自動車メーカーに義務付ける規制策を, 最終決定した。

regulators　(名)規制当局, 規制機関, 規制責任者
antitrust regulators　独占禁止規制当局, 反トラスト規制当局
federal and state regulators　連邦・州規制当局
financial regulators　金融当局
government regulators　規制当局
securities regulators　証券業務規制当局, 証券規制機関
self-regulators　自主規制機関
U.S. federal antitrust regulators　米連邦反トラスト規制当局
◆U.S. federal antitrust regulators have cleared the way for the proposed merger between Sony Music Entertainment and BMG, the music unit of the German media conglomerate Bertelsmann AG. 米連邦反トラスト規制当局 (米連邦取引委員会) は, ソニーと独複合メディア大手ベルテルスマンの音楽部門のBMGとの事業統合案を承認した。

regulatory　(形)規制上の, 法規制の, 規制当局の, 監督当局の, 取り締まる
regulatory approvals　規制上の許認可, 監督機関 [規制当局] の承認 [認可]
regulatory barrier　規制上の障害
regulatory body [agency]　規制機関, 監督機関, 規制当局
regulatory capital (adequacy) ratio　自己資本規制比率
regulatory certification　法規認証
regulatory environment　規制環境
regulatory provision　法令
regulatory relief　規制の適用除外
regulatory risk　規制上のリスク
regulatory sanction　規制当局による処分

regulatory authorities　規制当局, 監督当局, 規制機関, 監督機関
◆Amid Libor scandal, Britain's financial regulatory authorities have embarked on full-scale investigations into the matter. ライボー (ロンドン銀行間取引金利) の不正操作問題を受けて, 英金融

監督当局が(問題の)本格調査に乗り出した。

regulatory reform 規制改革
◆The framework of a Free Trade Area of the Asia-Pacific is aimed at liberalizing trade and investment as well as the elimination of nontariff barriers, regulatory reform and smoother logistics. アジア太平洋自由貿易地域(FTAAP)の枠組みは、貿易や投資の自由化のほか、非関税障壁の撤廃、規制改革、物流の円滑化などを目指している。

reimburse (動)経費などを返済する、弁済する、償還する、払い戻す、返還する、弁償する、賠償する
◆In the event that Supplier is requested to assist Distributor in arranging for transportation, Distributor shall reimburse Supplier for all costs relating to such arrangements, including, without limitation, insurance, transportation, loading and unloading, handling and storage following their delivery to Distributor. 供給者が販売店から運送手配の支援を要請された場合、販売店は、供給者が(本製品を)販売店へ引き渡した後の保険、運送、積み下ろし、貨物取扱い、保管料などの関連費用を、すべて供給者に償還するものとする。

reimbursement (名)返済、弁済、代金支払い、代金回収、償還、払戻し、精算、返還、補償、弁償、賠償
for reimbursement 代金回収のため、(注文などの)代金支払いのため
reimbursement bank (手形買取り金)償還銀行
reimbursement claim 還付請求
reimbursement credit 支払い条件付き信用(買取り銀行や割引銀行から発行銀行またはその指定銀行あてに手形を振り出して、資金回収を行うことを指定した信用状)
reimbursement draft 償還手形
reimbursement obligation 補償債務
reimbursement of expenses 経費の弁済(=expense reimbursement)
reimbursement service 補償サービス(損害が発生した場合に、保険者が被保険者に保険金を支払うこと)
◆For reimbursement, we have applied to our bankers for an L/C to be opened. (本注文に対する)代金支払いのため、当社は銀行に信用状の発行を申請しました。◆For reimbursement, we have drawn upon you through ABC Bank a draft at 90 d/s for $50,000 against your order No. 50. 代金回収のため、当社は貴社注文第50号に対しABC銀行を通じて50,000ドルの一覧後90日払い為替手形を貴社宛てに振り出しました。◆Through 2014 we expensed these reimbursements as incurred. 2014年度までは、この返済額を発生時に費用計上していました。

reimport (動)再輸入する、逆輸入する (名)再輸入、逆輸入
reimport entry 再輸入申告書

reimportation (名)再輸入、逆輸入

reinsurance (名)再保険、再保険額
excess of loss reinsurance 超過損害再保険
excess reinsurance 超過額再保険
obligatory reinsurance 義務再保険
reinsurance amount 再保険金額
reinsurance assets 再保険資産
reinsurance claims 再保険金
reinsurance collectibles 再保険請求権
reinsurance commission 再保険料、再保険手数料、再保険配当金
reinsurance contract 再保険契約 (⇒reinsurance company)
reinsurance for excess 超過額再保険
reinsurance losses 再保険金
reinsurance of second risk 第二次危険再保険
reinsurance policy 再保険証券
reinsurance rate 再保険料
reinsurance slip 再保険申込み書
reinsurance transaction 再保険取引
reinsurance treaty 再保険特約
treaty reinsurance 特約再保険
◆All reinsurances shall be effected in the original currency. 再保険は、すべて元受通貨で行うものとする。

reinsurance cession 出再契約
◆The Reinsurer agrees to accept all reinsurance cessions automatically up to the limits shown in the annexes to this Agreement. 再保険会社は、本協定書の補遺に示す限度まですべての出再契約を自動的に引き受けることに同意する。

reinsurance company 再保険会社
◆Nonlife insurance companies used to disperse the risk of large contracts with new corporate clients through reinsurance contracts with other insurance or reinsurance companies. 損保各社は従来、他の保険会社もしくは再保険会社と再保険契約を結んで、新規顧客企業と大型契約を結ぶリスクを分散してきた。

reinsurance conditions 再保険条件
◆The parties to this Agreement shall agree new reinsurance conditions in the case of significant changes. 重大な変更が生じた場合、協定当事者は、新たな再保険条件に合意するものとする。

reinsure (動)再保険をかける、再保険を付ける
risks reinsured hereunder 本協定に従って再保険された危険[契約]
risks reinsured under this agreement 本協定に従って再保険されている危険

reinsured (形)再保険に入っている、再保険付きの
reinsured portions 再保険部分
reinsured sum at risk 再保険危険保険金額

the reinsured　被再保険者

the sum at risk reinsured　危険再保険金額

reinsurer　（名）再保険会社

◆Any amounts exceeding the limits of automatic cover shall be offered to the Reinsurer for facultative acceptance. 自動再保険の適用限度を超える額は、任意受再のために再保険会社に申し出るものとする。◆The Company agrees to cede to the Reinsurer such shares of all insurances covered by this Agreement as are set forth in the annexes（Schedule and any Addenda）to this Agreement. 元受会社は、本協定対象の全保険のうち、本協定の補遺（特別条項や追加条項）に明記した部分を再保険会社に出再することに合意する。

reject　（動）拒絶する、拒否する、認めない、廃棄する、排除する　（名）廃棄物、拒絶品、不合格品

rejected samples or models　見本またはモデルの拒絶, 拒絶された見本またはモデル

rejected shares　拒絶された株式
　　（⇒bona fide offer）

◆In case any of samples or models submitted by the licensee is rejected by the licensor, the licensee shall not manufacture or distribute such rejected samples or models under the trademarks. ライセンシーが提出した見本またはモデルをライセンサーが拒絶した場合、ライセンシーは、拒絶された見本またはモデルを本商標で製造または販売しないものとする。

rejection　（名）拒絶, 拒否, 廃棄, 排除

◆Such inspection shall not, in any way, prejudice the purchaser's right of inspection of the products after the delivery at the final destination or rejection of the defective products. この検査は、最終目的地での引渡し後に本製品を検査する買い主の権利、または瑕疵（かし）ある製品を拒絶する買い主の権利をいかなる意味でも損なわないものとする。

rejection or disposal　拒絶または処分

◆The seller shall reimburse the purchaser for any loss, damages or expense incurred in connection with such rejection or disposal. 売り主は、買い主に対して当該拒絶または処分に関連して生じた損失, 損害または費用の補償をするものとする。

related to　～に関する、～に関連する、～に関して、～に近い

◆Commencing on the date of this agreement until the Closing, Buyer shall be permitted to perform such due diligence investigation related to the transactions contemplated by this agreement as Buyer deems necessary and appropriate in its discretion. 本契約締結日からクロージングまで、買い主は、本契約で意図されている取引に関して買い主が買い主の判断で必要かつ適切と考えるデュー・ディリジェンス調査を行うことができるものとする。

relations　（名）関係, 広報, リレーションズ

bilateral relations　両国関係, 二国間関係

business relations　取引関係, 業務上の関係, 事業上の関係, ビジネス関係

capital and business relations with　～との資本・業務関係

close cooperative relations　密接な協力関係

industrial relations　労使関係

international relations　国際関係

investor relations　対投資家関係, 投資家向け広報, 財務広報, インベスター・リレーションズ, IR

partner relations　提携先との関係

◆Lawmakers voted 260-170 to continue for a year what is now called normal trade relations（NTR）and used to be called most favored nations（MFN）trade status. 議員が260対170で票決して、これまで最恵国待遇と呼ばれていた（中国に対する）正常通商関係を1年間継続することになった。◆The value of South Korea's trade with China since it established diplomatic relations with Beijing has expanded to such an extent that it has surpassed its combined trade with Japan and the United States. 韓国が中国と国交を樹立して以来、韓国の対中貿易額は、対日・対米の貿易総額を凌駕（りょうが）するまでに拡大している。

relations with China　中国との関係

◆Japan's exports and production have been reduced because of the slowdown of foreign economies and the worsening of relations with China. 海外経済の減速と日中関係の悪化で、日本の輸出や生産は低迷している。

relationship　（名）関係, 関連, 結びつき, 取引先

arm's length relationship　商業ベースの取引関係

build relationships of trust with　～との信頼関係を築く

business relationship　取引関係

causal relationship　因果関係

collaborative relationship　協力関係

contractual relationship　契約関係

cooperative relationship　協力関係

corporate relationship　企業関係

currency relationships　為替相場, 為替レート

customer relationship　顧客関係, 顧客との良好な取引関係

debtor-creditor relationship　債権者・債務者関係, 債権債務関係

economic relationship　経済関係

interbusiness relationship　企業間関係, ビジネス相互間の関係

legal relationship　法的関係

principal-agent relationship　本人と代理人の関係

relationship of the parties　当事者の関係, 当事

者の関係条項

◆The relationship hereby established between Company and Distributor shall be that of seller and buyer on principal to principal basis. 本契約により会社と代理店が設定する関係は、本人対本人をベースとする売り主と買い主の関係とする。

relative documents 関連書類

◆Title with respect to each shipment of the products shall pass from the seller to purchaser when the seller negotiates relative documents and receives proceeds from the negotiating bank for such shipment with effect retrospect to the time of such shipment. 本製品の各船積みに関する所有権は、売り主が関連書類を手形買取り銀行に提出して本製品の代金を当該銀行から受領した時点で、当該船積み時に遡及して売り主から買い主に移転するものとする。

release （名）発表, 公表, 公開, 権利の放棄, 免責, 責任免除, 契約の解除, 債務の消滅, 解雇, 解任 （動）発表する, 公表する, 公開する, 権利などを放棄する, 譲渡する, 移転する, 責任を免除する, 義務などから解放する（=remise)

release and covenant not to sue　免除と訴訟を提起しない約束, 免除と提訴しない約束, 免除と訴訟を取り下げる約束

release of assigning party　譲渡人の免責

release of obligations　義務履行の免除

release one from one's debt　〜の債務を免除する

release order　航空貨物引渡し指図書

◆The guarantor hereby agrees that no such modification, amendment or supplement shall release, affect or impair its liability under this guarantee. 保証人はここに、このような変更、修正または補足が本保証書に基づく保証人の責任を免除せず、またその責任に影響を与えず、その責任を縮減するものでもないことに同意する。◆The TSE does not plan to release details on names of stock issues or methods of short selling. 東証は、空売りの対象の個別銘柄や空売りの手口などの詳細については、公表しない方針だ。

relevant （形）関連した, 関連する, 関係のある, 当該の, 適切な, 当を得た, 要点をついた, 的を射た

relevant and incidental matter　関連・付随事項

relevant copy of the Product　本製品の当該複製

relevant matters　関連事項

relevant period　当該期間, 当該年度

relevant provisions in this agreement　本契約書の関連条項, 本契約中の関連規定, 本契約書中の関連条項

◆Unless otherwise agreed, relevant provisions in this agreement shall be applicable to each individual contract to be made hereunder between the parties. 別段の合意がないかぎり、本契約書

の関連条項は、本契約に基づいて両当事者が締結する個別の契約にそれぞれ適用されるものとする。

reliability （名）信頼, 信頼性, 信頼度, 確実性

automobile reliability survey　自動車信頼度調査

product reliability　製品［商品］の信頼性

reliability survey　信頼度調査

◆Sony's battery recall problem hurts the company's reliability as a supplier. ソニーの充電回収問題は、同社のサプライヤーとしての信頼性を損ねている。◆The number of Twitter followers is used as a barometer of companies' popularity and reliability. ツイッターのフォロワー（閲覧者）の数は、企業の人気度や信頼度のバロメーターになっている。

relief （名）救済, 救済手段, 救済措置, 請求の趣旨, 軽減, 緩和, 除去　（⇒equitable relief)

equitable relief　エクイティ上の救済, 衡平法上の救済

injunctive relief　差止命令による救済, 差止救済

interim relief　仮処分や仮差し押さえなどの中間的な救済, 暫定的救済

relief demanded　請求の趣旨

◆The arbitrators shall have the authority to order such discovery and production of documents, including the depositions of party witnesses, and to make such orders for interim relief, including injunctive relief, as they may deem just and equitable. 仲裁人は、当事者の証人の宣誓証言［証言録取書］を含めて文書の開示と提出を命じる権限と、差止救済を含めて仲裁人が正義かつ衡平と見なす暫定的救済を命じる権限を持つものとする。

relieve （動）救済する, 解放する, 免除する, 解任する, 取り除く

◆The assignment under this assignment agreement shall not relieve ABC of any of its obligations under the original agreement. この譲渡契約に基づく契約の譲渡によって、ABCはその原契約上の債務履行の責任を免除されないものとする。

relocate （動）移す, 移動する, 移転する, 移設する, 再配置する, 配置転換する

◆As labor costs in China are expected to continue rising, labor-intensive industries such as fashion and electronics will keep relocating their manufacturing bases to Southeast Asia and other regions with cheaper labor. 中国の人件費上昇は今後も続く見通しなので、アパレルや家電などの労働集約型産業では、生産拠点を中国より低賃金の東南アジアなどに移す流れが続くものと思われる。◆Both foreign-capitalized and Japanese companies are forced to relocate their headquarters functions overseas. 外資系企業も日本企業も、本社機能を海外に移さざるを得なくなっている。

remain （動）〜のままである, まだ〜されないままだ, 依然として〜だ, 今なお〜だ, 〜から抜け出していない, 引き続き〜だ, 今後も〜

だ, 〜で推移する, 根強い

remain in effect 依然として有効である, 有効に存続する, 〜の間有効である, 〜まで効力が存続する

remain in force 有効に存続する （⇒as long as）

remain in force and effect 依然として有効である, 有効に存続する

remain responsible to 〜に対して引き続き責任を負う, 〜に対して引き続き責任がある

remain subject to all the terms of this agreement 継続して本契約の条件に従う
◆Bilateral relations between both Japan and South Korea will remain stalemated at least for the time being. 日韓両国の二国間関係は, 少なくとも当面, 停滞が続くと思われる。◆Even if Toyota is able to compete more effectively thanks to the weaker yen, competition with low-priced models and other makers in emerging countries will remain fierce. 円安でトヨタの競争力が上がっても, 新興国での低価格モデル・他社との競争はやはり激しい。

remain in full force and effect 完全に効力が存続する, 全面的に有効に存続する, 依然として完全に有効である, 継続して完全に効力がある
◆All the remaining terms of this agreement shall remain in full force and effect. 本契約の残存規定は, すべて完全に効力が存続するものとする。

remaining （形）残りの, 残存する, 残余の

remaining interest 残余権

remaining life 残存期間, 残存年数, 残存耐用年数

remaining loan balance ローン残高

remaining terms of this agreement 本契約の残存規定, 本契約の残りの条項
（=remaining provisions of this agreement）
◆Following the tender offer, Oji Paper would acquire the remaining Hokuetsu shares through a share swap to turn it into a wholly owned subsidiary. 株式公開買付け（TOB）後に, 王子製紙は, 株式交換で残りの北越製紙の株を取得して北越製紙を完全子会社化する。

remaining goods 残存商品, 未引渡しの商品
◆If some or all of the goods have not been received by the buyer on the termination of this contract, the buyer shall, in its sole discretion, cease to take delivery of the remaining goods and the seller shall return to the buyer any amounts paid in advance in respect of such goods. 本契約解除時に商品の一部または全部を買い主が受領していない場合, 買い主は, 買い主単独の選択で, 残存商品［未引渡し商品］の引取りを中止し, 売り主は当該商品に関して前払いで受領した代金を買い主に返還するものとする。

remaining provisions hereof 本契約の残存規定, 本契約の残りの規定

◆In case any one or more of the provisions of this agreement are held invalid, illegal or unenforceable in any respect, the validity, legality and enforceability of the remaining provisions hereof shall not be in any way affected or impaired thereby, except to the extent that giving effect to the remaining provisions would be unjust or inequitable. 本契約の一つ以上の規定がいずれかの点で無効, 違法または強制不能と判断された場合, 残存規定の実施が不公正または不均衡となる範囲を除いて, 本契約の残存規定の有効性, 合法性と強制可能性はその影響を受けることはなく, またそれによって損なわれることはないものとする。

remedial （形）（病気を）治療する, 治療の, 改善するための, 救済の, 矯正の, 矯正的な, 補習の

remedial action 救済措置, 改善措置

remedial expense 補償費用

remedial measures 救済策, 救済措置

remedial provision 救済規定

remedial punishment 矯正的処罰

remedy （名）対応策, 対策, 改善法, 薬, 治療, 治療法, 治療薬, 療法, 処方箋, 救済, 救済方法, 救済手段, 救済請求権, 救済措置, 措置, 補償, 権利回復手段

civil remedy 民事上の救済手段

court remedy 訴訟による救済方法

discretionary remedy 裁量的救済方法

equitable remedy 衡平法上の救済［救済手段］, エクイティ上の救済

explicit legal remedies 明示的な法的救済措置

injunctive remedy 差止命令による救済, 差止めによる救済

legal remedy 法律上の救済方法, 法的救済, コモン・ロー上の救済, 法的救済手段, 法的救済措置 （=remedy at law）

remedies cumulative 救済方法の非排他性［累積性］

remedies for the strong yen 円高対策 （⇒sourcing）

remedies or relief 救済, 救済手段, 救済方法, 救済手段または救済

remedy for economic stagnation 不況対策

remedy for the problem 問題への対策

remedy in equity エクイティ上の救済, 衡平法上の救済

remedy under 〜に基づく救済

seek remedy in court 裁判所に［裁判所に訴えて］救済を求める

trade remedies 貿易救済措置
◆The remedies under this clause shall be the sole compensation for the damages caused by such

delay. 本条項に基づく補償は、当該遅延で生じた損害の唯一の補償とする。

remind （動）〜に注意する, 〜に気づかせる
◆You are kindly reminded that this agreement will become null and void after the midnight of May 31, 2018. 本契約は2018年5月31日以降無効になることを、ご承知おきください。

remit （動）送金する
◆Within sixty（60）days after the end of March, June, September and December, Licensee shall remit the amount calculated in accordance with the preceding Article. 3月、6月、9月、12月の末日から60日以内に、ライセンシーは、前条に従って算定した金額を送金しなければならない。

remittance （名）送金, 外国送金, 振込み, 送金額, 送金高 （⇒guaranteed minimum royalty）
a ban on remittances from Japan to North Korea 日本から北朝鮮への送金停止
bank remittance　銀行送金為替, 送金為替
cash remittance　現金送金
ordinary remittance　並み為替
remittance advice　送金通知書, 送金案内書
remittance bill　送金為替, 送金伝票
remittance check　送金小切手
supply against remittance upon arrival of goods with 1% discount　着払い送金ベース1%引きで供給する
take steps to make the remittance　送金実施のための手を打つ
the amount of remittance　送金の金額, 送金する金額
the method of remittance　送金方法
◆The revised Foreign Exchange and Foreign Trade Law allows Japan to suspend or limit remittances and trade with North Korea. 改正外国為替及び外国貿易法によると、北朝鮮に関して日本は送金や貿易を停止・制限することができる。◆We enclose the shipping documents covering the goods and expect your remittance in due course. 契約品の船積み書類を同封し、期日どおりのご送金を期待しております。

remittance fees　送金手数料, 振込み手数料
◆Overseas remittance fees are currently several thousand yen per transfer. 海外への送金手数料は現在、送金1回に付き数千円かかる。

removal （名）除去, 撤去, 抹消, 移動, 移転, 免職, 罷免（ひめん）, 解任 （⇒resignation）

remuneration （名）報酬, 給料, 代償, 報償
◆The payment of the remuneration for Services shall be made by ABC within ten business days after the receipt of the invoice issued by XYZ. サービスに対する報酬の支払いは、XYZが発行した請求書の受領後10営業日以内に、ABCが支払うものとする。

render （動）提供する, 供与する, 与える, 提

出する, 交付する, 引き渡す, 納付する, 支払う, 返済する, 履行する, 行う, 判決を言い渡す, 宣告する
◆Commencing on the effective date and continuing throughout the term of this agreement, XYZ shall, upon ABC's request, render to ABC the services and assistance. 本契約の発効日から有効期間中を通して、XYZは、ABCの要請に応じてサービスと指導をABCに提供するものとする。◆The parties hereto agree to abide by and perform in accordance with any award rendered by the arbitrator in such arbitration proceedings. 本契約当事者は、上記の仲裁手続きで仲裁人が下した判断を遵守し、その判断に従って履行することに同意する。

renewal （名）刷新, 更新, 書換え, 書換え継続, 期限延長, 自動継続, 再開, 再生, 復活, 回復, 再燃, 再開発, リニューアル
automatic renewal　自動更新
renewal fee　更新料, 更新手数料, 書換え手数料
renewal fund　設備の更新資金
renewal note　書換え約束手形, 切替え手形［約束手形］
renewal notice　保険継続依頼通知書
renewal of a draft　手形の書換え
renewal of a loan　融資の借換え
renewal of an exchange contract　為替予約の更新
renewal of policy　保険契約の更新, 保険の更新
renewal option　更新選択権
renewal premium　更新保険料, 継続保険料
subscription renewal　予約の更新

renewal term　更新期間
◆This agreement may be terminated prior to the expiration of the initial term or any renewal term hereof by either party upon service of prior written notice to the other party. 本契約は、いずれかの当事者が他方当事者に事前通知書を送達することにより、本契約の当初期間または更新期間が満了する前に終了させることができる。

rent （名）地代, 家賃, 賃料, 賃借料, 不動産使用料 （=rental）

rental contract　賃貸借契約
◆A 20-year rental contract was concluded between the government and the landlord. 政府と所有者（地主）は、20年の賃貸借契約を結んだ。

reorganization, dissolution, liquidation or winding up　会社更生、解散、清算または整理

repay （動）払い戻す, 返済する, 返金する

repayment of the loan　借入金の返済, ローンの返済, 返済条項

repayment schedule　返済計画, 返済予定表

replace （動）〜に取って代わる, 入れ替える,

置き換える, 取り替える, 交換する
◆The whole provisions of Article V of the original agreement shall be wholly deleted and replaced by the following: 原契約第5条の全規定は, 全文削除して次の規定に置き換えるものとする。

replacement (名)後任者, 後継者, 交換, 取替え, 置き換え, 入れ替え, 代替, 交換要員, 代替品, 返済, 返却, 復職
◆In case of the death, resignation or other removal of a director prior to the expiration of his term, the parties hereto agree to cast their votes as shareholders, so as to appoint as his replacement a director nominated by the party hereto who has nominated the director whose death, resignation or other removal was the cause of such vacancy. 取締役の任期満了前に取締役が死亡, 辞任またはその他の理由で退任した場合, 本契約当事者は, その死亡, 辞任その他の理由による退任で当該欠員を生じさせた取締役を指名した本契約当事者が後任取締役を指名できるように, 株主としてその議決権を行使することに合意する。

replacements or substitutes 取替え品または代替品
◆The purchaser may at its option procure replacements or substitutes for the products for the seller's account from other sources at such price and time as the purchaser may deem reasonable. 買い主は, その裁量により, 買い主が合理的と見なす価格と時期に, 他の供給元から売り主の勘定で本製品の取替え品または代替品を調達できるものとする。

reply (動)答える, 返事をする, 応答する, 応じる, 応酬する, 応戦する, 再抗弁する (名)返事, 返答, 回答, 応答, 応酬, 応戦, 再抗弁
await a reply 返事を待つ
claim notice & its reply letter 事故通知書と運送人からの回答
closing date for replies 招請状への返答期限
give a reply 返事を出す
postpone a reply 返事を延ばす
reply for ～を代表して謝辞を述べる, ～を代表して挨拶(あいさつ)する
reply to a question 質問に答える
reply to the invitation 招待に対して返事を出す
send a reply 返事を送る
◆We are looking forward to a favorable reply from you pretty soon. 吉報を早急にいただけますよう, お待ち申しております。◆We would appreciate your immediate reply as time is running short. 時間がないので至急, ご返事をいただきたい。◆Your prompt reply would be highly appreciated. 早急にご返事いただければ, 有り難い。

report (動)報告する, 伝える, 報道する, 取材する, 公表する, 発表する, 通報する, 届け出る, 表示する, 計上する, (～の)監督下にある, 直属する

report back to ～に(折り返し)報告する, (調査後に)～に報告する
report directly to ～の直属である, ～の監督下にある
report heavy losses 巨額の損失を計上する
report the allowance for bad debts 貸倒れ引当金を設定する
◆In favorable settlements of accounts for fiscal 2013, companies one after another reported record high profits, buoyed by the weakening yen and a surge in demand just ahead of a hike in the consumption tax rate. 2013年度の好決算で, 円安や消費増税前の(駆け込み)需要増が追い風となって, 最高益を更新する企業が相次いだ。◆Shinsei and Aozora banks intend to report their decision to scrap the merger deal to the Financial Services Agency. 新生銀行とあおぞら銀行は, 両行の合併計画撤回[断念]の決定を金融庁に伝える意向だ。◆The company failed to report a total of about ¥5 billion including simple accounting errors. 同社は, 単純な経理ミスを含めて総額で約50億円を申告しなかった。

report (名)報告, 報告書, 申告書, 報道, レポート
accident report 事故報告
annual report 年次報告書, 年報, アニュアル・レポート
audit report 監査報告書
business report 営業報告書, 事業報告書, ビジネス・レポート
confidential report 秘密[秘密指定の]報告書
credit report 信用調査報告書, 信用調書
draft report 報告書案
earnings report 決算報告書
final report 最終報告書
follow-up report 追加報告書
funding report 収支報告書
half-year report 半期報告書, 中間事業報告書
import and export report 輸出入申告書
interim financial report 中間財務報告, 中間財務報告書
interim report 中間報告書
landing report 陸揚げ報告[報告書], 陸揚げ故障報告
management report 経営者報告, 経営者からのご報告
midterm report 中間報告, 中間決算
monthly report 月次報告書, 月報
offense report 被害届
preliminary report 暫定報告書, 速報, 速報値
press report 新聞報道
progress report 経過報告, 進捗度報告, 中間報告書

R

qualified report　限定意見

quarterly report　四半期報告書, 四季報

report card　成績通知表, 成績報告書, 通信簿, 成績

report of independent auditors　監査報告書

report stage　（英議会での）報告審議

sales report　営業報告書

statue report　現状報告, 現況報告

summary report　略式報告書

survey report　鑑定報告書

◆As a basis for its economic assessment, the report referred to increases in exports, progress in inventory adjustment and the bottoming out of industrial production. 景気判断の根拠として、同報告書は輸出が増加し、在庫調整が進展して、鉱工業生産も底を打ったことを挙げている。◆At the beginning of each calendar year, ABC shall make a report to XYZ on the sales of the Product during the previous year and general market conditions. 各暦年の初めに、ABCは、XYZに対して前年度の契約品の販売（実績）と市況全般について報告するものとする。◆The United Nations' World Intellectual Property Organization（WIPO）launched its World Intellectual Property Indicators 2012 report and said that global patent filings in 2011 swelled to a record 2.14 million. 国連の世界知的所有権機関（WIPO）は、「世界知的所有権指標2012年版」の報告書を発表し、2011年の世界の特許出願件数は増加して過去最高の214万件に達したと述べた。

reporting　（名）報告, 申告, 報道, 伝達
◆The false reporting by Barclays is a clear betrayal of investors' trust. 英金融大手バークレイズの虚偽申告は、明らかに投資家の信頼を裏切る行為だ。

represent　（動）表示する, 表明する, 意味する, 示す, 〜を表章する, 〜を表す, 〜の代理をつとめる, 〜を代表する, 〜を代行する, 〜に相当する, 〜に当たる
◆A committee of creditors was appointed to represent its business. 債権者委員会が、その事業を代表するために任命された。◆An aggregate market value represents a corporate value in terms of stock price. 時価総額は、株価による企業価値を示す。◆Since electronic money requires safeguards against unauthorized use and counterfeiting, encryption technology, on the software side, and IC cards, on the hardware side, represent essential technologies. 電子マネーには不正使用や変造を防ぐ技術が必要で、ソフト面では暗号化技術、ハード面ではICカードが、その代表的な技術とされている。◆The term "Subsidiary" shall mean a corporation, more than fifty percent（50%）of whose outstanding shares representing the right to vote for the election of directors, are, now or hereafter, owned or controlled, directly or indirectly, by a party hereto. 「子会社」という語は、

取締役選任のための議決権を表す発行済み株式の50%超が、本契約の一当事者によって直接・間接的に現在または今後所有されるか支配される法人を意味する。

represent A as B　AをBと表示する

represent and warrant（that）　〜を表明し保証する, 〜を表明しこれを保証する
（⇒own and possess, warrant and represent）
◆ABC represents and warrants the following as of the Closing Date: ABCは、クロージング日現在、以下の事実を表明しこれを保証する。

representation　（名）事実の表示, 表示事項, 表明,（保険契約での）告知, 陳述, 保証, 代表, 代表者, 代理, 代理人, 代行, 代行者, 代表団, 代議員

make any representation or warranties　事実の表明や保証をする

representations and understandings　事実の表明や了解事項, 説明・了解事項

representations and warranties　事実の表明とその保証, 現状表明・保証, 表示と保証

representations, warranties and indemnities　事実表明, 保証と免責

representations, warranties, terms, conditions, undertakings or oral agreements　表明、保証、条件、約束あるいは口頭での契約［合意］

◆Either party shall not be liable for or bound by any representation, act or omission whatever of the other party. いずれの当事者も、相手方の表明、作為または不作為に対して責任を負わず、これに拘束されないものとする。

representation or warranty　表明または保証
◆The seller shall indemnify and hold the buyer harmless from, and reimburse the buyer for, any damages, loss or expenses resulting from the inaccuracy as of the date hereof of any representation or warranty of the seller which is contained in or made pursuant to this agreement. 売り主は、本契約に明記したまたは本契約に従って行われた売り主の表明または保証が本契約現在で不正確であったことから生じた損害、損失または費用については、すべて買い主に補償し、買い主を免責し、買い主に弁償するものとする。

representative　（名）代表者, 代理人, 代理店, 代行者, 事務所, 駐在員事務所, 代議士, 米下院議員

accredited representative　信認する代理人

duly authorized representative　正式に権限を与えられた代表［代表者・代理人］

representative action　株主代表訴訟, 代表訴訟

representative director　代表取締役, 代表権のある取締役

representative promoter　（会社設立の）発起人総代

sales representative　販売代理店

◆IN WITNESS WHEREOF, the parties hereto have caused this instrument to be executed by their duly authorized representatives, as of the date and year first above written.　上記の証として、本契約の両当事者は、冒頭に記載した日付で正式に権限を与えられた代表者に本契約書［本証書］を作成させた。

repurchase of shares　株の買戻し, 株式の買戻し

repurchase the interest of　〜の権利を買い戻す

reputation　(名)評価, 評判, 信望, 信用

◆We are almost certain that these products will meet your requirements as the products have been enjoying a good reputation in EU markets. 本製品はこれまでEU市場で好評を博しており、かならずや貴社のご要望に沿うものと確信しております。

reputation and prestige　評判と威信

◆The licensed products manufactured and sold under this agreement are of high standard and such quality as to enhance the reputation and prestige of the Trademarks.　本契約のもとに製造、販売する許諾製品は水準が高く、本商標の評判と威信を高める品質である。

repute　(名)評判, 世評, 好評, 名声, 信望

◆ABC shall effect all risk (Institute Cargo Clauses) marine insurance with underwriters or insurance companies of good repute in an amount of one hundred and ten (110) percent of CIF value of the shipments of the products. ABCは、本製品積送品のCIF価格の110%の保険金額で、評判の良い保険引受業者または保険会社と全危険担保条件(協会貨物約款)の海上保険の保険契約をするものとする。

request　(名)要求, 要求書, 要請, 要請書, 依頼, 依頼書, 見積り依頼書, 委任, 委託　(動)要求する, 求める, 要請する, 依頼する

at the request of　〜の請求により, 〜の要請を受けて

at your specific request　貴社のたっての要請で

make an official request　公式な要請を行う, 公式に要請する

request and demand　要求する, 請求する, 要請する, 求める

request and require　要求する, 請求する, 要請する, 求める

requested modification　要請された変更, 変更の依頼, 変更依頼, 変更の要請

requests of any government　政府の要求

upon one's request　〜の要求のあり次第, 〜の要請がある場合には

◆We reduced our unit price by five percent at your specific request. 貴社のたっての要請で、当社は単価を5%引き下げました。

require　(動)必要とする, 要求する, 請求する, 求める, 義務付ける, 命じる

◆Guarantor hereby waives any right it may have of first requiring ABC to pursue its legal remedies against XYZ. 保証人は、保証人が持てる権利にして、まずXYZに対して法的救済を求めることをABCに要求する権利を、ここに放棄する。

requirement(s)　(名)要件, 条件, 必要条件, 資格, 必要量

meet the requirements　条件［必要量］を満たす, 条件に合致する, 条件に適合する

quality requirements　品質条件, 品質要件

ship all of your requirements　ご入用の品を全部出荷する［積む］

◆ABC shall, at all times during the term of this agreement, maintain an adequate stock of the products so as to enable it to meet the requirement and supply promptly all orders reasonably anticipated in the territory. 本契約の期間中つねに、合理的に予想される契約地域内の必要量をみたすことができるようにするため、またすべての注文品を迅速に供給できるようにするため、本製品の十分な在庫を維持するものとする。◆At least sixty days prior to the requested delivery date, the buyer shall provide the seller with a written estimate of its requirements of the product, which shall constitute a firm order. 希望渡し日から少なくとも60日前に、買い主は、本製品の需要予測書［需要見積り書］を売り主に提出し、これを確定注文とするものとする。◆We are almost certain that these products will meet your requirements as the products have been enjoying a good reputation in EU markets. 本製品はこれまでEU市場で好評を博しており、かならずや貴社のご要望に沿うものと確信しております。◆We regret to inform you that we may not be able to ship all of your requirements due to the unforeseen increase in the demand for the goods. 本品に対する需要が思いもかけず増大したため、遺憾ながらご入用の品全部の船積みは不可能になるかと思います。

resale price maintenance　再販売価格維持

research and development　研究開発, R&D　(⇒R & D)

joint research and development agreement　共同研究開発契約

research and development consignment agreement　研究開発委託契約

◆Research and development will become even more important to enable firms to make new products that give them a competitive edge in the future. 企業に将来の競争力を与える新製品を企業が生み出すにあたって、研究開発の重要性が今後一段と増すと思われる。

research and development center　研究開発センター, R&Dセンター, 研究開発拠点

◆This research and development center established in Kyoto will mainly handle product design and function improvements for new washing machines. 京都に新設されたこの研究開発 (R&D) センターは, 主に洗濯機の新製品の製品設計や機能向上などを担当する.

research and development spending [expenditure] 研究開発費

reserve (動) 留保する, 保留する, 保有する, 用意しておく, 確保する, 予約する
All rights reserved. 版権所有, 著作権所有 (=Copyrighted.)

reserve for [against] future losses 将来の損失に対して引当金を積む

reserve the right 権利を留保する, 権利を保有する, 権利を保持する, 権利を確保する
◆ABC reserves the right to replace on its own reasons any ABC Personnel so assigned with a competent substitute by giving XYZ a notice in advance. ABCは, XYZに事前通知を行って, 派遣したABC人員を自社の都合で適格交替人員と交替させる権利を持つ. ◆In case any dispute arises in connection with the above right, the seller reserves the right to terminate unconditionally this agreement or any further performance of this agreement at the seller's discretion. 上記権利に関して紛争が生じた場合, 売り主はその裁量で, 本契約または本契約のその後の履行を無条件で終了させる権利を留保する.

residual quantitative import restriction 残存輸入制限

resignation (名) 辞任, 辞職, 退任, 退職 (⇒replacement)

resolution (名) 決議, 決断, 決意, 決定, 裁決, 判定, 解決, 解明
extraordinary resolution 特別決議 (=special resolution)
Resolution Funding Corporation 整理資金調達公社
resolution of board of directors 取締役会の決議
resolution of disputes 紛争の解決, 紛争解決 (=dispute resolution)
resolutions of board of directors 取締役会議事録
shareholder resolution 株主決議
◆Each meeting of shareholders shall be convened by the president of the new company in accordance with a resolution of the board of directors. 各株主総会は, 取締役会の決議に従って新会社の社長が招集する. ◆Except as otherwise required by law, all resolutions of a meeting of shareholders shall be adopted by the affirmative vote of majority of the shares represented in person or by proxy at such meeting of shareholders. 法律で別段に要求されないかぎり, 株主総会の決議は, すべて当該総会で株主本人またはその代理人によって示される株式の過半数の賛成投票によっ

て採択されるものとする.

respect (名) 尊敬, 尊重, 敬意, 考慮, 配慮, 注意, 関心, 意識, 点, 箇所, 事項, 伝言, 差別, えこひいき (動) 敬 (うやま) う, 尊敬する, 尊重する, 重んじる, 遵守する
as respects ～については, ～に関しては
have no respect for the law 法律を守らない, 法律を遵守しない
in respect of ～に関しては, ～については, ～の代金として, ～の支払いとして
in respect that ～ということを考えると, ～を考慮して
pay one's respects to ～に挨拶に行く, ～のご機嫌をうかがう, ～を訪問する
with respect to ～に関しては, ～については, ～を考慮して, ～を念頭に置いて
without respect to [of] ～を考慮しないで, ～に構わずに
◆In case any one or more of the provisions of this agreement are held invalid, illegal or unenforceable in any respect, the validity, legality and enforceability of the remaining provisions hereof shall not be in any way affected or impaired thereby, except to the extent that giving effect to the remaining provisions would be unjust or inequitable. 本契約の一つ以上の規定がいずれかの点で無効, 違法または強制不能と判断された場合, 残存規定の実施が不公正または不均衡となる範囲を除いて, 本契約の残存規定の有効性, 合法性と強制可能性はその影響を受けることはなく, またそれによって損なわれることはないものとする.

respective (形) それぞれの, めいめいの, 各～
◆Unless specifically set forth herein, nothing in this agreement is intended to confer any rights or remedies upon any persons other than the parties and their respective successors and assigns. 本契約書に特に明記しないかぎり, 本契約の規定は, 契約当事者とその各承継人および譲受人以外の者に権利または救済方法を付与することを意図したものではない.

respondent (名) 被請求人, 被申立て人, 被控訴人, 被上訴人, 被上告人, 被告
◆The other party (the "Respondent") shall appoint its arbitrator within sixty (60) calendar days of receipt of the Demand and shall notify the Claimant of such appointment in writing. 相手方 (「被申立て人」) は, 仲裁申立て書の受領後60暦日以内にその仲裁人を指名し, その指名を書面で申立て人に通知するものとする.

responsibility (名) 責任, 職責, 義務, 責務, 債務, 負担, 契約義務, 履行能力, 支払い能力
◆Company executives have admitted responsibility in a class action suit filed on behalf of a firm. 株主代表訴訟で, 企業の幹部が責任を認めた.

responsible (形) 責任がある, 責任を負うべ

き, 信頼できる, 責任能力がある

◆One factor considered responsible for the recent stock market plunge is that foreign investors who purchased Japanese stocks in large quantities have started to sell their shareholdings. 今回の株安を招いたと思われる要因の一つは, 日本株を大量に買った海外投資家[外国人投資家]が, 保有株を売りに転じたことだ. ◆We may not have to add that we do not hold ourselves responsible for the corresponding delay in shipment if your actions should not be taken in time. 言うまでもなく[申すまでもなく], 貴社の打つ手が遅れたら, それに伴って生じる船積みの遅延に対して, 当社は責任を負いません. ◆We shall not hold ourselves responsible for the corresponding delay in shipment if the credit should fail to arrive in time. 万一信用状が間に合わない場合, その結果として起こる[それに伴って生じる]船積みの遅延に対して, 当社は責任を負わないものとする.

restrain (動)抑制する, 防止する, 禁止する, 拘束する, 規制する, 制限する
◆If I breach Article VI, ABC shall be entitled, in addition to all other remedies it may have, to injunctive or other appropriate relief to restrain any such breach without showing or proving any actual damages to ABC. 私が第6条に違反した場合, ABCが有する他のあらゆる救済手段のほかに, ABCは, ABCの実際の損害を証明または立証することなく, 当該違反を禁止するために差止めまたは他の適切な救済措置を受けられるものとする.

restraint (名)抑え, 抑制, 制止, 制限, 規制, 引締め, 自制, 控え目
　capital restraints on banks　銀行の自己資本比率規制
　credit restraint　信用引締め, 金融引締め, 信用規制
　dividend restraint　配当制約
　financial restraint　金融引締め
　fiscal restraint　財政引締め, 財政政策の引締め, 財政緊縮政策
　impose restraints on foreign trade　海外貿易に制限条項を課す
　monetary restraint　金融引締め
　price restraint　価格抑制
　production restraint　生産制限
　quantitative export restraint　輸出数量規制
　remove restraints on foreign trade　海外貿易の制限条項を撤廃する
　restraint of trade　取引制限, 貿易制限, 営業制限 (=trade restraint)
　restraint on bank lending　銀行貸出規制, 貸出規制, 融資規制
　restraint on economy　景気抑制
　self-restraint　自制, 自主規制, 自粛
　stock price restraint　株価規制
　voluntary restraint　自主規制

wage restraint　賃金抑制

restrict (動)制限する, 制約する, 限定する, 規制する, 禁止する, 打ち切る
◆The TSE will consider taking punitive measures, such as revoking trading licenses, restricting business or imposing fines if any violations of the law or TSE rules are found in the inspections of major securities firms. 主要証券会社への立ち入り調査で法令違反や東証ルール違反があった場合, 東証は, 取引免許の取消しや売買の制限, 過怠金(罰金)の賦課などの厳しい措置を取る[厳しい処分をする]方針だ.

restrict imports　輸入品を規制する
◆There has been a rising tide of protectionism among U.S. businesses and labor unions that want Washington to restrict imports that compete with domestic products. 米国の業界や労組の間には, 国産品と競合する輸入品の規制を政府に要請する保護主義的な動きが高まっている.

restrict imports of crude oil　原油輸入を規制する
◆Washington did not press Japan to restrict imports of crude oil from Iran. 米政府は日本に対して, イランからの原油輸入規制を強く求めなかった.

restriction (名)制限, 抑制, 規制, 制約
　credit restriction　信用規制, 信用制限
　currency restriction　通貨制限
　demand restriction　需要抑制
　exchange restriction　為替制限
　import restrictions　輸入規制, 輸入制限
　legal restrictions　法的規制
　output restriction　生産制限 (=restriction of output, restriction of production)
　qualitative restriction　質的規制
　quantitative restriction　量的規制
　quota restriction　輸入割当制限
　residual (quantitative) import restriction　残存輸入制限
　restriction on stock holding　株式保有制限
　restrictions in the use of power　権限行使制限
　restrictions on capital inflows　資本流入制限
　restrictions on capital movement　資本移動規制
　restrictions on share buyback　自社株買戻しに対する規制
　supply restriction　供給制限
　trade restriction　貿易制限 (=restriction of trade)
　transfer restriction　譲渡制限 (=restriction of transfer)
　voluntary restriction of export　輸出自主規制
◆ABC's obligation under this Article shall not apply to any information relating to the licensed products that is or becomes available without

restriction to the general public by acts not attributable to ABC or its employees. 本条に基づくABCの義務は、ABCまたはその従業員が引き起こしたと考えることができない行為によって一般公衆に制限なく知られている、または知られるようになった許諾製品に関する情報には適用されないものとする。◆Japan once provided patrol vessels to Indonesia as an exception to Japan's three principles on arms export restrictions. かつて日本は、日本の武器輸出規制[武器輸出]3原則の例外として、インドネシアに巡視船を供与したことがある。◆More than 90 percent of parts in North Korean missiles come from Japan despite strict restrictions on such exports. 北朝鮮のミサイル部品の90%以上は、厳しい輸出規制にもかかわらず日本から輸出されている。

restrictive （形）制限する，限定的な

restrictive agreement　制限の協定

restrictive budget　緊縮予算

restrictive business measures　制限的取引手段［商手段］

restrictive business practices　制限的商慣行，取引制限行為，RBP

restrictive covenant　不作為約款，制限契約（一定の行為をしないという約定）

restrictive credit policy　金融引締め政策，信用引締め政策，信用抑制政策

restrictive endorsement［indorsement］　制限裏書き，限定的裏書き，譲渡制限裏書き，譲渡禁止裏書き　（=qualified endorsement）

restrictive government policy　政府の引締め政策

restrictive injunction　禁止的差し止め命令

restrictive lending policy　貸出抑制策

restrictive measures　抑制政策，抑制策，制限的手段

restrictive monetary policy　金融引締め政策，金融引締め策

restrictive monetary policy stance　金融引締めのスタンス

restrictive policy　制限的政策，抑制政策，引締め政策，引締め策

restrictive practices　制限の慣行（企業間の競争を制限する協定），労働組合による組合員や使用者の行為の制限

restrictive tariff　制限的関税，制限的税率

restrictive trade　取引制限，貿易制限（=restraint of trade）

restrictive trade practices　制限の商慣習，制限的取引慣行，取引制限行為

restrictive trade system　制限的貿易主義

restructuring （名）事業の再構築，事業の再編成，再構成，再建，再編，改革，経営合理化，解雇，リストラ，リストラクチャリング

business restructuring　事業再編成，事業再編，

企業リストラ，リストラ

corporate restructuring　企業再編成，企業再編，会社再建，企業リストラ，事業機構の再編，経営再建，リストラ

corporate restructuring efforts　企業の事業再構築努力，企業再編努力，会社再建努力，会社再建策

debt restructuring　債務再編，債務再構成，債務の特別条件変更　（=refinancing debt）

economic restructuring　経済の再編成，経済の立て直し，経済のリストラ

financial restructuring　財務再編，財務再構築，金融のリストラ

fiscal restructuring　財政再編，財政再建

global economic restructuring　グローバルな経済構造改革

group restructuring　グループ再編

implement large-scale restructuring　大規模なリストラを実施する

launch a massive business restructuring　大規模なリストラに着手する［踏み切る］

management restructuring plan　経営健全化計画

operational restructuring　業務再編，事業の再構築，事業のリストラ

socioeconomic restructuring　経済社会の再編成

◆The firm envisioned negotiations with the U.S. equity fund over financing for restructuring in a reconstruction plan it formulated in June. 同社は、経営合理化の資金調達に関しては、6月に策定した再建計画でこの米国の投資ファンドとの交渉を見込んでいた。

results （名）成績，業績，決算，決算内容，実績，成果，結果，よい［素晴らしい］結果，効果，影響，影響額，統計

bottom line results　純利益

business results　業績，企業収益

company's results　会社の業績，会社の決算（=corporate business results, corporate results）

firm results　堅調な業績，手堅い業績

full year results　通期決算

good results　好決算

group results　連結決算，グループ企業の連結業績　（=consolidated results）

interim performance results　四半期決算，四半期決算の内容

management by results　目標管理，目標による管理　（=result management）

quarterly performance results　四半期決算の内容，四半期業績の内容

results announcement　決算発表

results for the first half of the current fiscal year 今年度上半期の業績［決算］

results of business　営業成績, 営業実績

results of operating activities　経営成績

results of ［from］operations　経営成績, 営業成績, 営業活動の成果, 業績, 損益計算書

results season　決算期, 決算シーズン

successful results　好業績, 好結果, 上首尾

retail　(名)小売り, 個人投資家, 小口投資家, 個人向け取引, リテール

◆France's Competition Commission has ordered Sony, Matsushita and Philips to pay fines for allegedly concluding price-fixing agreements on retail goods with their local distributors. フランスの競争評議会は、国内販売店と小売電気製品の価格維持協定を結んだとして、ソニー、松下電器産業とフィリップスに罰金の支払いを命じた。

◆Marubeni Corp. plans to choose a partner to assist in the rehabilitation of Daiei after negotiations with major retail chain operators such as Aeon Co. and Wal-Mart Stores Inc. 丸紅は、イオンや米ウォルマート・ストアーズなどの流通大手と交渉の上、ダイエー再建に協力する事業提携先を選ぶ方針だ。

retain　(動)保有する, 保持する, 留保する, 委任契約する, 弁護士に依頼する

◆With respect to such manufacturer, XYZ shall ensure that the manufacturer is not retaining any Licensed Products in order to sell them in its own name or to a third party. この製造者については、XYZは、製造者が「許諾対象製品」を製造者自身の名前で販売したり第三者に販売したりするために「許諾対象製品」を保有することのないようにしなければならない。

retainer agreement　弁護士依頼契約, 弁護士委任契約

retaliatory　(形)報復的な, 報復の

adopt retaliatory tariffs　報復関税を発動する

retaliatory duties　報復関税

retaliatory sanction　報復措置

take retaliatory steps ［action］against　〜に対して報復措置をとる

retaliatory measures　報復措置

◆The EU considers retaliatory measures as a last resort. 欧州連合（EU）は、報復措置を最後の手段と考えている。

retaliatory tariff　報復関税

adopt retaliatory tariffs　報復関税を発動する

be targeted for retaliatory tariffs　報復関税の対象として狙いをつけられる

impose retaliatory tariffs on　〜に報復関税を発動する

◆China's retaliatory tariffs on Japanese cars, cellular phones and air conditioners clearly ran counter to WTO rules. 日本の自動車、携帯電話とエアコンに課した中国の報復関税は、明らかに

WTOルールに違反していた。◆When Washington refuses to comply with the WTO's ruling, the EU will impose retaliatory tariffs on U.S. products. 米国が世界貿易機関（WTO）の決定に従わなかった場合、欧州連合（EU）は米国製品に報復関税を発動する方針だ。

retention　(名)保持, 保有, 保管

◆The second copy is for your retention. もう一部は、貴社の保管用です。

return　(動)返却する, 返還する, 申告する, 利益などを生む

◆If some or all of the goods have not been received by the buyer on the termination of this contract, the buyer shall, in its sole discretion, cease to take delivery of the remaining goods and the seller shall return to the buyer any amounts paid in advance in respect of such goods. 本契約解除時に商品の一部または全部を買い主が受領していない場合、買い主は、買い主単独の選択で、残存商品［未引渡し商品］の引取りを中止し、売り主は当該商品に関して前払いで受領した代金を買い主に返還するものとする。

return　(名)返却, 返還, 返報, 報酬, 報告, 報告書, 申告, 申告書

◆Risk of loss of the Equipment shall pass to User upon Lender's delivery to the carrier, and back to Lender upon Lender's receipt of this Equipment following its return. 「機器」の危険負担は、貸主が運送業者に「機器」を引き渡した時点でユーザーに移転し、ユーザーが「機器」を返還した後はそれを貸主が受領した時点で貸主が危険負担しなければならない。◆The term "net sales" shall mean gross sales less returns. 「純売上高」は、総売上高から返品分を差し引いたものを意味する。

reverse side　契約書などの裏面

◆All the terms and conditions set forth on the reverse side hereof are confirmed to be an integral part of this agreement. 裏面に記載する条件は、すべて本契約の不可分の一部であることを確認する。

reverse stock split　株式併合

◆Even if the company conducts a reverse stock split, it will safeguard shareholders' interest by changing the minimum trading unit from 1,000 shares to 500. 同社が株式併合をしても、最低取引単位を1,000株から500株に変更して、株主の権利は守る方針だ。

revise, amend and supplement　改訂、修正し補足する

◆The parties hereto desire to revise, amend and supplement certain provisions of the original agreement. 本契約当事者は、原契約の一部の条項を改訂、修正して補足することを望んでいる。

revise the price of　〜の価格を見直す

◆Every three months, McDonald's Japan revises the price of the beef it imports from Australia according to the exchange rate. 3か月ごとに、日本マクドナルドは、為替相場に応じてオーストラリアから輸入している牛肉の価格を見直している。

revised Foreign Exchange and Foreign

Trade Control Law 改正外為法
◆A revised Foreign Exchange and Foreign Trade Control Law has been enacted to enable the swift freezing of funds belonging to terrorist organizations. テロ組織の資金［資産］凍結を迅速に行うための改正外為法は、すでに成立して［制定されて］いる。

revision of assumed exchange rate 想定為替レートの修正
◆The revision of the firm's assumed exchange rate will translate into an additional ￥150 billion loss in its consolidated accounts for the six-month period through March 2015. 同社の想定為替レートの修正に伴って、同社の2014年度下半期(2014年10月～2015年3月)の連結決算では、追加で1,500億円の為替差損が生じることになる。

revocation or suspension 撤回または取消し、取消しまたは停止
◆This shall include without limitation any action, suit, proceeding or investigation involving the revocation or suspension of a license or permit of the Company to conduct any type of the business of the Company. これには、本会社のいずれかの種類の事業を行うために必要な本会社の免許または許可の取消しまたは停止を伴う訴え、訴訟、手続きまたは調査などが制限なく含まれるものとする。

right （名）権利, 正義, 正当, 公正, 公平, 正確, 的確, 善, 真相, 版権, 所有権, 新株引受権
◆Guarantor hereby waives any right it may have of first requiring ABC to pursue its legal remedies against XYZ. 保証人は、保証人が持てる権利にして、まずXYZに対して法的救済を求めることをABCに要求する権利を、ここに放棄する。

right, title or interest 権利, 権原または権益, 権利, 所有権または利権
◆ABC represents and warrants that it owns and possesses all rights, title, interest, in all of the Software Products, and any trademarks, logos, trade secrets and proprietary rights associated with the Software Products. ABCは本ソフトウエア製品の全部に対するすべての権利、権原、権益と、本ソフトウエア製品に関連する一切の商標、ロゴ、トレード・シークレットおよび財産権を所有していることを、ABCは表明しこれを保証する。

right to ～の権利, ～に対する権利, ～する権利
right to access 取得する権利, 情報取得権, 立ち入る権利, 面接する権利, 面接権, アクセス権, 私的公道利用権 (=right of access)
right to counsel 弁護人の援助を受ける権利
right to information 情報に対する権利
right to inspect account books 帳簿閲覧権
right to sublicense サブライセンスする権利
right to work 労働権

right to transfer copies 複製物の譲渡権
◆Original edition rights include the right to transfer copies to enable publishers to provide them to the public. 出版物［書籍］原版権には、複製物の譲渡によって出版社が複製物を公衆に提供できるようにする譲渡権も含まれている。

right to use 使用権
◆Mitsui & Co. and Mitsubishi Corp. struck an agreement with a local company over the right to use the LNG facility in Cameron Parish, La. in April 2012. 三井物産と三菱商事は2012年4月、米ルイジアナ州キャメロン郡にあるLNG基地の使用権を得ることで地元企業と合意した。

right to vote 議決権
◆The term "Subsidiary" shall mean a corporation, more than fifty percent（50％）of whose outstanding shares representing the right to vote for the election of directors, are, now or hereafter, owned or controlled, directly or indirectly, by a party hereto. 「子会社」という語は、取締役選任のための議決権を表す発行済み株式の50％超が、本契約の一当事者によって直接・間接的に現在または今後所有されるか支配される法人を意味する。

rightfully （副）正当に, 正しく, 合法的に
◆Such information was rightfully communicated to the receiving party free of any obligation of confidence subsequent to the time it was communicated to the receiving party by the disclosing party. 当該情報は、開示当事者が受領当事者に通知した時点以後に、秘密保持義務なしに受領当事者に合法的に通知された。

rights and liabilities of the parties 当事者の権利と義務
◆The rights and liability of the parties shall be determined in accordance with the laws of Japan. 当事者の権利と義務は、日本の法律に従って判断するものとする。

riot （名）暴動, 騒乱, 騒動, 混乱, 騒擾（そうじょう）, 乱舞, 多種多彩 （動）暴動に加わる, 騒ぐ, 浮かれ騒ぐ, 放蕩（ほうとう）する
◆Japanese-affiliated companies operating in China will have to be aware of "China risks" such as rising production costs as well as the stronger Chinese yuan and anti-Japan riots. 中国に進出している日系企業は今後、生産コストの上昇のほか、人民元高や反日暴動などのような「中国リスク」を意識せざるを得ない。◆To avert China risks such as the stronger Chinese yuan, surging labor costs and anti-Japan riots, some firms have shifted production lines to other countries in Southeast Asia and other regions with cheaper labor. 中国人民元高や人件費高騰、反日暴動などの中国リスクを回避するため、一部の企業は、中国より低賃金の東南アジアなどの地域に生産ラインの移管［分散化］を進めている。

rise in prices of imported raw materials 原材料価格の上昇, 原材料価格の高騰
◆Japanese small and midsize businesses have been tormented by the rise in prices of imported raw materials due to the weakened yen. 日本の

中小企業は、円安による輸入原材料価格の上昇で、苦しんでいる。

rise in the value of the yen 円相場の上昇, 円高
◆There was a time when the more we exported, the more money we lost, by eroding export profitability due to the excessive rise in the value of the yen. 超円高による輸出の採算悪化で、輸出すればするほど赤字になる時もあった。

rise in the yen 円高
(=the rise in the yen's value)
◆Reflecting the rise in the yen, Tokyo stocks, particularly exporter stocks, dropped Wednesday. 円高を受けて[反映して]、水曜日は、輸出企業の株を中心に東京株式市場の株価が下落した[東京株式市場の株が売られた]。

rising (形)増加する, 増大する, 上昇する, 向上する, 上り調子の, 出世している, 新進気鋭の, 伸び盛りの (名)上昇, 昇進, 出世, 増水, 出現, 復活, 蜂起, 反乱, 隆起
ever-rising 上昇し続ける
rising inflation pressure インフレ圧力の増大
rising interest rate 金利の上昇, 金利上昇
rising market [quotation] 上げ相場, 上向き相場
rising productivity 生産性の向上
rising rate environment 金利上昇局面
rising trend 上昇基調, 上昇傾向
rising unemployment 失業増大
the yen's rising value 円高
◆The yen's rising value could open up new strategies for Japanese firms, such as making it possible acquire top-rate foreign companies. 円高だと[円の価値が高まれば]、優良な海外企業の買収など、日本企業にとって新経営戦略の幅が広がる可能性がある。

rising interest income 金利収入の増加
◆Rising interest incomes from Japanese investments in dollar- and euro-denominated securities and growing dividends from overseas subsidiaries of Japanese companies were behind the increase in the income account. 所得収支が増加した背景としては、米ドル建て債やユーロ建て債の金利収入が増えたほか、日本企業の海外子会社からの配当が増えたことが挙げられる。

rising labor costs 労働コストの上昇, 人件費の高騰
◆Despite rising labor costs and anti-Japan riots, most of Japanese businesses are opting to stay in China as the county is still enormous market. 人件費高騰や反日暴動が起きても、中国は依然として巨大市場なので、日本企業の大半は中国での事業を続けている。

rising price 価格の上昇, 価格の高騰
◆Economic upturn is expected to continue in and after next fiscal year, with rising prices of crude oil, steel, nonferrous metals and other key materials pushing up consumer prices. 景気回復は来年度以降も続き、原油や鉄鋼、非鉄金属といった主要原材料の価格が上昇して消費者物価を押し上げるものと見られる。

rising protectionist sentiment 保護主義の高まり
◆The APEC's special statement sounded the alarm about the rising protectionist sentiment. アジア太平洋経済協力会議（APEC）の特別声明は、保護主義の台頭に警鐘を鳴らした。

risk (名)リスク, 危険, 危険負担, 損害のおそれ, 危険率, 危険の程度, 保険金額, 被保険者, 被保険物 (⇒all risks, ship's rail, SRCC)
absorb unforeseen risks 不測のリスクを吸収する
accept higher risks 高リスクを受け入れる, 高リスクを取る
add risk to ～のリスクを高める, ～のリスクを増す
address market risk 市場リスクに対応する
all risks 全危険担保
all risks whatsoever いかなる危険でも担保
alleviate the exchange risk 為替リスクを軽減する
assume the risk 危険を負担する, リスクを負う, リスクを取る (=bear the risk, take the risk)
at one's own risk 自分の責任で, 自分の危険負担で
at the buyer's risk 買い主の危険負担で
avoid the risk リスクを回避する, リスクを避ける
bad risk 不良危険
balance of payment risk 国際収支リスク
be at risk of ～の危険にさらされている, ～のリスクがある
be exposed to the risk of ～のリスクにさらされる
be subject to currency risk 為替リスクを負う
be subject to market risk 市場リスクにさらされる
bear the risk 危険を負担する, リスクを負う
bring added risks リスクを高める
business risks 事業リスク, 営業リスク
buyer's risk 危険買い手持ち
calculated risk 計算済みのリスク, 織り込み済みのリスク
commercial risk 商業危険, 事業リスク
constitute a risk to price stability 物価上昇リスクを招く
counterparty risk カウンターパーティー・リスク
country risk 国別信用度, カントリー・リ

スク

credit risk　信用リスク, 与信リスク, 貸倒れリスク

credit risk insurance　信用リスク保険

currency risk　為替リスク, 為替変動リスク (=exchange (rate) risk)

decrease the risk of　〜のリスクを軽減する, 〜のリスクを引き下げる

default risk　債務不履行リスク, 貸倒れリスク

directional risk　金利上昇リスク

diversify development risks　開発リスクを分散する

ease (foreign) exchange risks　為替リスクを軽減する

eliminate risk　リスクを除去する

emergency risk　非常危険

entail risks　リスクを伴う

exchange risk insurance　為替変動保険, 為替変動リスク保険

extraneous risks　付加危険

face risk　リスクに直面する

fair risk　普通危険

for a person's account and risk　〜の勘定と危険負担で

foresee risk　リスクを見越す

good risk　優良危険

have a risk　リスクがある

hedge interest rate risk　金利 (変動) リスクをヘッジする

implement a thorough risk management　リスク管理を徹底する

increase risk　リスクを高める

incur a risk　リスクを負う

introduce a new risk　新たなリスクをもたらす

inventory risk　在庫リスク

investment risk　投資危険

land risk　陸上危険

language risk　言語リスク

lay off risk　リスクを回避する, リスクを低減する

legal risk　法的リスク, 法務上のリスク, 法務リスク

limit risk (s)　リスクを減らす, リスクを最小限に抑える

liquidity risk　流動性リスク

manage risk positions　リスク・ポジションを管理する

manage the risk exposure　リスクを管理する

marine risk　海上危険

market risk　市場リスク

materialized risk　リスクの具体化

measure market risk　市場リスクを測る, 市場リスクを測定する

mercantile risk　商業危険, 商品危険, 商品リスク

minimize risks　リスクを最小限に抑える

mitigate risks　リスクを緩和する, リスクを軽減する

optimal-risk portfolio　最適リスク・ポートフォリオ

pass on interest rate risk　金利リスクを回避する, 金利変動リスクを回避する

personal risk　人的危険

physical risk　物的リスク

political risk cover　政治リスク保険

reduce the default risk　不履行リスクを軽減する [低減する, 低下させる, 抑える]

risk-adjusted return　リスク調整後収益率

risk assessment　リスク評価, リスク査定 (=risk evaluation)

risk attachment　危険開始

risk bearer　危険負担者, リスク負担者

risk bearing　危険負担

risk bearing capacity　リスク負担能力

risk capital　危険資本　(=venture capital)

risk control [management]　リスク管理

risk cost　危険費用

risk disclosure　リスク開示

risk limit　リスク許容限度, リスク許容枠

risk note　略式保険証券

risk of both craft　両艇危険

risk profile　リスク特性, リスク輪郭, リスク構造

risk rating　危険測定

risk sharing　リスク分散

risk-taking　危険負担, リスク負担, リスクテーキング

risk tolerance　リスク許容度

risk trade　自己勘定による取引

risk yield　危険利回り

risks covered　担保危険, 保険危険

run a risk　リスクを負う, リスクを招く

run the risk of　〜の危険を冒す, 〜のリスクを招く

sea risk　海上危険

settlement risk　決済リスク

sovereign risk　ソブリン・リスク (=country risk; ⇒sovereign risk)

spread risk　リスクを分散する

systematic risk　市場リスク, 分散不能リスク, システマティック・リスク

take the risk　危険を負担する, リスクを取る,

リスクを負う

take the risks involved in 〜に伴うリスクを取る

the risk of inflation pick-up インフレ再加速のリスク

the risk of loss of principal 元本割れのリスク　(=risk to principal)

the risk of nonperformance risk 売約不履行危険

the risk of quality 品質保険, 品質相違の危険

trading risk 取引リスク

transfer risk リスクを移転する, 決済リスク

transit risk 運搬リスク

unique risk 個別リスク　(=unsystematic risk)

valuation of market risk 市場リスクの評価

war risks 戦争危険

◆In expanding into India's market, Japanese companies must work out a strategy that includes possible infrastructure risks. インド市場に進出するにあたって, 日本企業は, 想定されるインフラ面でのリスクを念頭に置いた戦略を練る必要がある。◆Japanese companies can hedge exchange risks and improve their business image abroad through external bond financing. 日本企業は, 外債発行による資金調達で, 為替リスクを回避するとともに海外での企業イメージアップを図ることができる。◆Pursuant to concerned provisions of Contract, all risks of loss or damage to Machines shall be directly transferred from Supplier to Customer. 本契約の関連規定に従って, 本機械に関する損失または損害の全危険は, サプライヤーから顧客へ直接移転するものとする。◆The firm controls its exposure to credit risk through credit approvals, credit limits and monitoring procedures. 同社は, 信用供与承認や信用限度, 監視手続きを通じて信用リスクを管理している。

risk arbitrage リスク裁定取引, リスクを伴った裁定取引, リスク・アービトラージ（企業買収に伴う株価の動きを予想して, 一般に株価が上昇する買収対象会社の株式を買い, 一般に株価が下落する買収会社の株式を売る値ざや稼ぎの裁定取引）

risk arbitrage trade リスク裁定取引

risk asset リスク資産, リスク・アセット

low-risk asset 低リスク試算, 安全資産

risk asset ratio 自己資本比率

◆Great rotation refers to the shift of investment money from low-risk assets such as U.S. Treasuries and the yen into riskier assets such as stocks. 「グレート・ローテーション（大転換）」とは, 投資資金を米国債や円などの低リスク資産［安全資産］から株式などリスクの高い資産に移すことを言う。

risk aversion リスク回避, リスクを嫌うこと

◆The euro plunged below ¥97 level in Tokyo as it was bruised by accelerated risk-aversion moves amid persistent worries about the European debt crisis. 欧州の財政・金融危機への根強い懸念からリスク回避の動きが加速した影響で, 東京外国為替市場では, ユーロが急落して1ユーロ＝97円台を割り込む展開となった。

risk factor 危険要因, リスク要因, リスク・ファクター　(⇒protectionist sentiment)

◆Foreign investors, including Japanese firms, regard Thailand's political climate with its repeated coups as a risk factor for investing in the country. 日本企業など外国資本は, クーデターが繰り返されるタイの政治風土を, 対タイ投資のリスク要因と見なしている。

risk management 危機管理, リスク管理

◆Bitcoin traded in units of BTC currently stays outside the framework of financial regulations, so the risk management of the virtual currency is difficult. BTCの単位で取引されているビットコインは現在, 金融規制の枠外にあるため, 仮想通貨「ビットコイン」のリスク管理は難しい。

risk of exchange rate fluctuations 為替変動のリスク, 為替変動リスク

◆Yen-denominated trade frees domestic companies from the risk of exchange rate fluctuations. 円建て貿易は, 国内企業にとって為替変動のリスクがない。

risk of loss 危険負担, 損失の危険, 滅失の危険

◆Risk of loss of the Equipment shall pass to User upon Lender's delivery to the carrier, and back to Lender upon Lender's receipt of this Equipment following its return. 「機器」の危険負担は, 貸主が運送業者に「機器」を引き渡した時点でユーザーに移転し, ユーザーが「機器」を返還した後はそれを貸主が受領した時点で貸主が危険負担しなければならない。

rival （動）〜に劣らない, 〜に匹敵する, 〜と並ぶ, 〜と張り合う, 〜と競争する

◆By gaining Intel's equity participation, NEC and Hitachi aim to make Elpida one of top three makers of multipurpose DRAM（dynamic random access memory）chips in the world, rivaling Samsung Electronics Co. of South Korea and Micron Technology Inc. of the United States. インテルの資本参加を得ることにより［インテルの出資により］, NECと日立は, 汎用（はんよう）DRAM（記憶保持動作が必要な随時書き込み読み出しメモリ）の製造で, エルピーダ（NECと日立が折半出資する合弁会社）を韓国のサムスン電子, 米国のマイクロン・テクノロジー社と並ぶ世界3強の一角に押し上げる戦略だ。

rival （名）競争相手, 競争相手国, 同業他社, 好敵手, 対抗機種, ライバル

fierce competition from foreign rivals 海外のライバル企業との激しい競争

overseas rivals 海外のライバル［ライバル企業］, 海外勢

trading rivals　貿易の競争相手国, 取引のライバル企業

◆Domestic home electronics makers' gaps with foreign rivals, which have gone on the offense by expanding their business scale, have continued to widen. 事業規模の拡大で攻勢をかける海外勢と国内家電との差は、開くばかりだ。◆Information about advanced technologies is sold to overseas rivals in industrial espionage, which has become a common threat for Japanese manufacturers. 産業スパイでは先端技術情報が海外のライバル企業に売り渡されるので、日本のメーカーにとって産業スパイは、共通の脅威となっている。◆Japanese electronics makers are needed to shrug off the adversity of economic slowdowns overseas, a strongly appreciating yen, and ever-intensifying competition with foreign rivals by wielding their latent power. 日本の電機製造業各社は、底力を発揮して、海外経済の減速、超円高、海外勢との競争激化などの逆勢を跳ね返す必要がある。

roadshow　(名)投資家説明会, 投資家向け説明会, 募集説明会, 販売説明会, 巡回説明会, 巡回キャンペーン, ロードショー　(=road show: 証券発行会社の経営者と引受業者の担当者が、機関投資家や有力な個人投資家(アナリストやファンド・マネージャーなど)を対象にして行う証券購入のメリットに関する説明会。一般に、発行会社の財務状況や将来の収益見通しなどを説明する)

◆In an IPO roadshow, corporate executives talk to potential investors about why they should invest in the stock. 新規株式公開(IPO)の募集説明会[投資家説明会]では、会社経営者が、新規上場銘柄に投資するメリットについて潜在的投資家に説明する。

rock-bottom　(形)どん底の, 最低の, 奥底の
　rock-bottom airfare　超割安運賃
　　(=ultralow fare)
　rock-bottom price　最低値, 底値

round trip air ticket　往復航空切符
　(⇒on one's own account)

◆Licensee shall, on its own account, purchase and send an economy class trip air ticket for each engineer ten days prior to his or her departure from Tokyo. ライセンシーは、自己負担で、各技術者のためのエコノミー・クラスの往復航空切符を購入し、東京から出発する10日前に送付する。

royalty　(名)ロイヤルティ, 著作権・特許権・鉱区などの使用料, 権利の実施料, 許諾料, 採掘料, 印税　(⇒compensation, minimum royalty, running royalty)
　annual minimum royalty　年間最低ロイヤルティ
　annual running royalty　年間ランニング・ロイヤルティ
　copyright royalty　著作権料
　initial royalty　イニシャル・ロイヤルティ

　one time royalty　1回限りのロイヤルティ, 1回全額払いのロイヤルティ
　paid-up royalty　ロイヤルティの一括払い
　royalty due hereunder　本契約上、支払い期限のきたロイヤルティ, 本契約に基づいて支払う義務のあるロイヤルティ, 本契約に基づいて支払われるロイヤルティ
　royalty free license　ロイヤルティ無償の実施権
　royalty income　ロイヤルティ収入
　royalty payment　ロイヤルティの支払い, ロイヤルティの支払い金

◆Licensee agrees to pay to Licensor during the term of this agreement the minimum royalty for each contract year as set forth below. ライセンシーは、本契約期間中、以下に定める各契約年度のミニマム・ロイヤルティをライセンサーに支払うことに同意する。◆Provided Licensor delivers the software without any bug, by no later than the delivery dates, Licensee shall pay Licensor a minimum guarantee of royalties of one million U.S. dollars ($1,000,000). ライセンサーがバグのないソフトウエアを引渡し日以前に引き渡した場合、ライセンシーは、ロイヤルティの最低保証料としてライセンサーに100万米ドルを支払うものとする。

royalty statement　ロイヤルティ計算書, ロイヤルティ報告書

◆Keidanren's charter on ethical recruitments, which stipulates job-hunting rules for member companies, is nonbinding and has no penalties for violators. 会員企業に向けて就職活動のルールを定めている経団連の倫理憲章(新卒者の採用選考に関する企業の倫理憲章)には、拘束力がないし、違反企業への罰則もない。

rule of construction　解釈のルール

◆This agreement shall not be construed for or against any party based on any rule of construction who prepared the agreement. 本契約は、どちらの当事者が本契約書の起草をしたかによる解釈のルールに基づいて、一方の当事者に有利に解釈したり不利に解釈したりしないものとする。

run　(動)効力を持つ, 有効である, 進行する, 権利・義務が伴う, 範囲が及ぶ, 運営する, 管理する, 立候補する
　run a cartel　カルテルを結ぶ
　run a sizable trade deficit　かなりの貿易赤字を出す
　run an exchange rate risk　為替リスクを負う
　run an investment trust fund　投資信託を運用する
　run the shop　店を切り盛りする

◆The term of this agreement and the rights granted hereunder shall run from the Effective Date. 本契約期間と本契約に基づいて付与された権利は、「発効日」から有効とする。

running of the software　ソフトの実行, ソ

フトウエアの実行

running royalty ランニング・ロイヤルティ, 継続的使用料, 継続的の実施料, 継続実施料, 継続実施料法, 歩合制使用料

◆The amount of the minimum royalty paid by ABC to Licensor will be credited against the payment of running royalty accruing under this agreement. ABCがライセンサーに支払ったミニマム・ロイヤルティは, 本契約により生じるランニング・ロイヤルティの支払い金と相殺されるものとする。

S

safe (形)安全な, 危険がない, 危険な目にあわない, (〜しても)差し支えない, 無傷な, 無事な, リスクが少ない, 無難な, 当たり障りのない

safe deposit box 貸し金庫

safe harbor rule 安全条項(規則や法律に抵触しないためのガイドライン), 避難条項, 安全港規則, 安全港ルール, セーフ・ハーバー・ルール(「セーフ・ハーバー・ルール」は, 会社が自社株を買い戻すときの規則を定めた米証券取引委員会(SEC)規則10-bの通称)

safe port 安全港

◆Germany's 10-year government bonds are regarded as one of the safest assets in the eurozone. ドイツの10年物国債は, ユーロ圏で最も健全な[安全な]資産と見られている。

safe haven 資金の安全な逃避先, 安全な投資先

◆Gold is still becoming the safe haven as people fear recession in the U.S. and the eurozone debt problems. 米国の景気後退やユーロ圏の債務危機問題への懸念から, まだ金が安全な投資先[資金の逃避先]となっている。

safe navigation 安全な航行

◆Pirates are threatening the safe navigation of oil tankers and other ships in Southeast Asian waters. 東南アジアの海域では, 海賊が原油タンカーなどの船舶の安全な航行を脅かしている。

safeguard (名)保護, 保全, 保護手段, 予防手段, 安全装置, 緊急輸入制限, 緊急輸入制限措置, セーフガード措置, 保障条項, 保障規約, セーフガード

a safeguard against hostile takeovers 敵対的買収の防衛策

a safeguard emergency import control measure 緊急輸入制限(セーフガード)措置(⇒tariff)

a safeguard measure to raise tariffs 関税引上げのためのセーフガード措置

corporate safeguards 企業防衛策

impose safeguard on 〜に緊急輸入制限を課す

multinational safeguard 多角的セーフガード, 多面的セーフガード

safeguard clause 緊急輸入制限条項, 緊急避難条項, 例外条項, セーフガード・クローズ (=escape clause)

safeguard provisions セーフガード条項 (=escape clause)

selective safeguard 選択的セーフガード

◆Since electronic money requires safeguards against unauthorized use and counterfeiting, encryption technology, on the software side, and IC cards, on the hardware side, represent essential technologies. 電子マネーには不正使用や変造を防ぐ技術が必要で, ソフト面では暗号化技術, ハード面ではICカードが, その代表的な技術とされている。◆Under the World Trade Organization rules, emergency import limits, or safeguard, are permitted as a temporary measure if the volume of imports of a certain product drastically increases, causing serious damages to industries concerned in the country. 世界貿易機関(WTO)のルールでは, 緊急輸入制限措置(セーフガード)は, 特定製品の輸入量が増加して, 国内の関係業界に大きな被害が出ている場合には, 一時的な措置として認められる。

safeguard emergency import control measure 緊急輸入制限(セーフガード)措置

◆The government plans to raise its tariff on imported beef from August as a safeguard emergency import control measure in the wake of a steep year-on-year increase in imports of beef. 牛肉の輸入量が前年に比べて急増していることから, 政府は8月から緊急輸入制限(セーフガード)措置として輸入牛肉の関税を引き上げる方針だ。

safeguard measure(s) 緊急輸入制限措置, セーフガード措置, セーフガード (=safeguard curbs)

a 200-day safeguard measure to raise tariffs 関税を引き上げるための200日間のセーフガード措置

enact safeguard measures セーフガード措置を発動する, セーフガードを発動する

resort to safeguard measures セーフガード措置を発動する

◆Despite strong criticism from Washington's trading partners against high tariffs on steel imports to rescue the ailing U.S. steel industry, the USTR stressed the legitimacy of such safeguard measures. 不況の米鉄鋼業界を救済するための輸入鉄鋼製品に対する高関税について, 米国の貿易相手国から強い批判がなされているにもかかわらず, 米国通商代表はこの緊急輸入制限(セーフガード)措置の正当性を強調した。

safeguard tariffs 緊急輸入制限のための関税, セーフガード関税

◆The Economy, Trade and Industry Ministry has shown little reaction to the EU's imposition of

safeguard tariffs on imported steel. 経済産業省
は、輸入鉄鋼製品［外国製鉄鋼製品］に対する欧州連合 (EU) のセーフガード関税の適用について、冷静に受け止めている。

safely landed　安全な陸揚げ

safety　(名)安全, 安定, 安全性, 安全装置, 安全確保, 保全, セーフティ

　capital safety　資本の安全性

　financial safety　財政安定

　food safety　食の安全, 食品の安全性

　industrial safety　産業安全

　product safety　製品の安全, 製品の安全性

　safety and quality　安全［安全性］と品質

　safety goods　安全製品

　safety precautions　予防措置

　safety standard　安全基準

　safety work　安全作業

　the safety of food　食の安全

　the safety of genetically modified food　遺伝子組換え食品の安全性

　◆To prepare for unpredictable events by anti-Japan demonstrators, the Japanese government will strongly press the Chinese government to ensure the safety of Japanese people and Japanese-affiliated companies in China. 反日デモ隊による不測の事態に備えて、日本政府は、在留邦人や日系企業の安全確保を中国政府に強く求める方針だ。◆U.S. agricultural products have gained a greater competitive advantage in the Japanese market due to mounting concern toward the safety of food. 米国製農産物は、食の安全に対する不安の高まりから、日本市場での競争力が拡大している。

safety criteria　安全基準

　◆The ISO, a private organization that sets international standards for industrial products, will adopt Japan-led global safety criteria for nursing-care robots. 工業製品の国際規格を定める民間組織の「国際標準化機構 (ISO)」は、日本政府が主導する介護ロボットの国際安全基準を採用する方針だ。

safety of Chinese food products　中国産食品の安全性

　◆Concerns over the safety of Chinese food products are rising in Japan, but the percentage of safety violations involving food imports from China fell below the overall average for all imported foods in fiscal 2012. 日本では中国産食品の安全性への懸念が強まっているが、中国からの輸入食品のうち安全面での違反件数の割合は、2012年度は輸入食品全体の総平均を下回った。

safety standard　安全基準

　◆Nursing-care robots under the envisaged international safety standards of the ISO stop or go around such hazards as objects or bumps. 国際標準化機構 (ISO) の国際安全基準案に基づく介護ロ

ボットは、障害物や凹凸などの危険があれば、止まったり避けたりする。

said　(形)上記の, 前記の, 当該, その, この（theとほとんど同じ）

　said products　本製品, 上記製品, 前記製品

　said term of this agreement　本契約の上記期間

　said to be　数量無関係

　said to contain　不知約款（荷主がコンテナ詰めした場合、船会社は中身について免責であることを示す）

sailing　(名)航海, 航行, 出港, 出帆, 帆走航法, 航海術, 配船

　sailing agreement　配船協定

　sailing for a different destination　異なる仕向け港への出港

　sailing on or about　出港月日

　sailing schedule　配船表

　sailing ship［vessel］　大型帆船

　sailing terms　出港条件

sale　(名)販売, 売買, 売却, 証券などの発行, セール

　anniversary sale　記念セール

　bonus sale　ボーナス・セール

　cash sale　現金販売

　clearance sale　見切り売り, 蔵払い, 在庫一掃セール, 在庫一掃大売出し

　consignment sale (s)　委託販売

　cut-price sale　大安売り

　discount sale　割引販売, 割引売り出し, ディスカウント・セール

　forced sale　投げ売り

　funds gained from the sale of shares　株式売却で調達した資金, 株式発行で調達した資金

　go on sale　発売される

　offer for sale　募集売出し, 売出発行, 売出し, 間接発行

　sale by certificate　証明書売買

　sale by credit　掛け売り

　sale by description　説明売買

　sale by inspection　実見売買

　sale by sample　見本売買

　sale by specification　仕様書売買

　sale by standard　標準品売買

　sale by trademark［trade mark］　商標売買

　sale by type or grade　規格売買

　sale of bonds　社債発行

　sale of future goods　先物取引

　Sale of Goods Act　英国物品売買法

　sale of securities　証券発行

　sale on approval　承認売買

sale on consignment　委託販売

sale or other disposition　売却その他の処分

sale or return　期限付き委託販売, 残品引受条件付き売買契約

share sale　株式売却

wash sale　仮装売買

◆A party hereto proposing to effect a sale of any shares of the new company (the Offerer) shall give a written notice to the other parties hereto, or their assignee, who are then shareholders of the new company (the Offerees), of the Offerer's intention, the identity of the prospective third party purchaser, and the terms and conditions of the proposed sale.　新会社の株式の売却を申し出る本契約当事者（「申込み者」）は、他の当事者またはその時点で新会社の株主である譲受人（「被申込み者」）に対して、申込み者の売却意思、予定される第三者購入者の住所・氏名と申し出をした売却の条件を、書面で通知するものとする。

sale and distribution　販売と頒布（はんぷ）, 販売

◆The Exporter grants the Distributor and the Distributor accepts to be the exclusive distributor for the sale and distribution of the products of the Exporter in the defined sales territory.　輸出者は、販売店が指定販売地域内で輸出者の製品販売の総代理店となることを認め、販売店はこれに同意する。

sale and purchase　売買

◆In the circular sales transactions, Katokichi's affiliates and business clients recorded the repeated sale and purchase of products only on paper receipts.　循環取引で、加ト吉の関連会社と法人顧客は、繰り返し行われた商品の売買を架空の売上だけに計上していた。

sales　（名）売上, 売上高, 取引高, 航空会社などの営業利益, 販売, 売買, 売却, 商法, セールス

after-sales service　アフター・サービス

amount of sales　売上高

block sales　大量販売, 大量売却, 大量取引, 大量売り付け

bogus sales　架空の売上, 虚偽の売上

call sales　訪問販売

catalog [catalogue] sales　カタログ販売

cost sales　元値販売

demonstration sales　実演販売, デモンストレーション・セールス

export sales　輸出販売, 輸出売上高

foreign sales　海外売上高

route sales　巡回販売, ルート・セールス

sales agreement　売買契約, 売買契約書

sales and purchase contract　売買契約

sales assistance　販売支援

sales basis　販売基準

sales channel　販売経路, 販売チャネル

sales competition　販売競争

sales confirmation　販売確認書

sales discounts　売上割引, 現金割引

sales expansion　販売拡張

sales expense　販売費用, 販売経費, 販売費

sales incentive　販売奨励手当て

sales management　販売管理

sales motivation　販売の動機づけ

sales network　販売網

sales organization　販売組織

sales performance　販売実績, 販売成果

sales policy　販売方針

sales promotion　販売促進, 販促, 販促活動, セールス・プロモーション

sales promotion efforts　販売促進努力, 販促努力, 営業努力

sales returns　売上戻り, 売上戻り高, 売上戻り品, 売上返品

sales revenue　売上高, 売上収益, 総売上高

sales slip [check]　売上伝票

sales tax　売上税, 取引高税（物品の売価に課税）, 物品販売税, 消費税

shrinking sales　販売の減少

side-business sales　副業幹旋商法

side-by-side sales　側面販売

telephone sales　電話販売, テレホン・セールス

the average sales per customer　客単価, 顧客1人当たりの平均売上高

unit sales　販売数量, 販売台数

Web sales　ネット販売, ホームページ販売

◆A large increase in overseas sales made up for the ¥180 billion earmarked for settlements and other costs for the company's large-scale recalls in the United States.　海外での販売の大幅増で、同社が米国での大規模なリコール（回収・無償修理）訴訟の和解などの費用として計上した1,800億円が補填された。

sales growth　販売の伸び, 売上高の伸び

◆The recent M&A is a strategy with an eye on Asia, which has a great potential for sales growth.　今回のM&Aは、販売が伸びる可能性が大きいアジアを視野に入れた戦略です。

sales of medical devices　医療機器の販売

◆Because of the domestic lengthy process of approving production and sales of medical devices, some domestic medical device makers have been applying for product approval in Europe and the United States first.　国内での医療機器の製造販売承認手続きの遅れから、国内医療機器メーカーの一部は、製品の承認申請を欧米で先に行っている。

sales practice　販売手法

◆As the value of using big data, a sales practice prevailing in the mail-order business sector is to analyze purchase records of customers and then recommend products based on their tastes and preferences. ビッグ・データの利用価値として、通販業界で広がっている販売手法は、顧客の購入履歴を分析して、顧客の好みに合う商品を薦める方法だ。

sales promotion　販売促進
◆Distributor shall be responsible for the advertising and sales promotion of Products in Territory. 代理店は、契約地域での本製品（契約品）の宣伝と販売促進について責任を持つ。

sales territory　販売領域, 販売区域, 販売地域
◆The Exporter grants the Distributor and the Distributor accepts to be the exclusive distributor for the sale and distribution of the products of the Exporter in the defined sales territory. 輸出者は、販売店が指定販売地域内で輸出者の製品販売の総代理店となることを認め、販売店はこれに同意する。

sales, use or delivery of the products　本製品の販売、使用または引渡し
◆The seller shall not be responsible for any infringement with regard to patents, utility models, designs, trademarks, copyrights, trade secrets or any other intellectual property rights in any country, except for the seller's country, in connection with the sales, use or delivery of the products. 売り主は、本製品の販売、使用と引渡しに関連する特許、実用新案、意匠、商標、著作権、トレード・シークレットまたはその他の知的財産権に関する侵害に対しては、売り主の国を除いていずれの国においても責任を負わないものとする。

salvage loss　救難損失

salvage loss settlement　救助物差引填補方式

same　（形）同じ, 同一の, 同種の, 前記の, 上記の, 前述した　（名）同一物, 同種・同様の事物, 前述の人［もの、こと］

same as, similar to, or competitive with　〜と同種の, 類似の, または〜と競合する, 〜と同種, 類似または競合する
◆During the life of this agreement or extension thereof, if any, and for two (2) years thereafter, Licensee shall not manufacture any other products that are the same as, similar to, or competitive with, Products. 本契約の期間中またはその延長期間中とその後の2年間、ライセンシーは本製品と同種、類似の他の製品または本製品と競合する他の製品を製造してはならない。

sample　（名）見本, 試供品, サンプル
（⇒prior approval）
advance sample　先発見本
counter sample　対（たい）見本, 反対見本
duplicate sample　控え見本
（=file sample, keep sample）
original sample　原（もと）見本
sample discount　見本割引

sample invoice　見本用インボイス
sample of no value　無償見本
sample result　サンプル結果
sample software support agreement　サンプル・ソフトウエア・サポート契約
sample test　サンプル検査, 試供品テスト
shipping sample　船積み見本
similar sample　類品見本
◆The retail stores which form chain-store contracts with a large manufacturing firm deal with all the products of the manufacturer and receive various services such as design of stores, store arrangement and free supply of samples. ある大手メーカーとチェーン店契約を結ぶ小売店は、そのメーカーの全製品を取扱い、そのメーカーから店舗のデザインや店舗配列、サンプルの無料供給などの各種サービスを受ける。◆We enclose a few samples of our product and should be obliged if you would send us samples of the nearest quality you could offer from stock. 当社製品の見本を数点同封しますので、在庫から提供できるほぼ同品質の見本を送っていただけるとありがたいのですが［ほぼ同品質の見本があれば送っていただけないでしょうか］。◆We will supply you with our samples free of charge. 当方見本は、無料で差し上げます。

sanction　（名）制裁, 処罰, 制裁措置, 経済制裁措置, 許可, 認可, 承認, 支持, （社会的・道徳的）拘束力, （法の）強制力
apply [take] economic sanctions against [on]　〜に対して経済制裁を加える、〜に制裁手段を取る
arrears sanctions　延滞した場合の制裁措置
financial sanctions　金融制裁
give sanction to　〜を認可する、〜を是認する
have [obtain] the sanction of　〜の許可を得ている［得る］
heighten sanctions against　〜に対する制裁を強化する
implement economic sanctions against　〜に対して経済制裁を実施する［行う］
impose economic sanctions against　〜に対して経済制裁を科す、〜に対して経済制裁に踏み切る、〜に対して経済制裁措置を取る
lift [remove] economic sanctions against　〜に対する経済制裁［経済制裁措置］を解除する
receive official sanctions　公的許可［認可］を受ける
trade sanctions　貿易制裁, 貿易制裁措置
◆Pyongyang's accounts with Banco Delta Asia in Macao were frozen under U.S. financial sanctions. マカオの銀行「バンコ・デルタ・アジア」にある北朝鮮の口座が、米国の金融制裁を受けて凍結された。◆Russia opposes the enforcement of anti-Syria sanctions because Syria is an impor-

tant importer of weapons from Russia, and Syria provides the Russian Navy with supply bases. シリアはロシアにとって重要な武器輸出先であると同時に、ロシア海軍に補給拠点も提供しているため、ロシアは対シリア制裁の実施に反対している。◆This kind of rocket engine is on the list of items whose exporters are subject to U.N. sanctions because it could be used to manufacture banned missiles that have a range of more than 150 kilometers. この種のロケット・エンジンは、開発が禁止されている射程150キロ・メートル以上のミサイルの製造に使用される可能性があるため、その輸出業者は国連の制裁を受けることになっている。◆Washington has imposed powerful financial sanctions on Iran and it has had a certain level of effect. 米国はイランに対して強力な金融制裁を科して、一定の効果を上げている。

sanction(s) violation 経済制裁違反, 経済制裁規制違反
◆Mitsubishi UFJ Financial Group Inc. agreed to pay $8.6 million to the Treasury Department's Office of Foreign Assets Control to settle alleged U.S. sanction violations related to the transfer of funds to client accounts in Myanmar, Iran and Cuba. 三菱UFJフィナンシャル・グループは、ミャンマーやイラン、キューバなどの顧客口座に行った送金に関して、米国の経済制裁規制に違反した疑いで、米財務省外国資産管理局に860万ドルの和解金を支払うことで合意した。

Sarbanes-Oxley Act 企業改革法(サーベンス・オクスレー法), 企業会計改革法, サーベンス・オクスレー法, SO法 (=Sarbanes-Oxley Act of 2002)
◆The Sarbanes-Oxley Act directed the SEC to implement some of the reporting changes in an attempt to force companies and their executives to be more honest with investors. 企業と企業経営者に投資家への一段と誠実な対応を義務付けるため、サーベンス・オクスレー法は、SEC(米証券取引委員会)に報告規則変更の一部実施を求めた。

satisfaction (名)満足, 充足, 納得, 得心, 償い, 賠償, 返済, 弁済, 義務・債務の履行, 弁済証書
customer satisfaction 顧客の満足, 顧客満足度, CS
customer satisfaction management 顧客満足度経営, CS経営
demand satisfaction 賠償請求する
express satisfaction with ～への満足感を表明する
full of partial satisfaction of previous debts 債務の全額または一部の弁済
meet the satisfaction of ～の要求を満たす
satisfaction of mortgage 譲渡抵当消滅証書
satisfaction of senior obligations 優先債務の支払い
satisfaction piece 償還履行証書

◆We trust that the goods will open up to your entire satisfaction. 契約品[約定品]は、開装の上、十分ご満足いただけるものと思います。
satisfactory to ～が満足する, ～の期待・要求を満足させる, ～に十分な
(⇒irrevocable documentary letter of credit)

schedule (動)予定する, 予定を立てる, 計画を立てる, 予定表を作る
as scheduled 予定どおり
be scheduled to ～する予定だ, ～する方針である, ～する見通しである
full schedule 詰まっている予定, 予定が詰まっている[埋まっている]こと
go according to schedule 予定どおりに進む
investment schedule 投資表
issue schedule 発行時期
keep to a schedule スケジュールを守る
on schedule 予定どおり, スケジュールどおり
prepare a schedule 明細を作成する
price schedule 価格表, 値段表, 定価表 (=schedule of price)
production schedule 生産計画, 生産スケジュール, 生産[製造]予定表
progressive schedule 付属明細表, 追加的明細表
run ahead of schedule 予定[計画]より先に進む
schedule conflict 予定の重なり, ダブル・ブッキング
schedule control スケジュール管理, 進捗状況
schedule of capital 資本明細表, 資本金明細表
scheduled date 予定日
scheduled maintenance 定期保守
scheduled payment 予定支払, 約定支払い, 約定返済
scheduled production 予定生産, 計画的生産
scheduled purchasing 計画的購入, 計画購買
scheduled quantity 予定数量
scheduled rating 表定料率
scheduled territory 指定地域
SEC schedules SEC付属明細表
◆About ten major Japanese automakers are scheduled to take part in an industrial parts and materials exhibition and procurement negotiation fair in Seoul. 韓国・ソウルで開かれる工業部品・素材展示調達商談会には、日本の自動車メーカー約10社が参加する予定だ。◆The big U.S. semiconductor maker Qualcomm put Japanese firms on low priority when it fell behind schedule in parts shipments this summer. 米半導体大手のクアルコムは今夏、部品の出荷が予定より遅れた際、日本企業への出荷を後回しにした[日本企業への出

荷の優先順位を低くした]。

schedule (名)別表, 別紙, 付属書類, 明細表, 一覧表, 予定表, 法律の付則, 特別条項, 予定, 計画, スケジュール

adjust a schedule　スケジュールを調整する

ahead of schedule　予定より早く, スケジュールより早く[早めに], 前倒しで

arriving and sailing schedule　配船表

attached schedule　付表, 貼付の付属書類

audit schedule　監査手順書

behind schedule　予定より遅れて

book a schedule　予定を入れる, スケジュールを埋める

commission schedule　手数料明細表

cost schedule　費用予定表

customs schedule　税率表

delivery schedule　納品予定, 納品日程, 納期

dividend schedule　配当予定

draw up a schedule　予定を立てる, スケジュールを立てる　(=plan a schedule)

extend a schedule　スケジュールを延ばす

fall behind schedule　予定より遅れる, スケジュールより遅れる

schedule of concessions　関税譲許表

schedule of financial statements　財務諸表付属明細表, 財務書類付属明細表

schedule of rates and prices　料率単価表

schedule of royalties　ロイヤルティー明細表

schedule of terms and conditions　取引条件書

schedule price　表示価格, 表示定価

standard schedule　標準日程

supporting schedule　付属明細書

tariff schedule　関税表, 料金制度

tentative auction schedule　暫定的な入札予定

trading schedule　貿易表

work schedule　作業予定, 作業計画, 作業スケジュール

◆The big U.S. semiconductor maker Qualcomm put Japanese firms on low priority when it fell behind schedule in parts shipments this summer. 米半導体大手のクアルコムは今夏, 部品の出荷が予定より遅れた際, 日本企業への出荷を後回しにした［日本企業への出荷の優先順位を低くした］。◆The Company agrees to cede to the Reinsurer such shares of all insurances covered by this Agreement as are set forth in the annexes (Schedule and any Addenda) to this Agreement. 元受会社は, 本協定対象の全保険のうち, 本協定の補遺（特別条項や追加条項）に明記した部分を再保険会社に出再することに合意する。

scheduled date of shipment　船積み予定日, 出荷予定日

◆A letter of credit shall allow partial shipments and be valid for 15 days after the scheduled date

of shipment, and under which Company may receive payment for each partial shipment. 信用状は, 分割船積みを許容するもので, 船積み予定日後15日間有効とし, 会社が分割船積みごとにその支払いを受けることができるものとする。

scheduled shipping date　船積み予定日, 出荷予定日

◆This letter of credit shall be opened not less than 30 calendar days before the first scheduled shipping date for each order and shall be 90 days beyond the anticipated final shipping date. この信用状は, 各注文の最初の出荷予定日から30暦日以上前に開設するものとし, 最終出荷予定日から90日を超えて有効でなければならない。

scope (名)範囲, 領域, 対象, 枠組み, 構成, 区分, 余地, 機会, 可能性

scope and definitions　範囲と定義

scope of services　サービスの範囲

the scope of claims　特許請求の範囲

◆The METI has decided to expand the scope of government-backed trade insurance for overseas social infrastructure projects. 経済産業省は, 海外の社会基盤（インフラ）事業に対する政府保証付き貿易保険の対象を拡大することを決めた。

sea (名)海, 海洋, 波, 大波, 海辺, 海岸

by sea　海路で, 船で

ea pilot　港外水先人

North Sea Brent Spot　北海ブレント・スポット

sail on the sea　海上を航行する

sea accident　海難, 海上事故

sea accident inquiry　海難審判

sea bed　海底

sea B/L　海洋船荷証券　(=ocean B/L)

sea-borne commerce　海上通商

sea-borne trade　海上貿易

sea chart　海図

sea damage　海損

sea damaged terms　品質条件, 潮濡れ売り手持ち条件, S.D.

sea dumping operations　海洋投棄作業

sea farming　海洋養殖, 海洋栽培　(=mariculture)

sea insurance stamp act　海上保険印紙法

sea law　海事法規

sea letter　中立国船証明書　(=sea brief)

sea peril　海上危険, 海難　(=sea risk)

sea protest　海難報告書　(=sea report)

sea room　操船余地

sea terms　航海用語

sea water damage　潮濡れ

sea well　海底油田

sea wolf　海賊

seaworthy packing　耐航包装

territorial sea　領海

the high seas　公海

sea area　海域

◆The sea area of the Pacific Ocean off the coasts of Nagoya and Aichi prefectures has reserves of natural gas equal to more than 10 years worth of Japan's annual imports of liquefied natural gas. 愛知県と三重県の太平洋側沖合の海域には、日本の液化天然ガス（LNG）年間輸入量の10年分以上に相当する天然ガス埋蔵量がある。

sea lane　海上交通路，海上航路帯，常設航路，航路，シーレーン

sea-lane defense　シーレーン防衛

◆The South China Sea is an international sea lane that connects the Middle East with the Northeast Asia. 南シナ海は、中東と北東アジアを結ぶ国際的な海上交通路（シーレーン）である。

◆With intolerable acts of provocation, China has threatened U.S. allies and their sea lanes. 目に余る挑発行為で、中国は米国の同盟国やその海上交通路（シーレーン）を脅かしている。

SEC　米証券取引委員会

（⇒Securities and Exchange Commission）

◆Facebook disclosed its IPO price range of $28 to $35 per share in the paperwork filed with the SEC. フェイスブックは、米証券取引委員会（SEC）に提出した書類で、新規株式公開（IPO）に伴う［IPOの際の］株式の売出価格を1株当たり28〜35ドルに設定することを明らかにした。

secrecy agreement　秘密保持契約，秘密保持協定，守秘契約

◆When Licensee causes a third party to sub-assemble or sub-manufacture substantial portions of Products, Licensee shall enter into a secrecy agreement with such third party, prohibiting said third party from disclosing Know-How and other technical information to others. ライセンシーが第三者に契約品の重要な部分を下請け組立てまたは下請け製造させる場合、ライセンシーは、当該第三者がノウハウとその他の技術情報を他者に開示することを禁止する秘密保持契約を、当該第三者と締結しなければならない。

secure　（動）獲得する，手に入れる，得る，確保する，達成する，実現する，設定する，固定する，（支払いを）保証する，請け合う，（〜から）守る，安全にする，もたらす（bring about），確実にする，確固たるものにする，とりまとめる，（〜に）保険を付ける，（〜に）担保を付ける

be secured by　〜によって保証される，〜で担保されている，〜を担保にして，〜を裏付けとする

loans secured by export trade bills　輸出貿易手形を担保とする貸付け

loans secured by real estate　不動産抵当貸付け

secure a loan with a pledge　担保を付けて

ローン返済を保証する

secure against　〜に備える

secure bank financing　銀行融資を受ける

secure high returns　高利回りを確保する

secure human resources　人材を確保する

secure jobs　雇用を確保する

secure oneself against accidents　損害保険を付ける

secure profits　収益を確保する

◆The company will secure ¥270 billion in loans from the Development Bank of Japan and other lenders. 同社は、日本政策投資銀行などの金融機関から2,700億円の融資を受ける［2,700億円を借り入れる］。

Securities and Exchange Commission　米証券取引委員会，SEC　（⇒SEC）

◆Citigroup will buy back the auction-rate securities from investors under separate accords with the Securities and Exchange Commission and state regulators. 米シティグループは、米証券取引委員会（SEC）や州規制当局との個々の合意に基づいて投資家から金利入札証券（ARS）を買い戻す。

解説 米証券取引委員会（SEC）：証券関連法の運用と公正な証券取引の維持および投資家保護を目的として、1934年証券取引法に基づいて創設された米国の独立した連邦政府機関。委員会は、上院の同意を得て大統領が任命する任期5年の委員5人で構成されている。

SECの主な組織構成：

Directorate of Economic and Policy Analysis　経済分析室

Division of Corporation Finance　企業財務局　法人金融部

Division of Enforcement　法規執行局　執行部

Division of Investment Management　投資管理局　投資管理部

Division of Market Regulation　市場規制局　市場規制部

Office of Administrative Law Judges　行政訴訟審判官室　行政法審判官室

Office of EDGAR Management　エドガー管理室

Office of International Affairs　国際問題室　国際問題課

Office of Opinions and Review　意見起草室

Office of the Chief Accountant　主任会計官室

Office of the General Counsel　法律顧問室

securities firm　証券会社

◆This struggling auto producer is considering setting up a joint venture with an American major securities firm to engage in North American financing operations. 経営再建中のこの自動車メーカーは現在、米証券大手と北米で金融事業［販売金融事業］を手がける合弁会社の設立を検討している。

SECU 418

securities report 有価証券報告書

◆According to the Financial Instruments and Exchange Law, penalties for making false securities reports are tightened from up to five years in prison to up to 10 years in prison. 金融取引法によれば、有価証券報告書の虚偽記載の刑罰は、懲役5年以下から懲役10年以下に引き上げられている。

security （名）証券, 有価証券, 保証, 保証金, 担保, 抵当, 抵当物件, 安全, 安全保障, 保障, セキュリティ

as security for　〜の抵当［担保・保証］として　（＝in security for）

benefit security　給付保障

dilutive security　潜在的普通株式

interest bearing security　利付き証券

listed security　上場証券, 上場有価証券

on security of　〜を担保にして

risk security　リスク証券

security trade［export］control　安全保障貿易管理

social security benefits　社会保障給付

unrated security　格付けのない証券

◆Calling computer security one of the top problems in the United States, the government is forming special units to prosecute hacking and copyright violation. コンピュータのセキュリティを米国の最重要問題のひとつとして、米政府は現在、ハッキング（不正アクセス）や著作権侵害などを摘発する特別専門班を設置している。◆In the loans to be extended to the company by the Development Bank of Japan, accounts receivable will be taken as security. 日本政策投資銀行の同社への融資では、売掛金が担保に取られる。◆Japan-ASEAN ties are meaningful in ensuring regional security, particularly freedom of navigation at sea. 日本とアセアン（東南アジア諸国連合）との関係は、地域の安全保障、とりわけ航海の自由を確保するうえで重要である。◆We need to enhance the security of information networks by preventing leaks of personal information and averting the spread of computer viruses. われわれは、個人情報の漏洩を防ぎ、コンピュータ・ウイルスの流行を回避して、情報ネットワークの安全性を高める必要がある。

seizure （名）差し押さえ, 押収, 没収, 謄本保有地の没収, 逮捕

sell （動）販売する, 売る, 売却する, 売り渡す, 売り込む, 納入する,（電力などを）供給する, 処分する, 債券などを発行する, 譲渡する（自動）売れている, 売られている

buy low and sell high　安く買い高く売る, 安く買って高く売る

close and sell affiliated companies　関連会社［関係会社］を閉鎖・整理して売却する

sell by public tender　公開入札で売却する

sell common stock at book value　普通株式を

簿価で発行する

sell operating rights to　〜に営業権を譲渡する

sell out　売り切れる, 売り尽くす, 店じまいする, 事業を売却する, 自分の信念を曲げる, 信念［主義］に背く, 裏切る, 敵側につく

sell some subsidiaries　一部の子会社を売却する

sell steadily　着実に売れている

sell $3 billion in stock through an online auction　ネット・オークションで30億ドルの株式を発行する

◆According to a salesperson at the TV section of Bic Camera Inc.'s Yurakucho outlet, low-priced products are not selling well now. ビックカメラ有楽町店のテレビ売場の販売担当者によると、今は格安品［低価格品］の売れ行きはかんばしくない。◆Citibank Japan Ltd. is arranging to sell its retail banking business by the end of March 2015 if it can obtain approval from the Financial Services Agency, while it will maintain its corporate banking business. 米金融大手シティグループの日本法人「シティバンク銀行」は、金融庁の承認が得られれば、2015年3月末までに個人向けの小口取引銀行業務の売却を打診しているが、企業との取引を行うコーポレート銀行業務は続ける方針だ。

sell and deliver the products 本商品を販売して引き渡す

◆The product is being sold and delivered to the purchaser under this agreement "AS IS, WHERE IS". 本製品は、現状のまま、本契約に基づいて買い主に販売され引き渡される。

sell, assign, transfer, pledge, encumber or otherwise dispose of 〜を売却、譲渡、移転、質入れ、担保差入れ、その他の方法で処分する

◆Without first obtaining the written consent of other parties hereto, no party, nor its successors or assignees, shall sell, assign, transfer, pledge, encumber or otherwise dispose of, whether by operation of law or otherwise, any shares of voting of the new company or instruments convertible into such shares. 他の本契約当事者の書面による同意を最初に得ないで、いずれの当事者も、その承継人または譲受人も、法律の運用によるかその他の方法によるかを問わず、新会社の議決権付き株式またはこのような株式に転換できる証書を売却、譲渡、移転、質入れ、担保差入れ、その他の方法で処分することはしないものとする。

seller （名）売り主, 売り手, 売り方, 販売者, 輸入販売元

◆A major bone of contention in the trial of the lung cancer drug Iressa case was whether the importer and seller's provision of information on Iressa's side effects to medical institutions was sufficient. 肺がん治療薬「イレッサ」訴訟の裁判の大きな争点は、輸入販売元による医療機関へのイレッサの副作用に関する情報の提供が十分だったか、という点だ。◆If delivery is made under the terms of CFR or CIF, the Seller shall inform the Buyer of the name, nationality, age and other details of the carrying vessel by Fax or E-mail not later than fourteen（14）days before the time of delivery. 引渡しがCFR（運賃込み）またはCIF（運賃保険料込み）の条件で行われる場合，売り主は，引渡し期限の14日前までにファクスかEメールで本船の船名，船籍，船齢その他の詳細を買い主に通知するものとする。◆In case of a CIF contract, the seller shall, at its own expenses, arrange for ocean freight of the products from the port of shipment stated in this agreement to the port of destination of the products. CIF契約の場合，売り主は，本契約に定める船積み港から本商品の仕向け港までの本商品の海上輸送の手配を，自己負担でするものとする。

selling （名）販売，売り，売却

  selling agent　販売代理人
    （=sales agent, representative）

  selling commission［concession］　販売手数料

  selling contract　売り予約，売約

  selling date　売却日，販売日

  selling exchange　売り為替（輸入取引で銀行が外貨を売る場合の総称）

  selling offer　売り申込み　（=offer for sale）

  selling period　販売期間

  selling price　販売価格，売却価格

  selling rate　売り相場

  selling restriction　販売制限

  selling short　空売り　（=short selling）

  semi-exclusive selling agent　限定一手販売代理人
  ◆The TSE does not plan to release details on names of stock issues or methods of short selling. 東証は，空売りの対象の個別銘柄や空売りの手口などの詳細については，公表しない方針だ。

selling organization　販売組織
◆The point of origin（the location of the selling organization）of revenues and the location of the assets determine the geographic area. 地域別区分は，収益の源泉地（販売組織の所在地）と資産の所在地に基づいています。

semiannual　（形）年2回の，半年毎の，半年継続の

sensitive　（形）敏感な，左右されやすい，影響を受けやすい，不安定な，動揺しやすい高感度の，要注意の，細心の注意を要する，繊細な，極秘の，機密の，重要な

  be sensitive to　～に敏感である，～に大きく左右される，～に対する感応性が高い

  be sensitive to lower rates　金利低下に対する感応性が高い，金利低下に敏感である

  be sensitive to price movements　価格動向に左右される

  consumer-sensitive　消費者動向に敏感な

  cost-sensitive　コストに敏感な，コストに左右されやすい

  interest-sensitive instrument　金利感応商品（=interest-rate sensitive instrument）

  market-sensitive　市場に敏感な，市場に左右されやすい

  price-sensitive consumer　価格に敏感な消費者

  sensitive item　輸入要注意品目，センシティブ品目　（=sensitive product: 輸入自由化によって多大な損害を受ける国内産品）

  sensitive list　輸入制限品目表

  sensitive market　不安定市場，不安定相場，不安市況

  sensitive sector　センシティブ・セクター（外国製品の影響を受けやすい部門）
  ◆Sensitive products include rice in Japan's case. 重要品目には，日本の場合のコメが含まれる。

sensitive area　輸入要注意の分野
◆Japanese agriculture still remains a sensitive area. 日本の農業は，まだ輸入要注意の分野［センシティブ・セクター］にとどまっている。

separate and independent　個々の独立した，個別の独立した，独立した
◆In case of shipment in installment, each shipment shall be regarded as a separate and independent agreement. 分割船積みの場合，各船積み個別の独立した契約と見なされる。

separate business activities　個別の営業活動
◆Any tax arising out of the separate business activities conducted by XYZ and ABC pursuant to this agreement shall be born and paid by the party upon whom such tax is imposed by applicable law. 本契約に従ってXYZとABCが行う営業活動から発生する税金は，適用法によりその税金が課される当事者が負担して支払うものとする。

separately　（副）個別に，個々に，別途
◆The period, time, method, and reasonable details of such visits shall be determined separately through mutual consultation between the parties. このような訪問［視察］の期間，時期，方法と合理的な詳細は，当事者間の相互協議により別途決定するものとする。

serve　（動）務める，勤務する，働く，仕事をする，サービスなどを提供する，供給する，商品などを売る，運航する，文書を渡す，送付する，送達する，～の役に立つ，奉仕する，貢献する，利用できる，～の目的にかなう，～の要求などを満たす，～の機能を果たす，～の任務［職務］を果たす，～の手段として機能する，助長する，促進する，推進する，高める
◆A cheaper dollar does definitely serve to make U.S. producers more cost-competitive in international export markets. 国際輸出市場で米国の生産者の価格競争力を高めるには，間違いなくドル安のほうがよい。◆Any notice served by registered mail or by telex as aforesaid shall be deemed

served on the earlier of actual receipt or the expiry of 120 hours after posting. 上記のとおり書留郵便またはテレックスで送達された通知は、実際の受領日と投函から120時間後のうちいずれか早いほうの日に送達されたものと見なすものとする。

service (名)労務, 役務, 勤務, 服務, 公務, 事業, 業務, 施設, 訴状や呼出状の送達, 借入金の定期返済, 公債利子, サービス
customer service　顧客サービス
scope of services　サービスの範囲
◆At TEPCO's shareholders meeting, the Tokyo metropolitan government as a major shareholder in the utility, proposed to include in the articles of incorporation a provision stipulating that putting customer service first is the company's mission. 東電の株主総会で、同社の大株主としての東京都が、「顧客サービス第一を会社の使命とする」との規定を定款に盛り込むよう提案した。◆Other competitive factors in the market for the products are service, delivery, technological capability, and product quality and performance. 市場での製品の競争要因としては、サービスや納入、技術活用能力[技術力]、品質、性能なども挙げられる。

service account　貿易外収支, サービス収支　(=services account)
◆The deficit in the service account in August widened 6 percent, to ¥122.8 billion from a year earlier. 8月の貿易外収支の赤字は、前年同月比で6%拡大して、1,228億円となった。◆The services account posted a deficit of ¥5.1 trillion. サービス収支は、5兆1,000億円の赤字を計上した。

service balance　サービス収支, 貿易外収支　(=services balance)
◆The service balance was ¥5.32 trillion in the red. サービス収支は、5兆3,200億円の赤字となった。

service charges　手数料
◆Service charges or tax on crude oil futures trading should be raised to curb the inflow of speculative money not related to actual demand. 実需に関係ない投機マネーの流入を抑えるため、原油先物取引の手数料の引上げや課税強化をすべきだ。

service trade pact　サービス貿易協定
◆Taiwan needs to pass a contentious service trade pact with China, Taiwan President Ma Ying-jeou said. 物議を醸(かも)している[世間の論議を引き起こしている]中国とのサービス貿易協定は、(立法院で)可決する必要がある、と台湾の馬英九総統は述べた。

services and goods　モノとサービス
◆The emergence of a global trade dispute could hamper smooth transactions in services and goods. 世界的な貿易摩擦が激化すれば、モノとサービスの円滑な取引が阻害されかねない。

services trade　サービス貿易, サービスの取引, (国際収支での)サービス収支

services trade deficit　サービス収支の赤字
◆Japan's services trade deficit in July 2013 was reduced by about 40 percent to ¥196.5 billion

thanks to an increase in the number of visitors to Japan due to the weaker yen and a rise in patent royalty revenues. 2013年7月の日本のサービス収支の赤字は、円安で日本を訪れる外国人旅行者が増えたことや特許権使用料の収入が増えたため、約4割縮小して1,965億円となった。

set forth　定める, 規定する, 記載する, 詳述する, 記述する, 説明する, 明記する, 明示する, 確認する　(=provide, specify: レター形式の契約書の場合には、合意した内容を「確認する」という意味で使われることがある)
◆The particulars of the services and assistance are set forth in Exhibit A hereto. サービスと指導の詳細は、本契約書の付属書類Aに定める。

set forth above　上記の
◆The letter of credit set forth above shall be negotiable against a draft at sight signed by the seller upon the presentation of the following documents: 上記の信用状は、次の船積み書類の提示がある場合には、売り主が振り出した一覧払い手形と引換えに買い取られるものとする。

set forth below　下記の, 以下に定める
on the date set forth below　下記の日付に, 以下に記載する日付に
◆Licensee agrees to pay to Licensor during the term of this agreement the minimum royalty for each contract year as set forth below. ライセンシーは、本契約期間中、以下に定める各契約年度のミニマム・ロイヤルティをライセンサーに支払うことに同意する。

set forth herein　本契約に定める, 本契約に規定する
◆ABC desires to obtain an exclusive license to use the Trademark in order to manufacture and market the products in the territory set forth herein. ABCは、本契約で定める許諾地域で本製品を製造、販売するため、本商標を使用する独占的ライセンスを取得することを希望している。

set forth herein above　本契約に定める上記の
◆Licensee shall pay to Licensor the following guaranteed annual minimum royalties which shall be regarded as part of, and deducted from the running royalties set forth herein above. ライセンシーは、ライセンサーに次の年間保証ミニマム・ロイヤルティを支払うものとする。このミニマム・ロイヤルティは、本契約に定める上記ランニング・ロイヤルティの一部と見なされ、当該ランニング・ロイヤルティから差し引くものとする。

set off A against B　AをBと相殺する　(⇒amount of such claim)
◆Except as otherwise expressly provided for in this agreement, ABC shall not be entitled to set off or withhold any amount owing to ABC under this agreement, against any payment to XYZ for the performance by XYZ of this agreement. 本契約に別に明文の規定がないかぎり、ABCには、本契約に基づきABCに支払われる金額を、XYZによる本契約の履行に対するXYZへの支払い金と相殺

する権利はなく、またその支払いを保留する権利もないものとする。

settle (動) 解決する, 決定する, 清算する, 財産を分け与える

be settled in cash　現金決済する

finally settle a dispute by arbitration　最終的に仲裁で紛争を解決する

settle put option　プット・オプションを決済する

settle the balance　残金を支払う

◆Mitsubishi UFJ Financial Group Inc. agreed to pay $8.6 million to the Treasury Department's Office of Foreign Assets Control to settle alleged U.S. sanction violations related to the transfer of funds to client accounts in Myanmar, Iran and Cuba. 三菱UFJフィナンシャル・グループは、ミャンマーやイラン、キューバなどの顧客口座に行った送金に関して、米国の経済制裁規制に違反した疑いで、米財務省外国資産管理局に860万ドルの和解金を支払うことで合意した。

settle trade　貿易の決済をする

◆If Japan posts a current account deficit, it has to sell yen to buy U.S. dollars as the greenback remains the world's dominant currency for settling trade. 日本が経常収支の赤字を計上した場合、米ドルがまだ世界の貿易決済の主要通貨なので、米ドルを買うために円を売らなければならない。

settlement (名) 合意, 決着, 解決, 決定, 妥結, 処分, 決済, 清算, 借金の支払い, 決算, 和解, 調停, 示談, 財産の譲渡, 贈与財産, 定款, 入植地, 地盤などの沈下, 社会福祉事業団, 厚生施設

a cash settlement　現金による返済

a check in settlement　返済のための小切手

a negotiated settlement　交渉による解決

agree to an out-of-court settlement　示談に応じる

an out-of-court settlement　示談による和解

automatic settlement　自動決済

Bank of International Settlements　国際決済銀行, BIS

biannual settlement　半期決算, 半期決済

business settlement　取引決済

cash settlement　現金決済, 現物決済, 即日決済

dispute settlement procedures　紛争処理手続き, 紛争解決手続き

early settlement　早めの支払い［決済］

enter into a settlement　和解する

fiscal 2015 settlement　2015年度決算

import settlement bill　輸入決済手形

in settlement of one's claim　～の請求に対する支払いとして

March account settlement　3月期決算

midterm settlement in February　2月中間決算

monthly settlements　月ごとの返済［返済金］

out-of-court settlement　示談による和解, 示談, 和解

overnight settlement　翌日決済

reach［achieve, come to］a settlement with　～と合意に達する, ～と和解に達する

semiannual settlement　半期決算, 半期決済

settlement accord［agreement］　和解契約

settlement agreement and release　和解と免除

settlement, compromise or judgment　解決、和解または判決

settlement of business transactions　商取引の決済

settlement of difference　反対売買による差金決済, 紛争の解決

settlement of disputes　紛争解決, 紛争解決条項, 紛争処理, 紛争処理条項

settlement proposal　和解案

terms of settlement　決済条件

the settlement day　（株式清算取引の）決算日, 決済日

window dressing settlement　粉飾決算

work out an out-of-court settlement　示談にする

◆Six executives of Kobe Steel Ltd. agreed in an out-of-court settlement to pay back ¥310 million to the company. 神戸製鋼の幹部6人が、示談による和解で3億1,000万円を会社に返済することで合意した。

settlement of accounts　決算, 決算報告

◆In favorable settlements of accounts for fiscal 2013, companies one after another reported record high profits, buoyed by the weakening yen and a surge in demand just ahead of a hike in the consumption tax rate. 2013年度の好決算で、円安や消費増税前の（駆け込み）需要増が追い風となって、最高益を更新する企業が相次いだ。

settlement term ending on March 31　3月期決算, 3月期

◆The firm is expected to suffer more than ¥260 million in operating losses on a consolidated basis in the settlement term ending on March 31, 2016. 同社の2016年3月期の営業赤字は、連結ベースで2億6,000万円に達する見込みだ。

shale gas production　シェール・ガスの生産

◆The prices of U.S. natural gas currently are about $3 to $5 per million British thermal units (BTU) and they briefly dropped to the $2 range in 2012, while the gas was traded between $6 and $10 until about 2008 before U.S. shale gas production increased. 米国の天然ガスの価格は現在、100万BTU（英国式熱量単位）当たり3～5ドル程度で、2012年には一時2ドル台まで下落した。なお、米国の天然ガスは、シェール・ガスの増産前の2008年頃までは、6～10ドル前後で取引されていた。

shale gas resources　シェール・ガス資源,

シェール・ガス資源量, シェール・ガス資源
埋蔵量
◆According to the U.S. Energy Information
Administration, recoverable U.S. shale gas resources are projected to be 862 trillion cubic feet
(about 24 trillion square meters), the world's
second-largest after China. 米エネルギー情報局
によると、採掘可能な米国のシェール・ガス資源量
［埋蔵量］は、862兆立方フィート(約24兆平方メー
トル)と推定され、中国に次いで世界2位となって
いる。

shale oil　頁岩(けつがん)油, シェール・オ
イル
◆Sumitomo Corp., a Japanese major trading
house, lost $2.2 billion in investments, includ-
ing Texas shale oil and Australian coal mining.
日本の大手商社の住友商事は、米テキサス州での
シェール・オイルの開発や豪州での炭鉱事業など
への投資で、22億ドルの損失を出した。

shale revolution　シェール革命 (シェール
(頁岩)層と呼ばれる硬い岩盤層に含まれる
天然ガスや石油を採掘する技術の急速な進歩
を指す)
◆If reasonably priced oil and gas are exported
to Japan by the U.S. "shale revolution," the cost
of domestic thermal power generation would decrease. 米国の「シェール革命」で、安価な原油や
ガスが日本に輸出されれば、国内火力発電のコス
トは下がることになる。

shall　(助動)～しなければならない、～するも
のとする、～と定める　(=must: 単純未来を
表す助動詞ではなく、現在あるいは未来の義
務、命令を表す)
◆The bank shall have the right, as the obligations
become due, or in the event of their default, to
offset cash deposits against such obligations due
to the bank. 債務の期限が到来したとき、または
債務不履行の場合、銀行はその債務とその預金を
相殺する権利を持つものとする。

shall not　～してはならない、～しないものと
する、～を禁止する　(=must not:may notを用
いることもある)
◆The other party shall not disclose such confidential information to any third party. 他方当事
者は、この秘密情報を第三者に開示してはならない。

share　(名)共有、分担、負担分、割当て、割当て
分、分け前、取り分、持ち分、役割、割合、貢献、
株、株式、株券、持ち分株、株価、市場占有率、市
場占拠率、シェア
◆The Company agrees to cede to the Reinsurer such shares of all insurances covered by
this Agreement as are set forth in the annexes
(Schedule and any Addenda) to this Agreement. 元受会社は、本協定対象の全保険のうち、
本協定の補遺(特別条項や追加条項)に明記した部
分を再保険会社に出再することに同意する。

share of stock　株式
◆No director of the new company shall be required to own of record or beneficially any

shares of the stock of the new company. 新会
社の取締役は、登録株主としてまたは株式の受益
者として新会社の株式を保有することを要求され
ないものとする。

share patents　特許を相互利用する
◆The three major steel companies are expected
to share patents on basic techniques necessary to
process iron ore and other materials for steel production and for manufacturing steel. 鉄鋼大手3
社は、鉄鋼生産のための鉄鉱石などの原料加工や
鋼(はがね)の製造に必要な基本技術に関する特許
を相互利用する見込みだ。

share purchase agreement　株式買収契約,
株式譲渡契約
◆In consideration for the Shares, ABC shall pay
to XYZ at the closing, subject to the terms and
conditions of the share purchase agreement, the
amount of U.S. 500,000. 本株式の対価として、
ABCは、株式譲渡契約の条項に服することを条件
として、クロージング時にXYZに50万米ドルを支
払うものとする。

share swap　株式交換
◆Following the tender offer, Oji Paper would acquire the remaining Hokuetsu shares through a
share swap to turn it into a wholly owned subsidiary. 株式公開買付け(TOB)後に、王子製紙は、
株式交換で残りの北越製紙の株を取得して北越製
紙を完全子会社化する。◆The company acquired
six firms via a share swap in 2014. 同社は、2014年
に株式交換で六つの会社を買収した。◆The com-
pany and its three group companies established a
joint holding company through share swaps. 同
社と同社のグループ企業3社が、株式交換により共
同持ち株会社を設立した。

share swap deal　株式交換取引
◆The bank became a unit of the financial group
through a share swap deal. 同行は、株式交換取引
で同金融グループ系の企業になった。

share transfer　株式譲渡、株式名義書換え

shareholder　(名)株主　(=stockholder)
◆Each meeting of shareholders shall be convened by the president of the new company in
accordance with a resolution of the board of directors. 各株主総会は、取締役会の決議に従って
新会社の社長が招集する。

shareholder approval　株主の承認
◆Companies should obtain shareholder approval
when introducing methods to counter hostile
takeover attempts. 敵対的買収への対抗策を導入す
る場合、企業は株主の承認を得なければならない。

shareholder of record　登録株主、株主名簿
記載の株主、株主
◆Dividends may be paid to the shareholders of
the new company of record as of the last day of
each fiscal year of the new company. 配当は、新
会社の各事業年度の最終日現在の新会社の登録株
主に支払うことができる。

shareholders meeting　株主総会

(=shareholders' [stockholders'] meeting)

◆At TEPCO's shareholders meeting, the Tokyo metropolitan government as a major shareholder in the utility, proposed to include in the articles of incorporation a provision stipulating that putting customer service first is the company's mission. 東電の株主総会で、同社の大株主としての東京都が、「顧客サービス第一を会社の使命とする」との規定を定款に盛り込むよう提案した。

shareholders' interest 株主の権利

◆Even if the company conducts a reverse stock split, it will safeguard shareholders' interest by changing the minimum trading unit from 1,000 shares to 500. 同社が株式併合をしても、最低取引単位を1,000株から500株に変更して、株主の権利は守る方針だ。

shareholdings （名）持ち株, 保有株, 保有株式, 株式保有　(=stockholdings)

◆A law on banks' shareholdings bans banks in principle from owning share in excess of their capital base after Sept. 30, 2004. 銀行等の株式保有に関する法律は、2004年9月30日以降、自己資本を上回る株式の保有を原則として禁止している。

sharp appreciation of the yen 円の急騰, 急激な円高

◆Business sentiment and the willingness of household to spend may cool and stall the economy unless the sharp appreciation of the yen is checked. 円の急騰を止めないと、企業の心理や家計の消費意欲が冷え込み、景気が腰折れしかねない。

sharp increase in imports 輸入の急増, 輸入額の急増, 輸入額の大幅増

◆The record trade deficit in 2012 was caused by a decline in exports due to the European financial crisis and deceleration of the Chinese economy, together with a sharp increase in imports of liquefied natural gas and the rapid hollowing-out of the domestic manufacturing industry. 2012年の過去最大の貿易赤字の要因としては、欧州の金融危機や中国経済の減速などで輸出が減少する一方、液化天然ガス（LNG）の輸入が急増し、国内製造業の空洞化が加速していることも挙げられる。

sharp rise in imports 輸入の急増, 輸入額の急増

◆A slight increase in exports led by automobiles was more than offset by a sharp rise in imports of liquefied natural gas and crude oil for thermal power generation. 自動車を中心に輸出は若干伸びたものの、これは火力発電用の液化天然ガス（LNG）や原油などの輸入急増でかなり相殺された。

sheet （名）表, 報告書, 計算書, 板, (1枚の)紙, 印刷物, パンフレット, 敷布［シーツ］, いかがわしい新聞, (主に)タブロイド版の新聞, 印刷用刷り紙, シート

balance sheet　財務体質, 財務基盤, 貸借対照表, バランス・シート

confirmation sheet　確認通知表, 確認通知状

contract sheet　売買契約書, 契約書

export contract sheet　輸出契約書

import contract sheet　輸入契約書

income sheet　損益計算書

mark sheet　輸入報告書

offer sheet　見積書, オファー・シート

pro forma balance sheet　見積り貸借対照表

process sheet　工程表

work sheet　精算表

shelf registration 一括登録, 一括登録制度, シェルフ登録, 発行登録

◆The Corporation has US $300 million of debt securities registered with the U.S. Securities and Exchange Commission pursuant to a shelf registration program. 当社は、米国の証券取引委員会（SEC）の一括登録制度（シェルフ・レジストレーション）に基づき、3億米ドルの債務証券発行予定額をSECに登録しています。◆Through this shelf registration, the Corporation will be able to offer, from time to time, up to U.S. $300 million of its debt securities and warrants to purchase debt securities. この発行登録［SECの一括登録制度］により、当社は3億米ドルを上限として、債務証券と債務証券の引受権付きワラントを随時、発行することができます。

Sherman Antitrust Act シャーマン反トラスト法

shift （動）移す, 移し替える, 配置転換する, 振り向ける, 変更する, 変える, 転換する, 転嫁（てんか）する, なすりつける, 入れ替える, 繰り上げる, シフトさせる, ギアを変える, 取り除く　（自動）移る, 移動する, 変わる, 変化する, シフトする, ギアを入れ替える

shift a person from the factory to the shop　人を工場から店へ配置転換する

shift downward　下降に転じる

shift funds into other financial products　資金を他の金融商品に変える

shift manufacturing overseas　海外に生産［生産拠点］を移す

shift money　資金を移動する, 資金を切り替える［移し替える］, 資金をシフトする

shift off payment　支払いを延ばす

shift production base overseas　生産拠点を海外に移す

shift the blame (on) to　～に責任をなすりつける, 責任を～に転嫁する

shift the raised costs of plastic parts onto product prices　プラスチック部品のコスト高［コスト上昇分］を製品価格に転嫁する

shift the tax　脱税する

shift upward　上昇に転じる

◆Investors seem to be shifting their money from investment trusts to more secured time deposits in the face of global financial turmoil. 世界の金

融市場の混乱に直面して、投資家は資金を投資信託から安定性の高い定期預金に切り替えているようだ。◆To avert China risks such as the stronger Chinese yuan, surging labor costs and anti-Japan riots, some firms have shifted production lines to other countries in Southeast Asia and other regions with cheaper labor. 中国人民元高や人件費高騰、反日暴動などの中国リスクを回避するため、一部の企業は、中国より低賃金の東南アジアなどの地域に生産ラインの移管[分散化]を進めている。

shift （名）変化, 変動, 変更, 移動, 移行, 転換, 再構成, 勤務, 交替[交代], 交替勤務制, 交替制, シフト, 手段, 方法, 工夫, やりくり, 方便, 策略, 計略, ごまかし, 言い抜け, 逃げ口上, 輪作
◆Great rotation refers to the shift of investment money from low-risk assets such as U.S. Treasuries and the yen into riskier assets such as stocks. 「グレート・ローテーション（大転換）」とは、投資資金を米国債や円などの低リスク資産[安全資産]から株式などリスクの高い資産に移すことを言う。

ship （動）出荷する, 船積みする, 発送する, 発売する, 船で送る, 輸送する, 輸出する
ship out your order　貴社の注文の品を積み出す
ship the goods as contracted　約定品を契約どおり出荷する[契約どおりに積む]
◆About 5.08 million cell phones were shipped domestically in June—a year-on-year increase of 2.1 percent. 携帯電話の6月の国内出荷台数は、前年同月比2.1％増の約508万台だった。◆The Seller shall ship the product to the place designated by the Buyer from New Jersey, U.S.A. on the basis of FOB Yokohama, Japan. 売り主は、買い手が指定する場所に、米国ニュージャージーから日本国横浜港条件で本製品を出荷する。◆We regret to inform you that we may not be able to ship all of your requirements due to the unforeseen increase in the demand for the goods. 本品に対する需要が思いもかけず増大したため、遺憾ながらご入用の品全部の船積みは不可能になるかと思います。

ship （名）船, 船舶, 本船, 船側, 飛行船, 宇宙船
buy American and ship American policy　自国貨自国船主義
cargo ship　貨物船　（=freight ship）
chartering of foreign ships　外国用船
container ship　コンテナ船
conventional ship　在来船
dry-bulk ship　散積み船
ex ship　着船渡し
factory ship　工船, 工作船
flag-of-convenience ship　便宜置籍船
free alongside ship　船側渡し
fully-laden ship　船倉が満杯の船

lighter aboard ship　ラッシュ船
merchant ship　商船
mortgage of ship　船舶抵当権
nuclear ship　原子力船
out of ship　沖渡し条件
qualified ship contract　適格船舶建造契約
registration of ship　船舶登記
Ship American　米船優先使用方針, シップ・アメリカン政策
ship and vessel　船舶
ship bill of sale　船舶売買証
ship broker　海運仲立人, 船舶仲買い人, 用船仲立人
ship canal　船舶用運河
ship entry　船舶入港届け
ship financing　船舶融資
ship laden in bulk　バラ荷を積んだ船
ship's agent　海運代理店, 船荷取扱い店, 船会社代理店
ship's articles　船員雇用契約書, 船員契約書
ship's certificate　船舶登録証
ship's class [classification]　船級
ship's company　乗組員, 全乗組員
ship's days　荷役日数
ship's husband　船舶管理人
ship's manifest　積み荷明細書
ship's papers　船舶書類
ship's registry　船籍
ship's stores　船舶用品
specialized ship　専用船
supply ship　糧食運送船
take ship　乗船する
tanker ship　タンカー
the passenger ship industry　旅客船業界
tie-in ship　仕組み船
tramp ship　不定期船
transport ship　輸送船
unprofitable ship　不採算船
working ship　作業船

shipment （名）出荷, 積出し, 出荷量, 出荷台数, 発送, 輸出, 船積み, 積み荷, 船積み品, 船荷, 船積み量, 船会社への貨物の引渡し
（⇒mainstay export item, ship's rail）
collect a shipment　荷を引き取る
complete the shipment　船積みを完了する
completive shipment　追積み
consignment shipment　積送品
country of shipment　船積み国
delayed shipment　積み遅れ, 船積み遅延

(⇒delay in shipment)

delivery of order　注文品の納入

direct shipment　直航船積み

due of shipment　船積み期限

export shipments　輸出, 輸出の出荷
（=overseas shipments）

factory shipment　工場出荷

forward shipment　先積み

guarantee shipment　積出しを保証する

immediate shipment　直（じき）積み, 即時船
積み

inbound shipment　受入品　（=incoming
shipment）

insure all shipments on W.A.　積送品はすべて
単独海損担保条件で付保する（W.A.=with
average）

inventory to shipment ratio　在庫率, 在庫率
指数

July shipment　7月積み

last shipment　最終船積み

latest shipment　最終船積み期限

make a shipment　出荷する, 発送する

monthly shipment　毎月積み, 月間出荷

next month shipment　翌月積み

offshore shipment　沖積み

outbound shipment　出荷品

outgoing shipment　出荷品

overseas shipments　輸出

paid shipment　支払い済み積出し額

part shipment　部分積み

partial shipment　分割積み

place of shipment　積立地

port of shipment　輸出港, 船積み港, 積出し港,
陸揚げ港

prompt shipment　直（じき）積み, 早積み, 即
時船積み, 即時船積み条件, 即時出荷
（=as soon as possible shipment）

receive a shipment　荷を受け取る, 荷の引渡
しを受ける

return shipment　積戻し

shipment advice　出荷案内

shipment at dock　岸壁積込み渡し値段

shipment by air　空輸

shipment by rail　貨車積送り

shipment by vessel　船積み送り

shipment contract　船積み契約, 積地売買（船
積み地を契約履行地とする売買契約）

shipment from New York　ニューヨーク積込
み渡し値段

shipment in bond　保税積荷

shipment notice　出荷通知, 発送案内

shipment of cargo　船積み

shipment of goods　商品の出荷, 商品の発送,
商品の船積み

shipment out　積送品

shipment procedures　輸出入手続き

shipment restriction　出荷制限

shipment sample　船積み見本

shipment terms　積み期条件

shipment time　船積み期限

shipment to Yokohama　横浜向積送品

shipments policy　出荷保険, 出荷保険証券

short shipment　積残り, 積残り品, 品不足, 船
積み不足

the conclusive date of shipment　船積みの確
定日

the country of shipment　船積み国
（⇒place of business）

the date specified for shipment　船積みの特
定日

the goods are ready for shipment　貨物の船積
み準備ができている

the latest date of shipment　積み期

the possible time of shipment　積み期の見込み

the time of shipment　船積み期, 積み期

the time of shipment contracted　契約の船積み
期, 契約の積み期

transshipment　積替え

upon shipment　出荷時に, 発送と同時に

wrong shipment　誤送品

◆Exports are decreasing moderately recently due
to the decline in shipments to Europe and China.
輸出は, 欧州や中国への輸出減で, このところ緩やか
に減少している. ◆Please give us your best quotations in U.S. dollars for immediate shipment
and proforma invoices. 直（じき）積みでドル建て
の貴社の建て値と試算送り状を, お送りください.
◆The big U.S. semiconductor maker Qualcomm
put Japanese firms on low priority when it fell
behind schedule in parts shipments this summer.
米半導体大手のクアルコムは今夏, 部品の出荷が予
定より遅れた際, 日本企業への出荷を後回しにした
［日本企業への出荷の優先順位を低くした］. ◆The
credit reads that partial shipments are permitted.
信用状には, 「分割積み許可」とあります. ◆The
L/C shall be available for at least fifteen days after the latest date for shipment stipulated in the
contract. 信用状は, 本契約指定の積み期の後, 少な
くとも15日間は有効とする. ◆The shipment will
be made late in March as our subcontractors are
somewhat behind in completing your order.　貴
社注文の履行に下請けが少々遅れを出しているた
め, 積出しは3月末になる見込みです. ◆The ship-
ments will reach you in due course time. 積み荷

SHIP　　　426

は、やがて到着します。◆To cover this shipment, we have drawn upon you at sight for the invoice amount under the L/C opened by ABC Bank. この船積みに対して、当社はABC銀行発行の信用状に基づいて、一覧払い送り状額面金額の手形を貴社宛てに振り出しました。◆We are giving your order priority, but a slight delay in the shipment of yours will be unavoidable. 貴社の注文を優先的に扱っていますが、ご注文の船積みが少々遅れることは避けられません。◆We need to have the goods by the end of October at the latest, so punctual shipment is essential. 同品は遅くとも10月末には入手しなければならないので、積み期に遅れないことが肝要です。◆While Japan's mainstay export item to the U.S. market is vehicles, the shipments to China are mainly electronic parts for assembly. 日本の米市場向け輸出の主力製品は自動車なのに対して、中国向け輸出製品は組立用電子部品が中心だ。◆With the ongoing international division of manufacturing, there is increasing demand for the speedy shipment of parts for automotive and digital electrical appliance products. 国際分業化が進んで、自動車部品やデジタル家電の部品などを迅速に運ぶ需要が高まっている。

shipment in installment　分割船積み
（=installment shipment, shipment by installment）
◆In case of shipment in installment, each shipment shall be regarded as a separate and independent agreement. 分割船積みの場合、各船積み個別の独立した契約と見なされる。

shipment of vehicles　自動車輸出
◆The export growth was supported by robust shipments of vehicles to the Middle East and Russia. この輸出の増加を支えたのは、自動車の堅調な中東とロシア向け輸出だ。

shipment volume　出荷量
◆In the beer industry, a single day's shipment volume during the busiest season from June to August influences the annual performances of beer companies. ビール業界では、6～8月の書き入れ時の1日の出荷量が、ビール各社の年間業績を左右する。

shipments　（名）積み荷, 船積み品, 積送品
shipments of the products　本製品の積送品
◆ABC shall effect all risk（Institute Cargo Clauses）marine insurance with underwriters or insurance companies of good repute in an amount of one hundred and ten（110）percent of CIF value of the shipments of the products. ABCは、本製品積送品のCIF価格の110％の保険金額で、評判の良い保険引受業者または保険会社と全危険担保条件（協会貨物約款）の海上保険の保険契約をするものとする。

shipowner　（名）船主, 船舶所有者
shipowner's liability　船主の責務, 船主責任
shipowner's right　船主の権利, 船舶の権利
shipowners' society　船主協会

shipped　（形）船に積んだ, 船積みした, 船で運ばれた, 輸送された, 発送された
shipped B/L〔bill of lading〕　船積み船荷証券　（=on board B/L）
shipped quality　積込み時品質, 積込み品質, 積込み品質条件
shipped quality terms　船積み時品質条件, 船積み品質条件, 積出し品質条件（=shipping quality terms）
shipped weight　積出し数量
shipped weight final　積出し数量条件
shipped weight terms　積出し数量条件
◆In case the quality of Products shipped to Distributor turns out not to meet the above quality requirements, Distributor can claim a replacement against those inferior Products or cancellation of the individual contract. 販売店に発送した本製品の品質が上記品質基準に適合しないことが判明した場合、販売店は、これら品質の劣る本製品の交換〔これら粗悪品の交換〕またはその個別契約〔個々の契約〕の解除を請求することができる。

shipper　（名）荷主, 発送人, 輸出人, 船積み会社
export shipper　輸出出荷人
merchant shipper　輸出商
shipper cooperative　荷主協同組合
shipper letter of instructions　荷送人信用指図書
shippers' association　荷主組合
shipper's credit　輸出者信用貸し
shipper's export declaration　輸出申告書
shipper's manifest　荷主積み荷目録
shipper's measurement〔weight〕　出荷主の才量
shipper's risk and expense　危険および費用荷主負担, 荷主の危険・費用負担
shipper's tare　船積み風袋
shipper's usance　輸出（者）期限付き手形
◆A full set of negotiable bills of lading made out to order must be endorsed by shipper. 指図人式で作成された譲渡可能な船荷証券一式には、荷送人の裏書が必要である。

shipping　（名）船積み, 港湾荷役, 海運, 海運業
cargo shipping　貨物輸送
declaration for shipping　積出し申告
merchant shipping　貨客船
ocean shipping demand　海運需要
packet-line shipping　定期航路
shipping act　海運法
shipping advice　船積み通知, 船積み通知状, 船積み案内
shipping agent　船舶代理店, 船会社代理店, 船積み代理店, 船荷取扱い店, 荷受業者

S

SHIP

shipping and handling　送料

shipping application　船積み申込み, 船積み申込み書

shipping articles　船員雇用契約書, 船員契約書

shipping bill　船積み送り状, 輸出明細書, 船荷証券

shipping broker　船積みブローカー, 乙仲業者, 海運仲立業者

shipping business　海運業

shipping capacity　船積み能力, 載貨能力

shipping charge　送料, 船積み費

shipping clerk　積み荷事務員, 運送店員

shipping commission　船積み手数料

shipping conditions　船積み条件

shipping conference　海運同盟, 運賃同盟

shipping congestion　船舶滞貨

shipping cost　輸送費, 発送コスト［費用］, 出荷コスト

shipping day［date］　船積み日, 発送日

shipping dock　搬出口

shipping enterprise　海運企業

shipping exchange　海運取引所, 船舶取引所

shipping expenses　出荷費用, 発送費用

shipping freight　海上運賃

shipping freight rates　海上輸送費

shipping goods　船積み商品

shipping industry　海運業界, 海運業

shipping information　出荷データ, 発送データ

shipping instruction　船積み指図, 船積み指図書, 船積み依頼書

shipping invoice　船積み送り状, 船積みインボイス

shipping law　海上運送法

shipping line　海運会社, 船会社

shipping list　船積み明細書, 輸出品明細書

shipping log　出荷記録

shipping mark　荷印, 荷印条件

shipping market　海運市場

shipping memo　シッピング・メモ

shipping merchant　海運商

shipping note　船積み通知

shipping notice　船積み通知書, 発送案内

shipping order　出荷指図書, 船積み書類, 出荷命令書

shipping papers　船積み書類

shipping parcel receipt　船積み小荷物受取証

shipping permit　船積み許可, 船積み免状

shipping point　正貨現送点, 船積み地点, 出荷

地点, 出荷地渡し

shipping policy　海運政策

shipping pool　運賃同盟

shipping port　積出し港

shipping quality　船積み品質

shipping quantity terms　積載重量条件（=intaken weight final, shipped weight final）

shipping rate　輸送量, 輸送運賃

shipping receipt　積み荷受取証

shipping report　出荷報告書

shipping ring　海運同盟

shipping room　発送室, 運輸部

shipping sample　船積み見本

shipping schedule　船積み予定, 船積み予定表

shipping specification　積み荷明細書

shipping terms　船積み条件, 発送条件

shipping ton　運賃建てトン, 運賃トン, 積載トン

shipping tonnage　船腹量

shipping weight　船積み重量, 積み高

transshipment shipping bill　接積貨物積入れ証, 接積貨船積み証

shipping company　海運会社, 船会社
◆The South Korean shipping company operating the sunken ferry attached little importance to its crew's training for evacuation guidance and other emergency measures aimed at securing the safety of passengers. 沈没した旅客船を運航していた韓国の船会社は, 乗客の安全確保のための避難誘導など緊急措置の乗務員訓練を軽視していた。

shipping date　船積み日　（=date for shipment）
◆This letter of credit shall be opened not less than 30 calendar days before the first scheduled shipping date for each order and shall be 90 days beyond the anticipated final shipping date. この信用状は, 各注文の最初の出荷予定日から30暦日以上前に開設するものとし, 最終出荷予定日から90日を超えて有効でなければならない。

shipping documents　船積み書類　（船荷証券（B/L）と商業送り状のほか, CIF契約の場合は海上保険証券（insurance policy）または保険承認状（insurance certificate）。この他に包装明細書（packing list）、領事送り状、税関送り状、原産地証明書（certificate of origin）、検査証明書（inspection certificate）、貸方票（credit note）または借り方票（debit note）などで構成される）
◆Enclosed are the copies of the shipping documents covering this order as follows: 本注文の船積み書類の写しは, 次のとおり同封してあります。◆We enclose the shipping documents covering the goods and expect your remittance in due course. 契約品の船積み書類を同封し, 期日どおり

SHIP 428

のご送金を期待しております。

shipping space 船腹
◆If delivery is made under the terms of FOB, the Buyer shall book shipping space in accordance with the time of delivery stipulated in this agreement. 引渡しがFOBの条件で行われる場合、買い主は、本契約で定める引渡し期限に従って（本船の）船腹を予約するものとする。◆In case of a FOB contract, the purchaser shall give shipping instructions and provide shipping space. FOB契約の場合は、買い主が船積みの指図を行い、船腹を提供（確保）するものとする。◆Shipment within the time stipulated shall be subject to shipping space being available. 所定の船積み期間内の船積みは、船腹を確保できることを条件とする。◆We fear we have to advise you that we may not be able to dispatch in full your order due to the shortage of shipping space. 不本意ながら、船腹不足のため、貴社の注文が一部積み残しになる可能性があることをお伝えしなければなりません。

shipside （名）船側

shipside delivery 本船渡し, 自家取り
（=alongside delivery）

ship's rail 船の舷側欄干, 本船の欄干, 本船舷側欄干
◆Risks of and title to the products shall pass from the seller to the purchaser at the time when the products or any part of the products passes the ship's rail of the vessel at the port of the shipment. 本製品の危険負担と所有権は、本製品または本製品の一部が船積み港で本船の舷側欄干を通過した時点で、売り主から買い主に移転するものとする。

short （形）不足の, 品薄の, 短期の
short bill （30日払い以下の）短期手形
short bond 短期債券
short bunker 燃料不足
short cash 現金不足
short check 預金切れ小切手
short crop 不作
short delivery 不足配達, 受渡し品不足, 個数不足, 揚げ荷不足
short exchange 短期為替（手形）
short form B/L 略式船荷証券
（=short form of B/L）
short in dispute 不足詮議中
short landed 揚げ残り
short landed cargo 不足荷物
short landing 着荷不足, 揚げ不足
short measurement 寸法不足
short money 短期借入れ
short notice （代金決済の）期限経過通知
short sale 空売り
short shipment 積残り, 積残り品, 品不足, 船積み不足

short shipped 積残り
short stock 在荷薄
short supply 供給薄, 出回り薄
short ton 軽トン, 米トン
（=American ton, net ton）
◆We would appreciate your immediate reply as time is running short. 時間がないので至急、ご返事をいただきたい。

short selling 空売り （=short sale）
◆The TSE does not plan to release details on names of stock issues or methods of short selling. 東証は、空売りの対象の個別銘柄や空売りの手口などの詳細については、公表しない方針だ。

short term （名）短期 （形）短期の
short term contract 短期契約
short term finance 短期金融

shortage （名）不足
a shortage of cash 現金不足
a shortage of equity capital 自己資本不足
a shortage of money 金不足, 資金不足, 通貨不足 （=money shortage）
a shortage of raw material 原材料不足
dollar shortage ドル不足
excess or shortage of funds 資金の過不足
foreign exchange shortage 外貨不足
inventory shortage 在庫不足, 棚卸し減耗費
investment shortage 投資不足
labor shortages 労働力不足, 人手不足
manpower shortage 人的資源不足, マンパワー不足
shortage of petroleum, gas or other energy sources 石油, ガスなどのエネルギー不足
shortage of shipping space 船腹不足
shortage of transport 輸送力不足
shortages of supply 供給不足
◆GM's parts shortages are caused by a 10-day supplier strike. GMの部品不足は、10日間に及ぶ部品供給業者のストによるものだ。◆We fear we have to advise you that we may not be able to dispatch in full your order due to the shortage of shipping space. 不本意ながら、船腹不足のため、貴社の注文が一部積み残しになる可能性があることをお伝えしなければなりません。

shortages, defects or damage 不足、瑕疵（かし）または損傷
◆Within 10 days after the receipt of such notice, Supplier will investigate the claim of shortages, defects or damage and inform Distributor of its findings. この通知を受け取ってから10日以内に、供給者は、不足、瑕疵または損傷のクレームを調査して販売店にその調査結果を報告する。

shortship （動）積み残す
◆This consignment had to be shortshipped as part of it was badly damaged. この積み荷に積

み残しが出たのは、積み荷の一部がひどく破損したからです。

SIFI システム上重要な金融機関, 巨大金融機関（systematically important financial institutionの略。G20の合意のなかで、通常の銀行以上に厳しい自己資本規制基準などが適用される大規模金融機関）

G-SIFs［GSIFs］ 国際的な巨大金融機関, グローバルSIFI（global systemically important financial institutionsの略：大規模金融機関のうち、世界的金融システムに影響を及ぼす可能性のある金融機関）

SIFIs システム上重要な金融機関
◆According to the Financial Stability Board, 28 banks viewed as global systemically important financial institutions（G-SIFIs）will be subject to a new global rule requiring them to hold extra capital to prevent future financial crises. 金融安定化理事会（FSB）によると、金融システム上重要な国際金融機関（G-SIFIs）と考えられる世界の28行が、金融危機の再発を防止するため、資本の上積みを求める新国際基準［新国際金融規制］の対象になる。

sight （名）一覧 （⇒at sight, draw）
a bill payable at sight 一覧払い手形
a draft at sight 一覧払い手形
a sight credit 一覧払い信用状
a sight L/C 一覧払い信用状
at sight 一覧で, 一覧払い, A/S
draft at sight 一覧払い手形
draw a draft at 30 day's sight on you through ABC Bank for $5,000 ABC銀行経由で5,000ドルの一覧後30日払い手形を貴社宛に振り出す
draw a sight draft on New York on［upon］you ドル建て一覧払い手形を貴社宛てに振り出す
open a sight L/C 一覧払い信用状を開設する
sight bill 一覧払い手形
sight buying 一覧払い為替の買い相場
sight credit 一覧払い信用状
sight draft 一覧払い手形, 一覧払い為替手形
sight draft with bill of lading 船荷証券付き一覧払い為替手形
sight entry 仮輸入品
sight note 一覧払い約束手形, 一覧払い手形
sight rate 一覧払い（為替）相場
sight test 一覧検査

sign （動）署名する, 署名調印する, 調印する, ～と契約する
sign a confidentiality agreement 秘密保持契約書に署名する
sign a memorandum 覚書に調印する, 覚書に署名する, 覚書を取り交わす

sign a proxy statement 委任状に署名する
sign an agreement to borrow 借入れ契約を結ぶ, 借入れ契約を締結する
sign off on ～に正式に同意する
sign on ～雇用契約に署名する, ～を登録する
sign up for ～と契約する, ～に登録を申し込む
◆Japan and the United States will sign the open skies agreement, and carriers in both countries will be able to apply for U.S. antitrust immunity. 日米両政府がオープンスカイ協定を締結することによって、両国の航空会社は米国独占禁止法の適用除外申請が可能になる。◆No modification of this agreement shall be effective unless in writing and signed by both parties. 本契約の変更は、両当事者が署名した書面でないかぎり、有効とはならない。

sign a contract 契約を結ぶ, 契約書に署名する
sign a one-year contract 1年契約を結ぶ
◆KEPCO and Kyushu Electric Power Co. have signed a one-year contract with a U.S. firm to jointly buy a total of 1 million tons of U.S. coal in the one year. 関西電力と九州電力は、米国産の石炭を1年間で計100万トン共同購入［共同調達］する1年契約を、米国の企業と結んだ。

signature （名）署名, サイン, 特徴, 特質, 痕跡, 形跡
commend our signature to your（kind）protection （手形振出人が名宛て人に対して言う）何とぞこの手形をお引き受けください、この手形の支払いをよろしくお願いします （=recommend our signature to your protection）
put one's signature to［on］ ～に同意する
Signature: 署名欄
signature by procuration 代理署名
signatures 契約書の後文
◆To cover this shipment, we have drawn upon you at 60 d/s, in the amount $50,000, in favor of ABC Bank, and recommend our signature to your protection. この船積みに対して、一覧後60日払い、ABC銀行を取引人とする額面5万ドルの手形を貴社宛てに振り出しましたので、何とぞこの手形をお引き受けください。◆We negotiated our draft through the bank above-mentioned under L/C No. 5000 established by the ABC Bank, New York, and commend our signature to your protection. 当社は、ABC銀行（ニューヨーク）発行の信用状5000号に従って上記銀行で手形を買い取ってもらいましたので、この手形の支払いをよろしくお願いします。

simultaneously with ～と同時に
◆On all orders of fifty thousand U.S. dollars or under, payment shall be made simultaneously

with the giving of the order. 5万米ドル以下の
注文の場合、支払いはすべて発注と同時に行うも
のとする。

single arbitrator 単独仲裁人, 単独の仲裁
人 (=sole arbitrator)
◆Any controversy, claim or dispute between the
parties concerning this agreement shall be finally
settled by arbitration in San Francisco, California, before a single arbitrator. 本契約に関する当
事者間の論争、請求または紛争は、米国カリフォ
ルニア州サンフランシスコ市で単独仲裁人による
仲裁で最終的に解決する。

site (名)サイト, インターネット上の場所,
ホームページ (=homepage, Web page, Web
site)
auction site オークション・サイト
e-commerce site eコマース・サイト
EC site 電子商取引サイト, ECサイト
(=e-commerce site)
harmful site 有害サイト
shopping site ショッピング・サイト
Web site ウェブ・サイト
◆There is no such thing as an absolutely secure
site. 絶対安全なサイト、などというものはない。

slip (名)伝票, 票, 券
application slip 申込み票, 保険申込み書
exchange contract slip 為替予約票
gate slip コンテナ貨物搬入票
order slip 注文伝票
pay-in slip 払込み伝票
sales slip 売上伝票
transfer slip 振替伝票

slowdown in exports 輸出の鈍化
◆A slowdown in exports will be temporary. 輸
出の鈍化は、一時的なものだ。◆The slowdown in
exports has also drastically cut into Japan's current account surplus. 輸出の鈍化で、日本の経常
黒字も激減している。

sluggish increases in exports 輸出の伸び
悩み
◆The positive effects of the yen's depreciation have not yet fully appeared, but sluggish
increases in exports in the future due to a
slowdown in the economic growth of emerging economies are worried about by some
economists. 円安のプラス効果はまだ本格的に現
われていないが、新興国の経済成長の鈍化で、今後
の輸出の伸び悩みをエコノミストは懸念している。

slump in global demand 世界的な需要の
冷え込み
◆The decline in China's exports accelerated in
February as a slump in global demand worsened.
世界的な需要冷え込みの悪化で、中国の2月の輸出
減少は加速した。

small and midsize businesses 中小企業
◆Japanese small and midsize businesses have

been tormented by the rise in prices of imported
raw materials due to the weakened yen. 日本の
中小企業は、円安による輸入原材料価格の上昇で、
苦しんでいる。

smuggle (動)密輸する, 密輸入する, 密輸出
する, 密入国させる, 密出国させる, 〜をこっ
そり運ぶ
smuggle drugs into 〜に麻薬を密輸する
smuggle in arms 武器を密輸入する
smuggle out nuclear weapons 核兵器を密輸
出する
smuggled cash 海外からの資金持ち込み
◆U.S. authorities arrested a British national on
suspicion of trying to smuggle a surface-to-air
missile into the United States. 米政府当局は、米
国に地対空ミサイルを密輸しようとした容疑で英
国人を逮捕した。

smuggling (名)密輸, 密航
◆Japan and Russia inked a treaty on measures
to control poaching and smuggling of crabs and
other marine products in the Okhotsk Sea. 日本
とロシアは、オホーツク海のカニなど水産物の密
漁・密輸入対策に関する協定に署名した。◆The
United States, Japan and South Korea agreed to
take tough action against alleged illegal activities
by North Korea, including drug smuggling and
money counterfeiting. 米国、日本と韓国は、北朝
鮮によるとされる麻薬密輸や通貨偽造などの非合法
活動に断固対処することで合意した。◆Two drug
detection dogs were introduced from the United
States in 1979 by Tokyo Customs to fight illegal
drug smuggling. 麻薬探知犬は、違法薬物の密輸
入を阻止するため、東京税関が1979年に米国から
2頭を導入した。

so advise その旨通知する, その旨連絡する
◆In the event that the purchaser does not wish to
purchase all or any part of the products from the
seller, the purchaser shall so advise the seller and
shall not be obliged to purchase such quantities
of the products. 買い主が売り主から本製品の全部
または一部を購入することを希望しない場合、買
い主はその旨売り主に通知するものとし、買い主
は本製品の当該数量を購入する義務は負わないも
のとする。

so long as 〜するかぎり, 〜する間は, 〜さえ
すれば
◆You may count on our best efforts so long as
you can maintain moderate prices. 手頃な価格
[格安料金]を維持できるかぎり、当社は最大限の
努力を貴社にお約束します。

social security 社会保障, 社会保険料, 社会
保障制度
◆The payment of the above salaries shall be subject to withholdings for income tax and social
security and to any other withholdings required
by applicable law. 上記給与の支払いは、所得税、
社会保険料と、適用法によって要求されるその他
の源泉徴収の対象となるものとする。

sole (形) 単独の, 独占的な, 一手に扱う, 唯一の

  at one's sole option 〜単独の判断で

  in one's sole discretion 〜の単独の裁量で, 〜の単独の判断で, 〜のみの判断で (=at one's sole discretion)

  on one's sole responsibility 単独の責任で

  sole and true owner of the technical information 技術情報の単独かつ真実の所有者

  sole distribution right 独占販売権

  sole export agent 輸出総代理店

  sole owner 唯一の所有者

  sole right 独占権, 単独の権利

sole and exclusive 独占的な, 独占的, 唯一の, 唯一の排他的な

  sole and exclusive agency agreement 独占的代理店契約, 総代理店契約

  sole and exclusive distributor 独占販売店, 独占的な販売店

  sole and exclusive distributorship agreement 独占的販売店契約, 一手販売店契約

  ◆Licensee acknowledges that Trademarks shall remain the sole and exclusive property of Licensor. ライセンシーは, 本商標がライセンサーの独占的財産として存続することを認める。

sole arbitrator 単独仲裁人 (=single arbitrator)

  ◆If the Respondent fails to appoint an arbitrator within such 60 day period, the arbitrator named in the Demand shall decide the controversy or claim as a sole arbitrator. 被申立て人が上記60日の期間内に仲裁人を指名しない場合には, 申立て書[仲裁申立て書]で指名された仲裁人が, 単独仲裁人として紛争または請求を判断する。

sole discretion 単独の裁量, 単独の判断で

  ◆X's credit limit may be set by Z at its sole discretion. Xの与信限度額は, Zがその単独の裁量で設定できる。

solely responsible for 〜に対して単独責任がある, 〜について単独で責任を負う

solicit (動) 勧誘する, 募集する, 募(つの)る, 強く求める, 〜するように要請する, 資金などを集める, 訪問販売する, (人を) 悪事に誘う

  solicit clients 顧客を勧誘する

  solicit funds from 〜に資金提供を要請する, 〜に出資を勧誘する, 〜から資金を集める

  solicit investors 出資者を募る[募集する], 投資家を募集する

  solicit new customers 新規顧客を勧誘する

  solicit new investors 新規出資者を募集する [募る]

  solicit orders 注文を求める, 注文を取る

  solicit proxies 委任状を取り付ける

  ◆It may sound legitimate because it is a U.S. firm soliciting on the Internet. But you should not get tempted easily by a business that does not exchange contracts and provide substantial information about cancellation procedures. インターネットを使ってアメリカの企業が勧誘している[呼び掛けている]ことから法的に問題はない, と思えるかもしれない。でも, 契約書面を交わさず, 解約手続きなどの説明も事実上ないような商法にはすぐ飛びつかないようにしなければならない。◆These briefing sessions for soliciting new investors in the pyramid scheme were run by sales department staff including the firm's chairman. マルチ商法で新規出資者を募集するためのこれらの説明会は, 同社の会長を含めて営業部門の幹部が担当していた。

solvency margin ratio ソルベンシー・マージン比率

  ◆The solvency margin ratio indicates the ability of insurers to honor insurance claims and other payments. ソルベンシー・マージン比率は, 保険会社の保険金その他の支払い金の支払い能力を示す。

source (動) 入手する, 仕入れる, 調達する

  be sourced from 〜から入手する, 〜から仕入れる

  locally sourced 地元産の

  money sourced from 〜から提供される資金

  source from abroad 海外から調達する

  ◆Some foreign automakers began sourcing their auto parts in other Asian countries after the March 11 earthquake and tsunami. 2011年3月11日の東日本大震災後, 海外自動車メーカーの一部は, 自動車部品の調達先を日本からアジアに切り替えるようになった。

source(s) (名) 仕入れ先, 調達先, 情報源, ニュースソース, 筋, 取材源, 関係者, 関係筋, 資料, 出典, 出所, 水源, 源, 源泉, 種(たね), 利子・配当などの支払い者

  business sources 市場筋

  cheaper sources 安い仕入れ先

  deduction at source 源泉徴収

  double sourcing 供給源の分散

  industry sources 業界筋

  liquidity sources 資金源

  market sources 市場筋

  outside source 外部の調達先, 外部の仕入れ先

  source material 基礎資材, 原資材

  source of cash 外貨の獲得源

  source of financing 資金調達源

  sources of technology 技術の導入先

  supply source 供給源

  ◆As long as Japan depends on thermal power generation as an alternative electricity source, LNG imports will continue to increase and the nation's wealth will flow to countries rich in natural resources. 日本が代替電源として火力発電に依存するかぎり, 天然液化ガス (LNG) の輸入額は

増え続け、国富は天然資源の豊富な国に流出する。

sourcing （名）調達（procurement）, 業務委託, 供給, ソーシング （⇒outsourcing）

double sourcing　供給源の分散

global sourcing　グローバル・ソーシング

overseas sourcing　海外調達

parts sourcing　部品調達

raw material sourcing　原材料の供給

world sourcing　世界市場への製品供給

◆Japanese automakers will boost parts sourcing from South Korean suppliers as remedies for the strong yen. 円高対策として、日本の自動車メーカー各社は韓国製部品の調達［韓国部品メーカーからの部品調達］を拡大する方針だ。◆The recent surges in the yen's strength have made it imperative for Japanese carmakers to substantially bring down their parts procurement costs by overseas sourcing. 最近の円高で、日本の自動車メーカー各社は、海外調達による部品調達コストの大幅引下げが緊急課題となっている。

South Korea　韓国

◆In terms of trade volume, South Korea is currently among the top 10 countries partly due to its efforts to promote free trade agreements with the United States, the European Union and others. 貿易額で、韓国は現在、米国や欧州連合（EU）などとの自由貿易協定（FTA）推進策を軸に、世界トップ10入りを果たしている。

South Korea's trade with China　韓国の対中貿易

◆The value of South Korea's trade with China since it established diplomatic relations with Beijing has expanded to such an extent that it has surpassed its combined trade with Japan and the United States. 韓国が中国と国交を樹立して以来、韓国の対中貿易額は、対日・対米の貿易総額を凌駕（りょうが）するまでに拡大している。

South Korea's won currency　韓国の通貨ウォン

◆Amid the ongoing European financial crisis, the value of South Korea's won currency may steeply decline if foreign financial institutions and investors withdraw funds from the country. 今回の欧州金融危機の影響で、海外の金融機関や投資家が資金を引き揚げたら、韓国の通貨ウォンは急落する可能性もある。

Southeast Asia　東南アジア

◆As labor costs in China are expected to continue rising, labor-intensive industries such as fashion and electronics will keep relocating their manufacturing bases to Southeast Asia and other regions with cheaper labor. 中国の人件費上昇は今後も続く見通しなので、アパレルや家電などの労働集約型産業では、生産拠点を中国より低賃金の東南アジアなどに移す流れが続くものと思われる。◆Japanese companies' direct investment in Southeast Asia in the first half of 2013 posted a

fourfold year-on-year jump to about ¥1 trillion, which is twice as high as China-bound investment. 2013年上半期の日本企業の東南アジア向け直接投資は、前年同期比4倍増の約1兆円で、中国向け投資の2倍となっている。

sovereign debt crisis　財政危機, 政府債務危機, ソブリン債危機, 国家の財政危機［債務危機］

◆The economic slowdown in Europe due to the sovereign debt crisis and slackening growth of China as a major exporter to Europe have dealt a painful blow to Japan's exports and production. 債務危機に伴う欧州経済の減速と、欧州向け輸出の多い中国の成長鈍化が、日本の輸出と生産に耐え難いほどの打撃を与えている。

sovereign immunity　主権免責, 主権免除, 国家主権に基づく免責

the privilege of sovereign immunity from suit　国家主権に基づく裁判からの免除・免責特権

the waiver of sovereign immunity　主権免責の放棄, 国家主権免責の放棄

◆ABC National Corporation hereby waives and agrees to waive in any proceedings for the enforcement of this agreement, any and all privileges or sovereign immunity, including the privilege of sovereign immunity from suit or immunity of the property from attachment or execution, to which it may be entitled under international or domestic laws, as a procedural defense or otherwise. ABC国営会社は、本契約を実施するための一切の手続きにおいて、手続き上の抗弁その他として当該国営企業が国際法または国内法により有する一切の特権または主権免除（国家主権に基づく裁判からの免除特権や財産の差し押さえまたは強制執行からの免除を含む）を本契約により放棄するとともに、その放棄に同意する。

sovereign risk　ソブリン（政府債務）危機, ソブリン・リスク, カントリー・リスク（対外融資先が公的機関の場合の債権回収リスクで、これには国債の利払い・元本償還の不履行、資本移動の制限、課税の強化、投資先企業の破たんなどが含まれる）

sovereign wealth fund　政府系投資ファンド

◆Amid surging prices of crude oil and other resources, the sovereign wealth fund will invest mainly in solar power generation, fuel cells, and other new energy technologies and natural resources. 原油その他の資源価格の高騰を受け、同政府系投資ファンドは、太陽光や燃料電池などの新エネルギー技術や天然資源に投資の重点をおく方針だ。

SPA　自社ブランドの衣料品販売直営店, 製造小売り（speciality store retailer of private label apparelの略。顧客のニーズに効率的に対応するため、衣料品の企画、開発から素材の選定、製造、流通、販売にいたるまでを自社で一手

に取り扱う手法。自主企画商品（プライベート・ブランド）として販売する場合もある）

space （名）船腹，空間，余地，スペース

blank space　余白，空白

book the necessary（freight）space at our limit　当方指し値で必要な船腹を予約する

dead space　空荷船腹

secure space for your order　貴注文の船腹を確保［獲得］する

space allotment　船腹割当て

space book　船腹原簿

space broker　船腹仲立人　（=shipping broker）

space charter　共同運航，共同配給，スペース・チャーター

space occupied　使用船腹

space reservation　数量予約

space unoccupied　余剰船腹

specification （名）明記，詳述，仕様，仕様書，明細，（特許・設計の）明細書，規格，内訳，加工

a model as per the enclosed specifications　同封仕様書どおりの機種

specification cost　仕様書原価

specification for difference　差金決済取引

specification limit　仕様限界，規格限界

specifications and drawings　仕様書と図面

◆We are prepared to place a prompt trial order if you can guarantee supply of products strictly in accordance with our specifications. 貴社が当社の仕様書どおりの商品の供給［納入］を保証するなら，早速，試験注文を出します。

specify （動）明記する，明示する，記述する，列挙する，特定する，定める，指示する

the amount specified above　上記金額

◆Quantity is subject to a variation of 5% more or less than the contracted quantity at Seller's option unless otherwise specified. 数量は，他にとくに明記しないかぎり，売り主の裁量で契約数量より5%増減の変動が生じることがある。◆The seller warrants that the Goods will be free from defects in material and workmanship for a period as specified in this agreement. 売り主は，本契約で定める期間，本商品が材料と仕上げの面で欠陥がないことを保証する。◆We have valued upon you today for the amount specified above, at sight, and ask you to accord our draft your due protection. 当社は本日，貴社宛てに上記金額に対する一覧払い手形を振り出しましたので，この手形のお引受けをお願い致します。

speculative fund　投機資金，投機マネー

◆In light of complaints from emerging economies that a glut of speculative funds due to monetary easing measures taken by advanced countries have caused the appreciation of their currencies and asset inflation, the G-20 partici-

pants agreed that they will monitor and minimize the negative ripple effects of their respective financial policies. 先進国の金融緩和策でだぶついた投機マネーが新興国の通貨高や資産インフレを招いているという新興国の不満に配慮して，G20参加国は，それぞれ金融政策の負の波及効果を監視し，最小化することで合意した。

speculative investments　投機的な投資

◆The Chinese economy will become anemic and the world economy could suffer immense damage if China is faced with an unabated flight of capital due to speculative investments that its economic bubble has lured from abroad. 中国で，中国のバブル景気で海外から流入した投機マネーが大量に流出したら，中国経済は活気を失い，世界経済は甚大なダメージを受けることになろう。

speculative money　投機マネー

◆By being vigilant against excessive volatility in exchange rates, the G-20 will reduce the risk of speculative money causing appreciation of currencies and inflation in emerging countries. 為替相場の過度な変動を監視して，世界［主要］20か国・地域（G20）は，投機マネーが新興国の通貨高やインフレを招くリスクを軽減する方針だ。◆Erratic fluctuations of both stock prices and exchange rates have continued, reflecting the turbulent moves of speculative money on world markets. 世界的な投機マネーの激しい動きを反映して，株価と為替相場の乱高下が止まらない。◆Service charges or tax on crude oil futures trading should be raised to curb the inflow of speculative money not related to actual demand. 実需に関係ない投機マネーの流入を抑えるため，原油先物取引の手数料の引上げや課税強化をすべきだ。◆Speculative money has poured into emerging economies, causing an appreciation of their currencies and asset inflation because of drastic monetary easing by Japan, the United States and Europe. 日米欧の大胆な［大規模な］金融緩和で，投機マネーが新興国に流れ込み，新興国の通貨高や資産インフレを招いている。

spikes in prices　値上り，価格の高騰

◆The import prices of crude oil and grains have surged, causing spikes in the prices of food products and daily necessities that have dampened household spending. 原油や穀物の輸入価格高騰で，食品や日用品の価格が上昇し，個人消費も冷え込んでいる［個人消費の低迷を招いている］。

spot （形）即座の，現金の，現金払いの，現金取引の，現物の

spot and short selling of shares　株の現物売りと空売り

spot basis　現物決済

spot broker　現物仲買い，現物仲買人，現物ブローカー

spot cargo　現物荷

spot cash　即時現金，即金，即金払い

spot charter　不定期用船

spot check　現物相場（現金売買の値段）, 抜き取り検査, 抜き打ち点検・検査

spot commodity　現物
（=cash commodity, spot goods）

spot contract　現物即時渡し約定, スポット売買契約

spot crude　スポット原油

spot currency market　直物通貨市場

spot deal　直物取引, 現物取引, 直物為替取引

spot dealing　直物取引, 現物取引

spot delivery　現場渡し, 現物渡し

spot dollars　ドル直物

spot exchange　直物為替

spot exchange rate　直物為替相場, 現物相場

spot exchange transaction　直物為替取引, 現物為替取引

spot firm　現金取引会社

spot-forward transaction　直売先買取引

spot goods　現物, 現物取引

spot inspection　立入り検査

spot market　現物市場, 直物市場, 現金取引市場, 当用買い市場, スポット市場, スポット・マーケット　（=cash market: 現金の受け払いで商品が即時に受渡しされる市場のこと）

spot needs　急需要

spot next ［spot/next］　スポット・ネクスト（受渡し日が約定日から3日後となる取引。2営業日後（スポット）から翌日までの金利やスワップ・レートを意味することもある）

spot operation　直物取引, 現物取引, 直物操作

spot position　現物持ち高, 直物持ち高

spot price　現物価格, 直物価格, 直物商品価格, スポット価格　（=cash price: スポット市場（現物市場）で取引される商品の現在価格）

spot purchase　当用買い, 現金買い, 即時買い

spot quotation　現物相場, 現場渡し値段

spot rate　直物相場, 直物レート, 直物為替相場, 直物為替レート, スポット・レート

spot rate of exchange　直物為替相場, 現物為替相場

spot reproduction cost　時価再生産原価

spot sale　即売, 現金売り, 現物取引, 現場取引

spot selling　現物売り

spot share ［stock］　実株, 現株, 花形株

spot start　スワップの開始日（一般に約定日から2営業日後を開始日とする）

spot transaction　直物取引, 現物取引, 実物取引, 直物為替取引, 直物為替契約, 直物契約

spot rate　直物相場, 直物レート, 直物為替相場, 直物為替レート, スポット・レート
◆We acquired a 60-day forward exchange contract for US $1,000,000, in anticipation of an increase in the spot rates for US dollars. 当社は、米ドルの直物レートが上がるのを期待して100万米ドル、60日後の先物為替予約を取得した。

spot transactions of stocks　現物株取引
◆More than 90 percent of spot transactions of stocks are conducted on the Tokyo Stock Exchange. 現物株取引の9割以上が、東京証券取引所（東証）で行われている。

SRCC　ストライキ、暴動、騒乱
（=S.R. & C.C. Clause）
◆Upon the request of the purchaser, the seller shall, for the account of the purchaser, provide insurance covering war（Institute War Clause）and SRCC（Institute Strikes, Riots and Civil Commotion Clause）risks, and/or any other risks as may be requested by the purchaser. 買い主の要求がある場合、売り主は、買い主の負担［勘定］で戦争危険（協会戦争危険担保約款）、ストライキ、暴動、騒乱危機（協会ストライキ、暴動、騒乱危険担保約款）および/または買い主が要求するその他の危険を対象とする保険を付けるものとする。

stable supply　安定供給, 安定した供給
◆A prerequisite for the continued existence of industry in Japan is an affordable and stable supply of high-quality electricity. 日本の産業が生き残るための必要条件として、良質な電力の安価で安定した供給が挙げられる。◆In Japan, ensuring a stable supply of the fuel for thermal power generation and importing the gas from a wide array of countries have become important issues since the accident at the Fukushima No. 1 nuclear power plant. 日本では、福島第一原発事故以来、火力発電用燃料の安定供給確保［安定調達］とガス輸入先の多様化が重要な課題となっている。

stake　（名）出資, 出資比率, 投資金, 投資金額, 資本参加, 株式持ち分, 持ち株, 持ち株比率, 株, 株式, 利害関係

controlling stake　支配持ち分

equity stake　持ち分, 株式持ち分

equity stake rate　持ち分比率, 出資比率

increase one's stake in　〜の持ち株比率を引き上げる　（=raise one's stake in）

keep a majority stake　過半数株式を維持する

raise one's stake in　〜の持ち株比率を引き上げる、〜の出資比率を引き上げる

reduce one's stake in　〜の持ち株比率を引き下げる、〜の出資比率を引き下げる

take a stake in　〜に出資する
◆Several companies plan to buy back stock with the aim of effecting realignments by buying entire stakes in subsidiaries. 一部の企業は、子会社株を100%取得して事業再編を進めるために自社株買

いを計画している。◆The company will acquire a 25 percent stake in $2.3 billion nickel project in Madagascar and South Africa. 同社は、マダガスカルと南アフリカの23億ドルのニッケル開発事業に25%出資する。◆The foreign funds' total stake in the company surged to about 70 percent. 同社に対する海外ファンド全体の持ち株比率は、約70%に急増した。

standard form 標準書式
◆A copy of such standard form in use as of the date of this agreement is attached hereto as Exhibit C. 本契約締結日に使用されている当該標準書式の写しは、付属書類Cとして本契約書に添付してある。

standard packing procedure 標準梱包手続き
◆Supplier shall, at its expense, pack all Products in accordance with Supplier's standard packing procedure. 供給者は、供給者の費用で、供給者の標準梱包手続きに従って本製品をすべて梱包する。

state (動)述べる、明言する、明示する、公表する、公開する、表示する、記載する、定める、規定する、指定する、評価する
◆The arbitral award shall state the reasons for the award and relief granted. 仲裁判断は、その判断の理由と認められた救済理由を明らかにするものとする。

state emergency 国家の非常事態

state-of-the-art (形)最先端の、最新式の、最新鋭の、最高級の、高度の、最高水準の、最新技術の、最高技術水準の、技術水準 (=cutting-edge, leading edge, sophisticated, territorial waters, top of the line, up-to-the-minute)
◆The biotechnology industry is expected to use state-of-the-art life science, including gene modifications, in the production of chemicals, medicines and food. バイオテクノロジー産業は、遺伝子組換えを含めて、先端的な生命科学を化学、医薬品や食品などの生産に利用するものと期待されている。

state-of-the-art technology 最新技術, 最先端技術, 先端技術
◆Chinese companies are looking to enhance the value of their products in the market by acquiring Japan's state-of-the-art technology and brand names. 中国企業は、日本の先端技術やブランド力を得て、市場での自社製品の価値を高めようとしている。

state-owned (形)国有の, 国営の
  state-owned commercial bank 国営商業銀行
  state-owned company [enterprise] 国有企業, 国有会社
  state-owned industry 国営産業, 国営産業
  state-owned lender 国有銀行
  state-owned property 国有財産
◆Sumitomo Corp. agreed to jointly develop rare earths and import the metals with Kazakhstan's state-owned resource firm Kazatomprom. 住友商事は、カザフスタンの国営資源企業「カザトムプロム」と、レア・アースを共同開発して輸入することで合意した。◆The Bank of China, one of the country's biggest state-owned lenders, has shut the account of the Foreign Trade Bank of North Korea, the country's main foreign-exchange bank. 中国国有銀行最大手の中国銀行が、北朝鮮の主要外国為替銀行[貿易決済銀行]の「朝鮮貿易銀行」の口座を閉鎖した。

stated above 上記の
◆The express warranty stated above is in lieu of all liabilities or obligations of ABC for damages arising from or in connection with the delivery, use or performance of the licensed program. 上記の明示保証は、許諾プログラムの引渡し、使用または履行から生じる損害、またはこれに関連して発生する損害に対するABCの債務または責任に代わるものである。

statement (名)声明, 申告, 供述, 陳述, 声明書, 計算書, 報告書, 財務表, 一覧表
  business statement 営業報告書
  cash flow statement キャッシュ・フロー計算書, 現金収支計算書
  income statement 損益計算書
  mission statement 基本規約
  operation statement 営業報告書
  profit and loss statement 損益計算書
  shelf registration statement 一括登録届け出書
  statement of account 勘定照合表, 勘定一覧表, 売掛金計算書
  statement of changes in the fiscal position 財務状態変動表, 財政状態変動表
  untrue statement 不正記述, 不実の記載, 虚偽の供述, 不誠実な陳述
◆All insurance policies possessed or owned by the Company together with brief statements of the interest insured are complete and accurate. 本会社が所有または保有しているすべての保険証券とその被保険利益についての簡単な説明は、完全で正確である。◆Concurrently with the statements required under Article 10, Licensee shall pay to Company the total amount of the running royalty. 第10条に基づいて要求される計算書[報告書]と同時に、ライセンシーは、会社にランニング・ロイヤルティを総額支払わなければならない。◆The APEC's special statement came out in favor of the promotion of free trade. アジア太平洋経済協力会議（APEC）の特別声明は、自由貿易推進を打ち出した。

statement of intent 意図の表明
◆This agreement supersedes and replaces any prior understanding, agreement, statement of intent or memorandum of understanding, written or oral. 本契約は、書面または口頭による従前の一切の了解、合意、意図の表明または了解覚書に優先するもので、これらに代わるものである。

statistics (名)統計, 指標, 統計学
balance of payments statistics　国際収支統計
commercial statistics　商業統計
customs statistics　通関統計
dynamic statistics　動態統計
economic and price statistics　景気・インフレ指標
employment statistics　雇用統計
export and import statistics　外国貿易統計
export certification statistics　輸出認証統計
export letter of credit statistics　輸出信用状統計
financial statistics　金融統計
import license statistics　輸入承認統計
industrial statistics　工業統計, 業界統計
industry statistics　業界統計
labor statistics　労働統計
minor statistics　関心の薄い指標
national wealth statistics　国富統計
official statistics　政府の統計
social statistics　社会統計
static statistics of population　人口静態統計
strong economic statistics　堅調な景気指標
trade statistics　貿易統計
vital［dynamic］statistics of population　人口動態統計
◆A breakdown of the employment statistics by company size reveals that the number of people working for companies with fewer than 500 employees continued to decline in August. 雇用統計の企業規模別分析では、500人未満の中小企業の雇用者数は前月に続いて8月も減少している。

status (名)地位, 状態, 状況, 情勢, 事情, 構造, 身分, ランク, 資格, 信用, 権威, ステータス
benchmark status　指標銘柄の地位
economic status　経済状態
elevate the social status of women　女性の社会的地位を高める
financial status　財政状態
legal status　法的地位
most favored nations（trade）status　最恵国待遇
preferred creditor status　優先債権者の地位
tax status　税務上の取扱い
◆Japan must strengthen the competitiveness of its manufacturing industry which will lead to increasing exports in order to rebuild its status as a trading country. 貿易立国としての地位を立て直すには、日本は、輸出拡大につながる製造業の競争力強化が必要である。◆Lawmakers voted 260-170 to continue for a year what is now called normal trade relations（NTR）and used to be called most favored nations（MFN）trade status. 議員

が260対170で票決して、これまで最恵国待遇と呼ばれていた（中国に対する）正常通商関係を1年間継続することになった。◆The poor business performance of flat-screen TVs and personal computers was a major factor behind the Jan. 27, 2014 downgrading of Sony to speculative Ba1, or junk status, by Moody's Japan. 薄型テレビとパソコンの業績不振が、1月27日（2014年）にムーディーズ・ジャパン（格付け会社）がソニーの格付けを投機的水準の「Ba1」を引き下げる大きな要因となった。

statute (名)法, 法令, 法規, 法律, 規定, 規則, 定款
federal securities status　米連邦証券法
federal statute　連邦制定法
general statute　一般法, 公法　（=public statute）
private statutes　私法
revise one's statute　定款を改正する
state statute　州法
statute law　成文法, 制定法　（=statutory law）
statute mile　法令マイル
statute of frauds　詐欺防止法, 不正取引規則
statute or law　制定法または法律
the Statute of Monopolies　独占法
◆Nothing contained in this agreement shall be construed so as to require the commission of any act contrary to statute or law. 本契約に定めるいずれの規定も、制定法または法律に反する行為の実行を要求するものとは解釈しないものとする。

statute of limitations　出訴期限, 出訴期限法, 出訴期限法規, 消滅時効, 公訴時効, 時効　（=statute limits; ⇒illegal export）
◆The length of the statute of limitations for bribing foreign government officials was changed from three years to five years under the revised Unfair Competition Act. 不正競争防止法の改正で、外国公務員への贈賄罪の時効は、3年から5年に変更された。

statutory (形)法定の, 制定法上の, 制定法に関する
federal statutory rate　米連邦法人税率
outside statutory auditor　社外監査役
statutory audit　法定監査
statutory auditor　法定監査人, 常勤監査役, 監査役
statutory bar provisions　（米特許法の）権利喪失規定
statutory basis　根拠条文
statutory board　公的機関
statutory body　国家機関, 国策機関
statutory bond　制定法上の債務証書
statutory capital base　法定資本金
statutory company　国策会社

statutory condition　法的条件

statutory copyright　制定法による著作権

statutory corporation　特殊法人

statutory depletion　法定減耗償却法

statutory foreclosure　（裁判手続きによらな
い）簡易の担保物件執行手続き

statutory license　法定許諾

statutory lien　法定担保権

statutory meeting　法定株主総会, 創立総会

statutory merger　法的合併

statutory nonexclusive license　法定実施権

statutory notice　（企業の決算書などの）法定
公告

statutory records and books　法定帳簿

statutory requirement　法的要件

statutory reserve　法定準備金

statutory subject　法定主題

statutory tariff　法定税率, 固定税率

statutory trust　制定法上の信託

the United States statutory income tax rate　米
連邦所得税率

◆The foregoing warranties are exclusive and in
substitution for all other warranties, whether
oral, written, express, implied or statutory. 上
記の保証は排他的なものであり、口頭、書面、明
示、黙示、法定の保証を問わず他のすべての保証
に代わるものである。

statutory auditor　法定監査役, 会社法上の
監査役, 常任監査人

◆A statutory auditor shall be nominated by the
board of directors and elected by the shareholders. 法定監査役は、取締役会が指名して株主が選
任する。

statutory rights　制定法上の権利

◆The software and the game are original, and
neither the software nor the documentation
thereto infringes any common law or statutory
rights of any third party, including, without limitation, contractual rights, patents, copyrights,
trade secrets, right of privacy, right of publicity,
or other intellectual property rights. 本ソフトウ
エアとゲームはオリジナルなもので、そのソフト
ウエアと文書は、契約上の権利や特許権、著作権、
営業秘密、プライバシーの権利、パブリシティの
権利、その他の知的財産権などを含めて、第三者
のコモン・ローあるいは制定法上の権利を一切侵
害するものではない。

stealth marketing　ステルス・マーケティン
グ, ステマ　（=undercovering marketing: 消費
者に商品広告と気付かれないように宣伝する
こと）

◆As stealth marketing by postings is problematic, the Consumer Affairs Agency has revised
its guidelines for online transactions under the
Law for the Prevention of Unreasonable Pre-

miums and Misrepresentations concerning Products and Services. 書き込みによるステルス・マー
ケティングには問題があるので、消費者庁は、「景品
表示法 (不当景品類及び不当表示防止法)」のネッ
ト取引に関する指針を改正した。◆Stealth market-
ing refers to concealing the fact that it is an advertisement. ステルス・マーケティングとは、広
告であることを隠すことを言う。

sterilization　（名）殺菌, 滅菌, 消毒, 不妊, 不
妊化, 不胎化, 断種

gold sterilization policy　金不胎化政策

sterilization of gold　金の不胎化, 金の不妊化

sterilization policy　不胎化政策（通貨当局が
外為市場に円売り介入した後、介入で放出
した円資金を短期国債や手形で回収し、市
場金利等への作用がないようにする政策）

stipulate　（動）合意する, 約定する, 条件とし
て要求する, 明記する, 規定する, 定める, 指定
する　（⇒shipping space）

stipulate by contract　契約で明示する, 契約で
定める

stipulate for　～を条件として求める・要求
する

within the period stipulated on the contract　本
契約に定める期間内に, 契約所定の期間
内に

◆Keidanren's charter on ethical recruitments,
which stipulates job-hunting rules for member
companies, is nonbinding and has no penalties
for violators. 会員企業に向けて就職活動のルール
を定めている経団連の倫理憲章（新卒者の採用選考
に関する企業の倫理憲章）には、拘束力がないし、違
反企業への罰則もない。◆The Antimonopoly Law
stipulates that documents submitted to FTC hearings may be disclosed to certain concerned parties upon their request. 独占禁止法は、「公正取引
委員会の審判に提出された書類［記録］は特定の利
害関係人の請求に基づいて利害関係人に開示する
ことができる」と定めている。◆The L/C shall be
available for at least fifteen days after the latest
date for shipment stipulated in the contract. 信用
状は、本契約指定の積み期の後、少なくとも15日
間は有効とする。◆There is a contractual clause
stipulating that Japanese PC makers will take no
legal action even if Microsoft Corp.'s technologies are deemed to violate their patents. マイク
ロソフト社の技術が日本のパソコン・メーカーの
特許侵害にあたるとしても、日本のパソコン・メー
カーは法的措置を一切取らない［訴訟を起こさな
い］、と定めた契約条項がある。

stipulation　（名）契約書の規定, 契約条項, 約
定, 協定, 訴訟上の合意, 条件, 要求

◆If the purchaser fails to comply with the above
stipulation, the purchaser shall be deemed to
have waived such claim. 買い主が上記規定に従
わない場合、買い主は当該クレームを放棄したも
のと見なされるものとする。

stock　（名）在庫, 蓄え, 備蓄, 備品, 在庫品, 仕

STOC 438

入れ品, ストック

a large stock of knowledge　豊富な知識

accumulated stock　余剰在庫

base stock（method）　基準棚卸し法

be in stock　在庫がある

be out of stock　在庫がない, 在庫が切れている, 在庫切れとなっている, 品切れだ

buffer stock　緩衝在庫

build up stock　在庫を積み増す

buy in stock　在庫を仕入れる

closing stock　期末在庫

current stock　現行在庫

dead stock　売れ残り品, 動きのない在庫品

defective stock　仕損在庫

deliver from stock　在庫から発送する

deplete stock　在庫を取り崩す

distributor's stock　流通在庫

draw down existing stocks　在庫を取り崩す

excess stock　過剰在庫

finished goods［product］stock　製品在庫

frozen stock　滞留品

higher stocks　在庫の膨（ふく）らみ

intermediate stock　中間在庫

liquidate stock　在庫を処分する

maximum stock　最高在庫, 最高在庫量

minimum stock　最低在庫, 最低在庫量

obsolete stock　陳腐化在庫

opening stock　期首在庫

optimum stock　最適在庫, 最適在庫量

out-of-stocks　在庫切れによる欠品

periodic stock check　定期棚卸
　（=periodic stocktaking）

physically inspect the warehouse stock　倉庫の在庫品について実地棚卸をする

planned stock　計画在庫高

raw material stock　原材料在庫

replacement stock　在庫補充品

running stock　適正在庫, ランニング・ストック

safety stock　安全在庫

spare stock　予備部品の在庫

stock accumulation　在庫蓄積

stock appreciation　株式値上がり益, 在庫評価益, 在庫価値上昇

stock articles　在庫品, 手持ち品

stock control　在庫管理, 在庫調整

stock exhaust　品切れ

stock forecast［forecasting］　在庫予測

stock in hand［trade］　在庫品, 手持ち品

stock in process　仕掛品

stock in trade　流通在庫, 在庫品, 必要な営業用品

stock in transit　未達品

stock-keeping unit　在庫保管部, 在庫保管単位

stock level　在庫水準, 手持ち在庫水準

stock on hand　手持ち在庫

stock-out［stockout］　品切れ, 欠品

stock outs on basic merchandise　基本商品の在庫切れ［品切れ］

stock removal　在庫処分

stock turnover　棚卸し資産回転率

stock valuation adjustment　在庫品評価調整［評価調整額］

take stock　在庫の確認をする

unwanted stocks　意図しない在庫

◆For the purpose of display, demonstration and distribution, Distributor shall maintain at its own expense a stock of the Products. 展示, 宣伝と販売のため, 販売店は, 本製品の在庫を自己費用で［自己負担で］維持するものとする。◆We enclose a few samples of our product and should be obliged if you would send us samples of the nearest quality you could offer from stock. 当社製品の見本を数点同封しますので, 在庫から提供できるほぼ同品質の見本を送っていただけるとありがたいのですが［ほぼ同品質の見本があれば送っていただけないでしょうか］。

stock　（名）株, 株式, 株式資本, 証券, 銘柄, ストック　（=share）

active stock　人気株, 花形株

bank-held stocks　銀行保有株

blue chip stock　優良株, 値がさ株

capital stock　株式資本, 株主資本, 総株数, 資本ストック, 資本金

capital stock authorized　授権資本, 授権資本金

common stock　普通株式, 普通株

introduced stock［share］　公開株

issue and payment of stock　株式の発行および払込み

listed stock　上場株

nonconvertible preferred stock　非転換優先株式

preferred stock　優先株式, 優先株

stock appreciation　株式値上がり益, 在庫評価益, 在庫価値上昇

stock at par　額面株

stock dividend　株式配当

stock management　株の運用, 株式運用

stock manipulation　株価操作, 株価操縦

transfer of stock　株式の名義書換え, 株式の譲渡

treasury stock　自己株式, 金庫株

unlisted stock 非上場株 （=unquoted stock）

voting stock 議決権株

◆Great rotation refers to the shift of investment money from low-risk assets such as U.S. Treasuries and the yen into riskier assets such as stocks. 「グレート・ローテーション（大転換）」とは、投資資金を米国債や円などの低リスク資産［安全資産］から株式などリスクの高い資産に移すことを言う。

stock certificate 株券, 記名株券, 株式証券 （=share certificate）

◆ABC shall deliver to XYZ validly issued stock certificates representing the Shares being sold by ABC, affixing proper endorsement duly executed by ABC on the back of the certificates. ABCは、ABCが売り渡す本株式に当たる正当に発行された株券を、この株券の裏面にABCが正式に署名して適切に裏書きした上で、XYZに引き渡すものとする。

stock deal 株式取引, 株の売買 （=stock dealing）

◆According to a probe conducted by the Tokyo Stock Exchange, there was a series of questionable stock deals in which trading volume surged just after the capital increase announcements by listed companies. 東京証券取引所の調査によると、上場企業が増資［公募増資］を公表した直後に（その銘柄の）売買高が急増する不自然な株取引が、相次いでいた。

stock exchange 証券取引所, 株式取引所, 株式市場 （=securities exchange）

◆Japan Exchange Group Inc.（JPX）carried out the Tokyo Stock Exchange's merger with the Osaka Securities Exchange's cash equity market. 日本取引所グループ（JPX）が、東京証券取引所と大阪証券取引所の株式市場（先物以外の現物株市場）の統合を実施した。◆Nissay, the largest private institutional investor in Japan, has invested in about 1,800 companies listed on Japanese stock exchanges. 日本国内最大の民間機関投資家の日本生命保険は、日本の証券取引所に上場している企業約1,800社に出資している。◆Through the integration of the Osaka Securities Exchange's cash equity market into that of the TSE, Japan Exchange Group Inc. debuted the world's third-largest stock exchange. 大阪証券取引所の株式市場を東京証券取引所に一本化して、日本取引所グループ（JPX）は、（上場企業数で）世界第3位の証券取引所に浮上した。

解説 世界の主要証券取引所

American Stock Exchange アメリカン証券取引所（=AMEX）

Amsterdam Stock Exchange アムステルダム証券取引所

Australian Stock Exchange オーストラリア証券取引所

Brussels Stock Exchange ブリュッセル証券取引所

Frankfurt Stock Exchange フランクフルト証券取引所

Geneva Stock Exchange ジュネーブ証券取引所

Hong Kong Stock Exchange 香港取引所 香港証券取引所

International Stock Exchange of Great Britain and Ireland （連合王国およびアイルランド共和国）国際証券取引所（=International Stock Exchange（of the UK and the Republic of Ireland Ltd: ロンドン証券取引所の1986年以降の正式名称））

London Stock Exchange ロンドン証券取引所（⇒IAS）

NASDAQ OMX Group ナスダックOMXグループ

New York Stock Exchange ニューヨーク証券取引所 NYSE（=Big Board）

Osaka Securities Exchange 大阪証券取引所 OSE（2013年7月16日、現物市場（第一部、第二部、ジャスダック）を東京証券取引所に統合して、デリバティブ（金融派生商品）特化型の取引所となる）

Paris Stock Exchange パリ証券取引所

Shanghai Stock Exchange 上海証券取引所 SSE

Stock Exchange of Singapore シンガポール証券取引所

The Stock Exchange ロンドン証券取引所

TMX Group （カナダの）TMXグループ

Tokyo Stock Exchange 東京証券取引所 東証

Toronto Stock Exchange トロント証券取引所

stock exchange offer 株式公開買付け

stock issue 株式発行, 新株発行, 株式銘柄, 銘柄

◆The TSE does not plan to release details on names of stock issues or methods of short selling. 東証は、空売りの対象の個別銘柄や空売りの手口などの詳細については、公表しない方針だ。

stock market 株式市場, 証券市場, 株式相場, 株式市況, 株式売買, 株価 （=equity market）

domestic stock market 国内株式市場

help the stock market 株式市場を活性化する

sluggish stock market 株式相場の下落

stock market capitalization 株式市場の資本化, 株式市場で発行した株式の資本組入れ

stock market collapse 株式市場の崩壊［急落］, 株式相場の下落, 株価急落 （=stock market plunge, the collapse of the stock market）

stock market correction 株価の反落

stock market crash 株式市場の崩壊, 株式市場の暴落, 株価大暴落

stock market credibility 証券市場の信頼性

stock market credit 株式市場信用

stock market crisis 株式市場の暴落
（=stock market crash）

stock market decline 株価下落, 株安
（=decline in the stock market）

stock market gains 株式譲渡益
（=stock sale profits）

stock market level 株価水準

stock market movements 株式市場の動き, 株
価動向

stock market participant 市場参加者

stock market quotation［prices］ 株式相場

stock market turnover 株式出来高

the buoyant stock market 株式市場の活況

◆An increase in transactions that brokerages
handle has accompanied the brisk stock market business. 証券会社が扱う取引の増加は、そ
のまま株式相場の盛況と重なる。◆Insider trad-
ing, which is banned under the Financial Instruments and Exchange Law, harms ordinary investors and significantly damages stock market
credibility. 金融商品取引法で禁じられているイン
サイダー取引は、一般の投資家が不利益を被（こう
む）り、証券市場の信頼性を大きく損なう。◆With
the economic recovery gaining momentum, U.S.
companies have begun investing in the Japanese
stock market again, giving a lift to stock prices.
景気回復が力強さを増していることから、米国企
業が日本の株式市場に再び投資するようになり、株
価を押し上げている。

stock option plan 株式購入選択権制度, 株
式選択権制度, 自社株購入権制度, 株式オプ
ション制度, ストック・オプション制度
（=stock option scheme, stock purchase plan）

◆Shareholders of Toyota Motor Corp. approved
a company proposal for stock buyback and incentive stock option plans at an annual meeting.
年次株主総会で、トヨタ自動車の株主が、自社株
取得計画と奨励株式オプション制度の会社提案［会
社側の議案］を承認した。

解説 ストック・オプション制度とは：企業が
役員や従業員に、前もって決めた価格で一定
数の自社株を買う権利を与える制度。株価が
上がった時点でその権利を使って株を購入し、
市場で売ると株の値上がり分を手にできる仕
組みになっている。

stock price 株価 （⇒stock market）

◆At present, export industries including home
appliances and automobiles are raising their expectations for improved corporate performance
under the weak yen, which has also driven up
stock prices. 現在、家電や自動車などの輸出産業
は、円安で業績改善の期待を高めており、円安は
また株価も押し上げた。◆Erratic fluctuations of
both stock prices and exchange rates have continued, reflecting the turbulent moves of specu-

lative money on world markets. 世界的な投機マ
ネーの激しい動きを反映して、株価と為替相場の
乱高下が止まらない。

stock swap［swapping］ 株式交換
（=share swap）

◆Stock swaps allow the acquirer to purchase the
company it wants to control without preparing a
large sum of cash. 株式交換だと、買収企業は多
額の現金を用意しなくても、相手先企業（経営権を
握りたいと思う企業）を買収することができる。

stockholder （名）株主 （=shareholder）

◆The approval of numerous stockholders must
be gained for a retirement of 50 percent of common shares. 普通株式の50%消却については、多
くの株主の承認を得なければならない。

stocktaking （名）棚卸し, 在庫確認, 在庫調
べ, 在庫チェック, 在庫処分,（事業の）実績評
価, 実績調査, 現状把握

carry out stocktaking 棚卸しを実施する

do stocktaking 在庫調べをする, 在庫チェッ
クを行う, 在庫をチェックする

periodic stocktaking 定期棚卸し
（=periodic stock check）

physical stocktaking 現品棚卸し

stocktaking sale 在庫処分セール

storage （名）保管料

◆In the event that Supplier is requested to assist
Distributor in arranging for transportation, Distributor shall reimburse Supplier for all costs relating to such arrangements, including, without
limitation, insurance, transportation, loading and
unloading, handling and storage following their
delivery to Distributor. 供給者が販売店から運送
手配の支援を要請された場合、販売店は、供給者
が（本製品を）販売店へ引き渡した後の保険、運送、
積み下ろし、貨物取扱い、保管料などの関連費用
を、すべて供給者に償還するものとする。

stowage （名）（貨物の）積付け, 積み荷, 載貨

stowage capacity 載貨容積

stowage factor 積付け率, ストウェージ・
ファクター

stowage plan 本船積付け図, 載貨図

stowage planning 本船積付け計画

stowage survey 積付け検査

stowing （名）積付け作業

strategic （形）戦略的, 戦略上の, 戦略上重要
な, 戦略上役に立つ, 戦略に必要な

strategic business alliance 戦略的業務提携

strategic business unit 戦略的事業単位,
SBU （=business center）

strategic growth market 戦略的成長市場

strategic intent 戦略的意図

strategic management 経営戦略

strategic marketing planning 戦略的マーケ

ティング計画

strategic rival　戦略的競争相手

strategic target　戦略目標

strategic technology development program　戦略技術開発事業

strategic industry　戦略産業
◆Advanced countries proactively assist the production of passenger airplanes as a strategic industry. 先進諸国は、旅客機製造を戦略産業として積極的に支援している。

strategic location　地理的条件, 地理的に有利な条件
◆Toyota aims to benefit from economies of scale through the strategic location of production bases made possible by the international supplies network. トヨタは、国際的な供給のネットワークにより可能になった生産拠点の地理的条件を活用して、規模拡大効果を追求している。

strategic partnership　戦略的提携, 戦略的提携関係
◆Following the tie-up of Volkswagen AG and Suzuki Motor Corp., the alliance of Nissan and Renault SA of France announced a strategic partnership with Daimler AG. フォルクスワーゲンとスズキの提携に次いで［続いて］、日産・仏ルノー連合が、独ダイムラーとの戦略的提携を発表した。

strategically important product　戦略的商品
◆The keys to the revival of Japanese manufacturers are to discern the needs of emerging markets with strong growth potential and to develop strategically important products through originality and ingenuity. 日本の製造業各社復活のカギは、潜在成長力［成長率］が高い新興国市場のニーズの発掘と、創意工夫による重要な戦略的商品の開発である。

strategy　（名）戦略, 策, 手法, 方式, 方針, 方策, 政策, 作戦, 運営術, 長期計画, 計画, 計略, 策略, 兵法, ストラテジー　(⇒M & A)

acquisition strategy　買収戦略

administrative strategy　経営戦略

advertising strategy　広告戦略

basic strategy　基本戦略

brand strategy　ブランド戦略

build strategies　戦略を構築する

bundled strategy　一括販売戦略

business strategy　経営戦略, 事業戦略, 企業戦略, ビジネス戦略, 経営方針

competitive strategy　競争戦略

core strategy　主力戦略, 中核戦略, 基本戦略

corporate strategy　企業戦略, 経営戦略
◆In expanding into India's market, Japanese companies must work out a strategy that includes possible infrastructure risks. インド市場に進出するにあたって、日本企業は、想定されるインフラ面

でのリスクを念頭に置いた戦略を練る必要がある。
◆In step with the growing popularity of virtual engineering, the United States has launched a national strategy aimed at reinvigorating its manufacturing sector. バーチャル・エンジニアリング［仮想エンジニアリング］の普及とともに、米国は製造業の再活性化をめざした国家戦略を打ち出した。◆Japan's major automakers are capitalizing on improved quality at production plants overseas as part of their global strategies. 日本の大手自動車メーカーは、自動車各社の世界戦略の一環として、海外生産拠点での品質向上を活用している。◆The recent M&A is a strategy with an eye on Asia, which has a great potential for sales growth. 今回のM&Aは、販売が伸びる可能性が大きいアジアを視野に入れた戦略です。

strength　（名）力, 強さ, 強み, 力強さ, 体力, 勢い, 好調, 活況, 上昇, 伸び, 向上, 勢力, 兵力, 人数, 長所

brand strength　ブランド競争力

competitive strength　競争力

credit strength　信用力, 信用度, 信用の質

development strength　開発力

economic strength　経済力, 景気の力強さ, 景気の腰の強さ, 景気好調

financial strength　資金力, 財力, 財務力, 財務体質, 財務面での健全性, 支払い能力

financial strength rating　支払い能力の格付け

industrial strength　製造業の好調

international strength　国際的な力

marketing strength　販売力, マーケティング力

on the strength of　〜を根拠にして, 〜に基づいて, 〜を頼りにして, 〜の力で, 〜の影響で, 〜を背景に, 〜の勧めで

technological strength　技術力

yen's strength against the dollar　円高・ドル安, 円高ドル安
◆Japan must prevent the excessive strength of the yen from becoming the status quo due to the turmoil in the Europe as Japan has yet to experience a full-fledged economic recovery. 日本は本格的な景気回復が遅れているため、欧州の混乱による超円高の定着を防がなければならない。◆The company needs to enhance its development strength for such products as hybrid cars to maintain the competitiveness of its vehicles and auto parts domestically manufactured, in addition to improving export-driven profits. 同社の場合、輸出主導の収益改善にとどまらず、国内生産の車両や自動車部品の競争力を維持するには、ハイブリッド車などの製品の開発力を強化する必要がある。

strengthening　（名）強化, 上昇, 伸び, 高まり, 充実, 改善, 持ち直し, 好転

strengthening in sales　販売の伸び

the strengthening of the dollar　ドル高

the strengthening of the yen　円高　(=the strengthening yen, the yen's appreciation)

◆The recent strengthening of the yen may negatively affect exports. 最近の円高が、輸出に悪影響を与えかねない。

stress test　金融の特別検査, 金融機関の財務の健全性検査, 耐性検査, ストレス・テスト (=stress testing: ⇒financial stress test)

the EU's stress test　欧州連合 (EU) のストレス・テスト (特別検査)

the U.S. FRB's stress tests　米連邦準備制度理事会の特別検査

◆Europe's seven banks judged to have capital shortfall by the stress test will work on increasing their capital. ストレス・テスト (特別検査) で資本不足と認定された欧州の7銀行は、これから資本増強に取り組む。

strike　(名) 権利行使, 罷業 (ひぎょう), スト, ストライキ, (鉱脈などの) 発見, (石油などの) 掘り当て, 突然の成功, 攻撃, 空襲 (⇒force majeure)

be currently on strike　目下スト中である

be (out) on strike　ストをしている, スト中である

call [proceed with, stage] a strike　ストを決行する

call off a strike　ストを中止する

free from strikes, riots & civil commotions clause　罷業・暴動・内乱 [騒乱] 不担保約款

general strike　ゼネスト, 総同盟罷業, 総罷業

go ahead with a strike　ストに突入する

go on strike　ストをする, ストに突入する

gold strike　金鉱脈の発見

hunger strike　ハンガースト

official strike　公式ストライキ, 組合公認スト

protest strike　抗議スト

public sector strike　公務員スト

sit-down strike　座り込みスト

strike action　ストライキ

strike in waves　波状スト

strike price　(オプション取引の) 権利行使価格, 行使価格

strikebound [strike-bound] plant　従業員ストで動かなくなった工場

strikes exclusion clause　ストライキ免責約款

the strikes, riots, and civil commotions clause　罷業 (ひぎょう)、暴動および内乱条項, S. R.&C.C.C

◆GM's parts shortages are caused by a 10-day supplier strike. GMの部品不足は、10日間に及ぶ部品供給業者のストによるものだ。◆In the beer industry, a single day's shipment volume during the busiest season from June to August influences the annual performances of beer companies. ビール業界では、6〜8月の書き入れ時の1日の出荷量が、ビール各社の年間業績を左右する。

strike a low-interest loan deal with　〜から低利融資を受ける

◆Belarus is counting on striking a low-interest loan deal with the International Monetary Fund. ベラルーシは、国際通貨基金 (IMF) から低利融資を受けるのを期待している。

strike an agreement　契約を結ぶ [締結する, 取り決める], 合意する, 合意する

◆The company struck an agreement with its debtholder to win their support for reconstruction. 同社は、会社再建について債権者の支持を得ることで、債権者と合意に達した。

strike risks　ストライキ危険

解説 ストライキ危険に含まれるもの:

civil commotions　騒乱

riots　暴動

strikes　労働争議

strong euro　ユーロ高

◆The ECB's introduction of a negative deposit rate also aims to lower interest rate levels in general and redress the strong euro. ECB (欧州中央銀行) のマイナス (中銀預入) 金利導入には、金利水準全体の引下げとユーロ高是正の狙いもある。

strong yen　円高

◆Japanese automakers will boost parts sourcing from South Korean suppliers as remedies for the strong yen. 円高対策として、日本の自動車メーカー各社は韓国製部品の調達 [韓国部品メーカーからの部品調達] を拡大する方針だ。◆The fall in import prices that accompanies a strong yen could further prolong Japan's deflation. 円高に伴う輸入価格の下落で、日本のデフレがさらに長期化する可能性がある。◆The prices of Audi's all-new Q5 sport-utility vehicle range from ¥5.79 million to ¥6.37 million (consumption tax included), and it passed the benefits of the strong yen on to consumers by making high-grade aluminum wheels and car navigation systems standard features. 独アウディの全面改良したスポーツ用多目的車 (SUV)「Q5」の価格は、579万〜637万円 (消費税込み) で、高級アルミホイールや高性能カーナビゲーションを標準装備して、円高差益を消費者に還元した。

stronger yen　円高

◆A stronger yen has the favorable effect of stemming rises in import prices. 円高には、輸入物価の高騰を抑えるプラス面もある。

subcontract　(動) 下請負をする, 〜の下請け契約をする　(名) 下請け, 下請人, 下請業者, 下請 [会社] 企業, 下請契約, サブコントラクター

delaying in the payment of subcontracting charges　下請代金支払いの遅延

subcontract worker　下請業者

subcontracting factory［plant］　下請工場

subcontracting firm　下請会社

◆It is an entrenched bidding structure that allows irregularities such as influence-wielding, bid-rigging and subcontracting entire public works contracts. 口利きや談合、公共事業の丸投げなどの不正行為を許しているのは、旧態依然とした入札の構造だ。

subcontractor　（名）下請契約者, 下請業者, 下請企業［会社］

subcontractor relations　下請企業との関係

the Act against Delay in Payment, etc., to Subcontractors　下請法（下請代金支払い遅延等防止法）

◆The shipment will be made late in March as our subcontractors are somewhat behind in completing your order. 貴社注文の履行に下請けが少々遅れを出しているため、積出しは3月末になる見込みです。

subdistributor　（名）二次代理店, 副販売店

subdistributor discount　二次代理店割引

◆Subdistributor discount means the amount below the prices set forth in the price list, at which the subdistributor may purchase the products from Distributor. 「二次代理店割引」とは、価格表に記載する価格より低い金額のことで、二次代理店はこの金額で代理店から本製品を購入することができる。

subject　（名）対象, 目的, 主題, 内容

◆It shall constitute an event of default if either party is the subject of any proceeding relating its liquidation or insolvency which is not dismissed within 30 days. いずれかの当事者が清算または支払い不能手続きの対象となり、当該手続きが30日以内に取り下げられないときは、不履行事由となる。

subject matter　本件, 契約上の主題・内容, 目的物, 目的事項, 対象物, 対象事項, 裁判での係争物, 訴訟物

subject matter hereof　本契約の主題, 本契約の対象物, 本契約の目的事項, 本契約の目的とする事項, 本契約の対象事項

subject matter of insurance　保険目的物, 保険の対象, 保険の目的

◆The guarantor hereby waives, and agrees not to assert by way of motion as a defence or otherwise, in a suit, action or proceeding pursuant to this guarantee, any claim that this guarantee or the subject matter hereof may not be enforced in or by such courts. 保証人は、本保証書に従う訴訟、裁判または手続き［訴訟または訴訟手続き］で、抗弁として申し立てることによりまたは他の方法により、本保証書またはその主題を上記裁判所でまたはその裁判所が強制することはできないとの主張をここに放棄し、これを主張しないことに同意する。

subject to　〜に服する, 〜に従う, 〜に準拠する, 〜の影響を受ける, 〜を必要とする, 〜

を条件とする, 〜を条件として, 〜を前提として, 〜の場合に限って, 〜を免れない, 〜が適用される, 〜の適用を受ける, 〜次第で, 〜によって決まる, 〜を対象とする, 〜の対象となる, 〜を免れない, 〜にかぎり, 〜の場合にかぎって, 〜に従って, ただし〜

subject to no security interests, mortgage, pledge, lien, encumbrance, or charge　担保権, 抵当権, 質権, 先取特権, 不動産上の負担またはその他の負担の対象になっていない

subject to the conditions stated in this agreement　本契約に定める条件に従って

subject to the following Terms and Conditions　次の条件［取引条件］に従って

subject to the law　この法律の対象である

subject to the terms and conditions set forth herein　本契約に定める条件に従って, 本契約書に記載する条項に従って, 本契約に定める条項と条件に従って

◆A corporate merger plan is subject to legal screening by the Fair Trade Commission of Japan. 企業の合併計画は、公正取引委員会の法定審査を受けなければならない。◆If you find the terms of payment acceptable, please confirm the order subject to the modifications above. この支払い条件がのめるなら、上記の変更を条件として本注文の確認をお願いします。◆Quantity is subject to a variation of 5% more or less than the contracted quantity at Seller's option unless otherwise specified. 数量は、他にとくに明記しないかぎり、売り主の裁量で契約数量より5%増減の変動が生じることがある。◆The EU's 91 banks were subject to the stress test. 欧州連合（EU）の91行が、ストレス・テスト（特別検査）の対象となった。◆The prices are without engagement and subject to change with or without notice. 価格は確約なしで、予告の有無にかかわらず変更することがある。◆Trading of North Korea's weapons and other products of North Korea are subject to the U.N. embargo. 北朝鮮の武器などの取引は、国連の経済制裁の対象になっている。

subject to immediate confirmation by letter　書簡での至急確認を条件として

◆We accept your offer subject to immediate confirmation by letter. 書簡での至急確認を条件として、貴社のオファーを引き受けます。

subject to the fulfillment of　〜を達成することを条件に［条件として］

◆The obligations of Purchaser to effect the transactions contemplated hereby shall be, at the option of Purchaser, subject to the fulfillment, at or prior to the closing date, of the following additional conditions: 本契約で企図されている取引を実行する買い主の義務は、買い主の裁量で、クロージング日以前に以下の追加条件を達成することを条件とする。

sublicense　（動）サブライセンスする, 再実施する, 再許諾する　（名）再実施許諾, 再実施

権, サブライセンス

◆ABC may sublicense the proprietary information to its sublicensees to the extent of ABC's license under this agreement. ABCは、本契約に基づくABCのライセンスの範囲内で、そのサブライセンシーに専有情報を再許諾できるものとする。

sublicensee （名）再実施権者, 商標やソフトウエアなどの再使用権者, サブライセンシー（⇒sublicense）

submission （名）提出, 提示, 申告, 提示案, 提出物, 報告書, 服従, 降伏, 屈服, 従順, 送信, 送信内容, 考え, 意見, 付託, 依頼, 仲裁付託, 仲裁付託合意, 仲裁付託書

false submission　虚偽申告　(=false reporting)

in one's submission　～の考え[意見]では

the filing of regulatory submissions　規制機関への提出書類の申請

the submission of a dispute to arbitration　争議の仲裁付託

the submission of a report　報告書の提出

the submission of a scientific article　科学論文の提出, 科学論文の投稿

◆Barclays, one of Britain's top banking groups, has paid a huge fine over its false Libor submission. 英大手銀行・金融グループのバークレイズは、ライボー（ロンドン銀行間取引金利）の虚偽申告で、巨額の罰金を支払った。

submit （動）提出する, 提起する, 提示する, 付託する, 付す, 委（ゆだ）ねる, 具申する

◆The arbitration award shall resolve the questions submitted, award the relief to which each party may be entitled and allocate the cost of arbitration. 仲裁判断は、付託された問題を解決し、各当事者が受けることのできる救済を与え、仲裁費用を割り当てるものとする。

submit oneself to the jurisdiction of the courts of　～の裁判所にその裁判管轄を付託する

submit to　～に服従する, ～に服する, ～に従う, ～を受ける

◆Each party shall submit to the nonexclusive jurisdiction of the Courts of New South Wales. 各当事者は、ニューサウスウェールズの裁判所の非専属管轄権に服するものとする。◆The parties hereto shall submit to the nonexclusive jurisdiction of the Tokyo District Court of Japan with respect to all controversies arising from the interpretation and performance of this agreement. 本契約当事者は、本契約の解釈と履行から生じるすべての紛争については、東京地方裁判所（日本）の非専属管轄権に服するものとする。

subparagraph （名）契約書の条項の項

◆Even if the royalty computed pursuant to the preceding subparagraph b) of this Article does not amount to five million (5,000,000) Japanese yen, Licensee guarantees to pay Licen-

sor said sum as a minimum royalty. 本条の前期 b) 項に従って計算したロイヤルティの額が500万円に達しない場合でも、ライセンシーは、上記金額をミニマム・ロイヤルティとしてライセンサーに支払うことを保証する。

subrogation （名）保険代位, 債権などの代位, 代位弁済, 代位請求, 代位権

insurance subrogation　保険代位

letter of subrogation　権利移転書（=subrogation format）

right of subrogation　代位権

subrogation receipt　権利移転領収書

subscribe （動）署名する, 株を引き受ける, 買い取る, 寄付する, 予約する, 予約購読する

◆JVCO shall issue one hundred (100) shares of stock of the company, of which sixty (60) shall be subscribed by X and forty (40) shall be subscribed by Y. JVCOは同社の株式を100株発行し、このうち60株はXが、40株はYが引き受けるものとする。

subscribe for　株を引き受ける, 申込みを引き受ける

◆The parties hereto shall subscribe for, at par, shares of the common stock of the New Company to be issued at the time of its incorporation as follows: 本契約当事者は、新会社の設立時に発行される新会社の普通株式を、額面で次のとおり引き受けるものとする。

subscription and payment of the stock　株式の引受けと払込み

subsequent to　～の後, ～の後に, ～以後に　(=after)

◆Such information was rightfully communicated to the receiving party free of any obligation of confidence subsequent to the time it was communicated to the receiving party by the disclosing party. 当該情報は、開示当事者が受領当事者に通知した時点以後に、秘密保持義務なしに受領当事者に合法的に通知された。

subsequent year　次年度, 次年

◆The price of the products for any subsequent year commencing on the annual anniversary of this agreement shall be such as may be negotiated and agreed upon between the parties not later than 30 days prior to the commencement of such year. 本契約から1年後の応答日に始まる次年度の本商品価格は、当該年度が始まる30日前までに当事者間で交渉して合意する価格とする。

substantive law　実体法

◆This agreement shall be governed by the substantive laws of the State of California, U.S.A., excluding its choice of rules. 本契約は、適用法選択のルールを除いて、米国カリフォルニア州の実体法に準拠するものとする。

substitute （名）代用, 代用品, 交替, 代替, 代理, 代理人, 代役, 補欠　（形）代用の, 代替の, 代理の, 代役の　（動）～の代わりに用いる,

〜の代理になる［代理を務める］, 〜の代わり
をする

a competent substitute　適格交代人員

a poor substitute for　〜のお粗末な代用品

be no substitute for　〜の代用にならない

direct credit substitute　直接債務肩代わり契約

import substitute　輸入代替

substitute airliner　代替機

substitute contract　交替契約

substitute national holiday　振替休日

substitute premises　代替物件

substitute process agent　代わりの送達代理人

substitute security　代用証券

◆ABC reserves the right to replace on its own
reasons any ABC Personnel so assigned with a
competent substitute by giving XYZ a notice in
advance. ABCは、XYZに事前通知を行って、派遣
したABC人員を自社の都合で適格交替人員と交替
させる権利を持つ。

succeeding breach of such provision　そ
の後の当該規定違反, その後の同規定違反

successive consequent year or years　そ
の後に続く年度
◆Minimum purchase for the successive consequent year or years shall be decided upon by mutual negotiation before commencing such each
year. その後に続く年度の最低購入量は、当該各年
度の開始前に相互の協議により決定する。

successors and assigns　承継人と譲受人
◆Unless specifically set forth herein, nothing in
this agreement is intended to confer any rights or
remedies upon any persons other than the parties
and their respective successors and assigns. 本契
約書に特に明記しないかぎり、本契約の規定は、契
約当事者とその各承継人および譲受人以外の者に
権利または救済方法を付与することを意図したも
のではない。

such　(形) そのような, このような, 前述の, 上
記の, 当該の, この, そんなに〜な, とても［ひ
じょうに］〜な, 大変な, ひじょうな, 素敵な,
素晴らしい　(代) そのようなもの, そのよう
な類の人［もの, こと］, 〜のようなもの
and such　〜など, その他この種のもの

as such　そういう［そのような］ものとして,
それなりに, そういう資格で, それだけで,
それ自体は［で］

be not such as to　〜するほどのものではない

be such A as to do　〜するほどAである

be such as to　〜するほどである

be such that　〜のようなものである (be such
as to), ひじょうに良い［ひどい］ものなの
で〜, ひじょうに〜なので, 〜のような(種
類の)もの

or some such A　〜とかそういったA

such A as …　〜するようなA, 〜のようなA,

〜であるようなA

such A（that）…　とても［ひじょうに］Aな
ので〜, 〜であるほどAだ (such の後に名詞
が来る。同意表現のso A that…の場合は、
soの後に形容詞が来る)

such and such　これこれの

such as　〜のような, 〜など

such being the case　そういうわけで, こうい
うわけで

such that　ひじょうに〜なので, 〜のような
(種類)のもの, 〜のようなやり方で, 〜の
ような具合に (in a way that)

◆Commodity futures trading is based on contracts to buy or sell a specified quantity of an underlying asset, such as gold, at a particular time
in the future and at a price agreed when the contract was executed. 商品先物取引は、取引契約を結
ぶ時点で、一定量の金などの対象資産を将来の特定
の時期に合意した値段で売買する契約に基づいて
行われる。◆If the buyer fails to pay any amount
under this agreement when due, the buyer shall
be liable to pay to the seller overdue interest on
such unpaid amount from the due date until the
actual payment date at the rate of 15% per annum. 買い主が支払い期日に本契約に基づく代金
の支払いを怠った場合、買い主は、支払い期日か
ら実際の払込み日までの当該未払い金額に対する
年率15%の遅延金利を、売り主に支払わなければ
ならない。◆The board of directors may act at a
meeting at which a quorum is present by the affirmative vote of a majority of those present at
such meeting. 取締役会は、定足数の取締役が出
席した会議で、出席取締役の過半数の賛成投票に
より決議することができる。◆The total period of
such technical assistance and services shall not
exceed 90 man-days. この技術指導とサービスの
総期間（延べ日数）は、90人日（にんび）を超えない
ものとする。

**suit, action or proceeding pursuant to
this guarantee**　本保証書に従う訴訟、裁
判または手続き
◆The guarantor hereby waives, and agrees not to
assert by way of motion as a defence or otherwise, in a suit, action or proceeding pursuant to
this guarantee, any claim that this guarantee or
the subject matter hereof may not be enforced in
or by such courts. 保証人は、本保証書に従う訴
訟、裁判または手続き［訴訟または訴訟手続き］で、
抗弁として申し立てることによりまたは他の方法
により、本保証書またはその主題を上記裁判所で
またはその裁判所が強制することはできないとの
主張をここに放棄し、これを主張しないことに同
意する。

suit or charge　訴訟または請求

suit or proceeding　訴訟または訴訟行為
◆The guarantor hereby waives, and agrees not to
assert by way of motion as a defence or otherwise, in a suit, action or proceeding pursuant to

this guarantee, any claim that this guarantee or the subject matter hereof may not be enforced in or by such courts. 保証人は、本保証書に従う訴訟、裁判または手続き［訴訟または訴訟手続き］で、抗弁として申し立てることによりまたは他の方法により、本保証書またはその主題を上記裁判所でまたはその裁判所が強制することはできないとの主張をここに放棄し、これを主張しないことに同意する。

sum （名）金額, 金員, 合計金額, 総額, 総量, 合計

sums payable　支払わなければならない金額, 支払うべき金員, 未払い金

◆ABC shall pay to XYZ as the paid-up royalty the sum of ￥100,000,000, which shall be payable in five installments as follows: ABCは、ロイヤルティの一括払い（払込み済みロイヤルティ）として、XYZに次のとおり総額1億円を5回の分割で支払うものとする。

super cargo airship　大型貨物飛行船

Super 301 trade provision （米包括通商法）スーパー301条

supplement （名）補足, 追加, 補充, 補完, 付録, 追補

◆No supplement, modification or amendment of this agreement shall be binding unless executed in writing by both parties. 本契約の補足、変更または修正は、両当事者が書面で行わないかぎり、拘束力がないものとする。

supplier （名）供給者, 供給元, 供給業者, 仕入先, 買付け先, 提供者, サプライヤー

◆In comparison of your offer with that of our regular suppliers, their quotation is more favorable. 貴社のオファーと当社の常時買付け先のオファーを比べると、先方の価格のほうが有利です。◆Japanese automakers will boost parts sourcing from South Korean suppliers as remedies for the strong yen. 円高対策として、日本の自動車メーカー各社は韓国製部品の調達［韓国部品メーカーからの部品調達］を拡大する方針だ。◆Supplier shall be responsible for any claim of infringement or alleged infringement of patents, designs, trademarks, copyrights or other rights brought by a third party in relation to Products. 本製品に関して第三者が提起する特許、意匠、商標、著作権またはその他の権利の侵害または申し立てられた侵害の請求については、供給者がすべて責任を負う。◆The industrial sector welcomes the government's latest move to diversify rare earth suppliers as it will lead to stable rare earth supplies. レア・アース調達先の多角化については、レア・アース（希土類）の安定供給につながるとして、産業界は政府の今回の動きを歓迎している。◆Through diversifying rare earth suppliers, Japan will lessen the diplomatic pressure China is able to exert as it exclusively possesses heavy rare earth deposits. レア・アース調達先の多角化により、日本は、重レア・アース鉱床の独占を武器にした中国の外交圧力をかわす方針だ。

supply （動）供給する, 提供する, 不足分を埋め合わせる

◆ABC shall, at all times during the term of this agreement, maintain an adequate stock of the products so as to enable it to meet the requirement and supply promptly all orders reasonably anticipated in the territory. ABCは、本契約の期間中つねに、合理的に予想される契約地域内の必要量をみたすことができるようにするため、またすべての注文品を迅速に供給できるようにするため、本製品の十分な在庫を維持するものとする。◆Eight companies will jointly develop equipment and facilities to supply hydrogen to fuel cell vehicles. 企業8社が、燃料電池車に水素を供給する機器と設備を共同開発することになった。◆It would not be possible for us to supply the quantity you want at your bid. 貴社の指し値で貴社の必用量を供給することは、できません。◆We fear we may not supply exactly the same articles you want as they are not in our lines. 貴社お望みの商品は扱っていませんので、当社としてはお望みの品とまったく同じものを提供することはできないと思います。

supply （名）供給, 供給量, 需給, 供給品, 消耗品（複数形）, 貯蔵品, 政府の蔵出・経費（複数形）, 代理, 補欠, サプライ

be in good supply （～は）供給が潤沢である, （～の）供給は潤沢である

supplies　供給品, 供給量

◆A prerequisite for the continued existence of industry in Japan is an affordable and stable supply of high-quality electricity. 日本の産業が生き残るための必要条件として、良質な電力の安価で安定した供給が挙げられる。◆Japan has to import most of its fossil fuels from the Middle East in which supplies and prices remain unstable. 日本は、化石燃料の大半を、供給量も価格も不安定な中東からの輸入に頼っている。◆The following price list shows our best prices and rate of quantity discount for our supplies. 以下の価格表は、当社供給品の最低価格［勉強値］と数量割引率を示しています。◆The model you have in mind has been out of make for the moment, and we could not tell exactly when our supply might be made. 貴社ご要望の機種はここ当分、生産中止になっており、供給可能の時期は目下不明です。◆We are prepared to place a prompt trial order if you can guarantee supply of products strictly in accordance with our specifications. 貴社が当社の仕様書どおりの商品の供給［納入］を保証するなら、早速、試験注文を出します。

supply agreement　供給契約, 納入契約, 供給契約書, 納入契約書

supply and demand　需要と供給, 需給

◆Banks participating in direct yen-yuan trading in the Tokyo interbank foreign exchange market will trade the yen and the yuan at an exchange rate calculated on the basis of actual supply and demand. 東京外国為替市場で円・人民元の直接取引に参加する銀行は、実際の需給などをもとに算出

した取引レートで、円と人民元を銀行間で取引する。
◆Changes in exchange rates are a result of multiple factors, including the balance of international payments and market supply and demand. 為替相場の変動は、国際収支や市場の需給など複数要因によるものだ。

supply chain 供給連鎖, 供給体制, 供給網, 部品供給網, 供給経路, サプライ・チェーン
◆Due to the massive floods in central Thailand, the supply chains of parts for industrial products were disrupted, forcing factories in Thailand and neighboring countries to suspend production. タイ中部の大規模洪水で、工業製品のサプライ・チェーン（部品供給網）が寸断され、タイや周辺国の工場が生産停止を余儀なくされた。

supply chain management 供給連鎖管理, 供給体制管理, 供給網管理, サプライ・チェーン・マネジメント, SCM（情報技術（IT）を利用して、受注発注、資材や部品の調達、生産、製品の配達、在庫などを統合的に管理して、企業収益を高めるための管理手法）

supply of samples サンプルの供給
◆The retail stores which form chain-store contracts with a large manufacturing firm deal with all the products of the manufacturer and receive various services such as design of stores, store arrangement and free supply of samples. ある大手メーカーとチェーン店契約を結ぶ小売店は、そのメーカーの全製品を取扱い、そのメーカーから店舗のデザインや店舗配列、サンプルの無料供給などの各種サービスを受ける。

surcharge （名）割増料金, 追加料金, 付加料金, 上乗せ料金, 追徴金, 課徴金, 不足金不当請求, 荷物の積み過ぎ, 過載, サーチャージ
　bunker surcharge 燃料費割増, バンカー課徴料
　capital surcharge 資本の上積み, 自己資本の上積み, 資本の積み増し, 資本の上乗せ
　currency surcharge 通貨調整金 （=currency adjustment factor: 海上運賃に加算して徴収される割増料）
　export surcharge 輸出課徴金, 輸出税
　fuel surcharge 燃油特別付加運賃
　import surcharge 輸入課徴金, 輸入税
　inflation surcharge インフレ課徴金
　investment income surcharge 投資所得課徴金
　optional surcharge 揚地割増料
　out port surcharge 僻地割増運賃
　port congestion surcharge 船混割増
　solidarity surcharge 統一割増税
　tax surcharge 課徴金
　with no surcharge 追加料金なしで
◆According to a list of 28 global systemically important financial institutions published by the Financial Stability Board, Citigroup, Deutsche Bank and HSBC Holdings will be targeted for a capital surcharge of 2.5 percent. 金融安定化理事会（FSB）が発表した金融システム上重要な国際金融機関（G-SIFIs）28行のリストによると、米シティグループやドイツ銀行、英金融大手のHSBCなどが、2.5%の自己資本上積みの対象となる。◆After the delivery of the Goods, any taxes, customs duties, export or import surcharges or other governmental charges shall be for the account of the Buyer. 本商品の引渡し後、税金、関税、輸出・輸入税、その他政府が賦課する費用は、買い主の負担とする。

surety （名）保証, 保証人, 連帯保証
◆The guarantor shall be liable under this guarantee as if it were the sole principal obligor and debtor and not merely a surety. 保証人は、保証人が単なる保証人ではなく唯一の主債務者であるかのように本保証書上の責任を負うものとする。

surge in imports 輸入の急増
◆The deficit in goods trade in the first half of 2012 expanded sharply due to a surge in imports of fuel for thermal power generation following the suspensions of nuclear power plants. 2012年上半期のモノの取引を示す貿易収支の赤字は、原発停止に伴う火力発電用燃料輸入の急増で、急速に膨らんだ。

surges in the yen's strength 円高
◆The recent surges in the yen's strength have made it imperative for Japanese carmakers to substantially bring down their parts procurement costs by overseas sourcing. 最近の円高で、日本の自動車メーカー各社は、海外調達による部品調達コストの大幅引下げが緊急課題となっている。

surging prices 価格高騰, 物価高騰［急騰］, 物価の上昇
◆Amid surging prices of crude oil and other resources, the sovereign wealth fund will invest mainly in solar power generation, fuel cells, and other new energy technologies and natural resources. 原油その他の資源価格の高騰を受け、同政府系投資ファンドは、太陽光や燃料電池などの新エネルギー技術や天然資源に投資の重点をおく方針だ。

surplus （名）余剰, 過剰, 余剰分, 過剰分, 余剰金, 超過金, 剰余金, 積立金, 黒字, 歳入超過額, 残額
　balance of payments current account surplus 国際収支経常勘定黒字
　balance of payments surplus 国際収支の黒字
　be surplus to requirements 供給過剰である, もはや［もう］必要ない
　capital surplus 資本剰余金, 資本積立金
　cumulative［cumulated］surplus 累積黒字
　current account surplus 経常黒字
　export surplus 貿易収支の黒字
　external surplus 国際収支の黒字, 貿易収支の黒字, 経常海外余剰

S

SURP 448

financing surplus　資金余剰, 資金過剰

income surplus　所得収支の黒字［黒字額］
　（=income account surplus）

liquidity surplus　流動性過剰

massive［huge］international payments surplus
　巨額の国際収支の黒字

oil surplus　石油余剰, 石油黒字

primary surpluses　基礎収支の黒字

surpluses in Japan's current and trade accounts
　日本の経常収支と貿易収支の黒字額

trade surplus with the U.S.　対米貿易黒字, 対
　米貿易収支の黒字

◆Japan's current account balance remains in surplus, but it will eventually fall into the red if the
trade deficit continues. 日本の経常収支はまだ黒
字だが, 貿易赤字が続けば, 経常収支はいずれ赤
字に転落する。◆Japan's current account surplus
in July 2013 fell 12.9 percent from a year earlier to ￥577.3 billion, chiefly reflecting a wider
gap in goods trade as imports of LNG for thermal power generation swelled due in part to an
increase in electricity demand amid the hot summer. 2013年7月の日本の経常収支の黒字幅は, 前年
同月より12.9%減少して5,773億円となったが,
これは主に猛暑で電力需要が増えたこともあって火
力発電用の液化天然ガスの輸入が大幅に増加した
ため, モノの貿易での輸入超過［モノの貿易赤字］
が拡大したことを反映している。◆The balance of
trade in goods and services logged a surplus of
￥3.43 trillion in the April-September period. 4
～9月期のモノとサービスの貿易収支は, 3兆4,300
億円の黒字を記録した。◆The income surplus fell
24.5 percent, to about ￥1.1 trillion on a year-to-
year basis, on the back of declining interest rates
on foreign bonds. 所得収支の黒字額は, 外債の金
利低下の影響で（利子収入が減ったため）, 前年同
月比で24.5%減の約1兆1,000億円だった。

surplus fund　余剰資金, 剰余金（「剰余金」
は, 自己資本のうち資本金と資本準備金以外
の部分のことで, 過去の利益の蓄積を示す）
◆These surplus funds are moving into crude oil
and grain markets in search of profitable investments. これらの余剰資金は, 有利な運用先を求め
て原油や穀物市場に向かっている。

surplus in the current account　経常収支
の黒字, 経常黒字, 経常収支の黒字額
　（=the current account surplus）
◆The pace of decline in the surplus in the current
account was the steepest on a first-half basis. 経
常黒字［経常収支の黒字額］の減少率は, 上半期ベー
スで最大だった。

surplus in the income account　所得収支
の黒字, 所得収支の黒字額
◆The surplus in the income account that includes
dividend income from overseas subsidiaries narrowed to about ￥7.15 trillion in January-June
2012 from ￥7.28 trillion a year before. 2012年

上半期（1～6月）の所得収支（海外子会社からの配
当収入［配当受取金］などを示す）の黒字額は, 前
年同期の7兆2,800億円から約7兆1,500億円に縮小
した。

survey　（名）調査, 意識調査, 査察, 査定, 測量,
概観, 概説, サーベイ

a fact-finding survey　実態調査

a questionnaire survey　アンケート調査

business sentiment survey　企業景況感調査

establishment survey　事業所調査

fact-finding survey　実情調査, 実態調査

market survey　市場調査, 市場実査, 実態調査

marketing survey　市場調査, マーケティン
　グ・サーベイ

national purchasing managers survey　全米購
　買部協会景気総合指数

survey fee　鑑定請求書

survey report　鑑定報告書

surveyor　（名）検査人, 鑑定人, 輸入品検査
官　（⇒licensed surveyor）

authorized surveyor　公認鑑定人

licensed surveyor　公認鑑定人

Lloyd's surveyor　ロイズ［ロイド］鑑定人

surveyor of customs　税関検査官, 税関鑑定官,
　税関倉庫管理人

surveyor of weights and measures　度量衡検
　査官

surveyor's certificate　鑑定証明書

surveyor's report　鑑定報告書

◆The purchaser shall forward full particulars of
such claim, accompanied by an authorized surveyor's certificate of inspection of quality and
quantity of the products delivered in dispute, to
the seller by registered airmail within 30 days after such notification. 買い主は, 当該通知後30日以
内に, 引き渡された問題の製品の品質と数量に関す
る公認鑑定人の検査証明書を添付して, 当該クレー
ムの詳細を記載した書面を書留航空便で売り主に送
付するものとする。◆The quality and quantity of
the products shall be determined by a mutually
acceptable surveyor at the expense of the seller
prior to loading. 本製品の品質と数量は, 売り主
の費用で, 相互に受諾できる検査人が積込み前に
決定するものとする。

survival　（名）存続, 効力の維持, 継続

survive　（動）存続する, 効力を維持する, ～後
も存続［継続］する

survive any expiration or termination of this
　agreement　本契約の満了または終了後も
　存続する, 本契約の満了または終了後も効
　力を失わない

survive the termination of this agreement　本契
　約終了後も存続する, 本契約終了後も引き
　続き有効である, 本契約終了後も効力を失

わない

◆The provisions of Articles V（Confidentiality）and VIII（Arbitration）shall survive the termination of this agreement. 第五条（秘密保持）と第八条（仲裁）の規定は、本契約の終了後も存続するものとする。

survive the expiration, termination, or cancellation of this agreement 本契約の満了、終了または解除後も存続する、本契約の満了、終了または解除後も引き続き有効である

◆This provision shall survive the expiration, termination, or cancellation of this agreement. この規定は、本契約の満了、終了または解除後も存続する［引き続き有効であるものとする］。

susceptible to ～に左右されやすい、～に影響されやすい、～にかかりやすい、感染しやすい、～に敏感な、～に弱い

◆The yen's stable rate at about ¥110 against the dollar serves as a stabilizing factor for importers, exporters and others doing business susceptible to exchange fluctuations. 円の対ドル為替相場が110円台（前後）で安定していることは、輸出入業者など為替変動に左右されやすい仕事をしている者にとって安定要因となる。

suspend （動）停止する、一時停止する、中止する、中断する、差し止める、延期する、一時見合わせる、離脱させる、停職にする、休職させる、停学処分［出場停止処分］にする、休場させる、刑の執行を猶予（ゆうよ）する、（判決などを）保留する、吊り下げる、ぶら下げる

suspend judgment 判断を保留する

suspend payment 支払いを停止する

◆The revised Foreign Exchange and Foreign Trade Law allows Japan to suspend or limit remittances and trade with North Korea. 改正外国為替及び外国貿易法によると、北朝鮮に関して日本は送金や貿易を停止・制限することができる。

suspend factory operations 工場の操業を停止する

◆Some Japanese-affiliated companies and Japanese restaurants have been forced to suspend their factory operations or close their outlets due to the acts of destruction by Chinese demonstrators. 一部の日系企業や日本料理店は、中国のデモ隊による破壊行為で、工場の操業停止や店舗の休業に追い込まれている。

suspend operations 操業を停止する、営業を停止する、運転を停止する　（⇒suspension of operations）

◆By the instruction of the China Food and Drug Administration, the Shanghai city government suspended operations of Shanghai Husi Food and confiscated raw materials and products at the firm which had sold expired meat products. 中国の国家食品薬品監督管理総局の指示で、上海市は、品質保持期限切れの肉製品を販売していた上海福喜食品の営業を停止し、同社の原料と商品を差し

押さえた。

suspend production 生産を停止する

◆Due to the massive floods in central Thailand, the supply chains of parts for industrial products were disrupted, forcing factories in Thailand and neighboring countries to suspend production. タイ中部の大規模洪水で、工業製品のサプライ・チェーン（部品供給網）が寸断され、タイや周辺の工場が生産停止を余儀なくされた。

suspend transactions 取引を停止する

◆The firm has gone effectively bankrupt after banks suspended transactions with it on its second failure to honor a bill. 同社が2回目の不渡りを出して銀行取引停止となり、事実上倒産した。

suspension of operations 操業停止、営業停止、運転停止

◆The suspension of all operations at Nippon Steel Corp.'s Nagoya steelworks, following a gas tank explosion, could be a big blow to the motor industry, which depends on high-quality steel plates produced at the facility. ガス・タンク爆発事故の直後から新日本製鉄の名古屋製鉄所で行われている操業の全面停止は、同製鉄所で生産されている高級鋼板に依存している自動車業界に大打撃を与える可能性がある。

suspension of trade, capital transactions and remittances 貿易、資本取引と送金の停止

◆Under the current Foreign Exchange and Foreign Trade Control Law, the government must wait for the Security Council to pass a resolution before implementing sanctions against North Korea, including a suspension of trade, capital transactions and remittances. 現行の外国為替及び外国貿易法（外為法）では、政府が北朝鮮に対して貿易、資本取引と送金の停止などの制裁措置を実施するには、国連の安保理決議が必要だ。

suspension on imports 輸入差し止め

◆The Economy, Trade and Industry and Finance ministries will establish a system to allow companies and individuals to request suspensions on imports that infringe on their patent rights and designs. 経済産業省と財務省は、特許権と意匠権（デザイン権）を侵害した輸入品の輸入差し止めを日本の企業や個人が請求できる制度を創設する方針だ。

sustain （動）持続させる、維持する、保持する、存続させる、支える、支持する、裏付ける、～に耐える、養う、扶養する、援助する、激励する、（損失、負債、被害などを）被る［受ける］、妥当［正当］と認める、是認する

sustain a competitive edge 競争力を維持する

sustain a great loss 大損害を被る

sustain heavy damages 大損害を受ける

sustain objection 異議を認める

sustain one's claim ～の主張を認める

sustain organized efforts 組織的な取り組みを続ける

sustain overall economic growth　マクロ経済の成長を維持する

sustain the interest of　〜の興味をずっと引きつける

◆In a scenario for economic growth recovery drawn up by the government and the BOJ, domestic demand is sustained by reconstruction projects from the March 11 disaster and subsidies for environmentally friendly vehicles. 政府・日銀が描く成長回復シナリオでは、東日本大震災（2011年3月11日）の復興事業やエコカー補助金などで、内需を支える。◆In the event of the breach of this agreement by the seller, the limit of the seller's liability shall be for the actual damages directly sustained by the purchaser from such breach. 売り主が本契約に違反した場合、売り主の責任限度は、買い主が当該違反から直接被った実損額とする。

T

tactic［tactics］　(名)作戦, 作戦行動, 手段, 方策, 策, 手, 策略, かけ引き, 戦術, 戦法

adopt［use］the usual tactics　いつもの手を用いる

advertizing tactics　広告戦術

fraudulent business tactics　詐欺商法

marketing tactics　マーケティング戦術

money tactics　買収戦術

negotiating tactic　交渉戦術

poison pill defense tactics　ポイズン・ピル（毒薬条項）防衛策

sabotage tactics　（スト中の労働者による）破壊戦術, 器物損壊戦術

sales tactics　売上作戦, 販売戦術, 勧誘

scorched earth tactics　焦土作戦

sharp［brilliant, clever］tactics　巧妙な戦術

shift in tactics　戦術転換

strategies and tactics　戦略と戦術

◆Companies are allowed to use poison pill defense tactics more easily by the Business Organization Law, which went into effect in fiscal 2006. 2006年度から施行された「会社法」で、企業はポイズン・ピル（毒薬条項）防衛策を以前より容易に行使できるようになった。◆The company's aggressive sales tactics became a social problem. 同社の強引な勧誘は、社会問題化した。

take delivery of　〜を引き取る, 〜の引渡しを受ける

◆If some or all of the goods have not been received by the buyer on the termination of this contract, the buyer shall, in its sole discretion, cease to take delivery of the remaining goods and the seller shall return to the buyer any amounts paid in advance in respect of such goods. 本契約解除時に商品の一部または全部を買い主が受領し

ていない場合、買い主は、買い主単独の選択で、残存商品［未引渡し商品］の引取りを中止し、売り主は当該商品に関して前払いで受領した代金を買い主に返還するものとする。◆The seller shall sell and deliver the products and the buyer shall purchase and take delivery thereof. 売り主は本商品を販売して引き渡すものとし、買い主は本商品を買い取ってその引渡しを受けるものとする。

take effect　効力を発する, 効力を生じる, 発効する, 実施される, 施行される

◆This agreement shall take effect on August 1, 2015. 本契約は、2015年8月1日に発効する。

take out　ローンなどを組む, 保険に入る［加入する］, 保険を付ける［かける］, 契約する, 獲得する, 取得する, 取り出す, 持ち出す, （金を）下ろす, （預金などを）引き出す, （食事や散歩などに）連れ出す, 出かける, 出発する（set out）, （店で食べずに）持ち帰る, 削除する, 取り除く, 除去する, 破壊する, 無力化する, （訴訟を）起こす, （召喚状などを）発行する

take out a loan contract　ローン契約を結ぶ

take out a summons　召喚状を発行する

take out consumer loans　消費者金融から金を借りる

take out earthquake insurance　地震保険に加入する

take out provisions against loan losses　貸倒れ損失に備えて準備金を引き当てる

take out short-term loans　短期ローンを組む, 短期借入れを行う

◆Large firms such as trading and steel companies are taking out short-term loans to meet working capital needs. 商社や鉄鋼などの大企業は、運転資金のニーズを満たすため、短期ローンを組んでいる［短期借入れを行っている］。◆Many of the investors took out consumer loans to pay contract fees. 出資者の多くは、消費者金融から金を借りて契約料を支払った。

take over　企業を買収する, 取得する, 乗っ取る, 資産・業務などを引き継ぐ, 継承する, 経営権を獲得する

take over the assets of　〜の資産を継承する, 〜の資産を引き継ぐ

take over the business of　〜の事業を引き継ぐ

take over the collapsed bank　経営破たんした銀行を引き継ぐ

take over the operations of　〜の営業譲渡を受ける

◆The contract was taken over by successive owners. 契約は、承継人（歴代承継人・相続した所有者）に引き継がれた。◆The new company will take over all operations of the existing Yomiuri Shimbun. 現在の讀賣新聞本社の業務は、新会社が全部引き継ぐことになる。◆U.S. equity fund KKK & Co. will invest about ¥100 billion in struggling Japanese chipmaker Renesas Electronics Corp. in a bid to take over its management. 米投資ファンドのコールバーグ・クラビス・ロバーツ（KKR）が、経営再建中の日本の半導体大手ルネサスエレクトロニクスの経営権を獲得［取得］するため、ルネサスに約1,000億円を出資することになった。

takeover bid 株式公開買付け, 株式公開買付けによる企業買収, 買収提案, テイクオーバー・ビッド, TOB （=take-over bid, takeover offer, tender offer: 主に経営権を支配するため、株式の買取り業者が買付け期間と株数、買付け価格を公表して不特定多数の株主から株を買い取る方法。⇒TOB）

  agreed takeover 合意による公開買付け

  reverse takeover 逆買収

  takeover bid period 株式公開買付けの期間, TOBの期間 （=public tender offer period）

  takeover bid system 株式公開買付け制度

  unsolicited takeover 敵対的買収

  ◆A "white knight" is a friendly acquirer sought by the target of an unfriendly takeover. 「ホワイト・ナイト」とは、非友好的な買収の標的企業が探し求める友好的な買収者をいう。

talks （名）会談, 交渉, 協議, 話し合い, 議論, 講演

  alliance talks 提携協議, 提携交渉

  bilateral talks 二国間協議, 二国間交渉, 政府間協議

  debt restructuring talks 債務再編交渉

  direct talks 直接交渉, 直接対話

  exploratory talks 事前協議

  future talks 今後の協議

  multilateral trade talks 多角的貿易交渉, 多国間貿易交渉

  the latest round of multilateral trade liberalization talks 新多角的貿易交渉（新ラウンド）（=the new round of WTO talks）

  ◆Akira Amari, minister in charge of TPP negotiations, and U.S. Trade Representative Michael Froman started with around 30 minutes of one-on-one talks, with the aim of reaching a broad bilateral agreement before a Japan-U.S. summit meeting held on April 24, 2014. 甘利TPP担当相と米通商代表部のフロマン代表は、日米首脳会談（2014年4月24日）前に二国間の大筋合意を得るため、約30分の1対1の会談から始めた。◆By starting talks on a comprehensive partnership agreement, the EU and the United States will take the first step toward creating a giant free trade zone that would account for about 50 percent of the world's gross domestic product. 包括的連携協定の交渉を開始することで、欧州連合（EU）と米国は、世界のGDP（国内総生産）の5割近くを占める巨大な自由貿易圏の創設に一歩踏み出すことになる。◆Nissan Motor Co.'s board of directors gave its approval for exploratory talks on a proposal for struggling U.S. auto giant General Motors

Corp. 日産自動車の取締役会は、経営再建中の米自動車大手ゼネラル・モーターズ（GM）に対する提携提案の事前協議を承認した。◆The first official ministerial-level talks between China and Taiwan, at odds more than six decades since the 1949 creation of the People's Republic of China, mark a big step toward expanding cross-strait dialogue beyond economic and trade issues. 1949年の中華人民共和国の樹立［建国］以来60年以上も対立している中国と台湾が初めて行った公式の閣僚級会談（2014年2月11日）は、経済や貿易問題を超えた両岸対話拡大への大きな一歩を踏み出すものだ。◆The LDP will oppose Japan's participation in the TPP talks as long as the pact is premised on the elimination of all tariffs without exception. TPP（環太平洋経済連携協定）が聖域なき関税全廃を前提にしているかぎり、自民党は日本のTPP交渉への参加に反対する方針だ。◆The OPEC talks broke down in acrimony as Saudi Arabia failed to convince other member nations to raise production. 石油輸出国機構（OPEC）の協議は、サウジアラビアが増産［生産量の引上げ］について他の加盟国を説得できなかったため、険悪なムードのなかで決裂した。

tap the market 市場を開発［開拓］する, 市場に登場する, 市場で起債する, 市場で資金を調達する

  ◆Japanese companies actively tapped the stock market to raise fresh capital. 日本の企業が、新規資本を調達するため株式市場で積極的に起債した。

target （名）目標, 標的, 対象, の, （物笑いの）種, 目標額, 目標水準, 買収目標企業, 買収対象会社, 買収標的の会社, ターゲット

  ◆A "white knight" is a friendly acquirer sought by the target of an unfriendly takeover. 「ホワイト・ナイト」とは、非友好的な買収の標的企業が探し求める友好的な買収者をいう。

tariff （名）関税, 関税率, 税率, 料金表, 運賃表 （⇒European Union）

  across-the-board tariff reduction 関税の一括引下げ

  ad valorem tariff 従価関税

  additional tariff 割増料金

  adopt retaliatory tariffs 報復関税を発動する

  alternation tariff 選択関税

  antidumping tariffs 反ダンピング（不当廉売）関税, ダンピング防止関税

  autonomous tariff 国定税率

  bargaining tariff 交渉関税, 駆け引き関税

  cartel tariff カルテル関税

  common external tariff 対外共通関税, 域外共通関税

  common tariff 共通関税

  compensatory tariff 相殺関税 （=countervailing tariff）

  competitive tariff 競争関税, 競争税率

compound tariff 複合関税

concession of tariff 関税譲許

conventional tariff 協定関税, 協定税率 (WTOの取決めで、国際的にこれ以上引き上げてはならない責務を負わされた関税率)

counter tariff 対抗関税

custom tariff 関税

customs tariff 関税, 関税率, 関税定率

customs tariff law 関税定率法

customs tariff schedules (関税の)実行税率 (各国が実際に適用している関税率)

customs tariff table 関税率表

differential tariff 差別関税, 差別税率

discriminative tariff 差別的関税, 差別税率

double tariff 二重関税, 複関税

drug tariff 薬価基準

effective tariff 実効関税

elastic tariff 弾力関税

elimination of tariffs 関税の撤廃, 関税撤廃

emergency tariffs 緊急関税

financial tariff 資金調達税

flexible tariff 伸縮的関税

freight tariff 運賃表

General Agreement on Tariffs and Trade 関税貿易一般協定(ガット)

general tariff 一般税率, 国定関税

import duties tariff 輸入税表

import tariff 輸入関税

impose tariff barriers on ～に関税障壁を設ける

impose tariffs on ～に関税をかける

increased tariffs 関税引上げ

internal tariff 域内関税

legal tariff 法定関税

lift tariff barriers on ～に対する関税障壁を撤廃する

lower tariffs 関税を引き下げる, 関税の引下げ

maximum tariff 最高税率

minimum tariff 最低税率

mixed tariff 混合税率

multiple tariff 複式税率, 複関税

national tariff 国定税率

non-discriminative tariff 無差別関税

non-tariff barriers 非関税障壁

nuisance tariff 定率関税

off-peak tariff 閑散時間割引料金 (=restricted tariff, time-of-day tariff)

optimum tariff 最適関税

overall tariff rate 関税率水準

phasing out of tariffs 関税の段階的撤廃

preferential tariff treatment 特恵関税(率) (=preference treatment tariff)

prohibitive tariff 禁止関税, 禁止的税率

protective tariff 保護関税, 保護税率

punitive tariffs 制裁関税, 報復関税

raise tariffs 関税を引き上げる, 関税率を引き上げる

retaliatory tariffs 報復関税 (=punitive tariffs)

revenue tariff 収入関税, 財政関税

safeguard tariffs セーフガード関税

simple tariff 単一税率 (=single-line tariff)

sliding scale tariff 伸縮関税

sliding tariff スライド関税

specific tariff 従量税

tariff agreement 関税協定, 運賃協定

tariff association 保険料同盟

tariff autonomy 関税自主権

tariff barrier 関税障壁 (=tariff wall)

tariff changes 料金体系の変更

tariff classification 関税分類

Tariff Commission 米関税委員会

tariff company 協定会社, 協定加入会社

tariff concession rate 関税譲許率

tariff elimination 関税撤廃

tariff equivalent 関税等価

tariff escalation 傾斜関税

tariff exemption 関税免除, 関税減免

tariff factory 関税工場

tariff negotiations 関税交渉

tariff policy 関税政策

tariff quota 関税割当て

tariff rate 関税率, 表定運賃(率), 許認可料金

tariff schedule 関税表, 料金制度

Tariffs Act 関税法

tit-for-tat tariffs 報復関税

tonnage tariff トン税

uniform tariff 統一関税

◆A free trade agreement is a treaty between two or more nations and territories seeking to reduce or abolish tariffs on industrial, agricultural and other products. 自由貿易協定(FTA)は、鉱工業品や農産品［農産物］の関税の引下げや撤廃を求める2か国以上の国や地域間の協定だ。◆Canada and the European Union have already decided to impose tit-for-tat tariffs on U.S. products. カナダと欧州連合(EU)は、米国の製品に報復関税をかけることをすでに決めている。◆China's retaliatory tariffs on Japanese cars, cellular phones and air conditioners clearly ran counter to WTO rules. 日本の自動車、携帯電話とエアコンに課した中国の報復関

税は、明らかにWTOルールに違反していた。◆Despite strong criticism from Washington's trading partners against high tariffs on steel imports to rescue the ailing U.S. steel industry, the USTR stressed the legitimacy of such safeguard measures. 不況の米鉄鋼業界を救済するための輸入鉄鋼製品に対する高関税について、米国の貿易相手国から強い批判がなされているにもかかわらず、米国通商代表はこの緊急輸入制限（セーフガード）措置の正当性を強調した。◆FTAs are a regime under which import tariffs are eliminated bilaterally or regionally. 自由貿易協定（FTA）は、2国間で、または地域で輸入関税を撤廃する制度だ。◆The EU's high tariff policy toward three IT-related import items reflects its desire to encourage foreign electronics manufacturers to set up factories in EU member nations. 欧州連合（EU）のIT関連輸入機器3品目に対する高関税政策は、外国の電機業界にEU加盟国への工場立地を促すEUの狙いを反映している。◆The government plans to raise its tariff on imported beef from August as a safeguard emergency import control measure in the wake of a steep year-on-year increase in imports of beef. 牛肉の輸入量が前年に比べて急増していることから、政府は8月から緊急輸入制限（セーフガード）措置として輸入牛肉の関税を引き上げる方針だ。◆The LDP will oppose Japan's participation in the TPP talks as long as the pact is premised on the elimination of all tariffs without exception. TPP（環太平洋経済連携協定）が聖域なき関税全廃を前提にしているかぎり、自民党は日本のTPP交渉への参加に反対する方針だ。◆The meeting between TPP minister Akira Amari and U.S. Trade Representative Michael Froman centered on Japanese tariffs on 586 items in five major farm product categories, including rice and wheat. 甘利TPP相とフロマン米通商代表部代表との会談では、コメや麦など重要な農産品5項目の586品目にかける日本の関税に焦点が当てられた。◆The new tariff on beef imports favors producers rather than consumers. 牛肉の輸入に対する新関税は、消費者ではなく生産者寄りの対応だ。◆The WTO was inaugurated in 1995, as an outgrowth of the General Agreement on Tariffs and Trade, with the aim of promoting a framework for multilateral free trade toward 21st century. 世界貿易機関（WTO）は、21世紀に向けた多角的な自由貿易体制の推進を目的に、ガット（関税・貿易一般協定）を発展改組して1995年に発足した。

tariffication of rice import コメ輸入の関税化, コメの関税化

tax （名）税金, 税, 租税, 税務
　bear the tax　税金を負担する
　for tax purposes　税務上
　income tax　所得税
　inventory tax　資産税
　property tax　資産税（資産評価額に課税）
　sales tax　売上税, 取引高税（物品の売価に課

税）, 物品販売税, 消費税
tax authorities　税務当局
tax certificate　納税証明書
tax holiday　免税措置, 免税期間, 減税期間
tax incentive　税制上の優遇措置
tax receipt　税金受領書
tax returns　確定申告
tax system on transfer prices　移転価格税制
tax treaty　租税条約
taxes and duties　税金と関税
use tax　使用税（物品の売価に課税）
value added tax　付加価値税, VAT
◆ABC shall pay all import duties or sales, use, value added or property taxes or any other taxes of any nature, assessed upon any Product or Service purchased by ABC from XYZ. ABCは、ABCがXYZから購入した本製品またはサービスに課されたすべての輸入関税, 売上税, 使用税, 付加価値税, 資産税または他のあらゆる種類の税金を支払うものとする。

tax avoidance 節税, 租税回避, 課税逃れ, 税金逃れ, 税逃れ
◆In a report released by the U.S. Senate Permanent Subcommittee on Investigations, Apple was held up as an example of legal tax avoidance. 米上院行政監察小委員会が公表した報告書で、米アップル社は、合法的課税逃れの典型例と指摘された。

tax credit 税額控除, 税負担の軽減
foreign tax credit　外国税額控除, 税額控除
tax credit on losses　損失による税負担の軽減
◆Should these undistributed earnings be distributed, foreign tax credits would reduce the additional U.S. income tax which would be payable. これらの未処分利益を仮に分配した場合、米国で追加的に生じる法人税等の金額は、外国税額控除により引き下げられます。◆The DPJ executives added the creation of a tax credit system, including tax breaks and cash benefits, to the bills to raise the consumption tax rate as relief measures for low-income earners. 民主党執行部は、消費税率引上げ関連法案に、低所得者対策として減税や現金給付などを行う「給付付き税額控除制度」の導入を追加した。

tax evasion 脱税, 税金逃れ
◆Oil tycoon Mikhail Khodorkovsky, Russia's richest man and held in jail on tax evasion and fraud charges, has quit as head of oil giant YUKOS. ロシア一の大富豪で、脱税や詐欺の罪で拘置されている石油王のミハイル・ホドルコフスキーが、石油大手のユコス社の社長を辞任した。

tax haven 租税回避地, 租税逃避地, 租税避難国, 税金天国, タックス・ヘイブン（=tax shelter: カリブ海のケイマン諸島や英領バージン諸島など、法人税や所得税がかけられないか税率が著しく低い国や地域が多い。その特徴として、各国の税務当局との情報交換を妨

T

げる制度や慣行があり、不正資金の洗浄（マ
ネーロンダリング）に利用されることもある）
◆Investment advisory company AIJ started investing in financial derivatives through funds based in the Cayman Islands, a tax haven, since 2002. 投資顧問会社のAIJは、2002年から、租税回避地の英領ケイマン諸島を営業基盤とするファンドを通じて金融派生商品への投資を始めた。◆The Cayman Islands, a British colony in the Caribbean, are a tax haven noted for their extremely low tax rare. カリブ海にある英国の植民地のケイマン諸島は、極端に低い税率で有名なタックス・ヘイブン（租税回避地）である。

taxable year 課税年度

technical （形）技術の, 技術的な, 工業技術の, 科学技術の, 専門的な, 技巧的な, 実務上の, 実用の, 市場の内部要因による, 人為的な, 操作的な, テクニカル
　　technical advisor 技術顧問, 技術アドバイザー
　　technical balance of trade 技術貿易収支
　　technical collaboration fee 技術提携料
　　technical conditions テクニカル要因（=technical factors, technical forces）
　　technical cooperation [collaboration] 技術提携, 技術協力
　　technical data 技術資料
　　technical education 技術教育
　　technical factors テクニカル要因, 市場内部要因（=technical conditions, technical forces: 信用取引残高, 投資家の売買動向, 新株発行による資金調達状況, 株価規制など, 動向株価を動かす要因のうち株式の需給に直接かかわる要因を「市場内部要因」とか「内部要因」という）
　　technical gap 技術格差
　　technical guidance 技術指導, 専門的指導
　　technical improvement 技術革新（technical innovation）, 技術の改良, 技術の改良, 改良技術
　　technical invention 技術的革命, 技術革新
　　technical license fee 技術実施料, 技術ライセンス料
　　technical monopoly 技術の独占
　　technical personnel 技術要員
　　technical problem 実務上の問題
　　technical rebound 自立反発
　　technical renovation [innovation] 技術革新
　　technical results 技術的成果, 技術成果
　　technical review 技術調査
　　technical specification 技術仕様
　　technical support 技術援助, 技術サポート, テクニカル面からの下支え, テクニカル・サポート
　　technical tie-up 技術提携

technical assistance 技術協力, 技術援助, 技術支援, 技術指導（=technical aid, technical cooperation）
　　give technical assistance to ～に［～に対して］技術指導を行う
　　technical assistance agreement 技術援助契約, 技術援助契約書, 技術指導契約
　　◆The total period of such technical assistance and services shall not exceed 90 man-days. この技術指導とサービスの総期間（延べ日数）は、90人日（にんび）を超えないものとする。

technical documentation 技術書類, 技術文書（=technical documents）
　　◆Licensor shall deliver the Software with the technical documentation for the Software to Licensee in accordance with the procedures set forth in the schedule attached hereto. ライセンサーは、本契約書の添書類に明記した手順に従って、本ソフトウエアと本ソフトウエアの技術文書をライセンシーに引き渡さなければならない。

technical information 技術情報
　　◆In consideration for the license of the trademark and the technical information granted under this agreement, Licensee shall pay to Licensor the minimum royalty for each contract year as set forth below: 本契約で付与する商標と技術情報の使用許諾の対価として、ライセンシーは、下記の各契約年度のミニマム・ロイヤルティをライセンサーに支払うものとする。◆Knowhow shall mean technical information and data useful for manufacturing Products. ノウハウとは、契約品製造のために有用な技術情報とデータを意味する。

technical training 技術訓練, 技術指導, 技術教育, 技術研修（=technology training）
　　◆Corporations must work on job training for those people who will lead future industries, through improved technical training and other human resources development programs. 企業は、技術訓練の強化や他の人材開発プログラムなどで、これからの産業の担い手の職業訓練に取り組まなければならない。

technique （名）技術, 技法, 手法, 技巧, 技量, 技, テクニック
　　◆The three major steel companies are expected to share patents on basic techniques necessary to process iron ore and other materials for steel production and for manufacturing steel. 鉄鋼大手3社は、鉄鋼生産のための鉄鉱石などの原料加工や鋼（はがね）の製造に必要な基本技術に関する特許を相互利用する見込みだ。

technological （形）科学技術の, 技術的な, 工芸の, テクノロジカル

technological capability 技術力, 技術活用能力
　　◆Other competitive factors in the market for the products are service, delivery, technological capability, and product quality and performance. 市場での製品の競争要因としては、サービスや

納入、技術活用能力[技術力]、品質、性能なども挙げられる。◆Through the merger, the two firms will strengthen the development of energy-saving ships, offsetting high production costs with improved technological capabilities. 合併により、両社は省エネ船舶の開発を強化し、技術力の向上で生産のコスト高を補う方針だ。

technological cooperation 技術提携, 技術協力 (=technical cooperation)
◆The company will help support struggling U.S. automakers through price hikes and technological cooperation. 同社は、値上げや技術提携などで、不振にあえぐ米自動車メーカーを支援する方針だ。

technological edge 技術的優位, 技術的優位性, 技術的に先を行くこと
◆The United States and European countries have a technological edge in the field of 3-D printers which are expected to revolutionize the world's manufacturing industries. 世界の製造業に革命をもたらすと期待されている3D(3次元)プリンターの分野で、欧米は技術で先を行っている。

technology (名)技術, 科学技術, 工業技術, テクノロジー (⇒encryption technology)

advanced technology 先端技術, 先進技術, 高度技術, ハイテク

competitiveness in technology 技術競争力

efficiency-enhancing technology 省力化技術

higher technologies ハイテク

import technology 技術を輸入する

imported technology 輸入技術, 導入技術, 技術輸入, 技術の導入

intellectual technology 知的技術

labor-saving technology 労働節約的技術, 省力技術

leading-edge technology 先端技術

licensing of technology 技術供与

net technology exporter 技術の純輸出国

production technology 生産技術

proprietary technology 独自の技術, 自社技術

sources of technology 技術の導入先

state-of-the-art technology 最新技術

technology company ハイテク企業

technology development 技術開発

technology license agreement 技術ライセンス契約

trade in technology 技術貿易

upgrade technology 技術水準を引き上げる
◆ABC possesses certain technology for the design, manufacture, use, and distribution of the products and certain intellectual property pertaining thereto. ABCは、本製品の設計、製造、使用および販売のための特定の技術と、それに関する知的財産権を所有している。◆Abe advertised Japan at the New York Stock Exchange by explaining that introduction of a high-speed railway system using Japan's superconducting magnetic levitation technology could connect New York and Washington in less than an hour. 安倍首相は、ニューヨーク証券取引所で、「日本の超電導リニア技術を用いた高速鉄道を導入すれば、ニューヨークとワシントンは1時間足らずで結ばれる」と説明して、日本を売り込んだ。◆Information about advanced technologies is sold to overseas rivals in industrial espionage, which has become a common threat for Japanese manufacturers. 産業スパイでは先端技術情報が海外のライバル企業に売り渡されるので、日本のメーカーにとって産業スパイは、共通の脅威となっている。◆Russia sees Japan as a destination for its natural gas exports and a provider of medical and agricultural technology. ロシアは、日本をロシアの天然ガスの供給先[輸出先]、医療や農業技術の提供国と見ている。◆The most advanced technologies are often at stake in lawsuits over intellectual property. 知的財産を巡る訴訟では、最先端技術が争点になることが多い。

technology transfer 技術移転 (=transfer of technology)
◆The EU sanctions against Iran include prohibitions on investments and technology transfers related to oil refining and the production of liquefied natural gas. イランに対する欧州連合(EU)の独自制裁には、石油精製や液化天然ガスの生産に関する投資、技術移転の禁止も含まれている。

telegraphic transfer 電信送金, 電信為替, TT
◆Payment for the products shall be made by the purchaser by telegraphic transfer to the bank account(s) designated by the seller in United States Dollars within 20 days after the receipt by the purchaser of the seller's invoice. 本商品に対する支払いは、売り主の支払い請求書を買い主が受領後20日以内に、売り主が指定した銀行口座に買い主が米ドルで電信送金して行うものとする。

temporary (形)一時的な, 臨時の, 暫定的, 仮の

a temporary office 仮事務所

be on temporary assignment [posting] 出向中である

file (for) a temporary court injunction 差止めの仮処分を申し立てる

formation of temporary cartels 一時的カルテルの形成

impose temporary import restrictions 輸入制限措置を打ち出す, 輸入規制を加える, 輸入規制する

rate of temporary duty 暫定税率 (=temporary rate of duty)

temporary accommodation [loan] 一時貸付け, 一時融通

temporary admission （加工再輸出品の）仮通関

temporary assignment 出向（=temporary posting）

temporary borrowings 一時借入金

temporary business 仮営業

temporary difference 一時的な差異

temporary dock receipt 仮倉受証

temporary import restrictions 一時的輸入制限

temporary landing 仮陸揚げ

temporary repair 仮修繕

temporary residence 寄留地

temporary suspension of trading 取引の一時停止

Temporary Tariff Measures Law 関税暫定措置法

temporary works 仮設工事

temporary measure 一時的な措置
◆Under the World Trade Organization rules, emergency import limits, or safeguard, are permitted as a temporary measure if the volume of imports of a certain product drastically increases, causing serious damages to industries concerned in the country. 世界貿易機関（WTO）のルールでは、緊急輸入制限措置（セーフガード）は、特定製品の輸入量が増加して、国内の関係業界に大きな被害が出ている場合には、一時的な措置として認められる。

tenant （名）借地人, 借家人, 賃借人, 借主, 土地保有者, 不動産権所有者, 占有者, 現住者（occupant）, テナント

key tenant 核店舗, 核テナント, キー・テナント

life tenant 生涯不動産権者

tenant in common 財産共有者

tenant right 借地権, 借家権, 借用権, 賃借更新権, 小作権
◆The Landlord shall effect insurance by itself or have other tenants effect insurance against such accidents as aforementioned and indemnify the Tenant within the extent covered by the insurance.「貸主」は、前記の事故などに対して自ら保険を付けるか他のテナントに保険を付けさせ、その保険でカバーされる範囲内で「借主」に損害の補償をするものとする。

tender offer 株式公開買付け, テンダー・オファー （=public tender offer, takeover bid, takeover offer, TOB: 一般の証券取引市場の外で行われる大口証券購入の申込みのこと）

cash tender offer 現金公開買付け, 現金による株式公開買付け, キャッシュ・テンダー・オファー（買取先の会社の株式を現金で公開買付けする方法）

friendly cash tender offer 友好的現金公開買付け

hostile cash tender offer 敵対的現金公開買付け

proposed tender offer price 提示された株式公開買付け（TOB）価格, 株式公開買付け（TOB）の予定価格
◆Following the tender offer, Oji Paper would acquire the remaining Hokuetsu shares through a share swap to turn it into a wholly owned subsidiary. 株式公開買付け（TOB）後に、王子製紙は、株式交換で残りの北越製紙の株を取得して北越製紙を完全子会社化する。◆Hitachi Ltd. plans to buy Clarion Co. through tender offer. 日立製作所が、株式公開買付け（TOB）でクラリオン買収を計画している。

tender on the Internet ネット入札, インターネットでの入札 （=bidding on the Internet）

tenor （名）期限（債務発生の日から満期日までの期間。為替手形の場合は、手形の引受日から満期日までの期間）, 期間, 有効期間, 手形期間, 債券期間, 正確な文言, 文意, 大意, 趣旨, 写し, 写本, 謄本

first of the same tenor and date being unpaid 同期日・同振出日の第一券が支払われないことを条件にして、同日付け・同条件の第一券未払いの場合にかぎり、同一の手形振出日と手形期限を持つ第一券が未払いの場合にかぎり（2通1組の組手形（set bill）で振り出される為替手形の第二券に印字されている文言）

second of the same tenor and date being unpaid 同期日・同振出日の第二券が支払われないことを条件にして、同日付け・同条件の第二券未払いの場合にかぎり、同一の手形振出日と手形期限を持つ第二券が未払いの場合にかぎり（組手形で振り出される為替手形の第一券に印字されている文言）

tensions between Japan and China 日中間の緊張
◆The huge decline in business sentiment among large manufacturers has mainly been attributed to the global economic slowdown, a decrease in exports due to a recent flare-up in tensions between Japan and China, and a slump in domestic auto sales. 大企業・製造業の景況感の大幅悪化は、主に世界経済の減速や最近の日中間の緊張激化に伴う輸出の減少、国内の自動車販売の鈍化によるものだ。

term （名）期間, 契約期間, 専門用語, 用語, 定期不動産権, 条件（複数形で用いられることが多い）, 条項, 規定, 約定, 合意（⇒corporation）

during the term of this agreement 本契約の期間中

general terms 一般条項

principal terms 主要条項

remaining terms 残りの条項, 残存条項, 残存規定

such term of terms　当該条項

term and renewal　契約の期間と更新

term and termination　契約の期間および終了, 期間と解除

term insured　保険期間

◆All the remaining terms of this agreement shall remain in full force and effect. 本契約の残存規定は、すべて完全に効力が存続するものとする。◆ If the borrower shall default in the performance of any other term or agreement contained in this agreement, the lender may declare its commitment and its obligation to be null and void. 借主が本契約に定める他の条件または合意事項を履行しない場合、貸主は、貸主の約束と義務は無効であると宣言することができる。◆The price and terms of sale of Products shall be mutually agreed upon in writing by the parties. 本製品の販売の価格と条件は、両当事者が書面で合意する。◆The said term of this agreement shall be automatically extended for additional consecutive periods of three years each, unless terminated by either party hereto by giving the other party a written notice to that effect at least three months prior to the end of original term of this agreement or any extended term thereof. 本契約の上記期間は、少なくとも本契約の当初期間またはその延長期間が満了する3カ月前までに、本契約の当事者の一方が相手方に対して本契約を終了させる旨の書面による通知をして本契約を終了させないかぎり、さらに引き続き3年間ずつ自動的に延長するものとする。

term of office　任期

◆The term of office of a director shall expire at the close of the second ordinary general meeting of shareholders to be held subsequent to this election. 取締役の任期は、その選任後に開催される2回目の通常株主総会の終了時に満了する。

term of this agreement [Agreement]　本契約の期間, 本契約期間, 本契約の有効期間

◆As one of the main conditions prerequisite to the continuation of the Agreement, Distributor agrees to purchase the Products from Exporter in the quantity not less than 500 units for any contract year throughout the effective term of this Agreement. 本契約の継続に不可欠な主要条件の一つとして、販売店は、本契約の有効期間中、契約年に500台以上の数量の本製品を輸出者から購入することに同意する。

terminal　(名) 終着駅, 始発駅, 終点, 起点, 基地, 末端, 端末装置, 末期患者, ターミナル

aircargo terminal　航空貨物ターミナル

combined transport terminal　複合ターミナル

credit authorization terminal　信用照会端末装置, 加盟店端末機, クレジット専用端末, CAT

liquefied natural gas terminal　液化天然ガス(LNG)工場, LNG基地

manipulate a terminal of the online system　オンライン・システムの端末装置を操作する

◆Noda and Putin witnessed a signing ceremony of a memorandum on the construction of a liquefied natural gas terminal near Vladivostok. 野田首相とプーチン露大統領は、ウラジオストク近郊で進める液化天然ガス(LNG)工場の建設に関する覚書の署名式に立ち会った。

terminal　(形) 末端の, 最終の, 終点の, 末期の, 末端の, 一定期間の, 定期の, 毎期の, 胸像の形をした

a terminal payment on a loan　ローンの最終支払い

terminal accounts　期末決算

terminal airport　ターミナル空港

terminal capital　最終資本

terminal charges　荷役料金, 荷揚げ料金, 荷下ろし料金, 蔵置場利用料

terminal congestion　終着駅滞貨

terminal foreign debt　期末対外債務

terminal market　中央卸売り市場, 定期市場

terminal market association　定期市場協会

terminal operation　港湾事業

terminal operator　港湾事業者, ターミナル・サービス業者

terminal output　期末生産高

terminal pay allowance　退職金, 退職手当て

terminal service　貨物サービス

terminal demand　最終需要

◆The non-manufacturing industry has corrected its investment plan downward due to weak terminal demand. 非製造業は、最終需要の弱さを背景に投資計画を下方修正した。

terminal equipment　端末機器, 端末装置

◆The increase in local service revenues was offset partially by some competitive erosion in the provision of terminal equipment. 一部の端末装置市場で競争力が低下したため、地域通信サービス収益の増加分は一部相殺された。

terminate　(動) (契約を) 終了させる, 解除する, 解約する, 終了する

automatically terminate　自動的に終了する, 自動終了する, 自動的に解除し終了する

terminate this agreement or any part thereof　本契約またはその一部を解除する

unconditionally terminate　無条件で終了する, 無条件で終了させる, 無条件で解除する

unless earlier terminated as provided for in this agreement　本契約に定めるとおり早期終了しないかぎり、本契約に規定するとおり中途終了する場合を除いて

◆ABCD's obligations under Article 5 shall terminate when the party seeking to avoid its obligations under such Articles can document or otherwise prove that: 第5条に基づくABCDの義務は、当該条項に基づくその義務の回避を求める当事者が以下を文書その他で証明できる場合には、終了

するものとする。◆Unless other party cures such breach within 30 days after the receipt of such written notice of breach and intention of termination, this agreement shall be automatically terminated on the elapse of such 30-day period. 相手方が契約の違反と契約解除の意思に関する書面での通知を受けてから30日以内に当該違反を改めないかぎり、本契約は、この30日の期間が経過した時点で自動的に解除されるものとする。

terminate an agreement 契約を終了させる, 契約を解除する, 解約する
◆In the event of bankruptcy, insolvency, dissolution, modification, amalgamation, receivership proceedings effecting the operation of its business or discontinuation of business for any reason and/or reorganization by the third party in the other party, either of the parties hereto shall have the absolute right to terminate this agreement without any notice whatsoever to the other party. 本契約のいずれか一方の当事者は、相手方の破産、支払い不能、解散、改組、合併、事業運営に影響を及ぼす清算手続き、または何らかの理由による事業中止および/または第三者による会社整理の場合には、相手方に何ら一切の通知をしないで本契約を終了する絶対的な権利を持つものとする。

terminate merger talks 経営統合交渉を打ち切る
◆Kirin-Suntory merger talks were terminated due to a disagreement over the merger ratio and other conditions. キリンとサントリーの経営統合交渉は、統合比率などの条件が折り合わないため、打ち切られた。

terminate production [output] 生産を中止する, 生産を止める, 生産から撤退する
(=cease [wind down] production)
◆Due to the European financial crisis, Mitsubishi Motors Corp. will terminate production in the Netherlands and focus on emerging economies where demand is robust. 欧州の金融危機で、三菱自動車はオランダでの生産を中止し、需要が旺盛な新興国を重視する方針だ。

termination （名）契約の終了［満期］, 解約, 期間の満了, 解除, 権利の消滅, 解散
allow termination in the following events 以下の事由がある場合に契約の終了を是認する
effect of termination 契約解除の効果
intention of termination 解除の意思
noncompetition after termination 契約終了後の競業制限
notice of termination 解約通知, 解除の通知
survive the expiration, termination, or cancellation of this agreement 本契約の満了、終了または解除後も存続する, 本契約の満了、終了または解除後も引き続き有効である
survive the termination of this agreement 本契約終了後も存続する, 本契約終了後も引き

続き有効である, 本契約終了後も効力を失わない
termination agreement 解除契約
(=cancellation agreement)
termination by expiration 満了による終了
termination for cause 契約の途中解除
termination of adventure clause 運送打切り約款
termination of procuration 委任権の終了
termination of the corporate charter 定款の廃止
termination of the term 期限満了, 満期
termination of this agreement by cancellation 解除による本契約の終了
termination payment 契約終了時の支払い
termination provision 終了規定
upon expiration or termination of this agreement 本契約の満了または終了と同時に, 本契約が満了または終了したときは
◆Distributor or Supplier may terminate this agreement at will, at any time during the term of this agreement, with or without cause, by written notice given to the other party not less than 30 days prior to the effective date of such termination. 販売店または供給者は、この契約終了の効力発生日の30日以上前に相手方に書面で通知して、本契約中いつでも理由の有無を問わず自由に本契約を解除することができる。

terms （名）条件, 条項
express terms 明示条項
implied terms 黙示条項
the terms of a credit 信用状条件
the terms of agreement 契約条件
the terms of business 取引条件
the terms of delivery 引渡し条件
the terms of documentary draft 荷為替手形条件
the terms of sale 販売条件, 売買条件
the terms of service agreement 利用規約
the terms of use 利用規約（ウェブ上の法的通知）

terms and conditions 条件, 条項, 条項と条件
general terms and conditions of business 一般取引条件, 一般的取引条件
on the identical terms and conditions of ～と同一条件で
pursuant to the terms and conditions of a loan agreement 融資契約の条件に従って
terms and conditions of business 取引条件
terms and conditions of sale 販売条件, 販売規約
the terms and conditions of the proposed sale 申し出をした売却の条件

upon the terms and conditions set forth in this agreement 本契約に定める条件に従って
◆All the terms and conditions set forth on the reverse side hereof are confirmed to be an integral part of this agreement. 裏面に記載する条件は、すべて本契約の不可分の一部であることを確認する。

terms and provisions 条件と規定, 条件と条項
◆ABC hereby consents to such assignment and agrees for the benefit of XYZ to be bound by such terms and provisions. ABCは、ここに当該譲渡に同意し、XYZの利益のためにこのような条件と規定に拘束されることに同意する。

terms hereof 本契約の条件
◆The execution and performance of this agreement by Seller constitute legal, valid and binding obligations of Seller, enforceable in accordance with the terms hereof. 売り主による本契約の締結と履行は、本契約の条件に従って強制することができる法的、有効かつ拘束力のある売り主の義務を構成する。

terms of payment 支払い条件, 決済条件
◆If you find the terms of payment acceptable, please confirm the order subject to the modifications above. この支払い条件がのめるなら、上記の変更を条件として本注文の確認をお願いします。◆Our terms of payment are to value at 30 d/s under an irrevocable letter of credit to be opened in our favor for the corresponding value of an order. 当社の決済条件は、注文相当額につき、当社を受益者として開設された取消不能信用状に基づいて一覧後30日払いの手形を振り出すことです。

terms of trade 交易条件, 取引条件
barter terms of trade 商品交易条件, バーター交易条件
commodity terms of trade 商品交易条件
double factoral terms of trade 二重生産要素交易条件
factoral terms of trade 要素交易条件
gross barter terms of trade 総商品交易条件, 総交易条件
gross terms of trade 総交易条件
income terms of trade 所得交易条件
net barter terms of trade 純商品交易条件
net terms of trade 純交易条件
real cost terms of trade 実質費用交易条件
simple factoral terms of trade 単一生産要素交易条件
single factoral terms of trade 単一生産要素交易条件
terms of trade effect 交易条件効果
unfavorable terms of trade 不順な交易条件, 悪化交易条件
utility terms of trade 効用交易条件

terms or conditions 条件または条項
◆The failure of either party to insist upon strict adherence to any terms or conditions of this agreement on any occasion shall not be considered a waiver of any right thereafter to insist upon strict adherence to that term or condition or any other term or condition of this agreement. いずれかの機会に当事者の一方が本契約の条件または条項の厳格な順守を要求しなくても、これは本契約の当該条件・条項または他の条件・条項の厳格な順守を要求するその後の権利を放棄したとは見なされないものとする。

terms or provisions 条項または規定, 条項
◆The execution of this agreement and the consummation of the transactions contemplated hereby will not result in a breach of any of the terms or provisions of, or constitute a default under, any agreement, or other instrument to which Purchaser is a party or by which it is bound. 本契約の締結(本契約書の作成)と本契約により企図されている取引の完了は、買い主が当事者となっているまたは当事者が拘束される契約書その他の証書のいかなる条項にも違反せず、またその不履行にもならないものとする。

territory (名)販売区域, 販売地域, 販売領域, 担当区域(商標やソフトウエア・プログラムなど知的財産権の)使用許諾地域, 許諾地域, 契約地域, レベル, 領土, 領地, 領域, 主権, 分野, 区域, 範囲, ゾーン, テリトリー (⇒have manufactured, sales territory)
business territory 商圏, 商勢圏
distribution territory 販売区域
junk territory 投資不適格のレベル
manufacturing territory 製造地域
sales territory 販売領域, 販売区域, 販売地域
◆A free trade agreement is a treaty between two or more nations and territories seeking to reduce or abolish tariffs on industrial, agricultural and other products. 自由貿易協定(FTA)は、鉱工業品や農産品[農産物]の関税の引下げや撤廃を求める2か国以上の国や地域間の協定だ。◆ABC accepts such appointment and undertakes to use its best efforts, at its own expenses, to promote the sales of the products throughout the territory at all times during the term of this agreement. ABCは当該指定を受諾し、本契約期間中つねに、その自己負担で、契約地域全域で本製品の販売を促進するため最善の努力をすることを約束する。

terrorist attack テロリストの攻撃, テロ攻撃, テロ
◆The nonlife insurance industry wants all kinds of buildings and other properties not insured for terrorist attacks. 損害保険業界は、すべての物件をテロ免責にしたいと考えている。

terrorist organization テロ組織
◆A revised Foreign Exchange and Foreign Trade Control Law has been enacted to enable the swift freezing of funds belonging to terrorist organizations. テロ組織の資金[資産]凍結を迅速に行うための改正外為法は、すでに成立して[制定されて]

TEST 460

test (名)試験, 実験, 試査, 検査, チェック, 試金石, 検査用器具, 試薬, 試剤, (判断の)基準, 試練, テスト

consumer expectation test　消費者規定基準

deviation-from-norm test　標準逸脱テスト

field test　実地検査

private loan financing test　民間貸付け基準

private security or payment test　民間保証・支払い基

product test　商品テスト

risk-utility test　危険効用比較基準

sample test　サンプル検査, 試供品テスト

stress test　耐性検査, 特別検査

test marketing　試験販売

test run　試運転, テスト・ラン

◆Measures to tighten quality controls on Chinese food products, taken by many Japanese manufacturers in China, include more stringent tests on the amounts of agricultural chemicals used at Chinese farms and on the quality of processing materials used at Chinese factories. 中国の日系メーカーの多くが取っている中国産食品の品質管理強化策としては、中国農場での農薬使用量の検査や中国の工場で使用している加工原料の品質チェックの強化などが挙げられる。◆The IAEA gave the green light to the Nuclear and Industrial Safety Agency's review process of stress tests for nuclear reactors. 国際原子力機関(IAEA)が、保安院による原子炉のストレス・テスト(耐性検査)の審査方法を承認した。

testing procedures　検査手続き

◆Payment is not conditioned upon Products meeting any acceptance testing procedures Distributor may have. 支払いは、販売店が行う受入れ検査手続きに本製品が適合することを条件とするものではない。

text (名)本文, 原文, 主文, 条文, 正本

current text　原本

the official and controlling text hereof　本契約の公式の正本

◆The English language version of this agreement shall be the official and controlling text hereof. 本契約の英語版を、本契約の公式の正本とする。

theft (名)盗難, 窃盗

◆During the period when Products are in the custody of ABC, ABC shall keep Products insured at ABC's account for the benefit of XYZ against loss or damage by fire, theft or otherwise with extended coverage. 本製品[契約品]がABCが保管している期間中、火災、盗難、その他による滅失や損害を拡張担保するため、ABCはその勘定で、XYZを保険受取人として本製品に付保するものとする。

thereafter (副)その後, それ以降は, それ以降の　(=after that)

◆The licensee's obligation under this Article with respect to the confidential information shall not apply to information which is part of the public domain at the time of disclosure by the licensor, or thereafter becomes part of the public domain without fault on the part of the licensee. 本条に基づく秘密情報に関するライセンシーの義務は、ライセンサーによる開示の時点で公知であるか、その後ライセンシー側の過失なしに公知となる情報には適用されないものとする。

thereby (副)それによる, それにより, それによって, それについて[関して], その近くに[近辺に]

◆In case any one or more of the provisions of this agreement are held invalid, illegal or unenforceable in any respect, the validity, legality and enforceability of the remaining provisions hereof shall not be in any way affected or impaired thereby, except to the extent that giving effect to the remaining provisions would be unjust or inequitable. 本契約の一つ以上の規定がいずれかの点で無効、違法または強制不能と判断された場合、残存規定の実施が不公正または不均衡となる範囲を除いて、本契約の残存規定の有効性、合法性と強制可能性はその影響を受けることはなく、またそれによって損なわれることはないものとする。

therefor (副)その　(=for it, for that))

◆In case the borrower fails to pay any principal or interest payable under this agreement on the due date therefor, the borrower shall pay to the lender overdue interest on such overdue amount for each day for the period from and including the due date therefor up to and including the day immediately preceding the actual payment date. 借主が本契約に基づいて元本または支払い利息の支払い期日に元本の返済または支払い利息の支払いを怠った場合、借主は、その支払い期日から実際の払込み日の前日までの各日数について、その支払い遅延金額の遅延利息を貸主に支払うものとする。

thereof (副)それの, その, それについて, その契約書の, その文書の　(=of that, of it)

◆The seller shall sell and deliver the products and the buyer shall purchase and take delivery thereof. 売り主は本商品を販売して引き渡すものとし、買い主は本商品を買い取ってその引渡しを受けるものとする。

thereto (副・形)それに付随する, それに関する, それに対する, それに　(=to it, to that)

◆ABC possesses certain technology for the design, manufacture, use, and distribution of the products and certain intellectual property pertaining thereto. ABCは、本製品の設計、製造、使用および販売のための特定の技術と、それに関する知的財産権を所有している。

thermal power generation　火力発電, 火力発電所

◆Japan's trade deficit in April-September 2014 hit a record high due to increased demand for liquefied natural gas for thermal power generation and a rise in overall import prices stemming from the yen's depreciation. 日本の2014年度上半期（4〜9月）の貿易赤字は、火力発電所向け液化天然ガス（LNG）の需要増加と円安による輸入物価全体の上昇で、過去最大となった。

thermal power station 火力発電所
（=thermal power plant）
◆As an abnormal situation, imports of liquefied natural gas, the fuel needed for operating power companies' thermal power stations, have increased to a massive ￥6 trillion a year after the operations of nuclear reactors were suspended around the country. 異常事態として、原子力発電所の運転が全国で停止した後、電力各社の火力発電の稼働に必要な液化天然ガス（LNG）の輸入額が、年間で6兆円もの巨額に達している。

they （代）先方, 同社, 競争会社, 当局, 関係者, 店の人たち
◆In comparison of your offer with that of our regular suppliers, their quotation is more favorable. 貴社のオファーと当社の常時買付け先のオファーを比べると、先方の価格のほうが有利です。 ◆Our bid of $1,000 was higher than theirs of $900. 当社の1,000ドルの買いの指し値は、競争会社の900ドルより高かった。 ◆We were asked to send out tracers by them. 当社は、同社に揚げ荷事故照会状を出すよう依頼された。 ◆We will get in touch with them if you so wish. お望みとあれば、先方［同社］に連絡をとってみます。

third party 第三者, 当事者以外の人
third party contractor 第三者請負人
third-party equity［share］allotment 第三者株式割当て （=third-party equity allocation）
third party infringement 第三者侵害, 第三者による侵害
third-party insurance 第三者保険（被保険者以外の第三者の傷害に対する保険）
third-party products 第三者の製品
third-party support 第三者支援
◆The other party shall not disclose such confidential information to any third party. 他方当事者は、この秘密情報を第三者に開示してはならない。 ◆The parties hereto shall keep in strict confidence from any third party any and all important matters concerning the business affairs and transactions covered by this agreement. 本契約当事者は、本契約の対象である営業上の問題や取引に関するすべての重要事項については、どんな第三者に対しても一切極秘にする。

third-party allocation 第三者割当て
（=third-party allotment: 業務提携先や金融機関など特定の相手に新株を引き受けてもらう形の第三者割当増資に対して、一般投資家を引受先として新株を発行することを公募増資という）
◆Private placement of new shares is also referred to as third-party allocation. 新株の私募発行は、第三者割当てとも言われる。

third-party share allotment 第三者株式割当て
◆In an attempt to recapitalize itself, the bank raised ￥15 billion through a third-party share allotment. 資本再編のため、同行は第三者株式割当てで150億円を調達した。

threatened against 〜に対して提起される恐れがある
◆Exhibit D sets forth a complete and accurate list of all claims, suits, actions, arbitrations, legal or other proceedings or governmental investigations to which the Company is a party or which is, to the knowledge of ABC, threatened against the Company. 付属書類Dには、本会社が当事者である、またはABCが知るかぎり本会社が当事者になる恐れのある［本会社に対して提起される恐れがある］すべての請求、訴訟、仲裁、法的手続きもしくはその他の手続き、または政府調査の完全かつ正確なリストが記載されている。

threatened breach 違反の恐れ
◆In the event of a breach or threatened breach by ABC of this agreement, XYZ will have no adequate remedy at law. ABCによる本契約の違反または違反の恐れがある場合、XYZは、コモン・ロー上の十分な救済を受けられない。

Three T's 取引形態（type）、取引条件（terms）と販売技術（technique）の三つ（貿易取引を有利にまとめるための3要素）

thriving （形）盛況な, 好況の, 好調な, 繁盛する, 繁栄する, 栄える, 成功する, 成長［生長］する
◆Japanese exporting firms have been enjoying positive earnings, benefiting from thriving markets in the United States and the weak yen. 日本の輸出企業は、米国の好調な市場と円安を追い風に、好業績が続いている。

through （前）〜により, 〜を通して, 〜で, 〜を手段として, 〜中に （形）直通の, 通しの, 停止しない, 〜を終えた（finished）
through B/L 通し船荷証券
through cargo handling 一貫荷役
through carriage 通し運送 （=through transport）
through freight 通し運賃 （=through rate）
through manifest 通過目録

through a medium of 〜により
◆On orders over U.S. $50,000, payment shall be made through a medium of a Letter of Credit to be established by ABC at its expense. 5万米ドルを超える注文の場合、支払いは、ABCがその費用で開設する費用で信用状で行うものとする。

through no act or failure to act 作為ま

たは不作為によらずに

◆The confidential information shall not include information which is or becomes generally known or available through no act or failure to act by ABC. この秘密情報は、公知であるか一般に入手することができる情報、またはABCの作為または不作為によらずに公知となるか一般に入手することができる情報を含まないものとする。

through no fault of 〜の過失によることなく

◆Such information entered the public domain subsequent to the time it was communicated to the receiving party by the disclosing party through no fault of the receiving party. 当該情報は、受領当事者の過失によることなく開示当事者が受領当事者に通知した時点以後に公知になった。

throughout （前）〜を通じて、〜の間中、〜の間ずっと、〜の至る所に　（副）あらゆる点で、すっかり

◆Throughout this agreement, Warrantee shall attempt to maintain an insurance policy to cover any claim, demand, liability, suit, damage or expense caused by Warrantee negligence. 本契約期間を通じて、被保証人は、被保証人の過失によって生じるクレーム、要求、責任、訴訟、損害または費用を担保する保険証券の維持に努めるものとする。

TIBOR［**Tibor**］　東京銀行間取引金利、東京銀行間貸し手金利、タイボー（Tokyo interbank offered rateの略。⇒LIBOR［Libor］）

◆In order to dispel investors' mistrust over the benchmark rates such as the Libor and the Tibor, ceaseless efforts by bankers associations and their members are essential. ライボー（ロンドン銀行間取引金利）やタイボー（東京銀行間取引金利）などの基準金利に対する投資家の不信を払拭（ふっしょく）するには、銀行協会や銀行協会会員の不断の努力が欠かせない。◆The Japanese Bankers Association's investigation found all 18 banks involved follow rules for their submissions of reference rates to set Tibor. 全国銀行協会（全銀協）は、調査の結果、調査対象の銀行18行がすべて東京銀行間取引金利（TIBOR）算出［算定］の参照金利を申告する規定を順守していることを確認した。

tick （名）照合済みの印

tidal waves 高潮損害

tie-up agreement 提携契約, 業務提携契約

◆Tokio Marine and Fire Insurance Co. concluded a tie-up agreement covering five business fields with the leading Chinese nonlife insurance company, the People's Insurance Company of China（PICC）, and Samsung Fire and Marine Insurance, a South Korean nonlife insurance company. 東京海上火災保険は、中国最大手の損害保険会社の中国人民保険公司（PICC）および韓国最大手の損保、サムスン火災海上保険と、5業務分野での提携契約を結んだ。

tie-up negotiations 提携交渉

◆Tie-up negotiations between Wal-Mart and Seiyu began last summer when executives met at an international conference of the supermarket industry. ウォルマートと西友の提携交渉は、スーパー業界の国際会議で首脳陣が顔を合わせた昨年の夏に始まった。

tied （形）ひも付きの, 連動する, 特約の
　be tied to LIBOR　LIBORに連動する
　products with variable rates tied to LIBOR　LIBORベースの変動金利商品
　tied aid　ひも付き援助, タイド・エイド
　tied crude oil　ひも付き原油
　tied loan program　ひも付き借款
　tied store［shop］　連鎖店　（=chained store）
　tied transaction　ひも付き取引, 連結取引
　tied yen loan　ひも付き円借款

tied loan ひも付き借款, ひも付き円借款（tied yen loan）, ひも付き融資, ひも付き援助, タイド・ローン　（=tied yen loans）

◆In offering the special yen loans, the government adopted tied loans limited to three years. 特別円借款を供与する際、政府は3年間の時限措置としてひも付き円借款を導入した。

TIFA　貿易投資枠組み協定, TIFA協定（trade and investment framework agreementの略）

time （名）時間, 時期, 期限, 日時, 期間
　time and schedule for disbursement　融資実行時期
　time bill　期限付き手形, 期限付き為替手形（=term bill, usance bill）
　time charge　時間制, タイム・チャージ（米国法律事務所の弁護士報酬基準の一つ）
　time charter　期間用船契約, 定期用船契約
　time discount　期間割引
　time draft　一覧後定期払い手形
　time freight　定期用船料
　time loan　定期貸付け
　time loss provision　喪失時間約款
　time penalty clause　（積送貨物の）遅着約款
　time policy　船の期間保険証券, 定期保険証券, 定期保険
　time schedule of works　工事の工程表
　time sheet　勤務［作業］時間記録票, タイム・シート（航海用船契約の停泊期間の計算資料となる記録）

◆In case there is delay in delivery of all or any part of the Goods on the time as stipulated in this agreement, the buyer is entitled to claim liquidated damages at the rate of one-half of one percent（0.5%）of the amount of the delayed Goods for each complete week of delay. 本契約で定める期限に本商品の全部または一部に引渡し遅延が生じた場合、買い主は、遅延対象の各1週間につき引渡し遅延商品の代金の0.5%を損害賠償予定額として請求することができるものとする。◆In the event of such a Force Majeure, the time for performance or cure will be extended for a period equal to the duration of the Force Majeure. このような不可抗力が発生した場合、履行または違反是正の期限は、不可抗力の期間と同じ期間延長される。◆We may not have to add that we do not hold ourselves responsible for the corresponding delay in shipment if your actions should not be taken in time. 言うまでもなく[申すまでもなく]、貴社の打つ手が遅れたら、それに伴って生じる船積みの遅延に対して、当社は責任を負いません。

time is of essence 期限は絶対条件である、期限は重要な要素である
◆Time is of essence under the terms of this agreement. 本契約の規定では、期限は絶対条件である。

time of shipment 船積み日、船積みの日時、船積み時期
◆Time of shipment is of the essence of this agreement. 船積み時期は、本契約の重要な条件である。◆Time of shipment shall be, in principle, within ( ) days after Company's receipt of the letter of credit stipulated in the preceding Article. 船積みの日時は、原則として前条に定める信用状を会社が受領後( )日以内とする。

tit-for-tat tariffs 報復関税
◆Canada and the European Union have already decided to impose tit-for-tat tariffs on U.S. products. カナダと欧州連合(EU)は、米国の製品に報復関税をかけることをすでに決めている。

title （名）役職、所有権、権原、名称、肩書、称号、契約書の表題（「権原」は、資産を使用・享受・処分できる権利のこと）

title covenants　売り主による約定

title insurance policies　権利保険約款

title or rights　所有権やその他の権利、所有権または権利

title, ownership or interest　権原、所有権または権益

title search　不動産の権原調査

title to and the risk of the shipments of the products　本製品積送品の所有権と危険負担
◆The Company has good and marketable title to each item of personal property used by it in the business of the Company, free and clear of all liens or security interests. 対象会社は、対象会社の事業で対象会社が使用している各動産（担保権は一切付いていない）を売買できる正当な権原をもっている。

title to the shares 株式の所有権、株式に対する権原
◆Seller has good and marketable title to the Shares, free and clear of any and all covenants, conditions, restrictions, voting trust arrangements, liens, options and adverse claims or rights. 売り主は、一切の約束、条件、制約、議決権信託契約、担保権、選択権、不利益を及ぼすクレームや権利をまったく負担しない本株式を売

買できる正当な権原を持っている。

to （前）〜へ、〜の方向に、〜に対して、〜まで、〜に、〜にとって、〜の限りにおいて

to all intents and purposes　事実上、つまり、あらゆる点で

to arrive goods　未着品、未到着品

to arrive terms　到着条件　(=arrival terms)

to such extent as may be reasonably necessary　合理的に必要な範囲で

to the best of one's knowledge　〜の知るかぎり、〜の知るかぎりにおいて、〜の知識の及ぶかぎり　(=to the best knowledge of)

to the extent one considers necessary　〜が必要と判断する範囲で

to the extent possible　できるかぎり

to the fullest extent permitted by applicable law　適用法により許される最高の限度まで、適用法上許容される最大の範囲まで

to the order of　〜の指図人に（支払いまたは引渡しのこと）

to the reasonable satisfaction of　〜が合理的に満足するように、〜の合理的な満足の行くように

to order 指図人式
◆A full set of negotiable bills of lading made out to order must be endorsed by shipper. 指図人式で作成された譲渡可能な船荷証券一式には、荷送人の裏書が必要である。

to that effect その旨の、その趣旨の、そのような趣旨で
◆The said term of this agreement shall be automatically extended for additional consecutive periods of three years each, unless terminated by either party hereto by giving the other party a written notice to that effect at least three months prior to the end of original term of this agreement or any extended term thereof. 本契約の上記期間は、少なくとも本契約の当初期間または上記の延長期間が満了する3カ月前までに、本契約の当事者の一方が相手方に対して本契約を終了させる旨の書面による通知をして本契約を終了させないかぎり、さらに引き続き3年間ずつ自動的に延長するものとする。

to the contrary それと反対の[に]、その逆の[に]、別の、異なる
◆Date of marine bill of lading shall be proof of the date of shipment in the absence of the evidence to the contrary. 海上船荷証券の日付は、反対の証拠がない場合、船積み日の証拠となる。

to the extent of 〜の程度にまで、〜の範囲内で、〜の限界・限度まで、〜まで
◆The price or revised price provided for herein shall be subject to adjustment to the extent of: 本条に定める価格または改定価格は、次の範囲内で調整するものとする。

to the extent that 〜の範囲で、〜まで
◆In case any one or more of the provisions of

this agreement are held invalid, illegal or unenforceable in any respect, the validity, legality and enforceability of the remaining provisions hereof shall not be in any way affected or impaired thereby, except to the extent that giving effect to the remaining provisions would be unjust or inequitable. 本契約の一つ以上の規定がいずれかの点で無効、違法または強制不能と判断された場合、残存規定の実施が不公正または不均衡となる範囲を除いて、本契約の残存規定の有効性、合法性と強制可能性はその影響を受けることはなく、またそれによって損なわれることはないものとする。

to the knowledge of ～の知るかぎり
◆Exhibit D sets forth a complete and accurate list of all claims, suits, actions, arbitrations, legal or other proceedings or governmental investigations to which the Company is a party or which is, to the knowledge of ABC, threatened against the Company. 付属書類Dには、本会社が当事者である、またはABCが知るかぎり本会社が当事者になる恐れのある[本会社に対して提起される恐れがある]すべての請求、訴訟、仲裁、法的手続きもしくはその他の手続き、または政府調査の完全かつ正確なリストが記載されている。

TOB 株式公開買付け(take-over bid [takeover bid]の略。⇒takeover bid)
解説**TOBとは**：自社株の消却のほか、上場企業などが経営の支配権を強化したり子会社化したりする目的で、証券取引所の市場外で3分の1超の株式(新株予約権や新株予約権付き社債などを含む)を買い付ける場合、あらかじめ買付け価格や買付け期間、株数などを提示して、株主に対して平等に売却の機会を与える制度。応募が取得目標の株式数に達しない場合、TOBは不成立となり、応募された株式を返さなければならない。

Tokyo interbank foreign exchange 東京外国為替市場
◆Banks participating in direct yen-yuan trading in the Tokyo interbank foreign exchange market will trade the yen and the yuan at an exchange rate calculated on the basis of actual supply and demand. 東京外国為替市場で円・人民元の直接取引に参加する銀行は、実際の需給をもとに算出した取引レートで、円と人民元を銀行間で取引する。

Tokyo Stock Exchange 東京証券取引所、東証、東京株式市場、TSE(持ち株会社の東京証券取引所グループの下に、東証一部・東証二部・新興市場マザーズの運営会社や、上場審査・不正取引の監視をする「自主規制法人」、取引の清算業務を行う日本証券クリアリング機構がある)
◆According to a probe conducted by the Tokyo Stock Exchange, there was a series of questionable stock deals in which trading volume surged just after the capital increase announcements by listed companies. 東京証券取引所の調査による

と、上場企業が増資[公募増資]を公表した直後に(その銘柄の)売買高が急増する不自然な株取引が、相次いでいた。

Tokyo trading 東京外国為替市場の取引
◆The euro plunged below ￥97 for the first time in about 11 1/2 years in Tokyo trading. 東京外国為替市場の取引で、ユーロは約11年半ぶりに1ユーロ＝97円を割り込む水準まで急落した。

ton (名)トン
解説**重量トン(weight ton)の種類**：

long ton 重トン(=English ton, gross ton:1重トンは2,240ポンドを1トンとする)
metric ton メートル・トン(1メートル・トン＝1,000キログラム)
short ton 軽トン(=American ton, net ton:1軽トンは2,000ポンドを1トンとする)

tort (名)不法行為、不法侵害(他人の権利・利益を侵害する行為)
any obligation, liabilities, claim or remedies in tort 不法行為による義務、責任、請求または救済手段
tort claims 不法行為に基づく損害賠償請求
tort damages 不法行為による損害
◆The total liability of XYZ on any claim, whether in contract, tort (including negligence) or otherwise, arising out of the sale or use of any Product or the furnishing of the Service shall not exceed the price allocable to the Product or Service, which gives rise to the claim. 契約上か不法行為(過失を含む)その他の理由によるかを問わず、本製品の販売、使用または本サービスの提供から生じる請求に対するXYZの責任総額は、当該請求を発生させた本製品または本サービスに割り当てられた価格を超えないものとする。

touch (名)連絡、接触、感覚、感触、感じ、手ごたえ、筆致、手法、技法、仕上がり、仕上げ、少量、気味、軽い症状、簡単に金を出す人、触診、タッチ
apply the final [finishing] touches to ～の最後の調整をする
be [keep, stay] in touch with ～に通じている、～をよく知っている
be out of [lose] touch with ～と連絡が途切れる、～と連絡していない、～に通じていない
get in touch with ～と連絡をとる
lose touch with ～と接触がなくなる、～と接触を失う、～との交流がなくなる、～に関心を持たなくなる
◆SMFG is applying the finishing touches to a plan to invest in Goldman Sachs Group Inc. 三井住友銀行は現在、(米証券首位の)ゴールドマン・サックスに投資する計画の最終調整に入っている。◆We will get in touch with them if you so wish. お望みとあれば、先方[同社]に連絡をとってみます。

TPA 通商一括交渉権(Trade Promotion

Authorityの略。ファースト・トラック (fast track: 速い道筋) と呼ばれ、ブッシュ政権は2002年にTPA法を成立させたが、07年6月末に期限切れとなった。「通商一括交渉権」は米大統領権限で、外国政府と結んだ通商合意を、大統領は議会に対して無修正で承認するよう要求できる)

TPP negotiations TPP (環太平洋経済連携協定) 交渉
◆If it is not certain five agricultural items, including rice and wheat, will be treated as exceptions to free trade, the government will not hesitate to pull out from the TPP negotiations. コメや麦など農産品5項目を自由貿易の聖域として確保できなければ、政府はTPP (環太平洋経済連携協定) 交渉からの脱退も辞さない方針だ。◆Japan has yet to enter full-scale TPP negotiations, but the LDP has not presented concrete measures to prepare for the liberalization of trade, including steps to bolster competitiveness in the agricultural sector. 日本が環太平洋経済連携協定 (TPP) の本格交渉に入るのはこれからだが、自民党は、農業分野での競争力強化策など、貿易自由化に備えた具体策をまだ示していない。◆The Abe administration faces several major challenges such as lifting the economy out of deflation, reconstruction from the Great East Japan Earthquake and the TPP negotiations. 安倍政権は、デフレ脱却、震災復興やTPP (環太平洋経済連携協定) 交渉など、大きな課題にいくつか直面している。

tracer (名) 揚げ荷事故照会状、紛失物照会状
◆We were asked to send out tracers by them. 当社は、同社に揚げ荷事故照会状を出すよう依頼された。

trade (動) 売買する、取引する、商う、商売する、交易する、交換する、(冗談などを) 交わす、(砲火を) 応酬する、(選手を) トレードする
trade above par　額面以上で取引される
trade and do business　取引し事業を行う
trade at around　～近辺で取引される
trade away　売り払う、売る、(権利などを) 手放す
trade below　～を割り込んで取引される
trade down　(下取りに出して) 買い換える、値を下げる
trade for one's account　自己売買をする
trade in　下取りに出す
trade most frequently at　取引の中心値は～である
trade off　～と交換する、～と相殺する
trade securities　証券の売買を行う
trade to a record low　新安値を付ける
trade up　高い物と買い換える [交換する]
trade within a narrow range　もみ合いが続く
◆A turnover ratio of 50% means that it was traded once every two years. 売買回転率50%と

は、2年に1回売買されたことを意味する。◆Banks participating in direct yen-yuan trading in the Tokyo interbank foreign exchange market will trade the yen and the yuan at an exchange rate calculated on the basis of actual supply and demand. 東京外国為替市場で円・人民元の直接取引に参加する銀行は、実際の需給などをもとに算出した取引レートで、円と人民元を銀行間で取引する。◆Bitcoin, a virtual currency circulated on the Internet, is traded in units of BTC. The value of bitcoin fluctuates excessively, but bitcoin has hovered at about $800 per BTC lately. ネット上で流通している仮想通貨「ビットコイン」は、BTCの単位で取引されている。ビットコインの相場は乱高下があまりにも激しいが、最近は1BTC=800ドル前後で推移している。◆In foreign exchange margin trading, investors repeatedly trade U.S. dollars, euros and other currencies, aiming to profit from fluctuations in exchange rates. 外国為替証拠金取引では、為替の変動による利益を狙って、投資家が米ドルやユーロなどの外貨を繰り返し売買する。◆In FX margin trading, investors can trade around the clock via the Internet. 外国為替証拠金取引の場合、投資家はインターネットで24時間取引できる。◆JAL stock was the most actively traded Tokyo Stock Exchange's First Section issue in terms of trading value. 日航株は、売買高では東証1部の銘柄でとくに活発に取引された。◆The prices of U.S. natural gas currently are about $3 to $5 per million British thermal units (BTU) and they briefly dropped to the $2 range in 2012, while the gas was traded between $6 and $10 until about 2008 before U.S. shale gas production increased. 米国の天然ガスの価格は現在、100万BTU (英国式熱量単位) 当たり3～5ドル程度で、2012年には一時2ドル台まで下落した。なお、米国の天然ガスは、シェール・ガスの増産前の2008年頃までは、6～10ドル前後で取引されていた。

trade (名) 貿易、交易、通商、取引、ビジネス、商売、売買、市場、職業、同業者、業界、顧客 (customers)、得意先、取引先、(政党間の) 取引、妥協、談合、下取り、交換、トレード (⇒free trade, multilateral trade negotiations, regional free trade area, world trade)
accommodation trade　馴れ合い売買
account payable trade　買掛金
account receivable trade　売掛金
Act Concerning Prohibition of Private Monopoly and Maintenance of Fair Trade　独占禁止法
administered trade　管理貿易
adversarial trade　敵対貿易
adverse balance of trade　輸入超過, 貿易の入超 (=adverse trade balance)
aid to trade　貿易援助
an increase in trade　市場の拡大
anti-trade biased effect　逆貿易偏向的効果
anti-trade oriented　反貿易志向的

arms trade 武器貿易

articles of trade 商品

bad trade 貿易不振

balance trade 取引を清算する

barrier to trade 貿易障壁, 貿易の障害 (=trade barrier)

barter trade 求償貿易, バーター貿易

be engaged in trade 貿易に従事する

be shrewd in trade 商売に抜け目がない

bilateral trade 二国間貿易, 双務貿易

bilateral trade agreement [arrangement] 双務的貿易協定

blind trade めくら貿易

block trade 大口取引, 大量取引

Board of Trade 英国商務省, (米国の)商工会議所

border trade 国境貿易

caravan trade 隊商

carriage trade 商売の上客 [上等の客], 金持ちの得意客, 金持ち, 富裕階級の人々, 富裕階層

closed trade 反対売買

coast trade 沿岸貿易

colonial trade 植民地貿易

Commission on International Commodity Trade (国連)国際商品貿易委員会, CICT

commission trade 仲介貿易

Committee For a National Trade-Policy 米国家貿易政策委員会

commodity trade 商品貿易

compensation trade 求償貿易, 補償貿易

complementary trade 相補貿易

Comprehensive Trade Act 包括通商法

contraband trade 密貿易, 密輸

control of trade 貿易管理 (=trade control)

controlled trade 管理貿易

country trade 地方貿易

cross trade 相対売買 (=crossed trade)

custom of trade 商慣習

cyclical trade 周期的貿易

Department of Trade and Industry 英国の貿易産業省

depression trade 不景気

directional trade 方向性取引

discriminative trade 差別的貿易

distributive trade 販売業, 商業

do a roaring trade 事業を盛んに営む (=drive [make] a roaring trade)

do a roaring trade in ～で当てる

do an honest trade 誠実な取引をする

domestic [home] trade 国内取引, 国内商業

eastern trade 東方貿易

equilibrium of trade 貿易の均衡

execute a large trade 大口取引を執行する

expand trade 貿易を拡大する

export trade 輸出業, 輸出貿易, 輸出貿易業, 輸出取引

Export Trade Act 輸出貿易法, 輸出取引法

export trade bill 輸出貿易手形

export trade control laws 輸出管理法令

external trade 対外貿易, 貿易収支

external trade unit value 貿易単価, 貿易価格

fair trade 公正取引, 互恵貿易

fair trade items 公正取引商品

favorable balance of trade 貿易収支の黒字, 輸出超過

Federal Trade Commission 米連邦取引委員会, FTC

Federal Trade Commission Act 米連邦通商法

flexible trade 弾力的貿易

floating trade 海運業, 海上貿易

free trade agreement 自由貿易協定, FTA

free trade area 自由貿易地域, 自由貿易圏

frontier trade 国境貿易

future trade 先物取引

general balance of trade 全般的貿易差額

general trade 一般取引, 一般貿易, 総合取引

general trade union 一般労組

give A a good trade Aに有利な買い物をさせる

give trade credit 与信取引を認める

good trade 儲かる取引

goods in trade 商品, 棚卸し商品

goods trade モノの取引, モノの取引を示す貿易収支

government to government trade 政府間貿易

home trade 国内取引, 内国取引, 内国商業

horizontal trade 水平貿易

horse trade 抜け目のない取引

illegal trade 不法取引, 違法取引

import trade 輸入業, 輸入貿易業, 輸入取引

import trade bill 輸入手形

improvable trade 加工貿易 (=improvement trade)

increase trade credit 与信取引を拡大する

industrial trade specialization 工業品貿易特化

inland trade 内国貿易, 国内取引, 国内通商

intensity of trade 市場結合度, 貿易結合度

intermediary trade insurance 仲介貿易保険

intermediate trade 中継貿易 : 仲介貿易

international trade 国際取引

467 TRAD

international trade fair　国際見本市

International Trade Organization　国際貿易機構, ITO

interregional［inter-regional］trade　地域間貿易, 地域間交易

interregional trade coefficient　地域間交易係数

intra-area trade　域内貿易

intra-firm trade　企業内貿易

intra-industry trade　産業内貿易

intra-regional trade　地域内貿易, 域内貿易

intra-sectoral trade　部門内貿易, 産業内貿易

intra-trade　域内貿易

invisible trade　貿易外取引, 無形貿易（目に見えないサービス、海上運賃、海上保険料、観光、特許料、代理店手数料などの取引）

invisible trade balance　貿易外収支

laissez-faire trade　自由放任貿易

legal trade　合法貿易, 合法取引

liberal trade　自由貿易

liberal trade environment　自由貿易環境

liberalization of trade　貿易自由化（=trade liberalization）

liberalization of trade and exchange　貿易・為替の自由化

low wage trade　低賃金貿易

manage trade credit　与信取引を管理する

marginal terms of trade　限界交易条件

maritime trade　海運業

market-neutral trade　市場中立取引

market trade　市場取引

memorandum trade　覚書貿易

merchandise trade　モノの貿易, 財の貿易, 財の輸出入, 貿易取引

merchant trade　仲介貿易

monopoly of trade　貿易独占

Moon Trade　時間外取引, 時間外サービス

negative balance of trade　逆調貿易差額

net barter terms of trade　純商品交易条件

net terms of trade　純交易条件

new global trade rules　新たな国際貿易ルール

nondiscriminatory trade　無差別貿易

nonmerchandise trade　非商品取引, 貿易外取引

ocean trade　遠洋貿易

Omnibus Trade and Competitiveness Act　米包括通商法

one-side trade　片貿易　（=one-way trade）

open trade　新規取引, 新規売買,（証券の）未決済取引

optimum trade　最適交易

outer-oriented trade regime　外部志向貿易体制

outstanding trade balance　未決済貿易残高

overbalancing of trade　順なる貿易差額

overland trade　陸上貿易

overseas merchandise trade　海外商品貿易

overseas trade　外国貿易

particular balance of trade　個別的貿易差額

passive trade　受動貿易

preferential trade system　特恵制度

price index of foreign trade　貿易物価指数

primary trade specialization　第一次産品貿易特化

private trade　民間貿易

pro-trade-biased growth　順貿易偏向的成長

processing trade　委託加工貿易

protected trade　保護貿易　（=protective trade）

quantitative trade restriction　輸入数量制限

reexport［re-export］trade　再輸出貿易

registered trade mark　登録商標（=registered trademark）

restraint of trade　取引制限, 貿易制限, 営業制限　（=restrictive trade）

retail trade　小売業

retail trade area　小売商圏

roundabout trade　迂回貿易

send sample ads to the trade　見本広告を得意先に送る

separate trade　単独営業

service to trade　商業活動用役

service trade　サービス貿易

sheltered trade　保護産業, 庇護（ひご）産業

shipping trade　海運業

silent trade　沈黙交換

silver trade dollar　貿易銀

special trade　特別貿易

speculative trade　投機売買, 見越し売買

state-controlled trade　国営貿易

stock in trade　流通在庫, 在庫品, 必要な営業用品

stock trade　株取引

strengthen trade and economic linkages between the two countries　貿易と経済のつながりを強化する

switch trade　スイッチ貿易, スイッチ取引

tally trade　分割販売

technical balance of trade　技術貿易収支

technological gap trade　技術格差貿易

technological trade　技術貿易

the next round of multilateral trade negotiations

T

次期多角的貿易交渉(新ラウンド)

total trade 総貿易額, 貿易総額

tourist trade 観光業

trade acceptance 貿易引受手形, 商業引受手形, 引受済み荷為替手形

trade acceptance payable 引受手形

Trade Act of 1974 1974年米国通商法

trade advertising 産業広告

trade agency 商業興信所 (=mercantile agency)

trade allowance 同業割引

Trade and Development Board (国連)貿易開発事会, TDB

trade and manufacture 商工業

trade and service industries 商業サービス業

trade arbitration agreement 貿易仲裁協定

trade area 商業区域, 商圏, 貿易圏

trade arrangement 貿易協定

trade assets 営業資産, 棚卸し資産

trade association 業界団体, 同業者団体, 同業組合, 産業団体, 事業者団体, 商工団体

trade between third countries 3国間貿易

trade-biased effect 貿易偏向効果

trade-biased growth 貿易偏向的成長

trade board 労使協議会

trade books 商業帳簿

trade by agreement 協定貿易

trade by exchange 物々交換

trade by region 地域別貿易

trade card 名刺 (=business card)

trade cartel 貿易カルテル

trade catalog(ue) カタログ

trade center 貿易センター

trade channel 取引経路, 貿易系路

trade channel discount 業者割引

trade check トレード・チェック(取引状況, 支払い状況, 資金繰りなど営業活動に関する調査)

trade circular 商業引札

trade class 取引段階

Trade Commission (OECD)の貿易委員会

trade conflict 貿易摩擦, 通商摩擦, 貿易紛争 (=trade friction)

trade contraction 貿易の縮小

trade contractor 職別コントラクター

trade control 貿易統制, 貿易管理

trade coordination 取引の協同化

trade corporation 貿易商社, 商社, 貿易会社

trade council 労働組合協議会

trade creation [creating] effect 貿易創出効果

trade creditor 買掛金, 仕入先

trade currency 貿易通貨

trade date 約定日, 取引実施期日

trade deal 取引約定, 取引協定, 業者取引

trade debt 取引債務, 取引負債

trade debtor 売掛金, 得意先

trade dependence 貿易依存, 貿易への依存度

trade dependency 貿易依存度

trade depression 貿易不振, 不況

trade description 商品の記述

Trade Descriptions Act 英国の取引表示法

trade destruction 貿易破壊

trade developer 貿易斡旋(あっせん)者

trade directory 同業者人名録

trade discrimination 貿易差別

trade diversion 貿易転換

trade diversion effect 貿易転換効果 (=trade diverting effect)

trade edition 市販の出版物

trade elasticity 貿易弾力性

trade environment 取引環境, 貿易環境

trade execution 証券の売買執行

trade exhibit 展示会

trade expenses 営業費

Trade Facilitation Committee 貿易円滑化委員会

trade fair 見本市 (=trade show)

trade figures 貿易収支

trade finance 貿易金融

trade firm 貿易会社, 商社

trade fluctuation 景気変動

trade group カルテル集団, 同業集団, 貿易使節団(trade mission)

trade idea (証券の売り時や買い時)など証券売買の助言

trade impediment 貿易障害

trade in technology 技術貿易

trade indifference curve 貿易無差別曲線

trade information 貿易情報, 通商情報

trade inquiring 取引の引合い, 取引照会 (=trade inquiry)

trade intensity analysis 貿易結合度分析

trade intensity index 貿易結合度指数

trade interests 貿易業者

trade inventories 流通在庫

trade investigation 仕入先調査(最高与信額(high credit)や現在与信高(owe)、期日の経過した与信(past due)、販売条件(terms of sale)、支払い(payments)などについての調査)

trade investment 営業投資

trade journal 業界誌

trade leakage　通常の漏損	trade-related bill　貿易付帯手形
trade liability　営業債務	trade-related expenses　貿易付帯費
trade-limited　貿易制限的	trade report　貿易報告(書)，取引報告書，業界
trade loss　貿易赤字，貿易上の赤字（元地損	報告書
害(country damage)や油類の通常の漏損な	Trade Representative　米通商代表
ど）貨物固有の慣習的損失	trade restraint　貿易制限，取引制限
trade matrix　貿易マトリックス	trade rights　商権，営業権
trade matrix analysis　貿易連関分析	trade rival　商売敵
trade ministers' conference of four axis-nations	trade rivalry　貿易戦争
四極通商閣僚会議	trade round　貿易交渉
trade mission　貿易使節団	trade route　通商航路，通商路
trade monopoly　貿易独占，交易独占	trade sale　仲間販売，同業者販売
trade multiplier　貿易乗数	trade salesman　外交販売員，外交セールス
trade negotiation　貿易交渉	マン
trade note　貿易手形	trade school　職業学校，職業訓練所
trade notes receivable　受取手形	trade servicing　貿易補助業務
trade of goods　モノの取引	trade show　展示会，見本市，映画試写会
trade of non-equivalents　不等価貿易	trade sign　看板
trade-off　相反関係，トレード・オフ	trade sources　貿易筋
trade on commission　委託貿易	trade status　取引地位，取引上の地位，通商上
trade on the spot　出先貿易	の地位[ステータス]
trade optimism　輸出楽観主義	trade stocks　業者在庫，流通在庫
trade organization　同業者組織，同業組合，事	trade tax　営業税
業者団体（⇒trade pact）	trade tension　貿易摩擦
trade-oriented　貿易志向的	trade troubleshooter　貿易問題対策特使
trade outlet　貿易販路，貿易先	trade union　労働組合　(=labor union)
trade paper　業界紙，業界新聞，専門紙，商業手	trade unionist　労働組合員
形(trade bill)，貿易手形	trade-up strategy　上位機種移行戦略
trade pattern　貿易パターン	trade usage　取引慣行，商慣習
trade payables　買入れ債務，仕入債務	(=usage of trade)
trade pessimism　貿易悲観主義	trade value　貿易額
trade port　貿易港	trade velocity　交易速度
trade position　取引上の地位，業界での地位	trade waste　工場下水，工場廃棄物
[相対的地位]	trade within the area　域内貿易
trade position motive　取引上の地位の動機	trade without L/C　信用状なしの貿易
trade preferences　貿易特恵	trade zone　貿易圏，取引ゾーン
trade price　卸し値，卸し値段，卸売価格	Trades Union Congress　労働組合会議，TUC
trade proceeds　貿易収入	(英最大の労働組合の中央組織)
trade profit　貿易利益	transit trade　中継貿易
trade promotion　貿易振興，貿易促進，貿易	transshipment trade　積換え輸送業
推進	triangular trade　三角貿易　(=trilateral trade)
trade protection　貿易保護	two-way trade　2方向の貿易
trade quantity　貿易数量	unfair trade　不公正取引，不公正貿易
trade rate　業者間料金，仲間料金	unit price index of trade　貿易単価指数，輸出
trade ratio　貿易比率	入単価指数
trade receivables　売上債権，営業債権	unit price of trade value index　輸出入単価
trade reciprocity　通商相互主義	指数
trade reference　同業照会，同業者信用照会先，	unlimited trade　無制限貿易
信用照会先，商業興信所	(=unrestricted trade)
trade register　商業登記	use trade credit　与信取引を利用する
	vertical trade　垂直貿易

T

waterborne trade 海上貿易, 水上貿易

wholesale trade 卸売り業

world trade 世界貿易

yen-denominated trade 円建て貿易, 円建て取引

◆A free trade agreement can do much to expand trade. 自由貿易協定（FTA）は、貿易を拡大する効果がある。◆In commodity futures trading, prices are decided when buyers and sellers make deals. So they can execute trades at promised prices even if the value of goods has changed drastically in the meantime. 商品先物取引では、売り手と買い手が取引契約をする時点で価格を決める。そのため、契約期間中に相場が大きく変動しても、売り手と買い手は約束した値段で取引を執行できる。◆In processing trade, imported raw materials are manufactured into goods that are then sold to other countries. 加工貿易では、輸入された原材料が製品に仕上げられた後、製品は海外に販売される。◆The value of South Korea's trade with China since it established diplomatic relations with Beijing has expanded to such an extent that it has surpassed its combined trade with Japan and the United States. 韓国が中国と国交を樹立して以来、韓国の対中貿易額は、対日・対米の貿易総額を凌駕（りょうが）するまでに拡大している。◆To ensure fair international commercial trade, the law against unfair competition stipulates that both individuals involved in bribery and the corporations they belong to should be punished. 公正な国際商取引を確保するため、不正競争防止法には、贈賄（外国公務員への贈賄）に関与した個人と法人を罰する規定（両罰規定）がある。◆To liberalize trade further, it is imperative to arrest a decline in Japan's agriculture sector and improve its international competitiveness. 一層の貿易自由化に向けて、日本の農業衰退に歯止めをかけ、農業の国際競争力を高めるのが急務だ。◆Yen-denominated trade frees domestic companies from the risk of exchange rate fluctuations. 円建て貿易は、国内企業にとって為替変動のリスクがない。

trade account 貿易収支, 貿易勘定, 営業勘定

trade account payable 買掛金

trade account receivable 売掛金

trade account settlement formula 貿易勘定決済方式

trade accounts 売掛金 (=accounts receivable)

trade act 通商法 (=trade law)

Omnibus Trade Act 包括通商法

Omnibus Trade and Competitiveness Act of 1988 1988年米包括通商法

Section 301 of the Trade Act of 1974 （1974年）米通商法301条, スーパー301条

trade agreement [accord] 通商協定, 通商条約, 貿易協定(trade arrangement), 取引契約, （労使の）団体協約, 労働契約, 労働協約

(collective agreement)

bilateral trade agreement 二国間通商協定

multilateral trade agreement 多角的貿易協定

Trade Agreement Act 米通商協定法

trade around the clock 24時間取引する

◆In FX margin trading, investors can trade around the clock via the Internet. 外国為替証拠金取引の場合、投資家はインターネットで24時間取引できる。

trade balance 貿易収支, 貿易尻, 貿易の帳尻 (=balance of trade: 貿易収支 = 輸出額(exports) − 輸入額(imports))

be adverse for the trade balance 貿易収支に不利な材料となる[不利な材料として働く], 貿易収支にとってマイナスに作用する

invisible trade balance 貿易外収支

merchandise trade balance 貿易収支

outstanding trade balance 未決済貿易残高

trade balance on customs clearance basis 通関収支

unfavorable trade balance 貿易収支の赤字, 輸入超過

◆In the trade balance last year, exports fell 5.9 percent to ￥46.58 trillion. 昨年の貿易収支のうち、輸出は前年比5.9%減の46兆5,800億円となった。

trade ban 国際[商業]取引禁止, 取引禁止, 禁輸

◆A bluefin tuna trade ban was rejected by a large majority. クロマグロ禁輸案は、大差で否決された。◆The Appendix 1 of the CITIES lists species subject to trade bans. ワシントン条約の付属書1には、禁輸[商業取引禁止]の対象である動植物が表示されている。

trade barrier 貿易障壁, 貿易の障害 (=barrier to trade)

discriminatory trade barrier 差別的貿易障壁

liberalize trade barriers 貿易障壁を撤廃する

modestly reduce trade barriers 貿易障壁をわずかに低める

official trade barriers 公式の貿易障壁

overcome trade barriers 貿易障壁を乗り越える, 貿易障壁に対応する

overt trade barriers 目に見える貿易障壁

preexisting trade barriers 既存の貿易障壁

protectionist trade barriers 保護主義的な貿易障壁, 保護貿易障壁

put up trade barriers 貿易障壁を設ける (=erect trade barriers)

the elimination [removal] of trade barriers 貿易障壁の除去

the reduction of trade barriers 貿易障壁の削減

◆As a member country of the WTO, Moscow should first improve Russia's investment climate, including the abolition of trade barriers. 世界貿

易機関（WTO）加盟国として、ロシアはまず貿易障壁の撤廃など投資環境を改善する必要がある。

trade bill 貿易手形, 商業手形（輸入手形や輸出手形のこと）
　trade bills payable　支払い商業手形
　trade bills receivable　受取商業手形
trade claim 貿易クレーム　（=business claim）
　cancellation　解約
　解説 貿易クレームの主な原因：
　bad packing　不完全包装
　breach of contract　契約違反
　breakage　破損
　delayed shipment　船積み遅延
　different quality　品質相違
　different shipment　船積み相違
　illegal shipment　法令違反の船積み
　inferior quality　品質不良
　shortage　不足
trade commissioner 通商担当委員
　◆Karel De Gucht is a European Commission trade commissioner who serves on the EU-U.S. joint panel as the EU representative. カレル・デフフトは、EU・米作業部会でEU側代表を務める欧州委員会の通商担当委員だ。
trade control 貿易統制, 国際取引の規制
　◆The Appendix 2 of the CITIES lists species that are not necessarily threatened with extinction but may become so unless they are subject to trade control. ワシントン条約の付属書2には、必ずしも絶滅の恐れはないが、貿易統制「国際取引の規制」の対象にしないかぎり絶滅する可能性がある動植物が表示されている。
trade credit 商業信用, 貿易信用, 企業間信用, 企業信用, 与信取引, 輸出延べ払い, 輸入延べ払い, 商業信用状, 貿易信用状
　give trade credit　与信取引を認める
　increase trade credit　与信取引を拡大する
　manage trade credit　与信取引を管理する
　trade credit on exports　輸出延べ払い信用
　trade credit on imports　輸入延べ払い信用
　trade credit underwriting process　企業顧客向け与信の過程
　trade credits extended　延べ払い信用
　use trade credit　与信取引を利用する
trade cycle 景気変動, 景気循環　（=business cycle）
　monetary theory of trade cycle　貨幣的景気循環論
　political trade cycle　政治的景気循環
　trade cycle policy　景気循環政策, 景気政策
　trade cycle theory　景気循環論
trade deficit 貿易赤字, 貿易収支の赤字, 貿易欠損
　（⇒services trade deficit, trading balance）
　chalk up large trade deficits　大幅な貿易赤字を計上する
　massive trade deficit　大幅貿易赤字
　massive upward revision to [in] trade deficits　貿易赤字の大幅（な）上方修正
　run a trade deficit　貿易赤字を出す
　slight [modest] revision to [in] trade deficits　貿易赤字の小幅（な）下方修正
　the record trade deficit　過去最大の貿易赤字
　trade deficit with A narrows　Aに対する貿易赤字（幅）が縮小する, 対A貿易赤字（幅）が縮小する
　trade deficit with A widens　Aに対する貿易赤字（幅）が拡大する, 対A貿易赤字（幅）が拡大する
　◆Indonesia has chalked up large trade deficits due to the decline in primary commodity prices and the rupiah has weakened as much as 17 percent against the U.S. dollar as of September 2013. インドネシアは一次産品の価格の下落で大幅な貿易赤字を計上し、通貨ルピアは2013年9月現在、対ドルで17%安となっている。◆Japan's customs-cleared trade deficit in April-September 2014 came to ￥5.43 trillion, up 8.6 percent from a year before and the largest for any fiscal first-half period since comparable data became available in fiscal 1979. 日本の2014年度上半期（4〜9月）の通関ベースでの貿易収支の赤字額は、前年同期比8.6%増の5兆4,300億円となり、統計を比較できる1979年度以降で上半期としては過去最大となった。◆The record trade deficit in 2012 was caused by a decline in exports due to the European financial crisis and deceleration of the Chinese economy, together with a sharp increase in imports of liquefied natural gas and the rapid hollowing-out of the domestic manufacturing industry. 2012年の過去最大の貿易赤字の要因としては、欧州の金融危機や中国経済の減速などで輸出が減少する一方、液化天然ガス（LNG）の輸入が急増し、国内製造業の空洞化が加速していることも挙げられる。◆The record trade deficit of ￥6.9 trillion in 2012 far exceeded ￥2.6 trillion in 1980 that immediately followed the second oil crisis. 2012年の6.9兆円もの過去最大の貿易赤字は、第二次石油危機直後の1980年に記録した2.6兆円を大きく上回った。
trade deficit in April-September 4〜9月の貿易赤字[貿易収支の赤字], 上半期の貿易赤字
　◆Japan's trade deficit in April-September 2014 hit a record high due to increased demand for liquefied natural gas for thermal power generation and a rise in overall import prices stemming from the yen's depreciation. 日本の2014年度上半期（4〜9月）の貿易赤字は、火力発電所向け液化天然ガス（LNG）の需要増加と円安による輸入物価全体の上昇で、過去最大となった。

T

TRAD 472

trade discount 卸売り割引, 卸売り値引き, 商業割引, 同業割引, 業者間割引, 仲間割引, 数量値引き

take a trade discount 仕入れ割戻しを受ける

trade discounts or allowances 卸売り割引または値引き

◆Net Wholesale Price referred to in this agreement is defined as the amount of the gross sales by ABC of the licensed products to ABC's customers in the territory, less customary trade discounts, insurance premiums, transportation and delivery charges, taxes（VAT）and duties. 本契約書に記載する「純卸売り販売額」とは、ABCの顧客に対する契約地域内でのABCの許諾製品の総売上高（総販売額）から、通常の卸売り割引額、保険料、運送・引渡し費用、税金（付加価値税）と関税を差し引いた額のことをいう。

trade dispute 通商摩擦, 貿易摩擦, 貿易紛争 （=trade friction: 労働争議の意味もある。⇒global trade dispute, emergence）

◆The U.S. president's decision to scrap tariffs on steel imports does not guarantee an end to trade disputes between the United States and its trading partners. 輸入鉄鋼製品に対する関税撤廃を米大統領が決めたことで、米国と貿易相手国との通商摩擦がなくなったわけではない。

trade expansion 貿易拡大, 通商拡大, 取引拡大 （=expansion of trade）

Trade Expansion Act 米通商拡大法

trade expansion effect 貿易拡大効果

trade friction 貿易摩擦, 通商摩擦 （=trade conflict, trade dispute）

cause trade friction 貿易摩擦を引き起こす, 貿易摩擦をもたらす

ease [reduce] trade frictions 貿易摩擦を緩和する [軽減する]

◆The introduction of new tariffs would reduce trade further, leading to new trade frictions. 関税を新たに導入すれば、貿易は一段とひっ迫し、新たな貿易摩擦につながる。

trade gap 貿易赤字, 貿易収支の赤字, 貿易欠損, 輸入超過, 貿易ギャップ （=trade deficit）

shrinking trade gap 貿易赤字の縮小

soaring trade gap 貿易赤字の急拡大

trade gap ratio 貿易ギャップ比率

trade gap with Japan 対日貿易赤字

◆China's trade gap with the 27-nation European Union shrank by 51 percent in February. 中国の対EU（欧州連合）27か国貿易赤字は、2月は51%減少した。

trade imbalance 貿易不均衡, 輸出入不均衡 （⇒trade pact）

have a trade imbalance with ～に対して貿易不均衡になっている

rectify trade imbalances 貿易不均衡を是正する

◆Import growth outpaced export growth, thus producing the trade imbalance. 輸入の伸びが輸出の伸びを上回ったため、貿易の不均衡が生じた。

◆In the joint statement, the need to rectify the trade imbalance was emphasized as a result of ballooning U.S. deficits with China. 共同文書では、中国に対する米国の赤字が膨らんでいるため、貿易不均衡は是正の必要性が強調された。◆Rectifying trade imbalances mainly with China by devaluing the dollar is the top priority in Washington. ドル安により主に中国との貿易不均衡を是正するのが、米国の最優先課題だ。

trade insurance 貿易保険（保険の種類としては、普通輸出保険、輸出代金保険、輸出手形保険、海外投資保険、為替変動保険、輸出保証保険、前払い輸入保険、仲介貿易保険がある）

◆The METI has decided to expand the scope of government-backed trade insurance for overseas social infrastructure projects. 経済産業省は、海外の社会基盤（インフラ）事業に対する政府保証付き貿易保険の対象を拡大することを決めた。◆The trade insurance of Nippon Export and Investment Insurance previously only covered direct exports by domestic firms. 独立行政法人・日本貿易保険の貿易保険はこれまで、国内企業の直接輸出だけが対象だった。

trade issue 貿易問題

◆The first official ministerial-level talks between China and Taiwan, at odds more than six decades since the 1949 creation of the People's Republic of China, mark a big step toward expanding cross-strait dialogue beyond economic and trade issues. 1949年の中華人民共和国の樹立［建国］以来60年以上も対立している中国と台湾が初めて行った公式の閣僚級会談（2014年2月11日）は、経済や貿易問題を超えた両岸対話拡大への大きな一歩を踏み出すものだ。

trade law 通商法（trade act）, 商取引法

Exon-Florio provision of the 1988 trade law 1988年通商法のエクソン・フロリオ条項（米国の安全保障を損なう企業買収の禁止）

foreign trade law 貿易法 （=law on foreign trade）

United Nations Commission on International Trade Law 国連国際商取引法委員会

◆In the United States, the Exon-Florio provision of the 1988 trade law can prevent takeover bids that are deemed a threat to national security. 米国では、1988年通商法のエクソン・フロリオ条項で、国家の安全保障上、脅威と考えられる企業買収を阻止することができる。

trade liberalization 貿易自由化

◆Due to the IT revolution and trade liberalization, product specialization now is determined by comparative advantages not in finished products but in work unique to each country or region in the context of global value chains. 情報通信技術（IT）革命と貿易自由化で、製品の特化は、「最終

財」の比較優位ではなく、国際的価値連鎖との関連で国・地域にそれぞれ特有の「仕事」の比較優位で決まるようになった。

trade liberalization talks 貿易自由化交渉
◆The APEC forum leaders showed a willingness to complete the seven-year-long Doha Round of trade liberalization talks. APEC（アジア太平洋経済協力会議）の首脳は、世界貿易機関（WTO）の7年にわたる貿易自由化交渉（ドーハ・ラウンド：新多角的貿易交渉）の達成に、意欲を示した。

trade management agreement 貿易管理協定
◆The government will improve ties with Southeast Asian countries, including concluding trade management agreements with Hong Kong and Singapore. 政府は今後、香港、シンガポールと貿易管理協定を締結するなど、東南アジア諸国との連携を強化する。

trade mark ⇒trademark

trade name 商号, 屋号, 社名, 商標, 商標名 (brand name), トレードマーク

infringement of a trade name 商号権の侵害

register a trade name 商号を登記する

selling under our trade name 当社の商号での販売

similar trade name 類似商号

specified products incorporating certain of the trade marks and trade names of Licensor ライセンサーの特定の商標と商号を取り入れた特定商品

temporary registration of a trade name 商号の仮登記

trade or do business 取引または事業を行う
◆The New Company shall not trade or do business under any fictitious or assumed name or name (s) of any shareholders. 新会社は、架空、仮想な名前または株主の名前で取引または事業を行ってはならない。

trade pact 貿易協定, 通商協定
◆U.S. trade organization the UAW has urged the U.S. government to immediately begin talks with Japan to form a new auto trade pact as part of efforts to correct huge trade imbalances favoring Tokyo. 米国の同業者組織「全米自動車労組（UAW）」は、日本の大幅貿易黒字の是正策の一環として、日本と即時交渉を開始して新たな自動車貿易協定を結ぶよう米政府に要請した。

trade partner 貿易相手, 貿易相手国 (=trading partner)
◆China has a life-or-death influence over the North Korea as the largest donor country and trade partner of Pyongyang. 中国は、北朝鮮最大の支援国、貿易相手国として、北朝鮮の生殺与奪の権を握っている。◆The international community, particularly Europe, Israel's biggest trade partner, has been intensifying criticism of Israel's con-

tinuing construction of settlements in the West Bank. 国際社会、とりわけイスラエル最大の貿易相手の欧州は、イスラエルがヨルダン川西岸で入植活動を続けていることに、批判を強めている。

trade partnerships with Europe and the Asia Pacific 欧州やアジア太平洋地域との(自由)貿易協定
◆New trade partnerships with Europe and the Asia-Pacific will help exporters create more jobs. 欧州やアジア太平洋地域との新自由貿易協定は、輸出企業の雇用創出拡大につながる。

trade policy （名）通商政策, 貿易政策 (⇒multilayered trade policy)

trade policy issue 通商政策問題, 貿易政策問題
◆Japan's basic trade policy until now has been to give the highest priority to a multilateral free trade system centering on the World Trade Organization. 日本のこれまでの通商政策は、基本的に世界貿易機関（WTO）中心の多角的自由貿易体制を最優先してきた。

trade practice 取引

trade practice agreement 取引協定, カルテル協定

trade practice rules 取引規則, 取引準則

trade practices 貿易慣行, 取引慣行, 商慣行
◆The United States will continue to actively address anticompetitive activity, market access barriers, and or market-distorting trade practices. アメリカは、非競争的行為や市場参入障壁、市場を歪める商慣行に引き続き取り組んで行く方針だ。

Trade Promotion Authority 通商一括交渉権, 貿易促進権限, TPA（米国では憲法上、通商権限を結ぶ権限は議会にある。そのため、大統領のTPA（通商一括交渉権）がないと、通商合意の内容が議会の要求でひっくり返される可能性がある。⇒TPA）

trade relations 通商関係, 取引関係
◆Lawmakers voted 260-170 to continue for a year what is now called normal trade relations (NTR) and used to be called most favored nations (MFN) trade status. 議員が260対170で票決して、これまで最恵国待遇と呼ばれていた（中国に対する）正常通商関係を1年間継続することになった。

trade restriction 貿易制限, 取引制限, 貿易規制, 取引規制, 輸出規制 (=trade restraint)
◆The United States sought an early lifting of U.N. sanctions against Iraq that would suspend some trade restrictions Washington imposed more than a decade ago. 米国は、10年以上前に米国が課した貿易制限の一部を停止させるため、対イラク国連制裁の早期解除を要求した。

trade rule 貿易ルール
◆In the next round of negotiations, labeling and trade rules for food produced with genetically modified organisms (GMOs) are expected to be discussed. 次期交渉では、遺伝子組換え食品（遺

伝子組換え作物を使って生産される食品）の表示問題や貿易ルールづくりが話し合われる見通しだ。

trade sanctions 貿易制裁, 貿易制裁措置, 制裁措置
◆Japan and six other countries warned the U.S. government of their intention to impose trade sanctions unless Washington abolished the Byrd Amendment. 日本など7か国は、米国政府に対して、米国がバード法（反ダンピング関税分配法）を撤廃しなければ制裁措置をとる用意があると通告した。

trade secret 企業秘密, 営業秘密, 業務上の秘密, トレード・シークレット
convert a trade secret to one's own benefit　自己の利益のために他者の企業秘密を利用する
disclose a trade secret　企業秘密を開示する
the law of trade secret　企業秘密保護法
the owner of the trade secret　企業秘密の所有者, 企業秘密の権利主体
the theft of trade secrets　企業秘密の窃取［窃盗］
trade secret information　企業秘密情報
trade secret misappropriation　企業秘密の不正利用
trade secret owner　トレード・シークレット所有者, 企業秘密の権利所有者
Uniform Trade Secrets Act　統一トレード・シークレット法
◆ABC represents and warrants that it owns and possesses all rights, title, interest, in all of the Software Products, and any trademarks, logos, trade secrets and proprietary rights associated with the Software Products. ABCは本ソフトウエア製品の全部に対するすべての権利, 権原, 権益と、本ソフトウエア製品に関連する一切の商標, ロゴ, トレード・シークレットおよび財産権を所有していることを、ABCは表明しこれを保証する。◆Licensee acknowledges that all Software in Source Code form is a trade secret of Licensor. ソース・コード形式のソフトウエアはすべてライセンサーの営業秘密であることを、ライセンシーは認める。◆The seller shall not be responsible for any infringement with regard to patents, utility models, designs, trademarks, copyrights, trade secrets or any other intellectual property rights in any country, except for the seller's country, in connection with the sales, use or delivery of the products. 売り主は、本製品の販売, 使用と引渡しに関連する特許, 実用新案, 意匠, 商標, 著作権, トレード・シークレットまたはその他の知的財産権に関する侵害に対しては、売り主の国を除いていずれの国においても責任を負わないものとする。

trade strategy 通商戦略
◆Settlement of the issue requires that the leaders act decisively, because the issue affects each country's trade strategy. この問題は各国の通商戦略ともからんでいるため、問題の解決には各国首脳の決断力が要る。

trade structure 貿易構造
◆A counselor to the Japan Research Institute warned that under the current trade structure, the yen's depreciation might apply downward pressure on the Japanese economy. 現状の貿易構造では、円安で日本の景気が下げられる懸念がある、と日本総研の理事が警告した。

trade surplus 貿易黒字, 貿易収支の黒字
build up enormous trade surpluses　貿易黒字を計上する
chronic trade surplus　慢性的な貿易黒字, 貿易黒字の慢性化
current account and trade surpluses　貿易黒字と経常黒字
dollar-based customs-cleared trade surplus　ドル表示の通関ベース貿易黒字
expanding trade surplus　貿易黒字の拡大
FOB trade surplus　貿易黒字（FOBベース）, FOBベースの貿易黒字
invisible trade surplus　貿易外取引の黒字
massive［considerable, large］trade surplus　大幅貿易黒字, 巨額の貿易黒字
merchandise trade surplus　モノの貿易黒字, 財の貿易黒字, 貿易収支の黒字額, 商品貿易の黒字, 貿易黒字
narrowing trade surplus　貿易黒字の縮小
post a trade surplus　貿易黒字を計上する（=run a trade surplus）
recycle trade surpluses　貿易黒字を還流させる
visible trade surplus　貿易収支の黒字
yen-denominated trade surplus　円表示の貿易黒字
◆Both imports and exports decreased, but the drop in exports exceeded that of imports, resulting in the trade surplus shrinkage. 輸出も輸入も減少したが、輸出の減少額のほうが輸入の減少額を上回ったため、貿易黒字が減る結果となった。

trade talks 通商交渉, 貿易交渉（=trade negotiations）
◆The Japan-U.S. trade talks did not help slash U.S. trade deficits, and instead sent the dollar plummeting. 日米通商交渉は、アメリカの貿易赤字減らしになったわけではなく、それどころか急激なドル安を招いた。

trade term 貿易用語, 貿易条件の用語, 貿易条件
◆The trade term CIF shall be interpreted in accordance with INCOTERMS 2010 as amended. 貿易用語のCIFは、2010年版インコタームズ（改訂版）［インコタームズ2010（改訂版）］に従って解釈する。

trade terms 貿易条件, 取引条件, 貿易用語（⇒Incoterms）

agreement on trade terms　貿易条件協定書

◆The trade terms of this transaction to be F.O.B Yokohama, Incoterms 2010 Edition. この取引の貿易条件は、横浜港本船渡し（インコタームズ2010年版）とする。

解説 貿易取引の基礎条件として用いられる貿易条件：

CFR　運賃込み条件 cost and freightの略

CIF　運賃保険料込み条件 cost, insurance and freightの略

CIP　運送費保険料込み条件 carriage and insurance paid toの略

CPT　運送費込み条件 carriage paid toの略

DAF　国境持込み渡し条件 delivered at frontierの略

DDP　仕向け地持込み渡し・関税込み条件 delivered duty paidの略

DDU　仕向け地持込み渡し・関税抜き条件 delivered duty unpaidの略

DEQ　埠頭持込み渡し条件 delivered ex quayの略

DES　本船持込み渡し条件 delivered ex shipの略

EXW　工場渡し条件 ex worksの略

FAS　船側渡し条件 free alongside shipの略

FCA　運送人渡し条件 free carrierの略

FOB　本船渡し条件 free on boardの略

trade U.S. dollars　米ドルを売買する

◆In foreign exchange margin trading, investors repeatedly trade U.S. dollars, euros and other currencies, aiming to profit from fluctuations in exchange rates. 外国為替証拠金取引では、為替の変動による利益を狙って、投資家が米ドルやユーロなどの外貨を繰り返し売買する。

trade volume　貿易量,貿易額,取引量,取引高,出来高

◆In terms of trade volume, South Korea is currently among the top 10 countries partly due to its efforts to promote free trade agreements with the United States, the European Union and others. 貿易額で、韓国は現在、米国や欧州連合（EU）などとの自由貿易協定（FTA）推進策を軸に、世界トップ10入りを果たしている。

trade war　貿易戦争　(=trade battle)

◆Japan stood defiant in an escalating trade war with China. 過熱する中国との貿易戦争で、日本は一歩も引かない姿勢を示した。

trade weighted　実効為替レートによる,実効レートでの

real trade weighted value　実質実効為替レート

the trade weighted exchange rate of yen　円の実効為替レート

the trade weighted U.S. dollar　米ドルの実効為替レート

the trade weighted value of the dollar　ドルの実効為替レート

trade weighted value　実効為替レート

trade with North Korea　北朝鮮との貿易

◆The revised Foreign Exchange and Foreign Trade Law allows Japan to suspend or limit remittances and trade with North Korea. 改正外国為替及び外国貿易法によると、北朝鮮に関して日本は送金や貿易を停止・制限することができる。

traded　（形）貿易取引の対象となる,売買される,取引される,交換される

average daily traded values　1日の平均売買高

exchange-traded contract　上場商品,取引所で取引される商品

exchange-traded derivatives　上場派生商品

exchange-traded instruments　上場商品,取引所で取引される商品

exchange-traded option　上場オプション

traded commodity　貿易財　(=traded goods)

traded option　上場オプション,取引所売買可能オプション,オプション取引

traded option on the potato futures　ポテト先物オプション

traded options market　オプション取引市場

traded options on the Brent crude contract　ブレント原油オプション

traded services　貿易取引対象のサービス

trade-in　（名）下取り,下取り取引,下取り品,交換品

trade-in allowance　下取り割引

trade-in deal　下取り取引

trade-in discount　下取り割引

trade in goods and services　モノやサービスの取引

trade-in price［value］　下取り価格

trade-in stock　流通在庫,在庫品

trade-in terms　下取り取引の条件

trademark　（名）商標,商標権,トレードマーク　(⇒exercise, knowledge, own and possess, prior approval, procurement)

a registered trademark　登録商標

a similar trademark　類似商標

a trademark owner　商標権者,商標の権利者

a well-known trademark　周知商標,著名商標

an owner of a trademark right　商標権者

certificate of trademark registration　商標登録証

computerized retrieval system for trademark examination　商標機械検索システム

copy a trademark　商標を真似（まね）る

counterfeit a trademark　商標を偽造する

dilute a trademark　商標を希薄化する,商標の希薄化を招く

file for trademark registration　商標登録を出願する

genericized trademark　普通名詞化［一般名詞化］した商標（商標の普通名詞化により独占的使用が認められなくなった商標）

identicalness of trademark　商標の同一

indication of existence of trademark registration　商標登録表示

invalidation of a trademark registration　商標登録の無効

license a trademark　商標使用権を許諾する, 商標をライセンスする

licensed products bearing the trademark　商標を付した許諾品

lose the exclusive use of the trademark　商標の独占的使用権を失う

obtain trademark registration　商標登録を受ける

owner of a trademark right　商標権者

piggyback on a trademark　商標にただ乗りする

registration of trademark　商標登録

request for trademark application　商標登録願

tarnish the trademark　商標を汚す, 商標のイメージを汚す

the right of trademark　商標権（=trademark right）

the use of the trademark　商標の使用

trademark administrator　商標管理人

trademark application　商標登録出願（=application for trademark registration）

trademark counterfeiting　商標の不正使用

trademark examination guidelines　商標審査基準（=examination standards on trademark appellations）

trademark examination manual　商標審査便覧

trademark gazette　商標公報

Trademark Law Treaty　商標法条約

trademark protection　商標保護

trademark registration　商標登録

trademark right　商標権

trademark usage　商標の使用

◆A trademark, which is used in respect of goods by a person who produces, processes, certifies or assigns such goods in the course of trade, is composed of characters, figures, signs or any combination thereof with colors. 商品取引の過程で商品を生産、加工、証明、譲渡する者がその商品について使用する商標は、文字、図形、記号またはこれらと色彩との組合せから成る。

Trademark Law　商標法
　◆The Trademark Law was enacted to protect a trademark by giving a monopoly such as an ex-clusive right and a prohibitive right to an owner of a trademark right. 商標法は、商標権者に専用権や禁止権などの独占権を与えて商標を保護するために制定された。

trader　（名）証券業者, 売買担当者, ディーラー, 貿易業者, 取引業者, 同業者, 業者, 市場関係者, トレーダー

bearish traders　弱気筋

bullish traders　強気筋

commodity trader　商品取引業者

contraband trader　密輸商

currency trader　為替トレーダー

export trader　輸出業者

forex trader　為替トレーダー（=forex dealer）

free trader　自由貿易主義者

general trader　一般貿易業者

individual trader　個人トレーダー

international speculative traders　海外投機筋

online trader　オンライン・トレーダー, ネット・トレーダー

retail trader　小売業者

unethical trader　悪質業者

wholesale trader　卸売り業者

◆Bitcoin deals may be abused as they are highly anonymous and in the United States, a trader who gave bitcoin to an illegal drug dealer faced prosecution on charges of money laundering. ビットコインでの取引は、匿名性が高いので悪用される可能性があり、米国では、違法な麻薬取引の当事者にビットコインを提供した業者が、マネー・ロンダリング（資金洗浄）の罪で刑事訴追された。◆ We can cancel a contract unconditionally within a cooling-off period even if it is signed with an unethical trader. 仮に悪質業者と契約を結んだ場合でも、クーリング・オフ期間内なら、無条件で契約を解除できる。

trading　（名）取引, 売買, 商業, 貿易, 営業, トレーディング（⇒Internet trading）

active trading　大商い（=heavy trading）

after-hours trading　時間外取引

automated trading　自動取引

block trading　大口取引

bulk trading　一括取引

check trading　小切手取引

chummy trading　偽装売買

closed trading　閉鎖的な貿易

commodity futures trading　商品先物取引

commodity trading adviser［advisor］　商品取引［売買］顧問, 商品投資顧問会社

cross trading　相対売買, 三国間輸送

daily trading limit　日々の取引制限, 値幅制限（=daily limit, daily price limit）

TRAD

day trading　デイ・トレーディング, 日計り
商い
dual trading　二重取引, 二重勘定取引, 二者
取引
e-trading　電子商取引, 電子取引, 電子売買,
コンピュータ取引
electricity trading　電力取引, 電気の売買
electronic trading　電子取引, 電子商取引, 電
子売買, コンピュータ取引, 電子トレーディ
ング, システム売買　(=e-trading)
equity trading business　株式取引業務, 株売買
業務
excessive trading　過当取引
exclusive trading zones　排他的経済ブロック
foreign exchange trading　外国為替取引
free trading bloc　自由貿易地域, 自由貿易圏
futures trading　先物取引
half-year trading figures　中間決算
hedge trading　ヘッジ取引
in-house trading rules　自己売買規制
index-linked trading　インデックス取引
insider trading　インサイダー取引
Internet trading　インターネット取引, ネット
取引
last trading day　最終取引日
light trading　薄商い
mail-order trading via the Internet　ネット通販
major trading country〔nation〕　主要貿易国
margin trading　信用取引, 証拠金取引
multilateral trading system　国際貿易体制
Net trading　ネット取引　(=Internet trading)
night trading　夜間取引
online stock trading business　株のインター
ネット取引業務
online trading　オンライン取引
open trading　開放的貿易
open world trading system　自由貿易体制
option trading　オプション取引
prearranged trading　事前打合せ取引
preferential trading area　特恵的貿易地域
professional trading market　専門家取引市場
program trading　プログラム売買, プログラ
ム取引
proprietary trading　自己取引, 自己売買, 自己
勘定取引, ディーリング業務
proprietary trading system　私設取引システム
public trading　公募取引
real time option trading　リアルタイム・オプ
ション取引
regional trading bloc　地域経済ブロック

regulation of trading　売買規制
round-the-clock trading　24時間取引
seamless trading　切れ目のない取引
securities trading　証券取引, 証券売買
short-term trading　短期売買, 短期取引
spread trading　スプレッド取引
state trading　国営貿易
stock trading　株式売買, 株式取引, 株取引
suspended trading　未決取引
swap trading　スワップ取引
the afternoon trading　後場
trading account　(工場の)売買勘定, 販売勘
定, 商品勘定
trading account assets　商品勘定資産, 商品有
価証券
trading advantage　取引上の優位性
trading among wholesalers　仲間取引
trading area　商圏, 商業圏, 商勢圏, 商取引
地域
trading assets　事業資産
trading association　同業者組合, 事業者団
体　(=trade association)
trading authorization　取引認可証
trading body　取引団体
trading capital　商業資本
trading center　貿易センター, 取引の中心地,
商店集中地域
trading certificate　取引許可証
trading concern credit　商社金融
trading currency　貿易通貨
trading day　営業日
trading debut　初取引
trading deficit　貿易赤字, 貿易収支の赤字
(=trade deficit)
trading difference　(株式の)取引差額
trading division　販売部門
trading down　薄利多売, 高リスク投資への組
替え
trading environment　事業環境
trading error　売買過誤, エラー・トレード
trading estate　産業地区
trading exposure　取引リスク
trading floor　立会場
trading halt　取引停止
trading income　取引所得
trading information　取引情報
trading inventory　流通在庫
trading irregularities　不正取引
trading limit　取引制限, 取引枠, 取引限度, 値

T

幅制限

trading loss　営業損失

trading margin　取引マージン, 売買マージン

trading market　流通市場, 売買市場, トレーディング・マーケット

trading merchant　貿易商, 貿易商人

trading multiple　株価収益率

trading network　取引ネットワーク

trading on the curb　場外取引

trading over the counter　店頭取引

trading partnership　商事組合

trading pattern　株価動向傾向線

trading port　貿易港

trading post　(銘柄の)取引ポスト, 交易所

trading profit　営業利益, 売買益

trading profit and loss account　売買損益勘定

trading profit and loss section　(商品)売買損益区分

trading range　取引限度, 取引圏, 相場圏, ボックス圏, 価格帯

trading record　売買記録

trading restriction　取引制限, 売買制限

trading revenues　売買収入

trading right　商業権

trading ring　取引場

trading risk　取引リスク

trading schedule　貿易表

trading specialist　取引専門家

trading stamp　景品券, クーポン券

trading statement　売買計画明細書

trading stock　流通在庫, 在庫品

trading strategy　取引戦略, 売買戦略

trading subsidiary　貿易子会社, 商事子会社

trading transaction　売買取引

trading up　高利少回転, 低リスク投資への組替え

turnover ratio of trading　売買回転率

unit of trading　売買単位, 取引単位

warrant trading　新株引受権証券取引

wash trading　偽装売買

wrongful trading　不正取引

◆A bearish mood enveloped the Tokyo market Tuesday from the start of the day's trading. 火曜日の東京市場［東京株式市場］は、取引開始から全面安の展開となった。◆A former executive of the securities firm was arrested by the Yokohama District Public Prosecutors Office on suspicion of insider trading in violation of the Financial Instruments and Exchange Law. 同証券会社の元役員を、金融商品取引法違反のインサイダー取引

容疑で、横浜地検が逮捕した。◆Direct yen-yuan trading started on the interbank foreign exchange markets in Tokyo and Shanghai on June 1, 2012. 円と中国の通貨・人民元の直接取引が、東京、上海の銀行間外国為替市場で2012年6月1日から始まった。◆In commodity futures trading, prices are decided when buyers and sellers make deals. So they can execute trades at promised prices even if the value of goods has changed drastically in the meantime. 商品先物取引では、売り手と買い手が取引契約をする時点で価格を決める。そのため、契約期間中に相場が大きく変動しても、売り手と買い手は約束した値段で取引を執行できる。◆The Diet enacted laws to impose restrictions on foreign exchange trading with low margin requirements. 少ない証拠金での外国為替取引［外国為替証拠金取引］を規制する法律が、国会で成立した。◆Trading of North Korea's weapons and other products of North Korea are subject to the U.N. embargo. 北朝鮮の武器などの取引は、国連の経済制裁の対象になっている。

trading asset　事業資産, 販売資産

◆The deal does not include any trading assets and trading liabilities. この取引に、事業資産と営業上の債務は含まれていない。

trading balance　貿易収支

◆Japan's 2012 trading balance, or exports minus imports, ran up a record deficit of ￥6.9 trillion, 2.7 times more than the 2011 figure, the first trade deficit in 31 years due to the negative effects of the Great East Japan Earthquake. 輸出額から輸入額を差し引いた日本の2012年の貿易収支は、過去最大の6.9兆円の赤字で、東日本大震災の悪影響で31年ぶりに貿易赤字に転落した2011年と比べて2.7倍に増えた。

trading company　商社, 商事会社, 貿易会社　(=trading concern [corporation, firm, house])

a general trading company　総合商社

a major trading company　大手商社

an international trading company　国際商社

◆Large firms such as trading and steel companies are taking out short-term loans to meet working capital needs. 商社や鉄鋼などの大企業は、運転資金のニーズを満たすため、短期ローンを組んでいる［短期借入れを行っている］。

trading country [nation]　貿易国, 貿易立国

◆Japan must strengthen the competitiveness of its manufacturing industry which will lead to increasing exports in order to rebuild its status as a trading country. 貿易立国としての地位を立て直すには、日本は、輸出拡大につながる製造業の競争力強化が必要である。

trading firm　商社, 商事会社　(=trading house)

◆Japanese trading firms are interested in African countries because they are rich in mineral resources, including untapped crude oil, platinum and manganese. アフリカは未開発の原油やプラチナ、マンガンなどが豊富なため、日本の商社がアフリカ諸国に関心を寄せている。

trading hours 取引時間, 取引途中
◆Oil prices on the New York Mercantile Exchange soared to the $100 level a barrel for the first time during the trading hours. ニューヨーク・マーカンタイル取引所の原油価格は、取引時間中に初めて1バレル＝100ドル台まで上昇した。

trading house 商事会社, 商社　(=trading firm)
◆Sumitomo Corp., a Japanese major trading house, lost $2.2 billion in investments, including Texas shale oil and Australian coal mining. 日本の大手商社の住友商事は、米テキサス州でのシェール・オイルの開発や豪州での炭鉱事業などへの投資で、22億ドルの損失を出した。

trading license 取引免許, 取引資格
◆The TSE will consider taking punitive measures, such as revoking trading licenses, restricting business or imposing fines if any violations of the law or TSE rules are found in the inspections of major securities firms. 主要証券会社への立ち入り調査で法令違反や東証ルール違反があった場合、東証は、取引免許の取消しや売買の制限、過怠金(罰金)の賦課などの厳しい措置を取る[厳しい処分をする]方針だ。

trading partner 貿易相手国
◆Despite strong criticism from Washington's trading partners against high tariffs on steel imports to rescue the ailing U.S. steel industry, the USTR stressed the legitimacy of such safeguard measures. 不況の米鉄鋼業界を救済するための輸入鉄鋼製品に対する高関税について、米国の貿易相手国から強い批判がなされたにもかかわらず、米国通商代表はこの緊急輸入制限(セーフガード)措置の正当性を強調した。

trading unit 売買単位, 取引単位
(=unit of trading)
◆Even if the company conducts a reverse stock split, it will safeguard shareholders' interest by changing the minimum trading unit from 1,000 shares to 500. 同社が株式併合をしても、最低取引単位を1,000株から500株に変更して、株主の権利は守る方針だ。◆If a quoted company with a one-share trading unit changes its trading unit to 100 shares without changing the price of individual shares, the amount required for investment would rise 100-fold. 売買単位が1株の上場企業が、1株当たりの価格を変更しないで売買単位を100株に変更すると、投資(株の売買)に必要な金額は100倍になってしまう。

trading value 売買高
◆JAL stock was the most actively traded Tokyo Stock Exchange's First Section issue in terms of trading value. 日航株は、売買高では東証1部の銘柄でとくに活発に取引された。

trading volume 取引量, 取引高, 出来高, 商い　(=volume of trading)
◆According to a probe conducted by the Tokyo Stock Exchange, there was a series of questionable stock deals in which trading volume surged just after the capital increase announcements by listed companies. 東京証券取引所の調査によると、上場企業が増資[公募増資]を公表した直後に(その銘柄の)売買高が急増する不自然な株取引が、相次いでいた。

training (名)訓練, 養成, トレーニング
◆The period, time, method and reasonable details of the training shall be determined separately through mutual consultation between the parties. 訓練の期間、時期、方法と合理的な詳細は、当事者間の相互協議で別途決定する。

training period 訓練期間, 養成期間
◆Such visits for training shall be conducted one time only and the training period shall not exceed 6 man-months. 訓練のための当該訪問は1回限りとし、訓練期間は6人月を超えないものとする。

transact business 取引を行う, 事業を行う, 事業の取引をする, 取引する
◆For a period of 5 years from the Closing date, Seller shall not engage or be interested, whether directly or indirectly, in any business in any place in which the Company now transact its business that would be in competition with business as now transacted by the Company. クロージング日から5年間、売り主は、対象会社が現在その事業を行っている場所で、対象会社が現在行っている事業と競合する事業に直接間接を問わず従事せず、また係らないものとする。

transaction (名)取引, 取扱い, 業務処理, 業務, 商取引, 売買, 和解, 示談, 法律行為
(⇒contemplate)
◆An increase in transactions that brokerages handle has accompanied the brisk stock market business. 証券会社が扱う取引の増加は、そのまま株式相場の盛況と重なる。◆Errors in computing systems at financial institutions could lead to problems in making international fund transactions. 金融機関のコンピュータ・システムのエラーは、国際的な資金取引上、トラブルが生じる可能性がある。◆The obligations of Purchaser to effect the transactions contemplated hereby shall be, at the option of Purchaser, subject to the fulfillment, at or prior to the closing date, of the following additional conditions: 本契約で企図されている取引を実行する買い主の義務は、買い主の裁量で、クロージング日以前に以下の追加条件を達成することを条件とする。◆The parties hereto shall keep in strict confidence from any third party any and all important matters concerning the business affairs and transactions covered by this agreement. 本契約当事者は、本契約の対象である営業上の問題や取引に関するすべての重要事項については、どんな第三者に対しても一切極秘にする。

transaction of business 事業取引, 商取引, 議事進行

◆At each meeting of the board of directors, a majority of each of the Class A directors and Class B directors shall be necessary and sufficient to constitute a quorum for the transaction of business. 取締役会の各会議には、Aクラスの取締役とBクラス取締役の各過半数の出席が必要で、これを議事進行の十分な定足数とする。

transaction tax 取引税
◆Eleven euro states agreed to press ahead with a financial transaction tax. ユーロ[ユーロ圏]11か国が、金融取引税(の導入)を推し進めることで合意した。

transfer (動)移転する、移行する、移す、移管する、転送する、配置換換する、譲渡する、名義を書き換える、振り込む、送金する、繰り入れる (⇒multinational corporation)
the right to transfer copies 複製物の譲渡権
transfer golden shares 黄金株を譲渡する
transfer production operations overseas 生産拠点を海外に移す
◆If golden shares held by a friendly company are transferred to another party, such shares could be transferred again to a hostile bidder. 友好的な企業が保有する黄金株を第三者に譲渡した場合、その黄金株はまた敵対的買収者に譲渡される可能性もある。◆Original edition rights include the right to transfer copies to enable publishers to provide them to the public. 出版物[書籍]原版権には、複製物の譲渡によって出版社が複製物を公衆に提供できるようにする譲渡権も含まれている。◆Pursuant to concerned provisions of Contract, all risks of loss or damage to Machines shall be directly transferred from Supplier to Customer. 本契約の関連規定に従って、本機械に関する損失または損害の全危険は、サプライヤーから顧客へ直接移転するものとする。

transfer (名)財産などの譲渡、移転、商品の売買、権限などの委譲、継承、名義の書換え、転送、転任、配属、配置転換、出向、振替え、振込み、送金、繰り入れ
account transfer 口座振替え
balance of transfer service 移転収支
bank transfer 銀行振替え
business transfer 営業譲渡、企業移転 (=transfer of business)
cash transfer 現金振込み
mail transfer 郵便送金
money transfer 現金振込み、代金振込み、振替え
ordinary transfer 普通送金
ownership transfer 所有移転
physical transfer 物理的移転、物理的に移転すること
restriction of transfer 譲渡制限
stock[share]transfer 株式の名義書換え、株式譲渡

technology transfer 技術移転 (=transfer of technology)
telegraphic transfer 電信送金、電信為替
transfer of business 営業譲渡
transfer of claims 権利の移転
transfer of obligations 義務の移転
transfer of ownership 所有権の移転、企業移転
transfer of real estate holdings 保有不動産の譲渡
transfer of technology and knowhow 技術・ノウハウの移転
transfer of title 所有権譲渡
transfer pricing 移転価格、移転価格税制
transfer pricing taxation system 移転価格税制
transfer tax 有価証券取引税、流通税
transfer the shares of the new company 新会社の株式を譲渡する
transfers between geographic areas 地域間の商品売買
unilateral transfer 一方的取引
wire transfer 電信送金
◆Licensee must not transfer the Software, the technical documentation or related materials, by sublicense or otherwise, without the prior written consent of Licensor. ライセンシーは、ライセンサーの書面による事前の同意を得ないでサブライセンスまたはその他の方法で本ソフトウエア、技術文書またはその他の関連資料を譲渡してはならない。◆The development of cross-border infrastructure in the Greater Mekong Subregion (GMS) has prompted a number of multinational corporations to transfer some of their manufacturing processes to Laos, Cambodia and Myanmar to take advantage of cheaper labor costs. 大メコン圏での国境を越えたインフラ整備に伴い、多くの多国籍企業が、安い人件費[低賃金]の利点を生かして生産工程の一部をラオスやカンボジア、ミャンマーに移転している。◆The term "delivery" shall mean the physical transfer to Licensee of the documentation and Software. 「引渡し」という用語は、書類とソフトウエアをライセンシーに物理的に移転することを意味する。◆Transfers between geographic areas are based on "arm's length" prices. 地域間の1商品の売買は、第三者間との取引価格に基づいて行われている。◆You may not electronically transfer the software program from one computer to another over a network. 通信ネットワークでコンピュータ間のソフトウエア・プログラムを電子的に転送することはできない。

transfer of funds 資金移動、資金のシフト、口座振替え、送金 (=fund transfer)
◆Mitsubishi UFJ Financial Group Inc. agreed to pay $8.6 million to the Treasury Department's Office of Foreign Assets Control to settle alleged U.S. sanction violations related to the transfer of

funds to client accounts in Myanmar, Iran and Cuba. 三菱UFJフィナンシャル・グループは、ミャンマーやイラン、キューバなどの顧客口座に行った送金に関して、米国の経済制裁規制に違反した疑いで、米財務省外国資産管理局に860万ドルの和解金を支払うことで合意した。

transfer of patent right　特許権の移転
◆In lawsuits over patent rights, courts have increasingly awarded inventors compensation for the transfer of patent rights. 特許権をめぐる訴訟で、裁判所は裁定で発明者に特許権移転の対価［報酬］を認めるケースが増えている。

transfer of shares　株式譲渡, 株式の名義書換え
◆The transfer of the Shares hereunder shall become effective as of the first day of July, 2015. 本契約に基づく本株式の譲渡は、2015年7月1日に有効となる。

transfer of technology and knowhow [know-how]　技術・ノウハウの移転
◆The company supports the transfer of technology and knowhow that the developing countries need. 同社は、開発途上国が必要としている技術やノウハウの移転を支援している。

transfer one's production base overseas　生産拠点を海外に移す
◆Many Japanese electronics makers have withdrawn from the TV market, but some domestic manufacturers which have maintained their TV businesses have transferred their production bases overseas. 日本の電機メーカーの多くはテレビ市場から撤退したが、テレビ事業を続ける国内メーカーの一部も、生産拠点を海外に移している。

transferring date　譲渡日, 移転日

translate　(動)言いかえる, 換言する, 翻訳する, 訳す, 通訳する, 解釈する, 説明する, 変える, 変換する, 移す, 移行する, 換算する　(自動)翻訳する, 通訳する, 翻訳できる, 〜に変わる, 〜になる, (航空機やミサイルが)移動する
be translated at rates prevailing at the respective transaction dates　各取引日の実勢為替レートで換算されている
be translated at the exchange rates in effect at the balance sheet date　貸借対照表日［決算日］現在の実効為替レートで換算されている
be translated into U.S. dollars　米ドルに換算されている
be translated into U.S. dollars using current exchange rates　決算日レートで米ドルに換算する
translate … into action　〜を実行に移す, 〜を具体化する, 〜を反映させる
translate A as　Aを〜と解釈する
translate as　〜と解釈される, 〜と翻訳される, 〜となって現われる
translate into a flat year-on-year rate　前年同月比で横ばいとなる［横ばいに当たる］

translate the data into computer images　データ［情報］をコンピュータ画像に変換する
◆Nonmonetary balance sheet items and corresponding income statement items are translated at rates in effect at the time of acquisition. 貸借対照表の非貨幣性項目とこれに対応する損益計算書項目は、取得日の為替レートで換算されています。◆The revision of the firm's assumed exchange rate will translate into an additional ¥150 billion loss in its consolidated accounts for the six-month period through March 2015. 同社の想定為替レートの修正に伴って、同社の2014年度下半期（2014年10月〜2015年3月）の連結決算では、追加で1,500億円の為替差損が生じることになる。

Trans-Pacific Partnership（pact [agreement, framework]）　環太平洋経済連携協定, TPP
◆The Trans-Pacific Partnership framework to promote free trade among member countries is expected to invigorate the movement of human resources. 加盟国間の自由貿易化を進めるための環太平洋経済連携協定（TPP）で、人材の移動も盛んになることが予想される。◆The Trans-Pacific Partnership pact is designed to promote free trade among member countries. 環太平洋経済連携協定（TPP）のねらいは、加盟国間の貿易自由化にある。

transport　(名)運送, 輸送, 運輸, 運搬, 輸送機関, 交通機関, 輸送手段, 交通手段, 移動手段
air transport　航空輸送, 航空運送
air transport industry　航空運送業
bag for fresh-water transport　淡水輸送用大容量バッグ
bulk transport　バルク輸送
capacity for transport　輸送力
chilled transport　チルド輸送
city transport　都市輸送
combined transport document　複合一貫運送書類, 複合運送書類
combined transport operator　複合運送人
International Air Transport Association　国際航空運送協会, IATA
international multimodal transport　国際複合一貫輸送
local transport　現地の輸送機関
maritime transport　海上交通, 海洋交通, 海上輸送　(=ocean transport, water transport)
multimodal transport　複合運送
ocean transport　海上輸送
overland transport　陸上輸送
port transport industry　港湾運送事業, 港湾輸送事業
public transport　公共輸送機関
rail transport　鉄道, 鉄道輸送システム
road transport　道路輸送, 道路輸送システム

sea transport　海上輸送

surface transport　陸上輸送

transport boat　運送船, 輸送船

transport capacity　輸送能力, 輸送力
（=capacity for transport）

transport charges　輸送量

transport cost　輸送費, 運送費用

transport craft　輸送機, 運送船

transport dues　通行税, 通行料

transport efficiency　運送効率, 輸送効率

transport equipment　輸送機器

transport facility　交通機関

transport insurance　運送保険

transport machinery sector　輸送機器セク
ター, 輸送機械部門

Transport Minister　運輸大臣

transport of goods　貨物移送

transport of value　価値移転

transport of waste　ごみの運搬

transport plane　輸送機

transport route　運送経路, 輸送路

transport sector　運輸部門

transport service　輸送サービス

transport ship　輸送船

transport unit　輸送単位

water transport　水上輸送, 海上輸送, 水上交通

transportation　（名）運送, 輸送, 運輸

air cargo transportation　（航空機による）空路
輸送, ACT

air transportation　航空輸送, 空輸

bonded transportation　保税運送

conveyor transportation　コンベア輸送

freight transportation　貨物輸送

inland coast transportation　（船舶による）海
路運送, ICT

Intermodal Surface Transportation Efficiency
Act　陸上一貫輸送効率化法

intermodal transportation　複合一貫輸送, 協同
一貫輸送

land transportation　陸上輸送, 陸上運送

marine transportation　海上輸送

mass transportation　大量輸送

motor transportation　自動車輸送

overland transportation　（鉄道やトラックに
よる）陸路運送, OLT

passenger transportation　旅客輸送

pipeline transportation　パイプライン輸送

rail transportation　鉄道輸送

river transportation　河川輸送

shipping transportation cost　発送運賃

slurry transportation　スラリー輸送

surface transportation　陸上輸送, 船便

transportation and insurance charges　運送料
と保険料

transportation and logistics　輸送と物流, 輸
送・物流

transportation business　運送業, 運輸業

transportation charge　運搬費

transportation claim　運送クレーム

transportation cost　輸送費

transportation documents　運送書類, 輸送書類

transportation entry　運送申告

transportation equipment　輸送機器

transportation in　運賃着払い

transportation in bond　保税運送

transportation industry　輸送業界, 運送業界,
輸送業, 運送業

transportation machinery　輸送用機械, 輸送
機器

transportation out　発送運賃

transportation rates　運賃

transportation risk　運送リスク

transportation without appraisement entry　無
査定輸送通関

◆Distributor shall be responsible for arranging
all transportation of Products, but if requested
by Distributor, Supplier shall, at Distributor's expense, assist Distributor in making such arrangements. 本製品の運送の手配についてはすべて販
売店が責任を負うが, 販売店から要請があった場
合, 供給者は, 販売店の費用負担で, 販売店を支援
して運送の手配を行うものとする。◆In the event
that Supplier is requested to assist Distributor in
arranging for transportation, Distributor shall reimburse Supplier for all costs relating to such
arrangements, including, without limitation, insurance, transportation, loading and unloading,
handling and storage following their delivery to
Distributor. 供給者が販売店から運送手配の支援を
要請された場合, 販売店は, 供給者が（本製品を）
販売店へ引き渡した後の保険, 運送, 積み下ろし,
貨物取扱い, 保管料などの関連費用を, すべて供
給者に償還するものとする。

transportation and delivery charges　運
送と引渡し費用, 運送・引渡し費用
◆Net Wholesale Price referred to in this agreement is defined as the amount of the gross sales
by ABC of the licensed products to ABC's customers in the territory, less customary trade discounts, insurance premiums, transportation and
delivery charges, taxes（VAT）and duties. 本契
約書に記載する「純卸売り販売額」とは, ABCの
顧客に対する契約地域内でのABCの許諾製品の総

売上高（総販売額）から、通常の卸売り割引額、保険料、運送・引渡し費用、税金（付加価値税）と関税を差し引いた額のことをいう。

transship （動）積み換える、乗り換える
◆Your orders are arriving in Yokohama soon and will be transshipped on to m.s. "President Wilson" which is leaving Yokohama for your port on August 10. 貴注文は間もなく横浜に到着し、貴地に向けて8月10日に横浜を出港予定のディーゼル船「プレジデント・ウイルソン」号に積み換える予定です。

transshipment （名）積み換え、乗り換え
no transshipment clause　積み換え禁止条項
◆Partial shipment to be permitted. Transshipment not to be allowed. 分割積み可。積み換え禁止。

traveling, living and all other expenses
渡航・滞在費とその他のすべての費用
◆Travelling, living and all other expenses of the licensee's personnel for such visits or training shall be borne and paid by the Licensee. 当該視察（工場見学）または訓練を受けるためのライセンシーの人員の渡航、滞在費用とその他のすべての費用は、ライセンシーが負担して支払うものとする。

treasury stock　金庫株、自己株式
（=reacquired shares, reacquired stock, repurchased shares, repurchased stock, treasury shares）

treaty （名）条約, 条約議定書, 盟約, 盟約書, 協約, 協定, 取決め, 約束, 契約, 約定, 交渉, 協議
be in treaty with　～と交渉中である
climate change treaty　気候変動条約
commercial treaty　通商協定, 通商条約
（=treaty of commerce）
double taxation treaty　二重課税防止条約
ink a treaty　協定［条約］に署名する
make a treaty with　～と条約を結ぶ
nuclear nonproliferation treaty　核拡散防止条約
Patent Cooperation Treaty　特許協力条約
ratify the treaty　条約を批准する
tax treaty　租税条約
treaty of commerce and navigation　通商航海条約（貨物や船舶の往来、個人の居住や営業の自由、財産の取得、関税、裁判権などが含まれる）
◆A free trade agreement is a treaty between two or more nations and territories seeking to reduce or abolish tariffs on industrial, agricultural and other products. 自由貿易協定（FTA）は、鉱工業品や農産品［農産物］の関税の引下げや撤廃を求める2か国以上の国や地域間の協定です。
◆Japan and Russia inked a treaty on measures to control poaching and smuggling of crabs and other marine products in the Okhotsk Sea. 日本とロシアは、オホーツク海のカニなど水産物の密漁・密輸入対策に関する協定に署名した。

treble damages　3倍の損害賠償
（=trebling of damages）

trend （名）傾向, 動向, 基調, 趨勢, 大勢, 地合い, 市場の足取り, 推移, 流れ, 潮流, 波, 現象, 流行, トレンド
above-trend growth　トレンドを上回る経済成長
be in a bear trend　下降傾向にある, 下降トレンドから脱していない
be on an upward trend　上昇基調にある, 増加傾向にある
competitive trends　競争環境
deflationary trend　デフレ傾向, デフレ気味, 物価下落傾向
downward trend of stock prices　株価の下落基調, 株価の下落傾向
earnings trend　収益動向
economic trends　経済動向, 景気動向, 景気, 経済の潮流
falling trend　下降傾向, 下落傾向, 低下傾向
financial trend　金融動向
global economic trends　世界の景気動向, グローバル経済の潮流　（⇒corporate merger）
inflationary trend　インフレ傾向, インフレ動向, インフレ気味, 物価上昇傾向
major trend　大勢
negative trend　低下傾向
new technological trends　技術革新の波
prospective trends　今後のトレンド
reversal of the trend　トレンドの反転
rising trend　上昇基調, 上昇傾向
（=upward trend）
secular trend　長期的な傾向, 長期傾向, 長期トレンド
spinoff trend　分社化傾向
the overall trend in prices　物価の総合的な動向
the trend in sales volume　販売数量の推移
◆Export and import trends are influenced by various factors, including economic situations in and outside of the country, currency exchange rates and crude oil price movements. 輸出入動向は、国内外の景気や為替相場、原油価格の変動などの各種要因に左右される。

trial （名）試験, 試み, 試用, テスト, 試運転, 裁判, 公判, 審理
by way of trial　試しに
make（a）trial of A　Aを試す, Aを実験する　（=put A to trial）

on a trial basis　試験的に, 実験的に

on trial　試しに, 試験中で, 審理中で, 公判中で

trial and error　試行錯誤

trial balance（sheet）　試算表

trial boring　試掘

trial by jury　陪審による審理, 陪審審理, 陪審による裁判, 陪審裁判　（=jury trial）

trial consignments　委託品

trial cruise［trip］　船の試運転

trial employment period　試用期間

trial free　試用無料

trial kit　試供品, 試供品セット

trial manufacture　試作

trial operation　試運転, 試験操業

trial period　試験期間, 試用期間

trial piece　試売品, 試供品

trial pit　試掘坑

trial product　試作品

trial rate　当初使用率

trial run　試運転, 試乗, 試行テスト, 実験　（=test run）

trial sale　試売

trial sample　試験用見本

◆A major bone of contention in the trial of the lung cancer drug Iressa case was whether the importer and seller's provision of information on Iressa's side effects to medical institutions was sufficient. 肺がん治療薬「イレッサ」訴訟の裁判の大きな争点は, 輸入販売元による医療機関へのイレッサの副作用に関する情報の提供が十分だったか, という点だ。◆Nursing-care robots produced on a trial basis by some Japanese companies cost as much as 20 million yen per unit, but the government hopes to promote the robots priced at about 100,000 yen for widespread use across the nation. 一部の日本企業が試験的に生産している介護ロボットは, 1台2,000万円と高額だが, 政府は1台10万円程度の介護ロボットを全国に普及させたい考えだ。

trial order　試し注文, 試験注文, 試験的注文, 見本注文（order for samples）, 試買注文
◆We are prepared to place a prompt trial order if you can guarantee supply of products strictly in accordance with our specifications. 貴社が当社の仕様書どおりの商品の供給［納入］を保証するなら, 早速, 試験注文を出します。◆We hope that this trial order will be the beginning of good business relations between the two of us. この試験注文が両者間の良好な取引関係の始まりとなることを, 当方は願っております。◆We hope that this trial order will lead to future business. この試験注文は, 今後の取引につながるものと思います。

trilateral　（形）3者間の, 3者構成の, 3極の, 3角形の, 3角の

trilateral meeting　3者会議, 3か国会談

trilateral trade　3角貿易, 3極貿易　（=triangular trade）

trilateral trade negotiation　3極貿易交渉

trilateral cooperation　3者協力, 3者間協力, 3角協力
◆Trilateral cooperation between industry, academia and the government is crucial to steadily advance iPS R&D projects. iPS研究開発プロジェクトを着実に進めるには, 産学官の3者協力が大切だ。

TRIP　知的財産権の貿易的側面に関する協定（Agreement on Trade-Related Aspect of Intellectual Property Rightsの略）

tri-reserve-currency regime　3準備通貨体制
◆Financial exchanges between the BRICs group, Indonesia and South Korea will move toward a tri-reserve-currency regime by losing a dependency on the U.S. dollar. BRICsグループ（ブラジル, ロシア, インド, 中国）とインドネシア, 韓国の新興6か国間の金融取引は今後, 米ドルに依存しなくなるため, 3準備通貨体制に移行するものと思われる。

true and complete books and records　真正かつ完全な会計帳簿と記録
◆Licensee shall keep true and complete books and records covering all business done hereunder. ライセンシーは, 本契約に基づいて行われる業務をすべて対象とする真正かつ完全な会計帳簿と記録を保持する。

true and correct　真正な, 真正かつ正確な, 真実の, 正確な

true and correct copy　真正な写し, 真正かつ正確な写し, 正確な写し
◆Included in Schedule 5 are true and correct copies of the Articles of Incorporation and regulations of the Company in effect on the date hereof. 付属書類5には, 本契約日に効力をもっている対象会社の基本定款と関連規則の真正かつ正確な写しが含まれている。

true and fair view　真実かつ公正な見方
◆The annual financial statements for the financial year ending on December 31, 2015 present a true and fair view of the financial position as of the date thereof. 2015年12月31日に終了する事業年度［会計年度］の年次財務書類は, 同日現在の財政状態について真実かつ公正な見方を提示している。

trust account　信託勘定, トラスト勘定

trust fund　信託基金, 信託資金, 投資信託
◆In December 1998, trust funds became the first financial products offered by securities firms and life insurers that banks were allowed to sell. 1998年12月に, 投資信託は, 証券会社と生命保険会社が提供する金融商品のうち銀行窓口での販売が認められた最初の商品となった。

trust receipt 輸入担保貨物保管証, T/R

turnkey [turn-key] （形）完成品渡しの, 完成引渡し契約の, パッケージ・ディール契約の, ターンキーの

export by turnkey system　ターンキー方式輸出, ターンキー式輸出, ターンキー輸出

full turnkey　一括受発注方式, フルターンキー

full turnkey export　フルターンキー輸出

negotiated turnkey project　随意契約ベースのターンキー・プロジェクト

turnkey contract　ターンキー契約（＝パッケージ・ディール契約）, 完成品受渡し契約（設計から試運転までの業務を引き受け, 完成した段階で引き渡す方式）, 設備一括請負契約

turnkey export　ターンキー方式輸出, ターンキー（式）輸出

turnkey import　ターンキー方式輸入, ターンキー（式）輸入

twelve-month period　1年, 12か月期間

Twitter followers　ツイッターのフォロワー（閲覧者）
◆The number of Twitter followers is used as a barometer of companies' popularity and reliability. ツイッターのフォロワー（閲覧者）の数は, 企業の人気度や信頼度のバロメーターになっている。

type and kind　種類

U

UCC [U.C.C.]　統一商法典（Uniform Commercial Codeの略）

UCCC [U.C.C.C.]　統一消費者信用法

UCP　信用状統一規則（Uniform Customs and Practice for Documentary Credits（荷為替信用状に関する統一規則および慣習）の略）

UCP 500　信用状統一規則500, 荷為替信用状に関する統一規則および慣例（国際商業会議所出版物第500号）（Uniform Customs and Practice for Documentary Credits（1993 Revision）, ICC Publication No. 500の略）

ULCC　（30万重量トン以上の）超大型油槽船

ULIS　国際的物品売買契約に関する国連条約（United Nations Convention on the Contract for the International Sale of Goodsの略）

unaffiliated third party　無関係な第三者
◆Such information was communicated by the disclosing party to an unaffiliated third party free of any obligation of confidence. 当該情報は, 開示当事者が秘密保持義務なしに無関係な第三者に通知した。

unauthorized practice of law　無資格法律業務, 非弁行為

unauthorized use　不正使用

◆Since electronic money requires safeguards against unauthorized use and counterfeiting, encryption technology, on the software side, and IC cards, on the hardware side, represent essential technologies. 電子マネーには不正使用や変造を防ぐ技術が必要で, ソフト面では暗号化技術, ハード面ではICカードが, その代表的な技術とされている。

UNCITRAL Rules　国連国際商取引法委員会（UNCITRAL）規則

unconditionally　（副）無条件に, 無条件で

cancel a contract unconditionally　無条件で契約を解除する, 無条件で解約する

unconditionally guarantee　無条件に保証する
◆In case any dispute arises in connection with the above right, the seller reserves the right to terminate unconditionally this agreement or any further performance of this agreement at the seller's discretion. 上記権利に関して紛争が生じた場合, 売り主はその裁量で, 本契約または本契約のその後の履行を無条件で終了させる権利を留保する。◆We are pleased to accept your order unconditionally and are sending you our sales note. 貴社の注文を無条件で快諾し, 当社の売約書をお送りします。◆We can cancel a contract unconditionally within a cooling-off period even if it is signed with an unethical trader. 仮に悪質業者と契約を結んだ場合でも, クーリング・オフ期間内なら, 無条件で契約を解除できる。

UNCTAD　国連貿易開発会議（United Nations Conference on Trade and Developmentの略）

UNCTRAL　国連国際商取引委員会（the United Nations Commission on international Trade Lawの略）

under　（前）～の真下に, ～の下に, ～の指揮下に, ～の最中で, ～に基づく, ～に基づいて, ～に従って, ～によって, ～のもとに, ～以下の（less than）, ～未満の

under and subject to　～に従って

under no circumstances　どんなことがあっても～ない, 決して～ない

under separate cover　別便で

under the terms and conditions herein contained　本契約［本契約書］に記載する条件で, 本契約に定める条件で

under this agreement　この契約上, 本契約上, 本契約に基づいて, 本契約により, 本契約の下で
◆On all orders of fifty thousand U.S. dollars or under, payment shall be made simultaneously with the giving of the order. 5万米ドル以下の注文の場合, 支払いはすべて発注と同時に行うものとする。

under and by virtue of　～に基づいて
a corporation organized and existing under and by virtue of the laws of　～の法律に基づい

て設立され現存する会社

under the laws of 〜の法律に基づいて、〜の法律のもとに、〜法に準拠して
◆The parties hereto desire to establish a stock corporation under the laws of Japan to undertake and accomplish the manufacture and marketing of the products in the territory as described in Article 1. 本契約当事者は、第1条に定める地域で本製品の製造とマーケティングを引き受け、実行するために、日本法のもとに株式会社を設立することを望んでいる。

under the terms and conditions set forth herein 本契約に定める条件で、本契約書に記載する条件に従って、本契約書に記載する条項に基づいて
◆Distributor desires to act as an independent distributor of Products under the terms and conditions set forth herein. 販売店は、本契約書に記載する条件に従って本製品[契約品]の独立した販売店になることを希望している。

under the terms of FOB FOBの条件で
◆If delivery is made under the terms of FOB, the Buyer shall book shipping space in accordance with the time of delivery stipulated in this agreement. 引渡しがFOBの条件で行われる場合、買主は、本契約で定める引渡し期限に従って(本船の)船腹を予約するものとする。

underlying asset 原資産, 対象資産, 担保となる資産
◆Commodity futures trading is based on contracts to buy or sell a specified quantity of an underlying asset, such as gold, at a particular time in the future and at a price agreed when the contract was executed. 商品先物取引は、取引契約を結ぶ時点で、一定量の金などの対象資産を将来の特定の時期に合意した値段で売買する契約に基づいて行われる。

undersigned (形)下記の, 下名の, 下記に署名した, 末尾に署名した
the undersigned 下記署名者, 末尾署名者
◆For Value Received, the undersigned ("Borrower") promises to pay to ABC Co., Ltd. , a Japanese corporation ("Holder"), or order, in lawful money of the United States, the principal sum of Five million Eight hundred Fifty thousand dollars ($5,850,000), with interest on the principal balance remaining unpaid from the date hereof until paid, at the following rates. 「対価の受領」については、末尾署名者(以下「振出人」という)が、元本585万ドル($5,850,000)と本手形の振出日から決済日まで残存する元本の未払い残高利息を、日本法人のABC株式会社(以下「所持人」という)にまたはその指図人に、米国の法定通貨と以下の金利で支払うことを約束する。

understanding between parties 当事者間の了解, 両当事者間の合意

undertake (動)引き受ける, 約束する, 〜の義務・責任を負う, 保証する, 着手する,

undertake and agree, 合意する
undertake to manufacture and distribute 〜を生産、販売することを約束する
◆The assignee shall undertake to observe and perform this agreement and to be bound by the terms and conditions hereof in every way as if the assignee were named as a party in place of the assigning party. 譲受人は本契約を遵守し履行する義務を負い、譲渡人に代わって当initから当事者として指名されていたかのように、あらゆる点で本契約の条件に拘束されるものとする。

undertake and accomplish the manufacture and marketing of 〜の製造とマーケティングを引き受ける
◆The parties hereto desire to establish a stock corporation under the laws of Japan to undertake and accomplish the manufacture and marketing of the products in the territory as described in Article 1. 本契約当事者は、第1条に定める地域で本製品の製造とマーケティングを引き受け、実行するために、日本法のもとに株式会社を設立することを望んでいる。

undertaking (名)引受け, 請負, 事業, 企業, 約束, 約束事項, 約束ごと, 公約, 保証, 保証書 (⇒NOW, THEREFORE)
cash deficiency undertaking 不足資金負担
nonabandonment undertaking 出資維持保証
parent undertaking 親会社, 親企業
subsidiary undertaking 子会社
Undertaking on Rules and Procedures Governing the Settlement of Disputes 紛争解決に係わる規則と手続きに関する了解
undertakings and commitments 約束, 約束ごと
◆Such letter of credit shall be transferable and having the clause of definite undertaking by the issuing bank for unconditional payment against a draft at sight. この信用状は、譲渡可能で、一覧払い手形に対する無条件支払いに関して発行銀行が明確に約束した文言が入っているものとする。

underwriter (名)保険・証券の引受業者, 保険業者, 引受人
◆ABC shall effect all risk (Institute Cargo Clauses) marine insurance with underwriters or insurance companies of good repute in an amount of one hundred and ten (110) percent of CIF value of the shipments of the products. ABCは、本製品積送品のCIF価格の110%の保険金額で、評判の良い保険引受業者または保険会社と全危険担保条件(協会貨物約款)の海上保険の保険契約をするものとする。

unenforceable (形)強制することができない
◆In case any one or more of the provisions of this agreement are held invalid, illegal or unenforceable in any respect, the validity, legality and enforceability of the remaining provisions

hereof shall not be in any way affected or impaired thereby, except to the extent that giving effect to the remaining provisions would be unjust or inequitable. 本契約の一つ以上の規定がいずれかの点で無効、違法または強制不能と判断された場合、残存規定の実施が不公正または不均衡となる範囲を除いて、本契約の残存規定の有効性、合法性と強制可能性はその影響を受けることはなく、またれによって損なわれることはないものとする。

unfair (形)不公平な, 不当な, 不正な, 公明正大でない, 一方に片寄った, 卑劣な

unfair advantage 不当利益

unfair business practice 不正な商取引

unfair dismissal 不当解雇

unfair labor practice 不当労働行為

unfair practice 不正商慣行, 不正商慣習, 不正な取引方法, 不当営業行為, 不公正競争

unfair pricing policies 価格カルテル

unfair trade 不公正取引, 不公正貿易

unfair trade practices 不公正取引慣行, 不公正貿易慣行, 不公正な取引方法

unfair trading practices 不公正貿易慣行, 不公正取引慣行

unfair competition 不正競争

◆To ensure fair international commercial trade, the law against unfair competition stipulates that both individuals involved in bribery and the corporations they belong to should be punished. 公正な国際商取引を確保するため、不正競争防止法には、贈賄(外国公務員への贈賄)に関与した個人と法人を罰する規定(両罰規定)がある。

Unfair Competition Prevention Act 不正競争防止法

◆The Unfair Competition Prevention Act prohibits bribing foreign government employees. 不正競争防止法は、外国公務員への贈賄を禁止している。

unfair competitiveness 不正競争

◆To ensure fair international commercial trade, the law against unfair competition stipulates that both individuals involved in bribery and the corporations they belong to should be punished. 公正な国際商取引を確保するため、不正競争防止法には、贈賄(外国公務員への贈賄)に関与した個人と法人を罰する規定(両罰規定)がある。

unfavorable [unfavourable] (形)不利な, 好ましくない, 悪い, マイナスの

unfavorable balance 支払い超過

unfavorable developments 不利な展開, 好ましくない展開, 逆風

unfavorable effects on earnings per share 普通株式1株当たり利益に対する不利な影響額

unfavorable impact 不利な影響, マイナス影響, 悪影響

unfavorable market conditions 市況の悪化, 市

場環境の悪化, 不利な市場環境

unfavorable winds 逆風

◆A strong yen is generally unfavorable for Japanese exporters. 円高は、日本の輸出企業には好ましくない。

unforeseen (形)予期しない, 予測されない, 不測の, 予見し難い, 思いがけない, 意外な, 想定外の

a risk that is as yet unforeseen 未知のリスク

unforeseen circumstances 不測の事態, 予見し難い事態

◆We regret to inform you that we may not be able to ship all of your requirements due to the unforeseen increase in the demand for the goods. 本品に対する需要が思いもかけず増大したため、遺憾ながらご入用の品全部の船積みは不可能になるかと思います。

unfriendly takeover 非友好的買収

◆A "white knight" is a friendly acquirer sought by the target of an unfriendly takeover. 「ホワイト・ナイト」とは、非友好的買収の標的企業が探し求める友好的買収者をいう。

Uniform Commercial Code (米国の)統一商事法典, 統一商法典, U.C.C.[UCC](⇒proceeds)

◆Seller shall waive any claim against Buyer under the Uniform Commercial Code or otherwise, with respect to a claim asserted against Seller or Buyer for patent, trademark or copyright infringement or the like. 売り主は、特許・商標・著作権の侵害等について売り主または買い主に対してなされる請求に関しては、買い主に対する米国統一商事法典その他に基づく請求権をすべて放棄する。

Uniform Customs and Practice for Commercial Documentary Credits 商業荷為替信用状に関する統一規則および慣例, 荷為替信用状統一規則, UCP (1933年に国際商業会議所が制定。1994年1月1日に発行された「1993年版」が最新の改訂版。⇒confirmed and irrevocable letter of credit)

Uniform Limited Partnership Act (米国の)統一合資会社法, U.L.P.A.

Uniform Negotiable Instruments Law 米国統一流通証券法, U.N.L.L.

Uniform Partnership Act (米国の)統一合名会社法, U.P.A.

Uniform Rules for Combined Transport Documents 複合運送証券統一規則

Uniform Trade Secrets Act 統一トレード・シークレット法

unilateral (形)片側だけの, 一方的な, 片務的な, 単独の, 一国主義の

net unilateral transfers 純移転収支

unilateral benefit 一方的利益

unilateral commercial transaction 単独商行為

unilateral contract [agreement] 片務契約

（契約当事者の一方だけが債務を負う契約）

unilateral decision 一方的決定, 一方的決断, 独自の判断

unilateral dismissal notice 一方的解雇通知

unilateral mistake 契約当事者の一方の錯誤

unilateral monopoly 一方独占

unilateral step 一方的な処置

unilateral transaction 一方的な取引

unilateral transfer 一方的取引

unilateral development 単独開発, 一方的な開発
◆China attempted to resume the unilateral development of a gas field known as Chunxiao. 中国は、春暁（日本名・白樺）ガス田の単独開発を再開する動きを見せた。◆Moscow is Russianizing the northern territories off Hokkaido by faits accompli with unilateral development of them. ロシアは、一方的な北方領土開発の既成事実により、北方領土のロシア化を進めている。

unit （名）単位, 構成単位, 部門, 事業部門, 会社, 支社, 支店, 子会社, 設備一式, 台, 基, 装置, 部隊, セット, ユニット （⇒arm, middleman）
a unit of the financial group 同金融グループ系の企業
business unit 事業部, 事業単位
condominium unit マンション
economic unit 経済主体
European Currency Unit 欧州通貨単位
export unit value 輸出単価
government unit 政府機関
music unit 音楽事業部門
operating unit 事業体
property unit trust 財産契約型投資信託
reemployment services unit 再就職サービス部門
rental units starts 賃貸住宅の着工戸数
starts of built-for-sale units 分譲住宅の着工戸数
unit kilometers 走行台キロ
unit of GDP 国内総生産（GDP）単位
unit of measurement 測定単位
unit pricing 単位価格表示
unit sales price 販売単価
unit trust オープン型投資信託
unprofitable unit 不採算部門, 不採算事業
◆Bitcoin, a virtual currency circulated on the Internet, is traded in units of BTC. The value of bitcoin fluctuates excessively, but bitcoin has hovered at about $800 per BTC lately. ネット上で流通している仮想通貨「ビットコイン」は、BTCの単位で取引されている。ビットコインの相場は乱高下があまりにも激しいが、最近は1BTC=800ドル前後で推移している。◆Nursing-care robots produced on a trial basis by some Japanese companies cost

as much as 20 million yen per unit, but the government hopes to promote the robots priced at about 100,000 yen for widespread use across the nation. 一部の日本企業が試験的に生産している介護ロボットは、1台2,000万円と高額だが、政府は1台10万円程度の介護ロボットを全国に普及させたい考えだ。◆Suntory Holdings Ltd. is expected to use about ￥500 billion in estimated proceeds from the listing of its beverage and food unit to finance mergers and acquisitions abroad. サントリーホールディングスは、清涼飲料・食品子会社の上場により推定で5,000億円程度の資金を調達して、海外企業の買収に充てる見込みだ。◆The bank became a unit of the financial group through a share swap deal. 同行は、株式交換取引で同金融グループ系の企業になった。◆U.S. federal antitrust regulators have cleared the way for the proposed merger between Sony Music Entertainment and BMG, the music unit of the German media conglomerate Bertelsmann AG. 米連邦反トラスト規制当局（米連邦取引委員会）は、ソニーと独複合メディア大手ベルテルスマンの音楽部門のBMGとの事業統合案を承認した。

unit price 単位価格, 単価
◆We reduced our unit price by five percent at your specific request. 貴社のたっての要請で、当社は単価を5％引き下げました。

unitary tax [taxation] 合算課税, ユニタリー・タックス

United Auto Workers 全米自動車労組, UAW（United Automobile, Aerospace, and Agricultural Implement Workers of America（全米合同自動車・航空宇宙産業・農業機械製造労働者組合）が正式名）
◆The United Auto Workers ratified a four-year contract with Mitsubishi Motor North America. 全米自動車労組は、北米三菱自動車との4年労使協約を承認した。

United Nations Convention on Contracts for the International Sales of Goods 国連物品売買統一法条約
◆The parties agree to exclude the application of the United Nations Convention on Contracts for the International Sales of Goods (1980). 両当事者は、国連物品売買統一法条約（1980年）の適用を排除することに合意する。

universal standard 世界標準, 国際標準, ユニバーサル・スタンダード
◆The universal standard is determined by a majority vote among nations producing the products. ユニバーサル・スタンダードは、製品生産国間の多数投票によって決められる。

unjust or inequitable 不公正または不均衡な, 不公正または不衡平な, 不公正または不公平な
◆In case any one or more of the provisions of this agreement are held invalid, illegal or unenforceable in any respect, the validity, legality and enforceability of the remaining provisions

hereof shall not be in any way affected or impaired thereby, except to the extent that giving effect to the remaining provisions would be unjust or inequitable. 本契約の一つ以上の規定がいずれかの点で無効、違法または強制不能と判断された場合、残存規定の実施が不公正または不均衡となる範囲を除いて、本契約の残存規定の有効性、合法性と強制可能性はその影響を受けることはなく、またそれによって損なわれることはないものとする。

unlawful act　不法行為, 違法行為
◆The government has started discussions on establishing legislation to protect the rights of employees who blow the whistle on their firms' unlawful acts for the sake of protecting consumers. 消費者保護のため、政府は、企業の違法行為を内部告発した従業員の権利を守る法整備の検討をすでに開始した。

unless otherwise expressly provided for　とくに明示の規定がないかぎり, とくに明示の定めがないかぎり, 別途明確に規定しないかぎり
◆Unless otherwise expressly provided for in this agreement, the price and trade term "C.I.F." shall be interpreted in accordance with Incoterms 2000. 本契約に特に明示の規定がないかぎり（本契約で別段に明確に規定しないかぎり）、価格と貿易条件のCIFは、2000年版インコタームズに従って解釈する。

unless otherwise specified　他にとくに明記［明示］しないかぎり, 別段の記載［定め］がないかぎり
◆Quantity is subject to a variation of 5% more or less than the contracted quantity at Seller's option unless otherwise specified. 数量は、他にとくに明記しないかぎり、売り主の裁量で契約数量より5%増減の変動が生じることがある。

unless terminated by either party hereto　本契約当事者の一方が（本契約を）終了させないかぎり［解約しないかぎり］
◆The said term of this agreement shall be automatically extended for additional consecutive periods of three years each, unless terminated by either party hereto by giving the other party a written notice to that effect at least three months prior to the end of original term of this agreement or any extended term thereof. 本契約の上記期間は、少なくとも本契約の当初期間またはその延長期間が満了する3カ月前までに、本契約の当事者の一方が相手方に対して本契約を終了させる旨の書面による通知をして本契約を終了させないかぎり、さらに引き続き3年間ずつ自動的に延長するものとする。

unless the context requires otherwise [the context otherwise requires]　文脈上、他の意味が要求されないかぎり, 文脈上、他の意味に解釈されないかぎり
◆In this Agreement, the following words and expressions shall, unless the context otherwise requires, have the following meanings. 本契約で、

次の語句と表現は、文脈上、別段の意味を必要としないかぎり、次の意味を持つものとする。

unload　（動）荷揚げする, 陸揚げする, 荷卸し［荷下ろし］する
◆The foregoing warranties are conditional upon the Products being received, unloaded, installed, tested and maintained and operated by ABC in a proper manner. 上記の保証は、本製品をABCが適正な方法で受領、荷揚げ、設置し、試験、維持して運転することを前提条件とする。

unloading　（名）荷揚げ, 陸揚げ, 荷卸し［荷下ろし］
unloading charge　荷揚げ費, 荷揚げ費用, 陸揚げ費用, 荷卸し費用
unloading plan　揚げ荷計画
◆In the event that Supplier is requested to assist Distributor in arranging for transportation, Distributor shall reimburse Supplier for all costs relating to such arrangements, including, without limitation, insurance, transportation, loading and unloading, handling and storage following their delivery to Distributor. 供給者が販売店から運送手配の支援を要請された場合、販売店は、供給者が（本製品を）販売店へ引き渡した後の保険、運送、積み下ろし、貨物取扱い、保管料などの関連費用を、すべて供給者に償還するものとする。

unpacking　（名）開梱, コンテナから貨物を引き出すこと, アンパッキング
◆Any claim by the purchaser, except for latent defects, shall be made in writing as soon as reasonably practicable after the arrival, unpacking and inspection of the products, whether by the purchaser or any subsequent purchaser of the products. 買い主によるクレームは、隠れた瑕疵（かし）を除いて、買い主によるか本製品のその後の購入者によるかを問わず本製品の到着、開梱および検査後、合理的に実行可能なかぎり速やかに書面で行うものとする。

unpaid amount　未払い金額, 未払い額
◆If the buyer fails to pay any amount under this agreement when due, the buyer shall be liable to pay to the seller overdue interest on such unpaid amount from the due date until the actual payment date at the rate of 15% per annum. 買い主が支払い期日に本契約に基づく代金の支払いを怠った場合、買い主は、支払い期日から実際の払込み日までの当該未払い金額に対する年率15%の遅延金利を、売り主に支払わなければならない。

unpaid principal amount of the loan　借入金の未払い元本金額, 借入金の未返済元本, 未返還元本
◆If the borrower shall fail to pay when due the principal of or interest on the loan, or any other amount payable under this agreement, the lender may in its discretion at any time after the occurrence of such event by notice in writing to the borrower, declare the entire unpaid principal amount of the loan, accrued interest thereon and all other sums payable under this agreement to

be immediately due and payable. 借主が本契約に基づく借入れの元本もしくは借入金の利息の支払い、または他の支払い金額の支払いを期日に行わない場合、貸主は、当該事態の発生後いつでも、借主に書面で通知を行い、その裁量で借入金の未返還元本全額、発生利息と本契約に基づいて支払わなければならない他のすべての金員の即時支払いを宣言することができる。

unpredictable events　不測の事態
◆To prepare for unpredictable events by anti-Japan demonstrators, the Japanese government will strongly press the Chinese government to ensure the safety of Japanese people and Japanese-affiliated companies in China. 反日デモ隊による不測の事態に備えて、日本政府は、在留邦人や日系企業の安全確保を中国政府に強く求める方針で。

unprofitable business　不採算事業
◆Sanyo Electric Co.'s unprofitable businesses including production of solar power generation panels and lithium-ion batteries were acquired for about ¥670 billion by Panasonic Corp. 三洋電機の太陽電池パネルやリチウムイオン電池の生産などの不採算事業を、パナソニックが約6,700億円で買収した。

unreasonably withhold　不当に保留する
◆The nonassigning party's consent shall not be unreasonably withheld. 非譲渡人の同意は、不当に保留してはならない。

unstable　(形)不安定な、変わりやすい、分解しやすい
◆Japan has to import most of its fossil fuels from the Middle East in which supplies and prices remain unstable. 日本は、化石燃料の大半を、供給量も価格も不安定な中東からの輸入に頼っている。

up to and including　〜まで
◆In case the borrower fails to pay any principal or interest payable under this agreement on the due date therefor, the borrower shall pay to the lender overdue interest on such overdue amount for each day for the period from and including the due date therefor up to and including the day immediately preceding the actual payment date. 借主が本契約に基づいて元本または支払い利息の支払い期日に元本の返還または支払い利息の支払いを怠った場合、借主は、その支払い期日から実際の払込み日の前日までの期間の各日数について、その支払い遅延金額の遅延利息を貸主に支払うものとする。

up to the limits　(〜の)限度まで
◆The Reinsurer agrees to accept all reinsurance cessions automatically up to the limits shown in the annexes to this Agreement. 再保険会社は、本協定書の補遺に示す限度まですべての出再契約を自動的に引き受けることに同意する。

update　(動)更新する、最新式にする、最新のものにする　(名)更新、改訂、最新情報、最新版
◆All such Updates shall become part of Licen-

sor's Products and shall remain in the sole property of Licensor. この最新版は、すべてライセンサーの製品の一部をなし、ライセンサーの単独財産としてとどまるものとする。

upon any permitted assignment　譲渡の承諾を受けると同時に
◆Upon any permitted assignment, this agreement shall inure to the benefit of and be binding upon the successors and assigns of both parties. 譲渡の許諾を受けると同時に、本契約は両当事者の承継人と譲受人に適用され、承継人と譲受人を拘束するものとする。

upon expiration or termination of this agreement　本契約の満了または終了と同時に、本契約の満了または終了時に直ちに、本契約が満了または終了したときは
◆Upon expiration or termination of this agreement, Distributor will immediately cease all display, advertising and use of all of Supplier's names, trademarks and logos. 本契約が満了または終了したときは、販売店は、直ちに供給者の一切の名称、商標とロゴの陳列、宣伝と使用をすべて止める。

upon one's request　〜の要請に基づいて、〜の請求に基づいて、〜の要請[請求]がある場合には
◆The Antimonopoly Law stipulates that documents submitted to FTC hearings may be disclosed to certain concerned parties upon their request. 独占禁止法は、「公正取引委員会の審判に提出された書類[記録]は特定の利害関係人の請求に基づいて利害関係人に開示することができる」と定めている。

upon receipt of　〜を受け取り次第、〜の受領と同時に
upon receipt of this order　本オファー受領と同時に、本オファーを受取り次第
upon receipt of your L/C　貴社の信用状を受け取り次第
◆We will execute the order with best attention upon receipt of your L/C. 貴社の信用状を受け取り次第、当社は最善の注意を払って注文を履行します。

upon the demand of either party　いずれか一方の要求により
◆If the parties are unable to settle the matter within 30 calendar days after their first meeting, then upon the demand of either party, the matter shall be submitted to binding arbitration. 当事者が最初の会談から30暦日以内に当該事項を解決できないときは、いずれか一方の当事者の要求により、当該事項は法律的に拘束力のある仲裁に付託するものとする。

U.S. Commerce Department　米商務省
◆The U.S. Commerce Department set dumping penalty margins of 115.22 percent each for the two Japanese steelmakers. 米商務省は、日本の鉄鋼メーカー2社に対してそれぞれ115.22%のダンピング率を認定した。

491 USE

U.S. currency 米ドル, ドル, 米国の通貨
◆The effects of the recent depreciation of the dollar have not been seen yet, but if the U.S. currency depreciates further, it may lead to an increase in imported commodity prices, which in turn may become an inflationary factor. 最近のドル安の影響はまだ見られないが, 米ドルがさらに下落すれば, 輸入品価格の上昇を招き, これがまた逆にインフレ要因になる恐れがある。

U.S. Department of Commerce 米国商務省
◆Recipient shall not transfer any confidential information received hereunder or any product made using such confidential information, to any country prohibited from obtaining such data or product by the U.S. Department of Commerce Export Administration Regulations without first obtaining a validated export license. 受領者は, 本契約に従って受領した秘密情報またはこの秘密情報を使用して製造した製品を, 米国商務省の輸出管理規則により当該データまたは製品の提供が禁止されている国に対して, 最初に輸出承認の許可を得ないで譲渡することはないものとする。

U.S. dollar 米ドル (⇒spot rate)
◆Indonesia has chalked up large trade deficits due to the decline in primary commodity prices and the rupiah has weakened as much as 17 percent against the U.S. dollar as of September 2013. インドネシアは一次産品の価格の下落で大幅な貿易赤字を計上し, 通貨ルピアは2013年9月現在, 対ドルで17%安となっている。◆Interbank trading between the U.S. dollar and the Chinese currency yuan accounts for 99.3 percent of the Shanghai foreign exchange market. 米ドルと中国の通貨・人民元の銀行間取引 [銀行間為替取引] が, 上海外国為替市場の99.3%を占めている。◆The Japanese and Chinese currencies were mainly exchanged using the U.S. dollar before the start of direct yen-yuan trading on June 1, 2012. 2012年6月1日から円・人民元の直接取引 [直接為替取引] が始まる前には, 円と人民元は, 米ドルを介した取引がほとんどだった。◆The U.S. dollar has dropped sharply in value not only against the yen, but also against the euro, the South Korean won, the Thai baht and other currencies. 米ドル [米ドル相場] は, 円に対してだけでなく, ユーロや韓国ウォン, タイ・バーツなどに対しても, 急落している。

U.S. federal antitrust regulators 米連邦反トラスト規制当局
◆U.S. federal antitrust regulators have cleared the way for the proposed merger between Sony Music Entertainment and BMG, the music unit of the German media conglomerate Bertelsmann AG. 米連邦反トラスト規制当局 (米連邦取引委員会) は, ソニーと独複合メディア大手ベルテルスマンの音楽部門のBMGとの事業統合案を承認した。

U.S. Federal Trade Commission 米連邦取引委員会 (⇒Federal Trade Commission)
◆The U.S. Federal Trade Commission exercises jurisdiction over matters including consumer protection issues in the United States. 米連邦取引委員会 (FTC) は, 米国消費者保護などの問題を管轄している。

U.S. fiscal and trade deficits 米国の財政・貿易赤字
◆Such capital inflows have offset U.S. fiscal and trade deficits and boosted stock prices to record highs. これらの流入資金が, 米国の財政や貿易の赤字を埋め合わせ, 空前の株高を演出した。

U.S. FRB 米連邦準備制度理事会 (the U.S. Federal Reserve Boardの略)
◆Indonesia has enjoyed decent economic growth since the global financial crisis of 2008 due to the U.S. FRB's quantitative easing and higher prices of primary commodities such as coal and palm oil as the country's major exports. インドネシアは, 2008年の世界金融危機以降, 米連邦準備制度理事会 (FRB) の量的金融緩和とインドネシアの主要輸出品である石炭, パーム油など一次産品の高値に支えられ, 高い経済成長を享受している。

U.S. Trade Policy Committee 米貿易政策委員会

U.S. Trade Representative 米通商代表部代表, 米通商代表
Assistant U.S. Trade Representative for ～担当米通商代表補
Deputy U.S. Trade Representative 米通商副代表
Office of the United States Trade Representative 米通商代表部
◆Akira Amari, minister in charge of TPP negotiations, and U.S. Trade Representative Michael Froman started with around 30 minutes of one-on-one talks, with the aim of reaching a broad bilateral agreement before a Japan-U.S. summit meeting held on April 24, 2014. 甘利TPP担当相と米通商代表部のフロマン代表は, 日米首脳会談 (2014年4月24日) 前に二国間の大筋合意を得るため, 約30分の1対1の会談から始めた。◆The meeting between TPP minister Akira Amari and U.S. Trade Representative Michael Froman centered on Japanese tariffs on 586 items in five major farm product categories, including rice and wheat. 甘利TPP相とフロマン米通商代表部代表との会談では, コメや麦など重要な農産品5項目の586品目にかける日本の関税に焦点が当てられた。

U.S. treasuries 米国債
◆Great rotation refers to the shift of investment money from low-risk assets such as U.S. Treasuries and the yen into riskier assets such as stocks. 「グレート・ローテーション (大転換)」とは, 投資資金を米国債や円などの低リスク資産 [安全資産] から株式などリスクの高い資産に移すことを言う。

use (動) 使う, 使用する, 用いる, 充てる, 利用する, (商品などを) 愛用する, 行使する, 消費する, 費やす, 扱う, 取り扱う, 待遇する

◆Measures to tighten quality controls on Chinese food products, taken by many Japanese manufacturers in China, include more stringent tests on the amounts of agricultural chemicals used at Chinese farms and on the quality of processing materials used at Chinese factories. 中国の日系メーカーの多くが取っている中国産食品の品質管理強化策としては、中国農場での農薬使用量の検査や中国の工場で使用している加工原料の品質チェックの強化などが挙げられる。◆Music and images may not, in principle, be copied or used without the artists' prior permission. 音楽や映像は、原則として著作者の事前許可なしに複製・利用することはできない。◆Suntory Holdings Ltd. is expected to use about ￥500 billion in estimated proceeds from the listing of its beverage and food unit to finance mergers and acquisitions abroad. サントリーホールディングスは、清涼飲料・食品子会社の上場により推定で5,000億円程度の資金を調達して、海外企業の買収に充てる見込みだ。◆The Japanese and Chinese currencies were mainly exchanged using the U.S. dollar before the start of direct yen-yuan trading on June 1, 2012. 2012年6月1日から円・人民元の直接取引［直接為替取引］が始まる前には、円と人民元は、米ドルを介した取引がほとんどだった。

use　（名）使用,使用量,使用法,利用,活用,運用,採用,使途,用途,効用,有用,収益権,ユース（⇒unauthorized use）
◆A Foreign Ministry panel has proposed the relaxation of the blanket ban on the military-related use of official development assistance. 外務省の有識者会議は、政府開発援助（ODA）の軍事に絡む利用の全面禁止を緩和するよう提案した。◆ABC possesses certain technology for the design, manufacture, use, and distribution of the products and certain intellectual property pertaining thereto. ABCは、本製品の設計、製造、使用および販売のための特定の技術と、それに関する知的財産権を所有している。◆An international treaty to ban the use, development, production, stockpiling and transfer of cluster bombs entered into force on August 1, 2010. クラスター（集束）爆弾の使用、開発、製造、保有と移転を禁止する国際条約が、2010年8月1日に発効した。◆Copyrighted materials can be used freely under the U.S. law as long as it is considered "fair use." 著作権のある著作物は、「公正な利用」であれば、米国の法律では自由に利用することができる。◆Sharp Corp. will release its 90-inch liquid crystal display TVs, the world's largest for household use, in Middle Eastern and Persian Gulf states such as Bahrain, Kuwait, Oman, Qatar and Saudi Arabia. シャープが、家庭用としては世界最大サイズの90型.液晶テレビを、バーレーン、クウェート、オマーン、カタール、サウジアラビアなどの中東湾岸諸国で発売する。◆The seller expressly disclaims any warranty of conditions, fitness for use or merchantability. 売り主は、状態、用途適合性または商品性の保証を明確に否認する。

use big data　ビッグ・データを利用する,ビッグ・データを活用する
◆As the value of using big data, a sales practice prevailing in the mail-order business sector is to analyze purchase records of customers and then recommend products based on their tastes and preferences. ビッグ・データの利用価値として、通販業界で広がっている販売手法は、顧客の購入履歴を分析して、顧客の好みに合う商品を薦める方法だ。

use one's best efforts　最善の努力をする,最大限の努力をする
◆ABC shall not disclose any information it receives from XYZ to any third party, and shall use its best efforts to prevent inadvertent disclosure of any information it receives from XYZ to any third party. ABCは、XYZから受領した情報をいかなる第三者にも一切開示しないものとし、またXYZから受領した情報をいかなる第三者にも不用意に開示しないよう最善の努力をしなければならない。

user　（名）使用者,利用者,消費者,顧客,加入者,会員,投資家,ユーザー
active service user　使用頻度の高いユーザー
actual user　実需筋
end user　最終使用者,一般使用者,最終利用者,最終投資家,エンド・ユーザー
fake user　サクラ
major user　大口ユーザー
user account　ユーザー識別符号,ユーザー・アカウント（ユーザーのパスワードやユーザーID,所属するグループなどの情報）
user agreement　利用規約,利用契約
user authentication　ユーザー認証
user charge　利用者料金
user fee　受益者負担金
user-friendly　ユーザーに使いやすい,使いやすい,使い勝手がよい,操作が簡単な,ユーザーに親しみやすい,ユーザーに分かりやすい,利用者に親切な
user-hostile　使いにくい,使いづらい,ユーザーに親しみにくい,不便
user identification　ユーザー登録名,ユーザー識別コード,ユーザーID
user-oriented　ユーザー志向の
user［user's］registration　ユーザー登録
user-unfriendly　使いにくい,ユーザーに親しみにくい　（=user-hostile）
user's manual　取扱い説明書,ユーザー・マニュアル
◆A major Internet shopping mall program which began in March 2000 allows payments to be made immediately through the bank accounts of users. 2000年3月にスタートした大規模なインターネット上の仮想商店街プログラムは、利用者の銀行口座から即時決済できる。

USTR 米国通商代表, 米通商代表部 （=U.S. ［United States］Trade Representative）
◆Despite strong criticism from Washington's trading partners against high tariffs on steel imports to rescue the ailing U.S. steel industry, the USTR stressed the legitimacy of such safeguard measures. 不況の米鉄鋼業界を救済するための輸入鉄鋼製品に対する高関税について、米国の貿易相手国から強い批判がなされているにもかかわらず、米国通商代表はこの緊急輸入制限（セーフガード）措置の正当性を強調した。

usury law 利息制限法
◆Interest shall accrue on any delinquent amounts owed by Distributor for Products at the lesser of 18% per annum, or the maximum rate permitted by applicable usury law. 利息は、販売店が負っている本製品の延滞金について発生し、年18%の利率と適用される利息制限法で認められる最高利率のうちいずれか低いほうの利率によるものとする。

utility model 実用新案, 実用新案権, 新案特許権（物品の形状、構造や組合せに係わる考案）
application for utility model registration 実用新案登録出願
certificate of utility model registration 実用新案登録証
claim of utility model 実用新案登録請求の範囲
owner of utility model 実用新案権者
utility model gazette 実用新案公報
utility model law 実用新案法
utility model registration 実用新案登録
utility model right 実用新案権
◆The seller shall not be responsible for any infringement with regard to patents, utility models, designs, trademarks, copyrights, trade secrets or any other intellectual property rights in any country, except for the seller's country, in connection with the sales, use or delivery of the products. 売り主は、本製品の販売、使用と引渡しに関連する特許、実用新案、意匠、商標、著作権、トレード・シークレットまたはその他の知的財産権に関する侵害に対しては、売り主の国を除いていずれの国においても責任を負わないものとする。

utility or communication failures 共益設備または通信設備の不能

V

vacancy （名）空位, 空席, 欠員, 空き事務所, 空き部屋, 空き地, 空き家状態
◆In case of the death, resignation or other removal of a director prior to the expiration of his term, the parties hereto agree to cast their votes as shareholders, so as to appoint as his replacement a director nominated by the party hereto who has nominated the director whose death,
resignation or other removal was the cause of such vacancy. 取締役の任期満了前に取締役が死亡、辞任またはその他の理由で退任した場合、本契約当事者は、その死亡、辞任その他の理由による退任で当該欠員を生じさせた取締役を指名した本契約当事者が後任取締役を指名できるように、株主としてその議決権を行使することに合意する。◆The term of office of a director elected to fill a vacancy shall be the same term with the remainder of the term of office of his predecessor. 欠員補充のために選任された取締役の任期は、前任者の残りの任期と同じとする。

validated export license 輸出承認の許可
◆Recipient shall not transfer any confidential information received hereunder or any product made using such confidential information, to any country prohibited from obtaining such data or product by the U.S. Department of Commerce Export Administration Regulations without first obtaining a validated export license. 受領者は、本契約に従って受領した秘密情報またはこの秘密情報を使用して製造した製品を、米国商務省の輸出管理規則により当該データまたは製品の提供が禁止されている国に対して、最初に輸出承認の許可を得ないで譲渡することはないものとする。

validity （名）効力, 有効性, 正当性, 妥当性, 適法性, 合法性, 発効, 承認, 有効期間
the validity of this contract 本契約の効力
validity, construction or effect of this agreement 本契約の有効性、解釈もしくは効果, 本契約の効力、解釈または効果

validity of this Article 本条の効力
◆This in no way changes the validity of this Article. これは、決して本条の効力を変更するものではない。

value （名）価額, 価格, 評価額, 簿価, 金額 （動）（為替）手形を振り出す
book value 簿価
CIF value CIF価格
invoice value 送り状価格, 送り状金額, 請求金額
market value 市価, 時価
the corresponding value of an order 注文相当額
value in Japanese Yen 日本円に相当する金額
value upon you 貴社に手形を振り出す （=draw a draft upon you）
◆In global currency wars, central banks effectively lower the value of their countries' currencies to boost their countries' export competitiveness. 世界の通貨安競争では、自国の輸出競争力を高めるため、中央銀行が自国通貨の価値を事実上切り下げる［自国通貨の為替相場を事実上安くする］。
◆Our terms of payment are to value at 30 d/s under an irrevocable letter of credit to be opened in our favor for the corresponding value of an order. 当社の決済条件は、注文相当額につき、当社を受

益者として開設された取消不能信用状に基づいて一覧後30日払いの手形を振り出すことです。◆The value of South Korea's trade with China since it established diplomatic relations with Beijing has expanded to such an extent that it has surpassed its combined trade with Japan and the United States. 韓国が中国と国交を樹立して以来、韓国の対中貿易額は、対日・対米の貿易総額を凌駕 (りょうが) するまでに拡大している。◆We have valued upon you today for the amount specified above, at sight, and ask you to accord our draft your due protection. 当社は本日、貴社宛てに上記金額に対する一覧払い手形を振り出しましたので、この手形のお引受けをお願い致します。

value-added （形）付加価値の, 付加価値のある, 付加価値の高い, 高付加価値の

　innovative value-added goods　革新的な付加価値製品

　value added entity　付加価値再販売業者

　value added reseller　付加価値再販売業者

value-added goods 付加価値のある商品, 付加価値製品　(=value-added product)
　◆The investment fund is aiming to use dormant patents owned by companies and universities to produce high-value added goods across a wide range of industries. 同投資ファンドは、企業や大学が保有している休眠特許を利用して、幅広い産業分野での付加価値の高い商品作りを目指している。

value-added tax 付加価値税, VAT
　(⇒VAT)
　◆In Britain, the value added tax, a form of consumption tax, is set at 20 percent, but the rate for daily necessities such as groceries and newspapers is zero. 英国では、消費税にあたる付加価値税の税率は20%だが、食品や新聞など生活必需品の税率は0%だ。

value chain 価値連鎖
　◆Due to the IT revolution and trade liberalization, product specialization now is determined by comparative advantages not in finished products but in work unique to each country or region in the context of global value chains. 情報通信技術 (IT) 革命と貿易自由化で、製品の特化は、「最終財」の比較優位ではなく、国際的価値連鎖との関連で国・地域にそれぞれ特有の「仕事」の比較優位で決まるようになった。

value of agricultural exports 農産品輸出額
　◆The LDP aims at doubling agricultural income and the value of agricultural exports, but its road map to achieve this target is unclear. 自民党は農業所得や農産品輸出額の倍増を目指しているが、この目標実現への道筋は曖昧だ。

value of bitcoin ビットコインの相場
　(=the market value of bitcoin)
　◆Bitcoin, a virtual currency circulated on the Internet, is traded in units of BTC. The value of bitcoin fluctuates excessively, but bitcoin has hov-

ered at about $800 per BTC lately. ネット上で流通している仮想通貨「ビットコイン」は、BTCの単位で取引されている。ビットコインの相場は乱高下があまりにも激しいが、最近は1BTC=800ドル前後で推移している。

value of oil imports 原油輸入額
　◆The value of oil imports in September jumped 62 percent year-on-year. 9月の原油輸入額は、前年同月比で62%急増した。

value of South Korea's trade with China 韓国の対中貿易額
　◆The value of South Korea's trade with China since it established diplomatic relations with Beijing has expanded to such an extent that it has surpassed its combined trade with Japan and the United States. 韓国が中国と国交を樹立して以来、韓国の対中貿易額は、対日・対米の貿易総額を凌駕 (りょうが) するまでに拡大している。

value of the won ウォン相場, ウォンの為替相場, ウォンの価値
　◆Due to the ongoing European financial crisis, concern is mounting in South Korea that the value of its won currency［the value of the won］may steeply decline if foreign financial institutions and investors withdraw funds from the country. 今回の欧州の金融危機で韓国では、海外の金融機関や投資家が韓国から資金を引き揚げたら、ウォン相場が急落しかねないとの懸念が高まっている。

value of using big data ビッグ・データの利用価値
　◆As the value of using big data, a sales practice prevailing in the mail-order business sector is to analyze purchase records of customers and then recommend products based on their tastes and preferences. ビッグ・データの利用価値として、通販業界で広がっている販売手法は、顧客の購入履歴を分析して、顧客の好みに合う商品を薦める方法だ。

values of overseas earnings 海外収益の額
　◆As the yen's decline inflated the values of overseas earnings when converted into yen, the income account surplus in July 2013 hit a record high for July. 円安で円換算したときの海外収益額が膨らんだため、2013年7月の所得収支の黒字額は、7月としては過去最大だった。

vanning （名）コンテナ詰め
　vanning report　コンテナ詰め報告書
　　(=container certificate, vanning certificate)

variation （名）変動, 変化, 変更, 変異, 変種, 変形, 異形
　◆Quantity is subject to a variation of 5% more or less than the contracted quantity at Seller's option unless otherwise specified. 数量は、他にとくに明記しないかぎり、売り主の裁量で契約数量より5%増減の変動が生じることがある。

VAT 付加価値税 (value-added taxの略)
　◆Net Wholesale Price referred to in this agree-

ment is defined as the amount of the gross sales by ABC of the licensed products to ABC's customers in the territory, less customary trade discounts, insurance premiums, transportation and delivery charges, taxes（VAT）and duties. 本契約書に記載する「純卸売り販売額」とは、ABCの顧客に対する契約地域内でのABCの許諾製品の総売上高（総販売額）から、通常の卸売り割引額、保険料、運送・引渡し費用、税金（付加価値税）と関税を差し引いた額のことをいう。

venue （名）裁判地, 開催地, 会場

　a change of venue　裁判地の変更

　governing law and venue　準拠法と裁判地

verify （動）確認する, 証明する, 立証する

　verify or determine　確認または決定する

vessel （名）本船, 船舶

　a cargo vessel　貨物船

　approved vessel　標準規格船

　capesize vessel　大型船（ケープサイズ型）

　carrying vessel　本船, 運送船, 輸送船

　charter-in vessel　用船　(=chartered vessel)

　chartered foreign-flag vessel　外国用船

　class of vessel　船級

　coasting vessel　沿岸航行船
　　(=ocean-going vessel)

　combination vessel　貨客船

　flag-on-convenience vessel　便宜置籍船

　foreign vessel　外国船

　free vessel　フリー船

　handy（size）vessel　小型船　(=small
　　vessel)

　lighter aboard ship handling vessel　ラッ
　　シュ船

　medium-sized vessel　中規模船

　merchant vessel　商船

　ocean-going［sea-going］vessel　大洋航行船,
　　航洋船

　ocean vessel　外航船舶, 外航船

　subject to approval of quality on arrival of
　　vessel　本船到着後品質点検の条件付きで

　substituting vessel　代船

　the first available vessel　第一便船

　the rail of the sea-going vessel　本船の欄干

　vessel clearance　船舶出向手続き

　vessel construction contract　船舶建造契約

　vessel entry　船舶入港手続き

　vessel management company　船舶管理会社

　vessel number　便名

　vessel tonnage　船舶トン数

　vessel's discretion　本船の意向

　vessel's trim　荷ならし

　◆Risks of and title to the products shall pass

from the seller to the purchaser at the time when the products or any part of the products passes the ship's rail of the vessel at the port of the shipment. 本製品の危険負担と所有権は、本製品または本製品の一部が船積み港で本船の舷側欄干を通過した時点で、売り主から買い主に移転するものとする。◆The purchaser shall effect, at its own expense, marine insurance on each cargo of the products from the point where such cargo passes the rail of the vessel of the port of the shipment. 買い主は、買い主の自己費用で、本製品の各貨物が船舶積み港の本船の舷側欄干を越える時点から、当該貨物に海上保険を付けるものとする。

vessel's intake　本船の貨物受入口

　◆Risk of and title to the products shall pass from the seller to the purchaser when the products pass the flange connection between the delivery hose and the vessel's intake. 本製品の危険負担と所有権は、本製品が引渡し用ホースと本船の貨物受入口とのフランジ接続点を通過した時点で、売り主から買い主に移転する。

vest （動）権利・権限を与える, 付与する, 権利が帰属する

　◆Responsibility for the management and direction of the new company shall be vested in the board of directors of the new company. 新会社の経営と指揮に対する責任は、新会社の取締役会に帰属する。

violate （動）（約束などを）破る, 裏切る, （法律、契約、規則などに）違反する, 侵害する, 侵犯する, 犯す, 汚す, 冒瀆（ぼうとく）する, （条項などに）触れる, （睡眠などを）妨げる, 乱す

　◆Imports of pirated designer goods violate commercial brand rights. 偽ブランド品の輸入は、商標権の侵害に当たる。◆There is a contractual clause stipulating that Japanese PC makers will take no legal action even if Microsoft Corp.'s technologies are deemed to violate their patents. マイクロソフト社の技術が日本のパソコン・メーカーの特許侵害にあたるとしても、日本のパソコン・メーカーは法的措置を一切取らない［訴訟を起こさない］、と定めた契約条項がある。

violation （名）違反, 侵害, 妨害, 暴行, 意味の曲解

　serious violation of one's obligations　〜の義務の重大違反

　the problem of patent violation　特許侵害問題

　violation of antimonopoly law　独占禁止法違反

　violation of covenant　契約違反

　violation of law　法律違反

　◆Mitsubishi UFJ Financial Group Inc. agreed to pay $8.6 million to the Treasury Department's Office of Foreign Assets Control to settle alleged U.S. sanction violations related to the transfer of funds to client accounts in Myanmar, Iran and Cuba. 三菱UFJフィナンシャル・グループは、ミャンマーやイラン、キューバなどの顧客口座に行っ

た送金に関して、米国の経済制裁規制に違反した疑いで、米財務省外国資産管理局に860万ドルの和解金を支払うことで合意した。

virtual currency 仮想通貨
◆Bitcoin, an online currency, is illegal in Thailand and financial services involving bitcoin are banned in China, but the virtual currency has been spreading around the world online. ネット通貨のビットコインはタイでは違法で、ビットコイン関連の金融サービス［ビットコインを使った金融サービス］は中国では禁止されているが、この仮想通貨はネット上で世界に拡散している。◆Bitcoin, which has attracted great attention as it can be remitted at low fees, is a virtual currency circulated only on the Internet. 安い手数料で送金できるので大いに注目を集めているビットコインは、インターネット上だけで流通している仮想通貨である。

virtual engineering 仮想エンジニアリング，バーチャル・エンジニアリング
◆In step with the growing popularity of virtual engineering, the United States has launched a national strategy aimed at reinvigorating its manufacturing sector. バーチャル・エンジニアリング［仮想エンジニアリング］の普及とともに、米国は製造業の再活性化をめざした国家戦略を打ち出した。

visible （形）目に見える，見える，有形の，明らかな，はっきりした，目立った，よく目にする，よく登場する，出演する，面会できる，会う気のある（⇒invisible）
visible asset　有形資産
visible current item　貿易経常項目
visible current transaction　貿易経常取引
visible earnings stream　明白な増益見通し
visible effects　目立った効果
visible goods　有形財
visible imports　有形品輸入
visible payment　貿易支払い
visible receipt　貿易受取り
visible stock　市場在庫

visible trade 貿易取引，商品貿易，有形品貿易，貿易収支
balance of visible trade　貿易収支（=trade balance, visible balance, visible trade balance）
visible trade balance　貿易収支
visible trade deficit　貿易収支の赤字
visible trade surplus　貿易収支の黒字

visit （名）訪問，視察，滞在
◆The period, time, method, and reasonable details of such visits shall be determined separately through mutual consultation between the parties. このような訪問［視察］の期間、時期、方法と合理的な詳細は、当事者間の相互協議により別途決定するものとする。

void ab initio 遡及的に無効，当初から無効

（ab initio=from the beginning）

void or unenforceable 無効または実施不能
◆If any provision or any portion of any provision of this agreement shall be held to be void or unenforceable, the remaining provisions of this agreement and the remaining portion of any provision held void or unenforceable in part shall continue in full force and effect. 本契約の規定またはその一部が無効または実施不能と判断された場合、本契約の残りの規定と、一部が無効または実施不能と判断された規定の残りの部分は、すべて有効に存続するものとする。

volume of exports 輸出量
◆The yen's appreciation will not only reduce the volume of exports but also harm a wide variety of other areas. 円高は輸出の減少だけでなく、その弊害は広範に及ぶ。

volume of imports 輸入量
◆Under the World Trade Organization rules, emergency import limits, or safeguard, are permitted as a temporary measure if the volume of imports of a certain product drastically increases, causing serious damages to industries concerned in the country. 世界貿易機関（WTO）のルールでは、緊急輸入制限措置（セーフガード）は、特定製品の輸入量が増加して、国内の関係業界に大きな被害が出ている場合には、一時的な措置として認められる。

voluntarily or involuntarily 自発的または強制的に

voluntary dissolution 任意解散，自発的解散

voluntary proceedings in bankruptcy 自発的な破産手続き

voluntary recall 自主回収
◆Following the discovery of frozen food products tainted with a pesticide known as malathion, Maruha Nichiro Holdings Inc. announced a voluntary recall of the products made by its subsidiary Aqli Foods. マラチオンと呼ばれる農薬（殺虫剤）が混入した冷凍食品が検出されたのを受けて、マルハニチロホールディングス（HD）は、子会社のアクリフーズ社が生産［製造］した冷凍食品を自主回収すると発表した。

vote （動）投票する，票決する，投票で決める，議決する，株式の議決権を行使する，提案する，動議を出す，（世評）〜と認める，〜と見なす
◆The term "Subsidiary" shall mean a corporation, more than fifty percent （50%） of whose outstanding shares representing the right to vote for the election of directors, are, now or hereafter, owned or controlled, directly or indirectly, by a party hereto. 「子会社」という語は、取締役選任のための議決権を表す発行済み株式の50%超が、本契約の一当事者によって直接・間接的に現在または今後所有されるか支配される法人を意味する。

vote （名）投票，投票用紙，票，得票，票決，決

議, 投票権, 議決権, 票決権, 選挙権
affirmative vote　賛成投票
one vote for each share　1株につき1議決権
◆Each party hereto shall have one vote for each share of which it is the holder and may be present at any meeting of shareholders either in person or by proxy. 本契約の各当事者は、自ら所有する1株につき1票の議決権を持ち、本人またはその代理人が株主総会に出席することができる。◆The board of directors may act at a meeting at which a quorum is present by the affirmative vote of a majority of those present at such meeting. 取締役会は、定足数の取締役が出席した会議で、出席取締役の過半数の賛成投票により決議することができる。

voting　(名)投票, 投票権行使, 議決権行使
abstain from the voting　投票[採決]を棄権する
by voting in the aggregate　単純合計の投票により
electronic voting　電子投票
nonvoting delegate　投票権を持たない代表者
plural voting　連記投票
proxy voting　代理投票
single voting　単記投票
super voting share　複数議決権株式
voting agreement　議決権契約, 票決契約
voting bond　議決権付き社債
voting by ballot　秘密投票, 無記名投票
voting by proxy　代理人による議決権の行使
voting list　投票名簿
voting power　議決権, 投票権　(=voting right: 株主が会社の総会で各種の重要な決議に参加できる権利のこと。一般に、普通株式1株につき1個の議決権が与えられている)
voting register　選挙人名簿
voting trust　議決権信託
voting trust arrangement　議決権信託契約
voting upon stocks　株式に基づく投票

voting right　議決権
◆Each party shall exercise its voting rights so that the persons nominated by the other party shall be elected as directors. 各当事者は、その議決権を行使して、相手方が指名した者が取締役に選任されるようにしなければならない。

voting share　議決権付き株式, 議決権株式
(=voting stock)
◆Pursuant to the terms of the articles of association of the Joint Venture Company, ABC will have an initial ownership interest of forty percent of the voting shares of the Joint Venture Company. 合弁会社の定款の規定に従って、ABCの当初の出資比率は、合弁会社の議決権付き株式の40%とする。

W

waive　(動)権利などを放棄する
(⇒motion, sovereign immunity)
◆If the purchaser fails to comply with the above stipulation, the purchaser shall be deemed to have waived such claim. 買い主が上記規定に従わない場合、買い主は当該クレームを放棄したものと見なされるものとする。◆The guarantor waives any and all notices of nonpayment or nonperformance or demand for payment or performance of such obligations under the franchise agreement. 保証人は、フランチャイズ契約に基づく当該債務の不払いまたは不履行について一切の通知を受ける権利と、当該債務の支払いまたは履行について一切の催告通知を受ける権利を放棄する。

waiver of any claim, demand or right
請求、要求または権利の放棄
◆A waiver of any claim, demand or right based on the breach of any provision of this agreement shall not constitute a waiver of any other claim, demand or right based on a subsequent breach of the same or any other provision. 本契約の規定違反に基づく請求、要求または権利の放棄は、同じ規定または他の規定のその後の違反に基づく他の請求、要求または権利の放棄とはならないものとする。

waiver thereof or of any other right or remedy　その権利放棄またはその他の権利放棄、救済の権利放棄
◆No delay or omission in exercising any right or remedy hereunder shall operate as a waiver thereof or of any other right or remedy. 本契約に基づく権利または救済の行使の遅滞または不作為は、その権利放棄、その他の権利の放棄、または救済の権利放棄としては作用しないものとする。

war　(名)戦争, 紛争, 争い, 戦い, 競争, 運動, 活動
an act of war　戦争行為
avert a currency war　通貨戦争を回避する
civil war　内戦, 内乱
deposit war　預金戦争, 預金獲得競争
loan war　ローン戦争
price war　安売り競争, 安売り合戦, 値下げ競争
prolonged war　長引く戦争, 長期の戦い, 長期戦
tariff war　関税戦争
trade war　貿易戦争
turf war　縄張り争い
war chest　運動資金, 活動資金, 軍資金
war (declared or not)　戦争 (宣戦布告の有無を問わない)
war (declared or undeclared)　戦争 (宣戦布告されているか否かを問わない)

war of the elements　自然災害, 嵐

war situation　戦況

wars（declared or undeclared）　戦争（宣戦布告の有無を問わず）, 戦争（宣戦布告のあるなしを問わず）

◆A price war with its rivals rumbles on. ライバル［ライバル企業］との安売り合戦は, 続いている。◆Currency wars will cause turmoil in global markets and adversely impact the world economy if the wars become common practice. 通貨安戦争［通貨安競争］が広がれば, 世界の市場の混乱を招き, 世界経済に悪影響を及ぼすことになる。◆Home electrical appliances including TVs have been exposed to fierce price wars. テレビなどの家電製品は, 激しい価格競争にさらされてきた。◆In a currency war, countries intentionally devalue their currencies to boost exports. 通貨安戦争では, 各国が輸出に追い風となるように自国通貨の為替レートを意図的に安く誘導する。◆In global currency wars, central banks effectively lower the value of their countries' currencies to boost their countries' export competitiveness. 世界の通貨安競争では, 自国の輸出競争力を高めるため, 中央銀行が自国通貨の価値を事実上切り下げる［自国通貨の為替相場を事実上安くする］。◆Japan stood defiant in an escalating trade war with China. 過熱する中国との貿易戦争で, 日本は一歩も引かない姿勢を示した。

war risks　戦争危険, 戦争保険

解説 戦争危険に含まれるもの：

civil war　内乱

insurrection　反乱

rebellion　反逆

revolution　革命

war　戦争

warehouse　（名）倉庫

bonded warehouse　保税倉庫

commercial warehouse　営業倉庫

ex warehouse　倉庫渡し

warehouse charges　倉庫料

warehouse goods　倉荷, 入庫貨物

warehouse in　倉庫入れ

warehouse stock　製品在庫

◆For the purpose of this agreement, Licensor may from time to time inspect Licensee's plants, offices, or warehouses. 本契約の目的上, ライセンサーは, ライセンシーの工場, 営業所または倉庫の検査を随時行うことができる。

warrant　（動）保証する, 正当化する

◆The seller warrants that the Goods will be free from defects in material and workmanship for a period as specified in this agreement. 売り主は, 本契約で定める期間, 本商品が材料と仕上げの面で欠陥がないことを保証する。

warrant　（名）権限, 権能, 認可, 保証, 権限証書, 証明書, 許可書, 株式買取り請求権, 倉荷証券, 令状, ワラント

◆About 15 percent of the leading companies are studying the possibility of using a poison pill to counter a hostile takeover by using the issue of warrants. 主要企業の約15％は, 新株予約権の発行などで敵対的買収に対抗するポイズン・ピル（毒薬）の導入可能性を検討している。

warrant and represent　～を保証し表明する, ～を保証しこれを表明する

◆The seller warrants and represents that the products will conform to their descriptions set forth in Exhibit D. 売り主は, 本製品が付属書類Dに記載する本製品の明細に合致することを保証し, 表明する。

warrantee　（名）被保証人, 被担保人, 被担保提供者

◆Throughout this agreement, Warrantee shall attempt to maintain an insurance policy to cover any claim, demand, liability, suit, damage or expense caused by Warrantee negligence. 本契約期間を通じて, 被保証人は, 被保証人の過失によって生じるクレーム, 要求, 責任, 訴訟, 損害または費用を担保する保険証券の維持に努めるものとする。

warranties or representations　保証または表明

◆The seller makes no other warranties or representations with respect to the products and disclaims all warranties, including but not limited to implied warranties of merchantability, fitness for a particular purpose and noninfringement. 売り主は, 本製品に関する他の保証または表明は行わず, 商品性, 特定目的への適合性および非侵害の黙示の保証などを含めてすべての保証を否認する。

warranty　（名）保証, 保証責任, 担保, 担保責任, 瑕疵（かし）担保, 付随条項, 保険契約での真実性の保証（商品やサービスの品質についての保証で, 契約履行の保証やローン返済の保証には使われない）

exclusion of implied warranty　黙示的保証の除外

express or implied warranty　明示・黙示の保証

express warranty　明示の保証, 明示の担保, 明示の品質保証

implied warranty　黙示の保証, 黙示の担保, 黙示の品質保証

implied warranty of merchantability　商品性の黙示的保証

limitation and exclusion of warranties　保証の制限・排除

limited warranties　保証責任の限度, 保証の制限, 有限保証

without warranty of any kind　一切の保証なしで, 無保証で

◆Lender makes no warranty, express, implied or statutory with respect to the Equipment, including but not limited to the warranties of noninfringement, merchantability, title, and fitness for a particular purpose. 貸主は、権利の非侵害、商品性、所有権と特定目的適合性の保証などを含めて、「機器」に関して明示、黙示もしくは制定法上の保証は一切しない。◆The Purchaser, in reliance upon the covenants, representations and warranties of the Seller contained in this agreement, is willing to purchase from the Seller the said shares of the Company. 買い主は、本契約に定める売り主の約束、表明とその保証を信頼して、売り主から本会社の当該株式を買い受けることを希望している。

warranty of fitness for a [any] particular purpose 特定目的への適合性の保証, 特定目的への適合性の担保責任
◆No other warranties of any kind, whether statutory, written, oral, express or implied, including warranties of fitness for a particular purpose or merchantability shall apply. 特定目的への適合性または商品性の保証を含めて、法定か書面によるか口頭によるかを問わず、また明示・黙示を問わず、他のいかなる種類の保証も適用されないものとする。

warranty or consideration 保証または条件
◆The seller shall not be liable in respect of any warranty or consideration as to quality or fitness which would arise by implication of law. 売り主は、法律の運用により生じる品質または適合性に関する保証または条件については、責任を負わないものとする。

Wassenaar Arrangement ワッセナー協約, 新国際輸出管理機構, ワッセナー・アレンジメント（通常兵器と関連する民生品・技術の輸出を規制する国際的な枠組み。1994年に解散した対共産圏輸出統制委員会（ココム）に代わる体制として96年に発足し、ウィーンに事務局が置かれる。2014年12月の年次総会では、日米露独仏英など41か国が、軍事向けに転用できる民生品の国際取引の監視を強化することで合意した。輸出規制の対象となっている民生品には、ミサイルの胴体部分に使える炭素繊維などの先端材料や、全地球測位システム（GPS）、高性能コンピュータなどがある）

waybill （名）運送状, 貨物運送状, 乗客名簿
 air waybill 航空運送状, AWB
 sea waybill 海上運送状, SWB

we （代）当社, わが社, 当方
◆We were asked to send out tracers by them. 当社は、同社に揚げ荷事故照会状を出すよう依頼された。

weak yen 円安 （⇒cost of imports, import cost, yen's exchange rate）
◆As many domestic manufacturers have moved their production sites from Japan to Asian nations and elsewhere, the Japanese economy benefits less and less from the weak yen which lowers export costs. 国内製造業の多くが生産拠点を日本からアジアなどに移しているため、日本経済は、輸出コストが下がる円安メリットを享受しにくくなっている。◆At present, export industries including home appliances and automobiles are raising their expectations for improved corporate performance under the weak yen, which has also driven up stock prices. 現在、家電や自動車などの輸出産業は、円安で業績改善の期待を高めており、円安はまた株価も押し上げた。◆Japanese exporting firms have been enjoying positive earnings, benefiting from thriving markets in the United States and the weak yen. 日本の輸出企業は、米国の好調な市場と円安を追い風に、好業績が続いている。

weakening of the yen 円安
◆Toyota revised upward its consolidated operating profit estimates for the business year ending March 31, 2013, largely due to improved profitability in its exports from a weakening of the yen in response to "Abenomics," the economic policy of the Abe administration. トヨタは2013年3月期決算［2013年3月31日終了事業年度］の連結営業利益予想［連結業績予想］を上方修正したが、これは主に安倍政権の経済政策「アベノミクス」を好感しての円安で、輸出の採算が向上しているためだ。

weaker dollar ドル安
◆The United States is under pressure to make some difficult monetary policy decisions to cool down the overheating economy by countering the inflationary pressure stemming from higher import prices due to the weaker dollar. 米国は現在、ドル安での輸入価格の高騰によるインフレ圧力を抑えて、過熱気味の景気を鎮めるための難しい金融政策の決断を迫られている。

weaker yen 円安
◆Japan's services trade deficit in July 2013 was reduced by about 40 percent to ￥196.5 billion thanks to an increase in the number of visitors to Japan due to the weaker yen and a rise in patent royalty revenues. 2013年7月の日本のサービス収支の赤字は、円安で日本を訪れる外国人旅行者が増えたことや特許権使用料の収入が増えたため、約4割縮小して1,965億円となった。◆The weaker yen helps exporters, but close attention must be paid to the fact that the excessive depreciation of the yen will further increase the prices of imports of LNG and other foreign products. 円安は輸出企業にはプラスだが、円安が行き過ぎると、天然液化ガス（LNG）など海外製品の輸入額が一段と増えることにも、警戒が必要である。

weapons development 兵器開発
◆In April 2002, the government enforced socalled catch-all regulations aimed at controlling exports of goods and technology linked to weapons development. 2002年4月から政府は、兵器開発関連の機器と技術の輸出を取り締まるため、いわゆる「キャッチオール規制」を施行した。

website （名）サイト, ウェブサイト （=Web

site）

a mail order website　通販サイト

a paid website　有料ウェブサイト

an overseas website　海外サイト

◆About 70 websites which sold bogus pharmaceutical products on the Internet were forcibly shut down from April to September 2014 by the health ministry. インターネット上で偽造医薬品を販売していた約70サイトを、厚生労働省が、2014年4～9月に強制的に閉鎖した。

weight （名）重さ, 重量, 体重, 重荷, 負担, 圧迫, 重圧, 重要性, 有力, 勢力, 加重値, 厚み, 重み, 構成比率, ウェート

credit risk weight　与信リスクのウェート

dead weight ton　重量トン

gross weight　総重量

net weight　純重量, 正味重量

security weights　証券の組入れ比率

weights and measures　度量衡

whatsoever （副）まったく〜ない（=whatever:noなどの否定語を伴って at allの意味）

◆ABC shall take care of keeping its quality without any harm whatsoever as bona fide holder of Products on behalf of XYZ. ABCは、XYZを代理する契約品［本製品］の善意の保管者として、契約品［本製品］の品質保持上、どんな損害も生じないよう注意を払うものとする。

when due　支払い期日に, 期日に, 返済期日に, 期日が到来した, 満期が過ぎたとき

◆If the buyer fails to pay any amount under this agreement when due, the buyer shall be liable to pay to the seller overdue interest on such unpaid amount from the due date until the actual payment date at the rate of 15% per annum. 買い主が支払い期日に本契約に基づく代金の支払いを怠った場合、買い主は、支払い期日から実際の払込み日までの当該未払い金額に対する年率15%の遅延金利を、売り主に支払わなければならない。

whether by operation of law or otherwise　法律の運用によるかその他の方法によるかを問わず

◆Without first obtaining the written consent of other parties hereto, no party, nor its successors or assignees, shall sell, assign, transfer, pledge, encumber or otherwise dispose of, whether by operation of law or otherwise, any shares of voting of the new company or instruments convertible into such shares. 他の本契約当事者の書面による同意を最初に得ないで、いずれの当事者も、その承継人または譲受人も、法律の運用によるかその他の方法によるかを問わず、新会社の議決権付き株式またはこのような株式に転換できる証書を売却、譲渡、移転、質入れ、担保差入れ、その他の方法で処分することはしないものとする。

whether directly or indirectly　直接間接を問わず, 直接的にも間接的にも

◆For a period of 5 years from the Closing date, Seller shall not engage or be interested, whether directly or indirectly, in any business in any place in which the Company now transact its business that would be in competition with business as now transacted by the Company. クロージング日から5年間、売り主は、対象会社が現在その事業を行っている場所で、対象会社が現在行っている事業と競合する事業に直接間接を問わず従事せず、また係らないものとする。

whether express〔expressed〕or implied　明示・黙示を問わず

◆The seller does not make and hereby disclaim any warranty in respect of the products other than as provided above in this Article, whether express or implied, including without limitation any implied warranty of merchantability or fitness for any purpose. 売り主は、商品性または特定目的への適合性の黙示保証などを含めて、本条の規定以外に明示・黙示を問わず本製品に関する保証を一切行わず、本製品に関する保証を本契約により否認する。

whether or not in the ordinary course of business　通常の業務過程であるか否かを問わず

◆No material commitments, bids or bidding offers will be entered into by the Company in any case in excess of $10,000 whether or not in the ordinary course of business, except with the prior written consent of Purchaser. 買い主の書面による事前の同意がある場合を除いて、対象会社は、通常の業務過程であるか否かを問わずどんな場合でも1万ドルを超える重要な約束、入札、入札の申込みは行わないものとする。

whichever is greater　（〜と〜のうち）いずれか多いほう,（〜と〜のうち）いずれか大きいほう

◆At least the licensee shall in each year spend on advertising and promoting the licensed products as amount equal to ＿＿% of the total net sales amount of the licensed productsinvoiced in the previous year or ＿＿U.S. dollars, whichever is greater, in accordance with the advertisement plan to be approved by the licensor. 少なくともライセンシーは毎年、前年度に仕切った許諾製品の純売上総額の＿＿%に相当する金額と＿＿米ドルのうちいずれか多いほうの金額を、ライセンサーが承認する宣伝計画に従って宣伝と販売促進に使うものとする。

whichever is lower　（〜と〜のうち）いずれか低いほう

◆In the event the full amount of any invoice issued by the seller under this agreement is not paid by the purchaser when due, any unpaid amount shall bear interest from the due date until paid in full, at an interest of 14 percent per year or the maximum interest rate permitted by the usury law of the purchaser's country, if any, whichever is lower, on the basis of 360 days. 本契約に基づいて売り主が発行した請求書の全額を

買い主が支払い期日に支払わない場合、未払い金額には、この支払い期日から全額を支払うまで、1年を360日として年14％の利息と買い主の国の利息制限法で認められている最高利率のうちいずれか低いほうの利率で利息が付くものとする。

white knight 白馬の騎士, 友好的買収者, 善意の買収者, 友好的な支援者, 友好的な第三者, 友好的企業, 友好的株主, ホワイト・ナイト（ホワイト・ナイトは, 敵対的買収を防ぐ手法として, 敵対的なM&A（企業の合併・買収）にさらされている企業が, 友好的な関係にある別の企業に自社を買収してもらうこと。）
◆A "white knight" is a friendly acquirer sought by the target of an unfriendly takeover. 「ホワイト・ナイト」とは, 非友好的買収の標的企業が探し求める友好的買収者をいう。◆White knight is a company that saves another firm threatened by a hostile takeover by making a friendly offer. ホワイト・ナイトは, 友好的な買収により, 敵対的買収の脅威にさらされている他企業を救済する企業のことだ。

willing to ～する用意がある, ～する意思がある, ～する意図がある, ～したいと思う
◆The Purchaser, in reliance upon the covenants, representations and warranties of the Seller contained in this agreement, is willing to purchase from the Seller the said shares of the Company. 買い主は, 本契約に定める売り主の約束, 表明とその保証を信頼して, 売り主から本会社の当該株式を買い受けることを希望している。

win an order 受注する
◆Mitsubishi Heavy Industries Ltd. aims to win orders for commercial launches of foreign satellites with a current lineup of its core H-2A and H-2B rockets. 三菱重工業は, 現在の主力ロケットH2AとH2Bロケットの二本柱で, 外国の衛星の商用打上げ受注を目指している。

wind up 解散する, 清算する, 畳（たた）む, 閉鎖する, 事業停止する, 整理する, 中止する, 切り上げる, 終える, 辞める, ～で終わる, 結局～することになる, 結局～する羽目になる, 最後には～に行き着く［～で終わる］, 緊張させる, いらいらさせる
be wound up 閉鎖される, 中止される
wind up an account 口座を清算する
wind up an ailing company 経営不振の会社を解散する
wind up the meeting 会議を切り上げる
◆To wind up the ailing unit, its parent company sold some of its assets. 経営不振のこの子会社を解散するため, 親会社がその資産の一部を売却した。

wind-up （名）解散, 清算, 整理, 事業停止, 企業閉鎖 （=windup, winding up）

wind-up, dissolution, merger, or reorganization 清算, 解散, 合併または更生

WIPO 国連の世界知的所有権機関（⇒World Intellectual Property Organization）

◆Despite the sluggish economy, the number of global patent filings continued to grow, the United Nations' WIPO said. 国連の世界知的所有権機関（WIPO）の発表によると, 景気は低迷しているものの, 世界の特許出願件数の増加は続いている。

wire transfer 電信送金, 資金の電信振替え（⇒endorsement）
◆All bank charges, commissions and other costs associated with a bank wire transfer or establishing and maintaining a letter of credit associated with payments under this agreement shall be for the account of ABC. 本契約に基づく支払いにかかわる銀行の電信送金または信用状の開設・維持にかかわる銀行費用, 手数料, その他の費用は, すべてABCの負担とする。

with effect retrospect to ～に遡及（そきゅう）して
◆Title with respect to each shipment of the products shall pass from the seller to purchaser when the seller negotiates relative documents and receives proceeds from the negotiating bank for such shipment with effect retrospect to the time of such shipment. 本製品の各船積みに関する所有権は, 売り主が関連書類を手形買取り銀行に提出して本製品の代金を当該銀行から受領した時点で, 当該船積み時に遡及して売り主から買い主に移転するものとする。

with or without notice 通知の有無にかかわらず, 予告の有無にかかわらず
◆The prices are without engagement and subject to change with or without notice. 価格は確約なしで, 予告の有無にかかわらず変更することがある。

with respect to ～に関する, ～に関して, ～については
◆Seller shall waive any claim against Buyer under the Uniform Commercial Code or otherwise, with respect to a claim asserted against Seller or Buyer for patent, trademark or copyright infringement or the like. 売り主は, 特許・商標・著作権の侵害等について売り主または買い主に対してなされる請求に関しては, 買い主に対する米国統一商事法典その他に基づく請求権をすべて放棄する。

with strings attached 付帯条件付きで
◆Egypt's Morsi administration has concluded a basic agreement with the IMF on loans totaling $4.8 billion, with strings attached, in an effort to avert a default on debts. エジプトのモルシ政権は, 債務不履行を回避するため, 付帯条件付きで, 国際通貨基金（IMF）との間で総額48億ドルの融資を受けることで基本合意した。

withdraw （動）預金などを引き出す, 預金などを引き揚げる, 通貨などを回収する, 市場などから撤退する, 取り消す, 打ち切る, 撤回する

withdraw deposits 預金を引き出す, 預金を引き揚げる
◆It is natural for bank customers to withdraw de-

W

posits when they no longer trust financial institutions. 銀行預金者が銀行を信じられなくなったら、預金を引き揚げるのは当然のことだ。

withdraw from China 中国から撤退する
◆More and more business managers of Japanese-affiliated companies are thinking of withdrawing from China due to rising labor costs. 人件費の高騰で、中国撤退を考えている日系企業の経営者が増えている。

withdraw from the market 市場から撤退する (=pull out of the market)
◆Many Japanese electronics makers have withdrawn from the TV market, but some domestic manufacturers which have maintained their TV businesses have transferred their production bases overseas. 日本の電機メーカーの多くはテレビ市場から撤退したが、テレビ事業を続ける国内メーカーの一部も、生産拠点を海外に移している。

withdraw from the production of 〜の生産から撤退する
◆Matsushita Electric Industrial Co. plans to withdraw from the production of cathode-ray tube TVs in fiscal 2010 at the earliest. 松下電器産業は、ブラウン管テレビの生産から2010年度にも撤退する方針だ。

withdraw funds 資金を引き揚げる
◆Amid the ongoing European financial crisis, concern is mounting in South Korea that the value of its won currency may steeply decline if foreign financial institutions and investors withdraw funds from the country. 今回の欧州金融危機の影響で、韓国では、海外の金融機関や投資家が同国から資金を引き揚げたら、韓国の通貨ウォンの相場が急落しかねない、との懸念[危機感]が強まっている。

withdrawal (名) 撤退, 脱退, 離脱, 撤回, 回収, 預金の引出し, 引落し, 払戻し, 取消し, 解約, 出資者や株主に対する利益の分配, 資本の減少
double withdrawal 二重引落し
early withdrawal 期限前払戻し, 期限前解約
profit withdrawal 利益控除
the withdrawal of the company from Japan 同社の日本からの撤退
withdrawal from the core business 中核事業からの撤退, 主力事業からの撤退

withhold (動) 差し控える, 許さない, 与えない, 権利などを保留する, 妨害する, 阻止する, 控除する, 源泉徴収する, 差し止める
(⇒amount of such claim, unreasonably withhold)
◆All Japanese income taxes, if any, levied on the royalties to be paid by ABC to XYZ shall be born by XYZ and withheld by ABC in accordance with the tax laws of Japan. ABCがXYZに支払うロイヤリティに対して課税される日本国の所得税があれば、これはすべてXYZが負担するものとし、日本の税法に従ってABCが源泉徴収する

ものとする。◆The Seller may withhold delivery or cancel the Agreement if the Buyer fails to establish the letter of credit by the date stipulated in this Agreement. 買い主が本契約で定める期限までに信用状を開設することができない場合、売り主は、引渡しを保留するか契約を解除することができる。

withholding (名) 保留, 留保, 控除, 源泉徴収
income tax withholding 源泉所得税, 源泉所得税預り金
withholding at source 源泉徴収
withholding of delivery 引渡しの留保

withholding tax 源泉徴収税, 源泉課税
◆Any withholding tax lawfully levied by the Japanese tax authorities on any amount due to the licensor under this agreement shall be borne by the licensor. 本契約に基づきライセンサーに支払われるべき金額に対して日本の税務当局が合法的に課税する源泉徴収税は、ライセンサーが負担するものとする。

without fault 過失なしに
◆The licensee's obligation under this Article with respect to the confidential information shall not apply to information which is part of the public domain at the time of disclosure by the licensor, or thereafter becomes part of the public domain without fault on the part of the licensee. 本条に基づく秘密情報に関するライセンシーの義務は、ライセンサーによる開示の時点で公知であるか、その後ライセンシー側の過失なしに公知となる情報には適用されないものとする。

without notice 善意で, 通知なしで, 通知をしないで
◆Notwithstanding Paragraph 1 of this Article, this Agreement shall automatically terminate, without notice, by the occurrence of any one of the following: 本条1項にかかわらず、次のいずれかの事態が生じた場合、本契約は通知なしで自動的に終了する。

without one's written permission 〜の書面による許可なしで
◆Distributor shall not, without Supplier's written permission, require its customers to purchase other goods or services as a requirement for the purchase of Products. 販売店は、供給者の書面による許可なしに、本製品の購入の抱き合わせに[購入の条件として]他の商品またはサービスの購入を顧客に要求してはならない。

without prejudice (既得権の) 侵害なしに, 〜を損なうことなく
without prejudice to any of one's rights generally 〜の権利を一般的に損なうことなく
without prejudice to other rights and remedies 他の権利と救済手段を損なうことなく

without prejudice to, and not in limitation of 〜を損なうことなく、また〜に限定しないで

WORK

◆Without prejudice to, and not in limitation of, any other remedies or relief to which the buyer may be entitled under this agreement or otherwise, the seller agrees to pay to the buyer the amount in cash which would then be required to put the buyer in the position which it would have been in had such representation or warranty been true, correct and complete, or had such agreement been performed or fulfilled. 買い主が本契約によりまたは別段に権利を有する他の救済手段または救済を損なうことなく、またこれに限定することなく、売り主は、当該表明もしくは保証が真実、正確かつ完全であったなら、または当該合意事項が履行もしくは遂行されていたなら買い主が置かれていた立場に買い主を置くために、その時点で必要な金額を現金で買い主に支払うことに同意する。

without recourse 遡求（そきゅう）排除, 遡求［遡求権］なし, 遡求請求権のない, 無担保裏書きの, 二次的支払い義務のない, 償還請求義務のない, 償還請求義務のない, 償還義務を負うことなく, 非遡求型の
　project finance loans without recourse 二次的支払い義務のないプロジェクト・ファイナンス・ローン, 非遡求型の (nonrecourse) プロジェクト・ファイナンス・ローン
　without recourse, warranty or liability 償還義務, 担保責任や保証責任を負うことなく

without reference to 〜に関係なく, 〜に係 (かかわ) りなく, 〜を参照することなく, 〜を参照しないで, 〜を考慮しないで
◆This agreement shall be governed by and construed in accordance with the laws of England, without reference to its choice of law rules. 本契約は、法律選択のルールにかかわりなく、イングランド法に準拠し、同法に従って解釈するものとする。

without restriction 制限なく, 無制限に
◆ABC's obligation under this Article shall not apply to any information relating to the licensed products that is or becomes available without restriction to the general public by acts not attributable to ABC or its employees. 本条に基づくABCの義務は、ABCまたはその従業員が引き起こしたと考えることができない行為によって一般公衆に制限なく知られている、または知られるようになった許諾製品に関する情報には適用されないものとする。

without the other party's prior written consent 相手方の文書による事前の同意を得ないで, 相手方の書面による事前の承諾［承認］を得ないで
◆Neither party shall have the right to assign any of its rights or obligation provided hereunder to any third party without the other party's prior written consent. いずれの当事者も、相手方の文書による事前の同意を得ないで本契約に規定する権利あるいは義務を第三者に譲渡する権利を一切持たないものとする。

witness （名）証人, 立会い人, 署名人, 副署人, 目撃者
　bear witness to 〜を証明する
　in witness whereof 〜の立会いのもと, 上記の証として
◆IN WITNESS WHEREOF, the parties hereto have caused this agreement to be executed by duly authorized representatives of both parties on _____, 2015. 以上の証として、本契約当事者は、(両当事者の)正当な権限をもつ代表者により2015年 月 日、本契約を締結した。

won （名）ウォン（韓国と北朝鮮の通貨単位）
◆Amid the ongoing European financial crisis, concern is mounting in South Korea that the value of its won currency may steeply decline if foreign financial institutions and investors withdraw funds from the country. 今回の欧州金融危機の影響で、韓国では、海外の金融機関や投資家が同国から資金を引き揚げたら、韓国の通貨ウォンの相場が急落しかねない、との懸念［危機感］が強まっている。◆The U.S. dollar has dropped sharply in value not only against the yen, but also against the euro, the South Korean won, the Thai baht and other currencies. 米ドル［米ドル相場］は、円に対してだけでなく、ユーロや韓国ウォン、タイ・バーツなどに対しても、急落している。

work out a strategy 戦略を練る
◆In expanding into India's market, Japanese companies must work out a strategy that includes possible infrastructure risks. インド市場に進出するにあたって、日本企業は、想定されるインフラ面でのリスクを念頭に置いた戦略を練る必要がある。

workable （形）運用できる, 活用できる, 実行可能な (feasible), 実行できる, 採掘可能な, 耕作可能な, 加工できる, 実際的な
◆We refrained from making a counter offer as the price you offered is about seven percent higher than the level workable to us. 貴社がオファーされた価格は、当社の採算にのる水準よりも7%ほど高いので、カウンター・オファーを出すことを思いとどまりました。

workmanship （名）技量, 技術, 仕上がり, 仕上げ, 製作品, 製品, 製造方法, ワークマンシップ
　be free from all defects in title, design, material and workmanship 所有権, 設計, 材料と仕上がりの面ですべて瑕疵 (かし) がない
　be free from defects in materials and workmanship under normal use 通常の使用で材料の面でも仕上がりの面でも欠陥がない
◆The seller warrants that the Goods will be free from defects in material and workmanship for a period as specified in this agreement. 売り主は、本契約で定める期間、本商品が材料と仕上げの面で欠陥がないことを保証する。◆The seller warrants that the products are free from all defects in title, design, material and workmanship. 売り主は、本製品が所有権、設計、材料と仕上がりの面ですべ

W

て瑕疵（かし）がないことを保証する。

World Intellectual Property Organization 国連の世界知的所有権機関, WIPO
◆The United Nations' World Intellectual Property Organization（WIPO）launched its World Intellectual Property Indicators 2012 report and said that global patent filings in 2011 swelled to a record 2.14 million. 国連の世界知的所有権機関（WIPO）は、「世界知的所有権指標2012年版」の報告書を発表し、2011年の世界の特許出願件数は増加して過去最高の214万件に達したと述べた。

world market 世界市場 （=global market）
◆Erratic fluctuations of both stock prices and exchange rates have continued, reflecting the turbulent moves of speculative money on world markets. 世界的な投機マネーの激しい動きを反映して、株価と為替相場の乱高下が止まらない。

world trade 世界の貿易, 世界貿易
arena of world trade 世界貿易の舞台
decline in world trade growth 世界貿易の伸び悩み
world trade discussions 世界の貿易協議
world trade growth 世界貿易の伸び
world trade patterns 世界の貿易のルール
world trade prices 世界貿易価格

World Trade Organization 世界貿易機関, WTO （⇒WTO）
◆In the agricultural negotiations at the World Trade Organization, Japan has been under strong pressure from rice exporters to lower import tariffs on rice and to expand access for foreign rice. 世界貿易機関（WTO）の農業交渉で日本は、コメ輸出国から、コメの輸入関税率引下げや外国産米の輸入枠拡大への強い圧力を受けている。◆South Korea filed a complaint with the World Trade Organization over Japan's restrictions on imports of laver or nori seaweed. 韓国が、日本の食用のり輸入制限に対して世界貿易機関（WTO）に提訴した。◆The World Trade Organization has a long way to go before it can reach a consensus on a new set of rules governing free trade. 世界貿易機関（WTO）が貿易自由化の新ルールに関して合意が得られるまでの道のりは、まだまだ遠い。

World Trade Organization rules 世界貿易機関（WTO）のルール
◆Under the World Trade Organization rules, emergency import limits, or safeguard, are permitted as a temporary measure if the volume of imports of a certain product drastically increases, causing serious damages to industries concerned in the country. 世界貿易機関（WTO）のルールでは、緊急輸入制限措置（セーフガード）は、特定製品の輸入量が増加して、国内の関係業界に大きな被害が出ている場合には、一時的な措置として認められる。

worldwide retail exchange 小売業の国際電子取引市場, WWRE

WPA 単独海損担保（with particular averageの略。with averageともいう）

writing （名）書面, 文書
◆Such claims shall be dispatched in writing. このようなクレームは、書面で迅速に行うものとする。

written （形）文書にした, 書面にした, 文書［書面］による, 筆記の

written approval 書面による承認
◆Licensor must obtain written approval prior to use thereof. その使用に先立って、ライセンサーは書面による承認を得なければならない。

written consent 同意書, 承諾書, 書面による同意, 書面による承諾
◆This agreement shall not be assignable by either Licensor or Licensee without the other party's written consent, except to an assignee of either Licensor or Licensee of the entire business relating to the Products. 本契約は、本製品に関する全事業のライセンサーまたはライセンシーの譲受人に対する譲渡以外は、相手方の書面による同意を得ないでライセンサーもライセンシーも譲渡しないものとする。

written estimate 見積り書, 予測書
◆At least sixty days prior to the requested delivery date, the buyer shall provide the seller with a written estimate of its requirements of the product, which shall constitute a firm order. 希望渡し日から少なくとも60日前に、買い主は、本製品の需要予測書［需要見積り書］を売り主に提出し、これを確定注文とするものとする。

written notice 書面による通知, 書面通知, 通知書 （⇒default of this agreement）
◆A party hereto proposing to effect a sale of any shares of the new company（the Offerer）shall give a written notice to the other parties hereto, or their assignee, who are then shareholders of the new company（the Offerees）, of the Offerer's intention, the identity of the prospective third party purchaser, and the terms and conditions of the proposed sale. 新会社の株式の売却を申し出る本契約当事者（「申込み者」）は、他の当事者またはその時点で新会社の株主である譲受人（「被申込み者」）に対して、申込み者の売却意思、予定される第三者購入者の住所・氏名と申し出をした売却の条件を、書面で通知するものとする。

WTI （国際指標となる）テキサス産軽質油, ウェスト・テキサス・インターミディエート（West Texas Intermediateの略。米テキサス州西部とニューメキシコ州東南部で産出される軽質の原油。米国の市況動向を示す代表銘柄）
◆In the crude oil contract market of the New York Mercantile Exchange（NYMEX）, the price of January WTI, the benchmark U.S. crude oil, fell below $60 a barrel for the first time since June 2009 on December 11, 2014 due to the forecast of rising global oil production. 2014年12月11日のニューヨーク・マーカンタイル取引所の原

油先物市場では、指標となる米国産原油WTI（テキサス産軽質油）の1月渡し価格が、世界的な石油増産見通しから、2009年7月以来5年5か月ぶりに1バレル＝60ドルを割り込んだ。

WTO 世界貿易機関（World Trade Organizationの略。1995年に設立された国際機関。160か国・地域が加盟）

admission to the WTO　WTOへの加盟承認

enter the WTO　WTOに加盟する

file a petition with the WTO over the sanctions　制裁措置に対して世界貿易機関（WTO）に提訴する

launch a WTO case　WTOに提訴する

lose an appeal at the WTO　WTOで敗訴する

the new round of WTO talks　新ラウンド, 新多角的貿易交渉

trade dispute filed to the WTO　WTOに提訴の貿易紛争案件

WTO members　WTO加盟国

WTO panel　WTO紛争処理小委員会（パネル）

◆As a member country of the WTO, Moscow should first improve Russia's investment climate, including the abolition of trade barriers. 世界貿易機関（WTO）加盟国として、ロシアはまず貿易障壁の撤廃など投資環境を改善する必要がある。◆China lost an appeal at the WTO in a case about its export restrictions on raw materials including bauxite, magnesium and zinc. 中国によるボーキサイトやマグネシウム、亜鉛などの鉱物資源［原材料］輸出規制に関する問題で、中国は世界貿易機関（WTO）で敗訴した。◆Japan has filed a petition with the WTO over the sanctions, and the U.S. has promised a cross-complaint. 日本は、制裁措置に対して世界貿易機関（WTO）に提訴し、米国は逆提訴する見込みだ［逆提訴する構えを見せている］。◆The government decided to decrease the rate of a countervailing tariff by 18.1 percentage points, as the WTO recommend. 政府は、世界貿易機関（WTO）の勧告を踏まえて、相殺関税の税率を18.1％引き下げる方針を固めた。◆The new round of WTO talks to map out rules for promoting free trade has floundered since the failure of a key ministerial conference in September 2003. 自由貿易推進の新ルール策定をめざす新ラウンド（新多角的貿易交渉）は、2003年9月の主要閣僚会議の失敗以来、難航している。◆The United States, the EU and Mexico challenged China's export restrictions on raw materials and launched WTO legal cases in 2009. 米国、欧州連合（EU）とメキシコが中国の原材料（鉱物資源）輸出規制は世界貿易機関（WTO）の協定違反に当たるとして、2009年にWTOに提訴した。◆The WTO was inaugurated in 1995, as an outgrowth of the General Agreement on Tariffs and Trade, with the aim of promoting a framework for multilateral free trade toward 21st century. 世界貿易機関（WTO）は、21世紀に向けた多角的な自由貿易体制の推進を目的に、ガット（関税・貿易一般協定）を発展改組して1995年に発足した。

WTO accord［agreement］　WTO協定

◆Tokyo, Washington and Taipei have imposed no tariffs on liquid crystal display monitors for computers, all-in-one printers and set-top boxes under the WTO accord. 日本、米国と台湾は、WTO協定に基づき、パソコン用液晶モニター、一体型プリンターとセットトップ・ボックス（双方向テレビ向け家庭用通信端末）の3品目に、関税を課していない。

WTO General Council　WTO一般理事会

◆The WTO General Council meeting will be held from Tuesday with the participation of ambassadors of the 147 member states and regions. 147加盟国・地域の担当大使が参加して、木曜日から世界貿易機関（WTO）の一般理事会が開かれる。

WTO member　WTO加盟国

◆After both China and Taiwan became WTO members in 2002, Taiwan's investment in China, led by information technology firms, increased rapidly. 中国と台湾が2002年に世界貿易機関（WTO）に加盟してから、IT（情報技術）産業を中心に台湾の対中投資が急増した。

WTO rule　WTOのルール, WTOルール

◆China's retaliatory tariffs on Japanese cars, cellular phones and air conditioners clearly ran counter to WTO rules. 日本の自動車、携帯電話とエアコンに課した中国の報復関税は、明らかにWTOルールに違反していた。

WTO's ruling　WTOの決定

◆When Washington refuses to comply with the WTO's ruling, the EU will impose retaliatory tariffs on U.S. products. 米国が世界貿易機関（WTO）の決定に従わなかった場合、欧州連合（EU）は米国製品に報復関税を発動する方針だ。

Y

year in question　当該年

◆The amount of the guaranteed minimum annual royalty for each year shall be paid in advance by ABC to Licensor by remittance to the bank account as designated by Licensor on or before the 22nd day of December of the year in question. 各年度の年間最低ロイヤルティ保証額は、前払いで、ライセンサーが指定する銀行口座に当該年の12月22日までにABCが振り込むことによって支払うものとする。

yen　（名）円, 円相場

◆A recent plunge in the yen due to the economic and monetary policies of Prime Minister Shinzo Abe is a boon for domestic exporters. 安倍晋三首相の経済・金融政策による最近の円安は、国内の輸出企業にとっては追い風[恩恵]だ。◆At present, export industries including home appliances and automobiles are raising their expectations for improved corporate performance under the weak yen, which has also driven up stock prices. 現在、家電や自動車などの輸出産業は、円安で業績改善の期待を高めており、円安はまた株価を押し上げた。

yen-denominated trade　円建て貿易
◆Yen-denominated trade frees domestic companies from the risk of exchange rate fluctuations. 円建て貿易は、国内企業にとって為替変動のリスクがない。

yen-dollar rate　円・ドル［円ドル］相場，円・ドルレート，円・ドル為替レート，円の対ドル・レート
◆The competitive edge of Japanese exporters vying with U.S. firms is affected by the yen-dollar rate and the price levels in the two countries. 米企業と競合している日本の輸出企業の競争力は、円・ドルレートや日本と米国の物価水準の影響をも受ける。

yen fund　円ファンド
◆In a global carry trade, hedge funds borrow low-interest yen funds to invest in dollar-denominated assets. グローバル・キャリー・トレード［グローバル・キャリー取引］では、ヘッジ・ファンドなどが、低利の円資金を借りてドル建て資産に投資している。

yen-yuan trading　円・人民元の取引，円・人民元の為替取引
◆Banks participating in direct yen-yuan trading in the Tokyo interbank foreign exchange market will trade the yen and the yuan at an exchange rate calculated on the basis of actual supply and demand. 東京外国為替市場で円・人民元の直接取引に参加する銀行は、実際の需給などをもとに算出した取引レートで、円と人民元を銀行間で取引する。

yen's appreciation　円高
◆The recent yen's appreciation is not so painful as to deal a heavy blow to export-oriented industries. 最近の円高は、輸出企業に大きな打撃を与えるほどの痛手［大きな打撃を与える水準］ではない。
◆The yen's appreciation will not only reduce the volume of exports but also harm a wide variety of other areas. 円高は輸出の減少だけでなく、その弊害は広範に及ぶ。

yen's appreciation against the dollar　円高・ドル安
◆Rapidly increasing prices of primary commodities have had a positive influence on corporate performance with the yen's appreciation against the dollar. 円高・ドル安で、これまでのところ一次産品（原油や石炭など）の急騰が、企業の業績に好影響をもたらしている。

yen's depreciation　円安　(⇒positive effect)
◆A counselor to the Japan Research Institute warned that under the current trade structure, the yen's depreciation might apply downward pressure on the Japanese economy. 現状の貿易構造では、円安で日本の景気が押し下げられる懸念

がある、と日本総研の理事が警告した。◆A recovery will be export-driven, dependent on U.S. growth and the yen's depreciation, instead of being led by increased domestic consumption and capital investment. 今後の景気回復は、アメリカ経済の好転や円安を背景にした輸出主導型の回復で、国内の個人消費や設備投資の伸びがその牽引役となるわけではない。◆Japan's trade deficit in April-September 2014 hit a record high due to increased demand for liquefied natural gas for thermal power generation and a rise in overall import prices stemming from the yen's depreciation. 日本の2014年度上半期（4～9月）の貿易赤字は、火力発電所向け液化天然ガス（LNG）の需要増加と円安による輸入物価全体の上昇で、過去最大となった。◆The increase in the CPI in June 2013 is mainly attributed to a rise in gasoline prices and electricity charges as import prices of crude oil and liquefied natural gas were pushed up by the yen's depreciation. 2013年6月の消費者物価指数の上昇は、円安の影響による原油や液化天然ガス（LNG）の輸入価格上昇で、ガソリンや電気料金などが上昇したのが主因だ。

yen's exchange rate　円相場，円の為替相場，円の為替レート
◆The weak yen pushes up the cost of imports, so the yen's exchange rate will determine the degree to which declining crude oil prices will be a boon for Japan. 円安で輸入価格が押し上げられるため、原油安［原油価格の下落］がどの程度、日本にとって追い風になるかは、円相場に左右される。

yen's sharp climb　急激な円高
◆Aeon and Ito-Yokado started discount sales of foods imported from the United States to pass along to consumers the benefits of the yen's sharp climb against the dollar. イオンとイトーヨーカ堂は、急激な円高・ドル安による円高差益を消費者に還元するため、米国から輸入した食料品の値下げセールを開始した。

yen's steep appreciation　急激な円高
◆Losses from fluctuations of the currency market due to the yen's steep appreciation have added to Toyota's plight. 急激な円高による為替差損で、トヨタの経営状況が深刻化した。

yen's value　円相場，円価値
◆The rapid surge in the yen's value could deal a blow to Japan's export drive and export-related businesses. 急激な円高は、日本の輸出競争力の低下や輸出関連企業の業績悪化をもたらす［日本の輸出競争力と輸出関連企業に打撃を与える］可能性がある。

yield　(名)株式・債券などの利回り，歩留（ぶど）まり，収益，収穫量，収穫高，(核爆発の)威力，イールド
◆As European authorities failed to take swift action, the yields of Italian and Spanish government bonds rose, and there were violent fluctuations in the value of the euro. 欧州当局が迅速に対応しなかったので、イタリアやスペインの国債

流通利回りが上昇し、ユーロの為替相場が乱高下
した。

you （代）貴社, 御社, 貴方
◆We are certain that you will find it to be a very
good buy. 御社にとってこれは大変お買い得と思
われる、と確信します。◆We are giving your or-
der priority, but a slight delay in the shipment of
yours will be unavoidable. 貴社の注文を優先的に
扱っていますが、ご注文の船積みが少々遅れるこ
とは避けられません。

your good selves 貴社, 貴店

yuan （名）中国の人民元, 元
（＝the Chinese yuan）
◆Banks participating in direct yen-yuan trading
in the Tokyo interbank foreign exchange market
will trade the yen and the yuan at an exchange
rate calculated on the basis of actual supply and
demand. 東京外国為替市場で円・人民元の直接取引
に参加する銀行は、実際の需給などをもとに算出し
た取引レートで、円と人民元を銀行間で取引する。◆
Interbank trading between the U.S. dollar and the
Chinese currency yuan accounts for 99.3 percent
of the Shanghai foreign exchange market. 米ド
ルと中国の通貨・人民元の銀行間取引［銀行間為
替取引］が、上海外国為替市場の99.3％を占めてい
る。◆To avert China risks such as the stronger
Chinese yuan, surging labor costs and anti-Japan
riots, some firms have shifted production lines to
other countries in Southeast Asia and other regions with cheaper labor. 中国人民元高や人件費
高騰、反日暴動などの中国リスクを回避するため、
一部の企業は、中国より低賃金の東南アジアなどの
地域に生産ラインの移管［分散化］を進めている。

yuan's exchange rate 人民元の為替レート
◆Keeping in mind transactions with China,
which has yet to liberalize the yuan's exchange
rate completely, G-20 participants included in
the joint statement the necessity of swiftly shifting to exchange rate system determined by market. 人民元の為替レートをまだ完全に自由化して
いない中国との取引を念頭に、G20参加国は、市場
で決められる為替レートの体制に速やかに移行す
る必要性を、共同声明に盛り込んだ。

Z

zone （名）地域, 地区, 地帯, 範囲, 層, 圏, 区,
〜台, ゾーン
bonded zone　保税地区
business zone　商業地区
contiguous zone　接続水域
designated industrial zone　指定工業地域
economic development zone　経済開発区
enterprise zone　企業地区
exclusive economic zone　排他的経済圏, 排他
　的経済水域, 排他的経済ブロック
export processing zone　輸出加工区

free trade zone　自由貿易圏, 自由加工貿易
　地域
national strategic special deregulation zones
　国家戦略特区, 規制緩和を推進する国家戦
　略特区
polluted zone　汚染地帯
price zone　価格帯, プライス・ゾーン
regional economic zone　局地経済圏
special economic zone　経済特別区, 経済特区
target zone　目標相場圏, 目標圏, 目標範囲
target zone of exchange rates　目標圏相場
zone delivered pricing　地域別輸送価格
zone rate　区間運賃制
◆As the centerpiece of deregulation measures,
the government plans to create "national strategic special deregulation zones" to attract companies and talented workers from all over the world
by boldly relaxing regulations in the zones. 規制
緩和策の目玉として、政府は「国家戦略特区」を
創設し、特区内で大胆な規制緩和を断行して、世
界中から企業や有能な人材を集める方針だ。

編者略歴

菊地 義明（きくち・よしあき）：翻訳・校閲・辞書編纂家
現代文化研究所・海外情報担当主任研究員を経て、1979年（昭和54年）独立。モービル石油のオピニオン・リーダー誌『モービル文庫』の制作にあたる一方、サイマル・インターナショナル社翻訳部で校閲を務める。現在は辞書編纂に専念。文芸・評論のほか、アニュアル・レポート、四半期報告書、契約書などのビジネス文書翻訳を得意とする。

主な著書
『誤訳・悪訳・珍訳大研究』（日本実業出版社、1995年刊）
『これでいいのか、翻訳本！』（南雲堂、1997年刊）
『経営・ビジネス用語英和辞典』（IBCパブリッシング、2006年刊）
『財務情報英和辞典』（三省堂、2008年刊）
『ビジネス実務総合英和辞典』（三省堂、2009年刊）
『ビジネス時事英和辞典』（三省堂、2010年刊）
『経済・金融ビジネス英和大辞典』（日外アソシエーツ、2012年刊）
その他『モービル文庫』（モービル石油広報部、53冊）など多数

国際ビジネス英和活用辞典
―国際取引・貿易・為替・証券

2015年5月25日　第1刷発行

編　者／菊地義明
発行者／大高利夫
発　行／日外アソシエーツ株式会社
　　　　〒143-8550 東京都大田区大森北1-23-8 第3下川ビル
　　　　電話 (03)3763-5241(代表) FAX(03)3764-0845
　　　　URL http://www.nichigai.co.jp/
発売元／株式会社紀伊國屋書店
　　　　〒163-8636 東京都新宿区新宿3-17-7
　　　　電話 (03)3354-0131(代表)
　　　　ホールセール部(営業)　電話 (03)6910-0519

電算漢字処理／日外アソシエーツ株式会社
印刷・製本／光写真印刷株式会社

©Yoshiaki KIKUCHI 2015
不許複製・禁無断転載
〈落丁・乱丁本はお取り替えいたします〉
ISBN978-4-8169-2537-5　　　　**Printed in Japan,2015**

経済・金融ビジネス英和大辞典

菊地義明 編　B5・1,050頁　定価（本体23,800円＋税）　2012.5刊

銀行、証券、保険、財務会計分野の英和用例文例辞典。経済・金融ビジネスに関する各種公式文書、報告書、アナリスト・リポート、専門紙誌を読み解く上で必要な基本語、最新語、重要語句、関連語5万語と文例1.7万件を収録。既存の辞典には収録されていない言い回しや表現も豊富。

ビジネス技術 実用英和大辞典

海野文男＋海野和子 編　A5・1,330頁　定価（本体4,800円＋税）　2002.11刊

ビジネス技術 実用和英大辞典

海野文男＋海野和子 編　A5・1,210頁　定価（本体5,200円＋税）　2002.12刊

ネイティブによる自然な英語から取材した生きた用例を参考に、自在に英文を組み立てられる「英語表現集」。普通の辞書には載っていない表現を豊富に収録。取扱説明書、仕様書、案内書、報告書、プロポーザル、契約書、論文などの文書作成に、また、英字新聞・雑誌を読む時、海外のWebサイトを検索・閲覧する際に必携の辞書。

英和翻訳の原理・技法

中村保男 著　竹下和男 企画・制作

A5・280頁　定価（本体3,800円＋税）　2003.3刊

英語学習の盲点から翻訳の奥義まで、著者の半世紀にわたる経験から得られた翻訳理論・実践技法を伝授。豊富な文例・訳例により、「勘」と「こつ」を詳細に解説する貴重な一冊。

翻訳とは何か―職業としての翻訳

山岡洋一 著　四六判・290頁　定価（本体1,600円＋税）　2001.8刊

翻訳のありかた、歴史上の翻訳者の生涯から、翻訳技術、翻訳市場、現代の翻訳教育産業や翻訳学習者の問題点まで、総合的に「職業としての翻訳」を論じ、翻訳文化論を展開する。真の翻訳者とは何か、翻訳とは何か、を伝える翻訳学習者必読のロングセラー。

データベースカンパニー
日外アソシエーツ

〒143-8550　東京都大田区大森北1-23-8
TEL.(03)3763-5241　FAX.(03)3764-0845　http://www.nichigai.co.jp/